Introducing Advanced Macroeconomics:

Growth and Business Cycles

Second Edition

Second Edition

Introducing Advanced Macroeconomics:

Growth and Business Cycles

Peter Birch Sørensen

and Hans Jørgen Whitta-Jacobsen

Mc
Graw
Hill
Education

London Boston Burr Ridge, IL Dubuque, IA Madison, WI New York San Francisco
St. Louis Bangkok Bogotá Caracas Kuala Lumpur Lisbon Madrid Mexico City
Milan Montreal New Delhi Santiago Seoul Singapore Sydney Taipei Toronto

Introducing Advanced Macroeconomics: Growth and Business Cycles
Peter Birch Sørensen and Hans Jørgen Whitta-Jacobsen
ISBN-13 978-0-07-711786-3
ISBN-10 0-07-711786-7

Published by McGraw-Hill Education
Shoppenhangers Road
Maidenhead
Berkshire
SL6 2QL
Telephone: 44 (0) 1628 502 500
Fax: 44 (0) 1628 770 224
Website: *www.mheducation.co.uk*

British Library Cataloguing in Publication Data
A catalogue record for this book is available from the British Library

Library of Congress Cataloguing in Publication Data
The Library of Congress data for this book has been applied for from the Library of Congress

Acquisitions Editor: Natalie Jacobs
Development Editor: Tom Hill
Marketing Manager: Vanessa Boddington
Senior Production Editor: James Bishop

Cover design by Paul Fielding
Printed and bound in Great Britain by Bell and Bain Ltd, Glasgow

ISBN-13 978-0-07-711786-3
ISBN-10 0-07-711786-7

Dedication

To my wife, my children and my parents – Peter Birch Sørensen

To Charlotte, Alberte and Mads – Hans Jørgen Whitta-Jacobsen

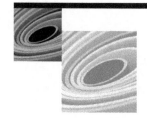

Brief Table of Contents

Detailed Table of Contents

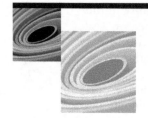

Preface

THE FIRST EDITION

The main challenges for macroeconomic theory are to explain the long-term economic growth and the short-term business fluctuations observed in the real world. This book offers an introduction to advanced economic analysis of these issues. In the following we will explain the philosophy underlying the book, its key features and target readership, and how it may be used for teaching purposes.

The main distinguishing feature of the book and the target readership

Our book seeks to bridge the gap between the typical intermediate macroeconomics text and the more advanced texts used at the graduate level. As examples of the typical intermediate level text, we have in mind well-known books such as those by N. Gregory Mankiw, Olivier Blanchard, J. Bradford DeLong, Rudiger Dornbusch and Stanley Fischer or Michael Burda and Charles Wyplosz, to mention but a few. Examples in the advanced category are the textbooks by David Romer, Ben J. Heijdra and Frederick van der Ploeg, Olivier Blanchard and Stanley Fischer, or a more specialized book like the one on open economy macroeconomics by Maurice Obstfeld and Kenneth Rogoff.

With respect to the level of abstraction and analytical sophistication and the technical skills required, we think that the gap between the typical intermediate and the typical advanced text is very wide, and for many students too wide to overcome in one step. One of our intentions is that a course based on this book (coming after an intermediate level course) should prepare well for the advanced texts. We think there are not many other textbooks aimed at this purpose, if any at all, and we believe there is a great need for such a book.

At many universities there are indeed macro courses between the intermediate and advanced level. This could, for instance, be a third-year undergraduate course where the second-year course was based on an intermediate level text. Personally we have had difficulties finding a well-suited coherent textbook for such a course. From conversations we have learned that colleagues in other countries have experienced similar difficulties. This book is intended to fit exactly such a course.

Other universities and business schools do not have courses between the two levels just described. Rather, their study programmes require graduate students to go directly from a typical intermediate text used in the final macro course at the undergraduate level to an advanced text used at the graduate level. Because of the gap we have described, we think that such a programme may be suboptimal for many students and that this book can be helpful also as a starter at the graduate level.

Thus, depending on the specific background of students, we imagine that the book may be studied during the one or two last years of undergraduate studies, or during the first year at the master's level, and a main intention of the book is that it should give students a strong background for pursuing further studies in macroeconomics at the graduate level.

Another intention is that the book should also be well suited for a final-year course for bachelor students who plan to leave the university with an undergraduate specialization in economics. In particular we think that the focus of the book on relatively few fundamental topics makes it appropriate for such a purpose.

What we expect from students

To give students a feel for the methodology of modern macroeconomics, the book uses formal mathematical analysis throughout, supplemented by graphical illustrations. However, the mathematics used are simple, and students are only required to have some training in basic calculus and some familiarity with first-order difference equations and with the concept of a stochastic variable. All steps in the mathematical derivations are carefully explained, and all results derived are given an intuitive explanation, so no student should feel that the models presented have the character of a 'black box'. In some empirical exercises we ask students to undertake Ordinary Least Squares regression analysis. A brief technical appendix provides the untrained student with the minimum knowledge needed to carry out OLS regressions.

Intuitive economic reasoning is important and indeed indispensable for understanding and interpreting the results of formal economic analysis. But in a complex world intuition can sometimes lead the analyst astray if it is not backed up by a mathematical analysis ensuring consistency. With this book we hope to demonstrate to students that even very simple mathematics can take them a long way towards understanding numerous key economic relationships and mechanisms.

Essential features of the text

1. Focus on fundamental and elementary models

Rather than offering a superficial coverage of a wide range of topics and different model types, we have chosen to provide an in-depth treatment of a limited number of basic workhorse macro models. We focus on models which are both fundamental and relatively elementary. The models are elementary in the sense that analysing them does not require mathematical skills which are out of line with a second-year or third-year undergraduate course. The models are fundamental in the sense that they have provided basic and lasting insights.

2. Finishing the job

Because the models in the text are basic, we can analyse them in depth without overburdening students with mathematical technicalities, but at the same time without sacrificing rigour, and we can use all models to their full potential. Hence the student can put some of the most important models in macroeconomics 'on the shelf' after having studied this text: he or she will not have to start over again studying, say, the Solow growth model at a more technical or general level in a later course. Instead, the student can move right on to more advanced models such as the Ramsey growth model, say.

3. Systematic confrontation of theory with data and continued emphasis on policy relevance

To justify the relevance of the models and the theoretical problems analysed, each part of the book starts by reviewing the stylized facts that we want our models to explain, and each chapter systematically confronts the model predictions with empirical data. Throughout the book we highlight how our models help to illuminate important economic policy problems, and we discuss what the models imply for economic policy.

4. Coherence and internal consistency

To help the student appreciate the big picture, the book is careful to point out how the models in different parts of the book are linked. For example, we illustrate how the aggregate supply curve in our short-run business cycle model may be derived from our models of long-run structural unemployment by introducing expectational errors and short-run nominal rigidities. As another example, we point out the link between our workhorse model of economic growth and the theory of real business cycles. In this way students do not have to move into entirely new 'model worlds' as they move from one chapter to another. In particular, we have chosen to specify all models in discrete time, including the growth models of Book One. This means that students do not have to go through the technicalities of the transition from discrete to continuous time. We do acknowledge that continuous time formulations of growth models can be very convenient and serve as a preparation for further studies. Throughout the growth chapters of Book One we have therefore included (heavily guided) exercises allowing more advanced students to become familiar with the parallel growth models in continuous time.

5. Respect for rigour, but avoidance of unnecessary technicalities

The combination of text and exercises will teach the student how to set up simple macroeconomic models, and how to derive the model implications through simple mathematics. In this way the student will learn the importance of being precise in stating one's assumptions, and he or she will learn to appreciate the importance of different assumptions. However, unnecessary technicalities are avoided, and a balance between formal and graphical analysis is maintained.

6. Complementarity between main text and exercises

We think that an unusual feature of this book is the extent of the system of exercises and the degree to which the exercises go hand in hand with the text. While solving the exercises systematically is in no way required for a fruitful reading, working through exercises should be very helpful for obtaining a deeper insight and an improved capacity for analysing macroeconomic problems independently. Our book is therefore very well suited for the type of course where lectures focused on theory are combined with smaller classes focused on solving problems.

Novelties

This book contains several features which we believe to be novel in a textbook context.

For example, Chapter 4 extends the Solow growth model to the open economy to allow an analysis of the long-run effects of international capital mobility. This model may serve as a basis for discussing some of the current issues in the ongoing debate on globalization. Moreover, in Chapter 7 we present a simple Solow model with scarce natural resources which may illuminate some of the issues in the debate on the environmental limits to growth.

In dealing with the macro economy in the short run, we apply and extend the modern AS–AD framework where the nominal variable is the rate of inflation rather than the price level, and where monetary policy is specified as a rule for setting the short-term interest rate. This set-up is gradually superseding the traditional IS–LM and AS–AD analysis and makes it easier to relate the model to real-world policy discussions. However, Chapter 16 on aggregate demand is careful to point out the link between our specification of monetary policy and the more traditional analysis of the money market, so students trained in IS–LM analysis should find it easy to make the transition to our modern AS–AD framework.

In Book Two we also illustrate the methodology of modern business cycle analysis by calibrating and simulating a simple stochastic AS–AD model to reproduce the most important stylized statistical facts of the business cycle. Furthermore, we present a detailed extension of the modern AS–AD framework to the open economy and introduce students to the problems of inflation targeting under flexible exchange rates.

The hard choices made

In our treatment of economic growth we have resisted the strong temptation to include fundamental workhorse models like the Ramsey model of economic growth and the

Diamond model of overlapping generations. A thorough treatment and full understanding of these models require mathematical techniques that go beyond those used in the present text. Furthermore, the Ramsey and Diamond models are typically core subjects in the advanced texts that this book prepares for. By devoting space to the Solow model and its various extensions, we can show in depth how successful this simple and elegant framework actually is in accounting for the stylized facts of economic growth and at the same time give a good preparation for the study of the more advanced models.

One cost of leaving out the Ramsey and Diamond models is that our analysis of public debt has to be kept rather brief. Chapter 15 does introduce the intertemporal government budget constraint in a two-period setting as a basis for discussing Ricardian equivalence, but we chose to leave an extensive treatment of government debt for a more advanced course which covers the OLG model.

Dealing with short-run fluctuations is even more difficult than presenting the theory of economic growth, since there is less consensus on the best way to model business cycles. Here we have also chosen to go carefully through our basic workhorse AS–AD model and its extensions to illustrate how far it can take us towards an understanding of business cycles. Thus we do not present an array of different short-run models, but we do show how a Solow model with stochastic productivity growth can generate real business cycles. In this way we confront our preferred AS–AD framework with real business cycle theory to give students a flavour of some of the controversies in the theory of short-run fluctuations.

Overview of contents

The text is divided into two 'Books'. Book One deals with the economy in the long run, covering economic growth and structural unemployment. Part I presents basic Solow growth models of capital and wealth accumulation for closed and open economies. Part II brings technological progress into the picture, first presenting the Solow model with exogenous technical progress, and then extending this model with human capital and with scarce natural resources.

Part III covers endogenous growth, starting with models based on the idea of productive externalities and increasing returns at the aggregate level, then moving on to a Romer-type model with endogenous R&D.

In Part IV the focus shifts to long-run structural unemployment. After some preliminary theorizing about frictional unemployment, we go through the efficiency wage theory and the trade union model of the labour market.

Book Two contains the analysis of short-run fluctuations. In Part V we develop the building blocks for our workhorse short-run model. While keeping the mathematics simple, we start by going through the life cycle-permanent income theory of consumption and Tobin's q-theory of investment, stressing the role of the stock market in the economy. The chapter on aggregate demand builds on the theories of consumption and investment and introduces monetary policy to derive the aggregate demand curve. This is followed by a chapter on aggregate supply which derives a micro-founded expectations-augmented Phillips curve and an aggregate supply curve from labour market theories consistent with those presented in Part IV.

Part VI puts the pieces together to assemble our basic dynamic AS–AD model for the closed economy. This model (with various amendments) is used to analyse short run fluctuations and optimal stabilization policy with backward-looking as well as forward-looking expectations. The analysis ends by highlighting credibility issues and the problems raised by time lags and uncertainty for stabilization policies.

Finally Part VII extends the AS–AD model to the open economy, developing model variants to study the effects of shocks and the scope for macroeconomic policy under fixed as well as flexible exchange rates. On this basis the last chapter discusses the choice of exchange rate regime, ending with a brief survey of optimum currency area theory.

How teachers may use the book

Although the book is written as a basis for a two- or three-semester course (or a sequence of courses) covering growth as well as business cycles, the structure of the book leaves a high degree of flexibility for teachers. First of all, the two 'Books' can serve as a basis for separate courses in Economic Growth and in Business Cycles, and teachers can choose to start with the short run before moving to the long run.

For the purpose of shorter courses, it is possible to skip some chapters without serious loss of continuity. For example, a relatively short course on Economic Growth should, we think, include Chapters 2, 3 and 5. The teacher can choose to include or exclude any one, two or three of Chapter 4 (on the open economy), Chapter 6 (on human capital), and Chapter 7 (on scarce natural resources). Likewise, Part III on endogenous growth can be skipped altogether if preferred, or one can skip Chapter 9 alone (the macro model of endogenous R&D). The remaining chapters would still constitute a coherent sequence on growth theory. Among the chapters on structural unemployment, Chapter 11 (on efficiency wages) can be read independently of Chapter 12 (on trade unions) and vice versa.

A short course on business cycles which does not intend to go deeply into the micro foundations for the aggregate demand curve could skip Chapters 14 and 15 on investment and consumption and start directly with Chapters 16 and 17 on aggregate demand and supply. It is even possible to start directly with Chapter 18 setting up our short-run model of aggregate supply and aggregate demand, provided the teacher spends a little time explaining the specification of the AD and AS curves. Moreover, a course which only seeks to cover the more basic points on stabilization policy could skip Chapters 19, 21 and 22. Finally, a course that does not have the ambition to cover both exchange rate regimes could skip either one of Chapters 24 and 25.

As another example of the flexibility offered by the book, a course on business cycles which digs deeper into the theory of unemployment could combine chapters from Book Two with one or more of the chapters on structural unemployment in Book One.

Although not absolutely necessary, we believe that students would benefit from starting out with Chapter 1, whether they follow a course on the long run or on the short run. In Chapter 1 we explain the different types of assumptions and modelling strategies used in long-run theory and short-run theory. Our experience is that such an introduction helps students to see how the various models fit into the 'big picture' of macroeconomic theory.

Special facilities

Each chapter ends with an extended summary highlighting the main points to be learned from that chapter. Moreover, each chapter is followed by a number of exercises intended to deepen the student's understanding of the material covered. Some of these exercises have the purpose of increasing the student's familiarity with the basic model encountered in the chapter text, while others invite the student to explore various extensions and modifications of the basic model version. Several exercises are empirical, asking students to undertake simple statistical analysis, typically running an OLS regression. The technical appendix to the book should provide students without prior statistical training with the minimum knowledge needed to solve these exercises (and serve as a useful brush-up for those students who already have some training). Book One also includes Table A reproducing growth relevant country data from various databases, most importantly from the Penn World Table 6.1.

One category of exercises asks students to implement and simulate simple dynamic macro models on the computer. This may be done by means of easily accessible software such as Excel. It is our experience that the process of implementing a simulation model increases the student's understanding of the model (and his or her motivation for model analysis). Because of this, we deliberately chose to ask students to program the models themselves rather than making the simulation models directly available on the internet.

THE SECOND EDITION

For this second edition we have chosen to maintain the key distinguishing features of the first edition, since the feedback we have received suggested that the book has in fact helped to fill a gap between the typical intermediate undergraduate text and advanced texts used at the graduate level. Thus we have stuck to the choice of topics and the technical level of the exposition in the first edition.

Contents: what is new?

Revising the book has not been easy, however. As we were working on the new edition, the worst financial and economic crisis since the Great Depression unfolded before our eyes, and the state of the business cycle and the stance and focus of macroeconomic policy changed at a breathtaking pace. Much empirical material updated just a few months earlier soon came to seem outdated. Like many other observers, we expect that the recent financial crisis will (and should) have a strong impact on macroeconomic research, hopefully leading to important new theoretical and empirical insights. For example, one may speculate that recent developments will accelerate the search for viable alternatives to the rational expectations hypothesis and for models that will deepen our understanding of the role of the financial sector in the macroeconomy. The enormous fiscal stimulus packages recently enacted in many countries should also allow new tests of competing theories of the effects of fiscal policy.

However, it is of course too early to say how the recent crisis experience will affect macroeconomic research and teaching. In this new edition we have made many references to the financial crisis and have updated several case stories to illustrate how our analysis can throw light on various aspects of the crisis. For example, we pay more attention to the challenges for stabilization policy arising when the nominal policy interest rate hits its zero bound, as it has (almost) done during the financial crisis. We have also included a critical discussion of Efficient Markets Theory and the roles of the housing market and monetary policy in the run-up to the crisis. Further, we now highlight how shocks to market risk premia fit into our AS–AD framework. Most importantly, we have completely rewritten our previous introductory chapter on stabilization policy, splitting it into two separate chapters containing a more thorough discussion of the welfare costs of business cycles and a more detailed analysis of optimal stabilization policy under alternative assumptions on the information available to policy makers. In this way we have brought the treatment of stabilization policy more up to date with recent research as well as with recent real-world events.

More generally, we have updated most of the empirical material and case studies in the book to account for new data and recent economic developments. To make room for the new material mentioned above, we decided to remove Chapter 10 from the First Edition, since this chapter on the microfoundations of R&D-based endogenous growth was more advanced than the rest of the book and hence may have been beyond the reach of many students. However, this chapter will be freely available from the website for the book for use by those teachers who find it useful. Further, we have eliminated the previous Chapter 26 on the choice of exchange rate regime as a separate chapter, but most of the material from that chapter has been written into Chapters 23 through 25 where it fits in more naturally.

A new pedagogical feature

In terms of exposition, an important new feature is that we have included a number of boxes in each chapter highlighting and summing up the most important definitions and results to help students keep track of the main insights and the chain of reasoning in the chapter. These boxes are complementary to the chapter summaries which we have maintained for the reader's convenience.

Peter Birch Sørensen and Hans Jørgen Whitta-Jacobsen
January 2010

Guided Tour

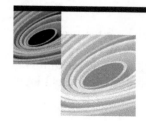

Book Openers

There are two Book Openers which introduce the topics and themes covered within the two Books of the text

Part Openers

There are seven Part Openers which, like the Book Openers, introduce the topics and themes covered throughout the Parts of the text

Figures and Tables

Each chapter provides a number of figures and tables to help you to visualise the various economic models, and to illustrate and summarise important concepts

Boxed Material

Key formulae and short summaries are pulled from the text and placed in boxes for easy reference

15.5 Summary

1. Private consumption is by far
and services. A satisfactory th
stylized facts that the average
disposable income in microecc
in long-run macroeconomic ti

2. The properties of the aggregate
behaviour of a representative c
over time, subject to his intert
this constraint implies that the
sum of the consumer's initial i
value of current and future dis

3. In the consumer's optimum, th
future consumption equals the
the real rate of interest. When
consumer will want to smooth

Summary

This briefly reviews and reinforces the main
topics you will have covered in each chapter to
ensure you have acquired a solid understanding of
the key topics

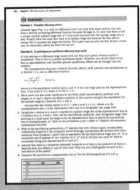

Exercises

These exercises encourage you to review and
apply the knowledge you have gained from each
chapter and can be undertaken to test your
understanding of key topics

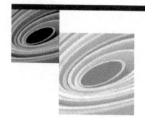

Technology to enhance learning and teaching

*Visit **www.mheducation.co.uk/textbooks/sorensen2** today*

Online Learning Centre (OLC)

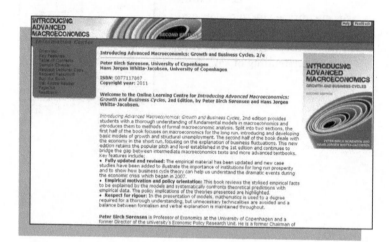

After completing each chapter, log on to the supporting Online Learning Centre website. Take advantage of the study tools offered to reinforce the material you have read in the text, and to develop your knowledge of economics in a fun and effective way. Resources include:

For Lecturers:
- Solutions to exercises in the book
- PowerPoint slides
- Artwork from the text
- Chapters removed from the first edition

For Students:
- Chapter summaries
- Exercises

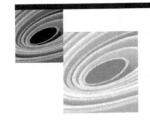

Custom Publishing Solutions: Let us help make our content your solution

At McGraw-Hill Education our aim is to help lecturers to find the most suitable content for their needs delivered to their students in the most appropriate way. Our **custom publishing solutions** offer the ideal combination of content delivered in the way which best suits lecturer and students.

Our custom publishing programme offers lecturers the opportunity to select just the chapters or sections of material they wish to deliver to their students from a database called CREATE™ at **http://create.mheducation.com/uk/**

CREATE™ contains over two million pages of content from:

- textbooks
- professional books
- case books – Harvard Articles, Insead, Ivey, Darden, Thunderbird and BusinessWeek
- Taking Sides – debate materials

Across the following imprints:

- McGraw–Hill Education
- Open University Press
- Harvard Business Publishing
- US and European material

There is also the option to include additional material authored by lecturers in the custom product – this does not necessarily have to be in English.

We will take care of everything from start to finish in the process of developing and delivering a custom product to ensure that lecturers and students receive exactly the material needed in the most suitable way.

With a Custom Publishing Solution, students enjoy the best selection of material deemed to be the most suitable for learning everything they need for their courses – something of real value to support their learning. Teachers are able to use exactly the material they want, in the way they want, to support their teaching on the course.

Please contact your local McGraw-Hill representative with any questions or alternatively contact **e:** custom.publishing@mheducation.com.

Improve Your Grades!
20% off any Study Skills book!

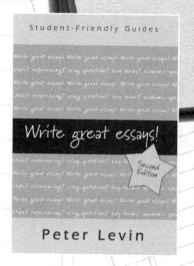

Our Study Skills books are packed with practical advice and tips that are easy to put into practice and will really improve the way you study. Our books will help you:

- Improve your grades
- Avoid plagiarism
- Save time
- Develop new skills

- Write confidently
- Undertake research projects
- Sail through exams
- Find the perfect job

Visit our website to read helpful hints about essays, exams, dissertations and find out about our offers.

www.openup.co.uk/studyskills

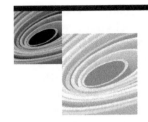

Acknowledgements

Many people have helped us in one way or another in preparing this manuscript. Our Copenhagen University colleagues Carl-Johan Dalgaard and Henrik Jensen provided very helpful critical comments on earlier drafts of many chapters of the book. Peter Allerup offered valuable comments on a previous version of Chapter 14 from the perspective of a statistician. We also received many useful suggestions from Michael Goldberg, Christian Groth and our teaching assistants Niels Christian Beier, Morten Dalgaard, Jakob Legaard Jakobsen, Søren Bjerregaard Nielsen, Søren Pedersen and Thorben Velling. In addition, we benefitted from numerous constructive comments from the many reviewers solicited by McGraw-Hill Education. Of course, none of these persons should be held accountable for any remaining errors or shortcomings.

Our research assistants Frederik Engholm Hansen, Jes Winther Hansen, Nicolai Kaarsen and Nicolaj Verdelin provided dedicated and invaluable help in gathering data, producing graphs and tables, and assisting in the empirical analyses presented in this book. We are very grateful for all their hard work. We are also grateful to the Institute of Economics at the University of Copenhagen for partly funding this research assistance.

Several colleagues were very helpful in providing us with data. These include Karsten Albæk, Anders Møller Christensen, Mette Ejrnæs, Henrik Hansen, Jesper Linaa, Heino Bohn Nielsen, Erik Haller Pedersen, Jan Overgaard Olesen, Torsten Sløk and John Smidt. Henrik Hansen also gave a helping hand with the appendix on regression analysis.

Throughout the preparation of the manuscript, the staff at McGraw-Hill Education has been most helpful and supportive.

When writing a textbook, one is of course standing on the shoulders of numerous intellectual giants, past and present. It would be onerous to mention all the colleagues in the profession who have inspired us, directly or indirectly. However, readers familiar with the works and textbooks by Charles I. Jones and by N. Gregory Mankiw will note that we have been particularly inspired by Jones' approach to and exposition of the theory of economic growth, and by Mankiw's approach to macroeconomics in general. While owing a lot to many other colleagues, we would like to acknowledge our special intellectual debt to Jones and Mankiw.

Finally, we are indebted to our families for their patience while we were working long hours to finish this project.

In revising the book we have benefited from excellent and enthusiastic research assistance from Mathias Bredkjær. We are very grateful to him for all his hard work. Thanks are also due to Niels Lynggaard Hansen from Danmarks Nationalbank and to John Smidt from the Secretariat of the Danish Economic Council who both provided us with valuable new data. Finally, we wish to thank Professor Neil Rankin from the University of York whose constructive review of the First Edition in the *Danish Economic Journal* provided inspiration for the revision. Thanks also go to reviewers of drafts for the chapters of the Second Edition and to Thomas Hill from McGraw-Hill for his patience as we struggled to finish this revision.

Our thanks go to the following reviewers for their comments at various stages in the text's development:

Giovanni Caggiano	University of Glasgow
Sanjit Dhami	University of Leicester
Per-Ola Maneschiöld	University of Skövde
Christopher Martin	Brunel University
Goncalo Monteiro	University at Buffalo
Ragnar Nymoen	University of Oslo
Roxana Radulescu	Newcastle University

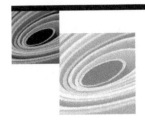

About the Authors

Peter Birch Sørensen is Chief Economist of the Danish central bank and a former Professor of Economics at the University of Copenhagen. From 2004 through 2009 he was Chairman of the Danish Economic Council, and he has served as a consultant on tax policy for the OECD, the European Commission and the International Monetary Fund.

Hans Jørgen Whitta-Jacobsen is Professor of Economics at the University of Copenhagen and Chairman of the Danish Economic Council. He has served as a consultant for the Danish government on tax reform and as a reporter on economic issues for the main Danish public service TV channel.

Macroeconomics for the long run and for the short run

What is the subject matter of macroeconomics? What methods and simplifying assumptions do macroeconomists use in their efforts to explain how the economy works? These are the issues addressed in this introductory chapter.

The chapter explains the philosophy underlying our course in macroeconomics. In particular, it explains why we have divided the main body of the text into two Books, one concerned with the long run, and another one dealing with the short run. Reading this chapter will help you to understand the links between the following chapters and to see where the material in each individual chapter fits into the big scheme. In addition, this chapter presents some important concepts and elements of macroeconomic models which we will use repeatedly in later chapters.

We start by discussing how to define macroeconomics. We then go on to explain why it is useful to develop separate macroeconomic theories for the long run and for the short run, and we present the essential assumptions underlying these two branches of macroeconomics as well as their main implications. In particular, we explain how the assumptions behind macroeconomics for the long run lead to the idea of a 'natural' level of economic activity. We also provide a theoretical foundation for the existence of nominal wage and price rigidities which are crucial for understanding fluctuations in economic activity in the short run.

1.1 What is macroeconomics?

It seems natural for a macroeconomic textbook to start by giving a general definition of macroeconomics. Yet you are not going to see a perfectly clear definition here; we simply do not think that there is one. In fact, economists have even found it hard to offer a clear-cut definition of the general science of economics.

The economist and Nobel Prize winner Gary Becker once said that 'economics is the study of the allocation of scarce resources to satisfy competing ends'.[1] This certainly says something essential about what (mainly micro) economics is. However, some parts of macroeconomics are concerned with situations where resources are *not* scarce, because the available supplies of labour and capital are not fully utilized. These important real-world situations would not fall within the realm of economics according to the above definition.

Given the difficulties of providing a brief and accurate definition of economics, one should not be surprised that a perfectly clear subdivision into micro- and macroeconomics

---

1. The idea behind this definition goes back to the nineteenth century, and the first scholar to give a comprehensive statement of it was Lionel Robbins in his famous *Essay on the Nature and Significance of Economic Science*, London, Macmillan, First edition, 1932.

is also elusive. It is sometimes said that macroeconomics is that part of economics which is concerned with the economy as a whole. This suggests that microeconomics focuses only on the small elements of the economy such as the single agent or the market for a particular product. Although much of macroeconomics *is* concerned with the economy in the large, this distinction between macro and micro is inaccurate. Important parts of macroeconomics are not (directly) concerned with the whole economy, but rather with understanding particular markets such as the labour market or the credit market. And a large and important part of microeconomics, general equilibrium theory, is concerned with the *interaction* among markets, that is, with the economy as a whole.

We therefore think that the best characterization of macroeconomics is one that simply states the main questions asked in this branch of economics.

A definition of macroeconomics by subject

What creates growth in aggregate output and income per capita in the long run? And what causes the fluctuations in economic activity that we observe in the short run? These are the basic questions in macroeconomics. At the risk of oversimplifying, we may therefore say that *macroeconomics is the study of economic growth and business cycles.* As we shall see later on, to explain the movements in total output we must also understand the movements in total consumption, investment and the rate of unemployment, as well as the interaction of these real variables with nominal variables such as the general level of wages, prices, nominal interest rates, foreign exchange rates, etc. Hence macroeconomics also includes the study of these variables.

A definition of macroeconomics by method

What we have offered above is a definition of macroeconomics by subject: macroeconomics is defined by the issues studied by macroeconomists. A strict 'empiricist' version of this definition, which also involves the choice of method, is to say that *macroeconomics is concerned with explaining observed time series for economic variables like GDP, consumption, investment, prices and wages, the rate of unemployment, etc.* This reflects the view that a scientific discipline should be defined in terms of the data it seeks to explain.

We do not agree completely with this view. We do think there are some purely theoretical scientific contributions that should be considered as part of the body of macroeconomics. However, like the rest of the macroeconomics profession, we are heavily influenced by the empiricist view. To secure the link between theory and the real world, theories should be evaluated by holding them up against the facts, and new theory should ideally be justified and accompanied by illustrative empirical material. You will see that our book very much reflects this approach.[2]

Why do macroeconomists aggregate?

The variables entering into macroeconomic models are typically *aggregate* variables covering the economy as a whole. For instance, in macroeconomics we often describe the entire production side of the economy as if a single commodity were produced by the use of just two different inputs, capital and labour, both one-dimensional variables which can be represented by a number. By contrast, microeconomics studies disaggregated models in which it is typically not 'allowed' to aggregate the production of, say, oranges and apples into the production of fruit.

The aggregation undertaken in macroeconomic models raises obvious problems. Take the concept of the aggregate capital stock, for example. Capital is defined as produced means

2. According to this view it is important that one is familiar with the definitions of the main statistical series on macroeconomic variables. We do not include the definitions in this book, since we assume that you know the basic concepts of national income accounting and the standard measures of inflation and unemployment, etc., from an earlier course in macroeconomics.

of production, so it includes, for example, buildings as well as computers. How should the quantities of these two capital goods be added into one number representing their combined productivity? In practice, the aggregate real capital stock is measured by multiplying the quantities of the different capital goods by their respective prices in some base year, and then adding up the values of the stocks of buildings, computers, etc., calculated at the fixed base-year prices. This would seem to be a sensible way of measuring the quantity of aggregate capital input provided the relative prices of the different capital goods remain reasonably constant over time. But we know that over the past decades the relative price of computers has decreased enormously, and at the same time computers have become tremendously more productive. Using relative prices to obtain an aggregate measure of capital representing the productivity of produced inputs is therefore a dubious procedure.

Nevertheless, the assumption that capital input as well as total output can be represented by single numbers is standard in macroeconomics. How can we defend, for instance, letting the production of myriads of different goods and services be represented by one number called 'aggregate output'? There are several lines of defence:

1. Over time the outputs of a lot of goods and services – including capital goods – do in fact tend to move in the same direction. Given that the production volumes of most industries tend to be positively correlated, it seems defensible to use concepts like aggregate output or aggregate investment, even if we do not have a method of measuring these aggregates which is fully correct in all circumstances.

2. The economy is such a complex mechanism that we cannot hope to explain and describe it in all detail. To understand at least some of the economic regularities observed, we have to make strong simplifications by abstracting from many details. Aggregation of variables is one convenient way of simplifying.

3. Whether a certain highly simplifying assumption is useful or not is ultimately an empirical question. If a model built on strong simplifications yields predictions which accord with observed movements in some economic variables, then that model seems useful for understanding (some of) the determinants of those variables. Presumably, it will then also be useful for evaluating the effects of economic policies intended to affect the variables considered.

Economist Robert Solow (of whom you will hear a lot more in this course) has put it the following way:

All theory depends on assumptions which are not quite true. That is what makes it theory. The art of successful theorizing is to make the inevitable simplifying assumptions in such a way that the final results are not very sensitive.[3]

The long run versus the short run

From our discussion it should be no surprise that in our view the best definition of macroeconomics is:

MACROECONOMICS: THE STUDY OF GROWTH AND BUSINESS CYCLES

Macroeconomics is the part of economics seeking answers to the questions: 'what creates growth in income per capita in the long run?' and 'what creates fluctuations in aggregate income in the short run?' It also tries to answer some related questions such as: 'what explains the level of long-run unemployment?', and 'what explains the short-run variations in unemployment?'

3. Robert M. Solow, 'A Contribution to the Theory of Economic Growth', *Quarterly Journal of Economics*, **70**, 1956, pp. 65–94.

Because these questions relate to different time horizons, we have organized the main body of this text in two Books, where the first is concerned with the long-run questions above, and the second is concerned with the short-run questions.

We find both parts of macroeconomics very important, but one can argue that the issues addressed in long-run macroeconomics are the most important ones. Consider a poor country like Uganda whose GDP per capita is only about 3 per cent of GDP per capita in the USA. A typical policy issue in long-run macroeconomics is: how could a country like Uganda initiate a growth process that would gradually take it up to, say, 20 per cent of the US level? A typical policy issue in short-run macroeconomics is: what could a government in, say, the UK, Sweden, Denmark or the Netherlands do to avoid an increase in the rate of unemployment from 5 to 8 per cent which would otherwise follow a negative shock to the economy? We do find the latter question very important, but for anyone concerned with the long-run welfare of human beings, the first type of question seems more essential.

1.2 Long-run and short-run macroeconomic phenomena

The distinction between long-run and short-run macroeconomics is first and fundamentally a distinction between the *phenomena we want to understand*. This leads to a distinction between the *fundamental characteristics of the models* we use, and of the *policies we analyse*. Below we will motivate these statements and explain the nature of the difference between long-run and short-run macroeconomic models.

Let us start by looking at some data. In Figs 1.1 and 1.2 we have chosen to focus on two countries, the USA and Denmark, since these two nations can be seen as polar cases: the USA is a large and relatively closed economy with a fairly small public sector (by European standards), whereas Denmark is a small and relatively open economy with a large public sector. We want to illustrate that, despite these differences, some important qualitative features of the data are shared between the two economies. Similar figures drawn for countries like the UK, Sweden, the Netherlands, and for practically any developed market economy would show the same qualitative features.

In Fig. 1.1 the natural logarithms of the annual real GDPs of the USA and Denmark are drawn up for the period from 1873 to recently, with the value in 1873 indexed to 100 for both countries. Figure 1.2 shows the average annual rates of unemployment for the two countries during the past and present century. In both figures the actual data are represented by the most solidly drawn zig-zagged curves.

The figures also include grey curves which are much more smooth. These are meant to express the *trends* of the relevant series. In Chapter 13 you will learn about a technique for constructing such a trend (that technique has in fact been used here). For now, let us just view the trend curves intuitively as the curves which a man in the street would draw with a pencil if he were asked to illustrate the 'underlying movement' or the 'underlying gravity level'.

In any event, the figures suggest that one way to interpret the movements of each of the series is to view them as being made up of two components: a *trend component* representing the overall evolution and captured by the smooth curves, and a *cyclical component* representing the year-to-year fluctuations and captured by the shifting vertical deviations between the actual data curve and the trend curve.

You may find that the cyclical components in Fig. 1.1 do not seem that great. To highlight the fluctuations (around the long-run trend), we have drawn Fig. 1.3 which shows the annual rate of change in real GDP, and the annual absolute change in the rate of unemployment for the USA and Denmark for the shorter period 1980–2008. The annual rate of change in GDP varies from sometimes higher than 6 per cent, down to sometimes around −2 per cent, and the rate of unemployment occasionally increases by up to two percentage points in just one year, and also sometimes drops by two points in one year. These cyclical movements are of considerable size. Final data for 2009 were not available at the time the manuscript for this book was completed, but the worldwide financial and economic crisis that exploded in the

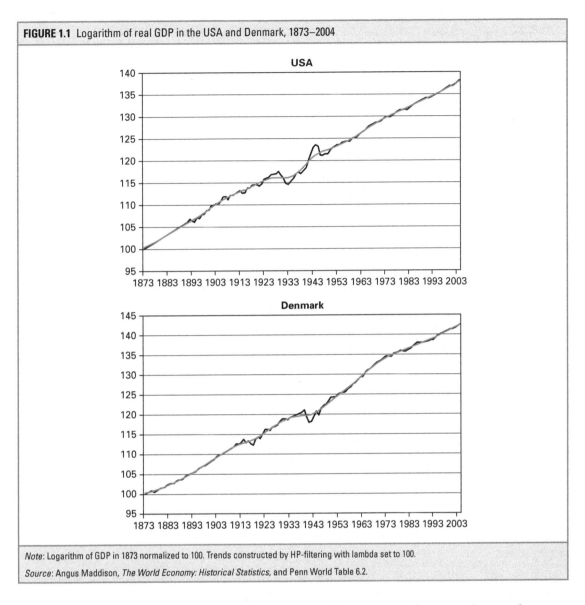

FIGURE 1.1 Logarithm of real GDP in the USA and Denmark, 1873–2004

Note: Logarithm of GDP in 1873 normalized to 100. Trends constructed by HP-filtering with lambda set to 100.

Source: Angus Maddison, *The World Economy: Historical Statistics*, and Penn World Table 6.2.

fall of 2008 implied negative values of GDP growth and increases in the rates of unemployment larger than the largest ones reported in the figure. Including the latest financial crisis period would only make the fluctuations appear larger.

The two main branches of macroeconomics are exactly divided by one being concerned with the trends of main economic time series, and the other with the considerable fluctuations around the trends:

THE SUBJECT MATTER OF MACROECONOMICS FOR THE LONG RUN AND FOR THE SHORT RUN

Macroeconomics for the long run is about understanding the **trends** in the most important macroeconomic series for GDP, consumption, investment, unemployment, etc., thus seeking explanations for long-run income levels and economic growth and so-called structural unemployment. Macroeconomics for the short run is about understanding the annual or quarterly **fluctuations** around trend in the most important macroeconomic series, thus seeking explanations for business cycles.

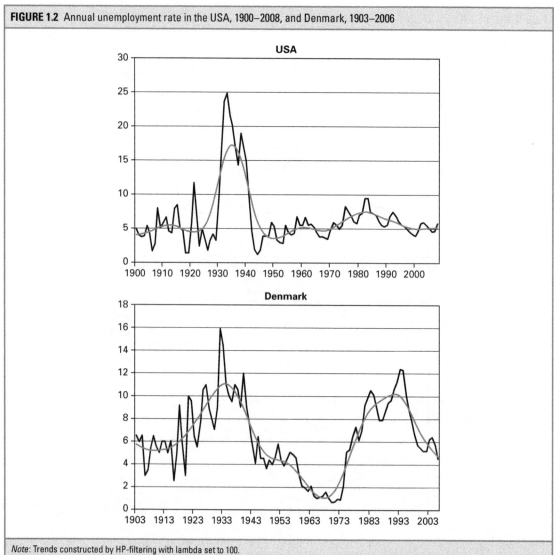

FIGURE 1.2 Annual unemployment rate in the USA, 1900–2008, and Denmark, 1903–2006

Note: Trends constructed by HP-filtering with lambda set to 100.

Sources: R.B. Mitchell, *International Historical Statistics*, Macmillan, 1998; US Bureau of Labor Statistics; S.A. Hansen, *Økonomisk Væksti Danmark*, Bind 2, 1914–83, Akademisk Forlag, 1984; Statistics Denmark (Statistisk Tiårsoversigt).

   Note how each part of macroeconomic theory corresponds to each of the main questions asked in our definition of macroeconomics.

   Most economists believe that an understanding of the trend requires a different type of explanation than an understanding of the fluctuations. The different macroeconomic models are formal expressions of these different explanations. The fundamental assumptions of the models for the long run and for the short run therefore differ, and hence the models themselves become different.[4] But why should there be different macroeconomic theories for understanding the trends and for explaining the fluctuations? We will now consider this question in more detail.

---

4. Not all economists think that different assumptions are necessarily needed to explain short-run and long-run macroeconomic phenomena. Some believe that one model can be used for understanding both growth and fluctuations, since they do not see the fluctuations as coming (only) from exogenous shocks, but (also) from forces within the economic system itself. This hypothesis of *endogenous* business cycles is too advanced for the present course.

1.3   Macroeconomic theory for the short run

It may be illuminating to start with an example. Consider the Danish economy in 1993 and 1994 as illustrated in Fig. 1.3. In 1993 Danish real GDP was completely stagnant, but in 1994 it increased by about 5.5 per cent! This dramatic shift affected the rate of unemployment which dropped by almost two percentage points in one year.

Exogenous shocks

A standard macroeconomic explanation for this short-run fluctuation would start by saying that in 1994 the Danish economy was hit by a positive *exogenous shock*, that is, by a sudden event which is viewed as coming from outside the (Danish) economic system. Such an event could be either a *supply shock* like a sudden increase in the productivity of resources, or a *demand shock* like a sudden rise in domestic consumption, investment or exports rooted, for example, in more optimistic expectations concerning the future, or in a more expansionary fiscal or monetary policy, or in a sudden increase in the demand for Danish exports. Danish fiscal policy was in fact relaxed in 1993–94, and the real interest rate fell at that time. Moreover, the Danish export markets in Europe started to grow more quickly in 1994. Thus we may assume that the 1994 shock was mainly a positive demand shock.

    To say that the sudden increase in Danish production was caused by an exogenous shock, basically an unexplained event, is not exactly deep. But note two things. First, economies *are* hit all the time by sudden events which are, perhaps, best considered as exogenous from the viewpoint of economic theory. For example, economists should not be concerned with explaining fluctuations in harvests due to shifting weather conditions, and probably they should not try to explain *all* sudden changes in the moods of consumers and investors. Focusing on the small economy of Denmark, a sudden increase in the demand for exports due to events in foreign countries should also be considered exogenous. Second, the occurrence of the shock is not the end of the story. A shock may be what *initiated* the change in economic activity, but it cannot itself explain all the subsequent economic reactions of households and firms. There is more explanation to do.

Nominal rigidities

For an increase in the aggregate demand for goods and services to lead to an increase in production, as observed in Denmark in 1994, it must have been profitable for Danish firms to increase their supply of output to accommodate the increase in demand. In the short run the capital stock is more or less given, so production can only increase if more labour is used. As more workers come to utilize the given capital stock, the marginal productivity of additional hours worked is likely to decline. If the marginal productivity of labour is indeed falling, it seems plausible that firms will only want to expand employment if the real wage falls. The real wage rate is defined as W/P, where W is the money wage rate and P is the price level. Presumably the higher demand for goods and services will lead to some increase in P. If the nominal wage rate W is rigid in the short run, this rise in prices will indeed cause a fall in the real wage, inducing firms to hire more labour to increase their supply of output.

    Thus another key ingredient in our explanation of the fluctuation is the assumption of some *short-run nominal rigidity*, in this case a rigid money wage. The assumption that nominal wage rates are fixed for a certain period of time is quite realistic. Firms and workers do not renegotiate their wage rates every day or every month, because negotiation is a time-consuming process involving the risk of unpleasant and costly industrial conflict.

    But experience also indicates that the nominal prices of most goods and services are only adjusted with certain time intervals. In an interesting empirical analysis of newsstand prices of American magazines, economist Stephen G. Cecchetti found that under an average general inflation of 4 per cent per year magazine prices were changed only every 6 years on average.

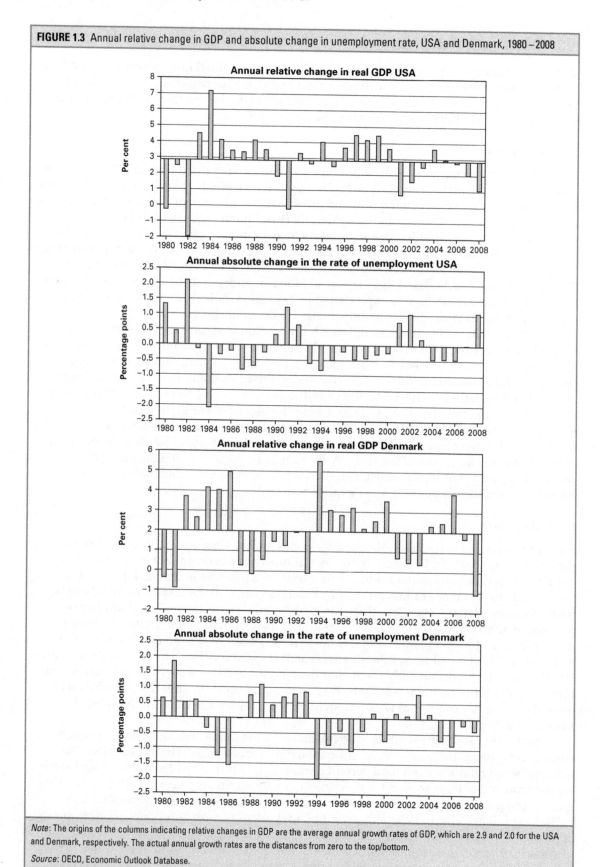

FIGURE 1.3 Annual relative change in GDP and absolute change in unemployment rate, USA and Denmark, 1980 – 2008

Note: The origins of the columns indicating relative changes in GDP are the average annual growth rates of GDP, which are 2.9 and 2.0 for the USA and Denmark, respectively. The actual annual growth rates are the distances from zero to the top/bottom.

Source: OECD, Economic Outlook Database.

This means that on average the real price of a magazine is eroded by about 25 per cent by inflation before the nominal price is changed.[5]

The rigidity of nominal magazine prices is not just a special case. In an empirical analysis of price rigidity, economist Alan Blinder asked a sample of business managers: 'How often do the prices of your most important products change in a typical year?' About 50 per cent of the managers responded that they changed their prices only once or less than once a year.[6] Explaining why (most) firms do not immediately adjust their prices in response to changes in demand and cost is an intriguing issue to which we return in Section 1.5 below.

We argued above that a rigid nominal wage in association with a flexible, upward-adjusting nominal price could create the fall in real wages that would make it profitable for firms to supply more output in response to a positive demand shock. If a fall in the real wage is the typical reason why firms want to increase their output in reaction to a positive demand shock, we should expect to observe a negative relationship between output and real wages 'over the business cycle'. However, output often increases without a simultaneous decrease in real wages. It is therefore important to ask if an increase in the demand for output can induce firms to increase their supply even if *all* nominal prices are fixed in the short run (so the real wage does not fall). The answer is 'yes', provided that prices are *above* marginal costs before the demand shock hits the economy. In practice, most markets are characterized by *imperfect competition* where firms have some monopoly power enabling them to charge prices which are indeed above marginal costs. In that case they will be able to increase their total profit by increasing their output in response to an increase in demand, even if they have to keep their prices fixed temporarily.

The basic point is that short-run nominal price or wage rigidity can explain why an exogenous increase in *nominal* aggregate demand leads to a short-run increase in *real* output and employment. If nominal prices are fixed, all of the increase in demand will be reflected in a rise in real output, because imperfectly competitive firms will be happy to increase their supply as long as their (fixed) prices remain above marginal costs. And even if prices increase in response to higher demand, a rigid nominal wage means that the price hike will drive down the real wage which in turn will stimulate employment and output. In practice, both nominal wages and nominal prices are rigid in the short run, although to different degrees in different markets.

Expectational errors

So far our explanation for the short-run fluctuation in Danish output has relied on two ingredients: exogenous shocks and short-run nominal rigidities. But there is a third ingredient which is essential for a full understanding of the fluctuation: *expectational errors*. To see this, consider the Danish boom in 1994 and suppose that there was in fact some fall in the Danish real wage, as some prices increased in response to growing demand and nominal wages lagged behind. Faced with falling real wages, why were Danish workers nevertheless willing to increase their supply of labour, thereby enabling firms to expand employment and output? One possible answer is that trade unions in the heavily unionized Danish labour market had pushed real wages above the marginal disutility of work so that some workers were involuntarily unemployed prior to the demand boom. By definition, a worker who is involuntarily unemployed is willing to take a job even if the real wage falls below its current level (provided it does not fall too much).

But this hypothesis only begs the question why trade unions faced with growing labour demand would allow the real wage to fall. If unions were bargaining in 1993 to achieve a

---

5. Stephen G. Cecchetti: 'The Frequency of Price Adjustment: A Study of the Newsstand Prices of Magazines', *Journal of Econometrics*, **31**, 1986, pp. 255–274.

6. Alan S. Blinder: 'On Sticky Prices: Academic Theories Meet the Real World', in N.G. Mankiw, ed., *Monetary Policy*, Chicago, University of Chicago Press, 1994.

certain real wage ω for 1994, why would they suddenly accept that the real wage fell below the target for 1994 at a time when labour demand was increasing? The most plausible answer is that the fall in real wages was *unintended* by unions. If unions had perfectly anticipated the positive 1994 demand shock and its effect on the price level, they would have bargained for a higher 1994 money wage rate to secure their target real wage ω, that is, they would have demanded a money wage satisfying $W = P \cdot \omega$.

However, since (most) wages had to be set *before* the occurrence of the shock, and since the shock was *not* perfectly foreseen, the negotiated money wage had to be based on the *expected* price level P^e which did not include the full inflationary effect of the shock: $W = P^e \cdot \omega < P \cdot \omega$. When the shock hit and prices increased above their expected level, unions were locked into their nominal wage contracts, and given the employer's right to hire more workers at the negotiated money wage, unions had to allow their members to supply additional labour even though the *realized* real wage, W/P, turned out to be lower than the *target* real wage, $W/P^e = \omega$.

This example illustrates our point that business fluctuations typically involve expectational errors, in this case errors made by workers (trade unions). In the case where some prices as well as money wages are rigid in the short run, an unanticipated shock will also cause some firms to err in their expectations. When firms pre-set their prices for a certain period, they will base their pricing decisions on their expected costs which will be influenced by the expected general price level P^e. When the unanticipated shock hits the economy, some firms (call them Group 1) will be just about to adjust their prices and will be able to account for the inflationary cost effect of the shock. But many other firms (Group 2) which have recently reset their prices will choose to maintain their existing prices for a while, even though the increase in the prices charged by Group 1 firms drives the costs of Group 2 firms above the previously expected level. As long as the shock does not push marginal costs above the pre-set prices, even Group 2 firms will want to expand their output to accommodate the unexpected rise in demand.

MODELLING ASSUMPTIONS OF MACROECONOMICS FOR THE SHORT RUN

Macroeconomic theory for the short run, intended to explain the economic fluctuations from year to year or from quarter to quarter, typically includes the following three modelling features:

1. exogenous shocks, i.e., sudden abrupt influences on the economy coming from changes in preferences, technology, or economic policies,

2. short-run nominal rigidity, i.e., some period after the occurrence of a shock during which some prices and/or wages are sticky, and

3. expectational errors, i.e., a period after the occurrence of a shock during which some prices are different from what was expected before the shock.[7]

---

7. Some short-run macroeconomic theories do not assume price rigidity, e.g. the theory of Milton Friedman presented in 'The Role of Monetary Policy', *American Economic Review*, **58**, 1968, pp. 1–17, and related more formal contributions such as Robert E. Lucas, Jr: 'Expectations and the Neutrality of Money', *Journal of Economic Theory*, **4**, 1972, pp. 103–124, or the real business cycle theory explained in Section 18.4. A main point in these theories is that fluctuations can be understood within a framework that only assumes shocks and possibly expectational errors. Hence one cannot conclude from the mere observation of fluctuations that wages or prices are rigid: fluctuations are theoretically compatible with all wages and prices being fully adjusted all the time, as we shall see in Chapters 17 and 18. In fact, a main point of real business cycle theory is that one and the same class of economic models can be used for understanding both long-run growth issues and short-run issues of fluctuations. The models in this class are much like the growth models to be dealt with in subsequent chapters. The only relevant element to add to the growth models to make them also models of fluctuations is, according to this view, exogenous supply shocks. We find this theoretically interesting, but today it is widely accepted that short-run price and wage rigidities are indeed important for understanding the economy's short-run reactions to shocks and that demand shocks are important.

1.4 Macroeconomic theory for the long run

While exogenous shocks, temporarily sticky wages or prices and erroneous expectations are required for an understanding of the changes from year to year in unemployment and GDP, most economists think that these features are best disregarded when we try to explain the 'gravity level' of the rate of unemployment and the trend-wise gradual growth of GDP over long periods. The smooth trend curves in Figs 1.1 and 1.2 could not possibly reflect a succession of random shocks over the more than 100 years considered. By definition, shocks have to go in opposite directions from time to time. If technology improves constantly each year to imply a 2 per cent increase in GDP per head, then this annual shift in technology should not be considered as a shock, but rather as a foreseeable gradual movement. Moreover, although nominal wages and prices may be sticky in the short run, they do adjust in the longer run. In macroeconomics for the long run we therefore abstract from the three features which define short-run macroeconomics.

Long-run modelling: the basic assumptions

In other words, *macroeconomic theory for the long run*, intended to explain the trend-wise movements of main economic variables around which the year-to-year fluctuations occur, portrays the economy **as if** *exogenous shocks do not occur*, i.e., the economic fundamentals like preferences and technology develop in a smooth and foreseeable way over time; *prices are fully adjusted* in all periods in accordance with the economy's full long-run price flexibility; and *expectations are correct* all the time.

You should carefully note the 'as if' in this definition. If the assumptions of macroeconomics for the short run give the right picture, then in (almost) every year the economy will be reacting to shocks, with prices still not fully adjusted and expectational errors still prevailing. This is because new shocks occur all the time. Nevertheless, certain phenomena may be better understood by considering the economy *as if* shocks did not occur, prices were always fully adjusted, and expectations always correct. Among such phenomena we include the long-run growth performance and the long-run gravity level of unemployment. Thus macroeconomic models for the long run describe the underlying long-run equilibrium towards which the economy is gravitating, even though recurring shocks and the time-consuming adjustment to these shocks imply that the economy is never exactly in this long-run equilibrium.

To put it another way, in explaining how economic growth in Denmark could change from zero per cent in 1993 to 5.5 per cent in 1994, and unemployment at the same time be significantly reduced, we have to allow for exogenous shocks, price rigidities and expectational errors. In an explanation of the average annual GDP growth of 2.9 per cent over the period from 1950 to 2004, or of the average rate of unemployment of 5.7 per cent over the same period, it is better to abstract from these three complicating features to focus attention on the fundamental forces governing the long-run evolution of the economy.

MODELLING ASSUMPTIONS OF MACROECONOMICS FOR THE LONG RUN

In macroeconomic theory for the long run, intended to explain the trends of economic variables over the long run, the economy is analysed **as if**:

1. the economic fundamentals evolve smoothly and predictably over time (no exogenous shocks),
2. prices are adjusted in accordance with the economy's full long-run price flexibility (no short-run nominal rigidity), and
3. expectations are correct (no expectational errors).

Static versus dynamic models

A macroeconomic model for the long run can be a single-period *static* model. This may seem surprising, but sometimes it is useful to focus on a single period which is viewed as an 'end period' in the sense that no new shocks have occurred for a long time and the economy has finished all its adjustments. One can then describe the state of the economy in the end period. The purpose is to characterize the equilibrium towards which the economy is tending in the long run, without complicating the theory with an explicit analysis of the dynamic process which takes the economy to the long-run equilibrium. The models of long-run structural unemployment presented in Part 4 of this book will be of this nature.

By contrast, *dynamic* models for the long run describe the process of capital accumulation explicitly, and typically they also describe the evolution of other important stock variables such as the labour force, the stock of natural resources, etc. These models, also called growth models, always contain the following dynamic link between the current flow of investment and the increase in the stock of capital:

$$K_{t+1} - K_t = I_t - \delta K_t, \tag{1}$$

where K_t is the amount of capital available in period t, I_t is gross investment in period t, and δ is the rate at which capital depreciates, $0 < \delta < 1$. In a closed economy the level of gross investment I_t must equal gross savings S_t. For a closed economy the capital accumulation equation therefore becomes:

$$K_{t+1} - K_t = S_t - \delta K_t. \tag{2}$$

Thus savings play a central role in growth models. In many models it is simply assumed that households always save an exogenous fraction s of total income so that in any period t we have $S_t = sY_t$. The growth models using this assumption are called Solow models.[8]

In more advanced growth models savings are derived from maximization of utility functions under appropriate budget constraints. We leave these more complicated models for a later macroeconomics course. Solow models are well suited and widely used for understanding many growth issues. However, for analysing the effects of economic policies, these models have the shortcoming that they do not contain utility functions and therefore do not allow an explicit evaluation of the welfare consequences of alternative economic policies. In Solow models one will just have to look at the policy implications for economic variables like GDP or the level of consumption, and simply assume that it is 'good' to have high per capita income or consumption.

1.5 Real rigidities and the natural rate in macroeconomics for the long run

The assumption in long-run macroeconomics that all wages and prices are fully adjusted in all periods means that there are no *nominal* rigidities in the long term. But there may well be permanent *real* rigidities preventing real prices and wages from adjusting to the values which would prevail under perfect competition. The economy's long-run wage and price flexibility can be different from the flexibility assumed in the traditional model of perfect competition. We will now go through a simplified example to illustrate what we mean. For concreteness, we will show how real rigidities may arise from the market power of trade unions, but we emphasize that even if unions are weak or non-existent, there are

---

8.   They have this name after the Nobel Prize Laureate Robert M. Solow who made fundamental contributions to growth theory. Some of Solow's contributions are the subjects of Chapters 3 and 5 below.

other mechanisms which may cause significant real rigidities, as our analysis in Chapter 11 will make clear.

Consider an economy divided into many different sectors, each represented by a firm producing a differentiated product, and each having an industry trade union which controls the supply of labour to firms in the sector. Suppose for simplicity that labour is the only variable factor of production and that it takes one unit of labour to produce one unit of output in each sector. The average and marginal cost of production for the individual firm will then be equal to the wage rate for its industry. We assume that the representative firm of each sector faces a demand curve with a constant price elasticity of demand and that this elasticity is the same in all sectors. It is well known from microeconomics that when the price elasticity of demand is constant, a profit-maximizing firm will set its price as a constant mark-up over its marginal cost. Hence, if the average nominal wage level across sectors is W, the average price level P may be specified as:

$$P = m^P W, \qquad m^P > 1, \tag{3}$$

where m^P is the mark-up factor of the representative firm.

Now consider the trade union monopolizing the supply of labour to a particular sector i. To simplify, suppose the union is so strong that it can effectively dictate the nominal wage rate W_i to be paid by the firm representing sector i. The trade union sets the wage rate with the purpose of maximizing the objective function Ω where:

$$\Omega = \left(\frac{W_i}{P} - v \right) L_i. \tag{4}$$

Here L_i is the level of employment in sector i, W_i/P is the real wage for union members employed in firm i, and v is the real income which members are able to earn elsewhere if they fail to find a job in sector i. The variable v is sometimes referred to as the workers' 'outside option' and will be specified below. Since $W_i/P - v$ is the rent (surplus) which the individual union member earns by being employed in firm i rather than having to look for a job elsewhere, the magnitude Ω is the total rent that union members gain from employment in firm i. In Chapter 12 we shall explain in detail why it is reasonable to assume that the trade union wants to maximize this total rent; for the moment we ask you to accept this plausible assumption.

When setting the wage rate W_i, the union must take into account that a higher wage will induce the firm to hire fewer workers. If the union charges an average wage rate so that $W_i/W = 1$, the firm in sector i will have the same cost level as its competitors in other sectors and will experience an average volume of sales. The union may then expect to gain a proportional share of total employment, so employment in sector i will be L/n, where L is aggregate employment and n is the number of different sectors. But if the union for sector i raises its relative wage rate, W_i/W, its employer will have to raise his relative output price, leading to a lower volume of sales and employment in the sector. Noting from (3) that $W = P/m^P$, we may thus specify the demand for labour in sector i as:

$$L_i = \frac{L}{n} \left(\frac{W_i}{W} \right)^{-\sigma} = \frac{L}{n} \left(\frac{m^P W_i}{P} \right)^{-\sigma}, \qquad \sigma > 1, \tag{5}$$

where the parameter σ measures the numerical wage elasticity of labour demand. Since the trade union for sector i is small relative to the rest of the economy, it takes the outside option v and the general price level P as given. By setting the nominal wage rate, W_i, the union thus implicitly chooses its real wage, W_i/P. Using (5) to eliminate L_i from (4), and differentiating the resulting expression for Ω with respect to W_i, we obtain a necessary (first order) condition for the optimality of the wage rate set by the union. Since the log-function is increasing we may as well differentiate the log of Ω, which is convenient here:

$$\frac{d\ln\Omega}{dW_i} = \frac{1}{\dfrac{W_i}{P} - v}\frac{1}{P} - \sigma\frac{1}{W_i} = 0 \quad \Leftrightarrow$$

$$\frac{W_i}{P} = m^w v, \qquad m^w \equiv \frac{\sigma}{\sigma - 1} > 1. \tag{6}$$

We see that the union will set the real wage as a constant mark-up over the outside option. Let us take a closer look at this option. If the unemployment rate is u, the representative union member has a probability $1 - u$ of finding another job if he has to look for work outside sector i. In that case he may expect to earn the average real wage W/P. There is also a probability u that the union member will remain unemployed if he does not obtain a job in sector i. In that situation the worker will receive a real unemployment benefit, b, assumed to be lower than the average real wage. The outside option, defined as the real income a worker may expect to earn outside sector i, may thus be specified as:

$$v = (1 - u)\frac{W}{P} + ub. \tag{7}$$

From (6) and (7) we may derive a simple theory of long-run unemployment which will help to clarify the concept of real rigidities. Inserting (7) into (6), and denoting the real wage rates inside and outside firm i by w_i and w, respectively, we get:

$$w_i = m^w[(1 - u)w + ub], \qquad w_i \equiv \frac{W_i}{P}, \qquad w \equiv \frac{W}{P}. \tag{8}$$

Assuming that the union mark-up factor m^w is the same across sectors, it follows from (8) that trade unions will charge the same wage rate in all sectors. Hence we may set $w_i = w$ in (6) and solve for w to get:

$$w = \frac{m^w u}{1 - m^w(1 - u)}b = \frac{1}{1 - \dfrac{m^w - 1}{m^w}\dfrac{1}{u}}b, \tag{9}$$

where we assume $u > (m^w - 1)/m^w$ for a meaningful expression. Equation (9) is the economy's so-called *wage curve* showing how the real wage claimed by unions depends on the unemployment rate and the rate of unemployment benefit: under the condition just stated, the real wage claim falls if unemployment goes up.

In a macroeconomic equilibrium the real wage claimed by unions must be consistent with the real wage implicitly offered by firms through their price setting. According to (3), firms implicitly offer the real wage $w \equiv W/P = 1/m^p$. Inserting this into (9) and solving for u, we get the *long-run equilibrium unemployment rate*, also called the natural (or the structural) rate of unemployment:

$$\bar{u} = \frac{\dfrac{m^w - 1}{m^w}}{1 - m^p b} = \frac{m^w - 1}{m^w(1 - m^p b)}. \tag{10}$$

It follows immediately that if $m^w = 1$, then $\bar{u} = 0$. In other words, if unions have no market power and labour markets are characterized by perfect competition (a situation arising as the demand elasticity σ goes to infinity), the natural rate of unemployment is zero. You may check for yourself that the equilibrium unemployment rate will be positive and smaller than one provided that $m^w m^p b < 1$ or, equivalently, $b/w < 1/m^w$. Hence, if unions do have market power, $m^w > 1$, and the 'replacement ratio' b/w offered by the system of unemployment insurance is not 'too' high, we get a strictly positive and meaningful solution for the equilibrium unemployment rate. (Our assumption $m^w m^p b < 1$ implies $w > b$ as well as $\bar{u} > (m^w - 1)/m^w$ as assumed above, which you should check.) The monopoly power of the trade unions implies a real rigidity in the sense that an excess supply of labour (i.e., unemployment) can exist without creating any downward pressure on real wages.

Note that a positive unemployment rate emerges even though we did not assume any *nominal* rigidities: the nominal variables W and P can be freely scaled up or down in the equations above.

The unemployment problem is rooted in the market distortions reflected in the mark-up factors m^p and m^w. If there were no unions and labour markets were perfectly competitive, workers could not drive wages above their outside option. According to our simplified model equilibrium unemployment would then be zero, as you can see by setting $m^w = 1$ in (10). But unions *do* exist and *do* have market power.[9] In the situation where $m^w > 1$, the unemployment generated by union monopoly power will be *exacerbated* by imperfect competition in product markets. This is because weaker product market competition implies a higher value of the price mark-up, m^p, and according to (10), this will increase the value of $\bar{u}$: when firms drive down the level of real wages by pushing prices above marginal costs, the amount of involuntary unemployment must rise to bring union wage claims down in line with the real wages implicitly offered by firms through their monopolistic price setting. We also see from (10) that a higher level of unemployment benefits will raise the equilibrium unemployment rate when unions have market power.

When economists speak of 'real rigidities', they often mean that market imperfections permanently distort the real prices and real wages claimed by firms and workers away from the competitive relative (real) prices which would ensure full resource utilization. Even in the long run, when all nominal wages and prices have had time to fully adjust to their desired levels, these structural market distortions will persist, leaving the economy in a state of permanent unemployment. Our analysis suggests that the degree of real rigidity in the economy may be measured by the size of the parameters m^w, m^p and b which contribute to equilibrium unemployment. Alternatively, we might simply measure the degree of real rigidity by the size of the equilibrium unemployment rate, since we have seen that $\bar{u} = 0$ in the benchmark case of perfect competition.

According to established tradition in macroeconomics, the long-run equilibrium unemployment rate implied by the economy's *real* rigidities is called the *natural rate*. This is the rate of unemployment emerging when all relative prices have fully adjusted in accordance with the economy's long-run wage and price flexibility. In line with this tradition, we will use the term 'natural rate of resource utilization' to denote the rate at which factors of production are utilized in long-run equilibrium when the economy has exhausted its potential for price adjustment. By definition, there are no real rigidities if perfect competition prevails, since real (relative) prices in a competitive economy adjust until the demand for each resource equals the full supply of that resource. This just means that the natural rate of resource utilization is 100 per cent. If real rigidities do exist, the natural rate of resource utilization will be less than 100 per cent.

We have suggested that the degree of real rigidity may be measured by the *level* of the natural unemployment rate. We should add that economists sometimes find it fruitful to work with a slightly different concept of real rigidity. In this alternative definition, the degree of real rigidity is measured by the *responsiveness* of real wages and real prices to a short-run *change* in the unemployment rate away from the natural rate. If this responsiveness is low, the degree of real rigidity is said to be high. In Section 1.6 we will adopt this alternative notion of real rigidity which will turn out to be useful for explaining short-run nominal rigidities. At any rate, real rigidity in a broad sense refers to the fact that the economy's degree of relative price flexibility is less than it would be in an ideal world of perfect competition.

---

9. You may ask why rational workers would want to form trade unions if unions create involuntary unemployment. Chapter 12 will offer an answer to this.

The crucial role of the supply side in long-run modelling

As indicated by the simple example in Eq. (10), the natural rate of employment, $1 - \bar{u}$, is given from the *supply side* of the economy, since the parameters m^w, m^p and b are characteristics of the economy's supply side structures. This has an important implication: in macroeconomic models for the long run, where wages and prices are assumed to be fully adjusted in all periods, output is determined solely from the supply side. In any given period there is a certain labour force L, and a certain (predetermined) capital stock K. Output is then completely constrained from the supply side, since it cannot exceed the volume which can be produced by means of 'natural' labour input $(1 - \bar{u})L$ and the predetermined capital input K (here assuming that the natural rate of utilization for capital is one).

By contrast, in short-run macroeconomic models nominal wage and price rigidities and/or expectational errors may cause employment to deviate from its natural rate. Hence we do not have the simple supply side determination of employment just described. Instead, employment is also influenced by the aggregate *demand* for goods and services. Thus, in long-run macroeconomic models employment always corresponds to the natural rate, whereas in short-run models employment is determined also from the demand side and fluctuates around the natural rate.

THE NATURAL RATE AND OUTPUT DETERMINATION IN THE LONG RUN AND IN THE SHORT RUN

In macroeconomics for the long run, long-run real price rigidities may prevail and imply that natural rates of resource utilization are smaller than one, so there can be structural unemployment in the long run. Output is determined from the supply side as what can be produced from available resources when these are utilized at their natural rates.

In macroeconomics for the short run, short-run nominal price rigidities can prevent price adjustment from continuously ensuring that resources are utilized at natural rates. Therefore output is not determined from the supply side alone, but rather by an interaction between supply and demand. In the short run output can therefore fluctuate around the natural rate of output.

1.6 Explaining the nominal rigidities of macroeconomics for the short run

We noted earlier that some form of nominal rigidity typically plays an important part in the explanation of short-run business fluctuations. As we shall demonstrate in this section, the phenomenon of *real* rigidity discussed in the previous section may help us understand how short-run *nominal* rigidity may be compatible with rational economic behaviour. Specifically, we will show that when target real wages are not very responsive to changes in the level of economic activity, even very small costs of nominal wage or price adjustment may be sufficient to induce rational agents to abstain from adjusting nominal wages or prices in the short run in response to fluctuations in economic activity.

It is not unreasonable to assume that there are some small costs of adjusting nominal wage rates. For example, union leaders may have to spend some time sitting down at the bargaining table with the employer to write a new wage contract. Moreover, when the demand for labour changes, wage setters may have to spend some resources estimating the exact magnitude of the change if they want to be sure that they set the optimal wage rate. Similarly, firms may incur small costs in resetting their nominal prices. For instance, they may have to print new catalogues or spend other resources communicating the new prices to the market.

The costs of adjusting nominal prices or wages are often referred to as 'menu costs', like the costs to a restaurant of having to print a new menu card. In most cases such costs are likely to be quite small, and hence they are usually neglected in economic models. But if we can show that even very small menu costs may be sufficient to induce economic agents not to adjust nominal wages or prices in response to even considerable shocks, we have a potential explanation for the nominal rigidities which seem to exist in the real world.[10]

Explaining nominal wage stickiness

We start by considering the circumstances in which nominal wage rigidity may be the outcome of optimizing economic behaviour. Our strategy is to measure the loss incurred by individual wage setters if they do *not* adjust their nominal wage rate in reaction to a change in the unemployment rate of a realistic magnitude. If this loss is very small, then the privately optimal behaviour may be to leave the wage rate unchanged to avoid the cost of wage adjustment.

We base our analysis on the simple model of wage formation developed in the previous section, adding to this a shock and small menu costs. For convenience, we now assume that the system of unemployment insurance offers a fixed compensation relative to the average wage level, $b \equiv cw$, where the replacement rate $c < 1$ is a constant. Recalling that $w \equiv W/P$, the outside option (5) may then be written as a function of the unemployment rate:

$$v = v(u) = [1 - (1 - c)u]w. \tag{11}$$

A higher unemployment rate implies a lower value of the outside option. We do not state explicitly that the outside option v is also a function of the average economy-wide real wage w, since we know from (3) that w will remain constant at the level $1/m^p$ as long as nominal *prices* are not rigid. Inserting (11) into (6) and remembering that $w_i \equiv W_i/P$, we get the optimal real wage which the union would choose in the *absence* of any costs of wage adjustment:

$$w_i = m^w v(u) = m^w[1 - (1 - c)u]w. \tag{12}$$

Without loss of generality, we may choose our units of measurement such that the total labour force is normalized to unity, implying $L = 1 - u$. Hence, from Eq. (5), labour demand in each sector will be: $L_i = [(1 - u)/n](m^p w_i)^{-\sigma}$. Substituting this expression into our expression for Ω in (4), and also inserting the expression (11) for v, we may write the objective function for the union organizing the workers in sector i as:

$$\Omega(w_i, u) = (w_i - v(u)) \overbrace{\left(\frac{1 - u}{n}\right)(m^p w_i)^{-\sigma}}^{L_i}. \tag{13}$$

You may want to check again that the first-order condition for maximization of Ω with respect to w_i gives (12). We can now analyse whether the union in a specific sector would actually want to adjust its own real wage w_i relative to the average real wage if the overall unemployment rate were to change due to a shock. If the union wanted to adjust its real wage it would do so by changing its *nominal* wage rate W_i, since this is the only way it can affect its real wage rate. And if all unions had an incentive to adjust their own real wage relative to the market real wage, this would initiate an economy-wide adjustment of nominal wage rates, so nominal wage rigidity would be absent, even though real wage rates would stay constant due to the mark-up price setting of firms.

---

10. A seminal contribution to the menu cost theory of nominal rigidity was made in the highly readable article by N. Gregory Mankiw: 'Small Menu Costs and Large Business Cycles: A Macroeconomic Model of Monopoly', *Quarterly Journal of Economics*, **100**, 1985, pp. 529–539. Later on, the menu cost theory was elaborated by Mankiw and several other so-called New Keynesians, including Laurence Ball and David Romer: 'Real Rigidities and the Non-Neutrality of Money', *Review of Economic Studies*, **57**, 1990, pp. 183–203.

Suppose that the union in sector i has initially set its wage optimally given some initial level of unemployment $\tilde{u}$, so that the real wage rate is $\tilde{w}_i = m^w v(\tilde{u})$. Suppose further that an exogenous shock drives unemployment to a new and higher level u. In the absence of any costs of nominal wage adjustment, the union would then want to adjust its nominal wage rate to secure a real wage of $w_i = m^w v(u)$, as given by (12). If it chooses *not* to change its wage rate, leaving it at the initial level $\tilde{w}_i$ to avoid the costs of wage adjustment, the union will suffer the following utility loss, UL, excluding adjustment costs:

$$UL = \Omega(w_i,\, u) - \Omega(\tilde{w}_i,\, u) \tag{14}$$

Since the union's objective function (and hence UL) is specified in terms of real income, the utility loss in (14) is directly comparable to the fixed real cost of nominal wage adjustment, denoted by C. Hence the union will want to maintain the real wage rate $\tilde{w}_i$ if $UL < C$, and in that case its nominal wage will be rigid. To estimate how high C will have to be to prevent wage adjustment, it is convenient to take a second-order Taylor approximation of $\Omega(\tilde{w}_i, u)$, calculated around the new optimum wage rate w_i:

$$\Omega(\tilde{w}_i,\, u) \approx \Omega(w_i,\, u) + \overbrace{\frac{\partial \Omega(w_i,\, u)}{\partial w_i}}^{\substack{=\,0 \text{ in} \\ \text{optimum}}}(\tilde{w}_i - w_i) + \frac{1}{2}\frac{\partial^2 \Omega(w_i,\, u)}{(\partial w_i)^2}(\tilde{w}_i - w_i)^2. \tag{15}$$

Note that since w_i is the new *optimal* wage rate (in the absence of adjustment costs), it must satisfy the first-order condition, $\partial \Omega / \partial w_i = 0$. Hence we may approximate the utility loss in (14) by:

$$UL \approx -\frac{1}{2}\frac{\partial^2 \Omega(w_i,\, u)}{(\partial w_i)^2}(\tilde{w}_i - w_i)^2. \tag{16}$$

Essentially (16) says that the trade union incurs no *first-order* utility loss of not adjusting its wage rate, but only a second-order loss. The second derivative in (16) may be calculated from (13). Doing this, using the definition $m^w \equiv \sigma/(\sigma - 1)$ plus the fact that (6) implies $(w_i - v)/w_i = 1/\sigma$, and expressing UL as a fraction of the union's total wage bill $w_i L_i = w_i((1 - u)/n)(m^p w_i)^{-\sigma}$, we find that:[11]

$$\frac{UL}{w_i L_i} \approx \left(\frac{\sigma - 1}{2}\right)\left(\frac{\tilde{w}_i - w_i}{w_i}\right)^2. \tag{17}$$

---

11. From (13) we have

$$\frac{\partial \Omega}{\partial w_i} = \left(\frac{1-u}{n}\right)\left[(m^p w_i)^{-\sigma} - \sigma m^p(w_i - v)(m^p w_i)^{-\sigma-1}\right] \quad \Rightarrow$$

$$\frac{\partial^2 \Omega}{(\partial w_i)^2} = \sigma m^p\left(\frac{1-u}{n}\right)\left[m^p(\sigma+1)(w_i - v)(m^p w_i)^{-\sigma-2} - 2(m^p w_i)^{-\sigma-1}\right]$$

$$= \sigma m^p\left(\frac{1-u}{n}\right)(m^p w_i)^{-(\sigma+1)}\left[(\sigma+1)\left(\frac{w_i - v}{w_i}\right) - 2\right].$$

Inserting $m^w = \sigma/(\sigma - 1)$ and $(w_i - v)/w_i = 1/\sigma$ into the latter expression, we get:

$$\frac{\partial^2 \Omega}{(\partial w_i)^2} = -\sigma\left(\frac{m^p}{m^w}\right)\left(\frac{1-u}{n}\right)(m^p w_i)^{-(\sigma+1)}.$$

Substituting this expression into (16), dividing by $w_i L_i = w_i((1 - u)/n)(m^p w_i)^{-\sigma}$, and using the definition of m^w again, we end up with (17).

Before the shock to unemployment, the union had set its wage rate $\tilde{w}_i$ optimally in accordance with (12) given $\tilde{u}$, and w_i is also given by (12) at u. Since the general wage level is the same in both situations ($w = W/P = 1/m^p$), it follows that:

$$\frac{\tilde{w}_i - w_i}{w_i} = \frac{(1-c)(u - \tilde{u})}{1 - (1-c)u}. \tag{18}$$

Not surprisingly, we see from (17) and (18) that the larger the rise in unemployment, $u - \tilde{u}$, and hence the larger the fall in the value of the outside option of union members, the larger is the union's utility loss from not adjusting the wage rate.

Armed with Eqs (17) and (18), we can calculate how high the costs of nominal wage adjustment will need to be to prevent such adjustment, assuming a set of parameter values which generate a realistic initial unemployment rate. First we note that when $b = cw = c/m^p$, the expression for the natural unemployment rate given in (10) simplifies to

$$\bar{u} = \frac{m^w - 1}{m^w(1-c)} = \frac{1}{\sigma(1-c)}. \tag{19}$$

As an example, suppose that the replacement rate c is equal to 0.5 (not unrealistic for the average worker in many OECD countries) and that the economy is initially in long-run equilibrium at an unemployment rate equal to 5 per cent. Inserting $\tilde{u} = \bar{u} = 0.05$ and $c = 0.5$ into (19), it follows that $\sigma = 40$. Finally, suppose that the increase in the unemployment rate is two percentage points, $u - \bar{u} = 0.02$, implying a large 40 per cent increase in unemployment. Inserting these parameter values into (17) and (18), one finds that $UL/w_iL_i \approx 0.002$ or 0.2 per cent. In other words, the costs of wage adjustment – broadly interpreted to include the costs and inconveniences of rewriting wage contracts plus the resource costs of re-estimating the optimal wage – only have to amount to about one-fifth of 1 per cent of the wage bill to make it suboptimal for the individual union to reduce its nominal wage claim, despite the sharp rise in unemployment. If the rise in the unemployment rate is only 1 percentage point (still a substantial 20 per cent increase in unemployment), our parameter values imply that the 'menu costs' of wage adjustment only have to make up a tiny 0.05 per cent of the wage bill to generate nominal wage rigidity. Adjustment costs of such small magnitude certainly do not seem unlikely.

To sum up, even very small menu costs may cause the individual trade union's nominal wage claim to be rigid in the short run, and as a consequence the general nominal wage level will be rigid.

The link between real and nominal rigidity

Nominal and real rigidities are linked in the sense that a stronger degree of real rigidity can imply more nominal rigidity: the term $(\tilde{w}_i - w_i)/w_i$ appearing in (17) measures how much the union would like to change its *real* wage rate if adjustment were costless, given a change in overall unemployment from $\tilde{u}$ to u. Hence $(\tilde{w}_i - w_i)/w_i$ may be seen as an inverse measure of the degree of real wage rigidity. The smaller this magnitude, the weaker is the desire for real wage adjustment in response to fluctuations in unemployment, so the higher is the degree of real wage rigidity, and vice versa. Eq. (18) shows that in this particular setting the degree of real rigidity is determined by the replacement ratio, and the larger c is, the stronger is the real rigidity. And the greater the degree of real wage rigidity, the smaller are the menu costs needed to prevent *nominal* wage adjustment, so the higher is the degree of nominal wage rigidity. On the other hand, if $(\tilde{w}_i - w_i)/w_i$ is large, reflecting a low degree of real rigidity, small menu costs are unlikely to prevent nominal wage adjustment, according to (17). In short, a relatively high degree of real wage rigidity tends to create relatively strong nominal wage rigidity.

Explaining nominal price rigidity

The menu cost theory may also explain the rigidity of nominal *prices*. Obviously, if firms set their prices in accordance with our mark-up price setting equation $P = m^p W$, and if the nominal wage rate is rigid, it follows that nominal prices will also be rigid.

But even if there is *no* nominal wage rigidity, there may still be nominal price rigidity. If we assume zero costs of nominal wage adjustment so that nominal wages are fully flexible, the labour market model set up above still implies considerable *real* wage rigidity for reasonable parameter values. This means that wage setters (unions) will not want to change nominal and real wage rates very much when economic activity changes, despite the fact that wage adjustment is costless. Consequently firms will experience only moderate fluctuations in their real wage costs over the business cycle. One can construct plausible examples in which this rigidity in the real production costs of firms will generate nominal price rigidity even when the menu costs of price changes are very small.

This parallel between the lack of incentives for wage and price adjustment may be explained as follows: in our model of union wage setting the outside option is the union's real opportunity cost of 'selling' an extra job to the owner of firm i through wage moderation (since the outside option is the real income a union member could have earned elsewhere in the labour market). Because the outside option is rather insensitive to changes in unemployment, the union loses little by not adjusting its wage rate. Similarly, if the firm's real labour cost of producing and selling an extra unit of output is insensitive to the business cycle, it has little incentive to adjust its real price, and hence it will often abstain from adjusting its nominal price in order to save menu costs.

Since the individual firm takes the prices set by all other firms as given, a decision by firm i to change its nominal price P_i is also a decision to change its real (relative) price, P_i/P. Hence nominal price rigidity is a reflection of real price rigidity, just as nominal wage rigidity arises from real wage rigidity.

Individual versus social costs of nominal rigidities

It should be emphasized that although the cost to the individual union (the private cost) of not adjusting its wage rate is likely to be small, the *social* cost of nominal wage rigidity may be substantial. The reason why the individual union estimates such a small gain from adjusting its own nominal wage is that it takes all other wages and prices as given. But if all unions could be induced to cut their nominal wage rates simultaneously in response to a drop in aggregate employment, they would collectively drive down the rate of inflation (via the price-setting equation $P = m^p W$), and as we shall see in Book Two, this will tend to increase real aggregate demand. In this way it might be possible to limit the fall in output and employment significantly. Take our first numerical example above: if a coordinated downward adjustment of wages and prices could secure an expansion of aggregate demand which would cut the two percentage point rise in unemployment in half, total output and real income would rise by more than one percentage point relative to the baseline scenario where no nominal adjustment takes place, given the assumption underlying our price setting equation that the production function is linear in labour input.[12] Against this significant income gain must be set the small menu cost of wage adjustment which is only 0.2 per cent of the wage bill, and hence an even smaller percentage of total GDP. Thus, since nominal wage rigidity causes a substantial loss of output, its social cost is many times as large as the perceived private cost of non-adjustment of nominal wages. For exactly the same reasons, the social cost of nominal price rigidity is likely to be many times as great as the private cost perceived by individual price setters. This is why the problem of nominal rigidity should be taken seriously.

---

12. With a linear production function, total GDP (Y) after the shock to unemployment is $Y = 1 - u = 1 - 0.07 = 0.93$, so if unemployment were to rise by one percentage point less, output would rise by $dY/Y = du/(1 - u) = 0.01/0.93 \approx 0.011$ relative to the baseline scenario where unemployment rises by two percentage points.

THE SMALL MENU COST FOUNDATION OF NOMINAL WAGE AND PRICE RIGIDITY

A menu cost associated with changing nominal prices (and wages) can, even if it is small, prevent price-setting imperfect competitors from adjusting their nominal prices in response to a shock even if this shock is of considerable size. The reason is that if the price is set optimally at the outset, a price adjustment will only have a second- (and higher-) order influence on the objective of the price setter, and when there are real rigidities these second- and higher-order effects will be small.

Although the cost (excluding menu costs) of not adjusting the nominal price in case of a shock is small for each individual price setter, given that other price setters also keep their nominal prices unchanged, the cost of nominal rigidities where many price setters are subject to small menu costs can be large, since there could be much to gain for everybody from a coordinated price reaction to the shock.

We should stress that the menu cost theory outlined here is only intended to explain *short-run* nominal rigidities. Over time as shocks accumulate, agents who keep their wages or prices constant are likely to be pushed ever further away from their optimal wages and prices. Eventually they will therefore find it optimal to pay the menu cost to realign their relative price position: in the long run wages and prices *do* adjust.

The role of shocks, expectational errors and nominal rigidities: a simple restatement

Our analysis of nominal rigidities assumed that unemployment could somehow deviate from its natural rate, but we did not explain how. We will now do so, since this will give us an opportunity to highlight the role of expectational errors. Going back to equations (4) and (6), we see that these equations assume that wage setters correctly anticipate the general level of wages and prices when they set the nominal wage rate for their particular sector. But in the short run the expected general wage level W^e and the expected price level P^e may deviate from the actual levels. For the purpose of short-run analysis, if B^u is the nominal rate of unemployment benefit, the wage-setting curve (6) should therefore be rewritten as

$$\frac{W_i}{P^e} = m^w \left[(1-u)\frac{W^e}{P^e} + u\frac{B^u}{P^e} \right] \Leftrightarrow \frac{W_i}{P}\frac{P}{P^e} = m^w \left[(1-u)\frac{W^e}{W}\frac{W}{P}\frac{P}{P^e} + u\frac{B^u}{P}\frac{P}{P^e} \right] \Leftrightarrow$$

$$\frac{W_i}{P} = m^w \left[(1-u)\frac{W^e}{W}\frac{W}{P} + ub \right], \tag{20}$$

where we have used the definition of the real unemployment benefit, $b \equiv B^u/P$. The price-setting equation (3) and the assumption that mark-ups are identical across sectors imply that $W_i/P = W/P = 1/m^p$. Inserting this into (20) along with the assumption that $b = c \cdot (W/P)$, we get:

$$1 = m^w \left[(1-u)\frac{W^e}{W} + uc \right]. \tag{21}$$

In a long-run equilibrium expectations must be fulfilled ($W^e = W$), so from (21) the natural unemployment rate must satisfy:

$$1 = m^w(1 - \bar{u} + \bar{u}c), \tag{22}$$

which is equivalent to (19). Subtracting (22) from (21) and rearranging, we find:

$$u - \bar{u} = \left(\frac{1-u}{1-c}\right)\left(\frac{W^e - W}{W}\right). \tag{23}$$

This shows how a misperception of the general wage level ($W^e \neq W$) can cause unemployment to deviate from its natural rate. Indeed, we see that such expectational errors are a *necessary* condition for deviations from long-run equilibrium. However, when shocks to the economy generate expectational errors, the existence of nominal rigidities will greatly *amplify* the resulting fluctuations of employment around the natural rate, as we shall explain in detail in Chapter 17.

1.7 Long-run versus short-run economic policies and some second thoughts on the traditional dichotomy of macroeconomics

Structural policy and stabilization policy

A main motivation for studying economic phenomena is the need to improve the basis for economic policy advice. For instance, we want to understand the sources of economic growth because this could be helpful in designing a growth-promoting policy for a low-income country trying to escape poverty.

The division of macroeconomics described above leads to a parallel division of economic policies into *long-run policies* aimed at promoting growth and long-run prosperity and at reducing long-run unemployment, and *short-run policies* aimed at mitigating economic fluctuations and their harmful consequences coming, for example, from sudden increases in unemployment.

However, the division of macroeconomics suggests more than this categorization of policies according to their aims. The basic and different assumptions underlying the two parts of macroeconomic theory have consequences for the channels through which long-run and short-run policies can affect the economy.

For example, recall that long-run macroeconomics assumes full nominal wage and price adjustment. As we saw from Eq. (10), this implies that long-run unemployment is determined exclusively by the parameters m^w, m^p and b which reflect the *structural* characteristics of labour and product markets. Because it is rooted in the basic structural features of the economy, the natural rate of unemployment is also referred to as the 'structural' unemployment rate. It follows that a policy intended to reduce long-run unemployment can only be successful if it affects the economy's basic structures. Specifically, our analysis suggests that such a policy must try to increase the degree of competition in labour or product markets (by lowering the values of m^w and m^p) and/or reduce the generosity of the system of unemployment insurance (lowering b).[13]

In a similar way, policies aimed at promoting long-run growth and prosperity must affect one or several structural characteristics of the economy such as the long-run propensities to save and invest, to engage in education and R&D, etc. In short, policies for the long run must be *structural* policies.

A short-run policy to mitigate business cycles, on the other hand, can be a monetary or fiscal policy of *demand management*. Such a policy can affect the rate of employment in the short run even if it does not influence the basic structures and incentives in the economy. The reason is that in the short run prices and expectations are not fully adjusted,

---

13. In richer models of the labour market there are other ways of reducing the natural unemployment rate, such as improving the level and composition of work skills through education and training to attain a better match between the skills possessed by workers and the skills demanded by employers.

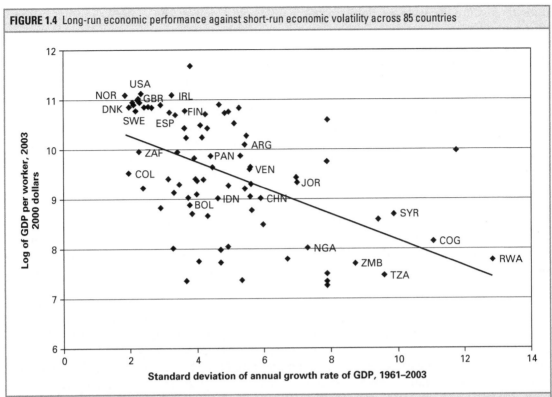

FIGURE 1.4 Long-run economic performance against short-run economic volatility across 85 countries

Note: Countries with data quality A, B or C according to the PWT 6.2 are included, except Ghana which was excluded due to an exceptionally large standard deviation in GDP growth (22.4). Ghana also had a low level of GDP per worker (8.0). The black line is estimated by ordinary least squares (OLS), and it is the uniquely determined line that minimizes the sum of the squared vertical distances between the points in the figure and the line. The estimate of the slope is −0.26. Additional information for the statistically proficient: The *t*-value is −5.5, and the *R*-square is 0.27. Country abbreviations can be seen in the appendix, Table A.

Source: Penn World Table 6.2.

and hence changes in nominal demand can affect real economic variables, as we explained earlier.

Discussing the relevance of the separation of macroeconomics in two branches

In our discussion of macroeconomics so far we have taken an orthodox view: macroeconomics for the long and the short run are almost distinct fields intended to explain separate phenomena (growth and business cycles, respectively) and using conflicting assumptions and qualitatively different models. From this dichotomy it follows that long-run structural policies and short-run stabilization policies are also considered as distinct. This strict dichotomy can be and has been challenged.

Consider Fig. 1.4. Each dot represents a country. Along the horizontal axis the standard deviation of the annual growth rate of the country's GDP between 1960 and 2003 is depicted. This is a measure of the volatility of the country's economic activity, that is, of the amplitude of the business cycle. Up along the vertical axis is the log of the country's GDP per worker (that is, per member of the labour force) in 2003. This is a measure of the country's long-run economic performance, i.e., its capability to create income for its inhabitants.[14] The figure includes a large number of countries for which

14. The figure and our discussion are inspired by the article by Valerie and Garey Ramey, 'Cross-Country Evidence on the Link Between Volatility and Growth', *American Economic Review*, **85**, 1995, pp. 1138–1151, and by subsequent research.

data of good quality were available from the relevant source, so the sample should be quite representative.

In short, the figure plots the long-run income-creating capability of the economy against its short-run volatility in economic activity across a large number of countries. The figure shows a relatively tight negative relationship between these two measures, as indicated by the downward-sloping regression line.

You will be warned repeatedly through this textbook about the importance of not confusing correlation with causality. It cannot be concluded from the figure alone that economic volatility affects long-run economic performance negatively. This is just one out of several alternative causal relationships that could underlie the correlation of Fig. 1.4. However, several of these causal interpretations would challenge the traditional dichotomy of macroeconomics.

First, the correlation could indeed reflect that short-run volatility affects the long-run economic performance negatively. This could be because instability creates an unfavourable environment for investment in capital and education. In this case an economic model that contributes to an understanding of business cycles would also contribute to an understanding of the economy's long-run performance. And a policy that affects short-run volatility would have an impact on the economy's long-run performance. Note that this could be an important motivation for stabilization policy. Stability could be a goal, not only because of the direct costliness of instability itself, but also because of the indirect positive effect of stability on the economy's long-run performance. Of course, no economist would claim that the degree of instability of the business cycle is the only factor that explains long-run performance. The article by Ramey and Ramey referred to in Footnote 14 finds that if one controls for (includes) other traditional explaining factors such as, e.g., the average share of investment in GDP, then one finds an even stronger connection between volatility and long-run performance.

Second, the correlation of Fig. 1.4 could be due to *reversed causality*, so that it is really a good long-run performance that causes a low volatility. It could be, for instance, that rich people and highly productive firms put more emphasis on, or have better possibilities for, creating relatively stable evolutions of consumption and investment over time. In that case, an economic model that contributes to an explanation of the economy's long-run capacity to create income would also deliver part of an explanation of the severity of short-run business cycles. This challenges once again the traditional dichotomy.

Finally, the tight relationship could be an expression of *spurious correlation*, where there is no causal link between the two measures of the figure, but a third factor, say the skilfulness of a country's inhabitants or the quality of its institutions, that explains both long-run and short-run performance. Different countries are skilful to different degrees. Going across countries the more skilful ones will exhibit more stable output *and* higher income per worker, both caused by the skilfulness. In this way a correlation such as that in Fig. 1.4 can arise without any of the variables along the axes affecting each other. If this is the true explanation, it would be all right to have separate models for the short and long runs, respectively, but the third factor mentioned should then be an explanatory factor in both types of models.

Despite these reservations, we will continue along a traditional line with a rather strict dichotomy between short-run and long-run analysis. We do, however, draw an important lesson from our discussion: although Fig. 1.4 is not a proof in itself, we think that there is more thorough evidence that relative economic stability in the short run causes relatively good economic performance in the long run. Hence, an important motivation for short-run stabilization policy is that success with such policy can have desirable long-run effects on income per capita.

1.8 Summary

This chapter has explained the ideas behind the structuring of our course in macroeconomics. Understanding these ideas is important for a good understanding of this book. Let us therefore summarize our main concepts and arguments, taking the key elements in a different sequence which will help to clarify the distinction between macroeconomics for the long run and macroeconomics for the short run:

1. The economy's *long-run equilibrium* is the combination of relative prices and quantities which would emerge in a general equilibrium where wages and prices have had time to adjust fully to past shocks and where no further shocks have occurred over a sufficiently long period.

2. If the long-run equilibrium is the outcome of perfect competition, all economic agents have taken wages and prices as given and found their optimal price-taking supplies and demands, and prices have adjusted to equate these supplies and demands market by market.

3. In practice, empirical studies often find that prices are above marginal costs, indicating that most markets – including the labour market – are characterized by *imperfect competition*. Still we can think of long-run relative prices as being determined by an underlying general equilibrium system, although not one that ensures equality between price-taking supplies and demands.

4. The *natural rate* is the rate of resource utilization emerging when relative prices have fully adjusted to their long-run equilibrium values. Imperfect competition typically means that the natural rate is less than 100 per cent. When this is the case, we say that *real rigidities* prevail. Real rigidities imply that individual agents do not wish to reduce their real (relative) wages and prices very much in response to unemployment or excess capacity. Hence real wages and prices do not adjust sufficiently to prevent permanent underutilization of resources.

5. *Macroeconomics for the long run* aims at explaining the trends in main economic time series and the effects of structural economic policies. In long-run macroeconomics the economy is analysed *as if* relative prices are fully adjusted to their long-run equilibrium values in each period, the fundamentals of the economy such as preferences and technology evolve smoothly and predictably, and expectations are correct all the time. One implication is that in long-run macroeconomics aggregate output is determined from the supply side alone, as the level of output that can be produced when available resources are utilized at their natural rates.

6. *Short-run nominal wage and price rigidities* mean that some money wages and/or prices are fixed over a certain period. Empirical evidence shows that most money prices and money wages are only adjusted with certain time intervals even under considerable inflation. Thus nominal rigidities prevail in the short run, and these may cause the rate of resource utilization to deviate from the natural rate for periods of sufficient length to be of interest.

7. Individual agents adjust their nominal wages or prices with the purpose of changing their real wages or prices. Because real rigidities imply that agents do not want to change their real prices very much in response to changes in economic activity, real rigidities also tend to generate nominal rigidities. When the degree of real rigidity is strong, short-run nominal wage and price rigidities can be privately optimal even if the *menu costs* of nominal wage and price adjustment are very small. At the same time the social cost of nominal rigidity can be many times as large as the perceived private cost for the individual agent.

▶

8. Short-run nominal wage and price rigidities may imply that some *relative* prices are also fixed in the short run. For instance, if both nominal wages and nominal prices are fixed, real wages are fixed. Short-run nominal rigidities can explain why it takes time for relative (real) prices to adjust to their long-run equilibrium levels.

9. *Macroeconomics for the short run* seeks to explain the fluctuations in main economic time series around their trends and the effects of stabilization policies. Economists believe that exogenous shocks (sudden unpredictable changes in factors such as business confidence, preferences and technology), short-run nominal wage and price rigidities, and expectational errors are fundamental for understanding short-run fluctuations. Because of nominal rigidities and expectational errors, the actual rate of resource utilization can deviate from the natural rate. In the short run aggregate demand is therefore just as important for economic activity as aggregate supply.

10. International evidence shows a clear positive correlation between economic stability in the short run and economic performance (income creation per capita) in the long run. Various causal relationships can explain this pattern, but one plausible explanation is that stability affects long-run performance positively. This constitutes an important motivation for stabilization policy.

1.9 Exercises

Exercise 1. Aggregation in macroeconomics

Discuss why macroeconomists typically work with aggregate variables and explain the arguments they use to defend this procedure. Do you find the arguments reasonable? Justify your answers.

Exercise 2. Short-run versus long-run macroeconomics

Explain the different assumptions underlying macroeconomics for the short run and macroeconomics for the long run. Do you find these assumptions reasonable? Justify your answers.

Exercise 3. Macroeconomic policies for the short run and for the long run

Explain the difference between structural policies and demand management policies. Explain the concepts of 'nominal rigidities', 'real rigidities' and the 'natural rate of resource utilization'. Try to give concrete examples of typical short-run policies and typical long-run policies.

Exercise 4. Fighting structural unemployment

Try to think of specific policies which might reduce the natural rate of unemployment. Explain why you think that these particular policies might reduce long-run unemployment.

Exercise 5. Menu costs and real and nominal rigidities

Explain and discuss the type of costs included in the concept of 'menu costs'. Explain why and in what sense so-called real rigidities are necessary to generate nominal wage and price rigidity.

Book One

The Long Run

Economic Growth, Long-run Unemployment and Structural Economic Policy

Some facts about prosperity and growth

*A*n *Inquiry into the Nature and Causes of the Wealth of Nations*. This was the title Adam Smith gave his famous book published in 1776, a book which greatly advanced economics as a scientific discipline. Already in the title Adam Smith stated what he considered to be the most important issue in economics: what is it that makes a nation prosperous, to the benefit of its citizens? Smith was clear from the very beginning about how prosperity should be measured:

> The annual labour of every nation is the fund which originally supplies it with all the necessaries and conveniences of life which it annually consumes, and which consists always either in the immediate produce of that labour, or in what is purchased with that produce from other nations.
>
>   According therefore as this produce, or what is purchased with it, bears a greater or smaller proportion to the number of those who are to consume it, the nation will be better or worse supplied with all the necessaries and conveniences for which it has occasion.
>
> (Opening remarks of 'Introduction and Plan of the Work' of
> *The Wealth of Nations*, 1776).

In modern economic language, Smith says that the average level of prosperity in a country can be measured by the country's GDP or income per person. It is not necessarily all of the annual income that is consumed during the year, but what is not consumed is saved, and becomes either investment or an export surplus. In both uses it adds to the national wealth and thereby becomes a source of future consumption. Consumption is thus always rooted in production and income, and in so far as consumption is a good proxy for the economic well-being of people, annual GDP or income per person is a relevant measure of prosperity. Clearly, not only the *average* income per person but also the *distribution* of income across persons is of interest. However, for a given degree of income inequality, an increase in average GDP per person is to the benefit of everybody.

According to Adam Smith's view, it is the annual *level* of GDP per person that is of importance. Nevertheless, in Book One we will be much concerned with economic growth, i.e. the annual *increase* in GDP per person. We are interested in growth, not as an end in itself, but because *the way a country can reach a higher level of income is through a process of growth*.

Figure 2.1 gives some clear illustrations of the importance of gradual growth for reaching higher, or falling to lower, levels of income per person.[1] Around 1970, three African nations,

---

1.   The figure shows GDP per worker (GDP per person in the labour force), not GDP per capita (GDP per person in the population) for reasons to be explained.

FIGURE 2.1 The importance of growth in GDP per worker for the level of GDP per worker

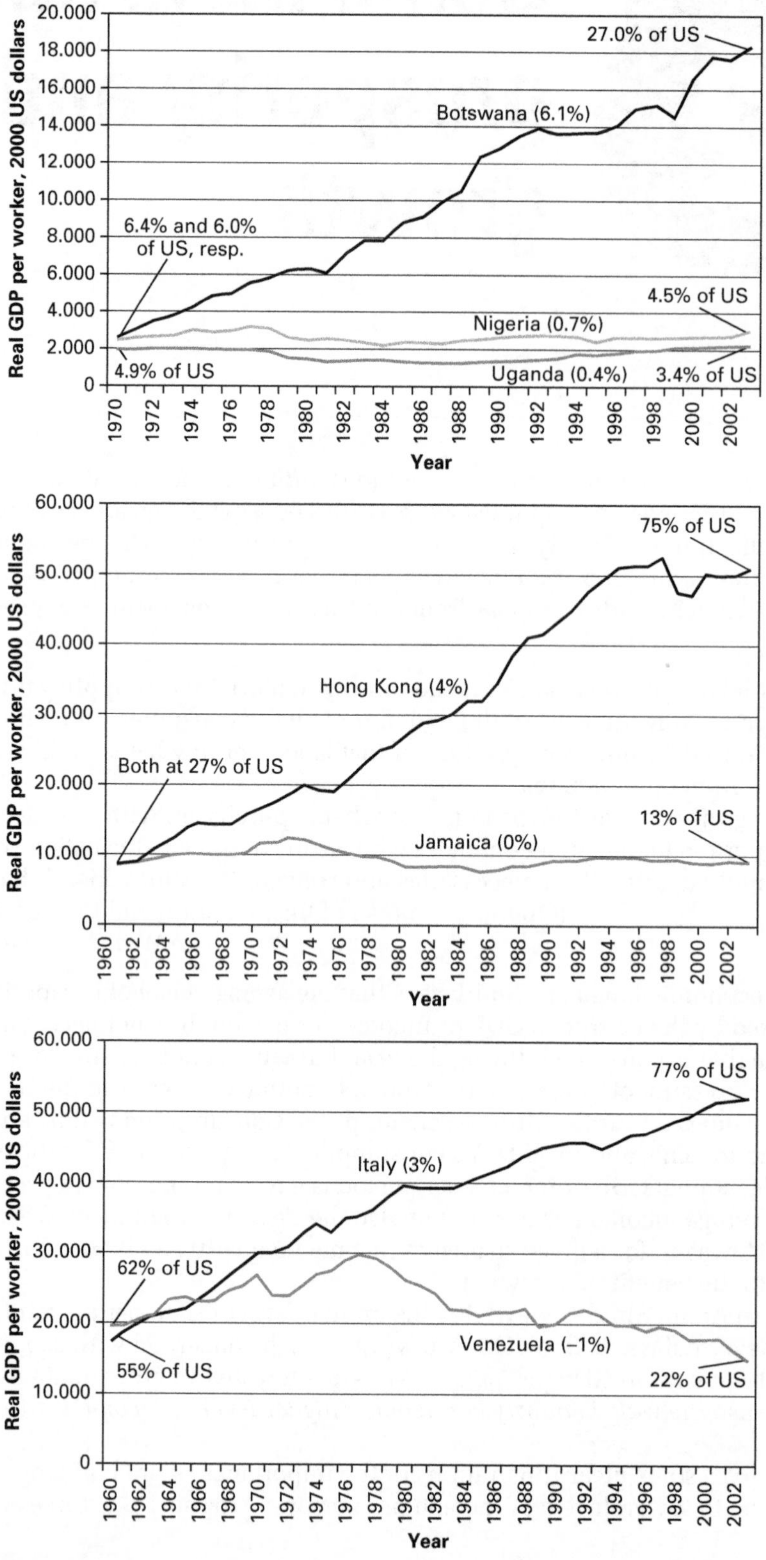

Source: Penn World Table 6.2.

Botswana, Nigeria and Uganda, were all at about the same level of GDP per worker, and this level was very low by international standards. Over the subsequent 33 years, GDP per worker in Botswana grew at an impressive average rate of about 6 per cent per year, while the growth rates of Nigeria and Uganda were 0.7 per cent and 0.4 per cent, respectively. This implied that in 2003 the *level* of GDP per worker in Botswana was 6 times greater than in Nigeria and 8 times greater than in Uganda. By 2003 Botswana had not become extremely rich, but rather than having, like Nigeria and Uganda, a GDP per worker at or below 4.5 per cent of the US level, Botswana had reached a level of 27 per cent of US income per capita. The differences in the conditions of life caused by these different growth experiences are not difficult to imagine.

Both Jamaica and Hong Kong had a GDP per worker of around 27 per cent of that in the USA in 1960. From that time until 2003, Jamaica grew at an average rate of 0.1 per cent a year, while Hong Kong grew at an annual rate of 4.2 per cent. Today Hong Kong is one of the world's rich areas, with a GDP per worker of about 75 per cent of the US level in 2003, while Jamaica is relatively poor at around 13 per cent of the US level.

In 1960 Venezuela was one of the world's rich countries with a GDP per worker of 62 per cent of the US level, while Italy was considerably behind at 55 per cent of the US level. However, until 2003, average annual growth in Italy was 2.6 per cent, but in Venezuela it was negative. In 2003 it is Italy, not Venezuela, that is one of the world's rich countries, with a GDP per worker at 77 per cent of the US level. Venezuela has fallen to 22 per cent of the US level.

What allows a country to escape from poverty, or to achieve prosperity, is a process of growth over a succession of years. Therefore one of the most important questions in economics, probably *the* most important one, is: what creates growth? Growth theory and growth empirics are fascinating subjects in economics. We start in this chapter by stating and discussing some empirical regularities concerning prosperity and growth. These 'stylized facts' constitute important knowledge in themselves. They will also be used later on as yardsticks: the growth theory to be presented will be held up against the empirical facts.

2.1 Measuring the wealth of a nation

Agreeing with Adam Smith that the ratio of the annual 'produce' to 'the number of those who are to consume it' is a relevant measure of the average standard of living in a nation, we will use GDP per person as a proxy for living standards. You are assumed to know about statistics such as GDP, total consumption, total investment, etc., from an earlier course in macroeconomics. We will therefore discuss only a few aspects of measuring economic welfare by GDP per person.

Suppose we would like to compare the standard of living between a highly developed country such as the USA, and a somewhat less developed country with relatively fewer transactions in the official market economy and relatively more self-sufficiency. The GDP of each country is the value of the 'official' marketed production.

First, a comparison between the two countries requires that their GDPs be measured in the same currency, say US dollars. For this purpose we need an exchange rate that converts amounts denominated in the currency of the less developed country, the peso say, into amounts in dollars. It may be misleading to use the official prevailing exchange rate between the peso and the dollar since prevailing exchange rates are volatile. A 10 per cent increase in the peso relative to dollars from one month to the next will typically not reflect that the less developed country has become 10 per cent richer compared to the USA in one month. It will rather be a reflection of some change in expectations. Current exchange rates are not appropriate for converting GDPs if one is interested in standards of living. Instead one should use a rate of conversion that reflects purchasing power. The total cost of a relevant bundle of goods representing the 'necessaries and conveniences' of life should be computed in the two countries, and the purchasing-power-adjusted exchange rate could then be defined as the relation between the two total costs. If the bundle has a total cost of 1000 dollars in the USA, and a cost of 100,000 pesos in the less developed country, the purchasing-power-adjusted exchange rate is one dollar for 100 pesos. One should use this computed exchange rate to convert the GDP of the less developed country into a purchasing-power-adjusted GDP in US dollars.

A second issue is whether GDP per person should mean GDP per capita, where the GDP is divided by the size of the total population, or whether it should mean GDP per worker, where the GDP is only divided by the size of the labour force, which is the population size times the labour force participation rate. The less developed country will typically have a larger informal sector and relatively more people living from non-marketed home production. If one divides the official GDP of the country, the value of the marketed production, by the size of the entire population, one will probably underestimate the prosperity of the country in comparison with the highly developed country. Dividing the official GDP by the size of the official labour force can be a way of correcting for this bias, since the official labour force does not include those working only in the informal sector. (If the productivity in the formal and informal sectors are identical, the correction should be perfect.) Generally, using GDP per worker as our measure of the standard of living makes at least some correction for cross-country differences in the degree of participation in the formal economy.

Table 2.1 shows that it may indeed make a difference whether one considers GDP per capita or per worker. For instance, measured by GDP per capita, Egypt and Pakistan are only 13 per cent and 7 per cent as rich as the USA in the year 2000, respectively. Measured by GDP per worker, they are still not rich compared to the USA, but they are considerably less poor, now at 18 per cent and 10 per cent of the US level, respectively. This reflects the low participation rates in Egypt and Pakistan.

According to GDP per capita, Ireland was 73 per cent as rich as the USA in 2000, but measuring by GDP per worker, Ireland was 88 per cent as rich. The difference is a reflection of the much higher participation rate in the USA. Also note that according to GDP per capita, Denmark is richer than the Netherlands, but according to GDP per worker it is a bit poorer, reflecting the higher participation rate in Denmark. For the examples of Ireland vs. the USA, and Denmark vs. the Netherlands, the differences in participation rates are probably not caused by differences in the relative sizes of the unofficial sectors, but rather by 'true' differences in labour force participation, e.g. by women. Nevertheless, it can still be argued

TABLE 2.1 GDP per capita and per worker (2000)

Country	Absolute, 2000 US dollars		Implicit participation rate[1]	Relative to US	
	GDP per capita	GDP per worker		GDP per capita	GDP per worker
USA	34,365	67,079	0.51	1.00	1.00
Denmark	27,827	50,448	0.55	0.81	0.75
Japan	23,971	44,563	0.54	0.70	0.66
Netherlands	26,293	56,691	0.46	0.77	0.85
Belgium	24,662	59,874	0.41	0.72	0.89
Sweden	25,232	46,544	0.54	0.73	0.69
UK	24,666	49,225	0.50	0.72	0.73
Ireland	24,948	59,103	0.42	0.73	0.88
Egypt	4,536	11,940	0.38	0.13	0.18
Pakistan	2,477	6,719	0.37	0.07	0.10

[1] Computed as GDP per capita divided by GDP per worker.
Source: Penn World Table 6.2.

that GDP per worker is a more appropriate measure of economic standards of living than GDP per capita, because home production and leisure should also count.

GDP per worker is closer to a *productivity* measure than GDP per capita. In the growth models presented in the subsequent chapters, average labour productivity is a key variable, and productivity has a closer correspondence to GDP per worker than to GDP per capita. Since we want a close correspondence between our empirical and theoretical variables, this is another reason for studying GDP per worker.[2]

The statistics used for international comparison in this book are of the purchasing-power-adjusted type, and we will mainly use GDP per worker as a proxy for the standard of living and for labour productivity. Data will, to a large extent, come from a database called the Penn World Table (PWT), which is an attempt to create internationally comparable statistics for the countries of the world for a considerable period (for many developed countries 1950–2003, and for most other countries 1960–2003).[3] The PWT does not cover all countries in the world. Among the exceptions are nations that were formerly part of the Soviet Union and other formerly planned economies of Eastern Europe.

2.2 The rich and the poor, the growing and the declining

We have already given some illustrations of the enormous differences between rich and poor countries, and of the fact that some countries have managed to develop from poor to not so poor through a good growth performance. We now go into more detail about the issues of poverty and prosperity, and about moving in and out of these categories.

The world income distribution

Some countries are poor and some are rich, but is there any sign that the world income distribution has become more equal? We can investigate this by means of so-called Lorenz curves. Figure 2.2 shows two Lorenz curves for the world, one for 1970 and one for 2003. A point (x, y) on a Lorenz curve indicates that the fraction x of the people in the world with the smallest incomes earns the fraction y of all the income in the world. For instance, the Lorenz curve for 1970 shows that in that year, the 60 per cent of the world population that lived in the poorest countries earned a bit more than 10 per cent of the world's income. In 2003 the corresponding figure was considerably above 20 per cent.

The curves are based on average GDP per worker and assume that *all* people living in a specific country, not just all people in the labour force, have an income equal to the average per worker GDP recorded in the PWT, in the country and for the year in question. We thus attribute to each individual in a country an artificial income equal to the recorded average GDP per worker. The Lorenz curves have been constructed from such personal incomes and population sizes (you will be asked to do a similar construction yourself in Exercise 2). The procedure may seem a bit odd, but in this way we can base the Lorenz curves on data for average GDP per worker.

Absolute equality corresponds to a Lorenz curve identical to the 45° line, or diagonal. The further the Lorenz curve is below the diagonal, the more unequal is the income distribution. Therefore the area between the diagonal and the Lorenz curve, as a fraction of the entire area below the diagonal, is an aggregate measure of inequality. This measure, called the Gini coefficient, is a number between zero and one, and the closer it is to one the more inequality

2. By this argument one should perhaps go all the way to GDP per work hour to allow not only for differences in participation rates, but also for differences in annual working time and unemployment rates. Lack of good internationally comparable statistics for annual work hours prevents this.

3. The PWT can be found on the internet at http://pwt.econ.upenn.edu/. At the time this second edition was prepared (2008), the most current version was PWT 6.2, from which most growth data in this book are taken. An extract from the PWT 6.2, and from other relevant databases, can be found in Table A at the end of Book One.

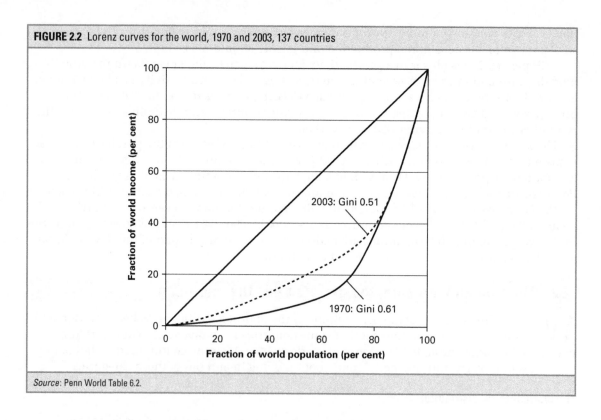

FIGURE 2.2 Lorenz curves for the world, 1970 and 2003, 137 countries

Source: Penn World Table 6.2.

there is. The Gini coefficients for 1970 and 2003 are shown in Fig. 2.2, and they are 0.61 and 0.51, respectively. Because of the particular construction of the Lorenz curves based on GDP per worker, these Gini coefficients are not comparable to traditional coefficients computed for the income distribution of a specific country. However, they should be comparable to each other.

Investigating the Lorenz curves and the Gini coefficients reveals that there were enormous income differences in the world both in 1970 and in 2003, but between these two years the world income distribution *does* seem to have become more equal.

Our investigation of the world income distribution is a bit crude. Most of the improvement indicated by Fig. 2.2 comes from the relatively good growth performances of some heavily populated countries, most importantly China and India (as illustrated in Table 2.3 below). This does not necessarily mean that Fig. 2.2 gives a distorted impression, but in the construction we have completely neglected the influence of inequality *within* countries by attributing the same income to all persons in each country. If, for instance, the personal income distribution in China has become more unequal over the period considered, Fig. 2.2 will exaggerate the degree to which the *personal* world income distribution has become more equal. It is interesting to note that more thorough studies of the evolution in the world income distribution, which account for inequality within countries, reach conclusions similar to the one appearing from our more crude analysis.[4]

---

4. One study is by economist Xavier Sala-i-Martin: 'The World Distribution of Income: Falling Poverty and . . . Convergence, Period', *Quarterly Journal of Economics*, 121, 2006, pp. 351–397. Sala-i-Martin emphasizes strongly the overall improvement in the world income distribution from 1970 to 2000, achieved mainly over the two decades from 1980 to 2000, but he also expresses a serious concern about 'the dismal growth performance of the African continent', writing: '. . . where poverty was mostly an Asian phenomenon 30 years ago . . . poverty is, today, an essentially African problem'.

STYLIZED FACT 1

Some countries are rich and some are poor, the differences are enormous, and it has pretty much stayed like that in relative terms for a long time. However, there is some tendency towards a more equal world income distribution over the past three to four decades, but not much at the very bottom.

Two features should be noted. First, the Lorenz curve and the associated Gini coefficient illustrate the income distribution in *relative* terms. If the Lorenz curve had been completely unchanged from 1970 to 2003 it would mean that the percentage change in income per capita in the world's poorest country would have been the same as in the richest country. In absolute terms the poorest country would be much less poor by 2003 than in 1970. Indeed, the world average income per worker (computed with population sizes as weights) increased from 1970 to 2003 by an average annual rate of 1.4 per cent, corresponding more or less to 60 per cent over the full period. The fact that the Lorenz curve is relatively unchanged at the very bottom means that the poorest countries have also enjoyed most of this increase. On the other hand, if the world income distribution is unchanged in relative terms, and incomes generally increase, then the *absolute* differences between the poorest and the richest increase.

Second, it is not exactly the same countries that are the poorest (or the richest) in 1970 and 2003. The fact that the 10 per cent of people living in the poorest countries earned only around 1.5 per cent of world income in 1970 as well as in 2003 does not mean that it is impossible to escape from poverty. There were some countries that did move out of the group of the poorest countries by having high growth (compared to the world). However, the other countries that took their place among the poorest had sufficiently bad growth experiences to ensure that the group of poorest countries did not increase their share of the world's income.

Prosperity and poverty, growth and decline

The movement in and out of the groups of the poorest and of the most prosperous countries is illustrated in Table 2.2. The table states some statistics for the countries that were among the 15 poorest in terms of GDP per worker in 1965 and in 2003, and for the 15 richest countries in these years. The average annual growth rates between 1965 and 2003 reported in Table 2.2 have been calculated as $(\ln y_{03} - \ln y_{65})/38$, where y_t is GDP per worker in year t: if the relative change in a variable is not too large, it is approximately equal to the variable's absolute change in (natural) logs.[5]

Table 2.2 illustrates again the enormous differences between the rich and the poor, but also a fair amount of income mobility. Some countries are among the 15 poorest both in 1965 and 2003, but other countries have left the group of the poorest. For instance, in 1965 China was among the poorest with a level of GDP per worker at 2.4 per cent of that in the USA. By 2003 China had advanced to 12.2 per cent of the US level. This was achieved by an average annual growth rate in GDP per worker of 6.1 per cent, bringing China safely out of the group of the 15 poorest nations in 2003, which all had a GDP per worker of less than 3.5 per cent of the US level.

Other countries that moved out of the bottom 15 are, for example, Lesotho and Ghana. Over the same 38 years countries such as Niger and Zambia moved the other way, into the group of the poorest, by having bad growth performances. Their GDP per worker relative to the US fell from around 7 per cent to 3.3 per cent or less.

---

5. The rate of change $(z - x)/x = z/x - 1$ is approximately equal to $\ln z - \ln x = \ln z/x$, since, as long as a number u is not too far from one, then $\ln u \approx u - 1$. The latter follows because $\ln 1 = 0$, and $d\ln u/du = 1/u$, so measured at $u = 1$, the slope of the log function is one. Hence, locally around $(1, 0)$, the function $\ln u$ goes like the function $u - 1$. If the relative change we are interested in is a growth rate in, e.g., GDP per worker, $(y_t - y_{t-1})/y_{t-1}$, then typically it is not too far from zero, so y_t/y_{t-1} is close to one, and then $(y_t - y_{t-1})/y_{t-1} \approx \ln y_t - \ln y_{t-1}$ is a good approximation.

TABLE 2.2 The world's prosperity 'top 15' and 'bottom 15', 1965 and 2003

	Real GDP per worker relative to USA		Average annual growth rate 1965–2003		Real GDP per worker relative to USA		Average annual growth rate 1965–2003
	Per cent	Per cent	Per cent		Per cent	Per cent	Per cent
Poorest in 1965	1965	2003	Per cent	**Poorest in 2003**	1965	2003	Per cent
Ghana	1.9	4.2	3.8	Guinea-Bissau	3.4	1.9	0.1
China	2.4	12.2	6.1	Burundi	3.1	2.1	0.6
Malawi	2.5	2.4	1.4	Ethiopia	2.5	2.3	1.3
Ethiopia	2.5	2.3	1.3	Madagascar	6.5	2.3	−1.1
Tanzania	2.8	2.6	1.4	Malawi	2.5	2.4	1.4
Burkina Faso	2.9	3.4	2.0	Tanzania	2.8	2.6	1.4
Burundi	3.1	2.1	0.6	Gambia	4.3	2.7	0.3
Mali	3.1	3.6	2.0	Niger	6.8	2.7	−0.9
Guinea-Bissau	3.4	1.9	0.1	Togo	6.2	2.7	−0.6
Nepal	4.1	4.5	1.9	Chad	6.3	2.9	−0.5
Rwanda	4.2	3.5	1.1	Zambia	6.9	3.3	−0.4
Lesotho	4.2	7.0	2.9	Burkina Faso	2.9	3.4	2.0
Mozambique	4.3	4.1	1.5	Uganda	4.7	3.4	0.7
Gambia	4.3	2.7	0.3	Kenya	6.8	3.4	−0.2
Uganda	4.7	3.4	0.7	Rwanda	4.2	3.5	1.1
Richest in 1965	1965	2003		**Richest in 2003**	1965	2003	
Switzerland	103.0	79.9	0.9	United States	100.0	100.0	1.6
United States	100.0	100.0	1.6	Ireland	44.0	97.1	3.7
New Zealand	99.1	65.3	0.5	Norway	76.4	96.8	2.2
Netherlands	91.5	83.7	1.4	Belgium	71.4	90.7	2.2
Canada	87.5	76.3	1.2	Austria	60.2	88.1	2.6
Denmark	81.9	75.9	1.4	France	67.0	83.9	2.2
Sweden	81.2	70.9	1.2	Netherlands	91.5	83.7	1.4
Australia	78.7	80.5	1.7	Australia	78.7	80.5	1.7
Norway	76.4	96.8	2.2	Singapore	35.7	80.0	3.8
Belgium	71.4	90.7	2.2	Switzerland	103.0	79.9	0.9
Iceland	71.2	68.1	1.5	Italy	59.1	76.8	2.3
United Kingdom	67.6	76.5	1.9	United Kingdom	67.6	76.5	1.9
France	67.0	83.9	2.2	Canada	87.5	76.3	1.2
Israel	66.6	69.9	1.7	Denmark	81.9	75.9	1.4
Venezuela	63.5	21.9	−1.2	Hong Kong	37.1	75.2	3.5

Note: Countries are chosen from a sample of 97 countries, for which data on real GDP per worker in 1965 and 2003 were available A lower limit of 1 mio. citizens was used.

Source: Penn World Table 6.2.

At the rich end there was also a substantial amount of mobility. Most impressively, Hong Kong, Singapore and Ireland, starting at levels of GDP per worker relative to the USA of 37, 36 and 44 per cent, respectively, moved into the top 15, and ended at levels 75, 80 and 97 per cent, respectively. Most spectacular drop-outs of the top 15 are Venezuela and New Zealand.

TABLE 2.3 World growth 'bottom 15' and 'top 15' 1965–2003

	Average annual growth rate of GDP per worker 1965–2003	Real GDP per worker relative to USA,	
		Per cent	Per cent
15 slowest growing	**Per cent**	**1965**	**2003**
Nicaragua	−1.9	48.9	12.7
Jordan	−1.3	50.8	16.8
Venezuela	−1.2	63.5	21.9
Madagascar	−1.1	6.5	2.3
Niger	−0.9	6.8	2.7
Togo	−0.6	6.2	2.7
Chad	−0.5	6.3	2.9
Zambia	−0.4	6.9	3.3
Peru	−0.3	33.9	16.3
Jamaica	−0.3	27.3	13.3
Kenya	−0.2	6.8	3.4
Senegal	−0.2	9.1	4.6
Bolivia	0.0	19.2	10.7
Guinea-Bissau	0.1	3.4	1.9
El Salvador	0.1	28.8	16.1
15 fastest growing			
China	6.1	2.4	12.2
Korea, Republic of	5.2	13.4	49.8
Thailand	4.2	6.9	18.0
Malaysia	4.0	16.9	41.2
Ghana	3.8	1.9	4.2
Singapore	3.8	35.7	80.0
Ireland	3.7	44.0	97.1
Romania	3.6	8.7	18.5
Hong Kong	3.5	37.1	75.2
Japan	3.2	37.0	66.4
Sri Lanka	3.1	7.7	13.7
Indonesia	3.1	7.1	12.2
India	2.9	6.0	9.9
Lesotho	2.9	4.2	7.0
Austria	2.6	60.2	88.1

Note: Sample of 97 countries as for Table 2.2. Botswana is missing for lack of 1965 to 1970 data, while Taiwan is missing for lack of 1998–2003 data. They would otherwise have been in the top of the top 15.

Source: Penn World Table 6.2.

Table 2.2 reveals another interesting, and perhaps surprising, fact: even among the world's 15 richest countries in 2003, there are substantial differences in income per worker, with the lowest levels of GDP per worker at around 75 per cent of the US level.

Since a country can move from poor to rich through a process of growth, and vice versa, it is of interest to look directly at growth performances. Table 2.3 shows the bottom 15 and the top 15 for growth in GDP per worker between 1965 and 2003. It is not surprising to find the so-called 'tiger economies' of East Asia in the top 15: South Korea, Thailand, Malaysia, Singapore, Hong Kong, and also Japan. It is perhaps more surprising to find the African countries Ghana and Lesotho in the top 15 (together with Botswana, see the note). The appearances of China and India should no longer be surprising these days.

The countries at the top of the top 15 are often called 'growth miracles'. Likewise, the countries in the bottom 15 can be called 'growth disasters'. Note that for many of these countries, average growth rates between 1965 and 2003 were actually negative.

The countries of the world that are neither in the growth top 15 nor the bottom 15 have had annual growth rates between the 2.6 per cent of the slowest-growing countries in the top 15 and the 0.1 per cent of the fastest-growing countries in the bottom 15; see for instance Table A at the end of Book One. Our insights can be summarized as follows:

STYLIZED FACT 2

Growth rates vary substantially between countries, and by the process of growing or declining quickly, a country can move from being relatively poor to being relatively rich, or from being relatively rich to being relatively poor.

Hidden in the data is another interesting fact. Consider the tiger economies, South Korea, Thailand, Malaysia, and Singapore (Taiwan could be included, but does not appear in Table 2.3 because of lack of data), which all grew very fast between 1965 and 2003, with average annual growth rates of GDP per worker in the range from 4 per cent and up. Up to around 1960 these countries grew much more slowly. In fact, in the 1960s some economists worried about the prospects for countries in South Asia.[6] All the growth miracles of South-East Asia experienced breaks in their growth rates from lower to higher values somewhere around the early 1960s. Similar growth breaks have occurred for several other countries in the growth top 15.

STYLIZED FACT 3

Growth can break in a country, turning from a high rate to a low one or vice versa.

You may perhaps think that this is a trivial fact: there is nothing inevitable about growth. However, it illustrates that the fight against poverty is not a hopeless one. In particular, one cannot point to a continent or part of the world in which the break in growth from low to high should be impossible. We stress this because sometimes in the public debate it is taken for granted that countries in some parts of the world, sub-Saharan Africa or the Middle East for instance, will never be able to grow out of poverty. The data simply do not support such an idea. There are no growth-preventing areas in the world, but there may be growth-preventing policies or circumstances (civil war, for instance).

Stylized fact 3 raises again the perhaps most important question in economics: *how* can a country create a positive growth break? What kinds of policies can do that? Growth theory and empirics, as presented in the coming chapters, can offer some possible answers.

---

6. In 1968 the Nobel Prize Laureate Gunnar Myrdal published the book (in three volumes, covering more than 2000 pages), *Asian Drama: An Inquiry into the Poverty of Nations*, Allen Lane, Penguin Press, London. The book was, as the title suggests, much concerned with why countries in South Asia, and in particular in South-East Asia, were not able to escape from poverty by a rapid growth process. At the time of publication several of these countries, but certainly not all, had started to grow fast.

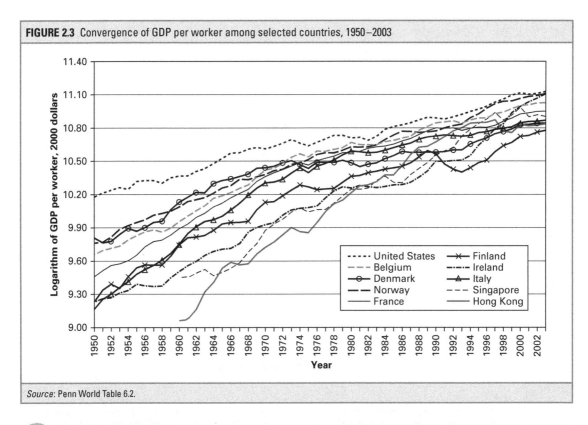

FIGURE 2.3 Convergence of GDP per worker among selected countries, 1950–2003

Source: Penn World Table 6.2.

2.3 Convergence

An interesting idea in economics would, if it were true, imply that poverty should disappear by itself.

Absolute convergence

Figure 2.3 plots the log of annual GDP per worker for the period 1950 to 2003 for a selection of countries. A glance at the figure suggests that all the countries tend to approach one and the same 'growth path'. Since $\ln y_t - \ln y_{t-1}$ is (approximately) the rate of growth in y_t, in a figure showing $\ln y_t$ against time t, constant growth corresponds to a straight line, and the slope of the line is the growth rate. Figure 2.3 suggests a tendency for countries to approach one and the same upward-sloping straight line, perhaps more or less a line corresponding to the USA.

Figures like Fig. 2.3 (drawn for even longer periods, up to 100 years and more) were presented by William J. Baumol in a famous article from 1986, suggesting some of the 'laws' discussed below.[7] Such figures open up the fascinating possibility that the differences with respect to output and income per person between the countries of the world automatically vanish in the long run. This possibility is sufficiently intriguing to have a name of its own:

THE HYPOTHESIS OF ABSOLUTE CONVERGENCE

In the long run GDP per worker (or per capita) converges to one and the same growth path in all countries, so that all countries converge on the same level of income per worker.

---

7. William J. Baumol, 'Productivity Growth, Convergence and Welfare: What the Long-Run Data Show', *American Economic Review*, **76**, 1986, pp. 1072–1085.

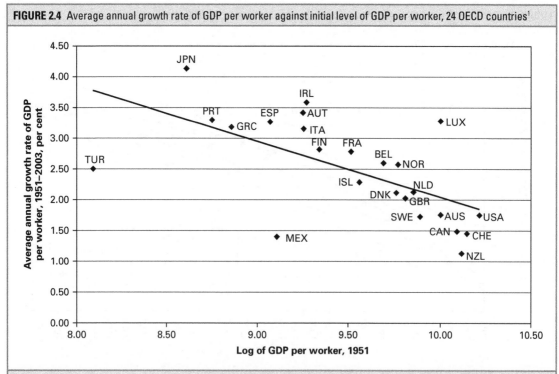

FIGURE 2.4 Average annual growth rate of GDP per worker against initial level of GDP per worker, 24 OECD countries[1]

Note: The countries behind the country codes can be found in Table A. The straight line is estimated by ordinary least squares (OLS), and it is the uniquely determined line that minimizes the sum of the squared vertical distances between the points in the figure and the line. The estimated line is $y = 11.10 - 0.91x$. Additional information for the statistically proficient: $R^2 = 0.39$, and $t = -3.72$ (standard error of the coefficient is 0.24).

[1] Members in 2003, except Germany, Hungary, Korea, Czech Republic, Poland, and Slovak Republic, which have been excluded due to lack of data.

Source: Penn World Table 6.2.

A main reason why this hypothesis is so fascinating is the implication that poverty should disappear by itself in the long run. It is worth thinking about what this would imply for the relevance of foreign aid policies. It would not make such policies irrelevant altogether. It could be argued that the speed by which poverty disappears is so slow, and the current poverty problems so severe, that foreign aid is currently needed. However, other things being equal, if poverty disappears by itself, it certainly makes foreign aid less necessary than if some countries are caught in poverty traps.

The hypothesis of absolute convergence implies that *countries with relatively low levels of GDP per worker in an initial year will grow relatively fast after that initial year*.[8] In other words, average growth in GDP per worker from year 0 to year T, say, should be negatively correlated with GDP per worker in year 0. Indexing countries by i, and denoting country i's GDP per worker in year t by y_t^i, the following equation (where the left-hand side is the approximate average annual growth rate in GDP per worker, β_0 is a constant, and β_1 is a positive parameter) should then be expected to fit well:

$$\frac{\ln y_T^i - \ln y_0^i}{T} \approx \beta_0 - \beta_1 \ln y_0^i \tag{1}$$

Figure 2.4 plots the average annual growth rate of GDP per worker from 1951 to 2003 against the log of GDP per worker in 1951 for all OECD member countries in 2003 for which data were available from the Penn World Table (PWT).

---

8. It cannot be concluded the other way round that a negative association between initial GDP per worker and subsequent growth is (necessarily) an indication of convergence! See the exercise on Galton's Fallacy at the end of the chapter.

The country points in Fig. 2.4 are nicely located along a decreasing straight line. The line that has been drawn in the figure is a best fit to the points according to a standard statistical method, ordinary least squares (OLS) estimation, which is described in the figure legend and in the statistical appendix to this book. The line has the particular formula:

$$\frac{\ln y_{03}^i - \ln y_{51}^i}{52} \cdot 100 \cong 11.10 - 0.91 \ln y_{51}^i \tag{2}$$

Figures 2.3 and 2.4 seem to support the hypothesis of absolute convergence, but they present data only for some countries. This would not be so much of a problem if those countries were randomly selected and representative. However, they are not. Both figures have, in different ways, selected countries which had relatively high and relatively similar GDPs per worker in 2003. Figure 2.4, for instance, focuses on the club of relatively rich OECD members in 2003. The countries in Fig. 2.4 that had relatively low GDPs per worker around 1950 must have grown relatively fast to be able to join the rich club in 2000. The selection of countries thus has a bias in favour of the hypothesis we are testing. This problem is known as the 'sample selection bias' problem, and was noted in the present context by the economist J. Bradford DeLong in an article in 1988.[9]

To avoid the sample selection bias problem one should try to get a more representative sample. We pick a sample as follows: in order to have good standardized data for a large number of countries, we consider the somewhat shorter period from 1960 to 2003. We include in the sample countries for which data on GDP per worker in 1960 and the average growth rate in GDP per worker between 1960 and 2003 (plus some additional data relevant for later purposes) can be obtained from the PWT. We exclude from the sample countries with less than two million inhabitants in 1960 (to avoid particular small country effects), countries for which oil production accounts for more than 30 per cent of the GDP (to avoid particularities due to very high dependence on oil), and countries for which the data quality is relatively poor according to the PWT itself.[10]

This leaves us with a relatively large sample of 65 countries that should be reasonably representative for the countries of the world. Figure 2.5 plots the average growth rate of GDP per worker from 1960 to 2003 against the log of GDP per worker in 1960 for the countries of this sample. The nice negative relationship has disappeared. The slope of the line of best fit has even become positive, but the line fits so poorly that we cannot attach any statistical significance to its slope. Since absolute convergence implies a clear negative relationship, we have to draw the sad conclusion: *the hypothesis of absolute convergence does not hold.*

Conditional convergence

Thinking a bit more about it, absolute convergence is too much to hope for. We know that the countries in Fig. 2.5 differ considerably with respect to basic structural characteristics. For instance, some countries have higher rates of saving and investment than others. Savings and investment accumulate as capital, and capital is productive. We should therefore expect countries with higher savings rates to have higher GDP per worker, but then GDP per worker cannot converge to one and the same level for all countries. Similarly, some countries spend a larger fraction of GDP on education (investing in human capital) than others, and education makes labour more productive. Countries with higher investment rates in human capital should therefore be expected to approach higher levels of GDP per worker. A third structural characteristic likely to be important is population growth. Higher population growth means (other things being equal) higher growth of the labour force and therefore, in turn, that a larger

9. J. Bradford DeLong, 'Productivity Growth, Convergence, and Welfare: Comment', *American Economic Review*, **78**, 1988, pp. 1138–1154.

10. Each country appearing in the PWT 6.2 is given a grade, A, B, C or D, for data quality. We exclude here countries with grade D.

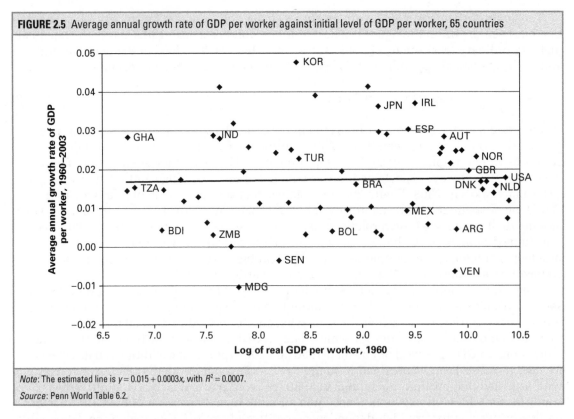

FIGURE 2.5 Average annual growth rate of GDP per worker against initial level of GDP per worker, 65 countries

Note: The estimated line is $y = 0.015 + 0.0003x$, with $R^2 = 0.0007$.

Source: Penn World Table 6.2.

number of people will come to share the capital accumulated in the past. Other characteristics being equal, this should pull GDP per capita down, again preventing absolute convergence.

Consider two countries with the same level of GDP per worker in an initial year zero, and suppose that the first country has more favourable structural characteristics than the second. Since the first country will then approach a higher level of GDP per worker than the second, it will also have higher average growth in GDP per worker over a period after year zero. Such reasoning has led to a weaker notion of convergence:

THE HYPOTHESIS OF CONDITIONAL CONVERGENCE

A country's income per worker (or per capita) converges to a **country-specific** long-run growth path which is given by the basic structural characteristics of the country. The further below its own long-run growth path a country starts, the faster it will grow. Income per worker therefore converges to the same level across countries **conditional** on the countries being structurally alike.

Again the convergence hypothesis implies a relationship between the initial level of and the subsequent growth in GDP per worker: *other things (basic structural characteristics) being equal, countries with relatively low levels of GDP per worker in an initial year will grow relatively fast after that initial year*. The crucial addition compared to the absolute convergence hypothesis is the phrase 'other things being equal'. According to the hypothesis of conditional convergence, it is only after controlling appropriately for structural differences that one should find a negative relationship between initial GDP per worker and subsequent growth. The correct equation would not be (1) above, but perhaps an equation like

$$\frac{\ln y_T^i - \ln y_0^i}{T} \cong \beta_0 - \beta_1 \ln y_0^i + \gamma(\mathbf{z}^i), \tag{3}$$

where $\mathbf{z}^i$ is a vector of variables capturing country-specific structural characteristics, and γ is a function expressing their influence.

The hypothesis of conditional convergence does not imply that poverty would disappear by itself in the long run. Nevertheless, conditional convergence is also a fascinating possibility. It *does* imply that if a poor country can manage somehow to achieve the same structural characteristics as rich countries, it *will* become as rich in due time. What are the implications of conditional convergence for the relevance of foreign aid? Certainly, conditional convergence gives more room for foreign aid than does absolute convergence, since conditional convergence means that a country may be caught in poverty due to bad structural characteristics. However, the kind of policy suggested is not so much a traditional one of transfers to the poor countries (with a reservation like the one we made in connection with absolute convergence). Rather, the conditional convergence hypothesis points to the importance of supporting poor countries in improving their internal structures. This could, for instance, be a policy of assisting a country in building up sound financial and educational systems.

To work seriously with an equation like (3), for example testing it against data, one must have an idea of how to handle the structural variables. Which economic variables should be included in $\mathbf{z}^i$, and what should the function γ look like? We have argued intuitively above that the rates of investment in physical and human capital and the population growth rate should probably be included, but this does not tell us how they should enter. A good answer will require some growth theory, as presented in the coming chapters. At this stage it will be illustrative to consider a specific version of (3), which is for now postulated, but will be rooted in theory later on. So, assume that (among) the relevant structural characteristics of country i are the rate of investment in physical capital (the GDP share of gross investment in physical capital), s^i, and the growth rate of the labour force, n^i. Assume further that (for reasons that will become clear in Chapters 3 and 5) the appropriate way they enter is:

$$\frac{\ln y_T^i - \ln y_0^i}{T} \cong \beta_0 - \beta_1 \ln y_0^i + \beta_2 [\ln s^i - \ln(n^i + 0.075)]. \tag{4}$$

Consider the same countries and years as in Fig. 2.5. Measure s^i and n^i as the country's average gross investment rate and its average labour force growth rate, respectively, over the period 1960 to 2003 (these can also be computed from data in the PWT, and are included in Table A of Book One). Assume that the appropriate value of the parameter β_2 is 0.016 (Chapter 5 will explain this value). Finally, create a diagram like Fig. 2.5, still with $\ln y_{60}^i$ along the horizontal axis, but now measure the growth rate *adjusted for country-specific structural characteristics*, $(\ln y_{03}^i - \ln y_{60}^i)/43 - \beta_2 [\ln s^i - \ln(n^i + 0.075)]$, up along the vertical axis. Figure 2.6 then results.

The points in Fig. 2.6 do seem to be clustered around a negatively sloped straight line. Hence, controlling for *some* structural differences makes the negative relationship between initial GDP per worker and subsequent growth visible again, and we have not even controlled for *all* the structural characteristics that should be important on *a priori* grounds. Education has not been taken into account, but will be later on. This will make the picture even more compatible with conditional convergence. Based on theoretical and empirical work, most economists believe that if one puts the right structural characteristics into $\mathbf{z}^i$, and takes account of these characteristics in the right way (assumes the right γ), then indeed one will end up with a significant and positive estimate of the β_1 in (3). That is, if one controls appropriately for the influence of structural characteristics, growth in GDP per worker *is* negatively correlated with the initial level of GDP per worker for the countries of the world. This accords with the hypothesis of conditional convergence.

Club convergence

According to the hypothesis of conditional convergence, the long-run growth path of each country is given entirely by the country's structural characteristics. It is independent of the country's initial level of GDP per worker: the starting point has no influence on the long-run

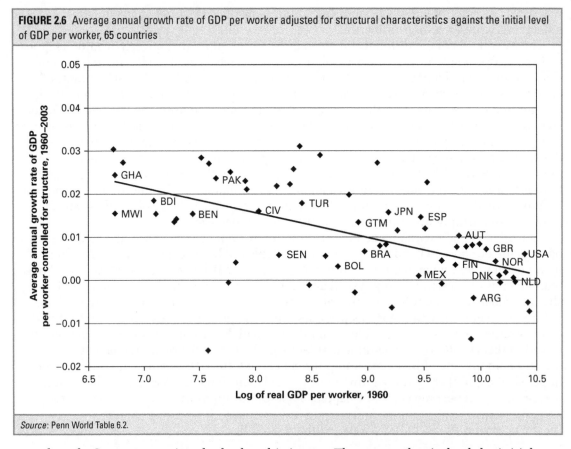

FIGURE 2.6 Average annual growth rate of GDP per worker adjusted for structural characteristics against the initial level of GDP per worker, 65 countries

Source: Penn World Table 6.2.

growth path. Some economists doubt that this is true. They argue that indeed the initial position of a country may have an influence on the level of the growth path that the country is approaching in the long run. In this way history can have a permanent impact – its influence is not washed out in the long run.

What these economists have in mind is that there is a certain threshold value of GDP per worker (or perhaps there are several thresholds, but here we present the idea in its simplest version), which may be country-specific, such that if a country happens to start below that value, it will converge to one growth path, and if it happens to start above, it will converge to another path. The two growth paths may have the same constant growth rate, but they differ with respect to their levels: the first path lies below the second. Figure 2.7 gives an illustration of club convergence.

The meaning of the term 'club' is that countries that start off on the same side of the threshold value are in the same category. Stating the hypothesis comprehensively, what must be changed from the definition of conditional convergence above is that the long-run growth path depends not only on structural characteristics, but also on the economy's starting point.

THE HYPOTHESIS OF CLUB CONVERGENCE ❗

A country's income per worker (or per capita) converges to a long-run growth path that depends on the country's basic structural characteristics and on whether its initial GDP per capita is above or below a specific threshold value. The further below the relevant growth path a country starts out, the faster it will grow. Income per worker therefore converges to the same level across countries **conditional** on the countries being structurally alike and on the countries starting on the same side of their respective threshold values.

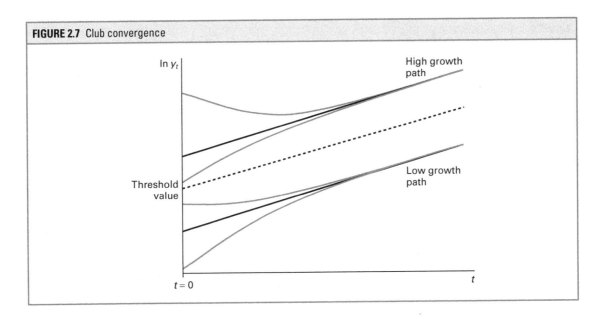

FIGURE 2.7 Club convergence

One can write down sound economic growth models that support the idea of conditional convergence, as well as models supporting the idea of club convergence. Likewise, some empirical analyses are in favour of conditional convergence, and some are in favour of club convergence. At present, the issue of conditional or club convergence is unsettled.

An interesting implication of the idea of club convergence is that it may provide a rationale for traditional foreign aid policy. Giving high transfers to a developing country over some period may bring the country's income per capita above the threshold level, and thereby initiate a growth process eventually leading the country to higher levels of income than would have been reached without the transfers, even after the transfers are no longer given. A foreign aid policy of giving *temporary* transfers to the poor countries can thus have *permanent* beneficial effects, according to the idea of club convergence.

We may sum up our discussion of convergence below in Stylized fact 4. The reader should be warned, however, that the issue of convergence is perhaps a bit more controversial than our use of the word 'fact' suggests:

STYLIZED FACT 4

Convergence: If one controls appropriately for structural differences between the countries of the world, a lower initial value of GDP per worker tends to be associated with a higher subsequent growth rate in GDP per worker. This accords with the idea that in the long run income and GDP per worker converge to a country-specific growth path which is given by the country's basic structural characteristics, and possibly also by its initial position.

2.4 The long-run growth process

The previous section was concerned with the relationship between the growth processes in different countries. Now we will focus on the long-run growth process within a single and steadily growing economy, that is, on growth along the country's own long-run growth path. To separate convergence to the growth path from the long-run growth path itself, we should look at very long series for GDP per person.

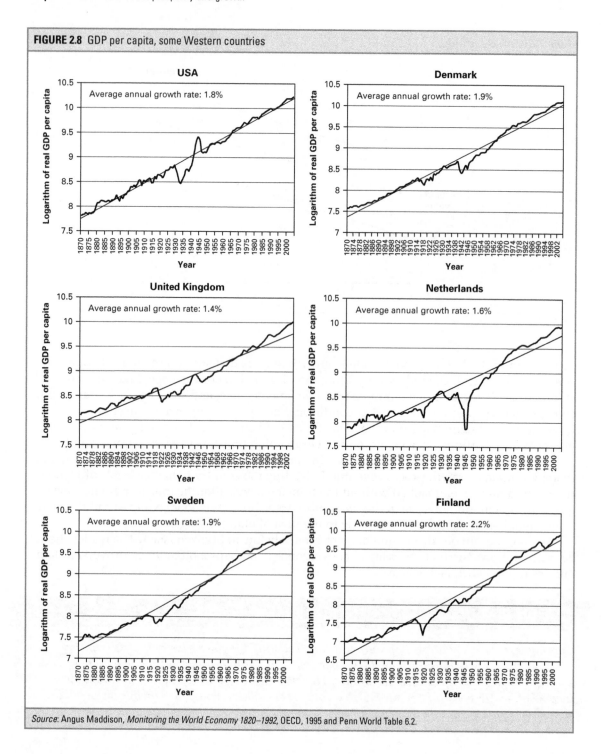

FIGURE 2.8 GDP per capita, some Western countries

Source: Angus Maddison, *Monitoring the World Economy 1820–1992*, OECD, 1995 and Penn World Table 6.2.

Steady long-run growth

Figure 2.8 shows the evolution of the log of GDP per capita in a number of Western countries for periods exceeding 100 years, and it also shows the linear trends. Disregarding shorter-run fluctuations and the influences from great wars and depressions, Fig. 2.8 shows for each country a remarkable tendency towards a constant and positive rate of growth in output per capita.

STYLIZED FACT 5

Over periods of more than 130 years, probably up to 200 years, many countries in Western Europe and North America have had relatively constant annual rates of growth in GDP per capita in the range 1.5–2 per cent.

Because of a lack of very long-run data for GDP per worker, Fig. 2.8 shows GDP per capita. However, there is good reason to believe that GDP per worker has also grown at constant (slightly lower) rates in the countries considered, since participation rates have typically increased gradually.

The countries that have experienced relatively constant growth have typically had remarkably constant factor income shares over long periods as well. The 'law' of stable income shares is illustrated in Fig. 2.9, which shows the evolution of the income share of labour for six OECD countries, five of which also appear in Fig. 2.8. Not only does labour's share not show any long-run trend, the relatively constant labour share turns out to be relatively close to 2/3 in all the countries. There *are* considerable short-run cyclical movements in labour's share (not so visible from Fig. 2.9), but the *long-run* evolution in the labour income share is fairly precisely described as being constant.

Consider a Western economy that has experienced steady annual growth in GDP per worker, $y_t = Y_t/L_t$, where Y_t and L_t are the GDP and the number of workers in year t, respectively. Labour's share in year t is $w_t L_t/Y_t$, where w_t is the average real wage per worker. We can rewrite labour's share as $w_t/(Y_t/L_t) = w_t/y_t$. Hence, if y_t has grown at a relatively constant rate, and labour's share has stayed relatively constant, the average real wage rate must have been increasing by more or less the same rate as GDP per worker. Steady growth in GDP per worker, and a constant labour income share, implies steady growth in the real wage.

STYLIZED FACT 6

During the long periods of relatively constant growth rates in GDP per worker in the typical Western economy, labour's share of GDP has stayed relatively constant, and (hence) the average real wage of a worker has grown by approximately the same rate as GDP per worker.

If labour's share has been relatively constant, so must the share of all other production factors since this latter share is one minus labour's share. Let us call the other factors 'capital', including into this category not only reproducible physical capital, but also, for example, land and other natural resources.

Let the total capital input in year t be denoted by K_t. If we denote the rate of return on capital by r_t, then capital's share is $r_t K_t/Y_t = r_t/(Y_t/K_t)$. Hence, constancy of capital's share implies that the real rate of return on capital, r_t, and the output–capital ratio, Y_t/K_t, must have been changing by the same rates.

Over long periods there should be no systematic differences between the trends in the real rates of return on different types of assets. If the rate of return on capital (as defined here) over a long period increased by one half of a per cent per year, say, while over the same period the real rate of interest on bonds stayed constant, investment in real capital would soon become much more advantageous than buying bonds. This would direct portfolios away from bonds and towards real capital, which would tend to equalize the rates of returns between bonds and capital.

In the long run the trend of the rate of return on capital must, therefore, be anchored by the trend of real interest rates on bonds. Figure 2.10 reports on the long-run behaviour of real interest rates over long periods in some Western countries. The figure shows that real

FIGURE 2.9 Labour's share of domestic factor incomes

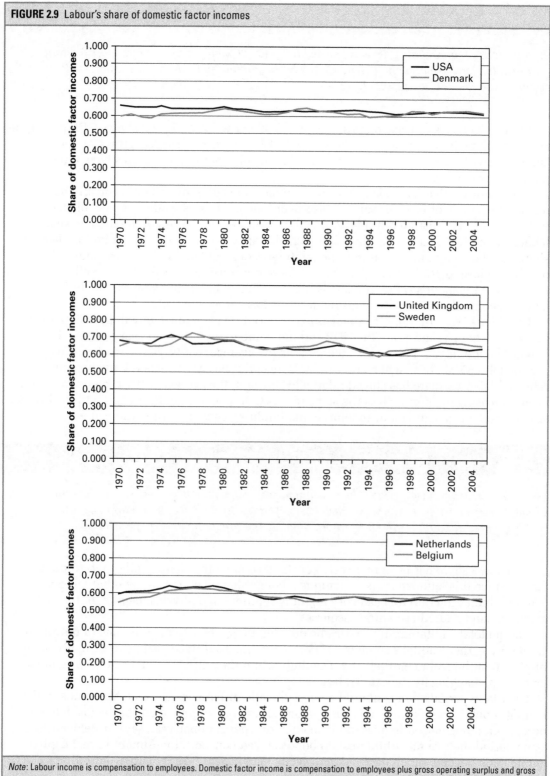

Note: Labour income is compensation to employees. Domestic factor income is compensation to employees plus gross operating surplus and gross mixed income.

Source: OECD, Annual National Accounts.

FIGURE 2.10 Real interest rates, Western countries

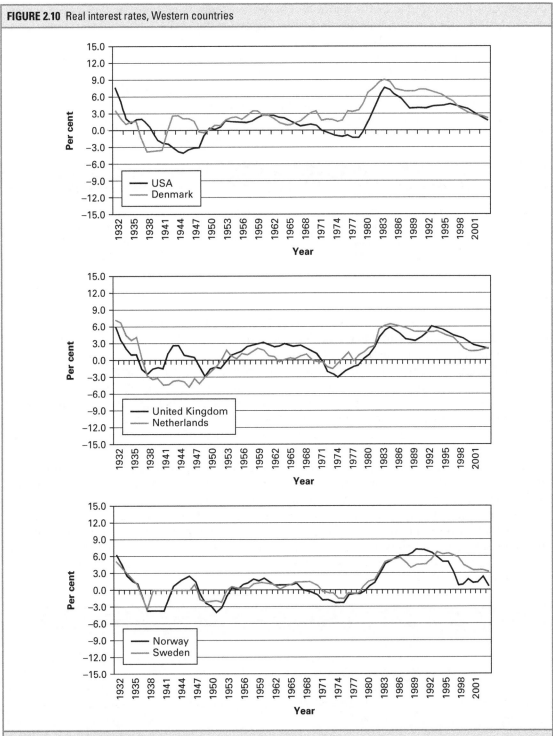

Note: The formula used for computing annual real interest rates is $(1 + r)(1 + p) = 1 + i$, where r is the real interest rate, i is the nominal interest rate, and p is the inflation rate measured as the relative change in average consumer prices from the current year to the next. The nominal interest rate used is the average annual yield on long-term government bonds. The figure shows five year moving averages of real interest rates computed this way.

Sources: Up to 1990–94, interest rates are from S. Homer and R. Sylla, *A History of Interest Rates*, Rutgers University Press, 1991, and consumer price indices are from B.R. Mitchell, *International Historical Statistics, 1750–1993*, Macmillan, 1998. For recent years interest rates and consumer price indices are from Source OECD.

interest rates (as computed in the figure) fluctuate, but there is no tendency for real interest rates to be systematically increasing or decreasing over long periods: they have no long-run trend, upwards or downwards. For purposes of long-run analysis, real interest rates, and hence the real rate of return on capital, may therefore be treated *as if* they were constant.

If capital's share, $r_t/(Y_t/K_t)$, and the rate of return on capital, r_t, have both been relatively constant, then the output–capital ratio, Y_t/K_t, and the capital–output ratio, K_t/Y_t, must also have been constant. We can rewrite the capital–output ratio as $K_t/Y_t = (K_t/L_t)/(Y_t/L_t) = k_t/y_t$, where we have denoted the capital–labour ratio, or capital intensity, K_t/L_t, by k_t. Constancy of K_t/Y_t implies that the capital intensity grows at the same rate as GDP per worker.

STYLIZED FACT 7

During the long periods of relatively constant growth in GDP per worker in the typical Western economy, capital's share and the rate of return on capital have shown no trend, (therefore) the capital–output ratio has been relatively constant, and the capital intensity has grown by approximately the same rate as GDP per worker.

Balanced growth

The empirical regularities in our Stylized facts 5–7 are much inspired by a famous lecture given by the British economist Nicholas Kaldor, who pioneered the approach of setting up the stylized facts and constructing theories to explain them.[11] All three facts can be expressed comprehensively by three fundamental constancies: the growth rate of GDP per worker is relatively constant, the functional income distribution between labour and 'capital' is relatively constant, and the rate of return on 'capital' is relatively constant. All the other features in our list of facts follow from these constancies (convince yourself of this).

The stylized facts have given rise to an idealized picture of the long-run growth process called 'balanced growth'. Consider an economy that fulfils the three constancies with an annual growth rate, g, in GDP per worker, a constant annual growth rate, n, in the number of workers, and for which total annual consumption is a constant fraction, $1 - s$, of total annual GDP (a realistic long-run feature for a typical western economy).

Since $Y_t = y_t L_t$, one has $\ln Y_t - \ln Y_{t-1} = (\ln y_t - \ln y_{t-1}) + (\ln L_t - \ln L_{t-1}) \approx g + n$, so GDP grows at a constant rate equal to the sum of the growth rate of GDP per worker and the population growth rate. Hence total consumption, $(1 - s)Y_t$, and total investment, sY_t, must also be growing at the rate, $g + n$. Finally, since $K_t = k_t L_t$, and k_t is growing at the same rate as y_t, total capital is growing at the rate, $g + n$.

BALANCED GROWTH[12]

T he growth process follows a balanced growth path if GDP per worker, consumption per worker, the real wage rate, and the capital intensity all grow at one and the same constant rate, g, the labour force (population) grows at constant rate, n, GDP, consumption, and capital grow at the common rate, $g + n$, the capital–output ratio is constant, and the rate of return on capital is constant.

---

11. You can find this lecture by Nicholas Kaldor, 'Capital Accumulation and Economic Growth', in *The Theory of Capital*, F.A. Lutz and D.C. Hague (eds), New York, St Martins, 1961.

12. Our definition of balanced growth is a relatively strict one. Often balanced growth is just meant to describe a situation where GDP, consumption, capital and population all grow at constant rates, which is implied by, but does not itself imply, our definition. We find the definition given here useful for how we are going to use the concept of balanced growth: as a comprehensive expression of the empirical regularities that we want our growth theories to explain.

Along a balanced growth path the capital–output ratio is constant. In fact, the constancy of the capital–output ratio is a main motivating factor behind the definition of balanced growth. We have argued indirectly for this constancy: it follows from constant income shares and the absence of a trend in the rate of return on capital, where we argued for the latter by pointing to the long-run behaviour of real interest rates. However, it should be mentioned that there is some controversy about whether long-run capital–output ratios are really constant. Direct estimates of the long-run evolution of capital–output ratios, most notably some by the British economist and economic historian Angus Maddison, suggest that the capital–output ratio may be close to constant in the US in the long run, but in several other countries the ratio seems to have been gradually increasing over the past 100 years.[13]

When we turn to growth models in the subsequent chapters, balanced growth will be of theoretical importance. If a growth model predicts that the economy will converge to or move along a specific long-run growth path, then this path should be a balanced growth path, because of the empirical plausibility of balanced growth. Long-run accordance with balanced growth will thus be used as an 'empirical consistency check' of growth models.

2.5 Summary

1. A country's GDP per worker may be used as a proxy for the average standard of living and the average productivity of labour in the country. In some countries the population participates much less in the formal market economy than in other countries. Focusing on GDP per member of the official labour force rather than on GDP per capita is a rough way of adjusting for this.

2. The empirical evidence on levels of GDP per worker reveals enormous income differences across countries. Combining data on GDP per worker with data on population size, we found that the relative cross-country income differences have declined over the past 30 years, but there was little reduction in international inequality at the very bottom of the world income ladder. The fact that the world income distribution has improved *in relative terms* means that *on average* poor countries have enjoyed percentage increases in income per worker at or above the percentage increase in income per worker in the world in general. *In absolute terms* poverty has therefore become less severe, but at the same time the *absolute* international income differences between the richest and the poorest countries have increased.

3. The evidence shows that growth rates vary substantially across countries. By the process of growing or declining quickly, a country can move from being relatively poor to being relatively rich, or from being relatively rich to being relatively poor. Moreover, growth can break in a country, turning from a high rate to a low one, or vice versa. These facts indicate that the fight against poverty is not hopeless. On the other hand, a relatively prosperous country will not automatically remain so regardless of the policies it follows. These observations point to the importance of structural policies to promote or maintain economic growth.

4. The evidence seems to support the hypothesis that the world's countries converge in a conditional sense: if one controls appropriately for structural differences across countries, a lower initial value of GDP per worker tends to be associated with a higher subsequent growth rate in GDP per worker. This accords with the idea that in the long run, income and GDP per worker converge to a country-specific growth path which is given by the country's basic structural characteristics (and possibly also by its initial position).

13. Angus Maddison, *Dynamic Forces in Capitalist Development: A Long Run Comparative View*, Oxford University Press, 1991.

▶

5. Over periods of more than 130 years, and probably up to 200 years, many countries in Western Europe and North America have had relatively constant annual rates of growth in GDP per capita in the range 1.5–2 per cent. During these long periods, labour's share of GDP has stayed relatively constant. Hence the average real wage of a worker has grown by approximately the same rate as GDP per worker. Furthermore, capital's share and the rate of return on capital have shown no trend, so the capital–output ratio has been relatively constant, that is, the stock of capital per worker has grown at roughly the same rate as GDP per worker.

6. The facts just mentioned have given rise to an idealized picture of the growth process called 'balanced growth'. In this book balanced growth will describe a situation where GDP per worker, consumption per worker, the (average) real wage rate, and the capital–labour ratio all grow at one and the same constant rate, and the rate of return on capital is constant. We will use long-run accordance with balanced growth as an empirical consistency check for the growth models to be presented in coming chapters.

2.6　Exercises

Exercise 1.　GDP per capita versus GDP per worker

Give some arguments why GDP per worker, rather than GDP per capita, should be used for a comparison of standards of living between countries.

Exercise 2.　The income distribution for the rich part of the world

Table 2.4 shows GDP per worker (in 2000 US dollars) and population size for 1951 and 2003 for the rich part of the world (defined here as the OECD countries for which data were available).

　　Construct Lorenz curves for the rich world for 1951 and 2003, respectively, assuming that everybody in the population earned the GDP per worker of the relevant year, and draw the two curves in one figure. Compute the Gini coefficient for each year. Comment on how inequality, or equality, among the rich has developed. Compare this to how the income distribution of the world has developed. Relate this to what you know about convergence from Section 2.3.

Exercise 3.　Time to double

Assume that in a specific country GDP per capita, or per worker, grows at the rate g each year over many years, where g is written as a percentage, e.g. 2 per cent. Show that GDP per capita, or worker, will then approximately double every $70/g$ years. Use this to set up a table showing for each of the 15 richest countries in the world in 2003, the country's average annual growth rate in GDP per worker from 1960 to 2003 (you can take these from Table 2.2), and the number of years it takes for the country's GDP per worker to double, if growth continues at the same rate as it averaged from 1960 to 2003.

Exercise 4.　Growth against ultimo level

In Section 2.3 there were figures showing across countries the log of GDP per worker in an initial year along the horizontal axis, and average annual growth in GDP per worker in a subsequent relatively long period along the vertical axis. For the OECD countries there was a clear negative relationship (see Fig. 2.4). Construct an 'opposite' figure for the same countries as in Fig. 2.4, where along the horizontal axis you have the log of GDP per worker, not in an initial year, but in a final year, 2003, and along the vertical axis you have the average annual growth rate in GDP per worker from 1960 to 2003. Comment on your findings. Data for this exercise can be taken from Table A at the end of Book One.

TABLE 2.4 Population size and GDP per worker, 1951 and 2003, OECD countries[1]

	1951			2003	
	Population (1,000)	**GDP per worker (2000 dollars)**		**Population (1,000)**	**GDP per worker (2000 dollars)**
Turkey	22,048	3,248	Turkey	71,252	11,812
Japan	85,118	5,496	Mexico	104,337	18,628
Portugal	8,393	6,312	Portugal	10,386	34,076
Greece	7,647	7,049	Greece	11,075	35,945
Spain	28,252	8,733	New Zealand	3,946	44,347
Mexico	28,438	8,996	Japan	127,736	45,030
Austria	6,930	10,435	Iceland	289	46,240
Italy	47,407	10,441	Spain	42,144	46,619
Ireland	2,966	10,629	Finland	5,220	48,016
Finland	4,050	11,358	Sweden	8,970	48,128
France	42,034	13,620	Denmark	5,397	51,499
Iceland	145	14,212	Canada	31,636	51,796
Belgium	8,673	16,213	United Kingdom	59,282	51,924
Denmark	4,310	17,355	Italy	57,961	52,097
Norway	3,299	17,541	Switzerland	7,226	54,256
United Kingdom	49,862	18,243	Australia	19,728	54,600
Netherlands	10,230	19,057	Netherlands	16,148	56,790
Sweden	7,076	19,736	France	60,008	56,909
Luxembourg	297	22,090	Austria	8,150	59,789
Australia	8,414	22,108	Belgium	10,379	61,541
Canada	14,133	24,118	Norway	4,575	65,699
New Zealand	1,948	24,834	Ireland	4,007	65,925
Switzerland	4,738	25,489	United States	292,617	67,865
United States	160,016	27,426	Luxembourg	453	117,759

[1] Members in 2003 except the Czech Republic, the Slovak Republic, Hungary, Poland, Korea & Germany.
Source: Penn World Table 6.2.

Exercise 5. Level convergence among the rich?

Commenting on Fig. 2.3 in Section 2.3 we said that it showed a tendency towards convergence to a common growth path with constant growth for the countries involved. Perhaps we were too hasty. The following figure will make level differences more visible if they are there. For the same countries and years as in Fig. 2.3, compute GDP per worker relative to GDP per worker in the USA over the period and illustrate in a figure with *relative* GDP per capita against years. The US will appear as a horizontal line. Comment on the issue if all countries other than the US seem to be approaching the US horizontal line. To find the data for this exercise, you will have to go to the PWT 6.2 yourself (http://pwt.econ.upenn.edu/).

Exercise 6. Growth and trade

This chapter has presented the stylized facts of growth that are most important for the theoretical developments in subsequent chapters. There is at least one more important fact, which relates growth to growth in trade. To draw the following figure you should go to the PWT 6.2 yourself (http://pwt.econ.upenn.edu/). First make sure that you understand what the variable 'openness' measures. For this you will need to go to the explanatory documents of the PWT. Across as many countries as possible, plot the average annual growth rate of GDP (not per worker) from 1960 to 2003, against the average annual growth rate of 'trade volume', where the latter is defined as the total value of exports and imports. Do an OLS estimation of the line of best fit. What has grown most, world GDP or world trade? Can it be inferred from the figure whether growth in trade causes growth in GDP, or growth in GDP causes growth in trade?

Exercise 7. Galton's Fallacy[14]

It is an implication of convergence that a lower initial GDP per worker should, other things being equal, imply a higher subsequent growth in GDP per worker. This was used in the chapter to test convergence: the lack of a negative relationship between initial GDP per worker and subsequent growth would imply a rejection of the hypothesis. Is it also true the other way around, that a clear negative relationship between initial GDP per worker and subsequent growth is necessarily an indication of convergence? The answer is no, as this exercise should teach you.[15]

To each of 26 imaginary countries attribute a GDP per worker in 1960 (measured in US 2000 dollars, say) as follows: 10,000 to Country 1, 12,000 to Country 2, 14,000 to Country 3, etc., up to 60,000 to Country 26. Now determine each country's GDP per worker in the year 2003 by *picking randomly* (without replacement) from the same set of values for GDP per worker, {10,000, 12,000, . . . , 60,000}, one value for each country (you can do this on the computer or by drawing values written on pieces of paper from a box). For each country you will now have an initial 1960 value for GDP per worker and an eventual year 2003 value. Plot across countries the average annual growth rate in GDP per worker against the initial level of GDP per worker. Why is it that there must be a negative relationship? Can we infer anything about convergence from this negative relationship?

---

14. The term 'Galton's Fallacy' comes from the English statistician Francis Galton who once, late in the nineteenth century, made a similar fallacy in connection with heights of sons and fathers. Galton noted a tendency that relatively tall fathers got sons shorter than themselves, and vice versa. He concluded from this, a tendency to 'convergence' towards a general intermediate height of everybody.

15. The exercise is based on Danny Quah, 'Galton's Fallacy and Tests of the Convergence Hypothesis', *Scandinavian Journal of Economics*, **95**, 1993, pp. 427–443.

PART 1

Basic Theory and Empirics about Prosperity and Growth

CHAPTER

3

Capital accumulation and growth

The basic Solow model

The previous chapter raised a basic economic question: how can a nation escape from poverty and ultimately become rich? Or more precisely: how can a country initiate a growth process that will lead it to a higher level of GDP and consumption per person?

This chapter presents a fundamental economic model that delivers some first answers. The model will show how the long-run evolutions of income and consumption per worker in a country are affected by structural parameters such as the country's rate of saving and investment and the growth rate of its population. The model is known as the Solow model of economic growth.

In 1956 the economist and Nobel Prize Laureate Robert M. Solow published a seminal article called 'A Contribution to the Theory of Economic Growth'. The article presented a coherent dynamic model with an explicit description of the process of *capital accumulation* by which saving and investment become new capital.[1]

In the Solow model, competitive clearing of factor markets implies that output in each period is determined by the available supplies of capital and labour. Furthermore, total saving and investment is assumed to be an exogenous fraction of total income, and the labour force is assumed to grow at a given rate.

The essential additional feature of the Solow model is that it incorporates the dynamic link between the flows of savings and investment and the stock of capital. Solow's model accounts for the fact that between any two successive periods, the stock of capital will increase by an amount equal to gross investment minus depreciation on the initial capital stock.[2]

The model describes how capital evolves as a result of capital accumulation, how the labour force evolves as a result of population growth, and how total production and income evolves as a consequence of the evolutions of the total inputs of capital and labour. The model therefore involves a certain evolution of income per worker as well. It thereby contributes to answering the fundamental question of what determines 'the wealth of nations'.

This chapter presents the Solow model in its most basic version where the focus is on capital accumulation, not on technological progress, as a source of economic growth.

---

1. Robert M. Solow, 'A Contribution to the Theory of Economic Growth', *Quarterly Journal of Economics*, **70**, 1956, pp. 65–94.

2. Solow was not the first to suggest a coherent formal framework with an explicit description of the capital accumulation process. Two famous predecessors are Roy. F. Harrod, 'An Essay in Dynamic Theory', *Economic Journal*, **49**, pp. 14–33, and Evsey D. Domar, 'Capital Expansion, Rate of Growth, and Employment, *Econometrica*, **14**, pp. 137–147. However, Solow was the first to suggest such a framework in a model with long-run substitution possibilities between capital and labour. The assumption that these inputs can substitute considerably for each other *in the long run* is empirically plausible.

Technological progress will be a main theme in coming chapters. Considering the simplicity of *the basic Solow model*, it will take us remarkably far in understanding potential sources of and limitations to economic growth and long-run prosperity: *the basic Solow model* makes a great contribution and is indeed an important workhorse model in economics.

3.1 The basic Solow model

The model presented in this chapter describes a closed economy (the next chapter will present a Solow model for an open economy). Initially we will not explicitly include the public sector in the model, but we will show that it can easily be interpreted as including government expenditure and taxation.

Agents, commodities and markets

The economic agents in the model are households, also referred to as consumers; firms, also called producers; and possibly a government. Time runs in a discrete sequence of periods indexed by t. A period should be thought of as one year. There are three commodities in each period, and for each commodity there is a market. The commodities are output, capital services and labour services.

In the market for output the supply consists of the total output of firms, Y_t. The demand is the sum of total consumption, C_t, and total investment, I_t. Hence output can either be used for consumption, or it can be transformed into capital via investment (at no cost, we assume). The model is thus a one-sector model and does not distinguish between production of consumption goods and production of capital goods. The price in the output market is normalized to one, so other prices are measured in units of output.

We may think of the accumulated stock of physical capital as being directly owned by the households who lease it to the firms. Hence, in the market for capital services the supply comes from the consumers. By a convenient definition of the unit of measurement for capital services (machine years), a capital stock of K_t units of capital can give rise to a supply of K_t units of capital services during period t. The demand for capital services, K_t^d, comes from the firms. The real price, r_t, in this market is the amount of output that a firm must pay to a consumer for leasing one unit of capital during period t. Thus r_t is a real *rental rate*.

This rental rate has a close association with, but is not equal to, the model's real *interest rate*. The reason is that capital depreciates. We assume that the use of one unit of physical capital for one period implies that an amount δ, where $0 < \delta < 1$, must be set aside to compensate for depreciation, that is, for the capital that is worn out by one period's use. The name for δ is the rate of depreciation. The model's real interest rate, ρ_t, is the return to capital *net of depreciation*, that is, $\rho_t = r_t - \delta$. This is the rate of return on capital comparable to an interest rate earned from a financial asset like a bond.

Alternatively, one can think of physical capital as being owned by firms who finance their acquisition of capital by issuing debt to consumers. In the latter case the real price of the use of a unit of capital for one period, also called the 'user cost', is the real interest rate on debt plus the depreciation on one unit of capital. In this interpretation one can think of the firm's 'rental rate' as $r_t = \rho_t + \delta$. For our purposes it does not matter whether the user cost of capital, r_t, is a direct leasing rate or the sum of an interest rate and a depreciation rate.

In the labour market the supply of labour services, L_t, comes from the households, while the demand, L_t^d, comes from the firms. We measure labour flows in man years, so a labour force of L_t can give rise to a labour supply of L_t. The real wage rate in period t is denoted by w_t.

All three markets are assumed to be perfectly competitive, so economic agents take the prices as given, and in each market the appropriate price adjusts so that price-taking supply becomes equal to price-taking demand. This implies that available resources are fully utilized in all periods or, in an alternative interpretation, that they are utilized up to the 'natural rate' defined in Chapter 1.

The production sector

The production side of the economy is modelled as if all production takes place in one representative profit-maximizing firm. The firm uses capital input, K_t^d, and labour input, L_t^d, to produce output (value added), Y_t, according to the production function:

$$Y_t = F(K_t^d, L_t^d).$$ (1)

The production function is assumed to display *constant returns to scale*. In mathematical terms this means that the function $F(K^d, L^d)$ is homogeneous of degree one, so $F(\lambda K^d, \lambda L^d) = \lambda F(K^d, L^d)$ for all $\lambda > 0$. In words, if we increase both inputs by, say, 100 per cent, output will also go up by 100 per cent. There is a *replication argument* for this assumption: it should be possible to produce twice as much from a doubling of inputs, since one could simply apply the same production process twice.

The marginal product of capital is the increase in output generated per extra unit of capital. Formally, it is the partial derivative $F_K(K^d, L^d)$ of $F(K^d, L^d)$ with respect to K^d. Similarly, the marginal product of labour is the partial derivative of the production function with respect to L^d, denoted by $F_L(K^d, L^d)$. We assume that F_K and F_L are positive for all input combinations (K^d, L^d). In accordance with standard microeconomic theory, the marginal products are also assumed to be decreasing in the amount of the factor used, so $F_{KK}(K^d, L^d) < 0$ and $F_{LL}(K^d, L^d) < 0$, where F_{KK} is the second derivative with respect to K^d, and F_{LL} is the second derivative with respect to L^d. Finally, when the input of one factor increases, the marginal product of the other factor is assumed to go up. This means that $F_{KL}(K^d, L^d) = F_{LK}(K^d, L^d) > 0$.

The variables K_t^d and L_t^d are the amounts of capital and labour *demanded* by the firm in period t. The firm faces the real factor prices r_t and w_t, and it will want to choose Y_t, K_t^d and L_t^d to maximize pure profits $Y_t - rK_t^d - wL_t^d$, subject to the technical feasibility constraint, $Y_t = F(K_t^d, L_t^d)$. From microeconomic theory we know that a competitive profit-maximizing firm will want to employ a factor of production up to the point where its marginal product is just equal to its real price. In our model, the necessary first-order conditions (resulting from differentiation, etc.) take the form:

$$F_K(K_t^d, L_t^d) = r_t,$$ (2)

$$F_L(K_t^d, L_t^d) = w_t.$$ (3)

Note that (2) and (3) do not determine the levels of K_t^d and L_t^d given r_t and w_t, even though they are two equations in two unknowns. If one combination (K_t^d, L_t^d) fits in the two equations, so does $(\lambda K_t^d, \lambda L_t^d)$ for any $\lambda > 0$. This is a consequence of the assumed homogeneity of the production function.[3] Nevertheless, a combination of factor inputs, K_t^d and L_t^d, must fulfil (2) and (3) to be optimal.

Because the factor markets are perfectly competitive, the rental rate, r_t, adjusts to equate capital demand with capital supply, and the wage rate, w_t, adjusts such that labour demand becomes equal to labour supply. We will argue below that as long as the rental rate is just slightly positive, it will pay for consumers to supply all of their capital to the market, so capital supply is equal to the capital stock, K_t. Furthermore, we are going to assume that consumers supply labour inelastically, so labour supply must equal the labour force, L_t. Inserting $K_t^d = K_t$ and $L_t^d = L_t$ into (2) and (3), respectively, gives:

$$F_K(K_t, L_t) = r_t,$$ (4)

$$F_L(K_t, L_t) = w_t.$$ (5)

---

3. If a function is homogeneous of degree k, then its first partial derivatives are homogeneous of degree $k - 1$. Since F is homogeneous of degree one, F_K and F_L are homogeneous of degree zero. Hence, $F_K(\lambda K^d, \lambda L^d) = F_K(K^d, L^d)$.

In each period t, the stocks of capital and labour are predetermined and given, as will be explained below. Therefore (4) and (5) determine the period's rental rate, r_t (and hence the interest rate, $r_t - \delta$), and the wage rate, w_t, respectively, as these depend on the given levels of capital and labour. This leads to a theory of the functional distribution of income.

The distribution of income and the Cobb–Douglas production function

Using (1), (4) and (5), we find that the shares of capital and labour in total income in any period t are:

$$\frac{r_t K_t}{Y_t} = \frac{F_K(K_t, L_t)K_t}{F(K_t, L_t)}, \tag{6}$$

$$\frac{w_t L_t}{Y_t} = \frac{F_L(K_t, L_t)L_t}{F(K_t, L_t)}. \tag{7}$$

Note that

$$\frac{F_K K}{Y} \equiv \frac{\partial Y}{\partial K}\frac{K}{Y}$$

is the elasticity of output with respect to the input of capital, and

$$\frac{F_L L}{Y} \equiv \frac{\partial Y}{\partial L}\frac{L}{Y}$$

is the elasticity of output with respect to labour input. Thus equations (6) and (7) say that the share of each factor in total income is equal to the elasticity of output with respect to that factor.

Notice also that the firm's pure profit measured in real terms is $Y_t - (r_t K_t + w_t L_t) = F(K_t, L_t) - [F_K(K_t, L_t)K_t + F_L(K_t, L_t)L_t]$. Since the production function is homogeneous of degree one, we have $F(K_t, L_t) = F_K(K_t, L_t)K_t + F_L(K_t, L_t)L_t$, implying that pure profits are zero. This is an appealing property of a perfectly competitive economy in long-run equilibrium, because if pure profits were positive, we would expect new firms to enter the market until profits were competed away, and if pure profits were negative, we would expect some failing firms to be driven out of the market until the remaining firms were able to break even.

In Chapter 2 we saw that in the long run the factor income shares are remarkably constant. How does this constancy fit with our theory of the income distribution? At first sight it does not seem to fit. According to (7), the labour income share is given as the output elasticity with respect to labour input, and this will generally depend on the input combination, (K_t, L_t), which is changing over time. More precisely, labour's share depends on the capital–labour ratio, K_t/L_t.[4] The capital–labour ratio has been systematically increasing over time in developed countries. Apparently this should have implied a changing labour income share, according to our theory.

A similar observation was already puzzling the economist Paul Douglas in 1927. He asked the mathematician Charles Cobb whether a production function exists which has all the properties assumed above, and which will produce constant income shares when factors are paid their marginal products. As we have seen in (6) and (7), this is the same as requiring the output elasticities with respect to capital and labour to be constant (and hence

---

4. Write labour's share as $F_L(K, L)/[F(K, L)/L]$. The numerator only depends on K/L, because F_L is homogeneous of degree zero, so $F_L(K, L) = L^0 F_L(K/L, 1) = F_L(K/L, 1)$, and the denominator only depends on K/L, because F is homogeneous of degree one, so $F(K, L)/L = L F(K/L, 1)/L = F(K/L, 1)$.

independent of K_t/L_t). Charles Cobb found that there exists one such function, since then called the Cobb–Douglas production function:

$$Y_t = F(K_t^d, L_t^d) = B(K_t^d)^\alpha (L_t^d)^{1-\alpha}, \qquad B > 0, \qquad 0 < \alpha < 1. \tag{8}$$

Here α and B are given parameters, and B is referred to as the total factor productivity, TFP. The TFP is often considered as a measure of technology, but it really captures the influence of all factors other than those explicitly present in the production function (here capital and labour), among these technology.

Note that the inputs of capital and labour are indexed by t, capturing that these amounts of input may vary over time. The total factor productivity, B, has no time subscript, so we have assumed here that there is no change in 'technology' over time. This is the sense in which the model in this chapter is the *basic* Solow model. The subject of Chapter 5 will be the Solow model with technological progress where TFP increases over time.

Taking partial derivatives in (8), and inserting the equilibrium conditions, $K_t^d = K_t$ and $L_t^d = L_t$, we find that Eqs (4) and (5) take the particular form:

$$F_K(K_t, L_t) = \alpha B \left(\frac{K_t}{L_t}\right)^{\alpha-1} = r_t, \tag{9}$$

$$F_L(K_t, L_t) = (1-\alpha)B \left(\frac{K_t}{L_t}\right)^{\alpha} = w_t. \tag{10}$$

Using (8), (9) and (10), you should check carefully that the Cobb–Douglas production function does indeed have *all* the properties attributed to F, and that it does imply constant income shares, a capital share of α, and a labour share of $1 - \alpha$.

The proximate constancy of income shares in the long run suggests that a production function of the Cobb–Douglas form is a reasonable approximation for an aggregate production function for long-run analysis. The fact that the labour income share stays rather close to $\frac{2}{3}$ (see again Chapter 2) suggests that we have a reasonable value for the α appearing in (8), namely a number around $\frac{1}{3}$. Both these features will be used extensively in the growth theory presented in this book. Aggregate production functions will be assumed to have the Cobb–Douglas form, and whenever we need an estimate of α, we will consider $\frac{1}{3}$ as a reasonable value.

The household sector

The number of consumers in period t is L_t, which is predetermined from the past evolution of the population. The behaviour of consumers is described by four features.

First, as mentioned, each consumer is assumed to supply one unit of labour inelastically in each period, so the total supply of labour is L_t. If households were trading off consumption against leisure so as to maximize utility, an inelastic supply of labour would follow if the income and substitution effects from a change in the real wage were exactly offsetting each other. Empirically, long-run labour supply is not too sensitive to changes in real wages, so the assumption of an inelastic labour supply is not a bad first approximation.

Second, the consumers own the capital stock K_t, which is predetermined from capital accumulation in the past. For any positive rental rate, $r_t > 0$, a consumer seeking to maximize his income will want to lease *all* his capital to the firms, because each consumer considers r_t as given. Therefore the supply of capital services in year t is inelastic and equal to the size of the capital stock K_t.

Third, each consumer must decide how much to consume and how much to save. We assume that the household sector behaves as one representative consumer who earns all the economy's gross income, $Y_t = r_t K_t + w_t L_t$. The representative consumer must decide on consumption, C_t, and hence on gross saving, $S_t \equiv Y_t - C_t$, respecting his intertemporal budget constraint. According to this constraint, the addition, $K_{t+1} - K_t$, to the consumer's real stock of capital from period t to $t+1$ must equal his gross saving in period t minus the depreciation, δK_t, on the capital leased to the firms during period t. Hence the intertemporal budget constraint is:

$$K_{t+1} - K_t = S_t - \delta K_t. \tag{11}$$

If we were deriving consumption and savings behaviour from explicit optimization, a utility function defined over streams of present and future consumption would be maximized under the intertemporal budget constraint (11). Here, however, we make a simplifying short cut. We assume that the outcome of the underlying optimization is a constant savings rate, i.e. the household sector saves the exogenous fraction, s, of total income in each period:

$$S_t = sY_t, \quad \text{where } 0 < s < 1. \tag{12}$$

We are going to show below that the assumption of a given, constant rate of saving and investment is empirically plausible in the long run. The intertemporal budget constraint, (11), is itself important in our model: it is the aggregate *capital accumulation equation* stating that new capital originates from net savings.

Fourth, the 'biological' behaviour of the households is described by an exogenous growth rate, n, of the population, or rather of the labour force:

$$L_{t+1} = (1 + n)L_t, \quad \text{where } n > -1. \tag{13}$$

The complete model

The basic Solow model consists of the six equations stated in the box below and all repeated from above. Note that as part of the model, initial values, K_0 and L_0, for the state variables capital and labour are stated in equations (18) and (19).

THE COMPLETE BASIC SOLOW MODEL   !

$$Y_t = BK_t^\alpha L_t^{1-\alpha}, \tag{14}$$

$$r_t = \alpha B\left(\frac{K_t}{L_t}\right)^{\alpha-1}, \tag{15}$$

$$w_t = (1-\alpha)B\left(\frac{K_t}{L_t}\right)^{\alpha}, \tag{16}$$

$$S_t = sY_t, \tag{17}$$

$$K_{t+1} - K_t = S_t - \delta K_t, \quad K_0 \text{ given} \tag{18}$$

$$L_{t+1} = (1 + n)L_t, \quad L_0 \text{ given} \tag{19}$$

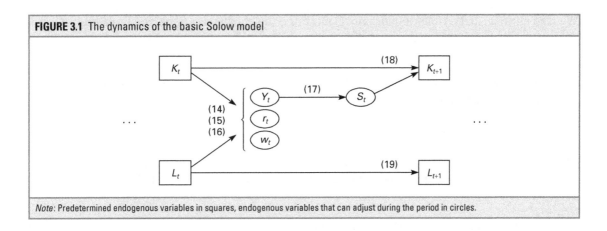

FIGURE 3.1 The dynamics of the basic Solow model

Note: Predetermined endogenous variables in squares, endogenous variables that can adjust during the period in circles.

The parameters of the model are α, B, s, n and δ. Given an initial input combination K_0, L_0 in some initial year zero, these six equations determine the dynamic evolution of the economy, as illustrated in Fig. 3.1.

In period t the inputs K_t and L_t are predetermined, so the first of the above equations gives the supply-determined output, Y_t, directly while the next two equations give the rental rate, r_t, and the wage rate, w_t, respectively. With Y_t determined, Eq. (17) gives the gross saving, S_t, in period t, and then from S_t and K_t, Eq. (18) determines the next period's capital supply, K_{t+1}. Finally, from the labour supply L_t of period t, Eq. (19) determines the next period's labour supply, L_{t+1}. Hence, K_{t+1} and L_{t+1} have been determined, and one can start all over again with period $t + 1$ etc.

We have chosen to present the fundamental *capital accumulation equation*, (18), as the representative consumer's intertemporal budget constraint. We could instead have explained the capital accumulation equation in the following more direct way: by definition, gross investment, I_t, minus depreciation, δK_t, is the addition to capital: $K_{t+1} - K_t = I_t - \delta K_t$. The national accounting identity for the output market, $Y_t = C_t + I_t$, is equivalent to $I_t = S_t$, since $S_t \equiv Y_t - C_t$. Inserting S_t for I_t in the definition of gross investment gives (18).

Government

The model can be interpreted as involving a government sector. Assume that the government collects a tax revenue of T_t in period t, and that government expenditure for public consumption and for public investment are C_t^g and I_t^g, respectively. Let expenditure behaviour be described by the ratio of public consumption to GDP, c_t^g, and by the ratio of public investment to GDP, i_t^g, respectively:

$$C_t^g = c_t^g Y_t, \qquad \text{where } 0 < c_t^g < 1,$$

$$I_t^g = i_t^g Y_t, \qquad \text{where } 0 < i_t^g < 1.$$

We allow c_t^g and i_t^g to be time dependent and assume $c_t^g + i_t^g < 1$. Assume further that the government balances its budget:

$$T_t = C_t^g + I_t^g.$$

Let c_t^p denote the ratio of private consumption, C_t^p, to private disposable income, $Y_t - T_t$. Then:

$$C_t^p = c_t^p (Y_t - T_t), \qquad \text{where } 0 < c_t^p < 1.$$

We also allow c_t^p to be time-dependent.[5] Combining the above equations one finds that:

$$C_t^p = c_t^p(1 - c_t^g - i_t^g)Y_t.$$

Thus private consumption as a fraction of GDP is $c_t^p(1 - c_t^g - i_t^g)$, which is not necessarily a constant. Total (national) consumption, $C_t = C_t^g + C_t^p$, is:

$$C_t = [c_t^g + c_t^p(1 - c_t^g - i_t^g)]Y_t.$$

The assumption we make is that the share of *total* consumption in GDP, $c_t^g + c_t^p(1 - c_t^g - i_t^g)$, is a given constant. Then national savings must be a constant fraction of GDP as well, $S_t = sY_t$, where:

$$s = 1 - c_t^g - c_t^p(1 - c_t^g - i_t^g) = (1 - c_t^p)(1 - c_t^g) + c_t^p i_t^g. \tag{20}$$

Again, national gross investment must equal national gross saving, $I_t = S_t$. Hence, all we need to do to interpret a government into our model (14)–(19) is to think of S_t as the sum of private and public saving and to think of the constant saving and investment rate, s, appearing in (17) as being given by underlying parameters as in (20). Note that s, the national investment rate, is decreasing in c_t^p and c_t^g, and increasing in i_t^g (explain, for instance, why i_t^g affects s through the term $c_t^p i_t^g$).

An essential assumption underlying the Solow model is that the sum of the GDP shares of private and public consumption, which is the share of total consumption in GDP, is a given constant. Figure 3.2 indicates that the ratio of total consumption to GDP has indeed stayed relatively constant over long periods in developed economies, with a tendency for C_t^p/Y_t and C_t^g/Y_t to move in opposite directions, keeping the sum, C_t/Y_t, relatively stable.

Table A at the end of Book One collects some data relevant for growth analysis, among them average (gross) investment rates (s_K in the table) over the period 1960 to 2003 for a large number of countries. You will see that values around, or somewhat above, 20 per cent are typical for developed countries, while less developed countries can have investment rates far below 20 per cent. For a typical Western developed country, a reasonable value for the model parameter s could thus be, say, 22 per cent.

We should emphasize that sometimes breaks in national saving and investment rates occur. For instance, Fig. 3.2 gives an indication that the Netherlands and Denmark experienced downward structural breaks in the consumption share of GDP in the early 1980s. We are not arguing that savings rates stay constant for ever, only that they tend to stay sufficiently constant over sufficiently long periods to justify a modelling assumption of an exogenously given savings and investment rate. Indeed, one important economic event that we want to be able to analyse in our growth model is a permanent structural change in the savings rate from one constant value to another.

Money?

There is no direct trace of 'money' in the Solow model. This is because most economists think that *in the long run money does not matter* for real economic variables. One should treat this statement with caution. Certainly the quality of the financial system can have a long-run impact, for instance by affecting our parameter s, as we will explain later in this chapter. Likewise, many economists think that the quality of monetary stabilization policy, that is, the systematic way that monetary authorities respond to economic events, can have economic consequences also in the long run, cf. the discussion in Chapter 1 of the

---

5. In Chapter 15 we shall see that c_t^p is actually quite stable in the long run.

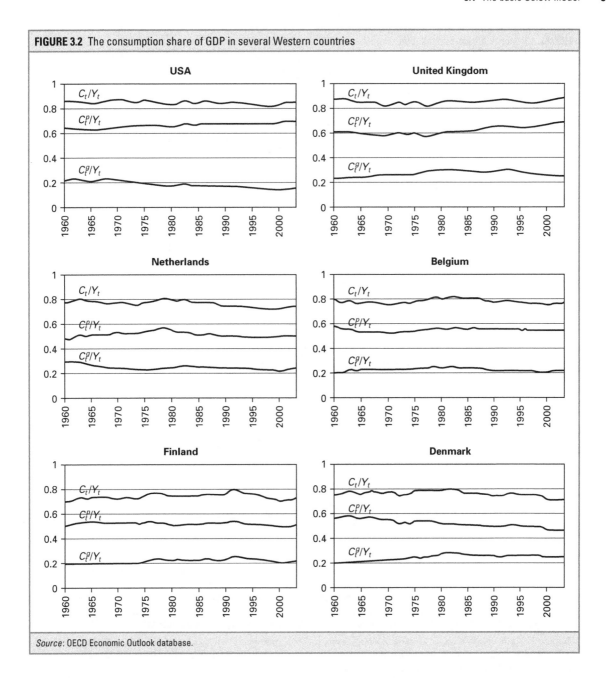

FIGURE 3.2 The consumption share of GDP in several Western countries

Source: OECD Economic Outlook database.

relationship between stability in the short run and growth in the long run. However, given the quality of the financial system, most economists think that the exact level or growth rate of the nominal money stock, or of the short-term nominal interest rate set by the central bank, do not affect real variables such as GDP in the long run.

Figure 3.3 gives a sharp illustration. Both in the USA and in Denmark a change in money growth of a given size goes hand in hand with a change in inflation of the same size in the longer run (note that the figure focuses on the long run by considering averages over periods of 10 years).

The figure does not *prove* that money growth has no real impact in the long run. There is, however, a rather sophisticated econometric literature on this issue. In his advanced textbook on monetary economics, the economist Carl E. Walsh gives an account of this

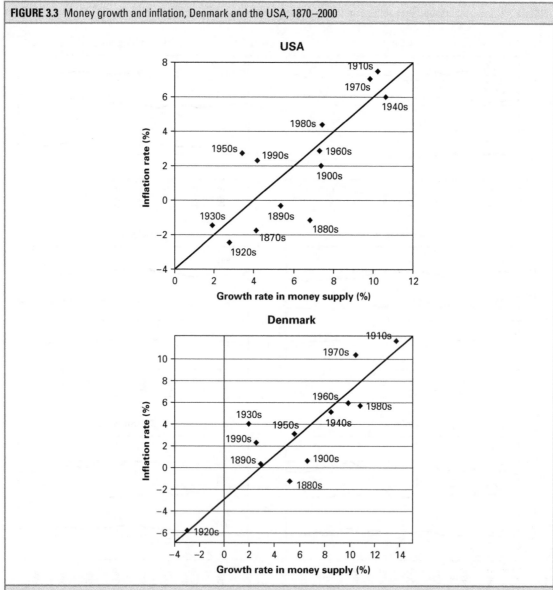

FIGURE 3.3 Money growth and inflation, Denmark and the USA, 1870–2000

Note: Money growth and inflation rates are average annual rates over each decade. Money supply is measured by M2.

Sources: For the USA: M. Friedman and A. Schwartz, *A Monetary History of the United States 1867–1960*, The University of Chicago Press, 1982 and IMF International Financial Statistics. For Denmark: Niels Kærgård, *Økonomisk Vækst: En Økonometrisk Analyse af Danmark 1870–1981*, Jurist-og Økonomforbundets Forlag, 1991 and OECD Economic Outlook (through EcoWin).

literature and summarizes as follows as regards the long run:[6] 'Money growth and inflation display a correlation of 1; the correlation between money growth or inflation and real output growth is probably close to zero…'. On the other hand, the conclusion '…on the short-run effects of money is that exogenous monetary policy shocks produce hump-shaped movements in real economic activity. The peak effects occur after a lag of several quarters (as much as two or three years in some of the estimates) and then die out'.

This should explain why you will hear no more of money in Book One of this text, while monetary policy will be at the heart of the analysis throughout Book Two.

---

6. Carl E. Walsh, *Monetary Theory and Policy*, Cambridge and London, MIT Press, 2000.

Time

In one respect our Solow model does not quite look as suggested by Solow himself. We have formulated time as running discretely like the integers 0, 1, 2, 3,... Perhaps it is more in accordance with how most people think of time to assume that time runs smoothly, or continuously, in an uninterrupted stream like the real numbers.

Often the Solow model is formulated in continuous time. In that case flow variables such as production, consumption, saving and investment are smooth functions of time to be interpreted as intensities. For instance, if the investment intensity at time t is $I(t)$, then total investment over the year from time $t = 0$ to $t = 1$ is $\int_0^1 I(t)\,dt$, so if the investment intensity stays constant at I over the full year, then the total investment during the year is I. Stock variables are also smooth functions of time with the obvious interpretation that $K(t)$, for instance, is the total capital stock at time t.

In continuous time the change in capital must be expressed as a time derivative,

$$\frac{dK(t)}{dt} \equiv \dot{K}(t) = \lim_{\Delta t \to 0} \frac{K(t + \Delta t) - K(t)}{\Delta t},$$

which measures the change in capital per unit of time (since there is a Δt in the denominator) at a specific *point* in time (at a nanosecond, so to speak). So, $\dot{K}(t)$ is the intensity of change in capital at time t. The counterpart of the discrete time expression, $K_{t+1} - K_t = I_t - \delta K_t$, is $\dot{K}(t) = I(t) - \delta K(t)$, stating that the intensity of change in capital at time t is the gross investment intensity minus the depreciation intensity at time t. When formulating the Solow model in continuous time, one often drops the explicit reference to time and one simply writes $\dot{K} = I - \delta K$, since the dot indicates change over time anyway.

With these conventions, the Solow model in continuous time consists of the following six equations, the counterparts of (14)–(19) above. The first one, for instance, says that the production intensity at any time is given as a Cobb–Douglas function of the intensities by which capital and labour are used at that time. The last one says that the growth rate of population is n at all times:

THE SOLOW MODEL IN CONTINUOUS TIME ❗

$$Y = BK^\alpha L^{1-\alpha}, \tag{21}$$

$$r = \alpha B \left(\frac{K}{L} \right)^{\alpha - 1}, \tag{22}$$

$$w = (1 - \alpha) B \left(\frac{K}{L} \right)^{\alpha}, \tag{23}$$

$$S = sY, \tag{24}$$

$$\dot{K} = sY - \delta K, \qquad K_0 \text{ given} \tag{25}$$

$$\frac{\dot{L}}{L} = n, \qquad L_0 \text{ given} \tag{26}$$

The exercises at the end of the chapter will ask you to analyse the Solow model in continuous time. This will help you to master both ways of modelling time, which will be important and useful in your further studies.

It is a matter of choice whether to formulate the Solow model in discrete time or in continuous time. The main argument in favour of continuous time is that it is sometimes mathematically more convenient. The case for discrete time modelling is that it is directly applicable to empirical data which are typically reported for discrete periods like a year or a quarter, and it is easier to do simulation exercises with a discrete time model on a computer.

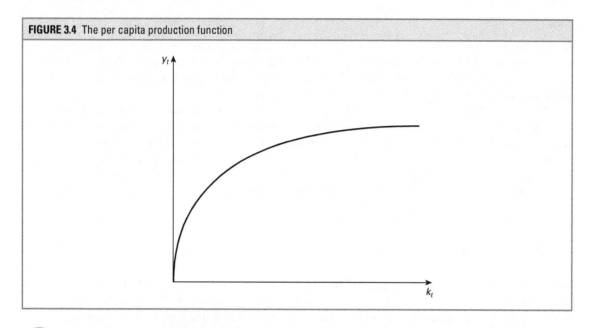

FIGURE 3.4 The per capita production function

3.2 Analysing the basic Solow model

Output and capital per worker

For the prosperity of a nation it is GDP per worker or per capita, not GDP itself, that is important. In the Solow model we are therefore interested in output per worker, $y_t \equiv Y_t/L_t$. Define similarly capital per worker in period t, also called the capital–labour ratio, or the capital intensity: $k_t \equiv K_t/L_t$. From the first equation of the Solow model, (14) above, it follows from dividing on both sides by L_t that:

$$y_t = Bk_t^{\alpha}. \tag{27}$$

This is like a production function where output is GDP per worker and input is capital per worker. This production function exhibits diminishing returns with the marginal product, $\alpha Bk_t^{\alpha-1}$, decreasing from infinity to zero as k_t increases from zero to infinity. The *per capita production function* is illustrated in Fig. 3.4.

One feature revealed directly by (27) is that in the basic Solow model (where B is assumed to be constant), an increase in production per worker can only come from an increase in capital per worker. Let the approximate growth rates of y_t and k_t from period $t-1$ to period t be denoted by g_t^y and g_t^k, respectively. Writing an equation like (27) for both period t and period $t-1$, taking logs on both sides, and subtracting gives:

$$g_t^y \equiv \ln y_t - \ln y_{t-1} = \alpha(\ln k_t - \ln k_{t-1}) \equiv \alpha g_t^k. \tag{28}$$

According to (28), the (approximate) growth rate in output per worker is proportional to the growth rate in capital per worker, and the proportionality factor is exactly the capital share, α. In the basic Solow model economic growth is thus completely linked to capital accumulation.

The law of motion

We can analyse the Solow model directly in terms of the variables we are interested in, the per capita (or worker) magnitudes, k_t and y_t. First, insert the savings behaviour (17) into the capital accumulation equation (18) to get:

$$K_{t+1} = sY_t + (1 - \delta)K_t.$$

Then divide this equation on both sides by L_{t+1}, on the right-hand side using that $L_{t+1} = (1 + n)L_t$. Using also the definitions of k_t and y_t, one gets:

$$k_{t+1} = \frac{1}{1+n}[sy_t + (1-\delta)k_t].$$

Finally, from the per capita production function, (27), we can substitute Bk_t^α for y_t to arrive at:

$$k_{t+1} = \frac{1}{1+n}[sBk_t^\alpha + (1-\delta)k_t]. \tag{29}$$

This is the basic law of motion, or the *transition equation*, for the capital intensity k_t following from the basic Solow model. Note that (29) has the form of a first-order, one-dimensional, non-linear difference equation. For a given initial value, k_0, of the capital labour ratio in year zero, (29) determines the capital–labour ratio, k_1, of year one, which can then be inserted on the right-hand side to determine k_2, etc. In this way, given k_0, the transition equation (29) determines the full dynamic sequence (k_t) of capital intensities.[7]

The four equations (14) and (17)–(19), which gave the dynamic evolution of Y_t, S_t, K_t and L_t, have thus been boiled down to the single equation (29) giving the dynamic evolution of k_t. With (k_t) determined, the factor prices will be given from (15) and (16):

$$r_t = \alpha Bk_t^{\alpha-1}, \tag{30}$$

$$w_t = (1-\alpha)Bk_t^\alpha. \tag{31}$$

The sequence for output per worker, (y_t), follows from (k_t) by $y_t = Bk_t^\alpha$. Total consumption in period t is $C_t = Y_t - S_t = (1 - s)Y_t$, so consumption per worker is $c_t = (1 - s)y_t$. Therefore (c_t) follows from (k_t) via $c_t = (1 - s)Bk_t^\alpha$. In this way the dynamic evolution of all the variables of interest can be derived, given an initial capital intensity.

There is another illustrative way to state the economy's law of motion, where one expresses the *change* in the capital intensity as a function of the current capital intensity. Subtracting k_t from both sides in (29) gives the so-called *Solow equation*:

$$k_{t+1} - k_t = \frac{1}{1+n}[sBk_t^\alpha - (n+\delta)k_t]. \tag{32}$$

This has a nice intuitive interpretation. On the left-hand side is the increase in capital per worker. On the right-hand side are the elements that can create such an increase: saving per worker in period t is $sy_t = sBk_t^\alpha$, which adds to capital per worker, depreciation per worker in period t is δk_t, which subtracts from capital per worker, and finally there is a subtraction, nk_t, which is the thinning-out of capital per worker caused by the fact that there are more workers in period $t + 1$ to share a given capital stock (if $n > 0$).

You may wonder why n enters (32) exactly as it does. Here is an explanation. Assume that the capital stock is unchanged from t to $t + 1$: $K_{t+1} = K_t$. This means that capital per worker will change from t to $t + 1$ by an amount caused by population growth, and by that alone. Using the definition of k_t, we have in that case: $k_{t+1}/k_t = (K_{t+1}/K_t)(L_{t+1}/L_t) = 1/(1 + n)$, so $k_{t+1} = k_t/(1 + n)$, and then $k_{t+1} - k_t = -[n/(1 + n)]k_t$. This shows how capital per worker evolves when there is no compensation for population growth. You should recognize the way n enters (32).

---

7. The notation (k_t) will be used for the full dynamic sequence for k_t, that is, (k_t) lists k_t for $t = 0, 1, 2, \ldots$

FIGURE 3.5 The transition diagram (top), and the Solow diagram (bottom)

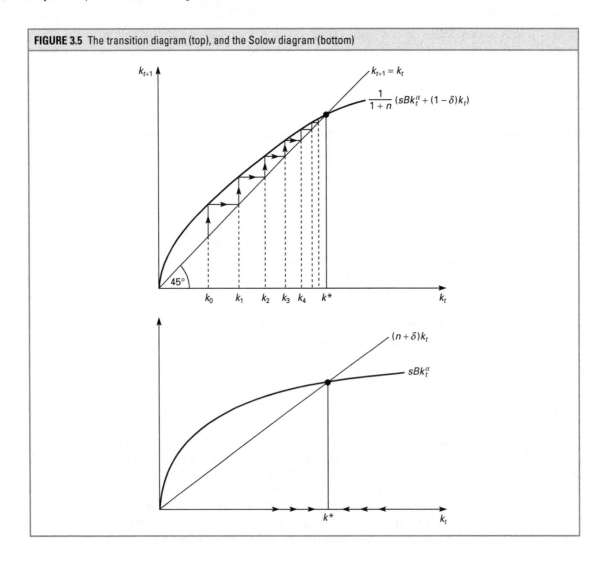

Convergence to steady state

Figure 3.5 illustrates the dynamics of the Solow model. The upper part of the figure, the *transition diagram*, shows the transition equation as given by (29). This curve starts at (0, 0) and is everywhere increasing. The 45° line, $k_{t+1} = k_t$, has also been drawn.

Differentiating (29) gives:

$$\frac{dk_{t+1}}{dk_t} = \frac{s\alpha Bk_t^{\alpha-1} + (1-\delta)}{1+n}.$$

This shows that the slope of the transition curve decreases monotonically from infinity to $(1-\delta)/(1+n)$, as k_t increases from zero to infinity. The latter slope is positive and less than one if $n + \delta > 0$, or $n > -\delta$, which is plausible empirically. Usually annual depreciation rates on capital are estimated to be between 5 and 15 per cent (there is some uncertainty here because there are many kinds of capital with different depreciation rates), while most often the lower end of the interval around 5 per cent is considered most plausible for *aggregate* capital. Annual population growth rates never slump to −0.05 (see, for instance, Table A at the end of Book One). We can therefore safely assume $n > -\delta$, implying that the slope of the transition curve falls monotonically from infinity down to a value less than one. Hence the transition curve must have a unique intersection with the 45° line (which has slope one), to the right of $k_t = 0$.

The lower part of Fig. 3.5, the so-called *Solow diagram*, illustrates the Solow equation (32). It contains the curve sBk_t^α, and the ray $(n + \delta)k_t$. The vertical distance between the first and the second, divided by $(1 + n)$, is $k_{t+1} - k_t$ according to (32). The two curves must intersect each other once to the right of $k_t = 0$, since the ray has constant slope $n + \delta > 0$, and the slope of the curve falls monotonically from infinity to zero. Where this intersection occurs, we have $k_{t+1} - k_t = 0$, or $k_{t+1} = k_t$. Hence the intersection must be at the same k_t at which the transition curve intersects the 45° line in the upper part of the figure.

The iterations of (29) described above appear in the transition diagram as follows. Assume an initial capital intensity $k_0 > 0$, as drawn. Then k_1 will be the vertical distance from the horizontal axis up to the transition curve, and by going from the associated point on the transition curve horizontally to the 45° line, and then vertically down, k_1 will be taken to the horizontal axis as shown. Now, k_2 will be the vertical distance up to the transition curve. The dynamic evolution of the capital intensity is given by the staircase formed of broken lines. It follows that over time, k_t will converge to the specific value k^* given by the intersection between the transition curve and the 45° line, and it will do so monotonically, getting closer and closer all the time and never transcending to the other side of the intersection point. Furthermore, the convergence is *global* in the sense that it holds for any strictly positive initial k_0.[8] Of course, as k_t converges to k^*, income per worker, $y_t = Bk_t^\alpha$, will converge to its steady state value, $y^* \equiv Bk^*$.

In the Solow diagram, when the curve is above the ray, one must have $k_{t+1} - k_t > 0$, or $k_{t+1} > k_t$, so k_t must be increasing over the periods, and vice versa. To the left of the intersection point, k_t is therefore increasing over time towards k^*, while to the right it is decreasing towards k^*, as indicated by the arrows along the k_t axis. Summing up:

CONVERGENCE TO STEADY STATE

Under the plausible stability condition, $n + \delta > 0$, the basic Solow model implies that the capital intensity (capital per worker) converges monotonically to a specific value k^*. This k^* is called the steady state value for the capital intensity. At the same time income per worker converges to a corresponding steady state value, y^*.

We have described the model's convergence to steady state in mathematical terms. The steady state is important and Section 3.3 below will focus on it. Before turning to that, we want to illustrate the properties of our model a bit further using the Solow diagram. This will, among other things, explain the convergence process in economic terms.

Comparative analysis in the Solow diagram

Figure 3.6 is a Solow diagram just like the lower part of Fig. 3.5. It contains the ray $(n + \delta)k_t$ and two different curves, sBk_t^α and $s'Bk_t^\alpha$, where $s' > s$. We imagine that the economy has first been characterized by the parameter values α, B, s, n and δ for a long time, but then from some year zero, the gross savings rate shifts to s' and stays at its new higher level thereafter, while no other parameters change. Remember that since $s = S_t/Y_t = I_t/Y_t$, we may as well say that it is the gross investment rate that has increased.

---

8. Mathematically, to establish global, monotonic convergence we have been using the following properties of the transition curve: it has a unique intersection with the 45° line for $k_t > 0$, everywhere to the left of this intersection (except in $k_t = 0$) it lies above the 45° line and everywhere to the right it lies below, *and* its slope is everywhere positive.

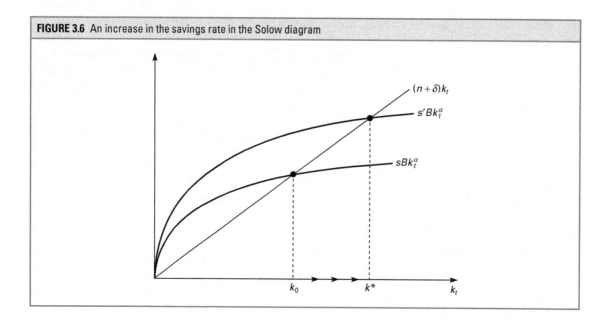

FIGURE 3.6 An increase in the savings rate in the Solow diagram

Since the old parameter values have prevailed for a long time, the economy should initially be at (or close to) the steady state corresponding to the old parameter values, k_0 in the figure. In this steady state current savings are just large enough to compensate capital per worker for depreciation and population growth, so k_t stays unchanged from period to period.

In year zero, when the increase in the savings rate occurs, the initial capital intensity will be unchanged, k_0, because it is predetermined and given by capital accumulation and population dynamics in the past, where the savings rate was s. Therefore output per worker stays unchanged at $y_0 = Bk_0^\alpha$ as well. In the short run, on impact, output and income per worker are thus unaffected. However, out of the unchanged income per worker, y_0, a larger part will now be saved, $s'y_0$ in period zero against sy_0 previously. Current savings will therefore more than compensate for depreciation and population growth. In the figure, $s'Bk_0^\alpha > (n+\delta)k_0$, so capital per worker will increase from period zero to period one. With $k_1 > k_0$, one will also have $y_1 > y_0$, and out of the increased income per worker will come even more savings per worker, $s'Bk_1^\alpha > s'Bk_0^\alpha$. Hence capital per worker will increase again, $k_2 > k_1$, and so on. In the long run successive increases in the capital intensity and in output per worker will make k_t converge to the new and higher steady state value k^*, and y_t will converge to the new and higher steady state value $y^* = B(k^*)^\alpha$. These increases reflect the economy's increased capacity for saving.

One can use the Solow diagram for another type of comparative analysis which does not involve a parameter shift. As above, assume that the economy is initially in steady state at parameters α, B, s, n and δ, so the capital intensity is k_0, etc. Suppose that the economy's capital per worker then drops to $\frac{1}{3}$ of its old value at the beginning of period one, say, because most of the capital is destroyed in a war or an earthquake during period zero, while the parameters stay unchanged. (This may illustrate something like what happened to Japan in the Second World War.) We can analyse this situation in the Solow diagram by keeping the curves in it unchanged, but reducing the capital intensity to $\left(\frac{1}{3}\right)k_0$ from period one. You should do this in a Solow diagram and convince yourself that the economy will immediately start a recovery back towards its initial steady state. Perhaps this recovery can partly describe the strong growth performance of Japan after the Second World War. In an exercise you will be asked to analyse further the remarkable recovery of the Japanese economy in the postwar period and investigate whether this seems to accord with the Solow model.

3.3 Steady state

Our model predicts that in the long run the capital intensity and GDP per worker converge to particular steady state levels, k^* and y^*, respectively. It is of interest to express k^*, y^* and other key variables of the steady state as functions of the model's parameters α, B, s, n and δ. This will show us which fundamental characteristics of an economy can create a high level of income and consumption per worker in the long run according to the basic Solow model. Furthermore, it will enable us to confront the model's steady state predictions with the data.

The key endogenous variables in steady state

The steady state capital–labour ratio is given as the unique constant solution, $k_{t+1} = k_t = k$, to (29) or (32) above. From the latter, such a k must fulfil: $sBk^\alpha - (n + \delta)k = 0$, or $k^{1-\alpha} = sB/(n + \delta)$. Hence:

$$k^* = B^{\frac{1}{1-\alpha}}\left(\frac{s}{n+\delta}\right)^{\frac{1}{1-\alpha}}. \tag{33}$$

Given the assumption $n + \delta > 0$, this is a meaningful expression.[9] Output per worker in steady state is found by inserting the particular value k^* for k_t in the per capita production function, $y_t = Bk_t^\alpha$:

$$y^* = B^{\frac{1}{1-\alpha}}\left(\frac{s}{n+\delta}\right)^{\frac{\alpha}{1-\alpha}}. \tag{34}$$

Consumption per worker is $c_t = (1 - s)y_t$ in any period t, so:

$$c^* = B^{\frac{1}{1-\alpha}}(1-s)\left(\frac{s}{n+\delta}\right)^{\frac{\alpha}{1-\alpha}}. \tag{35}$$

Likewise, inserting k^* into (30) and (31) gives the real factor prices in steady state:

$$r^* = \alpha\left(\frac{s}{n+\delta}\right)^{-1}, \tag{36}$$

$$w^* = (1-\alpha)B^{\frac{1}{1-\alpha}}\left(\frac{s}{n+\delta}\right)^{\frac{\alpha}{1-\alpha}}. \tag{37}$$

These simple and innocent-looking formulae contain some very sharp and important predictions about an economy's long-run performance. For instance, (34) gives a handy formula for how an economy's GDP per worker should depend on a few basic structural parameters, such as the rate of investment and the population growth rate, in the long run. Taking logs on both sides of (34) gives:

$$\ln y^* = \frac{1}{1-\alpha}\ln B + \frac{\alpha}{1-\alpha}\ln s - \frac{\alpha}{1-\alpha}\ln(n+\delta), \tag{38}$$

---

9. The fact that we have found exactly one positive solution confirms our earlier statement that there is a unique positive intersection between the transition curve and the 45° line in the transition diagram, or the curve and the ray in the Solow diagram.

from which, for instance, the elasticity of y^* with respect to s is $\alpha/(1 - \alpha)$, and the elasticity with respect to $n + \delta$ is $-\alpha/(1 - \alpha)$ (show this by differentiation on (38)). You will easily verify that the elasticity of w^* with respect to s is also $\alpha/(1 - \alpha)$ etc. Since α is around $\frac{1}{3}$, the elasticity, $\alpha/(1 - \alpha)$, should be a round $\frac{1}{2}$.

What can make a country rich in the long run? According to the basic Solow model, the answer is:

LONG-RUN INCOME PER CAPITA

A relatively high technological level, B, a high rate of gross saving and investment, s, a low population growth rate, n, and a low depreciation rate, δ, all tend to imply a relatively high GDP per worker in the long run according to the basic Solow model. The model predicts that the elasticity of long-run income per capita and of long-run real wages with respect to s should be around one half, and the elasticity with respect to $n + \delta$ should be minus one half, so, for instance, a 20 per cent increase in the investment rate, e.g. from 20 to 24 per cent, should imply an increase in people's average incomes of around 10 per cent in the long run.

The 'natural' interest rate: productivity and thrift

Just as (34) gives a prediction for the long-run GDP per worker, (36) gives a prediction for the real interest rate. Recall that the r^* of (36) is the steady state value for the rental rate for capital, while the steady state real interest rate is $\rho^* = r^* - \delta$, so:

$$\rho^* = \alpha \frac{n + \delta}{s} - \delta. \tag{39}$$

The ρ^* of (39) is sometimes referred to as the 'natural' rate of interest, following the Swedish economist Knut Wicksell who was the first to use this term.[10] We see that the natural rate of interest in the basic Solow model is determined by the forces of *productivity* and *thrift*. The parameter α measures the response of output to an increase in capital input. The higher the value of α, the higher is the productivity of capital, and the greater will be the demand for capital, and hence for replacement investment to compensate for depreciation and population growth in steady state. A higher value of $n + \delta$ increases the demand for replacement investment as well, and hence increases the equilibrium real interest rate, the price of capital. This is the influence of productivity on ρ^*. The influence of thrift is reflected in the appearance of s: the higher the national propensity to save, the greater the supply of capital, and the lower the equilibrium real interest rate, *ceteris paribus*.

As argued above and from our Table A, reasonable values by Western standards for the parameters entering into (39) could, on an annual basis, be: $\alpha = \frac{1}{3}$, $s = 0.22$, $n = 0.005$, and $\delta = 0.05$. You will easily compute that these parameters result in a value for the natural interest rate per annum of $\rho^* = 3.3$ per cent. This is very close to the long-run average values of annual real interest rates implied by the observed historical difference between nominal interest rates on long-term bonds and the observed rates of inflation. Although we are going to revise our formula for the natural real interest rate somewhat in more sophisticated models later on, it is promising that our extremely simple model predicts a long-run real interest rate that is so close to empirical estimates.

---

10. Knut Wicksell wrote at the turn of the twentieth century. Today he is considered as one of the great figures in the history of economic thought. His theory of interest rates is summarized in: Knut Wicksell, 'The Influence of the Rate of Interest on Prices', *Economic Journal*, **17**, 1907, pp. 213–220.

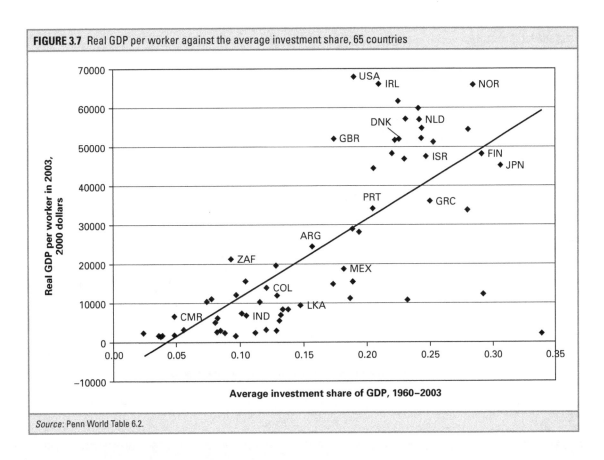

FIGURE 3.7 Real GDP per worker against the average investment share, 65 countries

Source: Penn World Table 6.2.

Testing the model's steady state prediction of GDP per worker

We can test our prediction of long-run GDP per worker empirically, for instance by considering cross-country data such as those in Table A. Here we run into the difficulty that it is not so easy to get reliable data for differences between countries in technological variables such as B and δ. However, we do have good data for GDP per worker and for the investment and population (or labour force) growth rates for many of the countries in the world, as evidenced by Table A. How well does the prediction of (34) fit with the data on these variables?

Figure 3.7 plots the GDP per worker in 2003 against the average gross investment rate between 1960 and 2003 across countries for the representative sample of 65 countries that we also studied in Figs 2.5 and 2.6. The selection criteria for the sample were described when we presented those figures. Basically the sample consists of countries that are not too small or too dependent on oil, and for which we have data of good quality from the Penn World Table 6.2. Figure 3.8 plots GDP per worker in 2003 against average labour force growth rates between 1960 and 2003 for the same countries. The increasing relationship in Fig. 3.7 and the decreasing one in Fig. 3.8 are in nice accordance with the basic Solow model. A high savings rate and a low labour force growth rate do seem to go hand in hand with a high level of GDP per worker.

Later we will discuss the goodness of these fits further. In particular, we will investigate whether the model prediction of a long-run elasticity of output with respect to $\ln s - \ln(n + \delta)$ of around $\frac{1}{2}$ stands up against the empirical evidence (and we ask you to do part of the job in the important Exercise 9 at the end of this chapter). For now we conclude:

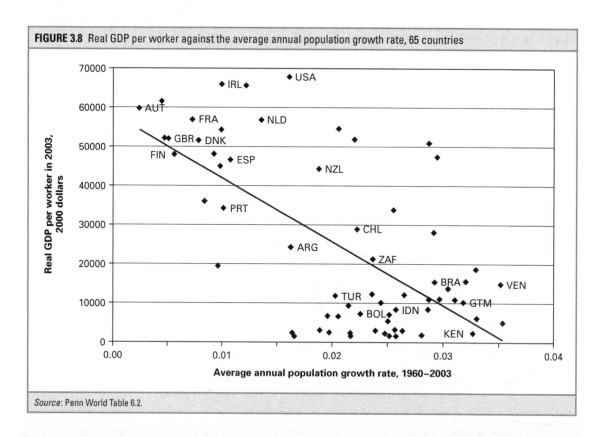

FIGURE 3.8 Real GDP per worker against the average annual population growth rate, 65 countries

Source: Penn World Table 6.2.

THE BASIC SOLOW MODEL EMPIRICALLY

Cross-country empirical evidence is consistent with the long-run predictions of the basic Solow model that a higher saving/investment rate and a lower growth rate of the labour force tend to increase income per capita.

This is promising for a research agenda building on the Solow model and it is the main reason we claimed in the introduction to this chapter that the model takes us remarkably far in understanding the sources of long-run prosperity.

3.4 Structural policy and the golden rule

Crowding out

Consider the model interpretation with a government, where the national savings and investment rate, s, is given by (20). Assume that government increases its propensity to consume, c_t^g, such that s decreases permanently to a new and lower constant level as given by (20). What will be the effects of such a policy according to our model starting from a steady state?

This is easy to answer since we have already studied the effects of an increase in s, and the effects are now just the opposite. Hence, in the short run (in the first period of the new and lower s), where K_t is predetermined by capital accumulation in the past according to the old investment rate, both K_t and L_t, and hence Y_t, will be unaffected by the policy change: Y_t will continue to grow at the rate n, ensuring that GDP per worker stays unchanged in the first period. This should remind you of lessons learned earlier, for example, in connection with the so-called classical macroeconomic model: in a period where output is determined from the supply side by the available amounts of resources, an increase in government demand has no influence on GDP, but private investment will be fully crowded out by the increase in government consumption.

In the long run, the policy change considered *will* have an effect on GDP and on GDP per capita. Out of the (unchanged) output and income in the first period of the new policy, a smaller fraction than before will be saved and invested, and therefore there will be less capital, and hence output, in the succeeding period, leading to a further fall in saving and capital accumulation, etc. Over time Y_t will thus develop more slowly than without the policy change, thus bringing output per worker to a new and lower steady state value, reflecting the economy's decreased potential for saving and investing. In the long run there is *more* than full crowding out, a result arising from the explicit consideration of the capital accumulation process. The decrease in capital supply caused by the government's increased propensity to consume also implies that the long-run equilibrium interest rate increases, as we noted in connection with (39) above.

It is an important and general insight that a government cannot create a positive influence on GDP or GDP per capita *in the long run* by boosting government consumption. However, it may be able to do so *in the short run* if the economy is not currently at the capacity constraint. In that case a rise in public consumption will lead to less than full crowding out of private spending, as we shall see in Book Two on short-run economic fluctuations and stabilization policies. Here we are concerned with the long run and with structural policies.

Should one conclude from the above analysis that in the long run government expenditure can have only a negative influence on economic activity and consumer welfare, because of its negative influence on capital accumulation? Certainly not, and for a number of reasons.

Government expenditure motivated by long-run concerns

First, instead of increasing its spending on consumption, the government could choose to spend an increase in tax revenues on investment in, say, infrastructure. In our model this possibility is represented by an increase in i_t^g rather than in c_t^g, and an increase in i_t^g has a positive influence on s, as shown by (20). Thus, a tax-financed increase in government's propensity to invest raises the national investment rate to a new and higher level, which has a positive long-run impact on GDP per worker.

Second, consumers may be willing to accept a fall in aggregate national income arising from an increase in government consumption if this increase enables the public sector to provide essential public goods which cannot be provided in adequate quantities by private, profit-motivated producers via the marketplace.

Third, if public consumption spent on, say, education and health is a near-perfect substitute for private spending on these items, a tax-financed increase in public spending on schools and hospitals will most likely reduce private consumption on education and health by a roughly similar amount, leaving total saving and investment, and thereby total output, unaffected.

Fourth, there may be distributional reasons for wanting part of, for example, health services to be publicly provided or financed. For educational services, both distributional concerns about equality of opportunity and the presence of positive externalities (e.g. the benefits to other citizens that a person is literate) may motivate public provision or financing.

Finally, much of what is normally categorized as public consumption may be seen as delivery of productive inputs to the private sector production process. For example, health and education services may improve the productivity of the labour force, and public institutions guaranteeing law and order (examples of essential public goods) may also be productivity-enhancing and encourage a higher private savings rate by safeguarding property rights. Thus part of public consumption may help to increase the productivity variable B as well as the private savings rate $1 - c_t^p$ in the Solow model.

Incentive policies

We have considered policies that influence the national savings rate, s, through the government's direct control over public consumption and investment. In addition, we can imagine that the government can influence the private savings rate (or the population growth rate or the depreciation rate, for that matter) through incentive policies, for instance policies that restructure the tax system. However, our model does not give any explicit description of the underlying incentive mechanisms.

Whether government is assumed to influence the model's basic parameters one way or the other, a main conclusion is that a government wishing to promote its citizens' long-run incomes should follow structural policies that can somehow improve technology, increase the national propensity to save and invest, and reduce population growth.

Certainly many countries use various programmes to enhance technology, and such activities may be meaningful according to the Solow model. However, if some technology is only adopted by private firms because it is subsidized, there should, from an economist's point of view, be a positive external effect associated with the technology, that is, a positive spillover effect on agents other than the firm investing in the technology. More advanced technology is not preferable at any cost. We will return to the discussion of policies to improve technology later in connection with models with endogenous technological innovation.

Policies to promote *private* savings can be of many types. Quite often these policies take the form of tax incentives for savings and investment. As mentioned, we cannot conduct an explicit analysis of such incentive policies, since we have not derived private savings behaviour from optimization. We can, however, point to some main issues. For example, is capital income overtaxed compared to labour income? Are the different types of capital income taxed in a uniform manner so as to prevent distortions in the pattern of savings and investment?

At the more basic level, a system of well-defined, secure property rights and a sound financial system are important prerequisites for large-scale private savings. There must be safe banks and assets in which savings can be placed. For some poor countries this is a serious issue, and the most essential policy to promote savings in such countries is the establishment of safe property rights and a good financial system. To achieve such a goal may be very difficult if, for instance, there is civil war in the country.

Because of its emphasis on capital accumulation, the basic Solow model strongly suggests that a good system for handling savings and channelling them into productive investment is important for prosperity. This is an example of a general and fundamental economic insight: institutions are very important for economic performance, and in some countries an improvement of institutions is the number one need for initiating positive economic development.

In Chapter 6, when we have extended the Solow model with technological development and human capital, we give a more explicit exposition of 'the importance of institutions'.

The golden rule of saving

One may get the impression from our discussion that it is good to have as high a savings and investment rate as possible. Equation (34) certainly says that a higher s gives higher long-run income per worker, y^*. However, it does not require much reflection to see that a maximal savings rate is not preferable. If s is close to one, GDP per worker will be maximal, but according to (35), consumption per worker will then be close to zero. If the ultimate purpose of production is to enjoy the highest possible level of *consumption* per worker, what should the savings rate be? Using (35) to maximize c^* with respect to s gives the savings rate: $s^{**} = \alpha$ (Exercise 7 will ask you to show and explain this). This consumption-maximizing savings rate, s^{**}, is called the *golden rule* savings rate. The capital income share, α, is around $\frac{1}{3}$. If policy makers are interested in consumption per person, they should not try to drive savings rates above $\frac{1}{3}$. Perhaps they should not even go close to that level, since the marginal increase in c^* obtained from an increase in s is small if s is already close to α (explain this), and since higher saving implies postponed consumption which represents a welfare cost if people have 'time preference', preferring to consume now rather than later.

As we notice from Table A at the end of Book One, many rich countries in the world have savings and investment rates somewhat above 20 per cent. Some of the East Asian 'growth miracle' countries had investment rates up to around $\frac{1}{3}$ at the end of the twentieth century. However, poor countries typically have much lower savings rates, down to around 10 per cent, and sometimes even considerably less than that. For the latter countries policies that could work to increase savings rates would seem to be important for raising the long-run level of economic welfare.

3.5 Economic growth in the basic Solow model

The macroeconomic dynamics outside steady state in the Solow model are of interest since this is where there can be economic growth.

Transitory growth

The long-run prediction of the Solow model is the steady state, and in steady state there is no growth in GDP per worker. There can be growth in the GDP itself, but only at the speed of population growth.

Why is it that growth has to cease in the long run according to the basic Solow model? Here, diminishing returns to capital plays a crucial role. The production function for output per worker, $y_t = Bk_t^\alpha$, has a 'marginal product', $\alpha Bk_t^{\alpha-1}$, which decreases with k_t because $\alpha < 1$. Assume that the economy is initially below steady state, $k_t < k^*$. Production and income per worker will be Bk_t^α in period t, and the resulting gross savings per worker, sBk_t^α, will exceed the amount $(n + \delta)k_t$ needed to maintain capital per worker in the face of population growth and depreciation (look again at the Solow diagram in the lower part of Fig. 3.5). Hence capital per worker will increase from one period to the next. As k_t increases, each unit of additional capital per worker will generate ever smaller increases in income and gross savings per worker (due to diminishing returns to capital). At the same time the additional savings needed to compensate for population growth and depreciation increase, since k_t is increasing. Therefore, ultimately (in steady state) gross savings per worker, sBk_t^α, will just cover what is needed to keep capital per worker unchanged, $(n + \delta)k_t$. In the Solow diagram diminishing returns is reflected by the function sBk_t^α being curved with a decreasing slope. (Try to envisage the growth process if sBk_t^α were instead a ray lying above $(n + \delta)k_t$, corresponding to $\alpha = 1$, which would mean constant returns to capital alone.)

As the steady state is approached (from below), both k_t and y_t will be growing. Hence, in the basic Solow model there is *transitory growth* in GDP per worker on the way to steady state, but no growth in steady state. During the transition phase, growth in k_t goes hand in hand with growth in y_t. As noted earlier, with the assumed aggregate production function, growth in GDP per worker has to be rooted in growth in capital per worker.

An example

It is relevant to investigate how fast or slow transitory growth is according to the basic Solow model. If growth fades within a few years, the model could not deliver much of an explanation of growth over decades.

Consider an economy that is initially described by the following parameter values: $B = 1$, $\alpha = \frac{1}{3}$, $\delta = 0.05$, $n = 0.03$ and $s = 0.08$. The value of B is just a normalization, while α and δ have been set at reasonable values, for δ assuming a period length of one year. The values for n and s, respectively, correspond to a high annual population growth rate and a low propensity to save, which could be descriptive of a typical poor country (see again

TABLE 3.1 Simulation output

Year	k_t	y_t	c_t	g_t^y, exact (%)*	g_t^y, approx (%)**
0	1.000	1.000	0.920		
1	1.000	1.000	0.760	0.00	0.00
2	1.155	1.049	0.797	4.93	4.81
3	1.310	1.094	0.832	4.28	4.19
4	1.463	1.135	0.863	3.76	3.69
5	1.614	1.173	0.892	3.33	3.27
6	1.762	1.208	0.918	2.97	2.92
7	1.907	1.240	0.942	2.66	2.63
8	2.048	1.270	0.965	2.40	2.38
9	2.184	1.298	0.986	2.18	2.16
10	2.317	1.323	1.006	1.98	1.97
⋮	⋮	⋮	⋮	⋮	⋮
∞	5.196	1.732	1.316	0	0
(new st.st.)					

Note: *computed as $((y_t - y_{t-1})/y_{t-1}) \times 100$, **computed as $(\ln y_t - \ln y_{t-1}) \times 100$

Table A). We assume that the economy is initially in steady state at these parameter values. Using (33) and (34) one finds steady state capital per worker and GDP per worker, respectively: $k^* = y^* = 1$.

Now suppose that from an initial year one, the savings rate increases permanently up to a level typically seen in rich countries, say, $s' = 0.24$, while the other parameters stay unchanged. The new steady state is easily computed: $k^{*\prime} = 5.20$, and $y^{*\prime} = 1.73$. In the long run, the very substantial increase in the savings rate of 200 per cent implies a 420 per cent increase in capital per worker and a 73 per cent increase in GDP per worker. (Try to explain why the increase in y^* is not 100 per cent, as an elasticity of y^* with respect to s equal to $\frac{1}{2}$ would suggest.) But how fast is the transition to the new steady state?

We can simulate the transition equation (29) with the savings rate equal to s' and the other parameters as given above over a number of periods $t = 2, 3, \ldots$, starting with $k_0 = k_1 = 1$. (In year one capital per worker will be at the old steady state level, since the increased savings rate during period one only has an effect on capital per worker from period two.) In this way a sequence, (k_t), can be constructed. From (k_t) one can derive a corresponding sequence (y_t) by using $y_t = k_t^\alpha$ in all years, and a sequence (c_t) by using $c_0 = (1-s)y_0$ and $c_t = (1-s')y_t$ for $t \geq 1$. For each year one can then compute the growth rate in GDP per worker, $y_t/y_{t-1} - 1$, or approximate by $g_t^y = \ln y_t - \ln y_{t-1}$. These operations are most easily done on a computer using a spreadsheet.

The simulation gives rise to the time series shown in Table 3.1, and illustrated graphically in Fig. 3.9, which depicts the evolution in y_t, c_t and g_t^y over some 50 years after the change in the savings rate.

There are several interesting features to note from Fig. 3.9. It illustrates the growth perspectives, according to the Solow model, for a poor country bringing its savings rate up to the standards of rich countries. For instance, there is a substantial initial sacrifice of consumption for some years, six to be precise (explain this). Furthermore, there is considerable transitory growth for a long time. It takes around 12 years to get half the way from the old to the new steady state level of GDP per capita. After 20 years the annual growth rate of GDP per worker is still close to 1 per cent, and this is still purely transitory growth arising from the permanent increase in the savings rate 20 years earlier.

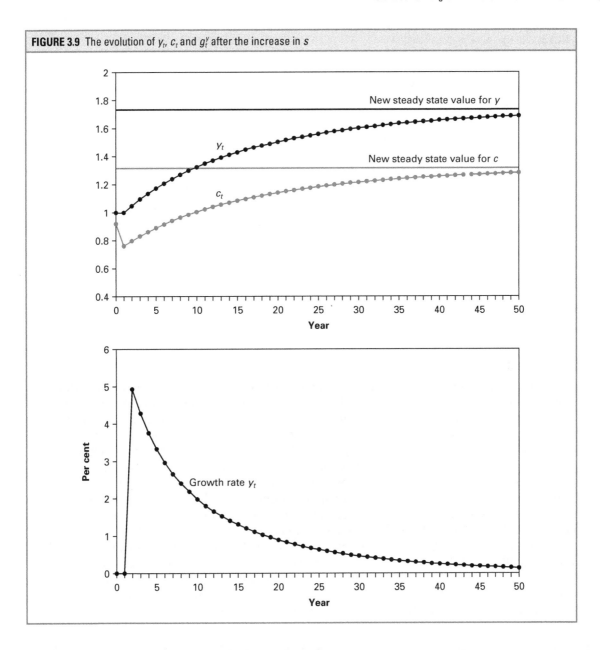

FIGURE 3.9 The evolution of y_t, c_t and g_t^y after the increase in s

Transitory growth in the Solow model takes place over decades for realistic parameter values. This relative slowness in the adjustment outside steady state is why it is justified to say that: *the basic Solow model is a growth model*.

A 'cousin' to the Solow diagram is useful for illustrating the growth process outside steady state. Dividing by k_t on both sides of (32) gives the *modified Solow equation*:

$$\frac{k_{t+1} - k_t}{k_t} = \frac{1}{1+n}[sBk_t^{\alpha-1} - (n+\delta)]. \tag{40}$$

In the modified Solow diagram, Fig. 3.10, the growth rate of the capital intensity is thus proportional to the vertical distance between the decreasing curve, $sBk_t^{\alpha-1}$, and the horizontal line at $n + \delta$. The steady state is, of course, where the curve and the line intersect.

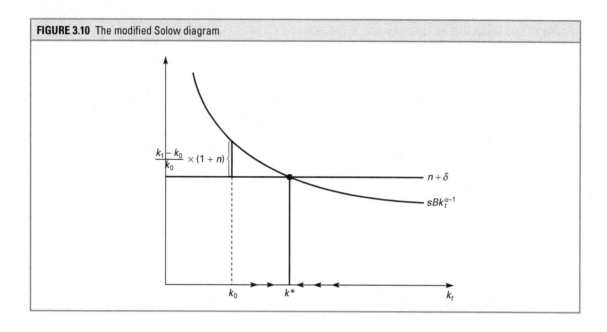

FIGURE 3.10 The modified Solow diagram

It follows that the growth rate in k_t will be higher (in absolute value) the further away from the steady state k_t is. The same will be true for the growth rate in y_t, since $g_t^y = \alpha g_t^k$. In the numerical example above this feature appeared. After the initial increase in the savings rate, the growth rate of y_t jumped up and then decreased monotonically back towards zero.

The model feature that growth is higher the further below steady state the economy is accords with the idea of conditional convergence discussed in Chapter 2. In a modified Solow diagram such as Fig. 3.10, the positions of the curve and the line depend on the structural characteristics of the economy. If one country has a higher savings rate than another, the countries being otherwise structurally alike, the decreasing curve of the first country will be situated above that of the second country. If the two countries start out with the same GDP per worker, the first country will grow faster and converge to a higher final level of GDP per worker. However, *conditional* on countries being structurally alike, the Solow model predicts that countries will converge to the same level of GDP per worker through a growth process where the countries that are initially most behind will grow the fastest. In other words, the Solow model supports conditional convergence.

THE CONVERGENCE PROCESS

For realistic parameter values the transitory growth of the basic Solow model is relatively slow and takes place 'over decades'. The further below steady state GDP per capita the economy starts out, the higher is its growth rate. This is an empirically appealing feature of the model because it accords with the idea of conditional convergence between the countries of the world.

The long-run increase in income per capita resulting from an increase in the investment rate can be viewed as modest. It also comes slowly and with a considerable consumption sacrifice. However, a central theme in chapters to follow will be that the effect of the investment rate on income per capita seems to be larger than predicted by the basic Solow model.

3.6 Summary

1. The basic Solow model studied in this chapter is characterized by the following features:

   - Aggregate output, GDP, is produced from aggregate capital and aggregate labour according to a Cobb–Douglas production function with constant returns to capital and labour and constant total factor productivity.

   - Competitive market clearing ensures that the amounts of capital and labour used in production in each period are equal to the predetermined available amounts and that factors are rewarded at their marginal products. An implication is that the income shares of capital and labour are equal to the elasticities of output with respect to capital and labour, respectively.

   - Capital evolves over time such that from one year to the next, the change in the capital stock equals gross saving (or investment) minus depreciation on the initial capital stock.

   - In each period gross saving is an exogenous fraction of total income or GDP. Depreciation on capital is given by an exogenous depreciation rate. The labour force changes over time at an exogenous growth rate.

2. The key assumptions of a Cobb–Douglas aggregate production function and a given rate of saving and investment are motivated empirically by the relative constancy of income shares in the long run and the relative long-run constancy of the GDP share of total consumption (private plus public), respectively.

3. The model implies that capital per worker and output per worker converge to particular constant values in the long run. The convergence point defines the economy's steady state. In steady state, consumption per worker, the real interest rate, and the wage rate are constant as well. The steady state has some empirical plausibility with respect to the predicted value for the long-run real interest rate and with respect to the long-run dependence of GDP per worker on the investment rate and on the labour force growth rate.

4. The expressions for the steady state values of the key variables contain some sharp predictions of how income per worker and consumption per worker depend on underlying parameters in the long run. These predictions are of importance for the design of structural policies to raise the standard of living. According to the model, policies to make a nation richer should mainly be policies that can increase the investment share of GDP and bring population growth under control, or policies to improve technology. To create a high level of consumption per person, the savings and investment rate should not exceed the golden rule value, which is equal to the elasticity of output with respect to capital.

5. In the model's steady state there is no positive growth in GDP per worker, consumption per worker, or the real wage rate. This is at odds with the stylized facts of growth (in developed economies). Remedying this shortcoming is one of the main purposes of the growth models to be presented later. These models will contain some form of technological progress, such that total factor productivity increases over time. The basic Solow model does give rise to (positive or negative) growth in output per worker during the transition to steady state. This transitory growth is relatively long-lasting for plausible parameter values. Furthermore, the process of transitory growth is such that the further below steady state an economy currently is, the faster it will grow. This is in accordance with the observed conditional convergence between the countries of the world.

▶ 6. Economics has much more to say about the sources of prosperity and growth than what can be inferred from the basic Solow model. For instance, human capital (the education and training embodied in people), and natural resources such as land, oil and metals are factors of production which could be as important as physical capital and 'raw' labour. Furthermore, the evolution of technology has to be an important determinant for long-run prosperity and growth as well. These factors will be dealt with in later chapters, but the basic Solow model is important as it stands. It is therefore worthwhile first modifying the model to take account of a fact we have neglected in this chapter, namely the openness of real-world economies. This openness implies that capital can flow between countries at least to some extent. A Solow model taking capital mobility appropriately into account and describing the accumulation of capital and national wealth in an open economy will be presented in the next chapter.

3.7 Exercises

Exercise 1. The elasticity of substitution between capital and labour and the income distribution

The Cobb–Douglas production function, $Y = BK^\alpha L^{1-\alpha}$ (omitting time subscripts and superscripts d for 'demand') implies a certain degree of substitution between the inputs. As a measure of this degree economists use the so-called elasticity of substitution. This is defined as the elasticity in the composition, K/L, of input demands with respect to the ratio, r/w, between the rental rates, when the firm maximizes profits (minimizes costs) given r and w.

1. Find the marginal rate of substitution between capital and labour (the marginal product of capital divided by the marginal product of labour) for the Cobb–Douglas production function. Show that profit maximization given r and w requires that this marginal rate of substitution is equal to r/w, and show that the elasticity of substitution between capital and labour is -1, independent of r and w.

    The so-called CES (constant elasticity of substitution) production function is:

$$Y = \left(\alpha K^{\frac{\sigma-1}{\sigma}} + (1-\alpha) L^{\frac{\sigma-1}{\sigma}} \right)^{\frac{\sigma}{\sigma-1}}, \qquad 0 < \alpha < 1, \sigma > 0, \neq 1,$$

    where α and σ are parameters.

2. Find the marginal rate of substitution between capital and labour for the CES production function, and show that the elasticity of substitution is $-\sigma$, independent of r and w.

    The CES function is more general than the Cobb–Douglas function, since the particular value $\sigma = 1$ (or the limit for $\sigma \to 1$) corresponds to the Cobb–Douglas function. Nevertheless, we have chosen to work with the more special Cobb–Douglas function, partly for simplicity, but also for the reason appearing from the answers to the next two questions.

3. Show that with the CES production function, the income share of labour under competitive market clearing is:

$$\frac{wL}{Y} = \frac{1-\alpha}{\alpha \left(\dfrac{K}{L} \right)^{\frac{\sigma-1}{\sigma}} + (1-\alpha)}.$$

4. In Chapter 2 it was shown that developed economies have experienced relatively constant positive growth rates in GDP per worker (annual rates around 2 per cent) and relatively constant capital–output ratios in the long run. Show that developed countries must then

also have experienced increasing capital–labour ratios in the long run. If K/L increases and eventually goes to infinity, how should labour's share evolve over time in the case of $\sigma < 1$, $\sigma = 1$ and $\sigma > 1$, respectively, according to the above formula? This gives an argument for considering $\sigma = 1$ most plausible in models for the long run. Explain why.

Exercise 2. The basic Solow model in continuous time

This exercise asks you to analyse the Solow model in continuous time as given by the six equations (21)–(26). The restrictions on the parameters α, B, s, n and δ are the same as in the model in discrete time, except we do not have to assume $n > -1$. It is assumed that $n + \delta > 0$. We use (for any point t in time) the definitions $k = K/L$ and $y = Y/L$ etc.

1. Show that from $k = K/L$ it follows $\dot{k}/k = \dot{K}/K - \dot{L}/L$. (Hint: You can do the 'log-dif-trick', that is, first take logs on both sides of $k = K/L$ and then differentiate with respect to time.) Then show that the Solow model in continuous time implies the Solow equation:

$$\dot{k} = sBk^\alpha - (n + \delta)k. \tag{41}$$

Compare with (32) for the model in discrete time and give an intuitive explanation like the one given for (32) in this chapter.

2. Illustrate the above Solow equation in a Solow diagram with k along the horizontal axis and the curve sBk^α as well as the ray $(n + \delta)k$ along the vertical axis. Demonstrate (from the Solow diagram) that from any initial value, $k_0 > 0$, the capital intensity, k, will converge to a specific steady state level, k^*, in the long run (as $t \to \infty$).

3. Compute the steady state values, k^*, y^* and c^*, for the capital–labour ratio, income per worker, and consumption per worker, respectively (use $\dot{k} = 0$). Explain and compare to the parallel expressions found in this chapter for the model in discrete time. Also compute the steady state values, r^* and w^*, for the real rental rates for capital and labour and compare again to the model in discrete time. How are r^* and w^* affected by an increase in s? Explain. What are the growth rates of y and Y in steady state?

4. Show that (it follows from the model that) the growth rate in k at any time is:

$$\frac{\dot{k}}{k} = sBk^{\alpha-1} - (n + \delta). \tag{42}$$

Illustrate this in a modified Solow diagram. Show that the growth rate, $\dot{y}/y$, at any time t is α times the growth rate, $\dot{k}/k$, of k. Assume that initially $k_0 < k^*$. Describe and explain qualitatively, in words, the transition to steady state. For instance, how do r and w develop along the transition, and when is the growth rate in k, and hence in y, largest?

Exercise 3. An analytical solution to the Solow model in continuous time

It was stated in this chapter that continuous time is sometimes mathematically more convenient than discrete time. For instance, although the differential equation (41) is not linear, we can actually solve it, that is, we can find the (closed form) function (for k as a function of t) that follows from (41), or from (42), and an initial value k_0. In the following assume for simplicity that $B = 1$. The trick is to define an auxiliary variable z, $z \equiv k^{1-\alpha}$. First show that z is actually the capital–output ratio, k/y. Then show by doing appropriate substitutions in (42), that:

$$\dot{z} = (1 - \alpha)s - \lambda z, \tag{43}$$

where $\lambda \equiv (1 - \alpha)(n + \delta)$. Note that (43) is linear. Show that the steady state value of z is $z^* = (1 - \alpha)s/\lambda = s/(n + \delta)$. Solve (43) by finding the characteristic roots, etc., and show that (given an initial capital–output ratio z_0) the solution is:

$$z = \frac{(1-\alpha)s}{\lambda}(1 - e^{-\lambda t}) + z_0 e^{-\lambda t}$$

$$= \frac{s}{n+\delta}(1 - e^{-\lambda t}) + z_0 e^{-\lambda t}.$$

In other words, at any time t, the capital–output ratio is the weighted average of its steady state value and its initial value, the weight going more and more to the first of these. Show that the solutions for k and y are:

$$k = \left(\frac{s}{n+\delta}(1 - e^{-\lambda t}) + k_0^{1-\alpha} e^{-\lambda t} \right)^{\frac{1}{1-\alpha}},$$

$$y = \left(\frac{s}{n+\delta}(1 - e^{-\lambda t}) + y_0^{\frac{1-\alpha}{\alpha}} e^{-\lambda t} \right)^{\frac{\alpha}{1-\alpha}}.$$

From the expressions verify that the larger λ is, the faster will convergence to steady state be, so that $\lambda \equiv (1-\alpha)(n+\delta)$ can be viewed a measure of the rate of convergence to steady state.

Exercise 4. The effects of a decrease in the population growth rate

1. Explain the economic effects according to the basic Solow model of a decrease (at some time) in the population growth rate from one constant level to a new and lower constant level: how does this affect the transition diagram and the Solow diagram? How does it affect the steady state values of capital, income and consumption per worker? Explain qualitatively the transition from the old steady state to the new one: what initiates the growth process, and what keeps it alive for some time?

    Now consider the same parametrization of the basic Solow model as in the example of Section 3.5, that is, $B = 1$, $\alpha = \frac{1}{3}$, $\delta = 0.05$, $n = 0.03$, and $s = 0.08$. Assume that in period zero the economy is in steady state at these parameter values, and then (working first time between period zero and period one) the population growth rate drops to 0.01, other parameters remaining unchanged. (This is illustrative for a developing country getting population growth down to Western rates.)

2. By how many per cent does the reduction by $\frac{2}{3}$ in the population growth rate increase the steady state values of capital, income and consumption per worker, respectively?

3. Carry out a simulation of the model over the periods 0 to 100, and show in a diagram the evolution of y_t, c_t, and the growth rate $(y_t - y_{t-1})/y_{t-1}$ (or the approximate one $\ln y_t - \ln y_{t-1}$), over the 100 periods. Comment with respect to what a developing country can obtain by birth control according to the Solow model. Does there seem to be any systematic difference with respect to the speed of convergence to the new steady state (or the speed by which the benefits arrive) between a decrease in the population growth rate as considered here, and an increase in the savings rate as considered in the example of section 5? For instance, for the two experiments (approximately from the figures) compare the number of periods it takes until half of the distance between the old and the new steady state values for y has been eliminated. Try to explain the difference (Exercise 3 may be useful).

Exercise 5. The effects of an increase in technology and the propagation mechanism

1. Do all you were asked to do in the previous exercise (there for a decrease in n) only this time for a *permanent* increase in B. First analyse the qualitative effects using the Solow diagram and explaining the transition mechanisms. Then consider a numerical example (e.g. $B = 1$, $\alpha = 1/3$, $\delta = 0.08$, $n = 0$, $s = 0.2$) and analyse by appropriate simulations the effects of a permanent increase in B from 1 to 1.2 taking place in period one, assuming the economy was in steady state up to period zero.

2. Now do the same for a *temporary* increase in B, where B goes up from 1 to 1.2 in period one and then falls permanently back to 1. Explain why GDP (per capita) increases compared to the old steady state also in the periods after period one. (Hint: the effect is referred to as propagation by capital accumulation.)

Exercise 6. A one-shot increase in L_t

Analyse in the Solow diagram the qualitative effects of a one-shot increase in L_t, starting in steady state at the prevailing parameter values. The event we are interested in here is that at the beginning of some period, period one say, L_t increases once and for all by a certain amount, for instance due to emigration. However, both before and after this event the population growth rate stays unchanged at n, say. How does this affect the Solow diagram and the capital accumulation process?

Exercise 7. Golden rule

In this chapter it was stated that the golden rule savings rate that maximizes steady state consumption per person as given by (35) is $s^{**} = \alpha$. Show this. To illustrate, draw a Solow diagram with the curve, sBk_t^α, and the ray, $(n+\delta)k_t$, as usual, and draw the curve Bk_t^α as well. For any given k_t, consumption per worker in period t is the vertical distance between Bk_t^α and sBk_t^α. Explain this. The particular steady state capital intensity is where sBk_t^α and $(n+\delta)k_t$ intersect. Hence, *in steady state* consumption per worker is the vertical distance between Bk_t^α and $(n+\delta)k_t$. Compute the particular value k^{**} of k_t that maximizes this distance. Illustrate the point in your Solow diagram: the slope of Bk_t^α should equal the slope of $(n+\delta)k_t$. Explain this. What is the requirement on s to ensure that the steady state capital intensity, k^*, becomes equal to the golden rule capital intensity, k^{**}? Illustrate again in your diagram.

Exercise 8. Balanced growth in the steady state

Show that *all* the requirements for balanced growth, as these are stated in Chapter 2, are fulfilled in the steady state of the basic Solow model. Why are we, nevertheless, not completely satisfied with the basic Solow model's steady state as a description of long-run growth?

Exercise 9. Further empirically testing the steady state prediction of the basic Solow model

This exercise anticipates some issues taken up in succeeding chapters, and it is a very useful empirical exercise. The data you will need can be taken from Table A. In Figs 3.7 and 3.8 we tested the steady state prediction of the Solow model by plotting, across 65 countries, GDP per worker in 2003 against investment rates (averaged over 1960 to 2003) and population growth rates (also averaged over 1960 to 2003). We concluded that the directions of the empirical relationships were nicely in accordance with the basic Solow model. However, the steady state prediction of the Solow model is more precise than 'y^* is increasing in s and decreasing in n': as shown by (38), there should be a linear relationship between $\ln y^*$ and $\ln s - \ln(n + \delta)$, and the slope in this relationship should be $\alpha/(1-\alpha)$.

Test this by creating a figure that plots $\ln y^i$ against $\ln s^i - \ln(n^i + \delta)$ across the same 65 countries i (indicated in Table A), using for y^i, s^i and n^i the same data that were used in Figs 3.7 and 3.8 (appearing in Table A), and setting $\delta = 0.075$. Does the relationship (by reasonable standards) seem to be a linear one? Estimate (by OLS) and draw the line of best fit through the points. What is the estimated slope of this line? How does this slope accord with the theory?

Exercise 10. The recovery of Japan after the Second World War

Table 3.2 shows GDP per worker for the USA and Japan for the period 1959 to 1996, measured in a common, purchasing-power-adjusted currency (1996 dollars). The table only goes to 1996 to avoid considering (in the present long-run context) the more recent years of economic crisis in Japan.

TABLE 3.2 GDP per worker, USA and Japan (1996 dollars)

Year	USA	Japan
1959	29,876	6,880
1960	30,304	7,689
1961	30,260	8,577
1962	31,520	9,164
1963	32,370	9,800
1964	33,710	10,782
1965	35,363	11,167
1966	36,900	12,184
1967	37,037	13,402
1968	38,302	15,047
1969	39,020	16,495
1970	38,432	18,098
1971	39,023	18,736
1972	40,477	20,119
1973	42,184	21,314
1974	41,367	20,735
1975	39,735	21,017
1976	41,469	21,681
1977	42,976	22,462
1978	44,583	23,510
1979	45,167	24,645
1980	44,217	25,252
1981	44,756	25,743
1982	42,741	26,254
1983	44,048	26,532
1984	47,159	27,353
1985	48,164	28,368
1986	49,271	28,960
1987	50,603	30,077
1988	52,174	31,920
1989	53,529	33,436
1990	53,887	35,079
1991	52,411	36,068
1992	53,268	36,184
1993	53,867	36,161
1994	55,361	36,362
1995	56,065	36,733
1996	57,259	37,962

Source: Penn World Table 6.1

To eliminate from these time series any underlying technological progress, this exercise will consider the two transformed series that appear for each year and country dividing GDP per worker by the GDP per worker in the USA and multiplying by 100. That is, we normalize for each year the GDP per worker in the USA to 100, and compute for Japan the GDP per worker as a percentage of that in the USA. The resulting series are called $(y_t^U)_{t=59}^{96}$ and $(y_t^J)_{t=59}^{96}$, where the first is just a list of 100s. We will take the view that the two transformed series are the relevant data on the two countries. The issue is how well the basic Solow model can explain these series and thereby how Japan was able to catch up the USA.

1. Compute the series $(y_t^U)_{t=59}^{96}$ and $(y_t^J)_{t=59}^{96}$ and plot each of them against years in a diagram. Give some qualitative description of the improvement in Japan's GDP.

   In the following we take (or perhaps test) the view that each country can be described by the basic Solow model with country-specific parameter values, and that the USA has been in steady state in all the considered years. We assume that for both countries $\alpha = \frac{1}{3}$ and $\delta = 0.05$. For the savings and population growth rates of the USA we assume $s^U = 0.21$ and $n^U = 0.015$, respectively. For Japan we assume $s^J = 0.34$ and $n^J = 0.012$. These parameter values are realistic annual values (for some as averages for the considered period). We will first, in Questions 2 and 3, assume that the two countries had the same technological level B over the period considered.

2. What must B be for the USA to be in steady state at $y^{*U} = 100$? What are the steady state values, k^{*J1} and y^{*J1}, of capital and output per worker, respectively, in Japan with this B? What must k_{59}^{J1} (capital per worker in Japan in 1959) have been? Describe roughly how far Japan was from steady state in 1959 according to these computations (what were the percentages in 1959 of capital per worker and output per worker, respectively, to the steady state levels?).

3. Starting with the computed k_{59}^{J1}, and assuming the computed B, simulate the model (the transition equation) for Japan over the period 1959 to 1996 and thereby create a model-based time series $(y_t^{J1})_{t=59}^{96}$ for GDP per worker in Japan. Plot the actual series, $(y_t^J)_{t=59}^{96}$, as well as the model-based one, $(y_t^{J1})_{t=59}^{96}$, against time in a diagram that also shows the steady state values, y^{*U} and y^{*J1}, as horizontal lines. How fast has Japan actually caught up to the USA compared to how fast it should have caught up according to the Solow model under the assumption of a *common technological level*?

   The assumption of the same B in the USA and Japan may be heroic. Another way to proceed in simulations is to rely on direct data for capital per worker in Japan in 1959 and compute an associated technological parameter B^J, which can be different from that in the USA (the B above). Data for capital are not the most reliable, but some empirical material suggests that in 1959 capital per worker in Japan was about one half of GDP per worker in Japan in the same year. In Questions 4 and 5 we therefore assume a level $k_{59}^{J2} = y_{59}^J/2$ of capital per worker in Japan in 1959.

4. What must B^J be? Compute the associated steady state values, k^{*J2} and y^{*J2}, for Japan. How far from steady state was Japan in 1959 according to these computations?

5. Simulate the model for Japan again, this time starting with k_{59}^{J2} and assuming the computed B^J, over the years 1959 to 1996, and thus create a new model-based series, $(y_t^{J2})_{t=59}^{96}$, for output per worker in Japan. Plot $(y_t^{J2})_{t=59}^{96}$ and $(y_t^J)_{t=59}^{96}$ against time in a diagram also indicating the steady state values, y^{*U} and y^{*J2}, as horizontal lines. Comment on the goodness of the model's fit and on the speed with which Japan actually caught up to the USA compared with the speed with which Japan should have caught up according to the Solow model under the assumption of *different technological levels*.

Exercise 11. Endogenous population growth and club convergence in the basic Solow model

Consider a growth model that consists of the same equations as the basic Solow model except that the n in Eq. (19) is no longer exogenous, but rather an endogenous variable that depends on prosperity. Hence, in (19), n is replaced with n_t, and an additional equation, $n_t = h(y_t) = h(Bk_t^\alpha)$, or just $n_t = n(k_t)$, states *how* the population growth rate depends on income per capita and hence on the capital–labour ratio. Show that the Solow equation that can be derived from the model defined this way is:

$$k_{t+1} - k_t = \frac{1}{1+n(k_t)}(sBk_t^\alpha - (n(k_t)+\delta)k_t),$$

and that the modified Solow equation is:

$$\frac{k_{t+1} - k_t}{k_t} = \frac{1}{1+n(k_t)}[sBk_t^{\alpha-1} - (n(k_t)+\delta)].$$

It seems reasonable to assume a shape of the function $n(k_t)$ as illustrated in the figure below. For low values of k_t, the function $n(k_t)$ is perhaps negative but increasing, since higher k_t and y_t mean better living conditions, less infant mortality, etc. This is true for k_t up to a certain value. From that value, $n(k_t)$ is decreasing, because as people get richer birth rates fall for various reasons. However, as k_t increases from the limiting value, $n(k_t)$ never falls below a certain positive value, n, in the figure.

Show by an appropriate illustration in the modified Solow diagram that with such a shape of $n(k_t)$, there may be three steady state values for k_t, that is, three intersections between the curve $sBk_t^{\alpha-1}$, and the curve $n(k_t) + \delta$. If this is the case, how does the (unmodified) Solow diagram look? Which of the steady states are stable in the sense that if k_t departs a little from the steady state in question, the dynamics of the model tend to bring it back towards the steady state, and which one is unstable? Relate the curves you have drawn in the Solow diagram (unmodified or modified) to the idea of club convergence explained in Chapter 2. Explain intuitively why it is that if k_t (and hence y_t) starts below a certain threshold value it converges to a low steady state value, while if it starts above the threshold value it converges to a high steady state value.

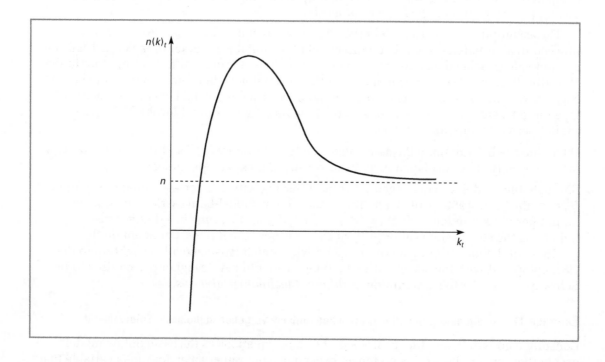

CHAPTER 4

Wealth accumulation and capital mobility

The Solow model for a small open economy

In the basic Solow model the only source of domestic investment is the volume of domestic saving. This is a good approximation to reality as long as international capital flows are relatively small. However, in recent decades the international mobility of capital has increased dramatically. In these circumstances a country may finance part of domestic investment via capital imports, or it may invest part of domestic savings abroad through capital exports.

In this chapter we will develop a Solow model of an open economy to study how the dynamics of wealth accumulation are affected by international capital mobility. The rapid growth of international trade and capital mobility are two of the most striking features of the process of *globalization*. Most economists believe that capital mobility tends to improve the long-run efficiency of the world economy, but the liberalization of international capital flows also creates new risks. Indeed, many critics of globalization have argued that increased capital mobility may destabilize the world economy and expose poor countries to the shifting moods of international investors. The potential for capital flows to generate short-run macroeconomic instability will be discussed in Part 7, whereas the model developed in the present chapter will highlight the potential long-run benefits and risks associated with capital mobility. Studying this chapter along with those in Part 7 should thus give you a better understanding of some of the contentious issues in the current debate on globalization.

We will start the chapter by documenting the trend towards growing trade volumes and increasing capital mobility. We will then set up a Solow model of a small open economy whose domestic capital market is perfectly integrated with the world capital market. This model will be used to analyse how an open capital account[1] modifies the dynamics of wealth accumulation in the individual country, and how capital mobility and the associated opportunity to incur foreign debt brings benefits as well as potential costs.

---

1. Countries allowing free capital mobility are said to have an 'open capital account' since their governments do not control the items on the capital account of the balance of payments.

4.1 The growing mobility of capital

Figure 4.1 illustrates trends in the degree of international economic integration. In Figure 4.1a, reaching from the late nineteenth century until the end of the twentieth century, the light columns associated with the left scale measure the volume of international trade (the sum of exports and imports) relative to world GDP. The dark columns associated with the right scale show the ratio of the total stock of foreign-owned assets to world GDP. Thus the light columns indicate the degree of trade integration, and the dark columns illustrate the degree of financial integration (or capital mobility). The figure documents an interesting fact which is often forgotten in the contemporary debate on globalization: before the First World War international capital mobility was very high, especially considering that the technological means of communication were less developed than today. Indeed, the average ratio of foreign assets to GDP was above 50 per cent in the early twentieth century, as a result of large capital exports from the most developed countries (particularly Great Britain) to the less developed regions in the world. This is why critics of the economic dominance of the industrialized countries often refer to this period as the heyday of Western imperialism.

The First World War marked the beginning of a long period of economic and political instability, culminating in the Great Depression of the 1930s and in the catastrophe of the Second World War. During this dark period in history national governments retrenched into inward-looking economic policies involving strong trade protection and controls on capital flows. In Fig. 4.1a this is reflected in the sharp drop in trade integration and financial integration after 1914. Even as late as 1960 the world's economies were still considerably less open to trade and capital flows than they were before the First World War. In particular, there was much less financial integration in 1960 than in 1900, because most countries still maintained extensive restrictions on private capital flows across borders, in an attempt to maintain national autonomy in the conduct of monetary policy. However, between 1960 and 1980 the degree of financial integration roughly doubled, and from 1980 to 1995 it almost doubled once again, reaching the highest level ever recorded. To some extent this remarkable increase in capital mobility was driven by the simultaneous increase in world trade, since a part of international capital flows takes the form of trade credits granted by exporters to the foreign importers. But most of the increase in capital flows stemmed from a combination of financial liberalization – with one government after another abandoning capital controls – and the rapid improvements in information and communication technologies which made it easier and cheaper to move capital across borders.

The increase in trade and financial integration has continued up to recently. Figure 4.1b shows how world trade (the sum of exports and imports for the countries of the world) and the stock of world portfolio investment have evolved since 1995. International portfolio investment involves international debt flows, e.g., the purchase of foreign bonds or the extension of bank credit across borders or the purchase of foreign shares for purposes of portfolio diversification. International portfolio investors do not acquire a controlling ownership share in foreign firms and therefore are not actively engaged in running a business firm abroad. This distinguishes portfolio investment, PI, from foreign direct investment, FDI. In Fig. 4.1b the stock of PI is used as measure of financial integration.

Between 1995 and 2007 world trade increased by 128 per cent, while the stock of PI increased by 511 per cent. In the same period world GDP rose by 58 per cent according to figures from the International Monetary Fund (IMF). Thus trade increased by more than twice as much as GDP and the stock of PI increased nine times the increase in GDP.

Figure 4.1b also shows the dramatic drop in world trade by more than 20 per cent from mid-2008 to mid-2009. This was a direct consequence of the great financial and economic crisis that exploded in the fall of 2008. This episode is, of course, of great interest theoretically and practically, but it is a business cycle episode and belongs to open economy macroeconomics for the short run dealt with in Part 7. Here our concern is with the long-run trend towards increased financial and trade integration.

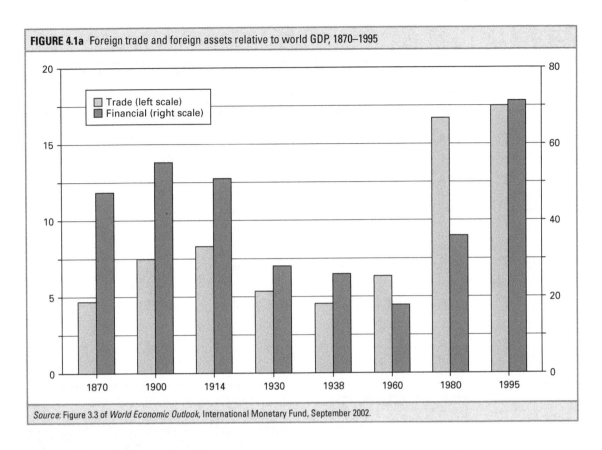

FIGURE 4.1a Foreign trade and foreign assets relative to world GDP, 1870–1995

Source: Figure 3.3 of *World Economic Outlook*, International Monetary Fund, September 2002.

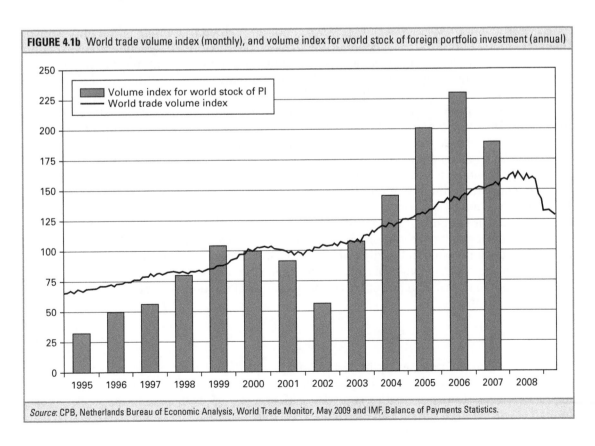

FIGURE 4.1b World trade volume index (monthly), and volume index for world stock of foreign portfolio investment (annual)

Source: CPB, Netherlands Bureau of Economic Analysis, World Trade Monitor, May 2009 and IMF, Balance of Payments Statistics.

TABLE 4.1 International investment, 1985–2002

	Stock of inward FDI % of GDP		Stock of outward FDI % of GDP		Stock of inward PI % of GDP		Stock of outward PI % of GDP	
	1985	2002	1985	2002	1986	2001	1986	2001
Australia	14.5	32.2	3.8	22.9	44.4	87.8	7.7	32.0
Austria	5.6	20.6	2.0	19.5	73.7	147.7	60.7	120.8
Canada	18.4	30.4	12.3	37.6	31.2	28.4	13.5	17.5
Denmark	6.0	41.7	3.0	43.4	–	120.3	–	89.6
Finland	2.5	27.0	3.4	52.8	30.7	153.8	22.9	81.2
France	6.9	28.2	7.1	45.8	2.8	74.7	2.8	58.7
Germany	5.1	22.7	8.4	29.0	20.6	62.9	11.7	60.0
Italy	4.5	10.6	3.9	16.4	19.9	62.5	13.3	56.3
Japan	0.3	1.5	3.2	8.3	10.9	18.0	14.6	33.3
Netherlands	18.8	74.9	36.1	84.7	71.0	181.2	78.5	220.1
Norway	11.7	17.4	1.7	20.0	54.8	–	23.3	–
Sweden	4.2	46.0	10.4	60.5	51.5	142.1	20.1	95.6
UK	14.1	40.8	22.0	66.7	40.4	116.2	51.3	112.1
USA	4.4	12.9	5.7	14.4	14.9	43.5	5.3	23.3
EU	9.3	31.4	10.5	41.0	–	–	–	–

Note: Definition of FDI: Investment in a lasting enterprise resident in another country. Definition of PI: Loans in foreign banks and cross-border investment in bonds, stocks, financial derivatives and other money market instruments.

Source: *World Investment Report 2003*, UNCTAD. IMF International Financial Statistics database.

As mentioned, international capital flows are often divided into foreign direct investment (FDI) and foreign portfolio investment (PI). FDI may take the form of 'greenfield' investment where a foreign multinational company sets up a new production plant in a country, but more often it involves the acquisition by a foreign company of a controlling ownership share in an existing domestic company. If an already established foreign-owned company retains and reinvests its profits in the host country, this is also counted as FDI. The distinguishing feature of FDI is that the investor is an active controlling owner who often brings along new production technologies and management know-how with the capital invested. Because FDI often implies an international transfer of technology and is typically undertaken by large multinational enterprises, it tends to attract special interest. Table 4.1 shows that FDI has become increasingly important relative to domestic economic activity in recent years. While FDI is a more visible form of investment, international portfolio investment (PI) still accounts for the bulk of international capital flows, as documented in Table 4.1.

In an open economy without restrictions on international capital flows, domestic saving, S, may either be invested in building up the domestic capital stock, K, or it may be used to build up foreign assets, F, via FDI or PI. In the open economy the intertemporal budget constraint of the domestic representative consumer (or of the domestic citizens together) is therefore given as:

$$F_{t+1} - F_t + K_{t+1} - K_t + \delta K_t = S_t, \tag{1}$$

where S_t is domestic gross saving in period t, $K_{t+1} - K_t + \delta K_t \equiv I_t$ is domestic gross investment in that period (which includes the replacement investment needed to compensate for the depreciation δK_t of the pre-existing capital stock), and $F_{t+1} - F_t$ is the rise in the stock of net foreign assets between period t and period $t + 1$. Thus:

$$F_{t+1} - F_t = S_t - I_t \qquad (2)$$

is the amount of capital exported during period t. We see that capital exports are given by the difference between domestic saving and domestic investment: that part of saving which is not invested at home must be invested abroad. Of course, $S_t - I_t$ may be negative. In that case part of domestic investment is financed by capital imports from abroad.

One way of measuring the degree of international capital market integration is to calculate the correlation between national savings rates and national investment rates across countries. This may be done by estimating the parameters α_0 and α_1 in a regression equation of the following form where Y_t is real GDP in year t, and where the superscript i refers to country i:

$$(I_t/Y_t)^i = \alpha_0 + \alpha_1 (S_t/Y_t)^i. \qquad (3)$$

In a closed economy aggregate investment must equal aggregate saving, $I_t = S_t$, implying $\alpha_0 = 0$ and $\alpha_1 = 1$ in Eq. (3). In an open economy with free capital flows, investment and saving may deviate from each other, leading to capital export or import as shown by (2). Part of an increase in domestic saving will typically be invested abroad, implying that $\alpha_1 < 1$. The reason is that an increase in domestic saving tends to reduce the level of domestic real interest rates as the supply of capital goes up, and this fall in domestic interest rates induces savers to invest abroad rather than at home. The greater the degree of integration of the domestic and foreign capital markets, the greater will be the tendency for domestic savings to flow out of the country in response to any given drop in domestic interest rates, so the lower α_1 will tend to be.

Alternatively, one can measure the degree of international capital mobility by focusing directly on the imbalances on current accounts between countries. A country with a savings surplus, $S_t/Y_t > I_t/Y_t$, will have a surplus on the current account of its balance of payments, whereas a country with a savings deficit will run a current account deficit. To see this, recall that goods market equilibrium in an open economy requires

$$Y_t + M_t = C_t + I_t + X_t, \qquad (4)$$

where C_t is total (private plus public) consumption, M_t is aggregate imports, and X_t is aggregate exports. If $\bar{r}$ is the international interest rate (assumed to be constant) and F_t is the stock of net foreign assets at the start of period t, then net asset income from abroad is $\bar{r}F_t$. We may rewrite (4) as:

$$Y_t + \bar{r}F_t = C_t + I_t + X_t - M_t + \bar{r}F_t. \qquad (5)$$

The magnitude $Y_t + \bar{r}F_t$ is total national income (the gross national product, GNP), consisting of gross domestic product, Y_t, plus net asset income from abroad, $\bar{r}F_t$. By definition, $X_t - M_t + \bar{r}F_t$ is the surplus on the current account of the balance of payments, consisting of the trade balance $X_t - M_t$ plus net foreign asset income, $\bar{r}F_t$. National saving is defined as national income minus total consumption, $S_t \equiv Y_t + \bar{r}F_t - C_t$. Denoting the current account balance by CA_t, we may therefore write (5) as:

$$CA_t = S_t - I_t = F_{t+1} - F_t, \qquad CA_t \equiv X_t - M_t + \bar{r}F_t, \qquad (6)$$

where (2) was used. This shows the well-known fact that the surplus on the current account and capital exports are just two sides of the same coin and both are equal to the savings surplus. The larger the average deviation between S_t and I_t across countries, the lower will be the estimated value of α_1 in (3). According to (6) a low value of α_1 therefore implies a large average imbalance on the current accounts of the countries considered.

Some years ago economists Martin Feldstein and Charles Horioka estimated a cross-country regression equation of the form (3), using average values of the investment rate,

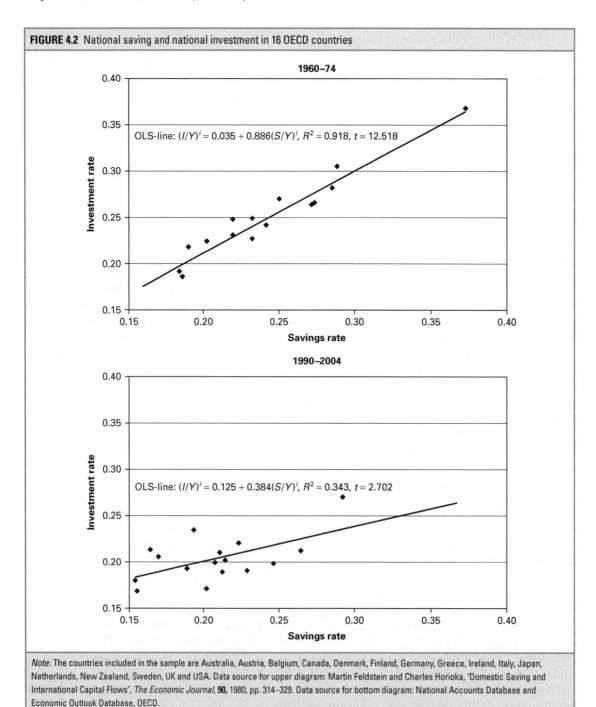

FIGURE 4.2 National saving and national investment in 16 OECD countries

Note: The countries included in the sample are Australia, Austria, Belgium, Canada, Denmark, Finland, Germany, Greece, Ireland, Italy, Japan, Netherlands, New Zealand, Sweden, UK and USA. Data source for upper diagram: Martin Feldstein and Charles Horioka, 'Domestic Saving and International Capital Flows', *The Economic Journal*, **90**, 1980, pp. 314–329. Data source for bottom diagram: National Accounts Database and Economic Outlook Database, OECD.

I_t/Y_t, and the savings rate, S_t/Y_t, for a sample of 16 OECD countries over the period 1960–74.[2] Their results are portrayed in the upper diagram in Fig. 4.2. The indicated line of best fit (estimated by OLS) has a slope as high as 0.89, suggesting a rather low degree of international capital mobility. The finding that savers apparently had a surprisingly high inclination to invest at home rather than abroad soon became known as 'the Feldstein–Horioka puzzle'. One possible explanation for the high correlation between domestic saving

2. Martin Feldstein and Charles Horioka, 'Domestic Saving and International Capital Flows', *Economic Journal*, **90**, 1980, pp. 314–329.

TABEL 4.2 The correlation between national savings rate and national investment rate, 1975–2002 (estimates of α_1)			
Period	**Old OECD**	**European Union**	**Euro area**
1975–2001	0.51	0.47	0.35
1975–1990	0.55	0.50	0.41
1991–2001	0.38	0.36	0.14

Source: Table 3 in Olivier Blanchard and Francesco Giavazzi: 'Current Account Deficits in the Euro Area: The End of the Feldstein-Horioka Puzzle?'. *Brookings Papers of Economic Activity*, **2**, 2002, pp. 147–209.

and domestic investment was that governments were eager to avoid large current account deficits because the OECD countries tried to maintain fixed exchange rates up until 1973. If a country started to build up a substantial current account deficit, its government would normally take steps to increase domestic saving and/or reduce domestic investment to redress its current account imbalance for fear that a large deficit would invite a speculative attack against its currency (by currency speculators believing that the country might have to devalue to rebalance its current account).

However, over the years the correlation between domestic saving and domestic investment has weakened. This is illustrated by the flatter regression line in the bottom part of Fig. 4.2, which shows a new estimation of Eq. (3) for the group of 16 OECD countries considered by Feldstein and Horioka, but using data for the period 1990–2004. We see that the slope coefficient α_1 for this recent period is less than one half the size of the original Feldstein–Horioka estimate, and the explanatory power of the regression as expressed by R-squared as well as the t-value is also considerably lower. Both of these findings suggest that international capital mobility has become significantly higher over time, thereby weakening the link between national saving and national investment.

Table 4.2 provides estimates of α_1 for three successive periods for a larger group of countries which are divided into the 'old' OECD (those OECD countries for which data are available for all the years back to 1975), the 15 countries which were members of the EU in 2001, and those EU countries which had adopted the euro in 2001. Again we see a clear tendency for α_1 to fall over time, indicating growing capital mobility. In particular, measured by the (low) value of α_1, capital mobility in the euro area seems to have become very high. This was also reflected in the fact that a country like Portugal ran a current account deficit as large as 10 per cent of its GDP in 2000–01, up from 2–3 per cent at the start of the 1990s. With an investment rate I_t/Y_t of around 20 per cent, this meant that about half of all gross investment in Portugal was being financed by foreign investors at the turn of the century. Similarly, in Greece the current account deficit in 2000–01 was 6–7 per cent of GDP, up from 1–2 per cent in the early 1990s.

FACTS ABOUT INTERNATIONAL ECONOMIC INTEGRATION

The empirical evidence shows that since the 1960s the world's economies have become much more integrated both with respect to trade and with respect to capital flows. In particular, capital mobility between the richest countries of the world has increased dramatically and reached an unprecedentedly high level in 2008. The great financial crisis exploding in 2008 brought the intensification to a halt, but nevertheless the long-run tendency is towards dramatically increased integration, financially and with respect to trade.

In Chapter 3 we considered the benchmark case of an economy with no cross-border capital mobility at all. In the present chapter we consider the opposite benchmark case of a small open economy whose capital market is perfectly integrated with the world capital market. The empirical evidence surveyed above suggests that capital mobility is neither absent nor perfect. Thus the 'truth' about capital mobility lies somewhere in between the two extreme cases studied in the previous and the current chapter, but looking at the two benchmark cases has the advantage of highlighting clearly what difference capital mobility can make for the dynamics of economic growth.

4.2 A Solow model of a small open economy

In this section we develop a growth model of a so-called small open economy with perfect mobility of commodities and capital, but with no labour mobility at all. This reflects the empirical fact that commodities and capital move much more across country borders than persons do. As examples of small open economies with free capital movements you may think of practically any of the countries in Western Europe, since even the larger economies like those of Britain, France or Germany are small compared to the size of the world economy.

The small open economy

The open economy considered is so small that its own economic activity does not significantly affect economic conditions in the rest of the world. In particular, the economy is so small that the volume of domestic saving and investment does not have any noticeable impact on world interest rates. Capital is assumed to be *perfectly mobile* between the domestic economy and the rest of the world. Under perfect capital mobility domestic and foreign assets are perfect substitutes, and domestic as well as foreign investors can instantaneously and costlessly switch between domestic and foreign assets. For concreteness, let us assume that foreign as well as domestic firms finance their investment in real capital by issuing bonds in the international capital market (alternatively we might assume that part of business investment is financed by issuing shares which are perfect substitutes for bonds in the eyes of financial investors). Under perfect capital mobility all of these bonds must then pay the same rate of interest. For example, if domestic bonds had a lower return than foreign bonds, international financial investors would immediately sell domestic bonds in order to buy foreign bonds, thereby driving down domestic bond prices until the rates of return were equalized. Given that this arbitrage can occur instantaneously and costlessly, bond returns (and hence effective foreign and domestic interest yields) must be equalized at any point in time.

For the small open economy this means that the domestic real interest rate is effectively given by the world real interest rate which the domestic economy cannot affect. Denmark is a good example of a small open economy in which the interest rate is more or less given from abroad. As shown in Fig. 4.3, the real rate of interest on Danish long-term bonds has followed the German real interest rate quite closely in recent years.[3]

Just as foreign and domestic assets are taken to be perfect substitutes, we assume that the goods produced in the small domestic economy are perfect substitutes for (some of the) goods produced in other countries. With free trade in commodities this means that the prices of domestic goods must equal the prices determined in the world market (with the possible addition of some exogenous transport cost). From the viewpoint of the small domestic economy the prices of exported as well as imported goods and services are thus exogenously given from abroad, that is, the ratio of the domestic to the foreign price level is exogenously fixed. For simplicity we will therefore set this exogenous relative price equal to unity. This is equivalent to assuming that all economies in the world produce the same single good.

---

3. Denmark has maintained fixed exchange rates vis-à-vis the German D-mark, and subsequently against the euro. As we shall see in Part 7, when exchange rates are flexible the domestic *nominal* interest rate may deviate from the world interest rate because exchange rate changes (currency gains or losses) are part of the total return on foreign bonds. However, with flexible exchange rates there will still be a tendency for the domestic *real* interest rate to follow the foreign *real* interest rate, at least over the longer run (as will be explained in detail in Part 7).

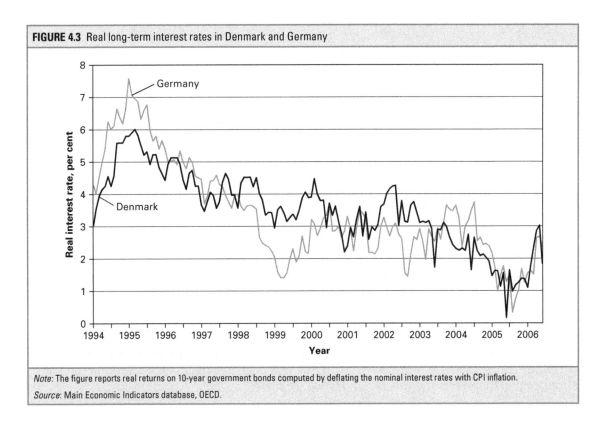

FIGURE 4.3 Real long-term interest rates in Denmark and Germany

Note: The figure reports real returns on 10-year government bonds computed by deflating the nominal interest rates with CPI inflation.

Source: Main Economic Indicators database, OECD.

With this assumption our model cannot explain the international pattern of commodity trade (i.e., which countries end up producing which types of goods) and the welfare gains from such trade. Our intention here is to understand the implications of international capital mobility for wealth accumulation and the potential gains from capital mobility.

Setting up the model

We are now ready to specify our long-run model of the small open economy. Since the rate of depreciation of the capital stock, δ, will not play any important role in our analysis, we will set it equal to zero. The intertemporal budget constraint, (1), then simplifies to:

$$F_{t+1} - F_t + K_{t+1} - K_t = S_t.$$

In the open economy it is important to distinguish between the country's *capital stock* and its total national *wealth*. National wealth, V_t, at the beginning of period t is the sum of the capital stock and the country's stock of net foreign assets at that time:

$$V_t \equiv K_t + F_t. \tag{7}$$

The capital stock is wealth invested at home by domestic citizens or foreigners, while net foreign assets are wealth invested abroad by domestic citizens minus the part of domestic capital owned by foreigners. With this definition, the intertemporal budget constraint may be written as:

$$V_{t+1} - V_t = S_t, \tag{8}$$

stating the simple fact that current savings imply a corresponding addition to national wealth.

As we have already seen, with capital mobility it is also necessary to distinguish between GDP, denoted by Y_t, and national income or GNP, denoted by Y_t^n. National income is defined as:

$$Y_t^n \equiv Y_t + \bar{r}F_t, \tag{9}$$

where $\bar{r}$ is the world real interest rate which is also the domestic real interest rate, given our assumption of perfect capital mobility. Since we are treating $\bar{r}$ as an exogenous constant, this variable does not carry any time subscript.

In accordance with the basic Solow model, we also assume a constant savings rate, s, but now aggregate national saving is a constant fraction of aggregate national *income* rather than a fraction of domestic product, since income from abroad can also be saved:

$$S_t = sY_t^n, \qquad 0 < s < 1. \tag{10}$$

Following the basic Solow model, aggregate output is given by the Cobb–Douglas production function:

$$Y_t = BK_t^\alpha L_t^{1-\alpha}, \qquad B > 0, \qquad 0 < \alpha < 1, \tag{11}$$

and the labour force, L_t, is growing at the constant rate n:

$$L_{t+1} = (1 + n)L_t, \qquad n > -1. \tag{12}$$

Maximizing profits under perfect competition, the representative domestic firm employs capital and labour up to the point where marginal products are equal to the real factor prices. Since we abstract from depreciation, the real user cost of capital (the rental rate) is simply equal to the real interest rate, $\bar{r}$. Hence we have:

$$\bar{r} = \alpha B\left(\frac{K_t}{L_t}\right)^{\alpha-1}, \tag{13}$$

$$w_t = (1-\alpha)B\left(\frac{K_t}{L_t}\right)^\alpha. \tag{14}$$

THE COMPLETE SOLOW MODEL OF THE SMALL OPEN ECONOMY

$$V_t \equiv K_t + F_t. \tag{7}$$

$$V_{t+1} - V_t = S_t, \qquad V_0 \text{ given} \tag{8}$$

$$Y_t^n \equiv Y_t + \bar{r}F_t, \tag{9}$$

$$S_t = sY_t^n, \tag{10}$$

$$Y_t = BK_t^\alpha L_t^{1-\alpha}, \tag{11}$$

$$L_{t+1} = (1 + n)L_t, \qquad L_0 \text{ given} \tag{12}$$

$$\bar{r} = \alpha B\left(\frac{K_t}{L_t}\right)^{\alpha-1}, \tag{13}$$

$$w_t = (1-\alpha)B\left(\frac{K_t}{L_t}\right)^\alpha. \tag{14}$$

Parameters: α, B, s, n and $\bar{r}$. Endogenous variables: V_t, L_t, K_t, F_t, Y_t, w_t, Y_t^n and S_t.

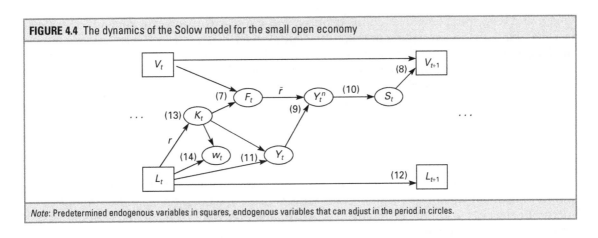

FIGURE 4.4 The dynamics of the Solow model for the small open economy

Note: Predetermined endogenous variables in squares, endogenous variables that can adjust in the period in circles.

The dynamics of the model are illustrated in Fig. 4.4. The predetermined variables in period t are national wealth, V_t, and the labour force, L_t, given from past accumulation of savings and from past population growth, respectively. The capital stock, K_t, is *not* predetermined since it can adjust within period t by capital export or import. Equation (7) shows that a larger capital stock, K_t, is associated with a lower value of net foreign assets, F_t. Given L_t, the domestic capital stock adjusts to the level K_t given by (13), ensuring that the marginal product of capital equals the world real interest rate, $\bar{r}$. Suppose for a moment that the domestic capital stock were lower than this level, implying a marginal product of capital above $\bar{r}$. The return to capital invested in the domestic economy would then be higher than the return offered in the international capital market. Capital would therefore flow into the domestic country, creating an increase in the capital stock until the marginal product of capital just became equal to $\bar{r}$. In this way (13) determines the domestic capital–labour ratio, K_t/L_t. With K_t determined and with the predetermined L_t, domestic output, Y_t, is determined by (11), and the marginal product of labour, and hence the real wage, is determined by (14). Given V_t and K_t, the net foreign asset position, F_t, follows from (7). With Y_t and F_t determined, national income, Y_t^n, is determined by (9), and Y_t^n, in turn, determines national savings, S_t, through (10). National savings add to national wealth determining V_{t+1} through (8), while L_{t+1} follows from L_t by (12). We can then start over with period $t + 1$, etc. From given initial values, V_0 and L_0, our model thus determines the dynamic evolution of all the endogenous variables.

4.3 Analysing the model: dynamics and steady state

As in Chapter 3 we will analyse our model in terms of per capita (or worker) variables, using the notation:

$$y_t \equiv \frac{Y_t}{L_t}, \ k_t = \frac{K_t}{L_t}, \ y_t^n \equiv \frac{Y_t^n}{L_t}, \ v_t \equiv \frac{V_t}{L_t}, \ f_t \equiv \frac{F_t}{L_t}. \tag{15}$$

Here, y_t is domestic product per capita, while y_t^n is national income per capita. Likewise, k_t is domestic capital per capita, while v_t is national wealth per capita, and f_t is net foreign assets per capita. It follows from (7) that $f_t = v_t - k_t$, and from (9) that $y_t^n = y_t + \bar{r}f_t$. The production function, (11), implies $y_t = Bk_t^\alpha$.

National income per capita

Equation (13) can be written $\bar{r} = \alpha Bk_t^{\alpha-1}$, and hence $\bar{r}k_t = \alpha Bk_t^\alpha = \alpha y_t$. Furthermore, from (14), $w_t = (1-\alpha)Bk_t^\alpha = (1-\alpha)y_t$. It follows that $y_t = \bar{r}k_t + w_t$. Thus GDP is fully used to reward the labour and the capital employed in the country, and the share of labour income in GDP, w_t/y_t, is $1 - \alpha$, while the income share of domestic capital in GDP, $\bar{r}k_t/y_t$, is α. These features are unchanged from the model for the closed economy of Chapter 3, but note that the share of labour income in *national* income, w_t/y_t^n, is not (necessarily) $1 - \alpha$. An exercise will ask you to analyse the income distribution further.

National income per capita is $y_t^n = y_t + \bar{r}f_t = y_t + \bar{r}(v_t - k_t) = y_t - \bar{r}k_t + \bar{r}v_t$. Using here that $y_t - \bar{r}k_t = w_t$ gives:

$$y_t^n = w_t + \bar{r}v_t. \tag{16}$$

In the open economy, national income (per capita) is the sum of wages (per capita) and the return to national wealth (per capita). This reflects that the labour force and the capital *owned by* the citizens in the country (not the capital *employed in* the country) are the country's sources of income.

The law of motion

We described above how capital exports or imports ensure that the capital stock and capital per worker adjust *within each period* to ensure that the marginal product of capital equals the international interest rate, $\bar{r} = \alpha B k_t^{\alpha-1}$. In other words, k_t adjusts *immediately* to the particular constant level k^* given by $\bar{r} = \alpha B(k^*)^{\alpha-1}$. The constant (steady state) value for the capital intensity is thus:

$$k^* = B^{\frac{1}{1-\alpha}} \left(\frac{\alpha}{\bar{r}} \right)^{\frac{1}{1-\alpha}}. \tag{17}$$

Consequently, domestic output per worker, $y_t = B k_t^{\alpha}$, and the wage rate, $w_t = (1-\alpha)B k_t^{\alpha}$, must jump immediately to the steady state levels:

$$y^* = B^{\frac{1}{1-\alpha}} \left(\frac{\alpha}{\bar{r}} \right)^{\frac{\alpha}{1-\alpha}}, \tag{18}$$

$$w^* = (1-\alpha)B^{\frac{1}{1-\alpha}} \left(\frac{\alpha}{\bar{r}} \right)^{\frac{\alpha}{1-\alpha}}, \tag{19}$$

and the capital–output ratio must jump to:

$$\left(\frac{K_t}{Y_t} \right)^* = \frac{k^*}{y^*} = \frac{\alpha}{\bar{r}}. \tag{20}$$

The constancy of the domestic capital intensity, k_t, and of GDP per capita, y_t, means that the capital stock, K_t, and the domestic product, Y_t, both grow steadily over time at a rate equal to the rate of population growth, and this occurs immediately without any adjustment time required (for the closed economy similar conditions held in the steady state, but not during the adjustment to steady state). In particular, $K_{t+1} = (1 + n)K_t$, so $I_t = K_{t+1} - K_t = nK_t$. It follows that the rate of accumulation of domestic capital, I_t/K_t, adjusts immediately to the constant level n, and, using (20), that the investment rate, $I_t/Y_t = n(K_t/Y_t)$, adjusts immediately to:

$$\left(\frac{I_t}{Y_t} \right)^* \equiv i^* = \frac{n\alpha}{\bar{r}}. \tag{21}$$

Thus, if cross-country variations in the ratio S_t/Y_t are driven mainly by variations in s, our Solow model of the small open economy suggests that the parameter α_1 in the Feldstein–Horioka equation (3) should be close to zero (since $(I_t/Y_t)^*$ is independent of s).

These properties contrast with the basic Solow model for the closed economy where capital and output per worker as well as factor prices depend on the domestic savings rate, s (in steady state and during the adjustment to steady state), and where capital and output per worker, and hence the rate of capital accumulation, only gradually converge on their steady state levels.

Instead of governing *capital* accumulation, the propensity to save now influences the accumulation of national *wealth*. To see this, start from Eq. (8), $V_{t+1} = V_t + S_t$, divide through by $L_{t+1} = (1 + n)L_t$, and use (9) and (10) to obtain:

$$v_{t+1} = \frac{1}{1+n}(v_t + sy_t^n).$$

Now insert the expression in (16) for y_t^n, and use $w_t = w^*$ to get

$$v_{t+1} = \frac{1}{1+n}(v_t + s(w^* + \bar{r}v_t)),$$

from which we obtain:

$$v_{t+1} = \frac{1+s\bar{r}}{1+n}v_t + \frac{sw^*}{1+n}. \tag{22}$$

Equation (22) is the *transition equation for the small open economy*. We have chosen to express the transition equation in terms of w^*, which is constant as long as $\bar{r}$ remains constant, but one can trace the transition equation back to parameters by substituting (19) for w^* in (22).

Equation (22) is quite intuitive. The sources of national wealth per capita in period $t + 1$ are the national wealth carried over from period t, adjusted for population growth, $v_t/(1 + n)$, plus the savings per capita in period t, $sy_t^n = s(w^* + \bar{r}v_t)$, adjusted for population growth, $s(w^* + \bar{r}v_t)/(1 + n)$.

Given an initial value, v_0, of wealth per capita, the transition equation determines v_1, which in turn determines v_2, etc., thus determining the full sequence (v_t). From (v_t), the sequences for all the endogenous variables may then be derived. For instance, the sequence for national income, (y_t^n), follows from $y_t^n = w_t + \bar{r}v_t$, (16) above, by using $w_t = w^*$ for all t. Then the sequence, (c_t), for consumption per capita follows from $c_t = (1 - s)y_t^n$.

Convergence to steady state

The transition equation is illustrated in the transition diagram, Fig. 4.5. The transition curve is a straight line that intersects the vertical axis at $sw^*/(1 + n) > 0$, and has a slope of $(1 + s\bar{r})/(1 + n)$. If this slope is smaller than one, as drawn, there is a unique positive intersection with the 45° line at a value for v_t denoted by v^*. From any predetermined initial wealth, $v_0 > 0$, v_t will converge towards v^*, as indicated by the iterations illustrated by the 'staircase' in Fig. 4.5. The convergence point, v^*, is the steady state value for national wealth per capita.

For the closed economy considered in Chapter 3, the transition curve (describing the accumulation of capital) was concave, reflecting diminishing returns to capital. In the small open economy, independently of how much wealth has already been accumulated, additional wealth always earns the international rate of return, $\bar{r}$. Hence, although there *are* diminishing returns to domestic capital, an increase Δv in current national wealth always creates the same increase $\bar{r}\Delta v$ in current national income and the same increase $s\bar{r}\Delta v$ in current savings, thus creating the same addition $(1 + s\bar{r})\Delta v/(1 + n)$ to national wealth next period after

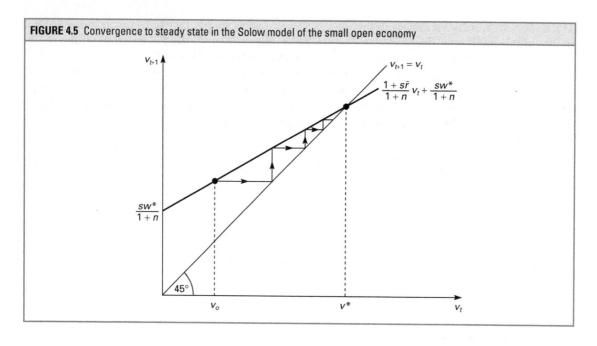

FIGURE 4.5 Convergence to steady state in the Solow model of the small open economy

adjusting for population growth. This is why the transition curve is a straight line with slope $(1 + s\bar{r})/(1 + n)$.

Figure 4.5 shows that the economy will converge on the steady state *only* if the transition line is flatter than the 45° line,[4] that is, if $(1 + s\bar{r})/(1 + n) < 1$. This requires fulfilment of the *stability condition*:

$$s\bar{r} < n. \tag{23}$$

In Western countries a long-run national savings rate around 0.2 is fairly common, and over the long run real interest rates in most Western economies have tended to fluctuate around a level of 3–4 per cent per annum, so a value of $s\bar{r}$ around 0.007 would not be unrealistic. In a literal interpretation of our model, n is the rate of population (labour force) growth which is rarely as high as 0.7 per cent per year in OECD countries (see Table A at the end of Book One). This seems to suggest that the stability condition (23) may not be met in practice.

However, this is an artefact of disregarding technological progress. In a more realistic setting with technological progress, we should measure the labour force, L_t, in so-called 'efficiency units', accounting for the fact that the rising level of technology gradually makes each unit of labour more productive. Effective labour input would then grow at a rate larger than the growth rate of the population and the stability condition would be just like (23) with n interpreted as the growth rate of effective labour, which is the sum of the rate of population growth and the rate of so-called 'labour augmenting' technological progress. Chapter 5 will present this extension of the Solow model in detail and explain, among other things, that the economy's long-run growth rate in GDP equals the growth rate of effective labour supply. Since long-run GDP growth rates in Western economies are considerably above 0.7 per cent per year, the stability condition would be met.

An appropriate way of evaluating (23) in the present context without technological progress is this: assume for a moment that the small economy considered is completely closed to the outside world. It should then work according to the model of Chapter 3, converging to a steady state in which the key variables would be given by the formulae in Section 3.3. In particular, the real interest rate established in the long run would be (recall that $\delta = 0$)

---

4. You may check this by doing a graphical analysis of the case where the transition line is steeper than the 45° line.

$$r_c^* = \frac{\alpha n}{s}, \tag{24}$$

where the subscript c refers to 'closed'. The world economy itself is closed, so in the long run the international interest rate should be $\bar{r} = \alpha \bar{n}/\bar{s}$, where $\bar{n}$ and $\bar{s}$ are the average international population growth rate and the international savings rate, respectively (and we have assumed a common α). If the small economy considered is structurally identical to the world economy ($n/s = \bar{n}/\bar{s}$), then $r_c^* = \bar{r}$, and (23) becomes equivalent to $\alpha < 1$, which is indeed one of our assumptions (realistically, α is much smaller than one, around $\frac{1}{3}$). In other words, as long as just the small economy we consider is not very different from the surrounding world economy (structurally), the stability condition, $s\bar{r} < n$, will be fulfilled.

Without apology, we will therefore assume that (23) is indeed satisfied, implying that v_t converges to the steady state value v^*. Consequently, since $y_t^n = w_t + \bar{r}v_t$, national income per capita must converge to $y^{n*} = w^* + \bar{r}v^*$, and consumption per capita, c_t, converges to the steady state level, $c^* = (1-s)y^{n*}$.

The key endogenous variables in steady state

Setting $v_t = v_{t+1} = v^*$ in (22) and solving for v^*, we find the steady state level of national wealth per capita,

$$v^* = \frac{s}{n - s\bar{r}}w^* = \frac{\frac{s}{n}}{1 - \frac{s}{n}\bar{r}}w^*, \tag{25}$$

which is positive under our stability condition, $(s/n)\bar{r} < 1$. The expression for w^* found in (19) can be inserted in place of the w^* in (25) to trace v^* back to parameters. Since w^* is independent of s and n, we see that the larger s/n is, the larger steady state national wealth per capita will be, reflecting that more savings and less erosion of per capita wealth by population growth both tend to create more wealth per person.

The net foreign asset position in steady state is $f^* = v^* - k^*$. From our solutions (17) and (19) for k^* and w^*, it follows that $k^* = (\alpha/\bar{r})w^*/(1-\alpha)$. Inserting this expression for k^* along with the expression in (25) for v^* into $f^* = v^* - k^*$, we get:

$$f^* = \frac{1}{1-\alpha}\frac{s}{n}\frac{1}{\bar{r}}\frac{\bar{r} - \frac{\alpha n}{s}}{1 - \frac{s}{n}\bar{r}}w^*. \tag{26}$$

This equation reveals that under our stability condition, net foreign assets are positive in steady state exactly if $\alpha n/s < \bar{r}$, while f^* is negative if $\alpha n/s > \bar{r}$. From (24), the condition $\alpha n/s < \bar{r}$ translates into $r_c^* < \bar{r}$. Hence the small open economy will become a net creditor if and only if the long-run interest rate it would create if it were closed is lower than the world interest rate. This is quite intuitive. If a country starts out from autarky, an opening of the capital account should lead to a capital export, and hence to a positive net foreign asset position, if the international capital market offers a higher rate of return than the domestic economy prior to the liberalization of capital flows. Conversely, if a country offers a rate of return above the international level before capital mobility is allowed, an opening of the capital account should lead to a capital import. Consequently, a country with a relatively strong propensity to save ($s/n > \bar{s}/\bar{n}$ and thus $r_c^* < \bar{r}$) will end up as a net creditor in the international economy, while a country with a relatively weak propensity to save ($s/n < \bar{s}/\bar{n}$) will become a net debtor.

The values for variables such as domestic capital per capita, GDP per capita, the wage rate, etc., that jump immediately to their steady state levels have been stated in (17)–(21)

above. The steady state value for national income per capita is $y^{n*} = w^* + \bar{r}v^*$, which we rewrite by inserting the expression in (25) for v^*:

$$y^{n*} = w^* + \bar{r}\frac{s}{n - s\bar{r}}w^* = w^*\left(1 + \frac{s\bar{r}}{n - s\bar{r}}\right) = w^*\frac{n}{n - s\bar{r}} = w^*\frac{1}{1 - \frac{s}{n}\bar{r}}.$$

We can then trace all the way back to parameters by inserting our solution, (19), for w^*:

$$y^{n*} = (1 - \alpha)B^{\frac{1}{1-\alpha}}\left(\frac{\alpha}{\bar{r}}\right)^{\frac{\alpha}{1-\alpha}} \cdot \frac{1}{1 - \frac{s}{n}\bar{r}}. \tag{27}$$

Note that y^{n*} is positive under our stability condition, $(s/n)\bar{r} < 1$. The terms in front of the dot on the right-hand side of (27) reflect the influence from the wage rate, w^*: the lower the world interest rate, $\bar{r}$, the more capital per worker will be built up in the domestic economy, and the higher the wage rate will be. The term after the dot in (27) includes the influence of the income from wealth, $\bar{r}v^*$. Here a low value of $\bar{r}$ has a negative influence, whereas a large value of the ratio s/n has a positive influence because it generates a high level of wealth per capita, v^*.

The steady state value for consumption per capita may be found as $c^* = (1 - s)y^{n*}$. In this model there is no meaningful golden rule value for the domestic savings rate, as you will be asked to explain in an exercise.

Issues of structural policy

Among the model parameters that domestic policy authorities should be able to influence are s and n. According to (27) a high value of s/n tends to create a high value of national income per capita. Hence, with respect to our fundamental question, 'what can make a nation rich?', our conclusions are qualitatively unchanged from Chapter 3. Attaining a high national savings rate and getting population growth under control will have a positive impact on income per capita in open as well as closed economies, reflecting that a high level of national wealth per capita will always contribute to a high level of national income. It is even true that the elasticity of steady state national income with respect to the savings rate is not too different between the closed economy and the small open economy as long as the latter is not too different structurally from the world economy. You will be asked to verify this in Exercise 1.

Likewise, an improvement of technology (an increase in B) increases income per capita in the open as well as in the closed economy.

CONVERGENCE, STEADY STATE AND STRUCTURAL POLICY !

Under a plausible stability condition, the Solow model for the small open economy implies convergence to a steady state. Economies with relatively strong savings propensities become net creditors in steady state, while economies with relatively weak savings propensities become net debtors. The structural policies required to generate a high long-run income per capita are similar in both the small open and the closed economy, and are policies ensuring a high savings ratio, a low population growth rate and a high technological level.

There is, however, an important structural policy issue which is not just a matter of appropriate values for structural parameters: should an economy choose to open itself to the outside world or is it better to be closed?

The open economy exposes itself to one type of shock that a closed economy avoids, namely international interest rate shocks. Does this feature represent a serious risk? And will a country benefit in the long run from an open capital account by obtaining higher income per capita? The answers to such questions are obviously important for decisions to liberalize capital flows.

4.4 Implications of an open capital account: advantages and drawbacks of globalization

Capital mobility, national income and the income distribution: a basic theorem

Will a country get richer if its government allows free capital mobility between the domestic economy and the rest of the world? In the first decades after the Second World War almost all governments in the capitalist world maintained strict capital controls.[5] As we have seen, capital was later on allowed to move much more freely between countries. Our first question is: from the viewpoint of the individual small open economy, should we expect the liberalization of capital movements to have contributed positively to national income per capita in the long run?

We will analyse this important policy issue by comparing the long-run level of national income under free capital mobility to the long-run income level attainable in a policy regime of 'autarky' where the government does not allow international capital flows. Our answer will be: yes, an open capital account does create a higher *average* income in a small economy, but domestic *wages* will fall in consequence of an opening if the domestic economy has a relatively high propensity to save. We will first give the intuition for our results and then prove them formally.

If the small economy were closed, the real interest rate established in the long run would be $r_c^* = \alpha n/s$, as stated in (24) above. Except for a knife-edge case, there are two possibilities. Either the interest rate that the small economy would experience if it were closed is lower than the international interest rate, or it is higher, that is, either $r_c^* < \bar{r}$ or $r_c^* > \bar{r}$. The first case materializes when the small economy has a relatively high savings rate relative to population growth, s/n, while the latter case corresponds to a relatively low s/n-value.

Consider the case $r_c^* < \bar{r}$, and assume that the small economy decides to open up and allow free movements of capital and commodities. The domestic owners of capital will then be able to earn more by investing their wealth in the international capital market rather than placing it in domestic capital as they had to do before the opening of the capital account. Hence, a country with a relatively high propensity to save will benefit from capital mobility by exporting capital, thus taking advantage of the higher international interest rate and earning more on its national wealth by becoming an international net creditor. After the international reallocation of portfolios has been completed there will no longer be a difference between the return on domestic capital and the international interest rate. As capital flows out of the domestic economy, domestic capital per worker decreases, creating a higher domestic marginal product of capital. This does not change the fact that domestic wealth owners benefit from the opening through a higher rate of return on wealth. However, as capital per worker decreases, the marginal product of labour goes down. Hence the capital account liberalization implies lower real wages in the domestic economy. If the small economy has a high savings propensity an opening should thus imply higher average income, but those who own no wealth and must live from their labour alone will be hurt.

Next consider the case $r_c^* > \bar{r}$. In this case an opening of the capital account will benefit the small economy via capital *import*, making it a net debtor. Since the rate of return on domestic capital is higher than the international interest rate, domestic residents can make

---

5. By decoupling the domestic interest rate from foreign interest rates, capital controls enable a government to pursue an independent national monetary policy even if exchange rates are fixed.

money by borrowing in the international capital market and investing the borrowed funds in domestic capital. This arbitrage is advantageous until the two rates of return have been equalized by the resulting increase in the domestic capital intensity which will imply higher domestic wages. In this case capital account liberalization will benefit domestic workers, but domestic wealth owners will be hurt by the fall in the rate of return on their wealth.

In the knife-edge case, $r_c^* = \bar{r}$, an opening of the capital account should have no influence on (steady state) average income or wages in the home country, according to our reasoning.

To prove formally that an open capital account always implies a higher long-run average income, and lower (higher) wages if the economy has a relatively high (low) savings propensity, we import expressions from Section 3.3 stating what national income per capita and the wage rate would be if the small economy were closed:

$$y_c^* = B^{\frac{1}{1-\alpha}}\left(\frac{s}{n}\right)^{\frac{\alpha}{1-\alpha}}. \tag{28}$$

$$w_c^* = (1-\alpha)B^{\frac{1}{1-\alpha}}\left(\frac{s}{n}\right)^{\frac{\alpha}{1-\alpha}}. \tag{29}$$

Define x as national income per capita under an open capital account *relative to* national income per capita under a closed capital account, and use our expressions for y^{n*} (in (27)) and for y_c^* to get:

$$x \equiv \frac{y^{n*}}{y_c^*} = (1-\alpha)\left(\frac{1}{\bar{r}}\frac{\alpha n}{s}\right)^{\frac{\alpha}{1-\alpha}}\frac{1}{1-\frac{s}{n}\bar{r}}.$$

From (24) we can replace $\alpha n/s$ by r_c^*, and s/n by α/r_c^* giving:

$$x = (1-\alpha)\left(\frac{1}{\tilde{r}}\right)^{\frac{\alpha}{1-\alpha}}\frac{1}{1-\alpha\tilde{r}}, \qquad \text{where } \tilde{r} \equiv \frac{\bar{r}}{r_c^*}. \tag{30}$$

We establish three features of x as a function of $\tilde{r}$. First, if $\tilde{r} = 1$ (corresponding to $\bar{r} = r_c^*$), we have $x = 1$, equivalent to $y^{n*} = y_c^*$. This confirms the intuitive insight that in case of $r_c^* = \bar{r}$, an opening of the capital account should have no influence on income per capita in the long run. Second, the derivative of $\ln x$ with respect to $\tilde{r}$,

$$\frac{d\ln x}{d\tilde{r}} = -\frac{\alpha}{1-\alpha}\frac{1}{\tilde{r}} + \frac{\alpha}{1-\alpha\tilde{r}},$$

is zero for $\tilde{r} = 1$. Third, the same derivative is strictly increasing in $\tilde{r}$, since we assume the stability condition, $(s/n)\bar{r} < 1$, now translating into $\alpha\tilde{r} < 1$.[6] These three properties imply that x as a function of $\tilde{r}$ attains its minimum for $\tilde{r} = 1$, and the minimum value is one. In other words, for any constellation of r_c^* and $\bar{r}$ other than $r_c^* = \bar{r}$, y^{n*} is larger than y_c^* (under our realistic stability condition). An open capital account thus implies a higher average income in the long run, except in the knife-edge case, $r_c^* = \bar{r}$.

Next consider the wage rate under an open capital account relative to the wage rate under a closed capital account. From (19) and (29) you will easily find that

6. Recall from (24) that $r_c^* = \alpha n/s$, so $\tilde{r} = \bar{r}/r_c^* = s\bar{r}/\alpha n$, implying $\alpha\tilde{r} = s\bar{r}/n$. Hence the stability condition $s\bar{r}/n < 1$ is equivalent to $\alpha\tilde{r} < 1$.

$$\frac{w^*}{w_c^*} = \left(\frac{\frac{\alpha n}{s}}{\bar{r}}\right)^{\frac{\alpha}{1-\alpha}} = \left(\frac{r_c^*}{\bar{r}}\right)^{\frac{\alpha}{1-\alpha}}, \tag{31}$$

from which follows that $w^* < w_c^*$ exactly if $r_c^* < \bar{r}$, which is the same as $\alpha n/s < \bar{r}$. The latter $\bar{r}$ could be replaced by $\alpha \bar{n}/\bar{s}$, so the condition would read, $n/s < \bar{n}/\bar{s}$ confirming that an opening of the capital account will lead to a fall (rise) in wages in a country with a relatively high (low) savings rate.

LONG-RUN IMPLICATIONS OF AN OPEN CAPITAL ACCOUNT !

If a small economy opens its capital account, allowing capital mobility to eliminate the difference between the domestic and the international real interest rate, the long-run implications according to the Solow model are: (i) Income per capita will increase. (ii) If the economy has a relatively high savings capacity, capital will flow out of the economy making it a net creditor, and the domestic capital intensity will fall, implying a higher rate of return on domestic capital and lower domestic real wages. (iii) If the economy has a relatively low savings capacity, capital will flow into the economy, making it a net debtor, and the domestic capital intensity will increase, implying a lower rate of return on domestic capital and higher domestic real wages.

Discussing the basic theorem on capital mobility

How large are the potential long-run effects of liberalizing capital movements according to our model? As shown by (30) and (31) above, this depends on r_c^*, $\bar{r}$, and α. A reasonable calibration is $\bar{r} = 0.03$, and $\alpha = 1/3$. For a relatively poor closed economy with a low savings capacity, a plausible domestic real interest rate could be $r_c^* = 0.06$. You will easily compute from (30) and (31) that in these circumstances the long-run effects of opening up would be a 13 per cent increase of domestic average national income, and a 41 per cent increase of domestic real wages. These effects are already considerable. Assuming instead $r_c^* = 0.09$, which would not be far-fetched for a poor country, would give an increase in average income of 30 per cent and an increase in domestic real wages of 73 per cent. For a relatively rich economy we may assume $r_c^* = 0.02$, giving an 8 per cent increase in national income of opening up, but also an 18 per cent cut in real wages. These are again considerable effects, mainly for real wages.

A liberalization of capital flows should thus imply an increase in average income in the long run, and possibly of considerable size, but, as we have emphasized, different types of income will be affected in different directions. In particular, if the initial domestic interest rate is lower than the world interest rate, a liberalization of capital movements makes capital flow *out of* the country. Domestic capitalists will then gain from a higher return to wealth whereas workers will lose from the drop in real wages resulting from the fall in domestic capital intensity, and the loss may be considerable under plausible parameter values. If wealth is evenly distributed among the domestic residents, the drop in wages will be more than offset by the increase in income from wealth for each and every person. However, people living from labour income alone will experience a drop in income when a country with a high savings rate opens up its capital account. This may be a perfectly 'rational' reason for workers in relatively rich, high-saving countries to be concerned about the implications of globalization. Note, however, that since average income increases, it may be possible to design a policy of redistribution through taxes and transfers such that everybody gains in all circumstances.

Our basic theorem says that free capital movements should imply higher national income from the point of view of a single small economy. It follows by the same reasoning, however, that if the world consisted of a collection of small economies then, if every economy opened its capital account, each and every economy would gain in the sense of attaining a higher national income. What is the basic intuition behind the feature that everybody can gain, that one country's gain is not another's loss? Where does the increase of the 'pie' to share basically come from? The answer is: from a more effective global allocation of capital. When all economies are closed, each will build up its own capital stock the size of which will reflect the economy's own savings capacity. Capital intensities will be different between different countries and therefore the marginal products of capital will be different in different countries. Whenever the marginal products are different in two different places, an increase in total production and income can be obtained by moving capital from where it has a low marginal product to where it has a high one without additional inputs being required. This is exactly what happens according to our theory when capital movements are liberalized, and the better use of the global capital stock explains why all countries can gain.

Just as international trade theory shows that free trade in goods and services generally tends to increase economic efficiency by enabling countries to exploit their comparative advantages, the theory of economic growth thus suggests that free trade in capital services (i.e. free international mobility of capital) tends to increase average long-run prosperity by implying a more effective global allocation of capital. This insight from our Solow models provides one explanation why most economists take a favourable attitude towards capital mobility, while realizing that redistributive policies may be needed to ensure that all groups in society enjoy the fruits of liberalization.

Our basic theorem is a pure steady state comparison. How fast do the effects of liberalization occur according to our theory? We have seen above that some variables adjust immediately, among these GDP per capita and real wages. So, the very important wage response should come fast. Some other variables have a gradual adjustment, among these national wealth and income per capita. An exercise will ask you to do simulations under plausible parameter restrictions for a relatively poor country to investigate how fast these more gradual affects occur. We may reveal that most of the adjustment of national income comes immediately and depends only a little on the gradual accumulation of national wealth. So, not only are the effects for a relatively poor country of opening its capital account beneficial and of considerable size (in particular for wages), they should also come very fast. We have to point to two reservations, however.

The very fast occurrence of the effects rests on our ideal assumption of *perfect* capital mobility. In the real world physical capital adjusts more slowly than required for an immediate equalization of marginal products across countries. In consequence the potential effects from liberalization come more slowly than our idealized model predicts.

Furthermore, when individual country risks are taken into account as we do below, the size and for some variables even the sign of the predicted effects of free capital mobility can be questioned.

Despite these reservations, our basic theorem does suggest a potential for highly beneficial effects of liberalizing capital movements. Moreover, in a more realistic setting with risk and uncertainty, capital mobility may even yield an additional type of welfare gain because it allows risk-averse savers to reduce the volatility (riskiness) of the rate of return on their wealth by holding foreign as well as domestic assets in their portfolios (assuming that the rates of return on foreign and domestic assets are not perfectly correlated).

On the other hand, a country opening its capital account exposes itself to a type of impact from the outside world that it would avoid if it remained closed, namely changes in the international interest rate, so-called interest rate shocks.

A permanent interest rate shock

It is of interest to analyse the *long-run* economic consequences of a *permanent* increase (or decrease) in the international interest rate, $\bar{r}$. Such an increase could, for instance, be caused by a permanent increase in government consumption in some of the larger countries in the world. The world economic system is closed and, as we explained in Chapter 3, a higher government propensity to consume implies a higher long-run interest rate in a closed economy. Hence a permanent expansion of public consumption in the rest of the world will affect the small domestic economy via a permanent increase in $\bar{r}$. What are the implications according to our model?

Our formulae (17), (18) and (19) reveal directly that steady state domestic capital intensity, GDP per capita and the real wage all decrease in response to a permanent increase in $\bar{r}$. Just after the interest rate shock (before any adjustments have taken place), the marginal product of domestic capital, and hence the return earned on domestic capital, will fall short of the new and higher international interest rate. Hence capital flows out of the country, implying a decrease in domestic capital per worker. The outflow ceases when the decrease in k_t has driven the marginal product of capital up to the level of the new and higher $\bar{r}$. This adjustment of k_t takes place immediately and is effected by capital export. A capital export should imply that the country's net foreign asset position improves. We will return to this issue below.

The fall in domestic capital intensity explains why domestic output per capita falls. Furthermore, the lower value of k^* implies a smaller marginal product of labour and therefore a lower wage rate. The rate of return on domestic capital increases with $\bar{r}$, but note that capital income created in the domestic economy ($\bar{r}k^*$) actually decreases, as can be seen by multiplying both sides of (17) by $\bar{r}$.

How about national income? Consider the formula (27) for the long-run value of income per capita, and remember that the term in front of the dot on the right-hand side is the steady state wage rate, w^*. We see that this term decreases in response to the increase in $\bar{r}$, reflecting the fall in the marginal product of labour caused by the drop in domestic capital intensity. The term to the right of the dot includes the return on national wealth, $\bar{r}v^*$, and this term increases (under our stability requirement). There are thus two opposing forces on y^{n*}. To determine which one is the strongest, we can differentiate (the log of) y^{n*} with respect to $\bar{r}$:

$$\frac{d \ln y^{n*}}{d\bar{r}} = -\frac{\alpha}{1-\alpha}\frac{1}{\bar{r}} + \frac{\frac{s}{n}}{1-\frac{s}{n}\bar{r}}.$$

This expression includes a negative and a positive term, reflecting the two opposing forces. Under the stability condition, the condition for the derivative being negative is that $\bar{r} < \alpha n/s$. This is exactly the condition for the country being initially a net debtor, $\bar{r} < r_c^*$. On the other hand, the derivative is positive exactly if $\bar{r} > \alpha n/s$, that is, if the country is initially a net creditor. The conclusion is that in the long run national income (and consumption) per capita will fall in response to an increase in the world interest rate if the country has a low propensity to save and therefore is a net debtor, while national income per capita will increase if the country has a strong savings capacity and is therefore a net creditor.

This is easy to understand intuitively. If a country has debt, its average income will be negatively influenced if a higher rate of interest must be paid on the debt (and we would expect the debt to decrease after all adjustments have taken place). On the other hand, if a country has positive net foreign assets, the domestic wealth owners will benefit from a higher rate of return on wealth (and we would expect the country to react by increasing further its net foreign assets).

As already explained, domestic wage earners will experience a drop in their wage income regardless of the country's net foreign asset position and regardless of their individual asset positions: a person without any debt or wealth will lose income after an increase in the international interest rate as a consequence of the domestic economy's reactions to the interest rate shock.

How are the long-run values for national wealth per capita, v^*, and net foreign assets per capita, f^*, affected by the negative interest rate shock? In the derivation of (27) we found that

$$y^{n*} = \frac{w^*}{1 - \dfrac{s}{n}\bar{r}},$$

(last equation before (27)), so (25) may be written as

$$v^* = \frac{s}{n}y^{n*}.$$

This shows that v^* is affected by $\bar{r}$ through the same terms as y^{n*}, so in the long run national wealth falls after the increase in $\bar{r}$ if the economy has a relatively low propensity to save, and vice versa. National wealth is affected in the same direction as national income because wealth comes from income through savings.

Finally, we can use (24) and (25) to rewrite (26) as

$$f^* = \left(\frac{1}{1-\alpha}\right)\left(\frac{\bar{r} - r_c^*}{\bar{r}}\right)v^*.$$

Thus f^* is influenced by $\bar{r}$ through the same terms as y^{n*} and v^*, *and* through the term $(\bar{r} - r_c^*)/\bar{r}$. If the country is initially a net debtor ($\bar{r} < r_c^*$), then this last term is negative, and as $\bar{r}$ increases it becomes smaller in absolute value. This reveals that net foreign assets per capita, f^*, altogether become smaller in absolute value. The domestic economy reacts to the increased price of debt by reducing its debt. On the other hand, if the country is initially a net creditor, an increase in $\bar{r}$ will make its positive net foreign assets even larger (show this).

In conclusion, a permanent interest rate shock where $\bar{r}$ increases has a negative influence on the domestic economy's long-run national income and wealth if the country is a net debtor and a positive influence if the country is a net creditor, while wages are negatively affected in all circumstances. A permanent decrease in $\bar{r}$ has, of course, just the opposite effects. If a country wants to avoid the ups and downs associated with international interest rate shocks, this may be a reason for *not* wanting to liberalize capital movements, although such a liberalization should have a positive long-run influence on national income on the average.

Country risk

So far we have assumed that the 'hurdle' rate of return required and accepted by investors for investing their wealth in the small economy is the same as the international interest rate, $\bar{r}$. However, in the real world investors will often require a *risk premium* on top of the international interest rate for investing in the assets of any particular small economy.

In August 1998 the American 'hedge fund', Long Term Capital Management, was in trouble (the reason is not important here) and had to sell off assets. It turned out that it had quite a lot of Danish mortgage bonds in its portfolio. Although the hedge fund was a small economic agent relative to the American or the European economy, it was relatively large compared to the Danish bond market and therefore its selling off caused a drop in Danish bond prices. This was bad news for the other investors who had (planned) to sell Danish bonds at that time. The wave could, of course, have gone the other way with investors being fortunate to sell Danish bonds at a time where large-scale buying by a big international investor had driven prices upwards. However, usually investors are risk averse, preferring a safe return of one million euros to a fifty-fifty chance of earning either two million euros or zero euros. Since the return on Danish assets can fluctuate a little depending on the particular circumstances of large international investors, investors in Danish bonds will require an expected return (slightly) in excess of the interest rate on the safest bonds traded in the international capital market. The 'thinness' of Danish asset markets may thus imply a risk premium in the Danish interest rate. Figure 4.3 indicates that the Danish real interest rate has indeed been a bit higher than the euro interest rate over longer periods, but not much in recent years, though.

There can be other (more severe) reasons for risk premia in interest rates. For instance, if investment in a country is not considered completely safe because of risks of, for example, civil war, coup d'états, nationalizations or widespread bankruptcies, investors will typically require large risk premia for investing in the country.

The risk premium on a country's real interest rate can change, and the change can be long lasting, for instance if international investors lose confidence in a country. A dramatic example of this was provided by the South-East Asian economic crisis in 1997–98 when foreign capital flows into the 'tiger' economies of Indonesia, Malaysia, South Korea and Thailand suddenly stopped, forcing these countries into drastic cuts in domestic consumption and investment as they could no longer finance their large current account deficits.[7] After such a loss of confidence investors sharply increase the risk premium they require in order to be willing to lend to the country.

In the great financial crisis of 2008 investors suddenly lost confidence in a lot of assets and financial institutions and capital therefore flowed massively into what was perceived to be risk-free assets issued by 'safe havens'. For this reason interest rates on the short-term government bonds of Germany and the USA fell to levels close to zero. At the same time the risk premia included in the interest rates of many other countries increased dramatically, not so much or not only because of reduced trust in these particular economies, but rather as a result of an extreme aversion to risk of any kind. Many so-called emerging market economies in Eastern Europe, South America and Asia experienced that capital fled their countries and that the real interest rates required to keep capital inside the country increased significantly.

Below we will analyse the effects of a long-lasting change in the risk premium on a country's real interest rate. Denoting, as before, the average international real rate of interest by $\bar{r}$, the hurdle real interest rate that investors require and accept for investing in a particular small economy may be $\bar{r} + \varepsilon$, where ε is a risk premium compensating for the risk associated with investing in the country's assets. In principle, ε could be negative if the country is considered very 'safe', but we will think of ε as positive.[8]

The risk premium, ε, can be influenced by certain types of domestic policy. For instance, if Denmark were to join the European Monetary Union, abandoning the Danish krone, Danish bonds denominated in euros would be very close substitutes for other euro bonds, and the market for Danish bonds would therefore no longer be thin. Hence, the risk we described above would be reduced and the (already small) risk premium in the Danish real interest rate should therefore also be reduced. Likewise, policies that promote the general safety of a country's assets, for instance an improvement of the financial system or of the system of corporate governance that reduces the risk of bankruptcies or fraud, should reduce the risk premium as well. Of course, a certain (bad) policy could imply an increase in the risk premium.

In our Solow model of the small open economy, (7)–(14), the interest rate, $\bar{r}$, appears in two places. One is in the arbitrage condition, (13), where $\bar{r}$ is obviously a hurdle interest rate and should be replaced by $\bar{r} + \varepsilon$ to take country risk into account explicitly. The other place is in the definition, (9), of national income. Should the $\bar{r}$ appearing here also be replaced by $\bar{r} + \varepsilon$?

---

7. In his highly readable book on *The Return of Depression Economics* (Allen Lane, The Penguin Press, 1999), Paul Krugman gives a breathtaking account of the Asian crisis as well as other recent international financial crises.

8. Just adding ε to $\bar{r}$ in the definition of the hurdle interest rate is an *ad hoc* way of dealing with country risks since it does not model uncertainty explicitly. Under uncertainty investors expect different rates of return from investment in the country with different probabilities. Since they are risk averse, they will require an *average* rate of return above the safe $\bar{r}$. We try to capture this by our ε, but without considering probability distributions explicitly.

This depends on the country's net foreign asset position. If it is a net debtor, $F_t < 0$, the foreign investors who have financed part of the country's capital stock will require a risk premium on their investment, so the interest rate that must be paid on F_t is indeed $\bar{r} + \varepsilon$. Hence, if the country is a net debtor, our model, (7)–(14), is amended to take country risk into account by writing $\bar{r} + \varepsilon$ instead of $\bar{r}$ wherever $\bar{r}$ appears.

If the country is a net creditor, it will earn only the international interest rate, $\bar{r}$ (without any risk premium), on its positive net foreign assets. In this case the appropriate model will therefore consist of (7)–(14), with the $\bar{r}$ in (9) kept unchanged, and with the $\bar{r}$ in (13) replaced by $\bar{r} + \varepsilon$.

We will consider a net debtor country that is initially in steady state. Our model is then simply (7)–(14), with $\bar{r}$ replaced by $\bar{r} + \varepsilon$. Mathematically the model is thus unchanged, with $\bar{r} + \varepsilon$ now taking the place of $\bar{r}$. We are interested in the long-run consequences of a permanent increase in the risk premium, ε. This situation could, for instance, be representative for a country that has developed by borrowing, thereby becoming a net debtor, and where some event suddenly causes a long-lasting lowering of investor expectations regarding the country's future long-term performance.

To analyse this situation we do not have to perform any new formal analysis. For a net debtor our model is unchanged with respect to mathematical structure, so in all our formulae for steady state values, transition curve, etc., we should just replace $\bar{r}$ by $\bar{r} + \varepsilon$. In the model with country risk, an increase in ε will have the same effects as an increase in $\bar{r}$ had in the old model, and for the same reasons. We have already analysed this and found that for a net debtor, wages, national income and national wealth would fall in the long run. Hence, this will be the long-run reaction of the small open debtor economy to an increase in the country risk premium, ε.

However, this time we cannot conclude that if the country is initially a net *creditor*, national income will increase in response to an increase in ε. Recall that the model including country risk is different for a net debtor and a net creditor. An exercise will ask you to analyse the case of a net creditor. The analysis will reveal that national income and wealth are negatively affected by an increase in the country risk premium in all circumstances. Summarizing with respect to interest rate and risk shocks:

LONG-RUN EFFECTS OF PERMANENT INTEREST RATE AND RISK PREMIUM SHOCKS

A higher international real interest rate will imply a higher national income in a small open creditor country and a lower income in a debtor country. Irrespective of the country's net foreign asset position, the domestic capital intensity and real wages will fall.

A higher risk premium on capital invested in a small open economy will cause the domestic real interest to increase and domestic national income, capital intensity and real wages to decrease.

The possibility of long-lasting interest rate shocks, caused by changes in international interest rates or by changes in country-specific risk premia, thus implies some risks for small open economies. However, the main risks of free capital movements lie in the economy's *short-run* reactions, and we should emphasize that our open economy Solow model cannot give a realistic description of the short-run effects of an interest rate shock. For example, although our model implies that workers must take a wage cut when the country is hit by an increase in $\bar{r}$ or ε, at least they keep their jobs. But in practice wages are not very flexible in the short run, so a higher interest rate will throw some people out of work for a while as firms reduce their investment.

As another example, in our model firms react to the higher interest rate by reducing their capital stock and output, but they 'stay in business'. However, in the real world a serious interest rate shock will cause many firms to go bankrupt, and investment will fall more dramatically in the short run than in the long run.

In summary, because our Solow model with fully flexible prices does not allow output and employment to deviate from their 'natural' rates, it does not capture all the drama of the recession that will occur in the short run when a country runs into an international financial crisis. In Part 7 of this text we shall develop business cycle models which can illuminate the short-run fluctuations generated by such a shock.

4.5 The costs and benefits of capital mobility: second thoughts?

Much of the ongoing international debate on globalization centres on the question whether free capital mobility is desirable or not. The analysis in this chapter suggests that capital mobility brings long-run benefits as well as potential costs.

An open capital account should enable a low-saving country with high investment needs to borrow more cheaply in the world capital market. It also allows wealth owners in high-saving countries to take advantage of more profitable investment opportunities abroad. In these ways capital mobility tends to raise a country's long-run national income and wealth.

On the other hand capital mobility also makes a country vulnerable to shifts in the moods of international investors. If investors suddenly lose confidence in a debtor country, the resulting increase in the country's borrowing rate of interest will cause a recession and sometimes even a depression, as illustrated by the Asian crisis in 1997–98. Recent economic history suggests that developing countries and emerging market economies tend to experience greater shifts in international borrowing conditions than the most developed Western market economies. This may explain why many developing countries still maintain some capital controls whereas the richest countries in the world have liberalized international capital flows.

If the risks associated with *shifting* risk premia are not too serious, there should be a strong case for a small economy to open its capital account. In particular, for a low-saving, poor country the consequence should be an inflow of capital creating a higher domestic capital intensity and higher real wages to the benefit of the country's wage earners. Many economists have seen this wage effect as a fundamental argument in favour of capital mobility as a means for poor countries to alleviate poverty. However, many of these economists have had second thoughts, and the example of Mexico is a perfect illustration.

Consider Fig. 4.6. This shows that Mexico has typically had a positive real interest rate differential to the USA, and this is particularly true for the years up to 1994 (consult the figure's note about the difficulties of measuring the interest rate gap). This is in line with our theory since the USA has typically had an s/n-ratio more than twice that of Mexico (consult Table A in the appendix for Book One). Up to 1994 there was strict control on capital movements between the two countries, but in 1994 the North American Free Trade Agreement, NAFTA, between Canada, the USA and Mexico began to take effect. NAFTA involved liberalizations of trade as well as removal of restrictions on investment and capital movements between the countries. Economists expected that this would cause a huge flow of capital from the USA into Mexico, the flip side of which would be a current account *deficit* of Mexico vis-à-vis the USA. The figure shows that the exact opposite happened: Mexico more or less immediately began to run a huge *surplus* on the current account with the USA, so capital was flowing out of Mexico and into the USA. The relatively poor Mexican economy was thus helping the rich USA, already with abundant capital, to increase its capital intensity. The idea that free capital flows would help poor Mexican workers turned out not to hold.

Our model *is* compatible with this evidence. The outflow of capital from Mexico can be explained by country risk: Mexican as well as international investors placed such a large

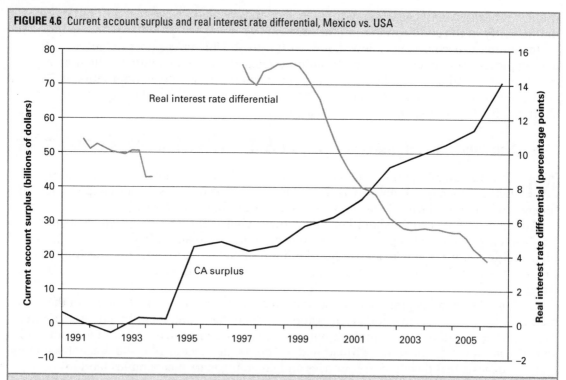

FIGURE 4.6 Current account surplus and real interest rate differential, Mexico vs. USA

Note: In lack of comparable longer interest rates, real interest rates have been computed from 1-year government bonds deflating nominal interest rates by CPI-inflation. The differential is computed as the difference between the two countries' 9-quarter smoothed real interest rates. A part of the curve is missing because during the Mexican (financial) crisis of 1995, short term nominal interest rates went to abnormally high levels without inflation going with it, so the interest rate differential as computed here would also go to extremely high, but atypical levels.

Source: Bureau of Economic Analysis and Economic Outlook database, OECD.

risk premium on investment in Mexico that, despite the apparently much higher Mexican real interest rates, investors considered investment in the USA more advantageous than investment in Mexico. When given the opportunity, rich Mexican wealth owners therefore began to move their capital to the USA. The perceived riskiness of investment in Mexico was confirmed by the Mexican crisis of 1995, but was probably also caused by a relative distrust in Mexican authorities and institutions at the time.

The Mexican case illustrates sharply that not only shifts in country risk, but also the presence of a large, constant country risk premium has important implications for the effects of capital mobility. In particular, one cannot take for granted that capital account liberalization will benefit the workers of poor labour-abundant countries through a capital inflow that raises the demand for labour.

Nevertheless, a modified version of our 'basic theorem' on capital mobility still applies even in the presence of country-specific risks. When Mexican wealth owners reacted to capital account liberalization by moving (some of) their capital to the USA, they did so because they expected a higher *risk-adjusted* return on investment in that country. Adjusted for risk, the net return to the capital owned by Mexicans therefore increased, and so did the 'risk-adjusted' Mexican national income, that is, national income adjusted for the welfare loss associated with investment risks. Even though Mexican GDP fell as capital fled the country, this was more than compensated by an increase in expected capital income from Mexican-owned investments in the USA and elsewhere, once the expected returns to capital were adjusted for risk. However, although total risk-adjusted income increased in Mexico as well as in the USA, the gains to Mexico were not equally shared, since Mexican workers faced less demand for their labour as capital was exported.

4.6 Summary

1. In an open economy which allows free international mobility of capital, part of domestic investment may be financed by capital imports from abroad, and part of domestic saving may be invested in foreign assets. It is then necessary to distinguish between the *domestic capital stock* (the stock of capital invested in the domestic economy) and *national wealth* (the total stock of assets owned by domestic residents). A country's stock of net foreign assets is equal to the difference between its national wealth and the domestic capital stock.

2. In parallel to the distinction between the domestic capital stock and national wealth, one must distinguish between *gross domestic product* (GDP) which is the total output produced by the factors of production employed in the domestic economy, and *national income* which is the total income earned by the factors of production owned by domestic residents. National income is equal to GDP plus the return to the country's net foreign assets.

3. The growth rate of a country's capital stock is given by its rate of domestic investment, whereas the growth rate of national wealth is determined by the national savings rate. In a closed economy saving and investment are identical and therefore perfectly correlated. In the open economy capital mobility reduces the correlation between saving and investment. The current account on the balance of payments represents the difference between national saving and national investment. As an accounting identity, the increase in a country's net foreign assets is given by the balance on its current account.

4. International capital mobility may take the form of international portfolio investment, where households or institutional investors (including banks) acquire foreign assets to diversify their portfolios, or it may take the form of foreign direct investment where the investor acquires a controlling ownership share of foreign business assets. In recent decades both forms of international investment have grown much more rapidly than world output and world trade, as many governments have liberalized capital flows, and as improvements in information and communication technologies have reduced the barriers to foreign investment. The growing mobility of capital has caused a fall in the correlation between national rates of saving and investment. In the euro area this correlation is now close to zero.

5. Capital is said to be perfectly mobile when domestic and foreign assets are perfect substitutes and investors can instantaneously and costlessly switch between the two asset types. In a small open economy which cannot affect the world interest rate or any other foreign macroeconomic variable, perfect capital mobility implies that the correlation between national saving and national investment tends to zero.

6. In our Solow model of a small open economy with perfect capital mobility, the domestic capital intensity adjusts instantaneously to its steady state level determined by the international interest rate. By contrast, national wealth per capita evolves gradually over time, since any increase in wealth generates an increase in capital income, thereby raising aggregate saving which in turn generates another increase in wealth, and so on.

7. The process of wealth accumulation in the small open economy is dynamically stable if and only if the (effective) labour force grows at a rate exceeding the product of the savings rate and the international real interest rate. When the labour force is measured in technology-adjusted efficiency units, this stability condition will be met for all realistic parameter values.

8. By allowing free international capital flows, a country will be able to increase its national income whenever the domestic steady state real interest rate in the absence

of capital mobility, r_c^*, deviates from the world real interest rate, $\bar{r}$. If $r_c^* > \bar{r}$, which will typically be the case in a country with a relatively low savings rate, capital mobility benefits the domestic economy by enabling firms to borrow at a world interest rate below the (initial) marginal return to domestic investment. If $r_c^* < \bar{r}$, which will tend to be the case in a country with a relatively high savings rate, domestic wealth owners gain because capital mobility allows them to invest their savings at a higher (initial) rate of return abroad than at home. If wealth is unevenly distributed, capital mobility will affect the distribution of income and may in fact hurt some domestic agents even though it raises aggregate income.

9. While capital mobility enables domestic agents to take advantage of rate-of-return differentials between the domestic and the foreign economy, it also makes countries more vulnerable to international interest rate shocks. In particular, a permanent increase in the real interest rate at which a net debtor country can borrow abroad will reduce the country's steady state level of national income and wealth. Moreover, if such an increase in the country risk premium occurs abruptly, as is often the case, it may create a serious domestic recession in the short run.

10. A risk premium on investment in a small economy may explain why capital flows out of the country, not into it, upon liberalization of capital movements, even if the country initially had a relatively high real interest rate. This is probably the background for the Mexican experience after NAFTA (and other similar incidences). This represents a serious challenge to the more orthodox view that capital mobility should lead to better living conditions for the working poor in low-saving countries through capital imports.

4.7 Exercises

Exercise 1. The elasticity of long-run national income per capita with respect to the savings rate in the small open economy

This exercise investigates how strongly national income per capita is influenced by the savings rate in the open economy compared to the closed.

1. First show from (27) that the elasticity of y^{n*} with respect to s is:

$$e_o = \frac{(s/n)\bar{r}}{1 - (s/n)\bar{r}}$$

(the stability condition, $(s/n)\bar{r} < 1$, should be assumed).

In the closed economy studied in Chapter 3, the elasticity of national income (equal to GDP) per capita with respect to the savings rate, s, was found to be $e_c = \alpha/(1 - \alpha)$. It seems difficult to compare these two elasticities since they involve different parameters. We can, however, apply a trick we used in this chapter as well. The real interest rate that would emerge in the long run in the small open economy if it were closed (given $\delta = 0$) as stated in (24) was: $r_c^* = \alpha n/s$.

2. Show that the elasticity, e_o, can be written as:

$$e_o = \frac{\alpha\tilde{r}}{1 - \alpha\tilde{r}}, \qquad \text{where } \tilde{r} \equiv \frac{\bar{r}}{r_c^*},$$

where the stability condition is now $\alpha \tilde{r} < 1$. Show that if the long-run real interest rate that the open economy would produce if it were closed is equal to the international real interest rate, then $e_o = e_c$. Then show that if the considered small economy has a stronger propensity to save (as measured by s/n) than corresponding to $r_c^* = \bar{r}$, then $e_o > e_c$, and vice versa.

3. Try to explain your result intuitively. (Hint: If the economy considered is 'savings strong', so that $r_c^* < \bar{r}$, then, when it has adjusted fully to the conditions of free capital movements it will have taken over a rate of return on wealth that is higher than the one it would produce itself if it were closed.)

Exercise 2. Golden rule in the open economy?

Show that in the small open economy's steady state, consumption per capita is:

$$c^* = (1 - s)\frac{1}{1 - (s/n)\bar{r}}w^*,$$

where the expression for w^* of (19) could be inserted (but, since w^* does not depend on s, this is not of importance for the present exercise). Show that as long as the stability condition, $(s/n)\bar{r} < 1$, is fulfilled, an increase in s has two opposing effects on c^*, and explain the origins of these.

   Given the two opposing effects it is natural to ask if there is a specific (golden rule) value of s that maximizes c^*. Show that this is not the case by demonstrating that as s increases up towards $n/\bar{r}$ (which is realistically assumed to be smaller than one), c^* goes to infinity.

   Try to explain intuitively what goes on here. Explain first, for instance, what happens to steady state national income when s increases towards $n/\bar{r}$. To understand this, in turn, explain what happens to the transition curve as s increases towards $n/\bar{r}$, and explain *why* the transition curve rotates as it does.

Exercise 3. The income distribution in the small open economy

As stated in this chapter, in any period t, the share of labour income in GDP, w_t/y_t, is equal to $1 - \alpha$, while the share of income earned on domestic capital in GDP, $\bar{r}k_t/y_t$, is α. These features are unchanged from the model for the closed economy of Chapter 3. However, from the point of view of the small open economy the income shares of the resources *owned by* domestic residents in *national income* (rather than GDP) are of more interest. That is, the income distribution is more relevantly described by the share of labour income in national income, w_t/y_t^n, and the share of income earned on national wealth in national income, $\bar{r}v_t/y_t^n$.

1. Show, using (16) and the fact that w_t jumps immediately to w^*, that labour's share in any period t is:

$$\frac{w_t}{y_t^n} = 1 - \bar{r}\frac{v_t}{y_t^n} = 1 - \bar{r}\frac{v_t}{w^* + \bar{r}v_t},$$

and show that as national wealth, v_t, converges towards its steady state level, v^*, from below (above), labour's share will converge to its steady state level from above (below).

2. Show that *in* steady state the shares in national income of labour and wealth, respectively, are:

$$\frac{w^*}{y^{n*}} = 1 - \frac{s}{n}\bar{r} \qquad \text{and} \qquad \frac{\bar{r}v^*}{y^{n*}} = \frac{s}{n}\bar{r}.$$

(As usual we assume the stability condition, $(s/n)\bar{r} < 1$.) Show that in an open economy, a relatively strong propensity to save (as measured by s/n) will tend to create a relatively low labour share in the long run. Will it also imply a lower long-run wage rate, w^*?

Explain your results intuitively. Should wage earners in open economies try to resist national saving?

3. To compare the functional income distribution just found to the income distribution in the closed economy, one can (once again) use the trick of rewriting some expressions in terms of the interest rate that the small economy *would* have created in the long run if it were closed, $r_c^* = \alpha n/s$. Show that the steady state functional income distribution in the open economy is given by:

$$\frac{w^*}{y^{n*}} = 1 - \alpha \tilde{r} \quad \text{and} \quad \frac{\bar{r} v^*}{y^{n*}} = \alpha \tilde{r}, \quad \text{where } \tilde{r} \equiv \frac{\bar{r}}{r_c^*},$$

where the stability condition, $\alpha \tilde{r} < 1$, is assumed. Show that if an economy has a relatively high propensity to save by international standards, an opening of the economy will imply a lower labour share in the long run. Explain why. Will an opening also imply a lower long-run wage, w^*? Do wage earners in savings strong economies have reasons to try to resist a liberalization of capital movements? Should they rather direct their political influence towards other aims?

4. How is the long-run functional income distribution in the open economy affected by a permanent international interest rate shock, where $\bar{r}$ increases permanently to a new and higher level? Explain your result.

Exercise 4. The effects of a permanent increase in the savings rate

Consider the Solow model of the small open economy and assume that as from some period the savings rate, s, shifts permanently upwards to a new and higher level, s'. The shift is sufficiently small to ensure that the stability condition is fulfilled after the change, and the country's position as net debtor or creditor in steady state (the sign of f^*) does not change.

1. Explain that this gives rise to a change in the transition curve that can be described as a combination of a parallel shift upwards and an anti-clockwise rotation around the intersection point with the v_{t+1} axis. Explain the economic background for each of these two movements.

2. Assume that the economy was in steady state before the shift in the savings rate. Using your transition diagram, explain qualitatively the economy's reactions over time to the permanent increase in the savings rate. Focus first on the first period with s'. How are GDP per capita, the wage rate, national income per capita, consumption per capita and savings per capita affected in that period? Then consider the subsequent sequence of periods. How do GDP per capita and the wage rate evolve over those periods? Describe how national wealth per capita evolves, that is, describe period by period the process of wealth accumulation. How do national income and consumption per capita evolve?

3. Compare the old to the new steady state. How (in what direction) are GDP per capita and national income per capita changed? Can we be sure in what direction consumption per capita has changed? How do the country's net foreign assets change from the old to the new steady state?

Exercise 5. The importance of capital movements for convergence and a permanent productivity shock in the open vs. the closed economy

In this chapter it was shown that if the small open economy, in the case where it was closed, were to create a long-run interest rate, $r_c^* = \alpha n/s$, equal to the international interest rate, $\bar{r}$, then its steady state national income per capita would be the same as if it were closed. One may get the impression that if $\alpha n/s = \bar{r}$, then it does not matter if the economy is closed or open. This is absolutely false. It is only the steady state that is unaffected. What happens outside steady state depends very much on the economy being closed or open, as this exercise illustrates. We will consider one and the same small economy as open and as closed.

We assume throughout that indeed $r_c^* = \alpha n/s = \bar{r}$, and that $\delta = 0$.

1. Show from (27) that under these assumptions steady state national income per capita is:

$$y^{n*} = B^{\frac{1}{1-\alpha}}\left(\frac{s}{n}\right)^{\frac{\alpha}{1-\alpha}}.$$

Then show, by comparing it to the relevant formula in Chapter 3, that this y^{n*} is equal to the steady state GDP per capita, y_c^*, for the closed economy. Show further that steady state national wealth per capita, v^*, for the open economy is equal to the steady state capital intensity, k_c^*, for the closed economy.

2. Consider the transition equation for the open economy (v_{t+1} as a function of v_t) and show that under our assumptions its slope is:

$$\frac{1+\alpha n}{1+n}.$$

Then consider the transition equation for the closed economy that we found in Chapter 3 (k_{t+1} as a function of k_t) and show that *at steady state* (for $k_t = k_c^*$) its slope is $(1 + \alpha n)/(1 + n)$ as well. On the basis of your findings in Questions 1 and 2, illustrate (in principle) the transition curves by drawing both in the same diagram (so you have both v_t and k_t along the horizontal axis, etc.). Assume that v_t and k_t for the open and the closed economy, respectively, start at a common initial value, $v_0 = k_0$, below steady state. For which economy will convergence towards steady state be fastest, the closed or the open, do you think? Explain intuitively *why* the fastest one is the fastest.

We will now assume that (initially) $B = 1$, which is just a normalization, and for the other parameters (except δ which has already been set equal to zero) assume some plausible values (on an annual basis): $\alpha = 0.4$, $n = 0.01$, $s = 0.2$. This implies that $r_c^* = \alpha n/s = 0.02$, so we assume that the annual international real interest rate is 2 per cent.

3. Compute the steady state values, $y^{n*} = y_c^*$ and $v^* = k_c^*$, under these specifications. Assume that both economies, the open and the closed, start in their steady states and then, as from period one, say, the total factor productivity increases permanently up to $B' = 2$. Compute the new steady state values for national income per capita and for wealth per capita for both economies. Describe in principle how the permanent productivity shock considered affects the transition diagrams and the accumulation of wealth and capital, respectively, in the open and the closed economy.

4. Now simulate each of the transition equations from period zero onwards (for a number of periods of your own choice, but be sure to have quite a few), thereby creating a sequence (v_t) for the open economy and a sequence (k_t) for the closed. From these sequences compute the associated sequences, (y_t^n) and (y_t), respectively, for national income per capita. Illustrate the output of your simulations by plotting each of y_t^n and y_t against periods in one and the same diagram that also has the old and the new steady states indicated by horizontal lines. Explain in words the differences and similarities between the series (y_t^n) and (y_t).

Exercise 6. Does the empirical evidence indicate that capital mobility is not important?

In this chapter we found that for a (small) economy with free capital movements, long-run GDP (not national income) per capita, y^*, is independent of s and n; see (18). In Fig. 3.7 we found a relatively clear positive correlation between average investment shares and GDP per capita across countries, and in Fig. 3.8 we found a negative correlation between average population growth rates and GDP per capita. The question we address in this exercise is whether we should conclude from the empirical evidence presented in Figs 3.7 and 3.8 that real-world economies behave more as closed than as open economies and that capital movements therefore are not so important for observed economic performance.

First, note that the variable indicated along the horizontal axis in Fig. 3.7 was *investment* shares of GDP, not *savings* shares. In a closed economy these coincide, but in an open economy they do not. Show, using (18) and (21), that for a small open economy in steady state there is the following necessary link between GDP per capita, y^*, the investment rate, i^*, and the growth rate of the labour force, n:

$$\ln y^* = \frac{1}{1-\alpha} \ln B + \frac{\alpha}{1-\alpha}(\ln i^* - \ln n).$$

Compare this to the expression for $\ln y^*$ we found in Section 3.3, and discuss whether the empirical evidence reported in Figs 3.7 and 3.8 indicates that capital movements are not important for economic performance across countries.

Exercise 7. Long-run national income in the small open economy as depending on domestic and international savings propensities

A certain restatement of (27) can be of interest. As argued in this chapter, the world economy is a closed system, so it should behave according to the model of Chapter 3 in the aggregate. This means that the formulae in Section 3.3 should be valid for the steady state of the world economy. If we assume that technology is the same in the domestic country and in the world (α is the same, and $\delta = 0$ in both), and we denote the average savings rate in the world by $\bar{s}$, and the world population growth rate by $\bar{n}$, then the steady state value for the world real interest rate is:

$$\bar{r} = \frac{\alpha\bar{n}}{\bar{s}}.$$

The meaning of the economy considered being *small* is exactly that, although it contributes to world savings and population growth, its impacts on $\bar{s}$ and $\bar{n}$ are so small that in practice $\bar{r}$ is given.[9]

Show, using (27), that steady state national income per capita is:

$$y^{n*} = (1-\alpha)B^{\frac{1}{1-\alpha}}\left(\frac{\bar{s}}{\bar{n}}\right)^{\frac{\alpha}{1-\alpha}} \cdot \frac{1}{1-\alpha\dfrac{s/n}{\bar{s}/\bar{n}}}.$$

Show that in the particular case, $s/n = \bar{s}/\bar{n}$, national income per capita is the same in the open economy as it would be if the economy were closed. What if $s/n > \bar{s}/\bar{n}$? Explain.

Exercise 8. The growth perspectives for a relatively poor, emerging market economy opening its capital account

This exercise considers a small economy that is relatively poor by world standards due to a relatively low savings capacity (as measured by s/n).

Our interest is in what the relatively poor economy might achieve, if anything, from opening its capital account, in particular the speed by which the effects occur.

Assuming a period length of one year, the economy has the following structural characteristics: $B = 1$, $\alpha = 1/3$, $\delta = 0$, $s = 1/6$, $n = 0.03$. The international real interest rate is $\bar{r} = 0.03$.

---

9. Note that if n is larger than $\bar{n}$, then the domestic economy will grow faster than the world economy, and at some point our assumption that the domestic economy is too small to affect the world economy will no longer be valid. We assume that this happens too far into the future to be of practical relevance.

1. The economy considered has a savings capacity, s/n, of around five and a half. Consult Table A to see if this seems reasonably descriptive for a typical poor economy.

   First assume that the small economy does not allow capital movements between itself and the world economy.

2. Describe the long-run economic outcome according to the basic Solow model of the closed economy in terms of the key macroeconomic variables: capital and GDP (income) per capita, consumption and investment per capita, real interest rate and real wage rate.

   Now assume that the small economy up to and including a specific year zero is in steady state as a closed economy, but liberalizes capital movements completely from period one and onwards, and thus comes to work as a small open economy (first with no country risk).

3. Is the stability condition fulfilled for the small and now open economy?

4. Describe the long-run (steady state) economic outcome of the small open economy in terms of all the variables mentioned in Question 2 and, in addition, in terms of national wealth, national income, net foreign assets, and interest payments on net foreign assets, all in per capita terms. Based on a comparison between the long-run outcomes of the small economy under a closed capital account and an open capital account, respectively, comment on the long-run perspectives for the small economy of opening up.

5. In this question, focus completely on period one, the first period of an open capital account for the small economy considered. For this period, state the values of all the variables that were mentioned in Question 4. (Be careful here: when you compute v_1, you cannot just apply formula (22) of this chapter with $t+1$ corresponding to one, and t corresponding to zero, because this formula assumes that the economy was open in period t. You can, however, use the formula four lines above.)

6. By simulating the appropriate model, create a table that reports the evolution over time of the central macroeconomic variables asked about in Questions 4 and 5 and, in addition, net capital inflow per capita and the growth rates of GDP per capita and of national income per capita, over years 0, 1, 2,…up to 25. Illustrate in (at least) two figures with time in years along the horizontal axis. One should have wealth per capita along the vertical axis, and another should have GDP per capita, national income per capita, and real interest payments per capita, respectively, along the vertical axis. Describe the economy's process of convergence towards steady state and comment on what you think the analysis importantly says about the short- and intermediate-run 'growth perspectives for a relatively poor, emerging market economy of opening its capital account'.

   As discussed by the end of this chapter, it is an important empirical observation that sometimes capital to a surprisingly small extent moves into, and sometimes out of, poor economies when they liberalize capital movements.

7. Set up a model for the small, open economy that includes country risk, assuming that the country is a net debtor. Assume an appropriate value for the country risk parameter, and show by doing relevant computations and simulations that, as a consequence of country risk, capital may move into the small economy to a (much) smaller extent after a liberalization of capital movements than found above. Comment on your results. Could country risk even imply that capital moves out of the small economy upon liberalization? How large would the country risk parameter have to be, and what would the appropriate model look like? (Don't analyse it, just describe it. Analysis comes in the next exercise.)

Exercise 9. Country risk and a risk premium shock if the small open economy is a net creditor

We argued in the chapter that to take country risk into account for a net creditor one should assume that the country earns the international interest rate without a risk premium on its net foreign assets since these are placed abroad. On the other hand the 'hurdle' rate of return on domestic capital that will make investors consider wealth placed in the small open economy and in the international capital market equally good should include a risk premium. The appropriate model is therefore (7)–(14), with the $\bar{r}$ in (9) kept unchanged, and with the $\bar{r}$ in (13) replaced by $\bar{r} + \varepsilon$. We will consider the most standard case of $\varepsilon > 0$, and for simplicity assume $B = 1$. Otherwise notation is as in the chapter.

1. Write down the complete model (for your convenience) and show that in any period t, GDP per capita is:

$$y_t = w_t + (\bar{r} + \varepsilon)k_t,$$

while national income per capita is:

$$y_t^n = w_t + \varepsilon k_t + \bar{r}v_t.$$

2. Show that domestic capital per capita and the wage rate, respectively, adjust immediately to:

$$k^* = \left(\frac{\alpha}{\bar{r} + \varepsilon}\right)^{\frac{1}{1-\alpha}} \quad \text{and} \quad w^* = (1-\alpha)\left(\frac{\alpha}{\bar{r} + \varepsilon}\right)^{\frac{\alpha}{1-\alpha}}.$$

3. Show that the transition equation for national wealth per capita is:

$$v_{t+1} = \frac{1 + s\bar{r}}{1 + n}v_t + \frac{s(w^* + \varepsilon k^*)}{1 + n}.$$

4. Using the above expressions for k^* and w^*, show that:

$$w^* + \varepsilon k^* = \left[1 + \frac{\varepsilon}{\bar{r} + \varepsilon}\frac{\alpha}{1-\alpha}\right](1-\alpha)\left(\frac{\alpha}{\bar{r} + \varepsilon}\right)^{\frac{\alpha}{1-\alpha}}.$$

5. Show that an increase in ε implies a decrease in $w^* + \varepsilon k^*$, whenever $\varepsilon > 0$ initially. How is the transition equation affected by an increase in ε?

6. Show that the steady state values for GDP per capita, the wage rate, wealth per capita and national income per capita all decrease in response to the increase in ε. (Hint: You don't have to solve the model for y^{n*}. From the shift of the transition curve you can infer how steady state wealth per capita, v^*, is affected. You can then use $y_t^n = w_t + \varepsilon k_t + \bar{r}v_t$, etc., to infer how steady state national income per capita, y^{n*}, is affected.) Explain your results intuitively.

Exercise 10. Free capital movements: pros and cons

On the background of what you have learned in this chapter, discuss arguments for and against liberalizing capital flows. Is your overall conclusion based on the theory (and empirics) of this chapter in favour of or against such liberalization?

PART  2 | Exogenous Growth

Technological progress and growth

The general Solow model

In one respect the basic Solow model presented in Chapter 3 did not perform well empirically: its long-run balanced growth path displayed zero growth in GDP per capita. This is at odds with the observed long-run growth in living standards in Western economies.

We want to develop a growth model whose long-term prediction is a balanced growth path with strictly positive growth in GDP per person. Obviously we can only trust the answers to our big questions, 'what creates prosperity in the long run?' and 'what creates transitory and long-run growth?', if these answers are grounded in a (growth) model that accords with the most basic empirical facts.

This chapter presents a growth model with the properties we are looking for: the steady state of the model exhibits balanced growth with positive growth in output per worker. We obtain this by a slight generalization of the basic Solow model. The resulting model is close to the one actually suggested by Robert M. Solow in his famous 1956 article referred to in Chapter 3.[1]

The essential new feature of the model is that total factor productivity is no longer assumed to be a constant, B. Instead it will be given as an exogenous sequence, (B_t), which may be steadily growing over time. In that case the model's steady state will display balanced growth with steady positive growth in GDP per worker.

Hence, according to the general Solow model (as we will call it) *the root of steady positive long-run growth in GDP per person is a steady* **exogenous** *technological progress.* This explanation of growth may not seem deep. However, it is not trivial that the consequence of steadily arriving technological progress should be a *balanced* growth path, and it *is* reassuring for the application of the model to issues of economic policy that its steady state mirrors a robust long-run growth fact. Of course, *explaining* the technological progress that creates growth in GDP per worker is a matter of great interest and it is the subject of Part 3 of this text.

Having obtained in this chapter a model that fits the basic stylized growth facts better, we are going to take the model through some more specific empirical tests. The tests will focus on the steady state prediction of the model as well as its outside steady state prediction concerning transitory growth or convergence.[2] Our conclusion will be that the general Solow

---

1. For your convenience, we give the reference to this pathbreaking article once again: Robert M. Solow, 'A Contribution to the Theory of Economic Growth', *Quarterly Journal of Economics*, **70**, 1956, pp. 65–94.

2. We could have done some of these more specific tests already in connection with the basic Solow model of Chapter 3, and, in fact, Exercise 9 of Chapter 3 asked you to do one of them yourself, but we think it is better to undertake them now that the model is in accordance with the basic fact of steady and positive long-run growth.

model does quite well empirically, both with respect to its steady state and its transitory growth predictions, although there will be some aspects still to be improved upon. The general Solow model is indeed a very important growth model.

5.1 The general Solow model

With respect to the qualitative features of the underlying 'micro world', the general Solow model is identical to the basic Solow model. It has the same commodities and markets, and the markets are again assumed to be perfectly competitive. There are also the same kinds of economic agents, and their behaviour is essentially the same. In particular, a representative profit-maximizing firm has to decide on the inputs of capital and labour services, K_t^d and L_t^d, in each period t, given the real rental rate of capital, r_t, and the real wage rate, w_t. The only difference is that the production function, which tells how much output can be produced from K_t^d and L_t^d, may now change over time so that, for instance, more and more output can be obtained from the same amounts of inputs.

The production function with technological progress

The total factor productivity will now be allowed to depend on time. The notation for it will therefore be B_t, where $B_t > 0$ in all time periods t. The full time sequence, (B_t), of total factor productivity is exogenous. Maintaining a Cobb–Douglas form, the production function in period t is:

$$Y_t = B_t K_t^\alpha L_t^{1-\alpha}, \qquad 0 < \alpha < 1. \tag{1}$$

This time we insert from the beginning the feature that the inputs demanded and actually used, K_t^d and L_t^d, must equal the (inelastic) supplies, K_t and L_t, because the factor markets clear. Since one particular assumption on (B_t) could be that B_t is constant, the general Solow model, or just the Solow model, is a *generalization* of the basic Solow model.

We may alternatively write the production function as:

$$Y_t = K_t^\alpha (A_t L_t)^{1-\alpha}, \tag{2}$$

where $A_t \equiv B_t^{1/(1-\alpha)}$. With the Cobb–Douglas form of the production function it makes no difference whether we describe technological change by a certain time sequence, (B_t), of the total factor productivity, or by an appropriately defined sequence, (A_t), of the labour productivity variable (not to be confused with the average labour productivity, Y_t/L_t).

With more general production functions it may make *some* difference. Generally, technological progress that appears as an increasing variable, A_t, in a production function, $F(K_t, A_t L_t)$, is called labour-augmenting or Harrod-neutral. If it appears as an increasing variable, D_t, in $F(D_t K_t, L_t)$, it is called capital-augmenting or Solow-neutral, while, when it appears as an increasing variable, B_t, in $B_t F(K_t, L_t)$, it is called Hicks-neutral.

Given the Cobb–Douglas specification one can simply choose the formulation of technological progress that is most convenient. For our present purposes this turns out to be the form with labour-augmenting technological change as in (2).

A full description of the production possibilities includes a specification of the exogenous sequence, (A_t). We will simply assume that the labour productivity variable, A_t, is changing at a constant rate:

$$A_{t+1} = (1 + g)A_t, \qquad g > -1. \tag{3}$$

Here g is the exact (not the approximate) growth rate of A_t. It follows that if the technological level in some initial period zero is A_0, then in period t it is $A_t = (1 + g)^t A_0$. For the approximate growth rate, $g_t^A \equiv \ln A_t - \ln A_{t-1}$, one has from (3), $g_t^A = \ln(1 + g) \approx g$ (where we use the approximation, $\ln v \approx v - 1$, as in Chapter 2).

We thus associate technology with the level of A_t and technological progress with an increase in A_t, but recall from Chapter 3 that A_t really has a residual interpretation as the influence of 'all other factors'. A positive value of g corresponds to a steadily arriving technological progress that comes exogenously to the economy without this requiring the use of economic resources. The production function just becomes ever more efficient period by period. It is sometimes said that technological progress comes as manna from heaven. The idea of the 'endogenous growth' models presented in Part 3 is exactly to change the description of technological progress, so that it will be the outcome of a use of economic resources.

We will again use the definitions of output per worker (average labour productivity) $y_t \equiv Y_t/L_t$, and capital per worker (the capital intensity) $k_t \equiv K_t/L_t$. Dividing by L_t on both sides of (2) gives the 'per capita production function':

$$y_t = k_t^\alpha A_t^{1-\alpha}, \tag{4}$$

and then, taking logs and time differences,

$$\ln y_t - \ln y_{t-1} = \alpha(\ln k_t - \ln k_{t-1}) + (1 - \alpha)(\ln A_t - \ln A_{t-1}), \tag{5}$$

or in the usual notation for approximate growth rates:

$$g_t^y = \alpha g_t^k + (1-\alpha)g_t^A. \tag{6}$$

These expressions reveal that an increase in output per worker can be obtained in two ways, by more capital per worker or by better technology. In fact, the (approximate) growth rate in output per worker is the weighted average of the rates of growth in capital per worker and in technology, the weights being α and $(1 - \alpha)$, respectively. There are now two potential sources of economic growth: capital accumulation and technological progress.

The complete model

Since the general Solow model is in all respects, other than the production function, identical to the basic Solow model, we can write down the full model consisting of seven equations without further delay:

THE COMPLETE GENERAL SOLOW MODEL !

$$Y_t = K_t^\alpha (A_t L_t)^{1-\alpha}, \tag{7}$$

$$r_t = \alpha \left(\frac{K_t}{A_t L_t}\right)^{\alpha-1}, \tag{8}$$

$$w_t = (1-\alpha)\left(\frac{K_t}{A_t L_t}\right)^\alpha A_t, \tag{9}$$

$$S_t = sY_t, \tag{10}$$

$$K_{t+1} - K_t = S_t - \delta K_t, \qquad K_0 \text{ given} \tag{11}$$

$$L_{t+1} = (1 + n)L_t, \qquad L_0 \text{ given} \tag{12}$$

$$A_{t+1} = (1 + g)A_t, \qquad A_0 \text{ given} \tag{13}$$

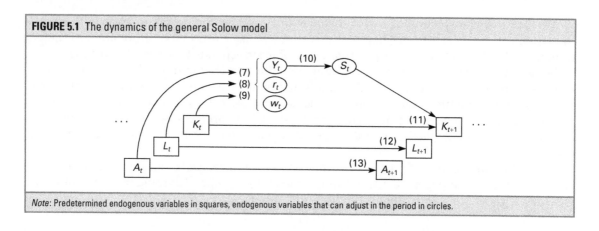

FIGURE 5.1 The dynamics of the general Solow model

Note: Predetermined endogenous variables in squares, endogenous variables that can adjust in the period in circles.

The first equation is a repetition of the production function with the input supplies inserted. The next two equations give the rental rates from the marginal products of the inputs. As in the basic Solow model this follows from competitive clearing of the input markets, but now the expressions for the marginal products are slightly different, since they are derived from the new production function. Note that we still have $r_t K_t / Y_t = \alpha$ and $w_t L_t / Y_t = 1 - \alpha$, so the functional income distribution is still given by α, and there are no pure profits. Equations (10), (11) and (12) are exactly as before, so there is no change in the assumed behaviour concerning savings or 'fertility'. Of course, the fundamental capital accumulation equation, (11), has to be respected as before. The last equation is just the addition of the assumption on technological change.

For given initial values, K_0, L_0, A_0, of the state variables, the model (7)–(13) determines the full dynamic evolution of the economic variables as illustrated in Fig. 5.1.

We have chosen to give a discrete time formulation of the general Solow model, but in an exercise you will be confronted with the counterpart model in continuous time.

5.2 Analysing the general Solow model

Comparing the general Solow model in the box above to the basic Solow model of Chapter 3, you will see that the two models are mathematically equivalent: in the general Solow model the product $A_t L_t$ has taken the place of L_t in the basic Solow model, and the exogenous growth factor of $A_t L_t$ is $(1 + n)(1 + g)$, rather than just $1 + n$. The analysis of the model should therefore more or less 'translate', letting $A_t L_t$ take the place of L_t from Chapter 3's analysis.

The law of motion

We analysed the basic Solow model in terms of the variables $k_t \equiv K_t / L_t$ and $y_t \equiv Y_t / L_t$, which turned out to converge to specific and constant steady state levels. A qualified guess is thus that the general Solow model can be analysed in terms of the variables:

$$\tilde{k}_t \equiv \frac{K_t}{A_t L_t} = \frac{k_t}{A_t} \quad \text{and} \quad \tilde{y}_t \equiv \frac{Y_t}{A_t L_t} = \frac{y_t}{A_t}, \tag{14}$$

that is, the technology-adjusted capital intensity (capital per *effective* worker) and the technology-adjusted average labour productivity (output per *effective* worker), respectively, and that these will converge to constant steady state values.

Note that this property would indeed be highly desirable, since if both k_t / A_t and y_t / A_t are constant in steady state, then both k_t and y_t must be increasing at the same rate as A_t, the rate g. We then get a steady state with a constant growth rate of income per worker *and* a constant capital–output ratio, k_t / y_t, in accordance with balanced growth.

Dividing on both sides of the production function (7) by $A_t L_t$ gives:

$$\tilde{y}_t = \tilde{k}_t^\alpha. \tag{15}$$

Now, start again from the capital accumulation equation with the savings behaviour inserted: $K_{t+1} = sY_t + (1 - \delta)K_t$. Divide on both sides by $A_{t+1}L_{t+1}$. On the left-hand side you will now have $\tilde{k}_{t+1}$. On the right-hand side use $A_{t+1}L_{t+1} = (1 + n)(1 + g)A_t L_t$ to get:

$$\tilde{k}_{t+1} = \frac{1}{(1+n)(1+g)}\left(s\frac{Y_t}{A_t L_t} + (1-\delta)\frac{K_t}{A_t L_t}\right) = \frac{1}{(1+n)(1+g)}(s\tilde{y}_t + (1-\delta)\tilde{k}_t).$$

Finally insert that $\tilde{y}_t = \tilde{k}_t^\alpha$ to find:

$$\tilde{k}_{t+1} = \frac{1}{(1+n)(1+g)}(s\tilde{k}_t^\alpha + (1-\delta)\tilde{k}_t). \tag{16}$$

This is the law of motion, or the *transition equation*, in the state variable $\tilde{k}_t$.

From given initial values of capital, labour and technology, K_0, L_0 and A_0, an initial value for capital per effective worker, $\tilde{k}_0 = K_0/(A_0 L_0)$, will be given. The first-order difference equation (16) will then determine $\tilde{k}_1$ and then the full sequence, $(\tilde{k}_t)$. An associated sequence, $(\tilde{y}_t)$, follows from $\tilde{y}_t = \tilde{k}_t^\alpha$. From these, the sequences for the economic variables in which we are interested follow. For instance, from (8) and (9):

$$r_t = \alpha \tilde{k}_t^{\alpha-1}, \tag{17}$$

$$w_t = (1 - \alpha)A_t \tilde{k}_t^\alpha. \tag{18}$$

Further, since income per worker is $y_t = \tilde{y}_t A_t$, and $A_t = (1 + g)^t A_0$ we have:

$$y_t = \tilde{k}_t^\alpha (1 + g)^t A_0,$$

and then consumption per worker follows as $c_t = (1 - s)y_t$. Given initial values K_0, L_0, A_0, the transition equation (16) and other model elements determine the full dynamic evolution of the economy.

Subtracting $\tilde{k}_t$ on both sides of (16) gives the *Solow equation*:

$$\tilde{k}_{t+1} - \tilde{k}_t = \frac{1}{(1+n)(1+g)}(s\tilde{k}_t^\alpha - (n+g+\delta+ng)\tilde{k}_t). \tag{19}$$

The transition equation (16) and the Solow equation (19) look much like their counterparts for the basic Solow model of Chapter 3, only now they incorporate technological change appropriately. Thus they involve $\tilde{k}_t$ rather than k_t, and the expressions involve the parameter g. However, qualitatively and with respect to interpretation the laws of motion are similar to those in the basic Solow model.

Convergence to steady state

The *transition diagram* associated with (16) and the *Solow diagram* associated with (19) also look much like their counterparts for the basic Solow model, as illustrated in Fig. 5.2. In particular, the slope of the transition curve shown in the upper part of the figure decreases monotonically from infinity to $(1 - \delta)/[(1 + n)(1 + g)]$, as $\tilde{k}_t$ increases from zero to infinity (show this). The limit slope as $\tilde{k}_t$ approaches infinity is less than one if $n + g + \delta + ng > 0$, which is highly plausible. Hence, under this realistic stability condition the transition curve

FIGURE 5.2 The transition diagram (top), and the Solow diagram (bottom)

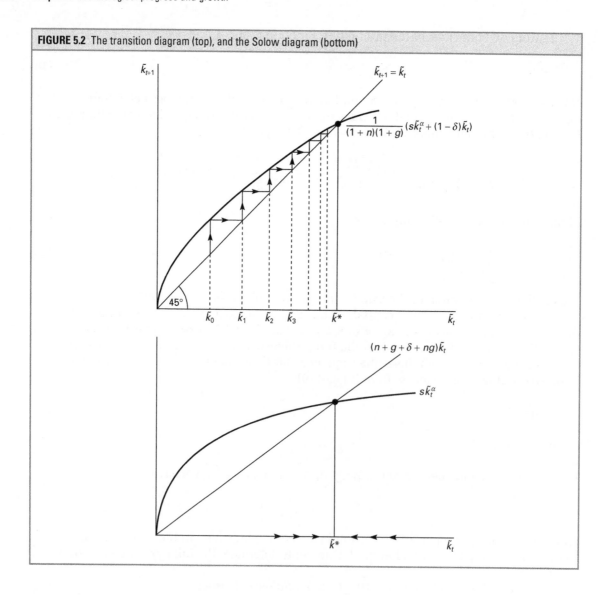

has the properties illustrated in the upper part of Fig. 5.2, and from these properties convergence to a steady state, given by the unique positive intersection between the transition curve and the 45° line, follows simply by 'staircase iteration' in the figure:

CONVERGENCE TO STEADY STATE ❗

Given the plausible stability condition, $n + g + \delta + ng > 0$, the technology-adjusted capital intensity, $\tilde{k}_t \equiv k_t/A_t$, will converge to a specific steady state value, $\tilde{k}^*$, and income per effective worker, $\tilde{y}_t \equiv y_t/A_t$, will converge to its steady state value, $\tilde{y}^* = (\tilde{k}^*)^\alpha$. Hence in the long run both capital per worker, k_t, and income per worker, y_t, converge on growing at rate g, implying that the capital–output ratio, $k_t/y_t = K_t/Y_t$, converges to a constant value in accordance with balanced growth.

The corresponding adjustments in the Solow diagram have been indicated by arrows in the lower part of Fig. 5.2. As long as the curve $s\tilde{k}_t^\alpha$ lies above the ray $(n + g + \delta + ng)\tilde{k}_t$, we must have $\tilde{k}_{t+1} > \tilde{k}_t$, so $\tilde{k}_t$ must be increasing, and vice versa.

FIGURE 5.3 An increase in the savings rate in the Solow diagram

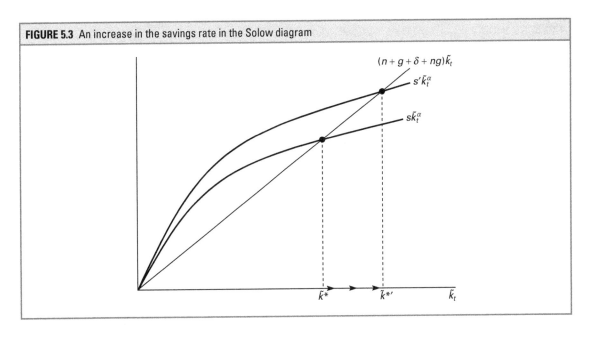

FIGURE 5.4 An increase in the savings rate in the modified Solow diagram

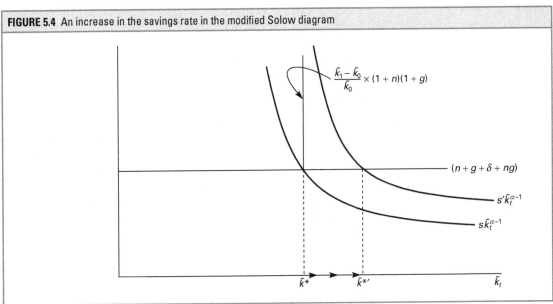

Comparative analysis in the Solow diagrams

Figure 5.3 illustrates the effects of an increase in the savings rate from s to s' in the Solow diagram. The curve $s\tilde{k}_t^{\alpha}$ shifts upwards to $s'\tilde{k}_t^{\alpha}$, implying a new and higher steady state level, $\tilde{k}^{*'}$, of capital per effective worker.

In Fig. 5.4 we illustrate the shift in s in the *modified Solow diagram* associated with the *modified Solow equation*, (20), which is derived from (19) by dividing by $\tilde{k}_t$ on both sides:

$$\frac{\tilde{k}_{t+1} - \tilde{k}_t}{\tilde{k}_t} = \frac{1}{(1+n)(1+g)} \left(s\tilde{k}_t^{\alpha-1} - (n+g+\delta+ng) \right) \tag{20}$$

Assume that the economy is initially in the old steady state where $\tilde{k}_t$ and $\tilde{y}_t$ are constant and equal to $\tilde{k}^*$ and $\tilde{y}^*$, respectively. In this situation capital per worker, k_t, and output per

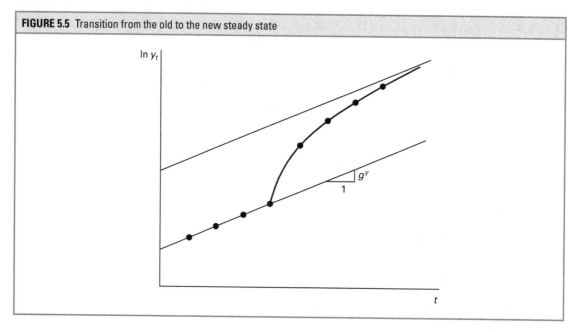

FIGURE 5.5 Transition from the old to the new steady state

worker, y_t, both change over time at the rate g which we assume to be positive. The growth path corresponding to the old steady state is illustrated by the lower upward-sloping line in Fig. 5.5.

From the first period after the savings rate has increased, $\tilde{k}_t$ begins to increase as illustrated in the Solow diagram as well as in the modified Solow diagram. From the modified Solow diagram, Fig. 5.4, one can see that the growth rate, $(\tilde{k}_{t+1} - \tilde{k}_t)/\tilde{k}_t$ of $\tilde{k}_t$ initially jumps up to a positive level and then decreases monotonically back towards zero. When $\tilde{k}_t = k_t/A_t$ increases, the numerator, k_t, must be increasing by a rate larger than the rate by which the denominator, A_t, increases, that is, by a rate larger than g. The approximate growth rate of k_t is $g_t^k \equiv \ln k_t - \ln k_{t-1} = (\ln \tilde{k}_t - \ln \tilde{k}_{t-1}) + (\ln A_t - \ln A_{t-1}) \equiv g_t^{\tilde{k}} + g_t^A$, so any relative increase in $\tilde{k}_t$ is equal to a relative increase in k_t *in excess of* the relative increase in A_t. As long as k_t increases faster than A_t, so does y_t, since $g_t^y = \alpha g_t^k + (1-\alpha)g_t^A$.

Along the adjustment to the new steady state, $\tilde{k}^{*\prime}$ and $\tilde{y}^{*\prime}$, represented by the upper straight line in Fig. 5.5, the capital intensity must be increasing all the time at a rate which is larger than g, but gradually falls back towards g. The same must then be true for y_t. The transition from the old to the new steady state is illustrated by the curve going from the lower to the upper straight line in Fig. 5.5. Figure 5.6 shows the adjustment of the growth rate of y_t during the transition from the old to the new steady state.

In the basic Solow model an increase in the savings rate implied that in the long run output per worker, y_t, changed from one constant level to a new and higher constant level. In the Solow model with technological progress the *growth path* of y_t shifts from one level to a new and higher level, with the long-run growth rate being the same before and after, namely g, as illustrated in Fig. 5.5. This happens through a transition where the growth rate of y_t first jumps up above g, and then falls monotonically back towards g, as shown in Fig. 5.6. One particular case is when $g = 0$. Then the growth paths of Fig. 5.5 will be horizontal, and the growth jump in Fig. 5.6 will occur around a long-run growth rate of zero. We are then back in the basic Solow model.

5.3 Steady state in the general Solow model

As we have seen, the steady state of the Solow model accords with the concept of balanced growth in *some* respects: the growth rates of capital per worker and of output per worker are constant and equal to each other. Furthermore, if $g > 0$, both growth rates are

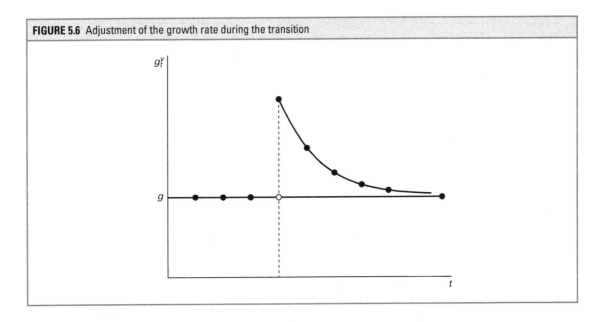

FIGURE 5.6 Adjustment of the growth rate during the transition

positive. We are going to show that the steady state is in accordance with balanced growth in *all* respects.

The key endogenous variables in steady state

The technology-adjusted capital intensity in steady state, $\tilde{k}^*$, is found by setting $\tilde{k}_{t+1} = \tilde{k}_t = \tilde{k}$ in (16) or (19) and solving for $\tilde{k}$. This gives:

$$\tilde{k}^* = \left(\frac{s}{n+g+\delta+ng}\right)^{\frac{1}{1-\alpha}}. \tag{21}$$

From $\tilde{y}_t = \tilde{k}_t^\alpha$ we then obtain the corresponding steady state value of $\tilde{y}_t$:

$$\tilde{y}^* = \left(\frac{s}{n+g+\delta+ng}\right)^{\frac{\alpha}{1-\alpha}}. \tag{22}$$

It is not really the *technology-adjusted* variables, $\tilde{k}_t$ and $\tilde{y}_t$, we are interested in. From the definitions, $\tilde{k}_t \equiv k_t/A_t$ and $\tilde{y}_t \equiv y_t/A_t$, it follows that when the economy has reached its steady state, capital per worker and output per worker in period t will be $k_t^* = A_t\tilde{k}^*$ and $y_t^* = A_t\tilde{y}^*$, respectively, or:

$$k_t^* = A_t\left(\frac{s}{n+g+\delta+ng}\right)^{\frac{1}{1-\alpha}}, \tag{23}$$

$$y_t^* = A_t\left(\frac{s}{n+g+\delta+ng}\right)^{\frac{\alpha}{1-\alpha}}. \tag{24}$$

Since consumption per worker in any period is $c_t = (1-s)y_t$, the steady state consumption path is:

$$c_t^* = A_t(1-s)\left(\frac{s}{n+g+\delta+ng}\right)^{\frac{\alpha}{1-\alpha}}. \tag{25}$$

The steady state expressions for the three variables above are all of the form A_t times a constant, and hence they all grow at the same rate g as A_t does. Note that substituting $A_0(1+g)^t$ for A_t will trace the three steady state growth paths above back to parameters and initial values. The steady state evolutions of the rental rates follow from inserting $\tilde{k}^*$ for $\tilde{k}_t$ in (17) and (18), respectively:

$$r^* = \alpha\left(\frac{s}{n+g+\delta+ng}\right)^{-1}, \tag{26}$$

$$w_t^* = A_t(1-\alpha)\left(\frac{s}{n+g+\delta+ng}\right)^{\frac{\alpha}{1-\alpha}}. \tag{27}$$

In steady state the rate of return on capital is a constant, r^*, so the real interest rate, $r^* - \delta$, is constant as well. The real wage rate, w_t^*, increases with A_t at rate g.

In fact all the requirements for balanced growth, as defined in Section 2.4, are fulfilled in the steady state: GDP per worker, capital per worker, consumption per worker, and the real wage rate all grow by one and the same constant rate, g. The labour force grows at the constant rate, n, and therefore (from $Y_t = y_t L_t$, $C_t = c_t L_t$, $I_t = S_t = sy_t L_t$, $K_t = k_t L_t$), GDP, consumption, investment and capital all grow at one and the same constant rate, approximately $g + n$. Finally, as we have shown, the rate of return on capital and the real interest rate are constant.

STEADY STATE

The Solow model passes the fundamental empirical test that its steady state prediction accords with balanced growth, and at the same time allows a strictly positive growth rate of GDP per worker ($g > 0$). The elasticity of long-run income per capita with respect to the investment rate s is $\alpha/(1-\alpha)$, the exponent in (24), and the elasticity with respect to $n + g + \delta$ is $-\alpha/(1-\alpha)$. Both elasticities should be around one half in absolute value given a labour's share of around $\frac{2}{3}$.

Structural policy for steady state

The above expressions and conclusions for output per worker and consumption per worker in steady state are reminiscent of what was found in the basic Solow model of Chapter 3. The similarity between the models implies that some of their policy implications and the relevant empirical tests of their predictive power are also quite similar.

With respect to structural policy, the general Solow model points to one type that could not be considered in the basic Solow model: a policy to increase the growth rate of technology. It is not easy to see from the present model what kind of policy could achieve this, and we will (again) defer further discussion of policies to affect technology to later chapters that consider models with endogenous technical innovation.

Otherwise, policies suggested by the general Solow model to increase income per person, now intended to elevate the whole growth path of income per person, are mainly policies that can increase the savings rate or decrease the population growth rate and possibly the depreciation rate. Note also from (25) that the value of the savings rate that maximizes consumption per person (by taking the consumption growth path to the highest possible level) is still $s^{**} = \alpha$. The golden rule savings rate is unchanged from the basic Solow model.

Empirics for steady state

Taking A_t and g as given, the implication of (24) is that higher s and lower n will generate higher steady state output per worker. In Chapter 3 we tested this prediction in Fig. 3.7, plotting GDP per worker against gross investment rates across countries, and in Fig. 3.8, plotting GDP per worker against population growth rates. Thus we tested the influences of

s and n on GDP per worker separately and found the model's prediction of the *directions* of these influences confirmed by the data. However, Eq. (24) implies a more precise theory of the influences of s and n on y_t than just their directions (the same was true for the counterpart equation for the basic Solow model). Taking logs on both sides of (24) gives:

$$\ln y_t^* = \ln A_t + \frac{\alpha}{1-\alpha}[\ln s - \ln(n + g + \delta + ng)]. \tag{28}$$

As far as empirics are concerned, this is the first of two important relationships resulting from the Solow model. This one concerns steady state, the other one (to be derived below) will concern convergence to steady state. Given the technological level, A_t, the steady state prediction of the model is that $\ln y_t^*$ should depend on $[\ln s - \ln(n + g + \delta + ng)]$, and the relationship should be a linear one with a positive slope equal to $\alpha/(1 - \alpha)$. The slope should therefore be around $\frac{1}{2}$, since the capital share, α, is around $\frac{1}{3}$.

In Fig. 5.7 we have put this prediction to a test by considering the representative sample of 65 countries studied and described in association with Figs 2.5 and 2.6. We assume, perhaps heroically, that the countries considered were all in steady state in 2003 and had the same technological level, A_{03}, in that year. The figure plots, across countries i, the log of GDP per worker in 2003, $\ln y_{03}^i$, against $\ln s^i - \ln(n^i + 0.075)$, where s^i is the average gross investment rate in country i over the period 1960 to 2003, and n^i is the average labour force growth rate over the same period. We have thus set $g + \delta + ng$ at 7.5 per cent for all countries. Since ng is the product of two small growth rates, it is very small. Thus, without sacrificing much precision, we could have excluded ng in the above formulae. Hence we are assuming that $g + \delta \approx 0.075$, an estimate that is often used. (Constructing Fig. 5.7 we are more or less doing what you were asked to do yourself in Exercise 9 of Chapter 3.)

The figure is in fairly nice accordance with a positive and linear relationship. The straight line that has been drawn is a line of best fit resulting from an OLS estimation of the regression equation:

$$\ln y_{03}^i = \gamma_0 + \gamma[\ln s^i - \ln(n^i + 0.075)] + \xi^i, \tag{29}$$

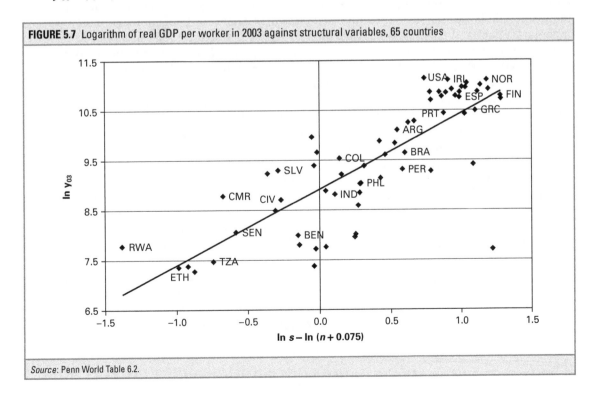

FIGURE 5.7 Logarithm of real GDP per worker in 2003 against structural variables, 65 countries

Source: Penn World Table 6.2.

where ξ^i is a random error term representing the influence of omitted variables (if necessary, consult the appendix on regression analysis regarding distributional assumptions on ξ^i etc.). The details of the estimation are:

$$\ln y_{03}^i = 8.92 + \underset{(se=0.14, t=10.5)}{1.52} [\ln s^i - \ln(n^i + 0.75)], \qquad R^2 = 0.64,$$

The estimate of γ, the slope of the line, is 1.52. This slope is considerably larger than the 0.5 it should be according to our theory. Note that the standard error of the estimate of γ is 0.14. The 95 per cent confidence interval for the estimate goes approximately from two standard deviations below to two standard deviations above the estimate of γ, giving a confidence interval of [1.24; 1.80]. This is not close to including the value 0.5, so the estimated slope is *significantly* larger than 0.5. In fact, for the fraction $\alpha/(1-\alpha)$ to equal 1.52, α would have to be 0.6. An α of around 0.6 is way above the capital share (around $\frac{1}{3}$) that α should correspond to.[3]

STEADY STATE AND THE CROSS-COUNTRY EMPIRICAL EVIDENCE   !

The steady state of the Solow model matches cross-country data quite well (even under an assumption of a common technological level): there is a clear positive correlation between $\ln y^i$ and $\ln s^i - \ln(n^i + 0.75)$ as predicted, and the linear form of the relationship is in nice accordance with the data. However, the model considerably underestimates the strength of the influences of the key parameters on GDP per person compared to the correlation found in the data.

The nice positive correlation in Fig. 5.7 is reassuring for our model, but it does not *prove* that the model's prediction of a positive long-run influence of the investment rate on income per capita is correct. In empirical analysis one must be careful not to confuse correlation with causation and about what is exogenous and what is endogenous. For instance, the picture would be consistent with a *reversed causality* where the exogenous variable was income per capita, the endogenous variable was the investment rate net of labour force growth, and income per capita had a positive influence on the investment rate net of labour force growth, perhaps through reducing population growth. It could also be *spurious correlation*, where there would be no causal relationship between the two in any direction, both would be endogenous, and a third exogenous factor, the 'entrepreneurial spirit' of a society, say, influenced both. Assume that entrepreneurial spirit is exogenous and affects both the investment rate and income per capita positively. Then more 'entrepreneurial' societies would tend to have higher investment rates *and* higher incomes per capita, so a positive correlation between the two would be observed without any causation between them. It may be, in fact, that there is indeed a positive influence of the investment rate net of labour force growth on income per worker *and* a positive influence of income per capita on the investment rate net of labour force growth *and* third factors influencing both systematically. In that case a picture like Fig. 5.7 will involve many different forces and viewed as a picture expressing the influence of the investment rate net of labour force growth on income per capita it will be highly distorted.

For now, just pick up that there is always a danger of misinterpreting correlation as causality. The positive correlation between the number of policemen and crime rates observed in many countries does not necessarily mean that more policemen imply more crime. It could be a simple reflection that more crime calls for more police.

---

3. The 95 per cent confidence interval for the implied α is [0.55; 0.64]. Show this.

5.4 Economic growth and convergence in the general Solow model[4]

It is reassuring that the Solow model can create balanced growth with a positive growth rate in steady state, but the model has transitory growth as well. As we have seen above, while the economy converges towards a steady state from below, the growth in GDP per worker will exceed the steady state growth rate, g, in such a way that the growth in excess of g decreases and goes to zero in the long run. The monotonically decreasing transitory growth means that the general Solow model accords with the idea of *conditional convergence* explained in Chapter 2. We will now examine the convergence process in detail.

Convergence according to the Solow model

Consider two countries that have the same structural characteristics, α, s, n, δ, A_0, g. They will then have identical modified Solow diagrams (see Fig. 5.4 for such a diagram). It follows that the country which is initially furthest below steady state will have the highest growth rate in $\tilde{k}_t$. As we showed above, this will imply that it has the highest growth rate in y_t as well. Through the process where each country approaches its own steady state, and does so faster the further away it is from steady state, the two countries will converge towards having the same level of GDP per worker.

Hence the Solow model supports conditional convergence. An implication is that if one controls appropriately for the structural differences between countries, there should be a negative relationship between GDP per worker in an initial year and the growth rate in subsequent years. In Chapter 2 we began to test the idea of convergence empirically by setting up growth in GDP per worker against the initial level of GDP per worker across countries, but there were things we could not do. When we wanted to control for structural differences between countries, we had to *postulate* an equation stating how the structural characteristics should enter (Eq. (4) of Chapter 2). Now that we have a real growth model we can explain how Eq. (4) is rooted in theory.

Furthermore, just as important as convergence itself is the *rate of convergence*, that is, the speed by which a country converges towards its long-run growth path. For a poor country that attempts to improve its structural characteristics (e.g., the savings rate) to approach a new and higher growth path, it is a matter of great concern whether it takes 10 or 50 years to go halfway to the new growth path, since this may be decisive for how fast poverty can be fought. In Chapter 2 we could not estimate rates of convergence, but now that we have a real growth model we can.

From the Solow model we will derive a 'convergence equation'. This will state how a country's average growth rate in GDP per worker over a period should depend on its structural characteristics and on its initial level of GDP per worker, that is, the Solow model's convergence equation will rationalize (4) of Chapter 2. Furthermore, the convergence equation will have a coefficient on the initial GDP per worker that is linked one-to-one to the rate of convergence, so an estimate of this coefficient will provide us with an estimate of the rate of convergence. Here is how to proceed.

Start from the transition equation (16). Write it in the generic form, $\tilde{k}_{t+1} = G(\tilde{k}_t)$, where the function $G(\tilde{k}_t)$ is given as the expression on the right-hand side of (16). The steady state value, $\tilde{k}^*$, stated in (23) fulfils $\tilde{k}^* = G(\tilde{k}^*)$. We now *linearize the transition equation around the steady state*. For any differentiable function $f(x)$, and for any given $\bar{x}$, we have $f(z) - f(\bar{x}) \approx f'(\bar{x})(z - \bar{x})$, as long as z is not too far from $\bar{x}$. This is really just using the definition of the

---

4. Some readers may find this section more difficult than the material presented up to now. It is possible to skip this section, and a corresponding one in Chapter 6, and still read the remainder of the book. It would be a pity, though, since these sections are concerned with convergence to steady state, which is just as important an element of our theory as steady state itself. The only additional mathematical element used in this section is how to solve a first-order linear difference equation. For those who do not yet know the technique, we will give a cookbook recipe for the solution.

derivative, $f'(\bar{x})$. If $\bar{x}$ is such that $\bar{x} = f(\bar{x})$, then we get $f(z) - \bar{x} \approx f'(\bar{x})(z - \bar{x})$. Using these properties for the dynamic equation, $G(\tilde{k}_t)$, measuring at the steady state value, $\tilde{k}^*$, we obtain:

$$\tilde{k}_{t+1} - \tilde{k}^* = G'(\tilde{k}^*)(\tilde{k}_t - \tilde{k}^*). \tag{30}$$

This is a new dynamic equation, a first-order difference equation in $\tilde{k}_t$ (or in the *absolute* discrepancy between $\tilde{k}_t$ and its steady state value). As long as we are not too far from steady state, the new dynamic equation approximately represents (16). Importantly, the new difference equation is linear, which means that we can solve it. Before doing so we will take it through some rewriting, but the linear structure, and hence the solvability, will be preserved.

The linearized dynamic equation includes $G'(\tilde{k}^*)$. We can derive an expression for $G'(\tilde{k}^*)$ in terms of model parameters by differentiating the right-hand side of (16) with respect to $\tilde{k}_t$, and then evaluating at $\tilde{k}_t = \tilde{k}^*$, where $\tilde{k}^*$ is given in (21):

$$G'(\tilde{k}_t) = \frac{1}{(1+n)(1+g)}[s\alpha(\tilde{k}_t)^{\alpha-1} + (1+\delta)] \Rightarrow$$

$$G'(\tilde{k}^*) = \frac{1}{(1+n)(1+g)}[\alpha(n+g+\delta+ng) + (1+\delta)]. \tag{31}$$

In the following we will still use the term $G'(\tilde{k}^*)$ for short, but $G'(\tilde{k}^*)$ has now been expressed in terms of model parameters, which can be used whenever wanted. From (31) it is easy to demonstrate that $0 < G'(\tilde{k}^*) < 1$ (do that). This implies that the linearized dynamic equation (30) is stable, so $\tilde{k}_t \to \tilde{k}^*$ as $t \to \infty$ according to it.

Our next step is to convert (30) into changes in natural log-values rather than changes in absolute values. This is easily done using (again) $f(z) - f(\bar{x}) \approx f'(\bar{x})(z - \bar{x})$, this time letting the function $\ln \tilde{k}_t$ take the place of f, and measuring at $\tilde{k}^*$: $\ln \tilde{k}_t - \ln \tilde{k}^* = (1/\tilde{k}^*)(\tilde{k}_t - \tilde{k}^*)$, or $\tilde{k}_t - \tilde{k}^* = \tilde{k}^*(\ln \tilde{k}_t - \ln \tilde{k}^*)$. Using this on both sides of (30) gives (note that $\tilde{k}^*$ cancels on both sides):

$$\ln \tilde{k}_{t+1} - \ln \tilde{k}^* = G'(\tilde{k}^*)(\ln \tilde{k}_t - \ln \tilde{k}^*). \tag{32}$$

We convert into log-differences of $\tilde{y}_t$ rather than $\tilde{k}_t$, applying that from $\tilde{y}_t = \tilde{k}_t^\alpha$, one has $\ln \tilde{y}_t = \alpha \ln \tilde{k}_t$, and then $\ln \tilde{y}_t - \ln \tilde{y}^* = \alpha(\ln \tilde{k}_t - \ln \tilde{k}^*)$. Using this on both sides of (32) gives:

$$\ln \tilde{y}_{t+1} - \ln \tilde{y}^* = G'(\tilde{k}^*)(\ln \tilde{y}_t - \ln \tilde{y}^*). \tag{33}$$

This is still a linear, first-order difference equation, now in $\ln \tilde{y}_t$, and since $0 < G'(\tilde{k}^*) < 1$, it implies that $\tilde{y}_t \to \tilde{y}^*$ as $t \to \infty$. The advantage of having transformed it into log-differences (or *relative* discrepancies between $\tilde{y}_t$ and its steady state value) is that the rate of convergence appears in a well-defined way. To see this, first subtract $\ln \tilde{y}_t$ and add $\ln \tilde{y}^*$ on both sides of (33) to obtain:

$$\ln \tilde{y}_{t+1} - \ln \tilde{y}_t = (1 - G'(\tilde{k}^*))(\ln \tilde{y}^* - \ln \tilde{y}_t). \tag{34}$$

Here we define $\lambda \equiv 1 - G'(\tilde{k}^*)$, where we must have $0 < \lambda < 1$, since $0 < G'(\tilde{k}^*) < 1$. Equation (34) then reads $\ln \tilde{y}_{t+1} - \ln \tilde{y}_t = \lambda(\ln \tilde{y}^* - \ln \tilde{y}_t)$, saying that in any period t, the relative change in $\tilde{y}_t$ (from period t to $t + 1$, the left-hand side) is the fraction λ of the current relative deviation between $\tilde{y}_t$ and its long-run equilibrium level, $\tilde{y}^*$. In other words, the remaining relative gap, $\ln \tilde{y}^* - \ln \tilde{y}_t$, is reduced by the fraction λ in any period, irrespective of how large the remaining gap currently is. Hence, λ is a time-independent measure of the rate at which $\tilde{y}_t$ converges to $\tilde{y}^*$, and we call λ the 'rate of convergence'. For instance, if λ is 0.02, then each year 2 per cent of the remaining distance to steady state is covered. Note that (34) has the 'convergence property': the growth rate of $\tilde{y}_t$ is larger (in absolute value) the further away from steady state $\tilde{y}_t$ is.

From (31) we can express the rate of convergence in terms of parameters as:

$$\lambda \equiv 1 - G'(\tilde{k}^*) = \frac{1}{(1+n)(1+g)}(1-\alpha)(n+g+\delta+ng) \approx (1-\alpha)(n+g+\delta). \tag{35}$$

For the latter approximation we have used the facts that since both n and g are small, the fraction $1/[(1 + n)(1 + g)]$ is close to one, and ng is close to zero. Thus we may conclude that, according to the Solow model, the rate of convergence is approximately $\lambda = (1 - \alpha)(n + g + \delta)$. For realistic parameter values such as $\alpha \approx \frac{1}{3}$ and $n + g + \delta \approx 0.075$ our model predicts a convergence rate of 5 per cent. A reasonable lower-bound estimate for λ would be around 4 per cent, e.g., corresponding to $\alpha = \frac{1}{3}$ and $n + g + \delta = 0.06$.

Inserting λ for $1 - G'(\tilde{k}^*)$ in (34) and rearranging a bit gives:

$$\ln \tilde{y}_{t+1} = \lambda \ln \tilde{y}^* + (1 - \lambda)\ln \tilde{y}_t, \tag{36}$$

which is a standard way of writing our linear, first-order difference equation in $\ln \tilde{y}_t$. To arrive at the Solow model's convergence equation we have to solve (36), that is, determine how $\ln \tilde{y}_t$ must depend on time t for (36) to be fulfilled in all periods. This is done using a standard 'cookbook procedure' involving the following steps.

First, one particular solution (a time path for $\ln \tilde{y}_t$ that makes (36) hold for all years) is the constant one: $\ln \tilde{y}_t = \ln \tilde{y}^*$ (check this).

Second, the so-called homogeneous equation, arising from setting the constant term $(\lambda \ln \tilde{y}^*)$ in (36) equal to zero, is: $\ln \tilde{y}_{t+1} - (1 - \lambda)\ln \tilde{y}_t = 0$. The characteristic polynomial associated with this is: $Q(x) = x - (1 - \lambda)$, with root $x = 1 - \lambda$ (the x that implies $Q(x) = 0$). The complete solution for the homogeneous difference equation is then: $\ln \tilde{y}_t = C(1 - \lambda)^t$, where C is an arbitrary constant.[5]

Third, the complete solution to (36) is the sum of a specific solution and the complete solution for the homogeneous equation: $\ln \tilde{y}_t = \ln \tilde{y}^* + C(1 - \lambda)^t$.[6]

Fourth, for the solution to be compatible with a given initial value $\tilde{y}_0$ for $t = 0$, we must have $C = \ln \tilde{y}_0 - \ln \tilde{y}^*$. Therefore, the unique solution to (36), given the initial value $\tilde{y}_0$, is:

$$\ln \tilde{y}_t = \ln \tilde{y}^* + (\ln \tilde{y}_0 - \ln \tilde{y}^*)(1 - \lambda)^t$$

$$= [1 - (1 - \lambda)^t]\ln \tilde{y}^* + (1 - \lambda)^t \ln \tilde{y}_0. \tag{37}$$

Evaluating for a specific year T and subtracting $\ln \tilde{y}_0$ on both sides gives:

$$\ln \tilde{y}_T - \ln \tilde{y}_0 = [1 - (1 - \lambda)^T](\ln \tilde{y}^* - \ln \tilde{y}_0).$$

Now using $\ln \tilde{y}_t = \ln y_t - \ln A_t$ for both $t = T$ and $t = 0$, and dividing by T on both sides gives:

$$\frac{\ln y_T - \ln y_0}{T} = \frac{\ln A_T - \ln A_0}{T} + \frac{1 - (1 - \lambda)^T}{T}(\ln A_0 + \ln \tilde{y}^* - \ln y_0). \tag{38}$$

Here we can (finally) insert from (24) how the steady state value $\tilde{y}^*$ depends on the structural characteristics. When we do that and also insert that $(\ln A_T - \ln A_0)/T$ is approximately equal to g, we get:

$$\frac{\ln y_T - \ln y_0}{T} \approx g + \frac{1 - (1 - \lambda)^T}{T}\left(\ln A_0 + \frac{\alpha}{1-\alpha}[\ln s - \ln(n+g+\delta+ng)] - \ln y_0\right). \tag{39}$$

This is the convergence equation of the Solow model. You may think that it looks complicated, but its content is simple: on the left-hand side is the average annual growth rate in GDP per

---

5. Check that $\ln \tilde{y}_t = C(1 - \lambda)^t$ fulfils the homogeneous equation for all t, irrespective of C.

6. Check again, this time that the stated solution fulfils (36) for all t irrespective of C.

worker over a period from year zero to year T. This growth rate is, according to (39) (or (38)), given as the sum of two terms: the first is simply the growth rate, g, *along* the steady state growth path, $A_t\tilde{y}^*$, for y_t. The other depends increasingly on the initial relative gap (the year zero log-difference) *between* the steady state growth path, taking the value $A_0\tilde{y}^*$ in year zero, and the actual GDP per worker, y_0. The dependence is such that as the number of years considered becomes large, as T goes to infinity, the second term will contribute very little to average growth. This is intuitively as it should be for an economy monotonically approaching an own long-run growth path with a constant growth rate, g.

CONVERGENCE THEORETICALLY

Convergence property: Income per worker converges towards a steady state growth path along which the growth rate is g, and which is fully characterized by the structural variables, s, n, g, δ, and A_0. The growth rate of income per worker is larger the lower the current level of income per worker.

Speed of convergence: The rate of convergence (to steady state), λ, is approximately $(1 - \alpha)(n + g + \delta)$, which on an annual basis should be in the range of 4 to 6 per cent for plausible parameter values. Each year 4 to 6 per cent of the remaining gap to steady state should thus be eliminated.

Testing the model outside steady state and estimating the rate of convergence

The theoretical convergence equation, (39), and an assumption that countries are technologically similar, having the same g and A_0, suggest a regression equation across countries i:

$$g_{T,0}^i \equiv \frac{\ln y_T^i - \ln y_0^i}{T} = \beta_0 - \beta_1 \ln y_0^i + \beta_2[\ln s^i - \ln(n^i + 0.075)], \tag{40}$$

where this time we do not bother to write an error term like the ξ^i of (29) explicitly. Eq. (40) is exactly the same as (4) of Chapter 2.[7] From appropriate data we can estimate the parameters β_0, β_1, and β_2 by OLS. We do that for the same sample of 65 countries considered in Figs 2.5 and 2.6, where, for example, s^i is the average investment rate between 1960 and 2003 of country i, etc. In fact, to create Fig. 2.6, we already did this estimation. The details of the estimation, with standard errors in parentheses below estimates, are:

$$g_{03,60}^i = 0.063 - \underset{(se=0.0015)}{0.006} \ln y_{60}^i + \underset{(se=0.0025)}{0.016} [\ln s^i - \ln(n^i + 0.075)], \qquad \text{adj. } R^2 = 0.38. \tag{41}$$

This is why we chose the parameter value $\beta_2 = 0.016$ in the construction of Fig. 2.6. We were then plotting $(g_{03,60}^i - 0.016[\ln s^i - \ln(n^i + 0.075)])$ against y_{60}^i, and we indicated the straight line, $0.063 - 0.006 \ln y_{60}^i$, resulting from our estimation. For convenience the figure is repeated here as Fig. 5.8.

The figure and the details of the estimation reported in (41) show that the explanatory power of our regression equation is not bad. Even under an assumption that the many countries considered are technologically similar, the model's convergence equation stands up quite well when confronted with cross-country data. One may take this as evidence that

---

7. In specifying this regression equation we are making a short-cut: according to (39) the parameters β_0, β_1 and β_2 in (36) all depend on λ, which in turn depends on n as stated in (35). Nevertheless, we hold β_0, β_1 and β_2 constant across countries in our estimations, ignoring that cross-country differences in n^i should imply cross-country differences in λ^i. We simply postulate a common rate of convergence λ and see how good our estimations become. The reason is that if we accounted for the influence of n on λ, the resulting non-linear equation would require more sophisticated methods to estimate.

FIGURE 5.8 Average annual growth rate of GDP per worker adjusted for structural characteristics against the initial level of GDP per worker, 65 countries

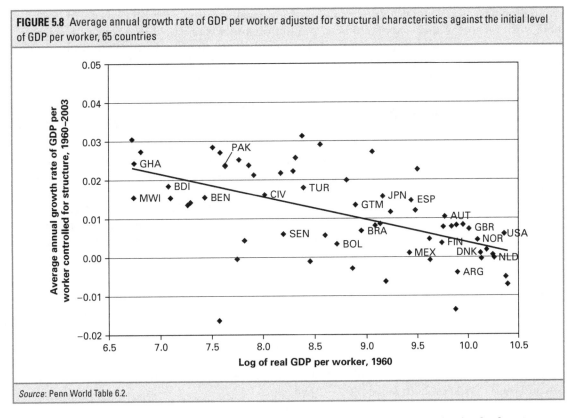

Source: Penn World Table 6.2.

the assumption that countries have equal access to technology is not as far-fetched as it may first seem, an issue we will return to in the next chapter where the convergence equation derived will perform even better.

Importantly, our estimation in (41) implies an estimate of the rate of convergence. According to (39), the parameter β_1 is equal to $(1 - (1 - \lambda)^T)/T$, implying that $\lambda = 1 - (1 - T\beta_1)^{1/T}$. Inserting $T = 43$ and our estimate of β_1 of 0.006 gives $\lambda = 0.007$. Thus our estimate of the annual rate of convergence based on our model and data for the 'countries of the world' is 0.7 per cent. Taking uncertainty into consideration, the 95 per cent confidence interval for λ goes from approximately 0.3 per cent to 1.1 per cent, computed (again) the simple way: go two standard errors down and two standard deviations up from the estimated β_1 to find (approximately) the 95 per cent confidence interval [0.003; 0.009] for β_1. Then insert the two end points of the interval into the formula for λ to find the 95 per cent confidence interval for λ. (Do this yourself.)

The estimated annual rate of convergence is substantially smaller than what it should be according to the model for realistic parameter values. Above we found that for plausible parameter values, predicted annual rates of convergence should be no less than 4 per cent. This suggests that the Solow model exaggerates considerably the speed of convergence compared to real-world convergence.

CONVERGENCE EMPIRICALLY   ❗

When confronted with real-world cross-country data, the general Solow model stands up quite well with respect to its out-of-steady-state convergence prediction: one does find a relatively clear negative relationship between the initial value of and the subsequent growth in income per worker across the countries of the world. However, the estimated speed of convergence is significantly lower than the one derived from the theoretical model.

In summary, the general Solow model performs well confronted with real-world data, both with respect to its steady state *level* prediction and with respect to its out-of-steady-state *convergence* prediction. For both of these predictions there is, however, a problem of magnitudes. In Chapter 6 we will present an extension of the Solow model that implies substantial improvements with respect to both of these empirical shortcomings.

5.5 Growth accounting

Growth accounting was suggested by Robert Solow in a paper that followed up on his famous 1956 article.[8] Growth accounting uses just one of the equations of the Solow model, the aggregate production function. We will still assume the production function to be of the Cobb–Douglas form. In growth accounting exercises one often expresses technical progress as (Hicks-neutral) changes in the total factor productivity, B_t, but one could equally well express it as labour-augmenting changes in an appropriately defined A_t, remembering that $A_t = B_t^{1/(1-\alpha)}$. So the aggregate production of a country in year t is assumed to depend on the inputs of capital and labour and on the level of technology as:

$$Y_t = B_t K_t^\alpha L_t^{1-\alpha} = K_t^\alpha (A_t L_t)^{1-\alpha}. \tag{42}$$

For another and later year $T > t$, we have:

$$Y_T = B_T K_T^\alpha L_T^{1-\alpha}. \tag{43}$$

If we take logs on both sides in each of the two above equations, subtract the first from the second, and divide on both sides by $T - t$, we get:

$$\frac{\ln Y_T - \ln Y_t}{T - t} = \frac{\ln B_T - \ln B_t}{T - t} + \alpha \frac{\ln K_T - \ln K_t}{T - t} + (1 - \alpha)\frac{\ln L_T - \ln L_t}{T - t}. \tag{44}$$

The left-hand side is the approximate average annual growth rate of GDP between t and T. The right-hand side is the approximate average annual growth rate of total factor productivity plus a weighted average of the approximate growth rates of capital and labour. Equation (44) thus splits up the growth in GDP into growth components.

If one has data for GDP and for the inputs of capital and labour for two years t and T, and if one sets the capital share α at $\frac{1}{3}$, (44) can be used to compute the contributions to total growth from each of the growth components. In particular, the contribution, $(\ln B_T - \ln B_t)/(T - t)$, of growth in the total factor productivity can be computed residually. This component is called the *Solow residual*.

How informative is a calculation of the average annual growth rate in total factor productivity of, say 3 per cent, over some period? In a way, not very informative, since we do not really know what B_t is. We have simply put all factors of importance for aggregate production other than physical capital and labour into B_t. Solow himself has expressed this by saying that the Solow residual may be viewed as 'a measure of our ignorance'. However, although we do not know exactly what an increase in B_t represents, growth accounting exercises may be useful. For instance, one could compare the Solow residuals between two different periods for one country, or between two different countries for the same period. If one residual is considerably larger than the other, the contribution to growth coming from unknown factors has changed from one period to the other, or has been larger in one country than in the other. Lower growth in B_t may be a first warning that productivity is not developing as favourably as it used to, or as favourably as in some other country.

---

8. The follow-up paper is: Robert M. Solow, 'Technical Change and the Aggregate Production Function', *Review of Economics and Statistics*, **39**, 1957, pp. 312–320.

One can also do growth accounting per worker. The production function (42) implies that $y_t = B_t k_t^\alpha$ in the usual notation. Taking logs and time differences, etc., gives:

$$\frac{\ln y_T - \ln y_t}{T - t} = \frac{\ln B_T - \ln B_t}{T - t} + \alpha \frac{\ln k_T - \ln k_t}{T - t}. \tag{45}$$

For $B_t = A_t^{1-\alpha}$, this equation may be rewritten in terms of A_t to give

$$\frac{\ln y_T - \ln y_t}{T - t} = (1 - \alpha)\frac{\ln A_T - \ln A_t}{T - t} + \alpha \frac{\ln k_T - \ln k_t}{T - t}, \tag{46}$$

expressing the growth rate of y_t as the weighted average of the growth rates of A_t and k_t, in accordance with (5) above. Equation (45) splits up the growth in GDP per worker into contributions from growth in capital per worker and growth in total factor productivity. Again, from data on GDP per worker and capital per worker, and setting $\alpha = \frac{1}{3}$, one can determine the growth contribution from technology (or other factors) residually.

Table 5.1 reports on a growth accounting exercise for six different countries. For each country and for five-year periods between 1960–65 and 1995–2000, the average annual growth rate in GDP per worker has been split up in components according to (45) assuming $\alpha = \frac{1}{3}$, that is, according to $g^y = g^B + g^k/3$ in our usual notation.

Consider first the figures for the USA. As you will see, over the full period from 1960 to 2000, capital and GDP (per worker) grew at almost the same rate. This indicates that the USA was close to balanced growth over the period (and so was Belgium, while for the other countries the capital–output ratio either decreased or increased substantially). In the first five-year period TFP (total factor productivity) growth in the USA was 2.9 per cent per year, which is high. To illustrate, note that a g^B of 2.9 per cent (per year) corresponds to g^A of 4.4 per cent for $\alpha = \frac{1}{3}$ (from $A_t = B_t^{1/(1-\alpha)}$ it follows that $g^A = g^B/(1 - \alpha)$, which you should show), and under balanced growth, g^A is directly comparable to g^y. Annual growth rates in GDP per worker of around 4.4 per cent are very high and unusual as averages over longer periods in Western, early industrialized countries. The internationally comparable data used for Table 5.1 only go back to 1960, but for the USA one can go further back, and doing so will reveal that high TFP growth was typical for a longer period following the Second World War.

The period of high TFP growth in the USA was followed by a considerable slowdown with quite low rates of TFP growth in the late 1960s and the 1970s, followed again by a partial return to higher TFP growth in the 1980s and 1990s. The downward movement in TFP growth in the middle of the period has been called the 'great productivity slowdown', and you will see from Table 5.1 that the UK, Belgium, Sweden and Denmark experienced similar slowdowns, while Ireland seems to have been developing quickly throughout the period. Economists have searched for reasons for the international productivity slowdown described.

Some have suggested that the oil crises of 1973 and 1979 were responsible (but note that the slowdown in the USA started before that). Others have stressed the relative shift in the production mix away from manufacturing towards the more labour-intensive production of services where productivity gains may be harder to achieve. Still others have claimed that declines in the quality of the labour force or of infrastructure caused the slowdown. Moreover, some have argued that it is not the low TFP growth of the 1970s and 1980s that needs explanation. Rather it is the high TFP growth in the 1960s that is unusual and needs to be explained. There are pros and cons for all these hypotheses. What we want to emphasize is that the evidence from a growth accounting exercise has induced economists to think hard about what was going on. This illustrates that growth accounting is a useful tool for economic analysis.

Growth accounting only uses a production function and some knowledge of parameters (like our α). The production function does not have to be as simple as (42) above. It is often argued that growth accounting should allow not only for the *quantity* of labour input, measured in hours or person-years, but also for the *quality* of labour input, measured by

TABLE 5.1 Growth accounting: the great productivity slowdown

	USA(%)					UK(%)			
Period	g^k	g^y	$g^k/3$	$g^B = g^y - g^k/3$	**Period**	g^k	g^y	$g^k/3$	$g^B = g^y - g^k/3$
1960–65	2.0	3.5	0.7	2.9	1960–65	–	3.0	–	–
1965–70	2.4	1.2	0.8	0.4	1965–70	–5.8	2.7	–1.9	4.6
1970–75	1.2	0.2	0.4	–0.3	1970–75	2.3	1.6	0.8	0.9
1975–80	1.0	1.0	0.3	0.7	1975–80	1.5	1.1	0.5	0.6
1980–85	1.7	1.6	0.6	1.0	1980–85	1.1	1.3	0.4	0.9
1985–90	0.8	1.5	0.3	1.2	1985–90	2.5	2.6	0.8	1.7
1990–95	1.0	1.3	0.3	1.0	1990–95	3.2	1.8	1.1	0.8
1995–00	2.2	2.5	0.7	1.7	1995–00	3.6	2.6	1.2	1.4
1960–00	1.5	1.6	0.5	1.1	1965–00	1.2	2.0	0.4	1.6

	Ireland(%)					Belgium(%)			
Period	g^k	g^y	$g^k/3$	$g^B = g^y - g^k/3$	**Period**	g^k	g^y	$g^k/3$	$g^B = g^y - g^k/3$
1960–65	–0.8	3.6	–0.3	3.9	1960–65	1.2	4.2	0.4	3.8
1965–70	1.2	4.6	0.4	4.2	1965–70	2.5	4.3	0.8	3.5
1970–75	0.9	3.7	0.3	3.4	1970–75	2.7	2.7	0.9	1.8
1975–80	2.4	3.4	0.8	2.6	1975–80	2.3	2.4	0.8	1.7
1980–85	1.9	1.2	0.6	0.6	1980–85	2.7	1.1	0.9	0.2
1985–90	2.3	4.6	0.8	3.8	1985–90	2.7	2.6	0.9	1.7
1990–95	0.3	2.8	0.1	2.7	1990–95	2.2	0.9	0.7	0.2
1995–00	1.1	5.5	0.4	5.2	1995–00	2.1	2.0	0.7	1.3
1960–00	1.2	3.7	0.4	3.3	1960–00	2.3	2.5	0.8	1.8

	Sweden(%)					Denmark(%)			
Period	g^k	g^y	$g^k/3$	$g^B = g^y - g^k/3$	**Period**	g^k	g^y	$g^k/3$	$g^B = g^y - g^k/3$
1960–65	–	4.6	–	–	1960–65	–	3.9	–	–
1965–70	2.7	3.2	0.9	2.3	1965–70	6.2	2.2	2.1	0.1
1970–75	2.9	1.5	1.0	0.5	1970–75	3.1	0.8	1.0	–0.2
1975–80	1.8	0.3	0.6	–0.3	1975–80	2.3	1.2	0.8	0.4
1980–85	1.9	1.6	0.6	1.0	1980–85	1.3	0.6	0.4	0.2
1985–90	2.4	1.6	0.8	0.8	1985–90	2.6	0.4	0.9	–0.5
1990–95	2.7	1.7	0.9	0.8	1990–95	3.0	2.4	1.0	1.4
1995–00	2.6	3.0	0.9	2.1	1995–00	3.0	2.3	1.0	1.3
1965–00	2.4	1.9	0.8	1.0	1965–00	3.1	1.4	1.0	0.4

Sources: OECD, Economic Outlook Database. For Denmark 1960–1970, Penn World Table 5.6.

the average level of education. It is natural to measure the average level of education in year t by the average number of years, u_t, that people in the year t labour force have spent on education (in school, say). The quality of labour would then be given by an increasing function $h(u_t)$, often referred to as a human capital function, and the aggregate production function would be modified to:

$$Y_t = B_t K_t^{\alpha}(h(u_t)L_t)^{1-\alpha}. \tag{47}$$

We cannot do growth accounting based on (47) until we know more about the function $h(u_t)$. Here some results from labour economics can be of use. Many labour economists have studied the relationship between education and wages. One of their findings (most often based on microeconomic data) is that a specific *absolute* change in the amount of education, one more year in school, say, seems to give rise to a specific *relative* change in the wage rate.[9] By assuming the functional form:

$$h(u_t) = \exp(\psi u_t), \qquad \psi > 0,$$

we obtain an increasing human capital function with exactly this property (just take logs on both sides and differentiate with respect to u_t):

$$\frac{dh(u_t)}{h(u_t)} \bigg/ du_t = \psi.$$

That is, one additional year of education yields a certain relative increase, ψ, in the level of human capital independently of the initial u_t. Let us now try to estimate ψ. If labour is paid its marginal product, then (47) implies that the wage rate, w_t, should be:

$$w_t = (1-\alpha)B_t K_t^\alpha h(u_t)^{1-\alpha} L_t^{-\alpha} = (1-\alpha)B_t \left(\frac{K_t}{L_t}\right)^\alpha \exp((1-\alpha)\psi u_t).$$

Taking logs on both sides and differentiating with respect to u_t gives (check this for yourself):

$$\frac{dw_t}{du_t} \bigg/ w_t = (1-\alpha)\psi.$$

Thus a one-year increase in schooling gives a relative increase in pay equal to $(1-\alpha)\psi$. A rather robust finding in empirical studies (mainly for the USA, but for some other countries as well) is that the percentage increase in pay generated by a one-year increase in schooling is around 7 per cent. If $(1-\alpha)\psi$ is roughly equal to 0.07, and α is $\frac{1}{3}$, then ψ must be approximately 0.1 (10 per cent). With the production function:

$$Y_t = B_t K_t^\alpha (\exp(\psi u_t)L_t)^{1-\alpha}, \tag{48}$$

and knowledge of the parameters α and ψ, we can do growth accounting again. In per worker terms the appropriate formula following from (48) is:

$$\frac{\ln y_T - \ln y_t}{T-t} = \frac{\ln B_T - \ln B_t}{T-t} + \alpha\frac{\ln k_T - \ln k_t}{T-t} + (1-\alpha)\psi\frac{u_T - u_t}{T-t}. \tag{49}$$

Derive this formula yourself and note that it is not the average *relative* change in schooling from year t to T that enters, but the average *absolute* change. From data on GDP per worker, capital per worker, and average years of schooling of the labour force in two different years t and T, one can again split up growth into the contributions from growth in capital per worker, growth in education, and the residual growth in TFP.

In particular, if a country has experienced a large increase in education over the period considered, one may tend to exaggerate the contribution from TFP growth if one does not include education in the growth accounting. This may be particularly relevant for an assessment of TFP growth in the growth miracle countries of East Asia. The East Asian tiger economies have typically experienced huge increases in educational effort. An exercise will ask you to try to get an impression of the TFP growth in the East compared to the West, taking education into account.

If one ends up finding that a certain country has had considerably higher TFP growth than another, controlling appropriately for differences in education, one can go on looking

9. A pioneering contribution is Jacob Mincer, *Schooling, Experience, and Earnings*, Columbia University Press, 1974.

for other neglected factors of production to explain the difference. The tiger economies do indeed tend to exhibit very high TFP growth even after one has controlled for education. One explanation which has been suggested is that over the periods most often considered, the West has experienced a larger shift of the production mix from manufacturing to services than East Asia. It is an open question whether, taking *all* relevant factors into account, East Asia has had above-average TFP growth, or whether its high growth is simply due to above-average factor accumulation.

A growth accounting exercise can split up growth in GDP or in GDP per worker into components, thus attributing total growth to various *sources*. However, this does not identify the *causes* of the growth. Here is why. Assume that the growth process of some economy can be described fully by the steady state of the Solow model with appropriate parameter values. In that case there will be positive growth in GDP per worker if and only if $g > 0$. In a causal sense, all growth in GDP per worker will then be rooted in the exogenous growth of the technological variable. On the other hand, if one conducts a growth accounting exercise, one will find that the growth in GDP per capita comes partly from technological growth and partly from growth in capital per worker. Both observations will be true. Without technological growth there would be no growth in GDP per worker, so technological growth is the ultimate source of long-run growth. However, when there *is* (steady state) growth in GDP per worker (and hence in technology), there will also be growth in capital per worker, so part of the growth observed comes from capital accumulation. An exercise will ask you to figure out exactly what a growth accounting exercise for an economy in Solow steady state will say.

5.6 Summary

1. In the basic Solow model the only source of long-run growth in economic activity is population (or rather labour force) growth. The basic Solow model cannot generate the long-run growth in GDP per capita that we observe in the data.

2. The general Solow model developed in this chapter generalizes the basic Solow model by introducing steady exogenous technological progress. This enables the model to generate long-run growth in GDP per capita. Technical progress may be labour-augmenting, increasing the efficiency of labour; it may be capital-augmenting, raising the productivity of capital, or it may take the form of an increase in total factor productivity. As long as the aggregate production function has the Cobb–Douglas form, all of these types of technological progress are equivalent and have the same implications for the evolution of the economy.

3. In the long run the general Solow model converges on a steady state with balanced economic growth, where total output, consumption, investment and the capital stock all grow at a rate equal to the sum of the exogenous growth rates of population and labour-augmenting productivity, where output per capita (worker), capital per capita, consumption per capita and the real wage rate all grow at the same rate as labour-augmenting productivity, and where the real interest rate is constant. Hence the long-run economic predictions of the general Solow model accord with the basic stylized facts about long-run growth. Outside steady state the general Solow model accords with the observation of conditional convergence.

4. The general Solow model implies that structural economic policies which succeed in raising the economy's savings rate or in reducing its rate of population growth will gradually take the economy to a higher steady state growth path characterized by a

higher level of steady state income and consumption. The general Solow model implies the same golden savings rule as the basic Solow model: long-run consumption per capita will be maximized when the savings rate equals the capital income share of GDP.

5. Structural policies which increase the savings rate or reduce the population growth rate cannot permanently raise the economy's growth rate. This can only be achieved via a policy that permanently raises the growth rate of factor productivity, but the general Solow model is silent about the factors determining technological progress.

6. Empirical data for a large sample of countries around the world confirm the steady state prediction of the Solow model, that real GDP per worker will tend to be higher, the higher the investment rate and the lower the population growth rate. However, for reasonable values of the capital income share of GDP, the theoretical Solow model underestimates the observed quantitative effects of these structural characteristics.

7. Outside the steady state the general Solow model predicts conditional convergence: controlling for cross-country differences in structural characteristics, a country's growth rate will be higher, the lower its initial level of real GDP per worker. The data for countries around the world support this prediction, but for reasonable parameter values the theoretical model significantly overestimates the rate (speed) at which economies converge.

8. Using an aggregate production function, one can estimate the contributions to aggregate output growth stemming from increases in factor inputs and from increases in total factor productivity. Such a decomposition of the overall growth rate is called growth accounting. In basic growth accounting, growth in output per worker can originate from growth in the capital stock per worker or from growth in total factor productivity. Still, in a causal sense the ultimate source of growth is technological progress, since long-run growth in capital per worker can only occur if there is continued growth in total factor productivity.

5.7 Exercises

Exercise 1. The general Solow model in continuous time

In continuous time the general Solow model consists of the seven equations:

$$Y = K^{\alpha}(AL)^{1-\alpha},$$

$$r = \alpha\left(\frac{K}{AL}\right)^{\alpha-1},$$

$$w = (1-\alpha)\left(\frac{K}{AL}\right)^{\alpha} A,$$

$$S = sY,$$

$$\dot{K} = sY - \delta K,$$

$$\frac{\dot{L}}{L} = n,$$

$$\frac{\dot{A}}{A} = g,$$

where the restrictions on the parameters α, s, n, g and δ are the same as in the model in discrete time, except that we do not have to assume $n > -1$ and $g > -1$. It is assumed that $n + g + \delta > 0$. We use (for any point t in time) the usual definitions, $k \equiv K/L$ and $y \equiv Y/L$, as well as the definitions, $\tilde{k} \equiv K/(AL)$ and $\tilde{y} \equiv Y/(AL)$.

1. Applying methods similar to those used in Exercise 2 of Chapter 3, show that the law of motion for $\tilde{k}$ following from the general Solow model in continuous time can be expressed in the Solow equation:

$$\dot{\tilde{k}} = s\tilde{k}^\alpha - (n + g + \delta)\tilde{k}.$$

Compare to (19) for the model in discrete time.

2. Illustrate the above Solow equation in a Solow diagram with $\tilde{k}$ along the horizontal axis. Demonstrate (from the Solow diagram) that from any initial value, $\tilde{k}_0 > 0$, capital per effective worker, $\tilde{k}$, will converge towards a specific steady state level, $\tilde{k}^*$, in the long run (as $t \to \infty$).

3. Compute the steady state values, $\tilde{k}^*$ and $\tilde{y}^*$, for capital per effective worker and income per effective worker. Compare to the parallel expressions found in this chapter for the model in discrete time. Also compute the steady state value and path (respectively), r^* and w^*, for the real factor prices and compare again to the discrete time model.

4. Show that (it follows from the model that) the growth rate in $\tilde{k}$ at any time is:

$$\frac{\dot{\tilde{k}}}{\tilde{k}} = s\tilde{k}^{\alpha-1} - (n + g + \delta).$$

Illustrate this in a modified Solow diagram. Show that the growth rate, $\dot{y}/y$, of output per worker at any time t is α times the growth rate of $\tilde{k}$ plus g. Assume that initially $\tilde{k}_0 < \tilde{k}^*$. Describe and explain qualitatively, in words, the transition to steady state. For instance, how do r and w develop along the transition, and when is the growth rate in y at its highest?

5. To solve the general Solow model analytically one can apply a trick as in Exercise 3 of Chapter 3. Define $z \equiv \tilde{k}^{1-\alpha}$. Show that z is the capital–output ratio, k/y. Then show that:

$$\dot{z} = (1 - \alpha)s - \lambda z, \tag{50}$$

where $\lambda \equiv (1 - \alpha)(n + g + \delta)$. Note that (50) is linear. Show that the steady state value of z is $z^* = (1 - \alpha)s/\lambda = s/(n + g + \delta)$. Solve (50) by finding the characteristic roots, etc., and show that (given an initial capital–output ratio z_0) the solution is:

$$z = \frac{(1-\alpha)s}{\lambda}(1 - e^{-\lambda t}) + z_0 e^{-\lambda t}$$

$$= \frac{s}{n + g + \delta}(1 - e^{-\lambda t}) + z_0 e^{-\lambda t}.$$

This says that at any time t, the capital–output ratio is the weighted average of its steady state value and its initial value, with the former variable carrying an increasing weight over time. Show that the solutions for $\tilde{k}$ and $\tilde{y}$ are:

$$\tilde{k} = \left(\frac{s}{n + g + \delta}(1 - e^{-\lambda t}) + \tilde{k}_0^{1-\alpha} e^{-\lambda t} \right)^{1/(1-\alpha)},$$

$$\tilde{y} = \left(\frac{s}{n + g + \delta}(1 - e^{-\lambda t}) + \tilde{y}_0^{\frac{1-\alpha}{\alpha}} e^{-\lambda t} \right)^{\frac{\alpha}{1-\alpha}}.$$

From these expressions, argue that λ is a measure of the speed of convergence and relate it to what was found for the rate of convergence (by considering a linear approximation around steady state) in Section 5.4.

Exercise 2. Analysing the Solow model in discrete time in terms of the capital–output ratio

(This exercise may be a useful preparation for Chapter 7, technically.) When analysing the general Solow model in this chapter, we were looking for some variables that would be constant in a steady state with balanced growth. We found that $\tilde{k}_t$ and $\tilde{y}_t$ had this property, and we analysed the model in terms of these variables. In steady state the capital–output ratio, $z_t \equiv K_t/Y_t$, must also be constant for the steady state to exhibit balanced growth.

1. Show that z_t as just defined fulfils: $z_t = k_t/y_t = \tilde{k}_t/\tilde{y}_t = \tilde{k}_t^{1-\alpha}$ with definitions as in this chapter, and show from the results of Section 3 that indeed z_t is constant in steady state and equal to:

$$ z^* = \frac{s}{n+g+\delta+ng}. $$

This gives the idea that the model could alternatively have been analysed in terms of z_t. In fact, the previous exercise showed that analysing the Solow model in continuous time in terms of the capital–output ratio had the advantage that the law of motion was a *linear* differential equation that could be solved. This exercise asks you to analyse the model in discrete time in terms of z_t, among other reasons to see whether the law of motion becomes a linear, and therefore solvable, first-order difference equation.

2. Show, using the per capita production function, that $z_t = (k_t/A_t)^{1-\alpha}$. Then show, by writing this equation for period $t + 1$, using the definition $k_{t+1} \equiv K_{t+1}/L_{t+1}$, and then using the model's equations, that:

$$ z_{t+1} = \left(\frac{1}{(1+n)(1+g)}\right)^{1-\alpha} (sy_t + (1-\delta)k_t)^{1-\alpha} \left(\frac{1}{A_t}\right)^{1-\alpha}. $$

From this equation show by appropriate manipulations that the law of motion for z_t is:

$$ z_{t+1} = \left(\frac{1}{(1+n)(1+g)}\right)^{1-\alpha} z_t^\alpha (s + (1-\delta)z_t)^{1-\alpha}. \tag{51} $$

(Hint: Start by taking k_t out of the middle parentheses and then utilize the fact that inside the parentheses you get $y_t/k_t = 1/z_t$, and outside you get a $k_t^{1-\alpha}$ that you can put together with the $(1/A_t)^{1-\alpha}$ to make z_t appear.)

Clearly, (51) is a non-linear difference equation, so we did not get solvability.

3. Now derive the steady state value z^* directly from (51). Sketch the transition diagram for z_t, and establish properties of the transition equation that imply global, monotone convergence to z^*, from any given initial $z_0 > 0$. (For this you must establish properties as listed in Footnote 8 in Chapter 3.) Finally show that in steady state k_t and y_t must be increasing at the same rate, and that the common approximate growth rate must be g.

Exercise 3. Time to halve

In Section 5.4 we arrived at the dynamic equation, $\ln \tilde{y}_{t+1} - \ln \tilde{y}_t = \lambda(\ln \tilde{y}^* - \ln \tilde{y}_t)$, which is (34) with the rate of convergence λ inserted for $1 - G'(\tilde{k}^*)$, and equivalent to (36). Show that it follows from this dynamic equation that the number of years, h, before half of an initial relative gap in year zero, $\ln \tilde{y}^* - \ln \tilde{y}_0$, has been covered is $h = -\ln 2/\ln(1 - \lambda)$, and this is independent of how large the initial gap is. (Hint: Use the solution (37) to our difference equation.) For realistic parameter values and the expression (35) for λ, what size is h? How large is h for our direct estimates of λ?

Exercise 4. The effects of an increase in the savings rate and convergence time

In this chapter an increase in the savings rate was analysed in the Solow diagram and in the modified Solow diagram, and the growth jump arising from the increase in s was described qualitatively. It follows from the chapter that the speed by which the economy adjusts from the old to the new steady state should (approximately) be measured by the rate of convergence, $\lambda \equiv (1 - \alpha)(n + g + \delta)$. This exercise asks you to do simulations and graphical representations to illustrate *numerically* the qualitative findings.

Let the parameters (before the shift) in the general Solow model be given by: $\alpha = \frac{1}{3}$, $s = 0.12$, $n = 0.01$, $g = 0.01$, $\delta = 0.05$. In the following, the *base scenario* is defined by the economy being in steady state at these parameter values from period zero through period 100.

1. Compute the steady state values $\tilde{k}^*$ and $\tilde{y}^*$ for $\tilde{k}_t$ and $\tilde{y}_t$ in the base scenario (all definitions are standard and as in the chapter). Illustrate the base scenario in three diagrams. Diagram 1 should plot $\tilde{y}_t$ against time t (the points are just situated on a horizontal line). Diagram 2 should plot $\ln y_t$ against t, and Diagram 3 should plot $\ln c_t$ against t. You have not yet been given sufficient information to do Diagrams 2 and 3. Explain why. Let $A_0 = 1$, and do Diagrams 2 and 3.

   The *alternative scenario* is defined by the economy evolving according to the base scenario from period zero through period nine (that is, all parameters, and A_0, are as in the base scenario from period zero to period nine, and the economy is in steady state at these parameter values). In period ten a permanent shift in the savings rate from $s = 0.12$ to $s' = 0.24$ occurs, working initially in period ten, while all other parameters remain unchanged.

2. Simulate the model using appropriate parameters and initial values, thus creating computed time series for relevant variables according to the alternative scenario. Extend Diagram 1 so that it shows the evolution in $\tilde{y}_t$ both according to the base scenario and according to the alternative scenario. Do the parallel extensions of Diagrams 2 and 3. In Diagrams 2 and 3 you should include the lines corresponding to the new steady state, that is, lines for $\ln y_t$ and $\ln c_t$ as if the economy had been in the new steady state in all periods. Now construct a Diagram 4 that shows the evolution in the growth rate, $g_t^y \equiv \ln y_t - \ln y_{t-1}$, over the periods $t = 1, \ldots, 100$, both according to the base and according to the alternative scenarios, and construct a Diagram 5 that shows the evolution in the capital–output ratio, K_t/Y_t (same periods, both scenarios).

3. From your simulations find the (approximate and rounded up) number of periods it takes for $\tilde{y}_t$ to move half the way from its old to its new steady state value. In Exercise 3 you were asked to derive a formula for the half-life, h, given a rate of convergence, λ. Relate the half-life you have just found to the one computed from the formula of that exercise, using $\lambda \equiv (1 - \alpha)(n + g + \delta)$. Why can there be a (slight) difference between these half-lives?

4. Do all of the above once more, but now with $g = 0.04$ throughout. So, the base scenario is now given by $\alpha = \frac{1}{3}$, $s = 0.12$, $n = 0.01$, $g = 0.04$, $\delta = 0.05$ and $A_0 = 1$, with the economy being in steady state at these parameter values in all periods, while the alternative scenario is given by an increase in the savings rate to 0.24 as from period ten, etc. Compare the two experiments in particular with respect to the half-lives of the adjustment from the old to the new steady state and relate to the 'theoretical' rate of convergence, λ.

Exercise 5. The effects of an increase in the rate of technological progress

Assume that the economy is initially in steady state at parameter values α, s, n, g, δ. Then from some period the rate of technological progress increases permanently to a new and higher constant level, $g' > 0$, but n, g and g' are relatively small, so $1/[(1 + n)(1 + g')]$ is approximately one, and ng' is approximately zero. This exercise asks you to conduct a qualitative analysis of the growth effects of the increase in the rate of technological progress. First, how are the Solow diagram and the modified Solow diagram affected by the change? In diagrams with t along the horizontal axis, illustrate how $\tilde{k}_t$ and the growth rate $g_t^{\tilde{k}}$ of $\tilde{k}_t$ adjust over time (all definitions as usual). You should find that in the first period after the change, $g_t^{\tilde{k}}$ falls to a certain negative value and then it increases monotonically back towards zero. Show that the value it first falls to is approximately $-(g' - g)$. Next, illustrate in a diagram how the approximate growth rate g_t^k of k_t evolves. In doing this, show that just after the change, g_t^k stays close to the original g, and then increases monotonically towards g' (here the formula $g_t^k = g_t^{\tilde{k}} + g_t^A$, following from $\tilde{k}_t = k_t/A_t$, is useful). Finally, show that the approximate growth rate, g_t^y, just after the change jumps from g to $\alpha g + (1 - \alpha)g'$, and from there increases monotonically towards g' (here $g_t^y = \alpha g_t^k + (1 - \alpha)g_t^A$ may be useful). Illustrate the adjustments of y_t in a $(t, \ln y_t)$ diagram.

Exercise 6. Deriving an estimate of α from the estimation of the convergence equation

In this chapter we derived an estimate of α from our estimation of the *steady state regression equation* (29). The γ in that equation was estimated to be 1.52 (see the displayed formula just after Fig. 5.7), and since $\gamma = \alpha/(1 - \alpha)$ according to the model, the value for α implied by the estimation had to be 0.6. Since α is capital's share of GDP, it should be around $\frac{1}{3}$, so we had to conclude that in this respect the model did not accord perfectly well with the data. From our estimation of the *convergence regression equation* (40) reported in (41) we derived an estimate of the rate of convergence, λ, and found a value of 0.7 per cent, which was low compared to the theoretical expression, $\lambda = (1 - \alpha)(n + g + \delta)$, since this is realistically around 5 per cent. We could also have derived an estimated value of α from our estimation of the convergence equation by using the estimated values of β_1 and β_2 and the theoretical equation (39). Find this implied value of α and compare it to the 'correct' value of around $\frac{1}{3}$, and to the value implied by the estimation of the steady state equation.

Exercise 7. Growth accounting: does your country keep up?

Table 5.2 shows GDP per worker, y_t, and non-residential capital per worker, k_t, for some countries and years. Use formula (45), assuming $\alpha = \frac{1}{3}$, to decompose for each country the average annual growth rate of GDP per worker over the full period 1966 to 1990 into components from growth in capital per worker and from TFP growth. Comment on how your own country has been doing (if your country is not there, just pick one as your home country for this exercise).

Next, use the same formula to do growth accounting for the sub-periods 1966–78 and 1978–90 for each country. Comment again with respect to how your country has been doing.

Exercise 8. Growth accounting: have the growth miracle economies experienced above-normal TFP growth?

Table 5.3 shows GDP per worker, y_t, capital per worker, k_t, and average years of education in the population aged 15 or more, for some East Asian and some Western countries for 1961 and 1990.

We all know that the East Asian countries included in the table have had very high growth in GDP per person compared to the West over the period considered, but have they also had relatively high technological growth? We argued in Section 5.5 that to give an answer via growth accounting, one would need to include education because some of the

TABLE 5.2 GDP per worker and non-residential capital per worker, 1985 – international prices

Year	USA y_t	USA k_t	Denmark y_t	Denmark k_t	UK y_t	UK k_t
1966	29,152	18,734	18,124	15,284	16,895	9,362
1978	32,773	26,549	21,459	26,824	21,341	15,811
1990	36,771	34,705	24,971	33,125	26,755	21,179

Year	Ireland y_t	Ireland k_t	Netherlands y_t	Netherlands k_t	Belgium y_t	Belgium k_t
1966	10,374	7,538	20,958	15,674	18,267	16,330
1978	17,849	15,604	29,142	27,513	26,474	29,792
1990	24,058	21,660	31,242	32,380	31,730	36,646

Year	Norway y_t	Norway k_t	Sweden y_t	Sweden k_t	Finland y_t	Finland k_t
1966	17,793	39,982	20,935	16,784	14,056	18,137
1978	23,984	41,875	23,935	28,173	19,244	32,496
1990	29,248	48,135	28,389	39,409	27,350	45,767

Note: This table is based on the older version 5.6 of Penn World Table. Some figures are substantially changed in later versions.
Source: Penn World Tables 5.6.

TABLE 5.3 GDP per worker, capital per worker, and years of education, East and West, 1961 and 1990

East Year	Japan y_t	Japan k_t	Japan u_t	Hong Kong y_t	Hong Kong k_t	Hong Kong u_t
1961	5,630	7,601	7.8	4,372	7,294	5.2
1990	22,624	65,741	9.0	22,827	30,553	9.2

Year	South Korea y_t	South Korea k_t	South Korea u_t	Singapore y_t	Singapore k_t	Singapore u_t
1961	2,724	2,034	4.2	5,225	8,445	4.3
1990	16,022	28,393	9.9	24,369	56,670	6.0

West Year	USA y_t	USA k_t	USA u_t	UK y_t	UK k_t	UK u_t
1961	24,431	52,113	8.5	15,077	21,214	7.8
1990	36,771	80,419	11.7	26,755	49,227	8.8

Year	France y_t	France k_t	France u_t	Italy y_t	Italy k_t	Italy u_t
1961	14,111	26,467	5.4	11,987	27,560	4.7
1990	30,357	80,194	7.0	30,797	78,026	6.5

Year	Netherlands y_t	Netherlands k_t	Netherlands u_t	Denmark y_t	Denmark k_t	Denmark u_t
1961	17,501	35,747	5.3	15,554	28,599	9.0
1990	31,242	72,234	8.7	24,971	64,480	9.6

Note: u_t is average years of education of people older than 15 years. y_t and k_t are measured in 1985 – international prices.

Sources: William Easterly and Ross Levine, 'It's Not Factor Accumulation: Stylized Facts and Growth Models', *The World Bank Economic Review*, **15**, No.2, 2001. Robert J. Barro and Jong-Wha Lee, International Data on Educational Attainment, Center for International Development at Harvard University (CID), 2000.

East Asian countries have had large increases in education standards, as also evidenced by the numbers in the table. This exercise asks you to do some growth accounting with education included. Let the aggregate production function for each country be:

$$Y_t = K_t^\alpha (A_t h(u_t) L_t)^{1-\alpha}, \qquad h(u_t) = \exp(\psi u_t),$$

where we have chosen this time to express technology in terms of the labour augmenting productivity variable, A_t.

1. Derive an appropriate growth accounting formula that splits up the average annual growth rate of GDP per worker into components coming from growth in A_t, growth in capital per worker, and growth in education.

2. Use the formula to split up the average annual growth rates of GDP per worker from 1961 to 1990 into the components described in Question 1 for the countries shown in the table, assuming $\alpha = \frac{1}{3}$, $\psi = 0.1$.

3. Discuss whether there seems to have been excessive technological progress in East Asia. Can this growth accounting exercise, by reasonable standards, be said to give a full answer to the question raised?

Exercise 9. Where growth comes from according to the Solow model and according to growth accounting

Assume that some economy behaves completely in accordance with the steady state of the Solow model presented in this chapter, where the assumed growth rate of A_t is g. From what you have learned in this chapter, what will the average annual growth rates of y_t, k_t and A_t be over some period from year t to year T? What creates growth in GDP per worker? If one did a growth accounting exercise for this economy, what would be the fractions of growth in GDP per worker attributed to growth in capital per worker and to growth in A_t, respectively? Again, what is the true source of growth in this economy?

Exercise 10. One (more) critical look at the empirical success of the Solow model's steady state prediction

In this chapter we concluded, based on Fig. 5.7 and the estimation of (29) going with it, that the steady state prediction of the Solow model did *quite* well empirically (but with some shortcomings concerning magnitudes of estimates). One thing to learn about empirical analysis is that there is always reason to be critical and to ask hard questions. This exercise illustrates one standard type of critical question: is the conclusion arrived at robust with respect to an appropriate division of the available data? All required data can be taken from Table A at the back of Book One. Proceed as follows.

Consider the countries in the sample of 65 countries. Split these countries into two subgroups: countries that in 2003 had a GDP per worker above 50 per cent of the US level, and countries that had GDP per worker below 50 per cent of the US level. For each of these groups, construct a figure like Fig. 5.7, and estimate by OLS the steady state equation (29) for each subgroup, that is, find the lines of best fit in your figures. Comment on your findings.

(Exercise 1 of Chapter 6 will illustrate another standard type of critical question one can ask, still in connection with the empirical success of the steady state prediction of the Solow model. If you wish you can, for your own interest, already do most of that exercise now, but it has a close relationship to the analysis in Chapter 6 as well.)

CHAPTER 6

Education and growth

The Solow model with human capital

The Solow model of Chapter 5 performed quite well by empirical standards, but we identified two systematic discrepancies between the international evidence and the predictions of the model: the steady state of the model seemed to substantially *underestimate* how strongly savings and population growth rates influence GDP per person, and the model seemed to substantially *overestimate* the speed by which economies converge to their steady states.

Is there a single modification of the Solow model that can redress *both* of its two empirical weaknesses? Indeed there is, and the idea behind it is brilliant. It is due to the economists, N. Gregory Mankiw, David Romer and David N. Weil, who presented it in an article entitled 'A Contribution to the Empirics of Economic Growth'.[1] We will now explain the idea intuitively.

Consider the problem concerning the speed of convergence. In the Solow model convergence is slower the larger the elasticity of output with respect to capital, α. We explained this fact in Chapter 5 where we found the rate of convergence to be $\lambda = (1 - \alpha)(n + g + \delta)$. If α could be chosen freely, we could simply set α sufficiently large to bring λ in accordance with the empirics, but α is one minus labour's share, so realistically α cannot be set much higher than $\frac{1}{3}$. However, suppose there were also another kind of capital with an output elasticity and 'income share' of its own, φ say, and that this capital were accumulated in the same way as physical capital (and therefore delayed convergence similarly). Furthermore, suppose the income share of this form of capital were accruing to workers. Then, for α maintained around $\frac{1}{3}$, one would have a slower convergence since $\alpha + \varphi > \frac{1}{3}$, *and* still a labour share, $1 - \alpha$, around $\frac{2}{3}$.

This suggests the idea of adding *human capital* to the model: each year there is a certain stock of human capital, which can be thought of as the sum of all the education and training the workers have had, and this stock (per worker) serves to increase the productivity of workers. Just like physical capital, total human capital is assumed to accumulate by a certain exogenous fraction of GDP being added to it each year. The income share of human capital goes to workers, because human capital (embedded education) is linked to workers and its services therefore sold inseparably together with work hours.

Since human capital accumulates like physical capital, the inclusion of it will lower the model's speed of convergence. Because the output elasticity of physical capital is

---

1. N. Gregory Mankiw, David Romer and David N. Weil, 'A Contribution to the Empirics of Economic Growth', *The Quarterly Journal of Economics*, **107**, 1992, pp. 407–437.

unchanged, the owners of physical capital will earn the same fraction of GDP. The fraction earned by human capital goes to the workers, so labour's share will also be unchanged. Thus, adding human capital should work to overcome the second of the empirical problems.

What about the first problem concerning the model's steady state prediction? Assume that the rate of investment in physical capital increases. This will create higher GDP per person in steady state because more physical capital per person is accumulated. If a certain fraction of GDP is invested in human capital, then the higher GDP first caused by the higher rate of investment in *physical* capital will also imply that more *human* capital per worker is accumulated. This reinforces the increase in output. Thus, the increase in GDP per person caused by a higher investment rate in physical capital is larger in a model including human capital than in one with only physical capital (other things, e.g. α, being equal).

The introduction of human capital should thus work to mitigate both of the empirical failures of the Solow model. How well a job it does in this respect is the subject of this chapter, and we will see that it does a very fine job.

6.1 The Solow model with human capital

The 'micro world' of the model to be presented is similar to that of the Solow models considered previously. There are the same kinds of economic agents, a representative profit-maximizing firm and consumers (government can again be interpreted into the model, a possibility that will be considered in an exercise). The production function of the firm is now different as it includes human capital, and the consumers will also have to decide on how large a fraction of income to accumulate as human capital each period. We assume that each unit of output can be used either as consumption, investment in physical capital, or as investment in human capital.

There are also the same competitive markets as before, one for output with real price normalized to 1, one for the services of physical capital with real rental rate, r_t, and one for labour with real wage rate, w_t. Hence we do not assume that there is a separate market for the services of human capital with a rental rate of its own. This is because human capital cannot be separated from workers. Its services have to be sold together with labour. So the services traded on the labour market will no longer be units of 'raw' labour, person-years, but person-years endowed with a certain level of human capital or education. This level is assumed to be the same for all workers. Hence the total stock of human capital, H_t, manifests itself as each worker in the labour force, L_t, holding a human capital of $h_t \equiv H_t / L_t$ that goes inseparably with the worker. Employing one more worker means hiring an additional unit of labour equipped with h_t.

The Solow model with human capital thus has two new features compared to the original Solow model: the inclusion of human capital in the production function and the accumulation of human capital by the consumers.

The production function with human capital

In period t the amounts of physical capital, K_t, and human capital, H_t, are predetermined by past accumulation. The aggregate production function is assumed to be:

$$Y_t = K_t^\alpha H_t^\varphi (A_t L_t)^{1-\alpha-\varphi}, \quad 0 < \alpha < 1, \quad 0 < \varphi < 1, \quad \alpha + \varphi < 1, \tag{1}$$

where A_t, the technological variable, is again assumed to follow an exogenous path given by a constant rate, g, of technological progress, where $g > -1$. Hence $A_t = A_0(1 + g)^t$ for all t.

The production function (1) assumes constant returns to the three inputs K_t, H_t and L_t. This accords with the replication argument. Given a technological level A_t, it should be possible to 'double production by doubling factor inputs', that is, by hiring $2L_t$ workers instead of L_t, each being supplied with the same amount, $k_t \equiv K_t/L_t$, of physical capital, meaning that physical capital doubles to $2K_t$, and each also being endowed with the same amount, h_t, of human capital, so human capital doubles to $2H_t$. It follows that there are diminishing returns to the two reproducible capital inputs, $\alpha + \varphi < 1$.

Hiring one more (marginal) unit of labour now means hiring one more unit endowed with the average amount, h_t, of human capital per worker. Hence, a firm cannot increase the input of 'raw' labour, L_t, without increasing proportionally the input of human capital, $H_t = h_t L_t$. When we compute the marginal product of labour we should therefore consider h_t (not H_t) as being given. Inserting $H_t = h_t L_t$ into (1) gives:

$$Y_t = K_t^{\alpha} h_t^{\varphi} A_t^{1-\alpha-\varphi} L_t^{1-\alpha}. \tag{2}$$

Profit maximization and perfect competition in the markets for the services of physical capital and labour imply that the rental rates, r_t and w_t, are given by the marginal products of K_t and L_t (taking h_t as given in the computation of the latter):

$$r_t = \alpha K_t^{\alpha-1} h_t^{\varphi} A_t^{1-\alpha-\varphi} L_t^{1-\alpha} = \alpha \left(\frac{K_t}{A_t L_t} \right)^{\alpha-1} \left(\frac{H_t}{A_t L_t} \right)^{\varphi}, \tag{3}$$

$$w_t = (1-\alpha) K_t^{\alpha} h_t^{\varphi} A_t^{1-\alpha-\varphi} L_t^{-\alpha} = (1-\alpha) \left(\frac{K_t}{A_t L_t} \right)^{\alpha} \left(\frac{H_t}{A_t L_t} \right)^{\varphi} A_t. \tag{4}$$

From (3) and (4) as well as (2), it is easy to verify that the income shares of the owners of physical capital and of the workers are $r_t K_t/Y_t = \alpha$ and $w_t L_t/Y_t = 1 - \alpha$, respectively.

Dividing on both sides of (2) by L_t, and using the usual definition of output per worker, $y_t \equiv Y_t/L_t$, we get the 'per capita production function':

$$y_t = k_t^{\alpha} h_t^{\varphi} A_t^{1-\alpha-\varphi}, \tag{5}$$

from which, taking logs and time differences, and using the usual notation for the approximate growth rates, for example $g_t^y \equiv \ln y_t - \ln y_{t-1}$, one gets:

$$g_t^y = \alpha g_t^k + \varphi g_t^h + (1-\alpha-\varphi) g_t^A \approx \alpha g_t^k + \varphi g_t^h + (1-\alpha-\varphi)g. \tag{6}$$

In the Solow model with human capital, growth in GDP per worker can come from three sources: more physical capital per worker, more human capital per worker, and better technology. The (approximate) growth rate of y_t is the weighted average of the growth rates of k_t, h_t and A_t, the weights being the appropriate exponents in the Cobb–Douglas production function.

The empirical observation that the income share of workers is around $\frac{2}{3}$ gives an estimate of α of around $\frac{1}{3}$. Is there an empirical observation that could be used to give an impression of the magnitude of φ? Mankiw, Romer and Weil suggest one in their paper. It may not give as firm a determination of φ as the relatively constant labour share does for α, but it does give *some* impression of the magnitude of φ. In US manufacturing the average wage has typically been around twice the minimum wage, perhaps somewhat larger. If we can interpret the minimum wage as the compensation for labour without education, and the average wage as the compensation for raw labour endowed with average education, this suggests that around one half of what a typical worker earns is really a compensation of raw labour, and the other half is a return to human capital. The income shares of physical capital, human capital and raw labour would then all be around $\frac{1}{3}$, with both of the two latter shares going to workers. Consider again the production function (1). It is evident that had we assumed that there was a separate market for the services of human capital with marginal product compensation, etc., then the implied income share of human capital would have been φ. If the share of human capital of $\frac{1}{3}$ computed above can be equalized with this implied share, then φ should be around $\frac{1}{3}$. Therefore, a realistic calibration of parameters could be that both α and φ, and hence $1 - \alpha - \varphi$, are around $\frac{1}{3}$.

Note that this calibration makes human capital as productive as physical capital in aggregate production. Omitting human capital may be a major source of error.

The accumulation of human capital

Each of the L_t households supplies one unit of labour inelastically in period t, and supplies all accumulated physical capital as long as the real rental rate, r_t, is positive. Again the number of households is assumed to change by an exogenous rate, n, where $n > -1$.

The representative consumer must decide how much to consume, C_t, and hence how much to save, $S_t = Y_t - C_t$, but this time also how to distribute total savings between gross investment in physical capital, I_t^K, and gross investment in human capital, I_t^H. Given these gross investments, the evolution in the capital stocks are:

$$K_{t+1} - K_t = I_t^K - \delta K_t, \qquad 0 \ll 1 \tag{7}$$

$$H_{t+1} - H_t = I_t^H - \delta H_t, \qquad 0 \ll 1 \tag{8}$$

where we have assumed that physical and human capital depreciate at the same rate. The intertemporal budget constraint that the choices of C_t (or S_t), I_t^K and I_t^H must obey, given Y_t, is:

$$I_t^K + I_t^H = Y_t - C_t = S_t. \tag{9}$$

Again we do not consider any explicit dynamic optimization, but simply assume that the results of the consumers' decisions are that a given and constant fraction, s_K, of income is invested in physical capital:

$$I_t^K = s_K Y_t, \quad 0 < s_K < 1, \tag{10}$$

and a given fraction, s_H, is invested in human capital:

$$I_t^H = s_H Y_t, \quad 0 < s_H < 1. \tag{11}$$

Hence from (9), $S_t = (s_K + s_H)Y_t$ and $C_t = (1 - s_K - s_H)Y_t$.[2] We assume $s_K + s_H < 1$.

The complete model

Since we have now described all the new model elements, we can write down the complete model consisting of the seven equations below. The first is the production function repeated from (1) above. The next two are the expressions for the factor prices, also derived above in (3) and (4). The following two are the capital accumulation equations that follow from (7) and (8) above with the assumed investment behaviour, (10) and (11), inserted. The last two equations contain the assumptions of given exogenous rates of change in labour force and technology, respectively.

---

2. The way we define consumption here does not correspond exactly to the usual national accounts definition where consumption is the excess of GDP over investment in *physical* capital only (and net exports).

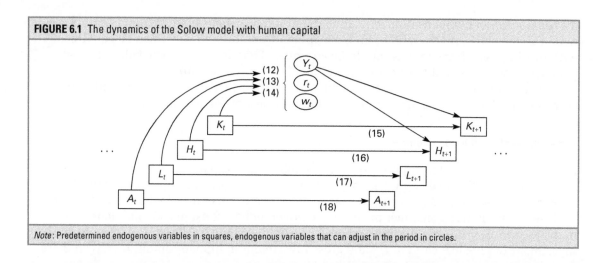

FIGURE 6.1 The dynamics of the Solow model with human capital

Note: Predetermined endogenous variables in squares, endogenous variables that can adjust in the period in circles.

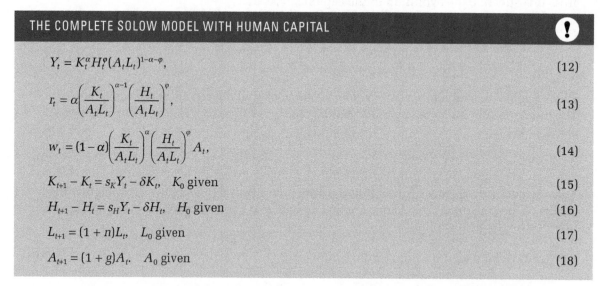

THE COMPLETE SOLOW MODEL WITH HUMAN CAPITAL

$$Y_t = K_t^{\alpha} H_t^{\varphi}(A_t L_t)^{1-\alpha-\varphi}, \tag{12}$$

$$r_t = \alpha\left(\frac{K_t}{A_t L_t}\right)^{\alpha-1}\left(\frac{H_t}{A_t L_t}\right)^{\varphi}, \tag{13}$$

$$w_t = (1-\alpha)\left(\frac{K_t}{A_t L_t}\right)^{\alpha}\left(\frac{H_t}{A_t L_t}\right)^{\varphi} A_t, \tag{14}$$

$$K_{t+1} - K_t = s_K Y_t - \delta K_t, \quad K_0 \text{ given} \tag{15}$$

$$H_{t+1} - H_t = s_H Y_t - \delta H_t, \quad H_0 \text{ given} \tag{16}$$

$$L_{t+1} = (1+n)L_t, \quad L_0 \text{ given} \tag{17}$$

$$A_{t+1} = (1+g)A_t. \quad A_0 \text{ given} \tag{18}$$

The parameters of the model are α, φ, s_K, s_H, δ, n, g. Given initial values, K_0, H_0, L_0, A_0, of the state variables, the model will determine the dynamic evolution of the economy as illustrated in Fig. 6.1.

The model is a *generalization* of the Solow model. If we set $\varphi = 0$, and consequently drop Eq. (16), the model of Chapter 5 appears (now denoting by s_K what was called s in Chapter 5). And if we also set $g = 0$, the basic Solow model of Chapter 3 appears. Just as in Chapter 5 we assume that $n + g + \delta + ng > 0$.

The law of motion

To analyse the Solow model with human capital it is again convenient to define 'technology adjusted' variables, physical capital per effective worker, $\tilde{k}_t \equiv k_t/A_t = K_t/(A_t L_t)$, human capital per effective worker, $\tilde{h}_t \equiv h_t/A_t = H_t/(A_t L_t)$, and output per effective worker, $\tilde{y}_t \equiv y_t/A_t = Y_t/(A_t L_t)$. Dividing both sides of (12) by $A_t L_t$ gives:

$$\tilde{y}_t = \tilde{k}_t^{\alpha} \tilde{h}_t^{\varphi}. \tag{19}$$

Writing the capital accumulation equations, (15) and (16), as $K_{t+1} = s_K Y_t + (1-\delta)K_t$ and $H_{t+1} = s_H Y_t + (1-\delta)H_t$, and dividing by $A_{t+1}L_{t+1}$ on both sides in each of them gives:

$$\tilde{k}_{t+1} = \frac{1}{(1+n)(1+g)}(s_K \tilde{y}_t + (1-\delta)\tilde{k}_t),$$

$$\tilde{h}_{t+1} = \frac{1}{(1+n)(1+g)}(s_H \tilde{y}_t + (1-\delta)\tilde{h}_t).$$

Inserting into these the expression for $\tilde{y}_t$ in (19) gives a law of motion for $\tilde{k}_t$ and $\tilde{h}_t$ consisting of the following two equations:

$$\tilde{k}_{t+1} = \frac{1}{(1+n)(1+g)}(s_K \tilde{k}_t^\alpha \tilde{h}_t^\varphi + (1-\delta)\tilde{k}_t), \qquad (20)$$

$$\tilde{h}_{t+1} = \frac{1}{(1+n)(1+g)}(s_H \tilde{k}_t^\alpha \tilde{h}_t^\varphi + (1-\delta)\tilde{h}_t). \qquad (21)$$

This law of motion is a bit more complicated than the transition equations you have seen before, since it consists of two coupled first-order difference equations (or a two-dimensional system of first-order difference equations). Given K_0, H_0, L_0, A_0 one can compute $\tilde{k}_0 = K_0/(A_0 L_0)$ and $\tilde{h}_0 = H_0/(A_0 L_0)$. Then $\tilde{k}_1$ can be computed from (20) and $\tilde{h}_1$ from (21). These two values can again be inserted into (20) and (21) to compute $\tilde{k}_2$ and $\tilde{h}_2$, etc. In this way the full sequences, $(\tilde{k}_t)$ and $(\tilde{h}_t)$, are determined. The new feature is that in each period t, the next $\tilde{k}_{t+1}$ depends on both $\tilde{k}_t$ and $\tilde{h}_t$, and likewise for $\tilde{h}_{t+1}$.

Given the sequences $(\tilde{k}_t)$ and $(\tilde{h}_t)$, the sequence $(\tilde{y}_t)$ follows from (19). The associated sequence (y_t) for GDP per worker follows from $y_t = \tilde{y}_t A_t$:

$$y_t = (1+g)^t A_0 \tilde{k}_t^\alpha \tilde{h}_t^\phi,$$

and the sequence (c_t) for consumption per worker follows from $c_t = (1 - s_K - s_H)y_t$, etc.

This time there is no simple diagrammatic way to demonstrate global convergence to a steady state. In fact, providing a global stability analysis of a two-dimensional system of *non-linear* difference equations is not easy. In the following we will limit ourselves to demonstrating convergence towards a steady state of the system (20) and (21) by doing a numerical simulation for realistic parameter values (and an exercise will ask you to do several more such simulations to check convergence), and by considering the linearization of the system around steady state to show convergence to steady state for the linearized system.

Before doing so we will *assume* stability and study the steady state in detail and develop a diagram that is useful for comparative analysis.

6.2 Steady state and comparative analysis in the Solow model with human capital

One can compute the steady state without first having established convergence to it over time. By definition a steady state is an economically meaningful 'resting point' for the dynamic system considered, in this case, two particular positive values for $\tilde{k}_t$ and $\tilde{h}_t$, which are such that if these values are ever reached, the economy stays at them forever.

The key endogenous variables in steady state

For the computation of steady state and for comparative static analysis it is convenient first to rewrite (20) and (21) as 'Solow equations' by subtracting $\tilde{k}_t$ from both sides of the first equation and $\tilde{h}_t$ from both sides of the second one:

$$\tilde{k}_{t+1} - \tilde{k}_t = \frac{1}{(1+n)(1+g)}(s_K \tilde{k}_t^\alpha \tilde{h}_t^\varphi - (n+g+\delta+ng)\tilde{k}_t), \tag{22}$$

$$\tilde{h}_{t+1} - \tilde{h}_t = \frac{1}{(1+n)(1+g)}(s_H \tilde{k}_t^\alpha \tilde{h}_t^\varphi - (n+g+\delta+ng)\tilde{h}_t). \tag{23}$$

A steady state is then a positive solution in $\tilde{k}_t$ and $\tilde{h}_t$ to the two equations that appear by setting the left-hand sides equal to zero:

$$s_K \tilde{k}_t^\alpha \tilde{h}_t^\varphi - (n+g+\delta+ng)\tilde{k}_t = 0, \tag{24}$$

$$s_H \tilde{k}_t^\alpha \tilde{h}_t^\varphi - (n+g+\delta+ng)\tilde{h}_t = 0. \tag{25}$$

Indicating the solution by an asterisk one has:

$$\tilde{k}^* = \left(\frac{s_K^{1-\varphi} s_H^\varphi}{n+g+\delta+ng}\right)^{\frac{1}{(1-\alpha-\varphi)}}, \tag{26}$$

$$\tilde{h}^* = \left(\frac{s_K^\alpha s_H^{1-\alpha}}{n+g+\delta+ng}\right)^{\frac{1}{(1-\alpha-\varphi)}}, \tag{27}$$

from which, also using (19), the steady state value for output per effective worker is:

$$\tilde{y}^* = \left(\frac{s_K^{1-\varphi} s_H^\varphi}{n+g+\delta+ng}\right)^{\frac{\alpha}{(1-\alpha-\varphi)}} \left(\frac{s_K^{1-\alpha} s_H^\alpha}{n+g+\delta+ng}\right)^{\frac{\varphi}{(1-\alpha-\varphi)}}$$

$$= \left(\frac{s_K}{n+g+\delta+ng}\right)^{\frac{\alpha}{(1-\alpha-\varphi)}} \left(\frac{s_H}{n+g+\delta+ng}\right)^{\frac{\varphi}{(1-\alpha-\varphi)}}. \tag{28}$$

(As an exercise, do the derivations leading to the second equality.) We assume, realistically, that $n+g+\delta > 0$, so all expressions above and below are meaningful.

With the constant steady state values of the technology-adjusted variables in hand, we can find the steady state growth paths of the more interesting variables such as k_t, h_t and y_t. For instance, from $y_t = \tilde{y}_t A_t$, it follows that in steady state:

$$y_t^* = A_t \left(\frac{s_K}{n+g+\delta+ng}\right)^{\frac{\alpha}{(1-\alpha-\varphi)}} \left(\frac{s_H}{n+g+\delta+ng}\right)^{\frac{\varphi}{(1-\alpha-\varphi)}}, \tag{29}$$

where A_t is growing according to $A_0(1+g)^t$. Likewise, since $c_t = (1 - s_K - s_H)y_t$, the growth path for consumption per worker in steady state is:

$$c_t^* = A_0(1+g)^t(1-s_K-s_H) \cdot \left(\frac{s_K}{n+g+\delta+ng}\right)^{\frac{\alpha}{(1-\alpha-\varphi)}} \left(\frac{s_H}{n+g+\delta+ng}\right)^{\frac{\varphi}{(1-\alpha-\varphi)}}. \tag{30}$$

Note from (29) that the exponent $\alpha/(1-\alpha-\varphi)$ is the elasticity of y_t^* with respect to s_K (show this), and this elasticity is larger than the $\alpha/(1-\alpha)$ of the general Solow model. This is as we wanted and it is due to the effect described in the introduction to this chapter. A higher s_K gives higher GDP per worker in steady state because of greater physical capital accumulation, but the increased GDP per worker now also generates more human capital per worker, reinforcing the increase in GDP per worker.

Notice also that the influence of n on y_t is now stronger than the influence of s_K (and of s_H), since n appears in both of the parentheses in (29). Disregarding the small product ng, the elasticity of y_t with respect to $(n + g + \delta)$ is $-(\alpha + \varphi)/(1 - \alpha - \varphi)$ (show this), which is larger in absolute value than both of the elasticities appearing directly as exponents in (29). The reason is that increased population growth now gives a thinning out of *both* physical *and* human capital. This feature, that the rate of population growth affects GDP per worker more strongly than investment rates, is consistent with the empirical evidence, as you will be asked to verify in an exercise.

STEADY STATE   ❗

According to the steady state of the Solow model with human capital, the elasticity of long-run income per capita with respect to the investment rate s_K in physical capital is $\alpha/(1 - \alpha - \varphi)$, with respect to the investment rate s_H in human capital it is $\varphi/(1 - \alpha - \varphi)$, and with respect to $n + g + \delta$, it is $-(\alpha + \varphi)/(1 - \alpha - \varphi)$. The two first elasticities should both be around one, and the last one should be around minus two, given reasonable parameter values, $\alpha = \varphi = \frac{1}{3}$.

The phase diagram and comparative analysis

Consider again the two equations (24) and (25) from which we computed the steady state. The first of these gives the restriction on $\tilde{k}_t, \tilde{h}_t$ that follows from requiring $\tilde{k}_{t+1} - \tilde{k}_t = 0$, or in other words, it gives all the combinations of $\tilde{k}_t, \tilde{h}_t$ such that $\tilde{k}_t$ stays unchanged. We can draw these combinations in a $\tilde{k}_t, \tilde{h}_t$ diagram (see the curve labelled $[\Delta \tilde{k}_t = 0]$ in Fig. 6.2). You should check by isolating $\tilde{h}_t$ from (24) that indeed this curve should look like a $\tilde{k}_t^2$ function in the $\tilde{k}_t, \tilde{h}_t$ diagram for realistic parameter values (e.g., $\alpha = \varphi = \frac{1}{3}$). Likewise, (25) gives all the combinations of $\tilde{k}_t, \tilde{h}_t$ such that $\tilde{h}_t$ stays unchanged, and the curve for it, $[\Delta \tilde{h}_t = 0]$ in Fig. 6.2, should look like a $\sqrt{\tilde{k}_t}$ function (demonstrate this). The steady state combination, $\tilde{k}^*, \tilde{h}^*$, is where the two curves intersect.

It is also easy to see from (22) that for every combination of $\tilde{k}_t, \tilde{h}_t$ above the curve $[\Delta \tilde{k}_t = 0]$, one has $\tilde{k}_{t+1} - \tilde{k}_t > 0$, so in this area $\tilde{k}_t$ must be increasing, while below the same curve it must be decreasing as indicated by arrows. Likewise, everywhere to the right of the curve $[\Delta \tilde{h}_t = 0]$

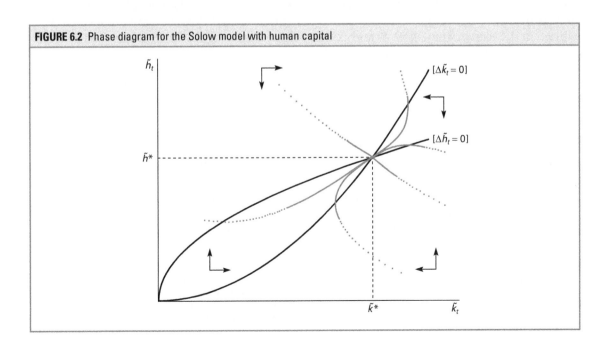

FIGURE 6.2 Phase diagram for the Solow model with human capital

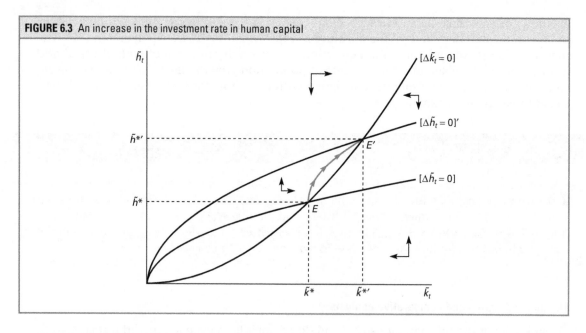

FIGURE 6.3 An increase in the investment rate in human capital

one has from (23) that $\tilde{h}_{t+1} - \tilde{h}_t > 0$, so in this area $\tilde{h}_t$ increases over time, while to the left of the curve, $\tilde{h}_t$ decreases as indicated by arrows.

From initial points $\tilde{k}_0$, $\tilde{h}_0$, like the alternative points shown in Fig. 6.2, $\tilde{k}_t$, $\tilde{h}_t$ will move along the trajectories as illustrated. These trajectories must respect the directions of change indicated by the arrows in the different regions. As Fig. 6.2 is drawn it suggests convergence to the steady state, but we emphasize that this does not follow just from the figure.

Figure 6.2 is called a phase diagram and it is useful for comparative analysis. Assume, for instance, that the economy is initially in steady state as illustrated by the intersection point E between the two curves $[\Delta\tilde{k}_t = 0]$ and $[\Delta\tilde{h}_t = 0]$ in Fig. 6.3. Suppose then that the investment rate in human capital, s_H, increases permanently, while the other parameters remain the same. You will easily show that this implies that the curve corresponding to unchanged $\tilde{h}_t$ shifts upwards as illustrated by $[\Delta\tilde{h}_t = 0]'$ in Fig. 6.3. As the phase diagram has now changed, the old steady state point E will be situated exactly on a boundary between two regions, and on this boundary $\tilde{k}_t$ does not change while $\tilde{h}_t$ increases. Once $\tilde{h}_t$ has increased, the economy will be in the region where both $\tilde{k}_t$ and $\tilde{h}_t$ increase and there could be convergence to the new steady state E' along the trajectory indicated.[3]

What happens is that the increased s_H in the very beginning implies more accumulation of human capital (and only that), but as soon as the increased stock of human capital begins to generate increases in output, more physical capital will also be accumulated because of the constant rate of investment in physical capital. This explains why, along the indicated trajectory, both $\tilde{k}_t$ and $\tilde{h}_t$ increase.

During the transition to the new steady state both $\tilde{k}_t$ and $\tilde{h}_t$ increase, so $\tilde{y}_t = \tilde{k}_t^\alpha \tilde{h}_t^\varphi$ must be increasing. Since $\tilde{y}_t = y_t/A_t$, output per worker, y_t, must, during the transition, be increasing at a rate which is larger than g, but which falls back towards g as the new steady state is approached. The jump in the growth rate of y_t caused by the increase in s_H is thus much like the growth jump caused by an increased s_K in the general Solow model. An exercise will ask you to do simulations suggesting that responses to parameter changes do have the 'growth jump character'.

---

3. Note that we are assuming that the initial jump upwards in $\tilde{h}_t$ is not so big that one ends in the upper region where $\tilde{k}_t$ is increasing and $\tilde{h}_t$ is decreasing. The (theoretical) possibility of such 'big jumps' is one reason why stability analysis is difficult here. Exercises will ask you to do numerical simulations that suggest that, for realistic parameter values, there will not be such big jumps, so the reaction to a parameter change is indeed as indicated by the grey curve in Fig. 6.3.

Empirics for steady state

To test the model's steady state prediction empirically, first take logs on both sides of (29) and use $ng \approx 0$:

$$\ln y_t^* \approx \ln A_t + \frac{\alpha}{1-\alpha-\varphi}[\ln s_K - \ln(n+g+\delta)] + \frac{\varphi}{1-\alpha-\varphi}[\ln s_H - \ln(n+g+\delta)]. \tag{31}$$

The relationship between $\ln y_t^*$ and the two explanatory variables, $[\ln s_K - \ln(n+g+\delta)]$ and $[\ln s_H - \ln(n+g+\delta)]$, is a linear one, and the relationship generalizes the one found in the general Solow model, the latter appearing by setting $\varphi = 0$. As already observed, if both α and φ are around $\frac{1}{3}$, then both the coefficients (or elasticities) in (31) should be around one.

With data for GDP per worker across countries i in year 2003 as well as data for s_K^i, s_H^i, and n^i, one will be able to estimate the regression equation:

$$\ln y_{03}^i = \gamma_0 + \gamma_1[\ln s_K^i - \ln(n^i + 0.075)] + \gamma_2[\ln s_H^i - \ln(n^i + 0.075)] + \xi^i, \tag{32}$$

suggested by the theoretical equation (31). The formulation of (32) assumes the same technological level A_{03} in year 2003 in all countries considered, the same technical parameters α and φ, as well as the same technological growth rate, g, and depreciation rate, δ. You may think these are heroic assumptions and we will discuss them further below.

We will consider the representative sample of 65 countries that we have used throughout Chapters 2, 3 and 5, and for which we have good data for y_{00}^i, s_K^i and n^i from the PWT 6.2. As before, we will for s_K^i use the average gross investment rate in physical capital between 1960 and 2003, and for n^i the average growth rate of the labour force between 1960 and 2003. But how can we get data for the investment rate, s_H, in human capital? This is required for an estimation of (32) and hence for testing the steady state prediction of our model.

In some countries most education costs are paid for by local and central public authorities, and for such countries one might consider measuring s_H as public expenditure on education divided by GDP. There are two problems with this. In many other countries much educational expenditure is paid privately, and in all countries the main part of the investment in education that consists of forgone income during education is paid privately. This leads to the idea of measuring s_H by a fraction that has as its denominator the GDP that *could* have been produced if all people of working age, including those in education, participated in production, and as its numerator, has the GDP that is *not* being produced because some people are in education. This fraction, the GDP lost due to education relative to potential GDP, would not include direct expenditure on education, but if this can be assumed to vary proportionally to lost GDP, one would have a good proxy.

It is not easy to get data for the fraction just described, but the fraction of people of working age in education to all people of working age should have a close relationship to it. The data available are such that even this latter fraction cannot be obtained directly. One *can*, however, get data across countries for the fraction of all people of school age (12–17) who attend secondary school. If we use this fraction as a proxy for the 'degree of education' among those who are of school age in a country, we can compensate for differences in the compositions of populations by multiplying it by the fraction of all people of working age who are of school age. For the latter we use the fraction of people between 15 and 19 to all people of working age (again because of available data). Our proxy for s_H is thus 'the fraction of the school age population (12–17) attending secondary school times the fraction of the working age population that is of secondary school age (15–19)'. This is how the investment rates, s_H^i, reported in Table A across countries, i, are computed (averaged over the years 1960, 1965, . . . , 1995).[4]

---

4. Our figures for s_H are taken from the data set from Ben S. Bernanke and Refet S. Gürkaynak, 'Is Growth Exogenous? Taking Mankiw, Romer, and Weil Seriously', NBER Working Paper 8365, July 2001.

TABLE 6.1 Steady state regressions

	Dependent variable: log of real GDP per worker, 2003 ($\ln y_{03}$)	
Model:	Solow model without human capital	Solow model with human capital
Observations:	65	65
Explanatory Variables:		
Constant	8.92	9.82
$\ln s_K - \ln(n + 0.075)$	1.52 (0.14)	0.59 (0.18)
$\ln s_H - \ln(n + 0.075)$		0.93 (0.14)
Adjusted R^2	0.63	0.79
Implied values:		
α	0.60	0.23
φ	–	0.37

Note: Standard errors in parenthesis.

Source: Estimations based on Table A.

These rates are not correct measures with respect to their levels since they ignore direct expenditure on education, but if a correct measure could be assumed to be a constant times s_H^i, the constant being the same in all countries, then with the rates, s_H^i, as defined, we would arrive at the correct *relative* investment rates between countries. In the regression equation (32) the log of this constant times γ_2 would enter the intercept variable, γ_0, by the same amount for all countries. Hence, an estimation of (32) based on the investment rates in human capital defined should give correct estimates of γ_1 and γ_2.

The procedure described can deliver data for s_H^i for the 65 countries of our sample. An OLS estimation of (32) across these countries gives:

$$\ln y_{03}^i = 9.82 + \underset{(se=0.18)}{0.59} [\ln s_K^i - \ln(n^i + 0.075)] + \underset{(se=0.14)}{0.93} [\ln s_H^i - \ln(n^i + 0.075)], \qquad (33)$$
$$\text{adj. } R^2 = 0.79,$$

where standard errors are indicated in parentheses below the estimates. This estimation is, in important respects, better than the corresponding one for the Solow model reported just after Fig. 5.7. For comparison we have included both regressions in Table 6.1 above, thereby also showing to you a way that multiple regressions are often presented.

The adjusted R^2, indicating the fraction of the cross-country variation in GDP per worker explained by the equation, has increased from 0.63 to 0.79. It is indeed impressive that the simple equation we are considering should explain 79 per cent of the per capita income variation in the world. Yet, the increase in R^2 is not the main reason for considering the present equation and estimation an improved one.

The main reason is that the sizes of the estimated parameters, the 0.59 and 0.93, respectively, are now in much better accordance with the values we would expect based on the empirical observations that suggest an α of around $\frac{1}{3}$, and (with less precision) a φ also around $\frac{1}{3}$. As mentioned, this implies a hypothesis that the coefficients, γ_1 and γ_2, are of equal size and both around one. Our estimates of γ_1 and γ_2 are not exactly equal and only the estimate of γ_2 is truly close to one, but taking uncertainty into account, one cannot reject the hypothesis considered. The 95 per cent confidence intervals for γ_1 and γ_2 (each of which goes approximately from two standard deviations below to two standard deviations above the estimate) overlap and the interval for γ_1 reaches up close to one.[5] Note that a similar accordance between theoretical and estimated values cannot be obtained for the γ of the Solow model considered in Chapter 5. The estimate was 1.52 with the 95 per cent confidence interval going down to 1.23, which is still far from the theoretical value for γ of 0.5.

Another way to illustrate the better accordance with the theory is to compute the estimates of α and φ implied by the estimates of γ_1 and γ_2. Since γ_1 should be $\alpha/(1 - \alpha - \varphi)$, and γ_2 should be $\varphi/(1 - \alpha - \varphi)$, we have two equations in two unknowns that can easily be solved to find:

$$\alpha = \frac{\gamma_1}{1 + \gamma_1 + \gamma_2} \qquad \text{and} \qquad \varphi = \frac{\gamma_2}{1 + \gamma_1 + \gamma_2}.$$

Inserting the estimated values for γ_1 and γ_2 gives, as also reported in Table 6.1, $\alpha = 0.23$ and $\varphi = 0.37$, which are not too far from the 'correct' values of *around* $\frac{1}{3}$ and $\frac{1}{3}$.

We can also give a graphical illustration of the improvement in our model obtained by including human capital. Consider first the steady state equation of the Solow model *without* human capital arising by setting $\varphi = 0$ (still using $ng \cong 0$):

$$\ln y_t^* = \ln A_t + \frac{\alpha}{1 - \alpha}[\ln s_K - \ln(n + g + \delta)].$$

We tested this in Chapter 5 by plotting $\ln y_{00}^i$ against $\ln s_K^i - \ln(n^i + 0.075)$, finding a nice linear relationship, but not with a slope of 0.5 as it should be. We could also have chosen to plot $\ln y_{00}^i$ against $0.5[\ln s_K^i - \ln(n^i + 0.075)]$, the difference being the addition of the factor 0.5. Assuming a value of $\frac{1}{3}$ for capital's share, α, the plotted points should be close to a straight line *with a slope of one* for the model without human capital to be correct. Fig. 6.4 shows the plot for the 65 countries of our sample. The grey line is an OLS regression line through the observations. The black one is a straight line with the same intercept as the grey one and with a slope of one. The figure shows that the data points may be situated along a straight line, but not along one with a slope of one.

Doing the same kind of graphical test for the Solow model *with* human capital consists of plotting $\ln y_{00}^i$ against $[\ln s_K^i - \ln(n^i + 0.075)] + [\ln s_H^i - \ln(n^i + 0.075)]$, where we have set both coefficients at one, which follows from $\alpha = \varphi = \frac{1}{3}$. The result is shown in Fig. 6.5. Compared to Fig. 6.4, the points are now clustered around a grey OLS line that has a slope that is relatively close to one (like the black line). To conclude:

STEADY STATE AND THE CROSS-COUNTRY EMPIRICAL EVIDENCE

The steady state prediction of the Solow model with human capital accords remarkably well with cross-country empirical evidence even under an assumption of a common technological level. We have explained about four-fifths of the cross-country variation in GDP per worker using a few explanatory variables, s_K, s_H and n, which have been constrained to appear in our regression equation as required by our theoretical model.

The good fit of Fig. 6.5 does not *prove* that the Solow model with human capital is correct. As warned also in Chapter 5, the problem of 'reversed causality' could be relevant here: is it really s_K, s_H and n that explain y, as the model assumes, or is it rather a high y that generates high values of s_K and s_H, and a low n? Or Fig. 6.5 could be a reflection of 'spurious

5. By including a bit of uncertainty with respect to the true values of α and φ, the accordance can be made even better. Based on empirical observations we can only say that α and φ should be *around* $\frac{1}{3}$. If they were both 0.3 say (rather than 0.333 . . .), then both of γ_1 and γ_2 should be 0.75, which is in both 95 per cent confidence intervals.

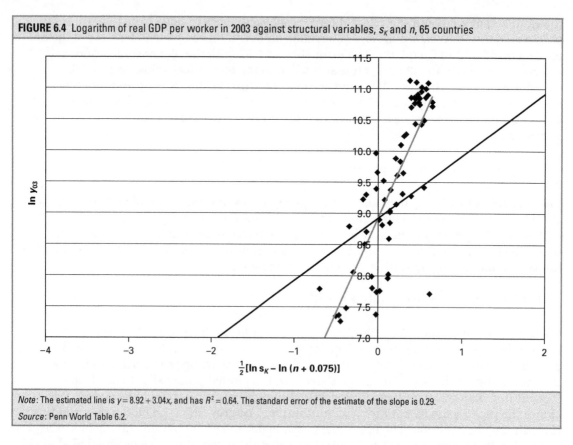

FIGURE 6.4 Logarithm of real GDP per worker in 2003 against structural variables, s_K and n, 65 countries

Note: The estimated line is $y = 8.92 + 3.04x$, and has $R^2 = 0.64$. The standard error of the estimate of the slope is 0.29.

Source: Penn World Table 6.2.

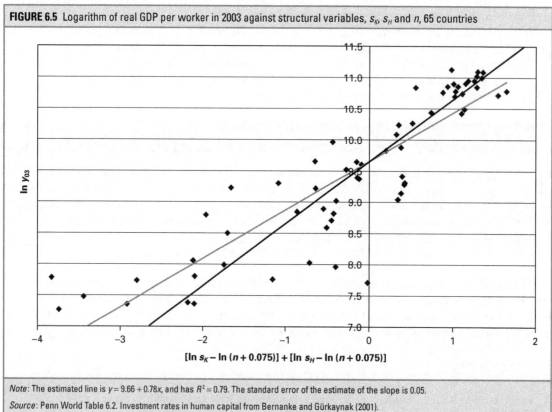

FIGURE 6.5 Logarithm of real GDP per worker in 2003 against structural variables, s_K, s_H and n, 65 countries

Note: The estimated line is $y = 9.66 + 0.78x$, and has $R^2 = 0.79$. The standard error of the estimate of the slope is 0.05.

Source: Penn World Table 6.2. Investment rates in human capital from Bernanke and Gürkaynak (2001).

correlation' where it is really omitted factors that cause s_K, s_H, n and y to move in a way that creates the correlation observed. Nevertheless, it is certainly reassuring for the model that its prediction fits the data so well.

The estimations and discussion above assume a common technological level, A_{03}, in 2003 among the countries considered. It is an important detail that this assumption does not seem to be strongly contradicted by the evidence: the points in Fig. 6.5 *do* seem to be situated along one and the same straight line with a slope close to one and this *is* evidence in favour of a common A_{03}. It may be surprising that in explaining the income differences in the world we do not necessarily have to rely strongly on 'technological differences', but can, to a large degree, see income differences as reflections of differences in investment rates and labour force growth rates. In other words, the income differences seem to a large extent to be explained by differences in the *amounts* of inputs (physical and human capital per worker), whereas differences in the *productivities* of these inputs appear to be less important. A rough way to state this conclusion (or hypothesis) is that computers and education in poorer countries are as advanced as in richer countries, there are just fewer computers and less education per capita in the poorer countries because of lower investment rates and higher population growth rates. In Section 6.4 below we return to this issue and investigate further how important 'technological differences' are in understanding the difference between rich and poor.

Structural policy for steady state

Since the model's steady state prediction fits as well as it does with the evidence, one can feel somewhat safe in using the model for recommendations concerning long-run structural policies. With respect to policies intended to affect investment rates in physical capital and population growth rates, the conclusions go in the same direction as in previous chapters. The present model may be more correct with respect to the sizes of the underlying elasticities, which is important for policy, but qualitatively the policy implications are not affected. It is worth repeating, however, that according to the present model, the elasticity of GDP per person with respect to population growth (or rather to $n + g + \delta$) is larger in absolute value than each of the elasticities with respect to the investment rates, s_K and s_H.

It is with respect to investment in human capital that the model may have new policy implications. First, note that according to (29), steady state GDP per worker is unambiguously increasing in the investment rate s_H, and according to the model as well as to the empirics investment in human capital seems to be at least as important for GDP per worker as investment in physical capital. This means that more investment in education may have desirable effects, but not under all circumstances. First, given the model's other parameters, the 'golden rule' values for s_K and s_H that will maximize the altitude of the growth path for consumption per worker are $s_K = \alpha$ and $s_H = \varphi$ (an exercise will ask you to show this). Raising the investment rates above these values is not meaningful.

Second, a public policy to provide for or subsidize education should be justified by specific reasons why leaving educational decisions to private individuals cannot be expected to yield optimal outcomes. In the case of education there are many such reasons. One is imperfect credit markets. If education were a completely private matter, people who would like to educate themselves would have to borrow money against their expected higher future labour incomes to provide for the costs of education and to compensate for the forgone income during education. However, there are strict limits to how much private banks will lend to a (poor) person based on this person's expected future income, for instance due to problems of 'adverse selection': a bank would probably be perfectly ready to lend to the able and honest people who will actually come to earn more and be able and willing to pay back after education, but not to other people. It may, however, be difficult for the bank to distinguish between the two types of people and therefore it will be reluctant to lend for educational purposes at all.

Another reason is imperfect insurance markets. More education does not yield a specific increase in future income with certainty, but rather with some probability. A decision on education may fail, so connected to education is an insurance problem. Few private insurance companies are prepared to sell insurance policies that pay out money in cases of failed education, this time due to 'moral hazard' problems: a person who is well insured against the event of failed education will not have so strong an incentive to work hard for making education a success since there will be payout under all circumstances. Therefore insurance companies will be reluctant to insure against failed education.

There are probably also strong positive externalities associated with education. Part of the return on an investment in education goes to other people. For instance, an engineer in a private firm is more productive if the other employees in the firm can read and write and do calculations. This means that part of the social return to the education invested in these employees appears as higher productivity of the engineer and is not appropriated by those who acquired the education. If left to private decisions, people will therefore probably educate themselves too little as compared to a social optimum.

The microeconomic arguments in favour of subsidizing education that we have presented are not part of the human capital growth model studied in this chapter, but the strong effects of investment in education that the model and the empirics point to indicate that these arguments are not just of academic interest. They are probably of interest quantitatively as well.

In any case, the issues of how and to what extent to provide for and subsidize education are among the most important concerns of public policy.

6.3 Convergence in the Solow model with human capital[6]

The steady state of the Solow model with human capital accords in all respects with positive balanced growth if $g > 0$. It is left to you as an exercise to demonstrate this in detail, but note that since $\tilde{k}_t$, $\tilde{h}_t$ and $\tilde{y}_t$ are all locked at constant values in steady state, k_t, h_t and y_t must all be increasing at the same rate as A_t, that is, at rate g.

The Solow model with human capital thus passes the 'long-run empirical growth check', but this time we have not shown that the steady state equilibrium is stable. Taking stability for granted (for the time being), as the economy converges to steady state there will be transitory growth in addition to the underlying technological growth, and the transitory growth seems to be more complicated than in the general Solow model since there are now two state variables, $\tilde{k}_t$ and $\tilde{h}_t$, in the dynamic system. For instance, outside steady state one variable could be below and the other one above its steady state value.

By conducting a numerical simulation exercise with the system (20) and (21), we will start by indicating that this system *does* imply convergence to steady state. We will then study the linear approximation of the system around steady state. Although this is a *two-dimensional* linear difference equation in $\tilde{k}_t$ and $\tilde{h}_t$, it turns out that it implies a one-dimensional linear difference equation in $\tilde{y}_t$, which has the same form as the corresponding equation for the general Solow model. This has three implications. First, the convergence process in terms of $\tilde{y}_t$ is like the one we have studied for the general Solow model: the model with human capital also supports conditional convergence. Second, we can show analytically that the linearized system is stable towards steady state. Third, we can test the convergence equation empirically and we will find that the rate of convergence predicted by the model is now in much better accordance with empirical evidence than was the case for the general Solow model.

---

6. Some readers may find this section difficult and it is possible to understand the remainder of the chapter and the book without reading it. Until the subsection 'The Convergence Process . . .' there should be no difficulties, however.

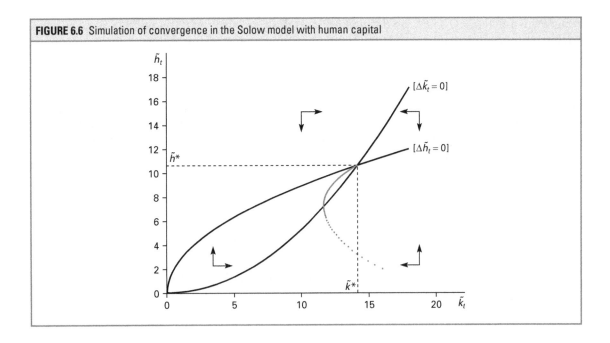

FIGURE 6.6 Simulation of convergence in the Solow model with human capital

Illustrating convergence to steady state by simulation

Let us specify some plausible parameter values: $\alpha = \varphi = \frac{1}{3}$, $s_K = 0.2$, $s_H = 0.15$, $\delta = 0.06$, $n = 0$ and $g = 0.015$. The steady state values $\tilde{k}^*$ and $\tilde{h}^*$ are easily computed from (26) and (27): $\tilde{k}^* = 14.22$ and $\tilde{h}^* = 10.67$. We consider a starting point where one of the state variables is above its steady state value and the other below: $\tilde{k}_0 = 16$ and $\tilde{h}_0 = 2$. Starting from these values we simulate the system (20) and (21) with the chosen parameter values. The result is shown in Fig. 6.6, a $\tilde{k}_t$, $\tilde{h}_t$ diagram where each dot corresponds to one period. The figure also has the two black curves $[\Delta \tilde{k}_t = 0]$ and $[\Delta \tilde{h}_t = 0]$, which makes it a phase diagram.

The sequence of dots in Fig. 6.6 converges to the steady state. An exercise will ask you to do simulations from other starting points and using other parameter combinations. You should find convergence to steady state. To construct Fig. 6.2 we actually simulated the model with alternative starting points and the same parameter values as considered here, so Fig. 6.2 contributes to the impression of general convergence and it suggests the type of picture you are supposed to find when you attempt the exercise.

CONVERGENCE TO STEADY STATE

The Solow model with human capital implies for reasonable parameter values convergence to the model's steady state. The steady state fulfils the requirements for balanced growth in all respects (Exercise 3).

The convergence process according to the Solow model with human capital

To obtain a linear approximation of the system (20) and (21), first write it in the generic form:

$$\tilde{k}_{t+1} = G(\tilde{k}_t, \tilde{h}_t),$$

$$\tilde{h}_{t+1} = L(\tilde{k}_t, \tilde{h}_t),$$

where the functions G and L are defined as the right-hand sides of (20) and (21), respectively. Linearizing around steady state turns the first of these equations into:

$$\tilde{k}_{t+1} - \tilde{k}^* = G_k(\tilde{k}^*, \tilde{h}^*)(\tilde{k}_t - \tilde{k}^*) + G_h(\tilde{k}^*, \tilde{h}^*)(\tilde{h}_t - \tilde{h}^*),$$

where G_k and G_h are the partial derivatives of G with respect to $\tilde{k}_t$ and $\tilde{h}_t$, respectively, and similarly for the other equation. If we use $\tilde{k}_{t+1} - \tilde{k}^* \cong \tilde{k}^*(\ln \tilde{k}_{t+1} - \ln \tilde{k}^*)$ etc. (just as in the previous chapter), we get that, *up to a linear approximation around steady state*, the system (20) and (21) is equivalent to:

$$\ln \tilde{k}_{t+1} - \ln \tilde{k}^* = G_k(\tilde{k}^*, \tilde{h}^*)(\ln \tilde{k}_t - \ln \tilde{k}^*) + \frac{\tilde{h}^*}{\tilde{k}^*}G_h(\tilde{k}^*, \tilde{h}^*)(\ln \tilde{h}_t - \ln \tilde{h}^*), \tag{34}$$

$$\ln \tilde{h}_{t+1} - \ln \tilde{h}^* = \frac{\tilde{k}^*}{\tilde{h}^*}L_k(\tilde{k}^*, \tilde{h}^*)(\ln \tilde{k}_t - \ln \tilde{k}^*) + L_h(\tilde{k}^*, \tilde{h}^*)(\ln \tilde{h}_t - \ln \tilde{h}^*). \tag{35}$$

This is a two-dimensional *linear* system of difference equations in the relative discrepancies (from steady state): $\ln \tilde{k}_t - \ln \tilde{k}^*$ and $\ln \tilde{h}_t - \ln \tilde{h}^*$. The coefficients in the system can be computed from the partial derivatives of G and L. Doing the differentiations and using $\tilde{y}^* = (\tilde{k}^*)^\alpha (\tilde{h}^*)^\varphi$ gives:

$$G_k(\tilde{k}^*, \tilde{h}^*) = R\left(s_K \alpha \frac{\tilde{y}^*}{\tilde{k}^*} + (1-\delta)\right), \qquad \frac{\tilde{h}^*}{\tilde{k}^*}G_h(\tilde{k}^*, \tilde{h}^*) = Rs_K \varphi \frac{\tilde{y}^*}{\tilde{k}^*},$$

$$\frac{\tilde{k}^*}{\tilde{h}^*}L_k(\tilde{k}^*, \tilde{h}^*) = Rs_H \alpha \frac{\tilde{y}^*}{\tilde{h}^*}, \qquad L_h(\tilde{k}^*, \tilde{h}^*) = R\left(s_H \varphi \frac{\tilde{y}^*}{\tilde{h}^*} + (1-\delta)\right),$$

where we have used R to denote $1/[(1+n)(1+g)]$. From the steady state expressions (26) to (28) we get:

$$\frac{\tilde{y}^*}{\tilde{k}^*} = \frac{n+g+\delta+ng}{s_K},$$

$$\frac{\tilde{y}^*}{\tilde{h}^*} = \frac{n+g+\delta+ng}{s_H},$$

$$\left(\frac{\tilde{k}^*}{\tilde{h}^*} = \frac{s_K}{s_H}\right).$$

Inserting into (34) and (35) then gives the linearized system:

$$\ln \tilde{k}_{t+1} - \ln \tilde{k}^* = R[\alpha(n+g+\delta+ng)+(1-\delta)](\ln \tilde{k}_t - \ln \tilde{k}^*) + R\varphi(n+g+\delta+ng)(\ln \tilde{h}_t - \ln \tilde{h}^*),$$

$$\ln \tilde{h}_{t+1} - \ln \tilde{h}^* = R\alpha(n+g+\delta+ng)(\ln \tilde{k}_t - \ln \tilde{k}^*) + R[\varphi(n+g+\delta+ng)+(1-\delta)](\ln \tilde{h}_t - \ln \tilde{h}^*).$$

It turns out that this system implies a specific one-dimensional and linear difference equation in $\ln \tilde{y}_t - \ln \tilde{y}^*$, to which we will limit our attention. From $\tilde{y}_t = \tilde{k}_t^\alpha \tilde{h}_t^\varphi$, it follows that in any period, $\ln \tilde{y}_t = \alpha \ln \tilde{k}_t + \varphi \ln \tilde{h}_t$. Hence, multiplying the first of the above two dynamic equations by α, and the second by φ, and then adding the two gives:

$$\ln \tilde{y}_{t+1} - \ln \tilde{y}^* = R[(\alpha+\varphi)(n+g+\delta+ng)+(1-\delta)]\alpha(\ln \tilde{k}_t - \ln \tilde{k}^*)$$
$$+ R[(\alpha+\varphi)(n+g+\delta+ng)+(1-\delta)]\varphi(\ln \tilde{h}_t - \ln \tilde{h}^*),$$

and then, moving the common factor on the right-hand side outside the bracket we get:

$$\ln \tilde{y}_{t+1} - \ln \tilde{y}^* = R[(\alpha + \varphi)(n + g + \delta + ng) + (1 - \delta)](\ln \tilde{y}_t - \ln \tilde{y}^*). \tag{36}$$

This is a first-order linear difference equation in $\ln \tilde{y}_t - \ln \tilde{y}^*$. The coefficient on the right-hand side is positive and you will easily (and should) verify that it is smaller than one if $\alpha + \varphi < 1$ and $n + g + \delta + ng > 0$, which are among our assumptions. Hence (36) implies stability, so according to it $\tilde{y}_t \to \tilde{y}^*$ as $t \to \infty$. You will recognize that (36) has exactly the same structure as (33) in Chapter 5.

Subtracting $\ln \tilde{y}_t$ and adding $\ln \tilde{y}^*$ on both sides of (36), and after that inserting for R gives:

$$\ln \tilde{y}_{t+1} - \ln \tilde{y}_t = \{1 - R[(\alpha + \phi)(n + g + \delta + ng) + (1 - \delta)]\}(\ln \tilde{y}^* - \ln \tilde{y}_t)$$

$$= \frac{(1+n)(1+g) - (\alpha + \varphi)(n + g + \delta + ng) - (1 - \delta)}{(1+n)(1+g)}(\ln \tilde{y}^* - \ln \tilde{y}_t),$$

which, using $(1 + n)(1 + g) - (1 - \delta) = n + g + \delta + ng$ (check) gives:

$$\ln \tilde{y}_{t+1} - \ln \tilde{y}_t = \frac{(1 - \alpha - \varphi)(n + g + \delta + ng)}{(1+n)(1+g)}(\ln \tilde{y}^* - \ln \tilde{y}_t). \tag{37}$$

Just as in Chapter 5, we have arrived at a dynamic equation of the form $\ln \tilde{y}_{t+1} - \ln \tilde{y}_t = \lambda(\ln \tilde{y}^* - \ln \tilde{y}_t)$, now with the rate of convergence:

$$\lambda = \frac{(1 - \alpha - \varphi)(n + g + \delta + ng)}{(1+n)(1+g)} \approx (1 - \alpha - \varphi)(n + g + \delta), \tag{38}$$

where $0 < \lambda < 1$ (since λ is one minus the coefficient we found above to be between zero and one). Consequently our dynamic equation, (37), has the convergence property, that the further below steady state the economy is, the larger is the growth rate of $\tilde{y}_t$, and hence of y_t. The model thus supports conditional convergence.

In Chapter 5 we found the solution to the dynamic equation, $\ln \tilde{y}_{t+1} - \ln \tilde{y}_t = \lambda(\ln \tilde{y}^* - \ln \tilde{y}_t)$, after having written it in the standard form, $\ln \tilde{y}_{t+1} = \lambda \ln \tilde{y}^* + (1 - \lambda)\ln \tilde{y}_t$ (equation (36) of Chapter 5), and applied a cookbook solution procedure. The solution we found was (38) of Chapter 5, repeated here:

$$\frac{\ln y_T - \ln y_0}{T} = \frac{\ln A_T - \ln A_0}{T} + \frac{1 - (1 - \lambda)^T}{T}(\ln A_0 + \ln \tilde{y}^* - \ln y_0).$$

Inserting the steady state value $\tilde{y}^*$ from (29) and $(\ln A_T - \ln A_0)/T \approx g$ we get:

$$\frac{\ln y_T - \ln y_0}{T} \approx g + \frac{1 - (1 - \lambda)^T}{T}\ln A_0 - \frac{1 - (1 - \lambda)^T}{T}\ln y_0$$

$$+ \frac{1 - (1 - \lambda)^T}{T}\frac{\alpha}{1 - \alpha - \varphi}[\ln s_K - \ln(n + g + \delta + ng)] \tag{39}$$

$$+ \frac{1 - (1 - \lambda)^T}{T}\frac{\varphi}{1 - \alpha - \varphi}[\ln s_H - \ln(n + g + \delta + ng)].$$

This is the convergence equation for the Solow model with human capital. It tells how growth should depend on the structural characteristics and on the initial position. Note from (38) that we have obtained a lower rate of convergence than for the Solow model without human capital, $(1 - \alpha - \varphi)(n + g + \delta)$ instead of $(1 - \alpha)(n + g + \delta)$. Realistic parameter values, e.g. $n + g + \delta$ between 0.06 to 0.09, and α and φ both around $\frac{1}{3}$, now imply a rate of convergence between 2 and 3 per cent, which should be compared to the 4 to 6 per cent from the general Solow model. The model-based rate of convergence has thus come much closer to our earlier empirical estimates, but these were not rooted in the present model. We should now do an estimation based on the new convergence equation (39) and see how well the equation describes the data and how well the estimate of λ, implied by the estimation, fits with the model-based values. We will do this shortly, but first sum up:

CONVERGENCE THEORETICALLY

Convergence property: Income per worker converges towards a steady state growth path along which the growth rate is g, and which is fully characterized by the structural variables, s_K, s_H, n, g, δ, and A_0. The growth rate of income per worker is higher the lower the current level of income per worker.

Speed of convergence: The rate of convergence (to steady state), λ, is approximately $(1 - \alpha - \varphi)(n + g + \delta)$, which on an annual basis should be in the range of 2 to 3 per cent for plausible parameter values.

Testing the convergence equation and estimating the rate of convergence

The theoretical equation (39) suggests a regression equation across countries i:

$$g_{T,0}^i = \beta_0 - \beta_1 \ln y_0^i + \beta_2 [\ln s_K^i - \ln(n^i + 0.075)] + \beta_3 [\ln s_H^i - \ln(n^i + 0.075)] + \xi^i, \tag{40}$$

where $g_{T,0}^i$ is the observed growth rate of GDP per worker from year 0 to year T. The coefficients β_1, β_2 and β_3 should be linked to the parameters of the model as given by (39). Moreover, β_0 should depend on the underlying rate of technological progress, g, and the initial level, A_0, as in (39). Hence, (40) assumes this latter technological influence on growth to be the same for all countries.

An OLS estimation of (40) based on the 65 countries of our representative sample gives:

$$g_{03,60}^i = 0.097 - \underset{(se=0.002)}{0.009} \ln y_0^i + \underset{(se=0.003)}{0.011} [\ln s_K^i - \ln(n^i + 0.075)] + \underset{(se=0.003)}{0.008} [\ln s_H^i - \ln(n^i + 0.075)],$$
$$\text{adj. } R^2 = 0.45. \tag{41}$$

For comparison Table 6.2 includes the corresponding growth regression of Chapter 5 based on the Solow model without human capital, the estimation in (41), plus one where the explanatory variables, $\ln s_K^i$, $\ln s_H^i$, and $\ln(n^i + 0.075)$ have not been restricted to enter exactly as the model says, but appear separately and linearly on the right-hand side.

There are several nice features about the estimation in (41). First note that the adjusted R^2 is 0.45, so apparently the simple equation explains almost half of the cross-country variation in growth rates. This is pretty good, and better than the 40 per cent we arrived at in the general Solow model. However, the increase in R^2 is not the main reason for considering this estimation a much improved one. The main reason is that the estimated coefficients are now in better accordance with the underlying model.

First, note that according to the theory, still assuming that α and φ are of equal size, β_2 and β_3 should also be of equal size and their estimates, the two coefficients on the square bracket terms in (41), are indeed roughly equal taking uncertainty into account. Furthermore, we can derive the magnitudes of λ, α, and φ from the estimation. The parameter β_1 should be $(1 - (1 - \lambda)^T)T$, implying (as in Chapter 5) $\lambda = 1 - (1 - T\beta_1)^{1/T}$. Inserting $T = 43$, and $\beta_1 = 0.009$, gives $\lambda = 0.011$. Hence, our estimate of the (annual) rate of convergence is now 1.1 per cent

TABLE 6.2 Growth regressions

Dependent variable: average annual growth rate of real GDP per worker, 1960–2003, (g^y)		
Model:	**Solow without human capital**	**Solow with human capital, restricted**	**Solow with human capital, unrestricted**
Observations:	**65**	**65**	**65**
Explanatory Variables:			
Constant	0.062	0.095	0.039
$\ln y_0$	−0.006 (0.001)	−0.009 (0.002)	−0.01 (0.002)
$\ln s_K - \ln(n + 0.075)$	0.016 (0.002)	0.011 (0.003)	
$\ln s_H - \ln(n + 0.075)$		0.008 (0.003)	
$\ln s_K$			0.009 (0.003)
$\ln s_H$			0.009 (0.003)
$\ln(n + 0.075)$			−0.045 (0.013)
Adjusted R^2	**0.38**	**0.45**	**0.48**
Implied values:			
α	0.73	0.39	–
φ	–	0.30	–
λ	0.007	0.011	–

Note: Standard errors in parenthesis.
Source: Estimations based on Table A.

as also reported in Table 6.2. The 95 per cent confidence interval for λ ranges from 0.6 per cent up to 1.8 per cent (compute this yourself). Our estimate of the rate of convergence is clearly in better accordance with the 'theoretical' value arising from the present model's rate of convergence, 2 to 3 per cent, than was the case for the Chapter 5 regression where the estimated λ of 0.7 per cent (with confidence interval from 0.3 to 0.9 per cent) did not accord well with the 'theoretical' 4 to 6 per cent arising from that model.

It is left to you as an exercise to find a way to derive α and φ from our estimation, and to find the implied magnitudes, but the solution is $\alpha = 0.39$ and $\varphi = 0.30$. These values are in nice accordance with the expected values based on empirical observations, both around $\frac{1}{3}$.

The unrestricted estimation reported in the last column in Table 6.2 confirms the restricted one in some respects: the estimates of the coefficients on $\ln y_0$, $\ln s_K$, and $\ln s_H$ are very close to their counterparts for the restricted estimation. However, the coefficient on $\ln(n + 0.075)$ is estimated to be −0.045, which is of the right sign, but five times larger in absolute value than the coefficients on $\ln s_K$ and $\ln s_H$, where, according to the model, it should only have been twice as large. This is a point where the unrestricted estimation seems not to confirm our model. The next chapter, which incorporates scarce natural resources into the Solow model, may contribute to an explanation why growth in the labour force has a stronger negative influence on economic growth than predicted by the present model.

CONVERGENCE EMPIRICALLY

The out-of-steady-state convergence prediction of the Solow model with human capital fits the cross-country data remarkably well: controlling for structural influences there is a clear negative relationship between the initial value of and the subsequent growth in income per worker across the countries of the world, and the estimated speed of convergence is now in better accordance with the theoretical prediction of the model than was the case for the Solow model.

Figure 6.7 illustrates the gradual improvement of the explanation of growth and convergence we have achieved. All three panels include the 65 countries of our sample. The top panel tests (again) unconditional convergence and simply plots average annual growth in GDP per worker from 1960 to 2003 against the log of GDP per worker in 1960. It is thus identical to Fig. 2.5 and shows no tendency that the initially poorest countries should grow fastest *unconditionally*.

The middle panel illustrates conditional convergence according to the general Solow model. It is close to, but not the same as, Figs 2.6 and 5.8. Based on our estimation of the convergence equation of the general Solow model, Fig. 5.8 plotted the 'growth rate controlled for structural characteristics' $g_{03,60}^i - 0.016[\ln s^i - \ln(n^i + 0.075)]$ against $\ln y_{60}^i$. The middle panel in Fig. 6.7 does almost the same, but plots the 'growth rate controlled for structural characteristics' (defined the same way) *plus the average of structural influence over all the countries* against $\ln y_{60}^i$. The difference lies in the addition of the average, which makes the scales along the vertical axes in the panels of Fig. 6.7 comparable.

The bottom panel does for the Solow model with human capital what the middle panel does for the general Solow model, that is, it plots the growth rate $g_{03,60}^i$ minus the structural influence, $0.011[\ln s_K^i - \ln(n^i + 0.075)] + 0.008[\ln s_H^i - \ln(n^i + 0.075)]$, plus the average of these structural influences over all the countries against $\ln y_{60}^i$.

In the two lowest panels the data points do seem to be clustered around the negatively sloped straight lines, and mostly so in the bottom panel. This panel is evidence that countries that start off poor tend to grow faster (structural characteristics being equal). Particularly, in so far as the points in the bottom panel can be said to be 'represented' by one and the same straight line, it supports the hypothesis that the technological influence on growth should be roughly the same in all countries. This is a striking conclusion and we should emphasize that there is no consensus among economists concerning this view.

6.4 The importance of institutions

We have emphasized that both the steady state, level prediction, and the convergence, growth prediction of our model perform remarkably well empirically even assuming the same influence from technology across countries. We will now take a deeper look at the issue of whether technological influence can really be assumed to be similar in rich and poor countries. We will proceed as follows.[7]

First, we will focus on explaining differences in *levels* of income per worker, not in growth rates. After all, it is the level of income that is important for welfare through its impact on consumption. Income growth can be seen as a means of achieving a high level of income. Second, we will consider only the world's richest and poorest countries, aggregating

---

7. This section is much inspired by the article of Robert E. Hall and Charles I. Jones, 'Why do some Countries Produce so Much More Output per Worker than Others?', *Quarterly Journal of Economics*, **114**, 1999, pp. 83–116. However, our method of growth accounting based on the Mankiw–Romer–Weil model differs from the method used by Hall and Jones so our conclusions are also somewhat different. Compared to us, Hall and Jones find that a larger part of the income gap between the poorest and the richest nations must be ascribed to 'technological differences'.

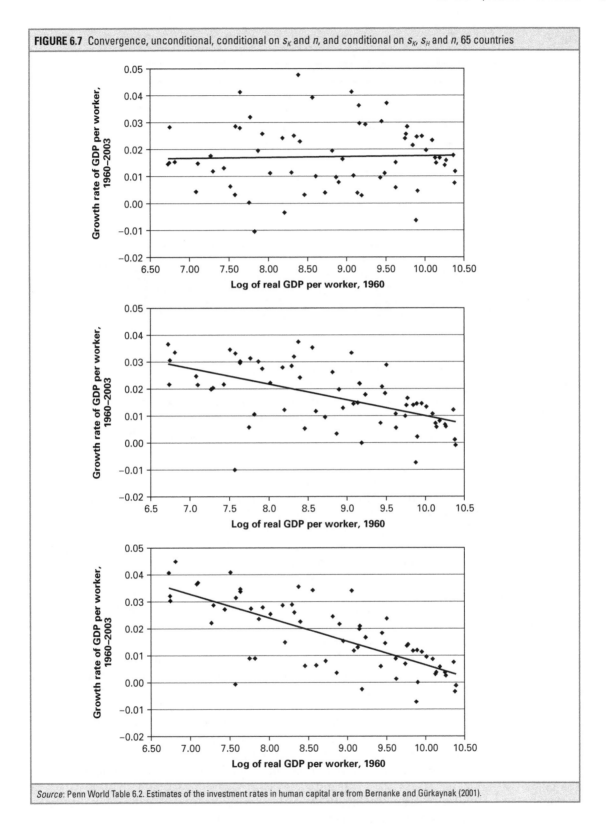

FIGURE 6.7 Convergence, unconditional, conditional on s_K and n, and conditional on s_K, s_H and n, 65 countries

Source: Penn World Table 6.2. Estimates of the investment rates in human capital are from Bernanke and Gürkaynak (2001).

TABLE 6.3 The gap between the world's richest and poorest countries

Group	y_{03}	s_K	s_H	n	A
USA	1.000	0.190	0.115	0.016	
Rich 17	0.825	0.248	0.099	0.013	
Poor 17	0.033	0.094	0.023	0.022	
Rich 17 compared to Poor 17					
Factor to be explained:	24.9				
Factor explained by:	–	2.6	4.2	1.2	1.8
USA compared to Poor 17					
Factor to be explained:	30.2				
Factor explained by:	–	2.0	4.9	1.1	2.6

Note: The countries in the group Rich 17 are USA, Ireland, Norway, Belgium, Austria. France, Netherlands, Australia, Singapore, Switzerland, Italy, United Kingdom, Canada, Denmark, Hong Kong, Sweden, Finland. The countries in the group Poor 17 are Cote d'Ivoire, Congo Rep. of, Senegal, Nigeria, Nepal, Benin, Ghana, Mali, Rwanda, Kenya, Burkina Faso, Zambia, Tanzania, Malawi, Madagascar, Ethiopia, Burundi.

Source: Computations based on Table A.

each of these groups into one observation, and eliminating countries in between. The focus will thus be entirely on understanding the difference between the world's very richest and very poorest countries. Third, this time we will not *assume* that these two groups have the same level of input productivity. Rather we will try to identify how much technological difference one must assume in order to explain the full income gap on the basis of our Solow model with human capital.

Consider Table 6.3 which has been constructed from data in Table A in the Appendix to Book One. The first row reports basic data measured as hitherto for the USA. Since GDP per worker in 2003 is measured relative to the USA, there is a '1' in the y_{03} column. In the following we will sometimes identify the rich world with the USA. Should one find this too narrow, the table's second row reports the same types of data as simple averages across the 17 richest countries in the world for which the required data were available, including the USA. This amounts to defining the rich world as countries with a GDP per worker of at least 70 per cent of that of the USA. The 16 remaining countries are listed in the note for the table. The third row reports average data for the 17 poorest countries in the world for which data were available, still excluding countries with grade D for data quality in the PWT. These countries all have GDPs per worker of 7 per cent or less of the US level and they are almost all African, see again the table's note.

In the two rows under the heading 'Rich 17 compared to Poor 17', the y_{03} column reports the ratio between average GDP per worker in the 17 richest and the 17 poorest countries. So, GDP per worker is almost a factor 25 larger in the richest part of the world as compared to the poorest. If one associates the rich world with the USA the ratio is 30, as shown under the heading 'USA compared to Poor 17'. These are the factors to be explained. Their values of 25 to 30 mean that the amount of output that it takes the workers in the poor countries one year to produce are produced in less than a fortnight in the rich.

Consider the steady state prediction of our model, given by Eq. (29) above, and assume the plausible parameter values $\alpha = \varphi = \frac{1}{3}$ and $g + \delta = 0.075$, implying that both of the exponents in Eq. (29) equal one. Writing the equation for the rich and for the poor, dividing the first by the second, and omitting time subscripts on y and A gives:

$$\frac{y^{\text{rich}}}{y^{\text{poor}}} = \frac{A^{\text{rich}}}{A^{\text{poor}}} \cdot \frac{s_K^{\text{rich}}}{s_K^{\text{poor}}} \cdot \frac{s_H^{\text{rich}}}{s_H^{\text{poor}}} \cdot \left(\frac{n^{\text{poor}} + 0.075}{n^{\text{rich}} + 0.075} \right)^2 \tag{42}$$

Return to Table 6.3, the section headed 'Rich 17 compared to Poor 17'. The row labelled 'Factor explained by' reports under s_K the value of the ratio $s_K^{\text{rich}}/s_K^{\text{poor}}$ between the 17 richest and the 17 poorest countries. This ratio is 2.6, so differences in investment rates in physical capital can, according to our model, account for a factor 2.6 out of the factor 25 of income difference. Likewise, under s_H one finds the ratio $s_H^{\text{rich}}/s_H^{\text{poor}}$, so a factor 4.2 should be explainable by differences in investment in education. In the column labelled n, the ratio $([n^{\text{poor}} + 0.075]/[n^{\text{rich}} + 0.075])^2$ is shown, so a factor 1.2 can be attributed to differences in population (labour force) growth rates. Finally, the column labelled A shows what the ratio $A^{\text{rich}}/A^{\text{poor}}$ needs to be in order for Eq. (42) to explain the full income difference. According to our model and data, differences in 'technology' should account for a factor 1.8. The corresponding figures if one compares the USA to the 17 poorest countries are found in the bottom row of Table 6.3. Here, taking our model seriously, one must attribute a factor 2.6 to differences in productivity to account for the full income gap.

Roughly, income seems to differ between the richest and the poorest in the world by a factor 25–30. According to our model with reasonable parameter values, a factor 2–3 seems to be attributable to differences in (investment rates in) physical capital input, a factor 4–5 to differences in (investment rates in) human capital, and a factor 1.1–1.2 to differences in population growth rates, which leaves, finally, a factor 2–3 for differences in the productivity of the inputs of physical and human capital per worker. Our conclusion is that differences in technology are certainly of importance for income-level differences between rich and poor, but still, according to the exercise we have performed, differences in factor productivity only account for income differences to the same extent as differences in physical capital do and less than differences in human capital do. This is probably less than commonly believed.

If investment rates in physical and human capital and total factor productivity are the main determinants of income levels, deeper questions arise: 'why do some countries invest more than others in physical and human capital? And why are some countries so much more productive than others?' These questions are quoted from the article of Hall and Jones (1999) who argue that a one-step-deeper explanation could be found, at least partly, in differences in 'social infrastructure' or 'institutions'.

By social infrastructure they mean 'the institutions and government policies that determine the economic environment within which individuals accumulate skills, and firms accumulate capital and produce output'.

To be more specific, the presence and quality of a *financial system* with safe banks and assets in which to place one's wealth is essential to the savings and investment performance of an economy. The quality of the system of *government rules and regulations*, for instance a high degree of protection of individuals and their property, and a smooth and uncorrupted public bureaucracy in connection with starting and running businesses are important for the incentive to start up a business firm. A well-functioning system of *laws and courts* that create fast and fair decisions in case of disputes between firms and individuals promotes productivity. A sound *fiscal policy* of the government with a *fair and well-designed tax system* and an *uncorrupted expenditure side* is fundamental for the provision of essential public facilities and services such as health services and infrastructure. A good *educational system* is, of course, essential for the accumulation of skills. The general idea can be illustrated as follows:

Quality of institutions and social infrastructure

↓

Propensity to save and invest, s_K, to educate, s_H, and the ability to turn inputs into output, A

↓

Output and income per worker, y

The causality indicated by the second arrow is exactly the content of the model of this chapter with the overall conclusion that the basic parameters s_K, s_H, and A are decisive for output per

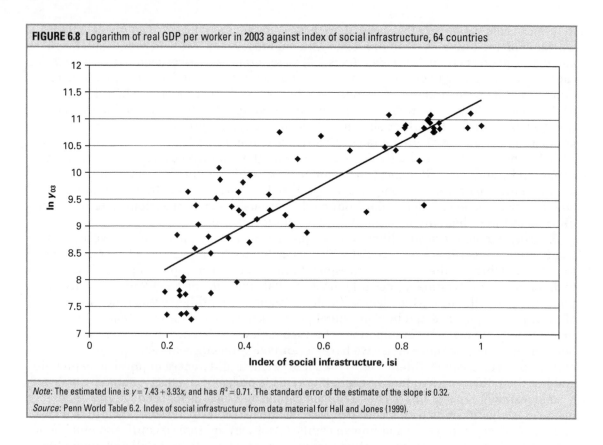

FIGURE 6.8 Logarithm of real GDP per worker in 2003 against index of social infrastructure, 64 countries

Note: The estimated line is $y = 7.43 + 3.93x$, and has $R^2 = 0.71$. The standard error of the estimate of the slope is 0.32.

Source: Penn World Table 6.2. Index of social infrastructure from data material for Hall and Jones (1999).

worker. The first arrow represents the idea that the quality of institutions affects these basic parameters. Putting it all together implies a positive influence of the quality of institutions on output per worker.

Testing such a connection involves the difficult issue of how to measure the quality of institutions, which may seem a hopeless task at first sight. However, different agencies and persons do set up indices of the quality of government, the degree of corruption, etc. across countries. Hall and Jones combine two different indices.

One comes from a private firm, Political Risk Services, that creates an 'International Country Risk Guide' rating 130 countries in a number of categories including the following five: 1) 'law and order', 2) bureaucratic quality, 3) corruption, 4) risk of expropriation, and 5) government repudiation of contracts. In each category the firm creates, from knowledge of government practices in a country, an index with a value between zero and one that is higher the more effective government policies are deemed to be. From the five indices one can define a single one by taking the average.

The other indicator is an index of openness suggested by the economists Jeffrey D. Sachs and Andrew Warner.[8] It simply measures the fraction of years during 1950 to 1994 (a number between zero and one) that a country has been open according to some criteria, among these that average tariff rates are less than 40 per cent, that non-tariff barriers cover less than 40 per cent of trade, and that the government does not monopolize major exports. The idea is that openness and free trade are institutions that improve productivity by allowing a country to take part in international specialization and by exposing the domestic production sector to competition thereby enhancing its effectiveness.

---

8. Jeffrey D. Sachs and Andrew Warner, 'Economic Reform and the Process of Global Integration', *Brookings Papers on Economic Activity*, **1**, 1995, pp. 1–95.

As their final index of social infrastructure Hall and Jones take the simple average of the two indices described. Figure 6.8 shows a scatter plot of GDP per worker against this combined index of social infrastructure, called '*isi*'. There is a very clear positive correlation.

The positive correlation could well be evidence that the quality of basic institutions affects income per worker positively, but as warned several times, and perhaps even more important here than elsewhere, one should be aware of the possibility of reversed causality: perhaps the positive correlation simply reflects that richer countries can afford better institutions.

Statistical methods to correct for reversed causality do exist and the article by Hall and Jones seeks to do such a correction. As a result they find an even stronger causal effect of institutions on performance than suggested by Fig. 6.2. The slope of the line of best fit in Fig. 6.8 is around four, suggesting that an increase in the *isi* of ten percentage points should give rise to a 40 per cent increase in income per worker. This is already a strong effect and if the true causal effect is even stronger, certainly institutions are very important for economic performance.

This has important implications for structural economic policy. Perhaps this should, more than anything else, be concerned with creating productive institutions such as good government conduct, protection of individuals and their property, well-functioning educational and financial systems, etc.

6.5 Summary

1. The quality and skills of the labour force are of obvious importance in human production. In this chapter we amended the Solow model to include human capital, defined as the stock of skills accumulated by workers through education and training. The stock of human capital was included among the essential inputs besides physical capital and 'raw' labour.

2. In some respects human capital was treated just like physical capital: we assumed that in each period there is a certain stock, H_t, of human capital, that human capital enters into an aggregate production function with constant returns to scale, $Y_t = K_t^\alpha H_t^\varphi (A_t L_t)^{1-\alpha-\varphi}$, parallel to the way physical capital enters, and that human capital accumulates by a certain fraction, s_H, of GDP being added to it each year. While empirical estimates of investment rates in physical capital are directly available from national accounts, nothing similar is true for s_H. We argued that since the most important part of investment in human capital is the GDP and income forgone while people educate themselves, the fraction of people of working age in education should give a good approximation of s_H. Using this idea, empirical estimates of s_H can be obtained across countries.

3. In one important respect human capital must be treated differently from physical capital: since human capital is embodied in persons, a firm cannot change its input of human capital and of (raw) labour independently. We made the simplifying assumption that each worker is equipped with the same amount of human capital, so each worker embodies a human capital of $h_t = H_t/L_t$, and hiring one worker means increasing raw labour input by one unit *and* increasing the input of human capital by h_t. Hence there is no separate market for the services of human capital: these are traded together with raw labour, and the return to human capital appears as a part of the real wage which is thus really a mix of a reward to raw labour and a return to human capital. Furthermore, in the computation of the marginal product of labour that determines the real wage, one should take human capital per worker, not total human capital, as given.

4. Our considerations on how to deal with human capital led to a model characterized by the following features:

   - The aggregate production function was as stated above. From empirical evidence on labour's share and on average wages compared to the wages of unskilled workers, we inferred that plausible parameter values could be $\alpha = \varphi = \frac{1}{3}$.

   - The prices of capital and labour were given by the marginal products.

   - The stocks of physical and human capital accumulated as implied by given investment rates, s_K and s_H, respectively, and a common depreciation rate.

   - The labour force as well as the technological variable A_t, grew at exogenously given rates.

5. The model implied convergence to a well-defined steady state in which GDP per worker follows a specific growth path with constant growth rate (equal to the exogenous growth rate of A_t). The 'steady state equation' told how the growth path depends on model parameters. According to the steady state equation:

   - An increase in s_K has a larger positive impact on GDP per worker than in the general Solow model because the rise in GDP occurring as more physical capital is accumulated will cause more human capital to be accumulated, reinforcing the increase in GDP.

   - An increase in the population growth rate has a stronger negative impact on GDP per worker than was the case in the general Solow model, because population growth now means the thinning-out of both physical and human capital.

   - An increase in s_H has a positive impact on GDP per worker similar to that of an increase in s_K.

   These features were promising for an empirical test since they appeared to remedy the empirical shortcomings of the general Solow model's steady state prediction that we had identified.

6. Confronting our model's steady state prediction with cross-country empirical evidence under the heroic assumptions that the countries considered were in steady state in year 2000 and all had the same technological level in that year, we found that the model did remarkably well and actually went a long way towards solving the empirical problems with the general Solow model's steady state prediction. This was evidence that countries are perhaps not as technologically different as usually thought.

7. The steady state analysis supported policy recommendations of ensuring adequate savings and investment rates and keeping population growth rates down, the latter now being even more strongly supported than earlier. The really new issue was government policies to provide for or subsidize education. Such policies are recommendable according to our model in so far as one cannot fully trust private decision making and markets to devote a sufficient amount of resources to educational purposes. We gave several reasons why a market-determined allocation would not be optimal, implying that educational policies should be at the forefront of structural policies to promote prosperity and growth (as indeed they are in many countries).

8. The general prediction of economic performance derived from the Solow model with human capital is the convergence process implied by the model. From the model one can derive a 'convergence equation' telling how a country's average annual growth rate of GDP per worker over some period should depend on parameters and on the country's initial GDP per worker. The structure of the equation is such that the growth rate equals the underlying technological growth rate adjusted upwards for how far below steady

state the country was initially, and for the speed by which the country converges to steady state. The rate of convergence depends in a simple way on model parameters and (*ceteris paribus*) it is smaller for the Solow model with human capital than for the general Solow model. The reason is that capital accumulation takes time and delays convergence, and there is more capital to accumulate when there is also human capital. This was again promising from an empirical point of view since we have found the general Solow model to overestimate the rate of convergence.

9. Estimating the model's convergence equation on cross-country data gave a remarkably good result and in particular a much improved accordance between the estimated rate of convergence and the one predicted by the model. The good result was strongly in support of the idea of conditional convergence among the countries of the world and gave an indication that countries are perhaps also more similar with respect to their technological growth rates than usually thought.

10. Although technology and input productivity may not be as different across countries as usually believed, the empirical evidence suggests that differences in total factor productivity do contribute to explaining the income differences between rich and poor countries, along with differences in physical and human capital per worker. For explaining these factors in turn, the quality of a society's institutions and social infrastructure seems to be of great importance.

6.6 Exercises

Exercise 1. One more empirical improvement obtained by adding human capital

We opened this chapter by summarizing two main empirical shortcomings of the general Solow model. One was that its steady state prediction tends to understate the influences of saving and population growth rates on GDP per person. There may be another one that also concerns the general Solow model's steady state prediction which is (setting $ng \approx 0$):

$$\ln y_t^* = \ln A_t + \frac{\alpha}{1-\alpha}[\ln s_K - \ln(n + g + \delta)].$$

The elasticity of y_t^* with respect to s_K is the same as the elasticity with respect to $n + g + \delta$ in absolute value. Show that both are $\alpha/(1 - \alpha)$, and hence should be around 0.5. To check empirically whether the two elasticities are approximately equal, construct two figures, taking data from Table A and only considering countries in the sample of 65 countries indicated in Table A (the figures are reminiscent of, but not the same as, Figs 3.7 and 3.8):

One figure should plot $\ln y_{00}^i$ against $\ln s_K^i$ across countries i. Estimate (by OLS) and draw the line of best fit through the points and identify its slope. The other figure should plot $\ln y_{00}^i$ against $\ln(n^i + 0.075)$, and include the line of best fit through the points. The slope of the line should be identified. Do the two slopes seem to be of equal size (in absolute value), or does one seem to be greater than the other? In case of the latter, which of the estimated elasticities is largest? How do your findings accord with the general Solow model's steady state prediction? How do they accord with that of the Solow model with human capital?

Another way to proceed is to do an OLS estimation of the regression equation:

$$\ln y_{00}^i = K + \gamma \ln s_K^i + \upsilon \ln(n^i + 0.075),$$

where we have *not* restricted the coefficients of $\ln s_K^i$ and $-\ln(n^i + 0.075)$ to be equal. If you know how to do an OLS estimation with more than one explanatory variable on the right-hand side, do an estimation of the above equation and compare your estimates of γ and υ. Are they of about equal size in absolute value (taking uncertainty on the estimates into account)? If one is larger than the other, how does that accord with each of the two models?

Exercise 2. Government in the Solow model with human capital

When we were setting up the basic Solow model in Chapter 3 we were careful to explain that the savings rate, s, in $S_t = sY_t$ could be interpreted as $s = (1 - c^p)(1 - c^g)$, where we now assume $i_t^g = 0$, and constant values for the private propensity to consume out of disposable income, c^p, and for the spending share, c^g, of government that balanced its budget each period. The model could thus be interpreted to include a government and obviously a government could be interpreted into the general Solow model considered in Chapter 5 in exactly the same way. This exercise asks you to show how government can be included in the model of this chapter.

Assume that the government always taxes all income by the constant rate τ, and in each period spends the constant fraction s_H^g of the tax revenue on education and the remaining tax revenue on government consumption (thus balancing its budget each period and not investing in physical capital). What the government spends on education accumulates as human capital with the households.

Assume that out of their disposable incomes households invest the fraction s_K^p in physical capital and the fraction s_H^p in human capital. In all remaining respects the model is as in this chapter. Show that the model presented in this chapter can be interpreted to cover the case with a government if the parameters of the chapter are: $s_K = (1 - \tau)s_K^p$ and $s_H = \tau s_H^g + (1 - \tau)s_H^p$.

Exercise 3. Balanced growth in steady state

Show that growth in the steady state of the Solow model with human capital in *all* respects accords with the concept of balanced growth. In particular, derive an expression for the steady state real rental rate, r^*, and show that this is constant. Also compare the expression to the corresponding one in the general Solow model. How is it possible that r^* does not depend on s_H? This is difficult to explain intuitively, but we only ask you to try to identify some counteracting factors that together can imply that r^* is not sensitive to s_H.

Exercise 4. Golden rule

Show that, given the values of the model's other parameters, the sizes of the investment rates, s_K and s_H, that will maximize the altitude of the growth path of consumption per worker in the steady state of the Solow model with human capital are $s_K = \alpha$ and $s_H = \varphi$.

Exercise 5. Further simulations to investigate stability

In Section 6.3 we ran a simulation of the Solow model with human capital to check stability of $\tilde{k}_t$, $\tilde{h}_t$ towards the steady state $\tilde{k}^*$, $\tilde{h}^*$. We considered only one starting point, $\tilde{k}_0 = 16$, $\tilde{h}_0 = 2$, which resulted in convergence to steady state, but in an interesting way that included some non-monotonicity ($\tilde{k}_t$ first decreases, then increases). Run some simulations yourself where (first) you consider the same parameter values as in Section 6.3, but you choose different initial points. Make diagrams like Fig. 6.6, including the two curves corresponding to constant state variables. Be sure that you have initial points in each of the figure's four regions (preferably several in each region which are spread out in a 'representative' way) and that you simulate over a sufficient number of periods to be able to judge whether there seems to be convergence to steady state. Choose some changed, but still realistic parameter values (obeying all stated parameter restrictions), and do the same again. Do your simulations seem to support convergence to steady state generally?

Exercise 6. The effects of various parameter changes

Let a *base scenario* be defined by the economy being, in all periods from 0 to 200, say, in steady state of the Solow model with human capital at parameter values $\alpha = \varphi = \frac{1}{3}$, $s_K = 0.12$, $s_H = 0.2$, $\delta = 0.055$, $n = 0$, $g = 0.02$, and with an initial value of the technological variable $A_0 = 1$.

We will consider various *alternative scenarios*, each one defined by the economy evolving according to the base scenario from period zero through period nine, while (working first time) in period ten a permanent shift in one (or several) parameters occurs, while other unmentioned parameters stay unchanged.

For each alternative scenario the qualitative effects of the parameter shift should be described and illustrated by showing how it affects the phase diagram and by explaining intuitively the transition towards the new steady state. The quantitative effects should be computed and illustrated by conducting the appropriate simulations and creating the following figures:

- A Diagram 1 showing the evolution of $\ln y_t$ against periods $t = 0, 1, \ldots, 200$ according to 1) the base scenario (the old steady state), 2) the new steady state (as if the economy had, in all periods, been in steady state at the new parameter values and with $A_0 = 1$) and 3) the alternative scenario.

- A Diagram 2 showing $\ln c_t$ the way Diagram 1 illustrates $\ln y_t$.

- A Diagram 3 showing the growth rate $g_t^y \equiv (y_t - y_{t-1})/y_{t-1}$ over periods $t = 1, \ldots, 200$, otherwise as Diagram 1.

- A Diagram 4 showing K_t/Y_t and H_t/Y_t, otherwise as Diagram 1.

Alternative 1 is defined by the investment rate in physical capital increasing to $s_K' = 0.24$. In particular, what is the half-life for $\tilde{y}_t$ (the number of periods it takes for $\tilde{y}_t$ to go half the way from the old to the new steady state)? Compare to the half-life you found in Exercise 4 of Chapter 5, and explain the difference.

Alternative 2 is defined by the investment rate in human capital increasing to $s_H' = 0.25$.

From your two analyses comment on the development perspectives from increasing the investment rates, in particular with respect to the duration of the consumption sacrifice.

Alternative 3 is defined by the investment rate in physical capital increasing to $s_K' = 0.24$, and the investment rate in human capital decreasing to $s_H' = 0.15$.

Does the economy always seem to react to parameter changes with a 'growth jump'?

Exercise 7. Inferring α and φ from the estimation of the convergence equation

First find a way to estimate values for α and φ from the information gathered in (39), (40) and (41). Then show that the implied values are $\alpha = 0.39$ and $\varphi = 0.30$. Comment.

Exercise 8. Illustrating further the improvement of the convergence equation obtained by adding human capital

In this chapter we created Figs 6.4 and 6.5 to illustrate the improvement in the steady state equation of the model with human capital over that of the model without human capital. A line of best fit should have a slope around one for the model to be correct. The line in the model with human capital had such a slope, but the model without human capital did not. This exercise asks you to make a similar illustration with respect to the convergence equations. You should consider the same 65 countries considered in Figs 6.4 and 6.5. Data can be taken from Table A at the back of Book One.

1. First consider the convergence equation of the general Solow model:

$$g_{T,0}^y \cong V - \frac{1-(1-\lambda)^T}{T}\ln y_0 + \frac{1-(1-\lambda)^T}{T}\cdot\frac{\alpha}{1-\alpha}[\ln s_K - \ln(n+g+\delta)],$$

where we have denoted the 'technological influence' by V and set $ng = 0$. Assuming as usual $\alpha = \frac{1}{3}$ and $n+g+\delta = 0.075$ (and remembering $\lambda = (1-\alpha)(n+g+\delta)$), what are the 'theoretical' sizes of the two coefficients, $\beta_1 = (1-(1-\lambda)^T)/T$ and $\beta_2 = \beta_1\alpha/(1-\alpha)$, in this equation if $T = 43$? In a figure, plot $g_{03,60}^i$ against $-\beta_1\ln y_{60}^i + \beta_2[\ln s_K^i - \ln(n^i + 0.075)]$ with β_1 and β_2 so computed and check if the line of best fit seems to have a slope of one.

2. Then consider the convergence equation of the Solow model with human capital:

$$g_{T,0}^y \cong V - \frac{1-(1-\lambda)^T}{T}\ln y_0 + \frac{1-(1-\lambda)^T}{T}\frac{\alpha}{1-\alpha-\varphi}[\ln s_K - \ln(n+g+\delta)]$$

$$+ \frac{1-(1-\lambda)^T}{T}\frac{\varphi}{1-\alpha-\lambda}[\ln s_H - \ln(n+g+\delta)].$$

Assuming $\alpha = \varphi = \frac{1}{3}$ and $n+g+\delta = 0.075$ (and remembering $\lambda = (1-\alpha-\varphi)(n+g+\delta)$), compute the 'theoretical' sizes of the three coefficients β_1, β_2 and β_3 in the equation given $T = 43$. In a figure, plot $g_{03,60}^i$ against $-\beta_1\ln y_{60}^i + \beta_2[\ln s_K^i - \ln(n^i + 0.075)] + \beta_3[\ln s_H^i - \ln(n^i + 0.075)]$ and check if the line of best fit seems to have a slope of one.

Exercise 9. An alternative Solow model with human capital

You may have been wondering why we have built human capital into the model of this chapter in a way that is different from how it was brought into the picture in Section 5.5 on growth accounting. In fact, there is an alternative growth model with human capital that incorporates human capital in the way it was done in Chapter 5.

This alternative model with human capital consists of the same equations as the general Solow model, that is, Eq. (7)–(13) of Chapter 5, with the following exceptions: the production function (7) is changed to:

$$Y_t = K_t^\alpha (A_t h L_t)^{1-\alpha},$$

where:

$$h = \exp(\psi u),$$

and ψ is a given productivity parameter in the production of human capital and u is the average number of years that people in the labour force have been to school (the same in all periods). The 'rental rate equal to marginal product' conditions (8) and (9) should be modified appropriately, but are not used in the following.

Both ψ and u are positive and constant parameters and to be thought of as rates like α and s, respectively. Realistically ψ should be around 0.1 (see again Section 5.5). Note that in this model human capital per worker, h, is simply a constant. The difference between this alternative model and the one considered in this chapter is that in the alternative model human capital per worker is not being built up gradually through an accumulation process where additions come from investing a given fraction of GDP each year, but rather is simply a given constant throughout. Nevertheless, *how* this constant depends on education as measured by u may be important.

The full model is conveniently analysed in terms of the auxiliary variables $\tilde{y}_t = y_t/(hA_t)$ and $\tilde{k} \equiv k_t/(hA_t)$, where y_t and k_t are output per worker, Y_t/L_t, and capital per worker, K_t/L_t, respectively.

1. Show that $\tilde{y}_t = \tilde{k}_t^\alpha$ and that the law of motion for $\tilde{k}_t$ is:

$$\tilde{k}_{t+1} = \frac{1}{(1+n)(1+g)}(s\tilde{k}_t^\alpha + (1-\delta)\tilde{k}_t).$$

2. Show that $\tilde{k}_t$ and $\tilde{y}_t$ converge to constant steady state values and that in steady state output per worker evolves as:

$$y_t^* = A_t\left(\frac{s}{n+g+\delta+ng}\right)^{\alpha/(1-\alpha)} \exp(\psi u).$$

3. The 'steady state equation' derived from the above is:

$$\ln y_t^* = \ln A_t + \frac{\alpha}{1-\alpha}[\ln s - \ln(n+g+\delta+ng)] + \psi u.$$

Test this empirically as follows. Consider our sample of 65 countries for which also data on u^i are available from Table A. Consider first the model without human capital ($\psi = 0$). Assuming $\alpha = \frac{1}{3}$, plot $\ln y_{03}^i$ against $0.5[\ln s^i - \ln(n^i + 0.075)]$ across countries i. This is almost what we did in Fig. 6.4, but not for exactly the same countries. Estimate the line of best fit and judge if it seems to have a slope of one. Next, plot $\ln y_{03}^i$ against $0.5[\ln s^i - \ln(n^i + 0.075)] + 0.1u^i$. Estimate again the line of best fit and see if it has come closer to having a slope of one. Is the improvement of the steady state prediction comparable to the one obtained in the model of this chapter?

4. By linearizing the above law of motion around steady state, etc., show that the 'convergence equation' of this model is:

$$\frac{\ln y_T - \ln y_0}{T} \cong g + \frac{1-(1-\lambda)^T}{T} \times \left(\ln A_0 + \frac{\alpha}{1-\alpha}[\ln s - \ln(n+g+\delta+ng)] - (\ln y_0 - \psi u)\right),$$

where $\lambda \cong (1-\alpha)(n+g+\delta)$. A regression equation suggested by this convergence equation is:

$$g_{03,60}^i = \beta_0 - \beta_1(\ln y_{60}^i - 0.1u^i) + \beta_2[\ln s^i - \ln(n^i + 0.075)].$$

Estimate this by OLS, taking data from Table A. Are the estimated parameters significant and do they have the right signs? What are the values for α and λ that can be derived from the estimated parameters? By introducing human capital, does this model bring a better accordance between the model's rate of convergence (an evaluation of λ for realistic parameter values) and the estimated rates as compared to what was found in the general Solow model? Is the improvement comparable to the one obtained in the chapter's model with human capital? Why not?

5. Discuss the advantages and disadvantages of the two models with human capital. For instance, which data do you think are most reliable, those for u^i used in the model of this exercise or those for s_H^i used in this chapter? Which of the models do you think has the nicest properties? Is there a trade-off with respect to which model to prefer?

Exercise 10. An empirical shortcoming of the Solow model with human capital?

Exercise 1 above pointed to an(other) empirical shortcoming of the Solow model without human capital. The model's prediction that the investment rate in physical capital and the population growth rates should affect GDP per worker equally strongly (but in opposite directions) does not seem to hold true empirically. Rather, there seems to be a stronger influence from the population growth rate than from the investment rate, a feature indeed found in the Solow model with human capital. Let's now take this latter model through a similar direct challenge. The steady state prediction of the Solow model with human capital is (setting $ng \cong 0$):

$$\ln y_t^* \approx \ln A_t + \frac{\alpha}{1-\alpha-\varphi}[\ln s_K - \ln(n+g+\delta)] + \frac{\varphi}{1-\alpha-\varphi}[\ln s_H - \ln(n+g+\delta)].$$

Find the elasticities of y_t^* with respect to s_K, s_H and $n+g+\delta$, respectively. Show that if $\alpha = \varphi = \frac{1}{3}$ (as we more or less believe) then the elasticities with respect to s_K and s_H should be of equal size and both should be one, while the elasticity with respect to $n+g+\delta$ should be twice as large in absolute value.

Taking data from Table A and considering the sample of 65 countries, do an OLS estimation of the following regression equation (requires that you can do an OLS estimation with more than one explanatory variable on the right-hand side):

$$\ln y_{00}^i = K + \gamma \ln s_K^i + \varepsilon \ln s_H^i + \upsilon \ln(n^i + 0.075),$$

where we have *not* imposed any model-based restrictions on the coefficients to $\ln s_K^i$, $\ln s_H^i$, $\ln(n^i + 0.075)$. How do your estimates of γ, ε and v accord with what the elasticities should be? Take the uncertainty of your estimates into account when you answer.

Exercise 11. Institutions and the intermediate explanatory variables

According to the reasoning of Section 6.4, the quality of institutions should be important for the 'intermediate' explanatory variables s_K, s_H and A, which in turn should be important for y. We tested this in Fig. 6.8 by plotting y against *isi*, finding a clear positive correlation. For the theory to be correct there should, however, be a positive influence of *isi* on each of the variables s_K, s_H and A, which was not tested. This exercise seeks to take a step in the direction of such a test.

Consider Table A and the 64 countries that are in our sample of 65 countries and for which the *isi* is available (we don't have the *isi* for Nepal). Let the USA be 'country of comparison'.

1. For each of the remaining 63 countries decompose the income per worker relative to the USA, y^i/y^{US}, into components the way it was done for rich vs. poor in Section 6.4, thereby among other things creating relative technology levels, A^i/A^{US}, for the 63 countries other than the USA.
2. Plot y^i/y^{US} against A^i/A^{US} across the 63 countries and comment with respect to whether technological differences seem to be important for understanding income differences.
3. In three figures, plot each of s_K^i, s_H^i and A^i/A^{US} against *isi* across the 63 countries. Comment with respect to the issue of this exercise.

CHAPTER 7

Limits to growth?
The Solow model with scarce natural resources

So far our presentation of growth theory has been a bit like 'playing Hamlet without the Prince of Denmark'. The theory of economic growth was initiated by the great classical economists, Adam Smith, Thomas Malthus and David Ricardo. They thought that the presence of land as a fixed factor in production implied a severe constraint on the economy's long-term growth potential. In their time agriculture accounted for a much greater share in total production than today, so it is no wonder that the economists of the time considered land to be essential.

Today, land is still in fixed supply and remains an important input to aggregate production. Not only is agriculture still of importance, but any kind of production requires at least some space and hence land. Moreover, if we interpret the services of 'land' in a broad sense to include all the life support services of the natural environment – such as its ability to generate clean air and water and to absorb the waste products of human activity, e.g., nature's and the atmosphere's (limited) capability to absorb CO_2 – it should be clear that 'land' is vital for economic activity.

The analysis of the classical economists taught them that the presence of an irreplaceable factor in fixed supply would imply a tendency towards long-run decline in income per capita and eventually stagnation at a low income level. In modern terms their argument was the following.

Assume there is some population growth and disregard technological progress for a moment. Assume further that the economy manages to build up capital at the same speed as the population increases. Note that this is exactly what we found in the basic Solow model's steady state: capital and labour were growing at the same rate (the capital–labour ratio was constant). Because of *constant returns to capital and labour*, this implied that output was also growing at this rate, leaving output per worker constant, possibly at a high level.

Assume now, realistically, that there are three inputs in the aggregate production function: capital, labour and land. Suppose further that land is in fixed supply. From the replication argument this production function should have constant returns to capital, labour *and* land, implying *diminishing returns to the combination of capital and labour*. Now, as the inputs of capital and labour increase proportionally, as we assume they do, while land stays fixed, output will grow less than proportionally to labour and capital, and hence output per worker will decline in the long run. In a nutshell, this is the classical argument why income per capita has to decline in the long run as a consequence of population growth. The ultimate root of this decline is the diminishing returns to capital and labour arising from the presence of a fixed factor, land.

This is not even the end of the story according to the classical economists. As income per capita falls, savings per capita would also fall, so capital would not really be able to increase at the same speed as labour in the long run. This would imply an even faster economic decline.

Furthermore, with decreasing incomes, population growth would also eventually be brought to a halt. Fertility might stay unchanged, but because of the miserable living conditions of workers, mortality would be so high that the labour force would stay constant. This would eliminate population growth, the original source of declining incomes, but in the 'end state' income per capita would have stagnated at a subsistence level. In the words of Malthus:

> Population, when unchecked, increases in a geometrical ratio. Subsistence increases only in an arithmetical ratio. A slight acquaintance with numbers will show the immensity of the first power in comparison of the second . . . This implies a strong and constantly operating check on population from the difficulty of subsistence . . . its effects are . . . Among mankind, misery and vice.
>   *(From Chapter I of Thomas Malthus' famous book, An Essay on Population, 1798)*

The labelling of economics as the 'dismal science' arose from this idea. The economic history of the past 200 years suggests that the pessimism of the classical economists was unwarranted. Income per capita has been growing at rates around 2 per cent per year over very long periods in many Western countries. This does not mean that the classical economists were wrong in their reasoning, only that there were perhaps some other factors to which they did not pay enough attention. In fact, the modelling of this chapter will show that the classical economists were in some sense right: land *does* imply a growth drag such that population growth leads to negative growth in income per capita *in the absence of technological progress.*

The possibilities of prolonged technological progress and birth control were not emphasized by the classical economists. As we saw in Chapter 5 and in Chapter 6 as well, technological growth is a source of long-run growth in income per capita. Fixed natural resources and technological progress seem to be two countervailing influences on long-run growth. Which one will be the strongest in the long run is a crucial issue and a central theme in this chapter.

We will study a Solow growth model that also includes a fixed factor, 'land', as an input in the aggregate production function. This will enable us to take a stand on the essential issue whether fixed land or technical progress has the strongest influence on long-run growth. The model we consider comes from an article by the economist William D. Nordhaus,[1] taking up a discussion about the limits to growth provoked by the pessimistic views expressed in some famous books from 1972 and 1992 known as the 'Limits to Growth' reports.[2]

Like Nordhaus, we will go one step further and also present a model with exhaustible natural resources. If a fixed factor such as land, the supply of which stays unchanged as it is used in production, can imply a drag on growth, one should expect that exhaustible resources such as oil and gas, which disappear as they are used, can imply even more of a growth drag. Our model will show that this intuition is indeed correct. We will again use the model to address the essential question: is the growth drag so strong that it will ultimately bring growth in income per capita to a halt despite continued technological progress?

7.1 The Solow model with land

The production function of the representative, profit-maximizing firm will now include three inputs: capital, labour and land. The consumers own the land as well as the capital

---

1. William D. Nordhaus, 'Lethal Model 2: The Limits to Growth Revisited', *Brookings Papers on Economic Activity*, **2**, 1992, pp. 1–59.

2. The most well known of these reports was *The Limits to Growth* published in 1972 by a group of scientists gathered in the Club of Rome. In neo-Malthusian fashion, this book predicted that economic growth and population growth would be brought to an abrupt halt some time in the present century, either as a result of acute shortages of food or raw materials, or as a consequence of an ecological breakdown arising from man-made pollution.

and labour, and the amount of land is fixed and does not change with its use in production. Consumers sell the services of capital, labour and land to the firm in competitive markets where the real factor prices are denoted by r_t, w_t and v_t, respectively. The consumers as a group (or consumers and government together) save a fraction s of total income which is the sum of interest earned on capital, wage income and rent from land. We should note that although the fixed factor is referred to as 'land' for convenience, its services could be interpreted broadly to include all the life support services of the natural environment.

The model

Equation (1) is a Cobb–Douglas aggregate production function with land and exogenous, constant technical coefficients α, β and κ:

$$Y_t = K_t^\alpha (A_t L_t)^\beta X^\kappa, \qquad \alpha > 0,\ \beta > 0,\ \kappa > 0,\ \alpha + \beta + \kappa = 1. \tag{1}$$

The input X of land does not carry a time subscript since land is in fixed supply. The competitive market for the services of land implies, by adjustment of v_t, that all land supplied is also demanded. The production function exhibits constant returns to the three inputs – capital, labour and land – as it should according to the replication argument. Hence there will be diminishing returns to any single factor, and also to the combination of any two factors. In particular, a doubling of both K_t and L_t will imply that output, Y_t, is multiplied by $2^{\alpha+\beta}$, which is less than two, since $\alpha + \beta$ ($= 1 - \kappa$) is less than one. The degree to which $\alpha + \beta$ is below one, or the size of κ, measures *how much* the returns to capital and labour diminish.

Equation (2) is the capital accumulation equation, assuming given rates of gross investment in physical capital (now disregarding human capital) and of depreciation:

$$K_{t+1} = sY_t + (1 - \delta)K_t, \qquad 0 < s < 1,\ 0 < \delta < 1. \tag{2}$$

Finally, Eqs (3) and (4) assume given growth rates for the labour force, L_t, and for the labour-augmenting productivity factor, A_t, respectively. Thus n is the growth rate of the labour force, and g reflects the rate of labour-augmenting technological progress. We assume that both of these rates are at least zero:

$$L_{t+1} = (1 + n)L_t, \qquad n \geq 0, \tag{3}$$

$$A_{t+1} = (1 + g)A_t, \qquad g \geq 0. \tag{4}$$

In each period the values of the state variables, K_t, L_t and A_t, are predetermined, so for given initial values the four equations above will determine the full time sequence for the state variables and for Y_t.

The competitive factor markets imply that, in each period, each factor will earn its marginal product which depends on the predetermined levels of K_t, L_t, A_t and X:[3]

$$\left(\frac{K_t}{A_t L_t}\right)^{\alpha-1} \left(\frac{X_t}{A_t L_t}\right)^\kappa, \tag{5}$$

$$\left(\frac{K_t}{A_t L_t}\right)^\alpha \left(\frac{X_t}{A_t L_t}\right)^\kappa A_t, \tag{6}$$

---

3. In the introduction and in this section we have opted for a broad interpretation of 'land' to include nature's ability to absorb waste, etc. In connection with a market for the services of land a more literal interpretation is appropriate since nature's ability to absorb waste is typically not owned or marketed by private people. Note, however, that the dynamics of Eqs (1)–(4) are independent of the real factor prices, so as long as we include only Eqs (1)–(4) in our model, the broader interpretation of X remains valid.

$$\left(\frac{K_t}{A_t L_t}\right)^{\alpha}\left(\frac{X_t}{A_t L_t}\right)^{\kappa-1}.\tag{7}$$

These three latter equations complete the description of the model, and you can easily verify that in the special case of $\kappa = 0$, where land is of no importance, the model boils down to the Solow model of Chapter 5. You can also easily show that the income *shares* of capital, labour and land ($r_t K_t/Y_t$, etc.) are α, β and κ, respectively, so the model is again one of constant income shares.

Some production function arithmetic

As with the other Solow models we have analysed, let us first see what can be said about the sources of economic growth from the production function alone. Defining output per worker as $y_t \equiv Y_t/L_t$, capital per worker as $k_t \equiv K_t/L_t$, and land per worker as $x_t \equiv X/L_t$, and dividing on both sides of (1) by L_t, one gets:

$$y_t = k_t^{\alpha} A_t^{\beta} x_t^{\kappa},\tag{8}$$

and hence, by taking logs and time differences, the approximate growth rates, $g_t^y \equiv \ln y_t - \ln y_{t-1}$ etc., must fulfil:

$$g_t^y = \alpha g_t^k + \beta g_t^A - \kappa g_t^n \approx \alpha g_t^k + \beta g - \kappa n.\tag{9}$$

Equation (8) shows that an increase in income per worker can now be obtained (only) by an increase in capital per worker, by better technology, or by an increase in land per worker. With our assumptions the latter effect can only give a decline in growth since the supply of land is constant and we have assumed that population growth is at least zero. In fact, Eq. (9) shows that the approximate growth rate of output per worker, g_t^y, is (approximately) the weighted average of g_t^k, g and $-n$, with weights α, β and κ.

The dynamics of the Solow growth models we considered earlier were such that the economy converged towards a steady state in which the capital–output ratio was constant. Let us assume for a moment that the dynamics of the Solow model with land have the same implication. If K_t/Y_t converges towards a constant steady state level, so must k_t/y_t, and then the steady state growth rates of capital per worker and of output per worker must be identical. In other words we must have $g_t^k = g_t^y$. Inserting this equality into (9) above and solving for g_t^y shows that g_t^y converges towards a constant g^y fulfilling:

$$g^y \approx \frac{\beta g - \kappa n}{1-\alpha} = \frac{\beta g - \kappa n}{\beta + \kappa}.\tag{10}$$

We have already arrived at an expression for the steady state growth rate in output per worker. It is not entirely correct to say that this was derived only from 'production function arithmetic'. It was derived from the production function *and* an assumption of a constant capital–output ratio in steady state (and constant growth rates for technology and the labour force). For a proper analysis we should now demonstrate convergence of the capital–output ratio to a constant steady state level. We will do exactly that in the next subsection. Having established a firm foundation for our expression, we will discuss it at length.

Convergence to steady state

The Solow model with land can conveniently be analysed directly in terms of the capital–output ratio, $z_t \equiv K_t/Y_t = k_t/y_t$, for which we want to establish convergence to a constant steady state level. We could have chosen to analyse the Solow model of Chapter 5 in z_t as well, as you were in fact asked to do in an exercise. It is often a matter of choice, whether the dynamic system associated with a growth model should be expressed in variables such as capital per effective worker or in the capital–output ratio. This way you will come to see examples of both.

From the per capita production function, $y_t = k_t^\alpha A_t^\beta x_t^\kappa$, we get $z_t = k_t/y_t = k_t/(k_t^\alpha A_t^\beta x_t^\kappa)$, or:

$$z_t = k_t^{1-\alpha} A_t^{-\beta} x_t^{-\kappa}. \tag{11}$$

Leading this expression for z_t one period and inserting appropriate model equations gives:

$$z_{t+1} = k_{t+1}^{1-\alpha} A_{t+1}^{-\beta} x_{t+1}^\kappa = \left(\frac{K_{t+1}}{L_{t+1}}\right)^{1-\alpha} A_{t+1}^{-\beta} \left(\frac{X}{L_{t+1}}\right)^{-\kappa}$$

$$= \left(\frac{sY_t + (1-\delta)K_t}{(1+n)L_t}\right)^{1-\alpha} (1+g)^{-\beta} A_t^{-\beta} \left(\frac{X}{(1+n)L_t}\right)^{-\kappa}$$

$$= \left(\frac{1}{(1+n)(1+g)}\right)^\beta (sy_t + (1-\delta)k_t)^{1-\alpha} A_t^{-\beta} x_t^{-\kappa}$$

$$= \left(\frac{1}{(1+n)(1+g)}\right)^\beta \left(s\frac{y_t}{k_t} + (1-\delta)\right)^{1-\alpha} k_t^{1-\alpha} A_t^{-\beta} x_t^{-\kappa}$$

$$= \left(\frac{1}{(1+n)(1+g)}\right)^\beta \left(\frac{s}{z_t} + (1-\delta)\right)^{1-\alpha} z_t,$$

where for the last equality we used the expression in (11) for z_t, and where we have exploited the fact that $\alpha + \beta + \kappa = 1$. We have thus arrived at a transition equation for z_t, most conveniently written as:

$$z_{t+1} = \left(\frac{1}{(1+n)(1+g)}\right)^\beta [s + (1-\delta)z_t]^{1-\alpha} z_t^\alpha. \tag{12}$$

To show that this transition equation implies convergence of the capital–output ratio, z_t, to a particular and constant steady state level, z^*, from any strictly positive initial level, z_0, it suffices to demonstrate the following four properties of the transition curve:

1. It passes through $(0, 0)$. This follows directly from (12) setting $z_t = 0$.
2. It is everywhere strictly increasing. This also follows directly from inspection of (12).
3. It has exactly one strictly positive intersection with the 45° line. We show this by solving the transition equation (12) for $z_{t+1} = z_t = z$. This gives:

$$z^{1-\alpha} = \left(\frac{1}{(1+n)(1+g)}\right)^\beta [s + (1-\delta)z]^{1-\alpha} \Leftrightarrow$$

$$z = z^* \equiv \frac{s}{[(1+n)(1+g)]^{\beta/(\beta+\kappa)} - (1-\delta)} > 0, \tag{13}$$

where we have used $1 - \alpha = \beta + \kappa$, and the inequality follows from $n \geq 0$, $g \geq 0$, and $\delta < 1$. We have thus found a unique value, z^*, for the intersection with the 45° line.

4. It has a slope at $(0, 0)$ which is strictly larger than one, the slope of the 45° line.[4] By differentiation of (12) with respect to z_t we get:

---

4. We could alternatively show that the slope at z^* is smaller than one (do that and explain why this is also sufficient), but here the procedure suggested is the simplest.

$$\frac{dz_{t+1}}{dz_t} = \left(\frac{1}{(1+n)(1+g)}\right)^{\beta} \cdot \{(1-\alpha)(1-\delta)[s+(1-\delta)z_t]^{-\alpha}z_t^{\alpha} + [s+(1-\delta)z_t]^{1-\alpha}\alpha z_t^{\alpha-1}\}.$$

This goes to infinity as z_t goes to zero because of the presence of $z_t^{\alpha-1}$, where $\alpha - 1 < 0$.

One can now sketch the transition diagram for z_t as it must look given the four properties, and convince oneself by 'staircase iteration' that z_t indeed converges to z^* in the long run from any initial $z_0 > 0$ (do this).

In the particular case of $\kappa = 0$, the steady state capital–output ratio z^* becomes $s/(n + g + \delta + ng)$, the same as that in the Solow model (just compute k_t^*/y_t^* from the appropriate equations in Section 5.3).

The steady state growth rate

Summarizing, we have established that the capital–output ratio, $z_t = k_t/y_t$, converges towards the constant steady state level z^*. This means that the growth rates of k_t and y_t must converge towards the same rate. Above we found the expression (10) for the common value of the approximate growth rates. This value was:

$$g^y \approx \frac{\beta}{\beta+\kappa}g - \frac{\kappa}{\beta+\kappa}n. \tag{14}$$

An exercise at the end of this chapter will ask you to find the exact growth rate of y_t in steady state and show that this is indeed close to the expression in (14). The same exercise will ask you to verify that the steady state of the Solow model with land meets the requirements for balanced growth formulated in Chapter 2.

Since total output is $Y_t = y_t L_t$, and total capital is $K_t = k_t L_t$, the approximate growth rates of Y_t and K_t in steady state are both close to $g^y + n$, or:

$$g^Y = g^K \approx \frac{\beta}{\beta+\kappa}(g + n). \tag{15}$$

It is illuminating to compare the steady state growth rate g^y in output per worker that we have arrived at here to that of the general Solow model, which was equal to the rate g of labour-augmenting technological progress. In the particular case of $\kappa = 0$, the growth rate g^y in (14) also takes the value g, which should be no surprise. However, when land has some importance in production so that $\kappa > 0$, the g^y in (14) is smaller than g (whenever $g > 0$ or $n > 0$), and the more important land is (the larger κ is), the more g^y will fall below g.

In the 'classical case' where there is no technological progress, $g = 0$, but some population growth, $n > 0$, economic growth will be negative according to (14). The growing input of labour will inevitably press on the limited amount of land. As land becomes more and more scarce relative to labour (and capital), diminishing returns will imply that income per worker will decline. Note from (15) that the input of capital will not be growing at the same rate as labour, but at a somewhat lower rate. Again this reflects the diminishing returns to capital and labour which imply that income per worker, and hence savings per worker, cannot keep pace with the labour force. As you will be asked to show in an exercise, the real wage will fall by the same rate as output per worker, while the real rent on land will be increasing at the same rate as total output, Y_t. The classical economists thought that decreasing wages would ultimately bring population growth to a stop. When that happened, wages would be at a subsistence level while the rent on land would be at a maximum. Working people would be poor while the landlords would live rich and idle lives, an unfortunate state of affairs much emphasized by the classical economists.

If there is no population growth, $n = 0$, but there is some technological growth, $g > 0$, (the 'modern case'), then $0 < g^y < g$. There will be growth in income per worker, but the growth rate will be smaller than the rate of labour-augmenting technological progress. Technological progress means that the *effective* labour input, A_tL_t, increases at rate g, while capital, K_t, will increase at a somewhat lower rate than g (see again (15)). The increased amounts of effective labour and capital will press on the fixed amount of land, implying, through diminishing returns to capital and effective labour, that income per worker cannot keep pace with labour-augmenting technological progress.

We can conclude that the classics were right on their own assumptions and perhaps more right than they thought. Not only does land imply a drag on growth in the presence of population growth, it also implies a drag on growth in the sense that technological progress is less effective in creating economic growth than it would have been if land had no importance for aggregate production.

Technological progress *does* have a positive influence on growth in income per capita according to (14), but will it, realistically, be enough to outweigh the negative influence from population growth? The condition for strictly positive growth in GDP per worker is $\beta g > \kappa n$. Is this likely to be fulfilled? A lower bound for labour's share, β, would be approximately 0.6, which would leave 0.4 to the sum of capital's share α and land's share κ. At the very most, κ could thus be close to 0.4. So, in an absolutely worst case, the condition for positive economic growth would be $g > (2/3)n$. With an annual population growth rate of 1 per cent, which is between plausible and high by Western standards, an annual growth rate of labour-augmenting technological progress of $\frac{2}{3}$ per cent would suffice for positive long-run growth in income per worker according to our model, and $\frac{2}{3}$ per cent is well below empirical estimates of long-run annual growth rates for labour-augmenting technological progress in Western countries.

We have just derived a worst-case condition for long-run economic growth. If we consider more realistic parameter values such as $\beta = 0.6$ and $\alpha = \kappa = 0.2$,[5] we get $g^y = (3/4)g - (1/4)n$. Hence, if the annual rates are, say, $g = 2$ per cent and $n = 0.5$ per cent, which could be typical for a Western economy, then g^y would be 1.375 per cent per year, which is a decent long-run growth rate and certainly far from zero. The fact that GDP per capita has grown at annual rates of around 2 per cent in many Western countries may suggest that technological growth rates (our model's g) have been somewhat above 2 per cent per year. Note, on the other hand, that if a country has little control over population growth and experiences annual values for n of around 3 per cent (which is the case in some developing countries, see Table A), then the drag on growth caused by population growth could be as large as $\frac{3}{4}$ of a percentage point, and rates of technological growth, g, above 1 per cent would be needed just to overcome the negative influence of population growth.

MODERN GROWTH THEORY AND THE GROWTH PESSIMISM OF THE CLASSICAL ECONOMISTS

The Solow model with a fixed factor such as land implies convergence to a steady state with two drags on long-run economic growth: 1) population growth will tend to cause a negative growth in income per capita and wages, and 2) technological progress will generate less growth in income per capita than in a fictitious situation where land is of no importance. However, continuing positive economic growth does not seem to be ruled out for rates of technological progress and population growth that are reasonable by Western standards: two hundred years of economic growth in the West suggest that the classics paid too little attention to the possibilities for long-run technological progress and birth control not caused by 'misery and vice'. Still, the classical pessimism may be sadly relevant for many developing countries that have not got population growth under control.

5. In the article by Nordhaus cited earlier in this chapter (see Footnote 1), a labour share of 0.6 and a capital share of 0.2 are considered realistic. This leaves another 0.2 for land's share.

The steady state balanced growth path

One may get the impression that to have much land is bad. Land implies drags on growth (compared to a fictitious situation where land is not important) and more so the more important land is. Isn't there anything good about an abundance of land? A glance at the production function will reveal that there is. For given inputs of other factors, a larger amount of land, X, will imply higher output and average income. The amount of land does not affect the *growth rate* in output per worker along the steady state growth path, but it does affect the *level* of this path. We can see this as follows.

Start again from the per capita production function, $y_t = \kappa_t^\alpha A_t^\beta x_t^\kappa$, as stated in (8). To get the capital–output ratio on the right-hand side, divide both sides by y_t^α, thereby getting $y_t^{1-\alpha} = z_t^\alpha A_t^\beta (X/L_t)^\kappa$. In steady state the capital–output ratio, z_t, is constant and equal to the z^* of (13), so the steady state growth path for y_t is (remembering that $1 - \alpha = \beta + \kappa$):

$$y_t^* = (z^*)^{\alpha/(\beta+\kappa)} A_t^{\beta/(\beta+\kappa)} \left(\frac{X}{L_t}\right)^{\kappa/(\beta+\kappa)}. \tag{16}$$

If we want to trace the growth path back to parameters (including those entering z^*) and initial values, we can insert $A_t = A_0(1 + g)^t$ and $L_t = L_0(1 + n)^t$ to get:

$$y_t^* = (z^*)^{\alpha/(\beta+\kappa)} A_0^{\beta/(\beta+\kappa)} \left(\frac{X}{L_0}\right)^{\kappa/(\beta+\kappa)} (1+g)^{\beta/(\beta+\kappa)t} (1+n)^{-\kappa/(\beta+\kappa)t}. \tag{17}$$

Note that in line with our discussion in the previous subsection, the growth rate along this path is affected by both g and n. In fact, it appears that the growth rate must be the g^y of (14). Taking g and n as given, the growth path lies higher the larger X/L_0 is, that is, the more land there is per worker in some base year. Furthermore, (16) shows that in any given year steady state income per worker, y_t^*, depends positively on X/L_t.

We can test these predictions empirically using data for the value of natural resources from the World Bank's Wealth Estimates. Here one can find year 2000 data for the values of 'crop land' and of 'pasture land' per capita. Adding these gives a measure of land per capita. We can combine these data with data from the Penn World Table (PWT). Taking logs on both sides of (16) gives:

$$\ln y_t^* = \frac{\beta}{\beta+\kappa}\ln A_t + \frac{\alpha}{\beta+\kappa}\ln z^* + \frac{\kappa}{\beta+\kappa}\ln\left(\frac{X}{L_t}\right).$$

Here we should insert the expression for z^* from (13), but taking the log of z^* does not give a handy expression because of the exponent in the denominator of z^*. Since β is realistically at least 0.6, and κ is relatively small, 0.2 say, we may crudely approximate the exponent $\beta/(\beta + \kappa)$ to be one, in which case $\ln z^* \cong \ln s - \ln(n + g + \delta)$, here also using $ng \cong 0$. Hence from the above formula for $\ln y_t^*$:

$$\ln y_t^* \approx \frac{\beta}{\beta+\kappa}\ln A_t + \frac{\alpha}{\beta+\kappa}[\ln s - \ln(n+g+\delta)] + \frac{\kappa}{\beta+\kappa}\ln\left(\frac{X}{L_t}\right). \tag{18}$$

We have arrived (more or less) at the steady state equation for the general Solow model corrected for the presence of land (setting $\kappa = 0$ in (18) gives the steady state equation of Chapter 5 with $ng = 0$). With our usual short-cuts, that is, assuming that the basic parameters α, β and κ as well as A_t are the same in all countries, (18) suggests the following regression equation across countries i:

$$\ln y_{03}^i = \gamma_0 + \gamma_1[\ln s^i - \ln(n^i + 0.075)] + \gamma_2 \ln x_{00}^i,$$

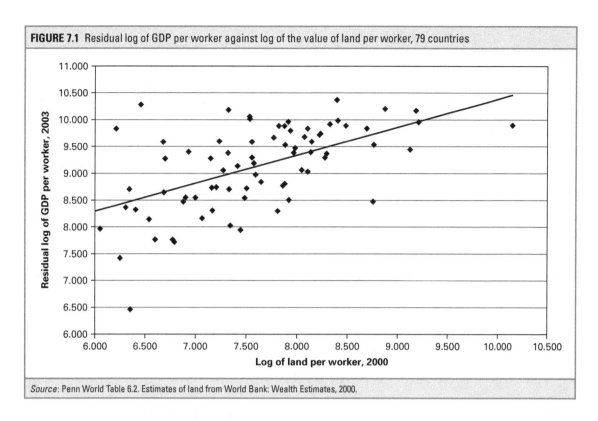

FIGURE 7.1 Residual log of GDP per worker against log of the value of land per worker, 79 countries

Source: Penn World Table 6.2. Estimates of land from World Bank: Wealth Estimates, 2000.

where x_{00}^i is the year 2000 value of land per capita for country i derived from the World Bank data, and, as usual, y_{03}^i is the GDP per worker in year 2003, while s^i and n^i are annual averages over the period 1960 to 2003 of investment rates and labour force growth rates, respectively. Strictly speaking, (18) suggests using the same year for GDP per worker and for land per worker, but 2000 is so close to 2003 that our inaccuracy should not be serious. We consider a sample of the 79 countries that have at least grade C for data quality in the PWT, had at least 2 million inhabitants in 1960, and for which data are available from the PWT and the World Bank. This time we do not want to exclude countries that are dependent on natural resources. An estimation based on this sample gives:

$$\ln y_{03}^i = 5.16 + \underset{(se=0.14)}{1.02} [\ln s^i - \ln(n^i + 0.075)] + \underset{(se=0.11)}{0.52} \ln(x_{00}^i), \qquad \text{adj. } R^2 = 0.61. \tag{19}$$

There seems to be a positive and significant influence from land per worker on GDP per worker, and the influence from $\ln s - \ln(n + g + \delta)$ is also estimated to have the 'correct' sign. An exercise will ask you if the estimates of γ_1 and γ_2 seem reasonable in view of plausible values for the parameters α, β and κ.

Figure 7.1 gives an illustration. It plots the 'residual value' of the log of GDP per worker, $\ln y_{03}^i - 1.02[\ln s^i - \ln(n^i + 0.075)]$, that is, the part not explained by the structural parameters s^i and n^i, against land per worker, $\ln x_{00}^i$, across countries. The figure gives an indication of a relatively tight positive relationship.

AN ABUNDANCE OF LAND IS GOOD . . .   ❗

Cross-country empirics are consistent with the prediction of the Solow model with land that more land per capita leads to higher income per capita in the long run.

7.2 The Solow model with oil

L and is not the only natural resource of importance for aggregate production. Non-renewable resources such as oil, gas, coal, metals, etc., are also important. Unlike land, the amount of which stays constant when used in production, non-renewable resources are depleted as they are used. Intuitively this should imply even more of a drag on growth than does land. We will investigate this intuition by analysing a Solow model with 'oil', using the term 'oil' generically for exhaustible resources. The model will abstract from the presence of land, but in the next section we will consider a model with both land and oil.

The underlying micro world one should now have in mind is like the one for the Solow model with land, with one exception: the natural resource owned by consumers is no longer a constant amount of land but rather, at the beginning of any period t, the total *remaining* stock, R_t, of an exhaustible resource, oil. The part of this stock that is used as energy input during period t will be denoted by E_t. An important resource depletion equation will state that the stock of oil will be reduced from one period to the next by exactly the amount used in production in the first of the periods.

The model

The production function of the representative firm is now:

$$Y_t = K_t^\alpha (A_t L_t)^\beta E_t^\varepsilon, \quad \alpha > 0, \ \beta > 0, \ \varepsilon > 0, \quad \alpha + \beta + \varepsilon = 1. \tag{20}$$

In line with the replication argument, this production function has constant returns to scale with respect to the three inputs, K_t, L_t and E_t, that can be varied at the firm level within a period. The equations describing capital accumulation, population growth and technological progress are as before:

$$K_{t+1} = sY_t + (1 - \delta)K_t, \quad 0 < s < 1, \quad 0 < \delta < 1, \tag{21}$$

$$L_{t+1} = (1 + n)L_t, \quad n \geq 0, \tag{22}$$

$$A_{t+1} = (1 + g)A_t, \quad g \geq 0. \tag{23}$$

The depletion of the natural resource is described by:

$$R_{t+1} = R_t - E_t. \tag{24}$$

This leaves us with the question: how much of the remaining stock, R_t, of the exhaustible resource will be used in production as the input, E_t, in each period t?

For a proper micro-founded answer (as given for the inputs of labour and capital) we should assume a market for oil, let us say, for simplicity, a competitive one with a real price, u_t, per unit of oil. The demand in this market would come from the representative firm and would in any period obey a usual marginal product (of energy E_t) equal to real price condition. The supply would, under the not quite realistic assumption of a perfectly competitive market, come from many small suppliers (possibly 'represented' by one) who would in total own R_t, and each of whom would have negligible influence on the current and future prices of oil and on the total future stock of oil. A supplier would be faced with a basic trade-off. Since the stock of oil is gradually used up, energy prices would and should be expected to increase over time, which speaks for not selling too much off today, but for saving it for later use. The possibility of placing a revenue from the sales of oil in interest-bearing capital speaks, on the other hand, for selling off more now.

The interaction between demand and supply involving current and (correctly foreseen) future prices would solve the full problem of how a given remaining stock of the exhaustible resource would be allocated over time. This problem is complex and we will not present a solution here. Instead we will postulate that the counteracting forces described can result in the 'rule' that in each period a certain and constant fraction s_E of the remaining stock is used in production, that is:

$$E_t = s_E R_t, \qquad 0 < s_E < 1. \tag{25}$$

Alternatively, we can view our analysis as simply exploring the *consequences* of a constant extraction rate, s_E, without bothering about the microfoundations for such a rule.

In (25) we have assumed $s_E < 1$, which is, of course, required. In Nordhaus' article an annual value for the extraction rate s_E of 0.005 is considered reasonable, corresponding to one half of a per cent of the remaining stock of exhaustible resources being used each year. At any rate, an assumption of $s_E < \delta$ is plausible as annual depreciation rates for aggregate capital are usually estimated to at least 0.05. We will therefore make this assumption, which will be of relevance for what you are asked to demonstrate in Exercise 5 at the end of the chapter.

Our model consists of the six equations above. It is easy to see that for given initial values of the state variables, K_t, L_t, A_t and R_t, the six equations determine the full evolution of all the endogenous variables (convince yourself of this). Note that the two equations (24) and (25) imply that $R_{t+1} = (1 - s_E)R_t$. Given our resource extraction rule, the growth rate of the stock of the resource is constant and equal to $-s_E$. This means that just like technology, A_t, and population, L_t, the stock of resources, R_t, lives a dynamic life of its own and evolves over time as $R_t = (1 - s_E)^t R_0$ from an initial value R_0.

Having assumed a specific rule for the use of the exhaustible resource, it is easy to complete the model with equations stating the prices of the factors, r_t, w_t and u_t, respectively, in terms of the state variables. An exercise will ask you to do so and to think about how the factor rewards evolve over time. It should be no surprise that the income shares of capital and labour will be constant, α and β, respectively. Similarly, energy's share, $u_t E_t/Y_t = u_t s_E R_t/Y_t$, remains constant at ε in all periods as the stock of oil is run down.

The steady state growth rate

Inserting $E_t = s_E R_t$ into the production function gives: $Y_t = K_t^\alpha (A_t L_t)^\beta (s_E R_t)^\varepsilon$. Dividing both sides by L_t gives:

$$y_t = k_t^\alpha A_t^\beta \left(\frac{s_E R_t}{L_t}\right)^\varepsilon = s_E^\varepsilon k_t^\alpha A_t^\beta R_t^\varepsilon L_t^{-\varepsilon}. \tag{26}$$

From the latter equality, taking logs and time differences, one gets in the now familiar notation:

$$g_t^y = \alpha g_t^k + \beta g_t^A + \varepsilon g_t^R - \varepsilon g_t^L \approx \alpha g_t^k + \beta g - \varepsilon s_E - \varepsilon n, \tag{27}$$

which uses the fact that g_t^R is approximately equal to $-s_E$. Assuming again that the dynamics of our full model are such that the capital–output ratio, k_t/y_t, converges towards a constant steady state level, the growth rates of output and capital per worker must converge towards the same rate. Setting $g_t^y = g_t^k$ in (27) and solving shows that both rates must converge towards a common constant level, approximately given by:

$$g^y \approx \frac{\beta}{\beta+\varepsilon}g - \frac{\varepsilon}{\beta+\varepsilon}n - \frac{\varepsilon}{\beta+\varepsilon}s_E. \tag{28}$$

We should demonstrate (rather than assume) that the dynamics of our model imply convergence towards a steady state with a constant capital–output ratio. An exercise will ask you to do this yourself. It is done in much the same way as for the Solow model with land.

The growth rate, g^y, of (28) is in two respects just like the one obtained in (14) for the Solow model with land. First, a given rate, g, of labour-augmenting technological progress is less effective in creating economic growth than in a hypothetical situation where natural resources are not important in production, i.e., $\beta/(\beta + \varepsilon)$ is less than one. Second, population growth implies a drag on economic growth of the size $-[\varepsilon/(\beta + \varepsilon)]n$. These two features occur for the same reasons as in the model with land. Increasing amounts of effective labour in association with increasing amounts of capital will press on the limited amount of the natural resource and therefore, through diminishing returns, imply a slower (and possibly negative) growth in income per worker than with no natural resource. This time, however, the natural resource is in even more limited supply as it disappears gradually through its use in production. This means that over time, the diminishing returns to capital and effective labour arising from the scarcity of the natural resource become more and more severe, implying even more of a drag on growth than in the case of a fixed factor. The last term, $-[\varepsilon/(\beta + \varepsilon)]s_E$, in (28) is explained by this increased scarcity of natural resources. Clearly, the larger is the extraction rate, s_E, the faster the exhaustible resource will be depleted, and the faster the negative influence from diminishing returns to the other factors will grow.

We could proceed as in the model with land, trying to make a numerical evaluation of g^y assuming realistic values for α, β, ε and s_E, etc. You should do such numerical exercises around (28) yourself. However, doing so would result in an 'error' that tends to overestimate the negative influence on growth of land and exhaustible resources. The reason is as follows. First we considered a model with land, but no exhaustible resource. We assumed plausible shares of capital and labour ($\alpha = 0.2$ and $\beta = 0.6$) and then gave the remaining share 0.2 to the remaining factor, land. Now we consider a model with an exhaustible resource but without land, and we are again about to give all of the remaining share, the 0.2, to this last factor. In the real world there are both fixed natural resources and exhaustible ones and with constant returns to all factors, we cannot give all of the income share that is left after capital and labour's shares to each of them. In other words, for a really meaningful numerical exercise there is no way around the job of setting up a model with both land and exhaustible resources.

This is exactly what we do in the next section. You can view the model of this section as a building block on the way, but a very important one, since it demonstrates the *isolated effects* of the presence of an exhaustible natural resource.

The steady state balanced growth path

Consider again (26). Dividing on both sides of the first equality by y_t^α one gets, as in the model with land, the capital–output ratio $z_t = k_t/y_t$ on the right-hand side: $y_t^{1-\alpha} = z_t^\alpha A_t^\beta s_E^\varepsilon (R_t/L_t)^\varepsilon$. An exercise will ask you to show that in this model z_t also converges towards a constant steady state level, z^*, and to find the appropriate expression for z^*. Inserting z^* for z_t, raising to the power of $1/(1 - \alpha)$ on both sides, and using that $1 - \alpha = \beta + \varepsilon$, gives the steady state balanced growth path for y_t:

$$y_t^* = (z^*)^{\alpha/(\beta+\varepsilon)} A_t^{\beta/(\beta+\varepsilon)} s_E^{\varepsilon/(\beta+\varepsilon)} \left(\frac{R_t}{L_t}\right)^{\varepsilon/(\beta+\varepsilon)}. \tag{29}$$

If one wants to trace this back to parameters and initial values, one can insert $A_t = (1 + g)^t A_0$, $L_t = (1 + n)^t L_0$, $R_t = (1 - s_E)^t R_0$, and the correct expression for z^*. In any case, the growth path will be higher the higher R_0/L_0 is, given the rates n, s_E, etc. One can also see directly from (29) that y_t^* is positively affected by R_t/L_t. Hence, according to our model, it is good to have an abundance of exhaustible resources, in a base year or left over in the current year, other circumstances being equal.[6]

As stated, finding the right expression for z^* is left to you as an exercise, but it should be no surprise that, as in the model with land, $\ln z^* \approx \ln s - \ln(n+g+\delta)$ should hold as a crude approximation. Hence, taking logs on both sides in (29), the steady state balanced growth path can be expressed as:

$$\ln y_t^* \cong \frac{\beta}{\beta+\varepsilon}\ln A_t + \frac{\varepsilon}{\beta+\varepsilon}\ln s_E + \frac{\alpha}{\beta+\varepsilon}[\ln s - \ln(n+g+\delta)] + \frac{\varepsilon}{\beta+\varepsilon}\ln\left(\frac{R_t}{L_t}\right). \tag{30}$$

With the usual short-cuts (assuming that the basic parameters α, β and ε as well as both A_t and s_E are the same in all countries), (30) suggests a regression equation across countries i:

$$\ln y_{03}^i = \gamma_0 + \gamma_1[\ln s^i - \ln(n^i + 0.075)] + \gamma_3 \ln\left(\frac{R^i}{L^i}\right)_{00}. \tag{31}$$

For $(R^i/L^i)_{00}$ we use data from the World Bank's Wealth Estimates for the value of 'subsoil assets' (including oil, gas, coal, metals, etc.) per capita in year 2000. Again, the error from mixing year 2003 data for GDP per worker with 2000 data for 'oil' per worker should be small. For some countries the Wealth Estimates report the value zero for subsoil assets and these countries are now excluded. An estimation of (31) based on a sample of 64 remaining countries gives:

$$\ln y_{03}^i = 8.62 + \underset{(se=0.16)}{1.08} [\ln s^i - \ln(n^i + 0.075)] + \underset{(se=0.04)}{0.09} \ln(R_{00}^i/L_{00}^i), \qquad \text{adj. } R^2 = 0.52.$$

The estimated coefficients have the expected signs and are significant, indicating indeed a positive influence of the amount of exhaustible resources on the level of GDP per capita. Figure 7.2 illustrates by plotting the 'residual log of GDP per worker' (that part of GDP which is not explained by the structural parameters s^i and n^i) in 2003 against the log of the value of subsoil assets per worker in 2000.

. . . AND AN ABUNDANCE OF NATURAL RESOURCES IS ALSO GOOD

Cross-country empirics are consistent with the prediction of the Solow model with oil that larger amounts of exhaustible resources lead to higher income per capita in the long run.

7.3 The Solow model with both land and oil

The model

The aggregate production function with both a factor in fixed supply, land, and an exhaustible resource such as oil, is (in the obvious notation):

---

6. Note that this is a statement about the influence of natural resources on the *level* of income, and not about the impact on the *growth rate*. Referring to the latter impact, some economists have spoken of 'the curse of natural resources'. By this they mean that in many resource-abundant countries, opposing interest groups have often been in political and even armed conflict to secure the rents from the exploitation of the resources for themselves. There is also a danger that resource abundance in a country will reduce the perceived need to invest in growth-enhancing activities such as education, research and development, etc. For whatever reason, it is a fact that many resource-rich countries have had a poor historical growth performance. Spectacular examples of this were given in Fig. 2.1 which showed that oil-rich countries like Nigeria and Venezuela have experienced very low and even negative growth in income per worker since 1960.

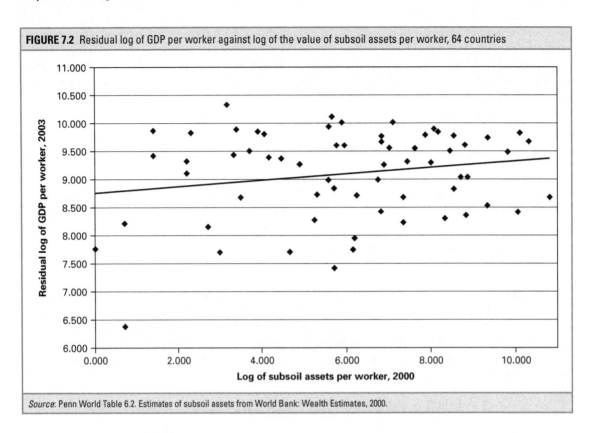

FIGURE 7.2 Residual log of GDP per worker against log of the value of subsoil assets per worker, 64 countries

Source: Penn World Table 6.2. Estimates of subsoil assets from World Bank: Wealth Estimates, 2000.

$$Y_t = K_t^\alpha (A_t L_t)^\beta X^\kappa E_t^\varepsilon, \qquad \alpha > 0, \ \beta > 0, \ \kappa > 0, \ \varepsilon > 0, \qquad \alpha + \beta + \kappa + \varepsilon = 1.$$

There are constant returns to the four factors, capital, labour, land and energy. Hence the sum of the income shares of the two latter factors, $\kappa + \varepsilon$, must be what is left over after capital's and labour's shares. The remaining equations of the model are again (21)–(25) above, where we continue to assume $s_E < \delta$. One can complete the model with equations for the factor reward rates, r_t, w_t, v_t and u_t, from which constant income shares would follow (show this).

The steady state growth rate

Inserting into the production function that $E_t = s_E R_t$ and dividing both sides by L_t now gives:

$$y_t = k_t^\alpha A_t^\beta \left(\frac{X}{L_t}\right)^\kappa \left(\frac{s_E R_t}{L_t}\right)^\varepsilon = s_E^\varepsilon X^\kappa k_t^\alpha A_t^\beta R_t^\varepsilon L_t^{-\kappa-\varepsilon}. \tag{32}$$

From the latter equality we get, taking log differences and in the usual notation:

$$g_t^y = \alpha g_t^k + \beta g_t^A + \varepsilon g_t^R - (\kappa+\varepsilon)g_t^L \approx \alpha g_t^k + \beta g - \varepsilon s_E - (\kappa+\varepsilon)n. \tag{33}$$

In the long run the capital–output ratio converges towards a constant steady state level, as you are again asked to show in an exercise. Therefore, g_t^y and g_t^k converge towards the same rate. Setting $g_t^y = g_t^k$ in (33), remembering that $1 - \alpha = \beta + \kappa + \varepsilon$, and calling the constant solution g^y gives:

$$g^y = \frac{\beta}{\beta+\kappa+\varepsilon}g - \frac{\kappa+\varepsilon}{\beta+\kappa+\varepsilon}n - \frac{\varepsilon}{\beta+\kappa+\varepsilon}s_E. \tag{34}$$

This formula is, in a sense, a perfect combination of the two formulae for g^y from the model with only land and from that with only oil. The explanations of the formula, in terms of the diminishing returns arising from the presence of land and the increasingly severe diminishing returns arising from the presence of oil, are also the same. There is an important difference in the model with just oil with respect to the negative influence of s_E. Taking capital's and labour's shares as given, e.g. $\alpha = 0.2$ and $\beta = 0.6$, one would have to set $\varepsilon = 0.2$ in the model with only oil, arriving, from (28), at a coefficient on s_E of $\frac{1}{4}$. In the present model κ and ε should share the remaining 0.2, e.g. $\kappa = \varepsilon = 0.1$, in which case the coefficient on s_E becomes $\frac{1}{8}$. With both land and oil in the model, the negative influence on growth from the extraction rate, s_E, is potentially much smaller.

Indeed, Nordhaus considers the values $\alpha = 0.2$, $\beta = 0.6$ and $\kappa = \varepsilon = 0.1$ to be realistic. With these values (34) becomes

$$g^y = 0.75g - 0.25n - 0.125s_E. \tag{35}$$

If we set $n = 0.01$ (which is a plausible *upper* estimate for developed countries) and, taking again a plausible value from Nordhaus's article, set $s_E = 0.005$, we get for the long-run growth rate of income per worker:

$$g^y = 0.75g - 0.0025 - 0.000625 \approx 0.75g - 0.003. \tag{36}$$

This equation can be said to involve two growth drags. The most serious one seems to be that (labour-augmenting) technological growth is only three-quarters as effective in creating economic growth as it would be in the (fictitious) absence of natural resources. However, a rate of technological progress of, e.g., 2.4 per cent per year will still contribute 1.8 percentage points to growth in GDP per capita. The other one, arising from the combined effect of increasing population and exhaustion of the limited resources, appears as a further drag (on the 'reduced' growth rate $0.75g$) of at most 0.3 percentage points. Hence, the Solow model with both land and oil seems to support:

GROWTH OPTIMISM IN THE DEVELOPED WORLD

According to modern growth theory the classical economists were correct in pointing out that scarcity of natural resources exerts a negative influence on economic growth. However, none of the drags on growth arising from natural resource scarcity will prevent growth altogether as long as there is a plausible amount of technological progress and population growth is under control, as typically seen in the most developed parts of the world.

This is indeed a major conclusion from our analysis. Still, one should again bear in mind that a population growth rate of, e.g., 3 per cent per year, as seen in some developing countries, would imply that the second of the above growth drags would be around 0.8 percentage points, so a g of around 1 per cent would be needed just to overcome the negative influence of population growth.

GROWTH PESSIMISM IN PARTS OF THE DEVELOPING WORLD

According to modern growth theory, if population growth is not under control, the drag on growth arising as the increasing number of people presses on the limited natural resources is of a serious, and possibly of a growth-preventing, magnitude.

Equation (35) above says that a one percentage point *change* in the population growth rate gives a quarter of a percentage point *change* in the growth rate of GDP per capita, other things being equal. This is an effect completely different from the level effect we discussed earlier. It is not (just) the *level* of the long-run growth path for GDP per worker that is negatively affected by population growth, it is also the *growth rate* along this path. Furthermore, it is an effect of potentially serious magnitude. For instance, *the observed differences in annual population growth rates between developed and developing countries of up to three percentage points would, according to our model, imply differences in annual growth rates of GDP per worker of 0.75 percentage points*. This is a big difference taking long-run compound interest effects into account.

Our model's steady state prediction of how economic growth should depend on population growth can be confronted with the usual type of cross-country data. One can simply plot long-run growth rates in GDP per worker against long-run labour force growth rates as in Fig. 7.3. Details of the estimation of the straight line are given in the figure's legend.

The figure and the estimation point to a relationship that is perhaps not too tight, but significantly negative. Note that the estimated slope is around –0.5, with a standard error of 0.14. Thus the estimated slope is within two standard deviations of the theoretical value of –0.25 predicted by our model (see the coefficient on n in (35)). Hence, both the direction and the magnitude of the influence of population growth on economic growth in our model's steady state are consistent with the data.

We should remind you once again of the warning concerning reversed causality that is very often important for the interpretation of empirical relationships in economics. Does Fig. 7.3 really illustrate a negative influence of population growth on economic growth across countries, or is it rather the other way around, that a better growth performance helps to get population growth under control? One simply cannot tell from the empirical evidence

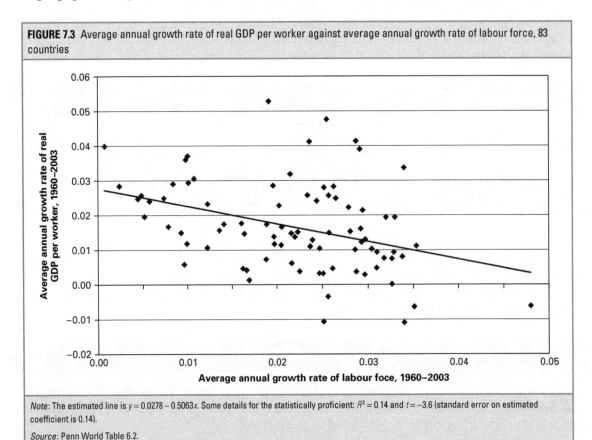

FIGURE 7.3 Average annual growth rate of real GDP per worker against average annual growth rate of labour force, 83 countries

Note: The estimated line is $y = 0.0278 - 0.5063x$. Some details for the statistically proficient: $R^2 = 0.14$ and $t = -3.6$ (standard error on estimated coefficient is 0.14).

Source: Penn World Table 6.2.

presented here. Our model provides theoretical reasons why the causality should run from population growth to economic growth, but there may well be other mechanisms which tend to generate a feedback from higher income growth to lower population growth. Indeed, the existence of such mechanisms might help to explain why our estimated correlation between population growth and income growth is somewhat higher than suggested by our theoretical model.

The steady state balanced growth path

If we divide both sides of the first equality of (32) by y_t^α, again to get the capital–output ratio on the right-hand side, we obtain: $y_t^{1-\alpha} = z_t^\alpha A_t^\beta (X/L_t)^\kappa s_E^\varepsilon (R_t/L_t)^\varepsilon$, where $z_t \equiv K_t/Y_t$. In steady state z_t has reached a constant value, z^*. Hence the steady state balanced growth path for y_t is:

$$y_t^* = (z^*)^{\alpha/(\beta+\kappa+\varepsilon)} A_t^{\beta/(\beta+\kappa+\varepsilon)} \left(\frac{X}{L_t}\right)^{\kappa/(\beta+\kappa+\varepsilon)} s_E^{\varepsilon/(\beta+\kappa+\varepsilon)} \left(\frac{R_t}{L_t}\right)^{\varepsilon/(\beta+\kappa+\varepsilon)}.$$

Getting an expression for z^* and demonstrating convergence towards it requires a dynamic analysis like that conducted for the model with only land, but it should be no surprise that again $\ln z^* \approx \ln s - \ln(n+g+\delta)$ can be used as a crude approximation (an exercise will ask you to demonstrate convergence and find z^*). Hence, by taking logs on both sides of the equation above, the steady state balanced growth path can be expressed as:

$$\ln y_t^* \cong \frac{\beta}{\beta+\kappa+\varepsilon}\ln A_t + \frac{\varepsilon}{\beta+\kappa+\varepsilon}\ln s_E + \frac{\alpha}{\beta+\kappa+\varepsilon}[\ln s - \ln(n+g+\delta)]$$

$$+\frac{\kappa}{\beta+\kappa+\varepsilon}\ln\left(\frac{X}{L_t}\right) + \frac{\varepsilon}{\beta+\kappa+\varepsilon}\ln\left(\frac{R_t}{L_t}\right). \tag{37}$$

This suggests a regression equation:

$$\ln y_{00}^i = \gamma_0 + \gamma_1[\ln s^i - \ln(n^i + 0.075)] + \gamma_2\ln\left(\frac{X^i}{L^i}\right)_{00} + \gamma_3\ln\left(\frac{R^i}{L^i}\right)_{00}, \tag{38}$$

across countries. Once again we take $(X^i/L^i)_{00}$ to be the 2000 value of 'crop land' plus 'pasture land' per capita for country i, while $(R^i/L^i)_{00}$ is measured as the value of 'subsoil assets' per capita in 2000, according to the data from the World Bank. An estimation based on 63 countries gives:

$$\ln y_{03}^i = 5.70 + \underset{(se=0.16)}{0.91}[\ln s^i - \ln(n^i + 0.075)] + \underset{(se=0.13)}{0.41}\ln\left(\frac{X^i}{L^i}\right)_{00} + \underset{(se=0.03)}{0.07}\ln\left(\frac{R^i}{L^i}\right)_{00}, \tag{39}$$

adj. $R^2 = 0.59$.

One should note that for both of the types of natural resources considered, the influence is in the expected direction, but with a bit of a significance problem regarding exhaustible resources (the t-value for the estimate of γ_3 is 2.1). Our earlier conclusions are thus generally confirmed.

7.4 Unlimited substitution? An important issue of concern

This chapter deals with the very important issue *whether sustained growth in per capita income can essentially go on for ever despite the limitations given by the natural environment*. Our main conclusions are repeated in the following:

TWO STATEMENTS ON THE PROSPECTS FOR ECONOMIC GROWTH

1 If underlying technological progress and population growth rates can be held at levels that have typically been seen over long (but recent) periods in Western countries, permanent economic growth seems to be sustainable, that is, not in conflict with nature's finiteness.
2 If population growth rates are at the highest levels seen in developing countries, the limited natural resources imply a serious drag on growth that may offset most or all of the positive influence of technological progress on income per capita.

The second of these statements means that for the poorest parts of the world the classical ('dismal science') views are still sadly relevant. Nevertheless, the overall conclusion with respect to the *possibility* of sustainable growth is optimistic because of the first statement.

The mainly optimistic conclusion is, of course, based on the premises of the models we have considered. It is now time to face one critical modelling assumption explicitly: our Cobb–Douglas production functions assume that there are no limits to the technological possibilities of substituting capital and technologically augmented labour for scarce natural resources. Indeed, we implicitly assumed that production can continue to grow even as the input of natural resources becomes infinitely small relative to other inputs. Much of the public debate on the possible limits to growth is really about the validity of this assumption, which is clearly not an innocent one.

Influenced by the economic history of Western countries over the past two centuries, most economists tend to be technological optimists, believing that the substitution possibilities in production are essentially unlimited in the long run. They point out that whenever a particular natural resource becomes scarce, its relative price will tend to go up, providing strong incentives for the development of alternative production techniques and consumption patterns which rely less on the scarce factor. According to this view the modelling assumption of unlimited substitution should not be taken literally, but should be seen as a metaphor for the described incentive effect. In other words, when the world has only one ton of copper left it is not that production will literally still use small amounts of the remaining copper in association with extremely sophisticated labour in accordance with an old production function. Rather, copper will have been replaced by a substituting product, as copper, because of its scarcity, became extremely expensive and the economic gains from developing a substituting product became very large. With just one or two types of natural resources in our production function we cannot describe this process explicitly, but the assumption of unlimited substitution can be seen as representing it.

The same (optimistic) economists also argue that the deterioration of the natural environment caused by the polluting activities of firms and consumers can be held in check by intelligent use of 'green' taxes and other economic instruments in environmental policy, e.g. tradable pollution permits.

On the other hand, many natural scientists and environmentalists argue that there are in fact limits to the possibilities of substituting other factors for certain essential raw materials and life support services offered by the environment. The more moderate critics doubt that the market mechanisms will always ensure the development of new substitute techniques in time to prevent serious disruptions stemming from environmental degradation. In particular, when it comes to environmental problems such as those caused by global warming, a fundamental difficulty is that measures taken by one country to reduce greenhouse gas emissions will mainly benefit other countries, thus reducing the incentive for individual countries to cut their emissions to the extent needed from a global perspective. Dealing with such truly global environmental problems requires international cooperation on a scale not previously seen in the history of mankind.

Passing a fully qualified judgement on these fundamental issues requires insight into the natural sciences as well as into economics and other social sciences. With this chapter we do not pretend to have given a definitive answer to the question: 'Are there limits to growth?' However, we hope to have shed some light on the basic assumptions one needs to make to warrant either growth optimism or growth pessimism.

7.5 Summary

1. Land and natural resources are important inputs into production. This is particularly the case if 'land' is interpreted in a broad sense to include all the life support services of the natural environment. This chapter has developed an extended Solow model where capital and labour are combined with natural resources in production. By the replication argument, an increase in all factor inputs yields constant returns to scale, but the need for natural resources implies diminishing returns to the combination of labour and capital. A crucial issue is whether technological progress is sufficient to generate perpetual economic growth despite the scarcity of natural resources.

2. In a three-factor Solow model where labour and capital are combined with a *fixed supply of land*, technological progress serves in part to offset the negative influence of increasing land scarcity on income per worker. Hence the growth rate of per capita income is lower than the rate of labour-augmenting technological progress even if there is no population growth. Positive population growth implies a further drag on growth in per capita income when land is in fixed supply and could even bring growth to a halt, as predicted by the classical economists. However, for parameter values characteristic of developed countries, a fixed supply of natural resources would not realistically prevent sustained positive growth in income per capita.

3. The Solow model with a fixed supply of land predicts that a country with a higher initial stock of land per worker will have a higher level of GDP per worker, all other things equal. The international empirical evidence is consistent with this prediction.

4. In a three-factor Solow model where labour and capital are combined with an *exhaustible* natural resource ('oil'), the gradual depletion of the natural resource creates even stronger diminishing returns to capital and effective labour than in the model with a fixed stock of land. Hence a higher rate of technical progress is required to outweigh the negative effect on growth arising from population growth and increasing natural resource scarcity.

5. The Solow model with oil implies that a larger initial stock of the exhaustible resource per worker should, *ceteris paribus*, yield a higher GDP per worker. Confirming this, the international evidence shows a positive relationship between the stock of subsoil assets and the level of real GDP per worker.

6. We also developed a four-factor Solow model where production uses a fixed stock of land as well as inputs of an exhaustible natural resource in combination with capital and labour. In such an economy positive economic growth is sustainable for parameter values typical for Western countries, but may not be attainable in poor developing countries which have not managed to bring population growth under control.

7. The Solow model with land and oil predicts that the average rate of growth in GDP per worker will be lower the higher the rate of population growth, other things equal. The international cross-country evidence does indeed show a negative relationship between population growth and economic growth, and the quantitative relationship is roughly in line with the prediction of the Solow model. However, causality may not only run from population growth to economic growth, but also in the opposite direction.

8. A crucial assumption in the Solow model with scarce natural resources is that there are unlimited technological possibilities of substituting capital and (educated) labour for increasingly scarce natural resource inputs. This assumption should not be taken literally, but should be seen as reflecting a belief that growing scarcity of a particular natural resource will generate an economic incentive to develop new substitute inputs. Much of the debate about the possible limits to growth is really about the validity of the assumption of unlimited substitution possibilities. Resolving this issue requires insight into natural as well as social sciences.

7.6 Exercises

Exercise 1. Exact growth rates, and balanced growth, in the steady state of the Solow model with land

1. Show that in the Solow model with land the exact (in contrast to the approximate) common growth rate g^{ye} of output per worker and of capital per worker in steady state is:

$$g^{ye} = (1+g)^{\beta/(\beta+\kappa)}\left(\frac{1}{1+n}\right)^{\kappa/(\beta+\kappa)} - 1.$$

(Hint: Start again from the per capita production function (8). This time, do not take logs, but write (8) also for period $t-1$, divide one by the other and proceed in terms of growth *factors*.) Show that g^{ye} is approximately equal to the g^y of (14) in Section 7.1. (Hint: Use repeatedly the approximation, $a-1 \approx \ln a$.)

2. Show that the steady state of the Solow model with land is in accordance with balanced growth, not only in the respect that the capital–output ratio is constant, but also in the following respects: the real wage rate, w_t, grows by the same rate as both output per worker and capital per worker, and the real interest rate, r_t, is constant. Show also that the real rate of rent on land, v_t, grows at the same rate as total output (not per worker), and that whenever $n > 0$, the real rent on land, v_t, grows faster than the real wage rate.

3. Assume that $n > 0$, but $g = 0$, more or less as considered by the classical economists. Describe how the real rates, r_t, w_t and u_t, evolve over time. If there is a fixed number of landlords owning the land, how will their life conditions evolve compared to the conditions of the workers?

Exercise 2. The Solow model with land in continuous time

Discrete time may be easier to grasp, but analysis in continuous time often runs more elegantly. The latter may be particularly true for the models considered in this chapter. Consider the following continuous time version of the Solow model with land (in obvious notation):

$$Y = K^\alpha (AL)^\beta X^\kappa, \qquad \alpha, \beta, \kappa > 0, \qquad \alpha + \beta + \kappa = 1,$$

$$\dot{K} = sY - \delta K, \qquad 0 < s, \delta < 1,$$

$$\frac{\dot{L}}{L} = n, \qquad n \geq 0$$

$$\frac{\dot{A}}{A} = g, \qquad g \geq 0.$$

1. Show that the per capita production function and the capital–output ratio (still in obvious notation, e.g. $x \equiv X/L$) are, respectively:

$$y = k^{\alpha} A^{\beta} x^{\kappa},$$

$$z = k^{1-\alpha} A^{-\beta} x^{-\kappa}.$$

2. Show that the law of motion for z following from the model is the following *linear* differential equation in z:

$$\dot{z} = (\beta + \kappa)s - \lambda z,$$

where $\lambda \equiv (\beta + \kappa)\delta + \beta(n + g)$. (Hint: Start from the expression for z you found in **1**. Take logs and differentiate with respect to time. In the equation you arrive at, use, e.g., that $\dot{k}/k = \dot{K}/K - n$, etc. Remember that $1 - \alpha = \beta + \kappa$.)

3. Show that the steady state value, z^*, for the capital–output ratio is:

$$z^* = \frac{s}{\dfrac{\beta}{\beta + \kappa}(n + g) + \delta},$$

and show that the above differential equation implies convergence of z to z^*. (For the latter you can just draw $\dot{z}$ as a function of z or you can solve the differential equation as in Exercise 3 of Chapter 3.)

4. Show that the growth rate of y in steady state is *exactly*:

$$\frac{\beta g - \kappa n}{\beta + \kappa},$$

and compare this to the approximate growth rate, g^y, found in Section 1 of this chapter.

Exercise 3. Golden rule in the Solow model with land

For the Solow model with land, find the value of the savings/investment rate, s, that will imply the highest possible position for the growth path of consumption per worker in steady state. Compare your result to the golden rule of the Solow model of Chapter 5, and explain the similarity. Why is the result nevertheless different here? From reasonable parameter values considered in this chapter, of what magnitude is the golden rule savings rate you have just found? Compare with empirical investment rates in typical developed countries (from Table A).

Exercise 4. Are the estimated coefficients in the Solow model with land reasonable?

Consider the estimation in (19). Are the estimated values of γ_1 and γ_2 reasonable given (18) and plausible parameter values? Why is γ_1 estimated to be smaller than the γ in Chapter 5? Does the fact that it is smaller tend to make it more reasonable? Is it enough? From (18) and (19) one can also find implied values of α, β and κ. Find these and judge their reasonableness. A major point in Chapter 6 was that by introducing human capital into the Solow model, the estimated coefficients in the model's steady state equation became much more reasonable. Does the introduction of land imply a similar improvement?

Exercise 5. Convergence to steady state in the Solow model with oil

For the Solow model with oil, set up the transition equation for the capital–output ratio, $z_t \equiv K_t/Y_t = k_t/y_t$ in usual notation, and show that this transition equation implies convergence of z_t towards a constant level z^*. State the expression for z^*. (Hint: You can go through a number of steps which are counterparts of the steps we went through for the model with just land in Section 7.1, in order to establish convergence to z^* and to find the value for z^*.) Show that the approximation we used in Section 7.2, $\ln z^* \approx \ln s - \ln(n + g + \delta)$, should not be far-fetched. (Note that for the latter you need one more approximation than we used in Section 7.1: not only $\beta/(\beta + \varepsilon) \approx 1$, but also $\varepsilon/(\beta + \varepsilon) \approx 0$ and/or $1 - s_E \approx 1$ should be used.)

Exercise 6. Golden rule in the Solow model with oil

State the steady state growth path for consumption per worker of the Solow model with oil. Does more oil per worker, in a base year or left over in the current year, given all other parameters, etc., imply a higher or lower position of this path? What is the golden rule value for the savings/investment rate, s, in this model? Comment.

Exercise 7. Balanced growth and the behaviour of the factor compensations in the steady state of the Solow model with oil

1. Consider the Solow model with oil. State expressions for the factor reward rates, r_t, w_t and u_t, as depending, in any period, on the state variables K_t, L_t, A_t and R_t. Show that the income shares are constant, in particular that the share of energy (or oil), $u_t E_t/Y_t = u_t s_E R_t/Y_t$, is equal to ε in all periods.

2. Consider now only the steady state of the same model. Show that the approximate growth rates of Y_t and K_t fulfil:

$$g^Y = g^K \cong \frac{\beta}{\beta + \varepsilon}(g + n) - \frac{\varepsilon}{\beta + \varepsilon} s_E.$$

   Show that there is balanced growth in steady state (also) in the respects mentioned in Exercise 1, Question 2.

3. Find expressions for the approximate growth rates, g^r, g^w and g^u, of the real interest rate, r_t, the real wage rate, w_t, and the real oil price, u_t, respectively, in steady state. How does u_t evolve compared to w_t?

Exercise 8. Convergence to steady state, and the steady state growth path, in the Solow model with both land and oil

For the Solow model with both land and oil, do what you were asked to do for the Solow model with just oil in Exercise 5 above. In particular, you are asked to justify equation (37) of Section 7.3, in the sense that the steady state growth path for y_t (involving the steady state value z^* for the capital–output ratio) with appropriate approximations leads to (37).

Exercise 9. Further numerical evaluation of g^y in the model with both land and oil

Consider equation (35), which assumes $\alpha = 0.2$, $\beta = 0.6$, $\kappa = \varepsilon = 0.1$, and (36), which assumes further $n = 0.01$ and $s_E = 0.005$. In the text we reminded you that a considerably higher population growth rate, e.g. $n = 0.03$, would change the conclusion that the growth drag from population growth is of a modest size. Is something similar true for the growth drag from depletion of the exhaustible resource? What would this drag be if, e.g., $s_E = 0.015$ were more realistic? Why is the trebling of the relevant rate less important for s_E than for n?

Exercise 10. Are the estimated coefficients in the Solow model with land and oil reasonable?

Consider equation (37) and the estimation in (38) based on it. Are the estimated values of γ_1, γ_2 and γ_3 reasonable for plausible parameter values? Back out implied values for α, β, κ and ε

from the estimation and judge their reasonableness. As in Exercise 3 above, discuss whether the introduction of both land and oil can substitute for the introduction of human capital.

Exercise 11. The Solow model with natural resources and human capital

In some exercises above you may have found that our parameter estimates based on the Solow models with natural resources are not too plausible. It is an obvious idea to build in human capital as well to see if this will make parameter estimates more reasonable. A full analysis of such a model is beyond the scope of this book, but finding the balanced growth rate should not be too complicated.

In a Solow model with both natural resources and human capital the production function would be:

$$Y_t = K_t^\alpha H_t^\varphi (A_t L_t)^\beta X^\kappa E_t^\varepsilon,$$

in an obvious combination of the notations of this chapter and the previous one. Assume that A_t grows at constant rate g, L_t at constant rate n, and that the exhaustion rate is a constant, s_E.

1. With usual notation like $y_t \equiv Y_t/L_t$, $k_t \equiv K_t/L_t$, $h_t \equiv H_t/L_t$, $x_t \equiv X/L_t$, $e_t \equiv E_t/L_t$, and $g_t^y \equiv \ln y_t - \ln y_{t-1}$, etc., show that the per capita production function is:

$$y_t = k_t^\alpha h_t^\varphi A_t^\beta x_t^\kappa e_t^\varepsilon,$$

and that:

$$g_t^y \approx \alpha g_t^k + \varphi g_t^h + \beta g - (\kappa + \varepsilon)n - \varepsilon s_E.$$

2. Define the physical capital–output ratio, $z_t \equiv K_t/Y_t$, as well as the human, $q_t \equiv H_t/Y_t$. Show that along a balanced growth path where both z_t and q_t are constant, the approximate growth rate of income per worker is:

$$g^y \cong \frac{\beta}{\beta + \kappa + \varepsilon} g - \frac{\kappa + \varepsilon}{\beta + \kappa + \varepsilon} n - \frac{\varepsilon}{\beta + \kappa + \varepsilon} s_E.$$

(Hint: $1 - \alpha - \varphi = \beta + \kappa + \varepsilon$.) Compare this expression for g^y with the corresponding one, (34), from the model without human capital. Although the expressions are algebraically identical, there is a difference. Why?

3. Assume that labour's share, $\beta + \varphi$, is 0.6 with raw labour and human capital having equal shares β and φ, respectively, and that capital's share is 0.2, while land's and oil's shares are both 0.1 (as we assumed in this chapter). Rewrite the formula for g^y using these values and comment with respect to growth drags. (Insert, for instance, also $s_E = 0.005$ and consider values of n typical for developed and developing countries, respectively.) In particular, how is the coefficient on n affected by also having human capital in the model? In view of what we found in Fig. 7.3, has the model become more realistic by introducing human capital?

PART 3 Endogenous Growth

CHAPTER

8

Productive externalities and endogenous growth

Although the Solow models studied so far are quite successful in accounting for many important aspects of economic growth, they have one major limitation: by treating the rate of technological change as exogenous, they leave the economy's long-run (steady state) growth rate unexplained. Solow models therefore belong to the class of so-called *exogenous growth* theories.

In this part of the book we will try to answer a very big question that remains unanswered: how can we explain the rate of technological change which is the source of long-run growth in income per capita? The search for an answer to this fundamental question takes us to the modern theory of *endogenous growth* where the long-run rate of growth in GDP per person is truly endogenous.

A model that 'explains' the long-run rate of growth in GDP per worker is one that endogenizes the underlying rate of technical change, that is, makes this rate depend on basic model parameters. Hence, by an endogenous growth model we mean a model in which the long-run growth rate of technology depends on basic model parameters such as the investment rates in physical and human capital, the population growth rate, or other fundamental characteristics of the economy. An endogenous growth model therefore allows an analysis of how economic policies that affect these basic parameters will affect long-run growth in income per capita. This is an important, and some will say the defining, feature of endogenous growth models: structural economic policy has implications for growth in output per capita in the long run.

In this chapter and the following one we will study endogenous growth theory. The models to be presented can be divided into two categories. In both categories there will be aggregate production functions involving a variable A_t that describes 'technology', but there will be no assumption of exogenous technological progress such as $A_{t+1} = (1 + g)A_t$, where g is exogenous.

One category contains models that include an explicit description of how technological progress, $A_{t+1} - A_t$ in period t, is produced through a specific production process that requires inputs of its own. Since we think of the production of technological progress as arising from research and development, we call such models *R&D-based models of endogenous growth*. These are the subject of the next chapter.

The other category does not have an explicit production process for technological improvement, but assumes that the A_t of the individual firm depends positively on the aggregate use of capital, or of output, because of so-called 'productive externalities'. This implies that the aggregate production function, as opposed to that of the individual firm, will have increasing returns to scale. As we will see, this will result in growth in GDP per worker in the long run without any exogenous technological progress being assumed.

The models in this category are referred to as *endogenous growth models based on productive externalities*, and they are the subject of this chapter.

8.1 A growth model with productive externalities

In Chapter 3 we explained why growth in income per worker had to vanish in the long run according to the basic Solow model. The explanation was related to *constant returns to capital and labour* and the associated *diminishing returns* to capital alone. Let us take the explanation once more in a way that is well suited to our present purposes.

The production function was $Y_t = K_t^\alpha L_t^{1-\alpha}$, exhibiting constant returns to K_t and L_t and diminishing returns to K_t alone ($\alpha < 1$). Consequently there were also diminishing returns to capital per worker in the production of output per worker: $y_t = k_t^\alpha$. Now, assume that there is some growth in the labour force, say at 1 per cent per year. If capital also increases by 1 per cent per year, as in the steady state of the basic Solow model, then because of constant returns to capital and labour, output will increase by 1 per cent per year. Hence output per worker will be constant.

How could there possibly be growth in output per worker? With the production function of the basic Solow model *only* if capital increases by more than 1 per cent per year. If capital increases at a given constant rate of more than 1 per cent per year, say at 2 per cent, then each year output will also increase by more than 1 per cent and hence there will be growth in output per worker. Indeed, the (approximate) growth rate of capital per worker, g_t^k, will be constant and equal to 1 per cent, and the (approximate) growth rate in output per worker, g_t^y, will be $g_t^y = \alpha g_t^k$. Hence, there will be a constant and positive growth rate in output per worker. However, the formula $g_t^y = \alpha g_t^k$ already reveals the problem. Since $\alpha < 1$, the growth rate of income per worker is smaller than the assumed growth rate of capital per worker. Therefore the continued constant growth rate in capital per worker cannot be sustained by savings. What happens is that as long as capital increases faster than labour there will be more and more capital per worker and this implies, due to diminishing returns, that additional units of capital per worker create less and less additional output per worker, and hence less and less additional savings per worker. As a consequence, growth in capital, and in GDP, per worker will have to cease in the long run.

This reasoning suggests that if there were *increasing* returns to capital and labour, then long-run growth in GDP per worker *would* be possible without exogenous technological progress. If both capital and labour were increasing at a rate of 1 per cent per year, then, simply because of increasing returns, output would be increasing by more than 1 per cent per year. And in this case growth would not have to cease in the long run, since it would be unnecessary to build up more and more capital per worker to sustain growth and hence diminishing returns would not be a problem.[1]

Increasing returns to scale at the aggregate level therefore seems to be a potential source of endogenous growth.

Constant returns at the firm level and increasing returns at the aggregate level

One may think that the idea of an endogenous growth model suggested by the above reasoning is simply the basic Solow model with the production function of the representative firm exhibiting increasing returns, that is, with the two exponents on capital and labour summing up to a number greater than 1 rather than exactly 1. For two reasons this is not an idea we will pursue. First, because of the replication argument, we believe that there should be close to constant returns at the firm level to the inputs that can be replicated. Second, the

---

1. In the models in this chapter that formalize this idea, capital and labour do *not* increase at the same rate in equilibrium. Rather capital increases at a greater rate than labour. The argument here is intended to show that increasing returns can work as a source of long-run growth in income per worker. The hypothetical assumption of equal growth rates in capital and labour is made for the sake of the argument.

idea of competitive markets, involving price-taking behaviour of the individual firms, is not compatible with increasing returns at the firm level. Here is why.

Under constant returns to scale and given input prices, total costs are proportional to total output. The reason is simply that an increase in output requires proportional increases in the inputs. Hence, under constant returns average and marginal cost are constant and both equal to the cost of producing one unit, $\hat{C}$, say. Under increasing returns, an increase in output requires less than proportional increases in the inputs, and therefore average and marginal costs will be decreasing in output. With a Cobb–Douglas production function with the exponents adding up to a number greater than 1, the marginal cost, $\hat{C}(Y_t)$, will be a decreasing function, and $\hat{C}(Y_t)$ will go to 0 as Y_t goes to infinity. If the firm takes the prices of inputs and outputs as given, to maximize profits it should want to produce an infinite amount of output. In other words, profit maximization does not imply well-defined behaviour of the individual firm. Price-taking behaviour and perfect competition are not compatible with increasing returns at the firm level.

There is a way to keep the assumption of constant returns at the firm level and at the same time have increasing returns at the aggregate level. In our model we only have one representative profit-maximizing firm, but this firm represents the aggregate behaviour of many firms each of which is small relative to the whole economy. The firm therefore takes aggregate magnitudes such as GDP or the aggregate use of capital as given, since it is too small to have more than a negligible influence on aggregates. In our model the aggregate use of capital has to be equal to the use of capital in the single representative firm, but we should nevertheless assume that *in making its individual decisions, the representative firm takes the aggregates as given*.

We assume that the *individual* production function of the representative firm (in its role as a small individual firm) is:

$$Y_t = (K_t^d)^\alpha (A_t L_t^d)^{1-\alpha}, \qquad 0 < \alpha < 1, \tag{1}$$

where the firm takes the labour productivity variable A_t as given and there are constant returns to the inputs of capital and labour, K_t^d and L_t^d. We assume further that the A_t of the *individual* firm depends positively on the *aggregate* stock of capital K_t as expressed by the constant elasticity function:

$$A_t = K_t^\phi, \qquad \phi \geq 0. \tag{2}$$

The special case $\phi = 0$ will bring us back to the basic Solow model of Chapter 3, but we will explain below why it may be reasonable to assume $\phi > 0$.

The individual firm has no influence on aggregate capital and takes A_t as given. The *aggregate* production function results from inserting (2) into (1) and using the facts that clearing of the input markets implies $K_t^d = K_t$ and $L_t^d = L_t$, where L_t is total labour supply in period t:

$$Y_t = K_t^\alpha (K_t^\phi L_t)^{1-\alpha} = K_t^{\alpha+\phi(1-\alpha)} L_t^{1-\alpha}. \tag{3}$$

When $\phi > 0$, the aggregate production function in (3) has increasing returns because the sum of the exponents, $1 + \phi(1 - \alpha)$, is larger than 1. A doubling of both aggregate inputs implies that aggregate output is multiplied by a factor $2^{1+\phi(1-\alpha)}$.

Since the individual firm takes aggregate capital as given, the marginal products entering the 'marginal product equal to real rental rate' conditions for optimal input demands should be those that appear when A_t is taken as given. Taking partial derivatives in (1), we therefore have:

$$r_t = \alpha \left(\frac{K_t^d}{A_t L_t^d} \right)^{\alpha-1} \qquad \text{and} \qquad w_t = (1-\alpha) \left(\frac{K_t^d}{A_t L_t^d} \right)^\alpha A_t, \tag{4}$$

in which we can insert the market-clearing conditions $K_t^d = K_t$ and $L_t^d = L_t$ as well as (2) to arrive at:

$$r_t = \alpha \left(\frac{K_t}{K_t^\phi L_t} \right)^{\alpha-1} \quad \text{and} \quad w_t = (1-\alpha) \left(\frac{K_t}{K_t^\phi L_t} \right)^\alpha K_t^\phi. \tag{5}$$

You will easily verify from (3) and (5) that $r_t K_t = \alpha Y_t$ and $w_t L_t = (1 - \alpha) Y_t$. Hence, we have achieved what we wanted: we have constant returns at the firm level (so perfect competition can be assumed), we have increasing returns at the aggregate level, and our theory of the functional income distribution still has the nice features of constant income shares and no pure profits, capital's share being α.

For this whole construction the assumption of a productive externality from the aggregate use of capital to labour productivity, Eq. (2), is crucial. What could be the motivations for this?

Empirically, the idea of increasing returns at the aggregate level is not implausible.[2] Estimates of the sum of our exponents, $1 + \phi(1 - \alpha)$, are systematically greater than 1, pointing to $\phi > 0$. Furthermore, they vary widely across investigations, ranging from just above 1 to levels way above 2. There is perhaps a tendency that most estimates (and the most reliable ones) should be found in the (lower) range, 1.1–1.5. A value for the sum of exponents, $1 + \phi(1 - \alpha)$, around 1.3, say, corresponds (with α around $\frac{1}{3}$) to ϕ being around 0.45, while a value of 1.5 would mean that ϕ should be 0.75. This may give an indication of largest possible plausible values for ϕ. Taking the great uncertainty of the estimations into account, however, one cannot completely exclude larger values for the sum of the exponents, for instance values close to $\frac{5}{3}$ (1.67). The latter corresponds to a ϕ around 1, a possibility that will be of importance below.

For the theoretical motivations the key phrase is *learning by doing*. There may be a bit of hand waving involved here, but the idea is that the use of (additional) capital in an individual firm will have a direct effect on production as expressed by the individual production function (1), but in addition it will have an indirect, positive effect on the capabilities of workers who gain new knowledge by working with the new capital. The benefit from this effect does not only accrue to the firm that increases its capital stock, but to firms in general, because knowledge is a public good circulating freely among workers as workers circulate between firms bringing their acquired knowledge and capabilities with them.

This should explain why the additional capability effect spills over to firms in general and hence should be modelled as an externality. But why should there be a capability effect in the first place? Here the idea is that one way workers get more skilful and sophisticated is through the installation of new capital in the firms, since new machinery is a carrier of new technological knowledge. Thus, working with new capital, learning by doing, makes workers more sophisticated. Taking this idea literally, the capability effect should arise from accumulated gross investment rather than from the stock of capital, but we may let the latter approximate all the gross investment undertaken in the past (in this connection ignoring depreciation).[3]

The complete model

The above explanations have focused on the crucial and only new feature of the growth model we are constructing. In all other respects the model is just like the basic Solow model. We can therefore write down the complete model without further delay.

2. A survey of empirical estimates of returns to scale in aggregate production functions can be found, for example, in Stephanie Schmitt-Grohé, 'Comparing Four Models of Aggregate Fluctuations due to Self-Fulfilling Expectations', *Journal of Economic Theory*, **72**, 1997, pp. 96–147.

3. The important idea of productive externalities due to learning by doing comes from a famous article by the economist and Nobel Prize winner Kenneth J. Arrow, 'The Economic Implications of Learning by Doing', *Review of Economic Studies*, **29**, 1962, pp. 153–173. Arrow constructs a model that involves a distinction between old and new capital and in which the idea of a capability effect from the use of *new* capital is perhaps better placed.

Equation (6) below is the individual production function of the representative firm taking A_t as given, but with the equilibrium conditions of the factor markets, $K_t^d = K_t$ and $L_t^d = L_t$, inserted. Equation (7) states the assumption that labour augmenting productivity, A_t, potentially (if $\phi > 0$) depends on aggregate capital because of learning-by-doing productive externalities. The two last equations, (8) and (9), describe capital accumulation and labour force growth, respectively, and are essentially unchanged from the basic Solow model. The parameters are assumed to fulfil $0 < \alpha < 1$, $\phi \geq 0$, $0 < s < 1$, $0 < \delta < 1$, and $n > -1$.

THE COMPLETE GROWTH MODEL BASED ON PRODUCTIVE EXTERNALITIES

$$Y_t = (K_t)^\alpha (A_t L_t)^{1-\alpha}, \tag{6}$$

$$A_t = K_t^\phi, \tag{7}$$

$$K_{t+1} = sY_t + (1-\delta)K_t, \qquad K_0 \text{ given} \tag{8}$$

$$L_{t+1} = (1+n)L_t, \qquad L_0 \text{ given} \tag{9}$$

We have chosen not to restate the expressions for the real factor prices this time, but whenever needed they can be taken from (5) above. From given initial values, K_0 and L_0, of the state variables, the model will determine the paths of all the endogenous variables Y_t, K_t, L_t and A_t, and hence, using (5), of the real factor prices.

Sometimes it is assumed in similar models that the external learning-by-doing effect on labour productivity really arises from total production rather than from capital use. This would amount to the formulation, $A_t = Y_t^\phi$, rather than (7) above, the remaining model being the same. An exercise will ask you to verify that this alternative model works qualitatively exactly as the one above. We could also have chosen to let the external effect from capital use (or production) affect total factor productivity rather than the labour-augmenting productivity variable, A_t, without any effect on our conclusions.

8.2 Semi-endogenous growth

As mentioned, in the special case of $\phi = 0$, the model above is just the basic Solow model. We will therefore assume $\phi > 0$, and the aggregate production function (3) will then have increasing returns to K_t and L_t. Note from (3) that if $\phi < 1$, there will be diminishing returns to capital alone, since $\alpha + \phi(1 - \alpha)$ will be smaller than 1, while if $\phi = 1$, the aggregate production function will have constant returns to K_t alone. Whether there are diminishing returns or constant returns to capital alone turns out to make an important difference. We will first consider the case $\phi < 1$.

The law of motion

Assuming $\phi < 1$, we can again analyse the model in terms of the technology-adjusted variables, $\tilde{k}_t \equiv k_t/A_t \equiv K_t/(A_t L_t)$ and $\tilde{y}_t \equiv y_t/A_t \equiv Y_t/(A_t L_t)$, but A_t is no longer growing at an exogenous rate. Instead, the evolution of A_t is endogenous and depends, through (2), on how aggregate capital evolves.

It follows straightforwardly from the production function (6) that:

$$\tilde{y}_t = \tilde{k}_t^a, \tag{10}$$

and (7) implies that:

$$\frac{A_{t+1}}{A_t} = \left(\frac{K_{t+1}}{K_t}\right)^{\phi}. \tag{11}$$

These two equations will be used in the following. From the definition of $\tilde{k}_t$ we have:

$$\frac{\tilde{k}_{t+1}}{\tilde{k}_t} = \frac{\dfrac{K_{t+1}}{K_t}}{\dfrac{A_{t+1}}{A_t}\dfrac{L_{t+1}}{L_t}} = \frac{\dfrac{K_{t+1}}{K_t}}{\left(\dfrac{K_{t+1}}{K_t}\right)^{\phi}\dfrac{L_{t+1}}{L_t}} = \frac{1}{1+n}\left(\frac{K_{t+1}}{K_t}\right)^{1-\phi}, \tag{12}$$

where we have used (11) and (9). Inserting that $K_{t+1} = sY_t + (1-\delta)K_t$, we get:

$$\begin{aligned}
\frac{\tilde{k}_{t+1}}{\tilde{k}_t} &= \frac{1}{1+n}\left(\frac{sY_t + (1-\delta)K_t}{K_t}\right)^{1-\phi} \\
&= \frac{1}{1+n}\left(\frac{s\tilde{y}_t}{\tilde{k}_t} + (1-\delta)\right)^{1-\phi} \\
&= \frac{1}{1+n}(s\tilde{k}_t^{\alpha-1} + (1-\delta))^{1-\phi},
\end{aligned}$$

where we have used (10) for the latter equality. Multiplying on both sides by $\tilde{k}_t$ gives the transition equation:

$$\tilde{k}_{t+1} = \frac{1}{1+n}\tilde{k}_t[s\tilde{k}_t^{\alpha-1} + (1-\delta)]^{1-\phi}, \tag{13}$$

which we can also write in the form:

$$\tilde{k}_{t+1} = \frac{1}{1+n}\left[s\tilde{k}_t^{\frac{\alpha+\phi-\alpha\phi}{1-\phi}} + (1-\delta)\tilde{k}_t^{\frac{1}{1-\phi}}\right]^{1-\phi}. \tag{14}$$

(You should check this reformulation.) Note that since we have assumed $\phi < 1$, the exponents in (14) are all well defined and positive. Also note that if we set $\phi = 0$, both of the equations (13) and (14) become the transition equation of the basic Solow model (the model of Chapter 3 with $B = 1$).

Convergence to steady state

The transition equation has the form of a one-dimensional first-order difference equation in $\tilde{k}_t$. We will establish properties of the transition equation implying that in the long run $\tilde{k}_t$ converges to a specific value $\tilde{k}^*$.

From either of (13) or (14), it is clear that the transition curve passes through $(0, 0)$. From (14) it follows that it is everywhere increasing. Further, from (13) follows that it crosses the 45° line for exactly one positive value $\tilde{k}^*$ of $\tilde{k}_t$: inserting $\tilde{k}_{t+1} = \tilde{k}_t$ into (13) and solving for $\tilde{k}_t$ gives

$$\tilde{k}_t = \tilde{k}^* \equiv \left(\frac{s}{(1+n)^{1/(1-\phi)} - (1-\delta)}\right)^{\frac{1}{1-\alpha}}, \tag{15}$$

verifying a unique positive intersection if $(1+n)^{1/(1-\phi)} > 1 - \delta$. The latter is assumed; note that it follows, e.g., from n positive (larger than or equal to zero).

Finally, for convergence to $\tilde{k}^*$ it is important that at $\tilde{k}^*$ the transition curve intersects the 45° line from above, as illustrated in Fig. 8.1. To show this, one can differentiate the transition function given in (13) with respect to $\tilde{k}_t$, insert $\tilde{k}^*$ for $\tilde{k}_t$ to find the slope of the transition curve at $\tilde{k}^*$, and then derive the condition for this slope being less than 1. You should do this and find the condition $(1+n)^{1/(1-\phi)} > 1 - \delta$, that we have just assumed.

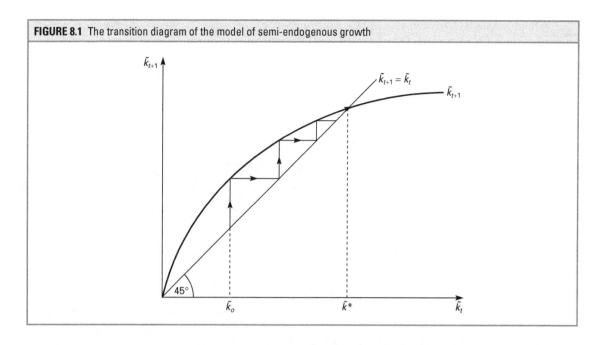

FIGURE 8.1 The transition diagram of the model of semi-endogenous growth

The properties established and illustrated in Fig. 8.1 imply that in the long run $\tilde{k}_t$ will converge to $\tilde{k}^*$. Consequently, $\tilde{y}_t = \tilde{k}_t^{\alpha}$ will converge to the associated:

$$\tilde{y}^* \equiv \left(\frac{s}{(1+n)^{1/(1-\phi)} - (1-\delta)}\right)^{\frac{\alpha}{1-\alpha}}. \tag{16}$$

We have demonstrated long-run convergence of $\tilde{k}_t$ and $\tilde{y}_t$ to $\tilde{k}^*$ and $\tilde{y}^*$, respectively. This defines the steady state.

Semi-endogenous growth in steady state

Our conclusions so far seem reminiscent of those we arrived at in Chapter 5 for the general Solow model. The auxiliary variables are defined in the same way, $\tilde{k}_t \equiv k_t/A_t$ and $\tilde{y}_t = y_t/A_t$, respectively, and we have found again that these variables converge to constant steady state values. When they are locked at these constant values in steady state, both k_t and y_t must grow at the same rate as A_t. In the Solow model this sufficed for determining the steady state growth rates of k_t and y_t. Both had to be equal to the exogenous growth rate, g, of A_t. This time we do not have an exogenous growth rate of A_t, so to determine the steady state growth rate of y_t we must determine the *endogenous* growth rate of A_t in steady state.

This is easy to do. Consider (12) above. In steady state the left-hand side, $\tilde{k}_{t+1}/\tilde{k}_t$, is equal to 1. Therefore the right-hand side must also equal 1:

$$\frac{1}{1+n}\left(\frac{K_{t+1}}{K_t}\right)^{1-\phi} = 1 \Leftrightarrow \frac{K_{t+1}}{K_t} = (1+n)^{\frac{1}{1-\phi}}.$$

Using (11) then gives:

$$\frac{A_{t+1}}{A_t} = (1+n)^{\frac{\phi}{1-\phi}} \Leftrightarrow \frac{A_{t+1} - A_t}{A_t} = (1+n)^{\frac{\phi}{1-\phi}} - 1 \equiv g_{se} \tag{17}$$

Hence, in steady state the growth rate of A_t is $(1+n)^{\phi/(1-\phi)} - 1$, and we call this growth rate g_{se}. (The constant approximate growth rate, $g_{se}^A \equiv \ln A_{t+1} - \ln A_t$, is $g_{se}^A \approx \phi n/(1-\phi)$, as you should verify.) Note that g_{se} is determined endogenously and depends on model parameters.

In steady state the growth rates of capital per worker, k_t, and GDP per worker, y_t, must then also be g_{se}. Hence from (17), if the growth rate of the labour force is 0, then the steady state growth rate of GDP per capita is also 0. For the growth rate of GDP per capita to be positive, a positive population (labour force) growth rate is required. This should not be surprising in view of the remarks in Section 8.1. To exploit the increasing returns in the aggregate production function an increasing labour force is required. The term 'semi-endogenous' growth refers to the fact that we only have (endogenous) growth in GDP per worker if there is (exogenous) population growth.

SEMI-ENDOGENOUS GROWTH

Under the highly plausible stability condition, $(1 + n)^{1/(1-\phi)} > 1 - \delta$, and under the assumption that the elasticity from aggregate capital use to labour-augmenting productivity is smaller than 1, the growth model based on productive externalities implies that capital per effective worker, k_t/A_t, and income per effective worker, y_t/A_t, converge to certain steady state values. Hence in the long run capital per worker, k_t, and income per worker, y_t, must both converge on growing at the same rate as does A_t, implying that the capital–output ratio, $k_t/y_t = K_t/Y_t$, converges to a constant value in accordance with balanced growth. In steady state, the common growth rate, g_{se} of A_t and y_t depends critically on the growth rate, n, of the labour force. In particular, g_{se} is strictly positive if and only if n is strictly positive.

Note that in steady state the inputs of capital and labour are not growing at the same rates. Labour input grows at rate n, but since $k_t \equiv K_t/L_t$ grows at the rate g_{se}, capital must be growing at approximately the rate $n + g_{se}$. Only if $n = 0$ are these growth rates equal.

Is the endogenous growth rate g_{se} of GDP per person derived from this model of a realistic size for plausible parameter values? Annual population growth rates of around 0.5 per cent are typical for Western countries (see Table A at the end of Book One) and according to the empirical studies mentioned earlier, realistic values of ϕ could be up to 0.5–0.75. As you will easily verify from (17), these parameter values result in steady state growth rates, g_{se}, in the range from 0.5 per cent to 1.5 per cent, which is not far-fetched.

The steady state growth path and structural policy

Let us now turn to the steady state growth path. From the definition of $\tilde{y}_t$, the steady state growth path of y_t must be $y_t^* = \tilde{y}^* A_t$. The evolution of A_t obeys $A_t = K_t^\phi$, so $y_t^* = \tilde{y}^* K_t^\phi$. Furthermore, when the economy is *in* steady state there is a necessary link between K_t and L_t. This follows because in steady state the variable $\tilde{k}_t$, defined as $K_t/(A_t L_t) = K_t^{1-\phi}/L_t$, is locked at the value $\tilde{k}^*$, so in steady state:

$$K_t = (\tilde{k}^* L_t)^{\frac{1}{1-\phi}}.$$

Inserting this expression for K_t into the steady state growth path, $y_t^* = \tilde{y}^* K_t^\phi$, for output per worker gives:

$$y_t^* = \tilde{y}^* (\tilde{k}^* L_t)^{\frac{\phi}{1-\phi}} = (\tilde{k}^*)^{\alpha + \frac{\phi}{1-\phi}} L_0^{\frac{\phi}{1-\phi}} (1 + n)^{\frac{\phi}{1-\phi}t},$$

where we have used that $\tilde{y}_t = \tilde{k}_t^\alpha$, and $L_t = (1 + n)^t L_0$. We can now finally insert $\tilde{k}^*$ from (15), and from (17) that $(1 + n)^{\phi/(1-\phi)} = 1 + g_{se}$:

$$y_t^* = \left(\frac{s}{(1+n)^{\frac{1}{1-\phi}} - (1-\delta)} \right)^{\left(\alpha + \frac{\phi}{1-\phi}\right)/(1-\alpha)} L_0^{\frac{\phi}{1-\phi}} (1 + g_{se})^t. \tag{18}$$

This gives the steady state growth path (y_t^*) for output per worker. The corresponding steady state growth path (c_t^*) for consumption per worker is obtained by multiplying by $1 - s$ on both sides of (18).

Structural economic policies for steady state must work to affect the positions of these paths or the growth rates along them (or both). With respect to the positions, the policy implications are somewhat similar to those in the basic Solow model. For example, a higher investment rate, s, shifts the growth path for y_t upwards. Note, however, that the golden rule value for s, implying the highest possible position of (c_t), is now $\alpha + \phi(1 - \alpha)$, which is greater than the α we have arrived at for the basic Solow model. (As an exercise, show that the golden rule saving rate is $\alpha + \phi(1 - \alpha)$ and try to explain intuitively why for a given α we must now get a higher golden rule savings rate.)

The really new feature is that the steady state growth rates of y_t and c_t depend endogenously on model parameters: both are equal to $g_{se} \equiv (1 + n)^{\phi/(1-\phi)} - 1$. Taking ϕ to be a given technical parameter (not easily affected by policy), the conclusion from this model's steady state is that to promote long-run growth in GDP and consumption per capita, one should try to *promote* population growth! There are reasons why one would be cautious about such a policy.

Empirics for semi-endogenous growth

The model's steady state predicts that a higher growth rate in the labour force, or the population, should give higher growth in GDP per capita. One way to test this prediction is to plot average annual growth rates in GDP per worker over some period against average annual labour force growth rates over the same period across countries, just as we did in Fig. 7.3, finding a negative, rather than a positive, relation. Figure 8.2 does more or less the same, focusing on a longer period and fewer countries.

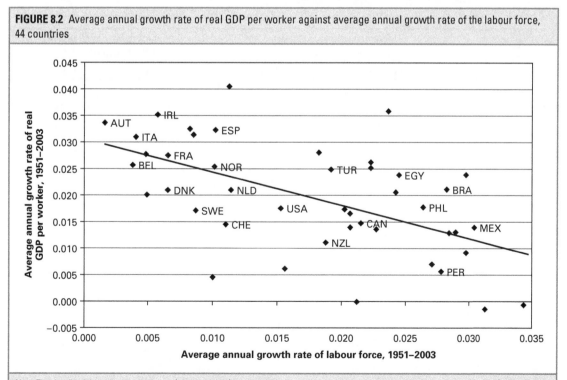

FIGURE 8.2 Average annual growth rate of real GDP per worker against average annual growth rate of the labour force, 44 countries

Note: The details of the estimated line are: $g^i = 0.03 - 0.62n^i$, the standard error of the estimate of the slope is 0.14 ($t = -4.4$), and adj. $R^2 = 0.30$. The countries considered are the countries from our main sample of 65 countries considered in Chapters 2 through 6 for which data all the way back to 1951 were available.

We find (again) a rather clear *negative* relationship between labour force growth and economic growth across countries in the period considered. The OLS-estimated straight line has a significantly negative slope (the details of the estimation are reported in the figure legend). This does not necessarily mean that the model of semi-endogenous growth is wrong, however.

First, it is not clear exactly what kind of area the model covers, a region, a country, or perhaps the (developed) world, since it is not easy to tell how wide the crucial external, spillover effect of the model reaches. If the firms and workers in one country learn from experiences with production and capital use in other countries, then perhaps the model should be considered to cover the world. It is therefore not clear if cross-country evidence as reported in Fig. 8.2 is relevant.

Second, the model we consider has a steady state *and* it has convergence to the steady state in the long run. During the convergence period there will be transitory growth in addition to the underlying (endogenous) steady state growth, and the transitory growth depends negatively on population growth, just as in the Solow models, and for the same reason: a decrease in the rate of population growth shifts the steady state growth path up but reduces its slope (see Eq. (18)). Hence, during the transition to the new steady state growth path there will, for some time, be a positive transitory contribution to growth arising from the lower population growth. Furthermore, convergence in the model we consider may be quite slow due to the presence of the productive externality. As ϕ comes close to 1, convergence will be very slow. (Exercises 1 and 2 at the end of the chapter will ask you to look in more detail at the convergence process, both numerically and analytically.) What we have found in Fig. 8.2 may be interpreted as an expression of long-lasting transitory growth that should indeed depend negatively on population growth according to our model.

These remarks seem to call for (even) longer-run empirical evidence that does not go across countries. Table 8.1 reports for each of the two sub-periods 1870–1930 and 1930–90

TABLE 8.1 Average annual growth rates in population and real GDP per capita in 17 industrialized countries, 1870–1990

	Average annual population growth rate (%)		Average annual growth rate of GDP per capital (%)	
	1870–1930	1930–90	1870–1930	1930–90
Australia	2.3	1.6	0.4	2.0
Austria	0.7	0.2	1.1	2.6
Belgium	0.8	0.4	1.0	2.1
Canada	1.7	1.6	1.7	2.4
Denmark	1.0	0.6	1.6	2.1
Finland	1.1	0.6	1.4	3.1
France	0.1	0.5	1.5	2.3
Germany	1.0	0.7	1.2	2.5
Italy	0.6	0.6	1.1	2.9
Japan	1.0	1.1	1.5	3.9
Netherlands	1.3	1.1	1.2	1.8
New Zealand	2.7	1.4	1.2	1.6
Norway	0.8	0.7	1.6	2.7
Sweden	0.6	0.6	1.4	2.5
Switzerland	0.7	0.8	1.7	2.1
UK	0.7	0.4	0.8	1.9
USA	1.9	1.2	1.5	2.1

Source: Angus Maddison, *Monitoring the World Economy 1820–1992*, Paris, OECD, 1995.

the average annual population growth rate and the average annual growth rate of GDP per capita for a number of countries. For all of them economic growth increased substantially from the early sub-period to the later one, while for all countries but three, population growth decreased, for many of the countries substantially. So, also if we consider quite long periods and 'stay' within each country or within the group of all countries, the evidence shows little sign that growth in GDP per capita should be positively related to population growth.[4]

EMPIRICS AND POLICY CONCERNING STEADY STATE

The position of the long-run, balanced growth path of the model of semi-endogenous growth depends on structural parameters in a way that supports the same kind of policy conclusions as were derived from the Solow model of exogenous growth: high investment rates and low labour force growth rates will elevate the growth path to a high position, now with a golden rule savings rate that exceeds capital's share, reflecting the positive spillover effect from capital use. However, the way that the growth rate along the balanced growth path depends on parameters suggests that promoting population growth will promote economic growth. The prediction of a positive association between population growth and economic growth is not easy to reconcile with the empirics.

We can still not conclude from the empirics above that the model of semi-endogenous growth is wrong. It could be that convergence according to the model is so slow that transitory growth really takes place over periods as long as 120 years. In that case the general picture found in Table 8.1 could be compatible with the model. However, if convergence to steady state is that slow, then the model's steady state is not very descriptive for periods of interest, so we should consider the very slow convergence process itself as the model's main prediction. This is exactly the perspective taken in the next section. We will apply a specific assumption that makes the convergence period not just very long, but infinite. We will then consider the model's infinite, outside steady state behaviour as an approximation of a very long-lasting convergence process.

8.3 Endogenous growth

In Exercise 2 (which is an important exercise) you are asked to find an analytical expression for the rate of convergence for y_t^* according to our model with $\phi < 1$. For the case where population growth is small, $n \approx 0$, the rate is $\lambda \approx (1 - \alpha)(1 - \phi)\delta$. This verifies the claim above that a large ϕ less than 1 implies very slow convergence. Below we will indeed set $n = 0$, since we now want to investigate the possibility that over periods of interest, such as centuries, population growth is *not* the factor that causes economic growth. The size of the labour force is then constant, equal to L, say. The idea is to consider the growth model of this chapter with $\phi = 1$. This gives a zero rate of convergence and hence an everlasting convergence process. We consider the everlasting convergence resulting from $\phi = 1$ to be of interest because it approximates the very long-lasting convergence that would result from a ϕ that is large, but still less than unity.[5]

---

4. It should be noted that Table 8.1 states population, rather than labour force, growth rates, and growth rates of GDP per capita rather than of GDP per worker, so it does not take changes in the evolution of participation rates into account.

5. It is *only* as an approximation of the case of a large ϕ less than one that $\phi = 1$ is of interest. There is no reason to believe that a parameter value should take one particular knife-edge value.

The AK model

In the analysis in the previous section the term $1 - \phi$ appeared in many places, including in some denominators, and several expressions would be meaningless for $\phi = 1$. Hence we cannot simply set $\phi = 1$ in all the equations above. For what we did in Section 8.1, on the other hand, it was not important whether ϕ was smaller than or equal to 1, so the expressions for the real factor prices we found there and the associated theory of the income distribution are also relevant when $\phi = 1$. With $L_t = L$ and $\phi = 1$ we get from (5) that:

$$r_t = r \equiv \alpha L^{1-\alpha} \quad \text{and} \quad w_t = (1-\alpha)K_t/L^\alpha, \tag{19}$$

so the real interest rate, $r - \delta$, is constant and the wage rate, w_t, evolves proportionally to K_t, and hence to $k_t \equiv K_t/L$.

In addition to the above expressions for the real factor prices the model can be condensed to the two equations:

$$Y_t = K_t L^{1-\alpha} \equiv AK_t, \tag{20}$$

$$K_{t+1} = sY_t + (1-\delta)K_t, \tag{21}$$

where the first equation is the aggregate production function resulting from (6) and (7), or directly from (3), with $\phi = 1$, while the second equation is the usual capital accumulation equation repeated from (8). The model's last equation, (9), has been replaced by $L_t = L$. Note that in (20) we have used the definition $A \equiv L^{1-\alpha}$. This is a bit of an abuse of notation, but it should cause no confusion if we denote $L^{1-\alpha}$ by an A *without* a subscript t. We apply this notation because the model we consider is so often referred to as the 'AK model'.

Growth according to the AK model

It is easy to see that the model above can result in permanent growth in GDP per worker. Dividing both sides of the production function (20) by L, in order to transform variables into per worker terms, gives $y_t = Ak_t$. Dividing also both sides of the capital accumulation equation (21) by L, and inserting Ak_t for y_t, then gives the transition equation:

$$k_{t+1} = (sA + 1 - \delta)k_t, \tag{22}$$

Subtracting k_t from both sides gives the Solow equation:

$$k_{t+1} - k_t = sAk_t - \delta k_t, \tag{23}$$

and then dividing both sides by k_t gives the modified Solow equation:

$$\frac{k_{t+1} - k_t}{k_t} = sA - \delta \equiv g_e. \tag{24}$$

The latter equation directly gives the constant and endogenous growth rate, g_e, in capital per worker, k_t, and hence in capital, K_t, since $k_t = K_t/L$. Furthermore, since y_t is a constant times k_t, the growth rate of output per worker is g_e, and hence the growth rate of consumption per worker, $c_t = (1 - s)y_t$, must be g_e. Finally, the technology variable A_t (not to be confused with the constant $A \equiv L^{1-\alpha}$) must increase at rate g_e, since with $\phi = 1$, we have $A_t = K_t$.

It follows that according to the AK model, $g_e = sA - \delta$ is the common endogenous growth rate of all the variables we are interested in (we assume that $sA - \delta > 0$). Hence, everlasting economic growth is possible in this model without an assumption of exogenous technological growth and without population growth. To understand this result it may be useful to draw some well-known diagrams.

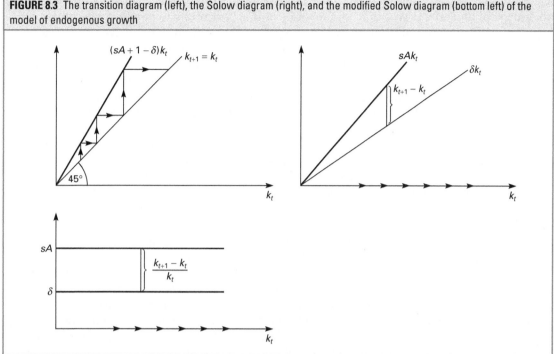

FIGURE 8.3 The transition diagram (left), the Solow diagram (right), and the modified Solow diagram (bottom left) of the model of endogenous growth

Figure 8.3 shows the transition diagram associated with (22), the Solow diagram associated with (23), and the modified Solow diagram associated with (24). The diagrams illustrate that in this model there is no steady state and k_t (and hence y_t and Y_t) grow at a constant rate forever.

The 'curves', which are straight lines in Fig. 8.3, would in Solow models be true curves due to diminishing returns to capital per worker ($\alpha < 1$). The linearity of the curves in the present model reflects that there are no diminishing returns to capital *at the aggregate level*. Rather there are constant returns to capital per worker: $y_t = Ak_t$.

The 'growth brake' from the Solow models, diminishing returns to capital, is simply no longer present in the aggregate production function. The source of growth is thus aggregate constant returns to the reproducible factor, capital.

Implications for structural policy and the scale effect

The main conclusion from the model is that *a higher savings (investment) rate, s, gives rise to a permanently higher growth rate in GDP and consumption per worker*. This differs from our earlier conclusions since a higher s no longer just gives a higher *level* of output per worker in the long run and a *temporarily* higher transitory growth rate in the intermediate run, but it results in a *permanently* higher rate of growth in output per worker. Since our model with $\phi = 1$ should be seen as an approximation of the semi-endogenous growth model with a large ϕ smaller than 1, we should remember that strictly speaking the correct statement is that an increase in s gives *very* long-lasting transitory growth in GDP per worker. The implications for economic policy are obvious: policies that stimulate savings now give a very long-lasting boost to growth.

A decrease in δ has an effect similar to that of an increased s, but it may be more difficult to achieve through economic policy. More effective aggregate investment should, however, lead to a lower rate of depreciation, and a lower rate of depreciation leads, in the model of endogenous growth, to a permanently higher growth rate in GDP per worker. If, somehow, a government can take actions that make net investment more 'effective', it can perhaps take advantage of this effect. This may be most relevant for countries where the government is heavily involved in production so that a large part of investment is not driven by private incentives, but decided upon by government bureaucracies. Historically this method of making investment decisions has often led to inefficient and rapidly worn out (sometimes even useless) investment. By relying more on private, profit-motivated incentives in investment decisions, such a country could probably attain higher prosperity and growth in the long run, although there may be transition costs involved in changing from one type of economic system to another.

Policies for more effective investment are not only relevant in connection with endogenous growth. In the Solow model a lower depreciation rate results in a higher *level* of GDP per capita in the long run, which is also important. Note the general tendency that parameter changes that give a long-run *level* effect on GDP per worker in the Solow models give a long-run effect on the *rate of change* in GDP per worker in the model of endogenous growth.

There is one odd feature of the AK model which casts doubt on any policy recommendation derived from it. Remember that $A \equiv L^{1-\alpha}$. Hence the growth rate $g_e = sA - \delta$ is higher the larger the constant population size L is, and the growth rate would even increase and indeed explode over time if population increased by a constant rate. This is the so-called 'scale effect', which is rather controversial. Empirical evidence does not support a hypothesis that larger countries should have larger long-run growth rates, but again it is not clear what geographical area the model covers. Perhaps it is the world, but then during the past 200 years the world population has increased rapidly while economic growth rates have not shown a similarly strong increase.

It is possible to get rid of the scale effect. Assume that the productive externality, which is the driving force of endogenous growth in this chapter, arises from capital *per worker* rather than from capital itself, so that Eq. (7) in our model should be replaced by:

$$A_t = \left(\frac{K_t}{L_t} \right)^{\phi}.$$

You will easily verify that with $\phi = 1$ the aggregate production function becomes $Y_t = K_t$, that is, the A (without subscript t) is equal to 1 and independent of L. Consequently the endogenous growth rate of the model will be $g_e = s - \delta$, and the scale effect has been eliminated. However, aggregate production (not production in the individual firm) is now completely insensitive to labour input. The positive effect on production of a higher labour input, L_t, arising at the firm level is exactly offset by the negative external effect of a lower K_t/L_t at the aggregate level (when $\phi = 1$).

Either endogenous growth models have the unattractive scale effect or they assume, unattractively, that labour inputs are unproductive at the aggregate level. There is no way around this problem.

Empirics for endogenous growth

As mentioned, a main prediction of the model of endogenous growth is the positive influence of the savings or investment rate on the long-run growth rate of GDP per worker. Let us put this prediction to a test by considering cross-country evidence. Figure 8.4 plots average annual growth rates, g^i, from 1960 to 2000 against average investment rates, s^i, over the same period across countries i. The sample of 65 representative countries is the one considered in earlier chapters as well.

The figure shows a quite good and tight positive relationship. This is a main reason why economists take the theories of endogenous growth seriously (still remembering that these should be seen as approximations of theories of very long-lasting transitory growth).

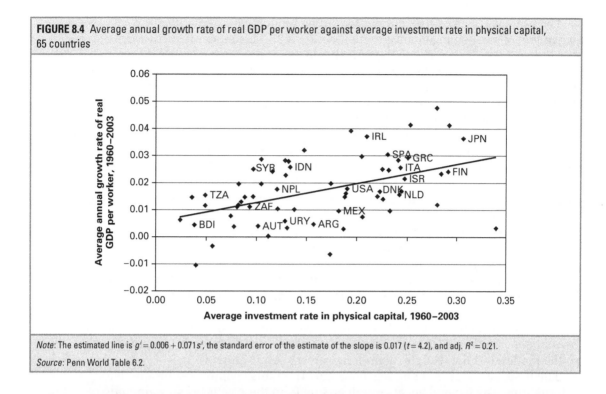

FIGURE 8.4 Average annual growth rate of real GDP per worker against average investment rate in physical capital, 65 countries

Note: The estimated line is $g^i = 0.006 + 0.071 s^i$, the standard error of the estimate of the slope is 0.017 ($t = 4.2$), and adj. $R^2 = 0.21$.

Source: Penn World Table 6.2.

ENDOGENOUS GROWTH

The growth model based on productive externalities with a unit elasticity from aggregate capital to labour-augmenting productivity gives rise to permanent growth in income per capita even without population growth. A higher savings rate gives rise to a permanently higher growth rate in GDP and consumption per worker. Hence, economic policy that stimulates saving not only has a permanent, positive effect on the level of GDP per capita – it also has a permanent, positive effect on the growth rate of GDP per capita. The model feature of a positive long-run association between the investment rate and the growth rate of GDP per worker is in nice accordance with cross-country empirics. However, the model suffers from an implausible scale effect according to which a larger labour force should result in a permanently larger growth rate of GDP per worker.

Yet the positive empirical relationship does not *prove* that the idea of endogenous growth is correct. As we have argued several times, it is not clear whether the model covers a country or the world, so cross-country evidence may not be the appropriate kind of empirics to study.

Furthermore, in no way does Fig. 8.4 contradict the traditional Solow models according to which an increase in the savings rate will imply a (higher) transitory growth in excess of the underlying exogenous growth. Perhaps the figure just shows that countries with a high average s^i over the period considered typically have experienced increases in s^i and therefore have had relatively high transitory growth rates. However, the next section will provide a reason for indeed viewing Fig. 8.4 as indicating endogenous growth.

8.4 Exogenous versus endogenous growth

In this chapter we have studied two distinct and alternative types of endogenous growth, semi-endogenous and endogenous growth, both fundamentally caused by productive externalities.

The presence of a positive, but not too strong productive externality, $0 < \phi < 1$, gave rise to a model of semi-endogenous growth (Section 8.2). This model had convergence to a steady state in the long run, and therefore it had the 'convergence property': growth is faster the further below steady state the economy is. Furthermore, in steady state economic growth was explained by growth in the labour force, and the long-run growth rate of GDP per worker was higher the higher the rate of population growth.

A strong productive externality, $\phi = 1$, resulted in a model of (genuinely) endogenous growth (Section 8.3). This model had no steady state and hence no convergence to one (or rather, in the appropriate model interpretation, very slow convergence to one). Therefore the model did not have the convergence property. Growth in GDP per capita could occur without population growth, but there was a scale effect: a larger labour force gave a higher rate of economic growth, and a fixed population growth would imply an exploding economic growth rate.

Both the model of semi-endogenous growth and the model of endogenous growth delivered explanations of economic growth: *the growth rate of GDP per worker depended on basic structural model parameters.*

In previous chapters we have studied models of exogenous growth. All these models had convergence to a steady state and the convergence property. In the long run the growth rate of GDP per worker was either independent of or negatively affected by the population growth rate (the latter in the realistic presence of natural resources). In these models *permanent growth in GDP per worker was a reflection of exogenous technological growth*, so the models did not really explain long-run economic growth.

The basic mechanism for endogenous growth in this chapter was productive externalities. The technological growth arising from these came as an unintended by-product of economic activity. No agents were concerned with deliberately producing technological progress. In the real world we know that a lot of research and development activities *intended* to create technological progress are undertaken in private companies as well as at universities. Therefore, perhaps the endogenous growth models of the next chapter in which technological progress is the outcome of an explicit and deliberate production activity will be more convincing.

However, the simple externality-based models of endogenous growth considered in this chapter share enough features with the more advanced endogenous growth models to be representative for endogenous growth theory. Therefore we can already present some main arguments from an ongoing and fascinating debate among growth theorists. The issue in this debate is whether the economic growth we see in the real world is best understood by exogenous growth models or by endogenous growth models. Here are some main arguments from the debate.

Explaining growth

Everybody agrees that it is good to have explanations of long-run economic growth, and since the endogenous growth models deliver much more of an explanation than exogenous growth models, this is certainly an argument in favour of endogenous growth models. However, it could be that at the present stage of knowledge the existing endogenous growth models were not convincing, so one would have to rely on exogenous growth models for understanding growth, although the understanding would be limited by technological progress being unexplained. Whether the growth explanations and other features of the endogenous growth models are sufficiently convincing is mainly an empirical matter, and some arguments presented below may be important for deciding this.

The knife-edge argument

Strictly speaking, the model of (genuinely) endogenous growth only pertains to a zero probability, knife-edge case ($\phi = 1$) which is uninteresting. Endogenous growth models are sometimes criticized on such grounds. However, as we have carefully argued, the model should rightly be interpreted as an approximation of a wider case (ϕ slightly smaller than 1), which does not have zero probability. On the face of it, this criticism is therefore not valid. The issue is really whether the relevant parameter (here ϕ) can realistically be assumed to be so close to a limiting value (here 1) that the model of endogenous growth can be seen as a good approximation. This is again an empirical matter. For the externality parameter ϕ considered in this chapter, empirical evidence seems to point to positive values of at most up to 0.75, which speaks in favour of models of semi-endogenous growth.

Population growth, economic growth and the scale effect

If the knife-edge property of the endogenous growth model does not represent a serious objection to it, the scale effect does. The feature that an increasing population implies an increasing growth rate in GDP per capita is simply not realistic. The presence of the scale effect is the single most important argument against models of (genuinely) endogenous growth.

According to the model of *semi*-endogenous growth there should be a positive relationship between the long-run growth rate of GDP per capita and the (constant) population growth rate. Based on the evidence presented in Fig. 8.2 and Table 8.1, one may have a hard time finding this feature convincing. There is, however, a counterargument: what Table 8.1 shows is true, but another fact is, according to this argument, more impressive and more important in a very long-run perspective. As we have seen, many countries in the West have experienced relatively constant average annual growth rates in GDP per capita of about 2 per cent during the past 200 years. Over the several thousands of years before that, the average annual growth rates in GDP per capita must have been close to 0 to fit with the level of income per capita around year 1800. So, thousands of years of almost no economic growth have been succeeded by 200 years of rapid economic growth. Population growth has behaved basically the same way, with the world population being close to constant for hundreds of years up to the eighteenth century and thereafter increasing rapidly.[6] This actually fits with semi-endogenous growth. Still, one may wonder if it is really the world's population growth that has caused economic growth, or the other way round. Furthermore, Table 8.1 shows that the areas in the world that have experienced the high (and even increasing) economic growth have had decreasing population growth. It is hard to believe that population growth in Africa, India and China should have caused economic growth in Europe, the USA and (other) parts of Asia, while it seems more plausible that economic growth in Europe and the USA has (indirectly) contributed to reduce mortality and create population growth in Africa and parts of Asia.

In the eyes of the authors of this book, the empirical relationship between population growth and economic growth seems to be mostly in favour of the models of exogenous growth, which predict a negative relationship when natural resources are included in the model.

Convergence

We saw in Chapter 2 that focusing on countries that can be assumed to be structurally similar, such as the OECD countries, there is a clear tendency for the countries that are initially most behind to grow the fastest and thus catch up to the initially richest.[7] In Chapters 5 and 6 we saw that if one controls for structural differences between countries in a way suggested by exogenous growth models, then also for larger, more representative groups of countries, the initially poorest tend to grow the fastest. There is thus evidence in support of convergence.

In the world of models the convergence among countries arises naturally in models with (an appropriate form of) convergence to a steady state. As the steady state is approached

---

6. For these 'facts' and an interesting discussion of them, we refer to Michael Kremer, 'Population Growth and Technological Change: One Million B.C. to 1990', *Quarterly Journal of Economics*, **108**, 1993, pp. 681–716.

7. This pattern is even more clear between states in the USA.

(from below), growth becomes slower and slower. Two different countries with similar characteristics will converge to the same steady state, so the country starting out with the lowest GDP per person will grow the fastest. The empirically observed convergence between countries is thus most naturally explained by models of exogenous or semi-endogenous growth.

The endogenous growth model considered in Section 8.3, on the other hand, did not have convergence to a steady state and showed no tendency for the initial position to be important for subsequent growth. The observed convergence thus contradicts the model and seems to speak against endogenous growth. It must be added, however, that quite natural modifications of the endogenous growth models can take account of convergence, for example by introducing a gradual technological transmission between countries into the framework.

The convergence between countries observed in the real world does not deliver a decisive answer to what kind of growth model does the best job.

Growth rates and investment rates

The single empirical regularity that speaks most strongly in favour of models of (genuinely) endogenous growth is the one illustrated in Fig. 8.4: the clear positive empirical relationship between investment rates and growth rates. The endogenous growth model predicts that a higher savings or investment rate should give a higher growth rate, and indeed high investment rates do go hand in hand with high growth rates.

In the models of exogenous or semi-endogenous growth a higher savings rate does not give a higher growth rate in the long run, but it does so in the intermediate run due to transitory growth. The positive association between investment rates and growth rates could thus be a result of transitory growth, and therefore it does not necessarily contradict the exogenous or semi-endogenous growth models.

However, in models of exogenous growth a higher savings or investment rate, s, could not possibly give a higher growth rate in the technological variable, A_t, exactly because this growth rate is exogenous. In the endogenous growth model a higher s *will* give a higher growth rate in A_t, since the growth rate of A_t is $sA - \delta$, and in the semi-endogenous growth model a higher s gives a higher *transitory* growth in A_t. It is thus of interest to find out whether investment rates are also positively related to growth rates in A_t. This is indeed an idea pursued in an article by the two economists Ben S. Bernanke and Refet S. Gürkaynak.[8] One can get an estimate of the average annual growth rate in the productivity variable A_t by growth accounting. In their article, Bernanke and Gürkaynak first do growth accounting for each of a large number of countries to get estimates of average annual growth rates of A_t. They then plot these rates against average investment rates across countries. Using the data of Bernanke and Gürkaynak the picture in Fig. 8.5 emerges. There is clearly a positive relationship. What is shown in Fig. 8.5 is the strongest empirical argument in favour of endogenous, or perhaps semi-endogenous, growth models that we know of.

The debate from which we have tried to present a few arguments is not settled. For what it is worth, the authors of this textbook find that the empirical results linking investment rates to growth rates are sufficiently convincing to make the endogenous growth research programme, and the existing models, highly promising. We also think that a serious challenge to endogenous growth theory, as it stands, comes from the empirical relationship between population growth rates and economic growth rates, which seems, if anything, to be a negative one. In contrast, semi-endogenous growth models predict a positive effect of population growth on economic growth, while endogenous growth models even predict that a constant positive population growth rate should give an exploding growth rate in GDP per capita (or that labour input is not productive at the aggregate level).

---

8. Ben S. Bernanke and Refet S. Gürkaynak, 'Is Growth Exogenous? Taking Mankiw, Romer, and Weil Seriously', NBER Working paper 8365, July 2001. And yes, this is the Bernanke who is now by 2010 the chairman of the US central bank, the so-called Fed.

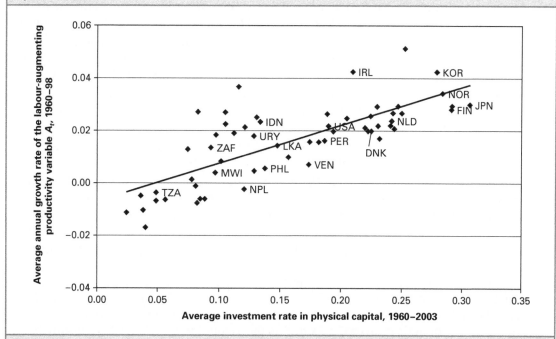

FIGURE 8.5 Average annual growth rate of labour-augmenting productivity against average investment rate in physical capital, 60 countries

Note: The estimated line is $y = -0.007 + 0.145x$, the standard error of the estimate of the slope is 0.016 ($t = 8.9$), and adj. $R^2 = 0.57$. The countries considered are the countries from our main sample of 65 countries considered in Chapters 2 through 6 for which data were available.

Sources: Penn World Table 6.2 and data set for Bernanke and Gürkaynak (2001).

8.5 Summary

1. In endogenous growth theory the growth rate of technology, which underlies the long-run growth in GDP per worker, is endogenous: it depends on basic behavioural model parameters and therefore on structural policies that affect these parameters.

2. According to the replication argument, the individual firm's production function should exhibit constant returns to the inputs of capital and labour at any given technological level. If there are productive externalities from the aggregate stock of capital (or from aggregate production) to labour productivity or total factor productivity in the individual firm, then there can be constant returns to capital and labour at the firm level and increasing returns to capital and labour at the aggregate level. With productive externalities one can therefore maintain the convenient assumption of perfect competition and the associated theory of the income distribution, and at the same time have a potential source of endogenous growth in the model.

3. There are theoretical as well as empirical motivations for productive externalities and aggregate increasing returns. The theoretical arguments are associated with learning by doing: by being involved with (new) capital, or with production in general, workers obtain better skills. Empirical motivations come, for instance, from attempts at estimating aggregate Cobb–Douglas production functions where the sum of exponents is often found to be considerably above one.

4. Building on the idea of productive externalities, we formulated in this chapter a base model with the following features:

- The representative firm was assumed to produce output (GDP) from the inputs of labour and capital according to a usual Cobb–Douglas production function with constant returns to capital and labour and a labour-augmenting productivity variable A_t.

- The labour productivity variable of the representative firm depended on the aggregate stock of capital as given by a function, $A_t = K_t^\phi$, $\phi \geq 0$. Since the firm should be thought of as small relative to the entire economy, it took K_t, and hence A_t, as given.

- Capital accumulated from savings the usual way, and the (gross) savings or investment rate was a given constant. The labour force was assumed to grow at a given rate, n.

- The real prices of capital and labour were determined by the marginal products, computed for a given level of the productivity variable.

5. It makes a qualitative difference in this model if the strength of the external effects is below, equal to, or above 1: $\phi < 1$ leads to semi-endogenous growth, $\phi = 1$ leads to (truly) endogenous growth, and $\phi > 1$ (a case we did not consider in the chapter, but which is considered in an exercise) leads to explosive growth and basically an ill-behaved model.

6. In the case $\phi < 1$, the model implies convergence of capital per effective worker and of output per effective worker to well-defined steady state levels. In steady state there was a common constant growth rate of output per worker and of technology. This growth rate depended in a specific way on ϕ and n, and it was strictly positive if and only if both of ϕ and n were strictly positive. The feature that growth in the labour force is required for economic growth motivates the term 'semi' in semi-endogenous growth. The intuition is that the increasing returns driving the (semi-)endogenous growth can only be exploited if some input increases by itself. Given that the labour force grows, the capital stock will grow by a rate higher than n.

7. For the policy implications of the model of semi-endogenous growth it is important that both the level of, and the growth rate along, the growth path for output (and consumption) per worker depend on behavioural model parameters. The levels of these paths are positively influenced by the rate of saving and investment and negatively influenced by the population growth rate. This speaks for policies to raise investment rates and dampen population growth. On the other hand, the growth rate along the steady state growth path was positively influenced by population growth, speaking for policies to promote population growth, since in the long run the positive growth effect will outweigh the negative level effect.

8. Empirically it seems hard to find a clear positive association between population growth and growth in income per capita, although there are both pros and cons in the debate over whether growth in the labour force really promotes growth in output per worker. Given that this issue is unsettled, one would be cautious about recommending policies to promote population growth, since it seems relatively certain that higher population growth will erode the stock of capital per worker and increase the pressure on scarce natural resources, thereby lowering the level of the basic growth path, whereas the positive effect on the growth rate along this path seems doubtful.

9. The negative association between population growth and economic growth found in the data does not contradict the model of semi-endogenous growth *per se*. If convergence to steady state is very slow, the negative level effect of higher population growth will dominate the positive growth effect for a long time. In this case, however, the steady state itself will not be very descriptive of the economy, rather the convergence process will be the relevant thing to study. The empirical evidence therefore suggests looking at the model with very slow convergence, which obtains as ϕ tends to 1.

10. We took this idea to the extreme and assumed $\phi = 1$, at the same time assuming a constant labour force. This gave us the so-called AK model. This model has constant returns to the reproducible factor, capital. It therefore implies a common and constant positive growth rate of capital per worker and output per worker, without any assumption of exogenous technological progress and without growth in the labour force being required. This is why the model's growth is called 'truly' endogenous. The everlasting balanced growth described by the model can be seen as approximating the very long-lasting transitory growth that would result if ϕ were smaller than, but close to 1. Importantly, the endogenous growth rate depended positively on the rate of saving and investment.

11. The main policy implication of the AK model was therefore that policies to promote saving and investment become even more attractive, now not only because of their level effects, but also for their permanent (or very long-lasting) effect on economic growth.

12. Empirically one finds across countries a rather strong positive relationship between, on the one hand, investment rates and, on the other hand, long-run growth rates in output per worker and in estimates of the productivity variable A_t. This is in very nice accordance with models of (truly) endogenous growth. On the other hand these models are plagued by an empirically implausible scale effect: according to endogenous growth models, a larger labour force gives higher economic growth and a growing labour force gives explosive economic growth. These features are highly counterfactual.

13. We closed this chapter by discussing the arguments for and against the theories of exogenous, semi-endogenous and endogenous growth. The scale effect implied by truly endogenous growth models speak against these models and in favour of models of semi-endogenous growth. Compared to endogenous growth models, models of exogenous growth seem easier to reconcile with the empirical evidence on convergence and on the relationship between population growth and economic growth. Nevertheless, endogenous growth models have made an interesting and promising contribution to the theory of economic growth, because of their ability to account for the observed positive relationship between investment rates and productivity growth, and because they have forced growth theorists to think harder about the forces underlying technological change.

8.6 Exercises

Exercise 1. The strength of productive externalities and the speed of convergence: simulations

This exercise illustrates *by numerical simulations* how the speed of convergence in the model of semi-endogenous growth ($0 < \phi < 1$) depends on the size of ϕ, and that for ϕ tending to 1 (here with $n = 0$), convergence becomes very slow so that the model tends to exhibit endogenous growth.

We consider the model consisting of Eqs (6)–(9), but we set $n = 0$ and we let the constant size of the labour force be $L = 1$. Hence we have excluded long-run growth due to population growth from the beginning.

1. Show that the steady state values, K^* and Y^*, of capital and output (also per worker), respectively, are:

$$K^* = \left(\frac{s}{\delta}\right)^{\frac{1}{(1-\alpha)(1-\phi)}} \quad \text{and} \quad Y^* = \left(\frac{s}{\delta}\right)^{\frac{\alpha+\phi(1-\alpha)}{(1-\alpha)(1-\phi)}}.$$

What is the steady state value of A_t?

In the following let $\alpha = \frac{1}{3}$ and $s = 0.24$ everywhere. Let $\delta = 0.08$ initially and after a shift, fall permanently down to $\delta = 0.06$. Consider three different values for ϕ: 0.5, 0.75 and 0.9.

2. For each value of ϕ, compute the steady state values for K_t and Y_t before and after the shift in δ.
3. For each value of ϕ, let the economy be initially in steady state for $\delta = 0.08$. After some periods, 10 say, δ shifts permanently down to $\delta = 0.06$. Simulate the model over the periods before the shift and 200 periods after to create series (K_t) and (Y_t). In one diagram plot the growth rate $(Y_t - Y_{t-1})/Y_{t-1}$ (or the approximate one, $\ln Y_t - \ln Y_{t-1}$) against periods t over the simulated periods for each of the three considered values for ϕ. Comment on the figure with respect to the opening statement of this exercise.

Exercise 2. The strength of productive externalities and the speed of convergence analytically

The transition equation, (13) or (14), we arrived at in this chapter for $\phi < 1$ can be written in the generic form $\tilde{k}_{t+1} = G(\tilde{k}_t)$ just as we did in Section 5.4 for the transition equation studied there. This is just a matter of defining G appropriately. Hence, using the same kind of operations that were used in Chapter 5 to arrive at that chapter's equation (34), a linear approximation around steady state of the transition equation studied in this chapter is:

$$\ln \tilde{y}_{t+1} - \ln \tilde{y}_t = \lambda(\ln \tilde{y}^* - \ln \tilde{y}_t), \text{ where } \lambda = 1 - G'(\tilde{k}^*).$$

1. Go through all the operations that lead to this equation yourself. (Of course, everything is the same as in Chapter 5 since there is no difference in the generic equation studied. It is important, though, that you can do the full linear approximation yourself.) Explain in what sense λ is a measure of the rate of convergence for $\tilde{y}_t$.

2. Show that the rate of convergence (for $\phi < 1$) is:

$$\lambda = (1 - \alpha)(1 - \phi)\frac{(1 + n)^{\frac{1}{1-\phi}} - (1 - \delta)}{(1 + n)^{\frac{1}{1-\phi}}}$$

$$= (1 - \alpha)(1 - \phi)\left[1 - \frac{1 - \delta}{(1 + n)^{\frac{1}{1-\phi}}}\right].$$

Convince yourself that in the special case $\phi = 0$, this rate is in accordance with the rate found in Chapter 5. Show that as ϕ goes to 1, λ goes to 0. Try to explain intuitively why a large ϕ implies slow convergence.

Exercise 3. The model of semi-endogenous growth ($\phi < 1$) and of endogenous growth ($\phi = 1$) with the productive externality arising from K_t/L_t rather than from K_t

In our discussion in Section 8.3 of the scale effect in connection with the model of endogenous growth ($\phi = 1$) we said that one can eliminate the effect by assuming a productive externality of the form:

$$A_t = \left(\frac{K_t}{L_t}\right)^\phi,$$

rather than the form $A_t = K_t^\phi$ mainly assumed in the chapter. We now consider the model of *semi*-endogenous growth ($\phi < 1$) with the alternative form of the external effect and we study the model of endogenous growth ($\phi = 1$) a little further to show that with the alternative formulation of the external effect one can have population growth in the model without getting exploding economic growth.

The model to be considered is (6)–(9), but with (7) replaced by the equation above. Our assumptions are the same as in the chapter, among them $s > n + \delta$.

Before turning to the more technical questions, try to think about whether you find the form $A_t = K_t^\phi$ or the form $A_t = (K_t/L)^\phi$ most convincing for the productive externality. Should the external effect on labour productivity from the use of machinery be expected to come from the amount of capital as such or from capital per worker? Think, for instance, of a firm with ten workers beginning to use computers. The direct (privately appropriated) productive effect will, of course, be stronger with ten computers than with one. How about the indirect (external) effect?

For questions 1–5 assume that $0 < \phi < 1$.

1. Show that now:

$$\frac{A_{t+1}}{A_t} = \frac{\left(\dfrac{K_{t+1}}{K_t}\right)^{\phi}}{(1+n)^{\phi}},$$

and that with the usual definitions, the transition equation is:

$$\tilde{k}_{t+1} = \left(\frac{1}{1+n}\right)^{1-\phi} \tilde{k}_t (s\tilde{k}_t^{\alpha-1} + (1-\delta))^{1-\phi}.$$

Convergence to positive steady state values, $\tilde{k}^*$ and $\tilde{y}^*$, follows from the properties of the transition equation the same way as in this chapter.

2. Find the steady state values, $\tilde{k}^*$ and $\tilde{y}^*$, for $\tilde{k}_t$ and $\tilde{y}_t$ respectively. Show that in steady state the common growth rate of A_t, k_t and y_t is 0 (also when $n > 0$).

3. What is the aggregate production function in this model? Is labour unproductive at the aggregate level (also when $\phi < 1$)? Why is it that in this case there is no positive, semi-endogenous type of growth in GDP per worker in steady state?

The fact that the presence of the external effects does not produce (semi-)endogenous growth in the steady state this time may give the impression that ϕ is not economically important, at least not for steady state. The size of ϕ is, however, important both for the steady state levels and for the convergence process outside steady state, as the answers to the following two questions should reveal.

4. Show that the constant levels of capital per worker and output per worker in steady state are:

$$k^* = \left(\frac{s}{n+\delta}\right)^{\frac{1}{(1-\alpha)(1-\phi)}} \quad \text{and} \quad y^* = \left(\frac{s}{n+\delta}\right)^{\frac{\alpha+\phi(1-\alpha)}{(1-\alpha)(1-\phi)}}.$$

5. By considering again the linear approximation around steady state, etc., find, also for this model, the rate of convergence λ for $\tilde{y}_t$ according to the linear approximation. Show that (again) λ goes to 0 as ϕ goes to 1. (The latter result means that the endogenous growth model ($\phi = 1$) without the scale effect approximates the behaviour of the model considered here for large ϕ.)

Now assume $\phi = 1$, and still $n > 0$.

6. Show that the Solow equation is:

$$k_{t+1} - k_t = \frac{1}{1+n}(s - \delta - n)k_t,$$

and that the endogenous growth rate of GDP per worker is $g_e = (s - \delta - n)/(1 + n)$. Comment with respect to scale effects.

Exercise 4. Balanced growth

Show that the steady state growth path of the model of semi-endogenous growth considered in Section 8.2 is one of balanced growth. Then show that the growth path of the model of endogenous growth considered in Section 8.3 (with $n = 0$) is one of balanced growth. (Essentially you are asked to show that all of capital per worker, output per worker and wages per worker (the wage rate) grow by one and the same constant rate and that the real rental (interest) rate of capital is constant along both of these growth paths. Since the models assume a constant growth rate of the labour force (possibly 0) the other requirements for balanced growth follow.)

Exercise 5. Explosive endogenous growth

You may have been wondering about some cases not dealt with in this chapter. For instance, when we were setting $\phi = 1$ in Section 8.3 (as an approximation of a large ϕ just below 1) we assumed at the same time $n = 0$. This was perhaps for a good reason, but $\phi = 1$ and $n > 0$ have not been considered. Furthermore, we have considered $\phi < 1$ and $\phi = 1$, but not $\phi > 1$. This exercise asks you to demonstrate that the uncovered cases lead, or may lead, to explosive growth, that is, to a growth rate in GDP per worker that increases over time and eventually goes to infinity. This is, of course, a *very* unrealistic feature.

Consider the growth model consisting of the equations (6)–(9).

1. In that model, let $\phi = 1$ and $n > 0$ (so that $L_t = (1 + n)^t L_0$ increases at a constant rate n). Show that the (exact) growth rates of k_t and y_t, respectively, in period t are:

$$\frac{k_{t+1} - k_t}{k_t} = \frac{1}{1+n}[sL_0^{1-\alpha}(1+n)^{(1-\alpha)t} - (n+\delta)]$$

and

$$\frac{y_{t+1} - y_t}{y_t} = \frac{1}{(1+n)^\alpha}[sL_0^{1-\alpha}(1+n)^{(1-\alpha)t} + 1 - \delta] - 1.$$

2. Now let $\phi > 1$ (but say also $\phi < 2$, not to be extreme) and $n = 0$ (so that L_t is constant, L say). Show that the aggregate production function can be written $Y_t = AK_t^{1+(1-\alpha)(\phi-1)}$, where $A \equiv L^{1-\alpha}$ (and since $\phi > 1$, the exponent on K_t is greater than 1). Write down the transition equation for K_t and show that K_t has a unique steady state value: $K^* = [\delta/(sA)]^{1/[(1-\alpha)(\phi-1)]}$. Is anything puzzling you about this value? Write down the Solow equation for K_t and sketch the Solow diagram. Is K^* stable or unstable? Also state the modified Solow equation and draw the modified Solow diagram. If K_t is initially greater than K^*, how does the growth rate of K_t evolve over time? How about the growth rates of k_t and y_t? What if $K_t < K^*$ initially?

Exercise 6. Endogenous growth with both physical and human capital

In this chapter we presented endogenous growth models with physical capital, but without human capital. The following three equations make up a model of endogenous growth including human capital:

$$Y_t = AK_t^v H_t^{1-v}, \qquad 0 < v < 1.$$

$$K_{t+1} = s_K Y_t + (1 - \delta)K_t$$

$$H_{t+1} = s_H Y_t + (1 - \delta)H_t.$$

Notation and parameter values are as usual if not explicitly stated. The first equation is the aggregate production function where the influence of the constant labour force, L, has been put into A and the sum of the exponents on physical and human capital add up to 1, so there is not diminishing, but constant returns to the reproducible factors taken together. The next two equations describe the accumulation of physical and human capital, respectively, just as in Chapter 6.

1. First show that if the production function of the individual firm is:

$$Y_t = (K_t^d)^\alpha (H_t^d)^\varphi (A_t L_t^d)^{1-\alpha-\varphi},$$

and an external productive effect implies:

$$A_t = (K_t^{\frac{\alpha}{\alpha+\varphi}} H_t^{\frac{\varphi}{\alpha+\varphi}})^\phi,$$

then if $\phi = 1$, the aggregate production function above results, where $A = L^{1-\alpha-\varphi}$, and $v = \alpha/(\alpha + \varphi)$. How should we view this model bearing in mind that a knife-edge case such as $\phi = 1$ is not of interest in itself?

2. Define the ratio between physical and human capital, $x_t \equiv K_t/H_t$. Show that the model above implies the following dynamic equation for this ratio:

$$x_{t+1} = \frac{s_k A x_t^v + (1-\delta)x_t}{s_H A x_t^v + (1-\delta)},$$

and demonstrate that this equation has properties that imply that in the long run x_t converges to $x^* = s_K/s_H$.

3. Show that according to the model above the growth rates of physical and human capital, respectively, in any period t are:

$$g_t^K \equiv \frac{K_{t+1} - K_t}{K_t} = s_k A \left(\frac{K_t}{H_t}\right)^{v-1} - \delta,$$

$$g_t^H \equiv \frac{H_{t+1} - H_t}{H_t} = s_H A \left(\frac{K_t}{H_t}\right)^{v} - \delta,$$

and then show that as $x_t = K_t/H_t$ tends to its long-run equilibrium value x^*, these two growth rates tend to the common value:

$$g = s_K^v s_H^{1-v} A - \delta.$$

Show that in long-run equilibrium g is also the constant and endogenous growth rate of Y_t and of y_t.

4. According to this model, growth in GDP per worker depends positively not only on s_K as tested in Fig. 8.4, but also on s_H. To test this, create a diagram that plots growth rates in GDP per worker, g^i, against investment rates in human capital, s_H^i, across countries i with data taken from Table A (includes countries from the sample of 65 countries). Comment.

   From the empirical observations we described in Chapter 6, α and φ should be of about equal size, which should here imply $v = \frac{1}{2}$. Put the model's full (endogenous) growth prediction to a test by plotting growth rates g_i against $(s_K^i)^{1/2}(s_H^i)^{1/2}$ again taking data from Table A. Estimate the line of best fit. Compare with Fig. 8.4 and to the figure plotting g^i against s_H^i. Comment.

Exercise 7. Semi-endogenous growth and endogenous growth if the productive externality arises from Y_t rather than from K_t

As mentioned in this chapter, sometimes models with productive externalities assume that the external learning-by-doing effect arises from workers being involved in production as such rather than (more narrowly) from their being involved with the use of capital.

   We therefore consider a growth model consisting of the four equations (6), (8), (9) and:

$$A_t = Y_t^\phi, \; 0 < \phi < \frac{1}{1-\alpha},$$

where the latter equation replaces (7).

1. Show that the aggregate production function in this model is:

$$Y_t = K_t^{\frac{\alpha}{1-\phi(1-\alpha)}} L_t^{\frac{1-\alpha}{1-\phi(1-\alpha)}}.$$

Why have we assumed $\phi < 1/(1-\alpha)$? Show that the aggregate production function has increasing returns to (K_t, L_t) whenever $\phi > 0$. Show also that if $\phi = 1$ it has constant returns to K_t alone.

2. Show that in this model:

$$\frac{A_{t+1}}{A_t} = \left(\frac{K_{t+1}}{K_t}\right)^{\frac{\alpha\phi}{1-\phi(1-\alpha)}} \left(\frac{L_{t+1}}{L_t}\right)^{\frac{\varphi(1-\alpha)}{1-\phi(1-\alpha)}}$$

Assume now that $\phi < 1$. Let $\tilde{y}_t$ and $\tilde{k}_t$ be defined as usual: $\tilde{k}_t \equiv k_t/A_t \equiv K_t/(A_tL_t)$ and $\tilde{y}_t \equiv y_t/A_t \equiv Y_t/(A_tL_t)$.

3. Show that the transition equation for $\tilde{k}_t$ is:

$$\tilde{k}_{t+1} = \left(\frac{1}{1+n}\right)^{\frac{1}{1-\phi(1-\alpha)}} \tilde{k}_t [s\tilde{k}_t^{\alpha-1} + (1-\delta)]^{\frac{1-\phi}{1-\phi(1-\alpha)}}$$

$$= \left(\frac{1}{1+n}\right)^{\frac{1}{1-\phi(1-\alpha)}} (s\tilde{k}_t^{\frac{\alpha}{1-\phi}} + (1-\delta)\tilde{k}_t^{\frac{1-\phi(1-\alpha)}{1-\phi}})^{\frac{1-\phi}{1-\phi(1-\alpha)}}$$

Find the steady state values for $\tilde{k}_t$ and $\tilde{y}_t$, and show that these are meaningful whenever $(1+n)^{1/(1-\phi)} > (1-\delta)$ (which we assume). Show also that the transition equation implies convergence to steady state.

4. Find the expression for the growth rate, g_{se}, of output per worker in steady state. Comment with respect to what creates growth in output per worker in this model (when $\phi < 1$).

Now assume $\phi = 1$, and $n = 0$, so L_t is equal to some L for all t.

5. Show that the model can be condensed to the two equations:

$$Y_t = AK_t, \qquad A \equiv L^{\frac{1-\alpha}{\alpha}},$$

$$K_{t+1} = sY_t + (1-\delta)K_t.$$

Find the growth rate, g_e, of output per worker. Comment, for instance, with respect to scale effects.

Exercise 8. Taxation and productive government spending: endogenous growth without productive externalities

There is a simple alternative to productive externalities as a mechanism for endogenous growth, which yields basically the same models as studied in this chapter: productive government expenditure financed by (proportional) income taxation. The model studied in this exercise comes from Barro (1990),[9] and consists of the five equations below.

The production function is as usual with a labour productivity variable A_t:

$$Y_t = K_t^\alpha (A_tL_t)^{1-\alpha}.$$

Income is taxed proportionally by the rate τ, $0 < \tau < 1$, in all periods, so the tax revenue in period t is τY_t. The budget is balanced, so government expenditure in period t is:

---

9. Robert J. Barro, 'Government Spending in a Simple Model of Endogenous Growth', *Journal of Political Economy*, **98**, 1990, pp. S103–S125.

$$G_t = \tau Y_t.$$

Government spending (on infrastructure, the legal system, health care, etc.) is assumed to be 'productive' in the sense that productivity is influenced positively by expenditure:

$$A_t = aG_t, \qquad a > 0.$$

Total savings and investment are given as a given fraction of total *net* income, so the capital accumulation equation is:

$$K_{t+1} = s(1 - \tau)Y_t + (1 - \delta)K_t.$$

Finally we assume a constant labour force:

$$L_t = L.$$

1. Show that the aggregate production function (where it is taken into account how A_t depends on Y_t through taxation, etc.) is:

$$Y_t = (a\tau L)^{\frac{1-\alpha}{\alpha}} K_t,$$

   and comment.

2. Show that the model is equivalent to an AK model (like (20) and (21) in the chapter) with appropriate relabelling of parameters. Find the growth rate of capital per worker and of GDP per worker that the model gives rise to.

3. Is there a scale effect? Assume alternatively that it is government expenditure per worker, G_t/L_t, that is productive, so that $A_t = aG_t$ above is replaced by $A_t = a(G_t/L_t)$. Analyse the model and find the growth rate of GDP per worker. Comment with respect to the scale effect and the aggregate productivity of labour.

4. What value of τ maximizes the rate of economic growth (for the case $A_t = aG_t$ as well as for $A_t = a(G_t/L_t)$)? Describe the opposing forces that determine the growth-maximizing tax rate. Discuss the policy implications of your analysis. How would policy implications be affected, do you think, if there were traditional distortionary effects of taxation, e.g., if labour supply was an increasing function of the after-tax real wage?

   Consider a generalization of the model where the equation $A_t = aG_t$ is replaced by $A_t = a(G_t)^\phi$, $0 < \phi \le 1$, and $L_t = L$ is replaced by $L_{t+1} = (1 + n)L_t$. The model above corresponds to $\phi = 1$, and $n = 0$, so let us now assume $\phi < 1$ and $n > 0$.

5. Analyse the resulting model as we have analysed models of semi-endogenous growth in this chapter, going through the following steps: find the aggregate production function and describe its returns to scale. Find the transition equation for $\tilde{k}_t \equiv k_t/A_t \equiv K_t/(A_t L_t)$, verify convergence to a steady state, and find the growth rate of output per worker and of A_t in steady state. Comment with respect to policy implications. (Hint: Exercise 7 can be of help here.)

Exercise 9. Exogenous or endogenous growth models?

You have now seen some models of exogenous growth and some of endogenous growth and you have been presented with some pros and cons for both types of models. At this stage, what kind of model do you think gives the best understanding of economic growth? This is not the type of exercise that has one correct answer. In fact, leading growth economists still discuss this issue between them. Get together with fellow students and line up the most important pros and cons for each type of model. Then discuss which arguments you find most important and convincing, and finally try to make up your own mind on the issue: exogenous or endogenous growth.

CHAPTER 9

R&D-based endogenous growth

In all our growth models the ultimate source of growth in GDP per worker is technological progress. Up to now technological progress has been either *unexplained* or *unintentional*. In this chapter we will study a growth model in which *technological progress is the endogenous and deliberate outcome of a production process which requires productive inputs.*

The exogenous growth models of Part 2 postulated a fixed growth rate in the technological variable A_t, so the driving force of economic growth was basically *unexplained*. In the externality-based endogenous growth models presented in the previous chapter, A_t was linked to aggregate capital (or income), so growth in A_t was endogenous and 'explained' by growth in capital, but technological progress was an *unintentional* by-product of economic activity in general. No agent was concerned with creating technological progress, and no inputs were used for the purpose of producing increases in A_t.

In the real world many people are occupied with producing better technology and production methods in private companies as well as at private and public universities and other organizations engaged in the creation of new knowledge.

In this chapter we study growth models that bring research and development, R&D, production processes explicitly into the picture. If economic growth is rooted in technological progress, then by better understanding the production process for technological progress we gain a deeper understanding of growth.

9.1 The role of ideas in economic development

In our models technological progress will have a very precise meaning: there will still be a technological variable, A_t, and technological progress will mean that A_t increases. The ultimate output of the R&D sector in period t is thus the total technological progress, $A_{t+1} - A_t$, from period t to period $t + 1$.

We view the production process in the R&D sector as follows. Economic resources in research and development (or in innovative effort in general) produce *ideas*. These ideas are what ultimately bring better technology, that is, increases in A_t. So, *better technology is created by new ideas*, where we interpret ideas in a broad sense. Ideas can be new insights in basic research, such as Newton's mechanics, calculus, Einstein's theory of relativism, Bohr's atomic theory, etc. They can also be more 'close-to-the-factory' inventions of new machinery, such as the steam engine or a new generation of computers, or better 'tools' for existing machinery, such as a new or improved piece of software for existing computers. Furthermore, they can be ideas for new and more productive ways to organize production, such as the assembly line, or they can be ideas for new intermediate or final products.

Ideas come from people, so the R&D production process has to be labour intensive. We assume that the only inputs in the R&D sector are the labour power of 'researchers' and the existing stock of knowledge, although in the real world also some capital is used in R&D activities. We thus view the R&D sector as follows:

Inputs: the innovative effort of labour and the existing level of technology

$\xrightarrow{\text{create as}}$

Direct output: new insights and ideas

$\xrightarrow{\text{which result in the}}$

Ultimate output: a new and higher level of technology.

The fact that the direct output of the R&D sector essentially consists of ideas makes the associated microeconomics more subtle than in the growth models we have considered earlier. The reason is that ideas, viewed as economic goods, are like *public goods*. They are *non-rival*: the fact that one person uses calculus or (the idea behind) a specific spreadsheet in no way limits another person's ability to use calculus or the same kind of spreadsheet. Ideas are also *imperfectly excludable*, varying from absolutely non-excludable (no person can be prevented from using calculus) to partly excludable (in principle people are excluded from using a spreadsheet they haven't paid for because using it without a licence is a violation of law, but pirate copying takes place).

The non-rival character of ideas implies that private production of ideas cannot take place under perfect competition. Imperfect competition is therefore a necessary condition for privately conducted R&D, but at the same time imperfect competition violates a basic condition for economic efficiency, namely the principle that consumer prices should equal the marginal costs of production. Furthermore, the imperfect excludability of ideas means that private for-profit production involving the creation of new ideas may not be a viable option at all. This is explained in Section 9.2 below.

The public goods nature of ideas thus gives reasons why the production of improved technology should be done by non-profit enterprises. Why then is not all production of ideas public in the real world? Certainly a lot of research and development takes place in government and non-profit organizations like universities and hospitals. This is particularly true for most basic research. However, a lot of R&D activities take place in private firms where the motive for creating new ideas is the profit that can be earned from the ideas being marketed and transformed into new technology. For instance, private medical companies have large and very expensive R&D departments struggling to create new, or improve upon existing, types of medicine. The motive is to earn profits from selling the new or improved medicine.

In capitalist market economies the profit motive is used as a device for the allocation of resources. If there is a shortage of potatoes the price goes up, which makes it more profitable to produce potatoes. Profit-seeking producers will therefore produce more, thereby working to eliminate the shortage. Each firm is motivated by its profit, but comes, through its attempts to maximize profits, to serve society, 'as if guided by an invisible hand' in Adam Smith's famous words. Most economists think that markets and the profit motive constitute a mechanism for the distribution of scarce resources over competing ends that is so effective that it should be widely used in actual resource allocation. (Most economists think as well that the market mechanism is not perfect and should be 'corrected' by various forms of government intervention to address imperfections such as externalities, public goods, abuse of market power, etc.)

If the market mechanism is useful in allocating resources between the production of potatoes and bread, say, it can perhaps also be effective in allocating resources to R&D activities. Private R&D firms create new ideas motivated by the profits that can be earned from selling the ideas, but thereby they come to act as technological developers to the benefit of everybody. Thus, society may have an interest in R&D activities being conducted privately in so far as the profit motive is considered an effective engine for technological development. However, the public goods nature of ideas implies difficulties for the working of this engine.

Section 9.2 explains and discusses the microeconomics of ideas and explains the difficulties of private production of new technology. It also describes some resolutions to these difficulties. From Section 9.3 an R&D-based growth model is presented. Since the microeconomics of (private) R&D production is too subtle for a textbook at this level, the model will abstract from these subtleties and be of a more conventional macroeconomic character. We simply lay out some relationships between technology and growth and study their implications. Although our model does not include an explicit treatment of the microeconomics of (private) production of ideas, this subtle microeconomics will be visible in the model, as we shall see.[1]

9.2 Ideas as economic goods

A private production of ideas requires that ideas can somehow create an income. In the real world income creation from ideas takes different forms. Sometimes an idea is invented by a pure R&D firm that does not intend to use the idea itself. The inventing firm will then want to sell the idea to another firm. This will most often take place by the selling of a *patent*, or by licensing (renting) out a patent in return for a royalty income paid period by period. In other cases ideas are created in research departments of firms that want to use the idea themselves in the production of commodities. The idea is then patented by the producing firm itself and creates an income through the selling of a good containing the idea. For instance, the main content in a new improved piece of software, like a new spreadsheet, is the idea of the computer code, but this is sold to the customer in a box containing a CD, a manual, etc. Likewise, the real novelty in a new generation of razors is the idea for an improvement (now with five blades and ball bearings), but the idea is sold packaged with a traditional good consisting of the razor itself and some blades. We may view the invention of an idea and its use in production as two separate activities. In any case, patents seem to play a crucial role in ensuring that ideas can generate income for those who developed them. This section explains why this is the case.

The non-rival nature of ideas

Once a new idea has been invented, the use of the idea in one activity does not in any way limit the extent to which it can be used in other activities. This feature gives ideas the nature of public goods. In relation to public goods, one important concept is *rivalry*. What we just said means that *ideas are non-rival*.

An economic good can be rival or non-rival. It is rival if the consumption or use of the good by one person or firm prevents other persons or firms from using it. Potatoes and bread, restaurant meals and cars are rival goods. A good is non-rival if its use by one agent does not limit the ability of other agents to use the same good. Classic examples of non-rival goods are national defence, the services of the legal system ('law and order'), the services of

1. The R&D-based growth model is known as the Romer model of endogenous growth and was developed by Paul M. Romer over several papers, in particular 'Endogenous Technological Change', *Journal of Political Economy*, **98**, 1990, pp. S71–S102. (We present a generalized version of the model due to Charles I. Jones, 'R&D-based Models of Economic Growth', *Journal of Political Economy*, **103**, 1995, pp. 759–784.) It is the full model, including the subtle microeconomics, that Romer has become famous for. Macro models close to the one we study in this chapter had been suggested before. One important conclusion of Romer's model with a true microeconomic foundation is that in a certain sense it implies the macro model we study in this chapter, making this much less *ad hoc* than it first appears.

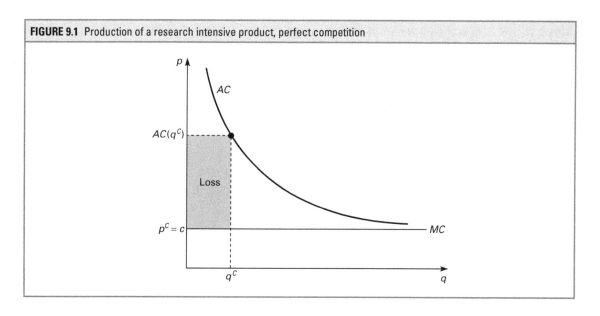

FIGURE 9.1 Production of a research intensive product, perfect competition

bridges and parks (in so far as they are not overcrowded), access to fresh air, great scenic views, etc. One aspect of a non-rival good is that its marginal cost of production is (close to) zero. One additional passage of a bridge, for instance, involves almost no additional cost (again provided it is not already congested), although the bridge may originally have been extremely costly to construct.

Ideas are non-rival. For instance, the big discoveries in basic research, like calculus, can be used by many different persons in many different places at the same time, and the extent to which it is used in one place at one time has no implication for the extent to which it can be used in other places at the same or at other times. The non-rival character of ideas has an important implication for the cost functions associated with the use of ideas, for instance in the production of a traditional good that embodies the idea.

Let us return to the example of a new generation of razors. The idea behind it has been developed either by an independent R&D firm or in the research department of the producing firm. In any case, acquiring the idea has given rise to a cost consisting mainly of the incomes of the developers. Once the idea has been fully developed, the use of the idea in one 'activity', the production of a specific razor unit, does not prevent the idea from being used in another activity, the production of another razor unit. Hence, the cost of acquiring the idea is to be considered as a fixed cost, F say, in the production of the new razors that carry the idea. Let us assume that in addition to this fixed cost there is a (small) constant unit cost, c, of producing razors, as would follow from the replication argument and given input prices (explain why). If we denote the firm's production of razors by q, the cost function is $C(q) = F + cq$, and hence the marginal and average cost functions, respectively, are $MC(q) = c$, and $AC(q) = F/q + c$. These are illustrated in Fig. 9.1.

Assume now that the producer is a small perfect competitor who takes the price of razors as given. The horizontal marginal cost curve will then also be the firm's supply curve: if the given razor price exceeds c, the supply will be infinite; if the output price is smaller than c, supply will be zero, and if the razor price is exactly c, any output level is an optimal supply. Once the idea has been fully developed, the development cost is 'sunk', and therefore optimal behaviour only depends on the variable cost component, c. In these circumstances market forces should imply a competitive equilibrium where the price, p^C, is equal to c, and the amount produced is given by demand, for instance for the small firm implying a production of q^C as indicated in Fig. 9.1. In this equilibrium the firm will earn a negative profit since average cost, $AC(q^C)$, exceeds the price, $p^C = c$. The total revenue $p^C q^C$ exactly

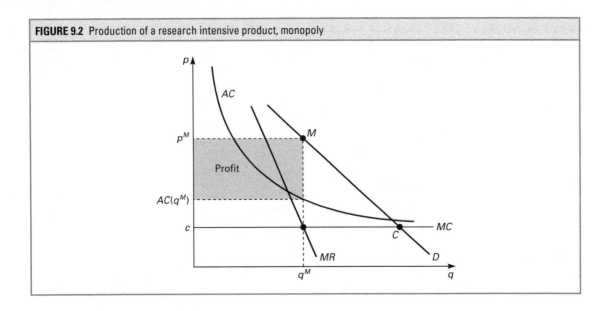

FIGURE 9.2 Production of a research intensive product, monopoly

covers the *variable* cost cq^C, but falls short of total cost by the amount $(AC(q^C) - c)q^C = F$. The fixed cost is uncovered and the production of razors involves a loss of F.

However, before the firm decides to develop or buy the idea behind the new razor it would be able to foresee what we have just explained: that the whole project can only end up yielding negative profits. The firm would therefore never decide to start such a project in the first place. The conclusion is that *under the conditions of perfect competition (price taking in the output market), one cannot have a private production of idea-based technological progress.*

Assume now instead that the firm is not small in the output market, but rather is the only producer of the particular new razor. Let the demand curve for this razor be as illustrated by D in Fig. 9.2. The cost curves are the same as in Fig. 9.1. With this demand curve the competitive equilibrium would be given by the point C involving the price c and a specific total output (of which we imagined the small firm above to supply q^C). When the firm is the sole supplier, it can take advantage of the fact that reducing output from the competitive level will imply a higher price (while the competitive firm's supply was assumed to be so small relative to the market that it had no significant influence on the price). It is well known from microeconomics that the monopoly firm should reduce output as long as marginal cost is larger than marginal revenue. This leads to the optimal point M in Fig. 9.2, where the marginal cost curve, *MC*, and the marginal revenue curve, *MR*, intersect. At the monopoly optimum, the price, p^M, could well be above average cost as illustrated, and the project of developing the idea and producing the new type of razor could thus imply positive profits. *Under conditions of imperfect competition (monopoly power in the output market) it is possible to have a private production of idea-based technological progress.*

The conclusion is that *in order to have a private production of idea-based technological progress it must somehow be ensured that the inventor of an idea holds monopoly over the use of the idea*, or in the production of a good that embodies the idea, at least for some period. This is indeed an important conclusion, and patent rights and other legal ways of protecting intellectual property rights serve as instruments for creating such monopoly power. Before turning to that, however, we should emphasize that this way of ensuring a profit-motivated development of ideas is highly imperfect, exactly because it works through giving monopoly power to the firm.

In the monopoly optimum given by point M in Fig. 9.2, the price is above marginal cost (otherwise there would not be positive profits). This means that the consumers are ready to pay more for additional units of the new razor than the additional cost that would result from producing additional units. Hence, from a social viewpoint, too few resources are devoted to the utilization of the idea behind the new type of razors: Monopoly implies a deadweight loss in the form of a foregone consumers' surplus, in the figure represented by the area of the triangle below the D-curve, above the MC-curve, and to the right of the vertical line at q^M. In other words, *if one ensures a private production of idea-based technological progress by giving monopoly in the use of ideas to the creators, then the resulting ideas will be used too little as compared to a social optimum.*

This might seem to suggest that research and development should mainly be conducted by public, or other non-profit, enterprises. These could supply ideas, or products embodying ideas, at marginal cost, thus ensuring an optimal utilization of the ideas and simply accept the implied negative profits. The losses would, however, have to be financed by taxes, and taxes have negative welfare effects too because they imply distortions. The social cost of having a less than optimal utilization of ideas under private R&D would have to be weighed against the social cost of distortionary taxation under public R&D. Furthermore, as mentioned earlier, we (the general public) may wish to have private R&D activities, and be willing to live with the monopoly power necessarily associated with it, in so far as we believe that sometimes the profit motive is an effective engine for technological development. The experiences of the formerly planned economies of Eastern Europe suggest that the more applied part of research and development is done most effectively in private enterprises. When it comes to developing the kind of razor, toothbrush, or blue jeans that people really want, or the kind of spreadsheet or catalyser that other firms can really use, private developers are, probably, more effective than public bureaucracies exactly because they are governed by market signals and the profit motive.

Private R&D activities may therefore be socially beneficial, and certainly in the real world we do observe a lot of R&D taking place in private firms. This state of affairs requires, as we have seen, that somehow the inventor of an idea obtains monopoly power over the use of the idea. Very often patents serve the purpose of ensuring such a monopoly. When Novo Nordisk, at huge development costs, has designed a new way of producing an improved form of insulin, it can protect its 'design' by taking out a patent on it. The patent gives Novo Nordisk the right to be the sole user of the design in production of insulin for some period. If another firm uses the same design in the production of insulin, it will violate the law. What the patent really does is thus to exclude other persons and firms from the use of the idea for a specific purpose. This leads us naturally to the discussion of another essential concept in relation to public goods, namely *excludability*.

The importance of excludability

A good is excludable if the owner of the good can exclude other persons or firms from using it (if they do not pay for it). Most traditional goods, like bread and potatoes, haircuts, restaurant meals and travels, etc., are excludable. They are only handed over the desk upon payment. A good is non-excludable if persons or firms cannot be excluded from the use of it. Classic examples of non-excludable goods are, again, national defence, 'law and order', clean air, etc. Since the access to a non-excludable good cannot be made conditional on payment, non-excludable goods cannot be produced and marketed by private, profit-motivated firms. Only public enterprises not motivated by profits can produce completely non-excludable goods.

Most economic goods are either both rival and excludable, or both non-rival and non-excludable. The first are the traditional goods like bread, potatoes, haircuts, restaurant meals, etc., and the latter are the pure public goods like national defence, law and order, fresh air, etc. However, rivalry and excludability are conceptually distinct. There are goods that are non-rival and excludable, for instance crossing a (not congested) bridge. One person's passage will (under normal circumstances) not limit other persons' possibilities of crossing the same bridge, so the good is non-rival. People can, however, be excluded from crossing a bridge if they do not pay, so the good is excludable. An example of a good that is rival, but non-excludable could be 'fish in the sea', since a fish caught by one person cannot be caught by another person too, but during most of history free access to catching fish in the open sea has been considered a right for everybody.

While a good is either rival or non-rival (again disregarding congestion), excludability can occur to different degrees. Furthermore, and relatedly, increased excludability can to some extent be ensured by law and by technology. These two features are important in connection with ideas.

Consider again the idea for a new way of producing an improved form of insulin. Each package of medicine will somehow contain the idea, but the exact recipe will not be directly visible and hence not completely open for use by everybody. The idea or design is therefore, by nature, somewhat excludable. On the other hand, a competitor with a research department of its own could probably, by analysing the product, break or read the code and in that way technically become able to produce the same medicine. Hence the design is not perfectly excludable.

The legal institution of patent rights can to some extent prevent direct copying and thus make the design more excludable than it was by nature. There may also be ways to produce the new medicine that can make it more difficult to detect the invention behind it, just like a TV transmission in the air (another non-rival good) can be made more excludable by encoding the signal. Both legal and technological devices can serve to make ideas more excludable.

Note carefully what a patent does, for example in connection with a new design for insulin: it prevents a competitor who can break the code from using the same design for the production of insulin. It does not prevent a competitor from analysing the product or from studying the application for the patent, thereby getting full insight into the design. In this way a competitor may obtain increased knowledge that can be used for a related idea not protected by the patent. The knowledge first created by Novo Nordisk can be useful for other developers even though the patent prevents them from using this knowledge for exactly the same purpose as Novo Nordisk.

While non-rivalry prevents private idea-based production under perfect competition, complete non-excludability prevents private production under any market structure. If one cannot prevent people who do not pay for a good from using it, no money can be made from producing the good. At least some degree of excludability is needed in order to have private production.

By nature, ideas vary between being absolutely non-excludable and being imperfectly excludable. Discoveries in basic research are non-excludable, while more down-to-earth ideas for new products or production methods most often are partly excludable: they can be copied, but at some cost. In the latter case, the degree of excludability can often be much increased by legal or technological arrangements.

For these reasons almost all basic research takes place at public universities or at other types of non-profit research institutions. On the other hand, a lot of R&D directed at creating new products and improved production methods takes place in private firms. The latter requires some degree of excludability, which is often ensured by the presence of a legal system protecting intellectual property rights. At the same time, this legal system, by giving (through a patent) the exclusive right to use a certain idea for a certain purpose to the inventor, creates the monopoly power in the use of the idea that is necessary to overcome the problem associated with the non-rival character of ideas. *A legal system of protection of intellectual property rights thus serves the double purpose of ensuring some excludability and ensuring some monopoly power in the use of new ideas.*

THE MICROECONOMICS OF PRIVATE PRODUCTION OF IDEAS

The non-rival character of ideas implies that idea-based technological progress driven by private R&D will only take place if the inventor of an idea holds monopoly over its use. This monopoly power means that ideas, once developed, will be used less than what is socially optimal.

The imperfect excludability of ideas threatens the commercial viability of private R&D, but legal and technical arrangements can increase excludability.

A legal system for the protection of intellectual property rights (patents) can work to ensure both a relatively large degree of excludability and the monopoly power required for a private production of ideas.

The role of intellectual property rights in economic development

Some economic historians, for instance Nobel Prize winner Douglass C. North, consider this point to be absolutely essential for understanding the unprecedented economic growth over the past 200 years. As we have touched upon before, the Western world has experienced average annual growth rates of GDP per capita of about 2 per cent during the past 200 years, while over the several thousands of years before that, the average annual growth rate of GDP per capita must have been close to zero to fit with the level of income per capita around year 1800. Apparently big changes must have occurred around the late eighteenth and early nineteenth centuries, changes that have worked to initiate and maintain technological progress and economic growth.

What kind of an event could that be? According to some (Marxian, for instance) historians the big event was the change in the mode of production from feudalism to capitalism. During centuries of feudalism a very slow technological evolution had taken place. Gradually during this process, technology came to be in increasing contradiction to the social relations of feudalism characterized by labour power being tied to rural estates and lots of rules and regulations preventing the free initiative to establish new firms in trade and industry. A social revolution had to occur, and the revolution that took place was the transition from the feudal to the capitalist mode of production. Among other features, this transition implied that labour power was set free from (or kicked out of) rural estates, thus obtaining 'freedom' to move to the cities looking for work in the growing manufacturing sector. Another feature was the abolition of rules and regulations that had hitherto prevented free enterprise. In this way the profit motive and the allocation of resources through markets became much more important than it had been earlier. The market mechanism thus came to work as a driving force for the creation of new technologies. Each firm, competing with other firms, would have an individual incentive to create new production methods that could increase productivity and reduce costs. After any such invention there would be a period where the competitors had not yet adopted the new technique. The output price would therefore, during this period, be determined by the higher costs of the competing firms, and the inventing firm would temporarily earn above-normal profits. In this way the profit motive would continuously work as an incentive for further technological progress.

This story certainly sounds appealing, but according to the economic historians mentioned above, one element is missing. If new inventions were in no way protected from being copied, then the time that an inventor would be alone with a new production method would be short, so there would not be much extra profit to reap. This state of affairs would prevent inventing in the first place (note that this argument is basically the same as our argument that there can be no private idea-based technological progress under perfect competition). The important feature missing from the Marxian story, still according to these economic historians, was an improvement in the legal protection of intellectual property rights that had occurred gradually up to the time we are talking about, at that time reaching the 'critical' level. By protecting through patents new ideas from being copied, a private return on the effort exerted in developing ideas was ensured. This may have improved greatly the incentives for a private production of ideas that in turn contributed to the technological progress witnessed over the past 200 years.

With these remarks in mind it seems worthwhile to set up a formal model which focuses on research and development as a source of technological evolution and growth. As mentioned, our model will be of a macroeconomic nature showing only some signs of the subtle microeconomics of the production of ideas.

9.3 An R&D-based macro growth model

The model we study in this chapter is meant to explain the relatively constant economic growth of around 1.5–2 per cent per year in the developed world, *considering the developed world as one large economy*. Since the economy we consider will produce all of its technological progress itself, and thus does not import technology developed elsewhere, it is implicit that the model covers the entire developed world.

There will be two types of output: 'new technology', and final goods that can be used for consumption or for investment in physical capital. We will now describe the production processes for each type of output.

The production of final goods

A representative firm produces final output in the amount Y_t according to the familiar Cobb–Douglas production function:

$$Y_t = K_t^\alpha (A_t L_{Yt})^{1-\alpha}, \qquad 0 < \alpha < 1. \tag{1}$$

Formally, the only new feature is that labour input is now denoted by L_{Yt} rather than by L_t. This is because there will also be a labour input, L_{At}, in the R&D sector and we have to distinguish between the two. Another input is capital services, the amount of which we assume to be proportional to the stock of capital, K_t. Finally the technological variable, A_t, enters as usual.

From now we will think of A_t more as an input in line with K_t and L_{Yt}. The variable A_t is the total productive effect of the stock of all innovative ideas that have come into existence up to period t. There are important differences between the input A_t and the inputs K_t and L_{Yt}: first, the representative firm cannot adjust its input of technology as it wishes. From the point of view of each individual firm, society's stock of ideas or technology, A_t, is given. Second, the fixed amount of technology, A_t, can be used in every firm because the general level of technology is non-rival.

According to the replication argument, the production function should have constant returns to the two *rival* inputs, K_t and L_{Yt}, as assumed in (1). Doubling production by undertaking the same activities twice means doubling the inputs of capital and labour *using one and the same input of technology twice*. As a consequence, the production function in (1) has *increasing returns* in the three inputs, K_t, L_{Yt} and A_t, a feature that is important for our conclusions.

The production of new technology

The R&D sector also has one representative firm. As usual we should distinguish between its two roles. On the one hand, it produces the entire output, $A_{t+1} - A_t$, of new technology in period t, since there is only this one firm. On the other hand, the firm is actually to be considered as one of many small firms and therefore it has only a negligible influence on the aggregates of the R&D sector, that is, on the total input of labour, L_{At}, and on the total output, $A_{t+1} - A_t$, produced in the sector in period t. Consequently, the representative firm in the R&D sector takes the stock of technology as given at any point in time, just like the firm in the final goods sector does.

The production function of the individual firm is:

$$a_t = \bar{\rho} A_t^\phi L_{At}^d, \qquad \bar{\rho} > 0, \tag{2}$$

where a_t is the number of innovative ideas produced by the individual firm, and L_{At}^d is the labour demand of the individual firm in period t. In equilibrium a_t and L_{At}^d have to equal the total production of ideas, $A_{t+1} - A_t$, and the total labour input, L_{At}, respectively.

As already explained, we make the simplifying assumption that capital is not required as an input in the R&D sector. Hence the production function should, according to the replication argument, have constant returns to the input of labour alone.[2]

The existing stock of knowledge, A_t, is an input for the R&D firms, just as it is for the producers of final output, its output elasticity being ϕ, and like the firms in the final goods sector, each individual firm in the R&D sector takes A_t as given. Just as existing insights, production methods, computer software, etc., are productive in the final goods sector, they are productive in research and development. Hence, existing technology may promote the production of new technology, an effect sometimes referred to as 'standing on shoulders'. This effect speaks for a positive ϕ, possibly equal to 1. On the other hand, it may be that the more ideas that have already been accumulated in the existing stock of knowledge, A_t, the more difficult it becomes to get new ideas. This 'fishing out' effect is based on the view that there is a given, large (possibly infinite) pool of potential ideas and the easiest ones are discovered first, so the more ideas that have already been harvested, the more difficult it becomes to find a new one. This effect speaks for a negative value of ϕ. For the time being we will not impose any restrictions on the size or sign of ϕ, but generally we will think of ϕ as positive.

At the aggregate level we will assume that there may be a negative externality from the aggregate use of labour, L_{At}, in the R&D sector:

$$\bar{\rho} = \rho L_{At}^{\lambda-1}, \qquad \rho > 0, \, 0 < \lambda \leq 1. \tag{3}$$

If $\lambda < 1$, then there is a negative spillover from the aggregate activity level in the R&D sector to the productivity of the individual firm, while if $\lambda = 1$, there is no such effect. The motivation for the possibility of such an effect is 'stepping on toes': the more research there is in the R&D sector, the more probable it is that several individual firms work with the same ideas. Two firms creating the same idea only count for one in the stock of knowledge, A_t.

In equilibrium one must have $a_t = A_{t+1} - A_t$, and $L_{At}^d = L_{At}$, so from (2) and (3) the aggregate production function for new technology is:

$$A_{t+1} - A_t = \rho A_t^\phi L_{At}^\lambda. \tag{4}$$

Note some particular cases. If there is no negative 'stepping on toes' effect, $\lambda = 1$, then also at the level of the whole R&D sector, the number of ideas produced is proportional to the labour input in the sector. If the combination of the 'standing on shoulders' effect and

---

2. We are abstracting from an important aspect of real-life R&D, namely the stochastic nature of the arrival of new ideas. By doubling labour inputs, an R&D firm cannot be sure of doubling the number of ideas it will produce *in a deterministic sense* since ideas arrive in a less predictable way. Rather, a doubling of labour inputs could double the stochastic arrival intensity of ideas (in a Poisson process describing the production of ideas). An explicit modelling of stochastic arrival of ideas would not change our results qualitatively.

the 'fishing out' effect is such that $\phi = 1$, then (4) gives the growth rate of technology as: $(A_{t+1} - A_t)/A_t = \rho L^\lambda_{At}$.

The complete model

Our complete model consists of the six equations below. The first two are the aggregate production functions for the final goods sector and the R&D sector, respectively. The third one is the usual capital accumulation equation assuming an exogenous savings (investment) rate, s, and an exogenous depreciation rate, δ. Both s and δ are between 0 and 1. Likewise, (8) is the familiar equation assuming that the labour force, L_t, grows at a fixed exogenous rate, n, where $n > -1$. The two last equations are new. Equation (9) says that the sum of the labour inputs in the two sectors has to be equal to the total amount of labour available. Equation (10) assumes that in all periods a given and exogenous fraction, s_R, of all labour is used in the R&D sector, where $0 < s_R < 1$.

THE COMPLETE R&D-BASED GROWTH MODEL

$$Y_t = K_t^\alpha (A_t L_{Yt})^{1-\alpha}, \tag{5}$$

$$A_{t+1} - A_t = \rho A_t^\phi L^\lambda_{At}, \qquad A_0 \text{ given} \tag{6}$$

$$K_{t+1} = sY_t + (1-\delta)K_t, \qquad K_0 \text{ given} \tag{7}$$

$$L_{t+1} = (1+n)L_t, \qquad L_0 \text{ given} \tag{8}$$

$$L_{Yt} + L_{At} = L_t \tag{9}$$

$$L_{At} = s_R L_t. \tag{10}$$

The parameter s_R, referred to as the R&D share, should be thought of as a behavioural parameter in line with s and n, while $\alpha, \rho, \phi, \lambda$ and δ are technical parameters.

The state variables of the above model are K_t, L_t and A_t. For given initial values K_0, L_0 and A_0, the model will determine the full dynamic evolutions of all endogenous variables as illustrated in Fig. 9.3.

Because our model does not have an explicit micro foundation, we will have to treat the R&D share as exogenous and look into the consequences, rather than the causes, of its size. Thus, taking s_R as a given parameter, how large should we typically expect it to be, and how does it seem to change over time? Table 9.1 reports on the so-called GERD (gross expenditure on research and development), as a percentage of GDP in some OECD countries.

Typically, R&D shares in OECD countries seem to be around 1–4 per cent in the year 2005, with a tendency to have increased over the period from 1981 to 2005. Averaging over the 18 OECD countries of the table, the R&D share has increased from 2.0 to 2.4 per cent over the period corresponding to an average annual rate of increase in the R&D share of 0.8 per cent. As a crude extrapolation this corresponds to the R&D share roughly doubling every 100 years.

On the suppressed microeconomics of the model

As mentioned, we do not deal explicitly here with the microeconomics of our growth model. However, the microeconomics and the microeconomic problems of the model are visible in certain respects as it now stands. For instance, note that labour inputs used in

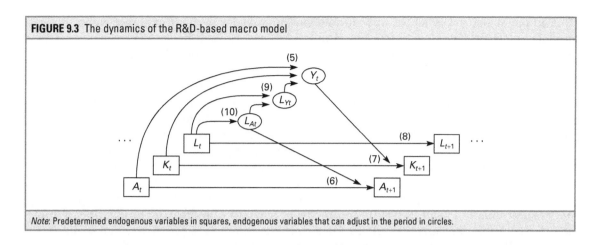

FIGURE 9.3 The dynamics of the R&D-based macro model

Note: Predetermined endogenous variables in squares, endogenous variables that can adjust in the period in circles.

TABLE 9.1 Gross expenditure on research and development (GERD) as a percentage of GDP, 18 OECD countries

Country	1981	2005	Average annual growth rate of GERD/GDP 1981–2005 (percent)
Austria	1.1	2.4	3.3
Canada	1.2	2.0	2.0
Denmark	1.0	2.4	3.6
Finland	1.2	3.5	4.7
France	1.9	2.1	0.5
Germany	2.2	2.5	0.6
Greece	0.2	0.6	5.7
Iceland	0.6	2.8	6.3
Ireland	0.7	1.3	2.7
Italy	0.9	1.1	1.0
Japan	2.3	3.3	1.5
Netherlands	1.8	1.7	−0.1
New Zealand	1.0	1.2	0.7
Norway	1.2	1.5	1.1
Spain	0.4	1.1	4.4
Sweden	2.2	3.8	2.3
UK	2.4	1.8	−1.2
USA	2.3	2.6	0.5
OECD average weighted by GDP in 1990	2.0	2.4	0.8

Source: OECD Science & Technology Data Base, 2007.

one sector cannot be used in the other, reflecting that labour power is a rival good, while the stock of knowledge can be used by all firms in both sectors simultaneously, reflecting that knowledge is non-rival. Furthermore, there is no equation for a factor reward rate in the model. In a more elaborate version of the model with an explicit description of its microeconomics, the wage rates and the other endogenous variables would adjust to ensure that real wages and the marginal products of labour are equalized across the two sectors.

You might also ask what the appropriate measure of GDP and national income in this model should be. There are two production sectors, so GDP will have to be some aggregate of the productions, Y_t and $A_{t+1} - A_t$, respectively, of the two sectors. Should it not be this aggregate income rather than just the Y_t that entered into the savings function? You may think of it as follows. The R&D sector is run by the government and its output is not marketed, but simply made freely available to everybody. People working in the R&D sector earn incomes, of course, but the government pays these incomes and finances its expenditure by taxing all income, so the total tax revenue equals the labour cost of running the research sector. Hence, total income after tax is the sum of the (values of the) productions in the two sectors minus the production in the R&D sector, that is, the Y_t of the final goods sector. This after-tax income enters into the savings function.

With respect to welfare, we will take the view that production of new technology does not create welfare in itself. It is only indirectly, as a means of increasing production of final goods, that technology creates welfare. Hence our measure of the prosperity of a society should (still) be the production of final goods per person, $Y_t/L_t \equiv y_t$, or rather the consumption of final goods per person, $c_t = (1 - s)y_t$.

9.4   The law of motion

We can describe the dynamics of the model by two difference equations that we now derive.

The dynamics of the rate of growth of technology

From (6) we can compute the growth rate in technology in any period by dividing both sides by A_t, and we can then, using (10), insert $s_R L_t$ for the L_{At} on the right-hand side:

$$g_t \equiv \frac{A_{t+1} - A_t}{A_t} = \rho A_t^{\phi-1} L_{At}^{\lambda} = \rho A_t^{\phi-1}(s_R L_t)^{\lambda}. \tag{11}$$

This shows that g_t is strictly positive in all periods. As long as just some labour input is used in the research sector there will be positive additions to knowledge all the time. If we write (11) for period $t + 1$ as well as period t and divide the first equation by the second, we get (with s_R constant):

$$\frac{g_{t+1}}{g_t} = \left(\frac{A_{t+1}}{A_t}\right)^{\phi-1}\left(\frac{L_{t+1}}{L_t}\right)^{\lambda}.$$

Here A_{t+1}/A_t is the growth *factor* of A_t, equal to the growth *rate* plus 1: $A_{t+1}/A_t = (A_{t+1} - A_t)/A_t + 1 = g_t + 1$. If we insert $(1 + g_t)$ for A_{t+1}/A_t, and insert $1 + n$ for L_{t+1}/L_t, we get:

$$\frac{g_{t+1}}{g_t} = (1 + g_t)^{\phi-1}(1 + n)^{\lambda},$$

which we can write as:

$$g_{t+1} = (1 + n)^{\lambda}g_t(1 + g_t)^{\phi-1}. \tag{12}$$

This is a first-order difference, or transition, equation in g_t alone. It has been derived exclusively from the three model equations that concern the research sector, (6), (8) and (10). A first conclusion from our model is thus that the growth rate, g_t, of technology has a dynamic evolution of its own: from any given initial value it develops independently of the other endogenous variables in a way that only depends on the parameters ϕ, λ and n (as long as s_R is constant).

The dynamic system also involving the economic variables

Let us define the usual auxiliary variables, $\tilde{k}_t \equiv K_t/(A_tL_t) = k_t/A_t$ and $\tilde{y}_t \equiv Y_t/(A_tL_t) = y_t/A_t$. Using (5), (9) and (10), we can write the production function as $Y_t = K_t^\alpha(A_t(1 - s_R)L_t)^{1-\alpha}$. Dividing both sides by A_tL_t gives $\tilde{y}_t = \tilde{k}_t^\alpha(1 - s_R)^{1-\alpha}$. From the capital accumulation equation, (7), dividing both sides by $A_{t+1}L_{t+1}$, we then get:

$$\tilde{k}_{t+1} = \frac{1}{(1+n)(1+g_t)}[s\tilde{k}_t^\alpha(1-s_R)^{1-\alpha} + (1-\delta)\tilde{k}_t]. \tag{13}$$

This has been derived in the same way that we derived transition equations in models considered earlier, but (13) is not a law of motion for $\tilde{k}_t$ since it has the endogenous g_t on the right-hand side. However, the system consisting of (12) and (13) is a law of motion in g_t and $\tilde{k}_t$. The two difference equations are only coupled in one direction: to compute $\tilde{k}_{t+1}$ from (13), one must know both $\tilde{k}_t$ and g_t, but to compute g_{t+1} from (12), one only needs to know g_t. This makes the dynamic system relatively easy to analyse.

Technological dynamics for $\phi = 1$ and for $0 < \phi < 1$

It will be highly illustrative and indicative for what goes on in this chapter to focus for the moment on the independent dynamics of technology, assuming a constant labour input in the research sector. Thus, assume that L_{At} is a constant, $L_A > 0$. In this case one gets from (11) the following growth rate of technology:

$$g_t = \rho A_t^{\phi-1}L_A^\lambda. \tag{14}$$

If $\phi = 1$, the technological growth rate, g_t, will be constant and positive and equal to ρL_A^λ in all periods. This implies that A_t will be ever increasing and go to infinity in the long run.

If $0 < \phi < 1$, the stock of knowledge, A_t, will also be increasing in all periods and go to infinity: in period t, the absolute change in technology is given directly by (6), $A_{t+1} - A_t = \rho A_t^\phi L_A^\lambda$, which is positive, and as A_t becomes larger and larger, the increase, $A_{t+1} - A_t$, in technology will also become larger and larger, implying that eventually A_t goes to infinity. This time, however, the *growth rate* of technology will decrease over time and eventually go to 0. This is easy to see from (14): as A_t goes to infinity, $A_t^{\phi-1}$ goes to 0 (remember $\phi < 1$). There will be increases in knowledge all the time, but when $\phi < 1$, the increases, $A_{t+1} - A_t$, cannot keep pace with the stock, A_t, because the existing stock of knowledge is not sufficiently productive in the creation of new knowledge. Hence, the growth rate of knowledge, $(A_{t+1} - A_t)/A_t$, has to fall.

It makes an important difference whether a fixed input of labour into the research sector creates a constant positive growth rate in technology ($\phi = 1$), or just an ever-increasing stock of knowledge with the growth rate of this going to 0 ($0 < \phi < 1$).

9.5 Semi-endogenous growth

In this section we consider $0 < \phi < 1$. For reasons that will become obvious we will, in this case, also assume that there is some growth in the labour force, $n > 0$.

Convergence to steady state

Let us repeat the dynamic system we have arrived at:

$$g_{t+1} = (1 + n)^\lambda g_t(1 + g_t)^{\phi-1}, \tag{12}$$

$$\tilde{k}_{t+1} = \frac{1}{(1+n)(1+g_t)}(s\tilde{k}_t^\alpha(1-s_R)^{1-\alpha} + (1-\delta)\tilde{k}_t). \tag{13}$$

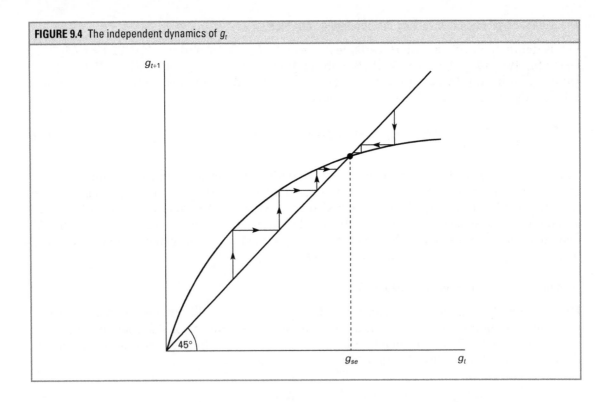

FIGURE 9.4 The independent dynamics of g_t

First, consider the independent dynamic equation (12) for g_t. You will easily verify that the transition curve defined by this equation has properties as illustrated in Fig. 9.4 (remember that $g_t > 0$, so Fig. 9.4 is only drawn for positive values of g_t and g_{t+1}). First, it passes through (0, 0). Second, for any g_t, its slope, $(1 + n)^\lambda (1 + g_t)^{\phi-2}(1 + \phi g_t)$, is strictly positive.[3] Third, because we assume $n > 0$ there is a unique *positive* intersection with the 45° line: setting $g_{t+1} = g_t$ in (12) gives $(1 + g_t)^{1-\phi} = (1 + n)^\lambda$, or

$$g_t = (1+n)^{\frac{\lambda}{1-\phi}} - 1 \equiv g_{se}, \tag{15}$$

where indeed $g_{se} > 0$, because $n > 0$. Fourth, the slope of the transition curve at $g_t = 0$ is $(1 + n)^\lambda$, and hence it is strictly larger than 1, because we assume $n > 0$.

The four features we have stated imply that g_t goes to g_{se} as t goes to infinity, as illustrated by the staircase-formed iterations in Fig. 9.4. This is one major conclusion from our model with $\phi < 1$ and $n > 0$: *in the long run the growth rate of knowledge converges monotonically to the particular value $g_{se} > 0$.* (You should note carefully how this conclusion depends on our assumption $n > 0$. An exercise will ask you to analyse the case $n < 0$ with respect to the evolution of g_t and the implied evolution of other endogenous variables.)

Next, consider the other dynamic equation, (13). As mentioned, this is not a real transition equation for $\tilde{k}_t$ because it has g_t on the right-hand side. However, we now know that in the long run g_t converges monotonically to the particular value g_{se}. We could therefore write down a new dynamic equation, setting the g_t in (13) constantly equal to g_{se}.

---

3. The slope of the transition curve (12) is found as follows:

$$\frac{dg_{t+1}}{dg_t} = (1+n)^\lambda [(1+g_t)^{\phi-1} + (\phi-1)g_t(1+g_t)^{\phi-2}]$$

$$= (1+n)^\lambda (1+g_t)^{\phi-2}[1 + g_t + (\phi-1)g_t]$$

$$= (1+n)^\lambda (1+g_t)^{\phi-2}(1 + \phi g_t).$$

If, according to this new equation, $\tilde{k}_t$ converges to a specific value $\tilde{k}^*$ in the long run, this will also be the implication of the correct dynamic system consisting of (12) and (13). The new equation would look almost exactly like our transition equations studied earlier, for instance the one in Chapter 5, and would, by similar reasoning, imply convergence of $\tilde{k}_t$ to a constant value $\tilde{k}^*$ (provided that $n + g_{se} + \delta + ng_{se} > 0$, which is fulfilled here because we assume $n > 0$).

Inserting g_{se} for g_t in (13) and solving for the constant solution, $\tilde{k}_{t+1} = \tilde{k}_t = \tilde{k}^*$, gives:

$$\tilde{k}^* = \left(\frac{s}{n + g_{se} + \delta + ng_{se}} \right)^{\frac{1}{1-\alpha}} (1 - s_R). \tag{16}$$

We can find the associated $\tilde{y}^*$ by using $\tilde{y}^* = (\tilde{k}^*)^\alpha (1 - s_R)^{1-\alpha}$:

$$\tilde{y}^* = \left(\frac{s}{n + g_{se} + \delta + ng_{se}} \right)^{\frac{\alpha}{1-\alpha}} (1 - s_R). \tag{17}$$

These expressions have well-known structures except for the $(1 - s_R)$ on the right-hand side, reflecting that now only this fraction of the labour input is used in the final goods sector.

We have shown that in the long run g_t converges to g_{se}, and $\tilde{k}_t$ and $\tilde{y}_t$ converge to $\tilde{k}^*$ and $\tilde{y}^*$, respectively. The situation where these variables are constant at their long-run values defines steady state.

We can illustrate the convergence process to steady state in two, one-way coupled diagrams. The first is Fig. 9.2 associated with the independent dynamic equation, (12), for g_t. The diagram shows how the technological growth rate, g_t, gradually converges to g_{se}. The other diagram is much like a modified Solow-diagram and it is associated with a rewriting of the other dynamic equation, (13), where one has the growth rate in $\tilde{k}_t$ on the left-hand side:

$$\frac{\tilde{k}_{t+1} - \tilde{k}_t}{\tilde{k}_t} = \frac{1}{(1+n)(1+g_t)} [s(1 - s_R)^{1-\alpha} \tilde{k}_t^{\alpha-1} - (n + g_t + \delta + ng_t)]. \tag{18}$$

For any fixed g_t this is like a modified Solow equation and we illustrate it in Fig. 9.5.

For a given g_t in period t, the growth rate in $\tilde{k}_t$ will be proportional to the distance between the decreasing curve, $s(1 - s_R)^{1-\alpha} \tilde{k}_t^{\alpha-1}$, and the horizontal line at $n + g_t + \delta + ng_t$, and $\tilde{k}_t$ will move towards the intersection between the curve and the line. This time, however, the intersection is a 'moving target', since the horizontal line moves when g_t changes. In the long run the movements in g_t become smaller and smaller as g_t eventually converges to g_{se}, so the horizontal line gradually comes to rest at the position corresponding to g_{se}, as illustrated.

These diagrams provide intuition for an important insight. Assume that the economy starts in an 'old' steady state given by the (final) intersection points in Figs 9.4 and 9.5. Consider a parameter change that only affects the second of the diagrams, say a change in the depreciation rate δ. This will have no impact on Fig. 9.4, so the growth rate of A_t will stay unchanged at its old steady state value. The horizontal line in Fig. 9.5 will shift once and for all and thus initiate a process of dynamic adjustments which are like those in the Solow model (since g_t does not change, there will be no further changes of the horizontal line in Fig. 9.5). The speed of convergence will therefore be as in the Solow model.

Consider now a parameter change that shifts the transition curve in Fig. 9.4, say a change in λ. This will initiate adjustments in g_t, gradually taking it towards its new steady state value. Every time g_t changes, the horizontal line in Fig. 9.5 will shift. Convergence in Fig. 9.5 will now be towards a moving target and the convergence time will therefore be longer for

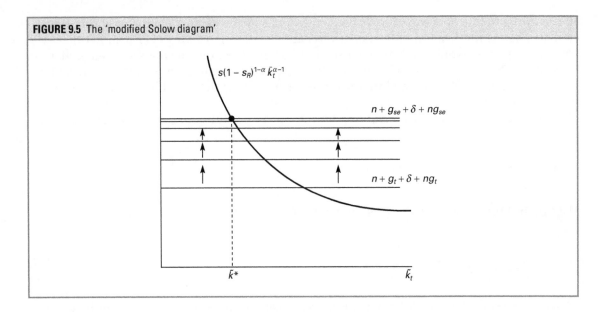

FIGURE 9.5 The 'modified Solow diagram'

this latter parameter change. In conclusion, a parameter change that initiates an adjustment process for g_t, that is, a change that somehow affects the research sector, will imply slower convergence to the new steady state than a parameter change that does not affect the research sector. This intuition is important for the theory we present in Section 9.7.

Growth in steady state

In steady state, when $\tilde{k}_t \equiv k_t/A_t$ and $\tilde{y}_t \equiv y_t/A_t$ have reached their long-run constant values, both k_t and y_t must be increasing at the same rate as A_t. In steady state this rate is g_{se}. Hence, in the long run, technology, A_t, capital per worker, k_t, and output per worker, y_t, converge towards growing at one and the same constant rate, g_{se}.

This is in accordance with the requirements for balanced growth. In particular, in steady state the capital–output ratio, $z_t \equiv K_t/Y_t = \tilde{k}^*/\tilde{y}^*$, will be constant and given by:

$$z^* = \frac{s}{n + g_{se} + \delta + ng_{se}}. \tag{19}$$

In steady state the rate of technological growth as well as the rate of economic growth is $g_{se} = (1 + n)^{\lambda/(1-\phi)} - 1$. This is only positive if $n > 0$. Because of this feature our growth model with $\phi < 1$ is referred to as one of *semi-endogenous* growth (explaining the subscript *se* on g).

The intuition for population growth being a requirement for economic growth is this: when $\phi < 1$, a constant labour input into the research sector will imply that the growth rate, g_t, of technology will go to 0 in the long run as explained in the previous section. To sustain a positive constant growth rate in A_t, an increasing labour input into the research sector is required, and with a constant fraction, s_R, of all labour used in the research sector, this can only result if the labour force increases all the time.

Our formula, $g_{se} = (1 + n)^{\lambda/(1-\phi)} - 1$, has the implication that $\lambda(1 - \phi) \approx g_{se}/n$.[4] For magnitudes to be reasonable by Western standards, annual population growth rates in the range between $\frac{1}{2}$ and 1 per cent per year should be compatible with a steady state growth in

---

4. The formula for the growth rate may be written as $1 + g_{se} = (1 + n)^{\lambda/(1-\phi)}$. Taking logs on both sides and using the approximation $\ln(1 + x) \approx x$, we get $g_{se} \approx \lambda/(1 - \phi)n$, or $g_{se}/n \approx \lambda/(1 - \phi)$.

GDP per worker of around 2 per cent per year. Hence, $\lambda(1 - \phi)$ should be in the range of 2–4. Assuming λ around 1 (not too much stepping on toes), ϕ should then be somewhere between $\frac{1}{4}$ and $\frac{1}{2}$.

As usual, we are more interested in output per worker, y_t, than in output per effective worker, $\tilde{y}_t$. From $y_t = \tilde{y}_t A_t$, output per worker must, in steady state, develop as $y_t^* = \tilde{y}^* A_t$. Furthermore, in steady state there is a necessary link between A_t and L_t. Note that (11) expresses the growth rate, g_t, as a function of A_t and L_t. In steady state $g_t = g_{se}$. In that case (11) reads: $\rho A_t^{\phi-1}(s_R L_t)^\lambda = g_{se}$, and therefore in steady state:

$$A_t = \left(\frac{\rho(s_R L_t)^\lambda}{g_{se}} \right)^{\frac{1}{1-\phi}}. \tag{20}$$

Using (17) and (20) plus the fact that $y_t^* = \tilde{y}^*/A_t$, it follows that steady state output per worker will evolve according to:

$$y_t^* = \left(\frac{s}{n + g_{se} + \delta + n g_{se}} \right)^{\frac{\alpha}{1-\alpha}} (1 - s_R) s_R^{\frac{\lambda}{1-\phi}} \left(\frac{\rho}{g_{se}} \right)^{\frac{1}{1-\phi}} L_t^{\frac{\lambda}{1-\phi}}, \tag{21}$$

where we can insert that:

$$L_t^{\frac{\lambda}{1-\phi}} = [L_0(1+n)^t]^{\frac{\lambda}{1-\phi}} = L_0^{\frac{\lambda}{1-\phi}}(1+n)^{\frac{\lambda}{1-\phi}t} = L_0^{\frac{\lambda}{1-\phi}}(1+g_{se})^t, \tag{22}$$

thus tracing output per worker in steady state back to initial values and parameters (some of which are in g_{se}). The steady state growth path for consumption per worker may be found as $c_t^* = (1-s)y_t^*$.

Structural policy and empirics for steady state

Structural policy aimed at improving the steady state should be concerned with the steady state growth path of consumption per worker, its *level* as well as the *growth rate* along it.

With respect to the *level* this is influenced by the savings and investment rate, s, in the same way as in our models of exogenous growth with a golden rule value of s (the value that maximizes the height of the growth path) equal to capital's share, α (show this). There is also a golden rule value for the research share, s_R, and an exercise will ask you to determine this and explain the counteracting forces of a larger s_R on consumption per worker in steady state. A conclusion is that up to a relatively large value of the research share, a higher such share will elevate the steady state growth path of consumption per worker. Hence, policies to obtain reasonable large values of the investment rate and the research share seem well motivated by the concern to create a high level of consumption per worker in the long run. Note that the growth rate, n, of the labour force affects the level of the steady state growth paths of income and consumption per worker negatively. This is due to the well-known thinning-out-of-capital effect.

Taking s_R as given, the *growth rate* along the steady state growth paths, that is g_{se}, can only be increased by a policy that manages to increase the labour force growth rate, n (taking the technical parameters ϕ and λ as given also). As we discussed at length in Chapter 8, it is hard to reconcile empirical evidence with the feature that economic growth should depend positively on population growth.

According to our model with a constant labour force, a gradual and steady increase in the research share, s_R, will, as long as it can take place, have an influence on growth similar to that of an increasing labour force at a constant research share. In both cases labour input in the research sector will be increasing, which creates technological growth. A policy intended to increase the research share gradually thus seems to be a cautious alternative to one intended to promote population growth, since such a policy avoids the erosion of capital and natural resources per worker implied by growth in the labour force. A deeper discussion of *how* to influence the research share would require an endogenous determination of s_R and therefore (again) an explicit incorporation of the microeconomics of idea production, but obviously some policy instruments to consider are government subsidies to, or tax deductions for, private research activities as well as direct public involvement in research and education and public investment in universities and other research and educational institutions.

R&D-BASED SEMI-ENDOGENOUS GROWTH AND STRUCTURAL POLICY

Assuming a strictly positive growth rate of the labour force, and assuming that the elasticity of existing knowledge in the production of new knowledge is positive, but less than 1, the R&D-based growth model implies that the technological growth rate converges to a specific steady state value, g_{se}, and that capital, income and consumption per worker converge on steady state growth paths along which the growth rate is g_{se}, so that the capital–output ratio converges to a constant value in accordance with balanced growth. The growth rate, g_{se}, is strictly positive if and only if the population (labour force) growth rate is positive.

The **levels** of the long-run balanced growth paths depend on structural parameters in a way that supports policies to establish a high investment rate, a low population growth rate, *and* a high research share. The **growth rate** along the balanced growth paths depends on parameters in a way suggesting that a policy promoting population growth should also promote economic growth. Given that a positive association between population growth and economic growth does not seem very plausible empirically, a cautious alternative policy that would avoid a negative impact on the level of the growth path and would instead gradually raise this level could be a policy securing a gradual increase in the research share.

If, on empirical grounds, one has problems accepting that the source of long-term economic growth should be growth in the labour force, one should not necessarily conclude that our model with $\phi < 1$ is wrong, but only that *its steady state* does not seem to be descriptive. We may therefore pursue an idea similar to that used in Chapter 8. If convergence in our model is very slow, the empirical evidence may be in accordance with the model. A decrease in the population growth rate, n, will raise the steady state growth path as given by (21) and (22), but also reduce the growth rate along it. The first effect gives a transitory additional growth, while the latter effect gives a lower growth rate in the long run. If it takes a long time to come close to the new steady state growth path, the first effect will dominate for a long time. However, if convergence is so slow that the transitory growth effect dominates over time horizons up to 100 years, then we would not be so interested in the model's steady state. We would be more interested in the convergence process itself.

As in Chapter 8, this suggests studying the model for parameter values that imply very slow convergence. Again, a large ϕ (below 1) will have that effect. Just look at the transition equation, (12), for g_t. As ϕ goes to 1, the transition curve will come close to a straight line with slope $(1 + n)^\lambda$ implying, for $n > 0$, a very long-lasting convergence of g_t to a very high value. At the limit, for $\phi = 1$, the technological growth rate, g_t, will, with $n > 0$, be exploding and go to infinity, which is, of course, absurd. We can eliminate the exploding g_t by considering $n = 0$. This is exactly what we will do next.

9.6 Endogenous growth

As an approximation of a large ϕ below 1, we will consider $\phi = 1$. To have a well-behaved model we will assume $n = 0$. We will denote the constant labour force by L.

It is easy to analyse the model that results from imposing these parameter restrictions on our base model consisting of Eqs (5)–(10). In fact, we have more or less analysed it before, since the model is almost identical to the Solow model considered in Chapter 5, with zero population growth and with a particular *endogenous* value for the growth rate of technology.

Equation (8), describing the evolution of the labour force, is now replaced by $L_t = L$ for all t. It follows from (9) and (10) that $L_{Yt} = (1 - s_R)L$ and $L_{At} = s_R L$ for all t. If we insert the latter of these into (6), we get

$$A_{t+1} - A_t = \rho A_t (s_R L)^\lambda,$$ (23)

or equivalently:

$$g_t \equiv \frac{A_{t+1} - A_t}{A_t} = \rho(s_R L)^\lambda \equiv g_e.$$ (24)

As stated earlier, when $\phi = 1$, a constant labour input $s_R L$ into the research sector gives a constant growth rate in technology, and this growth rate is now denoted by g_e (e for endogenous). Hence, $A_{t+1} = (1 + g_e)A_t$ for all periods t. Inserting $L_{Yt} = (1 - s_R)L$ in the production function for final goods, (5), and repeating the capital accumulation equation, (7), the full model reduces to the three equations

$$Y_t = K_t^\alpha (A_t(1 - s_R)L)^{1-\alpha},$$

$$K_{t+1} = sY_t + (1 - \delta)K_t,$$

$$A_{t+1} = (1 + g_e)A_t,$$

where one should bear in mind the endogenous value of g_e stated in (24). This model is like a Chapter 5, general Solow model with no population growth and an exogenous growth rate of technology g_e, with the one exception that only the fraction $(1 - s_R)$ of the constant labour force, L, is used in the production of final goods. With our usual definitions, $\tilde{y}_t \equiv Y_t/(A_t L_t) = y_t/A_t$, etc., it follows from an analysis similar to that in Chapter 5 (do this analysis) that $\tilde{y}_t$ converges to

$$\tilde{y}^* = \left(\frac{s}{g_e + \delta} \right)^{\frac{\alpha}{1-\alpha}} (1 - s_R),$$

and hence in the long run, y_t will converge towards the growth path:

$$y_t^* = \left(\frac{s}{g_e + \delta} \right)^{\frac{\alpha}{1-\alpha}} (1 - s_R)A_0(1 + g_e)^t.$$ (25)

Consumption per worker will consequently converge towards the growth path $c_t^* = (1 - s)y_t^*$.

The model considered in this section has some obvious merits. First, it is a model of 'truly' endogenous growth. Without assuming exogenous technological growth, we get a constant and positive technology growth rate, g_e, and in the long run the growth rate of GDP per worker converges to g_e. Second, we have an expression showing how the growth rate depends on behavioural model parameters. Third, as can be seen from the expression given in (24), population growth is not a prerequisite for economic growth.

The main potential implication for structural policy is that in order to obtain a high growth rate in output and consumption per worker, the government should try to obtain a high *level* of the R&D share, s_R (whereas, under semi-endogenous growth, an *increasing* R&D share was needed to promote growth in the long run). This could, for instance, be done by subsidizing or undertaking research activities, as most governments indeed do.

The growth rate g_e given by (24) does not depend on the investment rate s, in contrast to what was found in the externality-based endogenous growth model of Chapter 8. This feature is an artefact, however, arising from the assumption of an exogenous research share. In a properly micro founded model, where s_R is endogenous, this share turns out to depend positively on the investment rate, s. The mechanism is basically that a higher savings rate will create more capital and therefore a lower real interest rate. This in turn means that the capital value of a patent based on a new idea and giving rise to a future stream of income will increase, thus making the private research sector more profitable. Hence, according to an appropriate interpretation of the model, policies to stimulate saving and investment are growth promoting.

Another merit of the model is that it does have convergence (unlike the externality-based endogenous growth model we studied in Chapter 8). Whereas the growth rate of technology is constant, the growth rate of output per worker varies over time as y_t gradually approaches its long-run growth path given by (25). In particular, for given values of all the parameters in (25), a lower initial GDP per worker, y_0, will imply a higher growth rate in GDP per worker. The model can, therefore, be considered to be in accordance with the observed conditional convergence between the countries in the real world. Still, since the model is explicitly intended to describe the world economy, it does not literally have much to say about cross-country evolutions.

The model also has some less attractive features. First, there is the objection that the model only pertains to a knife-edge case ($\phi = 1$). Just as we did not think that the knife-edge property was a serious drawback of the endogenous growth model of Chapter 8, we do not think it is a serious problem in the present model because we only consider $\phi = 1$ as an approximation of a large ϕ below 1.

A main prediction of the model is that the long-run growth rate of GDP per worker and of technology should depend positively on the R&D share. The model is not intended to describe individual countries, but nevertheless it is tempting to look at cross-country evidence for growth rates and R&D shares. Figure 9.6 plots average annual growth rates in GDP per worker against GERD (recall this variable from Table 9.1) as a percentage of GDP across the 17 OECD countries of Table 9.1 for which we also have the data for GDP growth. Figure 9.7 plots average annual growth rates of A_t (using the same data as for the construction of Fig. 8.5) against GERD relative to GDP for the 14 countries for which we have the data needed.

Both figures suffer from having few observations and no clear relationship. They do not, however, point to a tight positive connection between growth rates and R&D shares across countries. As mentioned, the model does not describe individual countries, so cross-country evidence is, perhaps, not relevant.

The main problem of the model with $\phi = 1$ is the severe *scale effect* it implies. Equation (24) shows that a larger constant labour force, L, should, for a given s_R, give a higher growth rate in technology and then in the longer run also a higher growth rate in GDP per worker. If labour input in the research sector grows over time, either because L_t grows or because s_R grows or both, the result is a growing technological growth rate, g_t, as follows from (11) with $\phi = 1$. This will eventually lead to an increasing growth rate in output per worker. Empirical evidence suggests that indeed labour inputs into the research sectors in Western countries have been growing. Table 9.1 points to increasing R&D shares, and also independent longer-run evidence on the number of engineers and researchers employed in R&D activities, in particular in the USA, point to substantial increases. This should, according to the model with $\phi = 1$, have resulted in increasing growth rates in GDP per worker. However, this is not observed. The evidence points to constant long-term growth rates.[5]

5. The combination of gradually increasing labour input in the R&D sector and relatively constant long-run growth rates of GDP per worker is the opening observation of the article by Charles I. Jones mentioned in Footnote 1. Jones concludes that a value of ϕ equal, or close, to 1 is not realistic. For this reason he studies the model with ϕ (considerably) below 1, leading to semi-endogenous growth. Jones thinks that the very long-run evidence we discussed in Chapter 8 is supportive of the idea of semi-endogenous growth.

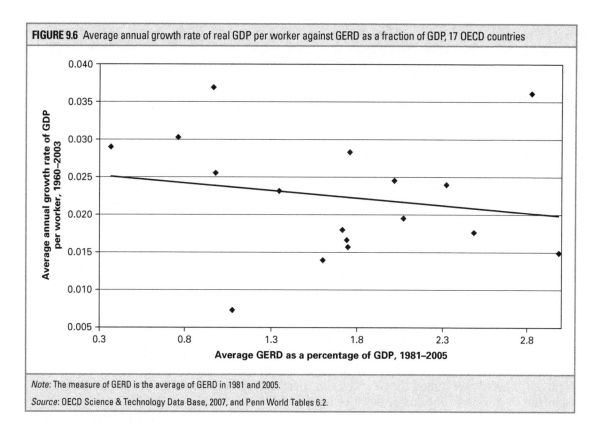

FIGURE 9.6 Average annual growth rate of real GDP per worker against GERD as a fraction of GDP, 17 OECD countries

Note: The measure of GERD is the average of GERD in 1981 and 2005.

Source: OECD Science & Technology Data Base, 2007, and Penn World Tables 6.2.

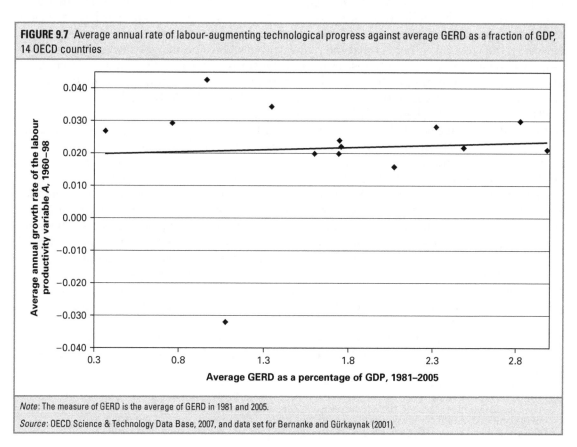

FIGURE 9.7 Average annual rate of labour-augmenting technological progress against average GERD as a fraction of GDP, 14 OECD countries

Note: The measure of GERD is the average of GERD in 1981 and 2005.

Source: OECD Science & Technology Data Base, 2007, and data set for Bernanke and Gürkaynak (2001).

> ## R&D-BASED ENDOGENOUS GROWTH AND STRUCTURAL POLICY
>
> The R&D-based growth model with an elasticity from existing knowledge to the production of new knowledge in the R&D sector's production function equal to one implies a constant technological growth rate, g_e, even with a constant research share and no growth in the labour force. The endogenous growth rate g_e depends positively on the research share and (under an additional plausible mechanism through which the research share depends positively on the savings rate) on the savings rate. Capital, income, and consumption per worker all converge gradually towards steady state growth paths along which the growth rate is g_e. Policies that increase the research share and the savings rate are thus growth-promoting policies. The model is, however, plagued by an implausible scale effect according to which a larger labour input in the R&D sector should result in a permanently larger growth rate of GDP per worker.

9.7 'Hemi-endogenous' growth[6]

The model we consider in this chapter paves the way for a third interpretation of the past 200 years of economic growth in the developed world, viewing this as neither semi-endogenous nor truly endogenous growth. We will use the term 'hemi-endogenous' growth for this third interpretation, because it may be seen as an attempt to explain the process of economic growth in the Western hemisphere.

It is (plausibly) assumed that $\phi < 1$, so an increasing labour input in the research sector is required to sustain economic growth for long periods. According to the hemi-endogenous growth interpretation, this increase in labour input does not primarily result from growth in the labour force, but mostly from steady ongoing growth in the research share. The model considered is like the model of semi-endogenous growth with $\phi < 1$, so it does have a steady state with a positive relationship between population growth and economic growth. However, the view taken here is that the real world is always on its way to steady state in response to new increases in the research share. Of course, steady growth in the research share cannot go on forever, as this share has a maximum of 1, but growth at a small positive rate can take place for a long time, particularly if the share is initially small.

The possibility of the hemi-endogenous growth interpretation is linked to a certain property of the model we have studied in this chapter: even if no parameter is initially at an extreme value (such as $\phi = 1$), certain parameter changes can have very long-lasting effects. We have already given the intuition for this in Section 9.3. If a parameter change does *not* affect the (independent) dynamics of the technological growth rate, g_t, the response to it will be as in the Solow model, also with respect to its duration. If a parameter change *does* affect the dynamics of g_t, the economy's response to it will potentially be longer-lasting since it implies all the types of adjustments found in the general Solow model *plus* the adjustments of g_t. The latter kind of adjustments give the first ones the character of 'convergence towards a moving target'.

To illustrate, we will conduct simulations with our model showing the economy's responses to a change in the investment rate, s, and to a change in the R&D share, s_R. The first of these changes does not affect the research sector and hence does not initiate an adjustment process for g_t, while the other does affect the research sector and therefore triggers adjustments in g_t.

Let us specify non-extreme initial parameter values that are reasonable for a period length of one year. First we set $\alpha = \frac{1}{3}$, $\delta = 0.06$, and $s = 0.2$, which are normal values. From

---

6. This section discusses an alternative interpretation of growth in the Western world during the past 200 years. The interpretation is related to the one suggested in Charles I. Jones, 'Sources of U.S. Economic Growth in a World of Ideas', *American Economic Review*, **92**, 2002, pp. 220–239. Reading the section is hopefully rewarding, but not required for further reading of the book.

Table 9.1 it could be reasonable to let $s_R = 0.02$. An annual population growth rate of 1 per cent also seems reasonable in a 200-year perspective, so we set $n = 0.01$, but note that assuming $n = 0.005$ would not change our conclusions substantially. For the parameters relating to the research sector we set $\rho = 1$ as a pure normalization, and we choose $\lambda = 1$ and $\phi = \frac{1}{2}$. This implies that the steady state annual growth rate, $g_{se} = (1 + n)^{\lambda(1-\phi)} - 1$, is around 0.02, which seems to be a reasonable anchor for our simulations.

Let us also say that in year 0 the economy is in steady state at these parameter values, and set the initial value of the state variable L_t at $L_0 = 1$. The initial values, K_0 and A_0, of the other state variables follow from the requirement that the economy is in steady state. First, A_0 should obey the necessary steady state link between A_0 and L_0 given in (20), here implying $A_0 \approx 0.99$. Finally, the capital–output ratio in steady state is given by (19) which imposes a restriction, $K_0 / Y_0 = z^*$, on the initial capital–output ratio, and K_0 and Y_0 must also fit in the production function, $Y_0 = K_0^\alpha (A_0(1 - s_R)L_0)^{1-\alpha}$. With our assumed parameter values and the already determined values for L_0 and A_0, solving the two equations in K_0 and Y_0 gives $K_0 \approx 3.20$ (verify this).

We now have values for all parameters and initial values for the state variables. We can then simulate the model consisting of Eqs (5)–(10) over a number of years. We will do so for 200 years, assuming a permanent parameter change in period 10. We first consider an increase in the investment rate from the initial value $s = 0.2$ up to $s' = 0.3$.

Before showing the results of the simulations, let us think about the qualitative effects using our diagrams, Figs 9.4 and 9.5 (do the drawing yourself). Since the dynamics for g_t are unaffected by s, as shown by the dynamic equation (12), the first of the diagrams is unaffected. Since g_t is initially at its steady state value g_{se}, it will stay at that value during all 200 years. In the second diagram the shift in the investment rate implies that the decreasing curve shifts upwards once and for all, which initiates a process of gradual increases in $\tilde{k}_t$, the growth rate of $\tilde{k}_t$ being largest at the beginning and then falling back towards 0 as $\tilde{k}_t$ approaches its new steady state value. Consequently, since $\tilde{k}_t = k_t/A_t$, the growth rate of k_t will jump up from g_{se} and then gradually return to g_{se}. The same will be true for the growth rate of y_t.

Figure 9.8 shows some output from the simulation and confirms the qualitative findings. It also gives an impression of the duration of the adjustments. Note that g_t stays at the unchanged steady state value g_{se} just above 0.02 all the time, while g_t^y (the approximate growth rate of y_t) jumps to around 0.035 and then starts to fall towards g_{se}. After 15 years it passes through the value 0.025, so at this point one half of a percentage point of the additional growth remains.

Now turn to a permanent change in the R&D share, assuming that it increases from the value $s_R = 0.02$ to $s_R' = 0.03$ in year 10, a 50 per cent increase as with the savings rate. How does this affect a diagram like Fig. 9.2 (you should draw the diagram yourself)? Looking at (12), you may first think that it does not affect it at all, since s_R does not enter into (12). However, in the derivation of (12) we assumed that s_R was constant, but now there is a change in this parameter in one period. In this one period, (12) does not hold. In the first period where the new s_R' works, that is, in period 10, the technological growth rate (up to the next period) as given by (11) is $g_{10} \equiv (A_{11} - A_{10})/A_{10} = \rho A_{10}^{\phi-1}(s_R'L_{10})^\lambda$, while in period 9, $g_9 = \rho A_9^{\phi-1}(s_R L_9)^\lambda = g_{se}$. Dividing the first by the second, etc., gives: $g_{10} = g_9(A_{10}/A_9)^{\phi-1}(s_R'/s_R)^\lambda(L_{10}/L_9)^\lambda = g_9(1 + g_9)^{\phi-1}(s_R'/s_R)^\lambda(1 + n)^\lambda$. Here, since in period 9 we are in steady state, it follows from (12) that $(1 + n)^\lambda g_9(1 + g_9)^{\phi-1} = g_{se}$. Inserting this gives $g_{10} = (s_R'/s_R)^\lambda g_{se}$. That is, in period 10 the technological growth rate, g_t, jumps by the factor $(s_R'/s_R)^\lambda$. After that, since the R&D share is again constant, the transition curve in Fig. 9.4 is unchanged and the associated dynamics gradually take g_t back towards the steady state value g_{se} around 0.02. In Fig. 9.5 this means that the horizontal line first jumps up and then gradually falls down towards its original position. Hence, eventually the growth rates of both A_t and y_t return to g_{se}.

Figure 9.9 reports on the simulation and gives an impression of the duration of the adjustments. Note how g_t jumps up once and then falls gradually back towards 0.02. The growth rate of final output per worker initially falls, reflecting that a first effect of the

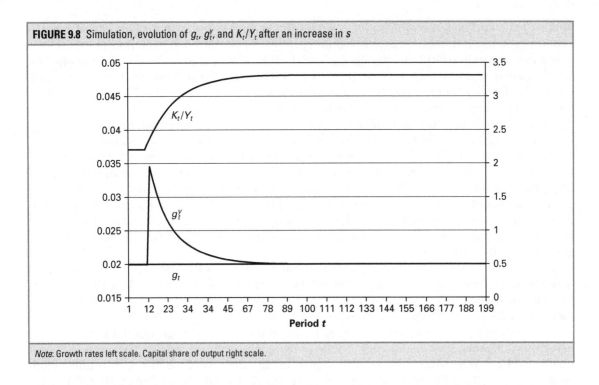

FIGURE 9.8 Simulation, evolution of g_t, g_t^y, and K_t/Y_t after an increase in s

Note: Growth rates left scale. Capital share of output right scale.

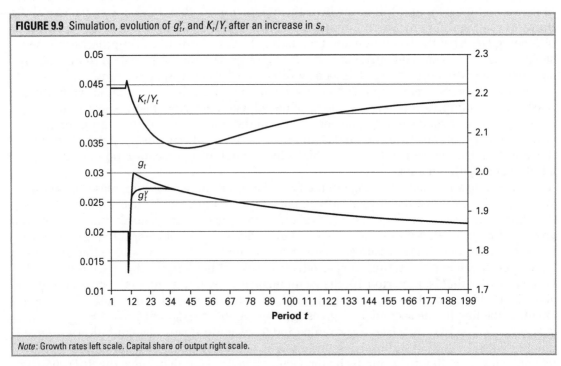

FIGURE 9.9 Simulation, evolution of g_t^y, and K_t/Y_t after an increase in s_R

Note: Growth rates left scale. Capital share of output right scale.

increased s_R is that relatively fewer people will be working in the final goods sector. After that the higher growth in A_t will pull up the growth in y_t. The phase where A_t grows faster than y_t corresponds to the phase where $\tilde{k}_t$ is decreasing in Fig. 9.5, and the later phase where y_t grows faster than A_t is when $\tilde{k}_t$ begins to increase again.

The main conclusion from Fig. 9.9 is that the adjustments following the increase in the research share are long lasting. For instance, although the jump upwards in g_t^y in the beginning is not as large as after the increase in s, it takes almost 50 years before the growth rate of y_t falls below 2.5 per cent. Of course, the duration of the adjustments depends on the parameter values, but these were deliberately chosen to avoid extreme cases.

If a once and for all change in the R&D share has long-lasting effects on growth, then perhaps a slow and gradual increase in s_R, which is not unrealistic by empirical standards, can sustain growth at reasonable levels for a long time? This is exactly the possibility of hemi-endogenous growth that we now turn to.

Let us first assume that $n = 0$, so that population growth is not the factor that keeps economic growth alive. Let us also assume that the R&D share increases at a pace earlier suggested as reasonable. It grows by a constant annual rate, g_{s_R}, implying a doubling every 100 years: $(1 + g_{s_R})^{100} = 2$, or $g_{s_R} = 2^{1/100} - 1 \cong 0.7$ per cent. As stated earlier, this cannot go on forever, but it could take place for 200 years, for instance by s_R increasing from 0.75 to 1.5 per cent over the first century and from 1.5 to 3 per cent over the next one. Consequently, the exogenous R&D share is no longer a constant, but an increasing sequence. How much growth in A_t can the assumed growth in s_R in itself sustain? Return to (11), write it down (once again) for period $t + 1$ as well as for period t, and divide the first equation by the second, this time remembering that s_R depends on time, while L_t is constant. You will easily verify that this gives:

$$g_{t+1} = (1 + g_{s_R})^{\lambda} g_t (1 + g_t)^{\phi - 1}.$$

The *constant* growth rate that can be sustained (inserting $g_{t+1} = g_t$) is thus:

$$g = (1 + g_{s_R})^{\lambda/(1-\phi)} - 1.$$

For the g_{s_R} assumed above, and $\lambda/(1 - \phi) = 2$, this is $g = 2^{2/100} - 1 \approx 1.4$ per cent. Interestingly, without any population growth at all, a plausible-looking gradual increase in the R&D share can sustain continuing growth in the technological parameter, A_t, that is not far from the observed relatively constant growth rates in GDP per capita over long periods.

Let us assume that in year zero s_R indeed has the value 0.0075, and then grows for 200 years at an annual rate of $g_{s_R} = 2^{1/100} - 1$. As mentioned, we consider $n = 0$ and, as a pure normalization, we fix the constant labour force at $L = 1$. For all other parameters we assume the same values as the initial ones above, $s = 0.2$, $\rho = \lambda = 1$, $\phi = \frac{1}{2}$, etc. Let us also assume that the initial value, A_0, of the technological parameter is such that already from year 0, g_t takes the constant value g. From (11) this requires, $g = A_0^{\phi-1} s_{R0}$, or $2^{2/100} - 1 = 0.0075 A_0^{-1/2}$, which gives $A_0 \approx 0.29$. This means that A_t will be growing at an annual rate of around 1.4 per cent over all 200 years. Finally we calibrate the initial value K_0 of capital so that the growth rate of output per worker also starts at around 1.4 per cent. We then simulate the model over 200 years. Figure 9.10 shows the results. The annual growth rate of output per worker stays very close to 1.4 per cent over the entire 200 years. The lower curve shows how the growth rate of output per worker would evolve if s_R stayed constant at the initial 0.75 per cent.

The assumed plausible-looking gradual increase in the research share can thus, over time spans like 200 years, 'explain' economic growth rates close to the observed ones. If we had assumed a slightly faster increase in s_R, we could also have rationalized technological and economic growth rates of 1.8–2 per cent per year. Hence, one possible interpretation of the growth in the developed world over the past 200 years is that it is really a transitory growth that is being maintained all the time by gradual increases in the research *share*.

This is neither semi-endogenous nor endogenous growth. Qualitatively hemi-endogenous growth is not so different from the growth one could have in a basic Solow model if the investment rate were increasing gradually. The difference is that the research share is initially so small, and the impact of increases potentially so strong and long lasting, that the research share can keep on growing at a small constant rate for a very long time, and this suffices for creating economic growth rates of realistic magnitudes for long times. It is this kind of interpretation of the growth process we refer to as hemi-endogenous growth.

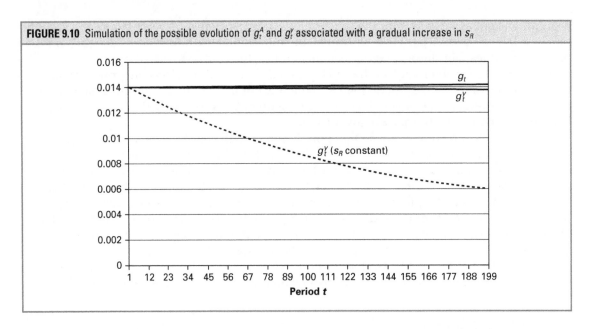

FIGURE 9.10 Simulation of the possible evolution of g_t^A and g_t^y associated with a gradual increase in s_R

One fascinating consequence of the hemi-endogenous growth interpretation is that *it cannot go on forever*. We may expect a few more centuries of growth in GDP per person based on a doubling of the research share every 100 years, but s_R cannot keep on doubling forever. According to the hemi-endogenous growth interpretation, some day growth will cease. At that time, however, the constant income per capita may be very high.

THE HEMI-ENDOGENOUS GROWTH INTERPRETATION ACCORDING TO THE R&D-BASED GROWTH MODEL

A possible and fascinating explanation – or interpretation – of long-run growth experiences like those of the developed world over the past 200 years is that the constant growth in GDP per capita of around 1.5–2 per cent per year is really due to a slow and gradual increase in the amount of resources used in R&D activities corresponding to roughly a doubling of the 'research share' every one hundred years. If this is the right explanation, one day economic growth will be over. At that time, however, mankind could be rich.

9.8 Summary

1. This chapter has studied the microeconomics of private idea (R&D) production. The fact that ideas are non-rival implies that to induce private R&D, market power is needed in the selling of ideas and idea-based products. Otherwise the fixed development cost cannot be covered. The fact that ideas are only imperfectly excludable necessitates some arrangements to increase excludability and prevent copying in order for private production to take place.

2. Patent laws as well as other legal rules for the protection of intellectual property rights can serve the double purpose of ensuring both excludability and monopoly in the production and selling of idea-based products. This way of obtaining private R&D activities is, however, imperfect. Ensuring monopoly power to the sellers of ideas implies that ideas are priced above marginal cost and therefore, from a social viewpoint, underutilized.

3. Even though a patent system is not a perfect way of ensuring private research and development, it is effective in the sense that much more private R&D will take place in the presence than in the absence of laws that protect intellectual property rights. According to some economic historians, the unprecedented economic growth during the past 200 years is partly due to the fact that the legal protection of intellectual property rights reached a critical level some two centuries ago.

4. The macro model of R&D-based endogenous growth studied in this chapter abstracted from the subtle microeconomics of idea production and had the following features:

- Final goods are produced from the inputs of capital, labour and (labour-augmenting) technology, A_t, according to a standard Cobb–Douglas production function.

- New technology is produced in the R&D sector from the inputs of labour and existing technology according to a production function with constant returns to labour at the firm level but possibly diminishing returns at the aggregate level, because firms in the R&D sector may be 'stepping on each other's toes' by working on the same ideas. There is a specific elasticity, ϕ, of the output of new technology, $A_{t+1} - A_t$, with respect to the input of existing technology, A_t.

- The labour force can be used in either production of final goods or in production of new technology, whereas existing technology can be used in both sectors, reflecting that ideas are non-rival. The fraction of labour used in the R&D sector is an exogenous parameter called the research (or R&D) share.

- In other respects the model is standard: capital accumulates from savings and investment (minus depreciation), and the labour force grows at an exogenous rate.

5. If ϕ is equal to 1, a constant input of labour in the R&D sector creates a constant and positive growth rate of technology, $(A_{t+1} - A_t)/A_t$. If ϕ is less than 1, reflecting that it becomes harder to generate new ideas as the more obvious ideas have already been discovered, a constant labour input in research will imply that the absolute production of technology, $A_{t+1} - A_t$, increases and goes to infinity over time, but the growth rate, $(A_{t+1} - A_t)/A_t$, goes to 0. To maintain a positive, constant growth rate of technology requires a positive, constant growth rate of the labour input into the research sector (when $\phi < 1$).

6. In the case $0 < \phi < 1$, the model implies convergence to a steady state where capital and output per worker both grow at the same constant rate as technology, and the growth rate of technology depends positively on the rate of growth of the labour force (or population) in such a way that there can only be economic growth if there is population growth. The reason is that given a constant research share, the labour input in the research sector can only grow at a constant rate if population grows at a constant rate. The semi-endogenous growth arising in this case suggests that a policy to promote economic growth should be one that stimulates population growth.

7. In the alternative case where $\phi = 1$, a constant labour force and a constant research share imply a constant positive growth rate of technology that depends positively, and in a simple way, on the size of the research share. The full model gives convergence to a steady state where capital and income per worker both grow at the same rate as technology. A growth-promoting structural policy is one that increases the research share, but the model is tacit about how this can be achieved since the research share is exogenous. The model of truly endogenous growth arising when $\phi = 1$ implies a highly implausible scale effect: a larger labour force should imply a higher rate of growth of GDP per worker, and if the labour force increases at a constant rate, the growth rate of income per worker should explode.

▶

8. Mainly because of empirical evidence concerning the links between population growth and economic growth, it can be hard to believe that the observed long-lasting economic growth in Western countries should be understood as either purely semi-endogenous growth (where growth in the labour force is needed for economic growth because the research share is constant, and $\phi < 1$) or as truly endogenous growth (where economic growth can occur for a constant labour force because $\phi = 1$, but an increasing labour force would imply increasing economic growth).

9. According to the model studied in this chapter there could be an in-between explanation of economic growth during the past 200 years. Hemi-endogenous growth, as we called it, is closely related to semi-endogenous growth (assuming $\phi < 1$), but explains the required growth of the labour input in R&D as the result, not of population growth given the research share, but of a gradually increasing research share possibly for a constant labour force. We showed that under reasonable parameter specifications, a realistic slow and gradual increase in the research share could, according to our model, explain annual growth rates of GDP per capita in the range 1.5–2 per cent over periods of 200 years and more. This makes the hemi-endogenous growth interpretation look plausible. Of course, the research share cannot grow at a constant rate forever, so one day hemi-endogenous growth will be over. When the research share reaches its maximum, increased labour input in the R&D sector (required for economic growth when $\phi < 1$) can only be achieved by increases in the labour force.

9.9 Exercises

Exercise 1. Rivalry and excludability

The figure below is taken with modifications from an article by Paul Romer.[7] It divides the plane of commodity characteristics according to two criteria: degree of excludability and degree of rivalry. While rivalry is a zero–one concept, excludability occurs more continuously in various degrees, in the figure reflected by three degrees. We have inserted a few commodities in the figure, according to their characteristics.

	DEGREE OF RIVALRY ←	
	RIVAL	**NON-RIVAL**
FULLY EXCLUDABLE (OR CLOSE)	Potatoes, bread, beers	Passage of a bridge
INTERMEDIATELY EXCLUDABLE	Fish in the sea? (think of quotas, etc.)	Computer code for spreadsheet
NON-EXCLUDABLE (OR CLOSE)	Fish in the sea	Fresh air, national defence

(DEGREE OF EXCLUDABILITY — vertical axis)

---

7. Paul M. Romer, 'Two Strategies for Economic Development: Using Ideas and Producing Ideas', in *Proceedings of the World Bank Annual Conference on Development Economics 1992*, supplement to the *World Bank Economic Review*, March 1993, pp. 63–91.

Your task is to discuss and suggest an appropriate placement of the following commodities:

- Drinking a beer in a bar
- Enjoying the atmosphere in a bar
- Bohr's atomic theory
- Travels
- Great scenic views
- The concept for a TV show
- TV transmissions 'in the air' (discuss encoded versus non-encoded and the extent to which excludability of non-encoded signals can be obtained by legal arrangements)
- Biscuits
- The idea of the assembly line
- Mozart's *Eine Kleine Nachtmusik*
- The services of a dentist
- Basic R&D, like discoveries in basic research
- Cable TV signals
- The idea for a new type of motor for cars (discuss legal and technical ways to ensure more excludability)
- Taxi rides
- Parking in a car park at a shopping centre (discuss the implication of the size of the cost of enforcing a payment system)
- Pythagoras' theorem.

Now use your own imagination and place other examples of commodities in the figure, at least one for each of the cells.

Exercise 2. The R&D-based macro model of endogenous growth in continuous time

In continuous time the model we have studied in this chapter would be:

$$Y = K^\alpha (AL_Y)^{1-\alpha},$$

$$\dot{A} = \rho A^\phi L_A^\lambda,$$

$$\dot{K} = sY - \delta K,$$

$$\frac{\dot{L}}{L} = n,$$

$$L_Y + L_A = L$$

$$L_A = s_R L.$$

Both notation and parameter restrictions are obvious and standard. We assume $\phi > 0$ and $\lambda \leq 1$.

1. Show that, at any time, the technological growth rate, $g_A \equiv \dot{A}/A$, according to this model is:

$$g_A = \rho A^{\phi-1} L_A^\lambda = \rho A^{\phi-1} (s_R L)^\lambda.$$

Explain for each of the two cases $\phi = 1$ and $\phi < 1$ how the output of the research sector $\dot{A}$, the technological level A, and the technological growth rate g_A evolve over time when the labour input into the research sector $L_A = s_R L$ is constant.

2. Still using standard notation and definitions, e.g. $\tilde{k} \equiv K/(AL) = k/A$ and $\tilde{y} \equiv Y/(AL) = y/A$, show that the model implies the two one-way coupled differential equations in g_A and $\tilde{k}$:

$$\dot{g}_A = (\phi - 1)g_A^2 + \lambda n g_A,$$

$$\dot{\tilde{k}} = s\tilde{k}^\alpha (1 - s_R)^{1-\alpha} - (n + g_A + \delta)\tilde{k}.$$

(Hint: for the first one take logs on both sides and then differentiate with respect to time in the above formula for g_A.)

Assume first that $\phi < 1$ and $n > 0$.

3. Illustrate the first of the above differential equations in a diagram with g_A along the horizontal axis and $\dot{g}_A$ along the vertical one. Show that g_A converges monotonically to:

$$g_{se} \equiv \frac{\lambda n}{1 - \phi}.$$

4. Illustrate the second equation in a 'Solow-type diagram' (and, if you wish to, also in a 'modified Solow-type diagram') and show that $\tilde{k}$ and $\tilde{y}$ converge to specific constant values, $\tilde{k}^*$ and $\tilde{y}^*$, respectively, in the long run. Show that the growth rates of capital per worker and of output per worker both converge to g_{se} in the long run.

Now consider the case $\phi = 1$ and $n = 0$, and let the constant labour force be denoted by $\bar{L}$.

5. Show that the technological growth rate is constantly $g_e = \rho(s_R \bar{L})^\lambda$ and that the growth rates of capital per worker and of output per worker both converge to g_e.

Exercise 3. Golden rule in the model of semi-endogenous growth

Consider the model studied in Section 9.5 where $0 < \phi < 1$ and $n > 0$, and the steady state growth paths for output per worker, y_t, (described in Eqs (21) and (22)) and for consumption per worker, $c_t = (1 - s)y_t$. What are the (golden rule) values of the fundamental rates, s and s_R, that will elevate the steady state growth path for consumption per worker to the highest position? Describe in words the two opposite effects of the R&D share, s_R, on the levels of the steady state growth paths. Say that reasonable values of λ and ϕ with a population growth rate of 1 per cent per year should imply a steady state growth rate g_{se} of 2 per cent per year. Show that this would mean that $\lambda(1 - \phi)$ should be around 2. What is the golden rule value for the R&D share under this assumption and how does it relate to the empirical GERD shares reported in Table 9.1?

Exercise 4. A scale effect also in the model of semi-endogenous growth

The model of endogenous growth studied in Section 9.6 was criticized for the scale effect it implied: an increasing labour input into the research sector, arising, for example, from population growth ($n > 0$), would imply ever-increasing technological and economic growth rates over time, which is empirically implausible. Consider now the model of semi-endogenous growth presented in Section 9.5. In this model, $n > 0$ does not imply increasing (but rather positive and constant) growth rates in the long run. Explain for yourself the basic intuition for this. The model can, nevertheless, be said to involve a 'scale effect', not on growth rates, but on levels. Explain this effect by stating how a larger level of the labour force, as measured by L_0, affects the level of the steady state growth path for output per worker given by (21) and (22). Do you find that this scale effect is as implausible as the one connected to the model of endogenous growth?

Exercise 5. The effects of an increase in research productivity

This exercise asks you to analyse qualitatively the effects of a once and for all, permanent increase in the productivity parameter ρ of the research sector. Consider the model of semi-endogenous growth ($0 < \phi < 1$ and $n > 0$). Assume that in all periods up to and including period 0 the economy has been in steady state at 'old' parameter values, among them $\rho > 0$. In particular, the growth rates $g_t \equiv (A_{t+1} - A_t)/A_t$ and $g_t^y \equiv (y_{t+1} - y_t)/y_t$ have been equal to $g_{se} = (1 + n)^{\lambda(1-\phi)} - 1$ in all periods up to and including period 0. Working first time in period 1 the productivity parameter jumps permanently to $\rho' > \rho$.

1. First show that this implies the technological growth rate from period 1 to 2: $g_1 = (A_2 - A_1)/A_1 = (\rho'/\rho)g_{se}$. (Hint: Write down Eq. (11) of Section 9.4 for period 1 and for period 0, divide the first by the second and proceed as in Section 9.4, remembering that $g_0^A = g_{se}$.)

2. Using a diagram like Fig. 9.4 for the independent dynamics of g_t, describe how g_t evolves over time. (Note that the transition curve does not move, but there is the initial jump in g_t you found in Question 1.)

3. Does the long-run growth rate of output per worker change as a result of the change in the research productivity parameter? What are the long-run effects on output and consumption per worker of the change?

4. In the model of endogenous growth ($\phi = 1$, $n = 0$), what is the long-run effect on the growth rate of GDP per worker of a permanent increase in ρ?

Exercise 6. Some special cases

Consider the transition equation (12) for g_t.

1. If $\phi = 1$ and $n > 0$, what does the transition curve look like and what is the evolution of the technological growth rate g_t in the long run? (Once again this is really just a description of the scale effect in the model of endogenous growth.)

2. Same questions for $\phi > 1$ and $n = 0$.

3. Same questions for $\phi < 1$ and $n < 0$, and for $\phi = 1$ and $n < 0$. For these ones, what is the long-run growth rate in output per worker according to the full model?

Exercise 7. The rate of convergence of the technological growth rate

Consider the transition equation (12) for g_t repeated here for convenience:

$$g_{t+1} = (1 + n)^{\lambda} g_t (1 + g_t)^{\phi-1} \equiv G(g_t).$$

Assume $\phi < 1$ and $n > 0$. Hence, in the long run g_t converges to $g_{se} = (1 + n)^{\lambda/(1-\phi)} - 1$. In this exercise we are interested in the speed of convergence.

1. Sketch the transition curve in a diagram and explain how it shifts as ϕ increases and eventually goes to 1. How will this affect the speed of convergence?

2. Consider the generic form $g_{t+1} = G(g_t)$ of the transition equation. Show that linearizing this around the steady state value g_{se} and changing into logs yields:

$$\ln g_{t+1} - \ln g_t \approx (1 - G'(g_{se}))(\ln g_{se} - \ln g_t).$$

Argue that $(1 - G'(g_{se}))$ can be viewed as the rate of convergence for the technological growth rate g_t *according to the linear approximation* of the transition equation for g_t. Show that:

$$1 - G'(g_{se}) = (1 - \phi)\left(1 - \frac{1}{(1+n)^{\frac{\lambda}{1-\phi}}}\right),$$

and that the rate of convergence goes to 0 as $\phi \to 1$.

3. Compute the range that the annual rate of convergence, $1 - G'(g_{se})$, will be in for values of λ between $\frac{1}{2}$ and 1, values of ϕ between $\frac{1}{4}$ and $\frac{3}{4}$, and values of n between 0.5% and 1% per year. Comment on the order of magnitude of $1 - G'(g_{se})$ for these non-extreme parameter

values, e.g., by comparing to the rate of convergence we typically find for output per effective worker in the Solow model. Figure 9.8 shows a relatively slow convergence of g_t for the particular parameter values $\lambda = 1$, $\phi = \frac{1}{2}$, and $n = 0.005$. Does this relatively slow convergence seem to be robust for parameters in the non-extreme region considered here?

Exercise 8. The effects of a decrease in the growth rate of the labour force

Consider a decrease in the growth rate n of the labour force in the model of semi-endogenous growth. We know from the chapter's analysis of the model that in the long run a lower n has a negative impact on economic growth, but due to transitory growth effects it may have a positive influence for some time. For some points in the chapter the duration of this positive effect can be considered important. If the positive impact can last for a long time (for reasonable parameter values), this may be what makes the model compatible with the empirical observation (Table 8.1) that over quite long periods lower population growth rates seem to go hand in hand with higher growth rates in GDP per capita within countries in the developed world.

Therefore, consider the model of semi-endogenous growth ($0 < \phi < 1$ and $n > 0$). Assume that in all periods up to and including an 'initial' one the economy has been in steady state at 'old' parameter values, among them $n > 0$. Working for the first time between the initial period and the next one, the growth rate of the labour force falls to a lower value $n' < n$, but still $n' > 0$.

1. To describe the qualitative effects, explain how diagrams like Figs 9.4 and 9.5 are affected by the parameter change and explain how g_t and $\tilde{k}_t$ adjust over time. Explain how there can be a positive contribution to growth in y_t in the beginning and why, in the long run, the growth rate of y_t has to fall.

   Assume parameter values, $\alpha = \frac{1}{3}$, $\rho = \lambda = 1$, $\phi = \frac{1}{2}$, $s = 0.2$, $\delta = 0.06$, $s_R = 0.03$ and initially $n = 0.015$. Starting between period 10 and 11, n drops permanently to $n' = 0.005$ while the other parameters stay unchanged.

2. Compute the steady state values for g_t, g_t^Y and K_t/Y_t before and after the parameter change. Simulate the model consisting of Eqs (5)–(10) over periods 0 to 200 assuming that from period 0–10 the economy is in steady state at the old parameter values. (As we did in Section 9.7, normalize, e.g., $L_0 = 1$, and find the initial values, A_0 and K_0, implied by the economy being in steady state in period zero.) Create figures like in Section 9.7 showing the evolution of g_t, g_t^Y and K_t/Y_t. Comment with respect to how long lasting the positive effect on g_t^Y is.

3. Assume that the decrease in the growth rate of the labour force comes gradually, so the change from 0.015 to 0.005 takes place over the 120 years following period 10 with an equal relative change each year. Simulate the model over 200 years and illustrate in the same type of diagram, again starting from the old steady state in periods 0–10. Comment again with respect to your simulations being able to 'explain' empirical observations on population growth rates and economic growth rates, as those reported in Table 8.1.

4. You may have found above that decreases in the growth rate of the labour force, whether they are once and for all or gradual, do not really (in the model of semi-endogenous growth with reasonable parameters) *by themselves* produce additional growth for long enough periods to provide an explanation for the empirical relationship. Does this mean that we should dispose of the model or could there be other explanations?

PART  Structural Unemployment

Some facts and introductory theory about unemployment

I n the growth models studied in the previous parts of this book, adjustments in the real wage ensured that labour demand was always equal to labour supply, because markets were assumed to be perfectly competitive. Literally speaking, we assumed that there was no unemployment at any point in time. In the real world there is always at least some unemployment.

Figure 10.1 shows average annual rates of unemployment for the USA and Denmark over a long historical period. As we explained in Chapter 1, the movements in the rate of unemployment can be viewed as consisting of two components: a *long-run trend* which could be described as a tendency towards a constant unemployment rate around 5–7 per cent over very long periods, and *cyclical fluctuations* around the trend. The fluctuations are sometimes large, and perhaps so large that one would really not call them fluctuations. Occasionally unemployment has gone to very high levels in both countries. For instance, in the 1930s the rate of unemployment went up to 25 per cent in the USA and above 15 per cent

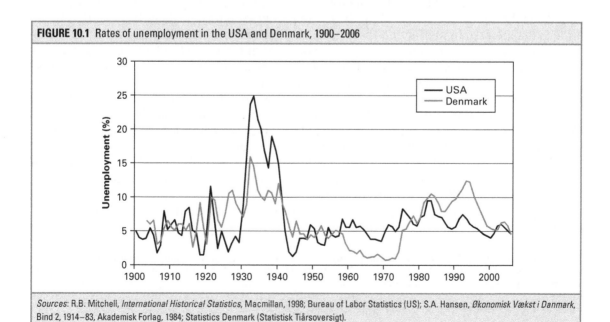

FIGURE 10.1 Rates of unemployment in the USA and Denmark, 1900–2006

Sources: R.B. Mitchell, *International Historical Statistics*, Macmillan, 1998; Bureau of Labor Statistics (US); S.A. Hansen, *Økonomisk Vækst i Danmark*, Bind 2, 1914–83, Akademisk Forlag, 1984; Statistics Denmark (Statistisk Tiårsoversigt).

in Denmark, and over the 1970s and early 1980s, unemployment rose to rates of around or above 10 per cent in both countries.[1]

The fact that the long-run 'gravity' rate of unemployment is not zero but is rather in the range of 5–7 per cent is not a problem for the growth theory presented in this book. We can simply reinterpret the L_t appearing in the growth models as total employment when the labour supply is used at a normal, or natural, rate. Our growth models were just silent about what determines the natural rate of utilization.

For society it is important how high the long-run rate of unemployment is. It makes a difference if the average rate of utilization of the most important economic resource, labour, is 96 or 92 per cent. This chapter and the two next are focused on the forces that determine the long-run or so-called natural rate of unemployment.

10.1 The social cost of unemployment

High unemployment is a major economic and social problem and a concern of economic policy makers mainly for two reasons. At the individual level, when unemployment is high many persons will have to go through long spells of joblessness. They therefore suffer substantial income losses that may force them and their families to move from their homes, change the children's schools, take a cut in their standard of living, etc. Although unemployment insurance is available in most countries, it does not insure a person's income fully, and it covers only a limited period.[2] In addition to the loss of income, longer periods of involuntary unemployment may inflict serious psychological costs on the jobless, because an unemployed person may feel excluded from society and therefore lose self-esteem. Unemployment thus gives rise to serious individual problems.

At the level of society, unemployment is a social waste, because income that could have been earned to the benefit of the individual as well as society is forgone. The income that unemployed persons would have earned, had they had jobs, would have been taxed, and the tax revenue could have been used to the benefit of other citizens. When unemployment is high, the associated loss of tax revenues will be substantial. Thus the income loss of an unemployed person is partly suffered by the unemployed himself and partly by other members of society. In any case it is a waste of resources to have people who are both qualified and willing to work at the going wage rates, unable to do so.

Economists explain the social waste associated with involuntary unemployment in more detail as follows. Let the marginal product of (a particular type of) labour be MPL, that is, MPL is the increase in production that will arise if one more worker is put to work, or the decrease that will result if one individual is taken out of work. We think of the marginal product of labour as being decreasing in employment because of the presence of fixed factors, e.g. capital or land, or because the most productive workers are hired first.

The marginal product of labour must be held up against the marginal rate of substitution between consumption and leisure, MRS, also referred to as the marginal disutility of work. A worker's MRS is the amount of goods needed to compensate him for the leisure and the value of the home production he must give up when taking a job. Typically different workers will have a different MRS. A person will obviously want to work if offered a real wage above the person's MRS, so the total labour supply induced by a given real wage is the number of workers having an MRS below that wage rate.

If a worker's marginal product is larger than his or her MRS, then a social loss occurs if he or she does not work, since putting him or her to work gives an additional amount of

---

1. The data underlying Fig. 10.1 are not completely comparable between the two countries. However, for both countries the rates represent all unemployed as a percentage of all workers rather than all *insured* unemployed as a percentage of all insured workers.

2. In Chapter 19, where we discuss the costs of the cyclical part of unemployment, we will go into more detail with the reasons why unemployment insurance typically cannot and does not fully cover the income losses arising from unemployment.

output sufficient to compensate the worker and to leave a surplus that can be shared with other members of society (through taxation) to the benefit of everybody. A situation where $MRS < MPL$ thus implies inefficiency in the use of labour resources.

Now, if there is involuntary unemployment and firms maximize profits, there will indeed be jobless workers with marginal products exceeding their disutilities of work. An involuntarily unemployed person would like to work at the going real wage rate, W/P, so this wage rate must be greater than his or her disutility of work, $MRS < W/P$. Profit maximization implies that the last worker hired has a marginal product at least as great as the going real wage rate, that is, $W/P \le MPL$, since otherwise the firm could increase its profits by firing the marginal worker. On the plausible assumption that the marginal product of labour decreases *gradually* with employment, there will be unemployed workers with marginal products close to that of the last worker hired. In other words, there will be unemployed workers for whom the condition $W/P \le MPL$ is (very close to being) fulfilled. Collecting what we have found, if there is involuntary unemployment, then there must be unemployed workers for whom $MRS < W/P \le MPL$, implying $MRS < MPL$. Hence their joblessness involves a social loss.[3]

For these reasons it is of great interest to know what determines the rate of structural unemployment and what policy measures could bring the natural rate of unemployment down from, say, 8 to 4 per cent. These are exactly the questions to which we now turn. This chapter lays the basis for answering these questions by going through some empirical regularities concerning unemployment and by presenting some introductory theories. The next two chapters will present two main theories of structural unemployment.

10.2 The rate of unemployment

Labour force, employment and unemployment

The rate of unemployment is a stock variable that can be measured at a given point in time, say on a specific day. Let the total number of persons who *would like to* work on day t be L_t. This is the labour force, which can be viewed as the size of the population of working age, P_t, times the participation rate, π_t, that is, $L_t = \pi_t P_t$. One can further subdivide into various groups such as women and men, $L_t = \pi_t^w P_t^w + \pi_t^m P_t^m$, where π_t^w and π_t^m are the participation rates of women and men, respectively. Total employment on day t, E_t, is the number of persons actually having a job on that day. The number of unemployed is then simply $U_t = L_t - E_t$, and the rate of unemployment is

$$u_t \equiv \frac{U_t}{L_t} = \frac{L_t - E_t}{L_t} = 1 - \frac{E_t}{L_t} \equiv 1 - e_t,$$

where we have denoted the rate of employment by e_t. Table 10.1 shows an estimate of the labour forces in the USA and Denmark for the month of January 2006, and it also shows the decomposition of the labour forces into employed and unemployed.

The rate of unemployment contains an element that is not as readily measurable as GDP, employment, inflation, etc., namely the number of persons, L_t, who *would like to* have a job. Out of these the E_t employed actually have a job, so we can infer that indeed these people want to work. The U_t unemployed, however, are persons who would like to work and yet do not do so. How do we measure the number of such people?

One way is to limit attention to those covered by unemployment insurance and to assume that individuals who plan to be active in the labour market will want to insure themselves against unemployment. One can then let L_t be the total number of people holding unemployment insurance, and let E_t be the number of insured people who have

---

3. An exercise will ask you to restate the explanation of the social cost of unemployment using a standard diagram.

TABLE 10.1 Labour market data, January 2006

(in 1000 persons)	USA	Denmark
Population in working ages*		
– Women	97,341	1,772
– Men	94,850	1,804
Participation rates		
– Women	69%	76%
– Men	81%	84%
Labour force		
– Women	66,951	1,348
– Men	76,797	1,515
Total labour force (L)	143,748	2,863
Employed (E)	136,320	2,755
Unemployed (U = L – E)	7,428	108
Rate of unemployment (U/L)	5.2%	3.9%

Note: *Population of working age is defined as those between 16 and 64 years of age in the USA, and between 16 and 66 years of age in Denmark.
Sources: Bureau of Labor Statistics (US) and Statistics Denmark (Statistisk Tiårsoversigt).

a job. Another way is to let L_t be the sum of all those who have a job (E_t) and all those who are registered at some kind of (public) institution as looking for a job but not having one (U_t). A third way is to let L_t consist of all persons who either have a job (E_t) or receive unemployment benefits or social assistance benefits motivated by joblessness (U_t). A fourth way is to estimate the number of unemployed by survey techniques asking a representative sample of individuals whether they are available for work. The three latter ways are the most common, and all the data for unemployment you will see in this chapter are of these types.

Although the rate of unemployment by definition pertains to a specific day, the data for unemployment most often shown are annual (or quarterly or monthly) rates. Fig. 10.1, for instance, shows annual rates. The annual rate of unemployment is simply the average over all the working days in the year of the daily rates of unemployment as defined above.

The duration of unemployment

When you hear that the annual rate of unemployment was 12 per cent in Denmark in 1993, you might think that 12 per cent of the people in the labour force were unemployed during all of 1993. This was not the case. Indeed, many more people than 12 per cent of the labour force experienced some unemployment during 1993, but most of these people were unemployed for considerably less than all of the year. Table 10.2 shows that in Denmark in 1993, the fraction of people in the labour force who experienced some unemployment was 29 per cent, but 21 per cent of these people were unemployed for less than five weeks, 44 per cent were unemployed less than 14 weeks, while 64 per cent were unemployed for less than half the year. A considerable 36 per cent of those affected by unemployment, that is, 10.4 per cent of all people in the labour force, were unemployed for more than half the year.

In the USA the annual rate of unemployment was substantially lower than in Denmark in 1993, namely 7 per cent, and the fraction of people in the workforce who experienced some unemployment was 20 per cent. Of these people, 20 per cent were unemployed for more than half the year, implying that only 4 per cent of the people in the labour force were unemployed for more than half the year.

This illustrates a general fact that we will return to below. Higher overall unemployment tends to raise the share of long-term unemployment in total unemployment. The figures for 2006 also confirm this. In Denmark the annual rate of unemployment had come down to

TABLE 10.2 Duration of unemployment

1993			2006		
Percentage of people experiencing unemployment during the year, who were unemployed for	USA	Denmark	Percentage of people experiencing unemployment during the year, who were unemployed for	USA	Denmark
Less than 5 weeks	37	21	Less than 5 weeks	37	38
5–14 weeks	29	23	5–14 weeks	32	27
15–26 weeks	14	19	15–26 weeks	15	16
27 or more weeks	20	36	27 or more weeks	16	19
	100	100		100	100
Persons having experienced unemployment as a percentage of the labour force	20	29	Persons having experienced unemployment as a percentage of the labour force	16	17
Unemployment rate, %	7	12	Unemployment rate %	5	4

Sources: Bureau of Labor Statistics (US) and Statistics Denmark (Statistisk Tiårsoversigt).

4 per cent, and now only 19 per cent of those affected by unemployment were unemployed for more than half the year, as opposed to 36 per cent in 1993 when the overall unemployment rate was 12 per cent.

If no people were ever unemployed for more than, say, one month during a year, the individual loss would not be so severe. However, those who are unemployed for long periods may be badly hurt by unemployment. A close positive relationship between the overall rate of unemployment and the rate of long-term unemployment provides one of the main reasons for trying to avoid high unemployment in general.

The Beveridge curve

If there is (involuntary) unemployment, can there be vacant jobs at the same time? At first, one would perhaps say no. If there are unemployed people truly seeking jobs, they should take the vacant jobs until there are no more vacancies. If there is unemployment there should be no vacancies, and if there are vacancies there should be no unemployment. This would correspond to a perfect matching in the labour market between people who want jobs and the employers who offer jobs. However, the matching is never that perfect.

Just as one can define a rate of unemployment at a given time, one can define a rate of vacancies. Let J_t be the total number of jobs offered by employers on day t, and let E_t be total employment on that day. The number of vacancies is then $V_t = J_t - E_t$, and the vacancy rate is $v_t \equiv V_t/J_t$.

To estimate vacancy rates we must be able to measure the number of vacant jobs, V_t. This involves even more practical problems than measuring the number of unemployed people, U_t, but one can try in different ways. In the USA a 'help wanted' index is published. This measures the number of job advertisements in major US newspapers. We may take this index as an imperfect measure of the vacancy rate. If the measurement error is the same at different dates, a time series for the help wanted index should give a correct indication of the direction in which the 'true' vacancy rate moves.

The perfect matching between 'people wanting jobs' and 'jobs wanting people' described above would imply that in a diagram with u_t along the horizontal axis and v_t along the vertical axis, only points (u_t, v_t) on one of the two axes would be observed. Fig. 10.2 shows how the points are situated for the US over the period 1960–2006, if one uses the help wanted index as a proxy for the vacancy rate.

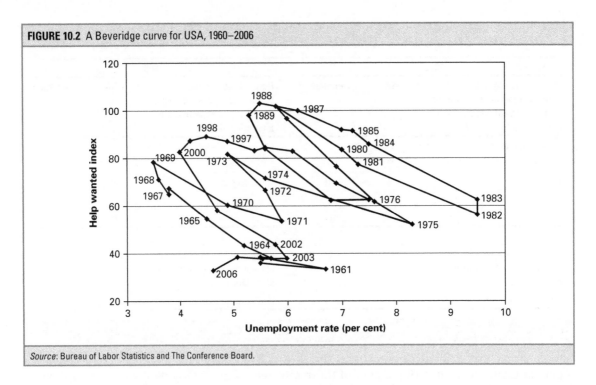

FIGURE 10.2 A Beveridge curve for USA, 1960–2006

Source: Bureau of Labor Statistics and The Conference Board.

The relationship between u_t and v_t is called a Beveridge curve. The fact that the curve does not just follow the axes is an indication of 'mismatch' in the labour markets. The further out to the northeast the curve is situated, the more severe are the problems of mismatch. The position of the Beveridge curve can thus be seen as an indicator of structural problems in the labour market. This is exactly why the Beveridge curve is useful. If the position of the curve shifts over time, this indicates shifts in the matching efficiency in the labour market. In Fig. 10.2 the points for the period from 1960 to 1969, for instance, are located on a nice downward-sloping curve. Then there is a shift outwards. The points for 1979 to 1988 seem again to be nicely situated on a downward-sloping curve, but this curve has shifted considerably to the north-east compared to the 1960–69 curve. This indicates that during the decade 1979 to 1988 people and jobs had much greater problems finding each other than during the decade 1960 to 1969. One would expect this to be part of the reason why there was more unemployment in the latter of these decades. From 1988 to 2006 there seems to have been an almost continually ongoing improvement of the basic structures of the American labour market.

10.3 Stylized facts about unemployment

We mentioned that the rate of unemployment contains an element that is not easy to measure, namely the number of people who do not have a job but *would have liked to have one*. For this reason there is some disagreement among economists about how much to trust statistics on unemployment rates. Should these be included among the time series that theories are held up against, or should one only include series of 'truly measurable' variables? Yet most economists believe that one can safely trust reported statistics of unemployment to give at least *some* indication of the extent of involuntary unemployment.

To see why, we may start by asking if there is a way to test if those who report that they are involuntarily out of work would actually take a job at the going wages if they were offered one. Assume that due to 'good times' there is a sudden increase in the demand for labour. If this reduces unemployment without driving up real wages too much, it can be taken as a sign that those who reported being unemployed actually did want jobs at the going wages, since they indeed took jobs at these wages when they had the chance. In other words, if we observe a clear relationship between increases in GDP and decreases in the rate of unemployment and, at the same time, do not observe that real wages increase sharply as soon as GDP goes up, then this suggests that the officially reported rates of unemployment indeed contain true information.

In Chapter 13 we return to the empirical facts of the business cycle. One fact reported is that real wages are not strongly correlated with GDP over the cycle, and in particular there is no strong tendency that increases in GDP are associated with increases in real wages. At the same time there is a clear tendency that increases in GDP are accompanied by decreases in reported unemployment, as shown in Fig. 10.3 for the USA and Denmark.

The relationship illustrated by Fig. 10.3 is both important and useful. It shows, for instance, that at a constant rate of unemployment, economic growth in the USA is around 3 per cent per year while for Denmark the corresponding intersection is just above 2 per cent (the difference being mainly due to a higher growth rate of the labour force in the USA). A one-time increase in the growth rate of GDP of 3 percentage points reduces unemployment by around 2 percentage points in Denmark and by slightly less in the USA (the difference again due to higher labour force growth in the USA). The relationship reported in Fig. 10.3 has a name: Okun's Law.

STYLIZED FACT 1

(Okun's Law). There is a tight negative relationship between the rate of growth in GDP and the absolute change in the rate of unemployment.

The rate of unemployment is a fraction and by definition it has to stay between 0 and 1. Therefore it cannot increase by a certain percentage each year over many years, since this would eventually make it larger than 1. It could have an increasing trend in other ways, for example it could tend to increase from one level to another higher level. Figure 10.4 (as well as Fig. 10.1) indicates that nothing like that is true. The figure uses the same data as Fig. 10.1 and shows the annual absolute change in the rate of unemployment for the USA and Denmark. Over time spans of 100 years, increases and decreases seem to offset each other so that there is no upward or downward long-run tendency.

STYLIZED FACT 2

There is no upwards or downwards trend in the rate of unemployment in the (very) long run.

Note, however, that over quite substantial periods there can be a tendency for unemployment to rise or fall. Consider Fig. 10.1 again and assume that for the USA you only had the data from the early 1940s to the early 1980s, a period of about 40 years. For this long period there seems to be a sustained upward movement in the rate of unemployment. Something similar is true for Denmark for the period from the early 1970s to the early 1990s.

Figures 10.1 and 10.4 also bring evidence of another fact which is well known:

STYLIZED FACT 3

There is a lot of variability in the rate of unemployment in the short run.

A fact that is perhaps not so directly visible from Figs 10.1 and 10.4 is the persistence in the rate of unemployment: if the rate of unemployment is high in a specific year, then

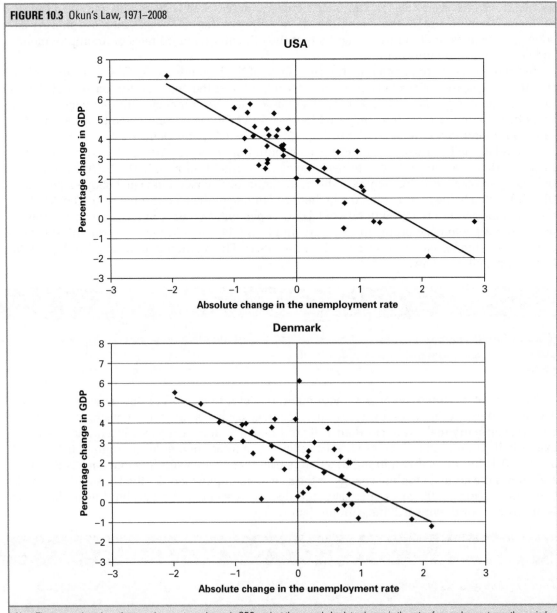

FIGURE 10.3 Okun's Law, 1971–2008

Note: The scatterplots show the annual percentage change in GDP against the annual absolute change in the rate of unemployment over the period from 1971 to 2008. Each dot corresponds to a single year. For the statistically proficient, the regression line for the USA has a slope of −1.8, $R^2 = 0.73$ and $t = −9.8$, while the line for Denmark has a slope of −1.5, $R^2 = 0.52$ and $t = −6.3$.

Source: OECD, Economic Outlook.

it was probably also high the year before (and will be the year after). We can measure this persistence by the coefficient of correlation between the current unemployment rate and its own past values. The coefficient of correlation between two time series, u_t and x_t, running through $t = 1, \dots, T$ and with averages $\bar{u} = (1/T)\sum_{t=1}^{T} u_t$ and $\bar{x} = (1/T)\sum_{t=1}^{T} x_t$ is:

$$\rho \equiv \frac{\sum_{t=1}^{T}(u_t - \bar{u})(x_t - \bar{x})}{\sqrt{\sum_{t=1}^{T}(x_t - \bar{x})^2} \cdot \sqrt{\sum_{t=1}^{T}(x_t - \bar{x})^2}}.$$

It should be visible from the formula that the coefficient ρ measures the degree of (linear) covariation between the two series, that is, roughly the degree to which one series is above

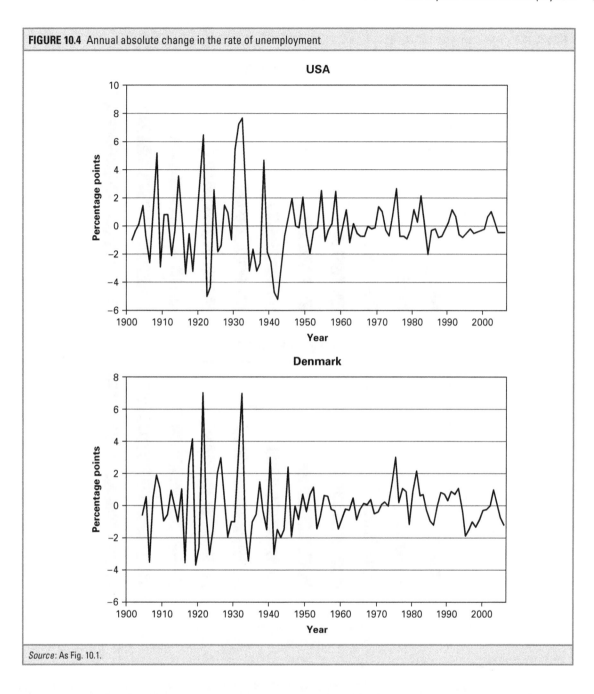

FIGURE 10.4 Annual absolute change in the rate of unemployment

Source: As Fig. 10.1.

average when the other is above average. One can show that $-1 \leq \rho \leq 1$, and $\rho = 1$ and $\rho = -1$ correspond to complete linear covariation along a straight line, $u_t = a + bx_t$, with positive and negative b, respectively. If u_t is the annual rate of unemployment and one lets $x_t = u_{t-1}$, and computes ρ for the two series u_t and x_t (for $t = 2, \ldots, T$), one gets the coefficient of correlation between the rate of unemployment in one year and the year before. One can then let $x_t = u_{t-2}$ to get the correlation with unemployment two years before, etc. Figure 10.5 shows such coefficients of correlation in unemployment for the USA and Denmark.

There is a clear positive correlation between the current rate of unemployment and the rates of unemployment in several previous years, and the degree of correlation decreases as one goes back in time. The tendency for high unemployment in one year to imply high unemployment in several previous and succeeding years is what we mean by the persistence in unemployment.

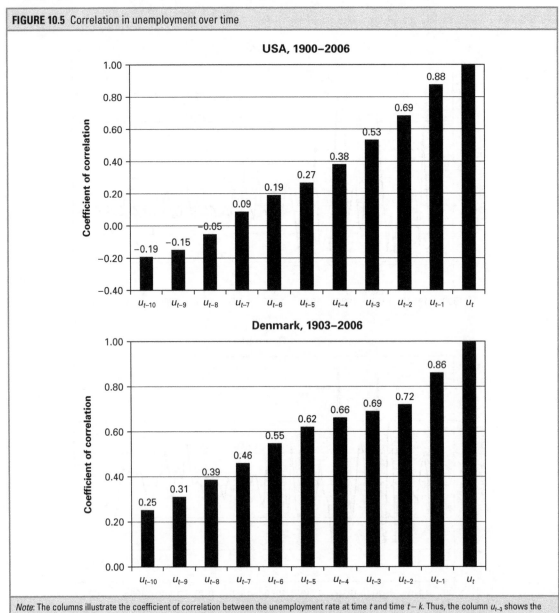

FIGURE 10.5 Correlation in unemployment over time

Note: The columns illustrate the coefficient of correlation between the unemployment rate at time *t* and time *t* − *k*. Thus, the column u_{t-3} shows the degree of correlation between the unemployment rate and the unemployment rate three years before.

Source: As Fig. 10.1.

STYLIZED FACT 4

There is a lot of persistence in annual rates of unemployment.

In connection with Table 10.2 we examined the relationship between overall unemployment and long-term unemployment. We can compute the annual rate of long-term unemployment over several years, defining this rate as, for example, the percentage of all people in the labour force who were unemployed for more than half of the year. We can then plot the rate of long-term unemployment against the overall rate of unemployment. This is done for the USA and for Denmark in Fig. 10.6.

The relationship is evidently tight and positive, with a relatively steep slope. This motivates:

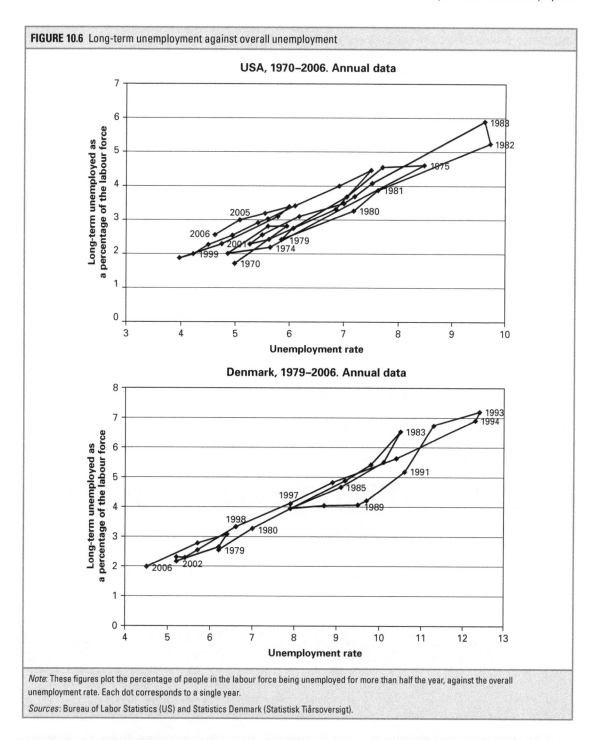

FIGURE 10.6 Long-term unemployment against overall unemployment

Note: These figures plot the percentage of people in the labour force being unemployed for more than half the year, against the overall unemployment rate. Each dot corresponds to a single year.

Sources: Bureau of Labor Statistics (US) and Statistics Denmark (Statistisk Tiårsoversigt).

STYLIZED FACT 5

Long-term unemployment varies tightly, positively and relatively strongly with overall unemployment.

As noted above, the most severe consequences of unemployment are felt by the long-term unemployed. Since higher unemployment means higher long-term unemployment, this may be one of the main reasons for fighting high unemployment.

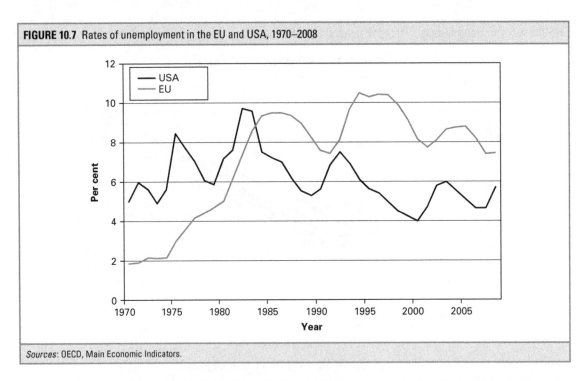

FIGURE 10.7 Rates of unemployment in the EU and USA, 1970–2008

Sources: OECD, Main Economic Indicators.

Does unemployment tend to be of equal size in different regions of the world? Perhaps it does in the very long run, as suggested by Fig. 10.1, but over substantial periods there can be considerable differences between major regions, as shown in Fig. 10.7. For a long time until the early 1980s, unemployment in Europe was lower than in America, but since then joblessness has been substantially higher in the EU than in the USA.

STYLIZED FACT 6

There can be large differences in unemployment across geographical areas for long periods of time.

Other systematic variations are also important. Fig. 10.8 shows rates of unemployment across educational groups for the USA and Denmark. Although different educational categorizations have been used for the two countries, the general picture is clear:

STYLIZED FACT 7

There are considerable and long-lived differences in rates of unemployment across educational groups with a broad tendency for higher education to mean lower unemployment.

Variations across other categories are of importance in different connections, e.g. across race or sex. However, a relatively high rate of unemployment for a particular section of the population may, at least partly, reflect that this group contains relatively many unskilled people compared to the general population.

The final 'law' we will focus on here is an important one, and the remainder of this chapter is more or less centred around it. Figure 10.9 shows in two panels annual rates of unemployment for the USA and Denmark for the postwar period from 1950 to 2007. For each country a trend constructed by the so-called 'HP filter' that you will learn about in Chapter 13 is shown. Fig. 10.9 is a close-up of the more recent part of Fig. 10.1 and Fig. 1.2.

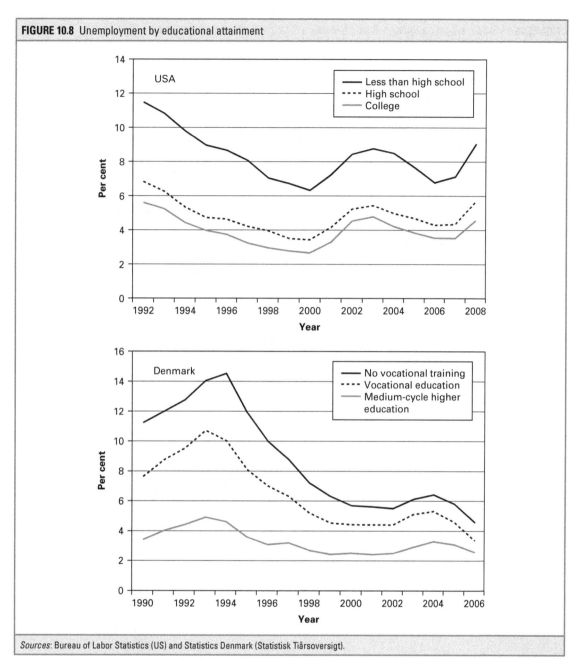

FIGURE 10.8 Unemployment by educational attainment

Sources: Bureau of Labor Statistics (US) and Statistics Denmark (Statistisk Tiårsoversigt).

Consider the upper panel for the USA. Even when the rate of unemployment is lowest, there is still a considerable amount of unemployment with annual rates normally above 4 per cent. Furthermore, the annual rate of unemployment fluctuates around a 'gravity level' that may change over time, but is normally not too far from 5–6 per cent. Also, for Denmark there seems to be a lower bound on the rate of unemployment and fluctuations around a gravity level, but the latter changes considerably more over time than for the USA. The period in the 1960s and early 1970s, when the unemployment rate in Denmark went far below 2 per cent, showed many signs that this was not a sustainable or equilibrium situation: inflation rose sharply. Accounting for this, the figures indicate that even in the best of times the lowest possible rates of unemployment are considerable, perhaps around 3–4 per cent, and gravity rates of unemployment are higher. Figure 10.9 gives a clear indication that the gravity or natural rate of unemployment can shift over time and differ between countries (and regions).

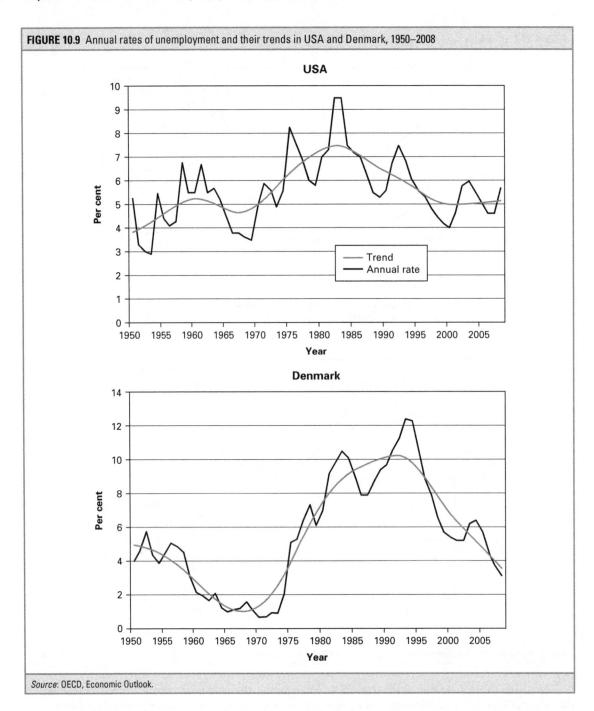

FIGURE 10.9 Annual rates of unemployment and their trends in USA and Denmark, 1950–2008

Source: OECD, Economic Outlook.

STYLIZED FACT 8

When rates of unemployment are at their lowest, there is still a substantial amount of unemployment, seemingly around 3–4 per cent, and the natural unemployment rate that the annual rates fluctuate around is higher. The natural rate of unemployment can shift over time and be different in different regions and countries.

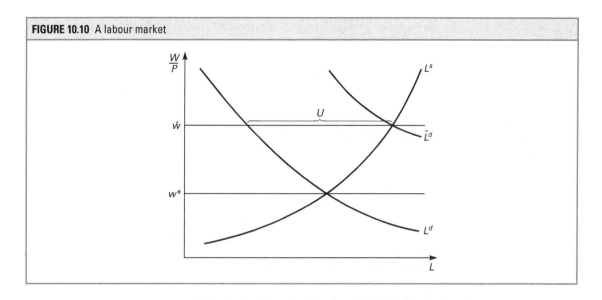

FIGURE 10.10 A labour market

10.4 Short-run cyclical and long-run structural unemployment

This section links the various types of unemployment, short-run cyclical and long-run structural, to the different types of wage and price rigidity that economists think are associated with them. The section will therefore contain some repetition of material from Chapter 1.

Unemployment and excess supply of labour

Figure 10.10 illustrates a situation of unemployment in a labour market (disregarding mismatching). The figure assumes that the *individual* suppliers of labour take the nominal wage rate, W, as well as the nominal price level, P, as given. The labour supply curve, L^s, is drawn as an increasing function of the real wage rate, W/P, but nothing in our arguments would change if the labour supply curve were vertical. The firms that demand labour are also assumed to take the nominal wage rate as given, and the demand curve for labour, L^d, is decreasing in the real wage rate.

If this labour market were perfectly competitive, the market forces (working on the nominal wage rate, W) would imply a real wage at the level w^*, where supply equals demand and there is no unemployment. A situation of unemployment, as illustrated in the figure, means that the real wage rate is at some level $\hat{w}$ at which the supply of labour exceeds the demand for labour by the amount U.

Should the excess supply of labour not imply downward pressure on the nominal wage rate, forcing the real wage down to w^*, thus eliminating unemployment? This is a key question that any theory of unemployment has to face. Let us first just state two trivial, but nevertheless important, and highly related points in connection to this question:

1 In a labour market characterized by full competitive wage flexibility, there can be no unemployment, since the nominal wage rate adjusts immediately to generate a real wage that equates the competitive (wage-taking) supply of and demand for labour.

2 For unemployment to be possible, there must be factors preventing the (real) wage from adjusting to a level that would equate the competitive supply of labour and the competitive demand for labour.

Wage rigidity in the short run and in the long run

If we define 'wage rigidity' as any factor that prevents a full, competitive equilibration of the labour market, we can also summarize the two above statements like this: *for unemployment*

to exist there must be some wage rigidity. Usually economists distinguish between two types
of wage rigidity and two associated types of unemployment.

Short-run nominal wage rigidity and cyclical unemployment
If a situation like the one illustrated by Fig. 10.10 prevails (for some time) for the mere
reason that it takes time for the nominal wage rate to adjust to circumstances, we say that a
short-run nominal wage rigidity is at work. The part of unemployment caused by short-run
nominal wage rigidity we call short-run, or cyclical, unemployment.

Short-run nominal wage rigidity can take different forms. One possibility is that the
adjustments of the nominal wage rate are really governed by competitive market forces, that is,
by discrepancies between wage-taking supply and demand, but it simply takes some time for
an excess supply of labour to bring about a full downward adjustment of the nominal wage rate.
The reason is that an excess supply of labour has to be there for some time before it can invoke
a downward pressure on the nominal wage rate. There will therefore be a period where the
real wage rate can be at a level such as $\hat{w}$ in Fig. 10.10 simply because the nominal wage
adjustments that should bring it down *have not yet occurred.* We would expect cyclical
unemployment caused by such a nominal wage rigidity to be eliminated by market forces
alone in the longer run when nominal wages have had time to adjust fully. However, if
the economy is hit by new shocks all the time, the nominal wage rate may be on a never-
ending job of adjustment, and during this continual adjustment, there will occasionally be
unemployment and occasionally excess demand for labour or 'overemployment'.

Another possibility that we introduced in Chapter 1 is that the nominal wage rate is really
set by an economic agent, let us say a trade union that organizes the wage-taking individual
workers. As we explained in Chapter 1, if the nominal wage rate is set optimally at the outset
and there are small 'menu costs' associated with nominal wage adjustments, it will be optimal
for the trade union *not* to react to shocks as long as these are not too large and of a temporary
nature.

The real wage, W/P, may be flexible under short-run nominal wage rigidity because the
nominal price level, P, may adjust in response to conditions in the product markets. The
implied adjustments in the real wage should not be expected to eliminate unemployment
since they do not come in response to circumstances in the labour market.

The dynamics of cyclical unemployment arising from short-run nominal wage rigidity
are one of the main subjects of Book Two and will not be dealt with further here.

Long-run real wage rigidity and structural unemployment
Consider again the situation in Fig. 10.10 where the wage-taking labour supply exceeds
employment, and assume that the real wage rate has already fully adjusted *in accordance
with the real wage flexibility that the economy possesses.* In that case we say that a long-run
real wage rigidity is at work, and the part of unemployment that is caused by long-run real
wage rigidity we call long-run, or structural, or natural unemployment.

Note that this is different from short-run nominal wage rigidity. It is not that the nominal
wage rate has not *yet* adjusted to circumstances or that wage-setting agents have *preferred* not
to react to temporary and opposing shocks. Here we assume (artificially) that the economy has
not been exposed to new shocks for a long time so that all relative prices have fully adjusted
to circumstances in accordance with the economy's long-run price and wage flexibility, and yet
excess supply of labour prevails. We should, of course, be interested in the exact reasons why an
excess supply of labour would not imply a downward adjustment of the real wage rate in the
long run. We briefly consider such reasons below, while Chapters 11 and 12 deal in depth with
two particular and important reasons for real wage rigidity and their macroeconomic implications.

The division of all unemployment into short-run and long-run unemployment is closely
related to the Stylized fact 8 above, and to the nature of the unemployment fluctuations
illustrated in Figs 10.1 and 10.9. From time to time there is a sudden increase in the rate of
unemployment, for instance by two percentage points over just one year. It is natural to see

this as caused by a negative shock to which the economy reacts not only with lower production, but also (temporarily) with higher unemployment because of short-run nominal wage rigidity. This can explain the fluctuations in the rate of unemployment, but not the trend level of 5–7 per cent that the unemployment rate fluctuates around. Over time spans such as the more than 50 years in Fig. 10.9, or the more than 100 years in Fig. 10.1, we cannot possibly view the economy as being all the time reacting to negative shocks. Sometimes the shocks must have been mainly positive, sometimes the labour market must have been close to equilibrium where wage rates are adjusted in accordance with the economy's wage flexibility. The permanent part of unemployment must therefore be due to long-run real wage rigidity, i.e., to the fact that the price and wage flexibility of the economy is simply not such that it tends to eliminate *all* unemployment, not even after a long time without new shocks. The box at the end of this section illustrates our categorization of unemployment and sums up other issues as well.

One of the main reasons why economists find it useful to distinguish between the fluctuating or cyclical part of unemployment associated with short-run nominal wage rigidity, and the permanent or 'natural' part of unemployment associated with long-run real wage rigidity, is that the kind of policies that can be expected to work in fighting the two types of unemployment are different. Long-run unemployment can only be affected by policy measures that have an impact on the price and wage flexibility of the economy. We call such policies *structural policies*. One example could be reforms of the unemployment insurance system designed to make the unemployed exert a stronger downward pressure on wage rates, but as we saw in Chapter 1, a policy which increases the degree of product market competition can also help to reduce structural unemployment. Short-run unemployment, on the other hand, can be affected by *stabilization policies*, such as traditional fiscal and monetary policy.

Causes of long-run structural unemployment

For long-run real wage rigidity and structural unemployment to exist, there must be some reason why unemployment does not impose a downward pressure on wages. The remaining part of this chapter, and Chapters 11 and 12, are focused on this issue.

Why should the presence of unemployed people not give rise to downward pressure on wage rates, not even in the long run? Let us go through some possible reasons.

Abuse
One potential reason is that some people registered as unemployed may not really be looking for jobs but may only be interested in collecting the publicly subsidized unemployment benefits. Hence they do not contribute any downward pressure on wages. There is hardly any doubt that such abuse occurs to some extent, but we have argued above that probably most of registered unemployment is not of this type, and in the following we will disregard it.

Frictional unemployment
Another reason is that some of the unemployed have already found a job, but have not yet started in it. Usually people are not hired immediately, but, say, from the first day of the next month. There will then be a period of time during which they are unemployed, and involuntarily so, but they do not look for jobs since they already have a job starting a few weeks later. Due to the natural development of the economy there will all the time be some people who lose their jobs. For instance, as time goes by the products of some firms become outdated, the firms must close, and the employees lose their jobs. Even at times when these people do not have difficulty finding new jobs, there will be some unemployment due to a number of people being on their way from one job to another, since the transition takes some time for technical and formal reasons beyond people's control. We call this *frictional* unemployment, and frictional unemployment is one part of structural unemployment. It is

of interest to try to estimate how much structural unemployment is frictional, and we will return to that in the next section. The conclusion will be that probably only a minor part of long-run unemployment is frictional. Hence there is still a lot of structural unemployment to explain, and indeed some economists view the non-frictional part of long-run unemployment as the 'true' structural unemployment.

Search unemployment

If the people who lose their jobs spend some time before taking a new job, not for reasons beyond their control, but as a matter of choice (they may turn down job offers for some time), we call the associated unemployment *search* unemployment. Just like frictional unemployment, search unemployment cannot be expected to exert downward pressure on wages. The two types of unemployment are closely related, differing only in the reason why the unemployed turn down job offers. In the case of frictional unemployment it is because they have already accepted a job offer. In the case of search unemployment it is because the unemployed choose to wait, or search, for better job offers. Who says that the first offer received is the best one the unemployed worker can get? Perhaps it is wise to spend some time searching. Search unemployment is thus closely related to uncertainty about available job offers: it is caused by imperfect information about job possibilities. Furthermore, search unemployment is voluntary.

The level of search unemployment depends on a basic trade-off for the unemployed person. On the cost side, longer search for a new job implies a larger income loss during the waiting time. On the benefit side, it implies a higher expected future income from the day employment starts, assuming that more search ultimately leads to a better job offer. The more important the benefit side is relative to the cost side, the more (voluntary) search unemployment there will be. Generous unemployment benefits help to keep the cost side down; they work as a subsidy to search. Therefore, lower benefits would tend to reduce search unemployment, and this is one example of a structural policy that could be used to fight a type of structural unemployment.

Should policy makers try to reduce search unemployment as much as possible? No, there are some positive aspects of search unemployment. It is in the general interest of society that the qualifications of the labour force are used optimally, that each individual is employed where his or her productivity is the highest, since this means higher incomes. The search by individuals may work to ensure that people are placed in jobs where they earn well because they have high productivity. So, for society there is also a basic trade-off related to search unemployment. When people are 'separated' from their jobs, we want them to search for some time in order for them to find new jobs where they have high productivity, but we do not want them to search for too long, because then the output loss during the search period will outweigh the productivity gain from further search.

The job for policy makers is thus not to reduce search unemployment to a minimum, but to create incentives through the tax and benefit systems for an *appropriate level of search unemployment*.

Search unemployment and structural policies intended to affect it are important issues in macroeconomics. However, the formal theory of search unemployment is quite complex, and for that reason we will not have (much) more to say about search unemployment in this book.

Efficiency wages

The efficiency wage theory of the coexistence of unemployment and fully adjusted wages represents a minimum departure from the fully competitive model of wage adjustment. Since it is the subject of Chapter 11, we will be brief about it here. Just note that there is a hidden assumption behind a supply and demand diagram like Fig. 10.10, or more precisely behind the labour demand curve in it. The labour demand curve is given by the decreasing marginal product of labour, since labour is demanded up to the point where the marginal cost of an additional unit of labour – the real wage – equals the marginal revenue product. However, behind this construction is the tacit assumption that the wage paid to the workers does not affect their productivity. In Chapter 11 we argue that if we keep all other characteristics of the competitive labour market, but add the feature that productivity may depend positively on real wages, then the traditional labour demand curve 'disappears', and firms may choose a combination of a real wage and a number of people demanded inside the labour supply curve. The result may well be unemployment without any tendency for falling wages. Wages fail to adjust because firms do not *want* lower wages, and unemployment is involuntary since individual unemployed workers would really like to work at the going wage rate.

Trade unions

Unionization of the labour market represents a more 'brutal', but realistic and therefore important, departure from the competitive model. It is simply assumed that the supply side of the labour market (and sometimes also the demand side) is not atomistic, since the workers are organized in a trade union that takes care of their interests. The trade union sets the wage rate and the labour market therefore does not work competitively, but more like a monopoly market. As we shall see in Chapter 12, this may well imply that the wage rate chosen by the trade union will be so high that the wage-taking labour supply of all the workers on the labour market exceeds the labour demand of the firms. Hence there is unemployment, but there is no tendency for falling wages, since the wage rate is what those who set it want it to be. The unemployment will be involuntary at the individual level, since the unemployed workers would really like to work at the wage rate set by the union. At the collective level, however, the unemployment has something voluntary about it, since it is due to the fact that workers have decided to organize to exert influence on the wage rate and, having obtained market power through a union, let this union *choose* a wage rate that is so high that unemployment results.

In this book we focus on efficiency wage setting and trade union behaviour to explain why real wages do not adjust to eliminate long-run unemployment. To motivate this focus, we will now argue that a large part of long-run unemployment cannot be explained by frictional or search unemployment.

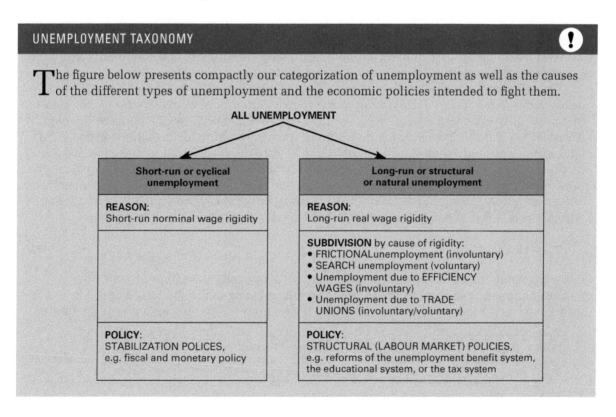

UNEMPLOYMENT TAXONOMY

The figure below presents compactly our categorization of unemployment as well as the causes of the different types of unemployment and the economic policies intended to fight them.

ALL UNEMPLOYMENT

Short-run or cyclical unemployment	Long-run or structural or natural unemployment
REASON: Short-run norminal wage rigidity	**REASON:** Long-run real wage rigidity
	SUBDIVISION by cause of rigidity: • FRICTIONALunemployment (involuntary) • SEARCH unemployment (voluntary) • Unemployment due to EFFICIENCY WAGES (involuntary) • Unemployment due to TRADE UNIONS (involuntary/voluntary)
POLICY: STABILIZATION POLICES, e.g. fiscal and monetary policy	**POLICY:** STRUCTURAL (LABOUR MARKET) POLICIES, e.g. reforms of the unemployment benefit system, the educational system, or the tax system

10.5 How large is frictional and search unemployment?

Let us now return to the simple formula that relates the number of unemployed workers to the labour force and the number of employed workers, say in a specific month, $U_t = L_t - E_t$. For simplicity assume that the labour force is constant, $L_t = L$ in all months t, so that the formula is $U_t = L - E_t$. How can the number of unemployed workers possibly change from month t to month $t + 1$? In exactly two ways.

Some people who are employed in month t may lose or quit their jobs from t to $t + 1$, causing an increase in unemployment. We denote by s_t the 'separation rate' of month t, that is, the fraction of the employed in period t who lose their jobs from t to $t + 1$. Then the increase in the number of unemployed coming from job separation can be written as $s_t E_t$. Some people who are unemployed in month t may find a job from t to $t + 1$, which gives a reduction in unemployment. If we denote the 'job finding rate' of month t by f_t, this reduction in unemployment is $f_t U_t$. The flow diagram in Fig. 10.11 shows the two ways the number of unemployed workers can change.

The total change in the number of unemployed workers from month t to $t + 1$ is thus:

$$U_{t+1} - U_t = s_t E_t - f_t U_t.$$

If we divide both sides by L and remember that in any month the rate of unemployment is $u_t = U_t/L$, we get:

$$u_{t+1} - u_t = s_t \frac{E_t}{L} - f_t u_t.$$

Now use $E_t = L - U_t$ to get:

$$u_{t+1} = (1 - s_t - f_t)u_t + s_t.$$

Given the evolution of s_t and f_t and an initial rate of unemployment, this equation describes how the rate of unemployment evolves over time. This law has nothing in particular to do with frictional or search unemployment. It is simply an identity that has to hold for unemployment in general (given a constant labour force).

We will now focus on a 'stationary environment' where both s_t and f_t are constant over time, that is, $s_t = s$ and $f_t = f$ in all months, t. You may find this assumption strange. Shouldn't the possibility of finding a job, the job finding rate f_t, depend on how much unemployment there is? We make this assumption deliberately since we want to focus entirely on frictional and search unemployment. We do not want it to be particularly difficult to find a job. We want to find out how much unemployment there will be if the only reasons for unemployment are that when people lose their job for some reason, they do not start in new jobs immediately, either for purely technical/practical/formal reasons, or because they decide to search for an attractive job offer. The dynamics of the rate of unemployment now simply become:

$$u_{t+1} = (1 - s - f)u_t + s. \tag{1}$$

Here we should think of s as a relatively small positive fraction, perhaps around 0.02, corresponding to 2 per cent of the employed workers losing their jobs each month.[4] If everyone who loses a job starts in a new one 'the first day of the next month', the job finding

---

4. In their article 'The Cyclical Behavior of the Gross Flows of US Workers', *Brooking Papers on Economic Activity*, **2**, 1990, Olivier Blanchard and Peter Diamond find a monthly job separation rate for the USA over the period January 1968 to May 1986 of 2.9 per cent. In the period from 1968 to 1986 there was an increasing trend in the rate of unemployment in the USA (see Fig. 10.9), so the separation rate under the stationary conditions we want to focus on here is probably somewhat smaller.

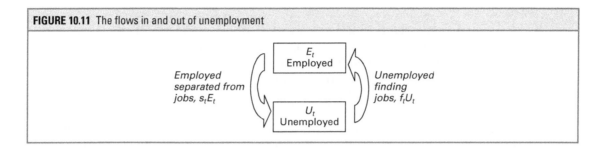

FIGURE 10.11 The flows in and out of unemployment

rate would be 1, but since voluntary job search will pull f down, we should probably think of f as a fraction that is somewhat smaller than 1, e.g. $f = 0.8$. This will imply that the parenthesis $(1 - s - f)$ in front of u_t in Eq. (1) is a positive number smaller than one, so the dynamics given by (1) are such that u_t converges monotonically to a constant level u (draw a diagram with u_{t+1} as a function of u_t and iterate) given by $u = (1 - s - f)u + s$, or:

$$u = \frac{s}{s + f}. \qquad (2)$$

One can compute the u given by (2) for various values of s and f. From the above, a value 0.02 for s could be realistic. If the value of f is to be explained only by frictions or search, a value of 0.8 seems small. A large s and a small f tend to make the u in (2) large, so inserting $s = 0.02$ and $f = 0.8$ should give an indication of a large rate of frictional and search unemployment. With these parameters the computed u is around 2.4 per cent. Even if we send f all the way down to 0.5, which is surely low, the computed u will still be lower than 4 per cent (3.8 per cent to be precise).

We conclude that there seems to be important elements of structural unemployment that cannot be explained by frictions or search. There seems, therefore, to be good reasons to investigate other explanations of structural unemployment.

10.6 Summary

1. Unemployment implies individual costs in the form of income losses that cannot be fully insured as well as psychological stress. Unemployment implies a social cost as well. For an involuntarily unemployed worker the real value of the goods and services needed to compensate for the sacrifice of leisure (*MRS*) is smaller than the going real wage. When firms maximize profits, the real wage equals or is smaller than the marginal product of labour (*MPL*). Hence involuntary unemployment implies $MPL > MRS$. This means that a social gain could be achieved if some unemployed workers got jobs, since the extra output generated by additional employment would more than suffice to compensate the newly employed workers. Because unemployment is a social waste, it is a main concern of economic policy makers.

2. The rate of unemployment is the fraction of unemployed in the total labour force, measured at a given point in time. The annual rate of unemployment is the simple average of the rates of unemployment in each day or month of the year. A large number of workers are affected by unemployment in each year, typically around 20 per cent of the labour force in countries like the USA and Denmark, but only some of the unemployed are out of work all of the year, whereas the rest have unemployment spells of varying but shorter duration.

3. The long-term unemployed during a given year are those who were unemployed more than a given fraction of the year, for example more than half of the year. Long-term unemployment is the part of overall unemployment carried by the long-term unemployed. It is mainly the long-term part of unemployment that causes serious individual costs, but for the social cost the overall (average) unemployment rate is also important.

4. Unemployment and vacancies can coexist because the labour market's match between 'people wanting jobs' and 'jobs wanting people' is not perfect. The Beveridge curve is a plot over time of the vacancy rate against the unemployment rate and gives an indication of the degree of mismatch in the labour market. For given structural mismatch problems, the Beveridge curve should be a stable decreasing relationship. If it shifts inwards or outwards, it can be an indication of decreased or increased structural problems in the labour market, respectively.

5. The empirical evidence shows that (i) there is a clear negative relationship between the rate of growth in GDP and the change in the rate of unemployment, (ii) there is no upward or downward trend in the rate of unemployment in the very long run, (iii) there is a lot of variability in the rate of unemployment in the short run, (iv) there is a lot of persistence in annual rates of unemployment, and (v) long-term unemployment varies positively and more than proportionally with overall unemployment.

6. When annual rates of unemployment are at their lowest, there is still a substantial amount of unemployment, seemingly around 4 per cent, and annual unemployment rates seem to fluctuate around a natural unemployment rate of about 5–7 per cent. The natural rate of unemployment seems to shift over time and can be different in different regions of the world.

7. The presence of unemployment reflects that wage rigidities prevent the real wage from adjusting to equalize supplies and demands for labour. Economists find it useful to distinguish between short-run nominal wage rigidities, which are fundamental for explaining the cyclical fluctuations in unemployment, and long-run real wage rigidities, which cause the positive and constant trend level of structural unemployment. This part of the book is focused on the natural rate of unemployment and long-run real wage rigidities.

8. This chapter briefly presented the following four causes of long-run real wage rigidity and structural unemployment: (i) labour market frictions, (ii) job search, (iii) efficiency wages and (iv) market power of trade unions. The last two of these potential causes for structural unemployment are dealt with in the following two chapters.

9. Studying a model of the flows in and out of unemployment, we derived a simple formula linking the rate of unemployment to the separation rate (the fraction of employed who lose their jobs in a month) and the job finding rate (the fraction of unemployed finding a job from one month to the next). Assuming a stationary environment with constant separation and job finding rates, and assuming realistic values for these rates, we found that only a minor part of structural unemployment seems to be due to labour market frictions or search. This gives good reason to study the explanation for structural unemployment offered by the theories of efficiency wages and trade unions presented in our two next chapters.

Exercise 1. The definition of unemployment

Exactly how is the rate of unemployment defined and measured in your own country according to the (most) official statistics? In particular, how is the number of unemployed counted? How is the labour force measured?

Exercise 2. The social cost of unemployment

This exercise asks you to explain the social cost of unemployment more or less as it was done in this chapter, but to do so using a standard diagram that you will see again in Chapter 19.

In the figure below, illustrating a particular labour market, the curve *MPL* depicts the marginal product of labour as this depends on the total number of workers employed. The curve is decreasing because of the presence of fixed factors or because of productivity differences among workers or both. For each worker there is a certain marginal rate of substitution of output for leisure, *MRS*, the amount of goods it takes to compensate the worker for the loss of leisure and home production resulting from having a job. The *MRS* curve in the figure shows how this marginal rate of substitution varies with employment when workers are lined up in order of increasing *MRS*.

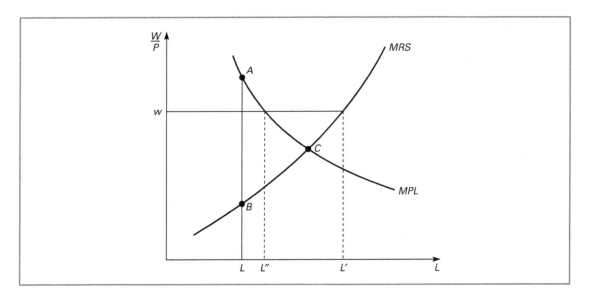

1. Explain that if the individual workers are wage and price takers then the *MRS* curve is identical to the labour supply curve, such that if the going real wage rate is the *w* indicated, total labour supply should be the *L'* indicated, that is, the labour supply coming from workers with an *MRS* below *w*.

2. Explain that if the firms that buy labour in the market considered are wage and price takers then their labour demand curve is given directly by the *MPL* curve, such that the labour demand arising from a wage rate of *w* is the *L"* indicated in the figure. Now assume that the firms take the nominal wage rate, *W*, as given, but, due to some kind of imperfect competition in the output market, profit maximization leads to the nominal price, *P*, being set as a mark-up over nominal marginal cost, that is, $P = m(W/MPL)$, where $m > 1$. Explain that to be in accordance with the profit-maximizing behaviour of firms, a combination of a real wage, *w*, and employment, *L*, must be such that at this combination, $W/P = MPL/m$, meaning that the labour demand curve is MPL/m. Indicate such a labour demand curve in the figure, and explain that under the circumstances described labour demand given *w* must be less than *L"*.

3. Explain that if there is involuntary unemployment (some workers, who would like to work at the going real wage, are without jobs) then the prevailing combination of real wage, w, and employment, L, must be strictly to the left of the MRS (labour supply) curve. Then explain that if firms are wage takers and maximize profits, the combination of w and L must be (weakly) to the left of the MPL curve.

4. Explain that if there is involuntary unemployment and the firms maximize profits then at the prevailing level of employment one must have $MPL > MRS$. Explain why the situation involves a social loss. Assume that the combination of real wage and employment is as indicated by w and L in the figure, a situation of involuntary unemployment compatible with profit maximization. Explain that the area of the triangle ABC represents the total social loss in the situation. Assume that the combination is instead w and L'', compatible with the firms being perfectly competitive, but still a situation of involuntary unemployment. Is there still a social loss and if so how large is it?

5. Return to the initial situation with real wage w and employment L, indicated in the figure. Assume that some marginal, hitherto unemployed workers are hired at the wage rate w, so that employment increases to a level above L, but below L''. Indicate the social gain that this gives rise to as an area in the figure. Is there a way to make everybody enjoy part of the gain?

Exercise 3. The duration of unemployment

Assume that you are told that in some year the (average) unemployment rate was 8.3 per cent. Does this mean that 8.3 per cent of the people in the labour force were without jobs the whole year, or does it mean that all people in the labour force were without jobs for one month during the year? Or does it mean something else, and if so what does it (typically) mean? We said in this chapter that with respect to the individual costs of unemployment it is long-term unemployment that is most severe. What is meant by long-term unemployment and why is this a particularly bad kind of unemployment?

Exercise 4. Coefficients of correlation

Below is a table showing the rate of unemployment in the USA for the period from 1965 to 1975.

t	u_t
1965	4.51
1966	3.78
1967	3.84
1968	3.55
1969	3.51
1970	4.98
1971	5.95
1972	5.60
1973	4.88
1974	5.62
1975	8.47

Source: OECD Economic Outlook.

1. Find u_{t-1} by lagging the numbers in the table, such that, for instance, $u_{1966-1} = u_{1965} = 4.51$. There are only 10 pairwise observations between u_t and u_{t-1}. Why?

2. Compute the coefficient of correlation between u_t and u_{t-1}, using the formula for the coefficient of correlation, where $x_t \equiv u_{t-1}$:

$$\rho = \frac{\sum_{t=1}^{T}(u_t - \bar{u})(x_t - \bar{x})}{\sqrt{\sum_{t=1}^{T}(u_t - \bar{u})^2} \cdot \sqrt{\sum_{t=1}^{T}(x_t - \bar{x})^2}},$$

and $\bar{u}$ and $\bar{x}$ are the averages, $\bar{u} = (1/T)\sum_{t=1}^{T} u_t$ and $\bar{x} = (1/T)\sum_{t=1}^{T} x_t$. In this case $\bar{u}$ and $\bar{x}$ are close to each other. Explain.

3. Next, compute the coefficient of correlation between u_t and u_{t+1}. How does it relate to the one between u_t and u_{t-1}? Explain your findings.

Exercise 5. Types of unemployment: reasons and policies

The box on page 295 presented a certain categorization of unemployment according to type. Explain the underlying motivations for this categorization, theoretical (in terms of different types of rigidities) as well as empirical. Explain also the figure's categorization of policies meant to fight unemployment, in particular why these policies are different for different types of unemployment.

Exercise 6. The size of frictional unemployment

Assume that due to normal 'job rotation', 2 per cent of workers lose or quit their jobs every month. Assume further that the only reasons why workers who are separated from their jobs do not find new jobs immediately are traditional labour market frictions, so all unemployment is frictional, and that these frictions are such that all workers who become unemployed in one month start in their new jobs the first working day in the next month. How large is the rate of frictional unemployment under these circumstances? How large is it if 2.9 per cent of all workers are separated from their jobs each month and only 90 per cent of those who are unemployed in one month find jobs in the next month? Why do we believe that not all structural unemployment is simply frictional?

CHAPTER 11

Efficiency wages and unemployment

This chapter is concerned with the causes and consequences of a minimal departure from the competitive labour market model. We keep all the traditional characteristics that are usually seen as underlying competitive market behaviour such as a multiplicity of buyers and sellers, a homogeneous product, etc. We then just add the feature that the productivity of labour may depend positively on the wage. We will demonstrate that there are good justifications for this idea, and that the macroeconomic consequences, mainly with respect to structural unemployment, are important.

We start out in Section 11.1 by giving a simple example of efficiency wages. In Section 11.2 we then consider the consequences of efficiency wages in a partial equilibrium framework, focusing on the optimal wage setting in the individual firm. Section 11.3 takes one step back to discuss the reasons for efficiency wages in more detail, that is, the reasons why paying higher wages may be a way for an employer to increase the productivity of his employees. This section also considers some empirical evidence in support of efficiency wage theory. Section 11.4 analyses efficiency wages in a macroeconomic setting, developing a general equilibrium model determining the equilibrium real wage and the structural rate of unemployment. On this basis we discuss some possible structural policies to fight involuntary unemployment.

11.1 Efficiency wages: a basic example

The idea that compensation is important for productivity could well be an old one. Consider a cotton farm where labour input comes from slaves owned by the landlord. Assume that the landlord does not care about the well-being of the slaves, but sees them only as labour power. The landlord provides food and shelter for the slaves and their families and will be faced with a basic trade-off when he decides on the quantity and quality of food and shelter to provide. Think of this amount as the slaves' 'wage'.

The wage has to have a certain level just to keep the slaves alive. Above this minimum level, a higher wage will mean less miserable lives and better health for the slaves, and better health means higher productivity. So, a higher wage has a positive influence on the profits of the farm due to the improved productivity of the slaves, and a negative influence due to the higher costs of providing the slaves with the necessities of life. When the wage is still close to the minimum level, the productivity effect should be large and dominate the cost effect, because a higher wage in this range will prevent the slaves from being physically weak and ill most of the time. The wage should thus, for pure profit reasons, be raised above this minimum. However, at sufficiently high wages, the cost effect of an increased wage will dominate the productivity effect, since only a little further improvement in the slaves' health conditions can be obtained by higher wages if the health conditions are already good. So the wage should, for pure profit reasons, be set lower than that. In between there has to be an 'optimal wage', a level of provision of food and shelter for the slaves at which the positive productivity effect and the negative cost effect just offset each other. Starting from this optimal wage, a 1 per cent increase in the wage, meaning a 1 per cent increase in the labour cost of one slave, must also imply a 1 per cent increase in the output of each slave. If the increase in productivity (production per slave) were larger than 1 per cent, then the 1 per cent increase in wage would increase profits, and the original wage could not be optimal. At the optimal wage the elasticity of productivity with respect to wage thus has to be exactly 1, a famous condition of which you will hear much more in this chapter.

Under slavery there are pure health reasons for a positive influence of wages on productivity. In modern economies health may still motivate such an influence, but as we shall see, there may be other reasons as well. In so far as there is a positive connection, a firm will be faced with a trade-off concerning wages similar to the one faced by the slave owner. This trade-off in wage determination may have serious macroeconomic implications, as this chapter will demonstrate.

A positive influence of pay on productivity can be the cause of structural unemployment and may therefore motivate structural policies intended to fight the permanent part of unemployment.

11.2 A first look at the consequences of efficiency wages in a partial equilibrium framework

A simple partial equilibrium model

Consider a single firm that produces output from labour input L. Let the total revenue of the firm be $zR(L)$, where we assume that $R'(L) > 0$, and $R''(L) < 0$, and where z is just a multiplicative shift parameter. We can think of revenue as price times production, so $zR(L) = zp(f(L))f(L)$, where $f(L)$ is the production function, $p(y)$ is price as a function of output $y = f(L)$, and z is a (demand) shock to p, or a (supply) shock to f. If the firm is a perfect competitor on the output market the function p is constant, and in that case the revenue curve R must have its property $R'' < 0$ from $f'' < 0$. If the firm is large on the output market, $p(y)$ can be a downward-sloping curve associated with a downward-sloping (inverse) demand curve.

For a clean argument we will first, and only temporarily, depart from the conditions usually seen as underlying wage-taking behaviour and assume that the firm is a monopsonist, the sole buyer, on the labour market. The firm faces an upward-sloping labour supply curve, $L^s(w)$, coming from many wage-taking workers, as illustrated in Fig. 11.1. The firm sets the (real) wage w, and it also decides how much labour L to buy. It must, of course, obey the restriction $L \leq L^s(w)$. The profits of the firm are $zR(L) - wL$.

Such a firm would never choose a combination (w, L) above the labour supply curve, like the point A in Fig. 11.1. From a position above the labour supply curve the firm can lower the wage rate and buy the same amount of labour, that is, it can move vertically downwards from A towards B, which lowers labour costs, wL, leaves revenue, $zR(L)$, unchanged, and hence unambiguously raises profits. Likewise, moving upwards from B means buying the same amount of labour more expensively, which unambiguously lowers profits. Therefore the firm will position itself *on* the labour supply curve which means that there will be no unemployment: the firm wants to buy the full amount of labour supplied at the going wage rate.

This argument assumes that productivity does not depend on pay. The wage rate does not enter the revenue curve. Assume now that there is a positive influence of the wage rate on the productivity of labour, and that the relationship is given by the function $a(w)$, where a is productivity and $a' > 0$. The revenue curve will then be $zR(a(w)L)$, which we can think

FIGURE 11.1 Positioning oneself above or on the labour supply curve

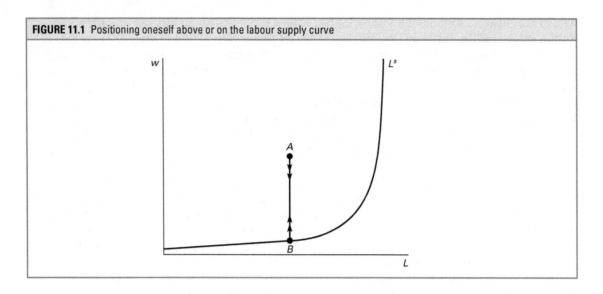

of as $zp(f(a(w)L))f(a(w)L)$. A first important insight is that it is no longer *necessarily* true that moving downwards from a point like A increases profits, or that moving upwards from a point like B decreases profits. Moving upwards from B still means that the firm buys the same number of hours of work at a higher price per hour, which raises labour costs wL, but it also means that the revenue, $zR(a(w)L)$, increases, because $a(w)$ increases. The latter effect may dominate, and in this case the firm will prefer a point above B to the point B itself.

Analysing the model

The phenomenon of a positive dependence of productivity on wage is called 'efficiency wages' (wages that work to promote productive efficiency). We have argued that efficiency wages may undermine the argument that a monopsonist wage setter would *never* position itself above the labour supply curve. To show that the firm's optimal combination of real wage and employment could actually be above the labour supply curve, one must study the full optimization problem of the firm which is to choose w and L to maximize profits $zR(a(w)L) - wL$, subject to the constraint $L \le L^s(w)$. It is a usual trick to first look at the unconstrained optimization (disregarding the constraint $L \le L^s(w)$). If this gives a combination (w^*, L^*) that fulfils $L^* \le L^s(w^*)$, the constrained optimum will also be (w^*, L^*).

The first-order conditions for an unconstrained maximization of $zR(a(w)L) - wL$ with respect to w and L are:

$$zR'(a(w)L)a'(w)L = L, \tag{1}$$

$$zR'(a(w)L)a(w) = w. \tag{2}$$

From the second of these, $zR'(a(w)L) = w/a(w)$. Inserting into the first condition gives:

$$\frac{a'(w)w}{a(w)} = 1. \tag{3}$$

You will recognize this as the condition we derived in the discussion of the slave economy above: the wage rate should be set at a point where the elasticity of labour productivity with respect to the real wage is 1 (if there is such a wage rate and if the optimum is interior). The intuition is also the same, but worth elaborating now that we have a formal framework.

In the absence of efficiency wages, output and revenue are produced by labour input measured *in hours*, L, and profits are $zR(L) - wL$. Whatever the optimal value of L turns out to be, it must be profit maximizing to buy that amount at the lowest possible cost, w, per unit, so the firm should set w at the lowest level required for buying L. In the presence of efficiency wages, output and revenue are produced by labour input measured in *efficiency units*, $a(w)L$, and profits are $zR(a(w)L) - wL = zR(a(w)L) - (w/a(w))a(w)L$. Whatever the optimal value of $a(w)L$ turns out to be (and note that for varying w one can keep $a(w)L$ fixed by adjusting L appropriately), it must be profit maximizing to acquire that amount of labour in efficiency units at the lowest possible cost, $w/a(w)$, per unit, so w should be set to minimize $w/a(w)$. The numerator here is the price of one hour of work, and the denominator is the number of efficiency units arising from one work hour, so the fraction is the price per efficiency unit. Hence, $w/a(w)$ should be minimized which, if the minimizing wage rate is interior (not 0 and not infinite), requires that a 1 per cent increase in w exactly gives a 1 per cent increase in a (if it gave more, $w/a(w)$ could be lowered by increasing w, etc.). This is exactly what is stated in (3), the so-called 'Solow condition'.[1]

THE SOLOW CONDITION

If the labour productivity of workers in a firm depends positively on the workers' pay through an efficiency function, $a(w)$, then an (interior) optimal wage rate w^* of the firm depends only on this efficiency function, and w^* is given by the condition that the elasticity of productivity with respect to real wage is 1, condition (3) above.

To find the optimal labour demand, L^*, one inserts w^* into (2) and solves for L. For w fixed at w^*, this equation is the usual one saying that the marginal cost of one *hour* of work should equal the marginal revenue that the hour gives rise to. Still assuming an interior optimum, (w^*, L^*) is simply given as the solution to the two equations (2) and (3). It may well be that $L^* < L^s(w^*)$, and in this case the unconstrained optimum is also the constrained optimum. Furthermore, *if it happens to be the case that $L^* < L^s(w^*)$, then there is unemployment in an equilibrium with a fully adjusted wage rate.*

Can one be sure that the unconstrained optimum is indeed interior and that it is given by the first-order conditions? This depends on the shapes of the functions R and a. Assume that the efficiency function, $a(w)$, looks like the thick curve shown in Fig. 11.2. The wage rate w has to be above a certain minimal level, v, to obtain positive productivity at all, and the marginal increase in productivity obtained by a given increase in the wage is decreasing in w, but possibly large for wages close to v.

For any given wage rate w, the fraction $a(w)/w$ is the slope of the ray through the origin and the point $(w, a(w))$. For profit maximization this slope should be maximized, since $w/a(w)$ should be minimized. The maximal slope is obtained just where the ray becomes a tangent to the a curve as indicated by the ray most to the left in Fig. 11.2, that is, at the wage rate w^* where the slope $a'(w^*)$ of the a curve is equal to the slope $a(w^*)/w^*$ of the ray. Note that $a'(w^*) = a(w^*)/w^*$ is equivalent to the Solow condition.

Given an efficiency curve as in Fig. 11.2, the optimal wage rate is indeed interior $(0 < w^* < \infty)$ and given by the Solow condition. Standard assumptions on the revenue curve, e.g. $R'(0) = \infty$ and $R'(\infty) \le 0$, ensure that the full unconstrained optimum is interior and given by the first-order conditions. The shape of the efficiency curve in Fig. 11.2 was not just chosen to ensure a well-behaved optimum. It seems reasonable, and it was the kind of shape that was implicitly argued in our slave economy example above.

---

1. The condition is named after the Robert M. Solow you know from growth theory. He once gave his students pretty much the profit maximization problem we study here as an exercise and asked them to derive the Solow condition.

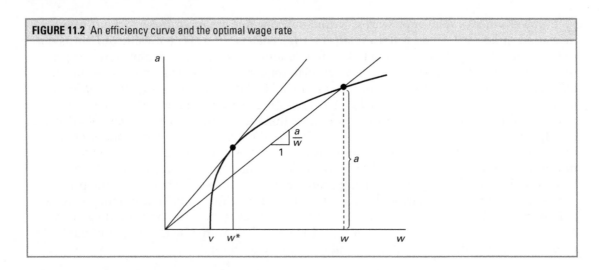

FIGURE 11.2 An efficiency curve and the optimal wage rate

We started this chapter by saying that we would consider a minimal departure from the competitive labour market and keep all the other characteristics usually seen as underlying wage-taking behaviour. We then, nevertheless, assumed that the firm was a monopsonist on the labour market. However, if there were many buying firms the labour market would, with the efficiency wage effect, work essentially as under monopsony.

Usually we would say that many firms should imply that each firm is a wage taker, so no firm sets a wage rate. The informal argument behind this is that if there are many buyers, *no buyer can get away with lowering the price* (compared to the 'going market price'), because then no one would want to sell to that buyer, and *no buyer would be interested in setting a higher price*, since the buyer already gets the demanded quantity at the going price. Therefore each buyer takes the price as given. Here, however, we have a situation where a buyer may *want* to pay a price above the market clearing level. Nothing prevents a buyer from setting a higher price. If there were many firms on the labour market, each identical to the firm considered above, then each of these firms would have an unconstrained optimum, (w^*, L^*), identical to the one described above, and total (unconstrained) labour demand would be L^* times the number of firms which could still be smaller than $L^s(w^*)$. There would then be unemployment in an equilibrium with fully adjusted wages. Thus we do not have to think of the labour market as a monopsony. All the characteristics usually seen as underlying perfect competition, many buyers and many sellers, etc., can be fulfilled, and still, with the efficiency wage effect, the labour market will work as described.

Discussion of the model's main implications

The partial equilibrium model above shows that efficiency wages can *potentially* cause unemployment in an equilibrium with fully adjusted wages if $L^s(w^*)$ happens to be greater than L^* times the number of firms. In the partial equilibrium model efficiency wages do not *necessarily* imply unemployment.

Assuming that there is unemployment in equilibrium, the model has the implication that variations in the supply/demand shift parameter z do not affect w, since the optimal wage rate is given entirely by the efficiency function $a(w)$. Changes in z only affect L, and high values of z go with high values of L.

This fits well with, and can be part of an explanation of, one of the most important empirical facts of the business cycle: that real wages are weakly correlated with output over the cycle, while employment varies positively and is strongly correlated with output. For this consideration we view z as a shock variable.

However, the same result does not fit well with the stylized fact of growth, that in the long run real wages increase in proportion to labour productivity. Now we view z as a long-run trend in productivity. In the model above, a steady and gradual increase in z will have no influence on the real wage rate. Counterfactually, the real wage will remain at a given level despite the steady growth in productivity.

One might think that this is a serious problem for the efficiency wage model. However, the phenomenon is an artefact of the simple partial equilibrium framework we have considered. We will argue below that the productivity of the workers in each firm should really depend on the excess of the wage paid in the firm over the 'normal income' in society. For instance, what makes workers provide more effort is not the wage as such, but a wage rate in excess of what could normally be expected. Furthermore, if there is a trendwise increase in normal incomes due to an increasing trend in productivity, it should be the *relative* excess of the wage over normal income that motivates effort. So the efficiency function should be like $a(w) = \tilde{a}([w - v]/v)$, where $\tilde{a}$ is an increasing function and v is 'normal income'. In that case the optimal wage in each firm will be determined relative to v, and if v increases, so will w, while as long as v stays relatively constant, so will w. Hence, if the expected normal income is not affected (much) by short-run shocks to z, but is affected by permanent trend changes in z, then we can have a situation where the real wage rate does not respond (much) to random fluctuations in productivity, but does increase proportionally to permanent productivity. Exercise 2 as well as Exercise 6 below will ask you to perform some further analysis highlighting this point.

The essence of the explanation of unemployment offered by efficiency wage theory is this: employers (not employees) drive up wages to attain an optimal level of productivity from each hired worker, and the wages thus determined (by the employers) may be so high that the employers do not want to hire all the workers who want jobs at those wages. The unemployment that results is truly involuntary. The workers really want to have jobs at the going wages, and they are in no way responsible for wages being so high.

UNEMPLOYMENT AND FLUCTUATIONS IN THE PARTIAL EQUILIBRIUM EFFICIENCY WAGE MODEL

A positive dependence of workers' productivity on their pay may imply that firms, in order to extract an optimal work effort from each worker, drive up wages to a level where employers do not want to hire all the workers who would like to work. Hence efficiency wages can help to explain structural unemployment, that is, the coexistence of some unemployment and fully adjusted prices and wages. In the partial equilibrium efficiency wage model with unemployment, temporary demand and supply shocks do not affect the real wage, but give rise to fluctuations in employment.

The plausibility of the efficiency wage explanation of structural unemployment stands and falls with the plausibility of the efficiency wage phenomenon. Are there good reasons to believe that productivity is positively affected by wages?

11.3 The causes of efficiency wages

The four traditional reasons

Besides the health argument, which may not be very important in developed economies, usually four reasons are given for why labour productivity depends positively on (above average) pay.[2]

---

2. For more about these reasons and their implications, consult the short and informative survey by Janet Yellen, 'Efficiency Wage Models of Unemployment', *American Economic Review*, **74**, 1984, pp. 200–205.

1. Keeping the workers in the firm

Paying wages that are high relative to what the workers could otherwise earn gives the workers an incentive not to quit their jobs so easily. This reduces labour turnover in the firm and saves the firm costs of recruiting new employees who are not fully productive until they have been trained. Thus, on average the productivity of the workers in the firm will be higher.

2. Getting good workers when hiring

Every now and then some workers quit their jobs for various reasons and the firm will want to hire new employees. It is realistic to assume that when it hires new workers, the firm cannot perfectly observe the abilities of each applicant, and that workers with higher ability will also demand a higher wage to be willing to accept a job offer. By offering relatively high wages, the firm will thus be able to recruit the more able applicants, thereby obtaining a more favourable composition of its workforce. This raises average labour productivity in the firm.

3. Making the workers in the firm work hard – 1

Assume realistically that the firm cannot perfectly monitor the effort exerted by each and every worker all the time, but that it can from time to time, by some control mechanism, observe the effort levels of some of the workers. Assume further that workers who are caught not exerting an effort level as required by the firm are fired. A relatively high wage will then create an incentive for the individual worker to work hard (as hard as required) since the cost of being fired is the difference between the wage paid in the firm and the income that could be earned outside the firm through unemployment benefits or alternative jobs. Working less hard than required by the employer is sometimes called 'shirking', but note that the effort level required by the employer could well be high. The model of efficiency wages based on the motive explained here is often called the 'shirking model'.

4. Making the workers in the firm work hard – 2

While the incentive effect just described builds fully on self-interested 'rationality' in the usual sense, it may also be that workers who are paid well compared to what is normal will work hard simply because they feel that they are treated well and want to be nice to people who are nice to them. Note that here it is not the risk of being fired that motivates the worker to work hard, but pure *reciprocity*: the wish to respond to nice behaviour with nice behaviour. This is not irrationality. What is argued is that 'treating others as they treat you' increases a person's well-being, and therefore reciprocity is in full accordance with utility maximization. It is not just individual income and consumption that give utility. The other side of reciprocity is that a low wage will be responded to by low effort.[3]

A closer look at the shirking model

We will present the shirking model of efficiency wages in a little more detail to illustrate how the positive effect of wages on productivity may be given a microeconomic foundation.[4] Consider a firm that is currently employing a certain number of workers. Assume that for each worker the utility of working in the firm at the wage rate w exerting the effort level a is

3. The reciprocity-based model of efficiency wages was presented in the article by George A. Akerlof and Janet L. Yellen, 'The Fair Wage-Effort Hypothesis and Unemployment', *Quarterly Journal of Economics*, **105**, 1990, pp. 255–283. The article reports plenty of evidence that high wages in a firm *relative to 'normal wages'* imply high effort in the firm in question, and that low wages tend to create low effort, for 'emotional' reasons based on feelings of loyalty, gratitude, anger, injustice, etc.

4. In this subsection we study some elements (the worker incentive part) of the theory suggested by Carl Shapiro and Joseph E. Stiglitz in 'Equilibrium Unemployment as a Worker Discipline Device', *American Economic Review*, **74**, 1984, pp. 433–444.

$w - c(a)$, where $c(a)$ is a convex effort cost function, $c' > 0$, $c'' > 0$, $c'(0) = 0$, and $c'(a) \to \infty$ as $a \to \bar{a} > 0$, where possibly $\bar{a} = \infty$. The worker's utility outside the firm would be v, which reflects what can be obtained by unemployment benefits, home production, alternative jobs, etc. The worker gets utility v if he or she is fired.

The employer presents the worker with a contract $(w, \hat{a})$ that specifies the wage w paid and the effort level $\hat{a}$ demanded, where $\hat{a} < \bar{a}$. The employer can only imperfectly monitor the worker's effort. Shirking, which means $\hat{a} < \bar{a}$, is discovered with probability q, where $0 < q < 1$. A worker who is discovered shirking will be fired. The expected utility of an *employed* worker in case $a \geq \hat{a}$, which is non-shirking, is $w - c(a)$, and in case $a < \hat{a}$, which is shirking, the expected utility is $(1 - q)[w - c(a)] + qv$.

Since $c(a)$ enters negatively in the worker's utility, it never pays to provide 'too much' effort, so if a worker does not shirk the effort will be exactly as required, $a = \hat{a}$, and if a worker does shirk the effort will be $a = 0$. Therefore the condition stating that non-shirking is at least as good as shirking is $w - c(\hat{a}) \geq (1 - q)w + qv$, or:

$$w \geq v + \frac{c(\hat{a})}{q}. \tag{4}$$

This is the *no-shirking condition*, and it is illustrated in Fig. 11.3. From the point of view of the employer this condition states how high a wage must be paid for its workers to provide a given demanded effort level $\hat{a}$. Note that the required wage is increasing in the demanded effort $\hat{a}$, decreasing in the probability q of detecting shirking, and larger than, and increasing in, the alternative income v.

Since it does not pay for the employer to offer a higher wage than required for a given effort, one may as well write the no-shirking condition with equality. This gives the combinations of $\hat{a}$ and w indicated by the curve in Fig. 11.3. One can read the condition inversely as stating how large an effort each worker will provide for a given wage rate w. This corresponds to 'reading' Fig. 11.3 from the w-axis, that is, with w as the independent variable, and from this point of view the curve in Fig. 11.3 looks exactly like the curve in Fig. 11.2 above. The curve in Fig. 11.3 emerges from solving the no-shirking equation for $\hat{a}$. With the assumed properties of the function $c(a)$, this can always be done. One will then arrive at a function giving the effort level as a function of w, v, and q, that is, a function $\hat{a}(w, v, q)$. This function will only assume positive values for w larger than v, it will be increasing in w, decreasing in v, and increasing in q.

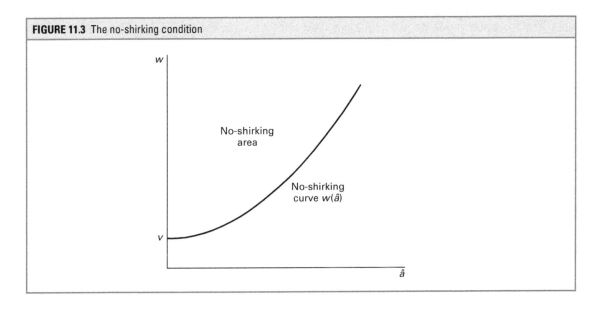

FIGURE 11.3 The no-shirking condition

One particular form of the effort cost function that fulfils all the assumptions above and allows us to solve the no-shirking equation analytically is $c(a) = \beta a^{1/\eta}$, where $\beta > 0$ and $0 < \eta < 1$. Using (4) with equality gives:

$$a = \hat{a}(w, v, q) = \left[\frac{q}{\beta}(w - v) \right]^{\eta}. \tag{5}$$

The efficiency function that was considered in the partial equilibrium model of Section 11.2 could well have taken the form $a(w) = k(w - v)^{\eta}$, where we have defined $k \equiv (q/\beta)^{\eta}$. Indeed, in Fig. 11.2 the efficiency function was drawn exactly that way.

The shirking model of efficiency wages studied in this section gives mainly three insights. First, it gives us an optimizing behaviour rationale for the idea of a positive effect of wages on productivity. Second, it suggests that it is only for wages above a certain base level that the positive effect on productivity starts to be felt. Third, it gives the interpretation of that base level as, more or less, the 'normal' income that a worker could obtain if separated from the firm. This normal income is therefore often referred to as the worker's 'outside option'.

Note that the other three motives for efficiency wages mentioned above have the same character. It is only if a firm's wage is above normal pay that workers will have a special incentive to stay in a firm, or to apply for a job in a firm, or have reason to feel particularly well treated by the firm. Therefore it is only for wages above an alternative or normal level that one should expect positive effort, and more effort for higher wages. So, all the motivations for efficiency wages point to efficiency functions like $a = k(w - v)^{\eta}$.

Empirical evidence in support of efficiency wages

We have already mentioned in Footnote 3 that Akerlof and Yellen have provided empirical evidence supporting their theory of efficiency wages based on reciprocity. A survey by the Swedish economists Jonas Agell and Helge Bennmarker is worth mentioning as well.[5] The paper presents the results from a survey among Swedish human resource managers. The survey is more representative than earlier surveys and includes many firms (1,200) and covers the relevant production sectors and firm size categories. The response rate obtained was very high (75.1 per cent).

An additional feature that makes the Swedish survey particularly interesting is that by the spring of 1999, when the survey was done, unemployment was high, around 10 per cent after having peaked at 13.6 per cent in 1994, while inflation was close to zero and had been very low for some years, on average 1 per cent per year over the preceding five years. This is a good environment for studying wage rigidity and resistance to wage reductions. Since unemployment was high, real wages should fall in the absence of real wage rigidity, and since inflation was low, real wage cuts of substantial size could only be achieved by nominal wage cuts. Hence, to see if firms resisted real wage cuts one could simply ask the human resource managers if they had cut (nominal) wages and related questions.

Table 11.1 presents some of Agell and Bennmarker's results in the form of some of the questions asked and some crude statistics on the answers obtained. From the table's first line it appears that only 3.2 per cent of the firms answered in the affirmative to the question whether they had cut regular base pay at any time during the crisis years of the 1990s (and most of the firms that had cut wages reported that they had done so for only a few employees, not for employees in general). This means that wage cutting by firms was not widespread despite very high unemployment.

---

5. Jonas Agell and Helge Bennmarker, 'Wage Incentives and Wage Rigidity: A Representative View from Within', *Labour Economics*, **14**, 2007, pp. 347–369.

TABLE 11.1 Selected results from Swedish survey by Agell and Bennmarker

Question	Answer
1. Cut base pay during crisis years of the 1990s?	3.2% affirmative
2. Encountered undercutters?	13.5% affirmative
3. Rejected offers by undercutters?	89.6% affirmative
4. Undercutting rejected because it 'violates firm's personnel policy; creates internal conflict'?	29.5–41.7% affirmative depending on sector
5. Extent to which it can be evaluated if an employee performs satisfactorily?	49.3% less than certain about performance
6. Implication for work effort if wages/salaries are increased in comparable firms?	65.9% answered impairment, great or small
7. Do employees who are dissatisfied with their pay normally reduce effort?	49.0% affirmative
8. Do employees who are dissatisfied with their pay normally seek employment elsewhere?	58.6% affirmative

Source: Jonas Agell and Helge Bennmarker, 'Wage Incentives and Wage Rigidity: A Representative View from Within', *Labour Economics*, **14**, 2007, pp. 347–369.

The next two lines are related to the first one. Active underbidding by workers (job seekers offering to work under conditions inferior to those normally offered to new employees) was quite rare despite the circumstances. Even more striking, when the firms were faced with undercutters a huge 89.6 per cent of them rejected the offers, which may explain why undercutting is so rare.

These findings are consistent with the theory of efficiency wages. As we have just seen, to induce an appropriate level of productivity each firm must pay an *individual* wage that is sufficiently high relative to *normal* pay, or the outside option. This outside option is, of course, heavily influenced by what other firms pay. Hence, the individual firm may be reluctant to be the first to cut wages because, as long as the other firms have not yet cut their wages, this will imply a substantial loss of productivity. If the firms could coordinate to cut wages simultaneously the productivity drop would not be large because normal pay would drop at the same time, but such a coordination task is too complex in an economy with hundreds of thousands of firms. Hence the theory of efficiency wages may imply some 'relative wage resistance' (reluctance to decrease one's own wage compared with the wages of other firms) that can provide an explanation for the findings in the first three lines of Table 11.1.

Other explanations could be possible, and therefore the survey of Agell and Bennmarker includes some questions that relate more directly to the theory of efficiency wages. As one can see from the fourth line of the table, when the managers were asked to explain *why* they would not accept the offers of undercutters, a substantial fraction of them indicated the reason that acceptance would 'violate the firm's personnel policy; create internal conflict', a motivation clearly related to how pay affects average productivity.

The managers were also asked how well they can monitor work effort. This is of importance for the shirking model where the assumption of imperfect monitoring is essential. The fifth line of the table shows that around half the firms indicated that they were less than certain about work performance.

The table's sixth line shows the question of most direct relevance for efficiency wages. It asks the subtle question how workers' effort would be affected by a wage increase in *other* firms. According to efficiency wage theory this should reduce effort by increasing the workers' outside option. As can be seen, a great majority of firms answered that a wage increase in other firms would indeed affect work effort in their own firm negatively.

The seventh and eighth lines of the table show that it is widely believed among managers that employees who feel their pay is too low will reduce their effort or seek employment elsewhere. These answers are in line with the reciprocity motivation and the labour turnover motivation for efficiency wages, respectively.

Overall the survey by Agell and Bennmarker provides a good deal of evidence that the productivity of a firm's employees is positively affected by the excess of the firm's wages over normal incomes.

FOUNDATIONS OF EFFICIENCY WAGES

Theory and evidence suggest that workers' productivity depends positively on their pay. From a theoretical as well as an empirical perspective, it is *the excess* **of** the firm's wages over normal incomes that should affect the productivity of employees positively. The positive dependence of productivity on above-normal pay is the central idea of efficiency wage theory.

11.4 Efficiency wages in a macroeconomic framework

In Section 11.2 we took the revenue curve of the individual firm as given. This was what made it a *partial equilibrium* analysis. We will now consider the full production side of the economy and be specific about how each firm's revenue is associated with the demand for its output, and how this demand is derived from the behaviour of the household sector of the economy. Our analysis will consequently be one of *general equilibrium*. This will enable us to show that the equilibrium unemployment rate in an economy with efficiency wages will indeed be positive; a result we could not establish with certainty in our partial equilibrium framework.

We will study a general equilibrium model intended to picture relevant aspects of the entire (macro)economic system, just as we did in Parts 1, 2 and 3 on growth theory. There will be an important difference, however. The model of this chapter will have only one period and hence no capital and no savings. The only input in production will be labour, and the only task of consumers will be to allocate their total income and consumption across different products. This is because our focus is not on growth and capital accumulation, but on the determination of the rate of structural unemployment in a single period. As usual in economics we simplify dramatically, so our model will involve only the few aspects we find most important for the problem we are analysing.

A macroeconomic framework

We will take the view that the product of each firm is a little different from the product of any other firm, so that each firm is the sole producer of a specific type of output. Hence each firm is a 'local monopolist' and sets the price of the commodity type it produces. This does not mean that each firm necessarily has a lot of market power. Its output may be in close substitution with the products of other firms, making demand highly sensitive to price, implying that the control over the price cannot be exploited much.

Since firms are not price takers, but set prices themselves, there is imperfect competition in product markets. The particular form of imperfect competition where each firm is a local monopolist is called *monopolistic competition*. To be specific, we assume that there are n firms each producing a separate type of output. The number of firms is large so *each firm is large in its own output market, but small relative to the entire economy.*

The demand (curve) for each output type $i = 1, \ldots, n$ is

$$D(P_i) = \left(\frac{P_i}{P}\right)^{-\sigma} \frac{Y}{n}, \qquad \sigma > 1, \tag{6}$$

where P_i is the money price of output type i, and P is a price index for, or an average of, the money prices P_j of all output types $j = 1, \ldots, n$, so $P = P(P_1, \ldots, P_n)$, and $P(x, \ldots, x) = x$ for all x. The variable Y is an indicator of total demand in the economy and taken as given by the individual firm, since each firm is small relative to the economy. Equation (6) says that total demand is distributed over the output types in a way that reflects their relative prices: each product type gets the fraction $(1/n)(P_i/P)^{-\sigma}$ of total demand. There is a specific formula for $P(P_1, \ldots, P_n)$ that is appropriate given that the demand curves in (6) are supposed to come from households optimizing with specific utility functions, but we do not need the exact formula for our present purposes.

Since all the n firms are faced with identical demand curves and will be assumed to have identical production functions, the optimal prices they set *in equilibrium* (to be derived below) will be identical, and hence the value of the price index will be equal to this common price. In equilibrium therefore $P_i/P = 1$ for all i, and hence in equilibrium the demand for each firm's output is Y/n. Since each firm satisfies all demand, Y/n will also be the production of each firm, and thus the total production, or the GDP, will be n times Y/n, that is, Y. Hence the indicator of total demand, Y, is the economy's GDP and it will be determined endogenously in our complete theory.

According to (6), the demand for output of type i does not only depend on P_i, as perhaps suggested by the notation $D(P_i)$, but on all of P_i, P, Y and n. However, the individual producer of output type i only has influence over P_i. The demand curve $D(P_i)$ is *iso-elastic* and its constant price elasticity is σ, that is, $-D_i'(P_i)P_i/D_i(P_i) = \sigma$ (show this by taking logs on both sides of (6) and differentiate with respect to P_i). Note that we assume $\sigma > 1$. Otherwise (if $0 < \sigma < 1$) our theory would not be meaningful.[6]

This description of the economy's demand side is compatible with utility maximization by a household sector with a particular type of utility function, a so-called constant elasticity of substitution, CES, utility function, where the (constant) elasticity of substitution is σ. For our purposes we do not need the exact derivation, but Exercise 3 will ask you to do it yourself. As a by-product you will also get the appropriate formula for the price index P.

From (6) it is clear that σ measures the degree of substitution between the commodities. The larger σ is, the more sensitive is the demand for output of type i to P_i/P, since a higher σ means that consumers are more willing to substitute away from any specific output type towards other types if its relative price increases. Therefore the market power of each firm is smaller the larger σ is. In the limit where σ goes to infinity the firm has no market power at all, since if it tries to set P_i above P, it will lose all demand. So, $\sigma \to \infty$ corresponds to price-taking competitive behaviour which is thus contained as a special case in our analysis.

The production function of each firm i is simply:

$$Y_i = a_i L_i, \tag{7}$$

where L_i is labour input and a_i is the productivity of labour input. All firms are assumed to use one and the same type of labour, and this comes from the household sector of the economy. In the labour market each firm is just one out of many buyers, and labour market conditions are similar to those underlying perfect competition (many buyers and sellers, homogeneous product, etc.). An efficiency wage effect can, nevertheless, make each firm a

---

6. From microeconomics it is well known that a monopolist faced with a demand curve with an elasticity that is smaller than 1 everywhere should let production go to 0 and sell its infinitesimal production at prices going to infinity. Explain why this is the case.

wage setter, as we explained in Section 11.2. In accordance with the idea of efficiency wages, the labour productivity, a_i, in firm i is assumed to depend on the real wage, $w_i \equiv W_i/P$, paid by firm i, and on the 'normal' real income, v, that a worker can obtain outside firm i:

$$a_i = a(w_i) = (w_i - v)^\eta, \qquad 0 < \eta < 1. \tag{8}$$

Compared to (5) we have normalized so that $k \equiv (q/\beta)^\eta = 1$. Again, a_i really depends on both w_i and v, but the firm only controls w_i, and has negligible influence over v, since the 'normal income' relates to the whole economy. This justifies using $a(w_i)$.

Price and wage setting by the individual firm

In Section 11.1 we assumed that the firm decided on wage and employment. We could proceed similarly here and derive the revenue curve of each firm from (6) and (7), express profits in terms of W_i and L_i, and find the optimal values for W_i and L_i. This time, however, it is most convenient to proceed by determining directly the optimal values for W_i and P_i. Of course, given these (and P and v), an optimal labour demand, L_i, follows.

The real profit of firm i is $\Pi_i = (P_iY_i - W_iL_i)/P = Y_i[P_i/P - (W_i/P)/(Y_i/L_i)]$ or, inserting for Y_i from the demand function, and $Y_i/L_i = (w_i - v)^\eta$ from the production and efficiency function:

$$\Pi_i = \left(\frac{P_i}{P}\right)^{-\sigma} \frac{Y}{n} \left(\frac{P_i}{P} - \frac{W_i/P}{(W_i/P - v)^\eta}\right). \tag{9}$$

This may be written in terms of the relative, or real, prices $p_i \equiv P_i/P$ and $w_i \equiv W_i/P$:

$$\Pi_i = p_i^{-\sigma} \frac{Y}{n} \left(p_i - \frac{w_i}{(w_i - v)^\eta}\right). \tag{10}$$

The task of the firm is to choose p_i and w_i to maximize real profits. (The firm really chooses the money price, P_i, and the money wage, W_i, such that at the given P, the desired p_i and w_i are established.) The first-order conditions for this optimization are necessary and sufficient.

Let us first take w_i as given – consider it as already chosen optimally – and look for the optimal p_i. This is a standard monopoly problem with iso-elastic demand and constant marginal cost. It is well known from microeconomic theory that the firm sets its price as a mark-up over marginal cost, where the mark-up factor is $m = \sigma/(\sigma - 1)$. To confirm, consider the first-order condition for maximizing Π_i with respect to p_i:

$$\frac{\partial \Pi_i}{\partial p_i} = -\sigma p_i^{-\sigma-1} \frac{Y}{n}\left(p_i - \frac{w_i}{(w_i - v)^\eta}\right) + p_i^{-\sigma}\frac{Y}{n} = p_i^{-\sigma-1}\frac{Y}{n}\left[-\sigma\left(p_i - \frac{w_i}{(w_i-v)^\eta}\right) + p_i\right] = 0.$$

Here the square bracket must be 0. This gives $p_i(\sigma - 1) = \sigma w_i/(w_i - v)^\eta$, or:

$$p_i = \frac{\sigma}{\sigma - 1}\frac{w}{(w_i - v)^\eta} = m\frac{w_i}{(w_i - v)^\eta}. \tag{11}$$

Note that unit labour cost is w_i/a_i, the cost w_i per hour of work divided by productivity a_i, where $a_i = (w_i - v)^\eta$.

Next consider p_i as already set (optimally) and look for the optimal w_i. The first-order condition is:

$$\frac{\partial \Pi_i}{\partial w_i} = -p_i^{-\sigma}\frac{Y}{n}[(w_i - v)^{-\eta} - \eta w_i(w_i - v)^{-\eta-1}] = -p_i^{-\sigma}\frac{Y}{n}(w_i - v)^{-\eta-1}[w_i - v - \eta w_i] = 0.$$

The square bracket must be 0, which is equivalent to:

$$w_i = \frac{v}{1-\eta}. \tag{12}$$

The optimal real wage is a mark-up over the alternative or normal real income v, and the mark-up factor, $1/(1-\eta)$, is larger the larger the productivity effect of higher wages.[7]

In view of Section 11.2, the expression for the optimal real wage in (12) should be equivalent to the Solow condition in the present setting. From (8) one gets for the elasticity of the efficiency function, $a'(w_i)w_i/a(w_i) = \eta w_i/(w_i - v)$. Equalizing this to 1 gives exactly (12). The intuition for this formula is thus as explained in Sections 1 and 2.

The wage curve

The normal real income v should measure what a worker in firm i could expect to earn in the rest of the economy if separated from firm i. This must depend on the risk of becoming unemployed and the income obtained in that case, and on the chance of getting employed and the real wage that can be expected in that case. We will focus on the simplest possible formulation where v is exactly the expected income of a person who becomes unemployed with probability u, the rate of unemployment in the economy, in that case receiving a real unemployment benefit b, and becomes employed with probability $1 - u$, in that case earning an expected real wage of w:

$$v = ub + (1 - u)w. \tag{13}$$

The rate of unemployment benefit b is (for now) assumed to be a fixed amount in real terms and, of course, measured in the same units as the real wage rate w, so if w is pay per day (or hour), so is b. We can interpret b to include the value of an unemployed person's home production.

The 'outside option', v, is the same from the point of view of all firms i. According to (12) all firms therefore set the same real wage rate which must then be equal to w, the expected real wage of an employed worker. Writing w for the w_i on the left-hand side of (12), and inserting the expression in (13) for v on the right-hand side gives:

$$w = \frac{ub + (1-u)w}{1-\eta},$$

which can be solved for w:

$$w = \frac{u}{u-\eta}b = \frac{1}{1-\dfrac{\eta}{u}}b. \tag{14}$$

The real wage is 'marked up' over the real rate of unemployment benefit with a mark-up factor of $u/(u - \eta) > 1$, so $w > b$.[8] Given b, the formula in (14) gives the real wage w as a *decreasing* function of the rate of unemployment, as illustrated in Fig. 11.4. Since $w > b$, higher unemployment means a lower value of the outside option in (13) and therefore the firms can obtain the same level of worker productivity for lower wages. In other words, if unemployment increases, wage pressure decreases. This is the essential incentive effect captured by the relationship in (14), a relationship called the 'wage-setting curve' or just the 'wage curve'.

---

7. As an exercise, show that the second-order conditions $\partial^2\Pi_i/\partial^2 p_i < 0$ and $\partial^2\Pi_i/\partial^2 w_i < 0$ are fulfilled at the p_i and w_i we have found.

8. For this to be meaningful one should have $u > \eta$, which we assume. It is demonstrated below that indeed in a full equilibrium of the model this condition is satisfied.

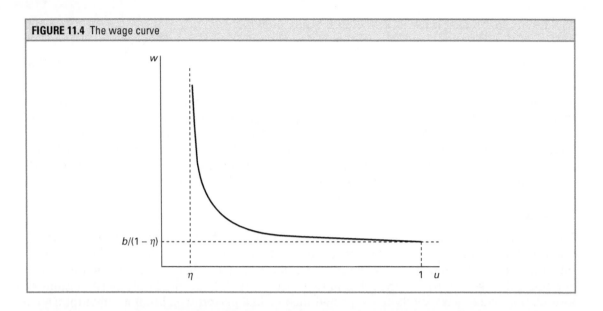

FIGURE 11.4 The wage curve

The general equilibrium efficiency wage model gives rise to a negative relationship between overall unemployment and real wages, a so-called wage curve: a lower rate of unemployment means that the alternative or normal income, the outside option, as viewed from each firm will be more favourable for workers. Firms will therefore have to pay higher wages to obtain the same level of effort and this creates increased wage pressure.

The economists David G. Blanchflower and Andrew L. Oswald have written a book entirely on the wage curve.[9] Much of the book is concerned with empirical tests and estimates. They find quite robustly (with varying methods of estimation and for several countries) that a wage curve exists, and estimates of the elasticity of the real wage with respect to the rate of unemployment are around −0.1, meaning that a 10 per cent increase in the rate of unemployment, e.g. from 5 to 5.5 per cent, should lead to a 1 per cent decrease in real wages. This magnitude also has an implication for how large one should expect η, the real wage elasticity of effort or productivity, to be. You will be asked to think about that in an exercise.

In the following it will be convenient to express the wage curve in terms of the rate of employment $e = 1 - u$, such that w is an increasing function of e:

$$w = \frac{1-e}{1-e-\eta}b = \frac{1}{1-\dfrac{\eta}{1-e}}b. \tag{15}$$

The wage curve in this form is illustrated as the curve labelled WS in Fig. 11.6 on page 318. Note that the wage curve will shift upwards if b or η increases (try to give the intuitive explanations yourself).

The price curve

Since all firms set the same wage rate w, it follows from (11) that they also set the same relative price $p_i = P_i/P$. Since P is given for each of them, this implies that they all set the

9.   David G. Blanchflower and Andrew L. Oswald, *The Wage Curve*, MIT Press, 1996.

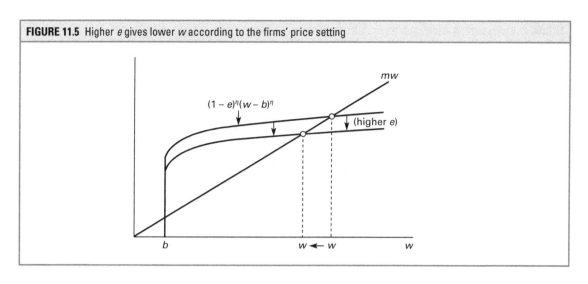

FIGURE 11.5 Higher e gives lower w according to the firms' price setting

same nominal price P_i, and hence the value of the price index P, an average of the individual nominal prices, must be equal to this common nominal price. Hence $p_i = P_i/P = 1$ for all firms i. It then follows from (11) that:

$$1 = m\frac{w}{(w-v)^\eta} \text{ or } mw = (w-v)^\eta.$$

Inserting the value of the normal income v from (13) gives:

$$mw = [u(w-b)]^\eta = (1-e)^\eta(w-b)^\eta. \tag{16}$$

A real wage w must fulfil this equation in order to be compatible with the mark-up pricing behaviour of firms. The equation does not give a closed form solution for w, but rather gives w as the intersection between the left-hand side, the straight line mw, and the right-hand side, the curved function $(1-e)^\eta(w-b)^\eta$ of w (see Fig. 11.5). For b not too large there will, for all sufficiently small e, be two intersections. However, it is only the upper one indicated by a small circle in Fig. 11.5 that corresponds to an optimum, because one can show from (15) and (16) that at an optimum the slope of the curved function must be smaller than the slope, m, of the line.[10]

The fact that the upper intersection is the right one means that an increase in e implies a decrease in w, since a higher e shifts the concave curve downwards (see Fig. 11.5 again). This is because a higher rate of employment increases the value of the outside option v (remember $w > b$), which decreases productivity so that unit labour cost, $w_i/(w_i-v)^\eta$, increases, pushing up real prices in accordance with (11), and hence reducing real wages. This is the basic incentive effect underlying the 'price curve' or 'price-setting curve', giving the real wage rate w as a decreasing function of the rate of employment e. The curve is illustrated in Fig. 11.6 and labelled PS. As explained, the price-setting curve is decreasing because of the way a change in the rate of employment (or unemployment) affects worker productivity through the value of the normal income, v. If one disregards that effect by assuming $\eta = 0$, then the price curve becomes flat: (16) with $\eta = 0$ gives $mw = 1$ or $w = 1/m$, simply expressing mark-up pricing by the firms, $P = mW$, when there is a constant labour productivity of unity.

A higher unemployment benefit, b, as well as more market power in product markets, a higher m, shifts the price-setting curve downwards, since both will shift the concave curve in Fig. 11.5 downwards for given e (give the intuitive explanations yourself).

---

10. The slope of the curved function is $(1-e)^\eta \ \eta(w-b)^{\eta-1} = \eta(1-e)^\eta/(w-b)^\eta(w-b)$, which, using (16), is equal to $\eta mw/(w-b)$. Inserting the optimal value for w from (15) gives the slope $(1-e)m$, which is smaller than m as long as $e > 0$.

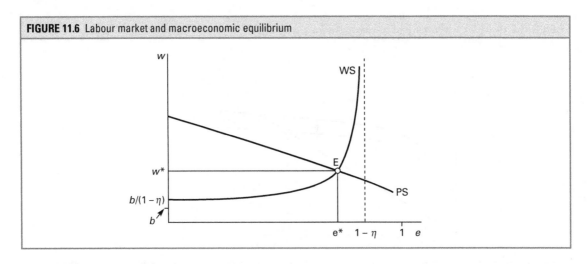

FIGURE 11.6 Labour market and macroeconomic equilibrium

Macroeconomic equilibrium

Figure 11.6 shows both the wage curve and the price-setting curve in the same diagram. The diagram assumes that the value of the benefit rate b is sufficiently low to ensure that the decreasing price-setting curve PS reaches far enough to the south-east to ensure an intersection with the wage curve WS. The full labour market equilibrium is at the point E, where the two curves intersect each other. Only the employment–wage combination (e^*, w^*) of the intersection is compatible with both the wage-setting and the price-setting decisions of the firms. In other words, e^* and w^* are the solutions in e and w to the two equations (15) and (16), repeated here for convenience:

$$w = \frac{1-e}{1-e-\eta}b, \tag{WS}$$

$$mw = (1-e)^\eta(w-b)^\eta. \tag{PS}$$

Thus in macroeconomic equilibrium e^* and w^* depend (only) on the parameters η, σ (through m), and b. Note from Fig. 11.6 that $e^* < 1 - \eta$, which is equivalent to $u^* = (1 - e^*) > \eta$. The condition mentioned in Footnote 8 is indeed fulfilled in equilibrium.

However, the labour market equilibrium illustrated in Fig. 11.6 also determines the GDP of the economy. Given a total (inelastic) labour supply, $\bar{L}$, total employment will be $e^*\bar{L}$. In equilibrium this is distributed evenly across the n firms, so employment in each firm will be $e^*\bar{L}/n$. Since w^* has also been determined, the productivity in each firm will be given by this w^* and the v implied by w^* and $u^* = 1 - e^*$, that is, $a^* = [(1 - e^*)(w^* - b)]^\eta$. Hence the GDP of this economy is $Y = [(1 - e^*)(w^* - b)]^\eta e^*\bar{L}$. This is the Y that entered the demand curves (6) from the very beginning. Just as in a classic macro model or in the Solow growth model, output is in each period determined entirely from the supply side.

It is worth noting how much Fig. 11.6 looks like a traditional demand and supply diagram for the labour market. Here we have the rate of employment rather than employment itself along the horizontal axis, and the wage curve has taken the place of the labour supply curve, while the price-setting curve has taken the place of the labour demand curve.

There is a particular case of some interest where the wage curve in Fig. 11.6 becomes vertical so the rate of employment (and unemployment) is determined by the wage curve alone. If the rate of unemployment benefit is not fixed as a given amount in real terms, but as a given fraction of the real wage rate, $b = cw$, $0 \le c < 1$, then the wage curve in (15) becomes: $w(1 - e - \eta) = (1 - e)cw$, giving:

$$e^* = \frac{1-c-\eta}{1-c} \quad \text{and hence} \quad u^* = 1 - e^* = \frac{\eta}{1-c}. \tag{17}$$

We arrive at an explicit expression for u^*, and we see that the natural rate of unemployment is increasing in the replacement ratio, c, and in the wage elasticity of effort, η. Furthermore, the formula can be used to say something about orders of magnitude. For a (realistically) small value of η of 1 per cent, $\eta = 0.01$, and a replacement ratio of $\frac{2}{3}$, one gets $u^* = 0.03$, while, for instance, $\eta = 0.01$ and $c = 0.5$ gives $u^* = 2$ per cent, and 2–3 per cent is a substantial part of real-world structural unemployment which is typically in the range 5–7 per cent. In Exercise 2 below you will be asked to investigate further the realism of the efficiency wage model as an explanation of the natural rate of unemployment.

Main implications and structural policy

One of the main conclusions from the macroeconomic efficiency wage model is that *there is necessarily unemployment in equilibrium*: as mentioned above, $u^* > \eta$ and by assumption $\eta > 0$. In the particular case of a fixed replacement ratio one can see from (17) that $u^* > 0$. Unemployment is thus not just a possibility, as in the partial equilibrium model considered in Section 2. Unemployment is a necessary property of the macroeconomic equilibrium. Why is it that there *must* be unemployment in the macroeconomic equilibrium?

The key lies in the fact that workers only deliver a positive level of productivity if they are paid above the normal income, $v = ub + (1 - u)w$. Each individual firm therefore has an incentive to set its real wage w_i above v; otherwise it will earn zero profits. If $u = 0$, then the normal income is given by the general wage, w, alone, $v = w$, so each individual firm wants to set its wage w_i above the general wage level w. Thus, whenever unemployment is zero there will be an upward pressure on wages. At a positive level of unemployment (created by firms driving up wages), it is possible for each firm's individual pay, w_i, to be above $v = ub + (1 - u)w$, even when the w entering in v is equal to the individual firm's wage, w_i, as it must be in equilibrium (this requires, of course, that $w > b$). Basically, employers bid wages up to a level that is so high that they do not want to buy all the labour supplied.

Other main conclusions come from comparative statics. We will consider changes in b and σ, which are naturally associated with labour market policy and competition policy, respectively. We will not consider changes in η, since it is difficult to imagine a kind of policy that can affect η.

Consider an increase in b. We have already noted that this shifts the wage curve WS upwards and the price-setting curve PS downwards, as illustrated in Fig. 11.7, where the wage and price-setting curves shift from WS_1 to WS_2 and from PS_1 to PS_2, respectively.

In the new equilibrium there has to be a lower rate of employment, that is, a higher natural rate of unemployment. (You should go carefully through the economic mechanisms underlying this result.) It does not follow from the directions of the shifts of the curves whether the wage rate goes up or down. It so happens that the wage rate is just unchanged, a fact you will be asked to show in Exercise 5. The most important conclusion is, however, that according to the macroeconomic efficiency wage model *more generous unemployment benefits mean higher structural unemployment*.

Next consider an increase in σ, which means more elastic demand functions and therefore less market power for the firms, reflected in lower mark-ups, $m = \sigma/(\sigma - 1)$. We can think of the reduction in market power as caused by an intensified competition policy by the government. This shifts the price-setting curve PS upwards, but it does not affect the position of the wage curve. (In this case we will leave both the figure and the intuitive explanations to you.) In the new equilibrium there will be less unemployment and higher real wages. According to the macroeconomic efficiency wage model *stronger competition in product markets means lower structural unemployment and higher real wages*. It is worth emphasizing that conditions in the *product* markets, namely the degree of competition, influence the rate of structural unemployment, since structural unemployment is often viewed as a pure *labour* market phenomenon that can only be affected by labour market policies.

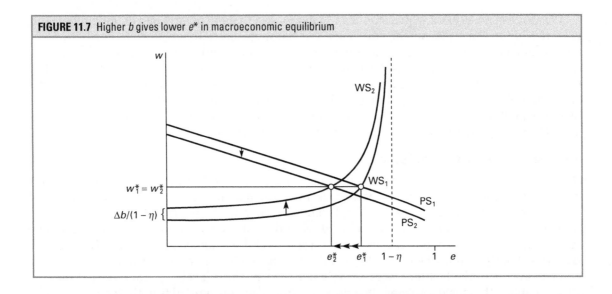

FIGURE 11.7 Higher *b* gives lower *e** in macroeconomic equilibrium

UNEMPLOYMENT AND STRUCTURAL POLICY IN THE GENERAL EQUILIBRIUM EFFICIENCY WAGE MODEL

- There is by necessity a strictly positive level of unemployment in the macroeconomic efficiency wage model. This is due to the positive dependence of worker productivity on *the excess* of pay over normal income and to the latter being a mix of average wages and income opportunities for the unemployed.
- According to the general equilibrium efficiency wage model, the rate of structural unemployment will be higher the more generous unemployment benefits are.
- According to the same model, more intense competition *on product markets* will imply lower structural unemployment as well as higher real wages.

11.5 Summary

1. Under the standard assumption that labour productivity does not depend on the wage rate, a profit-maximizing firm that can choose the wage it pays would never set the wage higher than strictly required for recruiting the workers it wants. Otherwise the wage could be lowered without reducing the labour supply to the firm, which would lower costs and raise profits. The firm would thus always position itself *on* the labour supply curve, creating full employment through its optimizing behaviour.
2. If labour productivity depends positively on pay, the above argument breaks down. Raising the wage above the level required to recruit the desired workforce has two counteracting effects on profits: the cost of labour increases, but at the same time productivity also increases. It may be that the second impact on profits is the strongest. The phenomenon that labour productivity (or effort) depends positively on the wage is referred to as efficiency wages. With a positive link from wages to productivity, it is a logical possibility that an individual firm will want to raise wages above the market-clearing level.

3. When labour productivity depends on real wages, each firm will set its real wage in accordance with the Solow condition saying that the elasticity of productivity with respect to the real wage should be equal to 1, and set employment at the optimal level given this wage rate. In a partial equilibrium model of the labour market, this behaviour could well imply a total level of employment smaller than the total labour supply induced by the efficiency wages set by firms. Under efficiency wages, unemployment in a full equilibrium with adjusted real wages is therefore a possibility, but in a partial labour market model unemployment is not a necessary feature of equilibrium.

4. In the partial labour market model analysed in the chapter, the equilibrium real wage rate is insensitive to supply and demand shocks to the revenue functions of firms, so employment bears the full burden of adjusting to such shocks. Efficiency wage models can therefore help to explain the fact that real wages fluctuate much less than employment over the business cycle.

5. There are at least four reasons why productivity should depend positively on pay. For the individual firm, setting a relatively high wage can be a way of (i) keeping good workers in the firm, thereby reducing recruiting and training costs, (ii) getting applications from relatively good workers in hiring situations, (iii) motivating workers to comply with a high level of required effort, because a larger difference between the wage paid and what can be earned outside the firm increases the cost to a worker of being fired for 'shirking', and (iv) motivating workers to exert a high level of effort for pure reasons of reciprocity.

6. Under plausible assumptions on the effort cost function, the 'shirking' model of efficiency wages implies that the efficiency function linking effort to pay should be an increasing, concave function of the excess of the real wage over the outside option, defined as the normal income a worker can expect to earn outside the firm where currently employed. The other motivating factors for the efficiency wage phenomenon point to similar curves.

7. The efficiency wage effect may be built into a general equilibrium macroeconomic model where the revenues of firms derive from consumer demand, and where the individual worker's outside option is a mixture of the general wage level and the unemployment benefit received in case of unemployment. In such a model unemployment is a necessary property of a macroeconomic equilibrium with fully adjusted real wages: if there were no unemployment, the outside option from the point of view of each firm would be the general wage level. To induce any effort at all, each firm would then have to set its own wage above the general wage level, but not all firms' wages can be above the average level. The upward pressure on wages would make labour so expensive that firms would not want to buy all the labour supplied. Unemployment would arise, and with positive unemployment it *is* possible for each firm to set a wage above the common outside option, since unemployment benefits are lower than wages.

8. The general equilibrium model with efficiency wages implies that more generous unemployment benefits will increase the natural rate of unemployment, whereas intensified competition in product markets will lower it. These features have implications for labour market and competition policies.

11.6 Exercises

Exercise 1. Plausible efficiency curves

Consider again Fig. 11.2 with an 'efficiency curve' and rays with slope $a(w)/w$. Can you draw a strictly increasing efficiency function that goes through $(0, 0)$, such that there is still a unique interior optimal wage rate, w^*? Also draw one such that the optimal wage rate is zero. Finally draw one such that there is no optimal wage rate because the firm would always like to increase the wage rate further. Try to give reasons why the first of your curves may be reasonable, while the latter two are not.

Exercise 2. A partial/general equilibrium efficiency wage model

In this exercise an efficiency wage model with one firm and a given revenue curve is considered. This is like in a *partial equilibrium* model. However, one should think of the firm as *representative*, and therefore *general equilibrium* effects can be brought into the analysis.

The representative firm has a revenue function, $zR(aL)$, with notation and assumptions as in Section 11.2, and an efficiency function:

$$a = \left(\frac{w' - v}{v}\right)^{\eta}, \qquad 0 \le \eta < 1,$$

where v is the employees' outside option, and w' is the real wage paid by the representative firm. (This is for $w' \ge v$, while a is 0 for $w' < v$.)

1. Write down the first-order conditions for the firm's profit maximization problem with respect to w' and L. Derive the Solow condition in this context and give the expression for the optimal wage as a function of z, v, and η.

    Assume that the outside option is $v = (1 - u)w + ucw$, $0 < c < 1$, where u is the unemployment rate, c is the replacement ratio, and w is the general real wage level.

2. Using how v relates to u, w and c, express the optimal wage rate of the representative firm as a function of η, u, w and c. Then use the 'equilibrium condition', that the general wage level entering in v must equal the wage set by the representative firm, to derive the equilibrium rate of unemployment, u^*. How do the parameters η and c affect u^*? Explain the economic mechanisms involved.

3. What is the equilibrium productivity, a^*? Assume that total labour supply is some fixed, inelastically supplied $\bar{L}$. By using your earlier findings, among them the relevant first-order condition from Question 1 above, find an expression for the equilibrium wage rate, w^*. (It is acceptable just to express w^* as a function of a^*, u^* and $\bar{L}$, but you can trace w^* back to parameters using your expressions for a^* and u^*.)

4. Assume that there is a trendwise movement upwards over time in the productivity factor z. Describe how this affects u^* and w^* over time. Why can your finding here be said to be a nice feature of the model?

5. Compute the equilibrium unemployment rate u^* for the following values of c and η:

C\η	0.01	0.02
0.8		
0.5		
0.2		
0		

Comment on your results with respect to the statement: 'Even for realistically small values of η, and for plausible values of the replacement ratio, the efficiency wage model can explain a substantial part of real world natural unemployment'.

6. Insert the expression you found for u^* into $v = (1 - u)w + ucw$, and write w^* for the w on the right-hand side. This expresses the outside option as a function $v(w^*)$ of the equilibrium general wage level. By inserting $v(w^*)$ in place of v, write down the effort a in each firm as a function, $a(w', w^*)$, of the firm's own wage, w', and the general wage level, w^*. How does the function look, e.g. for $\eta = 0.02$? To obtain any effort at all, how large a percentage of the general wage level, w^*, must the firm pay? Do you find this realistic?

Exercise 3. Deriving the demand side of the macro economy

Consider a representative consumer or household who has a utility function over the consumptions, $c_1, \ldots, c_n$, of n different commodities:

$$C(c_1, \ldots, c_n) = n \left(\frac{1}{n} \sum_{i=1}^{n} c_i^{\frac{\sigma-1}{\sigma}} \right)^{\frac{\sigma}{\sigma-1}}, \qquad \sigma > 0, \sigma \neq 1. \tag{18}$$

1. Show that this utility function is homogeneous of degree one with respect to $c_1, \ldots, c_n$.

   Let the money prices, $P_1, \ldots, P_n$, of the n commodities be given. Assume that the total amount of money that the representative consumer spends on the n commodities is M. Utility maximization must imply that the consumptions, $c_1, \ldots, c_n$, are chosen to:

   Maximize $C(c_1, \ldots, c_n)$ subject to $P_1 c_1 + \ldots + P_n c_n = M$.

   Because of the homogeneity of C, one can solve this problem in two steps. First one can find the consumptions, $c_i^*(P_1, \ldots, P_n)$ for $i = 1, \ldots, n$ by which one unit of utility can be bought as cheaply as possible, that is, one solves the problem of choosing $c_1, \ldots, c_n$ to:

   Minimize $P_1 c_1 + \ldots + P_n c_n$ subject to $C(c_1, \ldots, c_n) = 1$, \tag{19}

   and defines the price index $P(P_1, \ldots, P_n)$ as the total cost of one unit of utility:

   $$P = P(P_1, \ldots, P_n) \equiv \sum_{i=1}^{n} P_i c_i^*(P_1, \ldots, P_n).$$

   Then one can use that from homogeneity, the amount of money M can buy exactly M/P units of utility, and that the optimal way to acquire each unit is by the consumptions $c_i^*(P_1, \ldots, P_n)$, $i = 1, \ldots, n$, so that the demand for commodity i must be:

   $$c_i(P_1, \ldots, P_n, M) = c_i^*(P_1, \ldots, P_n) \frac{M}{P(P_1, \ldots, P_n)}.$$

   In everything that follows you can take as granted that the first-order conditions for the optimization in (19) are necessary and sufficient for a solution, $c_1^*, \ldots, c_n^*$.

2. Write down the Lagrange function for the cost minimization problem in (19) using the definition of C in (18), and show that the first-order conditions consist of the constraint $C(c_1, \ldots, c_n) = 1$, and for $i = 1, \ldots, n$:

$$P_i = \lambda \frac{c_i^{-\frac{1}{\sigma}}}{\sum_{j=1}^{n} c_j^{\frac{\sigma-1}{\sigma}}}, \tag{20}$$

where λ is a Lagrange multiplier. (Hint: on the way you must use once more how C is given by (18), and that $C = 1$.)

3. Multiplying by c_i on both sides of (20), find $P_i c_i$, and add up over all commodities, to show that the minimal total cost of one unit of utility must fulfil:

$$P = \sum_{i=1}^{n} P_i c_i = \lambda.$$

4. In the first-order condition (20) above, write P for λ, and also use that from (18), $C(c_1, \ldots, c_n) = 1 \Leftrightarrow \sum_{i=1}^{n} c_i^{(\sigma-1)/\sigma} = n^{1/\sigma}$, to show that:

$$c_i^*(P_1, \ldots, P_n) = \left(\frac{P_i}{P}\right)^{-\sigma} \frac{1}{n}.$$

5. Use the result in Question 4, and the definition of the price index to show that:

$$P(P_1, \ldots, P_n) = \left(\frac{1}{n} \sum_{i=1}^{n} P_i^{1-\sigma}\right)^{\frac{1}{1-\sigma}},$$

and that:

$$c_i(P_1, \ldots, P_n, M) = \left(\frac{P_i}{P}\right)^{-\sigma} \frac{1}{n} \frac{M}{P},$$

where we have (again) just written P for $P(P_1, \ldots, P_n)$.

(When all firms charge the same prices, $P_i/P = 1$ for all i, demand per commodity is $M/(nP)$, and hence total real demand is M/P. In a simple model where demand only comes from the households, this must in a symmetric equilibrium be the GDP. Writing Y for MP, we arrive at the demand functions (6) of the text.)

6. How does the ratio, c_i/c_j, between the consumptions of commodities i and j depend on the relative price, P_i/P_j, according to the consumer's demand? What is the elasticity of c_i/c_j with respect to the price ratio, P_i/P_j? Why is the utility function in (18) called a constant elasticity of substitution utility function?

Exercise 4. How large are realistic values of the wage elasticity of productivity?

Given the efficiency function $e(w_i) = (w_i - v)^\eta$ for individual firms, and the simple form $v = ub + (1 - u)w$ for the normal income or outside option, we found in Section 11.4 the particular form for the wage curve:

$$w = \frac{u}{u - \eta} b,$$

where b is a fixed amount (in real terms). Explain how this wage curve was found. Find the elasticity of the real wage, w, with respect to the rate of unemployment u, as this depends on η and u. According to estimates, this elasticity is realistically around -0.1, and rates of unemployment can be assumed to be more or less between 5 and 10 per cent. What is the implied interval for η, the elasticity of productivity with respect to real wage?

Exercise 5. Solving for the macroeconomic equilibrium

In Section 11.4, and in Exercise 2, it was shown how one can find an explicit expression for the equilibrium rate of unemployment, u^*, when the replacement ratio, c, is fixed. In the case where the benefit rate, b, is fixed one can also find an explicit expression for the equilibrium rate of unemployment, u^*, it is just a bit more cumbersome. The equilibrium rate of employment, e^*, and the equilibrium real wage, w^*, are the solutions in e and w to the two equations (15), the wage curve, and (16), the price-setting curve. One can solve directly for u and w using (14) and (16). Show that this gives:

$$u^* = \frac{\eta^{\frac{1}{1-\eta}}}{\eta^{\frac{1}{1-\eta}} - bm^{\frac{1}{1-\eta}}} \quad \text{and} \quad w^* = \frac{1}{\eta}\left(\frac{\eta}{m}\right)^{\frac{1}{1-\eta}}.$$

It is assumed that the parameters are such that the denominator in u^* is positive. This is really an important restriction (making the whole model meaningful) that we have not mentioned in the chapter. Show that the restriction is equivalent to $b < w^*$. The parameter restriction is thus equivalent to the condition underlying a positive mark-up of wage over benefit in equilibrium, so it is the parameter restriction underlying Footnote 8.

How do changes in b and m (coming from σ) affect u^* and w^*? Explain intuitively. What is the expression for u^* if you insert $b = cw^*$?

Exercise 6. Systematic productivity changes in the macroeconomic efficiency wage model

We said in this chapter that for the efficiency wage model to be in accordance with the stylized facts of growth, a systematic (trendwise) change in productivity should build itself fully into the real wage. We also said that an appropriately formulated general equilibrium macro model of efficiency wages would have this feature, but when we formulated our macroeconomic efficiency wage model in Section 11.4 we did not consider changes in productivity. This exercise considers the model of Section 11.4 with a productivity shift parameter included.

The model we will consider is the same as the model in Section 11.4 in all but three respects. The first change is that the production function in each sector i is changed into:

$$Y_i = za_iL_i,$$

where z is a productivity shift parameter common to all sectors. We interpret z as a systematic and predictable parameter, changing for instance permanently from one level to another, or increasing by a certain constant rate over time. Our second revision is that the efficiency (or effort) function of each firm i makes productivity depend on the *relative* excess of the real wage over the outside option:

$$a_i = \left(\frac{w_i - v}{v}\right)^{\eta}$$

Finally we assume that the benefit rate b changes proportionally with productivity:

$$b = \bar{b}z, \qquad \bar{b} > 0,$$

reflecting that empirically benefit levels do tend to evolve in line with general welfare in the long run.

1. Argue that in the presence of systematic productivity changes (e.g. a trendwise increase over time) it should, from the motivations for efficiency wages, be the *relative* excess of wage over outside option that governs effort.

2. Set up the profit maximization problem of firm i and show that its optimal (real) price and wage are now:

$$p_i = m\frac{w_i}{z\left(\dfrac{w_i - v}{v}\right)^{\eta}},$$

$$w_i = \frac{v}{1 - \eta},$$

where m has the same definition as in Section 11.4. Compare with the parallel expressions from the model of Section 11.4. Explain the differences.

3. Assume, as in Section 11.4, that the outside option for each sector is: $v = ub + (1 - u)w$, where w is the average wage level. Show that this leads to the wage curve:

$$w = \frac{u}{u - \eta}\bar{b}z.$$

Show that the price curve is:

$$mw = z\left(\frac{u(w - \bar{b}z)}{w - u(w - \bar{b}z)}\right)^{\eta},$$

where we assume that $w > \bar{b}z$. Compare again with the parallel expressions in Section 11.4.

4. Combining the wage curve and the price curve show that the macroeconomic equilibrium is:

$$w^* = \frac{z}{m}\left(\frac{\eta}{1 - \eta}\right)^{\eta}$$

$$u^* = \frac{\eta}{1 - \dfrac{\bar{b}m}{\left(\dfrac{\eta}{1 - \eta}\right)^{\eta}}}$$

Write down a parameter restriction ensuring our assumption $w^* > \bar{b}z$, and show that this also implies $u^* > \eta$. Comment on the macroeconomic equilibrium with respect to how the real wage and structural unemployment are affected by systematic productivity shifts. Given a total labour supply of $\bar{L}$, what is the GDP (Y) in the macroeconomic equilibrium and how is GDP affected by z?

5. Explain that the entire analysis in this exercise extends to the case, and therefore can be interpreted to cover the case, of a given replacement ratio where $b = cw$, if one sets the replacement ratio c as:

$$c = \frac{\bar{b}m}{\left(\dfrac{\eta}{1 - \eta}\right)^{\eta}}.$$

How are real wages and unemployment affected by changes in the replacement ratio? Write the natural rate of unemployment as a function of η and c. What is the condition for $u^* < 1$? Is this a realistic condition?

Exercise 7. 'Unemployment as a worker discipline device'

Carl Shapiro and Joseph E. Stiglitz gave their seminal paper on the shirking model of efficiency wages the title 'Equilibrium Unemployment as a Worker Discipline Device' (*American Economic Review*, **74**, 1984). Try to give an explanation of this use of language by going through (once more) the explanation why there has to be unemployment in equilibrium in the macroeconomic model of Section 11.4, and think of the motivation for the efficiency function, $a(w_i) = (w_i - v)^\eta$, as coming from the shirking model explained in Section 11.3.

Exercise 8. Taxes in the macroeconomic efficiency wage model

This exercise introduces an income tax in the macroeconomic efficiency wage model. The proportional income tax rate is τ, so the efficiency function of firm i is:

$$a(w_i) = ((1 - \tau)w_i - v)^\eta, \qquad 0 < \eta < 1.$$

Firms face demand curves as in (6), so the real after-tax profits of firm i are:

$$\Pi_i = (1 - \tau)p_i^{-\sigma} \frac{Y}{n} \left(p_i - \frac{w_i}{((1 - \tau)w_i - v)^\eta} \right).$$

The task of firm i is to choose p_i and w_i to maximize real profits, taking τ, Y, n and v as given.

1. Derive the firm's optimal wage and interpret the result. The real rate of unemployment benefit before tax is b, and b is assumed to be a constant fraction of the general wage level w, $b = cw$, $0 < c < 1$. If unemployment benefits are not taxed, the outside option is:

$$v = ub + (1 - u)(1 - \tau)w,$$

and we assume in this case that $1 - \tau > c$.

2. Derive the rate of structural unemployment, u^*, in the macroeconomic equilibrium. Explain how u^* is affected by the taxation and give the intuition.

3. Now assume that unemployment benefits are taxed by the same rate as other income. What is the value of the outside option, v? Find the natural rate of unemployment and explain how and why the result differs from what you found in Question 2.

CHAPTER

12

Trade unions and unemployment

In this chapter we consider another departure from the competitive labour market model. We will still think of the labour market as having many individual workers supplying labour, and perhaps also many buying firms, but the workers are now assumed to be organized in a trade union that takes care of their interests through its market power over the (real) wage rate.

The labour markets are thus no longer atomistic. In each sector of the economy the labour market has on the supply side a big agent, the trade union, and this big agent sets the wage rate in that market. The trade union will, however, be small in the total economy if there are many labour markets. If the total labour supply coming from the individual union members exceeds the total labour demand of the firms at the wage rate chosen by the union, then there will be unemployment. That is, there will be individual workers who would like to work at the going wage rate, but cannot find a job. The presence of these unemployed workers should be expected to exert a downward pressure on the wage rate. However, we will assume that the union has sufficient control over the labour supply to enforce the wage rate it has chosen. We thus assume that the labour market is effectively monopolistic.

In the real world trade unions are most often faced with large agents on the other side of the labour markets either in the form of big firms or of employers' organizations taking care of the interests of employers much the same way trade unions take care of the workers' interests. However, instead of considering explicitly labour markets with bilateral monopoly, we will simplify by assigning full market power to the supply side of labour markets, turning these into monopolies. An exercise will ask you to show that our theory could be modified to take account of bilateral monopoly and that qualitatively, although not quantitatively, most of our conclusions would remain unaffected.

The chapter is thus concerned with the economic consequences of labour markets being effectively monopolized by unions. We begin in Section 12.1 by discussing whether unions are important for wages in practice. Reaching an answer mostly in the affirmative, we continue in Section 12.2 by presenting a simple partial equilibrium model of a unionized labour market. This will give some basic insights with respect to the incentive effects implied by the presence of trade unions and into how a single unionized labour market functions. In Section 12.3 we extend the analysis to a general equilibrium macro model of the entire economy with many unionized labour markets. This will give additional insights that could not have been derived from partial equilibrium analysis. In particular, we will find that unemployment is a necessary implication of labour markets that are monopolized by unions.

This chapter takes a rather 'dry' view of trade unions: their only task will be to set wages in the interests of their members. In the real world trade unions are involved in many other tasks. For instance, they assist individual members with legal aid, help in negotiations, etc., when members have disputes or conflicts with their employers. This general presence of the trade unions may help to prevent individual members from being exploited or unfairly treated by their employer. Furthermore, trade unions take part in arranging general work conditions. For instance, agreements between unions and firms (or employer's organizations) often regulate the conditions of safety in the workplace. Other agreements lay down the rules for the process of negotiation of wages and other issues and may, in particular, establish the existence of a particular court for resolving conflicts between employers and employees. This may help to avoid 'wildcat strikes' and to create a general environment of security and predictability concerning the complex relations between employers and employees, leading to higher average productivity to the benefit of everybody. It may well be that these other tasks of trade unions are more important than the task of wage negotiation and that, historically, the general improvements that trade unions have helped to bring about are more associated with their influence on work conditions and rules in general than with their ability to influence wages. As economists we focus, nevertheless, on this latter aspect.

12.1　Are unions important?

There is no doubt that in a formal sense trade unions play an important role in many countries. Figure 12.1 reports two different measures of trade union influence in OECD countries. The 'union density rate' is roughly the percentage of all people in the labour force who are union members, while the 'coverage rate' is roughly the percentage of employed people whose work conditions, among them the wage rate, are influenced by trade unions. In the Scandinavian countries both membership and coverage are high. In several other countries the density rate is not so high, but the coverage rate is nevertheless high. France is an extreme such case where, according to the OECD figures, less than 10 per cent of

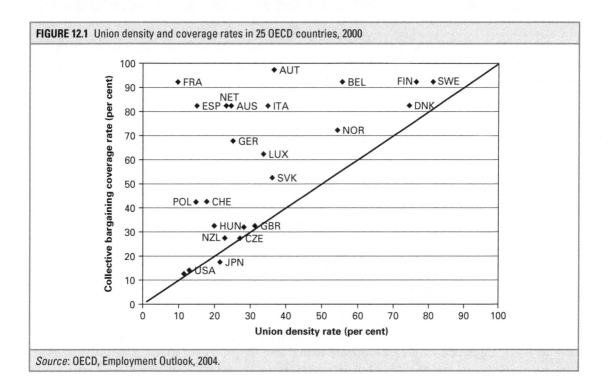

FIGURE 12.1 Union density and coverage rates in 25 OECD countries, 2000

Source: OECD, Employment Outlook, 2004.

TABLE 12.1 The evolution of union density rates over time

	1970	1990	2003	Change from 1990 to 2003	Change from 1970 to 2003
	(per cent)			(percentage points)	
Sweden	68	81	78	−3	10
Finland	51	73	74	2	23
Denmark	60	75	70	−5	10
Belgium	42	54	55[1]	2	13[2]
Norway	57	59	53	−5	−4
Austria	63	47	35[3]	−12	−27[4]
Ireland	53	51	35	−16	−18
Italy	37	39	34	−5	−3
UK	45	39	29	−10	−16
Australia	50[5]	41	23	−18	−27[6]
Germany	32	31	23	−9	−9
Netherlands	37	24	22	−2	−14
New Zealand	55[7]	51	22[8]	−29	−33[9]
Japan	35	25	20	−6	−15
Switzerland	29	24	17[10]	−7	−11[11]
Spain	–	13	16	4	3[12]
USA	23[13]	16	12	−3	−11[14]
Rep. Of Korea	13	18	11	−6	−1
France	22	10	8	−2	−13

Notes: [1]2002, [2]1970–2002, [3]2002, [4]1970–2002, [5]1976, [6]1976–2003. [7]1971, [8]2002, [9]1971–2002, [10]2001, [11]1970–2001, [12]1980–2003, [13]1973, [14]1973–2003.
Source: Table 3 of Jelle Visse, 'Union Membership Statistics in 24 Countries', *Monthly Labor Review*, January 2006, pp. 38–49.

people in the labour force are in unions, but unions negotiate the wages for more than 90 per cent of all employees. For all countries in the upper part of the figure trade unions are, at least formally, widespread and important. This covers most European countries. In some non-European countries like the USA and Japan both membership and coverage are substantially lower.

Is trade unionism increasing or decreasing over time? In particular, is there some indication that more and more people prefer not to be members of trade unions, thereby gradually making unions unimportant? Table 12.1 shows how union density rates have evolved over time in a number of countries. In many countries membership has indeed gone down between 1970 and 2003, but in some other countries density rates have increased over the same period. There is a surplus of decreases and particularly over the later period from 1990 to 2003 density rates have almost uniformly decreased. Nevertheless, density rates are still considerable in some countries in 2003, and as Fig. 12.1 revealed, in some of the countries where density rates have decreased to a rather low level, e.g., Australia, France and Austria, coverage is still high. Against this background we may conclude that in most European countries and in Australia trade unions appear to be a rather permanent feature, in terms of density or coverage or both.

Although unions are widespread and formally important in many countries, it is open for discussion how much influence they actually have on wages. The question is to what extent unions really influence wages and to what extent they have to give in to market pressures and, for instance, set wages where the market would have set them anyway.

The Swedish survey among human resource managers mentioned in Chapter 11 also posed the following question to the 1200 managers involved:[1] 'How common is it that your employees (or their union representatives) require wage rises because of high profits, or high ability to pay, in your firm/organization?' In the sectors of manufacturing and so-called skilled services, 43.5 per cent and 48.2 per cent, respectively, answered that workers or union representatives do demand higher wages when they think the firm has the ability to pay. This indicates that managers in firms do experience wage bargaining pressures from workers and unions.

Another way of measuring union influence on wage formation is to compare the wages of union members to the wages of non-union members, or to compare wage levels in unionized and non-unionized sectors of the economy, controlling for other factors likely to affect wages. Studies of this kind generally find a positive influence on wages of union membership; a relatively weak effect in some countries (in the UK 10 per cent higher wages for union members than for non-members), and a stronger effect in other countries (20 per cent in the USA, for instance).[2]

THE IMPORTANCE OF UNIONS

In many countries, and particularly in continental European countries, trade unions are widespread either in terms of density or coverage or both. Empirical investigations suggest that unions do have a substantial influence on wages.

Overall we think it is safe to assume that trade unions *do* influence wages. This chapter will indeed make such an assumption and investigate its potential consequences.

12.2 A partial equilibrium model of a unionized labour market

The labour market

We consider a labour market where each of N identical workers supplies (inelastically) one unit of labour in each period, and where the demand for labour as a function of the real wage w is $L^d(w)$. For simplicity we assume that the labour demand curve is iso-elastic, so $L^d(w) = zw^{-\varepsilon}$, where z is a shift parameter, $z > 0$, that can be interpreted as a demand or a supply shock to the firm's revenue function, and ε is the real wage elasticity of labour, $\varepsilon > 1$.[3]

We think of the N workers as naturally connected to the labour market considered. For instance, we may consider the market for carpenters' labour in a specific area. In that case the N workers are the active carpenters living in that area. Should one of the N workers not get a job in the 'local' labour market, he will be left with a real income $v \geq 0$, which we take as an exogenous variable in the partial equilibrium model. Like in the efficiency wage model, v reflects a mix of what can be earned in the economy in general via alternative work opportunities, unemployment benefits, home production, etc.

All of the N workers are organized in a trade union. We assume that this trade union controls the money wage rate W in the labour market considered, and that through this control the union also determines the real wage rate $w \equiv W/P$, because the general price level

1. Jonas Agell and Helge Bennmarker, 'Wage Incentives and Wage Rigidity: A Representative View from Within', *Labour Economics*, **14**, pp. 347–369.

2. See David Blanchflower and Richard Freeman, 'Unionism in the United States and Other Advanced OECD Countries', *Industrial Relations*, **31**, 1992, pp. 56–79.

3. Without the assumption $\varepsilon > 1$, the trade union equilibrium studied below would not be well behaved, since unions would in principle want to drive wages to infinitely high levels if $\varepsilon < 1$ (as our analysis unfolds, you may convince yourself of this).

is given from the point of view of the union, or because the union takes fully into account how the price level depends on W (the latter in the case of a large, economy-wide union).

One can think of labour demand as coming from a relatively large number of wage-taking firms that decide on how much labour to hire given a real wage rate w. Thus the union does not interfere with the firms' employment decisions, an assumption sometimes referred to as the firms having the 'right to manage'. Assume that employers in our 'local' labour market are described by a representative profit-maximizing firm with a given real revenue function $\hat{z}R(L)$, where $R'(L) > 0$ and $R''(L) < 0$, just as in Chapter 11. The parameter $\hat{z}$ can then be thought of as a supply or a demand shock that takes values around 1. Labour demand will be determined by a usual 'marginal cost equal to marginal revenue' condition, $\hat{z}R'(L) = w$. We will think of the labour demand curve, $L^d(w) = zw^{-\varepsilon}$, as arising from such an optimization.

The ingredients of the labour market are illustrated in Fig. 12.2. The labour supply curve L^s is vertical, but it is only for real wages above v that a positive labour supply emerges, since no one would want to work in the specific labour market considered if they could earn more elsewhere in the economy. Thus $L^s(w) = N$ for $w \geq v$, and $L^s(w) = 0$ otherwise. The labour demand curve may intersect the labour supply curve either at the labour supply curve's flat segment or at its vertical segment. We assume the latter, as illustrated in Fig. 12.2, an assumption that can be stated as $L^d(v) = zv^{-\varepsilon} > N$, or $v < (z/N)^{1/\varepsilon}$. This means that if the labour market were characterized by competitive wage flexibility, the real wage rate, w^c, determined by the intersection of supply and demand would fulfil $w^c > v$. Algebraically, w^c would be given as the solution in w to $L^d(w) = zw^{-\varepsilon} = N$, or

$$w^c = \left(\frac{z}{N}\right)^{1/\varepsilon}, \qquad \text{implying } L = L^c = N. \tag{1}$$

The condition $w^c > v$, or $(z/N)^{1/\varepsilon} > v$, is, of course, equivalent to our above condition for $L^d(v) > N$. Note that given this condition (ensuring $w^c > v$), if the labour market worked competitively, supply and demand shocks (changes in z) would imply no fluctuations in employment (which would always stay at N), whereas fluctuations in the real wage rate would be perfectly and positively correlated with z and hence with revenue (since employment is constant). With an elastic labour supply function, the shifts in the labour demand curve caused by shocks would give rise to fluctuations in both the real wage and in employment, but if the real wage elasticity of labour supply were small, the fluctuations in the real wage would be much larger than in employment. Empirically, the real wage elasticity of labour supply *is* small, and this is the situation approximated by the assumption of a

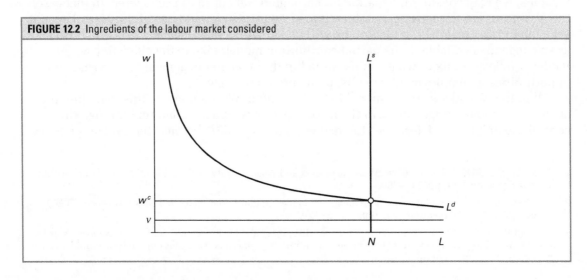

FIGURE 12.2 Ingredients of the labour market considered

completely inelastic labour supply. The resulting feature of the model, that fluctuations in the real wage are more closely correlated with fluctuations in output than are the fluctuations in employment, thus naturally arises from a competitive labour market, but accords badly with the stylized facts of the business cycle.

We assume that the labour market is not competitive, but monopolistic. One big agent, the trade union, decides on the real wage rate w. If the trade union sets a wage rate w larger than w^c, total employment will be given by labour demand, that is, $L = L^d(w)$, and there will be $N - L^d(w)$ unemployed workers. This means that the rate of unemployment will be given as:

$$u(w) = \frac{N - L^d(w)}{N} \qquad \text{if } w \geq w^c \text{, and } u(w) = 0 \text{ otherwise.} \qquad (2)$$

But will the union actually want to set $w > w^c$? To answer this crucial question, we must consider the objective of the trade union. What is the trade union trying to maximize?

The objective of the trade union

We will assume that the union's objective is derived from the members' utilities. Since the members are identical, this will give rise to an unambiguous criterion for the union: it should simply try to maximize the expected utility of its representative individual member. With identical union members, it is natural to assume that in any period where the rate of unemployment is u, the individual member's risk (probability) of becoming unemployed is also u. If the union sets the wage rate w, the expected income of each and every union member in that period will therefore be

$$\Omega(w) \equiv [1 - u(w)]w + u(w)v.$$

This will also be each union member's average income in the long run if the unemployment rate stays constant at $u(w)$. It is thus in the common interest of all the union members that in each period the expected, or long-run average, income $\Omega(w)$ is maximized.[4] Hence the union sets w in order to maximize $\Omega(w)$.

Such a w may involve unemployed members (if $L^d(w) < N$). In that case it will be in the individual unemployed member's *short-run* interest to take a job at a wage lower than the w chosen by the union, since this will increase the member's income in the short run where the alternative is unemployment. However, it will be in the individual member's *long-run* interest not to erode the market power of the union by such wage undercutting, since the union sets the wage rate so as to maximize each and every member's long-run (average) income. It is an underlying assumption here that members have realized this state of affairs and therefore, through the union, have made arrangements preventing undercutting.

The solution w^* to the problem of maximizing $\Omega(w)$ is unique (see below) and either $w^* = w^c$ or $w^* > w^c$ (explain why $w^* < w^c$ could not be optimal). In the latter case we say that the solution is interior. From the definition of $u(w)$, we have for $w \geq w^c$:

$$\Omega(w) = \frac{L^d(w)}{N}w + \frac{N - L^d(w)}{N}v = \frac{1}{N}(w - v)L^d(w) + v.$$

Since the trade union takes N and v as given, an interior solution is simply a w^* that maximizes $(w - v)L^d(w)$ with respect to w, where $w^* > w^c$. Note here that $(w - v)L^d(w)/N$ has

---

4. Strictly speaking, for the periodwise expected income, or the long-run average income, Ω to represent truly a member's interests, one must assume either that workers are risk neutral – having a utility function which is linear in income – or that they have access to perfect credit markets so that they can perfectly smooth their consumption over time via borrowing and lending.

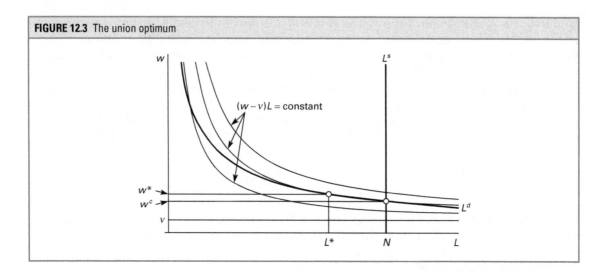

FIGURE 12.3 The union optimum

the interpretation that it is the excess of the expected income that the union ensures for a worker over what the worker could get in the general economy. Maximizing $(w - v)L^d(w)$ is the same as maximizing this surplus, or rent, from union membership.

Analysing the model

You may already have noticed yourself that setting w to maximize $(w - v)L^d(w)$ is equivalent to a traditional profit maximization problem of a monopolist firm, if this firm has constant marginal cost v and is faced with a demand curve identical to L^d. It is also well known that with an iso-elastic demand curve this problem has a unique solution where price is a mark-up over unit cost, and the mark-up factor is given by the elasticity of the demand curve as $\varepsilon/(\varepsilon - 1)$. Therefore, if the solution w^* to the union's maximization problem is interior it must be:[5]

$$w^* = \frac{\varepsilon}{\varepsilon - 1}v, \qquad \text{implying } L = L^* = z\left(\frac{\varepsilon}{\varepsilon - 1}v\right)^{-\varepsilon}. \tag{3}$$

Conversely, if the w^* given this way fulfils $w^* > w^c$, then indeed the union's optimum is interior and the unique optimal wage rate is w^*.

Drawing some indifference curves of the union in a diagram like Fig. 12.3 gives a good illustration of the union's behaviour, and verifies some of our claims. Combinations of wage and employment which ensure the same level of union utility are (w, L) such that $(L/N)w + ((N - L)/N)v = (1/N)[(w - v)L + Nv]$ is constant. These are, for a given N, hyperbolas of the form $(w - v)L = constant$, with the w-axis as vertical asymptote and $w = v$ as horizontal asymptote (see Fig. 12.3).

The union's optimum is where the highest indifference curve intersects the area below the labour demand curve, L^d, and to the left of the maximal labour supply, N. This could either be at the corner (w^c, N) or at an interior wage rate $w^* > w^c$. In the figure the latter is the case. In all circumstances the optimum of the union is unique, and if it is interior it is given by (3).

---

5. Just to confirm, set the derivative of $(w - v)L^d(w)$ with respect to w equal to zero:

$$L^d(w) + (w - v)L^{d'}(w) = 0 \quad \Leftrightarrow \quad L^d(w)\left(1 + \frac{w - v}{w}\frac{L^{d'}(w)w}{L^d(w)}\right) = 0 \quad \Leftrightarrow \quad 1 - \frac{w - v}{w}\varepsilon = 0,$$

which gives (3) when solved for w.

The unions's optimum may well be such that $w^* > w^c$, which implies unemployment in equilibrium: $L^* = L^d(w^*) < L^s(w^*) = N$. Using (1) and (3), the condition for unemployment to emerge, $w^* > w^c$, can equivalently be written:

$$\frac{\varepsilon}{\varepsilon - 1}v > \left(\frac{z}{N}\right)^{1/\varepsilon}. \tag{4}$$

This is indeed fulfilled for v or N large enough, or z small enough.

THE TRADE UNION OPTIMUM

If labour demand is sufficiently low relative to the number of union members, or the outside option is sufficiently attractive, the optimal wage rate chosen by the union will be greater than the 'competitive wage' and there will be unemployment in the labour market. In this case the union's optimal real wage is a mark-up over the outside option or normal income, and the mark-up factor is given by the real wage elasticity of labour demand in the standard way shown in Eq. (3) above.

Discussion of the model's main implications

A first conclusion from the partial equilibrium model is that there may well be unemployment in an equilibrium where the wage rate is fully adjusted in the sense that the wage-setting agent, the union, does not want it to be any different. Is there no pressure downwards on the wage rate in such an equilibrium? There are surely unemployed individuals who would like to work even at lower wages. For these workers not to imply a downward pressure on the wage, it must be assumed, as mentioned earlier, that the union has been given the power to hold back labour supply, that is, to order members not to take jobs at wage rates lower than the one set by the union. To delegate this power to the union is in the long-run interest of the members, since this is what makes it possible for them to appropriate the monopoly rent in the labour market. However, the presence of jobless workers whose short-run interest it is to take jobs at lower wages may give rise to difficulties holding the union together. These difficulties are of exactly the same nature as those facing any cartel.[6]

The unemployment in an equilibrium where $w^* > w^c$ is involuntary at the individual level. One could say that it is 'collectively voluntary', since it arises only because all the individual workers have decided to form a union that manages to hold the wage rate above w^c in the best long-run interest of the members.

A second conclusion is that when the equilibrium involves unemployment, that is, when (4) is fulfilled, the real wage rate is insensitive to demand and supply shocks while employment, and therefore output, vary in the same direction as z. This can be seen directly from (3), where the optimal wage rate, w^*, does not depend on z (as long as v is not affected by z), and employment L^* is proportional to z. Since employment co-varies closely with z, the rate of unemployment, $u^* = 1 - L^*/N$, will fluctuate as well and be negatively correlated with output and employment. At the same time the fundamentals of the labour market may well be such that if the market were competitive, demand and supply shocks would affect w, but not L. It was shown above that this requires that w^c, as determined by $L^d(w) = N$, is larger than v, or $v < (z/N)^{1/\varepsilon}$. So, if $v < (1/N)^{1/\varepsilon} < (\varepsilon/(\varepsilon - 1))v$, then for z fluctuating around 1, a competitive labour market would imply fluctuations in w in the same direction as the

---

6. For instance, exactly in so far as the OPEC organization of oil-producing countries manages to hold the price per barrel of oil above the marginal cost of producing one barrel, and in this sense is successful, individual OPEC members will have an incentive to sell more oil at lower prices.

fluctuations in output and no (or minor) fluctuations in employment, while a unionized labour market would imply no fluctuations in w and fluctuations in L in the same direction as those in output.

Thus, under a plausible assumption that permanent changes in productivity (z) are fully reflected in the normal income level v, while short-run random fluctuations in z are not, the trade union model may well, as (3) shows, have the property that the first type of productivity shock affects the real wage proportionally while the second type does not affect the real wage, but affects employment proportionally to the shock. These features are in good accordance with the stylized facts of growth and business cycles, respectively, so the trade union model (as well as the efficiency wage model) may contribute to bringing these two types of facts in accordance with each other.

UNEMPLOYMENT AND FLUCTUATIONS IN THE PARTIAL EQUILIBRIUM TRADE UNION MODEL

In a unionized labour market, the optimal real wage rate set by the trade union in the best long-run interests of the union members may well be so high that unemployment results. Hence trade union models may contribute to explaining structural unemployment, that is, the coexistence of some unemployment and fully adjusted prices and wages. In the partial equilibrium trade union model with unemployment, temporary demand and supply shocks do not affect the real wage, but give rise to fluctuations in employment.

12.3 Trade unions in a macroeconomic framework

We will now consider a macroeconomic framework with many labour markets, where the demand curves for each type of labour as well as the general income level v will be endogenized. This will give rise to a full macroeconomic equilibrium determining the real wage, total employment and GDP.

A macroeconomic framework

The framework considered is very close to the one studied in the previous chapter. Just as in the macroeconomic efficiency wage model, we will assume that there are n differentiated products and that the demand curve for each product $i = 1, \ldots, n$ is:

$$D(P_i) = \left(\frac{P_i}{P} \right)^{-\sigma} \frac{Y}{n}, \qquad \sigma > 1, \tag{5}$$

where P_i for $i = 1, \ldots, n$ are the nominal prices of the different products. This demand curve is in all respects as in Chapter 11: it can be viewed as arising from a representative household's optimization of a CES utility function (shown in Exercise 3 in Chapter 11), $P = P(P_1, \ldots, P_n)$ is the appropriate price index, Y is an indicator of aggregate demand that turns out to be the GDP of the economy, and σ is the elasticity of demand with respect to P_i or P_i/P (and equal to the elasticity of substitution between the different product varieties in the consumer's utility function).

For each product there is a single firm producing that type of output, so our framework is again one of monopolistic competition with one single firm representing the industry for each product. The production function of firm i is the simplest possible:

$$Y_i = L_i, \tag{6}$$

where L_i is labour input, and Y_i is output. All industries use the same kind of labour, but the firm in sector i has to hire labour only from members of the trade union that organizes all the workers presently connected to industry i. This framework is intended to represent an economy with *industry unions*.

In each industry's labour market a single firm thus faces a single trade union. This should define a bilateral monopoly and the wage, W_i, in labour market i should be determined in some form of negotiation between the firm and the trade union. For simplicity we will, nevertheless, assume that the trade union in each labour market has all the market power and sets the wage as a monopolist. Exercise 2 at the end of the chapter will ask you to conduct the parallel analysis with market power on both sides of each labour market and bargaining over the wage rate. As a consequence of our simplifying assumption of *monopoly unions*, each firm takes the money wage rate, W_i, as set by the union of sector i as given. The firm decides unilaterally how much labour it will employ at that wage, so in our trade union model the firms have the *right to manage*.

We will assume that in a given period a specific number, N_i, of workers are connected to production sector i. Each worker supplies one unit of labour inelastically. The workers of sector i are all gathered in the trade union that sets the money wage rate, W_i, in accordance with the members' interests. The union takes N_i as given as this number results from the number of workers seeking employment in sector i. Since there are many sectors, each union also takes economy-wide variables such as P, Y and n as given.

It will be part of our story that workers are not permanently tied to a sector, but can migrate to other sectors in between periods. In a full macroeconomic equilibrium it will be determined endogenously how many workers are connected to each sector. The condition determining this allocation will be a no-arbitrage condition stating that the expected income should be the same in all sectors since otherwise some workers would migrate. Because the sectors are symmetric, in the full macroeconomic equilibrium the number of workers in each sector will turn out to be the same.

Prices and wages in each industry

Using the fact that $Y_i = L_i$, the real profit of the firm in sector i is $\Pi_i = (P_i Y_i - W_i L_i)/P = Y_i(P_i/P - W_i/P)$. Given the definitions of the real or relative prices, $p_i \equiv P_i/P$ and $w_i \equiv W_i/P$, the profit of firm i can be written as $\Pi_i = Y_i(p_i - w_i)$. Inserting from (5) how output Y_i must relate to the relative price p_i, we get:

$$\Pi_i = p_i^{-\sigma} \frac{Y}{n}(p_i - w_i). \tag{7}$$

The firm in sector i takes the nominal wage rate, W_i, as well as the price level, P, as given, so it has no influence on w_i. It will set its price P_i, and hence, given P, its relative price p_i, so as to maximize Π_i. Maximizing Π_i is the same as maximizing the log of Π_i since the logarithmic function is everywhere increasing:

$$\frac{\partial \ln \Pi_i}{\partial p_i} = -\frac{\sigma}{p_i} + \frac{1}{p_i - w_i} = 0,$$

From this one easily derives:

$$p_i = m^p w_i, \quad \text{where } m^p \equiv \frac{\sigma}{\sigma - 1}. \tag{8}$$

(Check the second-order condition yourself, that is, show that $\partial^2 \ln \Pi_i/\partial^2 p_i$ is negative at the p_i we have found.) As we know from microeconomics, the optimal price p_i is a mark-up over the marginal cost w_i, and the mark-up factor, $m^p > 1$, relates to the elasticity of demand as shown. Given this price-setting behaviour, the labour demand function of firm i follows: if we insert the optimal value of p_i into the demand function (5), we get the optimal output of firm i: $Y_i = (m^p w_i)^{-\sigma} Y/n$. From our simple production function this output equals employment in firm i, so the labour demand function in each sector i is:

$$L^d(w_i) = (m^p w_i)^{-\sigma} \frac{Y}{n}. \tag{9}$$

This demand curve is iso-elastic, just like the one studied in Section 12.1. Its wage elasticity is the same as the price elasticity in the demand for products. Note also that the demand curve for labour is the same for all sectors. Hence each industry trade union is faced with the labour demand curve in (9).

As in Section 12.1, we will assume that the union maximizes the expected income of each of its N_i members. So the union chooses a w_i (or rather, it sets W_i so that, at the given P, it creates a $W_i/P = w_i$) that maximizes:

$$\Omega(w_i) \equiv \frac{L^d(w_i)}{N_i} w_i + \frac{N_i - L^d(w_i)}{N_i} v = \frac{(w_i - v)L^d(w_i)}{N_i} + v, \tag{10}$$

Again, v is a worker's 'outside option', which should be thought of as the average income a worker can expect to earn in the general economy if he is separated from sector i. Therefore v is the same from the point of view of all sectors. Note that $\Omega(w_i)$, as defined in (10), is only really the expected income of a worker if $L^d(w_i) \leq N_i$. However, in the macroeconomic equilibrium, the endogeneity of v will ensure that there is unemployment in equilibrium, $L^d(w_i) < N_i$, so the definition of Ω above is appropriate.

Since the union takes N_i and v as given, maximizing $\Omega(w_i)$ is the same as maximizing the 'union rent' $(w_i - v)L^d(w_i)$. This is independent of N_i, so an optimal wage for the union, and a wage in the members' interests, will be independent of how many members the union presently has.[7] We already know from Section 12.2 that there is a unique solution to maximizing $(w_i - v)L^d(w_i)$, given our iso-elastic labour demand function. The solution is:

$$w_i = m^w v, \qquad \text{where } m^w \equiv \frac{\sigma}{\sigma - 1}. \tag{11}$$

The optimal wage is a mark-up over the outside option v, where the mark-up factor $m^w \equiv \sigma/(\sigma - 1) > 1$ is given by the wage elasticity of labour demand in the usual way. Note that the price mark-up factor, m^p, and the wage mark-up factor, m^w, are identical because the elasticities of the product demand functions and the labour demand functions are the same. It is nevertheless useful to carry with us a logical distinction between the two.

This completes the description of equilibrium in each sector i. Everybody in the sector takes P as given. Given this P, the union sets a wage rate W_i that ensures $w_i \equiv W_i/P = m^w v$, and faced with this w_i, the firm sets a price P_i that ensures $p_i \equiv P_i/P = m^p w_i$, which implies a level of output and employment, $Y_i = L_i = (m^p w_i)^{-\sigma} Y/n$.

The wage curve, the price curve and the macroeconomic equilibrium

It follows directly from (11) that the real wage will be the same in all sectors, $w_i = w$, and this common w will, of course, be the general real wage level in the economy. Recalling that each individual union member faces a probability of unemployment equal to the general rate of unemployment, the outside option v should be tied to the unemployment rate, u, the real unemployment benefit rate, b, and the general real wage, w, as:

$$v = ub + (1 - u)w. \tag{12}$$

---

7. This uses $L^d(w_i) < N_i$, but again, this will be true in equilibrium.

Writing w for w_i on the left-hand side of (11), and inserting on the right-hand side the expression in (12) for v gives:

$$w = \frac{\sigma}{\sigma-1}[ub + (1-u)w],$$

where it is now convenient to insert the expression $\sigma/(\sigma-1)$ for m^w. Solving for w gives:

$$w = \frac{\sigma u}{\sigma u - 1}b = \frac{1}{1-\dfrac{1}{\sigma u}}b, \tag{13}$$

or expressed in terms of the rate of employment, $e = 1 - u$:

$$w = \frac{\sigma(1-e)}{\sigma(1-e)-1}b = \frac{1}{1-\dfrac{1}{\sigma(1-e)}}b. \tag{14}$$

At the aggregate level, the real wage is thus a mark-up over the rate of unemployment benefit, and (assuming $u > 1/\sigma$) the mark-up factor is larger than 1, implying $w > b$. Furthermore, the mark-up, and hence w, is larger the lower u is, or the larger e is.

The relationship in (13) or (14) is the 'wage curve' as derived from a macro model with trade unions. In the e–w diagram in Fig. 12.4 below, the wage curve is the increasing function labelled WS. This time the basic incentive effect behind the wage curve is that a higher rate of employment, from the point of view of each sector, means a better outside option, and hence each sectors's union must set a higher wage to defend the union rent.

An increase in the benefit rate b pushes the wage curve upwards, since, just like an increase in e, it improves the outside option. An increase in the elasticity of labour demand shifts the wage curve downwards. The more elastic labour demand is, the more costly, in terms of lost employment, it is for the union to push wages further up above v. So they will do this to a smaller extent, the larger σ is.

The expressions for the wage curve in (13) and (14) are, of course, only really meaningful if the mark-up factors involved are positive. This requires that $u > 1/\sigma$, or $e < (\sigma-1)/\sigma$. We therefore view the wage curve, as drawn in Fig. 12.4 for instance, as a function from employment rates e between 0 and $(\sigma-1)/\sigma$ to the associated wage rates, or, alternatively, as a function from unemployment rates u between $1/\sigma$ and one to the real wage. Unemployment rates above $1/\sigma$ will, of course, be quite large for elasticities σ close to 1. For the rates of unemployment coming out of the present model to be realistic, we must think of σ as

---

FIGURE 12.4 The macroeconomic equilibrium

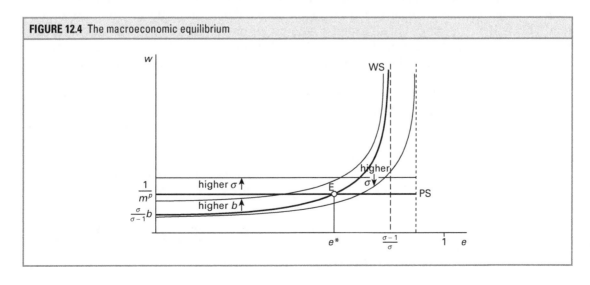

relatively large, e.g. σ has to be 20 to give a minimal rate of unemployment of 5 per cent. However, this is a consequence of the formulation given here where all market power lies with the unions. In Exercise 2 you will be asked to explore a model where both employees and employers have influence on the wage rate and negotiate it between them. One consequence will be that the wage curve may start at a more reasonable minimum rate of unemployment.

We found above that each sector's output price must fulfil $p_i = m^p w_i$. Since $w_i = w$ in all sectors, there will be one common real output price across sectors, $p_i = m^p w$ for all i. Hence P_i/P is the same for all i, implying that P_i has to be the same, and then since P is a price index, $P_i = P$ for all i. Thus $P_i/P \equiv p_i = 1$ for all i. It then follows that $m^p w = 1$, or:

$$w = \frac{1}{m^p}.$$

The line $w = 1/m^p$, illustrated as PS in Fig. 12.4, is the price curve in this model. We prefer not to insert how m^p depends on σ in order to preserve our logical distinction between market power in product markets and market power in labour markets. Nevertheless, an increase in σ, meaning stronger competition on the product markets, will of course give a lower value of $m^p = \sigma/(\sigma - 1)$, and therefore a higher position of the price curve, as illustrated in Fig. 12.4.

The full macroeconomic equilibrium is at the point E in Fig. 12.4 where the wage curve intersects the price curve. The associated rate of employment, e^*, or unemployment, u^*, can be found analytically by inserting $w = 1/m^p$ into the wage curve (14), or (13), giving (as you should check):

$$e^* = \frac{\sigma(1 - m^p b) - 1}{(1 - m^p b)\sigma} \quad \text{and} \quad u^* = \frac{1}{\sigma(1 - m^p b)}. \tag{15}$$

We assume that the parameters of our model are such that $(m^p)^2 b < 1$. This ensures a meaningful macroeconomic equilibrium where the rates of employment and unemployment are both between 0 and 1.[8]

The real wage of the macroeconomic equilibrium is $w^* = 1/m^p$. It is seemingly a striking result that w^* is given from the price-setting behaviour of the firms alone and is not at all influenced by the wage-setting behaviour of the unions, as reflected by the horizontal price-setting curve, PS, in Fig. 12.4. We should note that this is an artefact of our simplifying assumption of a constant marginal productivity of labour. Had we assumed diminishing returns to labour, the price curve in Fig. 12.4 would have been decreasing, meaning that both the wage and the price curve would be needed for determining the equilibrium wage rate. This will be the subject of an exercise below. Our model, as we have set it up here, can be said to show in a strong form the general insight that even though an economic agent may be large and influential in one part of the economy, the agent will, nevertheless, be constrained by the market forces of the entire economy.

The only element of the macroeconomic equilibrium we have not described is the allocation of workers across industries. What we have found above is that for any such allocation, the real wage rate in each industry will be $w^* = 1/m^p$, and hence the outside option as seen from any industry will be $v^* = u^* b + (1 - u^*)/m^p$. Given our assumption $m^p b < 1$, we have $v^* < w^*$, since $m^p v^* = u^* m^p b + (1 - u^*) < 1$, implying $v^* < 1/m^p = w^*$. This means that the income elements, w^* and v^*, that enter the expected income of a worker currently connected to industry i are the same in all sectors. Only the probabilities, $L^d(w^*)/N_i$ and $1 - L^d(w^*)/N_i$,

---

8. Note that $(m^p)^2 b < 1$ implies $m^p b < 1$, so both denominators in (15) are positive, implying $e^* < 1$ and $u^* > 0$. The condition for the numerator in the expression for e^* (and hence for e^*) being positive and for u^* being less than 1 is $m^p b < (\sigma - 1)/\sigma$. Using $m^p = \sigma/(\sigma - 1)$, this condition becomes $(m^p)^2 b < 1$. Note that $m^p b < 1$ also ensures that $u^* > 1/\sigma$, a condition mentioned above for our model to be meaningful.

by which w^* and v^* are achieved can differ between sectors. However, for the expected income to be the same in all industries, these probabilities, and hence N_i, must be the same in all industries. So, if the total number of workers is $\bar{L}$, there will be $N = \bar{L}/n$ workers in each industry union, and the GDP of the economy will be $Y = e^*\bar{L}$. This is the Y that entered into the demand curves (5).

Note that the macroeconomic equilibrium we have arrived at is worse with respect to welfare than an equilibrium with perfect competition in the labour markets, since under perfect competition all workers would be employed and the GDP would be $\bar{L}$, which is larger than the GDP with unions, $e^*\bar{L}$, since $e^* < 1$. This gives another important general equilibrium insight. Taking as given what happens in the remaining economy, the trade union in each industry does something good for its members by ensuring that they get a higher expected income than they would otherwise have had. These members would therefore be worse off if the trade union of that particular sector alone were dissolved. But when all unions in the economy have optimized on behalf of their members, the members are worse off than they would have been in a situation without trade unions at all. In our model this takes the drastic form that the equilibrium real wage rate is unaffected by the unions (the real wage is $1/m^p$, as follows from the price-setting behaviour of the firms with or without unions) and all that the unions really achieve *collectively* is to create some unemployment. We should note again, however, that with a decreasing price curve in Fig. 12.4, the presence of trade unions would imply both unemployment *and* higher real wages.

Main implications and structural policy

As can be seen directly from (15), or from Fig. 12.4, according to the macroeconomic trade union model *there is necessarily unemployment in equilibrium* (given our assumption, $(m^p)^2 b < 1$, that is required for a meaningful model). When unemployment is very low, the outside option $v = ub + (1 - u)w$ will be very close to the general wage level w. The unions only obtain rents for their members if they can attain a wage above v, so each union will seek to raise the wage in their sector above the general wage level, but of course not everybody can be above average. As all unions try to raise wages, the general wage level will be pushed up. Only when this has created some unemployment will all unions be able to ensure some rent for their members, since one can have $w > v = ub + (1 - u)w$ only when $u > 0$.

The comparative static results also follow easily, either from (15) or from shifting the wage and price curves appropriately as shown in Fig. 12.4. By either method one sees that according to the macroeconomic trade union model *more generous unemployment benefits mean higher structural unemployment*, a result that is naturally associated with structural labour market policy (reforms of the benefit system). At the same time, with our horizontal price curve the real wage rate is unaffected by b. When b increases, the outside option v increases, given u and w. Hence each union will set a higher real wage as reflected by the upward shift of the wage curve. However, in equilibrium the real wage is completely nailed down by the price-setting behaviour of the firms, so to keep each union satisfied with this (constant) real wage, the value of the outside option must fall back to its old level. This situation is brought about by an increase in unemployment. With a decreasing price curve, an increase in b would give both higher unemployment and higher real wages, as you will be asked to show in an exercise.

For our next results it may be convenient to replace the σ that appears in the equation for u^* in (15) with the equivalent expression, $m^w/(m^w - 1)$, written in terms of the mark-up $m^w = \sigma/(\sigma - 1)$:

$$u^* = \frac{1}{\dfrac{m^w}{m^w - 1}(1 - m^p b)}.$$

We can then see that according to the macroeconomic trade union model *more market power in the labour markets (a higher m^w, which must arise from a lower wage elasticity σ of labour demand) implies higher structural unemployment.*

What kind of policy does this result suggest if policy makers want to bring down structural unemployment? Perhaps a policy to make the union structure in the economy more decentralized would work to increase the elasticity of labour demand, and thus decrease market power and mark-ups for each trade union. The reason is that the more 'local' unions are, the easier it will be for firms to substitute away from the specific type of labour organized by a union if this particular union tries to increase the wage rate of its members. This may be part of an explanation why the union structure in many countries has become more decentralized in recent years.

We can also see that according to the macroeconomic trade union model *more market power in the product markets (a higher m^p, arising from a lower price elasticity σ of product demand) implies higher structural unemployment and lower real wages.* As in the previous chapter we arrive at the conclusion that structural unemployment is not only a matter of the structure of labour markets. Structural features of the product markets such as the degree of competition may also be important for the level of structural unemployment. Of course, this points to the relevance of competition policy as part of a policy package to fight structural unemployment.

UNEMPLOYMENT AND STRUCTURAL POLICY IN THE GENERAL EQUILIBRIUM TRADE UNION MODEL

- There is by necessity a strictly positive level of unemployment in the macroeconomic trade union model. This is due to the positive dependence of a decentralized union's rents on *the excess of* the real wage it obtains for its members over normal income and the feature that the latter is a mix of average wages and income opportunities as unemployed.
- According to the general equilibrium trade union model, the rate of structural unemployment is higher the more generous unemployment benefits are and the more market power unions have.
- According to the same model, more intense competition *on product markets* (less market power of firms) will imply lower structural unemployment as well as higher real wages.

12.4 Summary

1. In most European countries trade unions are widespread and large and even in countries where only a small fraction of workers are organized in unions, the agreements that trade unions enter into are often extended to cover a large part of the labour market. Furthermore, empirical investigations show that union members have higher wages than (otherwise comparable) non-union members. Unions thus seem to be important for wage determination.

2. Unions are involved in regulating many equally important working conditions, but this chapter concentrated on economic models where trade unions only have a role as wage setters. The models focused on *monopoly unions* with a market power so strong that they can dictate the wage rate to employers. In most respects, a model where employers are also assumed to have some market power generates the same qualitative results as the monopoly union model.

3. Under plausible assumptions, a union seeking to defend the interests of its members will want to maximize the expected, or long-run average, income of its representative member. This is equivalent to maximization of the total union 'rent', defined as the excess of the union wage over the income members could obtain elsewhere in the economy times the number of employed union members enjoying this excess.

4. In a partial equilibrium labour market model where firms have given revenue curves leading to downward-sloping labour demand curves, the wage rate set by the union to maximize the union rent could well be so high that labour demand falls short of the labour supplied by union members. The resulting unemployment is involuntary at the individual level, but voluntary from the collective long-run perspective of all union members, since the wage rate set by the union maximizes the long-run average income of the representative member. Those who are currently unemployed may have an interest in undercutting the wage set by the union in the short run, but if such undercutting leads to a breakdown of the union, the members are better off abstaining from undercutting. Trade unions thus face a 'cartel problem' like any other cartel. We assumed throughout the chapter that the union could impose sufficient discipline among its members to avoid breakdown due to the cartel problem.

5. If the labour market equilibrium in the partial equilibrium model with trade unions implies unemployment, shocks to the firms' revenue curves will have no impact on the real wage, but will be fully absorbed by fluctuations in employment and output, as long as the outside option (the income that union members can obtain elsewhere in the economy) is unaffected by the shocks. The trade union model may thus help to explain the business cycle fact that employment is much more closely correlated with output than real wages are.

6. The theory of monopoly union behaviour may be incorporated in a macro model with many production sectors and monopolistic competition and with a trade union in each sector. In such a general equilibrium model firms' revenues arise from consumer demand, and the outside option viewed from each production sector is a weighted average of the unemployment benefit and the general wage level, where the weights are given by the rate of unemployment. In a symmetric equilibrium the wage set by each union equals the general wage level, and the real (relative) output price of each sector is 1. Moreover, the equilibrium necessarily involves unemployment. The individual trade union can only create some rent for its members if there is a positive unemployment rate since, in the absence of unemployment, the wage set by each union equals the outside option.

7. In the general equilibrium macro model with trade unions the level of structural unemployment will increase if the market power of trade unions in the labour markets increases, if the market power of firms in the product markets goes up, or if the level of unemployment benefits is raised. These results are of obvious importance for labour market and competition policies.

12.5 Exercises

Exercise 1. The macro model of a unionized economy with a more general union objective

In the macro model of Section 12.3 as well as in the partial equilibrium model of Section 12.2 we assumed that the union maximized the union rent, $(w_i - v)L^d(w_i)$, a criterion derived from the interests of its members: it corresponded exactly to maximization of each member's expected or long-run average income (utility). The criterion includes a certain specification of how much the union cares about members' real wages relative to their employment. A more general criterion would be to maximize $(w_i - v)L^d(w_i)^\eta$, where the exponent η is a measure of the relative emphasis on employment, $\eta > 0$. Of course, $\eta = 1$ is the case considered in the chapter, but now we will also allow $\eta < 1$ or $\eta > 1$, corresponding to relatively less and relatively more emphasis on the employment aspect, respectively.

This exercise asks you to go through the macro model of Section 12.3 with the more general union objective function and no other changes. It should everywhere be assumed that $\sigma\eta > 1$.

1. Convince yourself by going through the description of firm behaviour that price setting and labour demand by firms are still given by (8) and (9).

2. Show that the optimal real wage rate set by trade union i is now:

$$w_i = m^w v, \quad \text{where } m^w = \frac{\sigma\eta}{\sigma\eta - 1}.$$

(Hint: You should actually go through the maximization of $(w_i - v)L^d(w_i)^\eta$ with $L^d(w_i)$ given by (9), using the first-order condition, etc. Here it may be helpful first to take log. When you have done that you should try to realize that you could have saved yourself the trouble since the maximization problem is just *as if* the union had been faced with a demand curve with constant elasticity of (minus) $\sigma\eta$, etc.).

3. Derive the wage curve as well as the price curve. Draw these in a diagram and explain how the position of the wage curve is affected by an increase in η. How is the macroeconomic equilibrium affected according to the figure? Show that in the macroeconomic equilibrium the real wage and the rate of unemployment are:

$$w^* = \frac{1}{m^p} \quad \text{and} \quad u^* = \frac{1}{\sigma\eta(1 - m^p b)}.$$

Confirm that the conclusion with respect to how the equilibrium rate of unemployment is affected by an increase in η is the same as you derived from your figure. Explain the incentive effect at work.

Exercise 2. A macro model with market power on both sides of the labour markets and wage bargaining

The macro model studied in Section 12.3 is modified such that in each sector the wage rate is negotiated between the trade union and the firm (or the firm's organization) who thus both have some influence on the wage rate. The model is otherwise the same as in Section 12.3, so among other unchanged features is the price-setting behaviour of the firms. While the interests of workers are naturally measured by their expected incomes as in Section 12.3, the interests of the firms must be associated with profits.

1. Show that given the price-setting behaviour of firm i, its real profit will vary with the wage rate w_i as given by:

$$\Pi(w_i) = (\sigma - 1)^{\sigma-1}\sigma^{-\sigma}\frac{Y}{n}w_i^{1-\sigma}.$$

Given a real wage rate w_i in sector i, we can measure firm interests by $\Pi(w_i)$, and we will, as in Section 12.3, measure workers', or union, interests by the union rent, $(w_i - v)L^d(w_i)$.

2. Show that given the labour demand curve in sector i as resulting from the behaviour of firm i, worker or union satisfaction with w_i is measured by:

$$\Omega(w_i) \equiv \left(\frac{\sigma - 1}{\sigma}\right)^\sigma \frac{Y}{n}w_i^{-\sigma}(w_i - v).$$

We will assume that the compromise wage between the conflicting interests of firms and workers is given by the so-called Nash bargaining solution, the wage rate w_i that maximizes the 'Nash product', $[\Omega(w_i)]^\beta[\Pi(w_i)]^{1-\beta}$, where β is a parameter, $0 < \beta \leq 1$, that measures the bargaining strength of the trade union.

3. Show that the negotiated wage rate in sector i is:

$$w_i = \frac{\sigma - 1 + \beta}{\sigma - 1}v,$$

and compare this expression to (11) for alternative β. Also describe the negotiated wage for $\beta \to 0$ and for $\sigma \to \infty$.

4. Show that the wage curve in the present context is:

$$w = \frac{u(\sigma - 1 + \beta)}{u(\sigma - 1 + \beta)}b - \beta = \frac{1}{1 - \dfrac{\beta}{u(\sigma - 1 + \beta)}}b,$$

and draw it in a diagram with u along the horizontal axis and w along the vertical, assuming that the mark-up factor in front of b is positive. This requires that u is above a certain value, at which the wage curve has an asymptote. Which value of u is that? Comment.

5. What is the price-setting curve in the present context? Assume that $b < (\sigma - 1)/\sigma$ and show that the rate of unemployment in the full macroeconomic equilibrium is:

$$u^* = \frac{\beta}{(\sigma - 1 + \beta)\left(1 - \dfrac{\sigma}{\sigma - 1}b\right)}.$$

Explain how the rate of structural unemployment is affected by changes in β, b, and σ and give the intuition in each case.

Exercise 3. The macro model of a unionized economy with a less extreme price curve

We mentioned several times in this chapter that the horizontal price curve arising from the assumption of constant marginal productivity of labour is a rather special feature of the macro model presented in Section 12.3: it means that the wage rate is determined by the price-setting behaviour of the firms alone and parameter changes that make the individual trade union require higher wages such as an increase in b (or, if you have solved Exercise 1, a decrease in η) leave the real wage unchanged. This exercise asks you to analyse the consequences of assuming a (possibly) decreasing marginal productivity of labour.

The macro model is changed in one respect. Instead of (6) we assume that the production function is:

$$Y_i = L_i^{1/\beta}, \qquad \text{where } \beta \geq 1,$$

which contains the old production function as the special case $\beta = 1$ (and β has nothing to do with the β of the previous exercise). Stated alternatively, the amount of labour required for producing an output of Y_i is $L_i = Y_i^\beta$. The model considered and the notation used is in all other respects as in Section 12.3.

1. Show that with the production function assumed here, the real profit of firm i can be written $\Pi_i = Y_i(p_i - w_iY_i^{\beta-1})$. Then show, using the demand functions (5) and the fact that output must equal demand, that Π_i can be rewritten as:

$$\Pi_i = p_i^{1-\sigma}\frac{Y}{n} - w_i\left(\frac{Y}{n}\right)^\beta p_i^{-\sigma\beta}.$$

2. Show, from the first-order condition for maximizing Π_i with respect to p_i, that the optimal real price, $p_i = P_i/P$, of firm i is:

$$p_i = \left(m^p \beta \left[\frac{Y}{n} \right]^{\beta-1} w_i \right)^{\frac{1}{\sigma(\beta-1)+1}}, \qquad \text{where } m^p \equiv \frac{\sigma}{\sigma - 1}.$$

Make sure that the second-order condition is fulfilled and that in the special case of $\beta = 1$ the formula for p_i accords with (8). A given relative increase in w_i gives rise to a larger increase in p_i if $\beta = 1$ than if $\beta > 1$. Explain this difference intuitively.

3. Show that trade union i will be faced with a labour demand function, $L^d(w_i)$, that has a constant elasticity of (minus) ε where:

$$\varepsilon = \frac{\sigma\beta}{\sigma(\beta - 1) + 1}.$$

(Hint: You should insert the p_i you have found in the demand function for product i to find how Y_i varies with w_i, and then use $L_i = Y_i^\beta$ to find how L_i varies with w_i). Show that $\varepsilon > 1$ under our assumption of $\sigma > 1$. Then show (by analogous operations to those we did in Section 12.3) that the wage curve of the economy expressed directly in terms of ε is:

$$w = \frac{\varepsilon u}{\varepsilon u - 1} b = \frac{\varepsilon(1 - e)}{\varepsilon(1 - e) - 1} b.$$

4. To derive the price curve first explain that in a symmetric equilibrium where all firms set the same price and produce the same amount of output, Y is the total production over all sectors, or the GDP of the economy, and must relate to the rate of employment as $Y = n(e\bar{L}/n)^{1/\beta}$, where $\bar{L}$ is the given size of the labour force. Then give reasons as in Section 12.3 to show that the price curve is:

$$w = \frac{1}{\beta m^p} \left(\frac{n}{e\bar{L}} \right)^{\frac{\beta-1}{\beta}}.$$

According to the price curve, w is decreasing in e. Explain why an increase in (the rate of) employment must be accompanied by a decrease in the real wage for the pricing behaviour of firms to be respected. Illustrate the wage curve as well as the price curve in a diagram and indicate the macroeconomic equilibrium, e^* and w^*.

5. How does an increase in b affect the wage curve, the price curve and the macroeconomic equilibrium? In particular, does the real wage increase? Explain the effects at work. Next, consider a decrease in σ. In which direction does this affect ε? How does it shift the wage curve? How does the decrease in σ shift the price curve, taking into account how m^p relates to σ? How is the equilibrium rate of employment affected? Explain the incentive effects at work.

Exercise 4. Taxes in the macro model of a unionized economy

Assume that labour income is taxed at a constant rate of τ, but at the same time an 'earned income tax credit' of a is given, so a person earning a wage income of w pays the tax $\tau w - a$, where $0 < \tau < 1$ and $a > 0$, and the net of tax wage income is $(1 - \tau)w + a$. The benefit rate b is fixed net of tax (it may be that benefits are taxed, but then the pre-tax level is set to keep the post-tax level at b). The credit a is only given to wage earners, and we assume $a < b$.

Each trade union realizes how labour income is taxed and takes the parameters of taxation, τ and a, as given. The objective of each union is then to maximize the union rent, $[(1 - \tau)w_i + a - v]L^d(w_i)$, where we assume $a < v$, and the outside option as seen from each sector is $v = ub + (1 - u)[(1 - \tau)w + a]$. In all other respects the model is as in Section 12.3.

In particular, the description of the firms is unchanged, so the pricing behaviour and the labour demand of firm i are still given by (8) and (9), respectively.

1. Show that the optimal wage rate set by union i is:

$$w_i = m^w \frac{1}{1-\tau}(v-a), \qquad \text{where } m^w = \frac{\sigma}{\sigma-1}.$$

Explain the incentive effects underlying that this wage rate increases with τ and decreases with a.

2. Show that the wage curve is:

$$w = \frac{\sigma u}{\sigma u - 1}\frac{1}{1-\tau}(b-a) = \frac{\sigma(1-e)}{\sigma(1-e)-1}\frac{1}{1-\tau}(b-a),$$

where we only consider $u > 1/\sigma$ (and assume that parameters are such that in equilibrium this condition is fulfilled). Illustrate the wage curve and the price curve (still $w = 1/m^p$) in a diagram and indicate the macroeconomic equilibrium, e^* and w^*. Explain how the wage curve shifts if τ is increased and if a is increased, and how the macroeconomic equilibrium is affected by each of these two policy changes. Explain the underlying incentive effects intuitively: why does an increase in a have a moderating effect on wage claims, while an increase in τ works opposite?

3. Show that in the macroeconomic equilibrium u^* and w^* depend on parameters as:

$$w^* = \frac{1}{m^p} \quad \text{and} \quad u^* = \frac{1}{\sigma\left(1 - m^p\frac{1}{1-\tau}(b-a)\right)}.$$

Show that an assumption of $(m^p)^2(b-a)/(1-\tau) < 1$, ensures $1/\sigma < u^* < 1$, that is, it makes the model meaningful. Show that the partial derivatives of the log of u^* with respect to τ and a are:

$$\frac{\partial \ln u^*}{\partial \tau} = \frac{1}{1 - m^p\frac{1}{1-\tau}(b-a)}\frac{m^p(b-a)}{(1-\tau)^2}$$

$$\frac{\partial \ln u^*}{\partial a} = -\frac{1}{1 - m^p\frac{1}{1-\tau}(b-a)}\frac{m^p}{(1-\tau)}$$

and make sure that their signs are in accordance with your findings in Question 2.

4. Now assume that from the old equilibrium, u^* and w^*, both the tax rate τ and the tax credit a are increased, by $d\tau$ and da, respectively, in such a way that tax payment (at the old equilibrium), $\tau w^* - a$, is unchanged, that is: $w^* d\tau - da = 0$. This change in the tax structure is a very simple example of a tax reform that increases marginal taxation, leaving total and average taxation unchanged. Using your partial derivatives from the previous question show that this tax reform implies *lower* structural unemployment according to the trade union model. (Hint: you should compute

$$\frac{\partial \ln u^*}{\partial \tau}d\tau + \frac{\partial \ln u^*}{\partial a}da$$

inserting the partial derivatives found above as well as $da = w^* d\tau$, remembering $w^* = 1/m^p$, and then use the parameter restriction for a meaningful equilibrium found in Question 3.) Try to explain the intuition for this somewhat striking result.

Exercise 5. Discussion: are unions bad?

The macro model with trade unions in Section 12.3 has the striking implication that the *general* prevalence of unions leads to unemployment and lower social welfare than could have been achieved without the unions (with perfectly competitive labour markets). This exercise asks you to discuss this result.

1. First let us take the macro model of Section 12.3 as it stands. Assume that initially the economy is in full equilibrium as described in Section 12.3 with real wage w^*, unemployment rate u^* > 0, and with workers evenly distributed across sectors. We assume that after this allocation of workers has been accomplished, workers are tied to their sectors for a long time. Assume that the workers of one sector i unilaterally consider dissolving their union, turning the labour market of sector i into a perfectly competitive market. Argue that this would actually hurt the workers in this sector by bringing them lower long-run average (or expected) incomes. Then argue that if *all* unions (of all sectors) are dissolved *simultaneously*, all workers will end up with higher long-run average incomes than in the equilibrium with unions.

2. Assume now that the price curve is not horizontal as in Fig. 12.4, but decreasing (in the same kind of $e-w$ diagram) because of diminishing returns to labour (as shown in Exercise 3 above). The macroeconomic equilibrium with unions is given by the intersection of the price curve and a wage curve as in Fig. 12.4. Give an illustration. Argue that if all unions are dissolved simultaneously and all labour markets thereby become perfectly competitive, the corresponding 'wage curve' will be a vertical line at $e = 1$. Indicate the macroeconomic equilibrium with perfect competition and show that in this model the prevalence of unions implies both unemployment and higher real wages. Discuss whether the fact that unions bring higher real wages means that the situation with perfectly competitive labour markets no longer Pareto dominates the situation with unions.

3. Broadening the view and taking into account functions of unions other than wage negotiations, do you think that historically trade unions have brought improved conditions of life for the working classes and, perhaps, for the general public?

Appendix

TABLE A Some growth-relevant country data

y_{03} Real GDP per worker relative to the USA in year 2003.
y_{60} Real GDP per worker relative to the USA in 1960.
g^y Average annual growth rate of real GDP per worker, 1960–2003. Logarithmic approximation.
s_K Average investment rate in physical capital (investment share of GDP), 1960–2003.
s_H Average 'investment rate' in human capital, 1960–95.
u Average number of schooling years in population above the age of 15 in year 2000.
isi   Index of social infrastructure
n Average annual labour force growth rate, 1960–2003.
Grade   Grading of data reliability from Penn World Table 6.1.

	Code	y_{03}	y_{60}	g^y	s_K	s_H	u	isi	n	Grade	In sample of 65
Luxembourg	LUX	1.735	0.966	0.031	0.256	–	–	0.900	0.008	A	0
USA	USA	1.000	1.000	0.018	0.190	0.115	12.049	0.973	0.016	A	1
Ireland	IRL	0.971	0.423	0.037	0.210	0.125	9.351	0.767	0.010	A	1
Norway	NOR	0.968	0.761	0.023	0.284	0.104	11.848	0.873	0.012	A	1
Belgium	BEL	0.907	0.664	0.025	0.225	0.101	9.338	0.866	0.005	A	1
Austria	AUT	0.881	0.555	0.028	0.240	0.095	8.354	0.864	0.002	A	1
France	FRA	0.839	0.623	0.025	0.231	0.095	–	0.871	0.007	A	1
Netherlands	NLD	0.837	0.909	0.016	0.242	0.113	9.355	0.894	0.014	A	1
Australia	AUS	0.805	0.837	0.017	0.243	0.102	10.922	0.810	0.021	A	1
Singapore	SGP	0.800	0.402	0.034	0.436	0.092	7.047	0.930	0.034	B	0
Switzerland	CHE	0.799	1.030	0.012	0.280	0.081	10.481	1.000	0.010	A	1
Italy	ITA	0.768	0.547	0.026	0.243	0.075	7.18	0.808	0.005	A	1
United Kingdom	GBR	0.765	0.705	0.020	0.174	0.094	9.42	0.856	0.005	A	1
Canada	CAN	0.763	0.895	0.014	0.225	0.105	11.617	0.966	0.022	A	1
Denmark	DNK	0.759	0.790	0.017	0.222	0.111	9.661	0.881	0.008	A	1
Hong Kong	HKG	0.752	0.271	0.041	0.253	0.073	9.413	0.896	0.029	A	1
Sweden	SWE	0.709	0.798	0.015	0.220	0.090	11.414	0.882	0.009	A	1
Finland	FIN	0.708	0.538	0.024	0.291	0.115	8.302	0.879	0.006	A	1
Israel	ISR	0.699	0.593	0.022	0.247	0.105	9.604	0.489	0.029	B	1
Spain	ESP	0.687	0.398	0.030	0.230	0.096	7.28	0.790	0.011	B	1
Iceland	ISL	0.681	0.670	0.018	0.251	–	8.83	0.896	0.020	B	0
Japan	JPN	0.664	0.299	0.036	0.306	0.109	9.467	0.833	0.010	A	1
New Zealand	NZL	0.653	1.018	0.007	0.205	0.118	11.737	0.593	0.019	B	1
Taiwan	TWN	0.628	0.122	0.056	0.170	–	8.764	0.767	0.022	D	0
Trinidad &Tobago	TTO	0.586	0.595	0.017	0.186	0.102	7.76	0.308	0.014	C	0
Mauritius	MUS	0.550	0.388	0.026	0.125	0.073	5.999	0.852	0.023	C	0
Greece	GRC	0.530	0.324	0.029	0.250	0.086	8.667	0.756	0.008	B	1
Portugal	PRT	0.502	0.301	0.030	0.205	0.073	5.873	0.795	0.010	B	1

TABLE A *Continued*

	Code	y_{03}	y_{60}	g^y	s_K	s_H	u	isi	n	Grade	In sample of 65
Korea, Rep. of	KOR	0.498	0.137	0.048	0.279	0.108	10.837	0.667	0.026	B	1
Chile	CHL	0.426	0.477	0.015	0.189	0.083	7.549	0.534	0.022	B	1
Barbados	BRB	0.415	0.562	0.011	0.049	–	8.732	0.869	0.012	C	0
Malaysia	MYS	0.412	0.164	0.039	0.194	0.079	6.8	0.844	0.029	C	1
Argentina	ARG	0.358	0.629	0.005	0.157	0.073	8.829	0.334	0.016	B	1
Gabon	GAB	0.317	0.374	0.014	0.076	–	–	0.287	0.020	C	0
South Africa	ZAF	0.312	0.414	0.011	0.093	0.068	6.138	0.414	0.024	C	1
Costa Rica	CRI	0.309	0.464	0.008	0.084	0.072	6.049	0.546	0.034	C	0
Panama	PAN	0.287	0.236	0.022	0.182	0.096	8.552	0.334	0.028	C	0
Uruguay	URY	0.287	0.478	0.006	0.128	0.081	7.558	0.337	0.010	B	1
Mexico	MEX	0.274	0.391	0.009	0.182	0.078	7.229	0.396	0.033	C	1
Iran	IRN	0.255	0.313	0.013	0.273	–	5.312	0.243	0.030	C	0
Algeria	DZA	0.240	0.395	0.006	0.157	0.124	–	0.265	0.030	D	0
Dominican Rep.	DOM	0.229	0.212	0.020	0.105	0.057	4.927	0.255	0.032	C	1
Brazil	BRA	0.228	0.243	0.016	0.189	0.049	4.884	0.385	0.029	C	1
Venezuela	VEN	0.219	0.616	−0.006	0.173	0.063	6.64	0.462	0.035	C	1
Colombia	COL	0.203	0.279	0.010	0.121	0.070	5.27	0.327	0.030	C	1
Romania	ROM	0.185	0.071	0.040	0.189	–	–	0.291	0.001	C	0
Paraguay	PRY	0.180	0.226	0.012	0.106	0.048	6.184	0.310	0.029	C	0
Thailand	THA	0.180	0.065	0.041	0.292	0.049	6.502	0.856	0.024	C	1
Cape Verde	CPV	0.180	0.134	0.024	0.149	–	–	0.229	0.023	D	0
Egypt	EGY	0.178	0.130	0.025	0.097	0.091	5.514	0.276	0.027	C	1
Turkey	TUR	0.174	0.140	0.023	0.129	0.062	5.289	0.367	0.020	C	1
Jordan	JOR	0.168	0.465	−0.006	0.131	0.146	6.914	0.615	0.048	C	0
Peru	PER	0.163	0.309	0.003	0.187	0.089	7.584	0.464	0.030	C	1
El Salvador	SLV	0.161	0.293	0.004	0.078	0.047	5.154	0.386	0.029	C	1
Ecuador	ECU	0.158	0.224	0.010	0.232	0.073	6.409	0.709	0.031	C	1
Guatemala	GTM	0.150	0.231	0.008	0.074	0.029	3.488	0.397	0.032	C	1
Morocco	MAR	0.148	0.112	0.024	0.116	0.045	–	0.504	0.024	C	1
Sri Lanka	LKA	0.137	0.075	0.032	0.147	0.091	6.866	0.432	0.022	C	1
Jamaica	JAM	0.133	0.269	0.001	0.170	0.112	–	0.483	0.017	C	0
Nicaragua	NIC	0.127	0.432	−0.011	0.088	0.063	4.579	0.428	0.034	C	0
Philippines	PHL	0.124	0.172	0.010	0.138	0.110	8.209	0.281	0.029	C	1
Indonesia	IDN	0.122	0.087	0.026	0.133	0.051	4.986	0.520	0.026	C	1
China	CHN	0.122	0.027	0.053	0.249	–	6.355	0.320	0.019	C	0
Bolivia	BOL	0.107	0.193	0.004	0.101	0.054	5.579	0.557	0.023	C	1
Pakistan	PAK	0.102	0.066	0.028	0.132	0.032	3.875	0.227	0.025	C	1
India	IND	0.099	0.062	0.029	0.105	0.056	5.063	0.306	0.020	C	1
Cameroon	CMR	0.096	0.126	0.011	0.049	0.026	3.54	0.359	0.021	C	1
Honduras	HND	0.090	0.157	0.005	0.125	0.039	4.796	0.390	0.031	C	0
Syria	SYR	0.089	0.082	0.020	0.082	0.090	5.775	0.412	0.033	C	1
Guinea	GIN	0.086	0.180	0.001	0.074	–	–	0.352	0.024	C	0

TABLE A *Continued*

	Code	y_{03}	y_{60}	g^y	s_K	s_H	u	isi	n	Grade	In sample of 65
Zimbabwe	ZWE	0.080	0.149	0.003	0.131	0.046	5.354	0.273	0.025	C	1
Cote d'Ivoire	CIV	0.072	0.096	0.011	0.081	0.027	–	0.313	0.035	C	1
Lesotho	LSO	0.070	0.040	0.031	0.174	–	4.232	0.552	0.016	D	0
Congo, Rep. of	COG	0.052	0.071	0.010	0.241	0.083	5.145	0.207	0.025	C	0
Senegal	SEN	0.046	0.115	−0.003	0.056	0.022	2.551	0.243	0.026	C	1
Nigeria	NGA	0.045	0.079	0.005	0.060	0.026	–	0.214	0.026	C	0
Nepal	NPL	0.045	0.045	0.018	0.120	0.036	2.428	NaN	0.019	C	1
Benin	BEN	0.044	0.053	0.013	0.085	0.020	2.335	0.244	0.024	C	1
Ghana	GHA	0.042	0.027	0.028	0.129	0.054	3.886	0.381	0.026	C	1
Mozambique	MOZ	0.041	0.046	0.015	0.030	0.009	1.105	0.268	0.019	D	0
Comoros	COM	0.040	0.090	−0.001	0.114	–	–	0.508	0.029	D	0
Mali	MLI	0.036	0.046	0.012	0.082	0.013	0.876	0.233	0.020	C	1
Rwanda	RWA	0.035	0.058	0.006	0.024	0.008	2.564	0.193	0.022	C	1
Kenya	KEN	0.034	0.073	0.000	0.112	0.033	4.197	0.313	0.033	C	1
Uganda	UGA	0.034	0.050	0.009	0.026	0.015	3.514	0.26178	0.027	D	0
Burkina Faso	BFA	0.034	0.038	0.015	0.088	0.006	–	0.249	0.016	C	1
Zambia	ZMB	0.033	0.061	0.003	0.339	0.029	5.457	0.234	0.025	C	1
Chad	TCD	0.029	0.071	−0.003	0.085	0.008	–	0.277	0.024	D	0
Togo	TGO	0.027	0.058	0.000	0.099	0.033	3.334	0.223	0.030	D	0
Niger	NER	0.027	0.072	−0.005	0.059	0.007	1.018	0.257	0.027	D	0
Gambia, The	GMB	0.027	0.041	0.008	0.068	–	2.312	0.395	0.033	C	0
Tanzania	TZA	0.026	0.029	0.015	0.049	0.007	2.705	0.276	0.028	C	1
Malawi	MWI	0.024	0.027	0.015	0.097	0.012	3.204	0.251	0.026	C	1
Madagascar	MDG	0.023	0.078	−0.010	0.040	0.031	–	0.238	0.025	C	1
Ethiopia	ETH	0.023	0.026	0.015	0.036	0.014	9.988	0.199	0.022	C	1
Burundi	BDI	0.021	0.038	0.004	0.038	0.005	–	0.264	0.017	C	1
Guinea–Bissau	GNB	0.019	0.030	0.007	0.132	–	0.839	0.259	0.016	D	0

Note: In order to be able to complete some of the exercises you need to know the level of GDP per worker in a common currency, 2000 dollars, for 1960 and 2003 for all the countries in this table. These numbers can be computed using the levels of US GDP given below.

	2003	1960	
Real GDP per worker, USA	67,865	31,691	(2000 dollars)

Sources: Average investment rates in human capital (s_H) from data set for Bernanke and Gürkaynak: 'Is Growth Exogenous? Taking Mankiw, Romer, and Weil Seriously', NBER Working Paper 8365, Juy 2001 (2001).
Average educational attainment (u) from Robert J. Barro and Jong-Wha Lee: 'International Data on Educational Attainment: Updates and Implications', Center for International Development Working Paper 42, 2000.
Index of social infrastructure (isi) from data set for Hall and Jones: 'Why do some countries produce so much more output per worker than others?', *Quarterly Journal of Economics*, 114, 2001.
All other data from Alan Heston, Robert Summers and Bettina Aten, Penn World Table Version 6.2, Center for International Comparisons at the University of Pennsylvania (CICUP), October 2002.

Book Two

The Short Run

Economic Fluctuations, Short-run Unemployment and Stabilization Policy

CHAPTER

13

Some facts about business cycles

Since the time of the Industrial Revolution the Western world has experienced a tremendous growth of total output. In Book One we focused on this long-run aspect of economic development. But history tells us that economic growth has been far from steady. In the short and medium term the growth rate fluctuates considerably, as you can see from Fig. 13.1 which plots quarterly data for the logarithm of real GDP for a number of Western countries. If the growth rate of the economy were constant, the log of GDP would follow the straight lines in Fig. 13.1. The fact that the graphs for the log of actual GDP are sometimes steeper and sometimes flatter than the straight lines reflects that periods of rapid growth tend to alternate with intervals of slow growth. Indeed, the graph has frequently had a negative slope, indicating that the growth rate sometimes even becomes negative. Note that the data underlying Fig. 13.1 are seasonally adjusted, so the fluctuations do not reflect the regular changes in business activity occurring with the changing seasons of the year, for example the seasonal swings in construction activity due to changing weather conditions. Thus there are more fundamental forces causing an uneven pace of economic growth.

The rest of this book studies these short-term fluctuations in economic activity, commonly known as *business cycles*. How can we explain that the state of the economy repeatedly alternates between business cycle *expansions* characterized by rapid growth, and business cycle *contractions* or *recessions* characterized by declining economic activity? To answer this question is one of the basic challenges of macroeconomic theory.

13.1 Why understanding business cycles is important

The fact that economic growth is repeatedly interrupted by recessions is a major source of concern for economic policy makers and the general public, since recessions bring considerable economic hardship to workers who lose their jobs, to entrepreneurs and homeowners who go bankrupt, and to ordinary consumers who suffer capital losses on their assets. Even for those who are not directly affected by layoffs and bankruptcies, recessions may cause a decline in well-being by generating fears of job losses and of future reductions in income and wealth. Understanding business cycles is therefore not only of academic interest; it may also help the economist to offer advice to policy makers on the possibility of reducing business fluctuations through macroeconomic *stabilization policy*, that is, active monetary and fiscal policy. At the very least an insight into the workings of the business cycle may enable the economist to suggest how policy makers can avoid *amplifying* the business cycle through misguided macroeconomic policies.

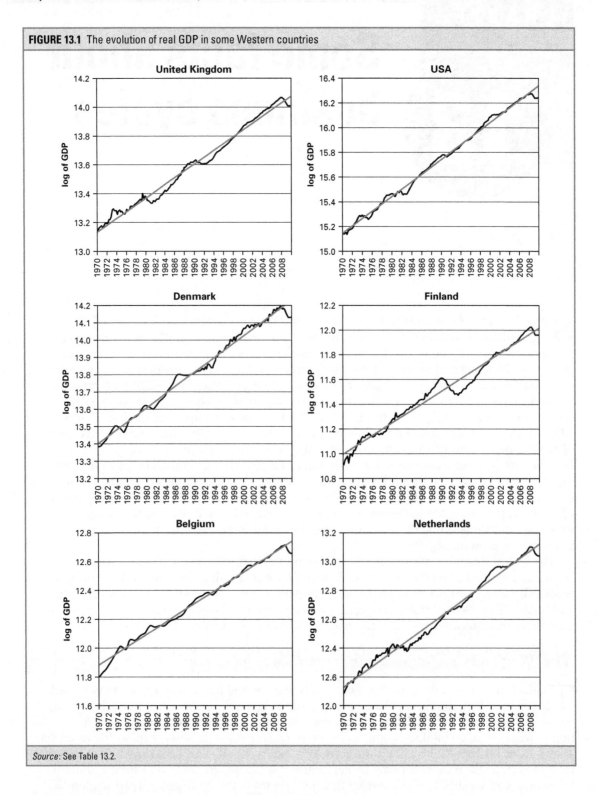

FIGURE 13.1 The evolution of real GDP in some Western countries

Source: See Table 13.2.

On several occasions in history, recessions have developed into severe economic *depressions* paving the way for social and political disaster. A glance at Fig. 13.2 should convince you why it is important to understand the causes of depressions and the means to avoid them. The figure shows a striking correlation between the unemployment rate in interwar Germany and the share of total votes in Reichstag elections going to Adolf Hitler's

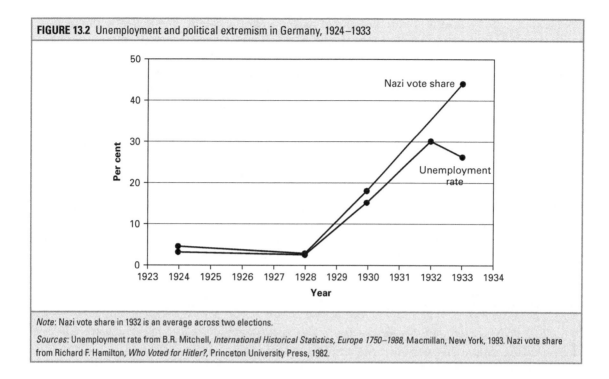

FIGURE 13.2 Unemployment and political extremism in Germany, 1924–1933

Note: Nazi vote share in 1932 is an average across two elections.

Sources: Unemployment rate from B.R. Mitchell, *International Historical Statistics, Europe 1750–1988*, Macmillan, New York, 1993. Nazi vote share from Richard F. Hamilton, *Who Voted for Hitler?*, Princeton University Press, 1982.

Nazi Party. In the 1928 election, when unemployment stood at the low level of 2.8 per cent, the Nazi Party captured only 2.6 per cent of the votes and were not considered a serious political force. But as the democratic system of the Weimar Republic proved unable to prevent the mass unemployment and human suffering caused by the Great Depression, a rapidly growing number of Germans became receptive to Hitler's radical critique of the parliamentary system. By 1933, with unemployment close to 30 per cent of the labour force, Hitler obtained a vote share of almost 44 per cent in the last free election before he established his Nazi dictatorship and steered Germany towards the Second World War. Although there were several other factors explaining Hitler's rise to power, there is no doubt that the economic depression made it easier for him to gather support.[1]

The Great Depression of the 1930s was exceptional in its severity and in its social and political consequences. Nevertheless, we have several recent examples of economic downturns which have caused social upheaval, including the South-east Asian crisis of 1997–98 which brought down the Indonesian government and led to serious civil unrest, and the economic crisis in Argentina in 2001 which forced the government to resign after riots in the streets. By studying business cycles we will not only learn more about the workings of a market economy; we will also improve our understanding of the general course of social and political events. In our later Chapters 19 and 20 on stabilization policy we will discuss in detail why business cycles generate a loss of economic welfare and how one may estimate the size of this loss. According to many estimates, the loss turns out to be considerable. It is therefore worthwhile to make an effort to understand business cycles.

The reason why it makes sense to theorize about business cycles is that, even though no two cycles are identical, they usually have some important features in common. Nobel laureate Robert Lucas of the University of Chicago made this point in the following way:

---

1. The Nazi leaders themselves were fully aware of the opportunities that economic depression played into their hands. Already in 1926 the later Nazi propaganda minister Joseph Goebbels wrote the following sentence in a pamphlet on *Die Zweite Revolution*: 'We can achieve anything if we can make hunger, despair and deprivation march in our ranks . . .' (quoted from Joachim C. Fest: *Das Gesicht des Dritten Reiches. Profile einer Totalitären Herrschaft*, Piper Verlag, München, 1980; quote translated by the present authors).

Though there is absolutely no theoretical reason to anticipate it, one is led by the facts to conclude that, with respect to the qualitative behavior of comovements among series (economic variables), *business cycles are all alike.* To theoretically inclined economists, this conclusion should be attractive and challenging, for it suggests the possibility of a unified explanation of business cycles, grounded in the *general laws* governing market economies, rather than in political or institutional characteristics specific to particular countries or periods.[2]

In the rest of this chapter we will describe some of those co-movements of economic variables which are characteristic of business cycles. Before we start theorizing about business cycles, we want to get some idea of the phenomenon which our theory is supposed to explain. We will begin in the next section by restating a definition of business cycles that has become familiar in the literature. We will then move on to the question how we can measure business cycles in quantitative terms. That is, how can we separate short-term business cycle fluctuations in economic activity from the long-term economic growth trend? Following this, we will be ready to describe in quantitative terms the co-movements of important economic variables during a 'typical' business cycle.

13.2 Defining business cycles

In a famous book which became a milestone in empirical business cycle research, the American economists Arthur Burns and Wesley Mitchell gave the following classic definition of business cycles:

> Business cycles are a type of fluctuations found in the aggregate economic activity of nations that organize their work mainly in business enterprises: a cycle consists of expansions occurring at about the same time in many economic activities, followed by similarly general recessions, contractions, and revivals which merge into the expansion phase of the next cycle; this sequence of changes is recurrent but not periodic; in duration business cycles vary from more than one year to ten or twelve years; they are not divisible into shorter cycles of similar character with amplitudes approximating their own.[3]

This definition of business cycles emphasizes several points:

- *Aggregate economic activity*: Business cycles are characterized by a co-movement of a large number of economic activities and not just by movements in a single variable like real GDP.

- *Organization in business enterprises*: Business cycles are a phenomenon occurring in decentralized market economies. Although they had several other economic problems, the former socialist economies of Eastern Europe did not go through business cycles of the type known in the Western world.

- *Expansions and contractions*: Business cycles are characterized by periods of expansion of economic activity followed by periods of contraction in which activity declines.

- *Duration of more than a year (persistence)*: A full business cycle lasts for more than a year. Fluctuations of shorter duration do not have the features characteristic of business cycles. This means that purely seasonal variations in activity within a year are not business cycles. We may also say that business cycle movements display *persistence*:

---

2. Robert E. Lucas, Jr., 'Understanding Business Cycles', in K. Brunner and A.H. Meltzer, eds, *Carnegie-Rochester Conference Series on Public Policy*, **5**, Autumn 1977, p. 10.

3. Arthur F. Burns and Wesley C. Mitchell, *Measuring Business Cycles*, National Bureau of Economic Research (NBER), New York, 1946, p. 1. Mitchell was a principal founder of the NBER, and Burns was a student of his who later became chairman of the US Federal Reserve Board from 1970 until 1978.

once an expansion gets going, it usually lasts for some time during which the expansionary forces tend to be self-reinforcing, and once a contraction sets in, it tends to breed further contraction for a while.

- *Recurrent but not periodic*: Although business cycles repeat themselves, they are far from being strictly periodic. The duration of cycles has varied from slightly more than a year to 10–12 years, and the severity of recessions has also varied considerably, with recessions sometimes (but not always) turning into *depressions*.

13.3 Dating business cycles

The contribution of Burns and Mitchell was to document the movements over time of a large number of economic variables. Through their work it became possible to *identify the turning points* in economic activity and hence to offer a *dating* of business cycles. Since the movements of the different economic variables are not perfectly synchronized, it is a matter of judgement to identify the point in time at which the business cycle reaches its peak and moves from expansion into contraction, and to determine when it reaches its trough, moving from contraction (recession) to expansion. Building on the tradition established by Burns and Mitchell, the US National Bureau of Economic Research (NBER) has for many years had a Business Cycle Dating Committee consisting of experts in empirical business cycle research. The NBER committee defines a recession (contraction) as a period of significant decline in total output, income, employment and trade, usually lasting from six months to a year, and marked by widespread contractions in many sectors of the economy. On this basis the committee has arrived at a dating of US business cycles between 1854 and 2001. This dating is reproduced in Table 13.1.

The length of the business cycle is measured from trough to trough, and the last column of the table measures the duration of the expansion phase relative to the duration of the contraction phase. Table 13.1 illustrates the point stressed by Burns and Mitchell: business cycles are far from regular and periodic. The duration of the cycle varies greatly, and though the expansion phase usually lasts longer than the contraction phase – reflecting the economy's long-term potential for growth – there are also examples of cycles where the contraction has lasted longer than the previous expansion. At the bottom of the Great Depression in March 1933, the US economy had been contracting for 43 months. During this economic nightmare, real GDP fell by almost 30 per cent, and unemployment rose to 25 per cent. Notice, however, that the contraction of the 1870s lasted considerably longer than the Great Depression, although economic historians tell us that the decline in activity was less catastrophic.

The dates in Table 13.1 indicate that business cycle expansions have tended to last longer and that contractions have on average been shorter after the Second World War than before that time. Until recently, the expansion from February 1961 to December 1969 was the longest economic boom in US history. That record was beaten by the ten-year-long expansion starting in March 1991. Although the subsequent recession lasted only eight months, this cycle was the longest business cycle on record in the USA.

The long US boom of the 1990s inspired many commentators to speculate about the arrival of a 'New Economy' in which the expansionary forces stemming from innovations in information technology were so strong that serious recessions would be a thing of the past, at least in the USA. Interestingly, the long boom of the 1960s gave rise to a similar unfounded optimism. In 1967, several leading US economists gathered for a conference asking: 'Is the Business Cycle Obsolete?'[4] But the recession in the USA and in many other countries at the beginning of this century and the dramatic international financial and economic crisis in 2008–09 – highly visible in Fig. 13.1 – show that the business cycle is still with us.

---

4. The conference participants tended to answer the question in the affirmative. The conference papers were published in Martin Bronfenbrenner (ed.), *Is the Business Cycle Obsolete?* Wiley, New York, 1969.

TABLE 13.1 US business cycle expansions and contractions

Business cycle reference dates			Duration in months			
Trough	Peak	Trough	1. Expansion	2. Contraction	Cycle[1]	1./2.
December 1854	June 1857	December 1858	30	18	48	1.67
December 1858	October 1860	June 1861	22	8	30	2.75
June 1861	April 1865	December 1867	46	32	78	1.44
December 1867	June 1869	December 1870	18	18	36	1.00
December 1870	October 1873	March 1879	34	65	99	0.52
March 1879	March 1882	May 1885	36	38	74	0.95
May 1885	March 1887	April 1888	22	13	35	1.69
April 1888	July 1890	May 1891	27	10	37	2.70
May 1891	January 1893	June 1894	20	17	37	1.18
June 1894	December 1895	June 1897	18	18	36	1.00
June 1897	June 1899	December 1900	24	18	42	1.33
December 1900	September 1902	August 1904	21	23	44	0.91
August 1904	May 1907	June 1908	33	13	46	2.54
June 1908	January 1910	January 1912	19	24	43	0.79
January 1912	January 1913	December 1914	12	23	35	0.52
December 1914	August 1918	March 1919	44	7	51	6.29
March 1919	January 1920	July 1921	10	18	28	0.56
July 1921	May 1923	July 1924	22	14	36	1.57
July 1924	October 1926	November 1927	27	13	40	2.08
November 1927	August 1929	March 1933	21	43	64	0.49
March 1933	May 1937	June 1938	50	13	63	3.85
June 1938	February 1945	October 1945	80	8	88	10.0
October 1945	November 1948	October 1949	37	11	48	3.36
October 1949	July 1953	May 1954	45	10	55	4.50
May 1954	August 1957	April 1958	39	8	47	4.88
April 1958	April 1960	February 1961	24	10	34	2.40
February 1961	December 1969	November 1970	106	11	117	9.64
November 1970	November 1973	March 1975	36	16	52	2.25
March 1975	January 1980	July 1980	58	6	64	9.67
July 1980	July 1981	November 1982	12	16	28	0.75
November 1982	July 1990	March 1991	92	8	100	11.5
March 1991	March 2001	November 2001	120	8	128	15.0
November 2001	December 2007	n.a.	73	n.a.	n.a.	n.a.
Average for pre-First World War period (15 cycles)[2]			25	23	48	1.10
Average for interwar period (5 cycles)[3]			26	20	46	1.30
Average for post-Second World War period (10 cycles)[4]			57	10	67	5.50

[1] The duration of the full business cycle is measured from trough to trough.
[2] December 1854 to December 1914.
[3] March 1919 to June 1938.
[4] October 1945 to November 2001.
n.a.: data not yet available at the time of writing.

Source: National Bureau of Economic Research.

Let us therefore move from the *dating* of business cycles to the problem of *quantitative measurement* of business fluctuations.

13.4 Measuring business cycles

Most economic time series fluctuate around a growing time trend. The growth trend reflects the forces described in the theory of economic growth, while the task of business cycle theory is to explain the fluctuations around that trend. For example, if Y_t is real GDP in period t, it is useful to think of Y_t as the product of a growth component Y_t^g indicating the trend value which Y_t would assume if the economy were always on its long-term growth path, and a cyclical component Y_t^c which fluctuates around a long-run mean value of 1:

$$Y_t = Y_t^g \cdot Y_t^c. \tag{1}$$

Our assumption on the mean value of Y_t^c implies that $Y_t = Y_t^g$ on average. Equation (1) also implies that as long as the amplitude of the fluctuations in the cyclical component remains constant, the *absolute* amplitude of the business cycle fluctuations in real GDP will rise in proportion to the trend level of output so that the *percentage* deviations of actual output from trend output over the business cycle will tend to stay constant over time.

It will be convenient to work with the natural logarithms of the various variables rather than with the variables themselves, because changes in the log of some variable X approximate percentage changes in X. Taking logs on both sides of equation (1) and defining $y_t \equiv \ln Y_t, g_t \equiv \ln Y_t^g$, and $c_t \equiv \ln Y_t^c$, we get:

$$y_t = g_t + c_t \tag{2}$$

In this section we will discuss how we can estimate the trend component g_t and the cyclical component c_t separately, given that we only have observations of y_t. Let us start by going back to Fig. 13.1. The straight lines in that figure are regression lines with a slope roughly equal to the average growth rate over the period of observation. Technically, the intercept and the slope of the regression line are chosen so as to minimize the sum of the squared deviations between the observed values of the log of GDP and the points on the line.

It might be tempting to let the straight regression line represent the trend value of output and to measure the cyclical component of GDP as the deviation from that hypothetical steady growth path. But a moment's reflection should convince you that this is not a satisfactory procedure. Recall that along the straight regression line the economy's real growth rate is constant. If we take the regression line to represent the trend growth path, we are therefore postulating that the economy would always be in a steady state equilibrium with a constant growth rate if it were not disturbed by business fluctuations.

However, the theory of economic growth gives no reason to believe that the economy is always in a steady state. Conventional growth theory tells us that the economy's growth rate will decline over time if it starts out with a capital–labour ratio below the steady state level, and vice versa. Moreover, the modern theory of endogenous growth suggests that the rate of technical progress may vary with the endogenous innovation activity of firms. Indeed, even if major technological innovations are exogenous to the economic system, they are unlikely to arrive at an equal pace over time, and this is sufficient reason to discard the assumption of a constant long-term growth rate. An inspection of Fig. 13.1 also suggests that the longer-term movement of the economy does not follow a straight line, even if we abstract from the short-term ups and downs of the graphs for real GDP.

Hence we need a more sophisticated method for separating the growth trend from the cyclical component of a variable like GDP. Since we do not perfectly understand how the economy works, we cannot claim that there is a single objectively correct way of separating

c_t from g_t. Still, our reasoning above suggests that we need a method which allows for variation over time in the underlying growth trend, but which nevertheless ensures that the short-term fluctuations are categorized as temporary cyclical deviations from trend. One such method which has become widely used in recent years is the so-called *Hodrick–Prescott filter*, named after American economists Robert Hodrick and Edward Prescott who popularized its use.[5] Under this method of 'filtering' (that is, detrending) an economic time series like $(y_t)_{t=1}^T$ for the log of GDP, the growth component g_t is determined by minimizing the magnitude:

$$HP = \sum_{t=1}^{T}(y_t - g_t)^2 + \lambda\sum_{t=2}^{T-1}[(g_{t+1} - g_t)-(g_t - g_{t-1})]^2 \tag{3}$$

with respect to all of the g_t, where observations are available for the time periods $t = 1, 2, \ldots, T$, and where λ is a parameter which is chosen by the observer. Note that since y_t is measured in logarithms, the magnitudes $g_{t+1} - g_t$ and $g_t - g_{t-1}$ are approximately the *percentage growth rates* of the trend value of real GDP in periods $t + 1$ and t, respectively. The term in the square bracket in (3) thus measures the change in the estimated trend growth rate from one period to the next. Note also that, by definition, the term $y_t - g_t$ in (3) measures the cyclical component c_t of log(GDP) in period t. Minimizing the expression in (3) therefore forces us to compromise between two objectives. On the one hand, we want to choose the g_t's so as to minimize changes in the estimated trend growth rate over time, since this will minimize the expression in the second term in (3). On the other hand, we want to bring g_t as close as possible to (the log of) actual output y_t so as to minimize the first sum in (3). The relative weight placed on each of these conflicting objectives depends on our choice of λ.

Consider first the extreme case where we set $\lambda = 0$. In this special case we will minimize *HP* by simply choosing $g_t = y_t$ for all $t = 1, 2, \ldots, T$, since *HP* will then attain its lowest possible value of zero. But this amounts to postulating that all observed fluctuations in y_t reflect changes in the underlying growth trend! This clearly does not make sense, unless we want to deny the existence of business fluctuations.

Consider next the opposite extreme where we let λ tend to infinity. In that case the first sum in (3) does not carry any weight, and *HP* will then attain its lowest possible value of zero if we choose the g_t's to ensure that the estimated trend growth rate is *constant* throughout the period of observation, that is $g_{t+1} - g_t = g_t - g_{t-1}$ for all $t = 2, 3, \ldots, T - 1$. This would give us the straight lines in Fig. 13.1, but we have already seen that it is unreasonable to assume that the trend growth rate is a constant.

Clearly, then, λ should be positive but finite. The greater the value of λ, the more we will try to avoid variation over time in the estimated trend growth rate, that is, the smoother will be our estimated growth trend (the closer it will be to a straight line). On the other hand, the smaller the value of λ, the smaller will be the deviation between our estimated g_t and the actual value of output y_t, that is, the greater is that part of the movement in actual output which we ascribe to changes in the underlying growth trend.

Among business cycle researchers using *quarterly* data, it is customary to set $\lambda = 1600$. This is basically a convention, based on a consensus that this value of λ produces a fitted growth trend that a 'reasonable' student of business cycles would draw through a time plot of quarterly data for (the log of) real GDP. Figure 13.3 shows the fitted growth trend for the countries included in Fig. 13.1 when the trend is estimated via the HP filter using $\lambda = 1600$. We see that the HP filter does indeed seem to capture the gradual changes in the growth trend which are apparent to the naked eye. However, researchers have found that the HP filter tends to give imprecise estimates of the trend at the end-points of a time series. For this reason the analysis throughout this chapter excludes the first and the last 12

---

5. Robert J. Hodrick and Edward C. Prescott, 'Post-war U.S. Business Cycles: An Empirical Investigation', *Journal of Money, Credit, and Banking*, **29**, 1997, pp. 1–16 (originally published as a working paper in 1980).

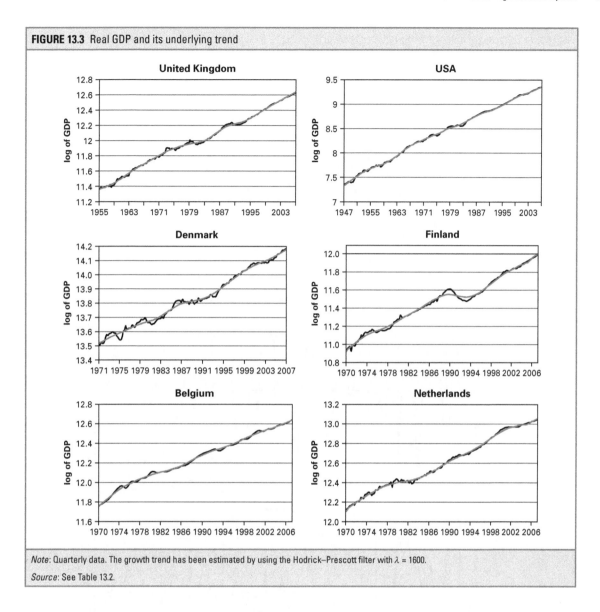

FIGURE 13.3 Real GDP and its underlying trend

Note: Quarterly data. The growth trend has been estimated by using the Hodrick–Prescott filter with $\lambda = 1600$.

Source: See Table 13.2.

estimated cyclical components of all quarterly time series, in line with common practice (this means that the severe recession of 2008 does not show up in Fig. 13.3 and subsequent diagrams).

Once we have fitted a growth trend using the HP filter, we immediately obtain an estimate of the cyclical component of the (log of) quarterly real GDP by rearranging equation (2) to get $c_t = y_t - g_t$. In Fig. 13.4 we have plotted the resulting estimates of business cycles, that is, the values of all the c_t's for our group of countries. The graphs confirm what we have already emphasized: periods of expansion and periods of contraction tend to alternate, but the business cycles are far from periodic and regular, and even within each longer cycle there are erratic quarterly fluctuations in activity.

It is tempting to offer a dating of recent business cycles based on Fig. 13.4, for although business cycles involve the co-movement of many economic variables (as we shall see in the next section), GDP is, after all, the most common single indicator of aggregate economic activity. We have inserted vertical lines in Fig. 13.4 to indicate business cycles measured from trough to trough. The identification of business cycle troughs and peaks is based on the following simple rules of thumb:

FIGURE 13.4a Cycles in real GDP in the UK, the USA and Denmark

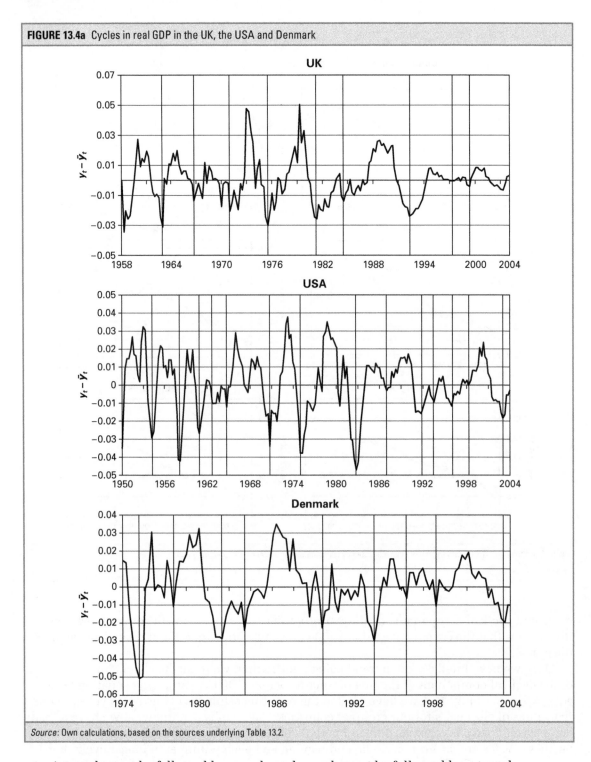

Source: Own calculations, based on the sources underlying Table 13.2.

1. A trough must be followed by a peak, and a peak must be followed by a trough.
2. The expansion phase as well as the contraction phase must last for a minimum of two quarters.
3. A business cycle must span a minimum of five quarters.

If the first criterion is not met, it does not make sense to speak of a 'cycle'. The second criterion implies that we require a minimum degree of persistence in the movement of

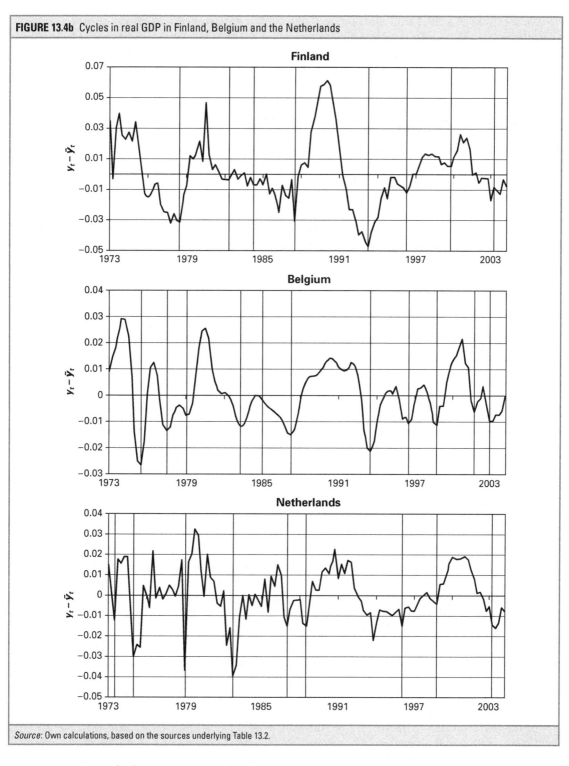

FIGURE 13.4b Cycles in real GDP in Finland, Belgium and the Netherlands

Source: Own calculations, based on the sources underlying Table 13.2.

economic activity before we can speak of a systematic tendency for activity to expand or contract. The last criterion reflects the convention that fluctuations spanning only a year or less do not count as business cycles.[6]

---

6. The computer algorithm used to date the business cycles was developed and kindly provided by Jesper Linaa from the secretariat of the Danish Economic Councils.

We see from Fig. 13.4 that all the countries shown experienced a serious contraction in the mid-1970s. All countries also fell into recession in the early 1980s, in the early 1990s, and in the early part of this century. In Exercise 1 we test your knowledge of recent economic history by asking you to mention some factors or 'shocks' which might help explain these downturns in economic activity.

13.5 What happens during business cycles?

The HP filter is a useful method of separating the growth trend from the cyclical component of an economic time series. In this section we will study the statistical properties of the estimated cyclical components of a number of time series for our group of countries. By doing so we will get more information on what happens during business cycles.

Our study is based on seasonally adjusted quarterly data going back as far as such data are available for our six countries. The data sets include the series for real GDP which we have already considered. The components of national income and product are measured in fixed prices, and all variables have been detrended by means of the HP filter, using the λ-value of 1600 which is customary for business cycle analysis of quarterly data. Variables displaying a growing time trend have been transformed into natural logarithms before detrending. Also, because the HP filter gives imprecise estimates of the trend at the end-points of a time series, we have excluded the first and the last 12 estimated cyclical components of each series from our statistical analysis, as mentioned earlier.

Volatility

The first question we will ask is: what is the magnitude of the variability in different economic variables during a 'typical' business cycle? We may quantify this variability by calculating the *standard deviations* of the estimated cyclical components of the various time series. The empirical standard deviation s_x of a series of observations of variable x_t over the time interval $t = 1, 2, \ldots, T$ is defined as:

$$s_x = \sqrt{\frac{1}{T-1}\sum_{t=1}^{T}(x_t - \bar{x})^2}, \qquad \bar{x} \equiv \frac{1}{T}\sum_{t=1}^{T}x_t, \tag{4}$$

where $\bar{x}$ is the empirical mean value of the x_t's. The empirical standard deviation measures the 'average' deviation of x_t from its mean over the period of observation. It is thus a natural indicator of the degree of *volatility* of the economic variable x_t.

In the middle columns of Table 13.2 we use the absolute standard deviation as a measure of the volatility of the cyclical components of some important macroeconomic variables. Recall that when variables are measured in logarithms, the absolute standard deviation of some variable $x \equiv \ln X$ roughly indicates the average *percentage* deviation of X from its mean. For example, the first figure in the middle column for the United Kingdom indicates that, on average over the UK business cycle, the cyclical component of real quarterly GDP deviates about 1.5 per cent from its mean value.

In the last columns in Table 13.2 we have measured the standard deviations of the various variables relative to the standard deviation of GDP. A figure in excess of (smaller than) 1 means that the variable considered tends to be more (less) volatile than GDP. One striking feature of Table 13.2 is that investment is between $2\frac{1}{2}$ and $4\frac{1}{2}$ times as volatile as GDP. The volumes of exports and imports also fluctuate a lot more than GDP, indicating that the foreign trade sector is relatively unstable. On the other hand, employment fluctuates considerably less than GDP. Private consumption is sometimes more and sometimes less volatile than GDP.

The main messages from Table 13.2 may be summarized as three stylized facts regarding business cycles.

TABLE 13.2a Macroeconomic volatility in the UK and the USA

UK	Average share in GDP	Absolute standard deviation (%)	Relative standard deviation[1]
GDP	100%	1.47	1.00
Private consumption	62%	1.64	1.11
Total fixed investment[2]	19%	3.75	2.54
Public consumption	20%	1.30	0.88
Exports	24%	2.99	2.03
Imports	25%	3.71	2.52
Employment		0.95	0.65

Note: Based on quarterly data from 1956Q1 to 2007Q1. 24 end-point observations excluded.
[1] Standard deviation relative to standard deviation of GDP.
[2] Includes both private and public investment.
Sources: UK Office for National Statistics, Ecowin and Datastream.

USA	Average share in GDP	Absolute standard deviation (%)	Relative standard deviation[1]
GDP	100%	1.64	1.00
Private consumption	64%	1.30	0.80
Private investment	16%	7.53	4.60
Public consumption	16%	3.30	2.02
Public investment	4%	5.85	3.58
Exports	8%	5.38	3.29
Imports	8%	5.09	3.11
Employment		1.40	0.86

Note: Based on quarterly data from 1947Q1 to 2007Q1. 24 end-point observations excluded.
[1] Standard deviation relative to standard deviation of GDP.
Sources: Bureau of Economic Analysis, Bureau of Labor Statistics, Federal Reserve Bank of St. Louis.

STYLIZED BUSINESS CYCLE FACT 1

Investment is much more volatile over the business cycle than GDP, typically three to four times as volatile. It is the most unstable component of aggregate demand.

STYLIZED BUSINESS CYCLE FACT 2

Foreign trade volumes are typically two to three times as volatile as GDP.

STYLIZED BUSINESS CYCLE FACT 3

Employment is considerably less volatile over the business cycle than GDP, typically 60–80 per cent as volatile.

TABLE 13.2b Macroeconomic volatility in Denmark and Finland

Denmark	Average share in GDP	Absolute standard deviation (%)	Relative standard deviation[1]
GDP	100%	1.61	1.00
Private consumption	51%	1.98	1.23
Private investment	16%	6.21	3.85
Public consumption	26%	1.15	0.72
Public investment	3%	7.12	4.42
Exports	35%	3.32	2.06
Imports	31%	3.44	2.13
Employment		0.82	0.51

Note: Based on quarterly data from 1971Q1 to 2007Q1. 24 end-point observations excluded.
[1] Standard deviation relative to standard deviation of GDP.

Sources: Danmarks Nationalbank and Ecowin.

Finland	Average share in GDP	Absolute standard deviation (%)	Relative standard deviation[1]
GDP	100%	2.18	1.00
Private consumption	52%	1.89	0.87
Private investment	19%	7.43	3.41
Public consumption	23%	1.24	0.57
Public investment	3%	5.13	2.36
Exports	30%	5.77	2.65
Imports	27%	5.81	2.67
Employment		1.75	0.80

Note: Based on quarterly data from 1975Q1 to 2007Q2. 24 end-point observations excluded.
[1] Standard deviation relative to standard deviation of GDP.

Sources: Statistics Finland and Bank of Finland.

Correlation, leads and lags

Table 13.2 tells us how much different variables fluctuate relative to the fluctuations in GDP. But we are also interested in studying whether and to what extent the cyclical component, x_t, of some economic variable moves in the same direction as or opposite to the cyclical component of real GDP, c_t. For this purpose we introduce the empirical *covariance* between x_t and c_t, defined as:

$$s_{xc} = \frac{1}{T-1}\sum_{t=1}^{T}(x_t - \bar{x})(c_t - \bar{c}), \qquad \bar{c} \equiv \frac{1}{T}\sum_{t=1}^{T}c_t, \tag{5}$$

where $\bar{c}$ is the mean value of the c_t's. The covariance measures the degree to which x and c move together, but its magnitude will depend on our choice of the units in which we measure x and c. To obtain an indicator which is independent of the choice of units, it is preferable to normalize the observations of $x_t - \bar{x}$ and $c_t - \bar{c}$ by the respective standard deviations s_x and s_c and to study the covariation of the normalized deviations, $(x_t - \bar{x})/s_x$ and $(c_t - \bar{c})/s_c$. Following this procedure, we obtain the *coefficient of correlation* between x and c, which we have already encountered in Chapter 11, and which is defined as:

TABLE 13.2c Macroeconomic volatility in Belgium and the Netherlands

Belgium	Average share in GDP	Absolute standard deviation (%)	Relative standard deviation[1]
GDP	100%	1.13	1.00
Private consumption	55%	1.09	0.97
Private investment	17%	4.55	4.01
Public consumption	24%	0.88	0.78
Public investment	2%	7.05	6.22
Exports	65%	2.78	2.46
Imports	63%	3.24	2.86
Employment		0.65	0.57

Note: Based on quarterly data from 1970Q1 to 2007Q2. 24 end-point observations excluded.
[1] Standard deviation relative to standard deviation of GDP.

Sources: Belgostat, Banque Nationale de Belgique and Ecowin.

Netherlands	Average share in GDP	Absolute standard deviation (%)	Relative standard deviation[1]
GDP	100%	1.33	1.00
Private consumption	52%	1.36	1.02
Private investment	17%	5.34	4.02
Public consumption	24%	1.05	0.79
Public investment	3%	5.20	3.91
Exports	54%	2.96	2.23
Imports	50%	3.21	2.41
Employment		0.80	0.60

Note: Based on quarterly data from 1970Q1 to 2007Q2. 24 end-point observations excluded.
[1] Standard deviation relative to standard deviation of GDP.

Sources: Statistics Netherlands, De Nederlandse Bank and Ecowin.

$$\rho(x_t, c_t) = \frac{s_{xc}}{s_x s_c} = \frac{\sum_{t=1}^{T}(x_t - \bar{x})(c_t - \bar{c})}{\sqrt{\sum_{t=1}^{T}(x_t - \bar{x})^2} \cdot \sqrt{\sum_{t=1}^{T}(c_t - \bar{c})^2}}. \tag{6}$$

It can be shown that the coefficient of correlation will always assume a value somewhere in the interval from −1 to +1. If $\rho(x_t, c_t)$ is equal to 1 we say that x_t and c_t are perfectly positively correlated, and if $\rho(x_t, c_t)$ equals −1 we say that the two variables are perfectly negatively correlated. In both cases there is a strict linear relationship between the two variables. If $\rho(x_t, c_t)$ is positive but less than 1, x and c will tend to move in the same direction, with the co-movement being more systematic the smaller the deviation of $\rho(x_t, c_t)$ from 1. On the other hand, a negative value of $\rho(x_t, c_t)$ indicates that the two variables tend to move in opposite directions. Clearly, if $\rho(x_t, c_t)$ is (close to) 0, there is no systematic relationship between x and c.

In the present context where c_t represents the cyclical component of real GDP, we say that x varies *procyclically* when $\rho(x_t, c_t)$ is substantially greater than 0, since the positive correlation indicates that x tends to rise and fall with GDP. By analogy, if $\rho(x_t, c_t)$ is negative, we say that x moves in a *countercyclical* fashion because x tends to move in the opposite direction of GDP.

As already noted, the co-movements of the different economic variables are not always synchronized over the business cycle: some variables may reach their turning point before others do. To investigate whether a variable x moves out of sync with real GDP, we may measure the coefficient of correlation $\rho(x_{t-n}, c_t)$ between c_t and the value of x observed n periods earlier (x_{t-n}), and the correlation coefficient $\rho(x_{t+n}, c_t)$ between c_t and the value of x observed n periods later (x_{t+n}). If $\rho(x_{t-n}, c_t)$ is significantly different from 0 and numerically greater than $\rho(x_t, c_t)$, we say that x_t is a *leading indicator*, because a change in x observed n periods earlier tends to be associated with a change in GDP in the current period. In other words, movements in x tend to *lead* movements in aggregate output, so a turnaround in x indicates a later turnaround in c. Similarly, we say that x is a *lagging variable* if $\rho(x_{t+n}, c_t)$ is significantly different from 0 and numerically greater than $\rho(x_t, c_t)$, since this is an indication that x tends to reach its peaks and troughs later than c.

In Table 13.3 we show coefficients of correlation between the logs of various variables and the log of GDP, including leads and lags. The middle columns headed '0' show the contemporaneous correlation coefficients, $\rho(x_t, c_t)$, where x_t is the relevant variable indicated in the left part of the table. The first two columns for each country show correlations between current GDP (c_t) and x_{t-2} and x_{t-1}, respectively, whereas the last two columns show correlations between y_t and x_{t+1} and x_{t+2}, respectively. Recall that the length of a time period is one quarter. From the second row for the United Kingdom we therefore infer that the coefficient of correlation between current GDP and private consumption two quarters earlier is 0.55, whereas the correlation between current GDP and private consumption one quarter later is 0.59.

Table 13.3 shows that whereas public consumption seems to be more or less uncorrelated with GDP, private consumption, private investment and imports are all *procyclical*, displaying a clear positive correlation with aggregate output. In particular, we see that private consumption and investment are strongly correlated with contemporaneous GDP.

Not surprisingly, we see that employment varies procyclically, since an increase in output requires an increase in labour input. The mirror image (not shown in the table) is that unemployment is countercyclical. We also see that employment is a *lagging variable*, since it is more strongly correlated with the GDP of the previous quarter than with contemporaneous GDP.

While employment displays a strong positive correlation with output, the correlation between real wages and real GDP is seen to be much weaker and less systematic. Average labour productivity (output per working hour) tends to be positively correlated with contemporaneous GDP, suggesting either that workers tend to work harder when the demand for output is high, or that productivity shocks are of some importance for the fluctuations in GDP. This may help to explain why employment is a lagging variable: if labour productivity rises as soon as output goes up, there is less need for firms to add to their stock of employees right from the start of a business cycle upswing.

While employment is clearly a lagging variable, there are only a few examples of leading variables in Table 13.3. In Finland the volume of exports seems to be a leading indicator, having a stronger positive correlation with GDP in the subsequent quarter(s) than with contemporaneous GDP. However, this pattern is not found in the other countries considered, so in general business fluctuations do not seem to be initiated by changes in export demand.

All the variables discussed so far have been defined in real terms. The bottom rows in Table 13.3 show the correlation between real output and some important *nominal* variables. In all countries except the UK the rate of inflation tends to be positively correlated with GDP, although the correlation is not particularly strong. As our theoretical analysis in later chapters will make clear, a positive correlation between output and inflation indicates that business cycles are driven mainly by shocks to aggregate demand. We also see a tendency for inflation to be a lagging variable, having a weaker correlation with GDP in the current

TABLE 13.3a Macroeconomic correlations. leads and lags in the UK and the USA

UK	Coefficient of correlation between GDP and X_t Quarterly leads and lags				
	−2	−1	0	1	2
X_t (Real variables)					
GDP	0.63	0.78	1.00	0.78	0.63
Private consumption	0.55	0.64	0.74	0.59	0.50
Private investment	0.35	0.48	0.65	0.62	0.54
Public consumption	−0.14	−0.09	−0.09	−0.15	−0.09
Exports	0.15	0.26	0.46	0.34	0.36
Imports	0.43	0.62	0.69	0.61	0.54
Employment	0.24	0.42	0.59	0.68	0.74
Real wage	0.15	0.24	0.36	0.25	0.24
Labour productivity	0.61	0.71	0.35	0.14	−0.05
X_t (Nominal variables)					
Inflation rate (CPI)	−0.22	−0.11	−0.04	0.19	0.21
Short-term nominal interest rate	−0.19	0.01	0.20	0.36	0.49
Long-term nominal interest rate	−0.33	−0.15	−0.01	0.11	0.24

Note: Based on quarterly data from 1956Q1 to 2007Q1. 24 end-point observations excluded.

Sources: See Table 14.2.

USA	Coefficient of correlation between GDP and X_t Quarterly leads and lags				
	−2	−1	0	1	2
X_t (Real variables)					
GDP	0.60	0.84	1.00	0.84	0.60
Private consumption	0.65	0.77	0.78	0.60	0.36
Private investment	0.57	0.75	0.85	0.66	0.40
Public consumption	−0.09	−0.02	0.11	0.19	0.25
Public investment	0.01	0.11	0.22	0.23	0.25
Exports	−0.04	0.17	0.37	0.46	0.45
Imports	0.46	0.62	0.69	0.61	0.39
Employment	0.27	0.57	0.81	0.89	0.83
Real wage	0.19	0.23	0.22	0.16	0.08
Labour productivity	0.50	0.49	0.45	0.13	−0.14
X_t (Nominal variables)					
Inflation rate (CPI)	0.03	0.17	0.31	0.39	0.39
Short-term nominal interest rate	−0.09	0.17	0.38	0.47	0.48
Long-term nominal interest rate	−0.28	−0.10	0.06	0.11	0.12

Note: Based on quarterly data from 1947Q1 to 2007Q1. 24 end-point observations excluded.

Sources: See Table 13.2.

TABLE 13.3b Macroeconomic correlations, leads and lags in Denmark and Finland

Denmark	Coefficient of correlation between GDP and X_t Quarterly leads and lags				
	−2	−1	0	1	2
X_t (Real variables)					
GDP	0.53	0.74	1.00	0.74	0.53
Private consumption	0.65	0.72	0.73	0.63	0.47
Private investment	0.48	0.65	0.76	0.73	0.61
Public consumption	−0.03	0.09	0.20	0.24	0.27
Public investment	0.31	0.41	0.49	0.53	0.53
Exports	−0.23	−0.21	−0.19	−0.24	−0.23
Imports	0.28	0.40	0.46	0.38	0.24
Employment	0.38	0.61	0.72	0.77	0.69
Real wage	−0.08	−0.04	−0.09	−0.23	−0.27
Labour productivity	0.04	0.08	0.36	0.09	−0.06
X_t (Nominal variables)					
Inflation rate (CPI)	−0.19	−0.10	0.10	0.24	0.24
Short-term nominal interest rate	−0.33	−0.18	−0.06	0.14	0.30
Long-term nominal interest rate	−0.39	−0.22	−0.04	0.09	0.10

Note: Based on quarterly data from 1971Q1 to 2007Q1. 24 end-point observations excluded.

Sources: See Table 13.2.

Finland	Coefficient of correlation between GDP and X_t Quarterly leads and lags				
	−2	−1	0	1	2
X_t (Real variables)					
GDP	0.80	0.87	1.00	0.87	0.80
Private consumption	0.74	0.80	0.82	0.77	0.73
Private investment	0.57	0.71	0.83	0.82	0.86
Public consumption	−0.01	0.13	0.26	0.39	0.52
Public investment	0.03	0.07	0.13	0.17	0.23
Exports	0.41	0.29	0.27	0.11	−0.01
Imports	0.62	0.66	0.75	0.64	0.55
Employment	0.42	0.59	0.70	0.80	0.85
Real wage	0.50	0.59	0.66	0.71	0.72
Labour productivity	0.64	0.58	0.67	0.36	0.20
X_t (Nominal variables)					
Inflation rate (CPI)	0.30	0.37	0.39	0.39	0.40
Short-term nominal interest rate	−0.19	0.00	0.14	0.25	0.37
Long-term nominal interest rate	0.03	0.15	0.26	0.34	0.37

Note: Based on quarterly data from 1970Q1 to 2007Q2. 24 end-point observations excluded.

Sources: See Table 13.2.

TABLE 13.3c Macroeconomic correlations, leads and lags in Belgium and the Netherlands

Belgium	Coefficient of correlation between GDP and X_t Quarterly leads and lags				
	−2	−1	0	1	2
X_t (Real variables)					
GDP	0.62	0.88	1.00	0.88	0.62
Private consumption	0.56	0.71	0.78	0.72	0.58
Private investment	0.49	0.64	0.70	0.64	0.49
Public consumption	0.09	0.07	0.04	0.01	0.00
Public investment	0.04	0.04	0.01	−0.08	−0.14
Exports	0.57	0.73	0.78	0.67	0.44
Imports	0.60	0.74	0.78	0.67	0.46
Employment	0.42	0.57	0.67	0.72	0.69
Real wage	−0.16	−0.16	−0.15	−0.13	−0.10
X_t (Nominal variables)					
Inflation rate (CPI)	0.00	0.14	0.25	0.32	0.38
Short-term nominal interest rate	0.15	0.38	0.55	0.61	0.57
Long-term nominal interest rate	0.17	0.36	0.49	0.53	0.49

Note: Based on quarterly data from 1970Q1 to 2007Q2. 24 end-point observations excluded.

Sources: See Table 13.2.

Netherlands	Coefficient of correlation between GDP and X_t Quarterly leads and lags				
	−2	−1	0	1	2
X_t (Real variables)					
GDP	0.44	0.58	1.00	0.58	0.44
Private consumption	0.47	0.57	0.62	0.51	0.44
Private investment	0.41	0.42	0.65	0.33	0.35
Public consumption	−0.17	−0.15	−0.12	−0.02	−0.10
Public investment	−0.02	0.01	0.24	−0.02	0.03
Exports	0.44	0.54	0.63	0.46	0.30
Imports	0.56	0.63	0.64	0.61	0.45
Employment	0.34	0.47	0.56	0.64	0.67
Real wage	−0.11	−0.06	−0.09	−0.09	−0.18
Labour productivity	0.05	0.05	0.29	−0.12	−0.27
X_t (Nominal variables)					
Inflation rate (CPI)	0.01	0.03	0.13	0.16	0.20
Short-term nominal interest rate	0.08	0.24	0.49	0.50	0.50
Long-term nominal interest rate	−0.05	0.12	0.30	0.33	0.32

Note: Based on quarterly data from 1970Q1 to 2007Q2. 24 end-point observations excluded.

Sources: See Table 13.2.

quarter than in the two subsequent quarters. Moreover, in all countries the short-term nominal interest rate tends to go up in the two quarters following a rise in GDP, reflecting that central banks typically tighten monetary policy in reaction to higher economic activity.

Let us sum up the main lessons from Table 13.3.

STYLIZED BUSINESS CYCLE FACT 4

Private consumption, investment and imports are strongly positively correlated with GDP.

STYLIZED BUSINESS CYCLE FACT 5

Employment (unemployment) is procyclical (countercyclical) and much more strongly correlated with GDP than real wages and labour productivity. Labour productivity tends to be procyclical, whereas real wages tend to be very weakly correlated with GDP.

STYLIZED BUSINESS CYCLE FACT 6

In most countries inflation is positively correlated with GDP, although the correlation is not very strong.

STYLIZED BUSINESS CYCLE FACT 7

Employment is a lagging variable; inflation and nominal interest rates also tend to be lagging variables.

Persistence

Another interesting property of an economic variable is its degree of *persistence*. As you recall, one characteristic of business cycles is that, once the economy moves into an expansion or a contraction, it tends to stay there for a while. Persistence in some variable x means that the observed value of x in period t, x_t, is not independent of the value, x_{t-n}, of x in some previous period $t - n$, where $n \geq 1$. In other words, if x assumed a high (low) value in previous period $t - n$, there is a greater chance that it will also assume a high (low) value in the current period t. We can measure such persistence in a time series $(x_t)_{t=1}^{T}$ by calculating the coefficient of correlation between x_t and its own lagged value x_{t-n}, for $n = 1, 2, \ldots$ This particular correlation coefficient $\rho(x_t, x_{t-n})$ is called the *coefficient of autocorrelation* and was already introduced in Chapter 10. If $\rho(x_t, x_{t-n})$ is significantly above zero for several positive values of n, there is a high degree of persistence: once x has been pushed above or below its mean value, it tends to continue to be above or below its mean for a long time.

Table 13.4 measures the persistence of business fluctuations by the coefficients of autocorrelation. The first figure in the first column for the UK (0.78) means that if real GDP goes up by one percentage point in the current quarter, then on average 0.78 percentage points of that increase will remain in the next quarter. We see from Table 13.4 that there is considerable persistence in the movements of GDP and of private consumption, but except in Denmark the most persistent variable is employment. The high persistence of

TABLE 13.4a Macroeconomic persistence in the UK and the USA

UK	Coefficient of autocorrelation			
	1-quarter lag	2-quarter lag	3-quarter lag	4-quarter lag
Real variables				
GDP	0.78	0.63	0.46	0.26
Private consumption	0.77	0.64	0.50	0.32
Gross domestic investment	0.72	0.53	0.39	0.19
Public consumption	0.63	0.50	0.41	0.23
Exports	0.39	0.30	0.10	−0.09
Imports	0.68	0.43	0.23	0.01
Employment	0.94	0.83	0.68	0.52
Real weekly earnings	0.53	0.18	0.00	0.03
Labour productivity	0.72	0.54	0.39	0.17
Nominal variables				
Inflation rate (CPI)	0.37	0.24	0.03	−0.09
Short-term nominal interest rate	0.81	0.57	0.32	0.13
Long-term nominal interest rate	0.78	0.48	0.28	0.11

Note: Based on quarterly data from 1956Q1 to 2007Q1. 24 end-point observations excluded.

Sources: See Table 13.2.

USA	Coefficient of autocorrelation			
	1-quarter lag	2-quarter lag	3-quarter lag	4-quarter lag
Real variables				
GDP	0.84	0.60	0.34	0.11
Private consumption	0.80	0.63	0.39	0.16
Private investment	0.80	0.55	0.29	0.05
Public consumption	0.88	0.73	0.53	0.30
Public investment	0.80	0.60	0.40	0.26
Exports	0.71	0.55	0.31	0.07
Imports	0.71	0.46	0.27	0.07
Employment	0.91	0.70	0.46	0.21
Real wage	0.79	0.58	0.39	0.21
Labour productivity	0.69	0.43	0.16	−0.01
Nominal variables				
Inflation rate (CPI)	0.48	0.25	0.29	0.01
Short-term nominal interest rate	0.81	0.55	0.41	0.24
Long-term nominal interest rate	0.80	0.53	0.29	0.05

Note: Based on quarterly data from 1947Q1 to 2007Q1. 24 end-point observations excluded.

Sources: See Table 13.2.

TABLE 13.4b Macroeconomic persistence in Denmark and Finland

Denmark	Coefficient of autocorrelation			
	1-quarter lag	2-quarter lag	3-quarter lag	4-quarter lag
Real variables				
GDP	0.74	0.53	0.29	0.13
Private consumption	0.88	0.73	0.56	0.38
Private investment	0.81	0.62	0.45	0.23
Public consumption	0.86	0.64	0.39	0.17
Public investment	0.86	0.73	0.60	0.42
Exports	0.81	0.61	0.35	0.13
Imports	0.82	0.49	0.06	−0.31
Employment	0.86	0.70	0.54	0.39
Real wage	0.74	0.51	0.37	0.18
Labour productivity	0.21	0.06	−0.06	−0.02
Nominal variables				
Inflation rate (CPI)	−0.11	0.05	−0.13	0.04
Short-term nominal interest rate	0.50	0.24	0.05	−0.23
Long-term nominal interest rate	0.79	0.45	0.13	−0.15

Note: Based on quarterly data from 1971Q1 to 2007Q1. 24 end-point observations excluded.

Sources: See Table 13.2.

Finland	Coefficient of autocorrelation			
	1-quarter lag	2-quarter lag	3-quarter lag	4-quarter lag
Real variables				
GDP	0.87	0.80	0.69	0.52
Private consumption	0.92	0.81	0.69	0.54
Private investment	0.89	0.80	0.69	0.54
Public consumption	0.93	0.82	0.66	0.48
Public investment	0.75	0.46	0.21	0.05
Exports	0.59	0.44	0.31	0.09
Imports	0.54	0.48	0.34	0.11
Employment	0.93	0.83	0.69	0.53
Real wage	0.92	0.79	0.67	0.52
Labour productivity	0.68	0.61	0.48	0.23
Nominal variables				
Inflation rate (CPI)	0.25	−0.01	0.25	0.46
Short-term nominal interest rate	0.73	0.51	0.32	0.18
Long-term nominal interest rate	0.83	0.57	0.29	0.07

Note: Based on quarterly data from 1970Q1 to 2007Q2. 24 end-point observations excluded.

Sources: See Table 13.2.

TABLE 13.4c Macroeconomic persistence in Belgium and the Netherlands

Belgium	Coefficient of autocorrelation			
	1-quarter lag	2-quarter lag	3-quarter lag	4-quarter lag
Real variables				
GDP	0.88	0.62	0.30	0.02
Private consumption	0.91	0.73	0.49	0.26
Private investment	0.88	0.66	0.40	0.19
Public consumption	0.90	0.65	0.33	0.06
Public investment	0.63	0.57	0.36	0.26
Exports	0.88	0.62	0.29	−0.04
Imports	0.90	0.67	0.37	0.08
Employment	0.96	0.83	0.67	0.48
Real wage	1.00	0.99	0.98	0.97
Nominal variables				
Inflation rate (CPI)	0.30	0.28	0.09	0.21
Short-term nominal interest rate	0.79	0.45	0.19	0.03
Long-term nominal interest rate	0.88	0.68	0.48	0.28

Note: Based on quarterly data from 1970Q1 to 2007Q2. 24 end-point observations excluded.

Sources: See Table 13.2.

Netherlands	Coefficient of autocorrelation			
	1-quarter lag	2-quarter lag	3-quarter lag	4-quarter lag
Real variables				
GDP	0.58	0.44	0.30	0.17
Private consumption	0.76	0.70	0.62	0.50
Private investment	0.44	0.48	0.32	0.27
Public consumption	0.51	0.46	0.33	0.25
Public investment	0.29	0.07	0.05	0.11
Exports	0.69	0.49	0.33	0.05
Imports	0.84	0.67	0.47	0.27
Employment	0.97	0.90	0.78	0.64
Real wage	0.63	0.56	0.34	0.18
Labour productivity	0.71	0.60	0.48	0.36
Nominal variables				
Inflation rate (CPI)	−0.17	0.33	−0.22	0.53
Short-term nominal interest rate	0.73	0.40	0.22	0.07
Long-term nominal interest rate	0.84	0.61	0.43	0.22

Note: Based on quarterly data from 1970Q1 to 2007Q2. 24 end-point observations excluded.

Sources: See Table 13.2.

employment may reflect that firms are reluctant to hire and fire workers because hiring and firing is costly.[7]

To sum up, we have

STYLIZED BUSINESS CYCLE FACT 8

There is considerable persistence in GDP and about the same degree of persistence in private consumption.

STYLIZED BUSINESS CYCLE FACT 9

Employment tends to be even more persistent than GDP.

13.6 Measuring and decomposing the output gap: the production function approach

The percentage difference between real GDP and its trend value is usually termed the *output gap*. Economic policy makers and business cycle researchers take great interest in this variable, since a significant positive output gap means that the economy is in a boom, whereas a substantial negative output gap indicates that the economy is in recession, or at least that resources are being underutilized.

As we have seen, the output gap may be measured by detrending the time series for the log of real GDP by means of the HP filter. However, there is another and more elaborate way of estimating the output gap which allows an interesting decomposition of the gap. We shall now sketch this method which makes use of the concept of the aggregate production function known from the theory of economic growth.

Specifically, suppose that real GDP is given by the following Cobb–Douglas production function:

$$Y_t = B_t K_t^\alpha L_t^{1-\alpha}, \quad 0 < \alpha < 1, \tag{7}$$

where K_t is the aggregate capital stock, L_t is the aggregate number of hours worked, and B_t is the 'total factor productivity' measuring the combined productivity of capital and labour. By definition, total working hours are given as:

$$L_t = (1 - u_t)N_t H_t, \tag{8}$$

where u_t is the unemployment rate, N_t is the total labour force, and H_t is the average number of working hours per person employed. Hence we can specify GDP as:

$$Y_t = B_t K_t^\alpha [(1 - u_t)N_t H_t]^{1-\alpha}. \tag{9}$$

Suppose now that Y_t, B_t, u_t, N_t and H_t all tend to fluctuate around some long-run trend levels denoted by $\bar{Y}_t$, $\bar{B}_t$, $\bar{u}_t$, $\bar{N}_t$ and $\bar{H}_t$, respectively. By analogy to (9), we may then write trend output (also referred to as *potential output*) as:

$$\bar{Y}_t = \bar{B}_t K_t^\alpha [(1 - \bar{u}_t)\bar{N}_t \bar{H}_t]^{1-\alpha}. \tag{10}$$

---

7. Because the Danish 'flexicurity' model of the labour market implies low hiring and firing costs, this may explain why employment is less persistent in Denmark than elsewhere.

Note that this specification does not distinguish between the actual capital stock and its trend level, since we assume for simplicity that the capital stock is always fully utilized.

The output gap may be approximated by $y_t - \bar{y}_t$, where $y_t \equiv \ln Y_t$ and $\bar{y}_t \equiv \ln \bar{Y}_t$. Taking logs on both sides of (9) and (10), subtracting the resulting expressions from one another, and using the approximation $\ln(1 - u) \approx -u$, we get:

$$y_t - \bar{y}_t \approx \ln B_t - \ln \bar{B}_t + (1 - \alpha)[(\ln N_t - \ln \bar{N}_t) + (\ln H_t - \ln \bar{H}_t) - (u_t - \bar{u}_t)]. \tag{11}$$

Thus the output gap may be found as the cyclical component of total factor productivity, $\ln B_t - \ln \bar{B}_t$, plus $1 - \alpha$ times the cyclical component of total labour input (the term within the square brackets). The latter may in turn be decomposed into the cyclical component of the labour force, $\ln N_t - \ln \bar{N}_t$, the cyclical component of average working hours, $\ln H_t - \ln \bar{H}_t$, and the amount of cyclical unemployment, $u_t - \bar{u}_t$.

Equation (11) may be used to estimate the output gap provided one has access to data on real GDP, the labour force, average working hours, unemployment, and the total capital stock. The cyclical components of labour supply and unemployment may be estimated by detrending the time series for $\ln N_t$, $\ln H_t$ and u_t by means of the HP filter. To estimate the cyclical component of (the log of) total factor productivity, one may proceed as follows. First, take logs on both sides of (7) and rearrange to find:

$$\ln B_t = \ln Y_t - \alpha \ln K_t - (1 - \alpha) \ln L_t, \tag{12}$$

where L_t may be calculated from (8) (or where data on L_t may be directly available). From the theory and empirics of economic growth we know that the magnitude $1 - \alpha$ should correspond roughly to the labour income share in total GDP which is close to $\frac{2}{3}$ in most countries. Hence we may set $\alpha = \frac{1}{3}$. Plugging the data for Y_t, K_t and L_t into equation (12), then, gives an estimate of total factor productivity.[8] In a second step, one may detrend the estimated time series for $\ln B_t$ through HP filtering to obtain an estimate of the cyclical component of total factor productivity. The estimates for $\ln B_t - \ln \bar{B}_t$, $\ln N_t - \ln \bar{N}_t$, $\ln H_t - \ln \bar{H}_t$ and $u_t - \bar{u}_t$ may finally be inserted into (11) along with $\alpha = \frac{1}{3}$ to give an estimated time series for the output gap.

Figure 13.5 shows an estimate and decomposition of the output gap in the United States, based on the method just described and using annual data.[9] The upper part of Fig. 13.5 shows the part of the fluctuations in the output gap that can be traced to cyclical fluctuations in total labour input. It follows from (11) that the vertical distance between the curve for the output gap and the curve $(1 - \alpha)(\ln L_t - \ln \bar{L}_t)$ measures the contribution of cyclical fluctuations in total factor productivity to the total gap. Note that if there are variations in the degree of utilization of the capital stock, this will tend to generate cyclical fluctuations in our measure of total factor productivity (TFP). Similarly, if work intensity varies over the business cycle, say, because people tend to work harder when there is more work to do, this will also be captured in the cyclical component of TFP. Hence the fluctuations in $\ln B_t - \ln \bar{B}_t$ not only reflect instability in the rate of technical progress; they also capture variations in the intensity with which factors of production are utilized.

We see from the top diagram in Fig. 13.5 that a large part of the variation in the output gap stems from the cyclical variation in total labour input. At the same time the cyclical component of TFP accounts for a large fraction of the output gap at business cycle peaks and troughs, presumably reflecting that work intensity and capacity utilization are unusually low in recessions and unusually high in boom periods.

---

8.   If you have already studied Chapter 5, you will note that this way of estimating total factor productivity is closely related to the method of 'growth accounting' used to identify the sources of economic growth.

9.   The value of the parameter λ in the HP filter has been set to 100, which is common practice in business cycle analysis of annual data. Since the HP filter gives imprecise estimates of the trend at the end points, we have excluded the first and the last three estimates of the cyclical components at the end points of each time series.

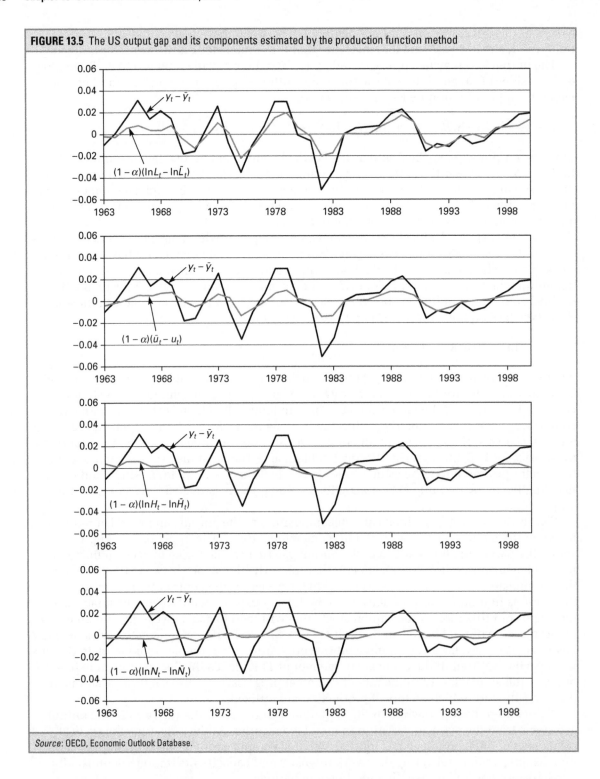

FIGURE 13.5 The US output gap and its components estimated by the production function method

Source: OECD, Economic Outlook Database.

The other diagrams in Fig. 13.5 show the separate contributions of the cyclical swings in unemployment, average working hours and the labour force to the swings in the output gap. Changes in cyclical unemployment account for the greatest part of the variation in labour input, but average working hours also tend to fluctuate in a procyclical manner, suggesting that employees tend to work longer hours when there is more work to be done. The labour force does not seem to respond very much to the business cycle, although there is a tendency for the workforce to vary in a slightly procyclical manner (while lagging a bit behind the output gap) from the early 1970s and onwards.[10]

We may sum up this analysis of the output gap as follows:

STYLIZED BUSINESS CYCLE FACT 10

Total labour input varies in a strong procyclical manner, explaining most of the variation in the output gap. Total factor productivity, TFP, also varies procyclically and the cyclical component of TFP accounts for a large fraction of the total output gap at business cycle peaks and troughs.

STYLIZED BUSINESS CYCLE FACT 11

Most of the cyclical variation in total labour input stems from fluctuations in cyclical unemployment, but average working hours, and to some extent the total labour force, also vary procyclically.

It is of interest to compare the estimate of the output gap based on the production function method to the estimate obtained by simply HP filtering the time series for the log of GDP. This comparison is made in Fig. 13.6. It is reassuring to see that the output gaps found from the two alternative methods are quite close to each other. Hence HP filtering of the real GDP series may be a quick and easy way of obtaining a first estimate of the output gap, but if one wants to identify the various contributions to the gap, one will have to use some version of the production function method, as international organizations like the OECD, the IMF and the European Commission actually do.

HP filtering: a final word of caution

Even more sophisticated versions of the production function method typically rely on the use of the HP filter, say, for the purpose of estimating the trend in TFP. Although convenient, the method of HP filtering is not unproblematic. We have already mentioned that the HP trend tends to be imprecisely estimated at the end points of the time series. Hence the serious researcher should disregard some end-point observations, as we have done above. However, this is unfortunate since one is often particularly interested in estimating the output gap for the most recent periods in order to evaluate the need for active macroeconomic policy to smooth the business cycle.

Another problem is that there is no objectively correct value of the parameter λ which determines the estimated HP trend. In Fig. 13.7 we have shown two different estimates of the US output gap, using the HP filter with $\lambda = 100$ and with $\lambda = 1000$, respectively. We see that the difference between the two measures is non-negligible in the 1960s and early 1970s, so the basic arbitrariness in the choice of λ adds another element of uncertainty to measures of cyclical fluctuations based on the HP filter.

A further problem is that the HP filter cannot capture structural breaks in the trends of economic time series. For example, if a labour market reform leads to a significant one-time shift in the level of the natural unemployment rate, this change in structural unemployment will only be slowly and gradually picked up by the estimated HP trend in unemployment.

Thus there is considerable uncertainty about the 'true' output gap, reflecting our imperfect knowledge of the way the economy works. As we shall discuss at length in Chapter 22, the uncertainty regarding the size (and sometimes even the sign) of the output gap creates difficulties when policy makers try to reduce the short-run fluctuations in output and employment through active fiscal and monetary policy.

---

10. The slightly negative contribution of the workforce to the output gap in the booming 1960s could reflect that many potential members of the labour force during that period were called up for military service in the Vietnam War.

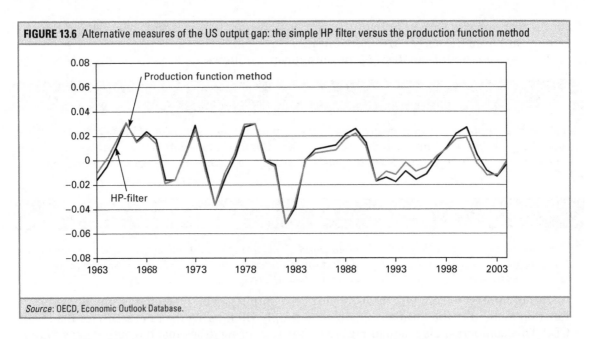

FIGURE 13.6 Alternative measures of the US output gap: the simple HP filter versus the production function method

Source: OECD, Economic Outlook Database.

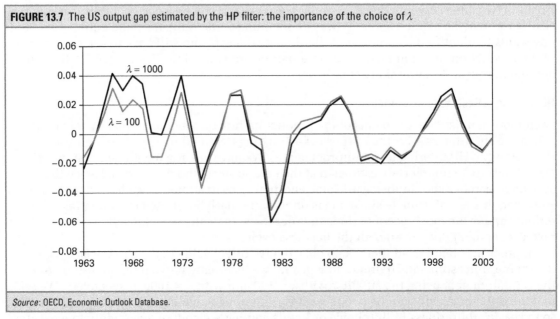

FIGURE 13.7 The US output gap estimated by the HP filter: the importance of the choice of λ

Source: OECD, Economic Outlook Database.

13.7 A look ahead

We have now described some facts about business cycles. In the rest of this book our main goal will be to construct an economic model that may explain short-run fluctuations in aggregate output, employment and inflation. Specifically, we will gradually build up a model which may be summarized in the manner depicted in Fig. 13.8, where real output and the rate of inflation are determined by the intersection of an upward-sloping aggregate supply curve and a downward-sloping aggregate demand curve. We will then use this model to study how the economy reacts over time to various shocks to the aggregate supply curve and the aggregate demand curve.

Our goal is to construct a model in which the effects of aggregate demand and supply shocks tend to *persist* over time due to so-called *propagation mechanisms* arising from the

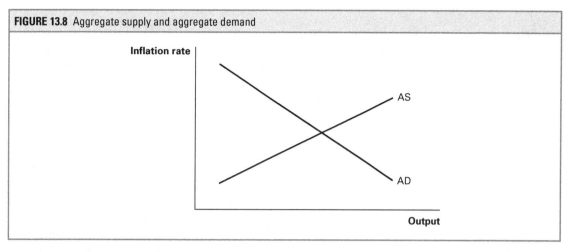

FIGURE 13.8 Aggregate supply and aggregate demand

links between central macroeconomic variables. In this view of the world business cycles are *initiated* by random shocks to the economy such as an unanticipated change in the oil price or a change in business confidence due, say, to unexpected political events. However, the *cumulative and systematic* character of business fluctuations documented in this chapter will be explained endogenously by the properties of our macroeconomic model. We hasten to add that we cannot promise to explain all the features of business cycles – economists are still far from having a perfect understanding of this complex phenomenon – but our model economy will at least have the property that random shocks tend to generate irregular cycles displaying a certain persistence.

As indicated in Fig. 13.8, the aggregate demand curve and the aggregate supply curve are the central building blocks of our model. To construct the aggregate demand curve we must build a theory of private investment and private consumption. This is our agenda for Chapters 14 and 15. In Chapter 16 we combine the insights from Chapters 14 and 15 with a study of monetary policy to derive the aggregate demand curve. Chapter 17 then analyses the relation between inflation and unemployment as a basis for constructing the aggregate supply curve. This enables us to set up our basic AS–AD model in Chapter 18 where we use the model to reproduce some of the stylized facts about business cycles. The subsequent Chapters 19 to 22 extend the basic model in order to analyse the problems of macroeconomic stabilization policy. In the last four chapters of the book we extend the AS–AD model to the open economy, studying regimes with fixed as well as flexible exchange rates, and end with a discussion of the choice of exchange rate regime.

13.8 Summary

1. Business cycles are periods of expansion of aggregate economic activity followed by periods of contraction in which activity declines. These fluctuations are recurrent but not periodic; in duration business cycles have varied from a little more than a year to 10–12 years. The severity of recessions has also varied considerably, with recessions sometimes turning into depressions where output and employment fall dramatically.

2. The expansion phase of the business cycle usually lasts considerably longer than the contraction phase, reflecting the economy's capacity for long-term growth. In the period since the Second World War business cycle expansions have tended to last longer, and recessions have tended to be shorter and milder than was the case before the war. For the post-Second World War period the average duration of the US business cycle expansions has been 57 months, while recessions have on average lasted 10 months. By contrast, the average recession lasted about 22 months before the war.

3. The business cycle fluctuation in a macroeconomic time series may be measured as the deviation of the actual time series from its long-term trend. The trend may be estimated by means of the HP filter which allows for smooth changes in the underlying (growth) trend in a series.

4. The volatility of the cyclical component in a macroeconomic time series may be measured by its standard deviation. By this measure, investment is a lot more volatile over the business cycle than GDP, whereas employment is considerably less volatile.

5. The co-movements in different economic variables over the business cycle may be measured by their coefficients of correlation with GDP. Private investment, consumption and imports all have a strong positive correlation with GDP. Employment also displays a clear positive correlation with GDP, but it is a lagging variable, being more strongly correlated with the GDP of the two previous quarters than with current GDP. Labour productivity tends to vary positively with GDP, and so does inflation in most countries, although the latter correlation is not very strong. The nominal short-term interest rate tends to go up in the two quarters following a rise in GDP, reflecting a tightening of monetary policy.

6. The degree of persistence in a macroeconomic variable may be measured by its coefficients of correlation with its own lagged values, the so-called coefficients of autocorrelation. There is considerable persistence in GDP and private consumption, and typically even more persistence in employment. This means that once these variables start to move in one direction, they will continue to move in the same direction for a while, unless they are significantly disturbed by new shocks.

7. The output gap is the percentage difference between actual GDP and trend GDP. The output gap may be estimated by means of the production function method which allows a decomposition of the gap into contributions from cyclical variations in unemployment, average working hours, the total labour force, and total factor productivity (TFP). Such a decomposition shows that fluctuations in TFP – capturing cyclical swings in work intensity and capacity utilization as well as an uneven pace of technical progress – account for a relatively large share of the fluctuations in output at business cycle peaks and troughs. The largest part of the cyclical variation in labour input comes from fluctuations in cyclical unemployment, but average working hours (and to a minor extent the labour force) also tend to vary positively with the output gap, reflecting that labour supply tends to increase when there is more work to do.

8. The method of detrending an economic time series by means of the HP filter should be used with care, because (i) the HP filter gives imprecise estimates of the trend at the end-points of the time series; (ii) the filter relies on an arbitrary choice of the λ-parameter which determines the smoothness of the estimated trend, and (iii) the HP filter cannot capture structural breaks in the data series. For these and other reasons there is considerable uncertainty associated with the measurement of business cycles.

13.9 Exercises

Exercise 1. Accounting for recent recessions

1. All of the countries included in Fig. 13.4 experienced serious recessions in the mid-1970s, in the early 1980s and in the early 1990s. Try to give a brief account of the factors and exogenous 'shocks' which are likely to have generated these contractions in economic activity.

2. According to Table 13.1 the US economy fell into recession in 2001. The same thing happened in most other countries in the world. Mention some factors and 'shocks' which in your view contributed to this economic downturn.

Exercise 2. Explaining the turning points in the US business cycle

In Table 13.1 we summarized the NBER datings of US business cycles. In an NBER Working Paper (no. 6692, August 1998) entitled 'The Causes of American Business Cycles: An Essay in Economic Historiography', economic historian Peter Temin attempts to explain the turning points in the chronology of US business cycles by identifying various demand and supply shocks to the US economy. Using Peter Temin's NBER Working Paper and your knowledge of the basic AS–AD model from introductory macro, explain some of the most spectacular turning points of the US business cycle in the twentieth century.

Exercise 3. Measuring the output gap by means of the HP filter

At the web page for the book you may get access to a computer facility performing HP filtering of economic time series (you will also find a brief guide on how to use this facility).

1. Find annual data for real GDP for your country, going back in time as far as consistent data are available (you may want to use the Penn World Table or some other easily accessible source). Transform the time series into natural logarithms and use the HP filter to estimate a series for the trend in the log of output and for the output gap, $\ln Y_t - \ln \bar{Y}_t$, setting $\lambda = 100$ (because of the imprecise end-point estimates produced by the HP filter, you should discard your estimates for the first and last three years in your estimated series). Perform the same exercise with $\lambda = 1000$. Are there significant differences in the estimated output gaps with the two alternative values of λ?

2. Use your estimated series for the output gap to offer a rough dating of recent business cycles in your country. Are the major peaks and troughs in your estimated output gap in line with your prior expectations, given your knowledge of the recent economic history of your country?

Exercise 4. Measuring and decomposing the output gap

In Section 13.5 of this chapter we explained how one may estimate and decompose the output gap by means of the production function method. In this exercise we ask you to use this method to estimate a time series for the output gap and its components using annual data for your own country (or for some other country of your choice for which data are available).

The production function method described in Section 13.5 requires data on real GDP (Y), the total capital stock (K), the total labour force (N), the average number of (annual) working hours per person employed (H), and the unemployment rate (u). One practical problem is that the available data on (some of) the variables K, N, H or u do not always cover the entire economy, but sometimes only, say, the private business sector. However, under certain assumptions the data K^e, N^e, H^e and u^e covering only *part* of the economy may be used as substitutes for the missing *economy-wide* variables K, N, H and u without generating a bias in the estimate of the output gap and its components. First, define the economy-wide rate of employment as $E \equiv 1 - u$ and the corresponding rate of employment recorded in the statistics as $E^e \equiv 1 - u^e$. Then suppose that:

$$K_t^e = c_K K_t, \qquad N_t^e = c_N N_t, \qquad H_t^e = c_H H_t, \qquad E_t^e = c_E E_t, \tag{13}$$

where c_K, c_N, c_H and c_E are all constant over time. If $c_X = 1$ we have the fortunate situation where the data for variable X covers the entire economy, but if $c_X < 1$ the available data for variable X only covers a subsector of the macroeconomy. With $\bar{X}$ denoting the trend value of variable X, it follows from (13) that:

$$\bar{N}_t^e = c_N \bar{N}_t, \qquad \bar{H}_t^e = c_H \bar{H}_t, \qquad \bar{E}_t^e = c_E \bar{E}_t. \tag{14}$$

Furthermore, define the following indicators of labour input measured in hours:

$$L_t \equiv E_t N_t H_t, \qquad \bar{L}_t \equiv \bar{E}_t \bar{N}_t \bar{H}_t, \qquad L_t^e \equiv E_t^e N_t^e H_t^e, \qquad \bar{L}_t^e \equiv \bar{E}_t^e \bar{N}_t^e \bar{H}_t^e. \tag{15}$$

1. The cyclical component of the macroeconomic variable X_t is defined as $\ln X_t - \ln \bar{X}_t$. Use Eqs (13)–(15) to show that the cyclical components of L_t^e, N_t^e, H_t^e and E_t^e are unbiased estimates of the cyclical components of the corresponding economy-wide variables L_t, N_t, H_t and E_t. Using the approximation $\ln(1 - x_t) \approx -x_t$ (which is valid for 'small' values of x_t), show that the magnitude $\bar{u}_t^e - u_t^e$ is a good approximation of $\ln E_t - \ln \bar{E}_t$.

   Given the assumption that the capital stock is always fully utilized (so that there is no need to distinguish between K_t and $\bar{K}_t$), it follows from Eq. (12) in the main text that:

$$\ln B_t = \ln Y_t - \alpha \ln K_t - (1-\alpha)\ln L_t,$$
$$\ln \bar{B}_t = \ln \bar{Y}_t - \alpha \ln K_t - (1-\alpha)\ln \bar{L}_t, \tag{16}$$

   where B_t and $\bar{B}_t$ are the actual and the trend level of total factor productivity (TFP), respectively. By analogy, if TFP is estimated on the basis of the available data, we have:

$$\ln B_t^e = \ln Y_t - \alpha \ln K_t^e - (1-\alpha)\ln L_t^e,$$
$$\ln \bar{B}_t^e = \ln \bar{Y}_t - \alpha \ln K_t^e - (1-\alpha)\ln \bar{L}_t^e. \tag{17}$$

2. Show by means of (13)–(17) that the magnitude $\ln B_t^e - \ln \bar{B}_t^e$ is an unbiased estimate of the 'true' cyclical component of TFP, $\ln B_t - \ln \bar{B}_t$.

3. Try to find annual data on Y, K, N, H and u for your country (as a default, you may also use the data for Denmark available at the web page for the book and apply the production function method described in Section 13.5 to these data to estimate the output gap and its components). If the available data for one or several of the variables K, N, H or u do not cover the entire economy, you may assume that assumptions (13) and (14) are satisfied (with c_K, c_N, c_H, and c_E all being constant over time) and use the available data K^e, N^e, H^e or u^e, since you have shown in Questions 1 and 2 that this will yield unbiased estimates of the true gaps. You may get access to a computer facility performing HP filtering at the web page for the book. To ensure comparability with Fig. 13.5, set $\lambda = 100$.

   Construct diagrams showing the evolution of the output gap and its components (because of the imprecise end-point estimates produced by the HP filter, you should discard your estimates for the first and last three years in each of your estimated series). Investigate whether the stylized business cycle facts 10 and 11 derived from US data (see Section 13.5) also hold for your country.

   If your data for K, N, H or u do not cover the whole economy, discuss briefly whether there is reason to believe that any of the parameters c_K, c_N, c_H and c_E may not be constant over time. If they are not, is this necessarily a problem?

4. Estimate a time series for the output gap for your country by running an HP filter through the time series for the natural log of real GDP with $\lambda = 100$ (you may also reuse your HP estimate from Exercise 3, assuming it is based on the same time series for real GDP as the one used in this exercise). Draw your estimate in a diagram and compare it to your estimate of the output gap based on the production function method. Are the two estimates as close as was the case for the USA in Fig. 13.6?

PART 5

The Building Blocks for the Short-run Model

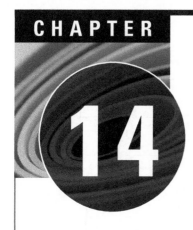

CHAPTER

14

Investment and asset prices

The previous chapter showed that private investment is often the most volatile component of aggregate demand and that it is highly correlated with total output. Understanding the forces driving private investment is therefore crucial for understanding business cycles. In this chapter we present a theory of business investment as well as a theory of housing investment. This will give us an opportunity to study two of the most important asset markets in the economy: the stock market and the market for owner-occupied housing. As we shall see, there is a systematic link between stock prices and business investment, and a similar systematic impact of housing prices on housing investment. To understand investment, we must therefore study how asset prices are formed.

A glance at Fig. 14.1 should make clear why we are interested in asset prices. The figure shows the link between the evolution of housing prices and stock prices and the evolution of the output gap in the USA. *There is a close relationship between asset price fluctuations and output fluctuations and a clear tendency for stock price movements to lead movements in output.* Data for most other OECD countries show a similar picture. Thus the evidence suggests that an increase in stock prices or in housing prices will trigger an increase in economic activity, whereas a significant drop in asset prices may be a signal of a future economic downturn. As we will show in this chapter and the next one, Fig. 14.1 reflects that higher asset prices tend to stimulate private consumption and investment. In particular, the present chapter will explain why higher stock prices tend to be followed by higher business investment, and why higher housing prices provide a boost to housing investment.

The basic idea underlying our theory of investment may be most easily illustrated by looking at the housing market. At any point in time there is a certain market price for houses of a given size and quality. This price may well exceed the cost of constructing a new house of similar size and quality (the replacement cost). The more the market price exceeds the replacement cost, the more profitable it will be for construction firms to build and sell new houses. Hence we will observe a higher level of housing investment the greater the discrepancy between the market price and the replacement cost of housing. Note that the market price can deviate from the replacement cost for a long time, since it takes time for new construction to produce a significant increase in the existing housing stock, and since it is time-consuming to shift economic resources into the construction industry if construction activity becomes more profitable due to a rise in the market price of housing.

For business investment a similar basic principle applies. The market price of the business assets owned by a corporation is reflected in the market price of the shares in the firm. The replacement cost of the firm's assets is given by the price at which it can acquire machinery, etc., from its suppliers of capital goods. If the stock market value of the firm's assets is higher than their replacement cost, the firm can increase the wealth of its shareholders by purchasing

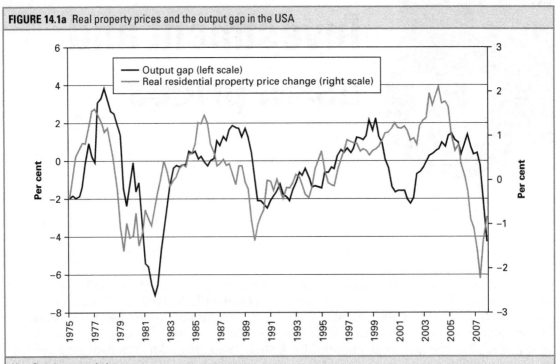

FIGURE 14.1a Real property prices and the output gap in the USA

Note: Based on quarterly data.

Data sources: Nominal property price index from Office of Federal Housing Enterprise Oversight, CPI from Bureau of Labor Statistics, and output gap from OECD Economic Outlook Database.

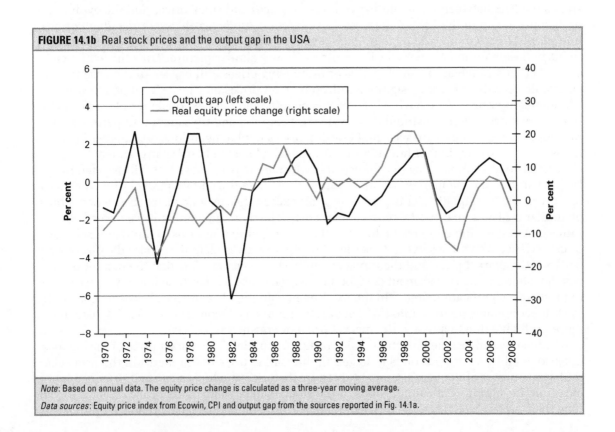

FIGURE 14.1b Real stock prices and the output gap in the USA

Note: Based on annual data. The equity price change is calculated as a three-year moving average.

Data sources: Equity price index from Ecowin, CPI and output gap from the sources reported in Fig. 14.1a.

additional capital goods, that is, by investing. The higher the stock price relative to the replacement cost, the greater is the incentive to invest, so the higher the level of investment will be. One might think that the firm would instantaneously adjust its capital stock so that any discrepancy between the stock market value and the replacement cost of its assets is immediately eliminated. However, this is not realistic since in practice the firm will incur various costs of adjusting the capital stock, and these costs are likely to increase more than proportionally to the level of investment. Hence it will be more profitable to allow a gradual adjustment of the capital stock, and during this (potentially long) adjustment period the stock market value of the firm will deviate from the replacement cost of its assets.

In the following sections we will explain this theory of the link between asset prices and investment in more detail, starting with the theory of the stock market and business investment.

14.1 The stock market

A few facts about the stock market

It is well known that stock prices are highly volatile and sometimes experience dramatic swings. For example, on 19 October 1987 the US Dow Jones index fell by 22.6 per cent in a single day. This was even more apocalyptic than the notorious crash in the 'Black October' of 1929 when the Wall Street stock market dropped by 23 per cent in the course of two days (however, the recovery of stock prices after October 1987 was much faster, so the macroeconomic effects of the crash of 1929 were much more serious).

Figure 14.2 illustrates the long-term trends in the US stock market, documenting the evolution of real (inflation-adjusted) stock prices and the so-called price–earnings ratio,

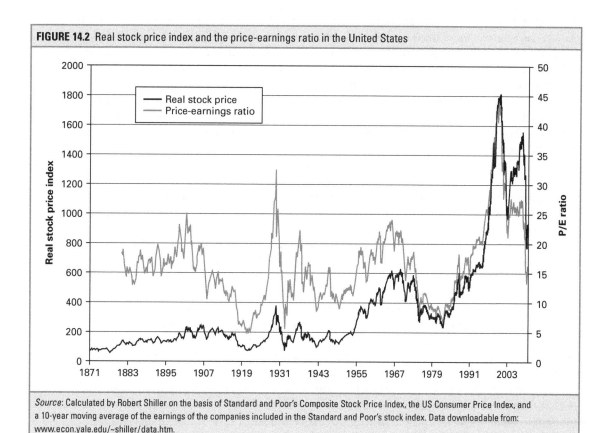

FIGURE 14.2 Real stock price index and the price-earnings ratio in the United States

Source: Calculated by Robert Shiller on the basis of Standard and Poor's Composite Stock Price Index, the US Consumer Price Index, and a 10-year moving average of the earnings of the companies included in the Standard and Poor's stock index. Data downloadable from: www.econ.yale.edu/~shiller/data.htm.

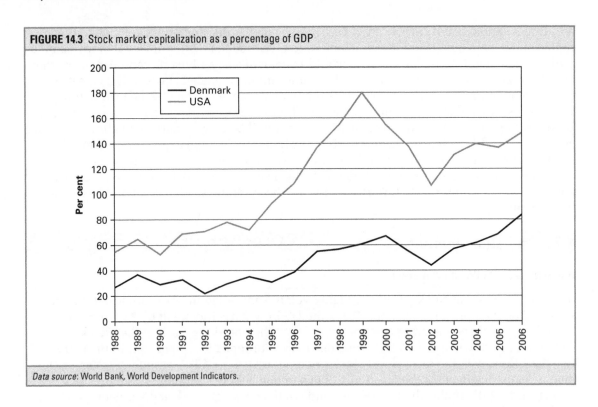

FIGURE 14.3 Stock market capitalization as a percentage of GDP

Data source: World Bank, World Development Indicators.

defined as the market value of shares relative to the profits of the companies which have issued the shares. The curve for the real stock price index highlights the enormous stock market boom of the 1990s which was followed by a sharp downturn after the turn of the new century and a subsequent strong recovery that was interrupted by a new dramatic drop in stock prices during the financial and economic crisis of 2008.

Mainly as a consequence of rising stock prices, the market value of outstanding shares (the 'stock market capitalization') as a percentage of GDP rose sharply during the 1990s, as shown in Fig. 14.3. In this way stocks became a much more important component of total financial wealth.

In many countries the booming stock market motivated a growing proportion of households to invest in shares, and half the adult US population owned stocks at the turn of the millennium, as indicated in Fig. 14.4. In a country like Sweden, the corresponding proportion was about one-third, whereas only about 15 per cent of the adult population in Denmark held shares at the start of this decade.

But the stock market is actually more important for households than Fig. 14.4 might suggest, since the numbers in the figure only include households who are *direct* owners of stocks. Households also channel a large part of their savings through pension funds, life insurance companies and other financial intermediaries which, in turn, invest a substantial part of their funds in shares. Hence the performance of the stock market directly or indirectly determines the return to a large fraction of household savings. In this way stock market developments may determine when people feel they can afford to retire from the labour market or when they can afford to buy new consumer durables. Moreover, the evolution of stock prices may have an important impact on the level of output and employment, because of its influence on consumption and business investment. In short, the stock market is important for individual consumers and for the macro economy, so it is worthwhile investing some effort in understanding how it works, and how it affects investment decisions.

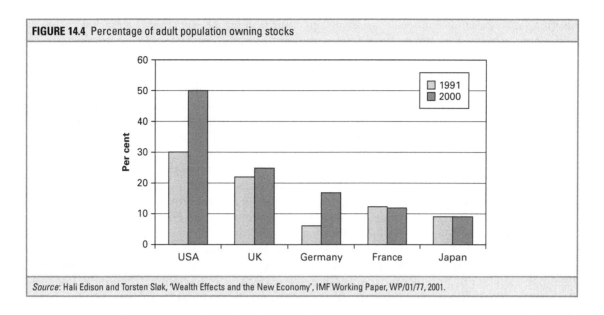

FIGURE 14.4 Percentage of adult population owning stocks

Source: Hali Edison and Torsten Sløk, 'Wealth Effects and the New Economy', IMF Working Paper, WP/01/77, 2001.

14.2 The price of stock

The value of a firm and the fundamental stock price

The starting point for our analysis is the assumption that business investment is guided by a desire to *maximize the wealth of the owners of the firm*. In modern Western economies where the bulk of business activity is carried out by firms organized as joint stock companies (corporations), maximization of the wealth of the firm's owners is equivalent to maximization of the market value of the outstanding shares in the corporation. This is the reason for our focus on the stock market. However, our theory of investment will also be relevant for unincorporated firms or for corporations which are not quoted in an official stock exchange. As we shall see, our theory of the stock market implies that *the market value of shares equals the discounted value of the expected future cash flow from the firm to its owners*. But this is exactly how a rational outside investor would also value an unquoted or unincorporated firm if he were contemplating buying or investing in such a firm. If the owner of an unincorporated firm wants to maximize the market value of his business assets, his investment behaviour will therefore be similar to the investment behaviour of a corporation whose shares are traded in a public stock exchange, as we shall explain in more detail later.

You may wonder why we assume that the objective of the firm is to maximize the *wealth* of its owners? The answer is that maximization of the current market value of the firm will also maximize the *consumption possibilities* of its owners. This will become clear in the next chapter where we show that a person's potential present and future consumption is constrained by the sum of his financial wealth and his current and discounted future labour income. Therefore, if a firm can change its operations so as to increase the market value of its assets, it will increase the financial wealth of its owners and enable them to increase their consumption either now or in the future. In both cases the owners will obviously be better off. In your basic microeconomics course you may have learned that firms maximize their profits rather than the market value of their assets. Fortunately, there is no contradiction between these two goals. A firm that maximizes its discounted stream of profits over time will also maximize its market value, as we shall demonstrate below.

If a corporation plans its investment with the purpose of maximizing the market value of its shares, we must base our theory of investment on a theory of the value of the firm. Our starting point for such a theory is an *arbitrage condition* which says that the market value of the shares in the firm must adjust to ensure that the investment of a certain amount of wealth in shares is equally attractive as investing a similar amount in bonds. Suppose that, at the beginning of period t, the shareholders in the firm expect to receive a dividend D_t^e at the end of the period, and that they expect the market value of their shares at the start of period $t + 1$ to be V_{t+1}^e. If V_t is the *actual* market value of shares in the firm at the beginning of period t, shareholders thus expect to earn a capital gain equal to $V_{t+1}^e - V_t$ during period t. Hence the total expected return on shareholding is $D_t^e + (V_{t+1}^e - V_t)$, composed of the expected dividend plus the expected capital gain.

In a capital market equilibrium this expected return must equal the 'required' return on shares. The required return consists of the opportunity cost of holding shares rather than bonds, plus an appropriate risk premium. If r is the market rate of interest on bonds (assumed for simplicity to be constant over time), the opportunity cost of shareholding is rV_t, since this is the interest income which the shareholder could have earned during period t if he had sold his shares at the inital market value V_t and invested the corresponding amount in bonds. Furthermore, since stock prices and dividends are generally more volatile than bond prices and interest payments, shares are a riskier investment than bonds. Because investors are risk averse, the expected rate of return on shares must therefore include a risk premium ε on top of the market interest rate to ensure that shareholding is considered just as attractive as the holding of bonds. Hence the total required return on the shares is $(r + \varepsilon)V_t$, and the arbitrage condition for capital market equilibrium may then be written as:

$$\overbrace{(r + \varepsilon)V_t}^{\substack{\text{required} \\ \text{return}}} = \underbrace{\overbrace{D_t^e}^{} + \overbrace{V_{t+1}^e - V_t}^{\substack{\text{expected} \\ \text{capital gain}}}}_{\substack{\text{total expected} \\ \text{return on shares}}} \tag{1}$$

If the current market value V_t is so high that the required return on the left-hand side of (1) exceeds the expected return on the right-hand side, financial investors will sell off their shares in the firm in order to buy bonds, and the market value V_t will drop. On the other hand, if the current share price (and hence V_t) is so low that shares in the firm promise a total rate of return in excess of $r + \varepsilon$, investors will shift from bonds to shares, thereby driving up the current market value V_t. Hence the stock market can only be in equilibrium when the arbitrage condition (1) is met. Since investors derive utility from their *real* consumption possibilities, we are measuring all variables in equation (1) in *real* (inflation-adjusted) terms, so r is the real rate of interest. We may rearrange (1) to get:

$$V_t = \frac{D_t^e + V_{t+1}^e}{1 + r + \varepsilon}. \tag{2}$$

This is a very important relationship in our analysis below. It says that the value of the firm at the beginning of any period equals the present value of that period's expected dividend plus the expected market value at the end of the period. We see that the rate at which future values are discounted includes the market interest rate r and the required risk premium ε.

As we have argued above, the firm will choose an investment plan which maximizes V_t. To characterize the firm's optimal investment policy we must therefore study how V_{t+1}^e and D_t^e and hence V_t depend on the firm's planned investment. This is the purpose of the following analysis.

Since arbitrage conditions similar to (2) must hold for all subsequent periods, rational financial investors will expect that future stock prices will satisfy the relationships:

$$V_{t+1}^e = \frac{D_{t+1}^e + V_{t+2}^e}{1 + r + \varepsilon}, \quad V_{t+2}^e = \frac{D_{t+2}^e + V_{t+3}^e}{1 + r + \varepsilon}, \quad V_{t+n}^e = \frac{D_{t+n}^e + V_{t+n+1}^e}{1 + r + \varepsilon}, \text{ etc.} \tag{3}$$

By successive substitutions of the expressions in (3) into (2), we find that

$$V_t = \frac{D_t^e}{1+r+\varepsilon} + \frac{D_{t+1}^e}{(1+r+\varepsilon)^2} + \frac{V_{t+2}^e}{(1+r+\varepsilon)^2}$$

$$= \frac{D_t^e}{1+r+\varepsilon} + \frac{D_{t+1}^e}{(1+r+\varepsilon)^2} + \frac{D_{t+2}^e}{(1+r+\varepsilon)^3} + \frac{V_{t+3}^e}{(1+r+\varepsilon)^3} \tag{4}$$

$$= \frac{D_t^e}{1+r+\varepsilon} + \frac{D_{t+1}^e}{(1+r+\varepsilon)^2} + \frac{D_{t+2}^e}{(1+r+\varepsilon)^3} + \ldots + \frac{V_{t+n}^e}{(1+r+\varepsilon)^n}.$$

It is reasonable to assume that investors do not expect future real stock prices V_{t+n}^e to rise indefinitely at a rate faster than $r+\varepsilon$, for if the opposite were the case, the current stock price V_t would become infinitely high according to (4). Hence we assume that

$$\lim_{n\to\infty} \frac{V_{t+n}^e}{(1+r+\varepsilon)^n} = 0. \tag{5}$$

If we continue the successive substitutions indicated in (4) and use our assumption (5), we end up with:

$$V_t = \frac{D_t^e}{(1+r+\varepsilon)} + \frac{D_{t+1}^e}{(1+r+\varepsilon)^2} + \frac{D_{t+2}^e}{(1+r+\varepsilon)^3} + \ldots \tag{6}$$

Equation (6) is our first important result:

THE FUNDAMENTAL SHARE PRICE

The market value of the shares in a firm equals the present discounted value of the expected future dividends paid out by the firm. This is sometimes referred to as the fundamental share price, because it is a price based on a 'fundamental' condition, namely the firm's ability to generate future cash flows to its owners.

Note that there must be a close correlation between a firm's dividends and its profits, since the latter are the source of the former. This observation is the basis for our earlier claim that maximization of (the present value of) profits is roughly equivalent to maximization of market value.

If investor expectations of future dividends are reasonably accurate, Eq. (6) predicts a fairly close link between the stock price observed at time t and the present discounted value (PDV) of the actual dividends paid out after that time. Figure 14.5 shows the evolution since 1871 of the Standard & Poor 500 stock price index for the USA and two alternative measures of the present value of future dividends (real dividends after 2007 were estimated by assuming that future dividends will grow at the average historical growth rate for dividends). The smooth line shows the PDV when future dividends are discounted at a constant rate equal to the observed average return on shares between 1871 and 2007. The graph 'discount rate = market interest rate' indicates the PDV when dividends are discounted by actual one-year interest rates plus a constant risk premium equal to the average actual risk premium on shares observed over the entire period. We see that at least up until the late 1990s, there is indeed a long-run link between stock prices and the PDV of dividends, as Eq. (6) would lead us to expect.

However, we also see from Fig. 14.5 that actual stock prices are much more volatile than our two measures of the PDV of dividends. This has led many observers to challenge the

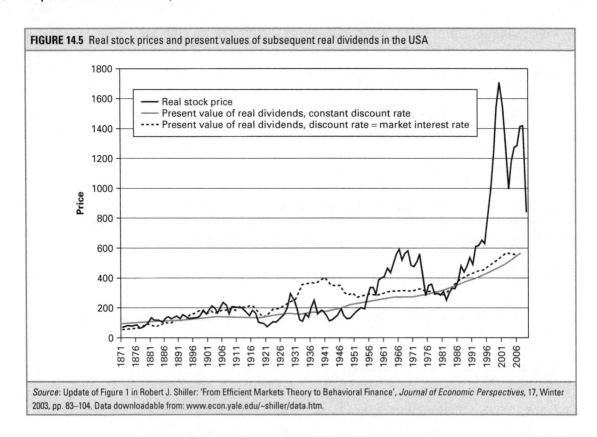

FIGURE 14.5 Real stock prices and present values of subsequent real dividends in the USA

Source: Update of Figure 1 in Robert J. Shiller: 'From Efficient Markets Theory to Behavioral Finance', *Journal of Economic Perspectives*, 17, Winter 2003, pp. 83–104. Data downloadable from: www.econ.yale.edu/~shiller/data.htm.

idea that the stock market works in an efficient manner. According to the so-called *Efficient Markets Theory* the stock price at any time t always reflects the present value of the best possible forecast of future dividends. In other words, investors always make optimal use of all information relevant for the forecasting of future dividends. In formal terms, the Efficient Markets Theory says that $V_t = E[V_t^*]$, where V_t is the actual share price, V_t^* is the PDV of the actual subsequent dividends accruing to that share (or portfolio of shares), and $E[V_t^*]$ is the mathematical expectation of V_t^*, calculated on the basis of all relevant information available at time t. By definition, the expected value of V_t^*, $E[V_t^*]$, must equal the actual value of V_t^* plus/minus the forecast error. The Efficient Markets Theory therefore implies that $V_t^* = V_t + u_t$, where u_t is a forecast error which is uncorrelated with V_t and with any other information available at time t (for if u_t were systematically correlated with V_t or with any other variables observable at time t, the forecast of V_t^* could be improved, which would contradict the assumption that markets make optimal use of all available information). But if $V_t^* = V_t + u_t$ and V_t and u_t are uncorrelated, the variance of V_t^* will equal the *sum* of the variances of V_t and u_t and hence must be *larger* than the variance of V_t. However, our two measures of V_t^* (the PDV of actual subsequent dividends) in Fig. 14.5 clearly have a *lower* variance than our measure of V_t (the Standard & Poor stock price index). Thus the high observed volatility of stock prices is a serious challenge to Efficient Markets Theory. Indeed, it seems that this theory can only be 'saved' if the measures of the PDV of future dividends in Fig. 14.5 are seriously wrong, that is, if the discount rate used by stockholders is much more volatile than we have assumed.

More generally, Fig. 14.5 invites the question:

Why are stock prices so volatile?

Equation (6) suggests three possible explanations for the observed volatility of stock prices:

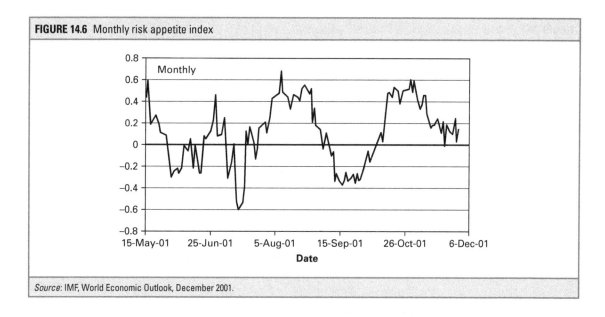

FIGURE 14.6 Monthly risk appetite index

Source: IMF, World Economic Outlook, December 2001.

1. Fluctuations in (the growth rate of) expected future real dividends

2. Fluctuations in the real interest rate r

3. Fluctuations in the required risk premium on shares, ε.

The great stock market boom of the 1990s seems to have been driven mainly by more optimistic expectations regarding future real dividends, as financial investors came to believe that the rapid innovations in information technology would create a 'New Economy' characterized by a significantly higher real growth rate in output and business profits. Presumably changes in the required risk premium on shares have also contributed to the recent turbulence on the stock market. There is some evidence that investors frequently change their attitude towards risk. This is illustrated by Fig. 14.6 which plots the movements of a so-called 'risk appetite index' for the major industrial and emerging market economies in most of 2001.

The idea behind the index is that if investors become willing to bear more risks, they will bid up the price of assets that have been risky in the past, and if they become more risk averse they will drive down the price of risky assets by selling them. Hence Fig. 14.6 assumes that movements in current asset prices which are systematically correlated with the observed past riskiness (the past volatility of returns) of those assets indicate a change in investor appetite for risk. The figure suggests that the terrorist attacks on 11 September 2001 caused a sharp temporary drop in investor appetite for risk. Following a recovery, risk appetite again began to weaken towards the end of 2001, perhaps as a reaction to the worsening news about the state of the world economy announced at that time.

As already mentioned, it is often asked whether the observed movements of the stock market are really consistent with rational investor behaviour. In the short run the stock market sometimes seems to overreact to news, showing signs of 'herd behaviour'. One may also wonder how the large longer-term stock market fluctuations observed during recent decades can be reconciled with realistic changes in the long-term earnings potential of firms.[1] Notice, however, that the theory summarized in Eq. (6) is compatible with the observation of frequent changes in stock prices, if investors frequently revise their forecasts

---

1. For a fascinating account of the less rational aspects of stock market behaviour, placing the bull market of the 1990s in historical perspective, see Robert J. Shiller, *Irrational Exuberance*, New York, Broadway Books, 2001 (paperback edition).

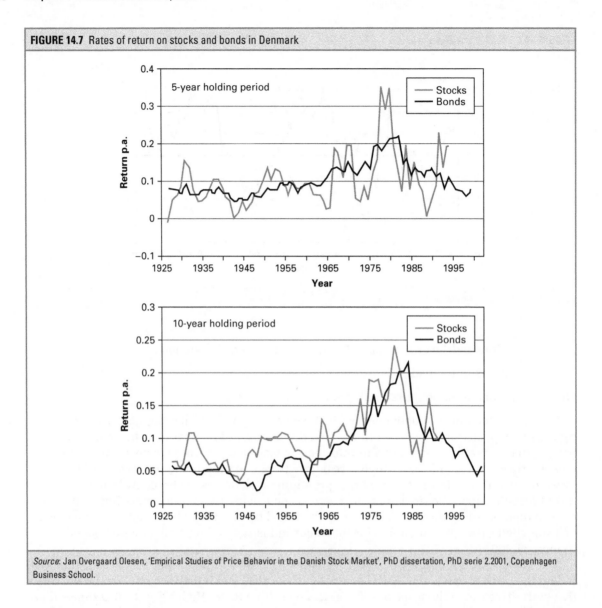

FIGURE 14.7 Rates of return on stocks and bonds in Denmark

Source: Jan Overgaard Olesen, 'Empirical Studies of Price Behavior in the Danish Stock Market', PhD dissertation, PhD serie 2.2001, Copenhagen Business School.

of future dividends and their appetite for risk, and if they are often faced with unanticipated changes in real interest rates. Notice also that we do not necessarily subscribe to the Efficient Markets Theory since our theory assumes only a weak form of rationality: all we assume is that investors require the holding of shares to be just as attractive as the holding of interest-bearing assets. We have *not* excluded the possibility that financial investors may at times hold unduly optimistic or pessimistic expectations about future dividends, and that they may sometimes require 'unreasonably' high or low risk premia due to an inability to make realistic forecasts of the riskiness of business investment. In short, Eq. (6) makes no assumptions regarding the formation of expectations and risk premia; it only assumes that the expected return on shares is systematically related to the return obtainable on bonds. According to Fig. 14.7 this does not appear to be a bad assumption for the longer run, since the realized returns on bonds and stocks in Denmark do indeed seem to move together when the rates of return are calculated over a five-year or a ten-year holding period.

Although Figures 14.5 and 14.7 suggest that the price of stocks is in fact linked to fundamentals in the long run, many observers of the stock market believe that stock prices can sometimes deviate from the fundamental value of firms. During such periods of 'speculative bubbles', stocks become objects of pure short-term speculation, and their prices cease to be pinned down by the discounted value of expected future dividends. We do not deny that speculative bubbles may sometimes occur, but in this chapter we will assume that stock prices do reflect expectations of future dividends, even if those expectations may not always be rational. As we shall see, the theory of the stock market outlined above can take us a long way towards understanding business investment.

14.3 Business investment

Stock prices and investment

Our working hypothesis is that the firm chooses its level of investment with the purpose of maximizing its market value V_t. From Eq. (2) we see that maximization of V_t is equivalent to maximizing the sum of its owners' expected dividends and expected end-of-period wealth, $D_t^e + V_{t+1}^e$, since the individual firm has no influence on r and ε. The question is: what level of investment will maximize $D_t^e + V_{t+1}^e$?

To answer this, let us introduce the variable q to indicate the *ratio between the market value of the firm and the replacement value of the firm's capital stock*. We thus have $q_t \equiv V_t/K_t$ or $V_t \equiv q_t K_t$, where K_t is the real capital stock, and where the acquisition price of a unit of capital has been normalized to 1 so that the replacement value of the capital stock is simply K_t. Note the direct link between stock prices and our q-variable: if the market price of shares in the firm goes up, the value of q increases correspondingly. The advantage of specifying our theory of investment in terms of q is that this variable can be measured empirically since stock market values as well as replacement values of business assets can in principle be observed, whereas the expected future dividends underlying V and q are very hard to measure. Introducing q, therefore, helps to make our theory of investment empirically testable.

Assuming that the firm communicates its investment plans for the current period to its owners, the shareholders will know the size of the firm's capital stock at the start of the next period (K_{t+1}), but they cannot know for sure what the level of the stock price q_{t+1} at that time will be. However, assume they expect the share price per unit of capital one period from now to be the same as the current share price so that $q_{t+1}^e = q_t$. We then have:

$$V_{t+1}^e = q_t K_{t+1}. \tag{7}$$

We have now expressed V_{t+1}^e in a form that will turn out to be convenient. Let us next consider the other determinant of current market value, $V_t = (D_t^e + V_{t+1}^e)/(1+r+\varepsilon)$, that is, the expected dividend D_t^e for period t. Suppose for the moment that the firm finances all of its current investment spending I_t via retained profits (we shall consider external financing later on). Furthermore, suppose realistically that increases in the firm's capital stock imply *adjustment costs*, including costs of installing new machinery, costs of training workers to use the new equipment, and possibly costs of changing the firm's organization. For convenience, all such costs will be called 'installation costs' and will be denoted by $c(I_t)$ to indicate that they are a function of investment spending.

With these assumptions, the expected dividend for period t will be equal to the expected profit in period t, denoted by Π_t^e and measured before deduction of installation costs, minus that part of profit which is retained in order to finance the expenditure $I_t + c(I_t)$ associated with new investment:

$$D_t^e = \Pi_t^e - I_t - c(I_t), \qquad c(0) = 0, \qquad c' > 0. \tag{8}$$

It seems reasonable to assume that installation costs will rise more than proportionately with investment spending. If investment is low, the changes in the capital stock are small and can be accommodated without significant changes in the firm's organization. But when investment is high, the firm may have to undertake significant organizational changes and extensive training of employees, and the attention of managers will be diverted from the firm's day-to-day business. Such an organizational overhaul is typically very expensive. A simple installation cost function capturing this assumption is:

$$c(I_t) = \frac{a}{2} I_t^2,$$

(9)

where a is a positive constant. Equation (9) implies that $dc/dI_t = aI_t$, that is, the *marginal* installation cost increases in proportion to the level of investment, reflecting that large changes in the capital stock are disproportionately more costly than small changes.

To derive our investment schedule, we finally need the bookkeeping identity:

$$K_{t+1} = K_t + I_t,$$

(10)

stating that the capital stock at the beginning of period $t + 1$ equals the capital stock existing at the beginning of the previous period plus the level of investment during period t. For simplicity, (10) abstracts from depreciation of the existing capital stock, but as you will learn from Exercise 2, our theory of investment can easily be generalized to allow for depreciation.

Starting from (2), and inserting (7)–(10) into (2), we now find that the firm's market value at the start of period t can be written as follows:

$$V_t = \frac{D_t^e + V_{t+1}^e}{1 + r + \varepsilon} = \frac{\overbrace{\Pi_t^e - I_t - c(I_t)}^{D_t^e} + \overbrace{q_t(K_t + I_t)}^{V_{t+1}^e}}{1 + r + \varepsilon}.$$

(11)

The firm chooses its level of investment I_t so as to maximize the initial wealth of its owners, V_t, *taking the stock market's valuation of a unit of capital (q_t) as given.* The first-order condition $\partial V_t/\partial I_t = 0$ for the solution to this maximization problem yields:

$$\overbrace{q_t}^{\substack{\text{expected} \\ \text{capital gain}}} = 1 + \overbrace{\frac{dc}{dI_t}}^{\substack{\text{forgone} \\ \text{dividend}}},$$

and then, noting from (9) that $dc/dI_t = aI_t$:

$$I_t = \frac{q_t - 1}{a}.$$

(12)

The investment rule $q_t = 1 + dc/dI_t$ may be explained as follows: to finance the acquisition and installation of an extra unit of capital in period t, the firm must reduce its dividend payout in period t by an amount equal to the acquisition cost of a unit of capital – which we have set equal to 1 – *plus* the marginal installation cost dc/dI_t. This forgone dividend $1 + dc/dI_t$ is the shareholder's marginal opportunity cost of allowing the firm to undertake an extra unit of investment. The shareholder's marginal benefit from investment is the gain q_t in the value of shares resulting from the installation of an extra unit of capital. At the optimal level of investment, the marginal dividend forgone is just compensated by the extra capital gain on shares. Clearly, the higher the market valuation q_t of an extra unit of capital, the further the firm can push its level of investment before the marginal installation cost reaches the threshold where the shareholder's additional capital gain is offset by the extra dividend forgone. Hence we obtain the simple investment schedule in (12) which says that investment

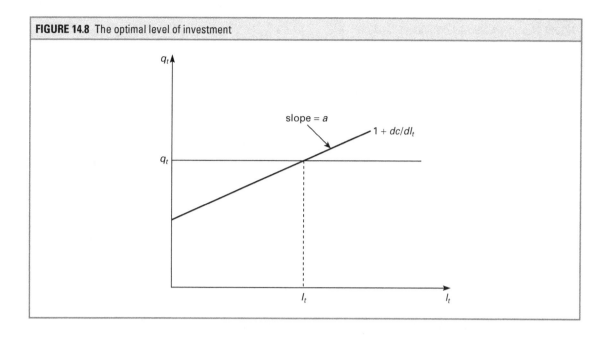

FIGURE 14.8 The optimal level of investment

will be higher the higher the level of the stock price q_t. Equation (12) also shows that high marginal installation costs (reflected in a high value of the cost parameter a) reduce the optimal level of investment, as one would expect. This is also clear from the graphical illustration of the determination of investment in Fig. 14.8: a higher value of a increases the slope of the curve $1 + dc/dI_t = 1 + aI_t$ and thereby reduces the value-maximizing level of investment where $1 + dc/dI_t = q_t$.

The investment schedule (12) also holds when investment outlays are financed by issuing new debt or new shares rather than by retaining profits. Regardless of the mode of finance, the installation of an extra unit of capital will increase the expected market value of the firm's assets by the amount q_t, still assuming that the current stock price gives an indication of the expected value. If the cost of buying and installing the extra unit of capital $(1 + dc/dI_t)$ is financed by an increase in the firm's outstanding debt or by the issue of new shares, the expected increase in the market value of the shares owned by the firm's *existing* shareholders will be equal to the rise in total market value q_t *minus* the value of the newly issued debt or equity, $1 + dc/dI_t$. Of course, it is optimal for existing shareholders to let the firm expand its investment until the expected marginal gain in the value of their shares is driven down to zero, that is, until $q_t - (1 + dc/dI_t) = 0$. But this is exactly the investment rule leading to the investment schedule in (12)! Hence we obtain the important result that the investment function $I_t = (q_t - 1)/a$ is valid *regardless of the method of investment finance*.

In summary, we have

THE q-THEORY OF BUSINESS INVESTMENT

Avalue-maximizing firm will invest up to the point where the rise in its market value induced by an extra unit of investment is just equal to the sum of the acquisition and installation cost of buying and installing an additional unit of capital. Because the marginal installation cost increases with the volume of investment, the optimal investment level is higher, the higher an increase in the firm's capital stock is valued by the stock market. An increase in the ratio of stock prices to the acquisition cost of the firm's assets (that is, a rise in q) will therefore stimulate its investment.

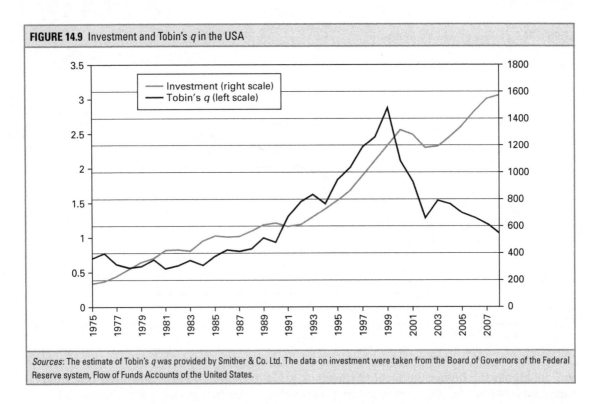

FIGURE 14.9 Investment and Tobin's *q* in the USA

Sources: The estimate of Tobin's *q* was provided by Smithers & Co. Ltd. The data on investment were taken from the Board of Governors of the Federal Reserve system, Flow of Funds Accounts of the United States.

The theory outlined above is known as Tobin's *q*-theory of investment, named after Nobel Laureate James Tobin who was the first economist to give a systematic formal account of the link between stock prices and business investment.[2] Figure 14.9 plots total fixed business investment in the USA against an estimate of Tobin's *q*, defined as the ratio of the stock market value of firms to the replacement value of their capital stock, as above.

We see that although total investment and the *q*-ratio do tend to move together over the longer run, they do not always change in the same direction in the short run. Part of the problem may be that, in practice, stock prices reflect many 'intangible' business assets besides physical capital, for example patents and know-how. Another part of the explanation for the sometimes weak relationship between investment and Tobin's *q* may be that the estimated value of *q* reflects the *average* ratio between the *total* market value and the *total* replacement value of the capital stock, whereas in theory, investment decisions depend on the *marginal* value of *q*, that is, on the *increase* in market value relative to the acquisition price of an *additional* unit of capital. In our analysis above, the marginal and average values of *q* were identical, because our simplifying assumptions implied proportionality between the firm's future capital stock and expected future profits. But if this proportionality breaks down, the marginal *q* will no longer coincide with the average *q*, and since only the latter can be measured empirically, this may make it difficult to test the *q*-theory of investment.

The role of interest rates, profits and sales

How does the *q*-theory of investment square with the conventional assumption that investment depends negatively on the real interest rate? The claim that investment varies positively with stock prices is fully consistent with the hypothesis that it varies negatively with the real interest rate.

---

2.   The classic statement of the theory was given in James Tobin, 'A General Equilibrium Approach to Monetary Theory', *Journal of Money, Credit, and Banking*, **1**, 1969, pp. 15–29. The theory was later refined and extended by Fumio Hayashi, 'Tobin's Marginal *q* and Average *q*: A Neoclassical Interpretation', *Econometrica*, **50**, 1982, pp. 213–224.

To see this, let us go back to Eq. (6) and let us assume for simplicity (since this will not affect our qualitative conclusion) that real dividends are expected to stay constant at the level D_t^e from period t and onwards. Equation (6) then becomes:

$$V_t = D_t^e \left[\frac{1}{1+r+\varepsilon} + \frac{1}{(1+r+\varepsilon)^2} + \frac{1}{(1+r+\varepsilon)^3} + \ldots \right]. \tag{13}$$

If we multiply both sides of (13) by $1+r+\varepsilon$ and subtract (13) from the resulting equation, we get:

$$V_t = \frac{D_t^e}{r+\varepsilon}. \tag{14}$$

Equation (14) is just a special version of the general formula stating that the value of the firm equals the present discounted value of expected future dividends. Now recall that by definition, $V_t = q_t K_t$. From this relationship and (14) it follows that:

$$q_t = \frac{D_t^e / K_t}{r+\varepsilon}. \tag{15}$$

According to (15) the market value of a unit of the firm's capital stock (q_t) equals the discounted value of the expected future dividends per unit of capital. Hence a rise in the real interest rate r will, *ceteris paribus*, reduce the stock price q_t, and this will reduce investment. From Figs 14.7 and 14.9 we have seen that stock prices do tend to adjust to keep the return on stocks in line with the return on bonds, and that investment tends to move in line with stock prices. This is indirect evidence of a negative impact of interest rates on investment.

Equation (15) implies that q will fluctuate not only with interest rates, but also with changes in the risk premium ε and in the expected dividend ratio, D^e / K. Let us take a closer look at the likely determinants of the latter variable. It seems reasonable to assume that expected dividends are positively related to the observed current profits of the firm, Π_t. For concreteness, suppose shareholders expect that the firm will pay out a fraction θ of its profits as dividends at the end of the period, so $D_t^e = \theta \Pi_t$. In that case the numerator of (15) may be written as $\theta (\Pi_t / K_t)$, where Π_t / K_t is the firm's current *rate* of profit (the profit to capital ratio). From (15) we would then expect to observe a positive correlation between (changes in) the current profit rate and (changes in) current investment. Figure 14.10 suggests that such a positive relationship does in fact exist.

We would also expect a positive relationship between the profit rate and the output–capital ratio. For example, we know from growth theory that if output Y is given by the Cobb–Douglas production function $Y = BK^\alpha L^{1-\alpha}$ (where L is labour input), and if markets are competitive, total profits will be equal to αY (see Section 3.1). In that case the *rate* of profit is $\alpha Y / K$ which is directly proportional to the output–capital ratio Y / K. Even if markets are not competitive, it is still reasonable to assume that the more firms can produce and sell on the basis of a given capital stock, the higher their profit rate will be. Figure 14.11 roughly confirms this expectation.

Although a higher current profit is likely to boost expected future dividends, it is too primitive to expect a mechanical one-to-one impact of the former on the latter variable. Firms and investors may sometimes have good reason to expect that future profitability will deviate from realized current profits. Indeed, the fact that the economy moves up and down in cycles suggests that intelligent investors will not mechanically extrapolate current earnings into the future. Instead they will revise their expectations regarding future sales and profits as they receive new information on relevant economic and political events. Most advanced countries publish indices of 'business confidence' to measure business expectations regarding the near future. Usually these indices build on survey data where a sample of business

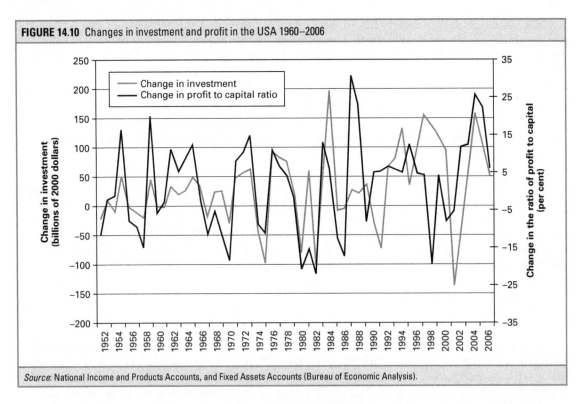

FIGURE 14.10 Changes in investment and profit in the USA 1960–2006

Source: National Income and Products Accounts, and Fixed Assets Accounts (Bureau of Economic Analysis).

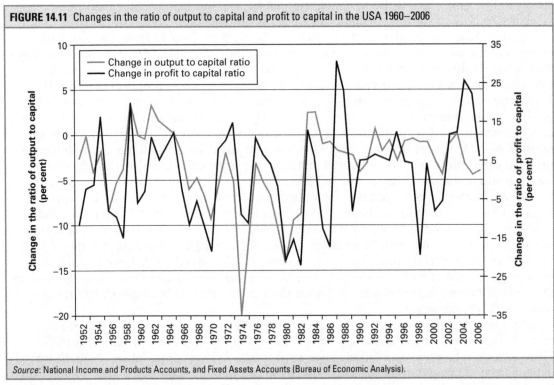

FIGURE 14.11 Changes in the ratio of output to capital and profit to capital in the USA 1960–2006

Source: National Income and Products Accounts, and Fixed Assets Accounts (Bureau of Economic Analysis).

managers report current and expected movements in their future output, sales, employment, investment, etc. Figure 14.12 shows the evolution of one such index of business confidence in the USA. We see that business confidence can fluctuate quite a lot and that it is sometimes significantly affected by unanticipated political events.

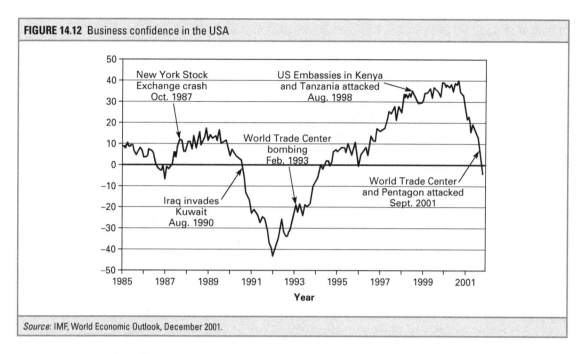

FIGURE 14.12 Business confidence in the USA

Source: IMF, World Economic Outlook, December 2001.

Hence, to understand the high volatility of investment spending, we have to allow for changes in expectations regarding the future. Our earlier discussion of Fig. 14.6 suggests that part of the impact of a change in expectations on investment may be caused by a change in the required risk premium ε.

To summarize, we have seen that the q-theory of investment is quite consistent with the hypothesis that business investment varies positively with the level of output (sales), whereas the existing capital stock and the real interest rate both have a negative impact on investment. Specifically, if E is an index of the 'state of confidence', we have argued that the expected dividend ratio D_t^e/K_t will be given by a function like $g(Y_t/K_t, E_t)$, where both of the first derivatives of the $g()$-function are positive. Using this relationship along with (12) and (15), we may thus write our investment function as:

$$I_t = \left(\frac{1}{a}\right)\left(\frac{D_t^e/K_t}{r+\varepsilon}-1\right) = \left(\frac{1}{a}\right)\left(\frac{g(Y_t/K_t, E_t)}{r+\varepsilon}-1\right),$$

or, in more general form, and dropping time subscripts for convenience:

$$I = f(\underset{(+)}{Y}, \underset{(-)}{K}, \underset{(-)}{r}, \underset{(+)}{E}), \tag{16}$$

where the signs below the variables indicate the signs of the corresponding partial derivatives of the $f()$-function. In terms of the q-theory, an increase in Y or E will stimulate investment by raising q_t through an increase in the expected dividend ratio $D_t^e/K_t = g(Y_t/K_t, E_t)$ (and possibly through a fall in the risk premium ε). An increase in the current capital stock K reduces investment by driving down D_t^e/K_t, and an increase in the real interest rate r likewise discourages investment via a negative impact on q_t.

In the case of firms whose market value is not directly observable because they are not quoted on the stock exchange, it is inappropriate to interpret Eq. (16) literally in terms of the q-theory. Nevertheless, as Exercise 3 will make clear, the investment behaviour of such firms may still be described by an equation like (16) if they invest with the purpose of maximizing the present value of the net cash flow to their owner (thereby maximizing his wealth). Equation (16) therefore summarizes our general theory of business investment. In words, we can sum up the insights from this important equation as follows:

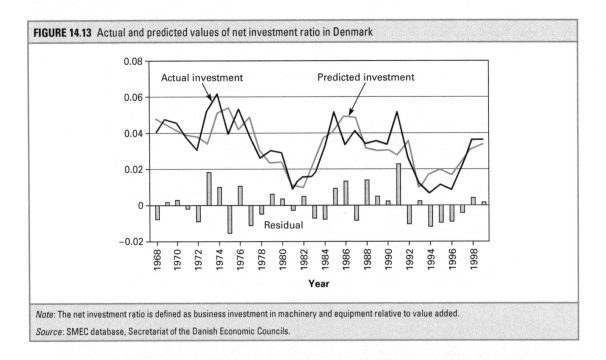

FIGURE 14.13 Actual and predicted values of net investment ratio in Denmark

Note: The net investment ratio is defined as business investment in machinery and equipment relative to value added.

Source: SMEC database, Secretariat of the Danish Economic Councils.

THE BUSINESS INVESTMENT FUNCTION

The value of Tobin's q reflects expected future dividends per unit of capital which are positively affected by a rise in the current profit rate. The profit rate in turn varies positively with the output–capital ratio. Hence investment is an increasing function of current output and a decreasing function of the current capital stock. A higher real interest rate or a higher risk premium increases the rate at which expected future dividends are discounted, thus depressing investment by reducing the value of Tobin's q.

Econometric research has confirmed that changes in Y, K and r influence investment in the manner indicated in (16). However, researchers have also found that it is quite difficult to explain fully all of the observed movements in investment. To illustrate, Fig. 14.13 plots actual investment against the predicted level of investment estimated on the basis of a sophisticated version of the investment function (16). To a large extent, the difficulties of predicting investment undoubtedly stem from the difficulty of finding reliable quantifiable proxies for 'the state of confidence', E. Because expectations are so hard to measure and may sometimes change abruptly, it is inherently difficult to forecast investment.

14.4 The housing market and housing investment

A q-theory of housing investment

Housing investment is an important component of total private investment, and as indicated in Table 14.1, it is strongly correlated with GDP. Hence fluctuations in residential investment often play an important role during business cycles. A basic factor contributing to the volatility of housing investment is the fact that housing capital is highly durable. In any year the construction of new housing is only a very small fraction of the existing housing stock. To accommodate even small percentage changes in consumer *demand* for

TABLE 14.1 The volatility of housing investment

	Average share of total private investment	Coefficient of correlation with contemporaneous GDP (same quarter)	Absolute volatility (standard deviation)	Volatility relative to volatiliy of total private fixed investment	Volatitity relative to volatility of GDP
Belgium	30%	0.79	0.30	0.93	1.28
Denmark	32%	0.62	0.27	0.66	1.17
Netherlands	36%	0.92	0.19	0.69	0.72
United Kingdom	36%	0.94	0.23	0.65	0.92
United States	32%	0.93	0.32	0.75	0.98

Sources: UK Office for National Statistics, Ecowin, Datastream, Bureau of Economic Analysis, Bureau of Labor Statistics, Federal Reserve Bank of St. Louis, Danmarks Nationalbank, Belgostat, Banque Nationale de Belgique, Statistics Netherlands and De Nederlandse Bank. The time periods considered roughly coincide with those reported for the various countries in the business cycle analysis of Chapter 13.

housing capital, construction activity may therefore have to undergo large relative changes.

In this section we will show that housing investment may be explained along lines which are similar to the q-theory of business investment.[3] The present section may therefore be seen as an illustrative special version of the q-theory, adapted to fit the housing market. As a by-product of our theory of housing investment, we will develop a theory of the formation of housing prices and identify the factors which may cause fluctuations in the market value of the housing stock. Since the stock of housing capital is an important component in total household wealth, and since the next chapter will show that private consumption depends on private wealth, the theory of the housing market developed below will also help us to understand fluctuations in private consumption.

We start by considering the production function of the construction sector. For concreteness, suppose that the construction of new housing, I^H, is given by the production function:

$$I^H = A \cdot X^\beta, \qquad 0 < \beta < 1, \tag{17}$$

where X is a composite input factor (to be specified below), and A is a constant which depends on the productive capacity of the construction sector. The assumption that the parameter β is less than 1 implies that, over the time horizon we are considering, production is subject to diminishing returns to scale.

For simplicity, we assume that construction firms combine labour L and building materials Q in fixed proportions. Specifically, each unit of the composite input X includes a units of labour and b units of materials:

$$L = aX, \qquad Q = bX. \tag{18}$$

If W is the wage rate and p^Q is the price of materials, it follows from (18) that the price P of a unit of the composite input X is equal to

$$P = aW + bp^Q. \tag{19}$$

---

3. The theory of the housing market we are about to present is inspired by the following influential article by James A. Poterba: 'Tax Subsidies to Owner-Occupied Housing: An Asset-Market Approach', *Quarterly Journal of Economics*, **99**, 1984, pp. 729–752. However, while Poterba assumed that homeowners rationally anticipate future capital gains or losses on their property, we simplify by treating the expected rate of capital gains as an exogenous variable.

We will refer to P as 'the construction cost index'. If p^H is the market price of a unit of housing, the sales revenue of the representative construction firm will be $p^H I^H$, and its profits, Π, will be

$$\Pi = p^H I^H - PX = p^H I^H - P(I^H/A)^{1/\beta}. \tag{20}$$

In deriving the second equality in (20), we have solved (17) for X and substituted the solution into the expression for profits. Taking the housing price p^H and the input price P as given, the construction firm chooses its level of activity I^H with the purpose of maximizing its profit. (We might also assume that the firm maximizes its market value. This would give the same results, but via a more cumbersome procedure.) According to (20), the first-order condition for profit maximization, $d\Pi/dI^H = 0$, implies:

$$p^H - \overbrace{\frac{P}{\beta A}\left(\frac{I^H}{A}\right)^{(1-\beta)/\beta}}^{\substack{d(PX)/dI^H=\text{marginal} \\ \text{construction cost}}} = 0 \quad \Leftrightarrow$$

$$I^H = k \cdot \left(\frac{p^H}{P}\right)^{\beta/(1-\beta)}, \qquad k \equiv \beta^{\beta/(1-\beta)} A^{1/(1-\beta)}. \tag{21}$$

Equation (21) is the *supply curve* for the construction sector. It is seen to be derived from the fact that profit-maximizing construction firms will push construction activity to the point where the marginal construction cost equals the market price of a housing unit. The relative price variable p^H/P is an analogue of Tobin's q. Thus, since $0 < \beta < 1$, Eq. (21) says that housing investment I^H will be larger the higher the q-ratio of the housing price to the construction cost index is.[4] Figure 14.14 shows that this theory of housing investment fits the facts very well.

Thus we have:

THE q-THEORY OF HOUSING INVESTMENT

When the market price of existing residential property rises relative to the cost of constructing a new unit of housing, it becomes profitable for firms in the construction industry to increase the supply of new housing. Hence housing investment goes up. This q-theory of housing investment is strongly supported by the data.

Housing investment, interest rates and income

Like the q-theory of business investment, our theory of housing investment is consistent with the hypothesis that investment varies negatively with interest rates and positively with total income. To demonstrate this, we will now develop a theory of housing demand in order to explain the housing price p^H.

Consider a representative consumer who has borrowed to acquire a housing stock H at the going market price p^H per unit of housing. Suppose the consumer expects to have to spend an amount $\delta p^H H$ on repair and maintenance each period to maintain the value of his house, and suppose the interest rate on mortgage debt is r. The consumer's total cost

---

4. In this theory of housing investment the assumption of diminishing returns to the composite input X has taken the place of the installation costs which we included in our model of business investment.

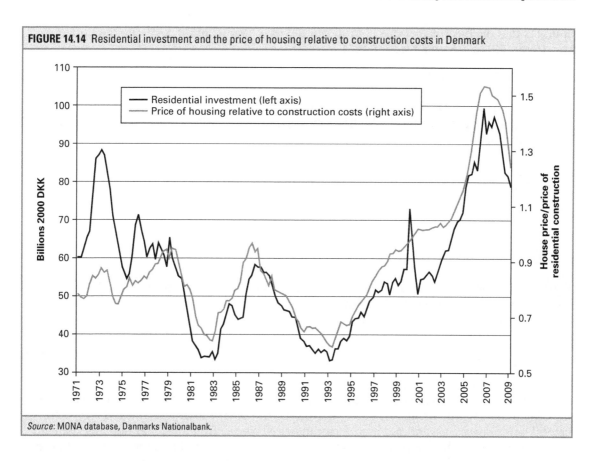

FIGURE 14.14 Residential investment and the price of housing relative to construction costs in Denmark

Source: MONA database, Danmarks Nationalbank.

of housing consumption will then be $(r + \delta)p^H H$. Note that if the consumer expects the market price of houses to increase (decrease) over the period considered, it will take a smaller (larger) spending on repairs etc. to maintain the value of the house. Hence we have $\delta = \hat{\delta} - g^e$, where $\hat{\delta}$ is the spending on housing repair needed to maintain the value of the house when housing prices are stable, and g^e is the expected rate of increase of housing prices (which could be negative). In the analysis below we will treat $\hat{\delta}$ as well as g^e as exogenous constants, but it is important to keep in mind that changes in expected capital gains or losses on houses (changes in g^e) will cause shifts in our parameter δ.

The consumer also consumes an amount C of non-durable goods. If his income is Y, and if we abstract from savings (which will not affect our qualitative results), the consumer's budget constraint may then be written as:

$$C + (r + \delta)p^H H = Y, \tag{22}$$

where we have set the price of non-durables equal to 1. This normalization implies that a rise in p^H represents an increase in the price of housing units relative to the general consumer price level, that is, a *real* capital gain on houses. In a similar way our variable r should be interpreted as a *real* interest rate.

The consumer wishes to allocate his total consumption between housing and non-durables so as to maximize his utility U which we assume to be given by the Cobb–Douglas function:

$$U = H^\eta C^{1-\eta}, \qquad 0 < \eta < 1. \tag{23}$$

In practice, the consumer will derive utility from the housing *service* flowing from the housing stock H, and not from the housing stock as such. The specification in (23) just assumes that the housing service is proportional to the housing stock. Using the budget constraint (22) to eliminate C from (23), we get:

$$U = H^{\eta}[Y - (r + \delta)p^H H]^{1-\eta}. \tag{24}$$

The consumer's optimal level of housing demand is found by maximizing the utility function (24) with respect to H. The first-order condition $dU/dH = 0$ for the solution to this problem is:

$$\overbrace{\eta H^{\eta-1}[Y - (r+\delta)p^H H]^{1-\eta}}^{\partial U/\partial H} - (r+\delta)p^H \overbrace{(1-\eta)H^{\eta}[Y - (r+\delta)p^H H]^{-\eta}}^{\partial U/\partial C} = 0, \tag{25}$$

or

$$\frac{\partial U/\partial H}{\partial U/\partial C} = (r+\delta)p^H. \tag{26}$$

Equation (26) says that, in the consumer's optimum situation, the marginal rate of substitution between housing and non-durables (the left-hand side) must equal the relative price of housing, $(r + \delta)p^H$. If we solve (25) for H, we get the *demand for housing*, now denoted as H^d:

$$H^d = \frac{\eta Y}{(r+\delta)p^H}. \tag{27}$$

The term $(r + \delta)p^H$ in the denominator of (27) is sometimes referred to as the *user-cost of housing*, reflecting the financial cost, r, as well as the costs of maintenance and expected capital gains or losses, captured by the parameter δ. We see from (27) that housing demand varies positively with income and negatively with the user-cost of housing. Note that even if the consumer has financed the acquisition of his house by his own past savings, the user-cost should still include the interest rate r as an opportunity cost, since this is the income the consumer forgoes by investing his savings in a house rather than in interest-bearing assets.[5]

While (27) gives the *demand* for housing, the aggregate *supply* of housing is fixed in the short run where the housing stock is predetermined by the accumulated historical levels of housing investment. In other words, at the start of each period there is a given predetermined housing stock, since the current construction activity determined by (21) does not add to the housing stock until the start of the next period. In the short run, the market price of houses must therefore adjust to bring the demand for housing, H^d, in line with the existing supply, H. Inserting the equilibrium condition $H^d = H$ into (27) and solving for p^H, we get the market-clearing price of houses:

$$p^H = \frac{\eta Y}{(r+\delta)H}. \tag{28}$$

Figure 14.15 illustrates how the equilibrium price of houses is determined in the short run where the supply of housing is fixed at the level H_o. *Ceteris paribus*, a higher preexisting housing stock will imply a lower current housing price. We also see from (28) that the housing price will be lower the higher the real interest rate r and the lower the level of income, Y.

Figure 14.14 showed that residential property prices can fluctuate quite a lot over time. From (28) one would attribute the shorter-term price fluctuations to fluctuations in incomes or real interest rates, since the housing stock evolves only gradually over time, as current construction activity typically makes up only a very small proportion of the existing

---

5. In practice, the tax system also affects the user-cost of housing (see Exercise 4).

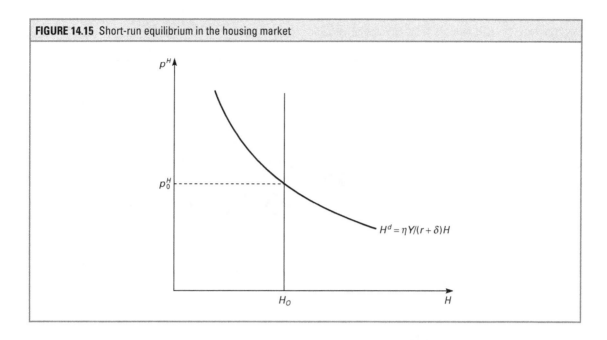

FIGURE 14.15 Short-run equilibrium in the housing market

housing stock. However, expectational factors may also contribute to instability in housing prices. Recall that the expected user cost of housing is $r + \delta = r + \hat{\delta} - g^e$, where g^e is the expected rate of real capital gain on a house. Thus, if for some reason households come to expect that house prices will rise less rapidly or even fall, the resulting drop in g^e will immediately reduce current property prices by driving up the user cost of housing. On the other hand, when expectations of large future capital gains on housing arise, there is an immediate boost to current property prices. When working with equation (28), it is therefore important to keep in mind that we are implicitly assuming a given state of expectations regarding future property prices.

Since we know from (21) that current construction activity varies positively with the housing price, we may combine (21) and (28) to get a housing investment function of the form

$$I^H = k \cdot \left[\frac{\eta Y}{(r + \delta)PH} \right]^{\beta/(1-\beta)},$$

or more generally:

$$I^H = h(\underset{(+)}{Y}, \underset{(-)}{H}, \underset{(-)}{r + \hat{\delta} - g^e}). \tag{29}$$

We may sum up the insights from the above analysis as follows:

HOUSING PRICES AND HOUSING INVESTMENT

In the short run where the housing stock is predetermined, property prices must adjust to keep housing demand equal to the existing housing stock. A larger housing stock puts downward pressure on property prices, thereby discouraging housing investment. A rise in income or a fall in the real interest rate will stimulate housing demand, thus raising property prices and the construction of new homes. By reducing the user cost of housing, expectations of future capital gains on residential property will also boost property prices and housing investment.

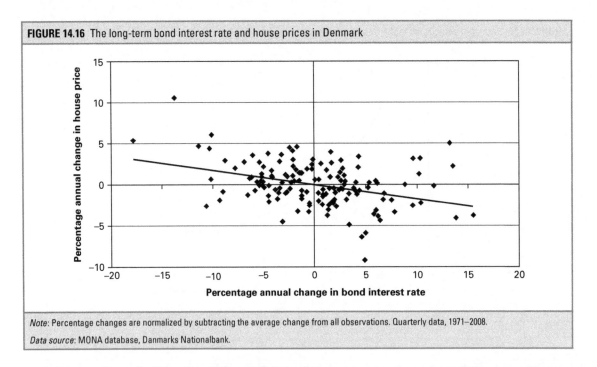

FIGURE 14.16 The long-term bond interest rate and house prices in Denmark

Note: Percentage changes are normalized by subtracting the average change from all observations. Quarterly data, 1971–2008.

Data source: MONA database, Danmarks Nationalbank.

The negative impact of the interest rate on housing investment in (29) is based on the theory that a higher interest rate will, *ceteris paribus*, reduce the market price of housing. The negatively sloped regression line in Fig. 14.16 confirms that housing prices do in fact tend to fall when the bond interest rate goes up, and vice versa.

Housing market dynamics

At the aggregate level, part of the current construction activity, I^H, serves to compensate for the physical depreciation of the existing housing stock. We have previously defined the parameter $\hat{\delta}$ as the spending on housing repair needed to maintain the value of a housing unit when housing prices are stable, so $\hat{\delta}H$ is a measure of the decline in the physical housing stock that would take place in the absence of any new construction activity (including maintenance and repair). The housing stocks in period t and in period $t + 1$ are therefore linked by the identity

$$H_{t+1} = H_t(1 - \hat{\delta}) + I_t^H. \tag{30}$$

Equations (21), (28) and (30) constitute a simple dynamic model of the housing market. For given values of Y and r, the predetermined housing stock, H_t, determines the housing price for period t via (28). Given the value of P, Eq. (21) then determines the current level of housing investment I_t^H which subsequently determines the next period's housing stock H_{t+1} via (30). We then get a new housing price p_{t+1}^H via (28) which enables us to determine I_{t+1}^H by use of (21), giving a new housing stock H_{t+2} via (30), and so on. This dynamic process will continue until the housing price has reached a level where construction activity is just sufficient to compensate for the depreciation of the existing housing stock so that the stock of housing remains constant. Thus, whereas an upward shift in housing demand is fully absorbed by a rise in house prices in the short run, over the longer run it will cause an increase in the housing stock which will dampen the initial price increase.[6]

If we allow for endogenous expectations formation, our housing market model (21), (28) and (30) may help to explain why housing markets tend to go through long cycles of boom

---

6. Exercise 4 asks you to explore these dynamics of the housing market in an extended model allowing for property taxes and income taxes.

FIGURE 14.17 Boom and bust in the US housing market 2000–09

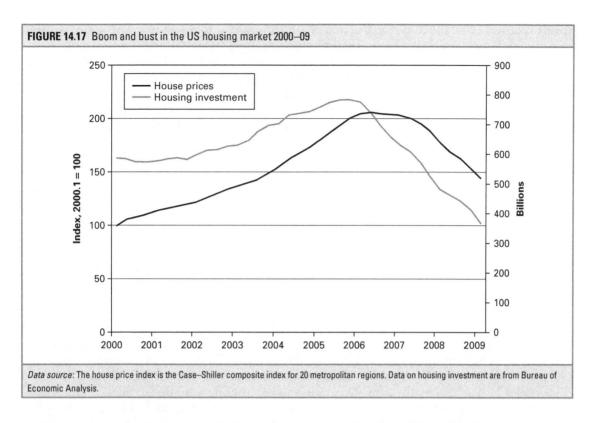

Data source: The house price index is the Case–Shiller composite index for 20 metropolitan regions. Data on housing investment are from Bureau of Economic Analysis.

and bust. For example, suppose the interest rate is cut, thereby shifting the housing demand curve in Fig. 14.15 outwards and driving up the short-run equilibrium housing price. Suppose further that this initial price increase generates expectations of further increases in house prices so that our parameter $\delta = \hat{\delta} - g^e$ decreases. According to (28) this will cause a further outward shift of the housing demand curve that will tend to initiate yet another round of price increases, thus confirming the expectations that drove up prices and helping to sustain expectations of further capital gains. Even though the rising prices of existing houses will induce construction of new houses (cf. (21)) which will help to keep the price increases in check over the longer run, it will take a while for the increased housing supply to catch up with the rising demand, since construction is time-consuming and since the existing housing stock is so large relative to the number of newly constructed housing units even in 'boom' years. Hence observed increases in actual house prices that generate expectations of further capital gains may keep a housing boom going for quite some time. However, as house prices continue to rise above construction costs, construction activity will continue to increase, and at some point the resulting increase in housing supply will bring the rise in housing prices to a halt and force a decline in the prices of existing homes. Once consumers observe a decline in prices, they are likely to revise the expected rate of capital gains g^e downwards, leading to a fall in housing demand as a result of a rise in the expected user cost $r + \hat{\delta} - g^e$ so that prices may have to fall even further, causing yet another reduction in housing demand via a fall in g^e, and so on. Note that such a self-reinforcing slump in the housing market may be quite prolonged, for even in an extreme case where the price decline completely eliminates all new construction activity, the annual decrease in total housing supply can never exceed the total physical depreciation $\hat{\delta}H$ (cf. (30)) which is small relative to the existing housing stock for any realistic value of the depreciation rate $\hat{\delta}$ (often estimated to be in the neighbourhood of 2 per cent).

Figure 14.17 illustrates the dramatic boom–bust cycle in the US housing market during the past decade. Supported by lax lending standards and a marked decline in interest rates between 2001 and 2004, American home prices rose sharply up until 2006, inducing a strong increase in residential construction. With the gradual increase in housing supply, the record high housing prices became unsustainable, and prices started to fall from 2006. As many so-called subprime (i.e. less creditworthy) borrowers in the US housing market relied on continuous price increases to be able to refinance their mortgage debts, the downturn in home prices left many new homeowners insolvent and caused a steep increase in the number of foreclosures and in defaults on many complex derivative financial assets backed by mortgage loans. This in turn triggered one of the worst financial crises in history. As the financial crisis weakened the real economy, causing income and employment to fall, the downturn in the housing market was exacerbated, and prices and construction took a further strong dive during 2008, thus contributing to the steepest economic downturn since the 1930s. As illustrated by this case study, instability in the housing market can be a major source of business fluctuations.

14.5 Summary

1. Empirically, changes in stock prices and in housing prices tend to be followed by changes in output in the same direction. In part this reflects that higher asset prices lead to higher investment. This chapter explains the links between asset prices and investment.

2. A firm seeking to maximize the wealth of its owners will choose an investment plan which maximizes the market value of the firm's assets. The value of the firm, referred to as the fundamental stock value, is the present discounted value of the expected future dividends paid out by the firm. This follows from the shareholder's arbitrage condition which says that the expected return to shareholding, consisting of dividends and capital gains on shares, must equal the return to bondholding plus an appropriate risk premium.

3. When share prices reflect the fundamental value of firms, there are three possible reasons for the observed volatility of stock prices: (i) fluctuations in (the growth rate of) expected future dividends, (ii) fluctuations in the real interest rate, and (iii) fluctuations in the required risk premium on shares. There is indirect evidence that the required risk premium fluctuates quite a lot.

4. The evidence suggests that the rate of return on stocks is tied to the rate of return on bonds over the long term. This accords with the view that stock prices reflect the fundamental value of firms. However, many observers believe that stock prices can sometimes deviate from fundamentals. The analysis in this chapter abstracts from such 'bubbles' in stock prices.

5. Increases in the firm's capital stock imply adjustment costs (installation costs), including costs of installing new machinery, costs of training workers to use the new equipment, and perhaps costs of adapting the firm's organization. These installation costs will typically increase more than proportionally to the firm's level of investment.

6. The value-maximizing firm will push its investment to the point where the shareholder's capital gain from a unit increase in the firm's capital stock is just offset by the dividend he must forgo to enable the firm to purchase and install an extra unit of capital. Because the marginal installation cost is increasing in the volume of investment, this investment rule implies that the firm's optimal level of investment will be higher, the higher a unit increase in the firm's capital stock is valued by the stock market. An increase in the ratio of stock prices to the replacement cost of the firm's assets will therefore stimulate its investment.

7. The market value of stocks relative to the replacement value of the underlying business assets is referred to as Tobin's q. Our theory of investment may be summarized by saying that business investment is an increasing function of Tobin's q.

8. Stock prices reflect expected future dividends which tend to be positively affected by a rise in current profits. The value of Tobin's q therefore tends to vary positively with current profits, which in turn vary positively with the output–capital ratio. Hence investment is an increasing function of current output and a decreasing function of the existing capital stock.

9. *Ceteris paribus*, a rise in the real interest rate implies that expected future dividends are discounted more heavily, leading to a fall in Tobin's q via lower stock prices. Thus a higher real interest rate tends to depress investment. A rise in the required risk premium on shares, generated by more uncertainty about the future, will have a similar negative impact on investment.

10. A version of the q-theory can explain investment in owner-occupied housing. When the market price of residential property increases relative to the cost of housing construction, it becomes profitable for firms in the construction sector to increase the supply of new housing units. As a consequence, housing investment (construction activity) goes up. There is strong empirical evidence in favour of this hypothesis.

11. In the short run, the market price of housing varies positively with current income and with the expected rate of capital gain on housing and negatively with the real interest rate and with the existing housing stock. Since construction increases with the market price of housing, it follows that housing investment is an increasing function of income and a decreasing function of the real interest rate and the current housing stock.

14.6 Exercises

Exercise 1. Stock market valuation and 'fundamentals'

The purpose of this exercise is to illustrate how our equation (6) for the fundamental stock price may be used to evaluate whether stock prices are unrealistically high or low, that is, whether the stock market is 'overvalued' or 'undervalued'. Suppose that real dividends are expected to grow at the constant rate g^e. If the actual real dividend for period t is D_t, the expected real dividend for future period n will then be given by:

$$D_n^e = D_t(1+g^e)^{n-t} \qquad \text{for } n = t+1, t+2, \ldots \tag{31}$$

1. Use Eq. (6) in the text to demonstrate that, when expected future dividends are given by (31), the value of shares will be given by:

$$V_t = \frac{D_t}{r+\varepsilon - g^e}. \tag{32}$$

Stock market analysts often focus on the so-called 'trailing dividend yield', D_t/V_t, defined as the current dividend relative to the current market value of shares. We will simply refer to this ratio as the 'dividend yield'.

2. Suppose you have information on the current dividend yield, D_t/V_t, the real interest rate, r, and the required risk premium on shares, ε. Use (32) to solve for the value of the expected real growth rate g^e which is necessary to justify current stock prices.

3. Suppose alternatively that, in addition to information on the current dividend yield and the current real interest rate, you have somehow obtained information on the expected future growth of real dividends whereas you do not know the required risk premium on shares. Use (32) to derive the value of the risk premium which will justify current stock prices.

4. In the USA in 1999 the average dividend yield was 1.2 per cent and the real interest rate on (approximately) risk-free ten-year government bonds was 3.4 per cent. Moreover, the average historical risk premium on shares in the period 1980–99 was 2.8 per cent per annum (all of these figures are taken from the IMF's World Economic Outlook, May 2000). What was the annual growth rate of real dividends which US financial investors expected in 1999 if they required a risk premium equal to the historical average? On the basis of your result, would you say that the US stock market was overvalued or undervalued in 1999? Justify your answer.

5. Over the period 1980–99 the average growth rate of US real GDP was 3.0 per cent. Suppose now that US investors in 1999 expected future real dividends to grow in line with historical GDP growth so that $g^e = 0.03$ (discuss whether this might be a reasonable assumption). Given the other pieces of information in the previous question, what was the risk premium on shares required by US investors in 1999? Would you say that this risk premium was 'reasonable'? Can you imagine any reasons why US investors in 1999 should require a lower or a higher risk premium than the average historical premium?

Exercise 2. A generalized *q*-theory of investment

Suppose that instead of Eq. (9) in the main text of this chapter, the installation cost function takes the more general form:

$$c(I_t) = \frac{a}{\eta+1} I_t^{\eta+1}, \qquad \eta > 0. \tag{33}$$

1. Derive an expression for investment as a function of q_t (a generalized version of Eq. (12)). Give a brief verbal explanation of the idea and economic mechanisms underlying the *q*-theory of investment. Explain why the *q*-theory is consistent with the well-documented fact that investment tends to vary negatively with the real interest rate and positively with economic activity.

   Suppose that during each period, a fraction δ of the capital stock has to be scrapped because of wear, tear and technical obsolescence, so the change in the capital stock is given by:

$$K_{t+1} - K_t = I_t - \delta K_t, \tag{34}$$

   where I_t indicates *gross* investment, including the replacement investment serving to compensate for depreciation. Suppose that only *net* additions to the capital stock generate adjustment costs. In that case installation costs will be determined by *net* investment $I_t - \delta K_t$ so that (33) must be replaced by:

$$c(I_t) = \frac{a}{\eta+1} (I_t - \delta K_t)^{\eta+1}. \tag{35}$$

2. Discuss whether it is reasonable to assume that only net investment (but not replacement investment) generates adjustment costs. Derive a revised expression for gross investment I_t, assuming that installation costs are given by (35).

   In a stationary economy with no long-run growth, a long-run equilibrium requires the capital stock to be constant over time. In such a situation where net investment is zero there is no need for firms to retain any part of their net profit. Hence all net profits will be paid out as dividends. According to Eq. (15) in the text, this implies $q_t = (\Pi_t/K_t)/(r + \varepsilon)$.

3. What is the ratio of the market value to the replacement value of the firm's capital stock in a stationary long-run equilibrium? Furthermore, what is the relationship between the profit rate Π_t/K_t and the required return on shares in such a long-run equilibrium? Try to provide some economic intuition for your results.

Exercise 3. Tax policy and investment

This exercise serves two purposes. First, you are asked to demonstrate that the investment behaviour of unincorporated firms is similar to the investment behaviour of corporations which are quoted on the stock market. Second, you are invited to study how various forms of capital income taxation will influence investment.

We consider an entrepreneur who owns a private unincorporated business firm. We divide the entrepreneur's time horizon into two periods which may be thought of as 'the present' (period 1) and 'the future' (period 2). At the beginning of period 1 the entrepreneur has accumulated a predetermined capital stock, K_1, which is invested in his firm. During period 1 he incurs gross investment expenditure, I, with the purpose of maintaining and increasing his capital stock. In each of the two periods, the capital stock depreciates at the rate δ, so at the beginning of period 2 the entrepreneur's capital stock will be given by:

$$K_2 = K_1(1-\delta)+I, \qquad 0 < \delta < 1. \tag{36}$$

The entrepreneur undertakes investment and employs labour with the purpose of maximizing the present value V of the net cash flows Π_1 and Π_2 withdrawn from the firm during periods 1 and 2, respectively. In other words, the entrepreneur wants to maximize:

$$V = \frac{\Pi_1}{1+r} + \frac{\Pi_2}{(1+r)^2}. \tag{37}$$

At the end of period 2 the entrepreneur plans to liquidate the firm and sell its remaining assets at their replacement value $(1-\delta)K_2$. For simplicity, we assume that there are no adjustment costs associated with changing the firm's capital stock. If Y_t is the firm's output, L_t is labour input, and w_t is the real wage rate, the cash flows from the firm to the owner during the two periods will then be:

$$\Pi_1 = Y_1 - w_1 L_1 - I, \tag{38}$$

$$\Pi_2 = Y_2 - w_2 L_2 + (1-\delta)K_2 - T_2. \tag{39}$$

where (39) includes the revenue from the sale of the firm's remaining capital stock at the end of period 2. Output in the two periods is given by the Cobb–Douglas production function:

$$Y_t = A_t K_t^\alpha L_t^\beta, \qquad 0 < \alpha < 1, 0 < \beta < 1, 0 < \alpha + \beta \le 1, t = 1, 2. \tag{40}$$

1. Demonstrate that the entrepreneur's optimal gross investment during period 1 can be written as:

$$I = \frac{\alpha Y_2}{r+\delta} - (1-\delta)K_1. \tag{41}$$

(Hint: use (36) to eliminate K_2 before you derive your first-order condition.) Does the investment function (41) have the same qualitative properties as the business investment function derived in the main text of the chapter? (Hint: note that the variable Y_2 must be interpreted as *expected* output in period 2.)

We now invite you to study the effects of a profits tax. In accordance with existing tax rules, suppose that the firm is allowed to deduct its labour costs and the depreciation on its capital stock from taxable profits. If the profits tax rate is τ, the firm's tax bill T then becomes:

$$T_t = \tau(Y_t - w_t L_t - \delta K_t), \qquad 0 < \tau < 1, \qquad t = 1, 2, \tag{42}$$

and the after-tax cash flows from the firm to the entrepreneur become equal to:

$$\Pi_1 = Y_1 - w_1 L_1 - I - T_1, \tag{43}$$

$$\Pi_2 = Y_2 - w_2 L_2 + (1 - \delta) K_2 - T_2. \tag{44}$$

2. Derive the analogue of the firm's investment function (41) in the presence of the profits tax. Explain how the profits tax affects investment.

   We have so far assumed that investment is financed by retained profits. Consider now the alternative case where only replacement investment δK is financed by retained earnings whereas net investment expenditure $I - \delta K$ is financed by debt. In that case the firm's stock of debt B will always be equal to its capital stock, that is:

$$B_t = K_t, \qquad t = 1, 2, \tag{45}$$

and the firm's revenue ΔB_1 from new borrowing during period 1 will be equal to its net investment during that period:

$$\Delta B_1 = I - \delta K_1. \tag{46}$$

Using (45) and (46) and noting that the firm's expenses on interest payments will be $rB = rK$, we may then write the cash flows to the entrepreneur as:

$$\begin{aligned}\Pi_1 &= Y_1 - w_1 L_1 - rB_1 - T_1 - I + \Delta B_1 \\ &= Y_1 - w_1 L_1 - (r + \delta) K_1 - T_1,\end{aligned} \tag{47}$$

$$\begin{aligned}\Pi_2 &= Y_2 - w_2 L_2 + (1 - \delta) K_2 - T_2 - (1 + r) B_2 \\ &= Y_2 - w_2 L_2 - (r + \delta) K_2 - T_2,\end{aligned} \tag{48}$$

assuming that the entrepreneur must repay all of his debt with interest at the end of the second period. Since the tax code allows interest payments as well as depreciation to be deducted from taxable profits, the tax bills for the two periods will be

$$T_t = \tau[Y_t - w_t L_t - (r + \delta) K_t], \qquad 0 < \tau < 1, \qquad t = 1, 2. \tag{49}$$

3. Derive the firm's investment function on the assumption that net investment is fully financed by debt. (Hint: remember to use (36) and (40).) Does the profits tax affect investment? Does it yield any revenue? Is the tax system neutral towards the firm's choice of financing method? Explain your results.

Exercise 4. Tax policy and the housing market

In this exercise we will extend our model of the housing market to allow for taxes. You are then asked to study how the housing market reacts to tax policy in the short run and the long run.

   We assume that the government levies a proportional property tax at the rate τ on the current value $p^H H$ of the consumer's housing stock H. We also assume that the government imposes a proportional income tax at the rate m but that it allows a fraction d of interest expenses to be deducted from taxable income, where $0 \leq d \leq 1$. Finally, we assume that the consumer has to spend an amount $\delta p^H H$ on repair and maintenance during each period to maintain the value of his house. The parameter δ may thus be interpreted as the depreciation rate for housing capital (for simplicity we ignore expected capital gains or losses on houses). Expenses on repair and maintenance are assumed not to be deductible from taxable income.

We consider a young consumer who starts out with zero financial wealth at the beginning of period t and who must therefore borrow an amount $p_t^H H_t$ to acquire the housing stock H_t at the going market price p_t^H. To keep the analysis simple we assume that the consumer's planned net saving is 0, so his current spending on non-durable consumption goods C_t is given by the budget constraint:

$$C_t = (1 - m)Y_t - [r(1 - dm) + \delta + \tau]p_t^H H_t, \qquad 0 < m < 1, \tag{50}$$

where Y is pre-tax labour income and where the term $[r(1 - dm) + \delta + \tau]p^H H$ reflects net interest payments on mortgage debt plus expenses on housing repair and property tax. Note that because interest expenses are deductible, it is the *after-tax* interest rate $r(1 - dm)$ which appears in the budget constraint (50).

The consumer's preferences are given by the Cobb–Douglas utility function:

$$U = H_t^\eta C_t^{1-\eta}, \qquad 0 < \eta < 1. \tag{51}$$

1. Demonstrate that the consumer's housing demand will be given by:

$$H_t = \frac{\eta(1 - m)Y_t}{[r(1 - dm) + \delta + \tau]p_t^H}, \tag{52}$$

and give your comments on this expression.

We will now set up a complete partial equilibrium model of the housing market. We start out by rearranging (52) to get an expression for the housing price:

$$p_t^H = \frac{\eta(1 - m)Y_t}{[r(1 - dm) + \delta + \tau]H_t}. \tag{53}$$

The supply side of the housing market is modelled in the same manner as in Section 14.4 in the main text. The construction of new houses I^H is therefore given by Eq. (21) which we repeat here for convenience:

$$I_t^H = k \cdot \left(\frac{p_t^H}{P_t}\right)^{\beta/(1-\beta)}, \qquad 0 < \beta < 1, \tag{54}$$

where we remember that k is an exogenous constant. From Section 14.4 we also recall that the evolution of the housing stock is given by:

$$H_{t+1} = (1 - \delta)H_t + I_t^H, \qquad 0 < \delta < 1. \tag{55}$$

Equations (53)–(55) constitute our model of the housing market where the exogenous variables and parameters are Y, P, r, η, β, k, δ, d, m and τ. At the beginning of each period the existing housing stock H_t is predetermined by the accumulated historical levels of housing investment. Given the initial housing stock, (53) may therefore be used to find the short-run equilibrium housing price P_t^H which may then be inserted into (54) to give the current level of housing investment I_t^H. Once I_t^H is known, we may insert its value into (55) along with the predetermined value of H_t to find the housing stock H_{t+1} at the beginning of the next period, which then determines p_{t+1}^H via (53), and so on.

2. Condense the housing market model (53)–(55) into a single non-linear first-order difference equation in the housing stock H (for convenience you may set $P_t = 1$, since we treat P as an

exogenous constant). State the condition under which this difference equation is locally stable so that the housing market will converge on a long-run equilibrium characterized by a constant housing stock. (Hint: the difference equation will be locally stable if dH_{t+1}/dH_t, is numerically smaller than 1. When you derive and simplify your expression for dH_{t+1}/dH_t, use Eqs (53) and (54) plus the fact that, in a local stability analysis, the derivative dH_{t+1}/dH_t is calculated in the long-run equilibrium point where $I_t^H = \delta H_t$ initially, because the housing stock is constant in long-run equilibrium.) Discuss whether the housing market is likely to be locally stable for plausible parameter values.

3. In a long-run equilibrium the housing stock is constant, $H_{t+1} = H_t$, implying from (55) that $I^H = \delta H$. Insert this condition for long-run equilibrium into (54) and invert the resulting equation to get a *long-run supply curve for the housing market*. Construct a diagram (with H along the horizontal axis and p^H along the vertical axis) in which you draw this long-run supply curve along with the housing demand curve given by (53). Identify the long-run equilibrium of the housing market and denote the long-run equilibrium housing stock by H^*. Insert a *short-run* housing supply curve for period 0 in your diagram, assuming that the housing market starts out in period 0 with a housing stock $H_0 < H^*$. (Hint: remember that in the short run the housing stock is predetermined. What does this imply for the slope of the short-run housing supply curve?) Provide a graphical illustration of the adjustment to a long-run housing market equilibrium. Give an intuitive verbal description of the adjustment process. How does the level of housing investment I_t^H evolve during the adjustment to long-run equilibrium?

4. Use the model (53)–(55) to derive expressions for the long-run equilibrium values of the housing price and the housing stock. Comment on the expressions.

5. Suppose now that the government permanently raises the property tax rate τ. Use your expressions from Question 4 to derive the long-run effects on p^H and H of a marginal increase in τ. Use a diagram like the one you constructed in Question 3 to illustrate the effects of the property tax increase in the short run (where the housing stock is predetermined) and in the long run when the housing stock has fully adjusted to the tax increase. Illustrate the gradual adjustment of the market to the higher property tax and provide a verbal explanation of the adjustment process.

6. Suppose next that the government permanently reduces the income tax rate m. How will this affect the housing market in the short run and in the long run? Give a graphical illustration and explain your results. In particular, explain how the effects depend on the policy parameter d.

7. Consider again a cut in the income tax rate m, but suppose now that the tax code allows property taxes as well as expenses on housing repair and *all* interest expenses to be deducted from taxable income. In these circumstances, how will the income tax cut affect the housing market? Explain your finding. (Hint: start by considering how the consumer budget constraint must be modified to allow for deductibility of expenses on property taxes and housing repair. Then use the revised budget constraint to derive a revised expression for housing demand and the housing price.)

You are now invited to simulate the housing market model consisting of Eqs (53)–(55) on the computer (you may use an Excel spreadsheet, for example). Your first sheet should allow you to choose the values of the parameters η, β, k and δ. We suggest that you set $\eta = 0.3$, $\beta = 0.9$, $k = 1$ and $\delta = 0.02$. Your second sheet should contain specified time paths for the exogenous variables P_t, Y_t, m_t, r_t, d_t and τ_t, say from period 0 to period 100. We propose that you choose $P = 1$, $r = 0.05$ and $Y = 100$ for all periods and that you assume $m_0 = 0.4$, $d_0 = 1$, and $\tau_0 = 0.015$ in period 0. You should assume that the housing market starts out in a long-run equilibrium in period 0 (and calculate the corresponding value of $H_{-1} = H_0$). Your subsequent sheets should draw diagrams of the simulated values of p^H, I^H and H (and possibly their respective relative rates of change, for further information).

8. Use your calibrated simulation model of the housing market to simulate the effects of the tax policy experiments defined in Questions 5 and 6 above over 100 periods. Check whether your simulation analysis accords with your previous theoretical and qualitative analysis.

Exercise 5. The housing market and the business cycle

To answer Question 8 in the previous exercise, you implemented a simulation model of the housing market on your computer (if you haven't gone through Exercise 4, you can still use the instructions above to construct your model and proceed with the present exercise). As you recall, the model consisted of the following equations (where we ignore expected capital gains or losses on houses):

Construction: $I_t^H = k \cdot \left(\dfrac{p_t^H}{P_t} \right)^{\beta/(1-\beta)}, \quad 0 < \beta < 1,$ (56)

Housing demand: $p_t^H = \dfrac{\eta(1-m_t)Y_t}{[r_t(1-d_t m_t)+\delta+\tau_t]H_t}, \quad 0 < \eta < 1.$ (57)

Dynamics of housing stock: $H_{t+1} = (1-\delta)H_t + I_t^H, \quad 0 < \delta < 1.$ (58)

You are now asked to use your calibrated simulation model as a basis for discussing how fluctuations in aggregate economic activity, Y_t, are likely to affect the housing market.

1. Suppose that $\eta = 0.3$, $\beta = 0.9$, $k = 1$, $\delta = 0.02$, $m = 0.4$, $d = 1$ and $\tau = 0.015$ in all periods. Furthermore, let the subscript 'o' denote the initial period and suppose $P_0 = 1$, $Y_0 = 100$ and $r_0 = 0.05$. Do you find that this calibration of the model produces a plausible initial equilibrium?
   (Hint: what is a plausible ratio of housing investment, I^H, to total GDP, Y? What is a plausible share of housing costs in consumer budgets?)

2. This question asks you to simulate the effects on the housing market of a stylized business cycle, using the parameter values specified in Question 1. For the moment we model the business cycle as a cycle in Y_t, keeping all other exogenous variables in the model constant at the levels assumed for the initial period. Starting with the initial value of aggregate income $Y_0 = 100$, suppose that total income assumes the following values over the subsequent periods: $Y_1 = 101$, $Y_2 = 103$, $Y_3 = 105$, $Y_4 = 103$, $Y_5 = 101$, $Y_6 = 99$, $Y_7 = 97$, $Y_8 = 95$, $Y_9 = 97$, $Y_{10} = 99$, $Y_{11} = 100$ and $Y_t = 100$ for all $t \geq 12$. Describe and comment on the way the housing market reacts to the business cycle in your simulation. Is housing investment more volatile than GDP?

3. Central banks usually try to drive up real interest rates in response to a rise in economic activity, and vice versa. Suppose therefore that, as a result of the time path of Y_t assumed in Question 2, the real interest rate displays the following time path: $r_1 = 0.05$, $r_2 = 0.051$, $r_3 = 0.052$, $r_4 = 0.051$, $r_5 = 0.05$, $r_6 = 0.049$, $r_7 = 0.048$, $r_8 = 0.046$, $r_9 = 0.047$, $r_{10} = 0.049$, $r_{11} = 0.05$, $r_t = 0.05$ for $t \geq 12$. Investigate and explain how these interest rate dynamics moderate the effects of the cycle in Y_t on the housing market.

4. In practice, construction costs usually move in a procyclical manner. Discuss why this is likely to be the case. Against this background, suppose for concreteness that the construction cost P_t varies in the following way, reflecting that P_t lags a little behind the cycle in Y_t: $P_1 = 1$, $P_2 = 1.01$, $P_3 = 1.02$, $P_4 = 1.02$, $P_5 = 1.01$, $P_6 = 1$, $P_7 = 0.99$, $P_8 = 0.98$, $P_9 = 0.98$, $P_{10} = 0.99$, $P_{11} = 100$, $P_t = 100$ for $t \geq 12$. To focus on the role of the dynamics of construction costs, let the real interest rate be constant over time at its initial level $r = 0.05$. Plug the time series for P_t into the model and investigate how it modifies the effects of the cycle in Y_t on the housing market. Explain your findings.

CHAPTER 15

Consumption, income and wealth

Private consumption is by far the largest component of aggregate demand for goods and services. Although Chapter 13 showed that consumption is less volatile than investment, changes in the propensity to consume are often the dominant source of changes in total demand, simply because private consumption is typically around three times as large as private investment. A theory of private consumption is therefore an essential building block in any theory of aggregate demand.

Studying private consumption will not only help us to build a short-run model of the business cycle. Since consumption is a basic determinant of economic welfare, our theory of the link between consumption and other macroeconomic variables will also help us understand how business cycles and economic policies affect consumer welfare. Moreover, our theory of consumption will imply a theory of saving, because saving is equal to income minus consumption. Since saving is the basis for capital accumulation, our analysis of consumption is also relevant for the theory of economic growth presented in Book One.

In the section on housing demand in the previous chapter we studied how the consumer allocates his total consumption between housing consumption and consumption of non-durables *within a given time period*. This chapter complements the previous one by analysing how the consumer will wish to allocate his total consumption *over time*. Since we now wish to explain *aggregate* consumption, this chapter will not elaborate on the previous chapter's analysis of the *composition* of consumption. Thus we will treat consumption as a single aggregate which, of course, must be thought of as a bundle of commodities, including housing services.

We will start this chapter by briefly restating and discussing the simple Keynesian theory of private consumption. We will then introduce a richer model of consumption to illustrate how consumption is linked to income, wealth and interest rates. In the final part of the chapter we will show how our theory of consumption can be used to analyse the effects of the government's tax and debt policies on aggregate demand.[1]

15.1 The consumption function

The simple Keynesian consumption function

In his famous *General Theory of Employment, Interest and Money*, published in 1936, John Maynard Keynes wrote that '...the propensity to consume is a fairly stable function so that,

---

1. This chapter borrows heavily from the teaching note by Henrik Jensen, 'Mikrofundament for konventionelle makroadfærdsrelationer', Københavns Universitets Økonomiske Institut, Marts 1996. We are grateful to Henrik for the inspiration, but of course he should not be held responsible for any shortcomings in our exposition.

as a rule, the amount of aggregate consumption mainly depends on aggregate income...'.
In other words, Keynes argued that real private consumption during period t, denoted by
C_t, is mainly determined by real disposable income Y_t^d during that period. In formal terms,
$C_t = C(Y_t^d)$. Keynes went on to argue that:

> The fundamental psychological law, upon which we are entitled to depend with great
> confidence both *a priori* from our knowledge of human nature and from the detailed
> facts of experience, is that men are disposed, as a rule and on the average, to increase
> their consumption as income increases, but not by as much as the increase in their
> income.

The claim made by Keynes in this passage is that the *marginal* propensity to consume,
$C' \equiv dC_t/dY_t^d$, is positive but less than 1. In a subsequent passage he asserted that

> ...it is also obvious that a higher absolute level of income will tend, as a rule, to widen
> the gap between income and consumption. For the satisfaction of the immediate
> primary needs of a man and his family is usually a stronger motive than the motives
> towards accumulation, which only acquire effective sway when a margin of comfort
> has been attained. These reasons will lead, as a rule, to a *greater proportion* of income
> being saved as real income increases.[2]

Thus Keynes believed that the *average* propensity to consume, C_t/Y_t^d, will decrease with the
level of income. In other words, the rich are assumed to have a higher average savings rate
than the poor.

A consumption function with all of these Keynesian properties is the simple linear one:

$$C_t = a + bY_t^d, \quad a > 0, \quad 0 < b < 1. \tag{1}$$

In this consumption function the marginal propensity to consume is the constant b, which
is less than 1, and the average propensity to consume is $C_t/Y_t^d = b + a/Y_t^d$ which is obviously
decreasing with income.

The consumption function (1) has the virtue of being simple, but there are at least two
problems with it. The first problem is theoretical: although it seems plausible that consumption
is positively related to current income, it is not clear why the current consumption of an
optimizing consumer should depend *only* on current income and not also on, say, expected
future income and the real rate of interest. Thus one must doubt whether a consumption
function like (1) is consistent with optimizing behaviour.

The second problem is empirical: although microeconomic *cross-section* data on the
relationship between consumption and income for different families within a given period
do indicate that the rich save a larger fraction of their current income than the poor,
macroeconomic *time series* data for most countries indicate that the ratio of aggregate
consumption to aggregate income is roughly constant over the long run. These apparently
contradictory stylized facts are illustrated in Fig. 15.1, where Fig. 15.1a indicates the
relationship between income and consumption for *different households within a given
period* such as a year, while Fig. 15.1b indicates the relation between *aggregate* household
income and *aggregate* consumption *over time*.

The rough long-run constancy of the average propensity to consume is illustrated for the
USA and Denmark in Fig. 15.2. Apart from a temporary drop due to consumption rationing
during the Second World War, the average propensity to consume in the USA has been

---

2. This quotation and the two previous ones can be found on pp. 96–97 of John Maynard Keynes, *The General
   Theory of Employment, Interest and Money*, London and Basingstoke, Macmillan Press, 1936. These brief
   quotations do not do full justice to Keynes' theory of consumption. He did in fact discuss a host of other factors
   likely to influence private consumption. Still, it is fair to say that as a first approximation, he believed that
   current consumption depends mainly on current income.

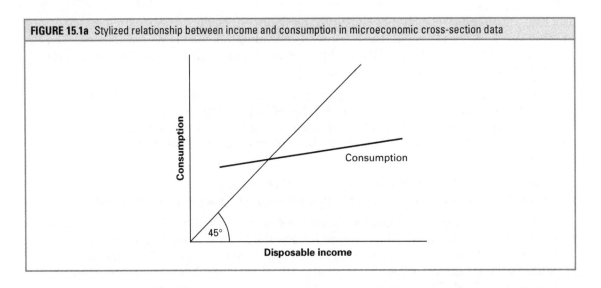

FIGURE 15.1a Stylized relationship between income and consumption in microeconomic cross-section data

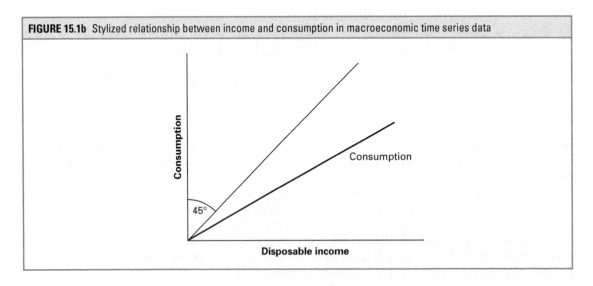

FIGURE 15.1b Stylized relationship between income and consumption in macroeconomic time series data

remarkably stable over the long run, despite the tremendous growth in income since 1929. The Danish propensity to consume has been more volatile, but without any systematic trend. Figure 15.2 clearly contradicts Eq. (1) which implies that the ratio of consumption to income should *decline over time* as income grows. Instead of Eq. (1), we therefore need a theory of consumption which has a solid theoretical foundation and which is able to explain why we observe different relationships between consumption and income in microeconomic cross-section data and in macroeconomic time series data. In the rest of this chapter we shall try to build such a theory.

Consumer preferences

The starting point for a micro-based theory of consumption is a specification of consumer preferences. Consider a consumer who plans for a certain finite time horizon. We will divide this time interval into two periods which may be thought of as 'the present' (the current period 1) and 'the future' (period 2). The limitation to only two periods is just a simplification; one can show that all our qualitative conclusions will continue to hold in a setting with many periods.

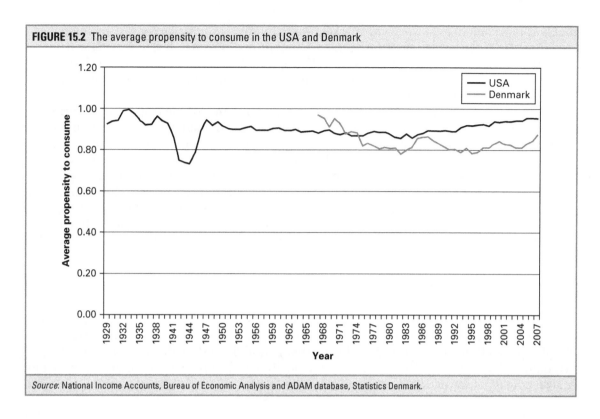

FIGURE 15.2 The average propensity to consume in the USA and Denmark

Source: National Income Accounts, Bureau of Economic Analysis and ADAM database, Statistics Denmark.

In each period t ($t = 1, 2$) the consumer derives utility $u(C_t)$ from consumption. However, because the consumer is 'impatient', he or she prefers a unit of utility today to a unit of utility tomorrow. When evaluated at the beginning of period 1, the consumer's *lifetime* utility U is therefore given by:

$$U = u(C_1) + \frac{u(C_2)}{1 + \phi}, \qquad u' > 0, \qquad u'' < 0, \qquad \phi > 0. \tag{2}$$

The consumer's impatience is captured by the parameter ϕ which is referred to as *the rate of time preference*. The positive rate of time preference means that if $C_1 = C_2$, a given additional amount of consumption today is valued more highly than a similar extra amount of consumption tomorrow. On the other hand, as long as ϕ is not infinitely high, the consumer is not indifferent about the future, and he or she will then have to decide how to allocate his or her consumption optimally over time. The assumptions $u' > 0$ and $u'' < 0$ reflect that the marginal utility of consumption in any period is positive but decreasing. An increase in consumption in any period will thus reduce the marginal utility gain from a further consumption increase in that period.

Our theory of consumption will be derived from the assumption that the consumer trades off present against future consumption so as to maximize the lifetime utility function (2). The terms of this trade-off will depend on the consumer's intertemporal budget constraint to which we now turn.

The intertemporal budget constraint

When specifying the consumer's budget constraints for the two periods, we will assume that *capital markets are perfect*. This means that the consumer can freely lend and borrow as much as he or she likes at the going market rate of interest. In practice some consumers may face *credit constraints* preventing them from borrowing as much as they would have preferred at the going interest rate. We will discuss credit constraints later in the chapter, and Exercise 3 asks you to consider their implications in detail, but for the moment we will assume perfect capital markets.

We specify the consumer's budget constraints in real terms. At the beginning of period 1 the consumer is endowed with a predetermined stock of real financial wealth V_1 (which could be negative if the consumer is indebted). During period 1 he or she earns real labour income Y_1^L, pays the real amount of taxes T_1, and spends the real amount C_1 on consumption. For convenience we assume that all payments are made at the beginning of the period.[3] After having received this income and incurred this expenditure on taxes and consumption, the consumer has an amount $V_1 + Y_1^L - T_1 - C_1$ left over for investment in interest-bearing financial assets. If the real interest rate is r, the consumer will therefore end up with a real stock of financial wealth $V_2 = (1+r)(V_1 + Y_1^L - T_1 - C_1)$ at the beginning of period 2. Hence the budget constraint for period 1 is:

$$V_2 = (1+r)(V_1 + Y_1^L - T_1 - C_1). \tag{3}$$

Note that V_2 may well be negative. In that case the consumer is a net borrower during period 1. Since he or she does not plan any consumption beyond period 2, the consumer will simply spend all his or her resources during that period, including the financial wealth accumulated during period 1. Using the same notation as before, we may therefore write the budget constraint for period 2 as:

$$C_2 = V_2 + Y_2^L - T_2. \tag{4}$$

Equation (4) states that the consumer will spend his or her initial financial wealth plus the after-tax labour income on consumption during period 2. Notice that if he or she has borrowed during period 1 so that $V_2 < 0$, the consumer must reserve part of the period 2 labour income for debt repayment.

It will turn out to be convenient to consolidate (3) and (4) into a single constraint. We therefore use (3) to eliminate V_2 from (4), divide through by $(1 + r)$ on both sides of the resulting equation and rearrange to get:

$$C_1 + \frac{C_2}{1+r} = V_1 + Y_1^L - T_1 + \frac{Y_2^L - T_2}{1+r}. \tag{5}$$

Equation (5) is the consumer's *intertemporal budget constraint*. It states that the present value of the consumer's lifetime consumption (the left-hand side) must equal the present value of his or her after-tax labour income plus the initial financial wealth (the right-hand side).[4] In other words, with a perfect capital market current consumption does not have to equal current income, but over the life cycle the consumer cannot spend any more than his or her total resources. These resources consist of labour income and the initial financial wealth.

We can write (5) in a simpler form by introducing

---

3. If some or all payments were made at the end of the period instead, we would obtain a consumption function with the same qualitative properties as those described below. However, the assumption that payments take place at the start of each period leads to slightly more elegant analytical expressions. Whenever we divide the time axis into discrete finite intervals, there is no objectively 'correct' assumption on the timing of payments (beginning-of-period versus end-of-period). Hence we are free to choose the assumption on timing that is most convenient for analytical purposes.

4. Of course, the consumer could choose to consume less than his or her total lifetime resources, but since an increase in consumption today or tomorrow will always increase lifetime utility, he or she will always choose to consume as much as the budget constraint permits. This is why (5) is written with an equality sign rather than an inequality sign.

$$H_1 \equiv Y_1^L - T_1 + \frac{Y_2^L - T_2}{1+r}. \tag{6}$$

The variable H_1 is the present value of the consumer's disposable lifetime labour income, and it is referred to as *human wealth* or *human capital* because it measures his or her capitalized earnings potential in the labour market. Note that H_1 carries the time subscript 1 because it includes labour income from period 1 and onwards. Inserting (6) into (5), we get

$$C_1 + \frac{C_2}{1+r} = V_1 + H_1, \tag{7}$$

where we assume throughout that $V_1 + H_1 > 0$. Hence the consumer's intertemporal budget constraint simply states that the present value of real lifetime consumption is constrained by *total real initial wealth*, consisting of the sum of financial wealth and human wealth.

We shall now study how consumers will wish to allocate consumption over time.

The allocation of consumption over time

The consumer chooses his or her time path of consumption so as to maximize the lifetime utility function (2) subject to the intertemporal budget constraint (7). The consumer's wage rate is taken as given, and we assume that his or her working hours are institutionally determined, say, by collective bargaining agreements or by law. This means that the labour incomes Y_1^L and Y_2^L and thereby H_1 are exogenously given to the consumer.[5] Since the market value of financial assets is also beyond the control of the individual consumer, it follows that the consumer's total initial wealth, $V_1 + H_1$, can be taken as given when optimizing consumption. Because we are mainly interested in studying the determinants of current consumption C_1, we will use the intertemporal budget constraint (7) to eliminate C_2 from the lifetime utility function (2). Doing that, we obtain:

$$U = u(C_1) + \frac{u((1+r)(V_1 + H_1 - C_1))}{1+\phi}. \tag{8}$$

The consumer's problem then boils down to choosing C_1 so as to maximize (8). The first-order condition for a maximum is:

$$dU/dC_1 = u'(C_1) - \frac{1+r}{1+\phi}u'((1+r)(V_1 + H_1 - C_1)) = 0,$$

which we can write as:

$$u'(C_1) = \frac{1+r}{1+\phi}u'(C_2), \tag{9}$$

or as:

$$\frac{u'(C_1)}{u'(C_2)/(1+\phi)} \equiv MRS(C_2 : C_1) = 1 + r. \tag{10}$$

Equations (9) and (10) are just two alternative ways of writing the consumer's optimum condition. Consider first the interpretation of (9). If the consumer increases consumption by

---

5. In Exercise 2 you will be asked to study the determination of consumption in the more complicated case where the consumer can choose his or her working hours and hence labour income.

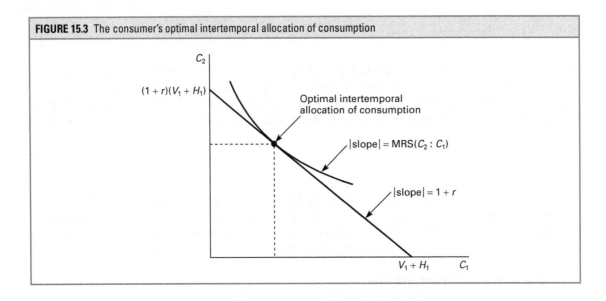

FIGURE 15.3 The consumer's optimal intertemporal allocation of consumption

one unit in period 1, his or her lifetime utility will increase by $u'(C_1)$. If he or she chooses instead to save an extra unit and invest the funds in the capital market to earn the real interest rate r, the consumer will be able to increase consumption in period 2 by $1 + r$ units. This will generate an increase in lifetime utility equal to $((1 + r)/(1 + \phi))u'(C_2)$. According to (9) these two alternatives must be equally attractive. In other words, in optimum the consumer must be indifferent between consuming an extra unit today and saving an extra unit today.

Equation (10) is a version of the usual optimum condition that the consumer's marginal rate of substitution, MRS, between any two goods must equal the price ratio between the two goods. In this case the two goods are 'present consumption', C_1, and 'future consumption', C_2. The optimum condition (10) is illustrated in Fig. 15.3.

To interpret the diagram, note that along any consumer indifference curve lifetime utility is constant. According to the lifetime utility function (2) a constant utility level implies:

$$dU = u'(C_1)dC_1 + \frac{u'(C_2)}{1 + \phi}dC_2 = 0,$$

or:

$$-\frac{dC_2}{dC_1} = \frac{u'(C_1)}{u'(C_2)/(1 + \phi)}. \tag{11}$$

Equation (11) shows that the numerical slope of the indifference curve is equal to the marginal rate of substitution between present and future consumption, $MRS(C_2 : C_1)$, defined as the ratio of the marginal lifetime utility of present consumption $u'(C_1)$ to the marginal lifetime utility of future consumption $u'(C_2)/(1 + \phi)$. Figure 15.3 also shows that the numerical slope of the consumer's lifetime budget constraint equals $1 + r$: if the consumer gives up one unit of present consumption, $1 + r$ additional units of future consumption will result because his or her saving earns the real interest rate r. Hence we can say that $1 + r$ is the *relative price of present consumption*, since it measures the amount of future consumption which must be given up to enable the consumer to increase present consumption by one unit. When the consumer attains the highest possible level of lifetime utility consistent with his or her lifetime budget constraint, we see from Fig. 15.3 that the slope of the indifference curve must equal the slope of the budget constraint, given by the relative price of present consumption. This is exactly what Eq. (10) says.

The optimum consumption and saving rule (9) or (10) is called the *Keynes–Ramsey rule* after its discoverers, and it may be restated as follows:

THE KEYNES–RAMSEY RULE OF OPTIMAL SAVING ❗

When consumers are impatient, the net utility gain from postponing a unit of consumption from the current to the next period is $-u'(C_1) + \gamma u'(C_2)$, where $\gamma = (1 + r)/(1 + \phi)$, r is the real interest rate and ϕ is the rate of time preference. In a perfect capital market, a consumer who optimizes the allocation of consumption over time will carry saving out of current income to the point where this net gain is zero.

Although formally derived by Cambridge economist Frank Ramsey in 1928,[6] this rule had been verbally anticipated by the very same John Maynard Keynes who later (in his *General Theory* of 1936) came to believe in a consumption function like (1)! As we will discuss later in this chapter (and in Exercises 1 and 3), for some households current consumption is indeed likely to depend only on current income, as postulated in the consumption function (1). But we shall also see that the consumption function implied by the Keynes–Ramsey rule (10) is consistent with several empirical observations on consumption which cannot be reconciled with the simple Keynesian consumption function.

One important implication of (10) is that consumers will typically want to use the capital market to smooth their consumption over time. This is seen most clearly in the benchmark case where the real interest rate equals the rate of time preference $(r = \phi)$ so that the consumer's impatience ϕ is exactly offset by the capital market reward r for postponing consumption. When $r = \phi$, condition (10) can only be met if $C_1 = C_2$, that is if consumption is constant over the consumer's life cycle. Suppose for simplicity that the consumer starts out in period 1 with zero financial wealth, $V_1 = 0$. Unless the consumer's labour income happens to be the same in periods 1 and 2, he or she will then have to engage in financial saving in one period and financial dissaving in the other period to keep consumption constant over time.

Figure 15.4a shows the case where labour income in period 1 is lower than labour income in period 2 (perhaps because the consumer spends a part of period 1 going through education rather than working in the labour market). The consumer will then want to borrow in period 1 to smooth consumption over the life cycle even though this means having to reserve part of the higher future labour income for payment of interest. Figure 15.4b shows the alternative case where future labour income is lower than current labour income (perhaps because the consumer plans to retire some time in period 2). In this case the consumer will want to save part of his or her current labour income and will partly finance period 2 consumption out of previous savings.

If there were no capital market allowing saving and dissaving, consumption would have to equal income within each period. If income is low in one period and high in another, the marginal utility of consumption would then differ across periods, because marginal utility decreases with increasing consumption. The consumer will therefore enjoy a welfare gain to the extent that he or she is able to smooth consumption by borrowing or saving through the capital market. Capital markets enable consumers to decouple current consumption from current income, and utility-maximizing consumers will typically want to take advantage of that in order to spread their consumption more evenly over time. Although total lifetime consumption is constrained by total lifetime resources (wealth), we should not necessarily expect to observe a close link between current consumption and current income.

Do consumers actually smooth their consumption over their working life? A glance at the upper two curves in Fig. 15.5 might suggest that the answer is 'No!'. The figure tracks data

---

6. Frank Ramsey, 'A Mathematical Theory of Saving', *Economic Journal*, **38**, 1928, pp. 543–559. This was one of two path-breaking articles published by the unusually gifted Frank Ramsey before his premature death at the age of 25.

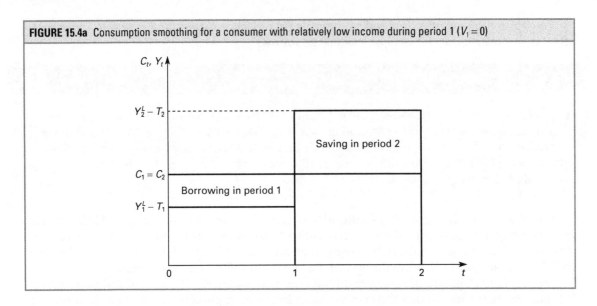

FIGURE 15.4a Consumption smoothing for a consumer with relatively low income during period 1 ($V_1 = 0$)

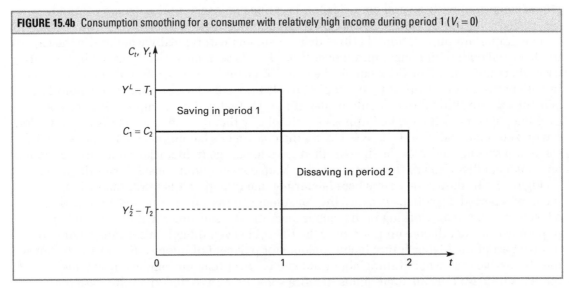

FIGURE 15.4b Consumption smoothing for a consumer with relatively high income during period 1 ($V_1 = 0$)

for the average consumption-age profile and the average income-age profile for a cohort of British married couples. The figures for income and consumption have been deflated by the consumer price index and transformed into logarithms. The age of the household is identified using the age of the female household member. We see that both consumption and income follow a hump-shaped pattern over the life cycle, peaking a little before the age of 50. In particular, current consumption seems to follow current income fairly closely, in apparent contrast to the hypothesis of consumption-smoothing.

However, using data from the UK Family Expenditure Survey, economists Martin Browning and Mette Ejrnæs have demonstrated that if one corrects the consumption figures for the systematic impact of differences in the number of children across households, consumers *do* actually tend to smooth their consumption over time. This is illustrated by the bottom curve in Fig. 15.5 which shows 'adjusted consumption', that is, the level of consumption adjusted for the estimated impact of the numbers and ages of children on the consumption needs of the household. We see that the adjusted consumption-age profile is much flatter than the income profile, suggesting that consumers do indeed prefer to smooth consumption per household member, in accordance with our theory.

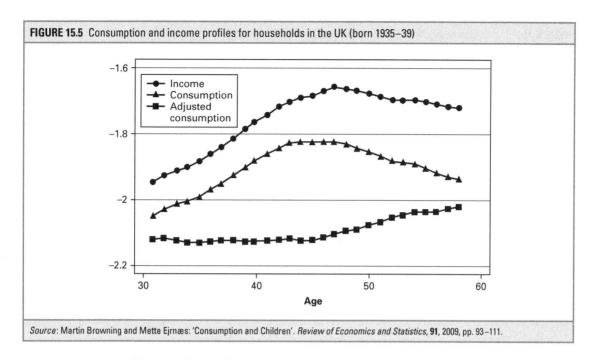

FIGURE 15.5 Consumption and income profiles for households in the UK (born 1935–39)

Source: Martin Browning and Mette Ejrnæs: 'Consumption and Children'. *Review of Economics and Statistics*, **91**, 2009, pp. 93–111.

The determinants of current consumption

The Keynes–Ramsey rule (10) only provides an implicit solution to the consumer's problem. To derive an explicit analytical solution for current consumption C_1, we need to specify the form of the consumer's utility function. One specification which has often been used in economic research is the following:

$$u(C_t) = \frac{\sigma(C_t^{(\sigma-1)/\sigma}-1)}{\sigma-1} \qquad \text{for } \sigma > 0, \neq 1, \tag{12}$$

$$u(C_t) = \ln C_t \qquad \text{for } \sigma = 1. \tag{13}$$

As you may easily verify, this specification satisfies the assumptions in (2) that $u' > 0$ and $u'' < 0$.[7] To interpret the parameter σ in (12), we introduce the concept of the *intertemporal elasticity of substitution in consumption*, IES, defined as the percentage change in the ratio of future to present consumption (C_2/C_1) implied by a 1 per cent change in the consumer's marginal rate of substitution, $MRS(C_2 : C_1)$:

$$IES \equiv \frac{d(C_2/C_1)/(C_2/C_1)}{dMRS(C_2 : C_1)/MRS(C_2 : C_1)} = \frac{d\ln(C_2/C_1)}{d\ln MRS(C_2 : C_1)}. \tag{14}$$

The *IES* measures the degree to which the consumer is willing to substitute future for present consumption. This is illustrated in Fig. 15.6 where we recall that $MRS(C_2 : C_1)$ measures the numerical slope of the consumer's indifference curve. The slope of the straight line from the origin through point E_0 measures the consumption ratio (C_2^0/C_1^0) prevailing when the marginal rate of substitution equals $MRS(C_2^0 : C_1^0)$. As we move up the indifference curve from point E_0 to point E_1, thereby raising the consumption ratio from (C_2^0/C_1^0) to (C_2^1/C_1^1), the consumer

---

7. To see that the functional form in (12) converges on the functional form in (13) when $\sigma \to 1$, note that the expression on the right-hand side of (12) may be written as $f(\sigma)/g(\sigma)$, where $f(\sigma) \equiv C^{1-(1/\sigma)} - 1$ and $g(\sigma) \equiv 1 - (1/\sigma)$. For $\sigma \to 1$ we see that $f(\sigma) \to 0$ and $g(\sigma) \to 0$. Using L'Hopital's rule, we then get $\lim_{\sigma \to 1}(f(\sigma)/g(\sigma)) = \lim_{\sigma \to 1}(f'(\sigma)/g'(\sigma)) = \ln C$.

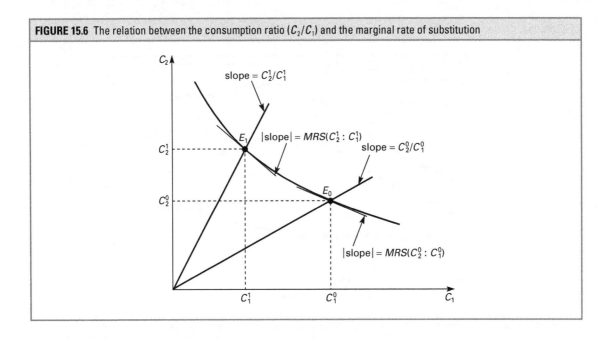

FIGURE 15.6 The relation between the consumption ratio (C_2/C_1) and the marginal rate of substitution

becomes less willing to trade present consumption for future consumption. This is reflected by the increase in the marginal rate of substitution, that is, by the fact that the numerical slope of the indifference curve is steeper at point E_1 than at E_0. It is obvious that, for any given increase in $MRS(C_2 : C_1)$, the rise in the consumption ratio (C_2/C_1) will be *greater* the *flatter* the indifference curve, that is, the easier it is to substitute future for present consumption. In other words, the more the consumer is willing to engage in intertemporal substitution in consumption, the greater will be the value of *IES* defined in (14).

Since $u'(C_t) = C_t^{-1/\sigma}$, we may now write the *MRS*, $u'(C_1)/(u'(C_2)/(1 + \phi))$, as:

$$MRS(C_2 : C_1) = (1 + \phi)\left(\frac{C_2}{C_1}\right)^{1/\sigma},$$

and hence:

$$\ln MRS(C_2 : C_1) = \ln(1 + \phi) + \frac{1}{\sigma}\ln\left(\frac{C_2}{C_1}\right),$$

from which:

$$IES = \frac{d\ln(C_2/C_1)}{d\ln MRS(C_2 : C_1)} = \sigma. \tag{15}$$

The utility function (12) thus has the property that the intertemporal elasticity of substitution is constant and equal to σ. By varying σ we may therefore study the effects of variations in the consumer's willingness to substitute consumption over time. As σ tends to zero, the consumer becomes quite unwilling to trade present for future consumption, and his or her indifference curves become rectangular, as shown in Fig. 15.7. On the other hand, as σ tends to infinity, substitution possibilities also become infinite, and the indifference curves converge to straight lines.

We are now ready to derive the consumption function. Substituting the expression $(1 + \phi)$ $(C_2/C_1)^{1/\sigma}$ for $MRS(C_2 : C_1)$ into the condition $MRS(C_2 : C_1) = 1 + r$ for an optimal intertemporal allocation of consumption, we get:

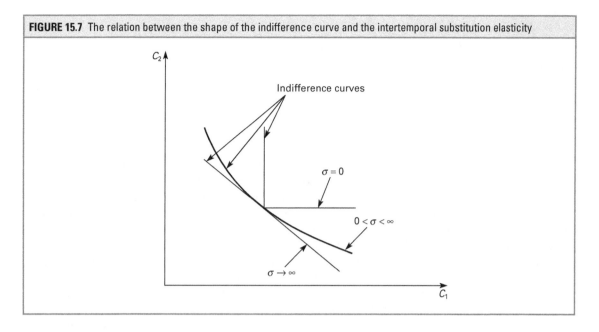

FIGURE 15.7 The relation between the shape of the indifference curve and the intertemporal substitution elasticity

$$C_2 = \left(\frac{1+r}{1+\phi}\right)^{\sigma} C_1. \tag{16}$$

Since (16) may also be written as $C_2/C_1 = (1+r)^{\sigma}/(1+\phi)^{\sigma}$, we see that the parameter σ measures the elasticity of future relative to present consumption (C_2/C_1) with respect to the relative price of present consumption $(1+r)$. This is in line with the interpretation of σ as the readiness of consumers to substitute consumption today for consumption tomorrow.

Equation (16) may be inserted into the lifetime budget constraint $C_1 + C_2/(1+r) = V_1 + H_1$ to give $C_1 + (1+r)^{\sigma-1}(1+\phi)^{-\sigma} C_1 = V_1 + H_1$, implying:

$$C_1 = \theta(V_1 + H_1), \qquad 0 < \theta \equiv \frac{1}{1+(1+r)^{\sigma-1}(1+\phi)^{-\sigma}} < 1. \tag{17}$$

Equation (17) is seen to be rather different from the simple Keynesian consumption function (1), and it contains the following important message:

CONSUMPTION AND WEALTH

When the intertemporal elasticity of substitution in consumption is constant, current consumption is proportional to total current wealth, consisting of the sum of financial wealth and human wealth. The propensity to consume out of current wealth (θ) is positive but less than one, and its magnitude will generally depend on the real rate of interest.

15.2 The properties of the consumption function

Consumption and income

Let us now explore the implications of (17) for the relationship between current consumption C_1 and current disposable labour income, $Y_1^d \equiv Y_1^L - T_1$. If we insert our definition of human wealth (6) into (17), we get:

$$C_1 = \theta\left(Y_1^d + \frac{Y_2^d}{1+r} + V_1\right), \qquad Y_t^d \equiv Y_t^L - T_t, \qquad t = 1, 2. \tag{18}$$

This may be rewritten as:

$$C_1 = \hat{\theta}Y_1^d, \tag{19}$$

$$\hat{\theta} \equiv \theta\left(1 + \frac{R}{1+r} + v_1\right), \qquad R \equiv \frac{Y_2^d}{Y_1^d}, \qquad v_1 \equiv \frac{V_1}{Y_1^d}, \tag{20}$$

where $\hat{\theta}$ measures the propensity to consume (out of) current income, R is the ratio of future to current income, and v_1 is the current wealth–income ratio. On the basis of (19) and (20) we may now explain the empirical puzzle that the average propensity to consume current income seems to decrease with income when we consider microeconomic cross-section data whereas it seems to be roughly constant when we consider macroeconomic time series data.

Consider first the observed cross-section relationship between individual household income and individual consumption suggesting that the rich have a higher average savings rate than the poor. Within any given time period, some of those individuals who record a high current income level cannot expect to earn similar high incomes in the future. One important reason is that workers must some day retire from the labour market in which case they will no longer earn income from labour. Moreover, for self-employed individuals a high current income will sometimes reflect that business has been unusually good during that year. Thus, if a high current income level is expected to be *temporary*, the ratio of future to current income (R) will be relatively low, and according to (20) this will imply a low average propensity to consume current income. In a similar way, some consumers with low current incomes may have good reason to expect that they will earn more in the future. This will typically be the case for university students and other young people who have not yet realized their earnings potential in the labour market, and for entrepreneurs who have just started up a business or who experience unusually bad business during the current year. For such individuals the ratio R in (20) will be high, and hence they will have a high propensity to consume out of their low current income. If some of the observed variation in income levels in a cross-section of consumers reflects such temporary factors, Eq. (20) may thus explain why the average propensity to consume appears to fall as income goes up.

In a celebrated article, Franco Modigliani and Richard Brumberg provided the first statement of the so-called *life cycle theory* of consumption according to which consumers in different stages of the life cycle will have different propensities to consume current income because of their desire to smooth consumption over time.[8] In a similarly famous contribution, Milton Friedman developed the so-called *permanent income hypothesis* which says that transitory changes in income will mainly lead to temporary changes in savings, whereas current consumption will depend on the consumer's *permanent* income, that is, his expected long-run average income (which is proportional to his total wealth).[9] Thus these writers pointed out that some of the high incomes observed during a given year are only temporarily high and hence will not induce high levels of current consumption, and some of the low incomes recorded in a given period are just temporarily low and thus will not cause similarly low levels of consumption. Because of this, a cross-section analysis of the relationship between current consumption and current income in any given year will give the impression that high-income people have a lower average propensity to consume than low-income people.

---

8. See Franco Modigliani and Richard Brumberg, 'Utility Analysis and the Consumption Function: An Interpretation of Cross-Section Data', in Kenneth K. Kurihara, ed., *Post-Keynesian Economics*, pp. 388–436, New Brunswick, NJ, Rutgers University Press, 1954.

9. Milton Friedman, *A Theory of the Consumption Function*, Princeton, NJ, Princeton University Press, 1957. Note that the consumer's stock of total wealth equals the discounted value of his expected future income. Permanent income is that hypothetical constant level of income which has the same present value as the consumer's expected future income stream.

Let us next see how Eqs (19) and (20) may explain the empirical observation that the average propensity to consume is roughly constant in the long run when we look at aggregate time series data. If we denote the growth rate of real income by g, we have $Y_2^d \equiv (1+g)Y_1^d$ which may by inserted into (20) to give:

$$\hat{\theta} = 1 + \frac{1+g}{1+r} + v_1. \tag{21}$$

While the growth rate g fluctuates in the short run, on average it has been fairly constant over the long run, as we saw in Fig. 2.8. Moreover, the real interest rate r shows no systematic long-run trend as we also saw in Fig. 2.10, and over the long run Chapter 2 found that the capital stock tends to grow at the same rate as income so that the long-run wealth–income ratio $v_1 \equiv V_1/Y_1^d$ is roughly constant. It then follows from (21) that the long-run average propensity to consume will also tend to be constant, as we do indeed observe.

To sum up, our reconciliation of the microeconomic cross-section data and the macroeconomic time series data runs as follows:

EXPLAINING THE EMPIRICAL CONSUMPTION PUZZLES

A temporary increase in income for an individual consumer will reduce his or her expected future income relative to current income and will also reduce his or her short-run wealth–income ratio. For these reasons the average propensity to consume will tend to fall with rising income levels in a cross-section of consumers. Over the long run, the average growth rate of income across all consumers is roughly constant, and wealth moves roughly in line with income. From the consumption function (21) this implies a constant long-run average propensity to consume at the macro level.

Consumption and wealth

While the average propensity to consume current income tends to be constant in the long run, it fluctuates quite a lot in the short run, as indicated in Fig. 15.8. Equation (21) suggests three possible reasons for this:

1. short-run changes in the expected growth rate of income (g),
2. short-run changes in the wealth–income ratio (v_1), and
3. short-run changes in the real rate of interest.

According to (21) a higher expected income growth or a rise in the market value of financial wealth relative to current income will increase the propensity to consume. Note that changes in g and v_1 will often go hand in hand, since a higher expected income growth is likely to drive up the market prices of stocks and owner-occupied housing, thereby increasing V_1, because a higher expected growth rate will tend to raise expected future corporate dividends and to drive up the demand for housing.

Figure 15.8 shows that there is indeed a fairly close empirical relationship between the wealth–income ratio and the average propensity to consume, as our theory of consumption would lead us to expect.[10]

---

10. It is worth noting that even though he did not include financial wealth as an explanatory variable in his basic consumption function, Keynes was fully aware of the potential influence of wealth on private consumption. On pp. 92–93 of his *General Theory* he wrote: 'Windfall changes in capital-values...are of much more importance in modifying the propensity to consume, since they will bear no stable or regular relationship to the amount of income. The consumption of the wealth-owning class may be extremely susceptible to unforeseen changes in the money-value of its wealth. This should be classified amongst the major factors capable of causing short-period changes in the propensity to consume.'

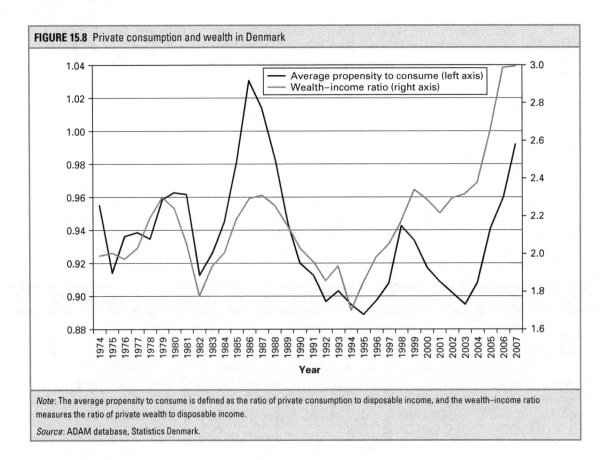

FIGURE 15.8 Private consumption and wealth in Denmark

Note: The average propensity to consume is defined as the ratio of private consumption to disposable income, and the wealth–income ratio measures the ratio of private wealth to disposable income.

Source: ADAM database, Statistics Denmark.

Consumption and interest rates

The third determinant of the propensity to consume current income is the real interest rate r. The interest rate affects consumption through three different channels. First of all, it influences the propensity θ to consume out of wealth. Second, it affects the market value of financial wealth. Third, the real interest rate also affects the value of human wealth. We will consider each of these channels in turn.

In (17) the propensity to consume wealth was defined as:

$$\theta \equiv \frac{1}{1+(1+r)^{\sigma-1}(1+\phi)^{-\sigma}}. \tag{22}$$

Clearly this propensity increases with r if $\sigma < 1$, and decreases if $\sigma > 1$, and we cannot say *a priori* which direction is correct as σ can be either smaller or larger than 1. The indeterminacy in how r affects the propensity to consume is due to offsetting substitution and income effects. On the one hand an increase in the real interest rate raises the relative price $1 + r$ of current consumption. *Ceteris paribus*, this will induce the consumer to substitute future for present consumption through an increase in current saving. Obviously this *substitution effect* will tend to reduce the propensity to consume in the current period. At the same time the higher interest rate also increases the amount of future consumption generated by a given amount of current saving. Hence the consumer can afford a higher level of current consumption without having to reduce future consumption. Other things equal, this *income effect* of the rise in the interest rate works in favour of a rise in current as well as future consumption and thus tends to increase θ.

Since σ measures the strength of the substitution effect, it is not surprising that the sign of the derivative $d\theta/dr$ depends on the magnitude of σ. We see that, for an intertemporal substitution elasticity equal to 1, the income and substitution effects will exactly offset each other, and the propensity to consume will be unaffected. Over the years many researchers have tried to estimate the empirical magnitude of the intertemporal substitution elasticity, σ. Most authors have found values of σ well below 1, suggesting that the propensity to consume wealth will *rise* when the real interest rate goes up.

However, a higher interest rate will also influence the level of wealth itself. As already mentioned, the stock of financial wealth, V_1, includes the value of stock and of housing capital. In Chapter 14 we saw that both of these important wealth components will be negatively affected by a rise in the real interest rate. Thus, a rise in r means that expected future dividends are discounted more heavily, leading to a fall in share prices. Moreover, by raising the user cost of owner-occupied housing, an increase in r reduces housing demand which in turn drives down the market value of the existing housing stock. For these reasons a rise in the real interest rate will reduce the wealth–income ratio, v_1.

In addition, the higher interest rate means that expected future labour income is discounted more heavily. As a consequence, the value of human wealth specified in (6) goes down. Intuitively, a higher real interest rate makes future labour income less valuable by making it easier to attain a given level of future consumption through saving out of current income.

The fall in human and financial wealth induced by a rise in the real interest rate clearly tends to reduce the propensity to consume current income, but since we have seen that there may be an offsetting increase in the propensity to consume wealth, θ, the net effect of a rise in r on the ratio of current consumption to current income, $\hat{\theta}$, is ambiguous. Against this background it is not surprising that empirical research has found it difficult to document a strong effect of real interest rates on consumption, although the dominant view is that a rise in r tends to reduce consumption because of the negative impact on wealth.

15.3 Consumption, taxation and public debt

We will now show how our theory of consumption can be used to derive the effects of the government's tax and debt policies on private consumption demand. This will give us an opportunity to highlight the importance of the way in which consumers form their expectations about the future. It will also enable us to illustrate the important distinction between temporary and permanent changes in tax policy.

Consumption and taxes: temporary versus permanent tax cuts

To focus on tax policy, we start by rewriting the consumption function (18) as:

$$C_1 = \theta\left(Y_1^L - T_1 + \frac{Y_2^L - T_2}{1+r} + V_1\right). \tag{23}$$

Suppose now that the government wishes to stimulate consumption demand by cutting net taxes T_1 during period 1, say, because the economy is in recession. For the moment, we assume that consumers expect the tax cut to be *temporary*, perhaps because the government has announced that it may have to raise taxes again once the recession is over. In that case consumers will expect T_2 to be unchanged, and according to (23) the immediate impact of the temporary tax cut will then be given by the derivative:

$$\frac{\partial C_1}{\partial T_1} = -\theta. \tag{24}$$

In other words, if the government cuts taxes temporarily by one unit, current consumption will go up by θ units.[11] Thus the temporary tax cut will indeed succeed in stimulating current consumption, but recalling from (17) that $\theta < 1$, we also see that part of the increase in disposable income will be saved for future consumption. Of course, this saving reflects the consumer's desire to smooth consumption over time.

For comparison, suppose instead that consumers expect the tax cut to be *permanent* so that T_2 goes down by the same amount as T_1. From (23) we then find the effect on current consumption to be:

$$\frac{\partial C_1}{\partial T_1} + \frac{\partial C_1}{\partial T_2} = -\theta\left(1 + \frac{1}{1+r}\right). \tag{25}$$

Not surprisingly, we see from (24) and (25) that *a permanent tax cut will have a stronger impact on current consumption than a temporary tax cut*. In the benchmark case where the real interest rate r equals the rate of time preference ϕ so that the consumer wants to consume equal amounts in the two periods, you may easily verify from (17) that $\theta = (1 + r)/(2 + r)$. In that case it follows from (25) that:

$$\frac{\partial C_1}{\partial T_1} + \frac{\partial C_1}{\partial T_2} = -1 \qquad \text{for } r = \phi. \tag{26}$$

In other words, when the consumer wants to smooth consumption perfectly over time, he or she will consume all of the period 1 tax cut during that period. There is no need to save any part of the increase in current disposable income to smooth consumption, since his or her expected future disposable income has gone up by a similar amount as his or her current net income.

The government budget constraint

In the analysis above we have not specified whether the tax cuts are associated with changes in public spending. As we shall argue below, the effects of a tax cut on private consumption may depend on whether or not it reflects a cut in public expenditure. To see this, we must make a slight detour to study the government's budget constraint. Let us assume for the moment that the government plans for the same time horizon as the household sector (later we will discuss the implications of relaxing this assumption). As before, we will divide this time horizon into two periods representing the 'present' (period 1) and the 'future' (period 2). At the beginning of period 1 the government starts out with a given real stock of public debt D_1 which is predetermined by the accumulated historical government budget deficits. In period 1 (at the beginning) the government spends a real amount G_1 on public consumption and collects a real net tax revenue T_1, where T_1 measures taxes net of government transfer payments (transfers are simply treated as negative taxes). If public spending exceeds tax revenues, the government must issue new government bonds in the real amount $\Delta D = G_1 - T_1$ in period 1.[12] Since debt carries interest, the government will then end up with a total amount of real debt $D_2 = (1 + r)(D_1 + \Delta D)$ at the beginning of period 2. Hence the government budget constraint for period 1 may be written as:

$$D_2 = (1 + r)(D_1 + G_1 - T_1). \tag{27}$$

---

11. Note that this is a *partial equilibrium* analysis. If the tax cut succeeds in stimulating economic activity, it will indirectly cause a further rise in consumption by raising aggregate labour income Y_1^L. However, our focus here is on the immediate direct impact on consumption, for a given level of activity.

12. We abstract from money printing (seigniorage) as a way of financing government consumption, since this plays very little role in developed countries.

In period 2 the government must run a budget surplus $T_2 - G_2$ which is sufficient to enable it to repay the public debt accumulated during the previous period. The government budget constraint for period 2 is therefore given by:

$$T_2 = D_2 + G_2. \tag{28}$$

In our simple two-period framework the relevant criterion for *sustainability of fiscal policy* is that the government pays back all debt at the end of period two: no one would lend to the government if the government did not pay back within the relevant time horizon. In a more general setting with many periods, long-run sustainability of fiscal policy still requires a balance between current and future tax payments on the one hand and initial debt plus current and future government spending on the other: the ratio of government debt to GDP must not 'explode', that is, it must not rise to such levels that lenders to the government no longer trust that it can pay back its debt by raising the necessary tax revenue. Since the future is not known with certainty, it may be difficult to judge at a given point in time whether fiscal policy is sustainable or not, but the government has to aim at sustainability to be able to finance its deficits, that is, it must convince the public that it has taken or will take actions that will ensure sustainability.

Inserting (27) into (28) and dividing through by $1 + r$, we obtain *the intertemporal government budget constraint:*

$$D_1 + G_1 + \frac{G_2}{1+r} = T_1 + \frac{T_2}{1+r} \tag{29}$$

Equation (29) makes a basic, but very important point:

THE INTERTEMPORAL GOVERNMENT BUDGET CONSTRAINT AND SUSTAINABILITY OF FISCAL POLICY

Fiscal policy is said to be **sustainable** if and only if the present value of current and future tax revenues cover the present value of current and future government spending plus the initial government debt. A government must aim at sustainability to finance its deficits.

As we shall now see, the intertemporal government budget constraint may have profound implications for the effects of tax policy.

Tax finance versus debt finance of government spending: the Ricardian Equivalence Theorem

It follows directly from (29) that if the government does not reduce its current or planned future spending – that is, if G_1 and G_2 are unchanged – a tax cut $dT_1 < 0$ in the current period must be followed by a future increase $dT_2 > 0$ in taxes so that:

$$dT_1 + \frac{dT_2}{1+r} = 0, \tag{30}$$

or $dT_2 = -(1 + r)dT_1$. To understand this relationship between current and future taxes, consider (27) and (28) once again. According to (27), if the government cuts current taxes by an amount $|dT_1|$ without reducing current public spending, G_1, the stock of real public debt will have risen by the amount $dD_2 = (1 + r)\,|dT_1|$ at the beginning of period 2. If the government does not cut back on its period 2 consumption, G_2, it follows from (28) that it will have to raise taxes in period 2 by the amount $dT_2 = (1 + r)\,|dT_1|$ to pay for the principal and interest on the extra debt created by the tax cut in period 1.

Suppose now that consumers have *rational expectations* in the sense that they look forward and understand the implications of the intertemporal government budget constraint. In that case they will realize that if the government reduces current taxes *without* reducing current or planned future public spending, the present value of future taxes will have to increase by as much as the cut in current taxes. It then follows from (23) and (30) that:

$$dC_1 = -\theta\left(dT_1 + \frac{dT_2}{1+r}\right) = 0 \tag{31}$$

The implication of (31) is striking: a cut in current taxes which is *not* accompanied by a cut in present or planned future public spending will have *no* effect on private consumption! In other words, a switch from tax finance to debt finance of current public spending leaves private consumption unaffected, since consumers realize that the tax cut today will be offset by the future tax increase needed to service the additional government debt. Indeed, because the present value of their lifetime tax burden is unchanged, consumers know that their net human wealth is also unchanged, and hence they feel unable to afford an increase in current consumption. Instead they will save the entire current tax cut and invest it in the capital market. This increase in current private saving will raise consumer cash receipts in period 2 by the amount $(1 + r)\,|dT_1|$ which is just sufficient to pay for the higher future tax bill. Hence future private consumption is also unchanged. The increased supply of government bonds in period 1 is thus matched by a similar increase in private demand for bonds, and the higher period 2 taxes are matched by an increase in private sector income from bond holdings.

The observation that tax finance and debt finance of government spending are in principle equivalent was first made as early as 1820 by the classical British economist David Ricardo. In a treatise on public debt Ricardo discussed three alternative ways of financing a war. For concreteness, he assumed that the war would generate military expenditure of £20 million per year. One financing option would be to impose additional taxes amounting to £20 million per year until the end of the war. Alternatively, the government could borrow £20 million every year during the war and increase tax collections by just £1 million each year to cover the interest payments on a £20 million loan, assuming an interest rate of 5 per cent. In this case the public debt would continue to rise until the war was over and would never be repaid, and taxes would be permanently higher. The third possibility considered by Ricardo was one where the war was mainly debt-financed, but where taxes would be raised by £1.2 million per year for every £20 million borrowed, enabling the government to pay off its debt in 45 years. Under the assumptions made, the present value of tax payments would be the same under the three modes of finance. As Ricardo put it: 'In point of economy, there is no real difference in either of the modes; for twenty millions in one payment, one million per annum for ever, or 1,200,000 pounds for 45 years, are precisely of the same value'.[13]

Because of this statement by Ricardo, the claim that taxes and debt are equivalent methods of public finance is referred to as the *Ricardian Equivalence Theorem.* Before you dismiss the theorem as being utterly unrealistic, take a look at Fig. 15.9. In that figure we have plotted private and public saving in Denmark as a percentage of GDP against time. As we have seen above, the Ricardian Equivalence Theorem implies that whenever the public sector reduces its saving, thereby increasing new issues of public debt (or reducing the rate at which public debt is retired), we should observe an offsetting increase in private saving, and vice versa. Figure 15.9 shows that there is indeed a clear tendency for private and public saving to move in opposite directions, suggesting that Ricardian equivalence may not be that unrealistic after all.

13.   See Ricardo's paper on the 'Funding System', *The Works and Correspondence of David Ricardo*, vol. IV, Piero Sraffa, ed., Cambridge University Press, 1951, p. 186. The subtle phrase: 'In point of economy...' has been interpreted to mean something like: 'From a rational economic perspective...'.

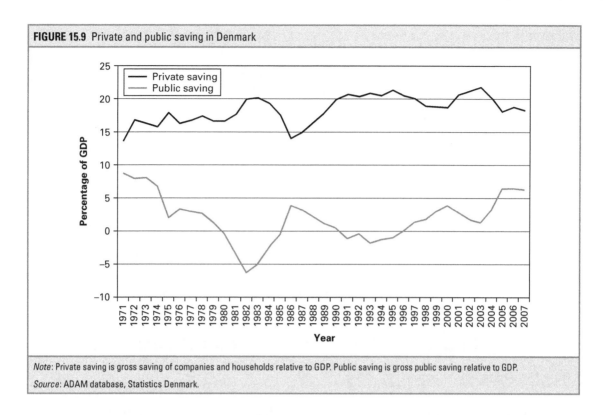

FIGURE 15.9 Private and public saving in Denmark

Note: Private saving is gross saving of companies and households relative to GDP. Public saving is gross public saving relative to GDP.

Source: ADAM database, Statistics Denmark.

However, while Fig. 15.9 does not seem inconsistent with Ricardian equivalence, it does not 'prove' that the theorem is correct, since there may be other explanations for the observed relationship between private and public saving. One potential Keynesian explanation is that Fig. 15.9 simply reflects the so-called automatic stabilizers built into the public budget: if the private propensity to save goes up for some reason, the resulting fall in consumption demand will tend to generate a fall in economic activity which in turn will increase the public budget deficit by automatically reducing government revenue from taxes on income and consumption and by automatically increasing public expenses on unemployment benefits. Alternatively, if the economy is hit by some other contractionary shock, say, a drop in investment, the resulting fall in economic activity may increase the private propensity to save at the same time as it increases the budget deficit via the automatic stabilizers. Thus, Fig. 15.10 suggests that reductions in the rate of employment are associated with reductions in the average propensity to consume, perhaps because higher unemployment reduces expected future income growth or increases uncertainty about the future.[14]

15.4 Towards a more realistic theory of consumption

Why Ricardian equivalence is likely to fail

Although Fig. 15.9 suggests that the Ricardian Equivalence Theorem cannot be dismissed so easily, most economists remain sceptical of the theorem in its strong form. Indeed, Ricardo himself did not believe in the practical relevance of his theorem. Right after having explained that his three alternative methods of war finance would imply the same present value of taxes (cf. the quotation above), he proceeded to write:

---

14. Of course, the fact that the employment rate and the propensity to consume move together does not necessarily mean that movements in employment *cause* movements in consumption. Causality could also run in the opposite direction, or the two time series could be driven by a common third factor not included in the figure.

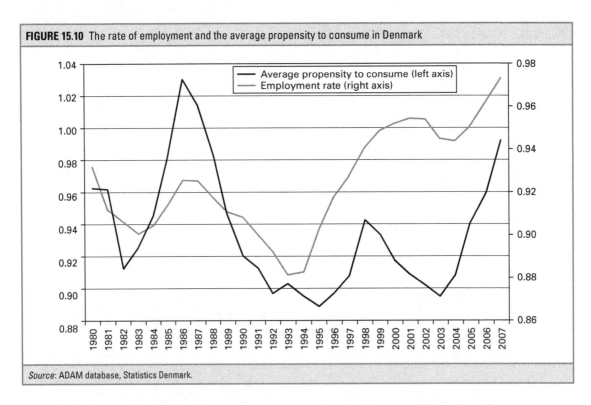

FIGURE 15.10 The rate of employment and the average propensity to consume in Denmark

Source: ADAM database, Statistics Denmark.

... but the people who pay the taxes never so estimate them, and therefore do not manage their private affairs accordingly. We are too apt to think that the war is burdensome only in proportion to what we are at the moment called to pay for it in taxes, without reflecting on the probable duration of such taxes.[15]

What Ricardo essentially says here is that ordinary taxpayers simply do not have the foresight or sophistication to calculate the present value of their expected future taxes. Hence they do not realize that lower taxes today (more government debt) must mean higher taxes tomorrow as long as the time path of public consumption is unchanged. Casual observation suggests that many people may indeed be myopic in this sense. But even if consumers are not irrational or myopic, there may still be several reasons why taxes and debt are not fully equivalent modes of public finance. Let us briefly consider these reasons.

Finite horizons and intergenerational distribution effects

Our analysis above assumed that the private and public sectors have identical planning horizons. In practice, the state will continue to exist beyond the finite lifetime of the individual consumer. Many current taxpayers (especially the elderly) may therefore rationally expect that some of the future taxes needed to service the existing public debt will be levied on future generations and not on those currently alive. In that case a shift from tax finance to debt finance is a way of shifting (part of) the burden of paying for current government spending onto future generations. A debt-financed tax cut will therefore increase the human wealth and consumption of the currently living generations.

This argument against Ricardian equivalence may sound plausible, but it was met by an ingenious objection from the American economist Robert Barro. He pointed out that parents care about their children. If the government tries to shift part of the tax burden from current to future generations through debt finance, parents may use their tax savings to increase their bequests to compensate their children for the higher future tax burden. When parents internalize the welfare of their children who in turn care about the welfare of *their* children

---

15. Ricardo, *op. cit.*, pp. 186–187.

and so on, the current generation will effectively behave as if it has an infinite time horizon. Any attempt by the government to redistribute resources across generations will then be neutralized by offsetting private intergenerational transfers, according to Barro.[16] However, this assumes that all parents actually plan to leave bequests to their children. In reality, some parents may not do so, for example if they believe that their children will be much richer than themselves. Moreover, the Barro argument abstracts from population growth. If population is growing, the future tax burden will be spread out across a larger number of taxpayers, and parents will not have to pass on all of their current tax savings to their children to compensate the latter for the higher future taxes needed to service the higher public debt. Still, Barro's analysis is an important reminder that human mortality as such is not a sufficient reason to dismiss Ricardian equivalence.

Intragenerational redistribution

The macro analysis of the preceding section hides the fact that most taxes are redistributive in nature. For the individual taxpayer or the individual family dynasty, a tax cut today may not be matched by an equivalent present-value tax increase tomorrow, even if the government obeys its aggregate intertemporal budget constraint. If a shift in the tax burden over time also involves a shift in the lifetime tax burdens across different individuals or families, the resulting *intragenerational* redistribution across agents belonging to the same generation may have macroeconomic effects. The reason is that different individuals or families have different characteristics and hence different propensities to consume so that redistribution of income does not necessarily leave aggregate consumption unchanged. However, intragenerational redistribution does not mean that a switch from tax finance to debt finance will necessarily raise current consumption. As a counter-example, if a lot of people fear that they will have to bear a disproportionate share of the higher future tax burden implied by an increase in public debt, a debt-financed cut in current taxes may actually *reduce* current private consumption by reducing expected aggregate human wealth.

Distortionary taxes

The Ricardian Equivalence Theorem assumes that taxes take the form of lump sum payments which are unrelated to individual economic behaviour. In practice, a person's tax bill is typically linked to his or her income or consumption. Taxes on income and consumption may discourage labour supply and savings and induce consumers to change their pattern of consumption. In particular, if a debt-financed cut in current income taxes generates expectations of higher future tax rates to service the higher public debt, consumers may want to increase their current labour supply and reduce their future labour supply to take advantage of the fact that marginal tax rates are lower today than they will be tomorrow. By inducing such *intertemporal substitution in labour supply*, the government may be able to stimulate current economic activity through a switch from tax finance to debt finance of current public spending.

Credit constraints

Our derivation of the Ricardian Equivalence Theorem relied on our assumption that capital markets are perfect so that no consumers are credit-constrained. In reality some consumers (such as university students!) may be unable to borrow as much as they would like at the going market interest rate. For example, a person may expect that he will earn much more

---

16. Robert J. Barro, 'Are Government Bonds Net Wealth?', *Journal of Political Economy*, **82**, 1974, pp. 1095–1117. This seminal article is the authoritative modern statement of the Ricardian Equivalence Theorem. Interestingly, even Barro's sophisticated reasoning was anticipated by Ricardo, for our previous quotation from Ricardo's text continues: 'It would be difficult to convince a man possessed of 20,000 pounds, or any other sum, that a perpetual payment of 50 pound per annum was equally burdensome with a single tax of 1000 pounds. He would have some vague notion that the 50 pounds per annum would be paid by posterity, and would not be paid by him; but if he leaves his fortune to his son, and leaves it charged with this perpetual tax, where is the difference whether he leaves him 20,000 pounds with the tax, or 19,000 pounds without it?'

in the future than today, but if his bank does not have the information necessary to estimate his future earnings potential, it may be reluctant to grant him a credit against his expected future labour income if he cannot produce any collateral. Such a credit-constrained consumer will wish to spend all of his current disposable income here and now, since he would prefer to increase his current consumption at the expense of future consumption if he could only obtain more credit. If the government implements a debt-financed tax cut, credit-constrained consumers will therefore increase their current consumption even if they realize that they will face higher taxes in the future. By means of the debt-financed cut in present taxes the government is using its access to the capital market to shift the consumption possibilities of credit-constrained consumers from the future to the present, thereby offsetting the imperfections in the private capital market. In this scenario Ricardian equivalence breaks down, as you are invited to demonstrate in Exercise 3.

Empirical research has found that current consumption tends to react more strongly to changes in current income than one would expect if consumption were governed only by expected lifetime income (of which current annual or quarterly income is usually only a small fraction). This so-called 'excess sensitivity' of current consumption to current income may reflect that many consumers are indeed credit-constrained and will hence wish to consume all of an increase in their current income, or it may reflect that they are simply short-sighted.

The debate on Ricardian Equivalence has been an important controversy in macroeconomics, so let us restate what we have learned:

THE RICARDIAN EQUIVALENCE THEOREM

The theorem says that a temporary switch from (lump-sum) tax finance to debt finance of public spending will not affect private consumption, since the intertemporal government budget constraint implies that the present value of future taxes will rise by the same amount as current taxes go down. Realizing this, rational forward-looking consumers will save all of the current tax cut and use the savings and the interest thereon to pay for their higher future tax bill. However, in practice the equivalence between tax finance and debt finance is likely to break down, as consumers may be short-sighted or may expect part of the higher future tax burden to fall on future generations, and as credit-constrained consumers will wish to spend their tax cut immediately even if they realize that future taxes will go up.

The generalized consumption function

We end this chapter by summarizing our theory of private consumption. Although we have just argued that the consumption of liquidity-constrained consumers will depend only on current disposable income, it is also realistic to assume that many consumers will not be credit-constrained in any particular year. For example, people with positive net financial assets are unlikely to be liquidity-constrained, since they can always sell off some of their assets if they want to increase their present consumption relative to planned future consumption. For these individuals we have seen that consumption depends on expected future income as well as on current income. In other words, aggregate consumption depends on current disposable labour income, Y_1^d, and on the expected rate of income growth (g) for those consumers who are not credit-constrained. We have also seen that consumption is affected by the real rate of interest, r, and by the market value of initial private wealth, V_1. We may therefore sum up our theory of consumption in the following generalized consumption function $C(\cdot)$:

$$C_1 = C(\underset{+}{Y_1^d},\ \underset{+}{g},\ \underset{(-)}{r},\ \underset{+}{V_1}). \tag{32}$$

The signs below the variables in (32) indicate the signs of the partial derivatives implied by our theory. The brackets around the sign of the derivative with respect to the interest rate indicates that the effect is in principle uncertain, but likely to be negative. In words, we have:

THE CONSUMPTION FUNCTION

Aggregate private consumption varies positively with current disposable income and with the expected rate of future income growth as well as with the current level of private wealth. Because of offsetting income and substitution effects, we cannot say for sure whether a rise in the real interest rate will raise or lower consumption, but once we recognize that the value of financial and human wealth varies negatively with the interest rate, it becomes likely that a higher real interest rate will cause private consumption to fall.

Notice how expectations feed into consumption. When consumers are optimistic about the future, they will expect a relatively high rate of income growth, g. This will have a direct positive effect on current consumption. A high expected growth rate will also tend to imply high stock prices and high prices of owner-occupied housing. This will further stimulate consumption by a positive impact on private wealth V_1.

In the next chapter we shall see how our consumption function (32) may be combined with our investment function from Chapter 14 to give a theory of aggregate demand for goods and services.

15.5 Summary

1. Private consumption is by far the largest component of the aggregate demand for goods and services. A satisfactory theory of private consumption must explain the paradoxical stylized facts that the average propensity to consume is a decreasing function of disposable income in microeconomic cross-section data, whereas it is roughly constant in long-run macroeconomic time series data.

2. The properties of the aggregate consumption function may be derived by studying the behaviour of a representative consumer who must allocate his consumption optimally over time, subject to his intertemporal budget constraint. With perfect capital markets, this constraint implies that the present value of lifetime consumption cannot exceed the sum of the consumer's initial financial and human wealth. Human wealth is the present value of current and future disposable labour income.

3. In the consumer's optimum, the marginal rate of substitution between present and future consumption equals the relative price of future consumption, given by one plus the real rate of interest. When disposable income varies over time, the optimizing consumer will want to smooth the time path of consumption relative to the time path of income. There is evidence that such consumption smoothing does indeed take place.

4. Given the assumption of perfect capital markets, the optimal intertemporal allocation of consumption implies that current consumption is proportional to total current wealth (the sum of financial and human wealth). The propensity to consume current wealth depends on the real interest rate, the consumer's rate of time preference, and on his intertemporal elasticity of substitution, defined as the percentage change in the ratio of future to present consumption implied by a 1 per cent change in the consumer's marginal rate of substitution.

5. A rise in the real interest rate will have offsetting income and substitution effects on the propensity to consume current wealth. If the intertemporal substitution elasticity

is greater than 1, reflecting a strong willingness of consumers to substitute future for present consumption, the substitution effect will dominate. A rise in the real interest rate will then reduce the propensity to consume current wealth. The opposite will happen if the intertemporal substitution elasticity is smaller than 1. Even if a rise in the interest rate does not significantly affect the propensity to consume a given amount of wealth, it may reduce current consumption by reducing the present value of future labour income, that is, by reducing human wealth, and by reducing the market value of the consumer's stockholdings and housing wealth.

6. For an optimizing consumer, the average propensity to consume current *income* will vary positively with the ratio of current financial wealth to current income. There is strong empirical evidence that such a positive relationship exists. The rough long-run constancy of the average propensity to consume observed in macroeconomic time series data may be explained by the fact that the wealth–income ratio, the growth rate of real income, and the real rate of interest tend to be roughly constant over the long run.

7. The negative correlation between income and the average propensity to consume observed in microeconomic cross-section data may be explained by the fact that, in any given period, many consumers will have a relatively low current income relative to their average income over the life cycle. Such consumers will therefore have a high level of current consumption relative to their current income, because they expect higher future incomes, or because they have accumulated wealth by saving out of higher past incomes.

8. A tax cut which is expected to be permanent will have a stronger positive impact on current consumption than a tax cut which is believed to be temporary. When the real interest rate equals the rate of time preference, a permanent tax cut will induce a corresponding rise in current consumption.

9. The government's intertemporal budget constraint implies that the present value of current and future taxes must be sufficient to cover the present value of current and future government spending plus the initial stock of government debt. For given levels of current and future government spending, a tax cut today must therefore be offset by a future tax increase of equal present value.

10. If consumers have rational expectations they will realize the implications of the intertemporal government budget constraint. This means that a cut in current (lump sum) taxes which is not accompanied by a cut in present or future public spending will have no effect on private consumption: consumers will save all of the current tax cut to be able to finance the higher future taxes without having to reduce future consumption. This equivalence between tax finance and debt finance of current public spending is referred to as Ricardian equivalence.

11. In practice, consumers are unlikely to save the full amount of a current tax cut, even if they realize that lower taxes today must imply higher taxes in the future. First of all, consumers may believe that some of the future taxes will be levied on future generations. Second, some consumers may be credit-constrained. A switch from current to future taxes will help these individuals to achieve a desired rise in current consumption at the expense of future consumption. The use of redistributive and distortionary taxes also means that a switch from tax finance to debt finance of current public spending is likely to have real effects on current consumption and labour supply.

12. The theory of private consumption is summarized in the generalized consumption function which states that aggregate consumption is an increasing function of current disposable income, of the expected future growth rate of income, and of the current ratio of financial wealth to income. A rise in the real interest rate has a theoretically ambiguous effect, although it is likely to reduce current consumption due to its negative impact on human and financial wealth.

15.6 Exercises

Exercise 1. Important concepts and results in the theory of private consumption

1. The theory of consumption presented in this chapter says that private consumption is proportional to private wealth. Explain the definition of wealth, including the concept of 'human wealth'. Explain the factors which determine the propensity to consume current wealth.

2. Explain the assumptions underlying our theory of consumption. Which assumptions do you find most important and problematic?

3. Empirical evidence suggests that many consumers tend to spend all of their current disposable income immediately. Is this irrational? Discuss.

4. Explain why we cannot say whether an increase in the real (after-tax) interest rate will raise or lower the propensity to consume. Explain the concept of the intertemporal elasticity of substitution in consumption and its role in determining the effect of a change in the interest rate on consumption. On balance, what do you consider the most likely effect of a rise in the real interest rate on consumption (positive or negative?). Justify your answer.

5. Explain the conflicting evidence on the relationship between the average propensity to consume and disposable income found in microeconomic cross-section data and in macroeconomic time series data. Explain how the theory of consumption presented in this chapter helps to resolve the apparent inconsistency between the two types of evidence.

6. Explain the consumer's intertemporal budget constraint and the government's intertemporal budget constraint and how the two constraints are linked, assuming that the representative consumer and the government have the same two-period planning horizon. (Hint: try to eliminate the consumer's lump sum tax payments from his budget constraint by using the government's intertemporal budget constraint.) What does your finding imply for the relationship between private and public spending? Explain and discuss.

Exercise 2. The consumption function with endogenous labour supply

In the main text of this chapter we made the simplifying assumption that the consumer's labour income is exogenously given to him, say, because wage rates as well as working hours are regulated by collective bargaining agreements. This exercise invites you to derive the consumption function when the representative consumer may freely choose his preferred number of working hours, h, while still taking the real wage rate w as given by the market.

To simplify, we will assume that the consumer is retired from the labour market during the second period of his life, earning labour income only during the first period. In real terms, his budget constraints for the two periods of life may then be written as:

$$V_2 = (1 + r)[V_1 + w(1 - \tau)h - C_1] \tag{33}$$

$$C_2 = V_2 \tag{34}$$

where τ is a proportional labour income tax so that $w(1 - \tau)h$ is disposable labour income. For concreteness, we assume that the consumer's lifetime utility is given by the function:

$$U = \ln C_1 + \beta \ln(1 - h) + \frac{\ln C_2}{1 + \phi} \tag{35}$$

where ϕ is the rate of time preference. In (35) we have assumed that the total time available to the consumer in the first period is equal to 1. Hence the magnitude $1 - h$ is the amount of leisure enjoyed during period 1, and β is a parameter indicating the strength of the consumer's preference for leisure. Furthermore, the after-tax real wage rate $w(1 - \tau)$ may be called the consumer's *potential* labour income (or the market value of his time endowment), since it measures the amount of wage income he could earn if he worked all the time. Note that $w(1-\tau)$ may also be seen as the 'price' of leisure, since it measures the net income forgone by the consumer if he chooses to consume one more unit of leisure.

1. Derive and interpret the consumer's intertemporal budget constraint. Does lifetime consumption depend on actual or on potential labour income? (Hint: for later purposes it may be useful for you to rewrite the lifetime budget constraint so that the value of the consumption of leisure, $w(1-\tau)(1-h)$, appears on the left-hand side as part of total lifetime consumption.)

2. Rewrite the utility function (35) and the intertemporal budget constraint by introducing the variable $F \equiv 1-h$, where F is leisure, and use the intertemporal budget constraint to eliminate C_2 from the utility function. Then show that the utility-maximizing choices of C_1 and F will be given by:

$$C_1 = \tilde{\theta}[V_1 + w(1-\tau)], \qquad \tilde{\theta} \equiv \frac{1+\phi}{1+(1+\phi)(1+\beta)}, \tag{36}$$

$$F = \frac{\beta C_1}{w(1-\tau)}. \tag{37}$$

Compare your consumption function to the consumption function (17) derived in the main text of the chapter and comment on the similarities and differences.

3. Derive an expression for the consumer's optimal labour supply h during period 1 (recall that $h = 1-F$). How does labour supply depend on the labour income tax rate τ? Give an intuitive explanation.

4. Suppose now that the consumer's desired working hours h exceed the amount of hours $\bar{h}$ that he is actually allowed to work as a member of his trade union. In that case he will work the maximum hours allowed, and his disposable labour income in period 1 will be $w(1-\tau)\bar{h}$. Derive his optimal period 1 consumption level in this case and compare with the consumption function derived in Question 2. Comment on the difference.

Exercise 3. Fiscal policy and consumption with credit-constrained consumers

In Section 15.3 we saw that the Ricardian Equivalence Theorem rests on the assumption of perfect capital markets. In this exercise you are asked to analyse the effects of a switch from tax finance to debt finance of public consumption when some consumers are credit-constrained.

For concreteness, suppose that all consumers in the economy earn the same labour income and pay the same amount of taxes in each period, but that one group of consumers ('the poor') enters the economy with a zero level of initial wealth at the beginning of period 1, whereas the remaining consumers ('the rich') start out with a level of initial wealth equal to V_1. Moreover, suppose that disposable labour income in period 1 is so low that the poor would like to borrow during that period, but that the banks are afraid of lending them money because they cannot provide any collateral. In that case the poor will be credit-constrained during period 1, and the consumption of a poor person during that period, C_1^p, will then be given by the budget constraint:

$$C_1^p = Y_1^L - T_1 \tag{38}$$

A rich consumer does not face any borrowing constraint, and his optimal consumption in period 1, C_1^r, will therefore be given by the consumption function (16) from the main text, that is:

$$C_1^r = \theta\left(V_1 + Y_1^L - T_1 + \frac{Y_2^L - T_2}{1+r}\right), \qquad 0 < \theta < 1 \tag{39}$$

Suppose that the total population size is equal to 1 (we can always normalize population size in this way by appropriate choice of our units of measurement). Suppose further that a fraction μ of the total population is 'poor' in the sense of having no initial wealth.

1. Derive the economy's aggregate consumption function for period 1, that is, derive an expression for total consumption $C_1 = \mu C_1^p + (1 - \mu)C_1^r$. Derive an expression for the economy's marginal propensity to consume current disposable income, $\partial C_1 / \partial(Y_1^L - T_1)$. Compare this expression with the value of the marginal propensity to consume in an economy with no credit-constrained consumers. Explain the difference.

   Suppose now that the government enacts a debt-financed reduction of current taxes T_1 by one unit, without cutting current or planned future public consumption. Assume further that the government and the private sector have the same planning horizons, and that the private sector understands that the tax cut today will have to be matched by a tax hike tomorrow of the same present value, due to the intertemporal government budget constraint. In other words, suppose that all consumers realize that:

$$dT_1 + \frac{dT_2}{1+r} = 0 \tag{40}$$

2. Derive the effect of the switch from tax finance to debt finance on aggregate private consumption in period 1. Compare with the situation with no credit-constrained consumers and explain the difference. Discuss whether the increase in public debt in period 1 will improve the lifetime welfare of consumers.

   Instead of financing the tax cut in period 1 by debt, the government may finance the tax reduction by cutting public consumption. In the question below we will distinguish between two scenarios. In the first scenario the fall in public consumption is expected to be *temporary*, that is, $dG_1 = dT_1$ and $dG_2 = dT_2 = 0$. In the second scenario the cut in public consumption is expected to be *permanent* so that $dG_2 = dG_1 = dT_1 = dT_2$.

3. Derive the effect on current private consumption C_1 of a temporary tax cut financed by a temporary cut in public consumption. Compare this to the effect on C_1 of a permanent tax cut financed by a permanent cut in public consumption. (In the latter case you may assume that $r = \phi$.) Explain the difference between your expressions. Does it make any difference for the effects of temporary and permanent tax cuts whether or not consumers are credit-constrained?

Exercise 4. Ricardian Equivalence?

1. Explain the content of the Ricardian Equivalence Theorem and its assumptions. Discuss whether the theorem is likely to hold in practice.

2. Try to find data for private saving and public sector saving as ratios to GDP in your country and plot the two series against each other. (If you are a Danish student, try to update Fig. 15.9 in the text.) Do the movements in the two time series seem consistent with the Ricardian Equivalence Theorem? Explain.

3. In many official statistics public sector saving is simply measured by the balance on the public sector budget (the negative of the budget deficit), defined as $T - C^g - I^g - rD$, where T is net taxes (taxes net of transfers), C^g is public consmption, I^g is public investment, and rD is the net interest payment on government debt. Discuss whether the ideal measure of public sector saving for the purpose of testing Ricardian Equivalence should include public investment, I^g. (Hint: if the budget deficit increases due to an increase in I^g, and if public investment yields a positive return, how will this affect the private sector's future tax liability?) Try to check if your empirical data for public sector savings include or exclude the public sector's net investment.

Exercise 5. Wage taxes versus consumption taxes versus wealth taxes

In the main text of the chapter we assumed for simplicity that taxes took the form of lump sum payments which were unrelated to the consumer's behaviour. Now we assume instead that the consumer must pay a proportional tax, τ^w, on his wage income, a proportional value-added tax, τ^c, on all his consumption expenditure, and potentially also a one-time tax, τ^v, on his initial wealth. This exercise asks you to consider some similarities and differences between these taxes.

We assume that the consumer's working hours are exogenously given to him and equal to 1 so that his total pre-tax labour income in period 1 is equal to the real wage rate w. We also assume that he is retired from the labour market during period 2. We begin with a situation without any taxes on wealth. The consumer budget constraints for the two periods of life are then given by:

$$V_2 = (1+r)[V_1 + (1-\tau^w)w - (1+\tau^c)C_1], \qquad 0 < \tau^w < 1, \qquad \tau^c \geq 0 \tag{41}$$

$$(1+\tau^c)C_2 = V_2 \tag{42}$$

1. Derive the consumer's intertemporal budget constraint and comment on your expression. From the consumer's perspective, what is the similarity and the difference between the wage tax and the consumption tax?

   The consumer has the lifetime utility function:

$$U = \ln C_1 + \frac{\ln C_2}{1+\phi}, \qquad \phi > 0 \tag{43}$$

2. Show that the consumer's optimal consumption is given by:

$$C_1 = \left(\frac{1+\phi}{2+\phi}\right)\left[\frac{V_1 + (1-\tau^w)w}{1+\tau^c}\right], \tag{44}$$

$$C_2 = \left(\frac{1+r}{2+\phi}\right)\left[\frac{V_1 + (1-\tau^w)w}{1+\tau^c}\right]. \tag{45}$$

   Comment on these expressions.

   Suppose now that the government needs to raise more tax revenue to finance additional public spending. The government presents two alternative proposals in parliament. The first proposal implies that the consumption tax rate (the VAT) will be raised from 20 per cent to 25 per cent while the wage tax rate will be kept unchanged at 50 per cent. The second proposal implies that the consumption tax rate is maintained at 20 per cent, while the wage tax rate is raised from 50 per cent to 52 per cent. In addition, the second proposal includes a one-time proportional tax of 4 per cent on existing initial wealth V_1. The government stresses that this is a once-and-for-all wealth tax which will not be imposed on future wealth V_2.

3. Would consumers prefer one of the government's proposals to the other one? (Hint: how do the two alternative tax plans affect the consumer's total wealth, including his human wealth?) What difference does it make to your answer whether the wealth tax is a one-time levy or a permanent tax?

Monetary policy and aggregate demand

16

According to the classical macroeconomic theory which dominated economic thought before the Great Depression of the 1930s, the total level of output and employment is determined from the economy's supply side. In the classical world, wages and prices adjust to ensure that the available supplies of labour and capital are utilized at their 'natural' rates determined by the structure of labour and product markets. In Chapter 1 we argued that this is a useful working assumption when we analyse the long-run economic phenomena which are the subject matter of the theory of economic growth. But in the short and medium term economic activity often deviates from its long-run growth trend. To understand these short-run macroeconomic fluctuations, we must explain why the aggregate demand for goods and services does not necessarily correspond to the aggregate supply which is forthcoming when all resources are utilized at their natural rates. Building on the previous two chapters, the present chapter therefore develops a theory of aggregate demand.

16.1 Keynes, the classics and the Great Depression

The classical economists did not literally claim that a capitalist market economy could never deviate from its natural rate of employment and output, but they did believe that if only market forces were allowed to work, such disturbances would be temporary and quite short-lived. The classical economists therefore saw no need for the government to engage in macroeconomic stabilization policy. In their view, the only role of monetary policy was to ensure price stability, and the task of fiscal policy was to avoid budget deficits which would crowd out private capital formation and thereby hamper economic growth. Winston Churchill, who was Secretary of the Treasury in Britain for several years during the 1920s, was very much in agreement with this classical view when he explained his approach to fiscal policy as follows: 'It is the orthodox Treasury dogma, steadfastly held, that whatever might be the political or social advantages, very little employment can, in fact, as a general rule, be created by state borrowing and state expenditure.'[1]

When the Great Depression of the 1930s struck the Western world, this classical laissez-faire position came under heavy attack. The Great Depression was an economic earthquake. Due to a catastrophic combination of negative shocks and macroeconomic policy failures, output in several countries fell by 25–30 per cent between 1929 and 1932–33, with disastrous consequences for employment (see Fig. 16.1). For a country like

---

1. Quoted in Richard T. Froyen, *Macroeconomics – Theories and Policies*, 6th edition, Prentice-Hall, Inc., 1999, p. 68.

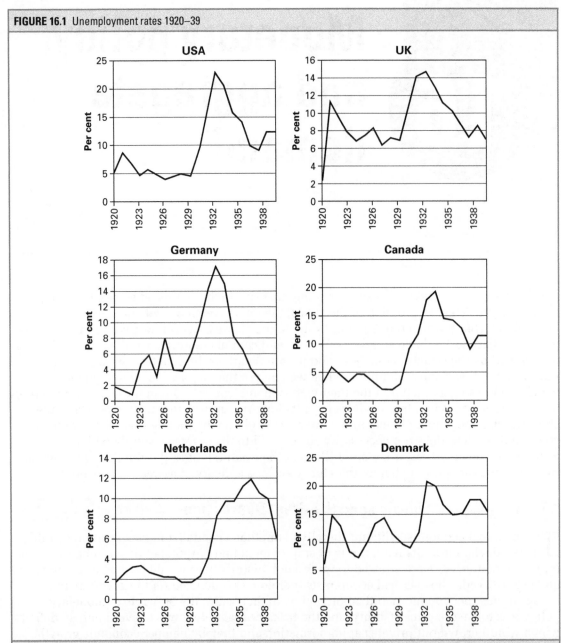

FIGURE 16.1 Unemployment rates 1920–39

Note: The unemployment rate is defined as the number of unemployed persons as a percentage of the total labour force. The source for this figure is not the same as for Fig. 1.2 and Fig. 10.1, which explains the differences.

Source: Macroeconomic database constructed by Jacob Brøchner Madsen, Monash University. The underlying sources are documented in: Jacob Brøchner Madsen, 'Agricultural Crises and the International Transmission of the Great Depression', *Journal of Economic History*, **61** (2), 2001, pp. 327–365.

the USA, it took almost a decade for output to return to its pre-1929 peak: a whole decade of economic growth lost!

Against this background the British economist John Maynard Keynes and several others attacked the classical view that resource utilization at natural rates is the normal state of affairs. Indeed, Keynes challenged the time-honoured definition of economics as 'the study of the allocation of scarce resources to satisfy competing ends'. Keynes' point was that resources are *not* always scarce; on the contrary they are often underutilized due to a lack of demand. In such circumstances the government will be able to raise total employment and output through a fiscal or monetary policy which stimulates aggregate demand. These ideas were laid out in 1936 in Keynes' famous book, *The General Theory of Employment, Interest and Money*. That book is often considered to mark the birth of modern macroeconomics, because it revolutionized the way economists thought about the problem of business cycles.

Today, most macroeconomists believe that economic activity in the short and medium run is determined by the interaction of aggregate demand and aggregate supply. In the long run the forces of aggregate supply stressed by the classical economists carry the day, but in the short run aggregate demand plays a key role in the determination of output and employment. As a step on the way to constructing a model of short-run macroeconomic fluctuations, we must therefore develop a theory of aggregate demand.

We have already seen that private investment as well as private consumption are influenced by the real rate of interest. In the long run the equilibrium real interest rate – the so-called natural rate of interest – is determined by the forces of productivity and thrift, as we explained in Chapter 3. However, in the short run monetary policy can have a significant impact on the real interest rate. Hence much of this chapter will focus on the conduct of monetary policy and how it affects aggregate demand.

We start our analysis by specifying the equilibrium condition for the goods market, drawing on the theory of consumption and investment developed in Chapters 14 and 15. We then move on to a study of the monetary sector and the conduct of monetary policy. Incorporating our specification of monetary policy into the equilibrium condition for the goods market, we then end up deriving a systematic link between the level of output and the rate of inflation which must hold whenever the goods market clears. This link is called the aggregate demand curve, and it will be one of the two central building blocks of the short-run macroeconomic model we set up in Chapter 18.

16.2 The goods market

Goods market equilibrium

For the product market to clear, the aggregate demand for goods must be equal to total output, Y. In this chapter we will focus on a closed economy (we will consider the open economy in later chapters). Aggregate demand for goods then consists of the sum of real private consumption, C, real private investment, I, and real government demand for goods and services, G. Hence goods market equilibrium requires:

$$Y = C + I + G. \tag{1}$$

In Chapter 14 we saw that private investment behaviour can be summarized in an investment function of the form $I = I(Y, r, K, \varepsilon)$, where r is the real interest rate, K is the predetermined capital stock existing at the beginning of the current period, and ε is a parameter capturing the 'state of confidence', reflecting the expected growth of income and demand. For the purpose of short-run analysis, we may treat the predetermined capital stock as a constant and leave it out of our behavioural equations.[2] We may then write private investment demand as:

$$I = I(Y, r, \varepsilon), \qquad I_Y \equiv \frac{\partial I}{\partial Y} > 0, \qquad I_r \equiv \frac{\partial I}{\partial r} < 0, \qquad I_\varepsilon \equiv \frac{\partial I}{\partial \varepsilon} > 0, \tag{2}$$

---

2. The dynamics of capital accumulation were dealt with in Book One. To include it here as well would complicate the formal analysis considerably, given that we also want to study the dynamics of output and inflation. We therefore leave the inclusion of capital stock adjustment in the economy's short-run dynamics for a more advanced macroeconomics course.

where the signs of the partial derivatives of the investment function follow from the theory developed in Chapter 14. Thus, investment increases with current output and with growth expectations, ε, whereas it decreases with the real interest rate.

Our theory of private consumption presented in Chapter 15 implies a consumption function of the form $C = C(Y - T, r, V, \varepsilon)$, where T denotes total net tax payments so that $Y - T$ is current disposable income, V is non-human wealth, and ε is the future income growth expected by consumers, assumed to equal the growth expectations of business firms, since firms are owned by consumers. Our analysis in Chapter 15 showed that the market value of non-human wealth is a decreasing function of r, since a rise in the real interest rate will, *ceteris paribus*, drive down stock prices as well the value of the housing stock. In other words, $V = V(r)$ and $dV/dr < 0$. To simplify exposition, we will use this relationship to eliminate V from the consumption function and simply write:

$$C = C(Y - T, r, \varepsilon), \qquad 0 < C_Y \equiv \frac{\partial C}{\partial (Y - T)} < 1, \qquad C_\varepsilon \equiv \frac{\partial C}{\partial \varepsilon} > 0. \tag{3}$$

The signs of the partial derivatives were explained in Chapter 15. From that chapter we recall that the real interest rate has an ambiguous effect on consumption, due to offsetting income and substitution effects, although the negative impact of a higher interest rate on private wealth suggests that the net effect on consumption is likely to be negative. The analysis in Chapter 15 also implied that the marginal propensity to consume current income is generally less than 1, as we assume above.

Our variable T measures 'net taxes', defined as total tax payments minus total transfers from the government to private households. In practice, net tax payments vary positively with economic activity, so we will assume that

$$T = \tau Y, \qquad 0 < \tau < 1. \tag{4}$$

We shall refer to τ as 'the net tax rate'. Note that this parameter captures the fact that unemployment benefits and social assistance to the unemployed vary negatively with output and employment as well as the fact that the revenue from taxes on income and consumption varies positively with GDP. In an extended modern welfare state, the value of τ can therefore be quite high. For example, in Denmark it is estimated that τ is in the neighbourhood of 0.85. We assume that the values of τ and G are set such that, on average over the business cycle, the government budget is balanced so that the government does not systematically accumulate or decumulate debt over time. This allows us to ignore complications arising from the dynamics of government debt accumulation. At the same time the specification in (4) allows for the fact that public revenues may deviate from public spending in the short run when actual GDP deviates from its trend value.

Let us denote total private demand by $D \equiv C + I$. It then follows from (2) through (4) that the goods market equilibrium condition (1) may be stated in the form:

$$Y = D(Y, \tau, r, \varepsilon) + G. \tag{5}$$

Properties of the private demand function

We will now consider the signs and magnitudes of the partial derivatives of the private demand function $D(Y, \tau, r, \varepsilon)$. Since $Y - T = Y(1 - \tau)$ and $D \equiv C + I = C(Y(1 - \tau), r, \varepsilon) + I(Y, r, \varepsilon)$, it follows that $D_Y \equiv \partial D/\partial Y = (1 - \tau)C_Y + I_Y > 0$. The derivative D_Y is the marginal private propensity to spend, defined as the increase in total private demand induced by a unit increase in (pre-tax) income. We will assume that the marginal spending propensity is less than 1 so that:

$$0 < D_Y \equiv \frac{\partial D}{\partial Y} = (1 - \tau)C_Y + I_Y < 1. \tag{6}$$

The assumption that $D_Y < 1$ guarantees that the *Keynesian multiplier, $\tilde{m} \equiv 1/(1 - D_y)$,* is positive. Recall from your basic macroeconomics course that the Keynesian multiplier measures the total increase in aggregate demand for goods generated by a unit increase in some exogenous demand component, provided that interest rates and prices stay constant. The Keynesian multiplier captures the phenomenon that as economic activity goes up, the resulting rise in output and income induces a further increase in private consumption and investment, which generates an additional rise in output and income that in turn causes a new round of private spending increase, and so on. Below we shall return to the role played by the Keynesian multiplier in our theory of aggregate demand.

The effect of a rise in the real interest rate on private demand is given by $D_r \equiv \partial D/\partial r \equiv C_r + I_r$. The derivative D_r measures the effect of a rise in the real interest rate on the private sector savings surplus. The private sector savings surplus is defined as $SS \equiv S - I$, where private saving is given by $S \equiv Y - T - C$. Hence we have $\partial SS/\partial r = -C_r - I_r = -(C_r + I_r) \equiv -D_r$. There is strong empirical evidence that a higher real interest rate raises the private sector savings surplus. For example, Fig. 16.2 illustrates a clear positive correlation between SS and a measure of the real interest rate in Denmark. Even though economic theory does not unambiguously determine the sign of the derivative C_r, we may therefore safely assume that:

$$D_r \equiv \frac{\partial D}{\partial r} \equiv C_r + I_r < 0, \qquad C_r \equiv \partial C/\partial r. \tag{7}$$

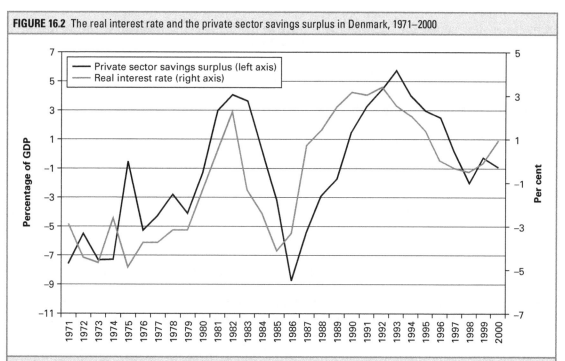

FIGURE 16.2 The real interest rate and the private sector savings surplus in Denmark, 1971–2000

Note: The real interest rate is measured as the after-tax nominal interest rate on ten-year government bonds minus an estimated trend rate of inflation which includes the rate of increase of housing prices.

Source: Data provided by Erik Haller Pedersen, Danmarks Nationalbank.

Finally we see from (2) and (3) that the effect on private demand of more optimistic growth expectations is:

$$D_\varepsilon \equiv \frac{\partial D}{\partial \varepsilon} \equiv C_\varepsilon + I_\varepsilon > 0. \tag{8}$$

Restating the condition for goods market equilibrium

It will be convenient to rewrite the goods market equilibrium condition (5) such that output, government spending and the confidence variable, ε, appear as percentage deviations from their trend values. We begin from an initial situation in which the economy is on its long-run growth trend so that initial output is equal to $\bar{Y} = D(\bar{Y}, \tau, \bar{r}, \bar{\varepsilon}) + \bar{G}$, where the magnitudes $\bar{G}$, $\bar{r}$ and $\bar{\varepsilon}$ are the trend values of G, r and ε prevailing in a long-run equilibrium. We then consider a small deviation from trend. Taking a first-order linear approximation of the goods market equilibrium condition (5), keeping τ fixed, we get:

$$Y - \bar{Y} = D_Y \cdot (Y - \bar{Y}) + D_r \cdot (r - \bar{r}) + D_\varepsilon \cdot (\varepsilon - \bar{\varepsilon}) + G - \bar{G} \quad \Leftrightarrow$$

$$Y - \bar{Y} = \tilde{m} \cdot [D_r(r - \bar{r}) + D_\varepsilon(\varepsilon - \bar{\varepsilon}) + G - \bar{G}], \quad \tilde{m} \equiv \frac{1}{1 - D_y} \equiv \frac{1}{1 - (1-\tau)C_Y - I_Y}. \tag{9}$$

Our next step is to rewrite (9) in terms of relative changes in Y, G and ε:

$$\frac{Y - \bar{Y}}{\bar{Y}} = \tilde{m} \cdot \left[\left(\frac{D_r}{\bar{Y}}\right)(r - \bar{r}) + \left(\frac{\bar{\varepsilon}D_\varepsilon}{\bar{Y}}\right)\left(\frac{\varepsilon - \bar{\varepsilon}}{\bar{\varepsilon}}\right) + \left(\frac{\bar{G}}{\bar{Y}}\right)\left(\frac{G - \bar{G}}{\bar{G}}\right)\right]. \tag{10}$$

In the final step we use the fact that the change in the log of some variable is approximately equal to the relative change in that variable. Defining

$$y \equiv \ln Y, \quad \bar{y} \equiv \ln \bar{Y}, \quad g \equiv \ln G, \quad \bar{g} \equiv \ln \bar{G}, \tag{11}$$

we may then write (10) in the form:

$$y - \bar{y} = \alpha_1(g - \bar{g}) - \alpha_2(r - \bar{r}) + v, \tag{12}$$

where

$$\alpha_1 \equiv \tilde{m}\left(\frac{\bar{G}}{\bar{Y}}\right), \quad \alpha_2 \equiv -\tilde{m}\left(\frac{D_r}{\bar{Y}}\right), \quad v \equiv \tilde{m}\left(\frac{\bar{\varepsilon}D_\varepsilon}{\bar{Y}}\right)(\ln \varepsilon - \ln \bar{\varepsilon}). \tag{13}$$

Eq. (12) says that the percentage deviation of output from trend (the output gap) can be approximated by a linear function of the percentage deviations of G and ε from their trend values and of the absolute deviation of r from its trend level.[3] Of course, (12) is just a particular way of stating that the aggregate demand for goods varies negatively with the real interest rate and positively with government spending and with expected income growth.

3. Using the linear approximation (12) implies that we are treating the coefficients α_1 and α_2 as constants. To justify the assumption that $\alpha_2 \equiv -\tilde{m}(D_r/\bar{Y})$ remains roughly constant despite the fact that $\bar{Y}$ is growing over time, we must assume that the derivative D_r takes the form $D_r = f(r)Y$, $f' < 0$. This is equivalent to assuming that the investment *ratio*, I/Y, will stay constant as long as the real interest rate stays constant. This assumption is warranted by our analysis of economic growth in Book One where we found that once the real interest rate has settled down to its long-run equilibrium value, the level of investment tends to grow at the same rate as output.

Note that the long-run equilibrium real interest rate $\bar{r}$ is the Wicksellian 'natural' rate of interest discussed in Section 3.3. Notice also the role played by the *Keynesian multiplier* $\tilde{m} \equiv 1/(1 - D_Y)$ in the definitions of the coefficients α_1 and α_2 given in (13). For example, if government consumption rises by one unit, the immediate impact is a net increase in aggregate demand equal to 1, but when the Keynesian multiplier effect is accounted for, the total increase in demand adds up to $\tilde{m} > 1$. Therefore, if public consumption increases by 1 per cent, the resulting percentage increase in total demand will be $\tilde{m}(\bar{G}/\bar{Y})$, given that the initial ratio of public consumption to total output is $\bar{G}/\bar{Y}$. This explains the coefficient α_1 on the percentage increase in government consumption, $g - \bar{g}$, in (12). Similarly, if the real interest rate goes up by one percentage point, the resulting *percentage* drop in total demand is $D_r/\bar{Y}$. When this initial fall in demand is magnified by the Keynesian multiplier, the total percentage fall in demand adds up to $-\tilde{m}(D_r/\bar{Y})$, as shown by the expression for α_2 in (13). Thus the familiar Keynesian multiplier theory is built into our theory of aggregate demand. Note from the definition of $\tilde{m}$ in (9) that the presence of the net tax rate τ reduces the size of the multiplier, thereby reducing the repercussion effects of shocks to aggregate demand such as changes in ε or G. Hence the net tax rate is a so-called *automatic stabilizer* which helps to reduce the fluctuations in aggregate demand even when the government does not actively change its fiscal policy. In a modern welfare state with high marginal tax rates and generous unemployment benefits (resulting in a high value of τ), the automatic responses of taxes and transfers to changes in economic activity may therefore play an important role in reducing the amplitude of business fluctuations.

Summing up our main findings so far, we have:

AGGREGATE DEMAND AND GOODS MARKET EQUILIBRIUM

The aggregate demand for goods and services varies positively with current income, with public consumption and investment and with the expected rate of income growth, whereas it varies negatively with the real rate of interest. In goods market equilibrium, any shock to aggregate demand is magnified by the Keynesian multiplier process but the presence of automatic stabilizers such as income taxes and unemployment insurance reduces the size of the multiplier.

Equation (12) is our preliminary version of the economy's aggregate demand curve. Below we will show that (12) implies a systematic link between output and inflation, once one allows for the way monetary policy is typically conducted. To understand this link, we must study the relationship between inflation and the real interest rate, and that requires taking a closer look at the money market and the behaviour of central banks.

16.3 The money market and monetary policy

The money market

From your basic macroeconomics course you will recall that equilibrium in the money market is obtained when

$$\frac{M}{P} = L(Y, i), \qquad L_Y \equiv \frac{\partial L}{\partial Y} > 0, \qquad L_i \equiv \frac{\partial L}{\partial i} < 0, \tag{14}$$

where $L(Y, i)$ is the demand for real money balances, i is the nominal interest rate, M is the nominal money supply, and P is the price level. The left-hand side of (14) is the supply of real money balances which must be equal to real money demand in equilibrium. Real money demand varies positively with income, since a rise in income leads to more transactions which in turn requires more liquidity. At the same time money demand varies negatively with the nominal interest rate, because a higher interest rate raises the opportunity cost of holding money rather than interest-bearing assets, inducing agents to economize on their money balances so as to be able to invest a larger share of their wealth in interest-bearing financial instruments. For concreteness, we will assume that the demand for real money balances can be approximated by a function of the form:

$$L(Y, i) = kY^{\eta}e^{-\beta i}, \qquad k > 0, \qquad \eta > 0, \qquad \beta > 0, \tag{15}$$

where e is the exponential function, η is the income elasticity of money demand, and β is the semi-elasticity of money demand with respect to the interest rate.[4] Notice that the interest rate i appearing in the money demand function should be interpreted as a *short-term* interest rate, since the closest substitutes for money are the most liquid interest-bearing assets with a short term to maturity.

The constant money growth rule

To find the link between output and inflation on the economy's demand side, we need to know how the real interest rate r appearing in (12) is related to these two variables. This depends on the way monetary policy is conducted. Monetary policy regimes vary across time and space. Here we shall focus on two benchmark monetary policy rules which have received widespread attention in the literature and in practical policy making. A monetary policy rule is a rule or principle prescribing how the monetary policy *instrument* of the central bank should be chosen. In practice, the main monetary policy *instrument* of the central bank is its short-term interest rate charged or offered vis-à-vis the commercial banking sector. Through their control of the central bank interest rate, monetary policy makers can normally control the level of short-term interest rates prevailing in the interbank market.[5] The interbank market is the market for short-term credit where commercial banks with a temporary surplus of liquidity meet other commercial banks with a temporary liquidity shortage. The interbank interest rate in turn heavily influences the level of market interest rates on all types of short-term credit.

Under the *constant money growth rule* for the conduct of monetary policy the central bank adjusts its short-term interest rate to ensure that the forthcoming money demand results in a *constant growth rate of the nominal monetary base*. Assuming a constant money multiplier (that is, a constant ratio between the broader money supply and the monetary base), this will also ensure a constant growth rate of the broader money supply which includes bank deposits as well as base money. In an influential book published in 1960, the American economist Milton Friedman argued that a constant money supply growth rate would in practice ensure the highest degree of macroeconomic stability which could realistically be achieved, since it would imply a stable increase in aggregate nominal income.[6] This argument was based on Friedman's belief in a stable money demand function with a low interest rate elasticity. To see his point most clearly, suppose for a moment that our parameter β in (15) is close to 0, and that the income elasticity of money demand η is equal to 1. Money market equilibrium then roughly requires $M = kPY$, where k is a constant. Hence aggregate nominal income PY must grow roughly in proportion to the nominal money supply M. Securing a stable growth rate of M will then secure a stable growth rate of nominal income.

4. The semi-elasticity β measures the *percentage* drop in real money demand induced by a one percentage *point* increase in the interest rate.

5. In times of financial crisis the ability of central banks to control interest rates in the interbank market may be weakened, though. We return to this issue below.

6. See Milton Friedman, *A Program for Monetary Stability*, New York, Fordham University Press, 1960.

Friedman pointed out that we have only limited knowledge of the way the economy works. His studies of American monetary history also suggested that monetary policy tends to affect the real economy with long and variable lags.[7] Friedman therefore argued that the central bank may often end up *destabilizing* the economy if it attempts to manage aggregate demand through activist monetary policy by constantly varying the growth rate of money supply in response to changing economic conditions. Moreover, according to Friedman, the self-regulating market forces are sufficiently strong to ensure that real output and employment will be pulled fairly quickly towards their 'natural' rates following an economic disturbance. Given that activist monetary policy may fail to stabilize the economy, and that the need for stabilization is limited anyway, Friedman concluded that his constant money supply growth rule would be the best way to conduct monetary policy.

Friedman's arguments did not go unchallenged, but they had a substantial impact on many central banks. In particular, the German Bundesbank adopted stable target growth rates for the money supply from the 1970s, and after the formation of the European Monetary Union the European Central Bank has maintained a target for the evolution of the money supply to support its target for (low) inflation.

What does the constant money growth rule imply for the formation of interest rates? To investigate this, suppose that the central bank knows the structure of the money market sufficiently well to be able to implement its desired constant growth rate μ of the nominal money supply through appropriate adjustment of the short-term nominal interest rate. Using (14) and (15), and denoting the rate of inflation by π so that $P \equiv (1 + \pi)P_{-1}$, we may then write the condition for money market equilibrium as:

$$\frac{(1+\mu)M_{-1}}{(1+\pi)P_{-1}} = kY^\eta e^{-\beta i}, \tag{16}$$

where M_{-1} and P_{-1} are the nominal money supply and the price level prevailing in the previous period, respectively. We want to study how the economy behaves when it is not 'too' far off its long-run trend. We therefore assume that the economy was in long-run equilibrium in the previous period. Ignoring growth for simplicity, a long-run equilibrium requires that the real money supply be constant, since the variables in the money demand function, Y and i, must be constant in a long-run equilibrium without secular growth. Constancy of the real money supply means that the inflation rate π must equal the monetary growth rate μ.[8] As we shall explain more carefully in Section 16.4, the approximate link between the nominal and the real interest rate is $i = r + \pi$, so in a long-run equilibrium where $\pi = \mu$ and $r = \bar{r}$, we have $i = \bar{r} + \mu$. If we denote the long-run value of the real money stock by L^*, our assumption that the money market was in long-run equilibrium in the previous period then implies that:

$$\frac{M_{-1}}{P_{-1}} = L^* = k\bar{Y}^\eta e^{-\beta(\bar{r}+\mu)}. \tag{17}$$

Taking natural logs of (16), remembering that $M_{-1}/P_{-1} = L^*$, and using the approximations $\ln(1 + \mu) \approx \mu$ and $\ln(1 + \pi) \approx \pi$, we get:

$$\mu - \pi + \ln L^* = \ln k + \eta y - \beta i, \tag{18}$$

---

7. Milton Friedman and Anna Schwartz, *A Monetary History of the United States, 1867–1960*, Princeton, NJ, Princeton University Press, 1963. In Chapter 20 we shall discuss the lags in monetary policy in more detail.

8. If we assume that trend output $\bar{Y}$ grows at the constant rate x, the real money supply would have to grow at the rate ηx in a long-run equilibrium with a constant interest rate. This in turn would imply an equilibrium rate of inflation π^* equal to $\pi^* = \mu - \eta x$. Nevertheless, for constant values of η and x, one can show that the nominal interest rate would still react to changes in inflation and output in accordance with our Eq. (20) derived below (see Exercise 2).

where (17) implies:

$$\ln L^* = \ln k + \eta \bar{y} - \beta(\bar{r} + \mu). \tag{19}$$

By inserting (19) into (18) and rearranging, you may verify that:

$$i = \bar{r} + \pi + \left(\frac{1-\beta}{\beta}\right)(\pi - \mu) + \left(\frac{\eta}{\beta}\right)(y - \bar{y}). \tag{20}$$

Equation (20) shows how the short-term nominal interest rate i must be adjusted in response to changes in inflation and output if monetary policy aims at securing a constant growth rate μ of the nominal money supply. Since η and β are both positive, we see that the interest rate varies positively with the output gap, $y - \bar{y}$. If the numerical semi-elasticity β of money demand with respect to the interest rate is not too high ($\beta < 1$), as Friedman assumed, we also see that the nominal interest rate will increase more than one-to-one with the rate of inflation, implying an increase in the *real* interest rate. Note that since the long-term equilibrium inflation rate equals the monetary growth rate, our parameter μ may be interpreted as the central bank's *target inflation rate.*[9]

Let us restate the main insights from this section:

THE CONSTANT MONEY GROWTH RULE

This is based on the belief that the best thing the central bank can do to secure a stable growth in nominal aggregate demand is to set its interest rate so as to achieve a constant growth rate of the nominal money supply. With a standard money demand function where the interest sensitivity of money demand is not too high, the constant money growth rule implies that the nominal interest rate should vary positively with the output gap and positively and more than one-to-one with the deviation of inflation from the target money growth rate.

The Taylor rule

As we have mentioned, some central banks have occasionally defined targets for the growth rate of the nominal money supply, in accordance with Milton Friedman's recommendation. However, one problem with this practice is that a constant monetary growth rate may not succeed in stabilizing the evolution of nominal aggregate demand if the parameters of the money demand function are changing over time in an unpredictable fashion. Such unanticipated shifts in the money demand function may occur when new financial instruments and methods of payment emerge as a result of financial innovation or when the appetite for risk in financial markets changes. An extreme example of instability of money demand was seen during the financial crisis of 2007–08 when the demand for liquid assets including bank reserves soared and central banks throughout the world allowed a drastic increase in bank reserves to keep interest rates down.

In an influential article, American economist John Taylor argued that rather than worrying too much about the evolution of the money supply as such, the central bank might as well simply adjust the short-term interest rate in reaction to observed deviations of inflation and output from their targets.[10] Assuming that policy makers wish to stabilize output around its trend level, and denoting the inflation target by π^*, we may specify the monetary policy rule proposed by Taylor as:

---

9. In Chapter 19 we shall discuss what an appropriate target inflation rate would be.

10. See John B. Taylor, 'Discretion versus Policy Rules in Practice', *Carnegie-Rochester Conference Series on Public Policy*, **39**, 1993, pp. 195–214.

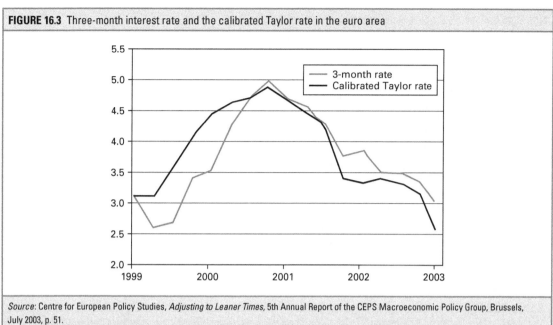

FIGURE 16.3 Three-month interest rate and the calibrated Taylor rate in the euro area

Source: Centre for European Policy Studies, *Adjusting to Leaner Times*, 5th Annual Report of the CEPS Macroeconomic Policy Group, Brussels, July 2003, p. 51.

$$i = \bar{r} + \pi + h(\pi - \pi^*) + b(y - \bar{y}), \qquad h > 0, \qquad b > 0. \tag{21}$$

Equation (21) is the famous *Taylor rule*. Recalling that the monetary growth rate μ may be interpreted as an inflation target, we see from (20) and (21) that the nominal interest rate follows an equation of the same form under the constant money growth rule and under the Taylor rule. Yet there is an important difference. Under the constant money growth rule the coefficients in the equation for the interest rate depend on the parameters η and β of the money demand function. In contrast, under the Taylor rule the parameters h and b in (21) are chosen directly by policy makers, depending on their aversion to inflation and output instability. According to Taylor it is important that the value of h is positive so that the real interest rate goes up when inflation increases. If $1 + h$ is less than 1, a rise in inflation will drive down the real interest rate $i - \pi$, and this in turn will further feed inflation by stimulating aggregate demand for goods, leading to economic instability. In fact, based on the US macroeconomic experience in the 1980s and early 1990s, Taylor suggested that the parameter values $h = 0.5$ and $b = 0.5$ would lead to good economic performance.

Empirical studies have found that although central bankers never mechanically follow a simple policy rule, central bank interest rates do in fact tend to be set in accordance with equations of the general form given in (21). To illustrate, Fig. 16.3 compares the evolution of the actual three-month euro area interest rate to the interest rate which would have prevailed if the European Central Bank had simply followed a Taylor rule of the form (21) with coefficients $h = 0.4$, $b = 0.6$, $\pi^* = 1.5$ per cent and $\bar{r} = 2$ per cent. We see that the Taylor rule gives a fairly good description of actual monetary policy in the euro area.

Fig. 16.4 shows the deviation between a 'Taylor interest rate' and the actual interest rate set by the central bank in four important countries. The 'Taylor rate' is assumed to be set in accordance with the following monetary policy rules:[11]

---

11. In the case of Germany, the actual interest rate is the one set by the German central bank (Bundesbank) prior to 1999 and the rate set by the European Central Bank after the formation of the European Monetary Union.

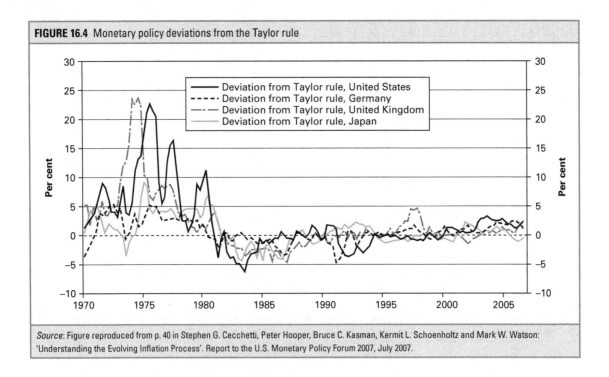

FIGURE 16.4 Monetary policy deviations from the Taylor rule

Source: Figure reproduced from p. 40 in Stephen G. Cecchetti, Peter Hooper, Bruce C. Kasman, Kermit L. Schoenholtz and Mark W. Watson: 'Understanding the Evolving Inflation Process'. Report to the U.S. Monetary Policy Forum 2007, July 2007.

Germany: $i = 2.88 + \pi + 0.25(\pi - 2.0) + 0.25(y - \bar{y})$

Japan: $i = 1.91 + \pi + 0.5(\pi - 1.0) + 0.25(y - \bar{y})$

United Kingdom: $i = 3.63 + \pi + 0.25(\pi - 2.0) + 0.5(y - \bar{y})$

United States: $i = 2 + \pi + 0.5(\pi - 2.0) + 0.5(y - \bar{y})$

From Fig. 16.4 we see that, during the 1970s, the actual central bank interest rates were much lower than prescribed by the Taylor rule whereas they were somewhat higher than the 'Taylor rates' during the early 1980s. However, from the mid-1980s the deviations of the actual interest rates from those predicted by the above Taylor rules have been relatively small. Note that all of these rules involve a positive value of the parameter h in (21), so in recent years all of the four central banks have indeed followed Taylor's recommendation that h should be substantially above zero to ensure a rise in the real interest rate in response to a rise in inflation.

In Chapter 20 we shall discuss whether the Taylor rule is in fact also an *optimal* monetary policy. In the meantime, let us sum up the important monetary policy principles advocated by John Taylor:

THE TAYLOR RULE

The rule says that the central bank interest rate should vary positively with the output gap and with the deviation of inflation from its target rate. In particular, the nominal interest rate should rise by more than one-to-one with the inflation rate to ensure that the real interest rate goes up when inflation increases. When output is at its trend level and inflation is at its target level, the central bank should set its nominal interest rate so as to achieve a real interest rate equal to the economy's estimated 'natural' interest rate. While this Taylor rule was originally advanced as a normative prescription for monetary policy, it has turned out to provide a rather good empirical description of the actual interest rate policies followed by central banks in recent decades.

Monetary policy and long-term interest rates: the yield curve

The central bank can normally control the current short-term interest rate via the choice of its own borrowing and lending rate. However, the incentive to invest in a real asset depends on the expected cost of capital over the entire useful life of the asset. This lifetime may be many years if the asset is, say, a building, a truck, or a piece of machinery. The crucial question is: to what extent can monetary policy affect the incentive to acquire the long-lived assets which make up the bulk of investment?

Consider a firm which is contemplating investment in a real asset with an expected lifetime of n periods. Suppose first that the firm plans to finance the investment with short term debt which is 'rolled over' in each period so that the interest rate varies with the movements in the short-term interest rate. For simplicity, suppose further that the firm does not need to pay any interest until time $t + n$ when the entire loan is paid back with interest. If one euro of debt is incurred in period t, the *expected* amount A^s to be repaid at time $t = n$ will be:

$$A^s = (1 + i_t) \times (1 + i_{t+1}^e) \times (1 + i_{t+2}^e) \times \ldots \times (1 + i_{t+n-1}^e), \tag{22}$$

where i_t is the current short-term (one-period) interest rate which is known at the time the debt is incurred, and i_{t+j}^e is the future short-term interest rate *expected* to prevail in period $t + j$.

As an alternative, the firm may finance the investment by a long-term loan with n terms to maturity (i.e., a loan lasting for n periods) where the long-term interest rate per period, i^l, is fixed at time t when the debt is incurred. Assuming again that no interest is paid until the loan expires at time $t + n$, the amount A^l to be repaid at that time will then be:

$$A^l = (1 + i_t^l)^n. \tag{23}$$

If the firm is risk neutral, it will not worry about the uncertainty pertaining to the future short-term interest rates but will simply choose the mode of finance with the lowest expected cost. Thus, if $A^l > A^s$, the firm will choose to finance the investment by a variable-interest rate loan, but if $A^l < A^s$ it will prefer the long-term loan with a fixed interest rate. In the latter case it would seem that monetary policy has no influence at all on the cost of investment finance, since the short-term interest rate controlled by the central bank does not enter the expression for A^l. However, this ignores that the arbitrage behaviour of financial investors creates a link between short-term and long-term interest rates.

We will now explore this link. Suppose that financial investors consider short-term debt instruments (with one term to maturity) and long-term debt instruments (with n terms to maturity) to be *perfect substitutes* for each other. Since short-term and long-term instruments have different risk characteristics, perfect substitutability requires that investors be risk neutral. In that case the effective interest rate on the long-term instrument must adjust to ensure that *the expected returns on short-term and long-terms instruments* are equalized. In a financial market equilibrium investors must thus expect to end up with the same stock of wealth at time $t + n$ whether they buy a long-term instrument and hold it until maturity, or whether they make a series of n short-term investments, reinvesting in short-term instruments every time the instrument bought in the previous period matures. At the beginning of period t we therefore have the financial arbitrage condition:

$$(1 + i_t^l)^n = (1 + i_t) \times (1 + i_{t+1}^e) \times (1 + i_{t+2}^e) \times \ldots (1 + i_{t+n-1}^e). \tag{24}$$

The term on the left-hand side of (24) is the investor's wealth at time $t + n$ if he invests in the long-term instrument at time t and holds on to his investment. The right-hand side of (24) measures the wealth he expects to accumulate if he makes a series of short-term investments, reinvesting his principal plus interest in each period until time $t + n$. In equilibrium the two investment strategies must be equally attractive, given the perfect substitutability of short-term and long-term financial instruments.

Equations (22)–(24) obviously imply that $A^s = A^l$, so under risk neutrality the cost of long-term finance is identical to the (expected) cost of short-term finance. This means that the long-term interest rate is influenced by the short-term interest rate controlled by the central bank. More precisely, according to (24) *the current long-term interest rate depends on the current and the expected future short-term interest rates*. This is referred to as the *expectations hypothesis*. If the length of our period is, say, a year, a quarter, or a month, the interest rates appearing in (24) will not be far above 0, and the approximation $\ln(1 + i) \approx i$ will be fairly accurate. Taking logs on both sides of (24) and dividing through by n, we then get:

$$i_t^l \approx \frac{1}{n}(i_t + i_{t+1}^e + i_{t+2}^e + \ldots + i_{t+n-1}^e). \tag{25}$$

Equation (25) says that *the current long-term interest rate is a simple average of the current and the expected future short-term interest rates*. This relationship assumes that investors are risk neutral. If they are risk averse, one must add a risk premium to the right-hand side of Eq. (25) to account for the greater riskiness of long-term bonds whose prices are more sensitive to changes in the market rate of interest and hence more volatile.

We have so far considered only two different debt instruments. In reality a large number of securities with many different terms to maturity are traded in financial markets. But the reasoning which led to Eq. (25) is valid for any $n \geq 2$, so (25) determines the entire *term structure of interest rates*, that is, the relationship between the interest rates on securities with different terms to maturity (different values of n).

From the term structure equation (25) one can derive the so-called *yield curve* which shows the effective interest rates on instruments of different maturities at a given point in time. According to (25) we have:

$$i_t^l = i_t \quad \text{if} \quad i_{t+j}^e = i_t \quad \text{for all} \quad j = 1, 2, \ldots, n-1. \tag{26}$$

In other words, if financial investors happen to expect no changes in future short-term interest rates – a situation sometimes described as 'static expectations' – the interest rates on long-term and short-term instruments will coincide, and the yield curve will be flat. Figure 16.5 shows that the yield curve in Denmark did in fact look this way in the beginning of January 2001.

As we move from left to right on the horizontal axis in Fig. 16.5, we consider instruments with increasing terms to maturity. The first point on the yield curve shows the market interest rate on interbank credit with 14 days until maturity. This interest rate is almost perfectly controlled by the interest rate policy of the Danish central bank (Danmarks Nationalbank). The last point on the yield curve plots the effective market interest rate on 30-year Danish government bonds. The flatness of the yield curve suggests that investors in Denmark roughly expected constant short-term interest rates at the beginning of 2001.

A rather flat yield curve is often considered to represent a 'normal' situation where investors have no particular reason to believe that tomorrow will be much different from today. But sometimes the situation is not normal. Figure 16.5 shows that short-term interest rates were far above long-term rates on 2 August 1993. Around that date Denmark and many other European countries suffered from a speculative attack on the European Monetary System, the fixed exchange rate system that existed before the formation of the European Monetary Union. To stem the capital outflow generated by fears of a devaluation of the Danish krone, Danmarks Nationalbank drove up the 14-day interbank interest rate to the exorbitant height of 45 per cent per annum! The fact that long-term interest rates remained

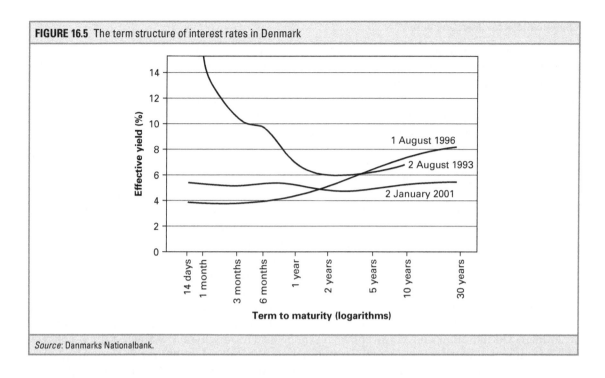

FIGURE 16.5 The term structure of interest rates in Denmark

Source: Danmarks Nationalbank.

much lower indicates that investors did not expect the extreme situation at the short end of the market to last long.

In contrast, the yield curve had an unusually steep upward slope on 1 August 1996, as illustrated in Fig. 16.5. At that time it was widely expected that the pace of growth in the European economy was about to increase significantly. Market participants therefore expected future monetary policy to be tightened to counteract inflationary pressures, and the expectation of higher future short-term interest rates drove current long-term rates significantly above the current short rate.[12]

The relationship between short-term and long-term interest rates is very important for the effectiveness of monetary policy. We therefore restate the theory of

THE TERM STRUCTURE OF INTEREST RATES

According to the expectations hypothesis, the current long-term interest rate is an average of the current and the expected future short-term interest rates. This arbitrage condition ensures that investors obtain the same expected return on long-term and short-term instruments. The expectations hypothesis implies that the yield curve (showing the interest rate on instruments with different terms to maturity) will be flat when investors expect the short-term interest rate to remain constant over time. When future short-term interest rates are expected to increase (fall), the yield curve will slope upwards (downwards). In practice, risk-averse investors will require a risk premium on longer-term assets, so even if the short-term interest rate is expected to remain constant, the yield curve will tend to slope upwards.

---

12. As mentioned earlier, in practice risk-averse investors will require some risk premium on long-term bonds to compensate for the fact that their market prices are more volatile than the prices of short-term bonds. In an equilibrium where the market does not expect any changes in future monetary policy, the yield curve will therefore typically have a slightly positive slope.

Complications for monetary policy

What does the expectations hypothesis imply for monetary policy? Recall that the left-hand side of (25) reflects the cost of financing investment by long-term debt while the right-hand side represents the cost of financing investment through a sequence of short-term loans. Moreover, even if a real investment is financed by equity, the cost of finance is still represented by either of the two sides of (25), since the opportunity cost of equity finance is the rate of interest which the owners of the firm could have earned if they had chosen instead to invest their wealth in the capital market. Regardless of the mode of finance, (25) thus implies that *monetary policy can only have a significant impact on the incentive to invest in long-lived real assets if it affects expectations about future short-term interest rates.* For example, if the central bank engineers a unit increase in the current short rate i_t which the market considers to be purely temporary, the expected future interest rates appearing on the right-hand side of (25) will be unaffected, and the interest rate on long-term debt with n periods to maturity will only increase by $1/n$. If the short-term rate applies to an instrument with a term of one month, and the long-term rate relates to a 10-year bond, n will be equal to $12 \times 10 = 120$. In that case a one-percentage point increase in the short term interest rate will only raise the long-term bond rate by a negligible 0.0083 percentage points, i.e., less than one basis point! Thus there is very little impact on the incentive to invest in long-lived real assets, regardless of whether the investment is financed by long-term bond issues or by a sequence of short-term loans. At the other end of the spectrum is the situation where a change in the current short-term interest rate is *expected* to be permanent. According to (25) the long-term interest rate will then rise by the full amount of the increase in the short rate. This corresponds to the assumption of static expectations in (26).

The difficulties of controlling the cost of long-term investment finance through central bank interest rate policy are illustrated in Figs 16.6a and 16.6b. For example, despite the many successive cuts in the target short-term interest rate of the US Federal Reserve Bank (the Federal funds target rate) undertaken during 2001 in reaction to economic recession, the interest rate on long-term government bonds was much more slow to come down, as shown by Fig. 16.6a. This suggests that market participants expected a quick economic recovery which would induce the Federal Reserve Bank to raise its interest rate again. As another example, even though central banks on both sides of the Atlantic kept their interest rates on hold, the summer of 2008 saw a rise in long-term interest rates in the euro zone as well as in the USA, apparently fuelled by fears that rising inflation rates would provoke central banks to raise future short-term interest rates.

The fact that monetary policy works to a large extent through its impact on market expectations explains why central banks care so much about their communication strategies, and why market analysts scrutinize every statement by central bankers to find hints about future monetary policy. As a former American central banker has put it, '*talking* about (monetary) policy is part of *making* it'.[13] In any given situation, the transmission from a change in the central bank interest rate to the change in long-term market interest rates will depend on market expectations. These in turn will depend on context and historical circumstances.

Another complication for monetary policy is that, in times of financial crisis, it may even be difficult for central banks to control the short-term market rates of interest. This is illustrated by Figs 16.7a and 16.7b. We see that normally there is a very tight link between the central bank interest rates and the three-month market interest rates formed in the interbank markets. But in August 2007, the financial crisis triggered by growing defaults on mortgage loans to 'subprime' (that is, less creditworthy) borrowers in the US housing market drove a highly unusual wedge between short-term market interest rates and the rates at which commercial banks could borrow from the central banks. Via complex securities backed by US mortgage loans, through sophisticated financial derivatives, and via (often

---

13. This saying is due to Alan Blinder, Professor of Economics and former member of the Board of Governors of the US Federal Reserve Bank System.

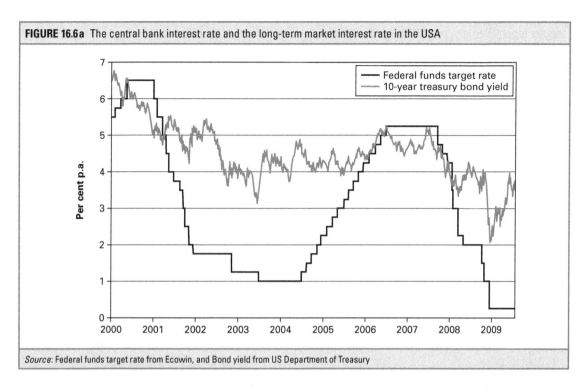

FIGURE 16.6a The central bank interest rate and the long-term market interest rate in the USA

Source: Federal funds target rate from Ecowin, and Bond yield from US Department of Treasury

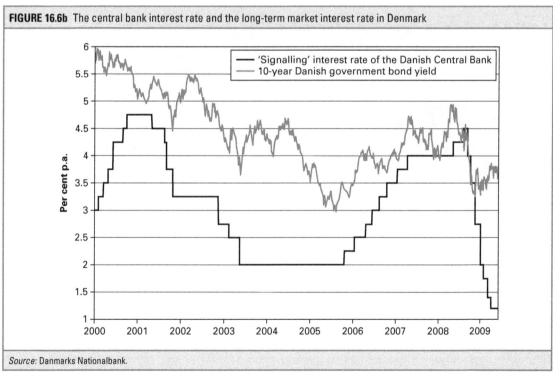

FIGURE 16.6b The central bank interest rate and the long-term market interest rate in Denmark

Source: Danmarks Nationalbank.

implicit) guarantees from one financial institution to another, the risks associated with lending to subprime debtors had been dispersed throughout the international banking system in a way that was hard to dissect. As a result, it became unclear which banks were most exposed to the expected losses created by the crisis, so the risk premium on short-term interbank credit – usually quite close to zero – suddenly rose to a very high and volatile

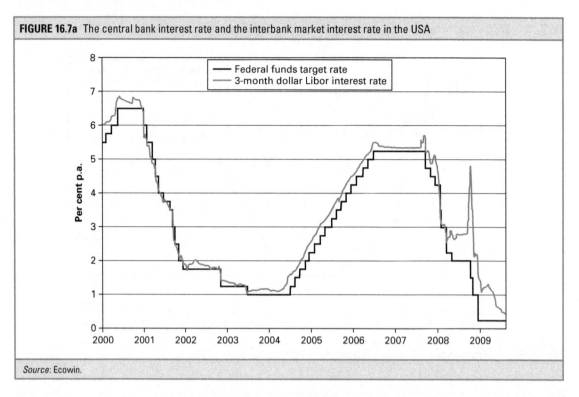

FIGURE 16.7a The central bank interest rate and the interbank market interest rate in the USA

Source: Ecowin.

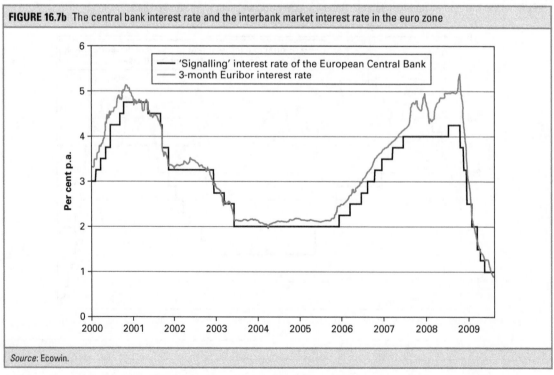

FIGURE 16.7b The central bank interest rate and the interbank market interest rate in the euro zone

Source: Ecowin.

level. In the fall of 2008 the size and volatility of the risk premium rose even further to historically unprecedented levels, following the bankruptcy of the large US investment bank Lehman Brothers in mid-September. In other words, the link between the central bank interest rates and the short-term market interest rates became much looser for an extended period, as shown by Figs 16.7a and 16.7b, and to stem the financial crisis central banks had to resort to unconventional instruments such as direct purchases of private and government securities and the extension of credit to private banks against risky types of collateral they would not normally accept.

If i^p is the official central bank interest rate ('the policy rate') and i is the short-term market interest rate, the recent experience thus suggests that $i = i^p + \rho$, where ρ is a risk premium which is roughly zero in normal times but which could take on a non-negligible and volatile value in times of financial crisis.

In the analysis below we will allow for a fluctuating risk premium in market interest rates, thereby recognizing that the central bank cannot perfectly control the level of interest rates prevailing in private markets. In particular, even in normal times without financial crisis, the market interest rates on longer-term instruments will typically include some risk premium which may change over time. However, for simplicity we will ignore the complication arising from the fact that a change in short-term interest rates engineered by the central bank may fail to affect the expected future short-term rates and hence may not spill over into long-term interest rates. In fact, we will assume that financial investors have static expectations so that $i_t^l = i_t$, in accordance with (26). As the preceding analysis makes clear, this may be a strong simplification at times. Still, it does not matter for the qualitative conclusions in the rest of this book whether or not the long-term interest rate literally moves one-to-one with the official central bank interest rate. The only important thing is that the two rates do tend to move in the same direction (see Exercise 5), and Fig. 16.6 indicates that this is indeed the case when we abstract from the very short-run fluctuations in the long-term rate.

16.4 The aggregate demand curve

The real interest rate: *ex ante* versus *ex post*

We are now ready to derive the relationship between the inflation rate and the aggregate demand for goods and services. This relationship, called the aggregate demand (AD) curve, will be one of the two cornerstones of our model of the macro economy.

The first step in our derivation of the AD curve is the specification of the relationship between the nominal interest rate, the real interest rate and inflation. We have previously used the popular definition according to which the real interest rate is given by $r = i - \pi$, but now we need to be more precise. For a saver or a borrower the actual real interest rate r^a earned or paid between the current period and the next one is given by:

$$1 + r^a \equiv \frac{1+i}{1+\pi_{+1}}. \tag{27}$$

The reasoning behind (27) is this: if the current price level is P, giving up one unit of consumption today will enable you to invest the amount P in the capital market. Your nominal wealth one year from now will then be $P(1 + i)$. With an inflation rate π_{+1} between the current and the next period, a unit of consumption tomorrow will cost you $P(1 + \pi_{+1})$, so the purchasing power of your wealth one year from now will be only $P(1 + i)/P(1 + \pi_{+1}) = (1 + i)/(1 + \pi_{+1})$. Thus your *real* rate of return is $r^a = (1 + i)/(1 + \pi_{+1}) - 1$, which is just another way of writing (27).

The variable r^a is called the *ex post* real interest rate, because it measures the real interest rate implied by the *actual* rate of inflation, measured *after* the relevant time period has passed ('*ex post*'). However, since saving and investment decisions must be made '*ex ante*', *before* the future price level is known with certainty, the real interest rate affecting aggregate demand for goods is the so-called *ex ante* real interest rate (r) which is based on the rate of inflation π_{+1}^e expected to prevail over the next period:

$$1 + r \equiv \frac{1+i}{1+\pi_{+1}^e}. \tag{28}$$

You may easily verify that:

$$r = \frac{i - \pi^e_{+1}}{1 + \pi^e_{+1}} \approx i - \pi^e_{+1}, \tag{29}$$

where the latter approximation holds as long as π^e_{+1} does not deviate too much from zero. In the special case of static inflation expectations where agents assume that the rate of price increase over the next period will correspond to the rate of inflation experienced between the previous and the current period, we have $\pi^e_{+1} = \pi$. It then follows from (29) that the *ex ante* real interest rate may be proxied by $r = i - \pi$, corresponding to the popular definition of the real interest rate. Still, you should keep in mind that the more correct specification of the real interest rate influencing saving and investment decisions is given by (29).

Deriving the aggregate demand curve

Since private demand depends on the *ex ante* real interest rate, it is important for the central bank to have a good estimate of inflation expectations. In many countries consumer and/or business surveys provide an estimate of the rate of inflation expected by the private sector. Several countries also have markets for indexed bonds whose principal and coupon payments are automatically adjusted in accordance with the change in some index of the general price level. For such bonds the interest rate does not have to include an inflation premium to compensate the creditor for the erosion of his real wealth caused by inflation. By comparing the interest rate on indexed bonds to that on conventional non-indexed bonds of similar maturity, one may therefore obtain an estimate of the expected rate of inflation.

In one of these ways the central bank will usually be able to measure the private sector's expected rate of inflation. We will therefore assume that the central bank can observe the expected inflation rate π^e_{+1}. Alternatively, we might assume that the central bank forms its own estimate of the future inflation rate and uses this as a proxy for the private sector's expected inflation rate. If the central bank and the private sector are using the same information, they will arrive at roughly the same value of π^e_{+1}.

Suppose now that the central bank sets its nominal policy interest rate i^p in accordance with the following slightly modified version of the Taylor rule:

$$i^p = \bar{r}^* + \pi^e_{+1} + h(\pi - \pi^*) + b(y - \bar{y}), \qquad h > 0, \qquad b > 0, \tag{30}$$

where $\bar{r}^*$ may be termed the *risk-free* equilibrium real interest rate, since it is the real interest rate on risk-free loans from or to the central bank in a long-run equilibrium where output is at its trend level ($y = \bar{y}$) and inflation is at its target rate ($\pi = \pi^*$). As already suggested, the nominal market interest rate may be specified as $i = i^p + \rho$, where ρ is a risk premium which may fluctuate over time. The real market interest rate affecting private demand is $r = i - \pi^e_{+1} = i^p - \pi^e_{+1} + \rho$, so in a long-run equilibrium where $y = \bar{y}$ and $\pi = \pi^*$ the real market interest rate may be written as

$$\bar{r} = \bar{r}^* + \bar{\rho}, \tag{31}$$

where $\bar{\rho}$ is the average long-run risk premium. Using (30) and (31) and the specifications of i and r, we get

$$r = \bar{r} + h(\pi - \pi^*) + b(y - \bar{y}) + \hat{\rho}, \qquad \hat{\rho} \equiv \rho - \bar{\rho}. \tag{32}$$

The variable $\hat{\rho}$ in (32) captures short-term shocks to market risk premia (deviations from the long-run trend value) such as those observed during the recent international financial crisis. By definition of the trend component $\bar{\rho}$ the value of $\hat{\rho}$ will fluctuate around zero. The size of the variance of ρ determines the degree of precision with which the central bank can control the *ex ante* market real interest rate in the short run via its control of the nominal policy rate i^p. Note that in the realistic case where the central bank does not slavishly follow the Taylor rule, we should include a residual additive 'error term' on the right-hand side of (30). This term would then become absorbed in ρ in (32). In a broader interpretation of our model the variable ρ thus reflects not only shifts in market risk premia, but also monetary policy eviations from the Taylor rule.

We may now insert (32) into the log-linearized version of the goods market equilibrium condition (12) to obtain:

$$y - \bar{y} = \alpha_1(g - \bar{g}) - \alpha_2 \overbrace{[h(\pi - \pi^*) + b(y - \bar{y}) + \rho]}^{r - \bar{r}} + v,$$

which is equivalent to *the aggregate demand curve*:

$$y - \bar{y} = \alpha(\pi^* - \pi) + z, \tag{33}$$

$$\alpha \equiv \frac{\alpha_2 h}{1 + \alpha_2 b} > 0, \qquad z \equiv \frac{v - \alpha_2 \rho + \alpha_1(g - \bar{g})}{1 + \alpha_2 b}. \tag{34}$$

We see from (33) and (34) that *the aggregate demand curve is downward-sloping* in the (y, π) space: a higher rate of inflation is associated with lower aggregate demand for output, as illustrated in Fig. 16.7 where the aggregate demand curve is denoted by AD. The reason for the negative slope is that higher inflation induces monetary policy makers to raise the real interest rate, given that the parameter h in the central bank's reaction function (30) is positive. The higher real interest rate in turn dampens aggregate private demand for goods and services.

Note that for $z = 0$, obtained, e.g., when $g = \bar{g}$ and $v = \rho = 0$, the AD curve passes through $(\bar{y}, \pi^*)$. To identify the determinants of the position and the slope of the AD curve in the (y, π) plane, it is convenient to rearrange (33) as:

$$\pi = \pi^* + (1/\alpha)z - (1/\alpha)(y - \bar{y}). \tag{33a}$$

The variable z on the right-hand side of (33a) captures *aggregate demand shocks*. From the definition of z given in (34) we see that aggregate demand shocks may come from changes in fiscal policy, reflected in g, from changes in private sector confidence affecting the variable v (see the definition of v in (12)), from shifts in risk premia or from changes in monetary policy (deviations from the Taylor rule) influencing the variable ρ. A more expansionary fiscal policy (a rise in g), more optimistic growth expectations in the private sector (a rise in ε) or a drop in market risk premia (a fall in ρ) will shift the aggregate demand curve *upwards* in the (y, π) plane. Given our definitions of v and z in (12) and (34), the value of z will be zero under 'normal' conditions where public spending and private sector growth expectations and risk premia are at their trend levels and monetary policy follows the Taylor rule.

According to (33a) the position of the aggregate demand curve is also affected by the central bank's inflation target π^*. If the central bank becomes more 'hawkish' in fighting inflation (if π^* falls), the aggregate demand curve will shift *downwards.*

Monetary policy influences the *slope* of the aggregate demand curve $(1/\alpha)$ as well as its position. If the central bank puts strong emphasis on fighting inflation and little emphasis on stabilizing output, the parameter h in the Taylor rule will be high, and the parameter b will be low. Since $\alpha \equiv \alpha_2 h/(1 + \alpha_2 b)$, this means that the aggregate demand curve will be flat (α will be high). On the other hand, if monetary policy reacts strongly to the output gap and only weakly to inflation, we have a low value of h and a high value of b, generating a steep aggregate demand curve. These results are illustrated in Fig. 16.8.

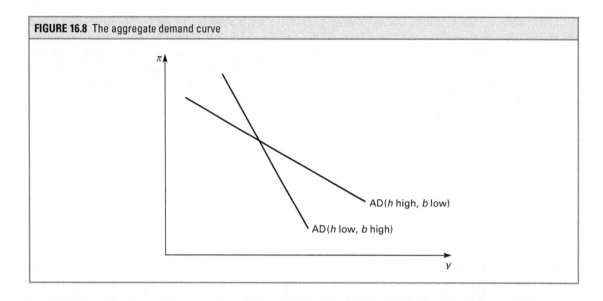

FIGURE 16.8 The aggregate demand curve

THE AGGREGATE DEMAND CURVE

The AD curve shows the relationship between the inflation rate and the aggregate demand for goods and services. The AD curve is derived from the goods market equilibrium condition and the Taylor rule for monetary policy. A rise in the rate of inflation reduces aggregate demand because it induces the central bank to raise the real interest rate, thereby reducing private investment demand and possibly also private consumption. The AD curve shifts upwards in case of a rise in public spending or an increase in the private sector's expected future income growth or a drop in market risk premia.

The aggregate demand curve is one of the two key relationships in our short-run model of the macro economy. To identify the point on the AD curve in which the economy will settle down, we need to bring in the aggregate supply side. This is the topic of the next chapter.

16.5 Summary

1. The aggregate demand curve (the AD curve) is derived by combining the aggregate consumption and investment functions with the goods market equilibrium condition that total output must equal the total demand for output consisting of private consumption, private investment and government demand for goods and services. Goods market equilibrium implies that aggregate saving equals aggregate investment. The AD curve assumes that the private sector savings surplus (savings minus investment) is an increasing function of the real rate of interest. The evidence supports this assumption.

2. Because aggregate demand depends on the real rate of interest, it is crucially influenced by the interest rate policy of the central bank. Historically some central banks have followed Milton Friedman's suggested constant money growth rule, setting the short-term interest rate with the purpose of attaining a steady growth rate of the nominal money supply. More recently, the interest rate policy of many important central banks has tended to follow the rule suggested by John Taylor according to which the central

bank should raise the short-term real interest rate when faced with a rise in the rate of inflation or a rise in output. If the money demand function is stable, the constant money growth rule has similar qualitative implications for central bank interest rate policy as the Taylor rule.

3. The central bank can normally control the short-term interest rate, but not the long-term interest rate. The *expectations hypothesis* states that the long-term interest rate is a simple average of the current and expected future short-term interest rates. If a change in the short-term interest rate has little effect on expected future short-term rates, it will also have little effect on the long-term interest rate. The ability of the central bank to influence the long-term interest rate therefore depends very much on its ability to affect market expectations.

4. The incentive to invest in a real asset depends on the expected cost of finance over the lifetime of the asset. Under debt finance a long-lived asset may be financed by a long-term loan or by a sequence of short-term loans. Risk neutral investors will choose the mode of finance which has the lowest expected cost. When the expectations hypothesis holds, the expected cost of finance is the same whether real investment is financed by equity, by long-term debt, or by a sequence of short-term loans. As a consequence, the ability of the central bank to influence incentives for long-term real investment depends on its ability to influence the long-term interest rate which in turn hinges on its ability to affect market expectations of future short-term rates.

5. When expectations are *static*, the expected future short-term interest rates are equal to the current short-term rate. A change in the current short-term rate will then cause a corresponding change in the long-term interest rate, and the *yield curve* showing the interest rates on bonds with different terms to maturity will be flat. The AD curve is derived on the simplifying assumption that expectations are static so that the central bank can control long-term interest rates through its control over the short-term rate.

6. Because of its empirical relevance, our theory of the aggregate demand curve also assumes that monetary policy follows the Taylor rule which implies that the central bank raises the real interest rate when the rate of inflation goes up. A higher rate of inflation will therefore be accompanied by a fall in aggregate demand, so the AD curve will be downward sloping in (y, π) space. The AD curve will shift down if the central bank lowers its target rate of inflation or if the economy is hit by a negative demand shock, due to a tightening of fiscal policy or a fall in private sector confidence or a rise in market risk premia.

16.6 Exercises

Exercise 1. Topics in the theory of aggregate demand

1. Explain the concepts of the *ex post* real interest rate and the *ex ante* real interest rate. Which of these measures is most relevant as an indicator of the incentive to save and invest? Which of the two measures is most relevant for judging how inflation affects the distribution of income between borrowers and lenders? How are the two measures of the real interest rate related to the popular measure $i_t - \pi_t$?

2. Why does the AD curve slope downwards? Which factors can cause the AD curve to shift? Which factors determine the slope of the AD curve? In particular, explain in economic terms why a higher value of the parameter b in the Taylor rule makes the AD curve steeper.

Exercise 2. Interest rate setting under a constant money growth rule

When we derived the central bank's interest rate reaction function (20) under the constant money growth rule, we assumed for simplicity that there was no growth in trend output. We will now assume instead that trend output grows at the constant rate x so that:

$$\bar{Y} = (1 + x)\bar{Y}_{-1} \quad \Rightarrow \quad \bar{y} \approx \bar{y}_{-1} + x, \quad \bar{y} \equiv \ln \bar{Y}, \quad \bar{y}_{-1} \equiv \ln \bar{Y}_{-1}, \tag{35}$$

where we have used the approximation $\ln(1 + x) \approx x$. Following Section 16.3 and the notation used there, we specify the demand for real money balances as:

$$L = kY^{\eta}e^{-\beta i}. \tag{36}$$

1. Show by means of (35) and (36) that the growth rate of the demand for real money balances in a long-run equilibrium is approximately equal to ηx. (Hint: approximate the growth rate in real money demand by $\ln L - \ln L_{-1}$.) Show that in long-run equilibrium, the rate of inflation will be given by $\pi = \mu - \eta x$, where μ is the constant growth rate of the nominal money supply, defined by $M = (1 + \mu)M_{-1}$. (Hint: you may approximate the growth rate of the real money supply by $\ln(M/P) - \ln(M_{-1}/P_{-1})$ using the fact that $P = (1 + \pi)P_{-1}$.)

   We now invite you to derive an equation showing how the central bank should set the short-term interest rate if it wishes to maintain a constant growth rate μ of the nominal money supply, in accordance with Milton Friedman's recommendation. You may assume that the economy is in long-run equilibrium in the previous period, with a nominal interest rate equal to $i_{-1} = \bar{r} + \mu - \eta X$. Given that the money market clears in every period, we then have:

$$\frac{M/P}{M_{-1}/P_{-1}} \equiv \frac{1 + \mu}{1 + \pi} = \frac{kY^{\eta}e^{-\beta i}}{k\bar{Y}_{-1}^{\eta}e^{-\beta(\bar{r}+\mu-\eta x)}}. \tag{37}$$

2. Use (35) and (37) to show that Friedman's constant money growth rule requires the central bank to set the nominal interest rate (approximately) in accordance with the rule:

$$i = \bar{r} + \pi + \left(\frac{\eta}{\beta}\right)(y - \bar{y}) + \left(\frac{1-\beta}{\beta}\right)[\pi - (\mu - \eta x)]. \tag{38}$$

   (Hint: take logs on both sides of (37) and use the approximation $(1 + \mu)/(1 + \pi) = \mu - \pi$.) Comment on the similarities and differences between (38) and Eq. (20) in the main text.

3. Friedman has argued that the interest sensitivity of money demand (β) is very low (although positive). What does this imply for the evolution over time in the nominal and real interest rate if monetary policy makers follow the constant money growth rule? Do you see any problem in this?

Exercise 3. Nominal GDP targeting

In the main text of this chapter we discussed the constant money growth rule which is intended to ensure a stable evolution of aggregate nominal income. Given this goal, some economists have proposed that the central bank should not focus on the evolution of the nominal money supply as such but rather adopt a target growth rate for nominal GDP. Such a rule would allow real GDP to grow faster when inflation falls and would require real growth to be dampened when inflation rises. In formal terms, if the target growth rate of nominal GDP is μ, the central bank must adjust the interest rate to ensure that:

$$\overbrace{y - y_{-1} + \pi}^{\text{nominal GDP growth}} = \mu, \tag{39}$$

where y is the log of GDP so that $y - y_{-1}$ is the growth rate of real GDP. Ignoring fluctuations in confidence and government spending ($z = 0$), and assuming static inflation expectations so that the *ex ante* real interest rate becomes equal to $i - \pi$, we may write the goods market equilibrium condition as:

$$y - \bar{y} = -\alpha_2 (i - \pi - \bar{r}). \tag{40}$$

Finally, suppose that trend output grows at the constant rate x so that:

$$\bar{y} \approx \bar{y}_{-1} + x. \tag{41}$$

1. Derive the policy rule for interest rate setting under nominal GDP targeting. How does the interest rate react to inflation? How does it react to the lagged output gap $y_{-1} - \bar{y}_{-1}$? Explain in economic terms why and how the parameter α_2 affects the central bank's interest rate response to changes in the rate of inflation and in the lagged output gap.

2. Compare interest rate setting under nominal GDP targeting to interest rate setting under the Taylor rule and under the constant money growth rule. Explain similarities and differences. Do you see any advantages of nominal GDP targeting compared to Friedman's constant money growth rule? Give reasons for your answer.

Exercise 4. Topics in monetary policy

1. Explain and discuss the arguments underlying the constant money growth rule for monetary policy. Explain the similarities and differences between the constant money growth rule and the Taylor rule. What could be the argument for choosing a Taylor rule rather than a constant money growth rule? Is it possible to determine by empirical analysis whether a central bank follows a constant money growth rule or a Taylor rule?

2. Explain the expectations hypothesis of the link between short-term interest rates and long-term interest rates. What is the crucial assumption underlying the expectations hypothesis? Is this assumption reasonable? Discuss the central bank's possibility of controlling long-term interest rates through its control of the short-term interest rate.

3. Discuss why financial market analysts study the official statements of central bankers so carefully and why central bankers seem to be so careful about what they say. Most observers argue that central banks should be as open and transparent about their analysis of the economic situation and their policy intentions as possible, but some argue that complete openness may not be the optimal policy. Try to think of arguments for and against maximum transparency of central banks. (As a source of inspiration, you may want to consult the article 'It's not always good to talk', *The Economist*, 24–30 July 2004, p. 65.)

Exercise 5. Embedding the yield curve and risk premia in the aggregate demand curve

The aggregate demand curve in Eq. (33a) assumes that long-term and short-term market interest rates always move in parallel and that the central bank always strictly follows the Taylor rule. This exercise invites you to analyse how the AD curve may be modified to account for the facts that long-term interest rates do not always move one-to-one with short-term interest rates and that the central bank does not always strictly adhere to a fixed monetary policy rule. We start by restating the term structure equation (25), where we drop the common time subscript t for convenience:

$$i^l = \frac{1}{n}(i + i^e_{+1} + i^e_{+2} + \ldots + i^e_{+n-1}) \tag{42}$$

Now subtract the expected inflation rate π^e_{+1} from both sides of (42) to get:

$$r = \frac{1}{n}(r^s + r^{se}_{+1} + r^{se}_{+2} + \ldots + r^{se}_{+n-1}),$$

(43)

$$r \equiv i^l - \pi^e_{+1}, \qquad r^s \equiv i - \pi^e_{+1}, \qquad r^{se}_{+j} \equiv i^e_{+j} - \pi^e_{+1} \qquad \text{for } 1 \leq j \leq n-1$$

The variable r is the current long-term real interest rate, r^s is the current short-term real interest rate, and r^{se}_{+j} is the expected short-term real interest rate for the future period $t+j$ on the simplifying assumption that the inflation rate is expected to stay constant. To keep things simple, suppose that

$$\begin{aligned} r^{se}_{+j} &= r^s \qquad \text{for } 1 \leq j \leq m-1, \\ r^{se}_{+j} &= \bar{r} \qquad \text{for } m \leq j \leq n-1. \end{aligned}$$

(44)

Thus we assume that the short-term real interest rate is expected to remain at its current level until period m, and that it will return to its long-run equilibrium level $\bar{r}$ from that time onwards. The parameter m indicates how quickly the market expects the economy to return to long-run equilibrium.

1. Suppose $\bar{r} > r^s$. Draw a diagram to illustrate the qualitative properties of the yield curve implied by (43) and (44).

2. Use equations (43) and (44) to show that

$$r = \omega(i - \pi^e_{+1}) + (1-\omega)\bar{r}, \qquad \omega \equiv \frac{m}{n}.$$

(45)

In the following, i^p denotes the official interest rate set by the central bank, while i denotes the current short-term interest rate formed in the interbank market. We assume that

$$i = i^p + \rho,$$

(46)

$$i^p = \bar{r} - \bar{\rho} + \pi^e_{+1} + h(\pi - \pi^*) + b(y - \bar{y}) + d, \qquad \bar{\rho} \equiv E[\rho], \ E[d] = 0.$$

(47)

The variable ρ is a risk premium and $\bar{\rho}$ is its long-run mean value, so $\bar{r} - \bar{\rho}$ is the risk-free equilibrium real interest rate introduced in Section 16.4. The random variable d captures so-called discretionary monetary policy, reflecting that central bankers do not rigidly and mechanically follow a fixed policy rule. However, by restricting the mean value of d to be zero, we assume that 'on average', the central bank does adhere to the Taylor rule.

3. Use (45), (46), (47) plus (12) from the chapter text to derive an AD curve of the same general form as (33) and (34). Specify how the definitions of α and z in (34) change when we incorporate the yield curve, risk premia and discretionary policy in the AD curve.

4. Write down a complete list of the types of shocks that may shift the AD curve derived in Question 3. Explain how the emergence of a risk premium in the interbank market will affect the AD curve. Explain also how a discretionary loosening of monetary policy (that is, a central bank interest rate cut that is not warranted by the Taylor rule) will affect the AD curve.

Inflation, unemployment and aggregate supply

Inflation and unemployment are two of the most important macroeconomic problems. Indeed, the main goals of macroeconomic stabilization policy are to fight cyclical unemployment and to avoid high and unstable inflation. In this chapter we explore the relationship between inflation and unemployment. As we shall see, understanding the link between these two variables is crucial for understanding how the supply side of the economy works in the short run and how the economy reacts to shocks. Therefore, studying the relationship between inflation and unemployment is fundamental for understanding business fluctuations.

17.1 Background: a brief history of the Phillips curve

For many years after the Second World War most economists and policy makers believed that there was an inescapable trade-off between inflation and unemployment: if you want less inflation, you have to live with permanently higher unemployment, and vice versa. Figures 17.1a and 17.1b, taken from a famous article published in 1958 by the New Zealand-born economist A.W. Phillips, suggest why most observers came to believe in a permanent unemployment–inflation trade-off. Figure 17.1a reproduces the curve which Phillips fitted to describe the relationship between unemployment and the rate of money wage inflation in the United Kingdom in the period 1861–1913. We see that he found a clear (although non-linear) negative correlation between the two variables. Phillips then showed that the curve fitted to the 1861–1913 data was able to explain the relationship between UK unemployment and wage inflation in the much later period 1948–57, shown in Fig. 17.1b. Apparently Phillips had discovered a very stable and fundamental trade-off. This trade-off was therefore quickly incorporated into macroeconomic models under the name of the Phillips curve.

As illustrated in Fig. 17.2a which is based on US data on unemployment and the rate of consumer price inflation, the Phillips curve trade-off also seemed to exist throughout most of the 1960s. However, in the 1970s the relationship broke down completely (see Fig. 17.2b). Many times during the 1970s the USA experienced a simultaneous rise in inflation and unemployment, much to the perplexity and frustration of economic policy makers. The same thing happened in practically all OECD countries during that decade. What was going on?

In this chapter we develop a theory of inflation and unemployment which offers an explanation for the apparently stable Phillips curve trade-off before the 1970s as well as the relationship between unemployment and inflation in the more recent decades. Our theory of wage and price formation will be consistent with the theory of structural unemployment

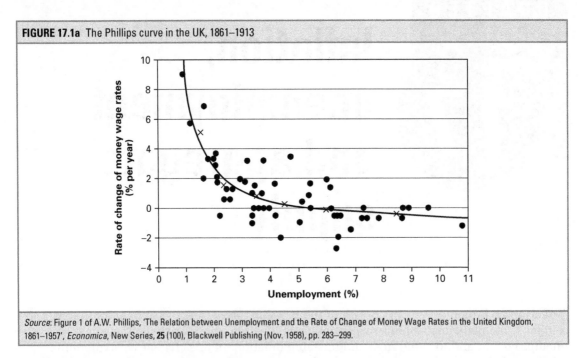

FIGURE 17.1a The Phillips curve in the UK, 1861–1913

Source: Figure 1 of A.W. Phillips, 'The Relation between Unemployment and the Rate of Change of Money Wage Rates in the United Kingdom, 1861–1957', *Economica*, New Series, **25** (100), Blackwell Publishing (Nov. 1958), pp. 283–299.

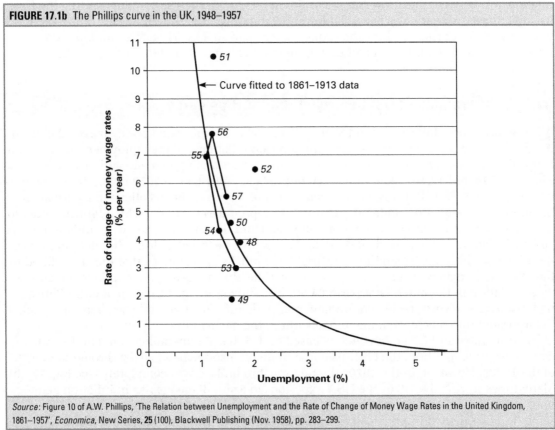

FIGURE 17.1b The Phillips curve in the UK, 1948–1957

Source: Figure 10 of A.W. Phillips, 'The Relation between Unemployment and the Rate of Change of Money Wage Rates in the United Kingdom, 1861–1957', *Economica*, New Series, **25** (100), Blackwell Publishing (Nov. 1958), pp. 283–299.

presented in Part 4. As we shall see, this framework can explain the short-run link between inflation and unemployment as well as the factors determining the long-run equilibrium rate of unemployment, the 'natural' rate. The relationship we shall arrive at is the so-called *expectations-augmented Phillips curve*,

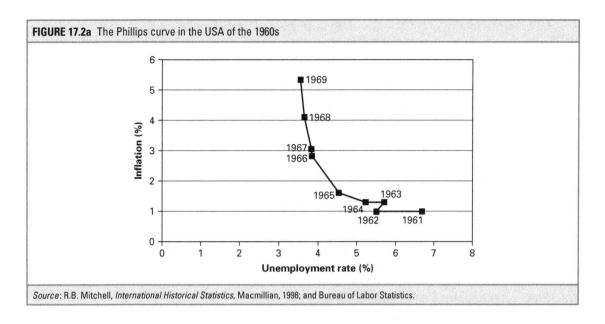

FIGURE 17.2a The Phillips curve in the USA of the 1960s

Source: R.B. Mitchell, *International Historical Statistics*, Macmillian, 1998; and Bureau of Labor Statistics.

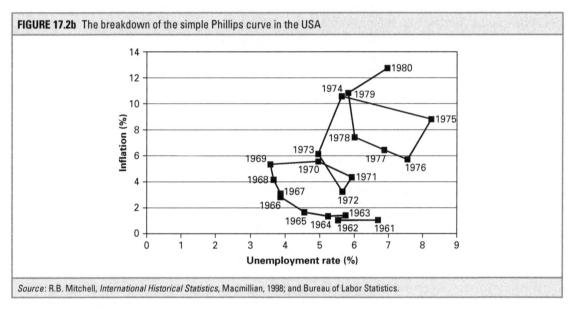

FIGURE 17.2b The breakdown of the simple Phillips curve in the USA

Source: R.B. Mitchell, *International Historical Statistics*, Macmillian, 1998; and Bureau of Labor Statistics.

$$\pi = \pi^e + \alpha(\bar{u} - u), \qquad \alpha > 0, \tag{1}$$

where π is the actual rate of inflation, π^e is the expected inflation rate, u is the actual rate of unemployment, and $\bar{u}$ is the natural unemployment rate.

Many roads lead to the expectations-augmented Phillips curve. This chapter will take you down some of these roads. In Section 17.2 we offer a theory of the expectations-augmented Phillips curve in line with the theory of trade union behaviour introduced in Chapter 12.[1] However, the same qualitative results may be obtained from the theory of efficiency wages presented in Chapter 11, as we shall see in Chapter 23.

---

1. The exposition in this chapter does not assume that you have already studied Chapter 12, so you should still be able to understand all parts of the present chapter even if you have not had the opportunity to go through Book One.

The baseline model of inflation and unemployment presented in Section 17.2 assumes that nominal wages are rigid in the short run. At the end of the section we extend the model to allow for the fact that many nominal prices may also be rigid in the short run. In Section 17.3 we show that the expectations-augmented Phillips curve may also be derived from a model of a competitive labour market with fully flexible wages and prices. By comparing the models in Sections 17.2 and 17.3, we are able to highlight how nominal rigidities exacerbate the employment fluctuations which occur when economic agents underestimate or overestimate the rate of inflation.

17.2 Nominal rigidities, expectational errors and employment fluctuations

Inflation is a continuous rise in the general price level. A theory of inflation therefore requires a theory of price formation. Since prices depend on the cost of inputs, and since labour is the most important input, our theory of price formation will build on a theory of wage formation. The theory will allow for imperfect competition in the markets for goods as well as labour. Introducing imperfect competition in output markets complicates the analysis, but in return it enables us to illustrate how structural changes in product markets affect inflation and the natural rate of unemployment.

In Book One, where we focused on the long run, we assumed that agents had correct expectations about the general level of wages and prices, as must be the case in any long-run equilibrium. By contrast, in the present short-run context we assume that people do not have perfect information about the current general price level. As we shall see, this means that employment and output may deviate from their long-run equilibrium levels.

This section assumes that nominal wages are 'sticky' in the short run, being pre-set by trade unions. We will therefore start with a description of trade union behaviour and wage formation.

The trade union's objective

Consider an economy which is divided into a number of different sectors each producing a differentiated product. Workers in each sector are organized in a trade union which monopolizes the supply of labour to all firms in the sector. Because of its monopoly position, the trade union in each sector may dictate the nominal wage rate to be paid by employers in that sector, but employers have the 'right to manage', that is, they can freely choose the level of employment. For simplicity, we assume that the number of working hours for the individual worker is fixed, so total labour input is proportional to the number of workers employed.

Workers in sector i are educated and trained to work in that particular sector, so they cannot move to another sector to look for a job. If a worker fails to find a job in his sector, he therefore becomes unemployed. His real income will then be equal to the real rate of unemployment benefit b.[2] An employed worker in sector i earns the real wage $w_i \equiv W_i/P$, where W_i is the sectoral money wage and P is (an index of) the general price level, so his *net* income gain from being employed is $w_i - b$. The trade union for sector i cares about this real income gain for its employed members, but it also cares about the total number of jobs L_i secured for the membership. We formalize this by assuming that the union sets the nominal wage rate with the purpose of maximizing a utility function Ω of the form:

---

2. In Chapters 11 and 12 and in Section 1.4, where we focused on the long run, we assumed that workers who fail to find a job in their initial sector have time to retrain so that they can move into other sectors to look for alternative employment opportunities. In that case the expected real income obtainable by a sector i worker who loses his initial job is $v = (1 - u)w + ub$, where u is the general unemployment rate, w is the average real wage outside sector i, and where the employment rate $1 - u$ represents the probability of finding a job outside sector i. In Exercise 1 you are asked to consider such a case with intersectoral labour mobility and to show that this case leads to the expectations-augmented Phillips curve as well.

$$\Omega = (w_i - b)L_i^{\eta}, \qquad \eta > 0. \tag{2}$$

The parameter η reflects the weight which the union attaches to high employment relative to the goal of a high real wage for employed union members. The more the union is concerned about employment relative to wages, the higher is the value of η. In the benchmark case where $\eta = 1$ (corresponding to the cases analysed in Chapters 1 and 12), the union is simply interested in the aggregate net income gain obtained by employed members.

When setting the wage rate, the union must account for the fact that a higher real wage will lower the employer's demand for labour. Our next step is to derive this constraint on the union's optimization problem.

Price setting and labour demand

The representative employer in sector i uses a technology described by the production function:

$$Y_i = BL_i^{1-\alpha}, \qquad 0 < \alpha < 1. \tag{3}$$

where Y_i is the volume of real output produced and sold in sector i, and B is a productivity parameter. Since we are concentrating on the short run where the capital stock is fixed, we have not included capital explicitly in the production function.[3] According to (3), the marginal product of labour, MPL, is:

$$MPL_i \equiv dY_i/dL_i = (1-\alpha)BL_i^{-\alpha}, \tag{4}$$

which is seen to diminish as labour input increases, due to the fixity of the capital stock.

The employer representing industry i produces a differentiated product and therefore has some monopoly power, so we assume that he faces a downward-sloping demand curve of the form:

$$Y_i = \left(\frac{P_i}{P}\right)^{-\sigma} \frac{Y}{n}, \qquad \sigma > 1, \tag{5}$$

This demand curve has a constant numerical price elasticity of demand equal to $\sigma = -(dY_i/dP_i)(P_i/Y_i)$, where P_i is the price charged per unit of Y_i. The variable Y is total GDP, and n is the number of different sectors in the economy. Aggregate output Y is a measure of the total size of the national market, and Y/n is the market share captured by each industry if they all charge the same prices (so that $P_i = P$).[4] The total revenue of firm i is $TR_i \equiv P_iY_i$, so according to (5) its marginal revenue (the increase in total revenue from selling an extra unit of output) will be:

$$MR_i \equiv \frac{dTR_i}{dY_i} = P_i + Y_i\left(\frac{dP_i}{dY_i}\right) = P_i\left(1 + \frac{dP_i}{dY_i}\frac{Y_i}{P_i}\right) = P_i\left(1 - \frac{1}{\sigma}\right). \tag{6}$$

From microeconomic theory we know that a profit-maximizing firm will expand output to the point where marginal revenue equals marginal cost, $MR_i = MC_i$. Because labour is the only variable factor of production, marginal cost is equal to the price of an extra unit of labour – the nominal wage rate, W_i – divided by labour's marginal product, MPL_i, since MPL_i measures the additional units of output produced by an extra unit of labour. Thus $MC_i = W_i/MPL_i$.

---

3. In Book One we worked with the Cobb–Douglas production function $Y = BK^{\alpha}L^{1-\alpha}$. Equation (3) is just a version of this production function where we have fixed the capital stock K at unity.

4. As we mentioned in Chapter 11, the demand curve (5) may be derived from the solution to the consumer's problem of utility maximization if utility functions are of the CES form. In that case the parameter σ is the representative consumer's elasticity of substitution between good i and any other good. See Exercise 3 in Chapter 11.

From (4) and (6), the necessary condition for maximization of profits, $MR_i = MC_i$, therefore becomes:

$$P_i\left(\frac{\sigma - 1}{\sigma}\right) = \frac{W_i}{(1-\alpha)BL_i^{-\alpha}},$$

which is equivalent to:

$$P_i = m^p \overbrace{\left(\frac{W_i}{(1-\alpha)BL_i^{-\alpha}}\right)}^{MC_i}, \qquad m^p \equiv \frac{\sigma}{\sigma - 1} > 1. \tag{7}$$

Equation (7) shows that the profit-maximizing representative firm in sector i will set its price as a mark-up over its marginal cost. Our previous assumption $\sigma > 1$ guarantees that the mark-up factor m^p is positive and greater than one. The price elasticity, σ, is a measure of the strength of product market competition. The higher the elasticity, the greater is the fall in demand induced by a higher price (the flatter is the demand curve), and the lower is the mark-up of price over marginal cost. In the limiting case where the price elasticity tends to infinity, the price is driven down to the level of marginal cost ($\sigma \to \infty \Rightarrow m^p \to 1$), corresponding to perfect competition.

We can now derive the labour demand curve of sector i, showing the relationship between the real wage W_i/P claimed by the union in sector i and the level of employment in that sector. Dividing by P on both sides of (7) gives the relative price, P_i/P, of sector i's product. Inserting this P_i/P into (5) then gives production, Y_i, in sector i. Finally, we can use (3) to compute how much employment, L_i, is needed to produce that level of output. Performing these operations, we end up with:

$$L_i = \left(\frac{Y}{nB}\right)^{\varepsilon/\sigma}\left(\frac{B(1-\alpha)}{m^p}\right)^{\varepsilon}\left(\frac{W_i}{P}\right)^{-\varepsilon}, \qquad \varepsilon \equiv \frac{\sigma}{1+\alpha(\sigma-1)} > 0. \tag{8}$$

The numerical real wage elasticity of labour demand at the sectoral level, defined as $-(dL_i/d(W_i/P))((W_i/P)/L_i)$, is equal to the constant ε. From the expression for ε you may verify that a higher numerical price elasticity of product demand (tougher competition in product markets) increases the wage elasticity of sectoral labour demand. This is intuitive: a rise in the wage rate will drive up the output price by raising the firm's marginal cost. The higher the price elasticity of output demand, the greater is the fall in sales and output, so the greater is the resulting fall in labour demand.

Wage setting

The labour demand curve (8) implies that employment in sector i is a declining function, $L_i(w_i)$, of the real wage, $w_i \equiv W_i/P$. The union's utility function (2) may therefore be written as:

$$\Omega(w_i) = (w_i - b)[L_i(w_i)]^{\eta} \tag{9}$$

Suppose for the moment that the union has perfect information about the current price level so that it may perfectly control the real wage $w_i \equiv W_i/P$ via its control of the money wage W_i. The union will then choose w_i so as to maximize $\Omega(w_i)$. The necessary condition for a maximum, $d\Omega(w_i)/dw_i = 0$, is $L_i^{\eta} + (w_i - b)\eta L_i^{\eta-1}(dL_i/dw_i) = 0$, which is equivalent to:

$$1 + \frac{\eta(w_i - b)}{w_i}\left(\frac{dL_i}{dw_i}\frac{w_i}{L_i}\right) = 0.$$

Using the fact that $(dL_i/dw_i)(w_i/L_i) = -\varepsilon$, we may rewrite this expression as:

$$w_i = m^w \cdot b, \qquad m^w \equiv \frac{\eta}{\eta\varepsilon - 1}. \tag{10}$$

According to (10) the union's target real wage is a mark-up over the opportunity cost of employment. The opportunity cost of employment is the rate of unemployment benefit b, since this is the income a worker forgoes by being employed rather than unemployed. To secure that (10) actually implies a positive real wage, we assume that $\eta\varepsilon > 1$ (note from the definition of ε given in (8) that since $\alpha < 1$, an assumption of $\eta \geq 1$ will indeed imply that $\eta\varepsilon > 1$). It then follows that the wage mark-up factor, m^w, is greater than 1.

Equation (10) implies that the union's real wage claim will be lower the greater the weight it attaches to the goal of high employment, i.e., the higher the value of η. It also follows from (10) that the target real wage will be lower the higher the elasticity of labour demand, ε. The reason is that a higher labour demand elasticity increases the loss of jobs resulting from any given increase in the real wage. Finally, we see from (10) that a higher rate of unemployment benefit drives up the target real wage because it reduces the income loss incurred by those union members who lose their jobs when the union charges a higher wage rate.

We have so far assumed that the union has perfect information about the current price level and therefore perfectly controls the real wage W_i/P through its control of the money wage rate, W_i. However, in practice, nominal wage rates are almost always *pre-set* for a certain period of time, that is, in the short run the nominal wage rate is *rigid*. Moreover, at the start of the period when wages are set, trade union leaders cannot perfectly foresee the price level which will prevail over the period during which the nominal wage rate will be fixed by the wage contract. A trade union setting the wage rate at the start of the current period must therefore base its money wage claim on its *expectation* of the price level which will prevail over the coming period. Given that the union strives to obtain the real wage specified in (10), it will then set the *money* wage rate so as to achieve an *expected* real wage equal to the target real wage m^wb.[5] If the expected price level for the current period is P^e, the nominal wage rate set by the union at the start of the period will thus be:

$$W_i = P^e \cdot m^wb. \tag{11}$$

Having developed a theory of wage and price setting as well as a theory of labour demand, we are now ready to derive the link between inflation and unemployment.

The expectations-augmented Phillips curve

Equation (11) implies that the *actual* real wage may be written as $W_i/P = (P^e/P)m^wb$. Inserting this expression into the labour demand curve (8) and rearranging, we obtain the level of employment in sector i:

$$L_i = \left(\frac{Y}{nB}\right)^{\varepsilon/\sigma} \left(\frac{B(1-\alpha)}{m^p m^w b} \frac{P}{P^e}\right)^{\varepsilon}. \tag{12}$$

The higher the actual price level relative to the expected price level, P/P^e, that is, the more the trade union underestimates the price level, the lower is its nominal wage claim relative

---

5. We assume for simplicity that the union has a correct estimate of the level of b. For example, we may assume that the nominal rate of unemployment benefit is automatically indexed to the current price level so as to protect its real value. The union will then be able to forecast the level of the real rate of unemployment benefit even if it cannot perfectly foresee the price level. In Exercise 1 you are asked to consider the alternative case where the union does not have perfect information about the real value of the nominal rate of unemployment benefit.

to the actual price level, so the lower is the real wage and the higher is the level of sectoral employment, as we see from (12).

We will now show that a similar qualitative relationship between employment and the ratio of actual to expected prices will prevail at the aggregate level. In doing so we will assume that all sectors in the economy are *symmetric* so that output and employment in each sector are given by Eqs (3) and (12), respectively, where all the parameters as well as the ratio P/P^e are the same across sectors. Total employment (L) will then be $L = nL_i$, and total GDP will be $Y = nY_i = nBL_i^{1-\alpha}$. Substituting the latter expression into (12) and computing $L = nL_i$, we get

$$L = nL_i = n \cdot \left(\frac{B(1-\alpha)}{m^p m^w b} \cdot \frac{P}{P^e} \right)^{1/\alpha}, \tag{13}$$

where we have used the definition of ε given in (8) according to which $1 - \varepsilon(1-\alpha)/\sigma = \alpha\varepsilon$. Note that since the real wage $w \equiv W/P$ is the same in all sectors and equal to $(P^e/P)m^w b$, we may also write (13) as:

$$L = n \left(\frac{B(1-\alpha)}{m^p} \right)^{1/\alpha} \left(\frac{W}{P} \right)^{-1/\alpha}. \tag{14}$$

This expression shows that at the *aggregate* level the numerical real wage elasticity of labour demand is $1/\alpha$, whereas at the level of the individual sector we found it to be equal to $\varepsilon = \sigma/[1 + \alpha(\sigma - 1)]$. In Exercise 2 we ask you to provide an intuitive explanation for this difference between the labour demand elasticities at the macro and the micro levels.

In a long-run equilibrium expectations must be fulfilled. Inserting $P^e = P$ into (13), we therefore obtain the long-run equilibrium level of aggregate employment, $\bar{L}$, also called the 'natural' level of employment:

$$\bar{L} = n \left(\frac{B(1-\alpha)}{m^p m^w b} \right)^{1/\alpha}. \tag{15}$$

Equation (15) gives the level of employment which will prevail when price expectations are correct so that trade unions actually obtain their target real wage. Dividing (13) by (15), we get a simple relationship between the actual and the natural level of employment:

$$\frac{L}{\bar{L}} = \left(\frac{P}{P^e} \right)^{1/\alpha}. \tag{16}$$

If the aggregate labour force is N and the unemployment rate is u, it follows by definition that $L \equiv (1-u)N$. Similarly, the 'natural' unemployment rate, $\bar{u}$, is defined by the relationship $\bar{L} \equiv (1-\bar{u})N$. Substitution of these identities into (16) gives $(1-u)/(1-\bar{u}) = (P/P^e)^{1/\alpha}$. Taking natural logarithms on both sides and using the approximations $\ln(1-u) \approx -u$ and $\ln(1-\bar{u}) \approx -\bar{u}$, we get:

$$p = p^e + \alpha(\bar{u} - u), \qquad p \equiv \ln P, \qquad p^e \equiv \ln P^e.$$

Subtracting $p_{-1} \equiv \ln P_{-1}$ on both sides finally gives:

$$\pi = \pi^e + \alpha(\bar{u} - u), \qquad \pi \equiv p - p_{-1}, \qquad \pi^e \equiv p^e - p_{-1}, \tag{17}$$

where the subscript '–1' indicates that the variable in question refers to the previous time period. Recalling that the change in the log of some variable roughly equals the relative change in that variable, it follows that π is the *actual* rate of inflation whereas π^e is the *expected* rate of inflation, assuming that agents know the previous period's price level p_{-1} when they form their expectation about the current price level.

Equation (17) is a key macroeconomic relationship called the *expectations-augmented Phillips curve*,[6] and it provides the link between inflation and unemployment we have been looking for. It shows that for any given *expected* rate of inflation, a lower level of unemployment is associated with a higher *actual* rate of inflation, and vice versa. More precisely, we see from (17) that *unanticipated* inflation ($\pi > \pi^e$) will drive unemployment below its natural rate. The reason is that an unexpected rise in the rate of inflation causes the real value of the pre-set money wage rate to fall below the target real wage of trade unions, thereby inducing firms to expand employment beyond the natural level.

Let us take stock of what we have learned so far:

THE EXPECTATIONS-AUGMENTED PHILLIPS CURVE AND THE NATURAL RATE HYPOTHESIS

According to the expectations-augmented Phillips curve, the actual rate of inflation varies positively and one-to-one with the expected rate of inflation and negatively with the excess of the actual rate of unemployment over the natural rate of unemployment. The natural rate of unemployment is the long-run equilibrium level of unemployment ensuring that actual and expected inflation coincide so that workers obtain their target real wages.

The simple versus the expectations-augmented Phillips curve

If we set the expected inflation rate in (17) equal to 0, we obtain a version of the *simple Phillips curve* presented in Section 17.1, describing the unemployment–inflation trade-off discovered by Phillips:

$$\pi = \alpha(\bar{u} - u). \tag{18}$$

We may now offer an explanation why the simple unemployment–inflation trade-off estimated by Phillips broke down in the USA and elsewhere in the OECD from around 1970. Over the long historical period considered by Phillips – from around 1860 to the 1950s – there was no systematic tendency for prices to rise for extended periods of time, as you can see from Fig. 17.3. Because of this long experience of approximate price stability, it was natural for economic agents to expect prices to be roughly constant. In such circumstances where $\pi^e = 0$, Eq. (17) does indeed predict that a lower unemployment rate will always be associated with a higher inflation rate, and vice versa.

However, towards the end of the 1960s inflation had been systematically positive and gradually rising for several years, so people started to consider a positive inflation rate as a normal state of affairs. As a consequence, the expected inflation rate started to increase. According to (17) this tended to drive up the actual rate of inflation associated with any given level of unemployment, just as portrayed in Fig. 17.2b which showed that many years during the 1970s were characterized by simultaneous increases in inflation and unemployment. There were also other reasons for these developments, such as dramatic increases in the price of oil due to turmoil in the Middle East, but rising inflation expectations probably played an important role in the breakdown of the simple Phillips curve from the end of the 1960s.

The implication of all this is that the simple negative Phillips curve relationship between inflation and unemployment is a *short-run* trade-off which will hold only as long as the

6. The theory of the expectations-augmented Phillips curve was developed almost simultaneously by the US economists Milton Friedman and Edmund Phelps. See Milton Friedman, 'The Role of Monetary Policy', *American Economic Review*, **58**, 1968, pp. 1–17, and Edmund S. Phelps, 'Money-Wage Dynamics and Labor Market Equilibrium', *Journal of Political Economy*, **76**, 1968, pp. 678–711.

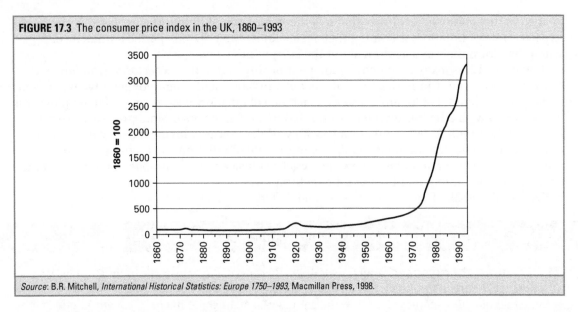

FIGURE 17.3 The consumer price index in the UK, 1860–1993

Source: B.R. Mitchell, *International Historical Statistics: Europe 1750–1993*, Macmillan Press, 1998.

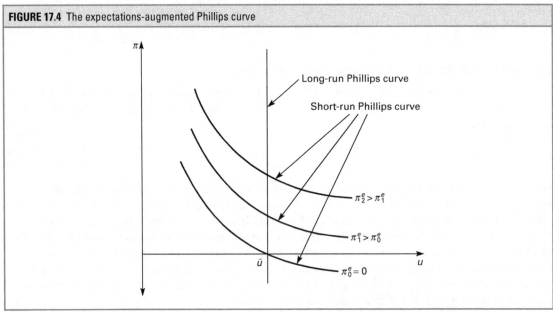

FIGURE 17.4 The expectations-augmented Phillips curve

expected rate of inflation stays constant. For this reason the simple downward-sloping Phillips curve (defined for a given expected rate of inflation) may also be called the *short-run* Phillips curve. Whenever the expected inflation rate π^e increases, the short-run Phillips curve will shift upwards, as illustrated in Fig. 17.4 which shows three different short-run Phillips curves, each corresponding to different levels of expected inflation. In a long-run equilibrium the expected inflation rate equals the actual inflation rate, $\pi^e = \pi$. According to (17) this means that only one unemployment rate – the natural rate $\bar{u}$ – is compatible with long-run equilibrium. We may say that *the long-run Phillips curve is vertical*, passing through $u = \bar{u}$, as indicated in Fig. 17.4. Hence there is no *permanent* trade-off between inflation and unemployment.

Outside long-run equilibrium, the expected inflation rate differs from the actual inflation rate. If such expectational errors persist, it is natural to assume that economic agents will gradually revise their expectations as they observe that their inflation forecasts turn out to be wrong. One simple hypothesis encountered in the previous chapter is that people have *static expectations*, expecting that this period's inflation rate will correspond to the rate of inflation observed during the previous period:

$$\pi^e = \pi_{-1}. \tag{19}$$

This hypothesis means that agents will change their inflation forecasts whenever they observe a change in last period's inflation rate. Substitution of (19) into (17) gives:

$$\Delta \pi \equiv \pi - \pi_{-1} = \alpha(\bar{u} - u), \tag{20}$$

which shows that inflation will *accelerate* when unemployment is *below* its natural rate, and *decelerate* when unemployment is *above* the natural level. To prevent inflation from accelerating (or decelerating), unemployment will thus have to be kept at its natural rate. For this reason the natural rate is sometimes called the 'Non-Accelerating-Inflation-Rate-of-Unemployment', or just the NAIRU, for short.

The feature that inflation will accelerate if unemployment is kept below the natural rate does not depend on the specific assumption of static expectations stated in (19). Accelerating inflation will occur whenever higher actual inflation *eventually* feeds into expected inflation.

Another important implication of the expectations-augmented Phillips curve (17) is that there is *nominal inertia*: if unemployment is at its natural rate, the inflation prevailing today will automatically continue tomorrow because it is built into expectations. To bring down inflation, it is necessary to push the actual unemployment rate above the NAIRU for a while. To recap:

THE SHORT-RUN PHILLIPS CURVE, THE LONG-RUN PHILLIPS CURVE AND THE NAIRU

In the short run where the expected rate of inflation is roughly predetermined, there is a trade-off between inflation and unemployment, described by the short-run Phillips curve. However, when the actual inflation rate deviates from the expected inflation rate, the latter will adjust over time, causing the short-run Phillips curve to shift. If the expected inflation rate varies positively with the actual inflation rates observed in the past, inflation will accelerate (decelerate) whenever actual unemployment is lower (higher) than natural unemployment. Hence a long-run equilibrium with constant inflation can only be established when unemployment is at its natural rate, also referred to as the Non-Accelerating-Inflation-Rate-of-Unemployment (NAIRU). Thus the long-run Phillips curve is vertical.

What determines the natural rate of unemployment?

It is obvious that the natural rate of unemployment plays an important role in our theory of inflation, given that inflation will tend to rise if unemployment is pushed below that level. But what determines the natural rate? Our expression (15) for the natural level of employment provides the key to an answer. Recall that $\bar{L} \equiv (1 - \bar{u})N$. For simplicity, let us set the number of workers in each sector equal to 1 so that the total labour force becomes $N = n$, implying $\bar{L} \equiv (1 - \bar{u})n$. Inserting (15) into this expression and rearranging, we get:

$$\bar{u} = 1 - \left(\frac{B(1-\alpha)}{m^p m^w b} \right)^{1/\alpha}. \tag{21}$$

Equation (21) shows that the natural unemployment rate depends on the level of the real unemployment benefit, b, among other things. It is reasonable to assume that the government allows the rate of unemployment benefit to grow in line with real income per capita, at least over the longer run. From Book One we know that the long-run growth rate of per capita income will equal the growth rate of total factor productivity B. We will therefore assume that the level of unemployment benefits is tied to the level of productivity so that $b = cB$, where $c > 0$ is a parameter reflecting the generosity of the system of unemployment compensation. Substituting cB for b in (21), we get the following expression for the natural rate of unemployment, where we assume that the combination of parameter values ensures a positive value of $\bar{u}$:

$$\bar{u} = 1 - \left(\frac{(1-\alpha)}{m^p m^w c} \right)^{1/\alpha}. \tag{22}$$

According to (22) the natural unemployment rate is higher the higher the mark-ups in wage and price setting, and the more generous the level of unemployment benefits (the higher the value of c). A rise in $m^p = \sigma/(\sigma - 1)$ reflects a fall in the representative firm's numerical price elasticity of demand (σ) which means that it takes a larger cut in the firm's relative price P_i/P to obtain a given increase in sales. To sell the extra output produced by an extra worker, the firm must therefore accept a larger price cut the lower the value of σ. For any given wage level, the profit-maximizing level of employment will thus be lower the lower the value of σ. This is why the natural unemployment rate will be higher the higher the mark-up factor m^p.

A fall in σ will also increase the wage mark-up, since the sectoral labour demand elasticity $\varepsilon \equiv \sigma/[1 + \alpha(\sigma - 1)]$ is increasing in σ, and since $m^w = \eta\varepsilon/(\eta\varepsilon - 1)$ is decreasing in ε. The intuition for this rise in the wage mark-up is that a lower price elasticity of demand for the output of the representative firm reduces the drop in sales and employment occurring when a higher union wage claim drives up the firm's marginal cost and price. Hence it becomes less costly (in terms of jobs lost) for the union to push up the wage rate, and this invites more aggressive wage claims.

The representative firm's price elasticity of demand reflects the degree of competition in product markets. The greater the number of competing firms in each market, and the greater the substitutability of the products of different firms, the tougher competition will be, and the greater will be the price elasticity of demand faced by the individual firm or industry. Thus our analysis shows that a lower degree of competition in product markets (a lower σ) will spill over to the labour market and raise the natural rate of unemployment, partly because it lowers labour demand, and partly because it induces more aggressive wage claims. This is an interesting example of how imperfections in some markets may exacerbate imperfections in other markets.

It is worth noting two more points from (22). First, a greater union concern about employment, reflected in a higher value of the parameter η, will reduce the natural rate of unemployment by lowering the wage mark-up $m^w = \eta\varepsilon/(\eta\varepsilon - 1)$. Second, the level of productivity B does not affect the natural rate of unemployment. This prediction is in line with empirical observations. As illustrated by Fig. 10.1, the unemployment rate tends to fluctuate around a constant level over the very long run despite the fact that productivity is steadily growing over time. However, as we shall see later in this chapter, short-run fluctuations in productivity growth do affect the short-run unemployment–inflation trade-off.

Let us restate these important points:

DETERMINANTS OF THE NATURAL UNEMPLOYMENT RATE

The natural rate of unemployment increases with the mark-ups in wage and price setting and with the replacement rate in the system of unemployment compensation. A greater union concern about employment relative to real wages reduces natural unemployment by reducing the wage mark-up. Stronger competition in product markets, reflected in a higher price elasticity of output demand in each production sector, lowers the natural unemployment rate in two ways. First, it reduces the optimal mark-up of price over marginal cost in the representative firm. Second, it reduces wage mark-ups because a higher elasticity of output demand increases the wage elasticity of labour demand, inducing unions to moderate their wage claims.

TABLE 17.1 The frequency of price changes and the average duration of prices (monthly basis)

Frequency of price changes (%)[1]	Euro area	Denmark
Unprocessed food	28.1	57.5
Processed food	13.0	17.6
Energy	77.8	94.6
Non-energy manufactures	7.4	8.3
Services	5.2	7.3
All products	14.2	17.5
Average duration of all prices[2]	13.0	15.5

[1] Percentage of prices within the product group which undergo a price change at least once a month. 2. Average number of months during which prices are kept unchanged (product groups weighted by HICP weights). Because of different weighting methods, the frequency of price changes for individual product groups do not add up to the overall frequency of price of price changes in the euro area.

Source: Bo William Hansen and Niels Lynggaard Hansen: 'Price Setting Behaviour in Denmark – A Study of CPI Micro Data 1997–2005. *Danish Economic Journal*, **145**, pp. 29–58.

Nominal price rigidity

For simplicity, we have so far assumed that while nominal wages are rigid in the short run, output prices adjust immediately to changes in demand and marginal costs. This is a way of capturing the stylized fact that nominal wages tend to be fixed for longer periods of time than most goods prices. But in reality many output prices are also held constant for considerable periods, as we noted in Chapter 1. In that chapter we also saw that small 'menu costs' of price adjustment – such as the costs of printing new price catalogues and communicating new prices to customers – may make it suboptimal for firms to adjust prices too frequently. Table 17.1 shows the frequency of price changes in Denmark and the euro area for a group of 50 products considered representative of the full expenditure basket of consumers. Wee see that only 14–18 per cent of all products undergo at least one price change every month, and on average prices are kept fixed for 13–16 months. We also see from the table that the frequency of price changes varies a lot across product categories. For example, while almost 78 per cent of the energy products included in the sample undergo price changes every month in the euro area, only about 5 per cent of all services have their prices changed at least once a month.

In this section we show how our model of wage and price formation may be extended to allow for nominal price stickiness. As we shall see, this extension does not alter the *qualitative* properties of the expectations-augmented Phillips curve, but it does change its *quantitative* properties in a potentially important way. To capture the fact that different products are characterized by different degrees of price rigidity, we now assume that firms are divided into a 'flex-price' group and a 'sticky-price' group. For firms in the flex-price group the menu costs of price adjustment are so small that they find it profitable to adjust their prices within each period as their cost conditions change, in the same way as we have so far modelled the price-setting behaviour of firms. By contrast, for firms in the sticky-price group the menu costs are so high that they choose to pre-set their prices at the beginning of each period and to keep their price fixed until the start of the next period, just as we have assumed that nominal wage rates are kept fixed within each period but may change between periods.[7] If ϖ is the fraction of firms belonging to the sticky-price group and these firms set a

---

7. Recall that even though nominal wages are assumed to be fixed within each period, the marginal costs of firms (including firms in the fix-price group) will nevertheless change when their level of output changes, so when menu costs are sufficiently small, firms do have an incentive to adjust their price within each period. However, as we explained in Chapter 1, when there are 'real rigidities', meaning that workers and firms do not wish to change their real (relative) wages and prices very much in response to a change in demand for labour and goods, even rather small menu costs may be sufficient to deter firms from frequent price adjustments.

price P^s for the current period whereas firms in the flex-price group charge an average price of P^f during the period, the average general price level in the current period will be

$$P = \varpi P^s + (1 - \varpi)P^f, \qquad 0 \le \varpi < 1. \tag{23}$$

The production function of firms is still given by (3), and all firms face the same pre-set nominal wage rate given by (11). Flex-price firms adjust their price instantaneously in accordance with (7), whereas fix-price firms must choose their price at the start of the period, before they know what their actual level of output – and hence their marginal cost – will be during the next period. Since the 'normal' or average level of employment and output is given by the natural rate, we assume that fix-price firms set their price at the level that maximizes their profit when their output and employment corresponds to the natural rate. From (7) and (11), fix-price firms will thus set a price equal to

$$P^s = m^p \cdot \overbrace{\frac{W}{\overline{MPL}}}^{=\,W} = \frac{m^p m^w b P^e}{(1-\alpha)B\bar{L}^{-\alpha}} = \frac{m^p m^w c \bar{L}^\alpha P^e}{1-\alpha}, \tag{24}$$

where $\overline{MPL}$ is the marginal productivity of labour at the natural employment level (which determines the marginal cost, $W/\overline{MPL}$, at that level), and where the last equality follows from our earlier assumption that the rate of unemployment benefit $b = cB$. Since flex-price firms adjust their price in accordance with their actual current level of employment, Eqs (7) and (11) imply that $P^f = m^p m^w c L^\alpha P^e/(1 - \alpha)$. Inserting this along with (24) into (23), we get

$$P = \left(\frac{m^p m^w c P^e}{1-\alpha}\right)\left[\varpi \bar{L}^\alpha + (1-\varpi)L^\alpha\right] \quad \Rightarrow$$

$$\frac{P}{P^e} = \left(\frac{m^p m^w c \bar{L}^\alpha}{1-\alpha}\right)\left[\varpi + (1-\varpi)\left(\frac{L}{\bar{L}}\right)^\alpha\right]. \tag{25}$$

The natural employment level may be found from (25) by setting $P = P^e$ and $L = \bar{L}$, yielding

$$\frac{m^p m^w c \bar{L}^\alpha}{1-\alpha} = 1 \quad \Leftrightarrow \quad \bar{L} = \left(\frac{1-\alpha}{m^p m^w c}\right)^{1/\alpha}, \tag{26}$$

which corresponds to (15) with $n = 1$. We now insert (26) into (25) to get

$$\frac{P}{P^e} = \varpi + (1-\varpi)\left(\frac{L}{\bar{L}}\right)^\alpha \tag{27}$$

and take logs on both sides of (27) to find

$$p - p^e = x, \qquad x \equiv \ln[\varpi + (1-\varpi)z^\alpha], \qquad z \equiv L/\bar{L}. \tag{28}$$

Making a first-order Taylor approximation of the auxiliary variable x around the point $z = 1$ (where $\varpi + (1 - \varpi)z^\alpha = 1$ and $x = 0$), we obtain

$$x \approx \alpha(1-\varpi)(z-1) = \alpha(1-\varpi)\left(\frac{L-\bar{L}}{\bar{L}}\right) \approx \alpha(1-\varpi)(\ln L - \ln \bar{L})$$

$$\approx \alpha(1-\varpi)(\bar{u}-u). \tag{29}$$

Combining (28) and (29) and using the approximations $\ln L \equiv \ln(1 - u) \approx -u$ and $\ln \bar{L} \equiv \ln(1 - \bar{u})$ $\approx -\bar{u}$, we finally end up with

$$\pi = \pi^e + \alpha(1 - \varpi)(\bar{u} - u). \tag{30}$$

We see that this equation has exactly the same form as our previous expectations-augmented Phillips curve (17), except that the introduction of nominal price rigidity lowers the slope coefficient on the unemployment gap from α to $\alpha(1 - \varpi)$. This is intuitive: since a fraction ϖ of firms do not change their prices in response to the cost changes generated by a change in activity within the current period, a change in output and employment now has a smaller short-run impact on the general price level. Since $1 - \varpi$ is the fraction of firms that have the opportunity to change their prices within any given period, the average length of the time span during which prices are fixed will be $1/(1 - \varpi)$. The data in Table 17.1 indicate that this time span is around 13 months in the euro area, that is, slightly longer than four quarters, so if the length of the time period in our model is one quarter, a realistic value of ϖ would be 0.75, since $1/(1 - 0.75) = 4$. Obviously such a high value of ϖ has a strong impact on the sensitivity of inflation to the unemployment gap. Hence we may conclude:

NOMINAL PRICE RIGIDITY AND THE PHILLIPS CURVE

Firms in different industries change their prices at different frequencies, presumably reflecting differences in menu costs and market structures. Allowing for a realistic degree of nominal price rigidity by distinguishing between 'flex-price' and 'fix-price' firms does not change the qualitative properties of the expectations-augmented Phillips curve but significantly reduces the slope of the short-run Phillips curve.

17.3 The importance of nominal rigidities for the short-run trade-off between inflation and unemployment

The theory of inflation and unemployment presented above included two elements which are typically used to explain how it is possible for economic activity to deviate from its long-run equilibrium level: expectational errors (erroneous price expectations) and nominal rigidity. We allowed for nominal rigidity by assuming that nominal wage rates and some nominal prices are *pre-set* at the start of each period and do not adjust within the period even if the demand for goods and labour changes. In other words, *within* each period the nominal wage rate and some prices are fixed, although they adjust *between* periods as price expectations and economic activity change.

In this section we will try to deepen your understanding of the importance of expectational errors and nominal rigidity for explaining fluctuations in employment. We will show that while expectational errors are both necessary *and* sufficient to generate deviations of unemployment from its natural rate, nominal rigidity is not necessary but will *amplify* the fluctuations in employment caused by expectational errors. To demonstrate this, we will analyse the response of employment to unanticipated inflation in a model with fully flexible nominal wages and compare this model with the one developed above where nominal wages and some prices are 'sticky' in the short run.

The link between inflation and employment in a competitive labour market: the worker-misperception model

To highlight the role of nominal rigidity, it is instructive to consider the link between inflation and employment which would prevail if the labour market were *perfectly competitive*, that is, if nominal and real wages were fully flexible, adjusting instantaneously to balance labour supply and labour demand.

In a competitive labour market there are no trade unions. Our wage-setting equation (11) specifying union wage claims is therefore replaced by a labour supply curve showing how workers adjust their labour supply in response to changes in the expected real wage. To facilitate comparison with the trade union model considered above, we continue to assume that each employed worker works a fixed number of hours which we may denote by H. Changes in aggregate labour supply will then take the form of more workers entering the labour market or some workers exiting the market. Suppose that worker j requires a minimum real wage w_j to be willing to sacrifice H hours of leisure by taking a job. In that case he will only enter the labour market if the expected real wage, W/P^e, is at least equal to w_j. Suppose further that different workers have different valuations of leisure, with some requiring only a low real wage to be willing to accept a job, while others require a high real wage to be willing to enter the labour market. If there is a continuum of required minimum real wages, the number of workers entering the labour market, L^s, will rise continuously as the expected real wage increases, implying an aggregate labour supply function of the form $L^s = f(W/P^e)$, $f' > 0$. For simplicity, let us assume that the distribution of the taste for leisure across workers (the distribution of required real wages) is such that the function $f(W/P^e)$ has a constant elasticity ϕ with respect to the expected real wage. We then get the aggregate labour supply function:

$$L^s = Z\left(\frac{W}{P^e}\right)^{\phi} = Z\left(w \cdot \frac{P}{P^e}\right)^{\phi}, \qquad Z > 0, \tag{31}$$

where Z is a constant reflecting the size of the population, and where we recall that $w \equiv W/P$ is the *actual* real wage. Equation (31) makes the reasonable assumption that the worker knows his nominal wage rate W when he accepts a job, but he does not have perfect information on the current price level when he makes his labour supply decision, so he must base his decision on his *expectation* of the current price level.

Aggregate labour demand L^d is still given by Eq. (14) which may be written as:

$$L^d = Xw^{-1/\alpha}, \qquad X \equiv n\left(\frac{B(1-\alpha)}{m^p}\right)^{1/\alpha}. \tag{32}$$

In a competitive labour market, the real wage w will adjust to balance supply and demand, $L^s = L^d$, implying:

$$w = \left(\frac{X}{Z}\right)^{1/(\phi+1/\alpha)}\left(\frac{P}{P^e}\right)^{-\phi(\phi+1/\alpha)}. \tag{33}$$

The equilibrium real wage found in Eq. (33) may be inserted into (31) to give the level of employment in the competitive labour market:

$$L = X^{\phi/(\phi+1/\alpha)}Z^{(1/\alpha)/(\phi+1/\alpha)}\left(\frac{P}{P^e}\right)^{(\phi/\alpha)/(\phi+1/\alpha)}. \tag{34}$$

Figure 17.5 illustrates how the equilibrium levels of w and L are determined by the intersection of the aggregate labour supply curve (31) and the aggregate labour demand curve (32). The natural employment level $\bar{L}$ is found at the equilibrium point $\bar{E}$ where price expectations are correct ($P^e = P$) so that the labour supply curve (31) collapses to $L^s = Zw^{\phi}$.

In the equilibrium E_0 employment is above the natural level because workers underestimate the price level ($P > P^e$). Whenever there is a change in the ratio of the actual

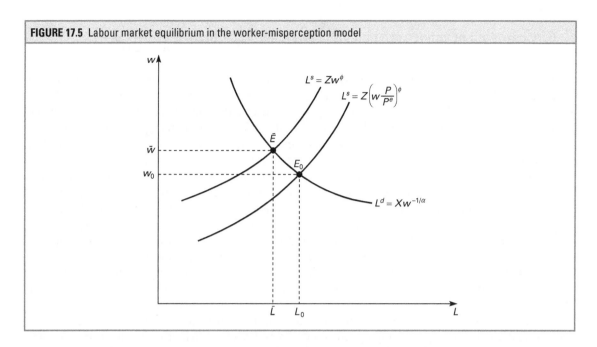

FIGURE 17.5 Labour market equilibrium in the worker-misperception model

to the expected price level, P/P^e, labour supply as a function of the actual real wage will shift, generating new short-run equilibrium levels of the real wage and employment. This model of the labour market is sometimes called 'the worker-misperception model' because it postulates that employment fluctuations are driven by workers' misperceptions of the price level, that is, by fluctuations in P/P^e.

Natural employment may be found from (34) by setting $P^e = P$. We then get:

$$\bar{L} = X^{\phi/(\phi+1/\alpha)} Z^{(1/\alpha)/(\phi+1/\alpha)}. \tag{35}$$

Dividing (34) by (35) gives:

$$\frac{L}{\bar{L}} = \left(\frac{P}{P^e}\right)^{(\phi/\alpha)/(\phi+1/\alpha)}. \tag{36}$$

We see that (36) has exactly the same form as our earlier (16) which was derived from the model with union wage setting. The only difference is that the coefficient $1/\alpha$ has now been replaced by $(\phi/\alpha)/(\phi + 1/\alpha)$. By taking logs on both sides of (36) and using the approximations $\ln(1 - u) \approx -u$ and $\ln(1 - \bar{u}) \approx -\bar{u}$, we can still derive an expectations augmented Phillips curve of the form $\pi = \pi^e + \hat{\alpha}(\bar{u} - u)$, where $\hat{\alpha}$ is a constant. This shows that the expectations-augmented Phillips curve is quite a general relationship which does not assume a particular market structure. But as we shall demonstrate below, it is quite important for the *quantitative* relationship between employment and unanticipated inflation whether nominal wages and prices are fully flexible or not.

The role of expectational errors and nominal rigidities

To see how unanticipated inflation affects employment in the competitive labour market and in the economy with nominal wage and price stickiness, we may rewrite (36) and (30) in the following way, using the usual definitions and approximations:

Economy with flexible nominal wages and prices: $\ln L - \ln \bar{L} = \left(\dfrac{1/\alpha}{1 + 1/\alpha\phi}\right)(\pi - \pi^e),$ (37)

Economy with nominal wage and price rigidities: $\ln L - \ln \bar{L} = \left(\dfrac{1}{\alpha(1-\varpi)}\right)(\pi - \pi^e).$ (38)

Since $(1/\alpha)/(1 + 1/\alpha\phi) < 1/\alpha(1 - \varpi)$, these equations show that for any given amount of unanticipated inflation, $\pi - \pi^e$, the percentage deviation of employment from its natural level, $\ln L - \ln \bar{L}$, will be smaller in the flex-price economy than in the economy with nominal rigidities: when nominal wages and prices only adjust slowly to a change in demand for goods and labour, it takes a larger change in economic activity to generate a given amount of (surprise) inflation than when nominal wages and prices are fully flexible.

To get a feel for the quantitative importance of nominal rigidities, recall from Book One that our production function parameter α may be estimated from the observed labour income share of GDP which is typically around 2/3.[8] The wage elasticity of the individual labour supply of voluntarily employed workers (ϕ) is usually estimated to be quite low, often around 0.2 as an average across males and females. Finally, we saw in the previous section that a realistic value of ϖ would be roughly 0.75 when the length of the time period is one quarter. With these parameter values, it follows from (37) that the elasticity of employment with respect to unanticipated inflation – given by the coefficient $(1/\alpha)/(1 + 1/\alpha\phi)$ – will be around 0.18 in the economy with fully flexible prices, whereas (38) implies that this same elasticity will be $1/\alpha(1 - \varpi) = 6$ in an imperfectly competitive economy with nominal rigidities. In other words, to achieve a one percentage point uanticipated drop in prices over the course of one quarter would require a dramatic 6 per cent drop in employment in our model economy with nominal rigidities, whereas it would only require a 0.18 per cent fall in employment in the flexible economy with a competitive labour market. This example suggests that short-run nominal rigidities can have a strong impact on the short-run volatility of employment.

We may sum up the insights from equations (37) and (38) as follows:

EMPLOYMENT FLUCTUATIONS, EXPECTATIONAL ERRORS AND NOMINAL RIGIDITIES

In competitive as well as non-competitive markets, expectational errors $(\pi \neq \pi^e)$ are both necessary and sufficient to cause deviations between the actual and the natural level of employment. Hence it is not necessary to assume nominal rigidities to explain why employment sometimes deviates from its trend level. However, once expectational errors occur, nominal rigidities will strongly amplify the resulting fluctuations in employment.

17.4 Supply shocks

Our expectations-augmented Phillips curve (17) postulates a strict deterministic relation between the unemployment rate u and the amount of unanticipated inflation $\pi - \pi^e$. In this section we shall see that the link between these two variables is not really that tight. The reason is that the labour market is frequently hit by shocks which generate 'noise' in the relationship between unemployment and inflation. These so-called supply shocks may take the form of short-run fluctuations in our parameters m^p, m^w and B around their long-run trend levels. Below we will extend our model of unemployment and inflation to account for supply shocks.

In Section 17.2 we assumed that the rate of unemployment benefit is tied to the level of B (since productivity determines long-run income per capita). In that case we should observe

---

8. Actually the equality between the labour income share and α only holds when competition in product markets is perfect. With imperfect competition in product markets, profit maximization implies that the labour income share will be lower than α. We ignore this complication here since assuming a somewhat lower value of α would not affect our conclusion that nominal rigidities are quantitatively very important for understanding short-run employment fluctuations.

substantial short-run fluctuations in unemployment benefits as B oscillates around its long-run growth trend. However, in practice, benefits do not move up and down in this way. It is reasonable to assume that benefits are instead linked to the underlying *trend* level of productivity, denoted by $\bar{B}$, which evolves gradually and smoothly over time. This is equivalent to assuming that benefits are allowed to rise in line with the underlying trend growth in per-capita income.

The magnitude $m^w b$ in the denominator on the right-hand side of (13) is the representative trade union's target real wage. Given our new assumption that $b = c\bar{B}$, the target real wage becomes $m^w c\bar{B}$. Inserting this in (13), we find that the actual level of employment is given by:

$$L = n \cdot \left(\frac{B(1-\alpha)}{m^p m^w c\bar{B}} \cdot \frac{P}{P^e} \right)^{1/\alpha}. \tag{39}$$

Our next step is to redefine the natural level of employment. Specifically, we now define natural employment as the level of employment which will prevail when expectations are fulfilled *and* when productivity as well as the wage and price mark-ups are all at their 'normal' long-run trend levels. Denoting the normal mark-ups by $\bar{m}^p$ and $\bar{m}^w$ and remembering that $b = c\bar{B}$, it follows that the natural employment level previously stated in (15) now modifies to:

$$\bar{L} = n \cdot \left(\frac{1-\alpha}{\bar{m}^p \cdot \bar{m}^w \cdot c} \right)^{1/\alpha}. \tag{40}$$

Dividing (39) by (40) and using the facts that $L \equiv (1 - u)N$ and $\bar{L} \equiv (1 - \bar{u})N$, we get:[9]

$$\frac{1-u}{1-\bar{u}} = \left(\frac{B \cdot \bar{m}^p \cdot \bar{m}^w}{\bar{B} m^p m^w} \cdot \frac{P}{P^e} \right)^{1/\alpha}. \tag{41}$$

Taking logs on both sides of (41) and using the approximations $\ln(1 - u) \approx -u$ and $\ln(1 - \bar{u}) \approx -\bar{u}$ plus the definitions $\pi \equiv \ln P - \ln P_{-1}$ and $\pi^e \equiv \ln P^e - \ln P_{-1}$, we end up with:

$$\pi = \pi^e + \alpha(\bar{u} - u) + \tilde{s}, \qquad \tilde{s} \equiv \ln\left(\frac{m^p}{\bar{m}^p}\right) + \ln\left(\frac{m^w}{\bar{m}^w}\right) - \ln\left(\frac{B}{\bar{B}}\right). \tag{42}$$

Equation (42) is an expectations-augmented Phillips curve, extended to allow for supply shocks. The specification of the supply shock variable, $\tilde{s}$, shows that a positive shock to inflation occurs if the wage mark-up or the price mark-up rises above its normal level, whereas a negative shock to inflation occurs if productivity rises above its trend level. By construction, $\tilde{s}$ will fluctuate around a mean value of 0, since $\bar{m}^p$ and $\bar{m}^w$ are the average values of m^p and m^w, respectively, and since B is on average on its trend growth path $\bar{B}$.

We are now ready to confront our theory of inflation and unemployment with some data.

17.5 Testing the Phillips curve theory

Does the Phillips curve theory fit the data?

If we insert our earlier assumption of static inflation expectations, $\pi^e = \pi_{-1}$, into (42), we obtain an equation of the form

---

9. For simplicity, we do not distinguish between the current labour force N and its trend level $\bar{N}$, implicitly assuming $N = \bar{N}$. In Chapter 13 we saw that the cyclical fluctuations in the labour force tend to be modest.

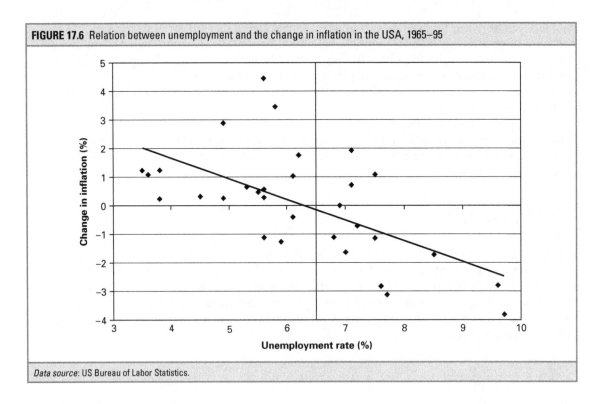

FIGURE 17.6 Relation between unemployment and the change in inflation in the USA, 1965–95

Data source: US Bureau of Labor Statistics.

$$\Delta \pi = a_0 - a_1 u + \tilde{s}, \qquad E[\tilde{s}] = 0, \tag{43}$$

where a_0 and a_1 are positive constants, and $E[\cdot]$ is the expectations operator. Thus our theory implies that the *change* in the rate of inflation should be negatively related to the rate of unemployment. If we have data for inflation and unemployment, we can use the econometric techniques described in the Appendix to estimate the magnitude of the parameters a_0 and a_1. In this way we can check whether the estimated parameter values have the 'correct' positive sign expected from theory, and we can test whether they are significantly different from zero in a statistical sense.

Figure 17.6 shows observations of the unemployment rate and the annual change in the rate of consumer price inflation in the USA in the period 1965–95. The downward-sloping straight line in the figure is a regression line indicating the 'average' relationship between unemployment and the change in inflation. The regression line has the following quantitative properties, where the figures in brackets indicate the standard errors of the estimated coefficients, and where R^2 is the so-called coefficient of determination measuring the share of the variation in $\Delta \pi$ which is explained by our estimated regression line:

$$\Delta \pi = \underset{(se=1.121)}{4.54} - \underset{(se=0.175)}{0.723} \cdot u, \qquad R^2 = 0.37. \tag{44}$$

The coefficients in (44) do indeed have the signs we would expect from theory. They are also significantly different from 0 in a statistical sense.[10] Figure 17.6 shows a fairly clear tendency for inflation to fall as unemployment goes up.

Note that the estimated coefficients in (44) enable us to offer an estimate of the natural rate of unemployment in the USA. According to (42) and (43) we have $\Delta \pi = \alpha(\bar{u} - u) = a_0 - a_1 u$ if

---

10. As a rule of thumb, the estimated coefficient should be numerically at least twice as big as its standard deviation to be statistically significant. This condition is easily met in our estimated equation (44). For the benefit of readers who are familiar with regression analysis, the value of the Durbin–Watson statistic is 1.515 which indicates that there are no serious problems of autocorrelation in our regression.

we set $\tilde{s}$ equal to its mean value of 0. Since $\Delta\pi = 0$ when $\bar{u} = u$, it follows that $\bar{u} = a_0/a_1$. Inserting the estimated parameter values from (44), we find that $\bar{u} = 4.54/0.723 \approx 6.3$. This implies that the natural unemployment rate in the USA averaged around 6.3 per cent in the estimation period 1965–95.

In summary, the theory of the expectations-augmented Phillips curve seems roughly consistent with the US data up until the mid-1990s. At the same time we also see that the observed change in inflation has often deviated quite a lot from the estimated regression line. Indeed, the value of R^2 suggests that variations in unemployment can only explain about 37 per cent of the variation in the annual change in the rate of inflation. According to our theory, the rest of the variation must be accounted for by the exogenous shocks incorporated in our supply shock variable $\tilde{s}$.

Given the strong simplifying assumptions we have made, it is not really surprising that our regression equation leaves a lot of the variation in inflation unexplained. Our assumption that inflation expectations are static is rather mechanical. For example, in periods where the fiscal or monetary authorities announce a significant change in economic policies, the private sector may have good reasons to believe that tomorrow's inflation rate will not simply equal the current rate of inflation.[11] As another example, our simple production function (3) abstracts from the fact that production requires inputs of raw materials as well as labour input. Hence our Phillips curve does not capture changes in inflation which are driven by changes in the international price of important raw materials such as oil.

Productivity growth, the Phillips curve and the 'New Economy'

Despite these weaknesses, the important message from Eq. (44) is that there seems to be a systematic and statistically highly significant negative relationship between the *level* of unemployment and the *change* in the rate of inflation. However, in the second half of the 1990s many observers began to question this relationship. The reason was the remarkable performance of the US economy during that period. As you can see from Fig. 17.7, having been located to the far northeast of the unemployment–inflation scatter diagram, during the 1990s the short-run Phillips curve seemed to shift almost all the way back to the favourable position it had occupied in the 1960s.

Apparently this shift was not a simple consequence of a fall in expected inflation generated by the observed fall in actual inflation since the early 1980s. This point is illustrated in Fig. 17.8. The figure compares the actual inflation rate with the rate of inflation predicted from our Phillips curve, (44), which was estimated from data for 1965–95. We see that from 1996 and onwards, the rate of inflation predicted from the historical link between unemployment and inflation systematically overshoots the actual inflation rate. For example, based on the behaviour observed during the 1965–95 period, one would have expected to see a US inflation rate of 8.5 per cent in 2000, but the actual inflation rate remained subdued at a level of 3.3 per cent, despite the low rate of unemployment. In other words, it seemed that a *structural shift* took place in the US economy around the mid-1990s, causing a breakdown of the expectations-augmented Phillips curve which had fitted the data reasonably well up until 1995.

At the same time as unemployment fell without driving up the rate of inflation, the growth rate of US labour productivity started to pick up. This is shown in Fig. 17.9. As indicated by the horizontal lines, the average growth rate of labour productivity during the period of the prolonged productivity slowdown from 1974 to 1995 was only 1.35 per cent per year, whereas the average productivity growth rate rose to 2.42 per cent per year during 1996–2001.

Impressed by these developments, many commentators argued that a 'New Economy' had arrived which did not obey the 'old rules of the game'. Some participants in the economic policy debate even claimed that it was time to scrap the established macroeconomic theory

---

11. In Chapter 21 we shall discuss the formation of private sector expectations in more detail.

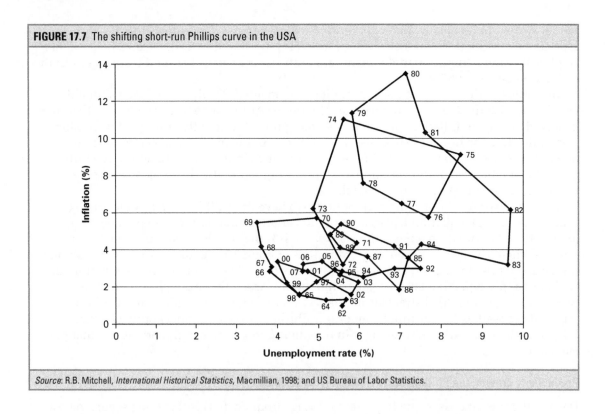

FIGURE 17.7 The shifting short-run Phillips curve in the USA

Source: R.B. Mitchell, *International Historical Statistics*, Macmillian, 1998; and US Bureau of Labor Statistics.

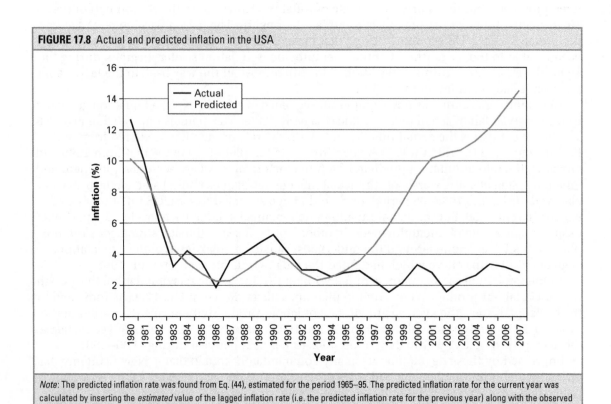

FIGURE 17.8 Actual and predicted inflation in the USA

Note: The predicted inflation rate was found from Eq. (44), estimated for the period 1965–95. The predicted inflation rate for the current year was calculated by inserting the *estimated* value of the lagged inflation rate (i.e. the predicted inflation rate for the previous year) along with the observed value of the unemployment rate into (44).

Data source: US Bureau of Labor Statistics.

FIGURE 17.9 Annual growth rate of labour productivity in the USA

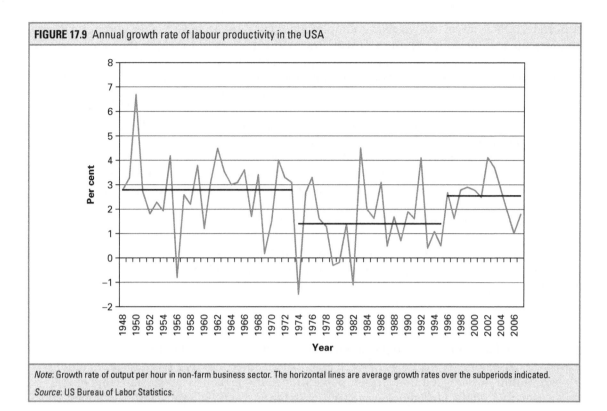

Note: Growth rate of output per hour in non-farm business sector. The horizontal lines are average growth rates over the subperiods indicated.

Source: US Bureau of Labor Statistics.

which apparently could no longer explain what was going on. However, we will now show that a slightly extended version of the expectations-augmented Phillips curve which allows for the impact of productivity growth may explain the recent behaviour of the US inflation rate. This extension will also provide an opportunity to illustrate yet another way in which the expectations-augmented Phillips curve may be derived.

For simplicity, let us consider the special case of the production function (3) where $\alpha = 0$ so that output is given by the linear technology $Y = BL$. With $\alpha = 0$ it follows from (7) that the price charged by the representative firm will be $P = m^p(W/B)$. Taking logs on both sides of this equation, computing first differences, and defining $w^n \equiv \ln W$, we get

$$\pi = \Delta w^n - g, \qquad \Delta w^n \equiv w^n - w^n_{-1}, \qquad g \equiv \ln B - \ln B_{-1}, \tag{45}$$

where Δw^n is the rate of wage inflation and g is the rate of growth of output per working hour, that is, the growth rate of labour productivity. In deriving (45), we have made the simplifying assumption that the price mark-up m^p is constant over time. With a linear technology, we then see that the rate of price inflation is simply the difference between the rate of wage inflation and the growth rate of labour productivity.

From (11) and the assumption $b = cB$ we have $W = P^e m^w cB$. Taking log-differences of this equation and treating m^w and c as constants, the theory of wage setting presented in Section 17.2 then implies that

$$\Delta w^n = \pi^e + g. \tag{46}$$

This simple wage equation has two key properties. First, the rate of wage increase does not depend on the level of unemployment. This property is due to the assumption in Section 17.2 that workers are not mobile across production sectors. But if workers can actually move between sectors in their search for jobs, we know from Chapters 11 and 12 that wage setters will reduce their target real wage if unemployment goes up, because higher unemployment reduces the earnings opportunities of workers outside the sector to which they are currently attached. The second property of the wage equation (46) is that the target rate of real wage growth $\Delta w^n - \pi^e$ adjusts immediately and one-to-one to the current rate of productivity growth g. In that case we see from (45) and (46) that changes in the rate of productivity growth cannot affect the rate of inflation, since the cost-reducing effect of higher productivity will be exactly offset by higher wage claims. However, in practice it may be that the target rate of real wage growth depends not only on current productivity growth, but also on the rate of real wage growth g^n that workers consider to be 'normal' or 'fair'.

Based on these observations, we will discard (46) and assume instead that wage setters set the rate of wage inflation so as to achieve a target rate of real wage growth equal to

$$\Delta w^n - \pi^e = a_0 - a_1 u + \eta g^n + (1 - \eta)g, \qquad 0 \leq \eta \leq 1, \tag{47}$$

where a_0 and a_1 are positive constants. Note that $a_1 > 0$ implies that wage setters moderate their wage claims when unemployment goes up. Substituting (47) into the first equation in (45), we get

$$\pi = \pi^e + a_1(\bar{u} - u) - \eta(g - g^n), \qquad \bar{u} \equiv a_0/a_1. \tag{48}$$

For $\eta = 0$ Eq. (48) boils down to the standard expectations-augmented Phillips curve (17). However, based on various types of evidence, American economists Laurence Ball and Robert Moffitt have argued that worker perceptions of what constitutes a 'fair' rate of real wage growth do in fact influence wage setting so that $\eta > 0$.[12] Ball and Moffitt assume that this 'aspiration' real wage increase adjusts gradually over time in response to the *actual* rate of real wage growth g^w_{-1} experienced during the previous period, that is:[13]

$$g^n = \beta g^n_{-1} + (1 - \beta)g^w_{-1}, \qquad 0 < \beta < 1. \tag{49}$$

In a long-run equilibrium, real wages must grow in line with productivity since labour's share of national income will otherwise change systematically over time. A long-run equilibrium also requires that g^n be constant over time. From (49) this implies $g^n_{-1} = g^w_{-1} = g$ in long-run equilibrium. Hence the variable $\bar{u}$ in (48) is the natural unemployment rate that will prevail in a long-run equilibrium where expectations are fulfilled, where actual real wage growth coincides with the aspiration real wage growth, and where labour's share is constant.

According to Ball and Moffitt, norms regarding the 'fair' rate of real wage growth are likely to change rather slowly, implying a value of the β-parameter not far below one. Assuming that $\beta = 0.95$ and applying annual US data on real wage growth and labour productivity growth for the period 1948–2007, we have used (49) to construct a time series for the explanatory variable $g - g^n$ appearing in (48).[14] Our estimates for this variable are displayed in Fig. 17.10 where we have applied the HP-filter to illustrate the underlying trend.

---

12. Laurence Ball and Robert Moffitt, 'Productivity Growth and the Phillips Curve', National Bureau of Economic Research, NBER Working Paper 8421, August 2001.

13. As you may verify by successive substitutions, the adjustment equation (49) implies that

$$g^n = \frac{1 - \beta}{\beta} \sum_{i=1}^{\infty} \beta^i g^w_{-i}.$$

In other words, the aspiration real wage increase is a weighted average of the historical rates of real wage growth, with geometrically declining weights for observations further back in the past so that more weight is put on the more recent experience.

14. Following Ball and Moffitt (2001), we have assumed that the value of g^n at the start of the observation period (1948) was equal to the trend rate of real wage growth for that year. Like Ball and Moffitt, we also adjusted the observed rates of labour productivity growth for the impact of cyclical variations in working hours. Fortunately our estimation results are not very sensitive to these specific procedures.

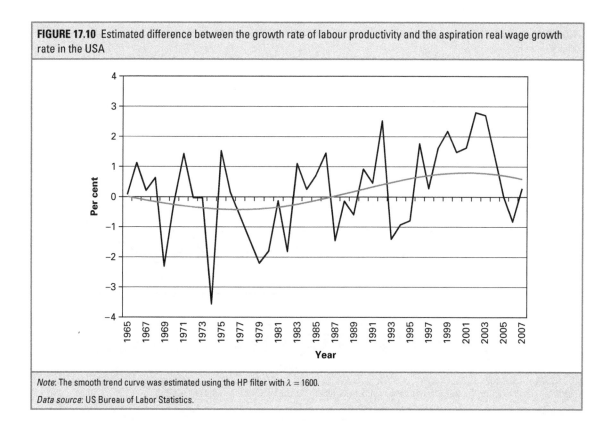

FIGURE 17.10 Estimated difference between the growth rate of labour productivity and the aspiration real wage growth rate in the USA

Note: The smooth trend curve was estimated using the HP filter with $\lambda = 1600$.

Data source: US Bureau of Labor Statistics.

Fig. 17.10 helps to explain why the US inflation rate has remained subdued in recent years: from the mid-1990s when productivity growth accelerated after a long period of slow growth, the aspiration real wage growth has tended to lag substantially behind the productivity growth rate, as workers had become accustomed to a rather low average rate of real wage growth. As a consequence, the term $g - g^n$ in the extended expectations-augmented Phillips curve (48) has tended to pull the inflation rate down over the past decade, provided the parameter η is indeed positive. To test whether this is in fact the case, let us maintain our previous assumption that $\pi^e = \pi_{-1}$ so that (48) yields a regression equation of the form

$$\Delta \pi = a_0 - a_1 u - \eta(g - g^n) + \tilde{s}, \qquad E[\tilde{s}] = 0, \tag{50}$$

where $\tilde{s}$ captures supply shocks other than those stemming from changes in productivity. Estimating (50) on our annual US data for the two periods 1965–95 and 1965–2007, using the constructed data for $g - g^n$ shown in Fig. 17.10, we obtain the following regression results, with standard errors indicated in brackets below the coefficients:

$$1965 - 95: \qquad \Delta \pi = \underset{(se=0.977)}{3.983} - \underset{(se=0.152)}{0.656} \cdot u - \underset{(se=0.180)}{0.608} \cdot (g - g^n), \qquad R^2 = 0.552, \tag{51}$$

$$1965 - 2007: \qquad \Delta \pi = \underset{(se=0.768)}{3.709} - \underset{(se=0.127)}{0.612} \cdot u - \underset{(se=0.132)}{0.483} \cdot (g - g^n), \qquad R^2 = 0.465. \tag{52}$$

Since the estimated coefficients on $g - g^n$ are far greater than their standard errors, this explanatory variable is clearly statistically significant, consistent with the hypothesis that wage formation is influenced by fairness norms. Measured by R^2, we also see that the extended version of the expectations-augmented Phillips curve in (51) has considerably more explanatory power than the standard version stated in (44). This is illustrated in

FIGURE 17.11 Actual US inflation and the inflation rate predicted by the extended version of the expectations-augmented Phillips curve

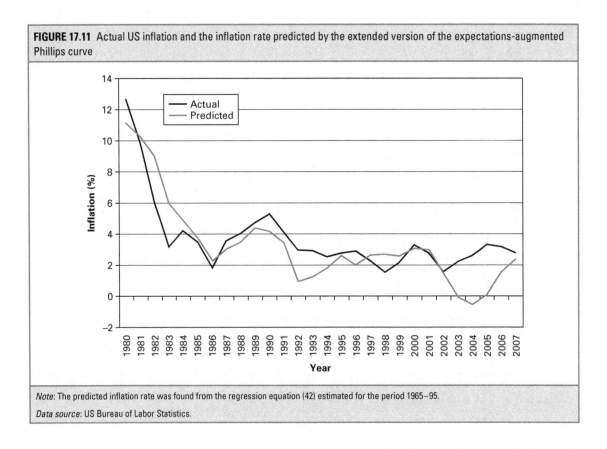

Note: The predicted inflation rate was found from the regression equation (42) estimated for the period 1965–95.

Data source: US Bureau of Labor Statistics.

Fig. 17.11 where we have used (51) to predict the inflation rate for the current year by plugging in the observed values of u and $g - g^n$ for the current year along with the estimated inflation rate for the previous year. Comparing Figs 17.8 and 17.11, we see that the extended version of the expectations-augmented Phillips curve produces much smaller forecast errors after 1995 than the standard version.

We may sum up these empirical findings as follows:

THE EMPIRICAL PERFORMANCE OF THE EXPECTATIONS-AUGMENTED PHILLIPS CURVE

The standard version of the expectations-augmented Phillips curve offers a reasonable description of the average relationship between inflation and unemployment in the USA from the mid-1960s until the mid-1990s, but since then it has predicted a much higher inflation rate than actually observed. An extended version of the expectations-augmented Phillips curve assumes that target real wage growth depends to a large extent on historical real wage growth. According to this theory, the short-run inflation-unemployment trade-off will improve during a period of accelerating productivity growth. This extended version of the expectations-augmented Phillips curve provides a fairly good fit of the US data on inflation and unemployment for the entire period 1965–2007.

While the extended version of the expectations-augmented Phillips curve performs better empirically than the standard version, it also complicates any theoretical macroeconomic analysis because it implies a complex and drawn-out pattern of inflation adjustment over time. To keep things simple we will therefore work with the standard version of the expectations-augmented Phillips curve in the rest of this book. Implicitly we are thereby assuming that the underlying trend rate of productivity growth is roughly constant, since in this case the standard and the extended versions of the expectations-augmented Phillips curve become identical, once real wage aspirations have adjusted to the constant rate of productivity growth.

17.6 The aggregate supply curve

Our theory of aggregate demand presented in Chapter 16 implied a systematic link between the output gap (the percentage deviation of output from trend) and the rate of inflation. We shall now show that our theory of inflation and unemployment implies another systematic link between these two variables.

Recall that in a symmetric general equilibrium, total GDP is $Y = nY_i$, and total employment is $L = nL_i$. From (3) we then have:

$$Y = nB\left(\frac{L}{n}\right)^{1-\alpha} = n^\alpha B L^{1-\alpha}. \tag{52}$$

Taking logs on both sides of (52) and using $L \equiv (1-u)N$ plus $\ln(1-u) \approx -u$, we get:

$$\begin{aligned} y &\equiv \ln y = \ln n^\alpha + \ln B + (1-\alpha)\ln[(1-u)N] \\ &\approx \ln n^\alpha + \ln B + (1-\alpha)\ln N - (1-\alpha)u \quad \Leftrightarrow \end{aligned} \tag{53}$$

$$u = \ln N + \frac{\ln n^\alpha + \ln B - y}{1-\alpha}.$$

Let us now define 'natural' output, $\bar{Y}$, as the volume of output produced when employment is at its natural level *and* productivity is at its trend level:

$$\bar{Y} = n^\alpha \bar{B} \cdot \bar{L}^{1-\alpha}. \tag{54}$$

In other words, natural output – sometimes also referred to as potential output – is the level of production prevailing when the economy is on its long-run growth trend. Defining $\bar{y} \equiv \ln \bar{Y}$ and using $\bar{L} \equiv (1-\bar{u})N$ plus $\ln(1-\bar{u}) \approx -\bar{u}$, we take logs in (54) and find an expression analogous to (53):

$$\bar{u} = \ln N + \frac{\ln n^\alpha + \ln \bar{B} - \bar{y}}{1-\alpha}. \tag{55}$$

Substituting (53) and (55) into our expectations-augmented Phillips curve (42) and collecting terms, we end up with the economy's *short-run aggregate supply (SRAS) curve*:

$$\begin{aligned} &\pi = \pi^e + \gamma(y - \bar{y}) + s, \\ &\gamma \equiv \frac{\alpha}{1-\alpha} > 0, \qquad s \equiv \ln\left(\frac{m^p}{\bar{m}^p}\right) + \ln\left(\frac{m^w}{\bar{m}^w}\right) - \frac{\ln(B/\bar{B})}{1-\alpha}. \end{aligned} \tag{56}$$

The magnitude $y - \bar{y}$ is the percentage deviation of output from trend, referred to as the *output gap*. From (56) we see that, *ceteris paribus*, the rate of inflation varies positively with the output gap. The reason is that a rise in output requires a rise in employment, and because of diminishing marginal productivity of labour, higher employment generates an increase in marginal cost which is translated into an increase in prices via the mark-up pricing

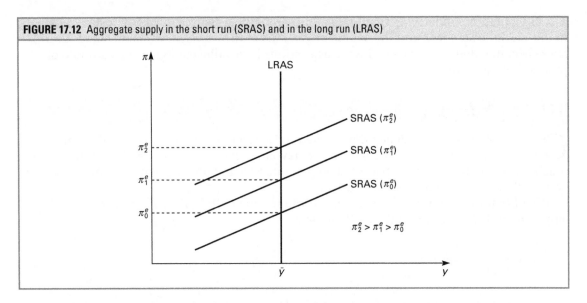

FIGURE 17.12 Aggregate supply in the short run (SRAS) and in the long run (LRAS)

behaviour of firms.[15] Equation (56) also implies that the actual rate of inflation varies positively with the expected rate of inflation and with the supply shock variable, s, capturing shocks to mark-ups and to productivity.

The short-run aggregate supply curve in (56) summarizes the supply side of the economy. Because the expected inflation rate is here taken as given, the curve is a *short-run* relationship. Over time, the expected inflation rate will gradually adjust in reaction to previous inflation forecast errors. When π^e changes, it follows from (56) that the short-run aggregate supply curve will shift upwards or downwards. This is illustrated in Fig. 17.12 which shows three different SRAS curves corresponding to three different levels of the expected inflation rate. In long-run equilibrium, when expected inflation equals actual inflation and there are no shocks ($s = 0$), we see from (56) that output must be equal to its 'natural' level, $\bar{y}$.

The natural rate of output is independent of the rate of inflation, since the natural unemployment rate $\bar{u}$ is independent of π. The *long-run aggregate supply (LRAS) curve* is therefore vertical, as shown in Fig. 17.12.

Apart from depending on the expected rate of inflation, the position of the short-run aggregate supply curve also depends on the supply shock variable, s. When $s = 0$, it follows from (56) that the SRAS curve passes through ($\bar{y}, \pi^e$). This is the situation depicted in Fig. 17.12. From (56) we see that the SRAS curve will shift upwards in the case of a positive shock to one of the mark-ups m^w or m^p, or in the case of a negative shock to productivity ($B < \bar{B}$). Note that several types of supply shocks may be modelled as productivity shocks. For example, a loss of output due to industrial conflict may be interpreted as a temporary fall in labour productivity. An unusually bad harvest due to bad weather conditions may likewise be seen as a temporary drop in productivity. An exogenous increase in the real price of imported raw materials such as oil will also work very much like a negative productivity shock. If the price of oil increases relative to the general price level, an economy dependent on imported oil will have to reserve a greater fraction of domestic output for exports to maintain a given volume of oil imports. Thus, for given inputs of domestic labour and capital, a lower amount of domestic output will be available for domestic consumption, just as if factor productivity had declined. More generally, any exogenous change in the economy's international terms of trade (a shift in import prices relative to export prices) may be modelled as a productivity shock in our AS–AD model.

---

15. Alternatively, the rate of inflation may rise with output because lower unemployment may induce higher wage claims which lead to higher prices as firms pass on their increased costs to consumers. According to the theory underlying the extended expectations-augmented Phillips curve (48), this mechanism is the reason why lower unemployment generates higher inflation. In practice, the positive slope of the SRAS curve may stem both from declining marginal productivity of labour and from the responsiveness of wage claims to unemployment.

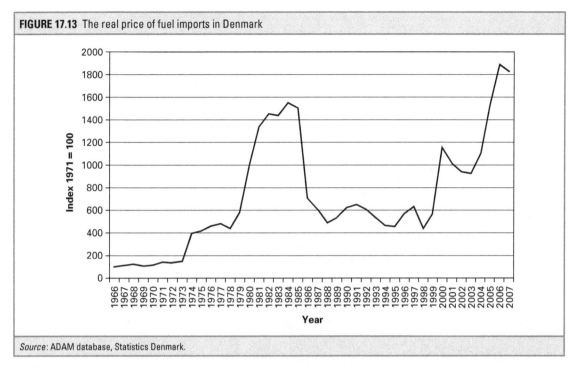

FIGURE 17.13 The real price of fuel imports in Denmark

Source: ADAM database, Statistics Denmark.

Over the last four decades, the real price of energy inputs has fluctuated considerably, as illustrated in Fig. 17.13. For example, following political upheaval in the Middle East, the OPEC cartel of oil-exporting countries was able to raise the real price of oil quite dramatically in 1973–74 and again in 1979–80. Because most OECD economies were large net importers of oil at the time, these oil price shocks worked like a significant negative productivity shock for the OECD area. On the other hand, the collapse of oil prices from around 1985 tended to boost real incomes in the OECD, just like a positive productivity shock. From the end of the 1990s the world saw another oil price hike, but this time it was fuelled mainly by a rapid increase in oil demand, due to strong economic growth in the OECD as well as in the emerging market economies, most notably the rapidly industrializing Chinese economy.

The aggregate supply curve is a cornerstone in our models of the macroeconomy, so let us recapitulate its properties:

THE AGGREGATE SUPPLY CURVE

The AS curve describes the relationship between total output and the rate of inflation. In the short run where the expected rate of inflation is predetermined, the actual rate of inflation varies positively with the output gap, as higher output and employment generates higher marginal production costs which are passed on to prices. This positive link between output and inflation defines the short-run aggregate supply curve (SRAS). The SRAS curve shifts upwards (downwards) one-to-one with a rise (fall) in the expected rate of inflation. The SRAS curve also shifts up in case of a negative supply shock. A negative supply shock may take the form of a rise in the price or wage mark-ups, a temporary drop in productivity or a fall in the country's international terms of trade. In long-run equilibrium inflation expectations must be fulfilled, and supply shocks must be zero. Output will then be at its 'natural' (trend) level, so the long-run aggregate supply curve (LRAS) is vertical.

This completes our theory of the aggregate supply side. In the next chapter we shall see how aggregate supply interacts with aggregate demand to determine total GDP as well as the rate of inflation.

17.7 Summary

1. The link between inflation and unemployment determines how the supply side of the economy works. Some decades ago most economists and policy makers believed in the simple Phillips curve which postulates a permanent trade-off between inflation and unemployment: a permanent reduction in the rate of unemployment can be achieved by accepting a permanent increase in the rate of inflation, and vice versa.

2. Empirically the simple Phillips curve broke down in the stagflation of the 1970s. This led to the theory of the expectations-augmented Phillips curve which says that the simple Phillips curve is just a short-run trade-off between inflation and unemployment, existing only as long as the expected rate of inflation is constant. When the expected inflation rate goes up, the actual inflation rate increases by a corresponding amount, other things equal.

3. The expectations-augmented Phillips curve implies the existence of a 'natural' rate of unemployment, defined as the level of unemployment which will prevail in a long-run equilibrium where the expected inflation rate equals the actual inflation rate. Since any fully anticipated rate of inflation is compatible with long-run equilibrium, the long-run Phillips curve is vertical. When the actual unemployment rate falls below the natural unemployment rate, the actual inflation rate exceeds the expected inflation rate, and vice versa.

4. Several different theories of wage and price formation lead to the expectations-augmented Phillips curve. One such theory is the 'sticky-wage model' in which nominal wage rates are pre-set at the start of each period. In the sticky wage model presented in this chapter, money wages are dictated by trade unions seeking to achieve a certain target real wage, given their expectations of the price level which will prevail over the next period. Given the wage rate set by unions, profit-maximizing monopolistically competitive firms set their prices as a mark-up over marginal costs and choose a level of employment which is declining in the actual real wage. According to this model, employment increases above its natural rate when the actual price level exceeds the expected price level, and vice versa. The model also implies that, in general, there is some amount of involuntary unemployment.

5. In the sticky-wage model the target real wage is a mark-up over the opportunity cost of employment which is given by the rate of unemployment benefit. The wage mark-up factor – and hence the target real wage – is higher the lower the wage elasticity of labour demand, and the lower the weight the union attaches to the goal of high employment relative to the goal of a high real wage. The mark-up of prices over marginal costs is higher the lower the price elasticity of demand for the output of the representative firm. The natural rate of unemployment is higher the higher the wage and price mark-ups and the more generous the level of unemployment benefits.

6. The evidence strongly suggests that, just as money wages are sticky, many nominal product prices are pre-set and held constant for a while, presumably because of menu costs of frequent price changes. The sticky-wage model can be extended to include a group of 'fix-price' firms that keep their prices fixed within each period, but adjusting them between periods, whereas the remaining 'flex-price' firms immediately adjust their prices to changing cost conditions within each period. This extension of the model does not change the qualitative properties of the expectations-augmented Phillips curve, but it reduces the short-run sensitivity of inflation to the unemployment gap.

7. Another theory leading to the expectations-augmented Phillips curve is the 'worker misperception model' which assumes a competitive clearing labour market with fully flexible wages. Labour demand is a declining function of the actual real wage, while labour supply is an increasing function of the expected real wage, since workers are

imperfectly informed about the current general price level. This model also implies that employment rises above the natural level when the actual price level exceeds the expected price level. However, for any given amount of unanticipated inflation, the increase in employment is smaller in the worker-misperception model than in the model with nominal wage and price rigidity. Even in the absence of nominal rigidities, unanticipated inflation will thus generate deviations of employment from the natural rate, but nominal rigidities will strongly amplify the fluctuations in employment.

8. According to the hypothesis of static expectations, the expected inflation rate for the current period equals the actual inflation rate observed during the previous period. Combined with the expectations-augmented Phillips curve, the assumption of static expectations implies that the rate of inflation will keep on accelerating (decelerating) when actual unemployment is below (above) the natural unemployment rate.

9. So-called supply shocks in the form of fluctuations in productivity and in the wage and price mark-ups create 'noise' in the relationship between inflation and unemployment. An unfavourable supply shock implies an increase in the actual rate of inflation for any given levels of unemployment and expected inflation. In the presence of supply shocks the natural unemployment rate is defined as the rate of unemployment prevailing when inflation expectations are fulfilled and productivity as well as the wage and price mark-ups are at their trend levels.

10. An expectations-augmented Phillips curve with static inflation expectations is consistent with US data on inflation and unemployment in the period from the early 1960s to the mid-1990s. In the 'New Economy' of the late 1990s inflation was surprisingly low, given the low rate of unemployment prevailing during that period. This experience may be seen as a result of a favourable supply shock arising from the fact that target real wages were lagging behind the accelerating rate of productivity growth.

11. The economy's short-run aggregate supply curve (the SRAS curve) implies a positive link between the output gap and the actual rate of inflation, given the expected rate of inflation. The SRAS curve may be derived from the expectations-augmented Phillips curve, using the production function which links the unemployment rate to the level of output. The SRAS curve shifts upwards when the expected inflation rate goes up, or when the economy is hit by an unfavourable supply shock. When there are no supply shocks and expected inflation equals actual inflation, the economy is on its long-run aggregate supply curve (the LRAS curve) which is vertical at the natural level of output corresponding to the natural rate of unemployment.

17.8 Exercises

Exercise 1. Intersectoral labour mobility and the expectations-augmented Phillips curve

In Section 17.2 we abstracted from intersectoral labour mobility by assuming that individual workers are educated and trained to work in a particular sector. In that case a worker's outside option (the income he could expect to earn if he were not employed by his current employer) is simply equal to the rate of unemployment benefit. In this exercise we ask you to show that one can still derive the expectations-augmented Phillips curve from a trade union model of wage setting even if unemployed workers can move between sectors in their search for jobs, as we assumed in our analysis of the labour market in Chapters 1, 11 and 12.

To simplify matters a bit, we now set our productivity parameter $B = 1$ and work with a linear production function with constant marginal productivity of labour, corresponding to

$\alpha = 0$ in Eq. (3) in the main text. For $\alpha = 0$ and $B = 1$, it follows from (7) in Section 17.2 that the representative firm will set its product price as:

$$P_i = m^p W_i, \qquad m^p > 1. \tag{57}$$

As in Section 17.2, an optimizing monopoly union for workers in firm (sector) i will set the nominal wage rate W_i to attain an expected real wage which is a mark-up over the expected real value of its members' outside option, denoted by v^e. The union expects the current price level to be P^e. Hence it will set the wage rate:

$$\frac{W_i}{P^e} = m^w v^e, \qquad m^w > 1. \tag{58}$$

This equation is a parallel to Eq. (11) in Section 17.2 where we assumed that v^e is simply equal to the real rate of unemployment benefit, b. Here we assume instead that workers who are initially members of the trade union for sector i are qualified to apply for a job in other sectors if they fail to find one in sector i. For an average job seeker, the probability of finding work is equal to the rate of employment, $1 - u$, where u is the unemployment rate which gives the probability that an average job seeker will remain unemployed. If the ratio of unemployment benefits to the average wage level is equal to the constant c, we thus have:

$$v^e = (1 - u)w^e + ub^e = (1 - u + uc)w^e, \qquad 0 < c < 1, \tag{59}$$

where w^e is the expected average level of real wages, and $b^e = cw^e$ is the expected real rate of unemployment benefit.

Since the outside option v^e is the same across all sectors and all unions are assumed to hold the same price expectations, it follows from (57) and (58) that all unions will charge the same nominal wage rate, W, and that all firms will charge the same output price, P:

$$W_i = W, \qquad P_i = P. \tag{60}$$

According to (57) the average real wage will then be $W/P = 1/m^p$. Let us suppose that union wage setters have a realistic estimate of the average real wage so that:

$$w^e = 1/m^p. \tag{61}$$

1. Show that the relationship between the actual and the expected price level may be written as:

$$P = m^w(1 - \gamma u)P^e, \qquad \gamma \equiv 1 - c > 0. \tag{62}$$

2. Use (62) to derive an expectations-augmented Phillips curve of the same form as equation (17) in Section 2. (Hint: use the approximation $\ln(1 - \gamma u) \approx -\gamma u$ and define $\bar{u} \equiv \ln m^w/\gamma$.) Explain intuitively what determines the natural unemployment rate, $\bar{u}$. Explain intuitively what determines the slope (γ) of the expectations-augmented Phillips curve.

3. Does the theory embodied in (57)–(62) assume short-run nominal wage rigidity?

4. The specification of the outside option (59) assumes that unions know the current aggregate unemployment rate when they set the wage rate. Suppose instead that unemployment statistics are published with a lag so that unions base their estimate of the outside option on last period's recorded unemployment rate, u_{-1}:

$$v^e = (1 - u_{-1})w^e + u_{-1}b^e = (1 - u_{-1} + u_{-1}c)w^e. \tag{63}$$

Derive the expectations-augmented Phillips curve on the assumption that the perceived outside option is given by (63) rather than (59). Do we now have nominal wage rigidity in the short run?

Exercise 2. Wage setting, labour demand and unemployment

1. Explain why union wage claims are moderated by a higher price elasticity in the representative firm's product demand curve.
2. In the text we found that the wage elasticity of labour demand is lower at the sectoral level than at the aggregate level. Explain why this is so.
3. 'Tougher product market competition will reduce structural unemployment.' Explain this statement. Discuss what the government could do in practice to promote fiercer product market competition.

Exercise 3. The Phillips curve with endogenous price mark-ups

In the main text we assumed for simplicity that the representative firm's mark-up m^p of price over marginal cost was an exogenous constant. However, empirical research for the USA suggests that price mark-up factors in that country tend to move in a countercyclical fashion. In other words, the mark-up tends to fall during business cycle expansions and to rise during recessions. There are several potential reasons for this countercyclical behaviour of mark-ups, including the possibility that during booms when the demand pressure is high, more new firms find it profitable to enter the market, thereby increasing the degree of competition and forcing existing firms to reduce their profit margins.

Since the rate of unemployment moves countercyclically, the countercyclical variation of the price mark-up means that m^p will tend to move in the same direction as the unemployment rate. For concreteness, suppose this relationship takes the form:

$$m^p = \tilde{m} \cdot e^{\varphi u}, \qquad \tilde{m} > 1, \qquad \varphi \geq 0, \tag{64}$$

where e is the exponential function, and φ is a parameter measuring the sensitivity of the mark-up to changes in the unemployment rate, u. In the main text of the chapter we focused on the case of $\varphi = 0$, corresponding to a constant mark-up. In this exercise we ask you to study the implications of assuming $\varphi > 0$ which is more in line with the empirical evidence for the USA.

As in Exercise 1, we consider an economy with intersectoral labour mobility, union wage setting and mark-up price setting. Hence we have (see Exercise 1 in case you need further explanation):

$$P_i = m^p W_i, \tag{65}$$

$$\frac{W_i}{P^e} = m^w \cdot v^e, \qquad m^w > 1. \tag{66}$$

$$v^e = (1-u)w^e + ub^e = (1 - u + uc)w^e, \qquad 0 < c < 1, \tag{67}$$

where w^e is the expected average level of real wages, $b^e = cw^e$ is the expected real rate of unemployment benefit, and v^e is the individual worker's expected outside option. The outside option is the same across all sectors, so all unions charge the same nominal wage rate and all firms charge the same price:

$$W_i = W, \qquad P_i = P. \tag{68}$$

Union wage setters assume that the average real wage is:

$$w^e = 1/\bar{m}, \qquad \bar{m} > 1, \tag{69}$$

where the constant $\bar{m}$ is the expected 'normal' price mark-up.

1. Show that the model consisting of (64)–(69) implies an expectations-augmented Phillips curve of the form:

$$\pi = \pi^e + (1 - c - \varphi)(\bar{u} - u), \qquad \bar{u} \equiv \frac{\ln \tilde{m} + \ln m^w - \ln \bar{m}}{1 - c - \varphi}, \tag{70}$$

where $\pi \equiv p - p_{-1}$, $\pi^e \equiv p^e - p^e_{-1}$, and $p \equiv \ln P$, and where you may assume that $1 - c - \varphi > 0$ to ensure a positive solution for the natural unemployment rate, $\bar{u}$. Explain intuitively how the parameter φ affects the sensitivity of inflation to unemployment. Explain and discuss the various factors determining the natural unemployment rate.

2. Suppose that union wage setters expect the 'normal' price mark-up $\bar{m}$ appearing in (69) to be

$$\bar{m} = \tilde{m} \cdot e^{\varphi \bar{u}}. \tag{71}$$

Discuss whether the assumption made in (71) is reasonable. Derive a new expression for the natural unemployment rate $\bar{u}$ on the assumption that (71) holds. Compare the new expression to the expression for $\bar{u}$ given in (70) and comment on the differences.

Exercise 4. The Phillips curve and active labour market policy

The model with intersectoral labour mobility presented in Exercise 1 assumes that all workers are competing on equal terms and with equal intensity for the available jobs. In that case it seems reasonable that any individual worker's probability of finding a job is simply equal to the overall rate of employment, $1 - u$, as we assumed when specifying a worker's outside option.

In the present exercise we assume instead that some of the workers recorded in the unemployment statistics are not fully 'effective' in competing for jobs, perhaps because their skills do not fully match the qualifications demanded by employers, or perhaps because they are not actively searching for a job all the time. We may model this in a simple way by assuming that only a fraction, s, of the registered unemployed workers contribute fully to the available labour supply in the sense of being immediately ready and able to accept the jobs available. Thus we may specify the 'effective' labour supply from the pool of unemployed workers as su. In the following, we will refer to s as the Job-Search-and-Matching-Efficiency parameter (the JSME parameter). For the moment, we will assume that s is an exogenous constant.

If we normalize the total labour force to equal 1, there are thus $(1 - s)u$ unemployed workers who are not really competing with their fellow workers for a job. Hence we may measure the 'effective' labour force as $1 - (1 - s)u$. For an average member of the effective labour force (a qualified person who is ready to accept the available jobs), the probability p^u of ending up in the unemployment pool is the ratio of the 'effective' number of unemployed to the 'effective' labour force, $p^u = su/[1 - (1 - s)u]$. By implication, a qualified person's probability of finding a job in the labour market is $1 - p^u$. If the expected average real wage is w^e, and if the ratio of the unemployment benefit to the average wage level is c, we may therefore specify the real value of a qualified worker's expected outside option as:

$$v^e = \left(1 - \frac{su}{1 - (1-s)u}\right) w^e + \left(\frac{su}{1 - (1-s)u}\right) \overbrace{cw^e}^{\substack{\text{unemployment} \\ \text{benefit}}} = \left(\frac{1 - (1-cs)u}{1 - (1-s)u}\right) w^e, \qquad 0 < c < 1. \tag{72}$$

The trade union for sector i expects the current price level to be P^e and sets its nominal wage rate W_i to attain an expected real wage W_i/P^e which is a mark-up over the outside option of the employable union members:

$$\frac{W_i}{P^e} = m^w v^e, \qquad m^w > 1. \tag{73}$$

The representative firm uses a linear production function with $\alpha = 0$ and $B = 1$, so according to Eq. (7) in the main text it sets its price P_i as:

$$P_i = m^p W_i, \qquad m^p > 1. \tag{74}$$

Since v^e is the same across all sectors, it follows from (73) and (74) that all unions will set the same wage rate and that all firms will charge the same price:

$$W_i = W, \qquad P_i = P. \tag{75}$$

In accordance with (74) and (75), the representative union expects the average real wage to be:

$$w^e = 1/m^p \tag{76}$$

1. Demonstrate through a logarithmic approximation that the model (72)–(76) leads to an expectations-augmented Phillips curve of the form

$$\pi = \pi^e + s\gamma(\bar{u} - u), \qquad \gamma \equiv 1 - c > 0, \qquad \bar{u} \equiv \frac{\ln m^w}{s\gamma}, \tag{77}$$

where $\pi \equiv p = p_{-1}$, $\pi^e \equiv p^e = p_{-1}$, and $p \equiv \ln P$. (Hint: use the approximations $\ln[1 - (1 - cs)u] \approx -(1 - cs)u$ and $\ln[1 - (1 - s)u] \approx -(1 - s)u$.) Explain in economic terms how the JSME parameter s affects the sensitivity of inflation to unemployment.

Let us now analyse the effects of active labour market policy. Suppose that a fraction l of the unemployed workers is enrolled in public education and training programmes aimed at improving their qualifications for the available jobs. Such programmes may increase the JSME parameter s partly by improving the match between the qualifications demanded by employers and the skills possessed by the unemployed, and partly by increasing workers' motivation to look for jobs (say, because it makes more attractive jobs available to them). Hence we assume that s is an increasing function of l:

$$s = \bar{s} \cdot l^\eta, \qquad 0 < \bar{s} < 1, \qquad \eta > 0, \qquad 0 < l < 1. \tag{78}$$

The elasticity η is a parameter measuring the degree to which the labour market programmes succeed in actually upgrading the skills and motivation of the unemployed. However, (78) does not capture all of the effect of active labour market programmes. When people are enrolled in such a programme, they will often not be immediately available for a job should they receive a job offer, or they may not have the time to look for a job. For simplicity, let us assume that only that fraction $1 - l$ of the unemployed who are not currently engaged in education and training are able to take a job. Moreover, let us assume that these job seekers have benefited from previous training so that their Job-Search-and-Matching-Efficiency corresponds to the value of s specified in (78). The 'effective' labour supply coming from the pool of unemployed workers is then given by:

$$\text{'Effective' unemployment rate} = s(1 - l)u \tag{79}$$

where s is determined by (78). The effective labour force consists of those unemployed workers who are effectively available for work, $s(1 - l)u$, plus those who are already employed, $1 - u$. Thus a qualified worker's probability of being unemployed is:

$$p^u = \frac{s(1-l)u}{1-u+s(1-l)u} = \frac{s(1-l)u}{1-[1-s(1-l)]u}. \tag{80}$$

In the questions below we will assume that l is a policy instrument controlled by the makers of labour market policy. Furthermore, we assume that workers enrolled in active labour market programmes receive the same unemployment benefits and enjoy the same utility as unemployed workers who are not enrolled in programmes. This implies that active labour market policy has no effect on the outside option other than the effect working through the impact of l on p^u.

2. Following the same procedure as in Question 1, demonstrate through a logarithmic approximation that when effective unemployment is given by (79) and the JSME parameter is given by (78), we obtain an expectations-augmented Phillips curve of the form:

$$\pi = \pi^e + \hat{\gamma}(\bar{u}-u), \qquad \hat{\gamma} \equiv (1-c)\bar{s}\,l^\eta(1-l), \qquad \bar{u} \equiv \frac{\ln m^w}{\hat{\gamma}}. \tag{81}$$

(Hints: start by using (80) to respecify v^e. Later on, when you take logs, use the approximations $\ln\{1-[1-cs(1-l)]u\} \approx -[1-cs(1-l)]u$ and $\ln\{1-[1-s(1-l)]u\} \approx -[1-s(1-l)]u$.)

3. How does the natural unemployment rate react to an increase in the proportion of the unemployed enrolled in active labour market programmes? (Hint: derive $\partial \bar{u}/\partial l$.) Explain the offsetting effects of an increase in l.

4. Suppose that the government wishes to minimize the natural rate of unemployment through its active labour market programmes. Derive the value of l which will achieve this goal. (Hint: remember that a necessary condition for minimization of is $\bar{u}$ is $\partial \bar{u}/\partial l = 0$.) Give an intuitive interpretation of your result. Discuss briefly whether the government should necessarily push active labour market policy to the point implied by your formula. (Hint: are there any costs and benefits of active labour market policy which we have not included in our analysis?)

5. Suppose that unemployed workers prefer not to be enrolled in active labour market programmes, say, because they consider enrolment to be stigmatizing, or because it reduces their leisure time. Discuss whether this would make active labour market policy more or less effective as a means of reducing structural unemployment.

Exercise 5. The Phillips curve with a time-varying NAIRU

Empirical estimates of the natural unemployment rate (the NAIRU) typically find that the evolution of the NAIRU tends to track the evolution of the actual rate of unemployment, at least in the short and medium run. This exercise extends our theory of the Phillips curve in order to explain why the NAIRU tends to move in the same direction as the actual unemployment rate in the shorter run.

We consider the following model with intersectoral labour mobility, where we apply the same notation as in Exercise 1, and where p^u is an average worker's probability of remaining out of work if he fails to find a job in his original sector:

Price formation: $P_i = m^p W_i, \qquad m^p > 1,$ $\tag{82}$

Wage claim of the representative union: $\dfrac{W_i}{P^e} = m^w v^e, \qquad m^w > 1,$ $\tag{83}$

The 'outside option' of union members: $v^e = (1-p^u)w^e + p^u b^e,$ $\tag{84}$

Expected average real wage: $w^e = 1/m^p,$ $\tag{85}$

Expected real rate of unemployment benefit: $b^e = cw^e$, $0 < c < 1$,   (86)

Probability of remaining unemployed in case of job loss:

$$p^u = u + \theta(u - u_{-1}), \qquad \theta \geq 0, \qquad p^u \leq 1 \tag{87}$$

The variables u and u_{-1} are the unemployment rates in the current and in the previous period, respectively. The new feature of the model above is Eq. (87) which says that, *ceteris paribus*, an unemployed worker has a smaller chance of finding a job if unemployment is rising than if unemployment is falling.

1. Discuss briefly whether the specification in (87) is plausible.
2. Use the model (82)–(87) to derive an expectations-augmented Phillips curve of the form:

$$\pi = \pi^e + \ln m^w - \gamma u - \gamma\theta(u - u_{-1}) \qquad \gamma \equiv 1 - c > 0, \tag{88}$$

where $\pi \equiv p - p_{-1}$, $\pi^e \equiv p^e - p^e_{-1}$ and $p \equiv \ln P$. (You may use the usual approximation $\ln(1 - x) \approx -x$ which is valid as long as x is not too far from zero.) Comment on the expression in (88) and compare with the expectations-augmented Phillips curve derived in the main text of the chapter.

   In the following we assume that inflation expectations are static so that $\pi^e = \pi_{-1}$.

3. Define the *long-run NAIRU* as the rate of unemployment $\bar{u}$ which will be realized when the rate of inflation as well as the rate of unemployment are constant over time, that is when $\pi = \pi_{-1}$ and $u = u_{-1}$. Derive an equation for the long-run NAIRU and use this expression to explain the factors which determine the equilibrium rate of unemployment in the long run.
4. Define the *short-run NAIRU* as the rate of unemployment $\bar{u}_s$ which will be compatible with a constant inflation rate in the *short* run where we do not necessarily have $u = u_{-1}$. (At the short-run NAIRU we thus have $\pi = \pi_{-1}$ but not necessarily $u = u_{-1}$). Derive an expression for the short-run NAIRU and show that $\bar{u}_s$ may be written as a weighted average of the long-run NAIRU and last period's actual rate of unemployment u_{-1}. Which parameter determines how much the short-run NAIRU is affected by last period's actual unemployment rate?
5. Assume that in period 0 unemployment increases from the long-run NAIRU ($\bar{u}$) to the level $\bar{u} + \Delta u_0$. Will it be possible to return to the unemployment rate $\bar{u}$ in period 1 without creating higher inflation? Give reasons for your answer.

Exercise 6. Estimating the time-varying NAIRU

In Section 17.5 we saw that the natural unemployment rate in the USA seems to have varied over time. In this exercise we invite you to estimate the level and variation in the NAIRU and to investigate whether changes in the underlying rate of productivity growth may help to explain the evolution of the NAIRU.

   If inflation expectations are static, the expectations-augmented Phillips curve allowing for supply shocks ($\tilde{s}$) takes the form:

$$\pi - \pi_{-1} = \gamma(\bar{u} - u) + \tilde{s}$$

which may be rearranged to give:

$$\bar{u} + \tilde{s}/\gamma = u + \Delta\pi/\gamma, \qquad \Delta\pi \equiv \pi - \pi_{-1}. \tag{89}$$

Thus we may see the movements in the magnitude $u + \Delta\pi/\gamma$ on the right-hand side of (89) to be a result of gradual movements in the NAIRU, $\bar{u}$, as well as a result of the shorter-term and more erratic supply shocks captured by $\tilde{s}$. If we have somehow obtained an estimate of the parameter γ, we may construct an estimate of $\bar{u} + \tilde{s}/\gamma$ by calculating $u + \Delta\pi/\gamma$, using available data on unemployment and inflation. We may then use the HP filter introduced in Chapter 13 to split our estimate of $\bar{u} + \tilde{s}/\gamma$ into a smooth underlying trend, which we interpret as an estimate of $\bar{u}$, and a residual term which we take to reflect $\tilde{s}/\gamma$. This is the methodology we ask you to follow below.

1. The first step is to obtain an estimate of our parameter γ. At the internet address http://highered.mcgraw-hill.com/sites/0077104250/student_view0/index.html you will find annual data on the unemployment rate and the rate of inflation in the USA for the period 1959–2003. Using these data, estimate a standard expectations-augmented Phillips curve of the form:

$$\Delta\pi = a_0 + a_1 u + \tilde{s}, \tag{90}$$

   by performing an OLS regression analysis for the period 1960–2003. (You may assume that $\tilde{s}$ is normally distributed with a zero mean and a constant variance.) Is your estimate of a_1 statistically significant and does it have the expected sign? Assuming you can answer in the affirmative, you may use your estimate of the numerical value of a_1 as an estimate of γ in your further analysis.

2. Armed with your estimate of γ and your data set, you can now calculate a time series for the magnitude $u + \Delta\pi/\gamma$. In this way you obtain an estimated time series for $\bar{u} + \tilde{s}/\gamma$ for the period 1960–2003. At the student web page for this book (http://highered.mcgraw-hill.com/sites/0077104250/student_view0/index.html) you will also find a link to a software facility enabling you to estimate a trend by means of the HP filter (plus a brief guide on how to use this program). Use this facility to estimate an HP trend in your time series for $\bar{u} + \tilde{s}/\gamma$, setting the λ parameter equal to 1000 to obtain a quite smooth trend. Interpret your HP trend as an estimate of $\bar{u}$ and construct a diagram in which you plot your estimated time series for the NAIRU. What is the range within which the NAIRU has varied?

   In Section 17.5 we argued that the trade-off between the level of unemployment and the change in the rate of inflation will tend to improve in periods of accelerating productivity growth, and vice versa. According to (89), a longer-lasting improvement in the trade-off between u and $\Delta\pi$ (that is, a fall in $u + \Delta\pi/\gamma$) must reflect a fall in the NAIRU, $\bar{u}$. Thus the NAIRU should tend to fall when the underlying rate of productivity growth accelerates, whereas $\bar{u}$ should tend to rise when underlying productivity growth slows down. The next question asks you to explore this relationship.

3. The internet address http://highered.mcgrawhill.com/sites/0077104250/student_view0/index.html contains annual data on the growth rate in output per hour worked in the USA for the period 1959–2003. Use the HP filter to estimate an underlying trend in this productivity growth rate, setting $\lambda = 1000$. Plot the resulting estimate of trend productivity growth against your estimate of the NAIRU. Do the two time series tend to move in opposite directions, as our theory predicts? Explain the theoretical reasons why accelerating productivity growth may be expected to reduce the NAIRU, at least temporarily.

   (Postscript: if you would like to know more about the likely reasons for the variations in the US NAIRU, you may want to consult the following readable article from which the idea for this exercise was taken: Laurence Ball and N. Gregory Mankiw, 'The NAIRU in Theory and Practice', *Journal of Economic Perspectives*, **16** (4), Fall 2002, pp. 115–136.)

PART

The Short-run Model for the Closed Economy

CHAPTER 18

Explaining business cycles

Aggregate supply and aggregate demand in action

Throughout economic history, the capitalist market economies of the world have gone through recurrent periods of boom and bust. This is the fascinating phenomenon of business cycles described in Chapter 13. Although long periods of high economic growth have sometimes led people to believe that the business cycle was dead, Figs 18.1 and 18.2 show that it is still very much alive: economic activity continues to fluctuate in an irregular cyclical manner around its long-run growth trend, and in the steepest economic downturn since the 1930s, output per capita in all the major developed economies fell sharply between 2008 and 2009. A fundamental challenge for macroeconomic theory is to explain why the economy goes through these cyclical movements rather than evolving smoothly over time.

The two previous chapters derived the economy's aggregate supply curve and its aggregate demand curve. In this chapter we bring the two curves together in a complete macro model which enables us to determine the levels of total output and inflation in the short run. This model allows us to investigate the causes of the fluctuations in economic activity which we observe in the real world. We will illustrate how business fluctuations may be seen as the economy's reaction to various shocks that tend to shift the aggregate supply and demand curves. We will also study the extent to which our model is able to reproduce the most important stylized facts of the business cycle.

The perspective on business cycles adopted here is sometimes referred to as the *Frisch–Slutsky paradigm*, named after the Norwegian economist and Nobel Prize winner Ragnar Frisch and the Italian statistician Eugen Slutzky who first introduced this way of interpreting business cycles.[1] The Frisch–Slutsky paradigm distinguishes between the *impulse* which *initiates* a movement in economic activity, and the *propagation mechanism* which subsequently *transmits* the shock through the economic system *over time*. In our model framework, the impulse is a sudden exogenous change in one of the 'shock' variables determining the position of the aggregate supply and demand curves. The propagation mechanism is the endogenous economic mechanism which converts the impulse into *persistent* business fluctuations. The propagation mechanism reflects the structure of the economy and determines the manner in which it reacts to shocks and how long it takes for it to adjust to a shock. Ragnar Frisch stressed that even though shocks to the economy may

---

1. See Ragnar Frisch, 'Propagation Problems and Impulse Problems in Dynamic Economics', in *Economic Essays in Honour of Gustav Cassel*, London, Allen and Unwin, 1933; and Eugen Slutsky, 'The Summation of Random Causes as the Source of Cyclic Processes', *Econometrica*, **5**, 1937, pp. 105–146.

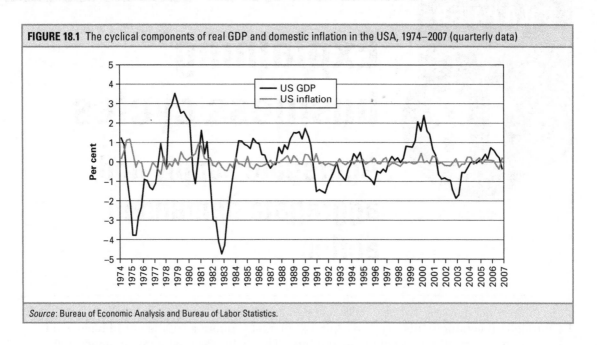

FIGURE 18.1 The cyclical components of real GDP and domestic inflation in the USA, 1974–2007 (quarterly data)

Source: Bureau of Economic Analysis and Bureau of Labor Statistics.

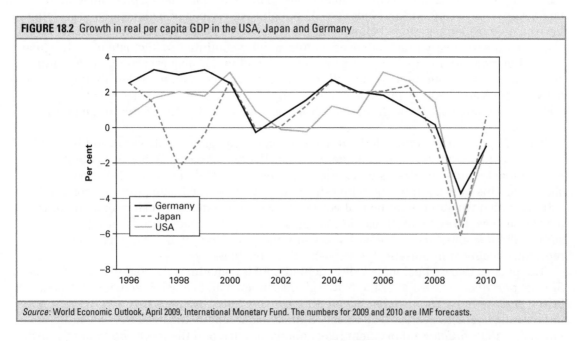

FIGURE 18.2 Growth in real per capita GDP in the USA, Japan and Germany

Source: World Economic Outlook, April 2009, International Monetary Fund. The numbers for 2009 and 2010 are IMF forecasts.

follow an unsystematic pattern, the structure of the economy may imply that it reacts to disturbances in a systematic way which is very different from the pattern of the shocks themselves. Frisch was inspired by the famous Swedish economist Knut Wicksell who used the following metaphor to explain the difference between the unsystematic impulse to the economy and the systematic business cycle response implied by the propagation mechanism: 'If you hit a wooden rocking chair with a club, the movement of the chair will be more or less regular because of its form, even if the hits are quite irregular'.[2]

---

2.   This statement by Wicksell was made in a discussion at a meeting of the Swedish Economic Association in Uppsala in 1924. See 'Nationalekonomiska Föreningens Förhandlingar 1924', Uppsala, 1925.

In short, this chapter raises two basic questions:

1. Why do movements in economic activity display persistence?
2. Why do these movements tend to follow a cyclical pattern?

We start out in Section 18.1 by setting up our model of aggregate supply and aggregate demand, termed the AS–AD model. In Section 18.2 we then use the model to illustrate how the economy reacts to demand and supply shocks in a so-called deterministic world. In this *deterministic* version of our AS–AD model, the demand and supply shocks are non-random, occurring either within a limited time span, or representing a permanent level shift in some exogenous variable. Following a qualitative graphical analysis, we will set up a quantitative version of the deterministic AS–AD model to study the *impulse-response functions* which show how the economy responds to various shocks over time. We find that the deterministic AS–AD model is capable of explaining the observed *persistence* of the movements in economic activity following a shock, but it cannot really explain why business fluctuations tend to follow a *cyclical* pattern. To deal with this problem, Section 18.3 sets up a *stochastic* version of the AS–AD model in which the exogenous demand and supply shock variables are *random variables*. As we shall see, this model is able to reproduce the most important stylized business cycle facts reasonably well. In Section 18.4 we discuss an alternative approach to business cycle analysis, the theory of 'real' business cycles, which claims that business fluctuations are caused by the irregular evolution of the technical progress underlying the process of long-term growth.

18.1 The model of aggregate supply and aggregate demand

Restating the AS–AD model

To prepare the ground for our analysis of business cycles, the first part of this chapter assembles the building blocks from the two previous chapters to form a model of aggregate supply and aggregate demand – the AS–AD model – which allows us to determine the short-run levels of output and inflation.

In extensive form, our AS–AD model may be stated as follows, where the subscript t indicates that we consider period t:

$$r_t \equiv i_t^p + \rho_t - \pi_{t+1}^e \tag{1}$$

$$y_t - \bar{y} = \alpha_1(g_t - \bar{g}) - \alpha_2(r_t - \bar{r}) + v_t, \qquad \bar{r} = \bar{r}^* + \bar{\rho} \tag{2}$$

$$i_t^p = \bar{r}^* + \pi_{t+1}^e + h(\pi_t - \pi^*) + b(y_t - \bar{y}), \tag{3}$$

$$\pi_t = \pi_t^e + \gamma(y_t - \bar{y}) + s_t \tag{4}$$

$$\pi_t^e = \pi_{t-1} \tag{5}$$

As you recall from Chapter 16, Eq. (1) is the definition of the *ex ante* market real interest rate, with ρ_t representing shocks to market risk premia. Eq. (2) is the condition for goods market equilibrium, where v_t captures shifts in private sector confidence, and $g_t - \bar{g}$ reflects shocks to public expenditure, and where the long-run equilibrium real market interest rate $\bar{r}$ is the sum of the risk-free equilibrium real interest rate $\bar{r}^*$ and the average long-run risk premium $\bar{\rho}$. Equation (3) is the Taylor rule describing how a central bank pursuing an inflation target π^* will set its nominal policy interest rate i^p. All of these equations were explained in Chapter 16. Equation (4) is the short-run aggregate supply curve derived in Chapter 17. The variable s_t captures supply shocks such as fluctuations in wage and price mark-ups and shifts in productivity. The final equation (5) restates the assumption of static expectations according to which the expected current inflation rate equals last period's observed inflation rate.

Chapter 16 showed how (1) and (3) may be inserted into (2) to give the economy's aggregate demand curve. Repeating this operation, we get the AD curve,

$$y_t - \bar{y} = \alpha(\pi^* - \pi_t) + z_t, \qquad \alpha \equiv \frac{\alpha_2 h}{1 + \alpha_2 b}, \qquad z_t \equiv \frac{v_t + \alpha_1(g_t - \bar{g}) - \alpha_2(\rho_t - \bar{\rho})}{1 + \alpha_2 b}, \tag{6}$$

which may be rearranged as:

$$\text{AD:} \qquad \pi_t = \pi^* - \left(\frac{1}{\alpha}\right)(y_t - \bar{y} - z_t). \tag{7}$$

Furthermore, we may write the short-run aggregate supply curve in the following form by merging (4) and (5):

$$\text{SRAS:} \qquad \pi_t = \pi_{t-1} + \gamma(y_t - \bar{y}) + s_t \tag{8}$$

Short-run macroeconomic equilibrium

Equations (7) and (8) summarize the AS–AD model in compact form. It is worth recalling the mechanisms underlying the AD and SRAS curves:

PROPERTIES OF THE AS–AD MODEL

The AD curve is downward-sloping in (y_t, π_t) space because a fall in the rate of inflation induces the central bank to cut the real interest rate, thereby stimulating aggregate demand. The SRAS curve slopes upwards in (y_t, π_t) space because a rise in output requires a rise in employment which drives down the marginal productivity of labour, thereby increasing marginal costs and inducing firms to raise their prices at a faster rate.

At the start of the current period t, last period's inflation rate π_{t-1} is a predetermined variable which may be taken as given. The shock variables z_t and s_t are also treated as exogenous. The current levels of output and inflation are then determined by the two equations (7) and (8). In graphical terms, the solution to the model is found at point E_0 in Fig. 18.3 where the SRAS curve intersects with the AD curve, that is, where firms' desired aggregate supply of goods and services matches aggregate demand.

The adjustment to long-run equilibrium

In Fig. 18.3 we have also included the long-run aggregate supply curve (LRAS). This curve shows the volume of output which is supplied in a long-run equilibrium where there are no shocks ($s_t = z_t = 0$) and where inflation is stable ($\pi_t = \pi_{t-1}$). It follows from (8) that $y_t = \bar{y}$ in long-run equilibrium, so the position of the LRAS curve is determined by the economy's natural rate of output, as we explained in Chapter 17.

The short-run equilibrium E_0 illustrated in Fig. 18.3 is characterized by cyclical unemployment, since actual output y_0 falls short of natural output. The question is: will the economy be able to work itself out of this recession? To focus on the economy's adjustment mechanism, suppose there are no further demand and supply shocks following the initial shock which created the recession.[3] Furthermore, remember that the position of the SRAS

---

3. Below we analyse more carefully how the economy may be pushed into a recession in the first place. Here we just take the economy's starting point as given, since we are currently focusing on its dynamic adjustment mechanisms.

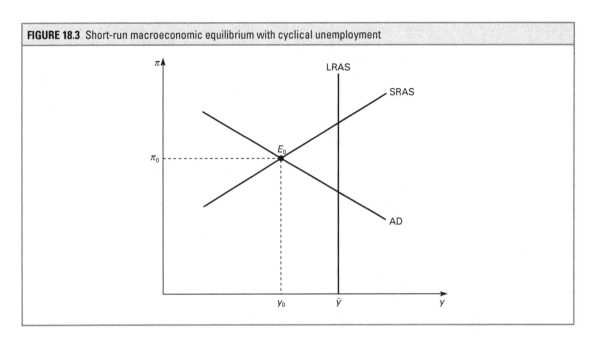

FIGURE 18.3 Short-run macroeconomic equilibrium with cyclical unemployment

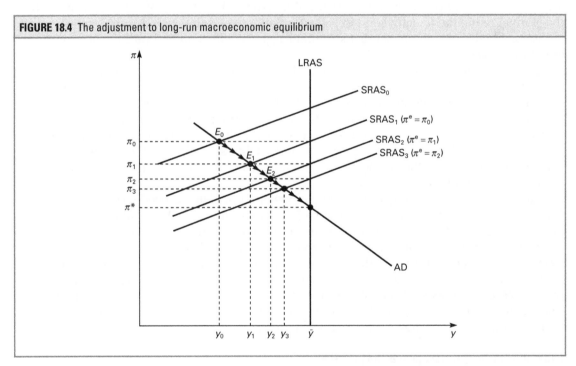

FIGURE 18.4 The adjustment to long-run macroeconomic equilibrium

curve depends on the expected rate of inflation π_t^e which is equal to last period's actual inflation rate π_{t-1}. Given that $s_t = 0$, and since $y_t = \bar{y}$ when the economy is on its LRAS curve, it follows from (8) that the SRAS curve for period t must cut the LRAS curve at an inflation rate equal to last period's inflation π_{t-1}.

Using this insight, Fig. 18.4 traces the economy's adjustment over time. In the initial time period $t = 0$ when the economy is in recession at point E_0, the inflation rate is π_0. In the next period $t = 1$ people expect the previous period's level of inflation to continue, so the SRAS curve for period 1 cuts the LRAS curve at the inflation rate π_0. Hence the SRAS curve shifts down from $SRAS_0$ to $SRAS_1$ between period 0 and period 1, generating a new short-run equilibrium at point E_1 where inflation is lower and output is higher than before. When the economy enters period 2, agents expect an inflation rate $\pi_1 < \pi_0$, so the SRAS curve shifts down again, cutting the LRAS curve at the inflation rate π_1. This creates a new short-run equilibrium at E_2 where inflation is even lower and output has risen once more. As illustrated in Fig. 18.4, this process of successive downward shifts in the SRAS curve will continue as long as $y_t < \bar{y}$. Thus the economy will gradually move down along the AD curve until it finally settles in the long-run equilibrium $\bar{E}$ where output is at its natural rate $\bar{y}$. In this long-run equilibrium inflation is at its target level, since it follows from (7) that $\pi_t = \pi^*$ when $y_t = \bar{y}$ and $z_t = 0$.

The economics underlying this macroeconomic adjustment mechanism may be explained as follows. When the economy is in recession, wage setters tend to overestimate the rate of inflation. This will motivate them to reduce their inflation forecasts over time, and as a consequence they will lower their required rate of increase in money wages. Hence firms will experience a lower rate of increase in marginal costs, and via mark-up price setting this will translate into a lower rate of price inflation. As inflation goes down, the central bank cuts the real interest rate, thereby ensuring that weaker inflationary pressure increases aggregate demand and output. As long as output and employment remain below their natural rates, wage setters will continue to overestimate the rate of inflation (although to a falling degree) and will therefore revise their inflation forecasts downwards, resulting in a lower rate of wage and price inflation which triggers another interest rate cut and generates yet another fall in expected inflation, and so on. In this way the gradual reduction in actual and expected inflation paves the way for successive reductions in the rate of interest that stimulate aggregate demand and pull the economy out of the recession.

Note the crucial importance of central bank behaviour for this macroeconomic adjustment process: to make sure that falling inflation actually increases aggregate demand, the central bank must cut the nominal interest rate by *more* than one percentage point for each percentage point drop in inflation, that is, our parameter h in the Taylor rule must be positive.[4] Otherwise falling inflation will cause the real interest rate to rise, exacerbating the initial recession. The stronger monetary policy reacts to falling inflation (the greater the value of h), the flatter is the aggregate demand curve, and the faster is the convergence of output to its natural rate.

The need to keep the monetary policy parameter h positive has been termed the 'Taylor Principle' because it was stressed by John Taylor himself. While adherence to this principle is crucial for the stability of the macro economy, our specific assumption of static expectations ($\pi_t^e = \pi_{t-1}$) is less important. The only thing needed to ensure convergence towards long-run equilibrium is that the expected inflation rate will fall over time when people learn that they have overestimated the rate of inflation, and that expected inflation will increase when people find out that they have underestimated the inflation rate. In that case the SRAS curve will gradually shift down when the economy is in recession, whereas it will shift up over time when the economy is in a boom (where $y_t > \bar{y}$).

Calibrating the model: how long is the long run?

According to the analysis above, the changes in the inflation rate generated by market forces will automatically pull the economy out of a recession as long as the central bank follows the Taylor Principle. In the long run the rates of output and employment will thus converge

---

4.   Inserting $\pi_{t+1}^e = \pi_t$ into (3), we get

$$i_t^p = \bar{r}^* + \pi_t + h(\pi_t - \pi^*) + b(y_t - \bar{y})$$

which shows that a one percentage point decrease in the current inflation rate will trigger a more than one percentage point decrease in the nominal policy interest rate when $h > 0$.

on their natural rates. But for workers who cannot find a job and for entrepreneurs struggling to avoid bankruptcy it may not be very interesting to know that the economy will eventually recover from a recession if the process of recovery is very slow. As John Maynard Keynes once said: 'In the long run we are all dead'. When deciding whether political action such as a tax cut or an increase in public spending is needed to fight a recession, it is obviously very important to know whether the economy's automatic convergence to the natural rate is relatively slow or relatively fast. In the former case fiscal policy intervention may be needed; in the latter case it may not.

To study the question 'How long is the long run?', we may consider a *quantitative* version of our AS–AD model. By assigning plausible values to the parameters of the model, we can investigate how fast the economy is likely to move from its short-run to its long-run equilibrium after having been hit by a shock. For this purpose we maintain the assumption that there are no further supply or demand shocks following the initial shock that created the recession. In formal terms this means that $s_t = z_t = 0$ for $t \geq 0$. Let $\hat{y}_t \equiv y_t - \bar{y}$ denote the relative deviation of output from trend (the output gap), and let $\hat{\pi}_t \equiv \pi_t - \pi^*$ indicate the deviation of inflation from the target inflation rate (the inflation gap). Setting $s_t = z_t = 0$, we may then restate our AS–AD model (7) and (8) as follows:

AD: $\quad \hat{\pi}_{t+1} = -\left(\dfrac{1}{\alpha}\right)\hat{y}_{t+1}, \qquad \alpha \equiv \dfrac{\alpha_2 h}{1 + \alpha_2 b},$ (9)

SRAS: $\quad \hat{\pi}_{t+1} = \hat{\pi}_t + \gamma \hat{y}_{t+1}.$ (10)

From (9) we have $\hat{\pi}_t = -(1/\alpha)\hat{y}_t$, which may be inserted into (10) along with (9) to give:

$$\hat{y}_{t+1} = \beta \hat{y}_t, \qquad \beta \equiv \frac{1}{1 + \alpha\gamma}.$$ (11)

It also follows from (9) that $\hat{y}_{t+1} = -\alpha\hat{\pi}_{t+1}$, which may be substituted into (10) to yield:

$$\hat{\pi}_{t+1} = \beta \hat{\pi}_t.$$ (12)

The linear first-order difference equations in (11) and (12) have the solutions:

$$\hat{y}_t = \hat{y}_0 \beta^t, \qquad t = 0, 1, 2, \ldots$$ (13)

$$\hat{\pi}_t = \hat{\pi}_0 \beta^t, \qquad t = 0, 1, 2, \ldots$$ (14)

where $\hat{y}_0$ and $\hat{\pi}_0$ are the initial values of $\hat{y}$ and $\hat{\pi}$, respectively.[5] According to the definition given in (11), $\beta \equiv 1/(1 + \alpha\gamma)$ is less than 1, so the term β^t on the right-hand sides of (13) and (14) will tend to 0 as time t tends to infinity. In other words, y_t will converge on $\bar{y}$ and π_t will converge on π^*. This proves that the economy is *stable* in the sense that it tends towards its long-run equilibrium.

Literally speaking, it will take infinitely long for the economy to reach the long-run equilibrium, but we may ask how long it will take before, say, half the adjustment to equilibrium has been completed. Let t_h denote the number of time periods that must elapse

---

5. To see that (13) is indeed the solution to (11), note that (13) implies

$\hat{y}_{t+1} = \hat{y}_0 \beta^{t+1} = \beta \hat{y}_0 \beta^t = \beta \hat{y}_t.$

In a similar way you may verify that (14) represents the solution to (12).

before half of the initial gap $\hat{y}_0$ between actual output and long-run equilibrium output has been closed. According to (13), the value of t_h may be found from the equation:

$$\hat{y}_t = \hat{y}_0 \beta^{t_h} \equiv \frac{1}{2}\hat{y}_0 \iff \beta^{t_h} = \frac{1}{2} \iff t_h \ln\beta = \ln(1/2) \iff \tag{15}$$

$$t_h = -\frac{\ln 2}{\ln\beta} = -\frac{0.693}{\ln\beta}, \qquad \beta \equiv \frac{1}{1+\alpha\gamma}.$$

Hence the economy's speed of adjustment is uniquely determined by the value of the parameter β which in turn depends on the values of γ and α. Our parameter γ measures the speed with which inflation adjusts to a change in the output gap. In Chapter 17 we estimated that (for the USA) a one percentage point unemployment gap $u - \bar{u}$ reduces the annual rate on inflation by about 0.6 percentage points (see Eq. (52) in Chapter 17), and Chapter 10 documented that (for the USA) it takes about a two percentage point output gap to generate a one percentage point unemployment gap ('Okun's Law'). This suggests that when the time period is one year, a realistic value of γ is around 0.3, so if the time period of our model corresponds to one quarter of a year, the value of γ should be set at around $0.3/4 = 0.075.$[6] According to Eq. (13) in Chapter 16, the parameter α_2 entering the expression for α in (9) can be written as:

$$\alpha_2 \equiv \frac{-D_r}{\bar{Y}(1-D_Y)} = \left(\frac{1-\tau}{1-D_Y}\right)\eta, \qquad \eta \equiv \frac{-D_r}{\bar{Y}(1-\tau)}, \tag{16}$$

where D_r is the marginal effect of a rise in the real interest rate on private goods demand, D_Y is the marginal private propensity to spend income on consumption and investment goods, and τ is the net tax rate (taxes net of transfers) levied on the private sector. The parameter η indicates the effect of a one percentage point rise in the real interest rate on the private sector's savings surplus (savings minus investment), measured relative to private disposable income. For Denmark, this parameter has been estimated to be roughly 3.6,[7] while plausible values for τ and D_Y would be $\tau = 0.2$ and $D_Y = 0.5$, implying $\alpha_2 = (0.8/0.5) \times 3.6 = 5.76$. If we use this value of α_2 and set the monetary policy parameters h and b appearing in (9) equal to 0.5 as proposed by John Taylor,[8] we get $\alpha = 0.742$, implying a value of β equal to 0.947. Inserting this into (15), we obtain $t_h \approx 13$. In other words, for reasonable parameter values our model implies that it will take roughly 13 quarters, that is, more than 3 years for the economy to complete half of the adjustment to its new long-run equilibrium after it has been hit by a shock. In a similar way one can show that it will take more than 10 years before the economy has completed 90 per cent of the total adjustment to long-run equilibrium. Thus our model implies that it will take quite a long time for the output gap to be closed if the economy is exposed to a permanent shock. This is just another way of saying that there is a

6. In our theoretical model of inflation in Chapter 17, we found that $\gamma = \alpha/(1-\alpha)$, where α is the elasticity of output with respect to capital input. When there is imperfect competition in product markets, as we assumed in Chapter 17, one can show that $\alpha = 1 - \lambda(1+m)$, where λ is the share of labour income in GDP, and m is the average mark-up of product prices over marginal costs. Empirical research for the USA suggests that the average mark-up could be as large as 20 per cent ($m = 0.2$), and a realistic value of the labour income share (λ) is 2/3. With these parameter values, we would have $\alpha = 0.2$ and $\gamma = \alpha/(1-\alpha) = 0.25$. However, our derivation of γ in Chapter 17 assumed that the capital stock is fixed and always fully utilized so that all of the burden of adjusting input factors to a change in production falls on labour. In practice, fluctuations in output are also associated with changes in the degree of utilization of the capital stock. We therefore prefer the more thoroughly empirical approach to the estimation of γ adopted in the text above.

7. See Erik Haller Pedersen, 'Development in and Measurement of the Real Rate of Interest', *Danmarks Nationalbank, Monetary Review*, 3rd Quarter, **40** (3), 2001, pp. 71–90.

8. See John B. Taylor, 'Discretion versus Policy Rules in Practice', *Carnegie-Rochester Conference Series on Public Policy*, **39**, 1993, pp. 195–214. In that article Taylor argued that $b = h = 0.5$ was a reasonably good description of actual US monetary policy since the early 1980s.

strong *persistence* in the deviations of output from trend. The reason for this persistence is that actual and expected inflation adjust only slowly over time, so in the short and medium run output and employment have to bear a large part of the burden of adjusting to a shock.

Note from the definitions of α and β in (9) and (15) that a high value of the monetary policy parameter h will push β towards 0, thereby speeding up the economy's convergence to long-run equilibrium. This confirms our earlier conclusion that the stronger the interest rate response to a change in the rate of inflation, the faster is the adjustment of output to its natural rate. It also follows from (9) and (15) that a lower value of the policy parameter b will tend to raise the speed of convergence. This might seem to suggest that the central bank should choose the highest possible value of h and the lowest possible value of b to minimize deviations from long-run equilibrium. However, through their influence on the slope of the AD curve, the magnitude of h and b also determine how far output and inflation are pushed away initially from their long-run equilibrium levels when the economy is hit by demand or supply shocks. Choosing the optimal values of h and b is therefore a complicated matter to which we return in Chapter 20.

For the moment, let us sum up the main insights from the above analysis:

THE MACROECONOMIC ADJUSTMENT MECHANISM IN THE AS–AD MODEL ❶

When the economy is in recession, wage setters tend to overestimate the rate of inflation and will therefore reduce their inflation forecasts and their required rate of increase in money wages. This will reduce the rate of inflation and will induce a central bank adhering to the Taylor Principle to cut the real interest rate. In this way the weaker inflationary pressure increases aggregate demand and output. In the absence of new shocks to the economy, the gradual fall in actual and expected inflation and the concomitant fall in the real interest rate will continue until the negative output gap is closed. If the economy starts out with a positive output gap, the reverse process will occur, with actual and expected inflation and the real interest rate gradually increasing until a long-run equilibrium is reached. For realistic parameter values, this macroeconomic adjustment process is likely to take a long time, since actual and expected inflation tend to adjust rather slowly. The stronger monetary policy reacts to a change in inflation, the flatter is the aggregate demand curve, and the faster is the convergence of output to its natural rate.

18.2 Business fluctuations in a deterministic world

The analysis above studied the economy's convergence on long-run equilibrium, but without explaining how output and inflation came to deviate from long-run equilibrium in the first place. In this section we will illustrate how the long-run equilibrium may be disturbed by shocks to aggregate supply and aggregate demand, and how the economy will react on impact and over time to such shocks. Although in practice new shocks occur all the time, we can learn about the workings of the economy by tracing the isolated effects of a single shock, so this is what we will do in the present section. Specifically, we will treat a shock as a one-time disturbance which hits the economy in a single period. In this way we are able to highlight how the economy's reaction to the shock will generate persistent (long-lasting) deviations of output and inflation from trend even if the shock itself is purely temporary. We assume that, after the initial shock, there are no further subsequent shocks. The economy will then evolve in a deterministic manner over time, that is, we can use our AS–AD model to calculate the exact values of the output gap and the inflation gap in each period following the shock. In Section 18.3 we will extend the model by assuming that the economy is repeatedly hit by random shocks which turn our AS–AD model into a stochastic system.

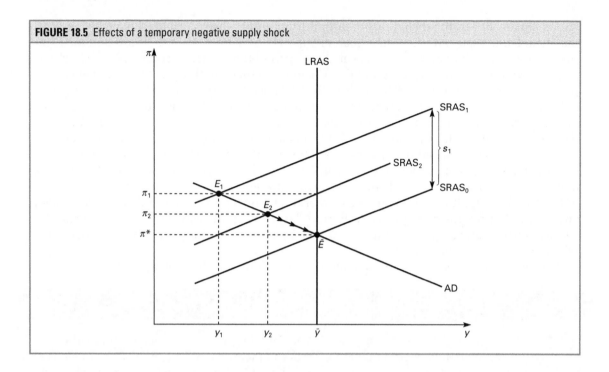

FIGURE 18.5 Effects of a temporary negative supply shock

A temporary negative supply shock

We start by studying the economy's reaction to a temporary negative supply shock such as an industrial conflict or a bad harvest. Let us assume that in period 0, before the shock, the economy is in the long-run equilibrium illustrated by point $\bar{E}$ in Fig. 18.5. Suppose then that the economy is hit by a temporary negative supply shock in period 1, causing the value of our shock variable s to rise from 0 to some positive number s_1 in period 1. Because of the temporary nature of the shock, it will not affect the long-run aggregate supply curve, but according to (8) the short-run aggregate supply curve will move up by the vertical distance s_1 from $SRAS_0$ to $SRAS_1$. The new short-run equilibrium for period 1 is therefore given by point E_1. In moving from $\bar{E}$ to E_1 we see that the economy goes through a period of *stagflation*, defined as the simultaneous occurrence of rising inflation and falling output. The fact that inflation goes up is not surprising, since a negative supply shock is essentially an exogenous increase in production costs. The reason why output falls is that the central bank reacts to the rise in inflation by raising the interest rate, thereby depressing aggregate demand.

Suppose next that the source of the supply shock disappears from period 2 onwards so that s returns to its original value of 0. One might then think that the SRAS curve would shift down to its original position $SRAS_0$, thereby restoring long-run equilibrium already in period 2. But since the inflation rate has risen to the level π_1 in period 1, our assumption of static expectations implies that the expected inflation rate for period 2 will be π_1, which is higher than the expected inflation rate π^* corresponding to the original SRAS curve. Because of this rise in expected inflation, the short-run aggregate supply curve only shifts down to the level $SRAS_2$ in period 2, even though s drops back down to 0. The result is the new short-run equilibrium E_2 illustrated in Fig. 18.5 where inflation is still above the target rate and output is still below its natural rate. Yet, since the actual inflation rate falls between periods 1 and 2, the expected inflation rate for period 3 also falls, generating a further downward shift in the SRAS curve in period 3, which in turn leads to a new short-run equilibrium with lower inflation, causing another downward shift in the SRAS curve, and so on. Thus the continued downward revision of the expected inflation rate enables the economy to move gradually down the AD curve back to the original long-run equilibrium $\bar{E}$.

However, the important point is that because of the dynamic adjustment of expectations, even a short-lived supply shock has a long-lasting effect on output and inflation. In summary,

A TEMPORARY NEGATIVE SUPPLY SHOCK

A temporary negative supply shock causes stagflation (a simultaneous increase in unemployment and inflation) in the short run. Even when the shock is temporary, economic activity will stay below its natural rate for a while, because the central bank will keep the actual real interest rate above the 'natural' real interest rate as long as inflation remains above the target rate.

A temporary negative demand shock

Let us now consider the effects of a shock to aggregate demand. Suppose that, after having been in long-run equilibrium in period 0, the economy is hit by a temporary negative demand shock in period 1, say, because private agents temporarily become more pessimistic about the prospects for income growth. Fig. 18.6 illustrates how the economy will react to the temporary weakening of private sector confidence. Between period 0 and period 1 the demand shock variable z changes from 0 to some negative number z_1. According to (7) the AD curve therefore shifts down by the distance $|z_1/\alpha|$, from AD_0 to AD_1 in Fig. 18.6. This drives the economy from the initial long-run equilibrium to the new short-run equilibrium E_1 where output as well as inflation are lower.

However, in period 2 private sector confidence is restored, pushing the aggregate demand curve back to its original position AD_0 as the variable z_t in (7) returns to its initial value of 0. You might think that this would immediately pull the economy back to its initial equilibrium $\bar{E}$. Yet this is not what happens, since the observed fall in inflation during period 1 causes a fall in expected inflation from π^* to the lower level π_1 as the economy moves from period 1 to period 2. Hence the short-run aggregate supply curve shifts down to $SRAS_2$ in period 2, generating a new short-run equilibrium at point E_2. Remarkably, we see

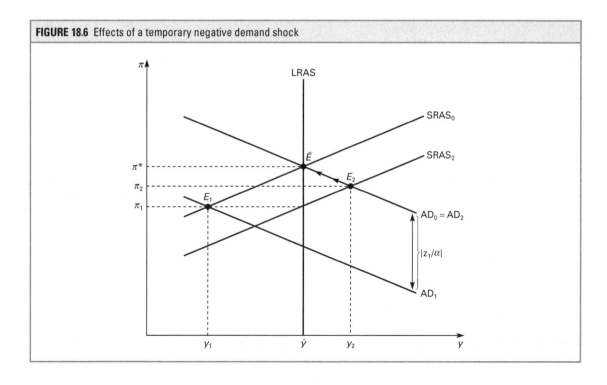

FIGURE 18.6 Effects of a temporary negative demand shock

that output in period 2 *overshoots* its long-run equilibrium value $\bar{y}$. Real GDP will only gradually return to its normal trend level as the above-normal level of activity drives up actual and expected inflation. As expected inflation goes up, the SRAS curve will gradually shift back towards its original position $SRAS_0$, and the economy will move back along the AD curve to the initial long-run equilibrium $\bar{E}$. The interesting point is that the initial recession generated by the temporary demand shock is followed by an extended economic boom. This shows how the economy's propagation mechanism may generate a pattern of adjustment which is rather different from the time pattern of the driving shock itself. In sum,

A TEMPORARY NEGATIVE DEMAND SHOCK

A temporary negative demand shock initially causes a recession where output and inflation are below their long-run equilibrium levels. However, when the aggregate demand curve returns to its original position, the economy enters a boom that will last for several periods, because the fall in actual and expected inflation caused by the initial recession allows the central bank to keep the real interest rate below the natural rate until actual and expected inflation catches up with the target inflation rate.

Impulse-response functions
In Section 18.1 we set up a quantified version of our model to study how long it will take the economy to converge towards long-run equilibrium. In a similar way, we may use a quantitative version of our AS–AD model to investigate how strongly the economy is likely to react to demand and supply shocks, assuming plausible values of the key parameters. For this purpose we must of course allow our shock variables z_t and s_t to deviate from 0. Using our previous notation for the output gap, $\hat{y}_t \equiv y_t - \bar{y}$, and our definition of the inflation gap, $\hat{\pi} \equiv \pi_t - \pi^*$, we may write the AD curve (7) and the SRAS curve (8) in the form:

$$\text{AD:} \quad \hat{\pi}_t = \left(\frac{1}{\alpha}\right)(z_t - \hat{y}_t), \tag{17}$$

$$\text{SRAS:} \quad \hat{\pi}_t = \hat{\pi}_{t-1} + \gamma \hat{y}_t + s_t. \tag{18}$$

From (17) we have $\hat{\pi}_{t-1} = (1/\alpha)(z_{t-1} - \hat{y}_{t-1})$. Inserting this plus (17) into (18), we find:

$$\hat{y}_t = \beta \hat{y}_{t-1} + \beta(z_t - z_{t-1}) - \alpha\beta s_t. \tag{19}$$

In a similar way we may use (17) to eliminate $\hat{y}_t$ from (18), yielding:

$$\hat{\pi}_t = \beta \hat{\pi}_{t-1} + \gamma\beta z_t + \beta s_t. \tag{20}$$

Using plausible parameter values, we may now simulate Eqs (19) and (20) from period 0 and onwards to obtain so-called *impulse-response functions* showing how output and inflation react over time to various shocks. Since output y_t is measured in logarithms, a unit increase in our demand shock variable z_t reflects an exogenous increase in demand corresponding to 1 per cent of initial GDP. Moreover, a unit increase in our supply shock variable s_t corresponds to an exogenous 1 percentage point increase in the rate of inflation.

In Fig. 18.7 we show the impulse-response functions for the output gap and for the inflation gap generated by a temporary increase in our supply shock variable s_t from 0 to 1 occurring in period 1. We use the same parameter values as before, except that we now assume that the length of the period is one year. For this reason we have set the parameter γ equal to 0.3, in line with our previous discussion of the likely magnitude of this parameter when the time period is one year. Not surprisingly, Fig. 18.7 confirms the qualitative analysis

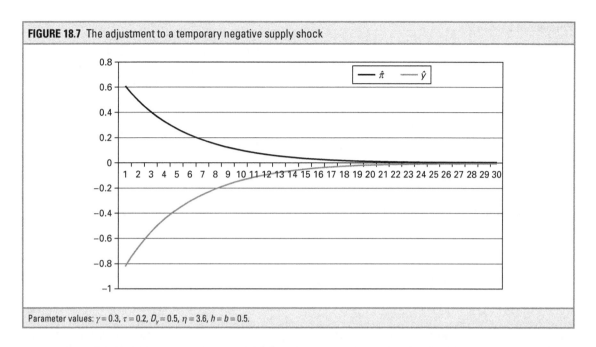

FIGURE 18.7 The adjustment to a temporary negative supply shock

Parameter values: $\gamma = 0.3$, $\tau = 0.2$, $D_y = 0.5$, $\eta = 3.6$, $h = b = 0.5$.

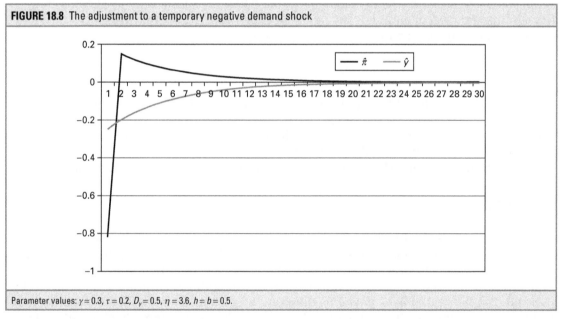

FIGURE 18.8 The adjustment to a temporary negative demand shock

Parameter values: $\gamma = 0.3$, $\tau = 0.2$, $D_y = 0.5$, $\eta = 3.6$, $h = b = 0.5$.

in Fig. 18.5: in the short and medium run, the temporary negative supply shock generates a positive inflation gap and a negative output gap. In period 1, the inflation rate does not quite rise by 1 percentage point, because the drop in output and employment reduces inflationary pressure a bit by driving down the marginal costs of production. The short-run decrease in output is quite substantial, amounting to more than 0.6 per cent.

Figure 18.8 shows the impulse-response functions emerging when our demand shock variable z_t temporarily falls from 0 to -1 in period 1. In the short run output falls by less than 1 per cent, since the drop in inflation and economic activity induces the central bank to cut the real interest rate to limit the fall in demand. When z_t returns to its normal level of 0 from period 2 onwards, we see that the output gap changes from negative to positive and then gradually falls back towards 0. This is quite in accordance with the qualitative analysis of a temporary demand shock in Fig. 18.6.

Permanent shocks

We have so far considered only temporary shocks, but sometimes a shock may be permanent. For example, a tax reform may permanently change the propensities to consume and invest, and a liberalization of international trade may permanently affect the markups of prices over marginal costs by changing the degree of product market competition.

Analysing the effects of permanent shocks is more complicated since such shocks will change the equilibrium real interest rate which enters into the central bank's monetary policy rule. Moreover, a permanent *supply* shock will change the economy's natural rate of output. We will now show how the economy's long-run equilibrium is affected by permanent shocks. Let $\bar{r}_0$ and $\bar{y}_0$ denote, respectively, the real market interest rate and the level of output prevailing in the *initial* long-run equilibrium before the economy is hit by a permanent shock. Since we have linearized the model around the initial long-run equilibrium, the goods market equilibrium condition (2) may then be written as

$$y_t - \bar{y}_0 = \tilde{v}_t - \alpha_2(r_t - \bar{r}_0), \qquad \tilde{v}_t \equiv v_t + \alpha_1(g_t - \bar{g}), \tag{21}$$

and the SRAS curve becomes:

$$\pi_t = \pi_{t-1} + \gamma(y_t - \bar{y}_0) + s_t. \tag{22}$$

In the initial equilibrium we have $\tilde{v}_t = s_t = 0$. Now suppose that the economy experiences a supply shock which permanently changes s_t from 0 to some constant $s \neq 0$. The *new* long-run equilibrium level of output, $\bar{y}$, may then be found from (22) by inserting $\pi_t = \pi_{t-1}$, $y_t = \bar{y}$, and $s_t = s$, and solving for $\bar{y}$ to get:

$$\bar{y} = \bar{y}_0 - \frac{s}{\gamma}. \tag{23}$$

Recall from Chapter 16 that the equilibrium real interest rate (the 'natural' interest rate) is the level of interest ensuring that the goods market clears at the natural rate of output. The *new* equilibrium market real interest rate, $\bar{r}$, may therefore be found from (21) by setting actual output y_t equal to the new natural rate of output $\bar{y} = \bar{y}_0 - (s/\gamma)$, and by setting $r_t = \bar{r}$. Assuming that no permanent demand shocks have occurred so that $\tilde{v}_t = 0$, it then follows from (21) that:

$$\bar{r} = \bar{r}_0 + \frac{s}{\gamma \alpha_2}. \tag{24}$$

The intuition for (24) is straightforward: a negative supply shock $(s > 0)$ which reduces the natural rate of output requires a fall in aggregate demand to maintain long-run equilibrium in the goods market. To curb aggregate demand, the real market interest rate must go up, as stated in (24). To steer the economy towards the new long-run equilibrium characterized by (23) and (24), the central bank must therefore revise its estimate of the risk-free equilibrium real interest rate entering the monetary policy rule (3). Thus the central bank must set its nominal policy rate on the basis of the estimate $\bar{r}^* = \bar{r} - \bar{\rho}$, where $\bar{r}$ is given by (24).

If the economy is instead hit by a permanent *demand* shock changing $\tilde{v}_t$ from 0 to some constant $\tilde{v} \neq 0$, we see from (23) that there is no effect on the natural rate of output (given that $s = 0$). We may therefore find the new equilibrium real market interest rate by setting $\bar{y} = \bar{y}_0$ and $\tilde{v}_t = \tilde{v}$ in (21) and solving for $r_t = \bar{r}$ to obtain:

$$\bar{r} = \bar{r}_0 + \frac{\tilde{v}}{\alpha_2}. \tag{25}$$

This result is also intuitive: since natural output is unchanged, an autonomous permanent increase in aggregate demand $(\tilde{v} > 0)$ must be offset by a rise in the real interest rate which reduces the interest-sensitive components of demand so that total demand does not exceed the constant long-run equilibrium level of output.

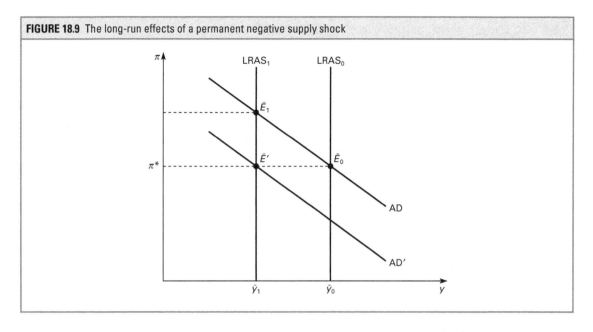

FIGURE 18.9 The long-run effects of a permanent negative supply shock

To achieve its objectives of keeping inflation close to its target rate and avoiding large output gaps, the central bank's estimate of the variables $\bar{r}^* = \bar{r} - \bar{\rho}$ and $\bar{y}$ entering the monetary policy rule (3) must try to account for any permanent demand and supply shocks occurring along the way. Otherwise the central bank will not be able to achieve its goals. For example, if a negative supply shock has permanently shifted the long-run aggregate supply curve from the position $LRAS_0$ to the position $LRAS_1$ in Fig. 18.9, and if the central bank does not account for the fact that the equilibrium real interest rate has increased, the economy will end up in the long-run equilibrium $\bar{E}_1$ where the inflation rate permanently exceeds the inflation target π^*. To prevent this systematic deviation of inflation from target, the central bank must revise its estimate of $\bar{r}$ upwards in accordance with (24). When this revision occurs, the AD curve will shift down to the level AD′ in Fig. 18.9 so that the new long run equilibrium $\bar{E}'$ becomes consistent with the inflation target.

Of course, requiring that the central bank should update its estimate of the equilibrium real interest rate to account for permanent shocks is much easier said than don̄ ˈnce it may take quite a while before it is possible to judge whether some ˢ˕ y or permanent in nature. When a permanent shock occurs, the economy's adjustment over time will depend on how long it takes for the central bank to discover the permanent character of the shock. In Exercise 2 we invite you to study the effects of permanent demand and supply shocks in more detail.

We may sum up these insights as follows:

PERMANENT SHOCKS

When the economy is hit by a permanent demand or supply shock which changes the 'natural' real interest rate, the central bank must adjust its estimate of the equilibrium real interest rate accordingly to ensure that inflation will stay on target in the long run. A permanent negative (positive) supply shock reduces (increases) natural output and increases (reduces) the natural real interest rate. A permanent negative (positive) demand shock does not affect natural output but reduces (increases) the natural real interest rate. In practice it may take a long time before the central bank is able to discover that a shock is permanent. In the meantime inflation may deviate substantially from its target.

18.3   Business cycles in a stochastic world

As we have seen, our deterministic AS–AD model does quite a good job in accounting for the observed *persistence* in the movement of output over time. But the deterministic model does not really explain the crucial feature of business cycles that economic booms tend repeatedly to be followed by recessions, and vice versa. A satisfactory model of the business cycle must be able to replicate the *recurrent fluctuations* in output and inflation, like those in Fig. 18.1 which illustrated the evolution of the cyclical components of real GDP and the rate of inflation in the USA in recent decades.

To explain the cyclical pattern of output and inflation, we will now set up a *stochastic* version of our AS–AD model in which our demand and supply shock variables z and s are assumed to be *random variables*. In taking this step, we are building on a remarkable discovery made in 1937 by the Italian economist-statistician Eugen Slutzky (see the reference in Footnote 1). Slutzky discovered that if one adds a stochastic term with a zero mean and a constant variance to a first-order linear difference equation, and if the coefficient on the lagged endogenous variable is not too far below unity, the resulting stochastic difference equation will generate a time series which looks very much like the irregular cyclical pattern of output displayed in Fig. 18.1!

To illustrate Slutzky's fundamental insight, suppose the variable a_t evolves according to the difference equation:

$$a_t = 0.9a_{t-1} + e_t, \tag{26}$$

where e_t is a random variable following a normal distribution with a zero mean. Note that (26) has the same general form as our previous equation (19) for the output gap if we treat the additive 'shock' terms $\beta(z_t - z_{t-1}) - \alpha\beta s_t$ in (19) as a single stochastic variable. Drawing a sample from the standard normal distribution with a zero mean and a unit variance to obtain a sequence of e_t, assuming e_t to be independently distributed over time and setting the initial value of a_t equal to zero, we simulated Eq. (26) over 100 periods, here thought of as quarters. In this way we obtained the time path for a_t displayed in Fig. 18.10. Comparing this to the graph for the evolution of the US output gap in Fig. 18.1, we see that the simple difference equation (26) is able to generate a time series which qualitatively looks remarkably like the recurrent business cycles observed in the real world.

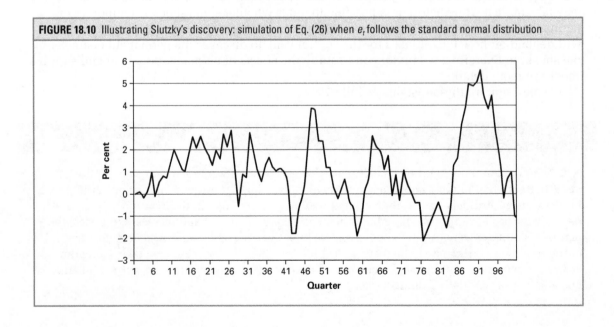

FIGURE 18.10 Illustrating Slutzky's discovery: simulation of Eq. (26) when e_t follows the standard normal distribution

Slutzky's discovery suggests that it may be fruitful to treat our shock variables z_t and s_t as stochastic processes. By nature, the shocks to demand and supply which we have been discussing are very hard to predict. Recall that supply side shocks include phenomena such as industrial conflicts, fluctuations in agricultural output due to changing weather conditions, oil price shocks due perhaps to military conflict or political unrest in oil-producing countries, changes in productivity stemming from irregularly arriving technological breakthroughs, etc. On the demand side, shocks may occur due to sudden shifts in market psychology, or due to political regime shifts involving significant changes in fiscal policies, among other things. Whether events such as these occur with deterministic necessity – that is, whether they were unavoidable, given the way things had developed – or whether they are fundamentally unpredictable, just like the outcome of the toss of a coin, is a deep scientific question. But as long as our understanding of the causes of such events – and hence our ability to predict them – is limited, it seems to make sense to treat the supply and demand shocks in macroeconomic models as random variables. In doing so, we admit that we can only predict what demand and supply will be on average, while acknowledging that the actual levels of demand and supply may deviate from their average positions in a way we cannot anticipate.

As mentioned earlier, this approach to analysing business cycles is sometimes referred to as the Frisch–Slutzky paradigm and it may be summarized as follows:

THE FRISCH–SLUTZKY PARADIGM FOR BUSINESS CYCLE ANALYSIS ❗

The paradigm sees business cycles as being initiated by stochastic demand and supply shocks. Even though these shocks (impulses) occur at irregular intervals in an unpredictable manner, they interact with the economy's endogenous persistence (propagation) mechanisms in a way that generates recurrent cycles in economic activity, provided the persistence mechanisms are strong enough.

Let us now investigate how far a stochastic version of our AS–AD model can take us towards explaining the stylized facts of business cycles.

The stochastic AS–AD model

The stylized business cycle facts which we would like our model to explain are summarized in the bottom row of Table 18.1. These figures are based on quarterly data for the USA from 1947 to 2007. We have chosen to focus on the relatively closed US economy because we still have not extended our AS–AD model to allow for international trade in goods and capital (we will do so in Chapter 23). The data in Table 18.1 show the degree of volatility and persistence in output and inflation, measured by the standard deviations and the coefficients of autocorrelation, respectively. In addition, the third column indicates the degree to which output and inflation move together, measured by the coefficient of correlation. Ideally, simulations of our stochastic AS–AD model should be able to reproduce closely these statistical measures of the US business cycle.

Economists have often debated whether demand shocks or supply shocks are the most important type of disturbances driving the business cycle. One way of resolving this issue is to investigate whether a model driven by demand shocks is better at replicating the stylized business cycle facts than a model driven by supply shocks, or vice versa. In the first row of Table 18.1 we consider a version of our AS–AD model with static expectations that includes only demand shocks. Thus we have set s_t equal to 0 in all time periods. The demand shocks are assumed to evolve according to the following first-order autoregressive stochastic process:

$$z_{t+1} = \delta z_t + x_{t+1}, \qquad 0 \le \delta < 1, \qquad x_t \sim N(0, \sigma_x^2), \qquad x_t \text{ i.i.d.} \tag{27}$$

TABLE 18.1 The stochastic AS–AD model and stylized business cycle facts

	Standard deviation (%)		Correlation between output and inflation	Autocorrelation in output				Autocorrelation in inflation			
	Output	Inflation		$t-1$	$t-2$	$t-3$	$t-4$	$t-1$	$t-2$	$t-3$	$t-4$
AS–AD model with static expectations and no supply shocks[1]	1.64	0.82	0.08	0.84	0.71	0.53	0.42	0.99	0.96	0.91	0.86
AS–AD model with static expectations and no demand shocks[2]	1.65	2.22	−1.00	0.91	0.83	0.75	0.69	0.91	0.83	0.75	0.69
AS–AD model with adaptive expectations and a combination of demand and supply shocks[3]	1.63	0.27	0.36	0.86	0.73	0.57	0.45	0.57	0.50	0.42	0.48
The US economy, 1947:I–2007:I[4]	1.64	0.21	0.31	0.84	0.60	0.34	0.11	0.48	0.25	0.29	0.01

[1] $\phi = 0, \sigma_c = 0, \sigma_x = 0.94, \delta = 0.8, \omega = 0.$

[2] $\phi = 0, \sigma_c = 0.97, \sigma_x = 0, \delta = 0, \omega = 0.$

[3] $\phi = 0.90, \sigma_c = 0.2, \sigma_x = 0.9, \delta = 0.8, \omega = 0.15.$

[4] The cyclical components of output and inflation have been estimated via detrending of quarterly data using the HP filter with $\lambda = 1600$.

Common parameter values in all AS–AD simulations: $\gamma = 0.075, \tau = 0.2, D_y = 0.5, \eta = 3.6, h = b = 0.5.$

The notation $x_t \sim N(0, \sigma_x^2)$, x_t i.i.d. means that x_t is assumed to follow a normal distribution with a zero mean value and a constant finite variance σ_x^2, and that it is identically and independently distributed over time (i.i.d.). Hence the probability distribution of x_t is the same in all time periods, and the realized value of x_t in any period t is independent of the realized value of x_j in any other time period j.[9] A stochastic process x_t with these 'i.i.d.' properties is called 'white noise'. Note from (27) that, by allowing the parameter δ to be positive, we allow for the possibility that a demand shock occurring in a given quarter may not die out entirely within that same quarter, but may be felt partly in subsequent quarters. At the same time the restriction $\delta < 1$ implies that demand shocks do not last forever.

To arrive at the numbers shown in the top row of Table 18.1, we go through the following steps:

1. Insert (27) into our AS–AD model given by Eqs. (19) and (20).
2. Set $\hat{y}_0 = \hat{\pi}_0 = z_0 = 0$ for $t = 0$ and $s_t = 0$ for all t.
3. Let the computer pick a sample of 100 observations from the standardized normal distribution $N(0, 1)$.
4. Use these observations as realizations of x_t and feed these values of x_t into Eqs (19) and (20), thus simulating the AS–AD model over the interval $t = 1, 2, 3, \ldots, 100$.
5. Use the resulting simulated values of $\hat{y}_t$ and $\hat{\pi}_t$ to calculate the standard deviations, cross-correlation, and coefficients of autocorrelation for the two endogenous variables over the 100 time periods.

In the simulations we use the same parameter values as those used to generate the impulse-response functions in the deterministic AS–AD model, except that we set $\gamma = 0.075$ because we are now trying to replicate quarterly (rather than annual) data. In addition, we

---

9. Formally, $E[x_t x_{t'}] = 0$ for all $t \neq t'$, where $E[\cdot]$ is the expectations operator.

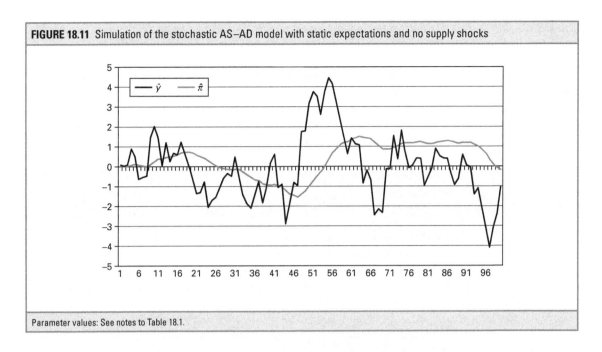

FIGURE 18.11 Simulation of the stochastic AS–AD model with static expectations and no supply shocks

Parameter values: See notes to Table 18.1.

assume the standard deviation σ_x of x_t to be equal to 0.94, and we set the value of the autocorrelation coefficient δ in (27) equal to 0.8. These values were chosen such that the model simulation generates a standard deviation of output equal to the one observed in the US economy. Comparing the top and bottom rows in Table 18.1, we see that our simulation without supply shocks reproduces the persistence (autocorrelation) in output reasonably well. However, the model simulation underestimates the positive correlation between output and inflation. In contrast, the simulation exaggerates the volatility (standard deviation) of inflation and particularly the degree of persistence (autocorrelation) in inflation. This impression is confirmed by a glance at Fig. 18.11 which plots the simulated values of $\hat{y}_t$ and $\hat{\pi}_t$ in our scenario without supply shocks. Comparing this figure to the actual US business cycle shown in Fig. 18.1, we see that while our model generates a reasonably realistic cyclical variability of output, it produces much too sluggish movements in the inflation rate. This suggests that an AS–AD model driven solely by demand shocks cannot give a fully satisfactory account of the business cycle.

In the second row of Table 18.1 we therefore focus on the opposite benchmark case where the stochastic disturbances occur only on the economy's supply side. By analogy to (27), we assume that the supply shocks follow a stochastic process of the form:

$$s_{t+1} = \omega s_t + c_{t+1}, \qquad 0 \le \omega < 1, \qquad c_t \sim N(0, \sigma_c^2), \qquad c_t \text{ i.i.d.} \tag{28}$$

To derive the figures in the second row of the table, we have followed the same steps as those explained above, except that we now set the demand shock variable $z_t = 0$ for all t. The standard deviation σ_c of the white noise variable c_t was chosen to ensure a simulated standard deviation of output roughly in line with the empirical standard deviation. The 'persistence' parameter ω in (28) was set to 0, since positive values of ω generate an even poorer fit to the data than that displayed in the second row of Table 18.1. Even so, we see that the purely supply-driven AS–AD model is inconsistent with the stylized business cycle facts in the bottom row. The model generates far too much persistence in output and particularly in inflation, far too much volatility of inflation, and a counterfactual perfect negative correlation between output and inflation. Of course, this negative correlation is not surprising, since we have previously seen that a positive supply shock, which shifts the SRAS curve downwards, will drive down inflation at the same time as it raises output. By contrast, in the US economy the correlation between output and inflation has been positive in recent decades, indicating that supply shocks cannot have been the only driver of the business cycle.

It should be stressed that the simulation results reported in Table 18.1 are *sample specific*, relying on particular samples from the normal distribution. If we feed different samples of x_t or c_t into the model, we get somewhat different sample statistics, but the general picture remains that neither a purely demand-driven nor a purely supply-driven AS–AD model can account fully for the stylized facts of the business cycle. To sum up:

THE STOCHASTIC AS–AD MODEL WITH STATIC EXPECTATIONS AND THE STYLIZED BUSINESS CYCLE FACTS

A stochastic AS–AD model with static inflation expectations where business fluctuations are driven solely by autocorrelated demand shocks can reproduce the observed volatility of output and the observed degree of output persistence reasonably well. It can also reproduce the observed positive correlation between output and inflation but it generates an unrealistically high volatility and persistence of inflation. A stochastic AS–AD model with static expectations where fluctuations are driven only by supply shocks produces a counterfactual negative correlation between output and inflation and far too much volatility and persistence of inflation.

These findings suggest that a satisfactory business cycle model will have to account for shocks to demand as well as supply, but without assigning too great a role to supply shocks. In the next section we will therefore consider an extended model allowing both types of shocks to occur at the same time.

The stochastic AS–AD model with adaptive expectations

Apart from allowing for simultaneous demand and supply shocks, we will also generalize our description of the formation of expectations, since this will improve the ability of our AS–AD model to reproduce the empirical business cycle. We have so far assumed that expectations of inflation are *static*, meaning that this period's expected inflation rate is equal to last period's observed inflation rate, $\pi_t^e = \pi_{t-1}$. Figure 18.12 indicates that this assumption may be too simplistic. The fat bold curve in the figure shows the *expected* inflation rate for the current quarter, π_t^e, calculated as an average of the inflation forecasts made by a number of professional economic forecasters in the USA. The forecasts were reported before the middle of the current quarter, at a time when the forecasters knew the *actual* inflation rate in the previous quarter, π_{t-1}. The latter variable is drawn as the grey line in Fig. 18.12. If expectations were entirely static ($\pi_t^e = \pi_{t-1}$), the two curves in the diagram would thus coincide completely. In reality, this is obviously not the case. Instead, we see from Fig. 18.12 that the expected inflation rate tends to fluctuate less than the lagged actual inflation rate.

This suggests that our AS–AD model will become more realistic if we replace the assumption of static expectations by a hypothesis which implies that the expected inflation rate fluctuates *less* than last period's actual inflation rate. We will therefore assume that expectations are *adaptive*, adjusting in accordance with the formula:

$$\underbrace{\pi_t^e - \pi_{t-1}^e}_{\substack{\text{revision of expected} \\ \text{inflation rate}}} = (1 - \phi) \underbrace{(\pi_{t-1} - \pi_{t-1}^e)}_{\substack{\text{last period's inflation} \\ \text{forecast error}}}, \qquad 0 \le \phi < 1. \tag{29}$$

Equation (29) says that the expected inflation rate is adjusted upwards (downwards) over time if last period's actual inflation rate exceeded (fell short of) its expected level. We also

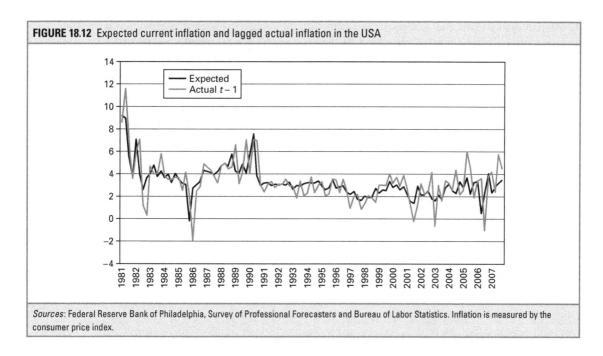

FIGURE 18.12 Expected current inflation and lagged actual inflation in the USA

Sources: Federal Reserve Bank of Philadelphia, Survey of Professional Forecasters and Bureau of Labor Statistics. Inflation is measured by the consumer price index.

see that a change in last period's actual inflation rate is not fully translated into a corresponding change in the expected inflation rate, provided $\phi > 0$. From (29) we get:

$$\pi_t^e = \phi \pi_{t-1}^e + (1-\phi)\pi_{t-1} \tag{30}$$

$$\pi_{t-1}^e = \phi \pi_{t-2}^e + (1-\phi)\pi_{t-2} \tag{31}$$

$$\pi_{t-2}^e = \phi \pi_{t-3}^e + (1-\phi)\pi_{t-3} \tag{32}$$

$$\vdots$$

and so on. From (30) we see that this period's expected inflation rate is a weighted average of last period's expected and actual inflation rates. We also see that static expectations $(\pi_t^e = \pi_{t-1})$ is that special case of adaptive expectations where the parameter ϕ is equal to 0. If we include the adaptive expectations hypothesis (29) in our AS–AD model, we can therefore easily reproduce all our previous results by simply setting $\phi = 0$. Note that ϕ is a measure of the 'stickiness' of expectations: a relatively high value of ϕ means that people tend to be conservative in their expectations formation, being reluctant to revise their expected inflation rate in response to previous inflation forecast errors. We can gain further insight into the implications of adaptive expectations if we use the expressions for π_{t-1}^e, π_{t-2}^e, etc., to eliminate π_{t-1}^e from the right-hand side of (30). Using such a series of successive substitutions we obtain:

$$
\begin{aligned}
\pi_t^e &= \phi^2 \pi_{t-2}^e + (1-\phi)\pi_{t-1} + \phi(1-\phi)\pi_{t-2} \\
&= \phi^3 \pi_{t-3}^e + (1-\phi)\pi_{t-1} + \phi(1-\phi)\pi_{t-2} + \phi^2(1-\phi)\pi_{t-3} \\
&\vdots \\
&= \phi^n \pi_{t-n}^e + (1-\phi)\pi_{t-1} + \phi(1-\phi)\pi_{t-2} + \phi^2(1-\phi)\pi_{t-3} + \cdots + \phi^{n-1}(1-\phi)\pi_{t-n}.
\end{aligned}
$$

Since $\phi < 1$, the term $\phi^n \pi_{t-n}^e$ will vanish as we let n tend to infinity. Hence we get:

$$\pi_t^e = \sum_{n=1}^{\infty} \phi^{n-1}(1-\phi)\pi_{t-n}, \qquad 0 \le \phi < 1. \tag{33}$$

Equation (33) shows that the expected inflation rate for the current period is a weighted average of all inflation rates observed in the past, with geometrically declining weights as we move further back into history. Thus adaptive expectations put more weight on the experience of the recent past than on the more distant past. But unlike the special case of static expectations, adaptive expectations imply that people do not base their expectations on only the experience of the most recent period. The higher the value of ϕ, the longer are people's memories, that is, the greater is the impact of the more distant inflation history on current expectations.

Our AS–AD model with adaptive expectations may now be summarized as follows:[10]

$$\text{AD:} \qquad y_t - \bar{y} = \alpha(\pi^* - \pi_t) + z_t, \tag{34}$$

$$\text{SRAS:} \qquad \pi_t = \pi_t^e + \gamma(y_t - \bar{y}) + s_t, \tag{35}$$

$$\text{Expectations:} \qquad \pi_t^e = \phi\pi_{t-1}^e + (1 - \phi)\pi_{t-1}. \tag{36}$$

Moving the SRAS curve (35) one period back in time and rearranging, we get:

$$\pi_{t-1}^e = \pi_{t-1} - \gamma(y_{t-1} - \bar{y}) - s_{t-1}, \tag{37}$$

which may be inserted into (36) to give:

$$\pi_t^e = \pi_{t-1} - \phi\gamma(y_{t-1} - \bar{y}) - \phi s_{t-1}. \tag{38}$$

Substituting (38) into (35) and using our previous definitions $\hat{y}_t \equiv y_t - \bar{y}$ and $\hat{\pi}_t \equiv \pi_t - \pi^*$, we may state the AS–AD model with adaptive expectations in the compact form:

$$\hat{y}_t = z_t - \alpha\hat{\pi}_t, \tag{39}$$

$$\hat{\pi}_t = \hat{\pi}_{t-1} + \gamma\hat{y}_t - \phi\gamma\hat{y}_{t-1} + s_t - \phi s_{t-1}, \tag{40}$$

where (39) is the AD curve and (40) is a restatement of the SRAS curve. As you may check, (39) and (40) imply:

$$\hat{y}_t = a\hat{y}_{t-1} + \beta(z_t - z_{t-1}) - \alpha\beta s_t + \alpha\beta\phi s_{t-1}, \tag{41}$$

$$\hat{\pi}_t = a\hat{\pi}_{t-1} + \gamma\beta z_t - \gamma\beta\phi z_{t-1} + \beta s_t - \beta\phi s_{t-1}, \tag{42}$$

$$a \equiv \frac{1 + \alpha\gamma\phi}{1 + \alpha\gamma} < 1, \qquad \beta \equiv \frac{1}{1 + \alpha\gamma} < 1. \tag{43}$$

In the third row of Table 18.1 we show the business cycle statistics generated by a simulation of the model (41) and (42). We assume that z and s are uncorrelated and that they follow the stochastic processes (27) and (28), respectively, with $\delta = 0.8$, $\omega = 0.15$, $\sigma_x = 0.9$ and $\sigma_c = 0.2$. To obtain realizations of the white noise variables x_t and c_t, we take the same samples from the standardized normal distribution as we used in the first and second columns of the table. The parameter ϕ has been set at 0.9, while the other parameter values are the same as those used in the AS–AD model with static expectations.

---

10. You may wonder if the AD curve is unaffected by the switch from static to adaptive expectations. The answer is 'Yes', provided the central bank has a good estimate of the expected inflation rate (such an estimate may be obtained through consumer and business surveys, or by comparing the market interest rates on indexed and non-indexed bonds). In that case the central bank can control the real (policy) interest rate $i_t^p - \pi_{t+1}^e$ regardless of the way inflation expectations are formed.

Comparing the third and fourth rows of Table 18.1, we see that the extended AS–AD model with adaptive expectations and simultaneous demand and supply shocks fits the empirical business cycle data fairly well, given the parameter values we have chosen. The simulated volatility of output and inflation and the correlation between the two variables are realistic, but the model tends to overestimate the degree of persistence in output and inflation, due to its simplified dynamic structure.

The model-generated time series for $\hat{y}_t$ and $\hat{\pi}_t$ are plotted in Fig. 18.13a. For convenience we have also reproduced Fig. 18.1 as Fig.18.3b. This shows the actual US business cycle for a recent time interval covering 100 quarters. The reader can thus compare the model-generated data with reality. Of course, since the timing of the random shocks hitting our model economy does not coincide with the timing of the historical shocks to the US economy, our model cannot

FIGURE 18.13a Simulation of the stochastic AS–AD model with adaptive expectations and a combination of demand and supply shocks

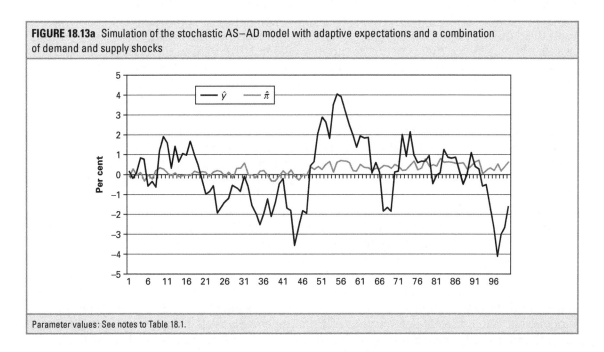

Parameter values: See notes to Table 18.1.

FIGURE 18.13b The cyclical components of real GDP and domestic inflation in the USA, 1974–2007

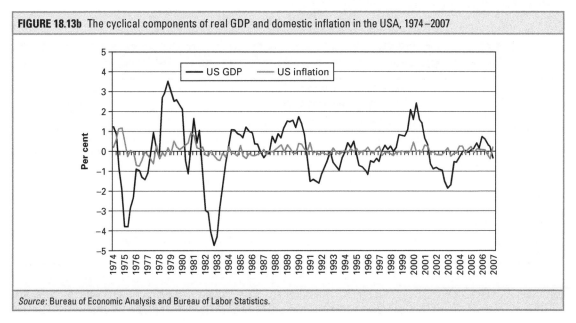

Source: Bureau of Economic Analysis and Bureau of Labor Statistics.

be expected to reproduce the historical turning points of the American business cycle. But a glance at Figs 18.13a and 18.13b suggests that the variance and persistence of output and inflation in our calibrated AS–AD model with adaptive expectations is fairly realistic.

We have tried to show that a simple stochastic AS–AD model allowing for shocks to supply as well as demand can provide a reasonably good account of the cyclical movements in output and inflation. In so doing, we have also tried to illustrate the basic methodology of modern business cycle analysis, showing how macroeconomists build dynamic stochastic general equilibrium models and calibrate these models to reproduce the stylized statistical facts of the business cycle.

We must emphasize once again that the simulation reported in the third row of Table 18.1 has the character of a numerical example, serving to illustrate that our AS–AD model may be able to fit the data for an appropriate choice of parameter values. But the example was based on two particular samples from the normal distribution. To analyse the model's ability to fit the data more systematically, one should either simulate the model over a very large number of periods, or run a very large number of simulations based on a correspondingly large number of samples from the probability distributions assumed for the stochastic shocks. In Table 18.2 we have taken the latter route. The upper row in the table shows the mean values of the results from 1000 simulations of our stochastic AS–AD model with adaptive expectations, where each simulation covers 100 time periods. The standard deviations (that is, average deviations from the mean) are indicated in brackets below the mean values. The parameter values in the simulation model are exactly the same as those assumed for the corresponding model in Table 18.1. For comparison, the bottom row in Table 18.2 repeats the stylized facts of the US business cycle between 1947 and 2007. We see that our AS–AD model seems to underestimate slightly the standard deviation and the autocorrelation of output when the model is simulated a large number of times with the parameter values that we used previously. Nevertheless, the overall impression remains that the model fits the data reasonably well, once we consider how simple it really is compared to the staggering complexity of the real-world economy.

Yet we must keep in mind that although our AS–AD model with adaptive expectations seems roughly consistent with the data on output and inflation, this does not imply that we have found *the* explanation for business cycles. It is possible to construct other types of models that match the data on output and inflation equally well. Hence we cannot claim to have found the only correct theory of the business cycle. All we can say is that our theory does not seem to be clearly rejected by the data.

	Standard deviation (%)		Correlation between output and inflation	Autocorrelation in output				Autocorrelation in inflation			
	Output	Inflation		$t-1$	$t-2$	$t-3$	$t-4$	$t-1$	$t-2$	$t-3$	$t-4$
AS–AD model with adaptive expectations and a combination of demand and supply shocks[1] (mean values of 1000 simulations, standard deviations in brackets)	1.35 (0.19)	0.27 (0.06)	0.25 (0.17)	0.75 (0.07)	0.57 (0.11)	0.42 (0.13)	0.31 (0.15)	0.48 (0.16)	0.37 (0.19)	0.33 (0.19)	0.31 (0.20)
The US economy, 1947:I–2007:I[2]	1.64	0.21	0.31	0.84	0.60	0.34	0.11	0.48	0.25	0.29	0.01

TABLE 18.2 The stochastic AS–AD model and the stylized business cycle facts

[1] $\gamma = 0.075$, $\tau = 0.2$, $D_y = 0.5$, $\eta = 3.6$, $h = b = 0.5$, $\phi = 0.9$, $\sigma_s = 0.9$, $\sigma_c = 0.2$, $\delta = 0.8$, $\omega = 0.15$

[2] The cyclical components of output and inflation have been estimated by detrending quarterly data using the HP filter with $\lambda = 1600$.

Let us sum up our latest findings:

The hypothesis of adaptive inflation expectations says that the expected rate of inflation is a weighted average of all inflation rates observed in the past, with a greater weight attached to more recent observations. A stochastic AS–AD model with adaptive expectations, where business fluctuations are mainly driven by demand shocks but where supply shocks also play some role, can reproduce the stylized business cycle facts reasonably well.

18.4 A different perspective: real business cycle theory

The theory of the business cycle offered by our AS–AD model emphasizes the role of expectational errors and sluggish wage adjustment, and the microfoundation for the SRAS curve developed in Chapter 17 implies that business fluctuations are associated with fluctuations in involuntary unemployment.

During the 1980s a group of researchers developed a very different approach known as 'real business cycle theory', henceforth termed RBC theory.[11] This school of thought seeks to explain the business cycle by fluctuations in the rate of technological progress. In the basic version of RBC theory, the impulse initiating the business cycle is a shock to productivity which is propagated through the economy via its impact on capital accumulation and the resulting effect on productive capacity. According to this view the employment fluctuations observed during business cycles reflect voluntary movements along individual labour supply curves, as workers choose to enter the labour market or to work extra hours when real wages are unusually high due to a high level of productivity, while reducing their labour supply when productivity and real wages are unusually low relative to their underlying growth trends. Thus markets are assumed to clear all the time, and the business cycle is seen as the economy's optimal response to the changing technological opportunities available to economic agents.

As we shall discuss later, this benign view of the business cycle is problematic in several respects, but its appeal is that it fully integrates business cycle theory with growth theory. To illustrate this, we will show how a slightly modified version of the Solow model of economic growth with technological progress can generate 'real' business cycles if we allow for stochastic shocks to the rate of productivity growth.

Technology

Suppose that aggregate output is given by the Cobb–Douglas production function:

$$Y_t = K_t^{\alpha}(A_t L_t)^{1-\alpha}, \quad 0 < \alpha < 1, \tag{44}$$

where K_t is the capital stock at the start of period t, L_t is total labour input during that period (measured in hours worked), and the parameter A_t captures so-called labour-augmenting technical progress increasing the productivity of labour over time.[12] The underlying growth

11. Important early contributions to RBC theory were made by Finn Kydland and Edward C. Prescott, 'Time to Build and Aggregate Fluctuations', *Econometrica*, **50**, 1982, pp. 1345–1370, and by John B. Long and Charles I. Plosser, 'Real Business Cycles', *Journal of Political Economy*, **91**, 1983, pp. 39–69. A good non-technical (but critical) introduction to the ideas underlying RBC theory can be found in N. Gregory Mankiw, 'Real Business Cycles: A New Keynesian Perspective', *Journal of Economic Perspectives*, **3**, 1989, pp. 79–90.

12. By defining $B_t \equiv A_t^{1-\alpha}$, we can easily rewrite the production function as:

$Y_t = B_t K_t^{\alpha} L_t^{1-\alpha},$

where B_t is the total factor productivity whose cyclical properties were studied in Chapter 13.

rate of A_t contains a constant trend component, g, but productivity is also affected by stochastic factors so that:

$$\ln A_t = gt + s_t, \tag{45}$$

where the stochastic variable s_t now measures the relative deviation of productivity from trend. When we simulate the model, we will assume that s_t follows the stochastic process, $s_{t+1} = \omega s_t + c_{t+1}$, specified in (28). In the following, we shall also need the concept of the *trend* level of productivity, $\bar{A}_t$, defined by:

$$\ln \bar{A}_t = gt. \tag{46}$$

If S_t denotes total gross saving which is invested in capital, and δ is the rate of depreciation of the existing capital stock, we have the bookkeeping identity that $K_t = (1 - \delta)K_{t-1} + S_{t-1}$. For convenience, we will now assume that all of the pre-existing capital stock depreciates within the course of one period, that is $\delta = 1$. We then have:

$$K_t = S_{t-1}. \tag{47}$$

The unrealistic assumption that the pre-existing capital stock fully depreciates within one period is by no means crucial for RBC theory, but in our context it greatly simplifies the formal analysis without affecting the qualitative conclusions.

Economic behaviour

At the research frontier, RBC theorists are careful to derive their behavioural equations from explicit intertemporal optimization of the objective functions of economic agents. However, since advanced RBC models require some sophisticated mathematics that go beyond the present book, we will make a short-cut and simply *assume* some behavioural relationships which yield a model whose fundamental properties are characteristic of the archetypical RBC model. Our first assumption is the standard Solow assumption that total saving is a constant fraction, $\bar{s}$, of total income:

$$S_t = \bar{s}Y_t, \qquad 0 < \bar{s} < 1. \tag{48}$$

Equations (44) and (48) are responsible for the *propagation mechanism* in the basic RBC model. When output and real income rise due to a positive productivity shock (a rise in A_t), total saving increases. This feeds into an increase in next period's capital stock, which in turn causes next period's output to remain above trend even if the positive technology shock has already died out. The high level of output keeps saving and capital accumulation above their normal levels, paving the way for yet another increase in output, and so on. In this way the initial impulse (the stochastic productivity shock) gets propagated through the process of saving and capital accumulation, generating *persistence* in total output and other macroeconomic variables. This is very different from our AS–AD model where persistence was generated by the sluggish adjustment of actual and expected inflation.

The next behavioural assumption in our RBC model is that aggregate labour supply, L_t^s, is given by:

$$L_t^s = \left(\frac{w_t}{\bar{w}_t}\right)^{\varepsilon}, \qquad \varepsilon > 0. \tag{49}$$

Here w_t is the current actual real wage, and $\bar{w}_t$ is the 'normal' trend real wage. For convenience, we have chosen our units such that the normal labour supply forthcoming when the real wage is on trend is equal to 1, so all the variables in the model may be interpreted as per-capita magnitudes. Equation (49) captures the important idea in RBC theory that there is *intertemporal substitution in labour supply*: when the real wage is unusually low ($w_t < \bar{w}_t$), workers react by working less and consuming more leisure, but when the wage is unusually high ($w_t > \bar{w}_t$), workers choose to work more than normal to take advantage of the extraordinarily favourable labour market opportunities. The elasticity ε reflects the strength of these intertemporal substitution effects. At the same time (49) implies that over the long run, where w_t and $\bar{w}_t$ grow at the same rate, there is no time trend in labour supply.[13]

Maximization of profits under perfect competition implies that the real wage will be equal to the marginal productivity of labour. From (44) we therefore have:

$$w_t = \frac{\partial Y_t}{\partial L_t} = (1-\alpha)A_t \left(\frac{K_t}{A_t L_t} \right)^{\alpha} = \frac{(1-\alpha)Y_t}{L_t}. \tag{50}$$

In Chapter 5 it was shown that the magnitude $K_t/(A_t L_t)$ will be equal to a constant $\tilde{k}^*$ when the economy is on its steady state growth path.[14] Using (50), we may therefore specify the trend real wage as:

$$\bar{w}_t = (1-\alpha)\bar{c}\bar{A}_t, \qquad \bar{c} \equiv (\tilde{k}^*)^{\alpha}. \tag{51}$$

The labour market is assumed to be competitive, so the fully flexible real wage adjusts to ensure that aggregate labour supply equals the amount of labour demanded, L_t. Hence we have the labour market clearing condition:

$$L_t = L_t^s. \tag{52}$$

This completes the description of our modified Solow model of growth and business cycles. We will now reduce the model to study the cyclical behaviour of output and employment.

The dynamics of output and employment

Our first step is to insert (49)–(51) into (52) and solve for L_t to get:

$$L_t = \left(\frac{Y_t}{\bar{c}\bar{A}_t} \right)^{\varphi}, \qquad \varphi \equiv \frac{\varepsilon}{1+\varepsilon} < 1. \tag{53}$$

Next we substitute (47), (48) and (53) into (44) and find:

$$Y_t = (\bar{s}Y_{t-1})^{\alpha} A_t^{1-\alpha} \left(\frac{Y_t}{\bar{c}\bar{A}_t} \right)^{\varphi(1-\alpha)}. \tag{54}$$

Taking logs on both sides of (54), inserting (45) and (46), and isolating $y_t \equiv \ln Y_t$ on the left-hand side, we obtain:

$$y_t = \frac{\alpha \ln \bar{s} - \varphi(1-\alpha)\ln \bar{c}}{1 - \varphi(1-\alpha)} + \left(\frac{\alpha}{1 - \varphi(1-\alpha)} \right) y_{t-1} + \frac{(1-\alpha)[(1-\varphi)gt + s_t]}{1 - \varphi(1-\alpha)}. \tag{55}$$

---

13. We are thus implicitly assuming that the income effect and the substitution effect of a higher real wage on labour supply cancel out when real wages grow at the normal rate.

14. The fact that we now allow for short-run variations in labour supply does not change the condition that $K_t/(A_t L_t)$ must be constant in the steady state.

We now want to focus on the *cyclical* component of output, y_t. For this purpose we define:

$$\hat{y}_t \equiv y_t - \bar{y}_t, \qquad \bar{y}_t \equiv \bar{y}_0 + gt, \tag{56}$$

where $\bar{y}_t$ represents the economy's steady state growth trend, i.e., the level of (log) output that would prevail if there were no productivity shocks and the economy had reached its steady state. The variable $\bar{y}_0 \equiv \ln \bar{Y}_0$ is the log of the output level $\bar{Y}_0$ which would have materialized in period 0 if the economy had been in steady state at that time. Since $w_t = \bar{w}_t$ and hence $L_t = 1$ in a steady state, it follows from (44) and our definition of $\bar{c}$ that a steady state in period 0 would have implied $\bar{Y}_0 / \bar{A}_0 = (K_0 / \bar{A}_0)^\alpha = (K_0 / \bar{A}_0 L_0)^\alpha = \bar{c}$ so that:

$$\bar{y}_0 = \ln \bar{c}, \tag{57}$$

since we have $\ln \bar{A}_0 = 0$ according to (46). In a steady state without productivity shocks and population growth, we also know from Chapter 5 that output is growing at the rate g. Hence we have $Y_{-1} = \bar{Y}_0 / (1 + g)$. Setting $t = 0$ and $A_0 = \bar{A}_0$ in (54), inserting $Y_{-1} = \bar{Y}_0 / (1 + g)$, taking logs, and using (57) plus the facts that $\ln \bar{A}_0 = 0$ and $\ln(1 + g) \approx g$, we find:

$$\bar{y}_0 = \left(\frac{\alpha}{1 - \alpha} \right) (\ln \bar{s} - g). \tag{58}$$

Exploiting (56), (57) and (58), you may verify that (55) simplifies to:

$$\hat{y}_t = \left(\frac{\alpha}{1 - \varphi(1 - \alpha)} \right) \hat{y}_{t-1} + \left(\frac{1 - \alpha}{1 - \varphi(1 - \alpha)} \right) s_t. \tag{59}$$

Since $\varphi \equiv \varepsilon / (1 + \varepsilon)$ is positive but less than 1, we see that the coefficient on $\hat{y}_{t-1}$ in (59) is also positive but less than 1. In the absence of productivity shocks, the economy would thus converge monotonically towards its steady state equilibrium where $\hat{y}_t = \hat{y}_{t-1} = 0$, and where output (per capita) is growing at the constant rate g, exactly as implied by the Solow model with technological progress described in Chapter 5.

Consider next the cyclical component of labour input, defined as $\hat{L}_t \equiv \ln(L_t / \bar{L})$, where $\bar{L}$ is the trend level of labour supply. Since $\bar{L} = 1$, it follows from (53) that $\hat{L}_t = \ln L_t = \varphi(y_t - (\ln \bar{c} + \ln \bar{A}_t))$. Since (46), (56) and (57) imply that $\ln \bar{c} + \ln \bar{A}_t = \bar{y}_0 + gt = \bar{y}_t$, this result may be written in the simple form:

$$\hat{L}_t = \varphi \hat{y}_t. \tag{60}$$

Equations (59) and (60) summarize our stochastic Solow model of real business cycles. In mathematical terms, (59) looks very much like the linear first-order difference equation for the output gap in our AS–AD model, but the underlying economic mechanisms are very different in the two models. In the AS–AD model the persistence in output and employment is generated by the sluggish adjustment of actual and expected inflation, and fluctuations in the output gap are associated with fluctuations in involuntary unemployment. In our RBC model persistence stems from the dynamics of capital accumulation, and employment fluctuations reflect that workers voluntarily adjust their labour supply in response to shifts in earnings opportunities.

In the previous section we saw that the AS–AD model does a reasonably good job of reproducing the most important stylized facts of the business cycle. Is our RBC model equally good at matching the data?

TABLE 18.3 The RBC model and the observed fluctuations in output and hours worked

	Standard deviation (%)		Standard deviation of hours worked relative to standard deviation output	Autocorrelation in output			Autocorrelation in hours worked		
	Output	Hours worked		$t-1$	$t-2$	$t-3$	$t-1$	$t-2$	$t-3$
RBC model[1]	3.42	2.84	0.83	0.75	0.50	0.23	0.75	0.50	0.23
The US economy[2]	3.47	2.88	0.83	0.76	0.38	0.08	0.73	0.29	0.06

Note: The cyclical components of output and employment have been estimated by linear OLS detrending of annual data.
[1] $\alpha = 0.33$, $\varphi = 0.83$, $\omega = 0.1$, $\sigma_c = 0.015$.
[2] Annual data for the business sector.
Source: Economic Outlook Database, OECD.

Taking the RBC model to the data

As the term indicates, the RBC model is indeed 'real', containing no nominal variables. Hence the model cannot be used to study the dynamics of inflation and the interaction of inflation and output, but it does enable us to simulate fluctuations in the cyclical components of output and labour input. In the bottom row of Table 18.3 we report summary statistics on the behaviour of these variables in the USA in the period 1960–2003, based on annual data on real private sector GDP and total hours worked in the private sector. We now use annual rather than quarterly data, since our simple RBC model is not designed to reproduce the slight lag in the correlation between output and total hours worked that one observes in quarterly data.[15] Because our theoretical RBC model measures the output and employment gaps as deviations from a constant linear growth trend, we have detrended the logs of output and hours worked by estimating a linear trend using Ordinary Least Squares regression analysis.

The top row in Table 18.3 shows the results of a simulation of our RBC model, using the parameter values stated in the notes to the table. The stochastic component in our productivity variable $\ln A_t$ is assumed to follow a first-order autoregressive process of the form in Eq. (28), and the simulation is based on a sample for c_t from the normal distribution, spanning 100 periods. Our simple RBC model is tightly specified, leaving us with the choice of only four parameters α, φ, ω and σ_c. We know from the theory and empirics of growth that the parameter α equals the capital income share of GDP which is roughly 1/3 in the USA. We therefore set $\alpha = 0.33$. Moreover, as indicated in (60), the parameter φ determines the ratio of the volatility of labour input to the volatility of output, so we set $\varphi = 0.83$ to reproduce the observed ratio between the standard deviation of total hours worked and the standard deviation of output. Given these choices, we have set the values of ω and σ_c to ensure that the simulated volatility and persistence of output matches the data as well as possible.

We see that, measured by the coefficients of autocorrelation, our simple RBC model produces too much persistence in output and labour input when we move more than one year back in time, but otherwise the model fits the data on output and hours worked quite well. In addition, we have seen in Chapter 5 that the Solow model does a good job of mimicking the most important stylized facts of long-term growth. Amended with stochastic productivity growth, this basic workhorse model thus seems able to describe the economy in the short run as well as in the long run.

---

15. This lag is documented in the highly readable article by Finn E. Kydland and Edward C. Prescott, 'Business Cycles: Real Facts and Monetary Myth', Federal Reserve Bank of Minneapolis, *Quarterly Review*, Spring 1990.

Some problems with basic real business cycle theory

From a theoretical perspective the great attraction of RBC theory is that it offers a unified and parsimonious explanation for growth and business cycles. According to the RBC model above, the economy's short-run fluctuations as well as its long-term growth are driven by the evolution of technology and the associated accumulation of capital. Thus it is not necessary to develop separate theories for the long run and for the short run. Furthermore, the basic RBC story of the business cycle is very simple, relying only on technology shocks: in our RBC model there was no need to postulate expectational errors and/or nominal rigidities to generate business fluctuations.[16]

Yet there are serious problems with the basic version of RBC theory presented above, despite the fact that it reproduces the data on output and labour input reasonably well. One issue is whether exogenous technology shocks really are the main driver of business cycles. Certainly we saw in Fig. 13.5 that the cyclical component of total factor productivity does account for a sizeable fraction of the total output gap at business cycle peaks and troughs. But are recessions really caused by periods of general technological regress? Why should firms and workers suddenly lose the ability to use the existing technologies and machinery as effectively as before?

One answer might be that negative shocks to productivity could reflect non-technological factors such as bad weather conditions affecting agricultural output, or sharp increases in the real price of imported raw materials such as oil (which were seen in Chapter 17 to work very much like a negative productivity shock). However, agriculture only accounts for a minor share of GDP in developed economies, and although some international recessions have in fact been preceded by dramatic increases in oil prices, most recessions seem to have been triggered by other events.

But if the observed fluctuations in total factor productivity do not reflect a highly uneven pace of technical progress, and if they only occasionally reflect commodity price shocks, how can they be accounted for? A plausible explanation is that most of the cyclical variation in factor productivity stems from changes in the degree of utilization of capital and labour caused by fluctuations in aggregate demand. In a recession firms may keep unnecessary and underutilized labour to be able to expand output quickly as soon as demand recovers. When demand picks up, the underutilized labour starts to put in more effort, resulting in higher productivity and enabling firms to increase output for a while without increasing their hirings. This straightforward mechanism may explain the procyclical variation in productivity as well as the fact that the number of persons employed lags behind the evolution of output, as documented in Chapter 13.

A second problem with basic RBC theory concerns the interpretation of the observed fluctuations in employment. The official unemployment statistics record substantial variations in the number of unemployed persons over the business cycle. According to our RBC model these shifts in recorded unemployment reflect that workers voluntarily opt for unemployment when real wages are relatively low, preferring to consume more leisure when work is not so well rewarded. Thus, while workers may be frustrated that market wages have fallen (relative to the expected normal growth trend), they are not involuntarily unemployed. This denial of the phenomenon of involuntary unemployment seems hard to reconcile with casual observation from serious recessions, in particular with episodes of mass unemployment like the Great Depression of the 1930s. As some critics have put it, if the standard RBC interpretation of unemployment were true, the Great Depression should be renamed as the 'Great Vacation'; hardly a convincing idea!

More generally, the idea that all employment fluctuations reflect intertemporal substitution in labour supply fits poorly with empirical labour market research. To explain

---

16. In more advanced RBC models expectational errors do occur, but they are not systematic and persistent, since agents are assumed to have rational expectations. Chapter 21 explains the concept of rational expectations.

the procyclical variation of employment as a result of voluntary movements along individual labour supply curves, the real wage must be procyclical. Table 13.3 showed that the real wage is indeed positively correlated with output in the USA, but the correlation is fairly low. To generate the large procyclical pattern of employment despite the very modest cyclical movements in the real wage, the wage elasticity of labour supply has to be very high. But empirical research suggests that labour supply elasticities are in fact quite low, at least for the core groups in the labour market.

To illustrate the problem, recall that we had to set our parameter $\varphi \equiv \varepsilon/(1 + \varepsilon)$ equal to 0.83 for our RBC model to reproduce the observed volatility of employment relative to the volatility of output. This implies that the wage elasticity of labour supply, ε, has to be as high as 4.9. The empirical labour supply elasticities estimated for the various groups in the labour market are much lower than this, even if one accounts for labour market entry and exit as well as variations in working hours for those who are permanently in the market. Moreover, while the US real wage is in fact (slightly) procyclical, as predicted by RBC theory, Table 13.3 documented that the real wage tends to be (slightly) *countercyclical* in several European countries, in direct contrast to the RBC story.

Our AS–AD model does not have this problem in dealing with the labour market, since its microfoundations imply that there is involuntary unemployment at the natural employment rate. As we explained in Section 17.3, this means that (some) workers are forced *off* their individual voluntary labour supply curves, and that aggregate labour supply in effect becomes infinitely elastic up to the point where the pool of involuntarily unemployed workers is depleted.

Let us sum up what we have learned about basic real business cycle theory:

THE THEORY OF REAL BUSINESS CYCLES

The theory unifies the theory of economic growth and the theory of business cycles by postulating that the growth in productivity underlying the long-run growth in income per capita is subject to stochastic short-run fluctuations that cause business activity to fluctuate in the short run. A negative productivity shock reduces the capital stock by lowering income and saving, and the fall in the capital stock causes a further drop in income, saving and capital accumulation in subsequent periods, thus propagating the effects of a temporary productivity shock through time. A Solow growth model with competitive markets and stochastic productivity growth embodies this propagation mechanism and is able to reproduce the observed volatility and persistence of output and hours worked reasonably well. Employment fluctuations in such a model reflect that workers voluntarily choose to supply less (more) labour when real wages are relatively low (high), and business fluctuations reflect the economy's optimal response to shifting technological opportunities. However, the basic real business cycle model requires an implausibly high elasticity of labour supply and implausibly postulates that recessions are caused by temporary spells of technological regress.

The lasting contribution of real business cycle theory

Of course, real business cycle theorists are not unaware of the problems mentioned above. In trying to reconcile their models with the stylized facts of the business cycle, RBC theorists have gradually modified and extended their models to account for various market frictions, in some cases including nominal rigidities. At the same time, practitioners of the more conventional AS–AD approach to business cycle analysis have tried to meet the challenge from RBC theorists by paying more attention to the potential role of supply side shocks and to the propagation mechanisms stressed by RBC theorists. They have also tried to provide more convincing microeconomic foundations for the various frictions causing output and employment to deviate from their natural rates.

As a result, recent years have seen a convergence of the different approaches to business cycle analysis. Today, most researchers recognize that RBC theorists have made valuable methodological contributions to the study of business cycles. First of all, RBC theorists introduced the practice of constructing and simulating stochastic dynamic general equilibrium models whose predictions could be compared with the stylized facts of the business cycle. In this way they introduced more rigorous theoretical and empirical standards for judging whether a particular theory of the business cycle is 'good' or 'bad'. The present book, as well as most modern macroeconomic research, is much inspired by this approach to business cycle analysis. Second, RBC theory has drawn attention to the fact that many mechanisms on the economy's supply side, such as the dynamics of capital accumulation, may help to explain the persistence observed in macroeconomic time series.

Thus real business cycle theorists have made important lasting contributions at the methodological level even if their specific early models were not very convincing.

18.5 Summary

1. The AS–AD model determines the short-run equilibrium values of output and inflation as the point of intersection between the upward-sloping short-run aggregate supply curve (the SRAS curve) and the downward-sloping aggregate demand curve (the AD curve). The model also determines the long-run equilibrium levels of output and inflation as the point of intersection between the vertical long-run aggregate supply curve (the LRAS curve) and the AD curve.

2. When expectations are static, the expected inflation rate for the current period equals the actual inflation rate observed during the previous period. Under this assumption the AS–AD model is globally stable, converging gradually towards the long-run equilibrium where output is at its natural rate and inflation is at its target rate. The adjustment to long-run equilibrium takes place through successive shifts in the SRAS curve, as economic agents gradually revise their inflation expectations in reaction to observed changes in the actual inflation rate. During the adjustment process the economy moves along the AD curve, as the central bank gradually adjusts the real interest rate in reaction to the changes in the inflation rate.

3. With plausible parameter values the AS–AD model suggests that it will take more than three years for the economy to complete half of the adjustment towards the steady state and more than ten years to complete 90 per cent of the adjustment. Hence output and inflation may deviate from their trend values for quite a long time, once the long-run equilibrium has been disturbed by a shock.

4. The AS–AD model may be specified in deterministic terms or in stochastic terms. In the deterministic version of the model, the demand and supply shock variables are non-stochastic. In the stochastic AS–AD model, the shocks to demand and supply are treated as random variables.

5. The deterministic model may be used to study the isolated effects of a single temporary or permanent shock to supply or demand. The stochastic AS–AD model may be used to generate simulated time series for output and inflation, allowing a calculation of the variance, covariance and autocorrelation in these variables. These statistics may then be compared to the statistical properties of empirical time series to investigate how well the stochastic AS–AD model is able to reproduce the stylized facts of the business cycle.

6. In the short run, a temporary negative supply shock generates stagflation, defined as an increase in inflation combined with a fall in output. Even after the negative supply

shock has disappeared, inflation will remain above the target rate and output will remain below the natural rate for many successive periods, because it takes time for inflation expectations to adjust back to the target inflation rate.

7. A temporary negative demand shock generates a bust–boom adjustment pattern in output. In the period when the negative demand shock occurs, there is a drop in output as well as inflation. But when the negative demand impulse disappears, output rises above its natural rate because the SRAS curve shifts down, due to a fall in expected inflation. In the subsequent periods, output gradually falls back to its trend level, and inflation gradually rises towards the target rate.

8. By quantifying the parameter values, the deterministic AS–AD model may be used to generate impulse-response functions showing how output and inflation will evolve over time in response to an impulse such as a temporary or permanent demand or supply shock.

9. The deterministic AS–AD model can explain the observed persistence (autocorrelation) in economic time series, that is, it can explain why even a temporary shock generates protracted, long-lasting deviations of output and inflation from their trend levels. However, the deterministic model cannot explain the observed recurrent cyclical fluctuations in macroeconomic variables. But if the demand and supply shock variables are treated as stochastic processes, the AS–AD model is able to generate irregular, cyclical fluctuations in output and inflation.

10. A calibrated stochastic AS–AD model with static expectations where all shocks take the form of demand shocks is reasonably good at reproducing the statistical properties of the empirical time series for output, but such a model generates an unrealistically high degree of persistence in the rate of inflation. A stochastic AS–AD model with static expectations where all shocks originate from the supply side is incapable of reproducing the statistical properties of the time series for output as well as inflation. This suggests that a model intended to explain the business cycle must allow for demand shocks as well as supply shocks and that the assumption of static inflation expectations may be too simple.

11. The hypothesis of adaptive expectations says that the expected inflation rate for the current period is a weighted average of all inflation rates observed in the past, with more weight being put on the experience of the recent past than on the more distant past. Static expectations are a special case of adaptive expectations where the weight given to last period's observed inflation rate is 100 per cent.

12. A calibrated stochastic AS–AD model with adaptive expectations allowing for demand shocks as well as supply shocks is able to reproduce the statistical properties of the time series for US output and inflation reasonably well. The stochastic AS–AD model offers an explanation for the business cycle in line with the Frisch–Slutzky paradigm. In this paradigm, business fluctuations are initiated by random demand or supply shocks which are then propagated through the economic system in a way that generates persistence in macroeconomic variables. In our AS–AD model, the persistence in the macroeconomic time series stems from the fact that the expected and actual inflation rates adjust sluggishly over time. However, one can construct other macroeconomic models with other persistence mechanisms, so our AS–AD model is not the only possible explanation for business cycles.

13. Real business cycle (RBC) theory seeks to explain business cycles by fluctuations in the rate of technological progress that is also driving the process of long-term economic growth. A Solow model in which the rate of productivity growth is stochastic does a fairly good job of reproducing the short-run dynamics of output and total hours worked

as well as mimicking the long-run facts of economic growth. The model generates endogenous persistence, since a positive productivity shock increases output which in turn increases saving, feeding into an increase in the capital stock which generates another round of increase in output and saving, and so on.

14. Despite its theoretical attraction, basic RBC theory has a problem explaining the observed fluctuations in aggregate employment as the outcome of intertemporal substitution in labour supply. The theory postulates that workers voluntarily choose to work less when real wages are relatively low, and vice versa. For this theory to fit the data, the elasticity of labour supply must be much higher than prevailing empirical estimates. Yet RBC theory has made an important methodological contribution by introducing the practice of setting up stochastic dynamic general equilibrium models which can be compared with the stylized facts of the business cycle.

18.6 Exercises

Exercise 1. Temporary shocks in the deterministic AS–AD model

1. Use the AS–AD model with static expectations to undertake a graphical analysis of the effects of a positive supply shock (a fall in s) which lasts for one period. You may assume that the economy starts out in long-run equilibrium in period 0 and that the temporary shock occurs in period 1. Explain the short-run effects as well as the economy's adjustment over time.

2. Suppose now that the positive supply shock emerging in period 1 also persists throughout period 2 before it goes away from period 3 onwards. Illustrate the effects of this two-period shock graphically and explain the difference compared to the one-period shock analysed in Question 1. Be careful to explain exactly how the SRAS curves shift in the two scenarios. (Hint: indicate precisely where the SRAS curves cut the LRAS curve in the various periods.)

3. Now use the AS–AD model with static expectations to perform a graphical analysis of the effects of a positive demand shock occurring in period 1 and dying out from period 2 onwards. Explain the mechanisms underlying the evolution of output and inflation over time.

4. Assume instead that the positive demand shock emerging in period 1 lasts for *two* periods before it dies out. Illustrate the effects graphically. Will the fluctuations in output and inflation be larger or smaller than those occurring when the shock lasts for only one period? Explain.

Exercise 2. Permanent shocks in the deterministic AS–AD model

1. Suppose that the economy is hit by a *permanent* negative demand shock, say, because a tax reform permanently raises the private sector's propensity to save. Illustrate by a graphical analysis that such a shock will lead to a permanent violation of the inflation target if the central bank does not adjust its estimate of the equilibrium real interest rate, $\bar{r}$.

2. Now suppose that the economy is in long-run equilibrium in period 0 and that the permanent negative demand shock hits the economy from period 1 onwards. Suppose further that it takes the central bank only one period to realize that the shock is permanent. From period 2 onwards, the bank thus revises its estimate of the equilibrium real interest rate from the original level to the new level given by Eq. (25) in the text. Analyse

mathematically and graphically how these developments will shift the AD curve in periods 1 and 2. Illustrate and explain the economy's adjustment over time. Compare your graphical analysis with the analysis of a purely *temporary* negative demand shock in Fig. 18.6. Is there any difference?

3. Suppose alternatively that it takes until period 3 before the central bank realizes the permanency of the negative demand shock and revises its estimate of the equilibrium real interest rate. Perform a graphical analysis of the economy's adjustment from period 0 onwards and compare with the analysis in Question 2. (Be precise in your indication of the shifts in the AD and SRAS curves.) How does the delayed adjustment of the estimate for $\bar{r}$ affect the magnitude of the fluctuations in output and inflation? Explain.

4. Suppose again that the economy starts out in long-run equilibrium in period 0 and assume that a *permanent negative supply shock* (a rise in s) occurs from period 1 onwards, reducing natural output from $\bar{y}_0$ to the new lower level $\bar{y} = \bar{y}_0 - (s/\gamma)$. Suppose further that the central bank realizes the permanency of the shock already in period 2 and hence revises its estimate of the equilibrium real interest rate in accordance with Eq. (24) from period 2 onwards so that the current real market interest rate is given by the following equation (where we abstract from shocks to market risk premia):

$$r_t = \bar{r}_0 + \frac{s}{\gamma \alpha_2} + h(\pi_t - \pi^*) + b\left[y_t - \left(\bar{y}_0 - \frac{s}{\gamma} \right) \right] \qquad \text{for } t \geq 2.$$

Derive the equation for the new AD curve which will hold for $t \geq 2$ (where will the new AD curve cut the new LRAS curve?). Illustrate the new short-run equilibria in periods 1 and 2. (Hint: note that from period 2 onwards, the SRAS curves will cut the *new* LRAS curve at the level of the previous period's inflation rate.) Illustrate by arrows along the new AD curve how the economy will evolve after period 2 and explain the economic adjustment mechanisms. Compare your results with the analysis of a purely temporary negative supply shock in Fig. 18.5.

Exercise 3. Interest rate smoothing in the AS–AD model

We have so far assumed that the interest rate adjusts immediately to the target level given by the Taylor rule. However, empirical research has found that central banks tend to adjust their interest rates only gradually towards the target level because they do not like to change the interest rate too abruptly. We may model such 'interest rate smoothing' by assuming that:

$$r_t = (1 - \lambda)r_t^* + \lambda r_{t-1} \iff r_t - r_{t-1} = (1 - \lambda)(r_t^* - r_{t-1}), \qquad 0 \leq \lambda < 1, \tag{61}$$

where λ is a parameter indicating the sluggishness of interest rate adjustment, and where r_t^* is the *target* real interest rate given by the Taylor rule (where we abstract from shocks to market risk premia):

$$r_t^* = \bar{r} + h(\pi_t - \pi^*) + b(y_t - \bar{y}). \tag{62}$$

In the main text we have analysed the special case where $\lambda = 0$, but here we will focus on the general case where $\lambda > 0$. The goods market equilibrium condition may still be written as:

$$y_t - \bar{y} = \alpha_1(g_t - \bar{g}) - \alpha_2(r_t - \bar{r}) + v_t, \tag{63}$$

and the economy's supply side is still given by:

$$\pi_t = \pi_t^e + \gamma(y_t - \bar{y}) + s_t. \tag{64}$$

As a new element, we will assume that economic agents are sufficiently sophisticated to realize that on average over the long run, the inflation rate must equal the central bank's inflation target. Hence we assume that the expected inflation rate is:

$$\pi_t^e = \pi^* \quad \text{for all } t. \tag{65}$$

This completes the description of our revised AS–AD model.

1. Discuss whether the assumption made in (65) is reasonable.

2. Define $\hat{y}_t \equiv y_t - \bar{y}$ and $\hat{\pi}_t \equiv \pi_t - \pi^*$ and show that the AD curve is given by the equation:

$$\hat{y}_t = \rho\hat{y}_{t-1} - \alpha\hat{\pi}_t + z_t - \lambda z_{t-1}, \tag{66}$$

$$\rho \equiv \frac{\lambda}{1 + \alpha_2 b(1 - \lambda)}, \qquad \alpha \equiv \frac{\alpha_2 h(1 - \lambda)}{1 + \alpha_2 b(1 - \lambda)}, \qquad z_t \equiv \frac{\alpha_1(g_t - \bar{g}) + v_t}{1 + \alpha_2 b(1 - \lambda)}.$$

3. Show that the model can be reduced to the difference equation:

$$\hat{y}_t = \beta\rho\hat{y}_{t-1} + \beta(z_t - \lambda z_{t-1}) - \alpha\beta s_t, \quad \beta \equiv \frac{1}{1 + \gamma\alpha}, \tag{67}$$

and prove that, in the absence of shocks, the economy will converge on a long-run equilibrium where $\hat{y}_t = \hat{\pi}_t = 0$. How does the parameter λ affect the economy's speed of adjustment? Explain.

4. Suppose that the economy starts out in a short-run equilibrium in period 0 where $y_0 < \bar{y}$. Give a graphical illustration of the initial short-run equilibrium and of the economy's adjustment to long-run equilibrium, assuming there are no further shocks. (Hint: note that the adjustment now takes place through successive *shifts in the AD curve* rather than through shifts in the SRAS curve.) Explain the economic mechanism which ensures convergence on long-run equilibrium.

5. Now assume that the economy is in long-run equilibrium in period 0 but is hit by a *temporary negative supply shock* (a rise in s_t) in period 1. The shock vanishes again from period 2 onwards. Give a graphical illustration of the new short-run equilibria in periods 1 and 2. Could y_2 be lower than y_1? (Hint: use (67) to justify your answer.) Indicate by arrows (along the SRAS curve) how the economy will evolve after period 2. Explain your findings.

6. Suppose again that the economy is in long-run equilibrium in period 0, but assume now that it is hit by a *temporary negative demand shock* which occurs only in period 1. Illustrate graphically how this will affect the economy in periods 1 and 2 and use arrows to indicate the economy's adjustment after period 2. Explain your findings. (Hint: you may want to use Eqs (66) and (67) to show that the AD curve for period 2 will lie *above* the AD curve for period 0.)

Exercise 4. Developing and implementing a stochastic AS–AD model

In this exercise you are asked to set up a stochastic AS–AD model, implement it on the computer, and undertake some simulations to illustrate the effects of monetary policy. In this way you will become familiar with the modern methodology for business cycle analysis which was described in Section 18.3.

Our starting point is a generalized version of the short-run aggregate supply curve. Many econometricians studying the labour market have found that wage inflation is moderated not only by the *level* of unemployment (u_t), but also by the *increase* in the unemployment rate between the previous and the current period $(u_t - u_{t-1})$. The reason is that, *ceteris paribus*, it is more difficult for a dismissed worker to find an alternative job when unemployment is rising than when it is falling. When labour is mobile across sectors, a rising unemployment rate thus reduces the value of the representative worker's outside option. Assuming static inflation expectations $(\pi_t^e = \pi_{t-1})$, we therefore get the following generalized version of the expectations-augmented Phillips curve:

$$\pi_t = \pi_{t-1} + \gamma(\bar{u} - u_t) - \gamma\theta(u_t - u_{t-1}), \qquad \gamma > 0, \qquad \theta > 0 \tag{68}$$

where $\bar{u}$ is the constant natural rate of unemployment, and the parameter θ indicates the degree to which the wage claims of workers are moderated by rising unemployment. We assume that current output is given by a simple linear production function of the form $Y_t = a_t L_t$, where a_t is the exogenous current average labour productivity, and L_t is current employment. If the constant labour force is N, we have $L_t \equiv (1 - u_t)N$. Using the approximation $\ln(1 - u_t) \approx u_t$ and the definition $y_t \equiv \ln Y_t$, we thus have:

$$y_t = \ln a_t + \ln N - u_t. \tag{69}$$

Trend output (natural output) is $\bar{Y} = \bar{a}\bar{L} = \bar{a}(1 - \bar{u})N$, where $\bar{L}$ is natural employment and $\bar{a}$ is the 'normal' (trend) level of productivity. Hence we have:

$$\bar{y}_t = \ln \bar{a} + \ln N - \bar{u}. \tag{70}$$

Let us define the supply shock variable:

$$s_t \equiv \ln \bar{a} - \ln a_t. \tag{71}$$

Note that s_t is *positive* when productivity is unusually low, that is, when unit labour costs are above their normal level.

1. Use (68)–(71) to demonstrate that the economy's short-run aggregate supply curve may be written as:

$$\hat{\pi}_t = \hat{\pi}_{t-1} + \gamma(1+\theta)\hat{y}_t - \gamma\theta\hat{y}_{t-1} + \gamma(1+\theta)s_t - \gamma\theta s_{t-1}, \tag{72}$$

$$\hat{y}_t \equiv y_t - \bar{y}, \qquad \hat{\pi}_t \equiv \pi_t - \pi^*.$$

How does Eq. (72) deviate from the SRAS curve in the model in the main text? Explain briefly why the lagged output gap $\hat{y}_{t-1}$ appears with a negative coefficient on the right-hand side of (72). Explain in economic terms how the parameter θ affects the sensitivity of inflation to the current output gap.

As usual, the economy's aggregate demand curve is given by:

$$\hat{y}_t = z_t - \alpha\hat{\pi}t, \qquad \hat{\pi}_t \equiv \pi_t - \pi^*, \tag{73}$$

where π^* is the central bank's inflation target.

2. Show that the solutions for the output gap and the inflation gap take the form:

$$\hat{y}_{t+1} = a_1\hat{y}_t + \beta(z_{t+1} - z_t) - a_2 s_{t+1} + a_3 s_t, \tag{74}$$

$$\hat{\pi}_{t+1} = a_1\hat{\pi}_t + c_1(z_{t+1} + s_{t+1}) - c_2(z_t + s_t), \tag{75}$$

where

$$\beta \equiv \frac{1}{1 + \gamma \alpha (1 + \theta)}, \qquad a_1 \equiv \beta(1 + \gamma \alpha \theta), \qquad a_2 \equiv \beta \gamma \alpha (1 + \theta), \tag{76}$$

$$a_3 \equiv \beta \gamma \alpha \theta, \qquad c_1 \equiv \beta \gamma (1 + \theta), \qquad c_2 \equiv \beta \gamma \theta. \tag{77}$$

(Hints: write Eq. (72) for period $t+1$, insert (73) into the resulting expression and collect terms to get (74). Then use (73) to write (74) in terms of $\hat{\pi}$ rather than $\hat{y}$ and collect terms to get (75).)

The demand and supply shock variables are assumed to follow stochastic processes of the form:

$$z_{t+1} = \delta z_t + x_{t+1}, \quad 0 \leq \delta < 1, \quad x_t \sim N(0, \sigma_x^2), \quad x_t \text{ i.i.d.} \tag{78}$$

$$s_{t+1} = \omega s_t + c_{t+1}, \quad 0 \leq \omega < 1, \quad c_t \sim N(0, \sigma_c^2), \quad c_t \text{ i.i.d.} \tag{79}$$

We also remember that:

$$\alpha_2 = \frac{\eta(1 - \tau)}{1 - D_\gamma}, \qquad \alpha = \frac{\alpha_2 h}{1 + \alpha_2 b}, \tag{80}$$

where the parameters are as defined and explained in the main text of this chapter.

3. *Implementing the model.* In order to undertake simulation exercises, you are now asked to program the model consisting of (74)–(80) on the computer, for example by using Microsoft Excel. From the internet address http://highered.mcgraw-hill.com/sites/0077104250/student_view0/index.html you can download an Excel spreadsheet with two different 100-period samples taken from the standardized normal distribution. You may take the first sample to represent the stochastic shock variable x_t, and the second sample to represent the shock variable c_t. In your first Excel spreadsheet you should list the parameters of the model as well as the standard deviations of the output and inflation gaps, the coefficient of correlation between the two gaps, and the coefficients of autocorrelation emerging from your simulations. It will also be useful to include diagrams illustrating the simulated values of the output gap and the inflation gap. We suggest that you use the parameter values:

$$\gamma = 0.075, \qquad \tau = 0.2, \qquad \eta = 3.6, \qquad D_\gamma = 0.5, \qquad h = b = 0.5, \qquad \theta = 0.5.$$

(All of these values except the one for θ were used in the main text.) To calibrate the magnitude of the demand and supply shocks, x_t and k_t, you must choose their respective standard deviations σ_x and σ_c and multiply the samples taken from the standardized normal distribution by these standard deviations. As a starting point, you may simply choose:

$$\sigma_x = 1, \qquad \sigma_c = 1.$$

You also have to choose the value of the parameters δ and ω. For a start, just set:

$$\delta = 0.5, \qquad \omega = 0.5.$$

Finally, you must choose the initial values of the endogenous variables in period 0. We assume that the economy is in a long-run equilibrium in period 0 so that:

$$\hat{y}_0 = \hat{\pi}_0 = z_0 = s_0 = 0 \qquad \text{for } t = 0.$$

Now program this model in Excel and undertake a simulation over 100 periods. Compare the model-generated statistics on the standard deviations and the coefficients of correlation and autocorrelation of output and inflation with the corresponding statistics for the USA given in the bottom row of Table 18.1 in the main text. Comment on the differences.

4. Experiment with alternative constellations of the parameters σ_x, σ_c, δ and ω until you find a constellation which enables your AS–AD model to reproduce the US business cycle statistics for output and for the correlation between output and inflation reasonably well. (You should not bother too much about the behaviour of inflation implied by the model, since we know from the text that a model with static inflation expectations is not very good at reproducing the statistical behaviour of inflation.) State a set of values for σ_x, σ_c, δ and ω which in your view gives a reasonable account of the behaviour of output and of the correlation between output and inflation. What does your choice of parameter values imply for the relative importance of demand and supply shocks? Comment.

5. The simulations above use the monetary policy parameter values suggested by John Taylor, that is, $h = b = 0.5$. Now suppose that the central bank decides to react more aggressively to changes in the rate of inflation by raising the value of h from 0.5 to 1.0. Simulate your model to investigate the effects of such a policy change. Try to explain the effects. Discuss whether the policy change is desirable.

6. Suppose again that the central bank decides to raise h from 0.5 to 1.0, but suppose also that supply shocks are very important so that $\sigma_c = 5$. Is the policy change now desirable? Discuss.

Exercise 5. Evaluating real business cycle theory

Discuss the main ideas and assumptions underlying the basic theory of real business cycles. Explain and discuss the differences between the basic RBC model and our AS–AD model of the business cycle. Explain and discuss the arguments for and against the real business cycle approach. (Hint: apart from the paper by Mankiw mentioned in Footnote 11 of this chapter, you may also want to consult the article by Charles I. Plosser, 'Understanding Real Business Cycles', *Journal of Economic Perspectives*, **3**, 1989, pp. 51–77.)

CHAPTER

19

Stabilization policy: Why?[1]

A re economic recessions and depressions a social evil that economic policy makers should try to prevent, or do they reflect the economy's optimal response to exogenous shocks? During the 1980s and early 1990s several economists actually defended the latter view, as we saw in the previous chapter. This school of real business cycle theorists claimed that shocks to productivity are the main driver of business cycles, and that the economy is reasonably well described by the general equilibrium model of a perfectly competitive economy. In such an economy Pareto-optimality always prevails, so even though policy makers may regret that economic activity falls in response to a negative productivity shock, there is nothing they can do to improve the situation, given that the economy always makes efficient use of the available resources and technologies.

Nowadays most economists believe that the competitive real business cycle model is an implausible theory of short-run business fluctuations, for the reasons given at the end of the previous chapter. The dominant view is that business cycles reflect market failures and that social welfare could be raised if business fluctuations could be dampened. A fundamental issue for macroeconomics is whether and how policy makers can indeed smooth the business cycle through macroeconomic *stabilization policy*.

Stabilization policy involves the use of monetary and fiscal policy to dampen fluctuations in output and inflation. In this chapter and the next one we offer an introduction to the problems of macroeconomic stabilization policy. The present chapter discusses the *goals* of stabilization policy, asking why business fluctuations cause welfare losses, and how the goals of stabilization policy should be defined.

To most observers of business cycles it may seem obvious that there is a need for stabilization policy. Indeed, how can anyone be against 'stabilization'? But the questions raised in this chapter deserve close scrutiny. Business cycles involve fluctuations in output, employment and inflation. By studying why these fluctuations generate welfare losses, we can offer an estimate of the magnitude of the economic welfare costs. This gives an idea of the importance of macroeconomic stabilization as a goal for public policy. The short-run inflation-unemployment trade-off described in the previous chapter also means that a rational stabilization policy cannot be designed unless policy makers have some idea of the welfare cost of an increase in the rate of unemployment relative to the welfare loss associated with an increase in the rate of inflation. The present chapter explains how economic theory and empirical analysis may help to answer this important question.

---

1. This chapter analyses the costs of business fluctuations and discusses *why* stabilization policy may be relevant. A reader who takes the need for stabilization policy as given can go directly to the next chapter analysing *how* to conduct stabilization policy. The 'how' part can be read independently of the 'why' part, but the latter is required for a more satisfactory understanding of the stabilization issue.

19.1 The goals of stabilization policy and the social loss function

The case for stabilization policy rests on the hypothesis that policy makers – and ultimately the general public – are averse to fluctuations in consumption, employment and inflation. Since employment and consumption tend to move together with output, this supposed aversion to fluctuations is sometimes formalized in the 'social loss function':

$$SL = \frac{a_y}{2}(y - \bar{y})^2 + \frac{a_\pi}{2}(\pi - \pi^*)^2, \tag{1}$$

where $y - \bar{y}$ is the gap between the (log of the) actual and the 'natural' output level, and $\pi - \pi^*$ is the gap between the actual inflation rate π and a 'target level', π^*, for the inflation rate. The parameters a_y and a_π determine the magnitude of the marginal social loss from changes in the output and inflation gaps, since $\partial SL/\partial(y - \bar{y}) = a_y(y - \bar{y})$ and $\partial SL/\partial(\pi - \pi^*) = a_\pi(\pi - \pi^*)$. Equation (1) can be used to calculate the average social loss from fluctuations in output and inflation by taking the mathematical expectation, $E[SL]$, to find

$$E[SL] = \frac{a_y}{2}\sigma_y^2 + \frac{a_\pi}{2}\sigma_\pi^2, \qquad \sigma_y^2 \equiv E[(y - \bar{y})^2], \qquad \sigma_\pi^2 \equiv E[(\pi - \pi^*)^2]. \tag{2}$$

Equation (2) postulates that society's average welfare loss from macroeconomic instability increases with the variance σ_y^2 of the deviations of output from its natural level and with the variance σ_π^2 of the inflation rate around its target level.

This social loss function raises a host of issues:

1. Why should society be concerned about the *variability* and not just the *average* values of output and inflation?
2. What determines the size of the weights a_y and a_π that should be attached to the goals of output stability and inflation stability?
3. Should output really be stabilized around its natural level regardless of the type of shocks hitting the economy?
4. What is the appropriate target level of inflation?
5. What are the properties of the optimal stabilization policy rules if policy makers wish to minimize the social loss function (1)?

In this chapter we address the first four of these challenging questions. The fifth issue – optimal stabilization policy – will be dealt with in the next three chapters.

Section 19.2 discusses the welfare costs associated with fluctuations in consumption and employment, thereby motivating the first term of the loss function (1). Section 19.3 focuses on the welfare costs of inflation and inflation volatility, thus explaining the background for the second term.

19.2 The welfare costs of output fluctuations

Laying the ground for analysing the welfare costs of fluctuations in consumption and employment: a simple model

We start by considering why fluctuations in output around its long-run growth trend are a social problem. For this purpose we set up a simple model intended to highlight the effects of volatility in consumption and employment on consumer welfare. The model illustrates the importance of market imperfections for the welfare effects of booms and recessions. It also shows how shocks to wage and price mark-ups can be drivers of business cycles. We start by focusing on such supply shocks since they represent the biggest challenge for stabilization policy, forcing policy makers into the tough choice between stabilizing output and stabilizing inflation. Later in this chapter and in the next one we shall explain how demand shocks can be incorporated into our model, so please keep in mind that the model we are about to set up is only the first step in our analysis, although an important one.

Consider an economy where the representative consumer engages in real consumption, C, and in labour, L. For concreteness, suppose the consumer's utility function $U(C, L)$ takes the form

$$U(C, L) = \frac{C^{1-\theta}}{1-\theta} - \frac{L^{1+\mu}}{1+\mu}, \qquad \theta > 0, \qquad \mu > 0, \tag{3}$$

where the first term measures the utility from consumption while the second term captures the disutility from work. Since $\partial U/\partial C \equiv U_C = C^{-\theta}$, we see that θ is the elasticity of the marginal utility of consumption with respect to consumption. The greater the value of θ, the stronger is the curvature of the utility function and the steeper is the rise in the marginal utility of consumption if the consumer experiences an unexpected drop in consumption. It is customary to refer to θ as the Coefficient of Relative Risk Aversion, for as we shall see below, the amount of consumption the consumer would be willing to forgo to avoid consumption risk is proportional to the size of θ.

Since $\partial U/\partial L \equiv U_L = -L^{\mu}$, we also see that μ is the elasticity of the marginal disutility of work. The inverse of μ is sometimes referred to as the Frisch labour supply elasticity. This elasticity measures how labour supply would respond to a rise in the after-tax real wage if the worker's income were adjusted to keep the marginal utility of consumption constant. In other words, the Frisch labour supply elasticity captures the pure *substitution effect* on labour supply of a change in the real net wage, since the income effect is assumed to be neutralized.[2] To illustrate, suppose the consumer receives real non-labour income I (which could include profit income and/or government transfers) along with real after-tax labour income $(W/P)(1-\tau)L$, where W is the nominal wage rate, P is the price level, and τ is a proportional tax rate on labour income. Thus the consumer's budget constraint is $C = (W/P)(1-\tau)L + I$. Using this to substitute for C in the utility function (3) and maximizing the resulting expression with respect to L, we get the following first-order condition for the consumer's optimal labour supply:

$$(W/P)(1-\tau)C^{-\theta} - L^{\mu} = 0. \tag{4}$$

Now suppose that we raise the after-tax real wage $(W/P)(1-\tau)$ a little bit while at the same time adjusting the consumer's exogenous income I so as to keep total after-tax income – and hence consumption and thereby the marginal utility of consumption $C^{-\theta}$ – constant. By implicit differentiation of (4), we then get (defining $w \equiv W/P$ and keeping $C^{-\theta}$ constant):

$$\frac{dL}{d(w(1-\tau))} = \frac{C^{-\theta}}{\mu L^{\mu-1}} = \overbrace{\frac{L^{\mu}/w(1-\tau)}{\mu L^{\mu-1}}}^{= C^{-\theta} \text{ from (4)}} = \frac{L}{w(1-\tau)\mu} \quad \Rightarrow$$

$$\frac{dL/L}{d(w(1-\tau))/w(1-\tau)} = \frac{1}{\mu}. \tag{5}$$

The insight that $1/\mu$ measures the wage elasticity of labour supply (adjusted for the income effect) is useful because it will help us to quantify the welfare costs of business cycles, as we shall see later on.

---

2. This concept of an 'income-compensated' labour supply elasticity was proposed by Ragnar Frisch, the Nobel Prize-winning Norwegian economist whose name we also encountered in the previous chapter.

Condition (4) for the consumer's desired labour supply may be written as $MRS(C:L) = (W/P)(1-\tau)$, where $MRS(C:L) \equiv -U_L/U_C = C^\theta L^\mu$ is the marginal rate of substitution between consumption and work, indicating how much extra consumption the worker requires to be willing to work an extra hour. If the labour market were competitive, ruling out the possibility of involuntary unemployment, the worker would thus work up to the point where the MRS just equals the after-tax wage rate. However, we assume that because of, say, union monopoly power or efficiency wage setting, the actual after-tax wage rate paid is a mark-up over the MRS, that is, a mark-up over the amount for which workers would be willing to put in additional hours. Thus we introduce the wage mark-up factor, m^w:

$$m^w \equiv \frac{(W/P)(1-\tau)}{MRS(C:L)} = \frac{(W/P)(1-\tau)}{C^\theta L^\mu} > 1. \tag{6}$$

This definition of the wage mark-up factor may seem different from the one encountered in Chapter 17, but the concept is essentially the same: in both cases m^w measures the mark-up of wages over the marginal opportunity cost of work. In Chapter 17 this opportunity cost was given by the unemployment benefit a worker forgoes when he moves from unemployment into employment. In the present model which does not explicitly incorporate unemployment benefits, the marginal opportunity cost of work is given by the value of the leisure that must be sacrificed to put in an extra hour, and this cost is exactly what the MRS measures.

Note that if individual working hours are fixed by law or by collective bargaining agreements, we can interpret the utility function (3) as representing the preferences of a collective household with many members each of whom has a different (psychological) cost of entering the labour market so that some household members prefer not to enter. In that interpretation the term $-L^{1+\mu}/(1+\mu)$ in (3) captures the sum of the disutility of work for all household members and the marginal disutility $-L^\mu$ reflects the cost of labour market participation for the 'marginal' worker with the highest disutility of work among those employed.[3] Thus our utility function (3) can capture the welfare effects of variations in individual working hours as well as fluctuations in the number of persons employed.

We turn now to the business sector. In line with Chapter 17, we assume that the output Y of the representative firm is given by the production function

$$Y = BL^{1-\alpha}, \qquad 0 < \alpha < 1, \tag{7}$$

where B is a parameter reflecting the exogenous level of productivity. Equation (7) implies that the marginal productivity of labour is $\partial Y/\partial L \equiv MPL = (1-\alpha)BL^{-\alpha} = (1-\alpha)(Y/L)$. In a perfectly competitive economy profit-maximizing firms would hire labour up to the point where $MPL = W/P$, but in Chapter 17 we saw that when product market competition is imperfect, the prices charged by firms will be a mark-up, m^p, over their marginal cost, that is, $P = m^p \cdot MC$, where the marginal cost is $MC = W/MPL$. Hence we have:

$$m^p \equiv \frac{MPL}{W/P} = \frac{(1-\alpha)BL^{-\alpha}}{W/P} = \frac{(1-\alpha)(Y/L)}{W/P} > 1. \tag{8}$$

From microeconomic theory we know that resource allocation in a perfectly competitive economy without tax distortions is Pareto-optimal, meaning that no consumer can be made better off without making at least one consumer worse off. In such an economy there are no mark-ups in the formation of wages and prices ($m^w = m^p = 1$) and the marginal tax rate is zero ($\tau = 0$), implying that $MPL = MRS$. Thus the amount of output produced by an extra unit of labour is just equal to the amount of additional consumption consumers require to be

---

3. In Exercise 1 you are invited to demonstrate exactly how a utility function of the form (3) can be derived when individual working hours are fixed while different members of the collective household have different psychological costs of labour market participation.

willing to put in an extra unit of labour. By contrast, in our model economy market imperfections and taxes drive the marginal product of labour above the marginal rate of substitution between consumption and labour, since it follows from (6) and (8) that

$$\delta \equiv \frac{MPL}{MRS} = \frac{m^p m^w}{1-\tau} > 1. \tag{9}$$

The parameter δ is a measure of the overall degree of market distortions caused by taxation and imperfect competition in labour and product markets. As we shall see, its size has important implications for the welfare effects of booms and recessions.

To close our small model, we assume for simplicity that all tax revenues are returned to consumers in the form of lump sum government transfers.[4] This is equivalent to assuming that, in so far as the government actually spends its revenue on purchasing goods and services, this government consumption is a perfect substitute for private consumption, taking the form of goods and services (say, education and health care) that consumers would have bought on their own account had they not been provided by the government. Since consumers also receive the profits earned by firms, it follows that total consumption equals total output, $C = Y$, since we abstract from saving and investment for the moment. We also assume for the moment that only the mark-up factors can fluctuate whereas all the other parameters of the model stay constant over time.

We may now solve our model for the 'natural' level of employment $\bar{L}$ that will prevail when the mark-up factors are at their 'normal' trend levels, $\bar{m}^p$ and $\bar{m}^w$. With $C = Y = BL^{1-\alpha}$ we have $MRS = C^\theta L^\mu = B^\theta L^{\theta(1-\alpha)+\mu}$, so Eq. (6) may be rearranged to give

$$\frac{W}{P} = \frac{\bar{m}^w B^\theta \bar{L}^{\theta(1-\alpha)+\mu}}{1-\tau}. \tag{10}$$

Eq. (10) describes the supply side of the labour market, showing the real wage that workers with market power (or their union representatives) will claim at the natural employment level $\bar{L}$. To find the real wage that firms will be willing to offer at that employment level, we rearrange (8) to get the labour demand curve:

$$\frac{W}{P} = \frac{(1-\alpha)B\bar{L}^{-\alpha}}{\bar{m}^p}. \tag{11}$$

Equating the right-hand sides of (10) and (11) and solving for $\bar{L}$, we obtain:

$$\bar{L} = \left[\frac{(1-\alpha)(1-\tau)B^{1-\theta}}{\bar{m}^p \bar{m}^w} \right]^{\frac{1}{\theta(1-\alpha)+\alpha+\mu}} = \left[\frac{(1-\alpha)B^{1-\theta}}{\bar{\delta}} \right]^{\frac{1}{\theta(1-\alpha)+\alpha+\mu}}, \qquad \bar{\delta} \equiv \frac{\bar{m}^p \bar{m}^w}{1-\tau}. \tag{12}$$

The (distorted) long run labour market equilibrium summarized in (12) is illustrated in Fig. 19.1 which also shows the (higher) employment level L^e that would prevail in a perfectly competitive economy with no distortionary taxes. By inserting (12) into the production function (7), we find the natural output level $\bar{Y}$ corresponding to the natural level of employment:

$$\bar{Y} = B^{\frac{1+\mu}{\theta(1-\alpha)+\alpha+\mu}} \left[\frac{(1-\alpha)(1-\tau)}{\bar{m}^p \bar{m}^w} \right]^{\frac{1-\alpha}{\theta(1-\alpha)+\alpha+\mu}} = B^{\frac{1+\mu}{\theta(1-\alpha)+\alpha+\mu}} \left[\frac{(1-\alpha)}{\bar{\delta}} \right]^{\frac{1-\alpha}{\theta(1-\alpha)+\alpha+\mu}}. \tag{13}$$

---

4. Of course, if all consumers were literally identical, it would not make sense for the government to introduce distortionary taxes simply to redistribute the revenue as lump sum transfers. But if consumers differ, say, in terms of their productivity and wage rates, the government can achieve a more equal distribution of income by imposing a proportional income tax and distributing the revenue in equal amounts to everyone.

FIGURE 19.1 The natural versus the efficient level of employment

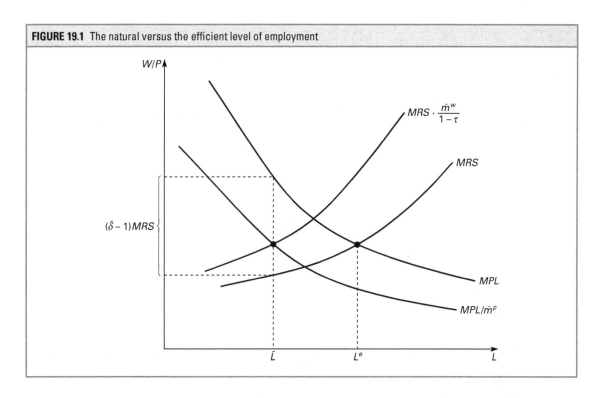

The welfare costs of mark-up shocks

Suppose that the mark-up factors fluctuate around their trend levels $\bar{m}^p$ and $\bar{m}^w$, causing employment and hence output and consumption to oscillate around the long-run equilibrium levels given by (12) and (13). From (3) we may calculate the impact of such business fluctuations on the utility of the representative consumer. In doing so, it will be convenient to approximate (3) by a second-degree polynomial, using the general result that a second-order Taylor approximation of the function $f(v, z)$ around the point $(\bar{v}, \bar{z})$ reads:

$$
\begin{aligned}
f(v, z) &\cong f(\bar{v}, \bar{z}) + f_v(\bar{v}, \bar{z})(v - \bar{v}) + f_z(\bar{v}, \bar{z})(z - \bar{z}) + \frac{1}{2}f_{vv}(\bar{v}, \bar{z})(v - \bar{v})^2 + \\
&\quad \frac{1}{2}f_{zz}(\bar{v}, \bar{z})(z - \bar{z})^2 + f_{vz}(\bar{v}, \bar{z})(v - \bar{v})(z - \bar{z}),
\end{aligned}
\tag{14}
$$

where f_i and f_{ii} are the first and second partial derivatives of f with respect to variable i, $i = v$, z, and f_{ij} is the cross-derivative of f with respect to variables i and j. Applying formula (14) to make an approximation of (3) around the long-run equilibrium point $(\bar{C}, \bar{L})$ and noting that (3) implies $U_{CL} = 0$, we get

$$
\Delta \equiv U(C, L) - U(\bar{C}, \bar{L}) \cong \bar{C}^{1-\theta}\left(\frac{C - \bar{C}}{\bar{C}}\right) - \bar{L}^{1+\mu}\left(\frac{L - \bar{L}}{\bar{L}}\right) - \frac{\theta \bar{C}^{1-\theta}}{2}\left(\frac{C - \bar{C}}{\bar{C}}\right)^2 - \frac{\mu \bar{L}^{1+\mu}}{2}\left(\frac{L - \bar{L}}{\bar{L}}\right)^2,
\tag{15}
$$

where Δ is the deviation of utility from its steady-state level. Equation (15) should give a good approximation of Δ as long as the economy is not pushed too far away from long-run equilibrium. If $c \equiv \ln C$, $\ell \equiv \ln L$, $\hat{c} \equiv c - \bar{c}$, and $\hat{\ell} \equiv \ell - \bar{\ell}$, the variables $\hat{c}$ and $\hat{\ell}$ measure the relative deviations of consumption and employment from their steady state levels, since $(C - \bar{C})/\bar{C} \cong \hat{c}$ and $(L - \bar{L})/\bar{L} \cong \hat{\ell}$. Further, from (3) it follows that $\bar{U}_C = \bar{C}^{-\theta}$. Dividing through by $\bar{C}^{1-\theta}$, we may therefore write (15) as

$$\frac{\Delta/\bar{U}_C}{\bar{C}} \cong \hat{c} - \frac{\theta\hat{c}^2}{2} - \left(\frac{\bar{C}^\theta \bar{L}^{1+\mu}}{\bar{C}}\right)\left(\ell + \frac{\mu\hat{\ell}^2}{2}\right). \tag{16}$$

Since $\bar{U}_C$ is the marginal utility of consumption, the magnitude $\Delta/\bar{U}_C$ in (16) measures the welfare effect of deviations from the steady state in terms of units of consumption. As you may verify from (6), (8) and (9), we have $\tilde{C}^\theta\bar{L}^{1+\mu}/\bar{C} = (1-\alpha)/\bar{\delta}$. Inserting this in (16), we get

$$\frac{\Delta/\bar{U}_C}{\bar{C}} \cong \overbrace{\hat{c} - \frac{\theta\hat{c}^2}{2}}^{\text{welfare effect of consumption fluctuations}} - \overbrace{\left(\frac{1-\alpha}{\bar{\delta}}\right)\left(\ell + \frac{\mu\hat{\ell}^2}{2}\right)}^{\text{welfare effect of employment fluctuations}}. \tag{17}$$

In our final step, we note that since $C = Y = BL^{1-\alpha}$ and B is assumed to be constant for the moment, we have $\hat{c} = \hat{y} = (1-\alpha)\hat{\ell}$, where $\hat{y} \equiv y - \bar{y}$. Using this in (17), we end up with

$$\frac{\Delta/\bar{U}_C}{\bar{C}} \cong \overbrace{\left(\frac{\bar{\delta}-1}{\bar{\delta}}\right)\hat{y}}^{\text{First-order welfare effect}} - \overbrace{\left[\theta + \frac{\mu}{\bar{\delta}(1-\alpha)}\right]\frac{\hat{y}^2}{2}}^{\text{Second-order welfare effect}}. \tag{18}$$

Equation (18) divides the welfare effect of (percentage) deviations of output from its 'natural' rate into a first-order effect and a second-order effect. The first-order effect is the impact of the output gap on welfare in the hypothetical case where the marginal utility of consumption and the marginal disutility from work are both constant so that $\theta = \mu = 0$. When markets are distorted by imperfect competition and/or by taxes so that $\bar{\delta} > 1$ (cf. the definition of δ in (9)), we see from (18) that an economic boom where $\hat{y} > 0$ is welfare-improving, whereas a recession $\hat{y} < 0$ reduces consumer welfare. The reason is that market distortions and taxes keep the marginal product of labour above the marginal rate of substitution between consumption and work, so a rise in output and employment always generates more additional consumption than the amount needed to compensate workers for their extra work effort. Hence booms are 'good times' while recessions are 'bad times'. Note that if competition were perfect and there were no distortionary taxes, the first-order effect would vanish since we would then have $\bar{\delta} = 1$. This reflects that $MPL = MRS$ in a non-distorted equilibrium, so to a first-order approximation consumers would be indifferent between working and consuming a little more or a little less. Notice also that if output fluctuates symmetrically around its natural rate so that $E[\hat{y}] = 0$, the first-order effect is zero on average, that is, the first-order welfare effects of booms and recessions wash out over the business cycle.

By contrast, the second-order effect in (18) unambiguously reduces consumer welfare. The second-order effect arises because the marginal utility of consumption is declining ($\theta > 0$) and the marginal disutility of work is increasing ($\mu > 0$). A positive output gap therefore generates a smaller net welfare increase than the welfare reduction caused by a negative output gap of the same magnitude.

Figure 19.2 illustrates the first-order as well as the second-order effects of business fluctuations driven by mark-up fluctuations. Mark-up shocks do not affect the MPL and the MRS, but a shock to the price mark-up shifts the labour demand curve MPL/m^p, and a shock to the wage mark-up shifts the wage curve $m^w MRS/(1-\tau)$. Suppose that such shocks cause employment to fluctuate symmetrically around its natural level within the interval $L_1 - L_2$ shown in Fig. 19.2. If employment increases from $\bar{L}$ to $\bar{L}_2$ and if (hypothetically) the marginal productivity of labour stayed constant at its steady state value given by point x_1 in Fig. 19.2, total output and consumption would increase by an amount equal to the area of the rectangle $x_1x_2L_2\bar{L}$. At the same time, if the MRS were to remain constant at its steady state level given by point x_5, the total disutility of work (measured in units of consumption) would increase by the area $x_5x_9L_2\bar{L}$, so the net welfare gain from the rise in employment

FIGURE 19.2 The welfare costs of employment fluctuations

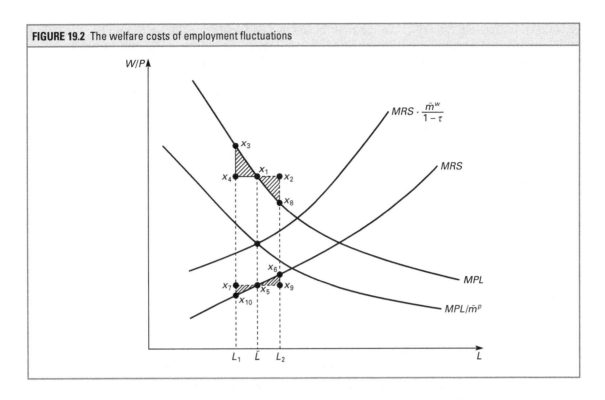

would equal the difference between areas $x_1 x_2 L_2 \bar{L}$ and $x_5 x_9 L_2 \bar{L}$ which is clearly positive. This is the first-order welfare gain from a boom with high employment. As you can see, the gain arises from the fact that MPL is initially above MRS, due to market distortions. By similar reasoning, if MPL and MRS were constant, the net welfare loss from a fall in employment from $\bar{L}$ to L_1 would equal the difference between areas $x_1 x_4 L_1 \bar{L}$ and $x_5 x_7 L_1 \bar{L}$. This difference measures the first-order welfare loss from a recession with low employment. Since $L_1 - \bar{L} = \bar{L} - L_2$ by assumption, the first-order welfare gain from the boom would thus be exactly offset by the first-order welfare loss from the recession, as implied by the first term in Eq. (18) when $E[\hat{y}] = 0$.

But as Fig. 19.2 clearly shows, the first-order effect gives an inaccurate approximation of the welfare effect of employment fluctuations, since MPL and MRS are not in fact constant. For example, when employment increases from $\bar{L}$ to $\bar{L}_2$, total output only increases by the area under the MPL curve in the interval $L_2 - \bar{L}$ (explain this to yourself) which is equal to the area of the rectangle $x_1 x_2 L_2 \bar{L}$ *minus* the area of the hatched triangle $x_1 x_2 x_8$. Similarly, since the rise in the (consumption value of) total disutility of work is given by the area below the MRS curve in the interval $L_2 - \bar{L}$ (explain this), the net increase in total disutility equals the area of the rectangle $x_5 x_9 L_2 \bar{L}$ *plus* the area of the hatched triangle $x_5 x_6 x_9$. Thus the net welfare gain from the boom is equal to the first-order effect *minus* the sum of the areas of the two triangles $x_1 x_2 x_8$ and $x_5 x_6 x_9$. The first of these triangles captures the fact that the marginal productivity of labour is declining, while the second triangle adjusts for the fact that the marginal disutility of labour is increasing. By a similar logic you see that the net welfare loss from the recession is given by the area of the rectangle $x_1 x_4 x_7 x_5$ *plus* the sum of the areas of the two hatched triangles $x_1 x_3 x_4$ and $x_5 x_7 x_{10}$, capturing that a fall in employment raises the marginal product of labour and reduces the marginal disutility of work.

It follows that the welfare gain from a boom is lower than the welfare loss from a recession involving a change in employment of the same magnitude. To be more precise, the net welfare loss from a business cycle where employment fluctuates between L_2 and L_1 is given by the sum of all the hatched triangles in Fig. 19.2. This welfare loss is reflected in the second-order term in Eq. (18).[5] We see that the second-order effect is larger the higher the value of α, since a higher α implies a faster decline in marginal productivity as employment goes up (recall that $MPL = BL^{-\alpha}$). The second-order effect also increases with θ and μ, because higher values of these parameters mean that the MRS increases faster with employment (since $MRS = C^{\theta}L^{\mu} = Y^{\theta}L^{\mu} = B^{\theta}L^{\theta(1-\alpha)+\mu}$). Interestingly, it follows from (18) that the second-order welfare loss from business fluctuations is smaller the higher the degree of market distortion, $\bar{\delta}$ (defined in (12)). The reason is that a higher value of $\bar{\delta}$ reduces the natural level of employment (see (12)), moving $\bar{L}$ to the left in Fig. 19.2 where the MRS curve is flatter. As you can see from the figure, a flattening of the MRS curve around the natural employment level will reduce the size of the second-order effect of employment fluctuations on the total disutility of labour.

From Eq. (18) we can calculate the *average* welfare loss from business cycles, using the assumption that output fluctuates symmetrically around the 'natural' level so that $E[\hat{y}] = 0$. Taking the mathematical expectation in (18), we then get

$$E\left[\frac{\Delta / \bar{U}_C}{\bar{C}}\right] \cong \left[\theta + \frac{\mu}{\bar{\delta}(1-\alpha)}\right]\frac{\sigma_y^2}{2}, \qquad \sigma_y^2 \equiv E[(y - \bar{y})^2]. \tag{19}$$

Equation (19) offers an answer to the first question posed in Section 19.1 above: why should society worry about the *variability* of output and not just about its average value? The answer is that the second-order effects of the fluctuations in consumption and employment caused by business cycles reduce the welfare of the average consumer-worker. He or she would therefore be better off if output and employment could be stabilized at their natural rates. As to the second question raised in Section 19.1, Eq. (19) shows that if policy makers are concerned about the welfare of the average citizen, the weight a_y attached to the goal of output stabilization in the social loss function (2) should depend on (the best estimates of) the parameters θ, α, μ, and $\bar{\delta}$ that affect the welfare loss from business cycles in the manner just discussed.

The analysis above assumes that mark-up shocks can be important drivers of business cycles. If this is true, our measure of distortion (δ) in (9) should be relatively high during recessions and relatively low during booms. Is that what we actually observe? To answer this question, economists Jordi Galí, Mark Gertler, and José López-Salido used formulas very similar to (6), (8) and (9) along with data on output, consumption, employment and real wages to construct a time series for the evolution of our 'distortion' variable δ in the USA, based on plausible estimates for the parameters α, θ, μ, and τ.[6] Their findings are illustrated in Fig. 19.3. The figure plots the estimated values of $(1/\delta)$ which should be rising during economic upturns and falling during downturns. The hatched areas are periods of recession according to the business cycle dating undertaken by the National Bureau of Economic Research (see Chapter 13), so the remaining areas are periods of economic upswing. We see that the 'inverse distortion variable' $(1/\delta)$ does in fact rise considerably during booms and falls substantially during recessions, as our simple model would predict. According to the estimates underlying Fig. 19.3, the fluctuations in δ are mainly caused by shifts in the wage mark-up specified in (6).

Allowing for demand shocks

While the evidence in Fig. 19.3 is consistent with our simple business cycle model, it does not 'prove' that business cycles are driven by mark-up shocks, as we shall show in this

---

5. This second-order term is an approximation which assumes that the MPL and MRS curves in Fig. 19.2 are linear in the interval considered. The stronger the curvature of the actual MPL and MRS curves, the less precise our second-order approximation will be.

6. See Jordi Galí, Mark Gertler, and José David López-Salido, 'Markups, Gaps, and the Welfare Costs of Business Fluctuations', *Review of Economics and Statistics*, **89**, 2007, pp. 44–59.

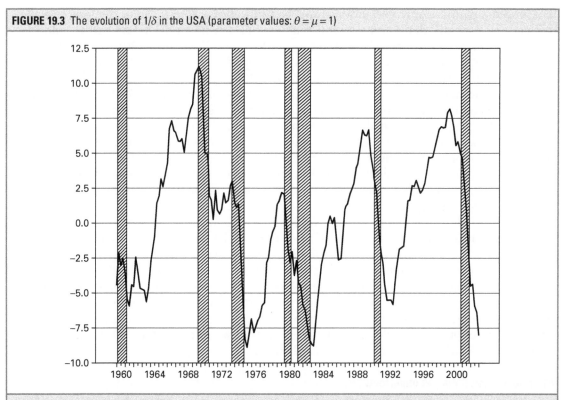

FIGURE 19.3 The evolution of $1/\delta$ in the USA (parameter values: $\theta = \mu = 1$)

Note: The hatched areas indicate periods of recession according to the business cycle datings of the National Bureau of Economic Research.

Source: Figure 2 in Jordi Galí, Mark Gertler, and J. David López-Salido: 'Markups, Gaps, and the Welfare Costs of Business Fluctuations'. *The Review of Economics and Statistics*, **89**, 2007, pp. 44–59.

subsection. Indeed, there are many types of evidence indicating that shocks to aggregate demand play an important and often a decisive role in initiating business cycles. We will now illustrate how demand shocks may be incorporated into our model. By doing so, we can offer a complementary explanation for the evidence shown in Fig. 19.3. At the same time we can explain how inflation and inflation instability may arise in our model, thereby laying the ground for a subsequent analysis of the welfare costs of inflation.

Let M denote the nominal money supply, and let us assume that the nominal demand for money is proportional to the total volume of nominal transactions which in turn is proportional to aggregate nominal income, PY. In money market equilibrium we then have

$$M = k \cdot PY, \qquad k > 0, \tag{20}$$

where the parameter k may fluctuate over time, say, due to financial innovations and/or shifts in the 'state of confidence' that affect the preference for liquidity.

If we maintain the previous specification of our model, it displays the classical dichotomy between nominal and real variables: Eq. (20) is just an addendum to the model which determines the price level once real income Y has been determined from the economy's supply side. However, this dichotomy rests on the assumption made in (6) that wage setters know the current price level when they set the nominal wage rate. As argued in Chapter 17, it is more realistic to assume that nominal wage rates are pre-set on the basis of the *expected* price level, P^e. Hence the target wage mark-up in (6) should be respecified as

$$m^w \equiv \frac{(W/P^e)(1 - \tau)}{MRS}. \tag{21}$$

In a long-run equilibrium expectations must be fulfilled (i.e. $P^e = P$), so in the long run all real variables are still determined by the 'real' business cycle model set up earlier, and the classical dichotomy still prevails. But in the short run it follows from (20) and (21) that a positive shock to the nominal money supply or a negative shock to the liquidity preference parameter k may drive the actual price level above the expected price level via its positive impact on nominal aggregate demand. In this way the *actual* real wage W/P will be driven below the target level given by (21), and the *actual* observed wage mark-up will fall below its target. By lowering the actual real wage, a positive shock to nominal demand will thus pull employment and output above the natural rate, while a negative nominal demand shock will push activity below the natural level by causing an unexpected drop in prices that raises the real wage above its target. During such business cycles generated by demand shocks, one will observe countercyclical movements in the realized wage mark-up even if the target wage mark-up stays constant.

Thus the evidence in Fig. 19.3 is not sufficient to establish that business cycles are driven by mark-up shocks, since a similar mark-up pattern will emerge if the cycle is caused by demand shocks. This is an example of the difficulties one often encounters when trying to discriminate between competing economic theories by simply 'letting the data speak for themselves'. Typically, one can only observe whether a given theory is consistent with the data, but one cannot exclude the possibility that another theory could explain the data equally well or even better. Fortunately, however, our expressions (18) and (19) for the welfare costs of business cycles are valid regardless of whether the fluctuations in output are caused by mark-up shocks or by demand shocks.[7]

The role of capital market imperfections

As we have seen, one of the sources of the welfare cost of business cycles is that fluctuations in real output generate fluctuations in real income and consumption. Since the marginal utility of consumption declines with increasing consumption, consumers put more value on avoiding low levels of consumption than on attaining very high consumption levels. Hence they prefer a smooth path of consumption to an unstable path, so if stabilization policy can even out the time path of consumption by smoothing fluctuations in output, a consumer welfare gain will result.

One objection to our analysis might be that our model leaves out the capital market, neglecting the fact that individual consumers can use the private capital market to smooth consumption over time, as we saw in Chapter 15. However, as we mentioned in that chapter, capital markets are hardly perfect, so some consumers may be subject to credit constraints. In particular, during a serious recession the market values of many assets may fall considerably and destroy much of the collateral that consumers normally use to obtain credit.

In addition to borrowing in the capital market, people can insure themselves against temporary income losses by taking out insurance in the private market, say, insurance against unemployment. But here again we run into problems with the functioning of markets. A person who is fully insured against any income loss from unemployment has little incentive to avoid joblessness. If he values leisure more than the social interaction obtained through his job, he may therefore choose to stay out of work for long periods of time. Because of this so-called *moral hazard problem* it is suboptimal for private insurance companies (as well as for the government) to offer full insurance against income losses from unemployment.

On top of this, the demand for unemployment insurance is likely to come mainly from those who face the highest risks of unemployment. If the premium for unemployment insurance is set to cover the *average* income loss from unemployment across a large group of

---

7. But as we shall see later, it will matter for the welfare cost whether cycles are initiated by productivity shocks or by other types of shock.

insured workers, individuals in very risky jobs have a strong incentive to buy insurance, because the present value of their expected unemployment benefits will exceed the present value of the insurance premium. But workers facing a relatively low risk of losing their jobs may find that the premium is too high relative to their expected unemployment benefits. Therefore they may decide to drop out of the insurance scheme. Because of this so-called *adverse selection problem*, private insurance companies may fear that those who want to take out insurance represent only the highest risks, and companies may therefore decide that offering insurance will not be profitable. Hence the adverse selection problem may cause too little unemployment insurance to be supplied by the market.

Thus the problems of moral hazard and adverse selection limit the scope for consumption smoothing through private credit and insurance markets. The moral hazard problem also makes it suboptimal for the government to offer full insurance against private income losses through the system of public transfer payments. A successful stabilization policy may therefore raise consumer welfare by evening out the time path of real income. We may say that effective stabilization policy provides a type of *income insurance* which cannot be delivered through the private market or the public transfer system.

These observations relate to an individual's opportunities for consumption smoothing in case a recession imposes a temporary income loss upon him. At the macro level it is clear that aggregate consumption has to fluctuate with aggregate output in our simple formal model of a closed economy where all output was assumed to be used for consumption in each period. But in a more realistic model including investment, it is conceivable that output fluctuations could be absorbed mainly by fluctuations in aggregate investment if well-functioning capital and insurance markets allow consumers as a whole to smooth their stream of consumption over time. Imperfections in these markets are therefore also important for consumption fluctuations at the macro level.

Quantifying the welfare costs of cycles in consumption and employment

Despite the simplicity of our model, it is tempting to use equation (19) to estimate the likely magnitude of the average welfare loss from business cycles to get an idea of the potential welfare gain from a successful stabilization policy. It is instructive to split (19) into the following two components:

$$E\left[\frac{\Delta/\bar{U}_C}{\bar{C}}\right] \cong \underbrace{\frac{\theta\sigma_y^2}{2}}_{\substack{\text{Welfare loss from} \\ \text{consumption fluctuations}}} + \underbrace{\frac{\mu\sigma_y^2}{2\bar{\delta}(1-\alpha)}}_{\substack{\text{Welfare loss from} \\ \text{employment fluctuations}}} \quad, \quad \bar{\delta} \equiv \frac{\bar{m}^p\bar{m}^w}{1-\tau}. \tag{22}$$

As indicated, the first term on the right-hand side of (22) captures the average welfare loss from consumption fluctuations (since the variance of consumption equals that of output, given that all output is consumed in every period), while the second term reflects the welfare cost of the employment fluctuations associated with the volatility of output.

To apply Eq. (22), we need to insert plausible estimates of the various parameters. Note that the first term on the right-hand side gives the maximum amount that consumers would be willing to pay (measured relative to the trend level of consumption) in return for perfect insurance against consumption fluctuations. In other words, it is the maximum amount consumers would pay to receive a constant consumption stream instead of the actual fluctuating stream of consumption. We see that this amount is proportional to the Coefficient of Relative Risk Aversion, θ. The size of this parameter can be estimated by studying consumer behaviour in situations involving risk. Empirical estimates of θ vary a great deal, depending on the data and the method of estimation. A recent study by economists Richard Layard, Guy Mayraz and Stephen Nickell applied survey data from more than 50 countries covering time periods between 1972 and 2005 to come up with an estimate of θ in the interval between 1.19 and

1.34, with a central estimate of 1.26.[8] Against this background, we set $\theta = 1.25$. As mentioned earlier, the magnitude $1/\mu$ is the income-compensated net wage elasticity of labour supply. Estimates of this parameter also vary a lot, but a value of $1/\mu$ in the neighbourhood of 0.2 is often considered to be realistic. Hence we set $\mu = 5$. As for the price mark-up, $\bar{m}^p$, a value of 1.15 to 1.2 has been estimated for the USA, so we choose $\bar{m}^p = 1.2$.[9] Less is known about the size of the wage mark-up, so we simply set it equal to the price mark-up ($\bar{m}^w = \bar{m}^p = 1.2$), thus assuming similar degrees of imperfection in the labour and product markets. Moreover, we set our tax rate τ equal to the average ratio of tax revenue to GDP in the OECD area which was around 0.36 in 2006. The parameter α in the production function (7) is usually considered to be around $\frac{1}{3}$. Finally, we need a plausible estimate for the variance of output around its natural level, σ_y^2. In mature OECD economies, the standard deviation of GDP around its trend level is typically close to 2 per cent, so we set $\sigma_y^2 = 0.02^2 = 0.0004$.

Given our assumed values of θ and σ_y^2, our estimate of the welfare loss from consumption fluctuations becomes $\theta \sigma_y^2 / 2 = 0.00025$, that is, a little less than 0.03 per cent of steady state consumption. This rather small number reflects that the volatility of output in the typical OECD country over longer time periods is not very large. Our estimate of the welfare loss from employment fluctuations is somewhat bigger, since our assumed parameter values imply that the second term in (22) is 0.00133, i.e. a little more than 0.13 per cent of steady state consumption. Nevertheless, the total estimated welfare loss of about 0.16 per cent of consumption must be said to be small.

However, this number measures the net effect of the offsetting welfare effects of booms and recessions. It therefore hides the fact that the welfare effects of booms and recessions can be quite substantial. For example, during the economic crisis of 2008–09, the output gap in many OECD countries has been estimated to be in the neighbourhood of minus 5 per cent or even more. According to Eq. (18), our parameter values imply that the sum of the first-order and the second-order effects of a deep recession involving $\hat{y} = -0.05$ is a fall in consumer welfare amounting to 3.4 per cent of steady state consumption, of which 2.8 per cent is due to the first-order effect. This is clearly a sizeable effect. In their study of mark-up shocks mentioned earlier in this section (see Footnote 5), Galí, Gertler, and López-Salido used a method similar to ours to estimate the cumulative welfare losses from the US recessions occurring in the last three decades of the twentieth century, assuming different combinations of values for θ and μ in order to span the range of uncertainty regarding these parameters. These estimates are summarized in Table 19.1. As you can see, they suggest that

TABLE 19.1 Estimated welfare costs of recession episodes in the United States

Value of		Percentage of one year's consumption		
θ	μ	1970s	1980s	1990s
1	1	4.6	4.7	2.3
1	5	6.2	6.4	3.2
5	1	2.9	7.2	0.4
5	5	4.9	8.0	1.7

Source: Table 5.2 in Jordi Galí, Mark Gertler, and J. David López-Salido: 'Markups, Gaps, and the Welfare Costs of Business Fluctuations', *The Review of Economics and Statistics*, **89**, 2007, pp. 44–59.

---

8. See Richard Layard, Guy Mayraz, and Stephen Nickell, 'The Marginal Utility of Income', *Journal of Public Economics*, **92**, 2008, pp. 1846–1857. It should be mentioned that several other authors have found estimates of the *CRRA* parameter that are considerably higher than those obtained in this article.

9. The evidence on price mark-ups and their cyclical behaviour is surveyed by Julio Rotemberg and Michael Woodford, 'The Cyclical Behaviour of Prices and Costs', in John Taylor and Michael Woodford (Eds.), *The Handbook of Macroeconomics*, Vol. 1B, 1999, Amsterdam: North-Holland.

the US recessions in the (early) 1980s could have caused a welfare loss of as much as 8 per cent of one year's consumption.

It is also important to stress that our relatively low estimate for the potential welfare gain from elimination of the business cycle could reflect that stabilization policy has already been quite successful in reducing the volatility of output so that the remaining gain from further stabilization is limited. For example, following the Keynesian revolution in macroeconomic thought that provided a rationale for active stabilization policy, and with the misery of the Great Depression still fresh in everybody's mind, the US Employment Act of 1946 prescribed that the government 'declares and establishes as a national goal the fulfillment of the right to full opportunities for useful paid employment at fair rates of compensation of all individuals able, willing, and seeking to work'. And macroeconomic volatility in the USA did indeed fall substantially after the Second World War: in the period 1920–40 the standard deviation of the annual growth rate of real GNP was as large as 7.1 per cent, but in the period 1948–97 it fell to 2.5 per cent.[10]

Let us sum up our main findings so far:

THE AVERAGE WELFARE COSTS OF CONSUMPTION FLUCTUATIONS

These are proportional to the variance of the output gap. The welfare loss from consumption fluctuations arises because risk-averse consumers prefer a stable consumption stream to a fluctuating one, and because problems of moral hazard and adverse selection in capital markets and insurance markets prevent perfect consumption smoothing. The welfare loss from consumption fluctuations varies proportionally with the consumer's degree of risk aversion. Because the variance of consumption is limited at the macro level, the average welfare loss from consumption volatility over the business cycle is likely to be small.

THE AVERAGE WELFARE COSTS OF EMPLOYMENT FLUCTUATIONS

These are also proportional to the variance of the output gap. They arise because the marginal disutility of work increases with the level of employment, causing workers to prefer a stable employment level to a fluctuating one. The welfare cost of employment fluctuations is higher, the higher the elasticities of the marginal disutility of work and of the marginal utility of consumption, and lower, the higher the degree of market distortions. For realistic parameter values the welfare loss from employment fluctuations is likely to be somewhat larger than the loss from consumption fluctuations. In particular, recessions can cause large welfare losses, although these losses are to a large extent offset by the welfare gained during boom periods.

The upshot of the above analysis is that the net welfare costs of business cycles are probably not very large. But this analysis ignores the possibility that business cycles may affect the trend level of output. Once we allow for this, the welfare loss from business fluctuations may be much larger, as we shall see in the next subsection.

The welfare costs of business cycles when the cycle affects the trend level of output

We have so far assumed that business cycles only affect the variance of output around its trend level, but not the trend level itself. But it may well be that a lower volatility of output and employment could raise the average level of real income. In fact, this possibility was discussed in Chapter 1 in connection with Fig. 1.4.

---

10. See Christina D. Romer, 'Changes in Business Cycles: Evidence and Explanations', *Journal of Economic Perspectives*, **13**, 1999, pp. 23–44.

To illustrate a specific way in which more stability could imply permanently higher income levels, recall from Figs 17.1 and 17.2 that the short-run relationship between unemployment and inflation appears to be non-linear: as the unemployment rate falls, the rise in inflation induced by a further one percentage point drop in unemployment accelerates, even if the expected inflation rate stays constant. Intuitively, as the labour market tightens, local labour shortages become more widespread, and at some point when the economy comes close to operating at full employment, it becomes very difficult to achieve a further fall in unemployment without creating strong upward wage pressures deriving from local 'bottlenecks' in the labour market. On the other hand, if wages are especially rigid in the downward direction, for example because fairness norms tend to prevent nominal wage cuts, a rise in unemployment may only have a small effect on wages if unemployment is already very high and wage inflation is already close to zero. To capture these non-linearities, economists have sometimes assumed that the expectations-augmented Phillips curve takes the form

$$\pi = \pi^e + a_0 + a_1(1/u), \qquad a_0 < 0, \qquad a_1 > 0. \tag{23}$$

For a given expected inflation rate π^e, this Phillips curve implies a convex relationship between unemployment and inflation much like the one observed in Fig. 17.1. According to (23), the natural unemployment rate $\bar{u}$ ensuring that inflation expectations are fulfilled ($\pi^e = \pi$) is $\bar{u} = -a_1/a_0$ (note from (23) that a_0 is assumed to be negative, ensuring $\bar{u} > 0$). Now define $f(u) \equiv 1/u$ and note that $f' = -1/u^2$ and $f'' = 2u/u^4 = 2/u^3$. Using these results in taking a second-order Taylor approximation of (23) around the point $u = \bar{u}$, we get:

$$\pi - \pi^e \approx a_0 + \overbrace{\frac{a_1}{\bar{u}}}^{= 0} - \frac{a_1}{\bar{u}^2}(u - \bar{u}) + \frac{a_1}{\bar{u}^3}(u - \bar{u})^2 = \frac{a_1}{\bar{u}^2}\left[\frac{(u - \bar{u})^2}{\bar{u}} - (u - \bar{u})\right]. \tag{24}$$

Now assume (as we did in the two previous chapters) that the expected inflation rate equals last period's actual inflation rate, $\pi^e = \pi_{-1}$, and suppose that inflation fluctuates around a stable level so that over the long run $E[\pi - \pi_{-1}] = E[\pi - \pi^e] = 0$.[11] It then follows from (24) that the mathematical expectation of the term in the square bracket will have to equal zero, that is

$$E\left[\frac{(u - \bar{u})^2}{\bar{u}} - (u - \bar{u})\right] = 0 \qquad \Rightarrow$$

$$E[u - \bar{u}] = \frac{E[(u - \bar{u})^2]}{\bar{u}} = \frac{\sigma_u^2}{\bar{u}} > 0. \tag{25}$$

Eq. (25) implies that on average unemployment has to lie somewhat *above* the natural rate to ensure a stable level of inflation in the long run. The reason is that the rise in inflation induced by a fall in unemployment below the natural rate is larger than the drop in inflation generated by a similar rise in unemployment above the natural rate. If unemployment fluctuated by equal amounts for equally long above and below the natural rate, the average rate of inflation would therefore tend to rise systematically over time. From (25) we see that the average (positive) deviation of actual unemployment from its natural rate varies in proportion to the variance of unemployment, σ_u^2, and inversely with the natural unemployment rate itself.

---

11. An alternative assumption generating the same result would be that people have *rational expectations*, meaning that they do not make systematic forecast errors. This also implies $E[\pi - \pi^e] = 0$. In Chapter 21 we explain and discuss the hypothesis of rational expectations.

The important message from Eq. (25) is that if policy makers could reduce *fluctuations* in unemployment, they could also reduce the average *level* of unemployment and thereby increase the trend level of output.[12] In OECD countries the standard deviation of unemployment is often in the neighbourhood of one percentage point, implying that $\sigma_u^2 = 0.01^2 = 0.0001$. If the natural rate of unemployment is, say, 5 per cent, Eq. (25) then implies that the average level of unemployment would fall by $0.0001/0.05 = 0.002$ or 0.2 percentage points if all fluctuations in unemployment could be eliminated. If the 'Okun's Law' coefficient is roughly 2, corresponding to our estimate for the USA in Chapter 10, a 0.2 percentage point drop in average unemployment would imply a 0.4 per cent increase in average output per year. Over a ten-year period, this would accumulate to a more than 4 per cent higher level of trend output and income; a sizeable gain. This analysis suggests that the welfare gain from a stabilization policy that succeeds in significantly reducing the volatility of unemployment could be considerably higher than indicated by our previous analysis. To sum up:

NON-LINEARITIES IN AGGREGATE SUPPLY AND THE WELFARE COST OF BUSINESS CYCLES

The evidence suggests that the short-run Phillips curve is convex to the origin, so that inflation reacts more strongly to a change in unemployment as the unemployment rate falls. A fall in the volatility of unemployment will then reduce the average level of unemployment and thereby increase the trend level of output. The resulting welfare gain from stabilizing unemployment is likely to be considerably larger than the estimated welfare gain from stabilization policy in a model that does not allow for an effect of employment volatility on average income.

Consumer heterogeneity and the welfare costs of business cycles

We have so far neglected the distributional aspects of business cycles. As we have seen, aggregate consumption does not fluctuate very much over the cycle, so an individual household whose consumption mirrored aggregate consumption would not be much better off if these fluctuations were smoothed out. But in a world with imperfect credit markets, the consumption of individual households may be far more volatile than aggregate consumption, and hence they would benefit more from the elimination of macroeconomic volatility. Economists Kjetil Storesletten, Chris Telmer and Amir Yaron have documented that the standard deviation of earnings across households in the USA more than doubles during a recession and that shocks to individual household earnings are highly persistent. When a household's earnings falls in the current year, its earnings are thus likely to be lower for quite a while.[13] The sharp rise in the dispersion of expected individual incomes during recessions means that the modest volatility of aggregate consumption does not fully capture the perceived risk to individual consumers caused by business cycles. When they account for the positive link between aggregate business cycle risk and the dispersion of individual earnings opportunities ('when it rains, it pours!'), Storesletten, Telmer and Yaron find that the welfare loss from business cycles could be as large as 2.5 per cent of average consumption, assuming a Coefficient of Relative Risk Aversion (θ) equal to 4.

Moreover, economic research has documented that the income losses caused by recessions tend to be concentrated among the poorer members of society. Manual workers –

---

12. This point was first made in a comment by N. Gregory Mankiw in the *Brookings Papers on Economic Activity*, 1988, pp. 481–485.

13. See Kjetil Storesletten, Chris Telmer and Amir Yaron, 'The Welfare Cost of Business Cycles Revisited: Finite Lives and Cyclical Variation in Idiosyncratic Risk', *European Economic Review*, **45**, 2001, pp. 1311–1339.

and in particular low-paid unskilled workers and young workers – tend to suffer a much larger decline in consumption than other people during times of recession.[14] For these groups who already earn low incomes while they are employed, recurring recessions and the associated spells of unemployment can imply a serious welfare loss. Hence a society concerned about inequality should also be concerned about instability of output and employment.

To recap:

CONSUMER HETEROGENEITY AND THE WELFARE COST OF BUSINESS CYCLES

The dispersion of individual earnings increases greatly during recessions and individual income losses caused by recessions (or other shocks) have a high degree of persistence. The resulting increase in uncertainty about individual earnings opportunities adds considerably to the welfare cost of business cycles. Moreover, the income losses from recessions tend to be concentrated among the poorer workers, thereby adding a social welfare cost to a society concerned about inequality.

Digging deeper: productivity shocks and the choice of output target

We have so far abstracted from shocks to the productivity variable B in our production function (7). When business cycles are driven by mark-up shocks and/or nominal demand shocks, we have seen above that stabilization of output around its natural rate is welfare-improving. This suggests a positive answer to the third question raised at the start of this section: should output really be stabilized around its natural level regardless of the type of shocks hitting the economy? But as we shall demonstrate below, the issue becomes more complicated once we allow for productivity shocks.

As mentioned earlier, a recent empirical study found that our *CRRA* parameter (θ) does not seem to be much greater than one. From now on we therefore simplify a bit by setting $\theta = 1$. This may also be justified by going back to (11) and (12). From (12) we see that when $\theta = 1$, the trend level of employment is independent of the level of productivity (B). It then follows from (11) that real wages will grow in line with productivity over the long haul. Both of these model properties are in line with the stylized facts of economic growth surveyed in Chapter 2.

Further, when analysing the welfare cost of deviations from the steady state in the presence of productivity shocks, it will be convenient to use the following second-order Taylor approximation. For any variable X we have:

$$\ln X \cong \ln \bar{X} + \frac{1}{\bar{X}}(X - \bar{X}) + \frac{1}{2}\left(\frac{-1}{\bar{X}^2}\right)(X - \bar{X})^2 \quad \Leftrightarrow \quad \ln X - \ln \bar{X} \cong \frac{X - \bar{X}}{\bar{X}} - \frac{1}{2}\left(\frac{X - \bar{X}}{\bar{X}}\right)^2$$

$$\Leftrightarrow \quad \frac{X - \bar{X}}{\bar{X}} \cong \hat{x} + \frac{1}{2}\hat{x}^2, \qquad x \equiv \ln X, \qquad \hat{x} \equiv x - \bar{x}, \tag{26}$$

where we have used the first-order approximation $(X - \bar{X})/\bar{X} \cong \hat{x}$ to arrive at the quadratic term in the last line of (26). We introduce the approximation (26) because it allows us to highlight the role of productivity shocks in a simpler and more elegant way, but neither our qualitative nor our quantitative results depend in any significant way on this approximation.

---

14.   See Kenneth Clark, Derek Leslie and Elizabeth Symons, 'The Cost of Recessions', *Economic Journal*, **104**, 1994, pp. 20–36.

We now insert $\theta = 1$ into (15) and note from (26) that $(C - \bar{C})/\bar{C} \cong \hat{c} + \frac{1}{2}\hat{c}^2$ and $(L - \bar{L})/\bar{L} \cong \hat{\ell} + \frac{1}{2}\hat{\ell}^2$. Recalling our earlier result that $\bar{C}^\theta \bar{L}^{1+\mu}/\bar{C} = (1 - \alpha)/\bar{\delta}$, and observing from (1) that $\bar{U}_C = 1/\bar{C}$ when $\theta = 1$, so that $(\Delta/\bar{U}_C)/\bar{C}$ becomes equal to Δ, Eq. (15) then modifies to:

$$\Delta \cong \hat{c} - \left(\frac{1-\alpha}{\bar{\delta}}\right)\left[\hat{\ell} + \left(\frac{1+\mu}{2}\right)\hat{\ell}^2\right], \tag{27}$$

When the (log of the) current productivity level $b \equiv \ln B$ deviates from its trend level $\bar{b} \equiv \ln \bar{B}$, it follows from our production function (7) that $\ell - \bar{\ell} = [y - \bar{y} - (b - \bar{b})]/(1 - \alpha) \equiv (\hat{y} - \hat{b})/(1 - \alpha)$. Moreover, since all output is consumed, we still have $\hat{c} = \hat{y}$. Inserting these relationships into (27), we end up with:

$$\Delta \cong \hat{b} + \left(\frac{\bar{\delta}-1}{\bar{\delta}}\right)(\hat{y} - \hat{b}) - \left(\frac{1+\mu}{2\bar{\delta}(1-\alpha)}\right)(\hat{y} - \hat{b})^2. \tag{28}$$

The important new insight from (28) is that an output gap which is caused by a productivity shock (i.e. a situation where $\hat{y} = \hat{b} \neq 0$) does not generate any welfare cost. To understand this result, recall that our output gap variable $\hat{y}$ measures the deviation of actual output from the 'natural' output forthcoming when both employment *and* productivity are at their 'normal' levels. But when for some reason productivity is temporarily above its normal level so that more output can be produced without additional work effort, consumers will obviously be better off if policy makers allow output and consumption to rise corresponding to the rise in productivity. On the other hand, if productivity temporarily falls below its normal level, there is no point in trying to keep output unchanged since this will require an additional work effort at a time when such effort is less rewarding. This is the intuition for the result in (28) that only output gaps which are *not* caused by productivity shocks will generate a welfare loss.

Another way of putting it is that actual output should ideally be allowed to fluctuate in line with the *efficient* level of output which would be produced in a perfectly competitive economy without any distortions. The efficient output level Y^e is the output corresponding to the efficient employment level L^e depicted in Fig. 19.1 where $MRS = MPL$. For $\theta = 1$ this condition implies $CL^\mu = (1 - \alpha)(Y/L)$. Solving this equation for L and remembering that $C = Y$, we get:

$$L^e = (1 - \alpha)^{1/(1+\mu)} \quad \Rightarrow \quad Y^e = B(L^e)^{1-\alpha} = B(1 - \alpha)^{(1-\alpha)/(1+\mu)}, \tag{29}$$

which shows that a change in the current productivity level B causes a proportionate change in the efficient output level. From (29) we may define the efficient steady-state level of output as the output that would be produced if there were no distortions and productivity were at its trend level: $\bar{Y}^e \equiv \bar{B}(1 - \alpha)^{(1-\alpha)/(1+\mu)}$. Defining $y^e \equiv \ln Y^e$ and $\bar{y}^e \equiv \ln \bar{Y}^e$, it then follows that $y^e - \bar{y}^e \equiv \hat{y}^e = \hat{b}$, so (28) may also be written as

$$\Delta \cong \hat{y}^e + \left(\frac{\bar{\delta}-1}{\bar{\delta}}\right)(\hat{y} - \hat{y}^e) - \left(\frac{1+\mu}{2\bar{\delta}(1-\alpha)}\right)(\hat{y} - \hat{y}^e)^2. \tag{30}$$

The gap-variable $\hat{y}^e = \hat{b}$ may be termed 'the efficient output gap', so according to (30) it is not the output gap ($\hat{y}$) as such – but rather the deviations between the actual and the efficient output gaps – which generate a welfare cost. To calculate the average welfare costs from business cycles, we may take the mathematical expectation of (30) to find:

$$E[\Delta] = -\left(\frac{1+\mu}{2\bar{\delta}(1-\alpha)}\right)\left[\sigma_y^2 + \sigma_{y^e}^2 - 2\text{cov}(y, y^e)\right], \qquad \text{cov}(y, y^e) \equiv E[(y - \bar{y})(y^e - \bar{y}^e)], \tag{31}$$

where σ_y^2 and $\sigma_{y^e}^2$ are the variances of y and y^e, and $\text{cov}(y, y^e)$ is the covariance between the actual and the efficient output levels. Note that if the economy were in fact perfectly competitive and there were no tax distortions, we would have $y = y^e$ and $\sigma_y^2 = \sigma_{y^e}^2$. The coefficient of correlation between y and y^e (defined as $\text{cov}(y, y^e)/(\sigma_y\sigma_{y^e})$) would then be equal to one, so the term in the square bracket in (31) would be zero, implying a zero welfare loss from output fluctuations. This result illustrates the claim made by the early real business cycle theory discussed in the previous chapter: in a competitive economy where business cycles are driven by productivity shocks, there is no need for macroeconomic stabilization policy, since business fluctuation represents the economy's optimal response to shifting technological opportunities.

However, in practice the economy is not perfectly competitive, and it may be hit by mark-up shocks and nominal demand shocks as well as by shocks to technology. In such a world Eq. (28) (and its equivalent (30)) suggests that policy makers should try to minimize output fluctuations caused by mark-up shocks and nominal demand shocks whereas they should allow output to fluctuate in line with productivity. In summary:

THE WELFARE COSTS OF OUTPUT FLUCTUATIONS

These costs are generated by deviations of the actual output gap from the efficient output gap. The efficient level of output is the output that would be produced in a perfectly competitive economy with no tax distortions, and the efficient output gap is given by the deviation of productivity from its trend level. Thus consumer welfare is harmed only to the extent that the deviation of actual from natural output exceeds the deviation of productivity from its trend, since it is welfare-improving to produce more (less) output when productivity is unusually high (low).

In practice it may be quite difficult to distinguish technology shocks from other types of shock. In the next chapter we shall discuss what this might imply for the optimal stabilization policy. But before we can characterize the optimal policy, we must study the welfare costs of (fluctuations in) inflation, for as we shall see in the next chapter, the presence of supply shocks creates a trade-off between the goal of stabilizing output and that of stabilizing inflation.

19.3 The welfare costs of inflation[15]

Nominal rigidities and the welfare costs of relative price distortions

To motivate why the squared inflation gap $(\pi - \pi^*)^2$ appears in the social loss function (1), we must explain why consumer welfare should be decreasing in this magnitude. In this subsection we take a first step in that direction by showing that when (some) nominal prices are rigid, inflation will distort the structure of relative prices which in turn will reduce consumer welfare. In the next subsection we will complete the argument by showing that this welfare loss is systematically linked to the squared inflation gap.

To understand the welfare effects of inflation, we must disaggregate total consumption. Suppose there is a total of n different consumer goods, and let C_i denote the consumption of good i. Further, suppose that our consumption aggregate C in the utility function (3) depends on the consumption of the individual goods in the following way:

$$C = n\left(\frac{1}{n}\sum_{i=1}^{n} C_i^{(\sigma-1)/\sigma}\right)^{\sigma/(\sigma-1)}, \qquad \sigma > 1. \tag{32}$$

---

15. Much of the analysis in this section is inspired by Michael Woodford, 'Inflation Stabilization and Welfare', NBER Working Paper 8071, January 2001.

Equation (32) is a so-called CES (Constant Elasticity of Substitution) utility function where the elasticity of substitution between any two different goods is equal to the parameter σ. In Exercise 3 in Chapter 11 we gave you guidelines on how to show that a cost-minimizing consumer with a CES utility function like (32) will allocate his or her spending across the different goods in accordance with the demand function

$$C_i = \left(\frac{P_i}{P}\right)^{-\sigma}\frac{C}{n}, \tag{33}$$

where P_i is the nominal price of good i, and P is a general consumer price index satisfying

$$P = \left(\frac{1}{n}\sum_{i=1}^{n}P_i^{1-\sigma}\right)^{1/(1-\sigma)} \quad \text{and} \quad PC = \sum_{i=1}^{n}P_iC_i. \tag{34}$$

To highlight the problem of relative price distortions in the simplest possible way, we have deliberately allowed each individual consumption good C_i to enter the utility function (32) in exactly the same way. We will also assume that the different goods are produced by means of the same technology. One might therefore think that in a market equilibrium all goods would sell at the same nominal price. But as we explained in Chapters 1 and 17, when individual firms face even small 'menu costs' of changing their prices, they may choose to keep their prices fixed for a certain period even if the average level of prices and costs is increasing over time. Moreover, different firms will generally change their prices at different points in time. Therefore, at any given point in time there will be firms that have very recently adjusted their price and firms that have kept their price constant for a while. When consumers go shopping, they will thus face some dispersion of prices because of the interaction between inflation and nominal price stickiness. We shall now show that such price dispersion reduces the welfare of the representative consumer.

Let us think of the process of production and marketing as consisting of two stages. In the first stage a representative competitive firm produces a large number of identical products which are sold to a number of different 'trading firms'. Each trading firm then gives its purchased products a special 'packaging' so that the final products marketed by different trading firms become imperfect substitutes in the eyes of consumers. Trading firm i thus sells a differentiated product C_i, facing the downward-sloping demand curve (33) in its market. However, all trading firms use exactly the same technology in 'packaging' their individual products, drawing on the same pool of labour. From an 'engineering' viewpoint all the different goods therefore remain identical, so when measured from the production side, total output (Y) may be counted as the simple sum ΣC_i of the production of the individual goods. In goods market equilibrium, this total output must equal the sum of the demands for the individual goods. From (33) we therefore have the goods market equilibrium condition:

$$Y = \sum_{i=1}^{n}C_i = \frac{C}{n}\sum_{i=1}^{n}\left(\frac{P_i}{P}\right)^{-\sigma} = C \cdot D, \qquad D \equiv \frac{1}{n}\sum_{i=1}^{n}\left(\frac{P_i}{P}\right)^{-\sigma}. \tag{35}$$

In a long-run equilibrium where all prices are fully adjusted one must have $P_1 = \ldots = P_n = P$, so that $D = \bar{D} = 1$ and $\bar{d} \equiv \ln\bar{D} = 0$. In our usual notation (where $d \equiv \ln D$), it then follows from (35) that $c - \bar{c} = y - \bar{y} - d$, or simply $\hat{c} = \hat{y} - d$. Moreover, we still assume that total output is given by the production function (7), implying that $\ell - \bar{\ell} = [y - \bar{y} - (b - \bar{b})]/(1 - \alpha) \equiv (\hat{y} - \hat{b})/(1 - \alpha)$. Inserting these relationships into (27) and recalling that $\hat{b} = \hat{y}^e$, we obtain the following slightly modified version of (30):

$$\Delta \cong \hat{y}^e + \left(\frac{\bar{\delta}-1}{\bar{\delta}}\right)(\hat{y}-\hat{y}^e) - \left(\frac{1+\mu}{2\bar{\delta}(1-\alpha)}\right)(\hat{y}-\hat{y}^e)^2 - d. \tag{36}$$

We will now offer an economic interpretation of the new term d in (36) by showing that

$$d \cong \frac{\sigma}{2} \cdot \sigma_p^2, \qquad \sigma_p^2 \equiv E[(p_i - p)^2] = \frac{1}{n}\sum_{i=1}^{n}(p_i - p)^2, \qquad p_i \equiv \ln P_i, \qquad p \equiv \ln P, \tag{37}$$

where σ still is the elasticity of substitution in the consumption index (32), and σ_p^2 is the (percentage) variance of price around their mean level, that is, a measure of the dispersion of prices. Before explaining the intuition behind (37), let us first establish that this approximation does in fact hold. We start by noting that the specification of P given in (34) implies:

$$Z \equiv \frac{1}{n}\sum_{i=1}^{n}\left(\frac{P_i}{P}\right)^{1-\sigma} = \frac{P^{-(1-\sigma)}}{n}\sum_{i=1}^{n}P_i^{1-\sigma} = 1. \tag{38}$$

Now define $X_i \equiv (P_i/P)^{1-\sigma}$ and use the fact that $X_i = \exp\{\ln X_i\} = \exp\{(1-\sigma)(p_i - p)\}$ to rewrite the expression for Z in (38) as:

$$Z = \frac{1}{n}\sum_{i=1}^{n}\exp\{(1-\sigma)(p_i - p)\}. \tag{39}$$

This expression may be further rewritten by taking a second-order Taylor approximation of $X_i = \exp\{(1-\sigma)(p_i - p)\}$ around $p_i = p$, exploiting the facts that $\exp\{0\} = 1$ and that $dX_i/dp_i = (1-\sigma)\exp\{(1-\sigma)(p_i - p)\} = 1 - \sigma$ for $p_i = p$:

$$Z \cong 1 + \left(\frac{1-\sigma}{n}\right)\sum_{i=1}^{n}(p_i - p) + \frac{(1-\sigma)^2}{2n}\sum_{i=1}^{n}(p_i - p)^2. \tag{40}$$

Since we know from (38) that $Z = 1$, it follows from (40) that

$$\left(\frac{1-\sigma}{n}\right)\sum_{i=1}^{n}(p_i - p) + \frac{(1-\sigma)^2}{2n}\sum_{i=1}^{n}(p_i - p)^2 \cong 0 \quad \Rightarrow$$

$$\frac{1}{n}\sum_{i=1}^{n}(p_i - p) \cong -\left(\frac{1-\sigma}{2n}\right)\sum_{i=1}^{n}(p_i - p)^2. \tag{41}$$

As a last step, we take a second-order Taylor approximation of the definition of D given in (35) to get:

$$D \equiv \frac{1}{n}\sum_{i=1}^{n}\left(\frac{P_i}{P}\right)^{-\sigma} = \frac{1}{n}\sum_{i=1}^{n}\exp\{-\sigma(p_i - p)\} \cong 1 - \frac{\sigma}{n}\sum_{i=1}^{n}(p_i - p) + \frac{\sigma^2}{2n}\sum_{i=1}^{n}(p_i - p)^2. \tag{42}$$

Inserting (41) in (42), we find:

$$D \cong 1 + \frac{\sigma}{2n}\sum_{i=1}^{n}(p_i - p)^2. \tag{43}$$

From (43) and the general approximation $\ln(1 + x) \cong x$, we finally obtain the result stated in (37) that $d \cong (\sigma/2) \cdot \sigma_p^2$.

Equations (36) and (37) thus imply that a greater variance of the price level reduces consumer welfare. To understand why, recall that since all consumer goods enter our CES utility function (32) in exactly the same way, they are 'equally good' at generating utility, and by assumption all goods are equally costly to produce, so there is no good reason why they should not all sell at the same price. If nominal price rigidities nevertheless cause price differences to emerge, cost-minimizing consumers will substitute towards goods with lower prices. The increased consumption of the cheaper goods and the reduced consumption of the more expensive goods will drive down the marginal utility derived from the former relative to the marginal utility obtained from the latter goods. Since all goods are equally costly to produce at the margin, it follows that total consumer utility could be increased without increasing total production costs if the production and consumption of the more expensive goods could somehow be expanded at the expense of production and consumption of the cheaper goods. But in a market economy with consumer sovereignty this does not happen since consumers have an incentive to consume relatively large quantities of the goods that are relatively cheap. Hence there is a loss of economic efficiency which translates into a loss of consumer welfare, since by definition economic (Pareto) inefficiency means that some consumers could be made better off without making anybody worse off.

Note how the expression $d \cong (\sigma/2) \cdot \sigma_p^2$ for the welfare loss from relative price distortions supports the intuitive explanation just given: the greater the size of the substitution elasticity σ, the stronger are the substitution effects induced by differences in consumer prices, and the greater is the distortion to the consumption pattern caused by any given variance of prices.

Notice also that the welfare-reducing effect of price stickiness is not just an artefact of our particular simplifying assumptions regarding consumer preferences and the technology of production. The welfare-reducing inefficiency arises whenever nominal price rigidities bring relative consumer prices out of line with the relative marginal production costs. When such a discrepancy exists, there will be pairs of goods for which the marginal rate of substitution (given by the price ratio) differs from the marginal rate of transformation (given by the ratio of marginal costs), and we then know from microeconomic theory that resources could be reallocated to raise the welfare of some consumers without hurting anybody else. In our simple model we have just 'rigged' our assumptions such that *all* of the variance of prices reflects a welfare-reducing distortion, but the negative welfare effect of the relative price distortions caused by price stickiness would still emerge in a more general model where only *some* of the variance of prices can be ascribed to nominal rigidities.

In our reasoning above we have taken for granted that the welfare-reducing dispersion of consumer prices stems from the interaction of nominal price stickiness with inflation. In the next subsection we shall show that there is indeed such a link.

The link between inflation and relative price distortions

To demonstrate the link, we may go back to the model with 'sticky-price' firms and 'flex-price firms' introduced at the end of Section 17.2. You may recall that for firms in the flex-price group the menu costs of price adjustment are so small that they find it profitable to adjust their prices within each period as their cost conditions change. By contrast, for firms in the sticky-price group the menu costs are so high that they choose to pre-set their prices at the beginning of each period and to keep their price fixed until the start of the next period. Apart from these differences in menu costs and the associated difference in price-setting behaviour, the two groups of firms are identical, facing similar cost and market conditions. Let ϖ denote the fraction of firms belonging to the sticky-price group and suppose all of these firms set a price P_s for the current period whereas all firms in the flex-price group charge an average price of P_f during the period. It then follows from (34) that the average general price level in the current period will be

$$P = \left[\varpi P_s^{1-\sigma} + (1-\varpi)P_f^{1-\sigma} \right]^{1/(1-\sigma)} \quad \Rightarrow$$

$$p = \left(\frac{1}{1-\sigma} \right) \ln \left[\varpi P_s^{1-\sigma} + (1-\varpi)P_f^{1-\sigma} \right]. \tag{44}$$

Now take a first-order Taylor approximation of (44) around the point $\bar{P}_s = \bar{P}_f = \bar{P}$, using $(X - \bar{X})/\bar{X} \cong x - \bar{x}$ to find (do this as an exercise):

$$p \cong \varpi p_s + (1-\varpi)p_f. \tag{45}$$

Since sticky-price firms face the same cost and market conditions as flex-price firms, the former firms will wish to keep their prices in line with the latter. We therefore assume that the price set by sticky-price firms at the start of the period corresponds to the average price p_f^e which they expect the flex-price firms to charge during the period:[16]

$$p_s = p_f^e. \tag{46}$$

Note that in a long-run equilibrium expectations must be fulfilled, $p_f^e = p_f$, implying from (46) and (45) that $p_s = p_f = p$. In long-run equilibrium all firms will thus charge the same prices, so in steady state our relative price distortion indicator D defined in (35) will indeed be equal to one (implying $\bar{d} \equiv \ln \bar{D} = 0$), as we assumed when we derived the welfare cost of deviations from the steady state in (36).

Since the 'sticky' price p_s is pre-set, it is known at the start of the current period, so $p_s^e = p_s$. Using this plus (45) and (46), we obtain the following expression for the amount of unanticipated inflation, where we use our usual notation that variables without subscripts refer to the current period, variables with a subscript '−1' refer to the previous period, and a superscript 'e' denotes an expected value:

$$\pi - \pi^e \equiv p - p_{-1} - (p^e - p_{-1}) = \overbrace{\varpi p_s + (1-\varpi)p_f}^{=p} - \overbrace{[\varpi p_s^e + (1-\varpi)p_f^e]}^{=p^e} \tag{47}$$

$$= \varpi p_s + (1-\varpi)p_f - [\varpi p_s + (1-\varpi)p_s] = (1-\varpi)(p_f - p_s).$$

According to (47), the amount of unanticipated inflation depends on the extent to which the prices of flex-price firms move ahead of those set by sticky-price firms, that is, on the extent to which sticky-price firms underestimate the prices set by flex-price firms, since $p_f - p_s = p_f - p_f^e$ (see (46)).

We may now derive an expression for the variance of prices (σ_p^2) to establish the link between inflation and relative price distortions. From (45) we have:

$$\sigma_p^2 \equiv \frac{1}{n}\sum_{i=1}^{n}(p_i - p)^2 = \varpi\{p_s - [\varpi p_s + (1-\varpi)p_f]\}^2 + (1-\varpi)\{p_f - [\varpi p_s + (1-\varpi)p_f]\}^2 \tag{48}$$

$$= \varpi(1-\varpi)^2(p_s - p_f)^2 + \varpi^2(1-\varpi)(p_f - p_s)^2 = \varpi(1-\varpi)(p_f - p_s)^2.$$

Combining (47) and (48), we get:

$$\sigma_p^2 = \left(\frac{\varpi}{1-\varpi}\right)(\pi - \pi^e)^2. \tag{49}$$

Thus the variance of prices is directly proportional to the (square of the) amount of unanticipated inflation, reflecting that the prices charged by sticky-price firms and flex-price firms will only differ to the extent that the former firms underestimate the pace at which the latter will raise their prices. Substituting (37) and (49) into (36), we can finally document the link between inflation and consumer welfare:

$$\Delta \cong \hat{y}^e + \left(\frac{\bar{\delta}-1}{\bar{\delta}}\right)(\hat{y} - \hat{y}^e) - \left(\frac{1+\mu}{2\bar{\delta}(1-\alpha)}\right)(\hat{y} - \hat{y}^e)^2 - \frac{\sigma}{2}\left(\frac{\varpi}{1-\varpi}\right)(\pi - \pi^e)^2. \tag{50}$$

Equation (50) shows that consumer welfare decreases with the square of the amount of unanticipated inflation, since higher unanticipated inflation combined with the presence of

---

16. This assumption about price setting is fully consistent with the one made in Chapter 17 if sticky-price firms assume that flex-price firms will operate at the natural level of output (just as sticky-price firms expect themselves to do in the model of Chapter 17). In that case sticky-price firms will expect to have the same marginal costs as the flex-price firms, so the expected profit-maximizing price for a sticky-price firm will equal the price such a firm expects the flex-price firms to charge. Hence a sticky-price firm's maximization of expected profits will lead to a price-setting equation like (46).

nominal rigidities generates stronger relative price distortions by increasing the variance of prices. Note that if the expected inflation rate corresponds to the policy makers' target inflation rate, the inflation term in (50) enters in the general form $(a_\pi/2)(\pi - \pi^*)^2$, that is, in exactly the same form as the inflation term in the social loss function (1). Equation (50) indicates the factors determining the weight a_π that policy makers should attach to the goal of stabilizing inflation: First, a_π should increase with the substitution elasticity σ, since a higher substitution elasticity means that the relative price distortions caused by inflation generate a bigger distortion of the pattern of consumption, as we explained earlier. Second, we see from (50) that a_π should increase with the degree of nominal price rigidity, captured by our parameter ϖ. Indeed, in the absence of nominal price rigidity ($\varpi = 0$) we see that there would be no welfare cost from inflation, since in this case all firms would be flex-price firms adjusting their prices instantaneously so that no relative price distortions would arise from inflation (note from (49) that the variance of prices would be zero for $\varpi = 0$). However, the role of nominal price rigidity is a little more subtle than suggested by (50), since it follows from (46) and (48) that the variance of prices is given by

$$\sigma_p^2 = \varpi(1 - \varpi)(p_f - p_f^e)^2. \tag{51}$$

This shows that the variance of prices would be zero either if there were no nominal rigidities, *or* if all firms had pre-set prices so that $\varpi = 1$. Thus it is not the existence of nominal rigidities *per se*, but rather the *mixture* of firms with *different* degrees of price flexibility (i.e. the fact that $0 < \varpi < 1$) which causes the welfare-reducing relative price distortions. In fact, for any given forecast error $p_f - p_f^e$, Eq. (51) implies that the variance of prices will be at a maximum when there are equally many sticky-price and flex-price firms ($\varpi = 0.5$). This is intuitive, for if firms tend to be concentrated in one group with the same price-setting behaviour, there is little scope for relative prices to become distorted by inflation.

One important implication of our model with sticky-price and flex-price firms is that only *unanticipated* inflation matters for consumer welfare. However, other forms of price rigidity may imply that *all* inflation causes welfare-reducing relative price distortions, whether it is anticipated or not. We will illustrate this by the so-called Calvo model of 'staggered' price setting which has been widely used in macroeconomic research.[17] In this model a random sample consisting of a fraction $1 - \varpi$ of all firms adjust their prices in the current period, whereas the remaining fraction of firms keep their prices unchanged. This means that on average firms keep their prices unchanged for a period of length $1/(1 - \varpi)$, so again the parameter ϖ is an indicator of the degree of price rigidity. Since the firms that do not adjust their prices represent an average of all firms (given that the group of price-adjusting firms is chosen at random), the average price they charge in the current period (p_s) will be equal to last period's average price level:

$$p_s = p_{-1}. \tag{52}$$

The firms that have the opportunity to adjust their price in the current period will set a price p_f at the level p^* which will maximize the expected present value of profits, given that these firms do not expect to be able to reset their price until a period of length $1/(1 - \varpi)$ has elapsed (for our present purpose we do not have to worry about the exact determinants of p^*):

$$p_f = p^*. \tag{53}$$

From (45), (52) and (53) the average current price level becomes

---

17. This popular model was first developed in Guillermo Calvo, 'Staggered Prices in a Utility-Maximizing Framework', *Journal of Monetary Economics*, **12**, 1983, pp. 383–398.

$$p \cong \varpi p_s + (1 - \varpi)p_f = \varpi p_{-1} + (1 - \varpi)p^*, \tag{54}$$

so the current inflation rate is:

$$\pi \equiv p - p_{-1} = (1 - \varpi)(p^* - p_{-1}). \tag{55}$$

Using (52) through (55), we now find the variance of the price level to be

$$\sigma_p^2 \equiv \frac{1}{n} \sum_{i=1}^{n} (p_i - p)^2 = \varpi \{p_s - [\varpi p_s + (1 - \varpi)p_f]\}^2 + (1 - \varpi)\{p_f - [\varpi p_s + (1 - \varpi)p_f]\}^2$$

$$= \varpi(1 - \varpi)^2 (p^* - p_{-1})^2 + \varpi^2(1 - \varpi)(p^* - p_{-1})^2 = \varpi(1 - \varpi)(p^* - p_{-1})^2 = \left(\frac{\varpi}{1 - \varpi}\right)\pi^2. \tag{56}$$

The last equality in (56) shows that the variance of prices now depends on (the square of) *total* inflation and not just on (the square of) *unanticipated* inflation. Inserting this result into (37), it follows that

$$\frac{\text{Welfare loss from inflation}}{\text{Steady-state consumption}} \equiv d \cong \frac{\sigma}{2} \cdot \sigma_p^2 = \frac{\sigma}{2}\left(\frac{\varpi}{1 - \varpi}\right)\pi^2. \tag{57}$$

Why does (57) predict that even fully anticipated inflation causes a welfare loss? The reason is that the firms adjusting their price in the current period know that they will not want to reset their prices until (on average) another period of length $1/(1 - \varpi)$ has passed. Therefore, the higher the expected rate of inflation, the higher the price-adjusting firms will want to set their own price relative to the average current price level in order not to be 'overtaken' by inflation during the subsequent period when their own price will remain constant. In any given period the difference between the prices set by the price-adjusting firms and the prices charged by those who keep prices unchanged will thus be higher – and consequently the variance of prices will also be higher – the higher the expected rate of inflation, regardless of whether the expectations come true or not.

To illustrate the link between our two models of the welfare costs of inflation, suppose the inflation rate fluctuates around a mean value corresponding to the target inflation rate π^*. Taking a second-order Taylor expansion of the expression on the right-hand side of (57) around the inflation target, we get

$$d \cong \sigma\left(\frac{\varpi}{1 - \varpi}\right)\left[\frac{(\pi^*)^2}{2} + \pi^*(\pi - \pi^*) + \frac{(\pi - \pi^*)^2}{2}\right], \tag{58}$$

from which it follows that the average welfare loss from inflation is

$$E[d] \approx \frac{\sigma}{2}\left(\frac{\varpi}{1 - \varpi}\right)(\pi^*)^2 + \frac{\sigma}{2}\left(\frac{\varpi}{1 - \varpi}\right)\sigma_\pi^2, \qquad \sigma_\pi^2 \equiv E[(\pi - \pi^*)^2], \tag{59}$$

where σ_π^2 is the variance of inflation. Suppose further that the central bank has credibility so that the expected inflation rate equals the announced inflation target, $\pi^e = \pi^*$. The second term on the right-hand side of (59) may then be interpreted as the average welfare cost of *unanticipated* inflation, while the first term captures the average loss from anticipated inflation. Further, from the last term on the right-hand side of (50) and our assumption that $\pi^e = \pi^* = E[\pi]$, it follows that the average welfare loss from unanticipated inflation is also the welfare loss caused by inflation *volatility* (Δ_π) in our model with sticky-price and flex-price firms:

$$\Delta_\pi \equiv E\left[\frac{\sigma}{2}\left(\frac{\varpi}{1 - \varpi}\right)(\pi - \pi^e)^2\right] = \frac{\sigma}{2}\left(\frac{\varpi}{1 - \varpi}\right)E[(\pi - \pi^*)^2] = \frac{\sigma}{2}\left(\frac{\varpi}{1 - \varpi}\right)\sigma_\pi^2. \tag{60}$$

How big is the welfare loss from inflation if we plug realistic parameter values into (59)? Recall that $1/(1-\varpi)$ is the average duration of the period during which individual product prices are kept constant. The evidence in Table 17.1 indicates that the average duration of prices in Western Europe is around 5 quarters = 1.25 years, so if the time period of our model is one year, a plausible value of ϖ may be found by solving the equation $1/(1-\varpi)=1.25$, yielding $\varpi=0.2$. According to (33) the substitution elasticity σ appearing in (59) is also the price elasticity of demand for the output of the representative firm. Recall from Chapter 17 that the target price mark-up of a profit-maximizing monopolistic competitor is $m^p=\sigma/(\sigma-1)$. As mentioned earlier in the present chapter, a realistic value of m^p would be 1.2, implying $\sigma=6$. With these parameter values it follows from (59) that if the annual inflation rate fluctuates around a 2 per cent inflation target with a standard deviation of 0.5 percentage point (and hence a variance of 0.000025), the resulting welfare cost would amount to a little more than 0.03 per cent of steady state consumption. It also follows that only a little more than 6 per cent of these costs would arise from unanticipated inflation (caused by inflation volatility), while the remaining costs would stem from anticipated inflation (equal to the average inflation rate). This rather small welfare loss is of the same order of magnitude as our earlier estimate of the welfare loss from consumption fluctuations. But note that with the same parameter values Eq. (59) would imply a sizeable welfare loss of more than 1.1 per cent of consumption if the average annual inflation rate were 12 per cent with a standard deviation of 3 percentage points (check for yourself). Inflation rates at that level and volatility were quite common in OECD countries during the 1970s (indeed, in several countries inflation peaked at much higher rates), so our analysis may help to explain why the experience of that decade pushed the fight against inflation to the forefront of the public policy agenda during the 1980s. The more general insight from the model is that while low inflation rates may not be much of a problem, the welfare costs are steeply rising with the rate of inflation.

It is time to take stock of the important lessons learned above:

NOMINAL RIGIDITIES AND THE WELFARE COSTS OF INFLATION

In an economy with nominal price stickiness where (some) firms keep their prices constant for a certain period and reset their prices at different points in time, inflation distorts relative prices by causing them to deviate from the relative marginal costs of production. The resulting economic inefficiency causes a loss of consumer welfare. If some firms adjust their prices instantaneously whereas other firms pre-set their prices on the basis of expected inflation in the flexible-price sector, only unanticipated inflation will generate a welfare loss. If instead all firms keep their prices constant for certain unsynchronized time intervals, even anticipated inflation will cause a welfare loss. The welfare loss tends to rise with the square of the inflation rate and will be greater the higher the elasticity of substitution between different consumer goods.

From a welfare perspective the distinction between anticipated and unanticipated inflation is irrelevant in the Calvo model. The model clearly suggests that the target inflation rate in the social loss function (1) should be zero, since (56) and (57) imply that relative price distortions and the associated welfare cost would then also be zero. However, in the next subsection we shall identify some good reasons to choose a positive inflation target after all. We shall also see that inflation may involve social costs other than those highlighted above.

Other costs of inflation and the choice of inflation target

The interaction of inflation with nominal rigidities tends to distort the relative prices of different consumer goods within each period of time. But inflation may also distort the relative price of *present versus future consumption* by distorting the real rate of return on nominal assets. A positive rate of inflation drives a wedge between the nominal and the real rates of return on saving and investment. The income tax is typically levied on the entire nominal interest rate, including that part which the investor must set aside to preserve the real value of his or her nominal asset. As a result, inflation may cause the return to nominal assets to be overtaxed relative to the return on real assets such as land and buildings, thereby inducing too much investment in the latter type of assets. Further, the tax code typically only allows business assets to be written down on the basis of the historical purchase price of the asset. Hence inflation tends to erode the real value of depreciation allowances, again implying a risk of overtaxation. In summary, the fact that the income tax system is not indexed for inflation means that inflation will tend to distort savings and investment decisions.

Further, recall that the nominal rigidities which interact with inflation to distort the relative prices of different consumer goods may be due to 'menu costs'. These include all of the resource costs of changing prices, such as the costs of printing new price lists and catalogues plus any other costs of communicating the new prices to the market. If the rate of inflation goes up, firms have to change their nominal prices more frequently to avoid an erosion of their real prices and profits. By increasing the frequency of price adjustments, a higher inflation rate therefore also increases the associated menu costs.

In addition, a higher inflation rate implies a higher nominal interest rate which induces households and firms to economize on their money balances. When people hold a lower average stock of real money balances, they have to make more frequent trips to the bank to withdraw money needed for transactions purposes. The resulting 'shoe-leather costs' (which include the value of the time spent on trips to the bank, the resources spent on cash management in firms, as well as other costs of exchanging non-liquid assets for money) are part of the social costs of inflation.

On top of all this, the historical experience shows that a higher *average* rate of inflation tends to go hand in hand with a *more unstable* inflation rate. If inflation becomes more volatile and hence less predictable as the average inflation rate goes up, people will make greater inflation forecast errors when the average inflation rate increases. When households and firms underestimate or overestimate inflation, they end up with different real rates of return to their labour and capital than they expected. Due to these miscalculations, they will regret some of the economic decisions they made and will therefore suffer a welfare loss. Moreover, unanticipated inflation (an unexpectedly low real rate of interest) implies an arbitrary redistribution of wealth from creditors to debtors, while an unexpectedly low rate of inflation generates a similarly arbitrary redistribution in the opposite direction. Such unintended redistribution may threaten the stability of society if it occurs on a large scale.

Adding all of these arguments to the insight from the Calvo price-setting model discussed earlier, there would seem to be a formidable case for choosing a zero target inflation rate π^* in the social loss function (1). Indeed, in a provocative essay, the late Nobel Prize winner Milton Friedman even argued that the target inflation rate ought to be *negative* and numerically equal to the long-run equilibrium real interest rate ($\bar{r}$) so that the nominal interest rate $i = \bar{r} + \pi^*$ would drop to zero.[18] His argument was that the marginal social cost of supplying money to the public is roughly zero, since printing money is virtually costless. To induce people to hold the socially optimal amount of money balances, the marginal private opportunity cost of money-holding – given by the nominal interest rate – should therefore also be zero. If the nominal interest rate is positive, people will economize on their money balances to hold more of their wealth in the form of interest-bearing assets. Hence they will incur socially wasteful 'shoe-leather costs' which may be avoided by driving the nominal interest rate to zero. This in turn requires a steady rate of *deflation* to ensure a real interest rate equal to the economy's 'natural' rate of interest.

---

18.   See Milton Friedman, 'The Optimum Quantity of Money', in *The Optimum Quantity of Money and Other Essays*, pp. 1–50, Chicago, Aldine Publishing, 1969.

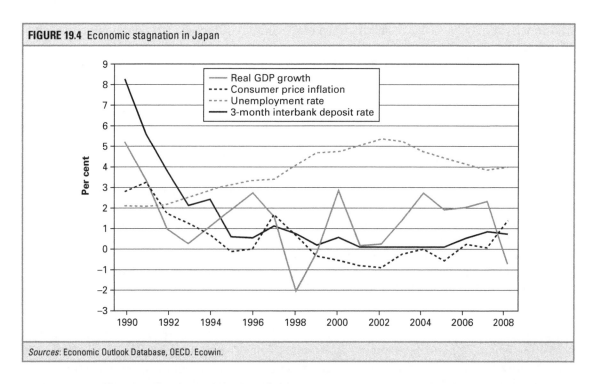

FIGURE 19.4 Economic stagnation in Japan

Sources: Economic Outlook Database, OECD. Ecowin.

However, if there are nominal price rigidities, it follows from the Calvo model that relative prices would be distorted by a negative as well as by a positive rate of inflation. Most economists also believe that a policy of deflation could be very dangerous in practice, since it might trigger a destabilizing wave of bankruptcies if debtors have not fully anticipated the future fall in prices and the resulting increase in their real debt burdens.

Indeed, rather than aiming at a negative inflation target as proposed by Friedman, or a zero inflation target as suggested by the Calvo model, modern central banks typically seek to keep the rate of inflation stable around a moderately positive level. The reason is that a zero inflation rate may impair the central bank's ability to stabilize the economy. With zero inflation, the short-term nominal interest rate will typically be rather low. In that situation the central bank will not be able to counter a severe recession by a large cut in the interest rate, since the nominal interest rate cannot fall below zero. If policy makers want interest rate policy to be an effective tool of stabilization policy, they may therefore have to accept a positive average rate of inflation to preserve room for substantial interest rate cuts in times of recession.

The inability to cut the nominal interest rate at very low rates of inflation is not just a theoretical possibility. In Japan, which has experienced economic stagnation and genuine *deflation* in many years during the past two decades, the short-term nominal interest rate has in fact been driven almost all the way to zero without putting an end to the economic malaise, as illustrated in Fig. 19.4. At times when a boost to aggregate demand was badly needed, the central bank of Japan thus lost its ability to stimulate demand through its interest rate policy.

A further argument against a zero inflation target is that nominal wage rates tend to be particularly sticky in the downward direction.[19] If the economy is hit by a negative shock which calls for a fall in real wages, this adjustment is therefore easier to achieve through price inflation than through a fall in nominal wages. This is one additional

---

19. There is a lot of evidence of downward nominal wage rigidity. See, for example, George A. Akerlof, William T. Dickens, and George L. Perry, 'The Macroeconomics of Low Inflation', *Brookings Papers on Economic Activity*, no. 1, 1996, pp. 1–59.

reason why it may be easier to stabilize the real economy if there is a moderate positive rate of inflation.

Finally, official price indices tend to overestimate the true rate of inflation since they cannot fully account for the fact that some price increases reflect improvements in product quality rather than genuine inflation.

For these reasons countries with explicit official inflation targets, such as Australia, Canada, New Zealand, Norway, Sweden, Switzerland and the UK, have typically accepted a positive target inflation rate of 2–2.5 per cent per annum. The European Central Bank also accepts an inflation rate of up to 2 per cent as being consistent with its goal of 'price stability'.

We started Section 19.1 by introducing the social loss function according to which fluctuations in the output and inflation gaps generate a social welfare loss. We then provided some welfare-theoretic reasons why it makes sense for policy makers to try to stabilize output and inflation around their target levels, and we saw that the proper choice of the output and inflation targets may depend on the type of shocks hitting the economy and on the way nominal prices and wages are set. In the next chapter we shall use these insights to characterize optimal monetary and fiscal stabilization policies.

19.4 Summary

1. Stabilization policy is the active use of monetary and fiscal policy to influence the aggregate demand for goods and services. The goal of stabilization policy is to minimize the social welfare loss from the volatility of output and inflation.

2. The instability of output and the associated fluctuations in real income impose a welfare loss on risk averse consumers who prefer a smooth to an uneven time path of consumption. Problems of moral hazard and adverse selection prevent consumers from insuring themselves fully against the unexpected temporary income losses caused by business cycles, and credit constraints often prevent unemployed consumers from borrowing against their expected future labour income. Hence the unanticipated income losses generated by recessions force some consumers into cutting their consumption, resulting in welfare losses which are not fully offset by the welfare gains from higher consumption during economic booms, due to diminishing marginal utility of consumption.

3. The employment fluctuations resulting from business cycles also create welfare losses for (some) workers. Market imperfections drive a welfare-reducing wedge between the marginal product of labour and the marginal rate of substitution between income and leisure. This wedge goes down when employment rises during a boom, but typically the wedge increases a lot more when employment falls during the subsequent recession. For this reason the average level of welfare could be increased if employment could be stabilized around its average (natural) rate.

4. Empirical evidence suggests that the welfare losses from recessions are considerable, but in the absence of non-linearities in the short-run aggregate supply curve these losses are to a large extent offset by the welfare gains reaped during boom periods. However, non-linearities in the Phillips curve imply that the trend level of output could be raised by stabilizing unemployment around its natural rate, and the welfare gain from this effect could be substantial. Empirical studies have also documented that the losses of income and consumption caused by recessions are borne disproportionately by low-paid unskilled workers. Hence business cycles tend to exacerbate the unequal distribution of income. This is another reason why society may wish to stabilize output and employment.

5. Ideally stabilization policy should aim at stabilizing output around the Pareto-efficient level that would prevail in a perfectly competitive economy without tax distortions. This

▶ means that output should be allowed to fluctuate in line with fluctuations in productivity whereas fluctuations arising from other shocks should be stabilized. However, in practice it may be difficult to distinguish productivity shocks from other shocks.

6. Nominal price rigidities mean that (some) firms keep their prices constant for a certain period and reset their prices at different points in time. Inflation will then distort relative prices by causing them to deviate from the relative marginal costs of production. The resulting economic inefficiency causes a loss of consumer welfare which tends to rise with the square of the inflation rate. Inflation also creates welfare costs stemming from an inefficiently low demand for cash balances, 'menu costs' due to frequent price changes, and a distorted measurement of taxable income due to an unindexed tax system. Unanticipated inflation arising from a volatile inflation rate is a particular problem since it causes relative prices (including real wages and real interest rates) to deviate from the expected levels on which household and business plans are based.

7. Apart from stabilizing output and employment, another goal for stabilization policy therefore is to minimize the volatility of the rate of inflation around its target rate. Though even anticipated inflation generates welfare costs, it is widely agreed that the target inflation rate should be kept above 0 to enable the central bank to cut the nominal interest rate significantly in a serious recession without hitting the zero bound for nominal interest, and to facilitate the downward adjustment of real wages to a negative shock in labour markets with downward nominal wage rigidity.

19.5 Exercises

Exercise 1. Household utility when individual working hours are fixed

(*Note: This exercise requires familiarity with integrals*)

This exercise asks you to prove the claim made in the main text that the household utility function (3) is also valid when the working hours of an individual worker are fixed, say, by law or by collective bargaining agreements. In this situation variations in our variable L must be interpreted as fluctuations in the number of persons employed.

To prove the claim, suppose the utility function (3) in the main text describes the preferences of a representative collective household with a continuum of members distributed over the unit interval (so that the total number of people in the household is 1). Household members have the same preferences for consumption and share all consumption goods equally among themselves. The individual household member enjoys utility $C^{1-\theta}/(1-\theta)$ from consumption. This is also the total utility from consumption for the household as a whole, given that the number of household members is 1. Further, household member number n ($0 \leq n \leq 1$) incurs an amount of disutility from work equal to n^μ in the case where he or she participates in the labour market, working a fixed number of hours. Thus we assign numbers to household members corresponding to the magnitude of their utility cost of work. Letting L denote the fraction of household members participating in the labour market, we may thus write the total utility of the collective household as follows, where the integral measures the total disutility of work aggregated over all household members who are active in the labour market:

$$U(C, L) = \frac{C^{1-\theta}}{1-\theta} - \int_0^L n^\mu, \qquad \mu > 0. \tag{61}$$

1. Show that (61) can be written in exactly the same form as (3) in the main text.

Exercise 2. The role of demand shocks as drivers of business cycles

The simple business cycle model set up in the first part of Section 19.1 focused on mark-up shocks as drivers of business fluctuations but we also mentioned that demand shocks undoubtedly play an important role in initiating business cycles. This exercise asks you to explore that role within the framework of the model in Section 19.1.

To focus on demand shocks, we assume throughout the exercise that mark-ups and productivity are constant over time. Total output is still given by

$$Y = BL^{1-\alpha}, \qquad 0 < \alpha < 1. \tag{62}$$

In accordance with (21) in the main text, wage setters set the nominal wage rate on the basis of the expected price level to achieve an expected after-tax real wage which is a mark-up over the MRS between consumption and work. We simplify by setting the $CRRA$ parameter θ equal to one in which case the model in the text implies $MRS = CL^\mu = YL^\mu$, given that all output is consumed. Thus we have

$$\frac{W}{P^e} = \frac{m^w}{1-\tau} \cdot MRS = \frac{m^w YL^\mu}{1-\tau} = \frac{m^w BL^{1-\alpha+\mu}}{1-\tau}, \qquad \mu > 0. \tag{63}$$

The demand for labour is still given by Eq. (8) in the text from which it follows that

$$\frac{W}{P} = \frac{MPL}{m^p} = \frac{(1-\alpha)BL^{-\alpha}}{m^p}. \tag{64}$$

Finally, we describe the economy's demand side by the simple money market equilibrium condition (20) in the text, where we recall that M is the nominal money supply, and k is an exogenous parameter which may fluctuate over time:

$$M = k \cdot PY, \qquad k > 0. \tag{65}$$

1. Define the natural level of employment ($\bar{L}$) as the level that prevails when price expectations are fulfilled ($P^e = P$). Use (63) and (64) to show that

$$\ell - \bar{\ell} = \left(\frac{1}{1+\mu}\right)(p - p^e), \qquad \ell \equiv \ln L, \qquad \bar{\ell} \equiv \ln \bar{L}, \qquad p \equiv \ln P, \qquad p^e \equiv \ln P^e. \tag{66}$$

Explain in economic terms why an actual price level above the expected level drives actual employment above natural employment.

2. Define natural output ($\bar{Y}$) as the output level corresponding the natural employment level, and use (62) and (66) to show that the economy's aggregate supply curve may be written as

$$p - p^e = \gamma(y - \bar{y}), \qquad \gamma \equiv \frac{1+\mu}{1-\alpha}, \qquad y \equiv \ln Y, \qquad \bar{y} \equiv \ln \bar{Y}. \tag{67}$$

Now suppose that the nominal money supply fluctuates stochastically around a trend level $\bar{M}$ which we assume to be constant for simplicity. If v is a stochastic 'white noise' variable with zero mean and constant variance σ_v^2, we thus have

$$\ln M = \ln \bar{M} + v, \qquad E[v] = 0, \qquad E[v^2] = \sigma_v^2. \tag{68}$$

We may now define the 'normal' price level $\bar{P}$ as the price level prevailing when the money supply is at its 'normal' level $\bar{M}$, when output is at its natural rate, and when the money demand parameter k in (65) is at its trend level $\bar{k}$. From (65) it then follows that the normal price level is $\bar{P} = \bar{M}/\bar{k}\bar{Y}$, implying:

$$\bar{p} = \ln \bar{M} - \ln \bar{k} - \bar{y}, \qquad \bar{p} \equiv \ln \bar{P}. \tag{69}$$

Using (65), (68) and (69), we may write the economy's aggregate demand curve in the form:

$$p - \bar{p} = \bar{y} - y - \hat{k} + v, \qquad \hat{k} \equiv \ln k - \ln \bar{k}. \tag{70}$$

Assume that when wage setters set the nominal wage rate, they expect prices in the current period to be at their normal level, that is:

$$p^e = \bar{p}. \tag{71}$$

3. Solve the AS–AD model consisting of (67), (70) and (71) for the output gap and illustrate the determination of output and the price level in a (y, p) diagram. Given that the money supply as well as the money demand parameter k fluctuate stochastically, describe how the model could explain the cyclical pattern of the ratio MRS/MPL illustrated in Fig. 19.3 in the text (hint: derive an expression for MRS/MPL as a function of P/P^e).

4. Use your solution for the output gap to derive an expression for the variance of output, $E[(y - \bar{y})^2]$, assuming that v and $\hat{k}$ are stochastically independent and that the variance of $\hat{k}$ is constant and equal to σ_k^2.

5. On the website for this textbook, www.mheducation.co.uk/textbooks/sorensen2, you will find an Excel spreadsheet containing a time series for the US money supply, M, and for US nominal GDP, PY. Let $\ln \bar{M}$ be represented by the linear time trend through the time series for $\ln M$, estimated by an Ordinary Least Squares regression, and let $E[v^2] = \sigma_v^2$ be represented by the variance of your estimated time series for $\ln M - \ln \bar{M}$. Similarly, calculate $\ln k = \ln(M/PY)$ and create a time series for $\hat{k}$ by calculating $\hat{k} = \ln(M/PY) - \ln(\overline{M/PY})$, where $\ln(\overline{M/PY})$ is your estimated OLS linear time trend through the time series for $\ln(M/PY)$. Let σ_k^2 be represented by the variance of your estimated time series for $\hat{k}$. Now use your estimates plus the formula you derived in your answer to Question 4 to calculate an estimate of the standard deviation of GDP that could be explained by fluctuations in M and k. Calculate the resulting welfare cost from formulas (12) and (19) in the main text, assuming parameter values $\mu = 1$, $\alpha = 1/3$, and $\bar{m}^p = \bar{m}^w = 1.2$. Is the welfare cost 'large' or 'small'?

   Now recall that wage setters set wages as a mark-up over the opportunity cost of work. In the model above, this opportunity cost is given by the value of the leisure which must be given up when engaging in work (the MRS). But suppose non-employed workers receive a benefit b^u which is higher than $MRS/(1 - \tau)$. Then the relevant opportunity cost of work is the benefit forgone when moving from non-employment to employment. Instead of being given by (63), it is then more plausible that nominal wages are set in accordance with

$$\frac{W}{P^e} = m^w b^u, \tag{72}$$

   as we assumed in Chapter 17.

6. Use the same procedures as above to derive an expression for the variance of output and use your estimates from Question 5 to calculate the welfare cost from output fluctuations when wages are set in accordance with (72) rather than (63). Compare the new estimate with that from Question 5 and try to give an economic explanation of the difference.

Exercise 3. The welfare costs of output fluctuations

The main text derived expressions allowing a quantification of the welfare costs of output fluctuations. In this exercise we ask you to study how sensitive the estimate of these welfare costs is to a plausible respecification of consumer preferences. For this purpose, suppose that instead of being given by Eq. (3) in the main text, the utility function of the representative consumer is:

$$U(C, L) = \beta \ln C + (1 - \beta)\ln(1 - L), \qquad 0 < \beta < 1, \tag{73}$$

where the consumer's total exogenous time endowment has been normalized at unity so that $1 - L$ is the consumption of leisure. Thus the parameter β measures the strength of the preference for material consumption relative to the preference for leisure.

1. Take a second-order Taylor approximation of (73) and show that

$$\Delta \equiv U(C, L) - U(\bar{C}, \bar{L}) \cong \beta\left(\hat{c} - \frac{\hat{c}^2}{2}\right) - (1 - \beta)\left(\frac{\bar{L}}{1 - \bar{L}}\right)\left[\hat{\ell} + \left(\frac{\bar{L}}{1 - \bar{L}}\right)\frac{\hat{\ell}^2}{2}\right], \tag{74}$$

$$c \equiv \ln C, \qquad \hat{c} \equiv c - \bar{c}, \qquad \ell \equiv \ln L, \qquad \hat{\ell} \equiv \ell - \bar{\ell},$$

where the bar superscripts indicate long-run equilibrium values. Explain that Δ equals the welfare effect of deviations from long-run equilibrium, measured in consumption units and expressed as a fraction of steady state consumption (hint: you may want to recapitulate how Eq. (16) in the main text was derived). Identify the costs of consumption fluctuations and the costs of employment fluctuations in (74).

From (73) it follows that the marginal rate of substitution between consumption and work is

$$MRS(C : L) = -\frac{U_L}{U_C} = \frac{(1 - \beta)C}{\beta(1 - L)}. \tag{75}$$

2. Suppose that the labour market can be described by equations (6) through (9) in the main text, except that $MRS(C : L)$ is now given by (75) instead of by the expression in the main text. Show that the long-run equilibrium level of employment relative to the long run equilibrium level of leisure is given by:

$$\frac{\bar{L}}{1 - \bar{L}} = \frac{\beta(1 - \alpha)}{(1 - \beta)\bar{\delta}}, \qquad \bar{\delta} \equiv \frac{\bar{m}^P \bar{m}^w}{1 - \tau}. \tag{76}$$

Try to provide an economic explanation for the way the various parameters on the right-hand side of (76) influence the solution. Does $\bar{L}$ correspond to the efficient level of employment? Explain.

3. Total output Y is given by the production function (7) in the main text. In every period all output is consumed. Define $y \equiv \ln Y$ and $\hat{y} \equiv y - \bar{y}$ and use (7) and (76) to express Δ in (74) as a function of $\hat{y}$ and $\hat{y}^2$, assuming that the productivity parameter B in (7) is constant. Use your result to explain the role of market imperfections for the welfare effect of deviations from long-run equilibrium.

4. Calculate the mathematical expectation of the formula for Δ derived in Question 3 to obtain an expression for the average welfare loss from output fluctuations. Compare your result to Eq. (22) in the main text and comment on the difference. In the chapter we argued that plausible parameter values would be $\bar{m}^P = \bar{m}^w = 1.2$, $\tau = 0.36$, and $\alpha = 1/3$. Recall that $\bar{L}/(1 - \bar{L})$ is the ratio of work to leisure. If we do not count time spent sleeping as 'leisure', a reasonable value of $\bar{L}/(1 - \bar{L})$ might be 0.5. With these parameter values you can use (76) to estimate a plausible value of β. Now use this information along with your formula for $E[\Delta]$ to calculate the average welfare cost of output fluctuations, assuming (as we did in the chapter text) that the standard deviation of GDP around its trend level is 2 per cent. Compare your estimate to the estimated welfare cost of output fluctuations based on formula (22) in the text. Is the difference large or small? Investigate the sensitivity of your welfare cost measure to plausible variations in the ratio $\bar{L}/(1 - \bar{L})$.

5. In the first step of the Taylor approximation undertaken in Question 1, you will have expressed Δ as a function of $(C - \bar{C})/\bar{C}$ and $\bar{L}/(1 - \bar{L})$. Recall from (26) in the chapter text that one can make the approximations

$$\frac{C - \bar{C}}{\bar{C}} \cong \hat{c} + \frac{\hat{c}^2}{2}, \qquad \frac{L - \bar{L}}{\bar{L}} \cong \ell + \frac{\ell^2}{2}. \tag{77}$$

Use (77) to derive an alternative expression for Δ comparable to (27) in the text. Now assume that the productivity parameter B fluctuates around the mean value $\bar{B}$ and define $b \equiv \ln B$ and $\hat{b} \equiv b - \bar{b}$. Use the production function (7) to express Δ as a function of the actual and the efficient output gaps so that you obtain an expression comparable to (30) in the main text. Explain why it is not the output gap as such, but only a deviation between the actual and the efficient output gaps that generates welfare effects.

Exercise 4. The goals of stabilization policy

In this exercise you are invited to restate and discuss some of the main results and arguments presented in this chapter. The case for macroeconomic stabilization policy rests on the assumption that it is desirable to stabilize the rates of output and inflation around some target values. This raises a number of questions.

1. Discuss why it is socially desirable to stabilize the rate of inflation around some constant target value. What are the costs of a fluctuating rate of inflation?

2. What are the arguments for avoiding fluctuations in output and employment? What factors determine the magnitude of the welfare costs of output and employment instability?

3. Explain why even a constant rate of inflation generates welfare costs. Do you consider these costs to be large or small? Discuss the factors which policy makers should take into account when they choose the target inflation rate. Is zero inflation an optimal inflation target?

4. Discuss the factors which should be considered when policy makers choose the target level of output. Should they choose the 'efficient' level of output or the trend level of output? Explain the difference between these two concepts.

Stabilization policy: How?

20

The previous chapter explained why fluctuations in output and inflation cause a net loss of economic welfare: the welfare gained during booms is more than offset by the welfare lost during recessions. Social welfare will therefore go up if policy makers succeed in reducing the volatility of output and inflation through active monetary and fiscal policy. But whether the government can indeed dampen the business cycle through active stabilization policy is a long-standing controversy in macroeconomics. For example, in Chapter 16 we reported the view of Milton Friedman that since monetary policy works with long and variable lags that are hard to predict, the best contribution that monetary policy can make to economic stability is to ensure a constant growth rate of the nominal money supply. Essentially Friedman argued that because the economy is such a complex mechanism which we do not understand very well, attempts by governments to manipulate aggregate demand will often fail as monetary or fiscal interventions may occur at the wrong time or in the wrong dosage. In this way active demand management policies may end up amplifying rather than dampening the business cycle. Some other economists have argued that if monetary or fiscal policy starts to follow a systematic pattern over the business cycle, rational private sector agents will come to anticipate this pattern and will adapt their behaviour in a manner that will tend to nullify the intended effects of stabilization policy.[1]

The debate on what macroeconomic stabilization policy can and should try to achieve continues and was recently stimulated by the severe financial and economic crisis of 2008–09 where monetary and fiscal policy makers intervened on a massive scale in their efforts to stabilize the economy. In this chapter we take a first step in the analysis of the optimal design of stabilization policy, building on the findings of the previous chapter. We start by discussing whether stabilization policy should be based on a fixed rule such as the Taylor rule or whether it should be 'discretionary', reacting to the particular circumstances of the day without following a predetermined pattern. We conclude that there are important advantages of following a policy rule. To get an idea of what stabilization policy could at best be expected to achieve, we then characterize the optimal monetary policy rule in an ideal world where the central bank has perfect information about the economy and can react instantaneously to any shocks. We then gradually relax these strong assumptions by analysing the optimal stabilization policy when information is imperfect and there are time lags in the economy's reaction to policy changes.

Most of the analysis in this chapter maintains our previous assumption that expectations are *backward looking*, i.e., that the expected future rate of inflation is determined solely by the actual rates of inflation observed in the past. In Chapters 21 and 22 we shall analyse the

---

1. Chapter 21 will explain this argument in detail.

scope for stabilization policy when expectations are *forward looking* in the sense that agents try to form the best possible estimate of future inflation, utilizing all the relevant information available to them at the time expectations are formed. Chapter 22 will also consider the challenges for stabilization policy arising when there is uncertainty in the measurement of the output and inflation gaps, and when the authorities have difficulties establishing the credibility of their commitment to a low and stable inflation rate.

In the present and the next two chapters we will thus gradually introduce many of the issues raised by those who are sceptical with regard to the government's ability to actively stabilize the economy. But our point of departure is that there is indeed an important role for macroeconomic stabilization policy. The crucial question is *how* such policy should be designed. Section 20.1 discusses the issue of policy rules versus discretion. Sections 20.2 and 20.3 deal with *monetary stabilization policy* in theory and practice, while Sections 20.4 and 20.5 will focus on *fiscal stabilization policy* in theory and reality.

20.1 Rules versus discretion

A basic issue in the debate on macroeconomic stabilization policy is whether policy makers should follow a fixed *policy rule*, or whether they prefer to be left with *discretion* in their policy choices.

Under the rules approach, stabilization policy is essentially automatic, since the policy rule prescribes how the policy instruments should be set in any given situation. The Taylor rule discussed in Chapter 16 is an example of a fixed monetary policy rule specifying how the central bank interest rate should be set, given the observed state of the economy. The Friedman rule prescribing a constant growth rate of the nominal money supply is another example of a fixed monetary policy rule. In an open economy a fixed exchange rate regime can also be seen as a monetary policy rule which requires the central bank to adjust its interest rate in reaction to any departure of the foreign exchange rate from its target value or interval.

By contrast, under discretion policy makers are free to conduct monetary and fiscal policy in any way that they believe will help advance the objectives of stabilization policy in any particular situation. The idea is that policy makers should use all the available information and take account of any special circumstances without necessarily following the same pattern of reaction from one period to the next.

It might seem that discretion should be preferred to rules, since reliance on a simple fixed policy rule reduces the ability of policy makers to react to all relevant information. A policy maker can always by discretion make exactly the choice that some policy rule would prescribe, so conducting policy by discretion simply allows more choice flexibility. Many economists nevertheless believe that stabilization policy should be based on simple rules. In Chapter 22 we discuss the issue of rules vs. discretion in detail, but for now the argument in favour of rules is essentially that they can help policy makers to establish *credibility* which will help them realize the goals of stabilization policy. For example, if the natural unemployment rate is rather high, the public may suspect that policy makers have an incentive to drive down the actual unemployment rate by creating surprise inflation. In these circumstances it may be difficult for policy makers to convince the private sector that they are committed to securing a low and stable rate of inflation. The fear of inflation will then keep the expected and actual inflation rate at an uncomfortably high level which can only be reduced by generating a serious recession. However, suppose policy makers put their reputation at stake by publicly announcing that they are bound by a policy rule requiring them to respond strongly to any increase in inflation. It may then be easier to convince the markets that inflation will indeed be kept low. In this way a policy rule may serve as an anchor for (low) inflation expectations. Similarly, if policy makers announce a rule which implies that policy is automatically tightened when output rises and automatically eased if output falls, this may help to stabilize the growth expectations of the private sector which in turn will help to stabilize aggregate demand.

Of course, policy makers can only 'buy' credibility by announcing a fixed policy rule if they can convince the public that they are really bound by the rule. This will be easier if the rule is written into the law or into the mandate or statutes of the central bank, and if policy makers face some kind of sanction if they break the rule. For example, the law regulating the central bank could specify that the central bank governor will be fired if he consistently misses the bank's inflation target. For a rule to be credible, it must also be reasonably simple so the public can easily understand the rule and check that policy makers actually stick to it.

The advocates of discretion argue that fixed policy rules can only establish credibility if they are overly simple and rigidly adhered to. Hence credibility can only be bought at the price of *flexibility*: by sticking to a simple policy rule no matter what the situation is, policy makers lose the ability to account for whatever special circumstances might prevail. For instance, suppose that because of some unexpected event the stock market suddenly takes an exceptional plunge which provides good reason to believe that the economy is headed for a deep recession. In that situation, should the central bank really keep the interest rate unchanged just because stock prices do not enter into the policy reaction function it has announced?

Most adherents of rules acknowledge that complete loss of flexibility would be a problem. For example, John Taylor has not argued that central banks should slavishly follow his rule. Rather, they should use it as a *guideline* to be followed under normal circumstances, but deviations from the rule would be acceptable when exceptional circumstances prevail.

In practice central banks do not announce a fixed quantified interest rate reaction function, presumably because they wish to preserve some amount of policy flexibility. Nevertheless, as we saw in Chapter 16, the interest rate policies of the most important central banks seem to be fairly well described by the Taylor rule. In the following we will therefore assume that stabilization policy is in fact based on rules. As we shall see in the next section, a version of the Taylor rule with appropriately chosen coefficients on the output and inflation gaps could indeed be an *optimal* monetary policy under realistic assumptions about the time lags with which interest rate changes affect the economy. The more general message of the next main section is that the optimal monetary policy rule depends crucially on the information available to monetary policy makers when they set the interest rate.

20.2 Monetary stabilization policy in theory

The social loss function

As you recall, our AS–AD model developed over Chapters 14–18 assumes that (in our usual notation) output is given by the production function

$$Y = BL^{1-\alpha}, \qquad 0 < \alpha < 1, \tag{1}$$

where B reflects the level of labour productivity. From (1) the natural output level is $\bar{Y} = \bar{B}\bar{L}^{1-\alpha}$, where $\bar{L}$ is natural employment and $\bar{B}$ is the trend level of productivity. As usual, we define the (relative) output gap as $\hat{y} \equiv \ln Y - \ln \bar{Y} \equiv y - \bar{y}$. Moreover, if the target inflation rate is π^*, the 'inflation gap' is: $\hat{\pi} \equiv \pi - \pi^*$. It follows from the analysis in Chapter 19 that the loss of economic welfare associated with the output and inflation gaps may be approximated by a 'social loss function' of the following form, where the welfare effect SL is measured as a fraction of GDP:[2]

$$SL = -a_d(\hat{y} - \hat{b}) + \frac{a_\ell}{2(1-\alpha)}(\hat{y} - \hat{b})^2 + \frac{a_\pi}{2}\hat{\pi}^2,$$

$$a_\ell > 0, \qquad a_\pi > 0, \qquad a_d \equiv 1 - \left(\frac{1-\tau}{\bar{m}^p \bar{m}^w}\right), \qquad \hat{b} \equiv \ln B - \ln \bar{B}. \tag{2}$$

---

2. In the notation of Chapter 19, we have $\hat{y}^e = \hat{b}$. Eq. (2) above then follows from Eq. (50) in Chapter 19 if we assume that $\pi^e = \pi^*$.

To understand why the social loss from business cycles takes the form (2), note that our production function (1) implies $\ln L - \ln \bar{L} = (\hat{y} - \hat{b})/(1-\alpha)$, so employment will deviate from its natural rate whenever $\hat{y} \neq \hat{b}$. The parameters $\bar{m}^p$ and $\bar{m}^w$ are the steady-state price and wage mark-ups and τ is the income tax rate. Hence the coefficient a_d reflects the degree of market distortion. As we explained in Chapter 19, it measures the wedge between the marginal product of labour (MPL) and the marginal rate of substitution (MRS) between consumption and work (recall that the MRS is the rise in net income needed to compensate workers for an extra hour of work).[3] When this wedge is positive, a rise in employment is welfare-increasing, and vice versa. Thus the first term on the right-hand side of (2) captures that an economic boom where $L > \bar{L}$ ($\hat{y} > \hat{b}$) generates a welfare gain (i.e. it *reduces* the social loss) because it creates more additional income than needed to compensate workers for their extra effort, whereas a recession where $L < \bar{L}$ ($\hat{y} < \hat{b}$) increases the social loss because the income lost exceeds the value of the additional leisure time available to (unemployed) workers.

If MPL and MRS were constant, symmetric fluctuations of employment around the natural rate would not cause a net social loss, since the welfare gained during booms would fully offset the welfare lost during recessions. But in fact MPL is decreasing whereas MRS is increasing with the level of employment, so employment fluctuations around the natural rate do create a net welfare loss, as we saw in Chapter 19. This is captured by the second term on the right-hand side of (2) which adds to the social loss whenever $\hat{y} \neq \hat{b}$ ($L \neq \bar{L}$). Further, we saw in Chapter 19 that fluctuations in the rate of inflation also generate welfare losses, in part by distorting relative prices. This explains the presence of the third term on the right-hand side of (2). The structural parameters determining the size of the parameters a_ℓ and a_π were identified in Chapter 19.

In the following we will define an optimal monetary policy as a policy that minimizes the social loss function (2). Our agenda will be to derive optimal monetary policy rules under alternative assumptions regarding the structure of the economy and the information available to the central bank.

Optimal monetary policy with a fully credible and perfectly informed central bank

We start by considering a central bank which can *perfectly observe* all the different types of shocks moving the economy and which can adjust its policy interest rate *instantaneously* to these shocks. In line with our AS–AD model, we also assume that the economy responds immediately to changes in the policy rate. Finally, we will assume for the moment that the central bank has *full credibility* in the sense that the private sector's inflation expectations are firmly anchored by the announced official inflation target so that $\pi^e = \pi^*$ in each period. These assumptions are not very realistic (and will be relaxed below), but as a benchmark it is useful to study their implications to understand what stabilization policy can at best be expected to achieve.

With $\pi^e = \pi^*$, the AS curve derived in Eq. (56) of Chapter 17 becomes:

$$\hat{\pi} = \left(\frac{\alpha}{1-\alpha}\right)\hat{y} + \hat{m} - \frac{\hat{b}}{1-\alpha}, \qquad \hat{m} \equiv \ln\left(\frac{m^p}{\bar{m}^p}\right) + \ln\left(\frac{m^w}{\bar{m}^w}\right). \tag{3}$$

According to (2) the marginal social loss from a change in the output gap is:

$$MSL_y \equiv \frac{\partial SL}{\partial \hat{y}} = \frac{a_\ell}{1-\alpha}(\hat{y} - \hat{b}) - a_d. \tag{4}$$

---

3.   In the notation of Chapter 19, $a_d \equiv (\bar{\delta} - 1)/\bar{\delta}$.

Note that since $\ln L - \ln \bar{L} = (\hat{y} - \hat{b})/(1 - \alpha)$, the parameter a_ℓ in (2) and (4) measures the marginal social cost of a (one percentage point) deviation of employment from its natural level. From (2) we may also derive the marginal social loss from a change in the inflation gap:

$$MSL_\pi \equiv \frac{\partial SL}{\partial \hat{\pi}} = a_\pi \hat{\pi}. \tag{5}$$

Now suppose the economy is in recession with a negative output gap and that the central bank cuts the interest rate to stimulate demand and output by one percentage point. The isolated welfare effect of the higher output is a social welfare gain equal to MSL_y. However, according to the aggregate supply curve (3) the rise in output induces a rise in the inflation gap amounting to $\partial \hat{\pi}/\partial \hat{y} = \alpha/(1-\alpha)$ percentage points which generates a social welfare loss equal to $MSL_\pi \cdot (\partial \hat{\pi}/\partial \hat{y})$. Under the optimal stabilization policy the marginal welfare gain from higher output is just offset by the marginal welfare loss from the higher inflation. Hence the optimal output gap may be found from the first-order condition:

$$\frac{dSL}{d\hat{y}} = 0 \implies MSL_y + MSL_\pi \cdot \frac{\partial \hat{\pi}}{\partial \hat{y}} = 0 \implies \overbrace{\frac{a_\ell}{1-\alpha}(\hat{y} - \hat{b})}^{MSL_y} - a_d + \overbrace{a_\pi \hat{\pi}}^{MSL_\pi} \cdot \overbrace{\left(\frac{\alpha}{1-\alpha}\right)}^{\partial \hat{\pi}/\partial \hat{y}} = 0 \tag{6}$$

$$\Leftrightarrow \quad \hat{y} = \hat{b} + (1-\alpha)\frac{a_d}{a_\ell} - \frac{\alpha a_\pi}{a_\ell}\hat{\pi}.$$

Using the AS curve (3) to substitute for $\hat{\pi}$ in (6) and rearranging, we obtain the optimal output gap expressed as a function of the shocks hitting the economy:

$$\hat{y} = \left(\frac{1-\alpha}{a_\ell + \alpha\gamma a_\pi}\right)a_d - \left(\frac{\gamma a_\pi}{a_\ell + \alpha\gamma a_\pi}\right)(1-\alpha)\hat{m} + \left(\frac{a_\ell + \gamma a_\pi}{a_\ell + \alpha\gamma a_\pi}\right)\hat{b}, \quad \gamma \equiv \frac{\alpha}{1-\alpha} > 0. \tag{7}$$

How can the central bank achieve an output gap equal to (7)? From the goods market equilibrium condition in Eq. (12) of Chapter 16 we have:

$$\hat{y} = \alpha_1 \hat{g} - \alpha_2(r - \bar{r}) + v. \tag{8}$$

With $\pi^e = \pi^e_{+1} = \pi^*$, the real market interest rate is $r = i^p - \pi^* + \rho$, where you recall that i^p is the central bank's policy interest rate, and ρ is a market risk premium. Inserting this into (8), and remembering from Chapter 17 that $\bar{r}^* \equiv \bar{r} - \bar{\rho}$ is the risk-free steady-state real interest rate, we get the output gap as determined from the economy's demand side:

$$\hat{y} = \alpha_1 \hat{g} + v - \alpha_2(i^p - \pi^* + \hat{\rho} - \bar{r}^*), \quad \hat{\rho} \equiv \rho - \bar{\rho}. \tag{9}$$

Equating the two output gaps in (7) and (9), we obtain *the central bank's optimal interest rate rule* which will generate an output gap representing an optimal trade-off between the goals of stable employment and stable inflation:

$$i^p = \bar{r}^* + \pi^* - \hat{\rho} + \frac{v + \alpha_1 \hat{g}}{\alpha_2} - \left(\frac{1-\alpha}{\alpha_2(a_\ell + \alpha\gamma a_\pi)}\right)a_d + \left(\frac{\gamma a_\pi}{\alpha_2(a_\ell + \alpha\gamma a_\pi)}\right)(1-\alpha)\hat{m} - \left(\frac{a_\ell + \gamma a_\pi}{\alpha_2(a_\ell + \alpha\gamma a_\pi)}\right)\hat{b}. \tag{10}$$

This policy rule has several important implications.

First, in contrast to the Taylor rule, Eq. (10) does not prescribe that the policy rate i^p should react directly to the output and inflation gaps. Instead, the central bank should exploit its perfect information about the various shocks to *adjust the policy rate in a way that depends on the specific type of shock hitting the economy.*

Second, *demand shocks should be perfectly stabilized*. Demand shocks may take the form of shocks to market risk premia ($\hat{\rho}$), 'confidence' shocks to private demand (v), or fiscal shocks ($\hat{g}$). Such shocks do not represent a dilemma for stabilization policy since they affect the output and inflation gaps in the same direction. Indeed, since the AS curve (3) is linear, the changes in the two gaps induced by a shift in the AD curve will be perfectly correlated. A policy response that fully neutralizes the impact on the output gap will therefore also fully neutralize the impact on the inflation gap, thereby preventing any welfare loss from the demand shock. For example, in case of a positive shock to the risk premium, (10) prescribes that the policy rate should be lowered correspondingly (assuming this can be done without hitting the zero interest rate floor). In this way market interest rates and hence aggregate demand are kept constant, and no change in the output and inflation gaps will occur. Similarly, according to (8) a one percentage point rise in the interest rate reduces aggregate demand by α_2 units, and therefore a positive confidence shock with a demand impact of magnitude v can be fully offset if the policy rate is raised by v/α_2 units, as indicated in (10). Note that since there is no conflict between stabilizing output and stabilizing inflation in the case of demand shocks, the appropriate interest rate response to such shocks does not depend on the respective social weights a_ℓ and a_π attached to the goals of stabilizing the two gaps.

Third, *mark-up shocks, $\hat{m}$, and productivity shocks, $\hat{b}$, although both supply shocks, call for different monetary policy reactions and these reactions should depend on the relative weights attached to the goals of stable employment and stable inflation*. Supply shocks raise a dilemma. For example, if employment is kept constant in the face of a temporary drop in productivity, inflation will go up. To avoid the higher inflation, employment will have to fall, thereby raising the marginal productivity of labour and reducing the marginal costs of production. Thus it is impossible to stabilize inflation and employment at the same time. To understand the policy reaction to a temporary mark-up shock ($\hat{m} \neq 0$) prescribed by the monetary policy rule (10), it is useful to take a look at Fig. 20.1. The lower AS curve in the diagram shows the relationship between the output and inflation gaps implied by the aggregate supply curve in (3) when there are no supply shocks, while the upper AS curve

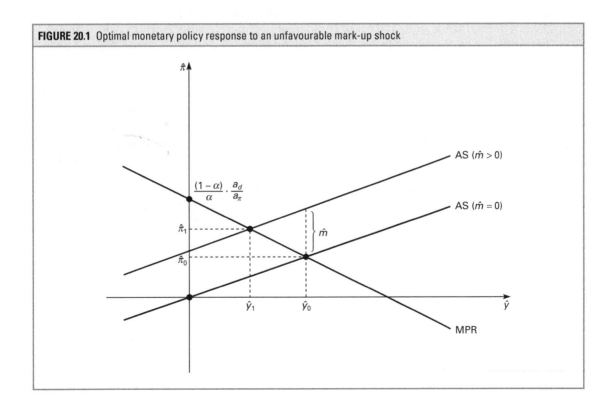

FIGURE 20.1 Optimal monetary policy response to an unfavourable mark-up shock

shows the relationship between the two gaps in the presence of a positive shock to wage or price mark-ups (but still assuming no productivity shocks). The curve MPR (where MPR stands for 'Monetary Policy Rule') shows the *optimal* combination of the output and inflation gaps when the central bank adjusts the interest rate to ensure that the marginal social gain from higher output (MSL_y) always equals the marginal social loss from the resulting rise in inflation ($MSL_\pi \cdot (\partial \hat{\pi}/\partial \hat{y})$). The general equation for the MPR curve is found by simple rearrangement of (6):[4]

$$\text{MPR curve:}\quad \hat{\pi} = \left(\frac{1-\alpha}{\alpha}\right)\frac{a_d}{a_\pi} + \frac{a_\ell}{\alpha a_\pi}(\hat{b} - \hat{y}). \tag{11}$$

Before the mark-up shock hits the economy, the central bank sets an interest rate that ensures the optimal combination $(\hat{y}_0, \hat{\pi}_0)$ of the output and inflation gaps. When a negative mark-up shock ($\hat{m} > 0$) hits, the AS curve shifts upwards, and the central bank therefore chooses the new combination $(\hat{y}_1, \hat{\pi}_1)$ of the two gaps where the MPR curve intersects with the new AS curve. We see that the socially optimal response to the mark-up shock is to accept some fall in output. This is intuitive: since the social loss rises more than proportionally with the inflation gap (indeed, it rises with the square of the inflation gap), it is optimal to absorb part of the shock by allowing output to fall rather than allowing the cost-push shock to be fully passed on to the rate of inflation. To induce a fall in output, the central bank must raise the policy interest rate to curb aggregate demand. This is exactly what the policy rule (10) prescribes when the economy is hit by an unfavorable mark-up shock.

Figure 20.2 illustrates the slightly more complicated case of an unfavourable productivity shock where $\hat{b} < 0$ (we now set $\hat{m} = 0$). According to (3) the cost-push effect of the negative productivity shock shifts the AS curve upwards by the vertical distance $|\hat{b}|/(1-\alpha)$. At the same time (11) shows that the MPR curve will shift downwards by the vertical distance $(a_\ell/\alpha a_\pi)|\hat{b}|$. Thus we see that the central bank will choose a lower output gap $\hat{y}_1$ in response to a negative productivity shock. This makes good intuitive sense, since output can only be sustained in the face of a negative productivity shock by requiring workers to put in more hours, and it is hardly optimal to let workers work unusually hard at a time when the output from their effort is unusually low. To dampen economic activity from $\hat{y}_0$ to $\hat{y}_1$ in Fig. 20.2, the central bank must reduce aggregate demand by raising its policy rate. Again this is what the policy rule (10) requires when $\hat{b} < 0$.

Note from the aggregate supply curve (3) that an unfavourable mark-up shock of size $\hat{m}(<0)$ has the same direct cost-push effect on the rate of inflation as a negative productivity shock of size $|\hat{b}| = (1-\alpha)\hat{m}$. Hence we see from the policy rule (10) that the policy interest rate should respond more strongly (thus inducing a larger change in output) when the economy is hit by a productivity shock than when it is hit by a mark-up shock with the same direct cost effect. The reason is that a productivity shock implies a change in the technological opportunities available to society whereas a mark-up shock does not. For example, a negative productivity shock implies a fall in the marginal productivity of labour whereas a rise in the price mark-up does not reduce the amount of output resulting from an extra hour of work. Thus it makes good sense to allow a larger drop in output in the former than in the latter case.

The above analysis described what monetary policy could achieve under ideal circumstances, and it rested on the following strong assumptions: 1) The central bank has perfect information about all the shocks hitting the economy. 2) Central bankers can react instantaneously on the basis of this information. 3) The economy responds immediately to a change in the policy interest rate. 4) The central bank has full credibility in the sense that

---

4. The MPR curve as a tool for graphical monetary policy analysis was introduced by Carl Walsh, 'Teaching Inflation Targeting: An Analysis for Intermediate Macro', *Journal of Economic Education*, **33**, 2002, pp. 333–347. However, in this subsection we differ from Walsh regarding the assumptions about the output target of the central bank and the information available to it, so our optimal monetary policy rule also differs from his.

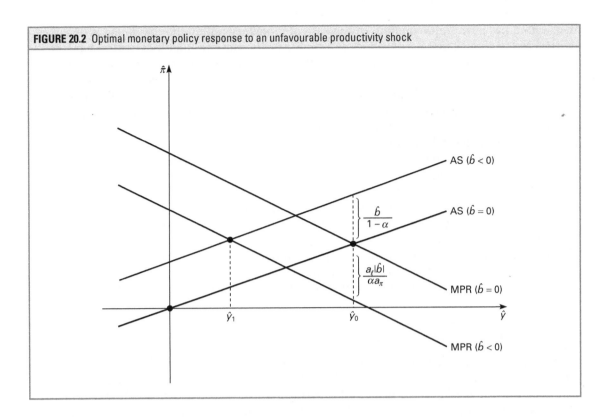

FIGURE 20.2 Optimal monetary policy response to an unfavourable productivity shock

inflation expectations are firmly anchored by its inflation target. Unfortunately these assumptions are not very realistic, for the following reasons.

Imperfect information: In practice many shocks cannot be directly observed right at the time when they hit the economy. Although the so-called leading economic (statistical) indicators may sometimes give a hint of shocks that are about to hit, the signals given by these indicators are typically 'noisy' and rather imprecise predictors of future economic developments. Moreover, in any given time period the economy may be exposed simultaneously to several different types of shock to demand as well as supply, so disentangling those shocks from each other right away and evaluating their relative importance by monitoring the current levels of output, employment and inflation (or other observable macroeconomic variables) is close to impossible. For instance, if the current rate of inflation is higher than might be expected from the current level of unemployment, this might indicate the presence of an unfavourable supply shock, but the data on inflation and unemployment do not reveal whether the inflationary pressure stems from a mark-up shock or from a productivity shock. And as we have seen, the optimal policy response to a supply shock depends critically on whether it is of one type or the other.

Time lags: As time passes, more information on the state of the economy at any given calendar time becomes available, making it easier to estimate the various shocks that have hit and to evaluate their relative size and degree of persistence. The problem of imperfect information described above is therefore sometimes referred to as the problem of the *recognition lag*. This is the difficulty that since the sufficient amount of information only becomes available with a time lag, it takes time before policy makers fully recognize that the state of the economy has changed. In addition to the recognition lag there may be a *decision lag*, because it may take some time to decide what change of policy is warranted by the change in the state of the economy. On top of that there may be an *implementation lag* in so far as the change in policy does not take effect immediately. The sum of the three lags just mentioned is sometimes referred to as the *inside lag*, covering the period from the time an economic disturbance arises until the time when a change in the economic policy instrument has been implemented. In the case of monetary policy the inside lag is usually considered to consist mainly of the recognition lag, since an independent central bank can typically decide and implement a change in the policy interest rate quite quickly once the need for a change has been recognized. But stabilization policy faces an additional complication in the form of the so-called *outside lag*. This is the period from the time the policy instrument has changed until this change achieves its (maximum) impact on the economy. The analysis above implicitly assumed that the outside lag is shorter than the length of the time period considered so that a change in the interest rate attains its full impact on aggregate demand within that period. But as we shall discuss in more detail later, the outside lag in monetary policy making may be quite long.

Credibility: The assumption of full credibility ($\pi^e = \pi^*$) is also problematic. The reason is that because of the market distortions which drive the natural output level below the *efficient* level that would prevail in perfectly competitive economy without tax distortions, a central bank seeking to minimize a social loss function like (2) will typically wish to keep output above the natural level. Hence the actual inflation rate will typically lie above the target rate. To see the problem, note that (7) gives the optimal output gap the central bank wishes to attain. Setting $\hat{m} = \hat{b} = 0$ in this equation and using the definition of a_d in (2), we get

$$\hat{y} = \left(\frac{1-\alpha}{a_\ell + \alpha\gamma a_\pi} \right) a_d = \left(\frac{1-\alpha}{a_\ell + \alpha\gamma a_\pi} \right) \left[1 - \left(\frac{1-\tau}{\bar{m}^p \bar{m}^w} \right) \right]. \tag{12}$$

In the presence of tax distortions ($\tau > 0$) and market imperfections ($\bar{m}^p \bar{m}^w > 1$), this expression is positive. By construction, the temporary shocks $\hat{m}$ and $\hat{b}$ fluctuate around a zero mean, so on average the output and inflation gaps will be at the levels ($\hat{y}_0$, $\hat{\pi}_0$) depicted in Fig. 20.1. On average inflation will thus be *higher* than the target rate. As the public learns that the central bank tends to systematically violate its announced inflation target, it is unlikely that the expected inflation rate can be kept down at the level π^*. Suppose instead that, having learned that the actual inflation gap fluctuates around the positive level $\hat{\pi}_0$ in Fig. 20.1, the public settles on an expected inflation rate corresponding to this gap. The AS curve will then shift upwards, intersecting the vertical axis in Fig. 20.1 at the point $\hat{\pi}_0$. But then it follows from the intersection between the MPR curve and the new AS curve that the central bank will aim at a higher inflation gap, so again the actual inflation rate will tend to exceed the expected rate, leading to another upward revision of the expected inflation rate that generates another rise in the average actual inflation rate, and so on until the AS curve intersects the vertical axis at point $(1 - \alpha)a_d/\alpha a_\pi$ in Fig. 20.1 (convince yourself of this). In short, a central bank aiming at an output target exceeding the natural rate will be unable to maintain the credibility of its inflation target over time.[5] Therefore it is usually argued that monetary and fiscal *stabilization policy* should aim at stabilizing output around its natural trend level, since this is consistent with maintaining a low and stable long-run rate of inflation. The government should then use *structural policies* such as labour market policies, tax policies and competition policies to alleviate the imperfections in labour and product markets, thereby pushing natural output closer to the efficient output level.

With all these criticisms the analysis in this subsection might seem quite irrelevant. Yet this conclusion would be too hasty. First of all, the above analysis illustrates what kind of information the monetary authorities would ideally like to have as a basis for their decision making. This type of analysis may therefore help to guide the collection and processing of relevant information that may serve to improve the foundations for policy making over time. Second, the analysis suggests that in cases where policy makers do actually possess (some) up-to-date information on the type of shocks hitting the economy, they should exploit this information when making their policy decisions. Since the amount of available information may vary from one situation to another, this insight may help to explain why actual monetary

---

5.   In Chapter 22 we shall analyse this credibility problem in greater detail and discuss how it can be alleviated.

policy often deviates somewhat from the policy choice dictated by simple mechanical rules like the Taylor rule. One might say that the above analysis could help to explain the statistical 'error terms' in the estimated monetary policy reaction functions of central banks.

Nevertheless, it is obviously relevant to ask what an optimal monetary policy rule would look like if we relax some of the strong assumptions made above. But let us first recapitulate the main lessons from this subsection:

OPTIMAL MONETARY POLICY WITH A FULLY INFORMED AND PERFECTLY CREDIBLE CENTRAL BANK

When the central bank can directly observe and instantaneously react to the different types of shocks hitting the economy and inflation expectations are firmly anchored by the announced inflation target, the policy interest rate should react directly to the various shocks rather than to the output and inflation gaps. Demand shocks should be perfectly stabilized by appropriate adjustment of the policy rate, since they do not represent a dilemma between output stability and inflation stability. Supply shocks do raise such a dilemma and should be allowed to affect both output and inflation. A productivity shock should be permitted to have a greater impact on output than a mark-up shock with the same direct cost effect. These policy principles represent a useful theoretical benchmark for what monetary policy can at best be expected to achieve, but in practice the central bank does not have perfect information. And even if it had, it would face a credibility problem because the optimal monetary policy rule will have an inflation bias when the monetary authority pursues an output target exceeding natural output.

Optimal monetary policy with limited information: inflation targeting

We now move towards a more realistic analysis of monetary policy. In particular, we assume that when it sets its policy rate for the current period, the central bank cannot directly observe all the different shocks currently hitting the economy, although it can observe the current output and inflation gaps. (In practice, the current output and inflation gaps may only be observable with a certain measurement error, but for simplicity we will postpone an analysis of the policy implications of measurement errors until Chapter 22.) Of course, if the central bank knows the slope of the AS curve and is able to observe the output and inflation gaps, it should be able to infer the size of aggregate supply shocks. Yet the bank cannot deduce whether this reflects a mark-up shock or a productivity shock. Further, the central bank must set its policy rate before it can observe the demand shocks occurring in the current period. As we argued above, the assumption that current shocks are not immediately observable seems reasonable in most situations. Moreover, motivated by our discussion of the credibility problem, we will assume that the central bank does not target an output level above the natural level. This is equivalent to assuming that the central bank acts as if natural output is equal to the efficient level of output so that the first term on the right-hand side of the social loss function (2) drops out. Further, when the central bank cannot observe the current productivity shock, the best it can do when it sets the policy rate is to assume that this shock will take its expected value of zero. Thus the central bank acts on the assumption that $\hat{y} - \hat{b} = \hat{y}$ in the current period. Instead of minimizing (2), the central bank thus seeks to minimize a modified social loss function of the form

$$SL = \frac{a_\ell}{2(1-\alpha)}\hat{y}^2 + \frac{a_\pi}{2}\hat{\pi}^2. \tag{13}$$

Comparing (13) to (2), you see that the objective function of the central bank no longer includes the term $-a_d(\hat{y} - \hat{b})$ which was responsible for the inflation bias in our previous model (note from (12) that the positive target for the steady state output gap in that model emerged because of the presence of the positive coefficient a_d). The assumption that the monetary authority does not try to keep output systematically above the natural rate is well in line with the declared policies of real world central banks. Note that even if they adopt the objective function (13), monetary policy makers may very well acknowledge that it would be socially desirable to raise the trend level of output above the current natural level. But given that the central bank does not possess the policy instruments needed to boost natural output, it is part of a rational division of labour among policy makers if the central bank focuses on minimizing fluctuations in the output and inflation gaps, leaving it to the government and parliament to implement the structural policy reforms that may move natural output closer to the efficient output level.

Finally, though our model no longer contains a source of inflation bias, we will go back to the assumption of static inflation expectations in previous chapters ($\pi = \pi_{-1}$) rather than assuming that the expected inflation rate equals the target inflation rate in each period. Thus we no longer assume that the central bank has full credibility in the sense defined earlier, since we wish to ensure that our conclusions do not rest on overly optimistic assumptions regarding the status of the central bank.[6]

When inflation expectations are static, policy makers must account for the fact that a change in the current output and inflation gaps will affect all future gaps. To see this, recall from Eqs (13) and (14) in Chapter 18 that when the future demand and supply shocks take their expected values of zero, our AS–AD model with static expectations implies that the output and inflation gaps will evolve according to the following linear first-order difference equations:

$$\hat{y}_t = \beta^t \hat{y}_0, \qquad \hat{\pi}_t = \beta^t \hat{\pi}_0, \qquad 0 < \beta < 1. \tag{14}$$

According to (14) a one percentage point rise in the current output gap $\hat{y}_0$ will cause the output gap t periods from now to be β^t percentage points higher than it would otherwise have been (this *ceteris paribus* assertion is also true even if there are future shocks to the economy). Now let (13) indicate the social loss incurred during each time period. A unit increase in the current output gap will then cause a marginal social loss amounting to $a_\ell \hat{y}/(1-\alpha)$ in the current period and hence a marginal social loss $\beta^t a_\ell \hat{y}/(1-\alpha)$ when the economy has moved t periods forward in time. Assuming a positive social discount rate ϕ, this future welfare loss has a present value of $(\beta/1+\phi)^t a_\ell \hat{y}/(1-\alpha)$. Thus the sum of the current and all discounted future marginal social losses arising from a unit increase in the current output gap (MSL_y^d) will be:

$$MSL_y^d = \frac{a_\ell \hat{y}}{1-\alpha}\left[1 + \frac{\beta}{1+\phi} + \left(\frac{\beta}{1+\phi}\right)^2 + \dots\right] = \left(\frac{a_\ell \hat{y}}{1-\alpha}\right)\left(\frac{1+\phi}{1-\beta+\phi}\right). \tag{15}$$

In a similar way we use (13) and (14) to derive the following expression for the present value of the marginal social losses from a unit increase in the current inflation gap (check this!):

$$MSL_\pi^d = a_\pi \hat{\pi}\left[1 + \frac{\beta}{1+\phi} + \left(\frac{\beta}{1+\phi}\right)^2 + \dots\right] = a_\pi \hat{\pi}\left(\frac{1+\phi}{1-\beta+\phi}\right). \tag{16}$$

We are now ready to derive the optimal monetary policy rule. Recall from Chapter 18 that, with static inflation expectations, we can write the AS curve embodied in the model underlying (14) as:

$$\pi = \pi_{-1} + \left(\frac{\alpha}{1-\alpha}\right)\hat{y} + s, \qquad s \equiv \hat{m} - \frac{b}{1-\alpha}, \tag{17}$$

---

6. In Exercise 1 you are asked to analyse how the results in this subsection are modified if we assume $\pi^e = \pi^*$.

where s captures mark-up shocks as well as productivity shocks. This AS curve implies that a one percentage point increase in the current output gap raises the current inflation rate by $\partial \pi / \partial \hat{y} = \alpha/(1-\alpha)$ percentage points. The optimal monetary policy is the policy that equates the present value of the marginal social gain from a unit increase in the current output gap with the present value of the marginal social loss from the resulting rise in the inflation gap. Using (15) and (16), this optimum condition may be written as:

$$MSL_y^d + MSL_\pi^d \cdot \frac{\partial \hat{\pi}}{\partial \hat{y}} = 0 \quad \Rightarrow \quad \left(\frac{1+\phi}{1-\beta+\phi} \right) \left(\frac{a_\ell \hat{y}}{1-\alpha} + a_\pi \hat{\pi} \frac{\alpha}{1-\alpha} \right) = 0 \quad \Leftrightarrow$$

MPR curve: $\hat{\pi} = -\left(\dfrac{a_\ell}{\alpha a_\pi} \right) \hat{y}.$ (18)

As indicated, (18) gives the MPR curve consistent with the modified social loss function (13), that is, the optimal combination of the output and inflation gaps, given that the central bank does not target an output level above the natural rate, and given that it cannot directly observe the supply shocks hitting the economy. The central bank knows that the aggregate demand curve is given by an equation like (9), but it must set its interest rate before it is able to observe the various demand shocks included in (9). The bank therefore assumes that these shocks $(\hat{g}, \hat{\rho}, v)$ will take their expected values of zero so that the output gap resulting from its interest rate decision will be

$$\hat{y} = -\alpha_2(i^p - \pi - \bar{r}^*).$$ (19)

Using (18) to substitute for $\hat{y}$ in (19) and solving for i^p, we obtain the optimal interest rate rule for the central bank, given the limited information available to it:

$$i^p = \bar{r}^* + \pi + h \cdot (\pi - \pi^*), \qquad h \equiv \frac{\alpha a_\pi}{\alpha_2 a_\ell}.$$ (20)

The policy rule (20) is a special case of the Taylor rule where the coefficient on the output gap is set equal to zero. Note the seeming paradox that even though this policy rule was derived from the social loss function (13), which includes a concern about output stability, the optimal policy rate does not react directly to the output gap. However, the concern about output and employment stability does enter the policy rule (20) via the coefficient a_ℓ in the denominator of the coefficient on the inflation gap. For example, if the inflation gap is pushed upwards by an unfavourable supply shock ($s > 0$), the rise in the central bank interest rate will be smaller the greater the concern about employment stability (a_ℓ), since an interest rate hike will reduce output and employment. It is also intuitive that the coefficient on the inflation gap in (20) varies positively with the welfare loss from inflation (a_π).

Our analysis provides a theoretical rationale for the widespread central bank practice of *inflation targeting* where the central bank seeks to stabilize the actual rate of inflation around an announced target inflation rate by raising the nominal interest rate when inflation is above the target, and vice versa.[7] It is useful to clarify the relation between the MPR curve (18), the inflation targeting rule (20) and the aggregate demand curve embodied in our AS–AD model. The general expression for the goods market equilibrium condition is given by Eq. (9) which includes demand shocks. If we insert the monetary policy rule (20) into (9) and rearrange, we get the

AD curve: $\hat{\pi} = \left(\dfrac{a_\ell}{\alpha a_\pi} \right)(z - \hat{y}), \qquad z \equiv v + \alpha_1 \hat{g} - \alpha_2 \hat{\rho},$ (21)

---

7. In Chapter 25 we shall discuss inflation targeting in more detail. See also the discussion in the next subsection.

FIGURE 20.3 Optimal monetary policy response to a temporary unfavourable supply shock

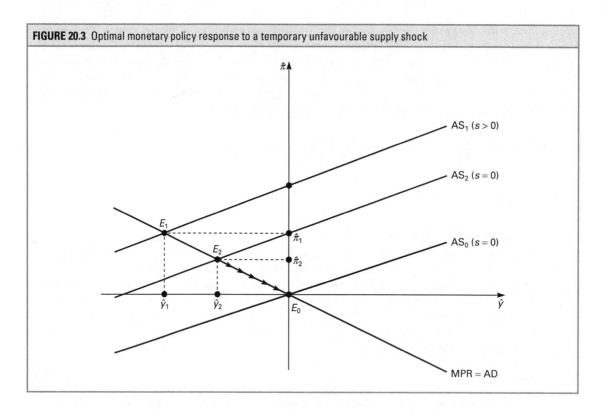

where z is the total aggregate demand shock. Comparing (18) and (21), we see that when the aggregate demand shock takes its expected value of zero, the AD curve coincides with the MPR curve. This is hardly surprising, since the inflation targeting rule (20) is designed to ensure that the level of aggregate demand will lead to a socially optimal trade-off between output stability and inflation stability, assuming that no unanticipated demand shocks hit the economy in the current period. When such shocks do in fact occur, we see from (18) and (21) that the economy will be pushed off the MPR curve, as the AD curve will undergo a parallel upward or downward shift whereas the MPR curve will stay put. This shift in the AD curve results from the fact that the central bank cannot immediately observe and react to new demand shocks. However, since the aggregate supply shock s does not appear in (18), it follows that the economy is *not* pushed away from the MPR curve when a new supply shock occurs. The reason is that the central bank can exploit its knowledge of the AS curve (17) to infer the size of the current supply shock by observing the current output and inflation gaps. As long as it can perfectly control aggregate demand (that is, when there are no unanticipated demand shocks), the central bank can therefore ensure that the economy stays on the MPR curve even if a supply shock hits.[8]

With this observation we can turn to Fig. 20.3 which illustrates the effect of a temporary unfavourable supply shock under an inflation targeting regime, given our assumption that the private sector's inflation expectations are static. In period zero the economy is in long-run equilibrium at point E_0 where the output and inflation gaps are zero, since we abstract from demand shocks. In period 1 the economy is hit by an unfavourable supply shock which could be a mark-up shock or a negative productivity shock (recall that the central bank has no way of distinguishing such shocks from each other and hence cannot condition its policy response on the exact nature of the shock). The AS curve therefore shifts upwards by the vertical distance $s > 0$ to the position AS_1, whereas the AD curve stays put at the

---

8. This optimistic conclusion rests on the strong assumption that the economy reacts immediately to a change in the policy interest rate. In the next subsection we shall study the implications of relaxing this assumption.

position of the MPR curve. The result is the new short-run equilibrium E_1 where inflation has risen while output has fallen. As agents observe the higher inflation gap $\hat{\pi}_1$ in period 1, they adjust their expected inflation rate for period 2 to this level, so even though the supply shock is assumed to disappear in period 2, the AS curve for that period does not shift all the way back to its original position but only moves down to the level AS_2 in Fig. 20.3. Thus we get the new short-run equilibrium E_2 which implies a lower inflation rate and a higher output level compared to period 1. In the subsequent periods, the economy moves further down the MPR (AD) curve back towards the original long-run equilibrium E_0 as agents gradually revise their inflation expectations downwards in reaction to the observed fall in actual inflation.

Figure 20.4 shows the effect of a temporary negative demand shock under the inflation targeting regime with static expectations. Initially the economy is in long-run equilibrium at E_0, but in period 1 a temporary negative demand shock hits the economy, pushing it off the MPR curve down to the new aggregate demand curve AD_1 and establishing a new short-run equilibrium at E_1 where output and inflation have fallen. In period 2 the demand shock goes away, so the AD curve shifts back to the position of the MPR curve, but at the same time the aggregate supply curve shifts down to the position AS_2, as the expected inflation rate adjusts to the lower inflation gap $\hat{\pi}_1$ observed in period 1. Hence a new short-run equilibrium is established at E_2 where the output gap has moved from negative into positive territory because of the expansionary effect of the downward shift in the AS curve. As the inflation rate goes up between periods 1 and 2, the expected inflation rate is gradually adjusted upwards in the following periods, so after period 2 the economy moves up along the MPR (AD) curve back towards the initial long-run equilibrium.

Let us sum up the insights from this subsection:

OPTIMAL MONETARY POLICY WITH IMPERFECT INFORMATION   (!)

When the central bank can only observe the output and inflation gaps, but cannot directly observe the shocks currently hitting the economy, and when the private sector's inflation expectations are static rather than being firmly pinned down by the official inflation target, the optimal monetary policy rule takes the form of an inflation-targeting regime where the policy rate is raised when inflation exceeds its target rate, and vice versa. The size of the optimal interest rate reaction to the inflation gap varies positively with the welfare loss from inflation instability and negatively with the social welfare loss from employment fluctuations. Since demand shocks cannot be immediately observed, they cannot be perfectly stabilized, but their effect on output and inflation is dampened by the inflation targeting rule. Mark-up shocks and productivity shocks are allowed to affect output and inflation in the same way since the central bank cannot distinguish between the two types of shock.

The outside lag, inflation forecast targeting, and the Taylor rule

The analysis in the previous subsection accounted for the so-called *inside lag* in stabilization policy by recognizing that the central bank cannot immediately observe and react to all new shocks hitting the economy. However, by assuming that the economy responds immediately to a change in the interest rate, we abstracted from the so-called *outside lag* mentioned earlier. The experience from many Western countries is that it takes about two years for a change in the interest rate to attain its maximum impact on the rate of inflation because of delayed behavioural responses in the private sector. While it may be possible to reduce the inside lag by investing more resources in the collection and improvement of economic data and by reforming the procedures for policy decision making, it is much harder for policy makers to do anything about the outside lag, since this lag is rooted in the

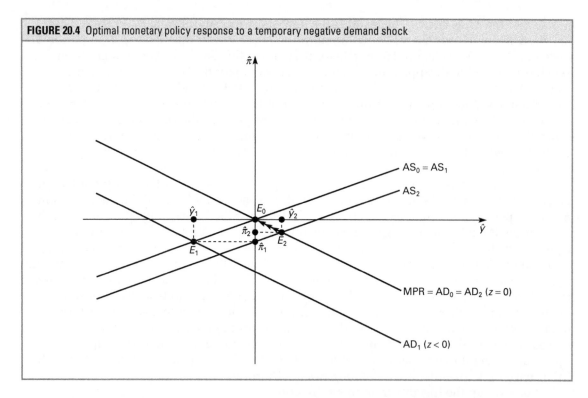

FIGURE 20.4 Optimal monetary policy response to a temporary negative demand shock

frictions and delays in the private sector's reactions to changes in the economic environment. Yet, if policy makers know the approximate length of the outside lag, they can account for it when designing the rules for stabilization policy. As an example, we will now demonstrate how a specific version of the *Taylor rule* for monetary policy may be an optimal way of coping with the outside lag.

Consider the following AS–AD model with static expectations, where we use our standard notation and time periods are indicated by subscripts:[9]

Goods market equilibrium: $y_{t+1} - \bar{y} = z_{t+1} - \alpha_2(i_t^p - \pi_t - \bar{r}^*),$ (22)

AS curve: $\pi_{t+2} = \pi_{t+1} + \gamma(y_{t+1} - \bar{y}) + s_{t+2}.$ (23)

The time period of the model may be thought of as one year. Thus Eq. (22) assumes that it takes one year before a change in the real interest rate attains its (full) impact on aggregate demand. This is not altogether unrealistic, since it takes time for firms to make new investment plans in response to a change in the cost of capital, and since it is time-consuming for firms in the investment goods sector to produce new equipment and (in particular) new business structures.

Equation (23) further assumes that it takes a year for a change in economic activity to affect the rate of inflation. Again, a certain delay in the impact of a change in activity on inflation is realistic, since nominal wages and prices tend to be sticky in the short run because of the menu costs of wage and price changes, or because workers and firms are temporarily locked into nominal contracts.

The model (22) and (23) captures the stylized empirical fact mentioned above that it typically takes about two years for monetary policy to achieve its full effect on the rate of

---

9. The model and the analysis in this subsection is a simplified version of the one found in Lars E.O. Svensson, 'Inflation Forecast Targeting: Implementing and Monitoring Inflation Targets', *European Economic Review*, **41**, 1997, pp. 1111–1146.

inflation. According to the model it takes one year for a change in the interest rate to affect aggregate demand, and then it takes another year before the resulting change in output and employment forces an adjustment of the pace of inflation.

Suppose now that the government has delegated monetary policy to an independent central bank which has been given the prime mandate of ensuring a low and stable rate of inflation at the target level π^*. As we shall explain in detail in Chapter 22, it may be quite rational for a government to give its central bank such a mandate even if the government also cares about employment stability, that is, even if the 'true' social loss function takes the form (13). And in practice many central banks have in fact been instructed to adopt 'price stability' (defined as a low and stable inflation rate) as their main goal. For example, Article 2 of the statutes for the European Central Bank says that the primary objective of the ECB shall be to maintain price stability. Given this one-dimensional goal, we may specify the central bank's loss function for period j as:

$$SL_j = \frac{1}{2}(\pi_j - \pi^*)^2. \tag{24}$$

The central bank must account for the fact that a change in the interest rate in year t will not affect the inflation rate until year $t + 2$. In year t the bank must therefore choose the nominal interest rate, i_t, so as to minimize the expected value of SL two years in the future. Of course, the bank is also concerned about the losses from the inflation gaps emerging after year $t + 2$, but since it can reset the interest rate at the start of each future period in the light of any new shocks which may have occurred since the previous period, the bank only needs to worry about the effect of i_t on π_{t+2}: the impact of monetary policy on inflation from year $t + 3$ and onwards can be optimized through the choice of future interest rates.[10]

To see how the current nominal interest rate affects the rate of inflation two years later, we note from (23) that $\pi_{t+1} = \pi_t + \gamma(y_t - \bar{y}) + s_{t+1}$. Inserting this into (23) along with (22), we get:

$$\pi_{t+2} = \overbrace{\pi_t + \gamma(y_t - \bar{y}) + s_{t+1}}^{\pi_{t+1}} + \gamma\overbrace{[z_{t+1} - \alpha_2(i_t^p - \pi_t - \bar{r}^*)]}^{y_{t+1}-\bar{y}} + s_{t+2}. \tag{25}$$

When the central bank sets the interest rate for the current period, it can observe the current inflation rate and the current output gap. The bank is also assumed to know the structure of the economy, summarized in Eqs (22) and (23), but obviously it does not know the magnitude of the future supply and demand shocks, s_{t+1}, s_{t+2} and z_{t+1}. Assuming that the stochastic shocks s and z have zero means and covariances and are independently distributed over time, the best that the central bank can do to forecast the inflation rate in year $t + 2$ on the basis of the information available in year t is to assume that the future shock variables, s_{t+1}, s_{t+2} and z_{t+1} in (25), will take their expected values of zero. Hence the best inflation forecast based on (25) is:

$$\pi_{t+2,t}^e = \pi_t + \gamma(y_t - \bar{y}) - \gamma\alpha_2(i_t^p - \pi_t - \bar{r}^*), \tag{26}$$

where $\pi_{t+2,t}^e$ is the central bank's inflation forecast for year $t + 2$, based on the information available in year t. Not surprisingly, the inflation forecast depends on the choice of the current policy interest rate. To minimize the *expected* social loss in year $t + 2$, we see from (24) that the central bank should choose i_t^p so as to ensure:

$$\pi_{t+2,t}^e = \pi^*. \tag{27}$$

Thus the central bank should follow a policy of *inflation forecast targeting*: if the forecast for the inflation rate two years ahead is higher than the inflation target, the nominal interest rate

---

10. To put it another way, by an appropriate future choice of i_{t+1}, i_{t+2}, i_{t+3}, etc., the central bank can always neutralize any potentially undesired effects of i_t on π_{t+3}, π_{t+4}, etc. Hence the bank only needs to account for the effect of i_t on π_{t+2}.

should be raised until $\pi^e_{t+2,t} = \pi^*$. If the opposite is the case, the interest rate should be lowered until the inflation forecast is on target. To find the interest rate which will ensure that the inflation forecast corresponds to the target inflation rate, we insert (27) into (26) and solve for the nominal interest rate to get:

$$i^p_t = \bar{r} + \pi_t + h(\pi_t - \pi^*) + b(y_t - \bar{y}), \qquad h \equiv \frac{1}{\gamma \alpha_2}, \qquad b \equiv \frac{1}{\alpha_2}. \tag{28}$$

Remarkably, we see that interest rate policy should follow a version of the Taylor rule! Indeed, our AS–AD model with an outside lag implies that *the Taylor rule is an optimal monetary policy* provided the coefficients on the inflation and output gaps reflect the way these variables affect the future inflation rate (through the parameters α_2 and γ). It is interesting to note that monetary policy should react to the output gap even though this variable does not enter the social loss function (24). The reason is that the current output gap is a *predictor* of future inflation. For example, if $y_t - \bar{y}$ rises by one unit, we see from (25) that this will, *ceteris paribus*, raise π_{t+1} and π_{t+2} by γ units. But if the central bank reacts to this by raising i^p_t by $1/\alpha_2$ units, it follows from (25) that this would reduce aggregate demand and output in the next period by one unit which in turn would reduce π_{t+2} by γ units. Thus, if the two-year-ahead inflation forecast is initially on target, the central bank can keep it there by raising the interest rate by an appropriate amount in response to a rise in the current output gap.

Similarly, if the current inflation rate were to rise by one percentage point, the (forecast for the) inflation rate two years ahead would, *ceteris paribus*, rise by $1 + \gamma \alpha_2$ percentage points, partly because of the direct impact of the rise in π_t on inflation expectations for years $t + 1$ and $t + 2$, and partly because of the indirect impact (captured by the term $\gamma \alpha_2$) through the fall in the real interest rate and the resulting increase in output in year $t + 1$. If it raises the current interest rate by $1 + h = (1 + \gamma \alpha_2)/\gamma \alpha_2$ units in response to the unit increase in π_t, we see from (25) that the central bank can neutralize the increase in π_{t+2}.

Let us draw some lessons from the above analysis:

THE OUTSIDE LAG, INFLATION FORECAST TARGETING AND THE TAYLOR RULE

The outside lag in monetary policy is the period from the time the central bank changes its policy rate until the (maximum) impact on the economy is felt. A central bank charged with the responsibility to maintain a low and stable inflation rate should target a **forecast** for the future inflation rate within a time horizon corresponding to the outside lag, adjusting the policy rate until the inflation forecast corresponds to the target inflation rate. This insight is reflected in the contemporary practice of many central banks who often justify their interest rate decisions by reference to inflation forecasts for the next couple of years, published in so-called inflation reports. A policy of inflation forecast targeting can lead to a version of the Taylor rule for monetary policy in which the coefficients on the current output and inflation gaps depend on the way these gaps affect the future inflation rate. This may help to explain the empirical finding that numerous central banks appear to follow some variant of the Taylor rule.

20.3   **Monetary stabilization policy in practice: Alan Greenspan, John Taylor and the financial crisis of 2007–09**

The monetary policy experience of the USA during the past half-century provides a good illustration of some of the policy principles discussed above. One main guideline is the so-called Taylor principle that the policy interest rate should vary more than one-to-one

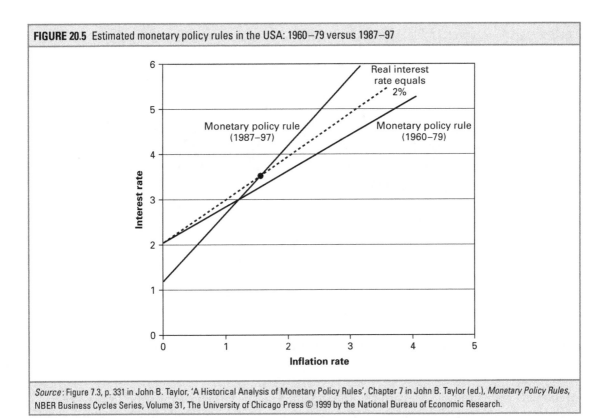

FIGURE 20.5 Estimated monetary policy rules in the USA: 1960–79 versus 1987–97

Source: Figure 7.3, p. 331 in John B. Taylor, 'A Historical Analysis of Monetary Policy Rules', Chapter 7 in John B. Taylor (ed.), *Monetary Policy Rules*, NBER Business Cycles Series, Volume 31, The University of Chicago Press © 1999 by the National Bureau of Economic Research.

with the rate of inflation, that is, the coefficient h on the inflation gap should be positive, as shown in the monetary policy rule (28).

The danger of choosing a negative h is illustrated by the two diagrams below. Figure 20.5 shows the estimated reaction of the nominal short-term policy interest rate to the rate of inflation in the USA for the two periods 1960–79 and 1987–97. The slopes of the two solid straight lines reflect the estimates of the coefficient $1 + h$ in the Taylor rule $i_t^p = \bar{r}^* + \pi_t + h(\pi_t - \pi^*) + b(y_t - \bar{y})$ in the two periods. We see that $1 + h < 1$ in 1960–79, implying a negative value of h. In other words, in this period a rise in inflation was typically allowed to reduce the *real* interest rate, and vice versa. Thus monetary policy did not succeed in curbing aggregate demand when inflation was rising during a boom period; nor did it systematically support aggregate demand during recessions when inflation tended to fall. By contrast, during the later period 1987–97 we see from Fig. 20.5 that h became positive, so in this period the short-term real interest rate did in fact rise and fall with the rate of inflation. The response of the policy interest rate to the output gap also increased between the two periods considered. A study by John Taylor found that the coefficient b on the output gap in the interest rate reaction function of the US Federal Reserve Bank doubled from about 0.25 in the first period to about 0.5 during the second period. At the same time the coefficient h on the inflation gap rose from around −0.25 to 0.5.[11] Other things equal, one would therefore expect the business cycle to be less volatile in the 1987–97 period than during the period 1960–79. Figure 20.6 clearly confirms this expectation.

In the intervening period 1980–86 not shown in Fig. 20.5, US monetary policy moved from being 'dovish' to being very 'hawkish' on inflation, reflecting the strong determination

---

11. See John B. Taylor: 'The Explanatory Power of Monetary Policy Rules'. The Adam Smith Lecture. Annual Meeting of the National Association of Business Economics, September 10, San Francisco. Available at: www. stanford.edu/~johntayl/

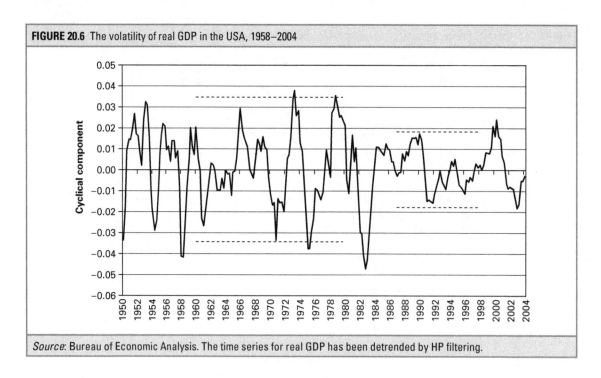

FIGURE 20.6 The volatility of real GDP in the USA, 1958–2004

Source: Bureau of Economic Analysis. The time series for real GDP has been detrended by HP filtering.

of the new Federal Reserve Board Chairman Paul Volcker to reduce inflation from the very high levels experienced during the 1970s. During this 'Volcker disinflation' period the short-term interest rate rose sharply above the rate prescribed by a Taylor rule with coefficients $h = b = 0.5$. This reversal of monetary policy was a main factor behind the deep US recession of 1981–82 recorded in Fig. 20.6, but Paul Volcker did succeed in permanently lowering the actual and expected inflation rate.

The transition to a less volatile business cycle after the mid-1980s is often referred to as 'The Great Moderation'. A lot of the credit for this improvement in macroeconomic stability has been ascribed to Alan Greenspan who became Chairman of the Federal Reserve Board from the start of 1987 when the Fed began to react more strongly and systematically to the output and inflation gaps, in accordance with the Taylor rule. When Alan Greenspan retired from the Federal Reserve in the beginning of 2006, he was hailed as one of the greatest central bankers the world has ever seen, mainly because the US economy experienced only two very short and mild recessions during his long term as chair of the Fed. But more recently John Taylor and several other economists have criticized the Fed's interest rate policy from 2003 to 2005 for having contributed to the severe financial and economic crisis of 2007–09.

To understand this criticism, take a look at Fig. 20.7. The figure shows the actual US policy interest rate (the Federal Funds rate) compared to the (smoothed) time path for the interest rate prescribed by the standard Taylor rule (with $h = b = 0.5$) that had worked so well during most of the Great Moderation. We see that the actual interest rate from late 2002 to 2006 was considerably below the 'Taylor rate'. The motivation for the low-interest-rate policy of this period was that the Fed worried about the danger of deflation, as inflation fell to very low levels in the aftermath of the bursting of the 'dot-com' stock market bubble (see Fig. 14.2) and the 2001 recession. Apparently the Fed was anxious to avoid falling into a Japanese-style deflation trap (see Fig. 19.4).

But the low-interest-rate policy contributed significantly to the record increase in US house prices between 2003 and 2006 and the resulting construction boom. The solid line in Fig. 20.8 illustrates the boom–bust cycle in US construction activity, measured by the number of new housing starts. The upper dotted line shows the number of housing starts

FIGURE 20.7 The Taylor rate versus the actual policy interest rate in the USA

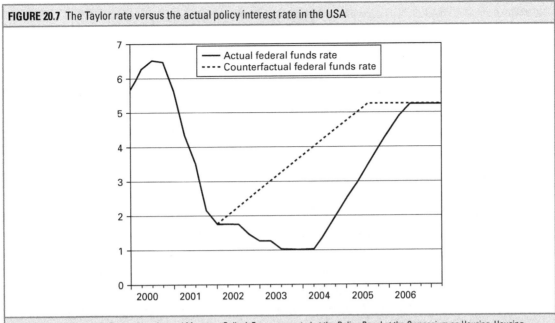

Source: Figure 1 in John B. Taylor: 'Housing and Monetary Policy'. Paper presented at the Policy Panel at the Symposium on Housing, Housing Finance, and Monetary Policy sponsored by the Federal Reserve Bank of Kansas City in Jackson Hole, Wyoming, September 2007. Available at: www.stanford.edu/~johntayl/

FIGURE 20.8 Actual and estimated housing starts in the USA

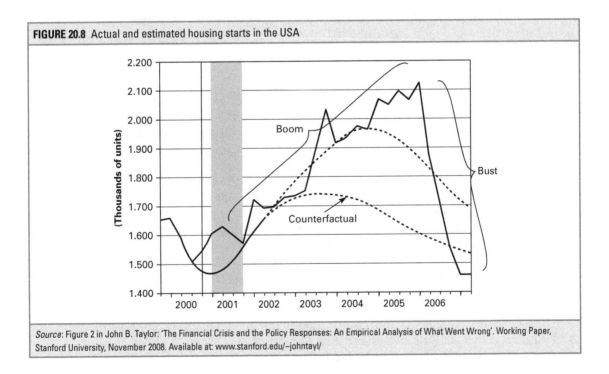

Source: Figure 2 in John B. Taylor: 'The Financial Crisis and the Policy Responses: An Empirical Analysis of What Went Wrong'. Working Paper, Stanford University, November 2008. Available at: www.stanford.edu/~johntayl/

predicted by a simple regression equation with the Federal Funds rate as the explanatory variable. We see that the Fed's interest rate policy can explain a large part of the boom–bust pattern of residential investment. The lower dotted line in Fig. 20.8 (labelled 'Counterfactual') shows the number of housing starts predicted by the regression equation if the Federal Funds rate had followed the Taylor rule illustrated in Fig. 20.7. We see that in such a counterfactual scenario the housing cycle would most likely have been significantly

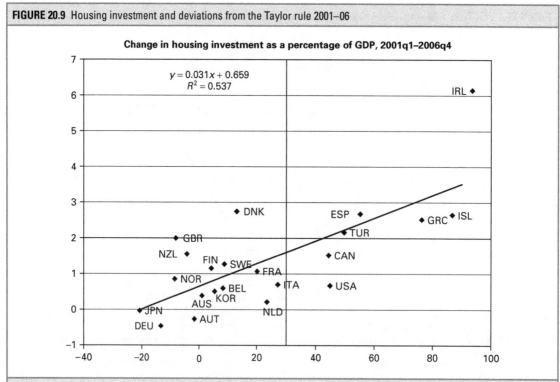

FIGURE 20.9 Housing investment and deviations from the Taylor rule 2001–06

Change in housing investment as a percentage of GDP, 2001q1–2006q4

$$y = 0.031x + 0.659$$
$$R^2 = 0.537$$

Horizontal axis: Sum of differences between the Taylor interest rate and the actual short-term interest rate, 2001q3–2006q4.

Source: Figure 9 in Rudiger Ahrend, Boris Cournède and Robert Price: 'Monetary Policy, Market Excesses and Financial Turmoil'. OECD Economics Department Working Paper No. 597, March 2008.

dampened. Since the strong increase in the supply of new housing units was a major factor behind the drop in housing prices from 2006 (see Fig. 14.17) – which in turn triggered the severe financial crisis starting in mid-2007 – many economists argue that the Fed's deviation from the Taylor rule unintendedly helped to pave the way for the crisis.

Many other countries also followed a loose monetary policy in the run-up to the financial crisis. These countries typically experienced the strongest housing booms and also suffered from the largest housing busts during the crisis. The horizontal axis in Fig. 20.9 measures the accumulated difference between the short-term interest rate prescribed by a standard Taylor rule and the actual short-term rate, calculated over the period from the third quarter of 2001 to the end of 2006. The greater this measure, the looser the country's monetary policy has been relative to the Taylor standard. The vertical axis in Fig. 20.9 shows the change in the ratio of housing investment to GDP over the same period. The regression line in the diagram reveals a clear positive correlation between the looseness of monetary policy and the rise in construction activity prior to the crisis.

Although many complex factors contributed to the financial and economic crisis of 2007–09, the above analysis suggests that an inappropriate monetary policy in many countries can help to explain why the crisis became so severe.

20.4 Fiscal stabilization policy

Fiscal versus monetary stabilization policy

Having studied monetary stabilization policy at length, we will now discuss how *fiscal* policy may help to stabilize the economy. Our AS–AD model from Chapter 18 includes two fiscal policy instruments, namely (the log of) government spending on goods and services (g) and the income tax rate τ. When we derived the AD curve in Chapter 16, we assumed for simplicity that the income tax rate was kept constant, but now we want to allow for the possibility that the tax rate may deviate temporarily from the trend level $\bar{\tau}$ needed to ensure long-run government budget balance. Starting from a long-run equilibrium, a unit rise in the income tax rate reduces disposable income by the amount $\bar{Y}$. On impact, private consumption therefore falls by the amount $C_Y\bar{Y}$, where C_Y is the marginal propensity to consume, but when the multiplier effect of the initial drop in demand is allowed for, the total fall in aggregate demand induced by the tax increase will be $\tilde{m}C_Y\bar{Y}$, where $\tilde{m}$ is the Keynesian multiplier. Measured relative to the initial level of GDP, a tax increase of magnitude $\tau - \bar{\tau}$ will thus reduce aggregate demand by the amount $\tilde{m}C_Y \cdot (\tau - \bar{\tau})$. Adding this 'tax shock' to total aggregate demand, the log-linearized goods market equilibrium condition derived in Ch. 16 modifies to

$$y - \bar{y} = \alpha_1(g - \bar{g}) - \tilde{m}C_Y(\tau - \bar{\tau}) - \alpha_2(i^p - \pi - \bar{r}^\star) + v - \alpha_2(\rho - \bar{\rho}),$$

$$\alpha_1 \equiv \tilde{m}\left(\frac{\bar{G}}{\bar{Y}}\right), \quad \alpha_2 \equiv -\tilde{m}\left(\frac{D_r}{\bar{Y}}\right), \quad v \equiv \tilde{m}\left(\frac{\bar{\varepsilon}D_\varepsilon}{\bar{Y}}\right)(\ln\varepsilon - \ln\bar{\varepsilon}), \quad \tilde{m} \equiv \frac{1}{1 - (1-\tau)C_Y - I_Y}, \tag{29}$$

where the 'confidence' variable ε reflects the expected rate of future income growth and $\rho - \bar{\rho}$ is the risk premium shock. From (29) we see that a 1 per cent rise in government spending on goods and services has the same impact on aggregate demand as an interest rate cut of α_1/α_2 percentage points. It follows that if fiscal policy makers have the same information on the state of the economy as the central bank and react with the same time lag to this information, a fiscal policy using the policy instrument g cannot achieve any stabilizing effect that could not have been achieved via monetary policy, or vice versa (assuming that monetary policy is not constrained by the zero bound on the interest rate).

The assumption that the fiscal and monetary authorities share the same information on the state of the macro economy is plausible, so fiscal and monetary policy is probably subject to roughly the same recognition lag. However, the *implementation lag* is generally assumed to be shorter for monetary than for fiscal policy. The reason is that the level and structure of taxation and public expenditure has important effects on resource allocation and income distribution, so large and abrupt changes in these variables may have considerable negative effects on the welfare of (some) citizens, even if they help to stabilize the macro economy. Hence changes in fiscal policy may require time-consuming political negotiations whereas the central bank can in principle change its policy interest rate very quickly after having recognized the need for a change in the monetary policy stance. On the other hand, once a change in government consumption or investment has been implemented, it has an immediate and direct impact on aggregate demand, whereas we have seen that a change in the central bank interest rate only achieves its maximum impact on demand with a considerable time lag. Thus the *outside lag* is typically longer in monetary than in fiscal policy.

As an alternative to public spending on goods and services, fiscal policy may be conducted via the choice of the tax rate τ. As emphasized in Chapter 16, even if fiscal policy is passive, the tax rate plays an important role as an *automatic stabilizer* which helps to dampen the impact of shocks to aggregate demand by reducing the size of the Keynesian multiplier. But sometimes governments also use temporary changes in tax rates as an active tool of fiscal stabilization policy. From (29) we see that τ affects aggregate demand via its impact on private consumption, an impact which depends on the marginal propensity to consume, C_Y. Again it is possible to replicate this fiscal impact on aggregate demand by an appropriate change in the policy interest rate, provided the zero bound on the interest rate is not binding. However, a change in the tax rate is likely to impact the economy's supply side as well. In particular, there is considerable evidence that a higher average tax rate on labour

income tends to drive up the pre-tax wage rate.[12] This evidence is easily reconciled with
the theory of wage formation presented in Chapter 17 if we account for the fact that trade
unions are likely to focus on the *after-tax* rather than the pre-tax wage rates accruing to their
members. For simplicity, we have assumed above that the tax rate τ is levied only on factor
incomes (wages and profits) but not on transfer incomes (this is just equivalent to assuming
that transfers are paid out on a net-of-tax basis). Thus, if b^u is the real rate of unemployment
benefit and unions care about after-tax rather than pre-tax wages, we may respecify the wage
setting equation (11) in Chapter 17 as follows:

$$W(1-\tau) = P^e \cdot m^w b^u \quad \Leftrightarrow \quad W = P^e \cdot m^{wn} b^u > 0, \qquad m^{wn} \equiv \frac{m^w}{1-\tau}. \tag{30}$$

This equation says that unions set the pre-tax nominal wage rate with the purpose of
securing a real after-tax wage rate which is a mark-up over the real rate of unemployment
benefit. In line with Chapter 17 we may assume that the real rate of unemployment benefit
makes up a fraction c of the trend productivity level $\bar{B}$, i.e., $b^u = c\bar{B}$. Thus the only difference
between the analysis in Chapter 17 and the analysis here is that while Chapter 17 assumed
$W = P^e m^w c\bar{B}$, we are now assuming $W = P^e m^{wn} c\bar{B}$, where m^{wn} is defined in (30). All results in
Chapter 17 therefore carry over to the present context if we just replace m^w by m^{wn} in the
relevant equations. Making this modification to Eq. (56) in Chapter 17, using the definition
of m^{wn}, and assuming static inflation expectations ($\pi^e = \pi_{-1}$), we obtain the following short-run
aggregate supply curve:

$$\pi = \pi_{-1} + \left(\frac{\alpha}{1-\alpha}\right)(y - \bar{y}) + s, \qquad s \equiv \ln\left(\frac{m^p}{\bar{m}^p}\right) + \ln\left(\frac{m^w}{\bar{m}^w}\right) - \frac{\ln(B/\bar{B})}{1-\alpha} - \ln\left(\frac{1-\tau}{1-\bar{\tau}}\right). \tag{31}$$

From (31) we see that a temporary tax cut driving τ below its trend value will work like a
favourable supply shock which reduces inflationary pressure by moderating pre-tax wage
claims.

Figure 20.10 illustrates the short-run effect of a temporary tax cut when the economy is
initially in recession at point E_0. According to (29) the tax cut will shift the AD curve
upwards while (31) implies that the SRAS curve will shift down. Thus a new short-run
equilibrium is established at point E_1 where output is unambiguously higher whereas the
inflation rate may be either higher or lower, depending on the relative magnitude of the
shifts in the AD curve and the SRAS curve.

A temporary tax cut will generate a temporary government budget deficit, thereby
increasing the stock of government debt. As we discussed in Chapter 15, the impact of a
temporary tax cut on private consumption will be dampened if consumers anticipate that
they will have to pay higher taxes in the future to enable the government to service the higher
debt. Moreover, the shorter the expected duration of the tax cut, the smaller is the impact on
human wealth and permanent income, so the smaller is the effect on aggregate demand.
However, in any given time period some consumers are likely to be credit-constrained, and
these people will want to spend all of a tax cut here and now.

Figure 20.10 highlights the fact that tax policies will influence the economy's supply side
as well as the demand side. Many forms of government expenditure may also have supply
side effects. For example, government spending on health and education may affect the size
and the productivity of the labour force; day care subsidies may encourage labour force
participation, and public infrastructure investment may increase the productivity of capital

12. Much of this evidence is surveyed in Peter Birch Sørensen: 'Public Finance Solutions to the European
Unemployment Problem?', *Economic Policy*, October 1997, pp. 223–264. This article also explains the
theoretical reasons to expect a positive effect of the average labour income tax rate (defined as the total tax
burden on a worker's labour income relative to his pre-tax earnings) on pre-tax wage rates in imperfect labour
markets.

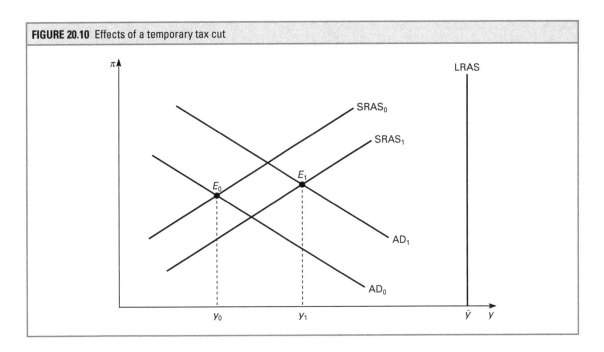

FIGURE 20.10 Effects of a temporary tax cut

and labour. However, these types of supply side effects are usually assumed to work with a considerable time lag.

By influencing the level of interest rates, monetary policy may also affect the supply of labour. In particular, if the interest rate is unusually high, some workers may increase their labour supply to earn and save more and thereby take advantage of the high return to saving, and vice versa. However, such interest rate effects on labour supply are not very well documented and are usually believed to be small. Of course, since changes in interest rates affect the level of investment, they will also affect the economy's productive capacity, but over time such supply side effects of short-term fluctuations in interest rates will tend to wash out.

In any case, it should be clear that monetary and fiscal policy have different effects on the economy's supply side. Since the two types of policy are not equivalent, it could be argued that there is a role for fiscal as well as monetary policy in stabilizing the economy. Given the impact of fiscal policy on the AD and AS curves, one may derive the optimal fiscal policy in the same way as we derived the optimal monetary policy rules in Section 20.2. Since the general methodology has already been explained in the previous section, we leave this analysis as an exercise (see Exercise 3).

However, as already noted, government tax and spending policies serve many important goals other than that of stabilizing the macro economy. Hence it may be socially costly to change these policies abruptly in response to changes in private sector economic activity. Also, because fiscal policy may involve a long implementation lag, a fiscal policy intervention may take effect at a time when the state of the business cycle is rather different from what was assumed when the intervention was decided. Indeed, as we shall see later in this section, the historical record indicates that the timing of active fiscal policy changes has generally been poor from a stabilization perspective. Many economists therefore believe that, apart from allowing the automatic fiscal stabilizers to work, fiscal policy should focus on the government's long-run goals regarding resource allocation and income distribution, thus leaving the task of active short-run macroeconomic stabilization to monetary policy.

In summary:

FISCAL STABILIZATION POLICY IN NORMAL TIMES

Government spending on goods and services may have important supply side effects in the long run, but in the short run it works mainly by affecting aggregate demand. Assuming that the policy interest rate is not constrained, public spending policies therefore cannot achieve any short-term stabilization effect that could not have been attained through monetary policy. However, a fiscal policy involving a cut (rise) in the net tax rate has a positive (negative) effect on aggregate supply as well as aggregate demand and hence is not equivalent to monetary policy. But since the implementation lag in fiscal policy tends to be long, many economists argue that the task of short-term stabilization policy is best left to monetary policy makers whereas fiscal policy should focus on the government's longer-term goals regarding resource allocation and income distribution.

Yet, while this division of labour between monetary and fiscal policy makers may work well in normal times, there may be times when monetary policy cannot handle macroeconomic stabilization on its own, as we shall see in the next subsection.

Depression economics: fiscal policy in a liquidity trap

We have already suggested how monetary stabilization policy may become impotent: if the economy is hit by a big negative demand shock causing a large drop in output and driving inflation close to zero, the nominal interest rate prescribed by monetary policy rules like (20) and (28) may be *negative*. But since the nominal interest rate cannot fall below zero, it follows that monetary policy cannot stimulate aggregate demand to the extent needed. Since the days of John Maynard Keynes such a situation is described as a 'liquidity trap', because the public's demand for money and other liquid assets is so large relative to their demand for real assets that the level of real investment is insufficient to pull the economy out of the recession. Note that even though the central bank loses its ability to boost demand via its interest rate policy, this does not mean that monetary policy becomes unimportant in a liquidity trap. On the contrary, such deep recessions often coincide with financial crises where the central bank plays a crucial role as a lender of last resort, providing financial institutions and the public with the liquidity and credit that private markets fail to supply. But although this vital policy of the central bank may help to prevent a complete meltdown of the economy, it does not by itself raise aggregate demand to the level needed to bring the economy back to the MPR curve that represents the optimal trade-off between the output and inflation gaps. Hence fiscal policy must come to the rescue.

During the Great Depression of the 1930s a lot of countries fell into the liquidity trap and almost all of them failed to adopt the appropriate countercyclical fiscal policy, because the prevailing fiscal orthodoxy of those days prescribed a balanced government budget as the only responsible policy. The Keynesian Revolution in macroeconomics following the publication of Keynes' *General Theory* in 1936 made countercyclical fiscal policy intellectually respectable, but the marked reduction in business cycle volatility after the Second World War generated a widespread belief that liquidity traps were a thing of the past. Thus, at the same time as deficit spending during recessions became the accepted norm, most economists gradually came to see monetary policy as the main tool of stabilization policy, for the reasons explained in the previous subsection. But in recent years the liquidity trap has come back with a vengeance! In Fig. 19.4 we have already seen how deflationary tendencies in the world's second largest economy (Japan) have kept the policy interest rate close to zero for a long time. And during the financial and economic crisis of 2007–09 central banks in many other countries cut their policy rates to near-zero levels, as shown in Fig. 20.11.

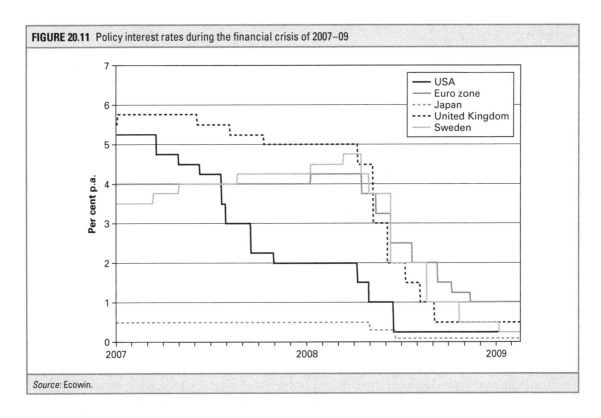

FIGURE 20.11 Policy interest rates during the financial crisis of 2007–09

Source: Ecowin.

Let us now analyse the effects of fiscal policy in a recession/depression where monetary policy makers have hit the zero-interest-rate floor. Going back to (29) and setting $i^p = 0$, we see that in such a liquidity trap the AD curve collapses to:

$$y - \bar{y} = v + \alpha_1(g - \bar{g}) - \tilde{m}C_Y(\tau - \bar{\tau}) + \alpha_2(\pi + \bar{r}^*) - \alpha_2(\rho - \bar{\rho}) \quad \Leftrightarrow$$

$$\pi = \rho - \bar{\rho} - \bar{r}^* + \frac{1}{\alpha_2}[y - \bar{y} - v - \alpha_1(g - \bar{g}) + \tilde{m}C_Y(\tau - \bar{\tau})]. \tag{32}$$

The unusual and striking feature of (32) is that the AD curve is now upward sloping! The reason is that, in a liquidity trap where the nominal interest rate is fixed at zero, a higher inflation rate necessarily reduces the real interest rate, thereby stimulating aggregate demand.

The short-run aggregate supply curve is still given by (31). Figure 20.12 combines this SRAS curve with the AD curve implied by (32). According to (31) the slope of the SRAS curve is $\gamma \equiv \alpha / (1 - \alpha)$, while (32) shows that the slope of the AD curve is $1/\alpha_2$. In Fig. 20.12 we have assumed that the AD curve is steeper than the SRAS curve. This accords with the parameter values reported in Chapter 18 where we saw that $\gamma \approx 0.075$ and $1/\alpha_2 \approx 1/5.76 \approx 0.174$ are plausible values in a short-run business cycle model with a time period equal to one quarter. In the initial equilibrium E_0 in Fig. 20.12, public spending is assumed to be at its trend level. As shown by the first equation in (32), for any given inflation rate, a rise in public spending on goods and services ($\hat{g} > 0$) will boost aggregate demand, thus shifting the AD curve to the right. Fig. 20.12 assumes that at the time when public spending goes up, inflation and hence inflation expectations have been stable for a while so that the SRAS curve does not shift between periods 0 and 1. In period 1 a new short-run equilibrium is therefore established at point E_1 where both output and inflation have increased. Note the unusual result that the rise in inflation actually helps to lift the level of output. If firms had been willing to satisfy the increased demand without any increase in prices, output would only have risen to the point E_1' in Fig. 20.12, but since a rise in output drives up the marginal

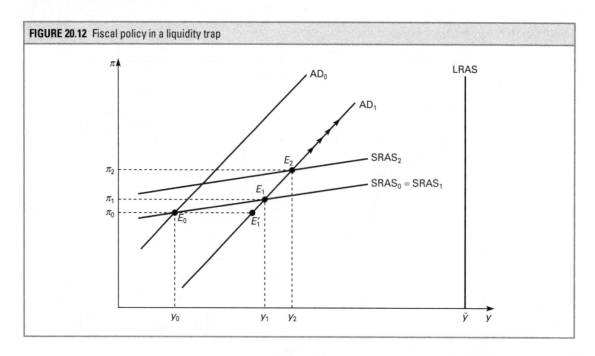

FIGURE 20.12 Fiscal policy in a liquidity trap

cost of production, the rate of inflation actually goes up, thereby reducing the real rate of interest and boosting aggregate demand, since the nominal interest rate is trapped at its zero bound. To satisfy this additional increase in demand, output must increase further from E_1' to E_1.

Notice also the benign dynamics triggered by the fiscal expansion illustrated in Fig. 20.12. As the rate of inflation rises from π_0 to π_1, the assumption of static inflation expectations implies that the SRAS curve shifts upwards from the level $SRAS_1$ to $SRAS_2$ between periods 1 and 2, so in period 2 there is a further rise in output as a result of a further drop in the real interest rate caused by yet another rise in inflation. As indicated by the arrows in Fig. 20.12, these expansionary dynamic effects of a rise in actual and expected inflation will continue until the economy escapes from the liquidity trap, that is, until output and inflation have risen to levels at which the monetary policy rule once again calls for a positive nominal interest rate. At that time the Taylor principle will be restored, i.e. the central bank will start to raise the nominal interest more than one-to-one with the rate of inflation, and the non-standard AD curve defined by (32) will be replaced by the normal downward-sloping AD curve (not shown in Fig. 20.12).

This analysis shows that active fiscal policy can play a critical role as a means of pulling the economy out of recession if monetary policy has been caught in a liquidity trap. However, the fiscal history of several OECD countries also suggests that there may be times when expansionary fiscal policy is not very effective in stimulating economic activity. In particular, if the public budget deficit and/or the level of public debt are already high and rapidly increasing, a fiscal expansion involving a further increase in the budget deficit may create increased uncertainty about future fiscal policy and cause doubts about the government's ability to keep the deficit under control. As a result of such increased uncertainty, the private sector's propensity to consume and invest may be weakened, thus offsetting the effect of the fiscal expansion on aggregate demand. Conversely, in a situation where the public finances are widely seen as being out of control, a fiscal tightening may give a boost to private sector confidence and paradoxically it may thereby stimulate demand, as countries like Denmark and Ireland experienced in the 1980s.[13] An

---

13. The experience of Denmark, Ireland and a number of other OECD countries with fiscal adjustments in times of crisis is analysed in Alberto Alesina and Silvia Ardagna: 'Fiscal Adjustments – Why They Can Be Expansionary', *Economic Policy*, October 1998, pp. 478–545.

expansionary fiscal policy therefore tends to be more effective in dragging the economy out of recession when the public finances are reasonably sound at the outset. To recap:

FISCAL POLICY IN A LIQUIDITY TRAP

When the economy is hit by a large negative demand shock, it may become stuck in a liquidity trap where the nominal policy interest rate reaches its zero bound so that monetary policy cannot further stimulate aggregate demand. In this situation a fiscal expansion can help to pull the economy out of recession, in part via its direct positive impact on aggregate demand, and partly by increasing the rate of inflation and thereby lowering the real rate of interest. The positive effect on aggregate demand is likely to be greater when the initial budget deficit and public debt are not too high.

20.5 Has fiscal policy been stabilizing?

During the international financial and economic crisis of 2008–09 a lot of countries resorted to large fiscal stimulus packages, against the background of near-zero central bank policy interest rates indicating that even a highly expansionary monetary policy was not sufficient to prevent a deep economic downturn. Although economists were (and still are) debating the size of the various fiscal multipliers, there is widespread agreement that active fiscal policy in 2008–09 helped to prevent an even greater loss of output and employment.

But has fiscal policy generally been countercyclical in a longer historical context, involving a tightening of policy when economic activity rises and a relaxation when the business cycle turns down? A tighter fiscal policy will appear as an improvement in the public budget balance, but we cannot measure the stance of fiscal policy by simply looking at the actual budget balance, since the budget deficit will automatically decrease when output and employment rise, due to the automatic stabilizers such as the marginal rates of direct and indirect tax, and the rates of unemployment benefits and social assistance benefits. These policy instruments imply that public revenue automatically rises and that public expenditures on transfer payments automatically fall when an economic expansion increases the tax base and reduces the number of unemployed workers. In this way the public budget improves even if fiscal policy makers remain passive, undertaking no active changes in any policy instrument. For fiscal policy to be actively countercyclical, policy makers must implement an increase in some tax rate or a cut in public spending that goes beyond the automatic fall in expenditure.

To measure such deliberate and active changes in fiscal policy, economists have developed measures of the so-called structural primary budget deficit, defined as the deficit which would arise in the primary public budget (the budget excluding net interest payments on the public debt) when economic activity is at its normal trend level. Thus a rise (fall) in the structural deficit indicates that fiscal policy has been relaxed (tightened) through active policy decisions. If $\bar{T}_t$ and $\bar{G}_t$ are the cyclically adjusted (or 'structural') levels of tax revenue and primary public spending, respectively, and $\bar{Y}_t$ is the trend level of output (natural output), the structural primary budget deficit as a share of potential output ($\bar{d}_t$) in period t is given by:

$$\bar{d}_t = \frac{\bar{G}_t - \bar{T}_t}{\bar{Y}_t}. \tag{33}$$

The structural levels of revenue and spending may be estimated by correcting the actually observed revenue and spending figures T_t and G_t in the following manner:

$$\frac{\bar{T}_t}{T_t} = \left(\frac{\bar{Y}_t}{Y_t}\right)^{\eta} \quad \Leftrightarrow \quad \ln\bar{T}_t = \ln T_t - \eta(y_t - \bar{y}_t), \qquad \eta > 0, \tag{34}$$

$$\frac{\bar{G}_t}{G_t} = \left(\frac{\bar{Y}_t}{Y_t}\right)^{\lambda} \quad \Leftrightarrow \quad \ln\bar{G}_t = \ln G_t - \lambda(y_t - \bar{y}_t), \qquad \lambda < 0. \tag{35}$$

These specifications account for the fact that tax revenues and public expenditures will, *ceteris paribus*, vary with the output gap, due to the automatic stabilizers. The revenue and spending elasticities η and λ have been estimated by the OECD, using information on the tax-transfer systems of OECD member countries.

Based on these estimates plus its estimates of the output gaps, $y_t - \bar{y}_t$, the OECD has produced time series for the structural budget deficits of its member countries. To study whether fiscal policies in the OECD have followed a procyclical or a countercyclical pattern, one may then estimate a regression equation of the form

$$\bar{d}_t = a_0 + a_1 E_{t-1}[y_t - \bar{y}_t] + a_2 b_{t-1} + a_3 \bar{d}_{t-1} + \varepsilon_t, \tag{36}$$

where ε_t is a white noise random variable, b_{t-1} is last year's stock of public debt, and $E_{t-1}[y_t - \bar{y}_t]$ is the *expected* output gap for the current year, estimated on the basis of relevant information which may include the previous year's output gap. By using the expected rather than the actual output gap as an explanatory variable, one allows for the possibility that fiscal policy decisions may have to be made before the current output gap is known. The rationale for including b_{t-1} and $\bar{d}_{t-1}$ on the right-hand side is that past debt and deficits may impose a constraint on current fiscal policy (for example, a higher inherited stock of debt may induce policy makers to pursue a tighter policy in order to bring down the debt burden). In the present context, we are particularly interested in the sign and magnitude of the coefficient a_1 in (36). If a_1 is negative, the country has tended to follow a countercyclical fiscal policy, as prescribed by economic theory, whereas a positive sign of a_1 indicates that the country's policy has been procyclical, involving more fiscal laxity in times of economic booms.

An analysis following this methodology has been undertaken by economists Antonio Fatas and Ilian Mihov.[14] Table 20.1 shows their estimated values of a_1 for a number of countries for the period 1970–98 (before the formation of monetary union in Europe) and for the period 1999–2007 (after the introduction of the euro). Separate estimates were made for these two subperiods to study whether the institutional framework for fiscal policy in the EMU (the so-called Stability and Growth Pact) has significantly affected the conduct of fiscal policy in the euro countries. Table 20.1 does not provide much support for this hypothesis. We see that both before and after the transition to monetary union many EU member states have followed a mildly *procyclical* fiscal policy, as indicated by the many positive estimates for a_1. In other words, fiscal policy in these countries has tended to *amplify* rather than dampen the business cycle, although this effect is statistically significant only in a few countries. Before 1999 we see that fiscal policy tended to be countercyclical in Australia, Canada and the four Nordic countries. After 1999 this countercyclical policy pattern still prevailed in Finland, Norway and Sweden, but not in Australia, Canada and Denmark. The most remarkable policy change took place in the USA where fiscal policy tended to be mildly procyclical before 1999 but became distinctly countercyclical after that time (with the countercyclical pattern being statistically highly significant). The shift to a countercyclical fiscal policy in the USA and the UK is the main explanation why the sign of the estimated average value of a_1 for all countries as a group changed from positive to negative.

14. See Antonio Fatas and Ilian Mihov: 'The Euro and Fiscal Policy'. National Bureau of Economic Research Working Paper 14722, February 2009. The details of the estimation technique in this paper differ a bit (but not in any important way) from the description above.

TABLE 20.1 The response of the structural primary budget deficit to the expected output gap			
	Estimates of a_1 (t-values in brackets)			
	Before 1999 (1970–98)		After 1999(1999–2007)	
EU countries				
Austria	0.002	(0.017)	0.059	(0.230)
Belgium	0.120	(0.424)	0.223	(1.000)
Denmark	−0.699	(−2.184)	0.242	(0.809)
Finland	−0.128	(−1.219)	−0.829	(−1.603)
France	0.196	(1.690)	−0.155	(−0.752)
Germany	0.212	(1.493)	0.305	(1.406)
Greece	0.429	(0.742)	−0.166	(−0.199)
Ireland	0.174	(0.967)	0.291	(0.507)
Italy	0.435	(2.771)	0.153	(0.595)
Netherlands	0.458	(2.009)	0.246	(1.352)
Portugal	0.119	(1.352)	0.211	(1.327)
Spain	0.088	(1.035)	0.951	(2.109)
Sweden	−1.118	(−2.788)	−0.662	(−1.651)
United Kingdom	0.186	(1.257)	−5.713	(−0.741)
Other OECD Countries				
Australia	−0.170	(−0.759)	2.014	(1.152)
Canada	−0.129	(−1.500)	0.553	(0.944)
Japan	0.072	(0.503)	−0.280	(−0.432)
Norway	−0.091	(−0.645)	−0.091	(−0.187)
United States	0.035	(0.263)	−1.326	(−4.966)
All countries	**0.010**		**−0.209**	

Source: Table 2 in Antonio Fatas and Ilian Mihov, 'The Euro and Fiscal Policy', NBER Working Paper 14722, February 2009.

The fact that fiscal policy has been procyclical rather than countercyclical in many countries may reflect that taxation and public spending serve several important goals other than that of stabilizing the macro economy, as we have already noted. This fact also explains why many economists have expressed scepticism regarding the possibility of using fiscal policy as a successful tool for countercyclical stabilization policy, given the way parliamentary political processes tend to work. But as we have seen, in times of severe crisis, when monetary policy may get caught in the liquidity trap, fiscal policy may play an important role as the only workable tool of demand management.

20.6 Summary

1. A monetary or fiscal policy rule prescribes how the instruments of stabilization policy should be set, given the observed state of the economy. Following a fixed policy rule may help policy makers to establish credibility and to increase the predictability of economic policy so as to minimize welfare-reducing expectational errors in the private sector. The alternative to fixed policy rules is discretionary policy. Under discretion, policy makers may conduct monetary and fiscal policy in any way they believe will help advance the goals of stabilization policy, taking account of any special

circumstances which might prevail. Discretion allows more flexibility than rules, but typically at the cost of reduced credibility and predictability. The evidence suggests that the monetary policy of the most important central banks is fairly well described by some form of Taylor rule, although policy makers never mechanically follow a fixed rule.

2. When the central bank can directly observe and instantaneously react to the different types of supply and demand shocks and inflation expectations are firmly anchored by the announced inflation target, the policy interest rate should react directly to the various shocks. Demand shocks should be perfectly stabilized since they do not raise a dilemma between output stability and inflation stability. Supply shocks do raise such a dilemma and should be allowed to affect both output and inflation. A productivity shock should be permitted to have a greater impact on output than a mark-up shock with the same direct cost effect.

3. In practice the central bank does not have perfect information about the current shocks hitting the economy, and even if it had, it would face a credibility problem if it pursued an output target exceeding natural output, since such a policy will have an inflation bias undermining the public's trust in the announced inflation target. Central banks therefore seek to stabilize output around its natural rate, leaving to government and parliament the task of implementing structural policies that may move natural output closer to the efficient output level.

4. When the central bank can only observe the output and inflation gaps but cannot directly observe the shocks currently hitting the economy, and when the private sector's inflation expectations are static, the optimal monetary policy takes the form of an inflation targeting regime where the policy interest rate is raised when inflation exceeds its target rate, and vice versa.

5. The outside lag in monetary policy is the period from the time the central bank changes its policy rate until the (maximum) impact on the economy is felt. A central bank charged with the responsibility to maintain a low and stable inflation rate should target a forecast for the future inflation rate within a time horizon corresponding to the outside lag, adjusting the policy rate until the inflation forecast corresponds to the target inflation rate. A policy of inflation forecast targeting can lead to a version of the Taylor rule in which the coefficients on the current output and inflation gaps depend on the way these gaps affect the future inflation rate.

6. Government spending on goods and services may have important supply side effects in the long run, but in the short run they work mainly by affecting aggregate demand. If the policy interest rate is not constrained, public spending policies therefore cannot achieve any short-term stabilization effect that could not have been attained through monetary policy. However, a fiscal policy involving a cut (rise) in the net tax rate has a positive (negative) effect on aggregate supply as well as aggregate demand and hence is not equivalent to monetary policy. But since the implementation lag in fiscal policy tends to be long, many economists argue that in normal times the task of short-term stabilization policy is best left to monetary policy makers whereas fiscal policy should focus on the government's longer-term goals regarding resource allocation and income distribution. Moreover, even if fiscal policy is not actively changed in response to changes in economic activity, the automatic stabilizers (income and consumption tax rates, unemployment benefits etc.) built into the public budget will dampen the activity effects of shocks by reducing the size of the Keynesian multiplier.

7. However, when the economy is hit by a large negative demand shock, it may become stuck in a liquidity trap where the nominal policy interest rate hits its zero bound so that monetary policy cannot further stimulate aggregate demand. In this situation a fiscal expansion can help to pull the economy out of recession, in part via its direct

> effect on aggregate demand, and partly by increasing the rate of inflation and thereby
> lowering the real rate of interest. The positive effect on aggregate demand may be
> dampened if the budget deficit and/or the level of public debt is already high and
> rapidly increasing, since in this case a further deterioration of the public finances may
> create uncertainty and fears of large future tax increases.

20.7 Exercises

Exercise 1. The optimal monetary policy of a credible central bank with limited information

Consider a central bank with an output target equal to natural output and an inflation target
equal to π^*. The bank seeks to minimize a social loss function of the following form (equal
to Eq. (13) in the main text):

$$SL = \frac{a_\ell}{2(1-\alpha)}\hat{y}^2 + \frac{a_\pi}{2}\hat{\pi}^2, \qquad \hat{y} \equiv y - \bar{y}, \qquad \hat{\pi} \equiv \pi - \pi^*. \tag{37}$$

The central bank has full credibility, so the public's expected inflation rate is firmly
anchored by the announced inflation target, that is, $\pi^e = \pi^*$. The economy's supply side is
therefore given by the following AS curve (equivalent to (3) in the main text), where s
captures mark-up shocks as well as productivity shocks:

$$\hat{\pi} = \left(\frac{\alpha}{1-\alpha}\right)\hat{y} + s. \tag{38}$$

When $\pi^e_{+1} = \pi^*$, the goods market equilibrium condition is given by Eq. (9) in the main text.
However, the central bank cannot directly observe the current demand and supply shocks,
so the best thing it can do when it sets the policy rate for the current period is to assume
that the current demand shocks will take their mean value of zero ($\hat{g} = v = \hat{\rho} = 0$). From (9)
the central bank therefore expects that the link between the current policy rate and the
current output gap is given by:

$$\hat{y} = -\alpha_2(i^p - \pi^* - \bar{r}^*). \tag{39}$$

1. Use (37) and (38) to derive the *MPR* curve showing the optimal combination of the output
   and inflation gaps. Does your expression for the *MPR* curve differ from Eq. (18) in the main
   text? Comment and explain.

2. Use your result in Question 1 along with (39) to derive the central bank's optimal interest rate
   rule. Compare this rule to Eq. (20) in the main text and explain similarities and differences.

3. Use your result in Question 2 plus Eq. (9) in the text to derive an expression for the economy's
   AD curve. Explain how the AD curve relates to the *MPR* curve.

4. Suppose the economy is in long-run equilibrium in period zero but is hit by an unfavourable
   temporary supply shock in period 1. Use a $(\hat{y}, \hat{\pi})$-diagram like Fig. 20.3 to illustrate the
   equilibrium positions of the economy in periods 0, 1 and 2, assuming that the supply shock
   disappears again in period 2. Explain the similarities and differences between your findings
   and the effects illustrated in Fig. 20.3.

5. Suppose the economy is in long-run equilibrium in period zero but is hit by a negative
   temporary demand shock in period 1. Use a $(\hat{y}, \hat{\pi})$-diagram like Fig. 20.4 to illustrate the

equilibrium positions of the economy in periods 0, 1 and 2, assuming that the demand shock goes away in period 2. Explain the similarities and differences between your findings and the effects illustrated in Fig. 20.4.

Exercise 2. The outside lag and inflation forecast targeting

Consider a central bank which has been charged with the main task of securing a low and stable inflation rate at the target level π^*. In accordance with Eq. (24) in the main text, the bank thus seeks to minimize the following loss function for any period j:

$$SL_j = \frac{1}{2}(\pi_j - \pi^*).\tag{40}$$

The private sector's inflation expectations are static ($\pi_t^e = \pi_{t-1}$), so the real policy interest rate in period t is $i_t^p - \pi_{t+1}^e = i_t^p - \pi_t$. Hence the goods market equilibrium condition for period t is (in our usual notation):

$$y_t - \bar{y} = z_t - \alpha_2(i_t^p - \pi_t - \bar{r}^*).\tag{41}$$

Because of short-run nominal wage and price rigidities, we assume that it takes one period before a change in economic activity affects the rate of inflation. In line with Eq. (23) in the text, the aggregate supply curve it therefore given by:

$$\pi_{t+1} = \pi_t + \gamma(y_t - \bar{y}) + s_{t+1}.\tag{42}$$

From (41) and (42) it follows that a change in the policy interest rate will affect the rate of inflation with a one-period time lag. The stochastic shocks z and s are assumed to have zero means and covariances and to be independently distributed over time ('white noise'), and the central bank is assumed to know that the economy's demand and supply sides are described by (41) and (42).

1. Show that the central bank's optimal interest rate rule is

$$i_t^p = \bar{r}^* + \pi_t + h(\pi_t - \pi^*), \qquad h \equiv 1/\gamma\alpha_2.\tag{43}$$

(Hint: Start by deriving the central bank's inflation forecast for period $t + 1$, given the information available in period t. Then explain why the central bank will adjust the policy interest rate until its inflation forecast equals the inflation target and use this insight to derive (43).) Explain why the coefficient h in (43) depends on the parameters γ and α_2 in the manner indicated. Does the policy rule (43) obey the Taylor principle?

As explained in the main text, it is realistic to assume that a change in the interest rate only affects aggregate demand with a certain time lag. Moreover, empirical research has found that it also takes a while before a change in income attains its full impact on aggregate demand. Suppose therefore that, instead of being given by (41), the equilibrium condition for the goods market is:

$$y_{t+1} - \bar{y} = z_{t+1} + \alpha_1(y_t - \bar{y}) - \alpha_2(i_t^p - \pi_t - \bar{r}^*), \qquad \alpha_1 > 0.\tag{44}$$

Thus a change in current income has some positive impact on demand in the next period, say, because it takes time before consumers adapt their consumption habits to a change in income. Equations (42) and (44) imply that it now takes two periods before a change in the interest rate affects the inflation rate.

2. Show that the optimal monetary policy is now given by the following version of the Taylor rule (hint: use the same procedure as the one used to derive (28) in the chapter text):

$$i_t^p = \bar{r}^* + \pi_t + h(\pi_t - \pi^*) + b(y_t - \bar{y}), \qquad h \equiv \frac{1}{\gamma\alpha_2}, \qquad b \equiv \frac{1 + \alpha_1}{\alpha_2}.\tag{45}$$

Compare (45) to (28) in the text and give an economic explanation for the difference. Explain why the various parameters enter the coefficients h and b in the manner indicated and why the central bank should react to the output gap even though the loss function (40) only includes the inflation gap.

The above analysis assumed static inflation expectations. Suppose instead that the central bank has full credibility so that the public's expected inflation rate is firmly anchored by the official inflation target, i.e. $\pi_t^e = \pi^*$. Given the time lags assumed in the previous question, the goods market equilibrium condition will then be

$$y_{t+1} - \bar{y} = z_{t+1} + \alpha_1(y_t - \bar{y}) - \alpha_2(i_t^p - \pi^* - \bar{r}^*), \tag{46}$$

while the aggregate supply curve modifies to:

$$\pi_{t+1} = \pi^* + \gamma(y_t - \bar{y}) + s_{t+1}. \tag{47}$$

3. Show that when the structure of the economy is given by (46) and (47), the optimal interest rate rule is:

$$i_t^p = \bar{r}^* + \pi^* + b(y_t - \bar{y}), \qquad b \equiv \frac{\alpha_1}{\alpha_2}. \tag{48}$$

Try to explain why the current inflation gap does not enter in (48). (Hint: does the current inflation gap affect the inflation rate two periods later?) Explain also why the policy interest rate should react to the current output gap and give an economic explanation for the determinants of the coefficient b in (48).

Exercise 3. Optimal short-run tax policy with limited information

Consider an economy where fiscal policy makers adjust the income tax rate τ with the purpose of minimizing the social loss function (identical to Eq. (13) in the main text):

$$SL = \frac{a_\ell}{2(1-\alpha)}\hat{y}^2 + \frac{a_\pi}{2}\hat{\pi}^2, \qquad \hat{y} \equiv y - \bar{y}, \qquad \hat{\pi} \equiv \pi - \pi^*. \tag{49}$$

The public's inflation expectations are tightly anchored by the official inflation target ($\pi^e = \pi^*$), so the AS curve is given by the following modified version of Eq. (31) in the main text:

$$\hat{\pi} = \left(\frac{\alpha}{1-\alpha}\right)(y - \bar{y}) + s, \qquad s \equiv \ln\left(\frac{m^p}{\bar{m}^p}\right) + \ln\left(\frac{m^w}{\bar{m}^w}\right) - \frac{\ln(B/\bar{B})}{1-\alpha} - \ln\left(\frac{1-\tau}{1-\bar{\tau}}\right). \tag{50}$$

To focus on fiscal policy, we assume that monetary policy is passive. In particular, the central bank is assumed to keep the real policy interest rate $i^p - \pi^e = i^p - \pi^*$ at the 'natural' level consistent with a long-run equilibrium:

$$i^p = \bar{r}^* + \pi^*. \tag{51}$$

Given that the real policy interest rate is constant, and abstracting for simplicity from shocks to risk premia and to public spending, the goods market equilibrium condition (29) in the chapter text simplifies to:

$$\hat{y} = v - \tilde{m}C_Y(\tau - \bar{\tau}). \tag{52}$$

In the questions below you are asked to characterize the optimal short-run tax policy, accounting for the fact that changes in the income tax rate τ will affect aggregate demand as well as aggregate supply.

1. Explain why the optimal short-run tax policy must satisfy the condition:

$$\frac{a_\ell \hat{y}}{1-\alpha} \cdot \frac{d\hat{y}}{d\tau} + a_\pi \hat{\pi} \cdot \frac{d\hat{\pi}}{d\tau} = 0.$$

(53)

2. Assume that $\tau = \bar{\tau}$ initially and use (50), (52) and (53) to show that the optimal short run tax policy involves the following relationship between the output gap and the inflation gap (where *TPR* stands for 'Tax Policy Rule'):

$$TPR \text{ curve:} \qquad \hat{\pi} = -\left(\frac{a_\ell \gamma \tilde{m} C_Y (1-\bar{\tau})}{\alpha a_\pi [\gamma \tilde{m} C_Y (1-\bar{\tau}) - 1]}\right)\hat{y}, \qquad \gamma \equiv \frac{\alpha}{1-\alpha}. \tag{54}$$

(Hint: when you derive $d\hat{\pi}/d\tau$ you must account not only for the direct effect of τ on $\hat{\pi}$, but also for the indirect effect via the impact of τ on $\hat{y}$.) Show that this *TPR* curve will have a negative slope in the $(\hat{y}, \hat{\pi})$-space if and only if $d\hat{\pi}/d\tau < 0$.

3. When fiscal policy makers set the tax rate, they cannot observe the demand shock hitting the economy in the current period. In their attempt to keep the economy on the *TPR* curve (54), policy makers therefore assume that the shock variable v in (52) will take its expected value of zero. On this basis, derive the optimal tax policy rule expressing τ as a function of the inflation gap. Give an economic explanation for the way the social preference parameters a_ℓ and a_π enter into the tax policy rule.

We have so far assumed that there are no costs of adjusting the tax rate, but according to public finance theory the distortionary effects of taxation tend to rise disproportionately with the marginal tax rate, i.e. the welfare loss from a tax rate increase is higher than the welfare gain from a tax rate cut of the same magnitude. Absent the need to stabilize the economy, society would thus have a preference for keeping the marginal tax rate stable. We may capture this preference by replacing the social loss function (49) by the extended loss function:

$$SL = \frac{a_\ell}{2(1-\alpha)}\hat{y}^2 + \frac{a_\pi}{2}\hat{\pi}^2 + \frac{a_\tau}{2}(\tau - \bar{\tau})^2, \tag{55}$$

where a_τ reflects the magnitude of the welfare loss from a fluctuating marginal tax rate.

4. Following the same procedure as above, derive the optimal tax policy rule when the social loss function is given by (55). Compare the new rule to the one derived in Question 3 and give an economic explanation for the difference. (Hint: should the tax rate respond more or less strongly to the inflation gap when the social loss is given by (55) rather than (49)?)

Exercise 4. Fiscal policy in a liquidity trap

Suppose a severe negative demand shock has driven the economy into a liquidity trap where the policy interest rate has hit its zero bound. The demand side of the economy is then described by the non-standard AD curve (32) while the supply side is given by (31), assuming static inflation expectations.

1. Carry out a graphical analysis similar to the one in Fig. 20.12 in which you compare the effects of an increase in public spending to the effects of a tax cut in a liquidity trap. On this basis, discuss which type of fiscal policy is likely to be most effective in pulling the economy out of the recession.

Exercise 5. Explaining time lags and their implications

Explain why there may be time lags in macroeconomic stabilization policy and why such lags reduce the ability of policy makers to stabilize the economy. Explain how monetary policy makers may try to cope with time lags through a policy of inflation forecast targeting. Discuss whether time lags are a more serious problem for fiscal than for monetary policy.

Stabilization policy with rational expectations

Economic activity today depends crucially on expected economic conditions tomorrow. A drop in the economy's expected future growth rate will tend to reduce the propensities to consume and invest by reducing the expected future earnings of households and firms. Hence the aggregate demand curve will shift down, causing an immediate fall in current output. As another example, a change in the expected rate of inflation will shift the aggregate supply curve by feeding into the nominal wages negotiated by workers and firms. It may also move the aggregate demand curve through its impact on the expected real rate of interest. The expected inflation rate is thus an important determinant of current economic activity.

Conventional macroeconomic models often assume that the expected future values of economic variables depend only on the past history of those variables. Indeed, in the previous chapters we typically postulated that the expected inflation rate for the current period is simply equal to the actual inflation rate experienced in the previous period. This assumption of *backward-looking expectations* may be plausible in 'quiet' times when the macroeconomy is not subject to significant shocks. When people have no particular reason to believe that the tightness of labour and product markets next year will be much different from what it is today, it seems reasonable for them to assume that next year's inflation rate will be more or less the same as this year's. However, if the economy is hit by an obvious and visible shock such as a dramatic change in the price of imported oil, or if there is a clear change in the economic policy regime, say, due to a change of government, it does not seem rational for people to assume that next year's economic environment will be the same as this year's. Instead of just mechanically extrapolating the past into the future, rational households and firms will seek to utilize all the relevant information available to them when they form expectations about the future state of the economy.

In the early 1970s, some macroeconomists took this idea of *forward-looking expectations* to its logical limit by advancing the *rational expectations hypothesis* (REH).[1] According to the REH, people use all the available information to make the best possible forecasts of the economic variables which are relevant to them. Moreover, *the available information includes information about the structure of the economy*. The idea is that, even though in

---

1. The rational expectations hypothesis was originally introduced in a microeconomic setting by John Muth, 'Rational Expectations and the Theory of Price Movements', *Econometrica*, **29**, 1961, pp. 315–335. Later on, the REH was introduced into macroeconomic theory by Robert E. Lucas, 'Expectations and the Neutrality of Money', *Journal of Economic Theory*, **4**, 1972, pp. 103–124, and by Thomas J. Sargent, 'Rational Expectations, the Real Rate of Interest, and the Natural Rate of Unemployment', *Brookings Papers on Economic Activity*, **2**, 1973, pp. 429–472; followed by many others.

practice the layman may not know much about the way the economy works, the economic forecasts produced by professional economists are available to the public through the media, so in this way people have access to the most competent forecasts of, say, next year's rate of inflation. Economists should therefore model the formation of expectations *as if* people use the relevant economic model to predict inflation and other economic variables which are important for their economic decisions. In other words, rational expectations are *model-consistent* expectations: they are identical to the forecasts one would make by using the available knowledge of the structure of the economy, as embodied in the relevant economic models. Another way of putting it is to say that economic analysts should not assume that they are smarter than the economic agents whose behaviour they are trying to predict. Instead, they should assume that agents form their expectations in accordance with the analysts' own description of the economy. If they did not, and if the analysts' model is correct, then agents would be making systematic expectational errors, and presumably this would induce them to change the rules of thumb by which they form their expectations until there is no discernible systematic pattern in their forecast errors.

This idea of rational expectations essentially revolutionized macroeconomic theory. The REH is obviously a very strong assumption, and as we shall see, it can be criticized on theoretical as well as empirical grounds. But before addressing these criticisms, this chapter will explain the case for the REH in more detail and derive some of its striking implications. Our main purpose is to illustrate the importance of the way expectations are formed. In particular, we will show how the effects of macroeconomic stabilization policy may differ significantly depending on whether expectations are rational or backward-looking. The final sections of the chapter will discuss the validity of the REH, drawing on theoretical arguments as well as empirical evidence.

21.1 Backward-looking versus forward-looking expectations

The case against backward-looking expectations

One way of justifying the assumption of rational expectations is to examine more carefully the implications of a macro model with backward-looking expectations. As we will illustrate in this section, in some circumstances the assumption of backward-looking expectations implies that economic agents are implausibly naïve.

We base our discussion on the model of aggregate demand and aggregate supply developed over Chapters 14 through 18, but we simplify by abstracting from shocks to public spending and from risk premia in market interest rates so that demand shocks only stem from our 'confidence' variable v_t (this simplification is in no way critical for our results). In the absence of risk premia we have $i_t = i_t^p$, so the central bank can fully control the nominal market interest rate i_t via its control of the policy interest rate i_t^p. In the usual notation, our AS–AD model may then be restated as follows:

Goods market equilibrium: $\qquad y_t - \bar{y} = v_t - \alpha_2(r_t - \bar{r})$, $\qquad\qquad$ (1)

Real interest rate: $\qquad r_t = i_t - \pi_{t+1}^e$, $\qquad\qquad\qquad\qquad\qquad\qquad$ (2)

Price formation: $\qquad \pi_t = \pi_t^e + \gamma(y_t - \bar{y}) + s_t$, $\qquad\qquad\qquad\qquad$ (3)

Monetary policy rule: $\qquad i_t = \bar{r} + \pi_{t+1}^e + h(\pi_t - \pi^*) + b(y_t - \bar{y})$, $\qquad$ (4)

Expectations: $\qquad \pi_t^e = \pi_{t-1}$. $\qquad\qquad\qquad\qquad\qquad\qquad\qquad$ (5)

Equation (5) assumes a particularly simple form of backward-looking expectations by postulating that the expected inflation rate for the current period equals the actual inflation rate observed during the previous period. We will now illustrate the implications of this assumption of 'static' expectations by solving the model (1)–(5).

For the moment, we will simplify by setting the exogenous aggregate demand and supply shock variables equal to their zero mean values, $v_t = s_t = 0$. On this assumption we find by substituting (2), (4) and (5) into (1) that the aggregate demand curve may be written as:

$$y_t - \bar{y} = \alpha(\pi^* - \pi_t), \qquad \alpha \equiv \frac{\alpha_2 h}{1 + \alpha_2 b}, \tag{6}$$

while substitution of (5) into (3) yields the aggregate supply curve:

$$\pi = \pi_{t-1} + \gamma(y_t - \bar{y}). \tag{7}$$

Inserting (6) into (7) and rearranging, we obtain the first-order linear difference equation:

$$\pi_t = \pi_{t-1} + \gamma\alpha(\pi^* - \pi_t) \iff \pi_t - \pi^* = \pi_{t-1} - \pi^* - \gamma\alpha(\pi_t - \pi^*) \iff$$

$$\pi_t - \pi^* = \beta(\pi_{t-1} - \pi^*), \qquad \beta \equiv \frac{1}{1 + \gamma\alpha}, \tag{8}$$

which has the solution:

$$\pi_t = \pi^* + \beta^t(\pi_0 - \pi^*), \qquad t = 0, 1, 2, \ldots \tag{9}$$

where π_0 is the predetermined initial value of the inflation rate in period 0. Since we see from (8) that $0 < \beta < 1$, it follows from (9) that the inflation rate will converge monotonically towards its target rate π^* as t tends to infinity.

From (9) we may calculate the *inflation forecast error*, defined as the difference between the actual and the expected inflation rate. Given the assumption of static expectations, $\pi_t^e = \pi_{t-1}$, the inflation forecast error during the phase of adjustment to long-run equilibrium is:

$$\pi_t - \pi_t^e = \pi_t - \pi_{t-1} = \beta^t(\pi_0 - \pi^*) - \beta^{t-1}(\pi_0 - \pi^*) \iff$$

$$\pi_t - \pi_t^e = \beta^{t-1}(\pi_0 - \pi^*)(\beta - 1). \tag{10}$$

Suppose now that at the end of period 0 the government appoints a 'tough' new central bank governor who announces a significant reduction in the target inflation rate from the start of period 1. For concreteness, suppose the inflation target π^* is reduced from 3 per cent to 0 per cent per year. Using empirically plausible parameter values like those reported in Chapter 18, we may then simulate the evolution of the inflation forecast error implied by Eq. (10), assuming that the initial inflation rate π_0 was equal to the previous inflation target of 3 per cent. The result of the simulation is shown in Fig. 21.1.

We see that throughout the period of adjustment to the new inflation target of 0, *the public systematically overestimates the actual rate of inflation*. The reason for these systematic mistakes in forecasting inflation is that the public mechanically extrapolates last period's observed inflation rate into the future. Thus, even though the central bank announces its determination to bring inflation down by setting a high interest rate as long as $\pi_t > \pi^*$, people nevertheless continue to believe period after period that next year's inflation rate will be the same as this year's. Clearly this behaviour is not very intelligent. Presumably, informed citizens will observe or at least gradually learn that the monetary policy regime has changed, and this should affect the way they form their expectations of inflation.

This is a statement of the case against the assumption of backward-looking expectations: if important aspects of the economic environment (such as the economic policy regime)

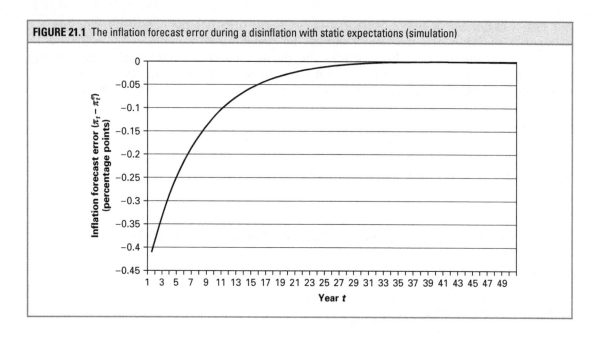

FIGURE 21.1 The inflation forecast error during a disinflation with static expectations (simulation)

change, rational agents are likely to realize that the future path of the economy cannot be projected by simply observing how the economy behaved in the past. To put it another way, rational economic agents will utilize all relevant information when they form their expectations about the future, including information about changes in economic policy and other new developments which are likely to influence the course of the economy.

Defining rational expectations

The rational expectations hypothesis takes the above line of reasoning one step further by suggesting that *economic agents do not make systematic forecast errors* of the kind illustrated in Fig. 21.1. To be sure, since the economy is often hit by stochastic shocks (which were ignored for simplicity in Fig. 21.1), agents usually *do* make mistakes when they try to predict the future state of the economy. But according to the REH there will be *no systematic bias* in these forecast errors. For example, sometimes the rate of inflation will be overestimated, and sometimes it will be underestimated, but on average people's inflation forecasts will be correct. The justification for this assumption is that economic actions based on erroneous expectations cause losses of profits and utility, and hence agents have an incentive to minimize their forecast errors. If the forecast errors revealed a systematic pattern such as persistent overestimation or underestimation, rational agents should be able to detect this pattern and would have an incentive to revise their methods of expectations formation to weed out systematic biases in their guesses about the future.

In an uncertain environment, the economic variables about which agents form their expectations may be seen as stochastic variables, as Chapter 18 explained. In such a setting we may formalize the hypothesis of rational expectations by saying that the *subjective* expectation of some economic variable X for time t, X_t^e, is equal to the *objective* mathematical expectation of X, conditional on all available information at the time the expectation is formed. Thus, if the expectation for period t is formed at the end of period $t - 1$, the expected value of X for period t is:

$$\underbrace{X_t^e}_{\substack{\text{subjective}\\\text{expectation}}} = \underbrace{E[X_t \mid I_{t-1}]}_{\substack{\text{objective}\\\text{conditional}\\\text{expectation}}} \tag{11}$$

where $E[\cdot]$ is the mathematical expectations operator, and I_{t-1} is the information set available to the agent at the end of period $t - 1$. Hence $E[X_t | I_{t-1}]$ is the mean value of the stochastic economic variable X for period t, calculated at the end of period $t - 1$ using all the information available at that time.

The definition of rational expectations can also be stated in slightly more general terms. If $f^e(X_j)$ is an agent's perceived probability that the stochastic economic variable X will assume the value X_j, and $f(X_j)$ is the true probability that one can calculate by using all the available information, the hypothesis of rational expectations says that $f^e(X_j) = f(X_j)$ for all possible values of X_j. In other words, the REH postulates that the agents' subjective probability distributions for the relevant economic variables are equal to the true objective probability distributions. The mean value of the subjective probability distribution of X and the mathematical expectation of the (conditional) objective distribution are, respectively:

$$X_t^e = \sum_j X_j f^e(X_i) \qquad \text{and} \qquad E[X_t | I_{t-1}] = \sum_j X_j f(X_j). \tag{12}$$

For $f^e(X_j) = f(X_j)$, (12) obviously implies (11).

The specification in (11) captures the idea that expectations are on average correct, even though they are hardly ever precisely correct, given the unpredictable stochastic shocks which are hitting the economy all the time. Formally, Eq. (11) states that economic agents know enough about the stochastic process determining X_t to be able to calculate the correct conditional mean value of X_t. In this sense rational expectations are *model-consistent*: the rationally expected value of X is equal to the mean value of this variable which one would calculate from the correct stochastic economic model describing the determination of X. Thus agents form their expectations *as if* they knew the 'correct' model of the economy (or the model of the subsector of the economy in which they are interested), even though in practice they may have arrived at their forecasting rules through a more intuitive trial-and-error learning process. In summary:

THE RATIONAL EXPECTATIONS HYPOTHESIS (REH) !

The REH says that agents optimally exploit all available information when they form their expectations of the values of future economic variables. Hence agents do not make systematic forecast errors, for if they did, they could use observations of past forecast errors to correct their forecasting rules so as to eliminate any systematic bias in their forecasts. Effectively the REH thus assumes that agents form their expectations as if they know the 'true' structure of the economy.

Later on we will discuss the realism of the REH, but first we will explore some of its striking implications.

21.2 Rational expectations and macroeconomic policy

We may use our model of aggregate demand and aggregate supply to study how rational expectations affect the scope for macroeconomic stabilization policy. For convenience, let us introduce the notation

$$X_{t,t-1}^e \equiv E[X_t | I_{t-1}] \tag{13}$$

to denote the rational expectation of variable X for period t, based on the information available up until the end of period $t - 1$.

The Policy Ineffectiveness Proposition

Now suppose that when the central bank sets the interest rate for period t, it does not know what the actual levels of inflation and output for that period will be. Instead, because macroeconomic data are only available with a time lag, the central bank has to base its interest rate decision on the *expected* inflation rates $\pi^e_{t,t-1}$ and $\pi^e_{t+1,t-1}$ and on the *expected* general activity level $y^e_{t,t-1}$. Since $r_t = i_t - \pi^e_{t+1,t-1}$, we may then respecify the monetary policy rule (4) as:

$$r_t = \bar{r} + h(\pi^e_{t,t-1} - \pi^*) + b(y^e_{t,t-1} - \bar{y}). \tag{14}$$

From (1) we still have the goods market equilibrium condition:

$$y_t - \bar{y} = v_t - \alpha_2(r_t - \bar{r}), \tag{15}$$

and using the notation in (13) the aggregate supply curve may be written as:

$$\pi_t = \pi^e_{t,t-1} + \gamma(y_t - \bar{y}) + s_t. \tag{16}$$

To complete the model, we must specify the stochastic properties of the exogenous demand and supply shock variables. For simplicity we assume that these variables are 'white noise', being identically and independently distributed over time, with zero means and constant variances σ^2_v and σ^2_s, respectively:

$$E[v_t] = 0, \qquad E[v^2_t] = \sigma^2_v, \qquad E[v_t v_j] = 0 \qquad \text{for } t \neq j, \tag{17}$$

$$E[s_t] = 0, \qquad E[s^2_t] = \sigma^2_s, \qquad E[s_t s_j] = 0 \qquad \text{for } t \neq j, \qquad E[v_t s_j] = 0. \tag{18}$$

To solve a model like (14)–(18) where expectations are rational, we must derive the expectations $\pi^e_{t,t-1}$ and $y^e_{t,t-1}$ which are consistent with the model, given the information available at time $t - 1$. We will solve the model by going through the following three steps:[2]

Step 1:   Solve the model for the endogenous variables y_t and π_t in terms of the exogenous variables and the expectations variables and $y^e_{t,t-1}$ and $\pi^e_{t,t-1}$.

Step 2:   Find the solutions for $y^e_{t,t-1}$ and $\pi^e_{t,t-1}$ by calculating the expected value of the expressions found in Step 1, given the information available at time $t - 1$.

Step 3:   Insert the solutions for $y^e_{t,t-1}$ and $\pi^e_{t,t-1}$ into the expressions found in Step 1 to obtain the final solutions for y_t and π_t in terms of the exogenous variables.

Let us illustrate the mechanics of this procedure.

Step 1. Inserting (14) into (15), we find:

$$y_t = \bar{y} + v_t - \alpha_2[h(\pi^e_{t,t-1} - \pi^*) + b(y^e_{t,t-1} - \bar{y})]. \tag{19}$$

If we substitute (19) into (16), we get:

$$\pi_t = \pi^e_{t,t-1} - \gamma\alpha_2[h(\pi^e_{t,t-1} - \pi^*) + b(y^e_{t,t-1} - \bar{y})] + \gamma v_t + s_t. \tag{20}$$

---

2.   The solution procedure described here works in simple models like the present one which includes expectations relating only to the current period. More general models typically also include expected values of variables for one or several future time periods. The solution of such models requires more advanced techniques which will be left for a future macro course.

We have now expressed the actual values of y_t and π_t as functions of the exogenous variables and of the expected values of y_t and π_t, as required in Step 1.

Step 2. The next step is to use (19) and (20) to calculate the rational expectations of y_t and π_t. The rationally expected value of output in period t is the mean value of the expression on the right-hand side of (19), calculated on the basis of information available at time $t-1$. In calculating this conditional expectation, we may use the facts that $E[\pi_{t,t-1}^e \mid I_{t-1}] = \pi_{t,t-1}^e$ and $E[y_{t,t-1}^e \mid I_{t-1}] = y_{t,t-1}^e$. This simply says that agents do, of course, know at time $t-1$ what their own expectations are at that time. We also recall from (17) that v_t has a zero mean value, so at time $t-1$, before 'nature' has drawn the value of v for period t, a rational agent's best guess is that this variable will assume its mean value of zero during the next period. From (19) we then find that the rationally expected value of output in period t is:

$$y_{t,t-1}^e = \bar{y} - \alpha_2[h(\pi_{t,t-1}^e - \pi^*) + b(y_{t,t-1}^e - \bar{y})], \tag{21}$$

given that agents are assumed to know the structure of the economy, including the values of the parameters appearing in Eq. (19). In a similar way, since $E[s_t] = E[v_t] = 0$, we may use Eq. (20) to calculate the rationally expected inflation rate for period t:

$$\pi_{t,t-1}^e = \pi_{t,t-1}^e - \gamma\alpha_2[h(\pi_{t,t-1}^e - \pi^*) + b(y_{t,t-1}^e - \bar{y})] \quad \Leftrightarrow$$

$$h(\pi_{t,t-1}^e - \pi^*) + b(y_{t,t-1}^e - \bar{y}) = 0. \tag{22}$$

Inserting (22) into (21), we get:

$$y_{t,t-1}^e = \bar{y}. \tag{23}$$

which may then be substituted into (22) to give the solution for the expected inflation rate (assuming that $h \neq 0$):

$$\pi_{t,t-1}^e = \pi^*. \tag{24}$$

Step 3. Now we need to insert (23) and (24) into (19) and (20) to get the final solutions for inflation and output in terms of the exogenous variables and parameters of the model. Taking this final step, we find:

$$\pi_t = \pi^* + \gamma v_t + s_t, \tag{25}$$

$$y_t = \bar{y} + v_t. \tag{26}$$

Notice that the policy parameters π^*, b and h do not appear in the solution for y_t given in (26). Hence systematic monetary stabilization policy does not affect the evolution of real output! This is the famous *Policy Ineffectiveness Proposition (PIP)* which says that *systematic demand management policies cannot influence real output and employment when expectations are rational.* To understand the intuition for this striking result, note that the aggregate supply curve (16) may be rearranged as:

$$y_t = \bar{y} + (1/\gamma)(\pi_t - \pi_{t,t-1}^e) + (1/\gamma)s_t. \tag{27}$$

Since $\bar{y}$ and s_t are exogenous, the supply curve (27) implies that monetary policy can only affect real output by influencing the inflation forecast error $\pi_t - \pi_{t,t-1}^e$, that is, by creating unanticipated inflation. But since wage and price setters have the same information on macroeconomic data as the central bank, and since they know the monetary policy rule (14) as well as the way the interest rate affects the economy through its impact on aggregate demand, *private agents can perfectly anticipate the effect of systematic monetary policy on the current inflation rate.* Thus systematic monetary policy (whether it takes the form of a Taylor rule or some other fixed policy rule) cannot generate surprise inflation, and hence it cannot cause output and employment to deviate from their natural rates.

THE POLICY INEFFECTIVENESS PROPOSITION

The Policy Ineffectiveness Proposition says that when expectations are rational, systematic monetary policy cannot influence 'real' economic variables such as output, employment, real wages and the real interest rate. Demand management policy can only influence these variables by generating unanticipated inflation. When agents have rational expectations, they fully anticipate the effects of any systematic policy on the rate of inflation. Hence systematic monetary policy can generate no inflation surprises, and consequently it cannot affect real economic variables.

Of course, purely erratic changes in the interest rate set by the central bank could create unanticipated inflation and thereby affect real output (you are asked to demonstrate this formally in Exercise 1). However, to be unpredictable, such policy changes would have to be purely random and completely unrelated to the state of the economy. Such a random policy would have negative welfare effects by creating expectational errors, inducing agents to make economic decisions they would probably regret *ex post.* Clearly, such central bank behaviour would not qualify as stabilization policy.

The PIP was a frontal attack on the conventional wisdom. Hence it created a strong controversy among macroeconomists when it was initially presented.[3] Because of its important implications for public policy, we will now discuss the robustness of the PIP.

Policy effectiveness under rational expectations

The model of the previous section assumes that the interest rate as well as the wages and prices for period t have to be set at the end of period $t-1$, based on the information available at that time. In other words, it is assumed that the central bank cannot act on the basis of more updated information than wage and price setters in the private sector. This is hardly realistic. Wage contracts often fix the nominal wage (or specify the evolution of the nominal wage) for a considerable period ahead, and many firms only change their prices at infrequent intervals. By contrast, the central bank can change its interest rate quite quickly if it feels that new information on the state of the economy warrants such a change. This means that the central bank can act *after* many wages and prices have been set, so even if private agents fully understand the effects of the interest rate change on the economy, they may not have the opportunity to adjust their wages and prices immediately to offset the effect of the policy change on the real economy, because they are temporarily locked into the existing nominal contracts.

A realistic macro model should therefore allow for the possibility that the central bank can react to economic developments occurring after (some of) the nominal wages and prices in the private sector have been set. To capture this, we will assume that the central bank interest rate can react to the *actual* levels of current output y_t and inflation π_t, whereas wages

---

3. The PIP was originally put forward by Thomas J. Sargent and Neil Wallace, 'Rational Expectations, the Optimal Monetary Instrument, and the Optimal Money Supply Rule', *Journal of Political Economy,* **83**, 1975, pp. 241–254; and in a paper by the same authors entitled: 'Rational Expectations and the Theory of Economic Policy', *Journal of Monetary Economics,* **2**, 1976, pp. 169–183.

and prices are set on the basis of *expectations* formed at the end of the previous period (so that $\pi_{t,t-1}^e$ is still the relevant expected inflation rate to include in the aggregate supply curve). The monetary policy rule (14) is then replaced by the more familiar equation:[4]

$$r_t = \bar{r} + h(\pi_t - \pi^*) + b(y_t - \bar{y}). \tag{28}$$

In practice, the central bank may not have perfect information on the current levels of output and inflation, but Eq. (28) is just a convenient way of modelling the fact that the central bank can react to observed economic developments occurring *after* (some of) the wages and prices in the private sector have been set. The qualitative results derived below will hold as long as the central bank can react to new information arriving after some of the wage and price setting decisons for the current period were made.

Let us now study the implications of the policy rule (28), assuming that the AD curve and the AS curve are still given by (15) and (16), respectively, and that the stochastic shocks have the properties stated in (17) and (18). Expectations are still rational, so we must solve this revised model by going through the three steps described in the previous section.

Step 1: *Solve the model for y_t and π_t in terms of the exogenous variables and the expectations variables.* If we insert (28) into (15) and rearrange, we get:

$$y_t - \bar{y} = \frac{v_t - \alpha_2 h(\pi_t - \pi^*)}{1 + \alpha_2 b}. \tag{29}$$

From (16) we have:

$$\pi_t - \pi^* = \pi_{t,t-1}^e - \pi^* + \gamma(y_t - \bar{y}) + s_t, \tag{30}$$

which may be inserted into (29) to give:

$$y_t - \bar{y} = \frac{v_t - \alpha_2 h s_t - \alpha_2 h(\pi_{t,t-1}^e - \pi^*)}{1 + \alpha_2(b + \gamma h)}. \tag{31}$$

Furthermore, we may substitute (29) into (30) to get:

$$\pi_t - \pi^* = \frac{(1 + \alpha_2 b)(\pi_{t,t-1}^e - \pi^*) + (1 + \alpha_2 b)s_t + \gamma v_t}{1 + \alpha_2(b + \gamma h)}. \tag{32}$$

Step 2: *Find $\pi_{t,t-1}^e$ by taking expected values in (32), conditional on information available at time $t-1$.* Performing this operation and remembering that $E[s_t] = E[v_t] = 0$, we get:

$$\pi_{t,t-1}^e - \pi^* = \frac{(1 + \alpha_2 b)(\pi_{t,t-1}^e - \pi^*)}{1 + \alpha_2(b + \gamma h)} \quad \Leftrightarrow \tag{33}$$

$$\pi_{t,t-1}^e = \pi^*.$$

---

4. Equation (28) assumes that the central bank sets the nominal interest rate as:

$$i_t = \bar{r} + \pi_{t+1,t-1}^e + h(\pi_t - \pi^*) + b(y_t - \bar{y}),$$

where $\pi_{t+1,t-1}^e$ is the private sector's expected inflation rate between the current and the next period, assuming that private spending decisions in period t are based on information available up until the end of period $t-1$. In other words, the central bank knows that the private sector's expected inflation rate is $\pi_{t+1,t-1}^e$, and hence it is able to control the *ex ante* real interest rate $r_t = i_t - \pi_{t+1,t-1}^e$ through its control of the nominal interest rate i_t.

Step 3: *Find the final solutions for π_t and y_t by inserting the solution for the rationally expected inflation rate (33) into (32) and (31).* Taking this last step, we obtain:

$$\pi_t = \pi^* + \frac{(1+\alpha_2 b)s_t + \gamma v_t}{1+\alpha_2(b+\gamma h)}, \tag{34}$$

$$y_t = \bar{y} + \frac{v_t - \alpha_2 h s_t}{1+\alpha_2(b+\gamma h)}. \tag{35}$$

The important message from (35) is that *real output is now influenced by systematic monetary policy*, since the policy parameters b and h appear in the solution for y_t. For example, we see that a more activist countercyclical policy (a higher value of b) will reduce the impact of demand and supply shocks on output. Hence the Policy Ineffectiveness Proposition breaks down, even though expectations are rational. The reason has already been suggested above: since the expectations governing the formation of wages and prices are formed *before* the central bank sets the interest rate, monetary policy can react to new information which was not available when the private sector formed its expectations for the current period. The inflation forecast error, $\pi_t - \pi_{t,t-1}^e$, is therefore affected by the central bank's systematic reactions to new events, and consequently systematic monetary policy will influence real output, according to the aggregate supply curve (27).

Since it seems realistic to assume that the central bank can indeed act after (some agents in) the private sector has temporarily locked itself into nominal contracts, most economists today consider the Policy Ineffectiveness Proposition as theoretically interesting, but not very relevant in practice. Summing up:

POLICY EFFECTIVENESS UNDER RATIONAL EXPECTATIONS

Since many nominal wages and prices are pre-set for a considerable period of time, the central bank can react to new information that was not available when (some of the) wage and price setters formed their inflation expectations for the current period. Hence the systematic reaction of monetary policy to new information can generate deviations between actual and expected inflation, thereby influencing output and other real economic variables.

In our AS–AD model with backward-looking expectations we have seen (in Chapter 18) how the gradual adjustment of expectations to observed changes in the actual inflation rate generates persistence in output and inflation. By contrast, in our model with rational expectations the expected inflation rate is pinned down by the central bank's target inflation rate, so there is no adjustment over time in expected inflation following a shock, and hence no persistence mechanism rooted in expectations formation. Indeed, we see from Eqs (35) and (34) that output will fluctuate randomly around the natural rate under rational expectations, and that inflation will fluctuate stochastically around the inflation target. As soon as a temporary shock disappears, and assuming that no new shocks occur, the economy immediately returns to its long-run equilibrium because there are no gradual shifts in the SRAS curve stemming from the updating of expectations.

In Chapters 14 and 19 we saw that many real-world macroeconomic time series display considerable persistence. The absence of such persistence in our simple model with rational expectations might seem to speak in favour of the assumption of backward-looking expectations. However, it is possible to generate persistence in macro models with rational expectations, for example by introducing autocorrelated supply shocks (see Exercise 4), or by allowing for the dynamics of capital accumulation. In such extended models the basic point remains that the way expectations are formed will influence the dynamics of the macroeconomy.

The Lucas Critique

The Policy Ineffectiveness Proposition played a prominent role in the so-called rational expectations revolution which swept through the field of macroeconomics in the 1970s. But as we have seen, the PIP is not robust to plausible changes in assumptions, so although it is regarded as an interesting theoretical benchmark, it is not really taken literally by today's macroeconomists.

A more lasting influence of the rational expectations revolution was the so-called Lucas Critique of macroeconometric policy evaluation, advanced by Nobel Laureate Robert Lucas.[5] The Lucas Critique says that *an econometric macro model with backward-looking expectations which was estimated under a previous economic policy regime cannot be used to predict economic behaviour under a new policy regime.* The reason is that a change in the policy regime will affect private sector behaviour, including the way in which expectations are formed, and this will change (some of) the parameters of the relevant economic model.

Our AS–AD model with rational expectations provides a simple illustration of the Lucas Critique. Consider Eq. (33) which shows that the rationally expected inflation rate equals the central bank's target inflation rate π^*. Suppose now that the government appoints an 'inflation hawk' as a new central bank governor to implement a more anti-inflationary monetary policy, implying a fall in π^*. According to (33) rational agents will then immediately *reduce* their expected inflation rate. If the economic analyst does not allow for this effect of the change in policy regime on expectations, he will miscalculate the effect of the policy change on inflation and output. For example, if the analyst assumes static expectations, we saw in Fig. 21.1 that he will predict a long period where agents will overestimate the inflation rate, following the downward revision of the inflation target. As a consequence, the analyst assuming static expectations will forecast a long and protracted recession. But if expectations are actually rational, and if the reduction in the official inflation target is considered to be credible, (35) shows that the cut in π^* can be implemented without any loss of output, because it is immediately translated into a corresponding fall in the expected inflation rate.

The Lucas Critique is relevant for structural policies as well as for stabilization policy. For example, the labour market models presented in Chapters 11, 12 and 17 imply that the natural rate of unemployment depends on the level of unemployment benefits, among other things. According to these models, a labour market reform involving a cut in unemployment benefits is likely to reduce structural unemployment. A macroeconomic model incorporating a Phillips curve estimated on historical data for periods when benefits were higher will then tend to overestimate the natural unemployment rate after the reform, leading to inaccurate economic forecasts.

The Lucas Critique is a warning that one cannot mechanically extrapolate past economic behaviour into the future. To avoid this problem, Lucas argued that the analyst must build economic models with rational expectations and explicit microfoundations. In such a setting it is possible to describe economic behaviour as functions of the government's policy instruments and of the 'deep' parameters representing tastes and technology which are not influenced by policy changes. Armed with such a micro-based rational expectations model, one can in principle predict how a change in the policy regime will affect the economy.

This methodological approach has had a profound influence on the way macroeconomists are nowadays trying to evaluate economic policies. The Lucas Critique also provides part of the motivation for our efforts in earlier chapters to offer a microtheoretic foundation for the behavioural relationships embodied in our AS–AD model.

---

5. See Robert E. Lucas, Jr, 'Econometric Policy Evaluation: A Critique', *Carnegie-Rochester Conference Series on Public Policy*, **1**, 1976, pp. 19–46.

Optimal stabilization policy under rational expectations

The analysis above showed that monetary policy can in fact influence real output and employment even if expectations are rational.[6] But what is the *optimal* monetary stabilization policy under rational expectations? In discussing this issue, we will assume that the central bank has decided to follow a Taylor rule like (4), since the empirical analysis in Chapter 16 showed that monetary policy in the most important countries seems to be quite well described by such a rule. By postulating that the central bank follows a Taylor rule, we are thus assuming that the bank can observe and react to the current inflation and output gaps whereas it cannot directly observe the shocks currently hitting the economy. The question then becomes: What are the optimal values of the coefficients on the inflation and output gaps (h and b) in the Taylor rule when expectations are rational so that the public can infer the monetary policy rule from observed economic outcomes? To answer this question, let us assume that the central bank takes the long view, choosing the parameters of its monetary policy rule so as to minimize the *expected average social loss* given by

$$E[SL] = E\left[\overbrace{(y - \bar{y})^2 + \kappa(\pi - \pi^*)^2}^{SL}\right] = \sigma_y^2 + \kappa\sigma_\pi^2, \qquad \kappa > 0, \tag{36}$$

where σ_y^2 and σ_π^2 are the variances of output and inflation which may be found from (34) and (35):

$$\sigma_y^2 \equiv E[(y_t - \bar{y})^2] = \frac{\sigma_v^2 + \alpha_2^2 h^2 \sigma_s^2}{[1 + \alpha_2(b + \gamma h)]^2}, \tag{37}$$

$$\sigma_\pi^2 \equiv E[(\pi_t - \pi^*)^2] = \frac{\gamma^2\sigma_v^2 + (1 + \alpha_2 b)^2 \sigma_s^2}{[1 + \alpha_2(b + \gamma h)]^2}. \tag{38}$$

The social loss function SL in (36) is identical to the one derived in Chapter 19 except that (for convenience and without loss of generality) we have normalized the coefficient on the output gap to be one so that the parameter κ measures the social loss from inflation volatility *relative to* the social loss from output volatility.

If business fluctuations were generated solely by demand shocks, i.e., if $\sigma_s^2 = 0$, we see from (37) and (38) that the variances of output and inflation will be smaller the higher the values of the policy parameters h and b. Regardless of the way expectations are formed, the central bank should thus react with a sharp decrease (increase) in the real interest rate when the inflation and output gaps fall (rise) in response to a negative (positive) demand shock, subject to the constraint that the nominal interest rate cannot become negative.

However, in the general case where the economy is hit by supply shocks as well as demand shocks, monetary policy makers face an inescapable trade-off between output stability and inflation stability. To see this, note from (36) that as long as the values of h and b are not constrained by the zero bound on the nominal interest rate, the first-order conditions for minimization of the social loss function with respect to h and b are:

$$\frac{\partial E[SL]}{\partial h} = 0 \quad \Rightarrow \quad \frac{\partial \sigma_y^2}{\partial h} + \kappa \frac{\partial \sigma_\pi^2}{\partial h} = 0, \tag{39}$$

$$\frac{\partial E[SL]}{\partial b} = 0 \quad \Rightarrow \quad \frac{\partial \sigma_y^2}{\partial b} + \kappa \frac{\partial \sigma_\pi^2}{\partial b} = 0. \tag{40}$$

---

6. In Exercise 2 we ask you to demonstrate that systematic *fiscal* policy can also be used to stabilize output under rational expectations, provided fiscal policy makers can act on information obtained after nominal wages have been set.

Since κ is positive, (39) and (40) imply that any change in h or b which reduces the variance of output will increase the variance of inflation, and vice versa. Therefore, if the policy parameters h and b are chosen appropriately so as to minimize the social loss from economic instability, policy makers will inevitably face a trade-off between output volatility and inflation volatility. The specific choice between the two types of instability will depend on the magnitude of the parameter κ measuring the social aversion to fluctuations in inflation relative to output volatility.

The derivatives of the variances of output and inflation may be found from (37) and (38). Inserting these derivatives in (39) and (40), one may then solve for the optimal values of h and b. However, the resulting expressions are quite complex, so to highlight the basic principles governing the choice of the optimal policy rule in a more transparent way, we will focus on the special case where the central bank's interest rate policy only reacts to the inflation gap. In this case where $b = 0$, it follows from (36) through (38) that the expected social loss can be written

$$E[SL] = \frac{\sigma_v^2 + \alpha_2^2 h^2 \sigma_s^2 + \kappa(\gamma^2 \sigma_v^2 + \sigma_s^2)}{(1 + \gamma \alpha_2 h)^2}. \tag{41}$$

According to (41) the optimal value of h that will minimize the expected social loss from instability of output and inflation may be found from the first-order condition:

$$\frac{\partial E[SL]}{\partial h} = 0 \implies \frac{2h\alpha_2^2 \sigma_s^2 (1 + \gamma \alpha_2 h)^2 - 2\gamma \alpha_2 (1 + \gamma \alpha_2 h)[\sigma_v^2 + h^2 \alpha_2^2 \sigma_s^2 + \kappa(\gamma^2 \sigma_v^2 + \sigma_s^2)]}{(1 + \gamma \alpha_2 h)^4} = 0$$

$$\Leftrightarrow \quad h\alpha_2 \sigma_s^2 (1 + \gamma \alpha_2 h) - \gamma[\sigma_v^2 + h^2 \alpha_2^2 \sigma_s^2 + \kappa(\gamma^2 \sigma_v^2 + \sigma_s^2)] = 0 \tag{42}$$

$$\Leftrightarrow \quad h = \frac{\gamma}{\alpha_2}\left[(1 + \gamma^2 \kappa)\frac{\sigma_v^2}{\sigma_s^2} + \kappa\right].$$

Equation (42) characterizes the *optimal inflation targeting rule under rational expectations*. Since (42) implies that $h > 0$, we see that the optimal monetary policy satisfies the Taylor principle discussed in earlier chapters. Further, when business fluctuations are mainly driven by demand shocks, the relative variance σ_v^2/σ_s^2 will be large, and a positive (negative) inflation gap will then typically be associated with a positive (negative) output gap (convince yourself of this). A strong interest rate reaction to the inflation gap will then typically serve to close the output gap as well as the inflation gap itself. This explains why (42) requires that h should be large when the relative variance σ_v^2/σ_s^2 is large. On the other hand, if supply shocks are important relative to demand shocks so that σ_v^2/σ_s^2 is low, a positive inflation gap will typically be associated with a negative output gap, and vice versa (again you should explain this to yourself). In this situation a rise in the interest rate in response to a positive inflation gap will serve to reduce that gap by reducing aggregate demand, but at the same time this fall in demand will further increase the size of the negative output gap. Since the central bank cares about both of the gaps, (42) prescribes that the interest rate should only react moderately to the inflation gap when supply shocks are relatively important, i.e., when σ_v^2/σ_s^2 is low. This is a reflection of the trade-off between output stability and inflation stability mentioned earlier.

Equation (42) also has several other intuitive implications. For example, a stronger inflation response to a change in the output gap (i.e. a greater slope of the Phillips curve, γ) calls for a stronger interest rate reaction to a change in the inflation gap to bring the volatility of inflation down to an acceptable level. On the other hand, the greater the sensitivity of aggregate demand to a change in the interest rate (the higher the value of α_2), the smaller is the optimal interest rate response to a change in the inflation gap, as shown by (42). Finally, it is very intuitive that the optimal interest rate reaction to the inflation gap is larger the more society loses from inflation volatility relative to output volatility, that is, the greater the value of κ.

To recap:

OPTIMAL MONETARY POLICY UNDER RATIONAL EXPECTATIONS

If business cycles are driven only by demand shocks, the central bank interest rate should react as strongly as possible to the inflation and output gaps, subject to the zero bound constraint on the nominal interest rate. In the general case where the economy is hit by supply shocks as well as demand shocks, the optimal interest rate policy faces a trade-off between output stability and inflation stability, and under inflation targeting the optimal interest rate reaction to the inflation gap is proportional to the variance of demand shocks relative to the variance of supply shocks. The greater the social loss from inflation volatility relative to the loss from output volatility, the stronger the interest rate should react to the inflation gap.

Monetary policy in a liquidity trap: does manipulation of forward-looking expectations offer an escape route?[7]

The previous subsection assumed that the parameters of the policy interest rate reaction function could be set freely without being constrained by the zero bound on the nominal interest rate. But as we saw in previous chapters, the zero bound may become binding when the economy is hit by a large negative demand shock. When expectations are backward-looking, an expansionary fiscal policy may then be the only way of pulling the economy out of recession, as we explained in Chapter 20. However, when expectations are forward-looking, there may still be ways in which the central bank can help to stimulate the economy in a liquidity trap.

We may demonstrate this through a slight respecification of our model. Recall from our derivation of the AD curve in Chapter 16 that the demand shock variable v_t reflects the expected future level of output and income which is one of the determinants of current consumption and investment. We may therefore assume that

$$v_t = y^e_{t+1,t} - \bar{y} + a_t, \qquad E[a_t] = 0, \qquad E[a_t a_j] = 0, \, j \neq t, \qquad E[a_t s_j] = 0, \tag{43}$$

where a_t is a stochastic 'white noise' variable. The goods market equilibrium condition is still given by

$$y_t - \bar{y} = v_t - \alpha_2(i_t - \pi^e_{t+1,t} - \bar{r}). \tag{44}$$

Since (43) implies $v^e_{t+1,t} = y^e_{t+2,t} - \bar{y}$, it follows from (44) that the rational expectation of next period's output gap is:

$$y^e_{t+1,t} - \bar{y} = v^e_{t+1,t} - \alpha_2(i^e_{t+1,t} - \pi^e_{t+2,t} - \bar{r}) = y^e_{t+2,t} - \bar{y} - \alpha_2(i^e_{t+1,t} - \pi^e_{t+2,t} - \bar{r}). \tag{45}$$

Substitution of (43) and (45) into (44) yields:

$$y_t - \bar{y} = y^e_{t+2,t} - \bar{y} - \alpha_2(i^e_{t+1,t} - \pi^e_{t+2,t} - \bar{r}) - \alpha_2(i_t - \pi^e_{t+1,t} - \bar{r}) + a_t. \tag{46}$$

7. The discussion in this subsection is inspired by Carl E. Walsh, 'Using monetary policy to stabilize economic activity'. Paper prepared for the Jackson Hole Symposium on *Financial Stability and Macroeconomic Policy*, 20–22 August, 2009.

But $y_{t+2,t}^e - \bar{y}$ is given by a relationship analogous to (45), so (46) may be written as

$$y_t - \bar{y} = \overbrace{y_{t+3,t}^e - \bar{y} - \alpha_2(i_{t+2,t}^e - \pi_{t+3,t}^e - \bar{r})}^{=y_{t+2,t}^e - \bar{y}} - \alpha_2(i_{t+1,t}^e - \pi_{t+2,t}^e - \bar{r}) - \alpha_2(i_t - \pi_{t+1,t}^e - \bar{r}) + a_t. \qquad (47)$$

Continuing to eliminate $y_{t+j,t}^e - \bar{y}$ from (47) in this way *ad infinitum*, we end up with the following expression for the current output gap:

$$y_t - \bar{y} = a_t - \alpha_2\left[i_t - \pi_{t+1,t}^e - \bar{r} + \sum_{j=1}^{\infty}(i_{t+j,t}^e - \pi_{t+j+1,t}^e - \bar{r})\right]. \qquad (48)$$

Equation (48) shows that under rational expectations the current output gap depends not only on the current real interest rate, but also on the *expected future* real interest rates and hence on the *expected future monetary policy*. If the economy has gut stuck in a liquidity trap where $i_t = 0$, (48) reduces to

$$y_t - \bar{y} = a_t + \alpha_2(\bar{r} + \pi_{t+1,t}^e) - \alpha_2\sum_{j=1}^{\infty}(i_{t+j,t}^e - \pi_{t+j+1,t}^e - \bar{r}). \qquad (49)$$

This analysis suggests two ways in which the central bank can help the economy to escape from a liquidity trap where the current nominal interest rate has hit its zero floor: it can promise to keep future nominal interest rates low and/or it can promise to create higher future inflation. To be more precise, the central bank can stimulate aggregate demand by promising to follow a *more expansionary* monetary policy in the future than the policy it pursued in the past – a policy that generated expected future real interest rates which were too high to prevent the economy from falling into the liquidity trap. In other words, the central bank must convince the markets that, at least for a certain period of time in the future, it will allow higher rates of inflation and economic activity than it would have allowed in the past. And this is the snag: is a promise to accept higher inflation than was acceptable in the past really credible? Will rational market participants really believe that the central bank will continue to allow higher future inflation and output gaps once the economy has escaped from recession? If markets do not believe that the central bank will stick to its promises, the announced change of future monetary policy will not work, since the variables $i_{t+j,t}^e$ and $\pi_{t+j+1,t}^e$ in (49) will then not be affected (sufficiently). This is the problem of (lack of) central bank *credibility* which will be analysed more rigorously in the next chapter.

As indicated by this discussion, central banks face an uncomfortable dilemma in a liquidity trap. On the one hand they may want to create expectations of higher future inflation to escape from the trap, but at the same time they hardly want inflation expectations to rise to levels that endanger their ability to keep future inflation rates under control. The dilemma is well illustrated by the statements of many central banks during the financial crisis of 2007–09. As the crisis unfolded central banks repeatedly stressed that they would keep their interest rates very low for as long as needed to stabilize the financial sector and the wider economy. But somewhat ambivalently, they also stressed their determination to keep inflation low and stable after the crisis. For example, in testimony before the US Congress in July 2009, Federal Reserve chairman Ben Bernanke said that '. . . it is important to assure the public and the markets that the extraordinary policy measures we have taken in response to the financial crisis and the recession can be withdrawn in a smooth and timely manner as needed, thereby avoiding the risk that policy stimulus could lead to a future rise in inflation'.

These observations suggest that central banks will not realistically be able to 'talk' the economy out of a liquidity trap, given the potential conflict between their short-term and their longer-term goals. Even if expectations are rational, fiscal policy may thus have to come to the rescue when the policy interest rate hits its zero bound, as indeed it did during the crisis of 2008–09. To sum up:

MONETARY POLICY IN A LIQUIDITY TRAP !

When aggregate demand depends on expected future income and expectations are rational, the current output gap will vary negatively with expected future real interest rates. Even if the economy is in a liquidity trap where the nominal interest rate has hit its zero bound, the central bank may therefore be able to stimulate demand by promising to keep future nominal interest rates low and to create higher future inflation. However, such a policy will only work if the central bank can persuade the markets that its future policy will be more expansionary than its past policies even after the economy has escaped from the recession. Such a promise is unlikely to be credible, and hence a fiscal expansion may still be needed to pull the economy out of a liquidity trap, even if expectations are forward-looking.

Announcement effects

The possibility of steering market expectations in a favourable direction during a liquidity trap is just one example of *announcement effects* of economic policies. In economies with forward-looking expectations, markets will react to *new information* on factors that are likely to affect the future course of the economy. Announcements of future changes in economic policy – or even just official statements which are interpreted as *signals* of future policy changes – will therefore influence the state of the economy even before the policy changes are implemented. To illustrate, financial market participants typically pay close attention to the public statements of central bankers and immediately react when they believe that these statements indicate future changes in monetary policy. A famous example of this was given on 5 December 1996, when the US Federal Reserve chairman Alan Greenspan gave a speech in which he argued that the booming stock prices at that time reflected the 'irrational exuberance' of stock market investors. This was interpreted as a sign that the Fed was ready to tighten monetary policy in order to bring stock prices down from an unsustainable level. As a result, stock prices immediately fell quite significantly, not only in the USA, but around the world, as illustrated in Figs 21.2a and 21.2b.[8]

To show how forward-looking expectations give rise to announcement effects in financial markets, we will consider a simple model of the stock market. As you recall from Chapter 14, the (fundamental) market value V_t of shares outstanding at the start of period t is given by the discounted value of expected future dividends. Assuming that dividends are paid out at the end of each period and that the representative shareholder's real discount rate is expected to stay constant over time at the value r, we thus have:

$$V_t = \frac{D_{t,t}^e}{1+r} + \frac{D_{t+1,t}^e}{(1+r)^2} + \frac{D_{t+2,t}^e}{(1+r)^3} + \ldots, \tag{50}$$

where $D_{t+n,t}^e$ is the *after-tax* real dividend which the shareholder expects to receive at the end of period $t + n$, given the information available at the beginning of period t. For simplicity, suppose that the pre-tax real dividend d fluctuates stochastically around a constant mean value $\bar{d}$ so that:

$$d_{t+n} = \bar{d} + \varepsilon_{t+n}, \tag{51}$$

---

8. In the end, as you probably know, the Fed was not willing to tighten monetary policy sufficiently to halt the stock market rally, so in the years after 1996 the stock market rose to even more exuberant heights before finally crashing in the year 2000.

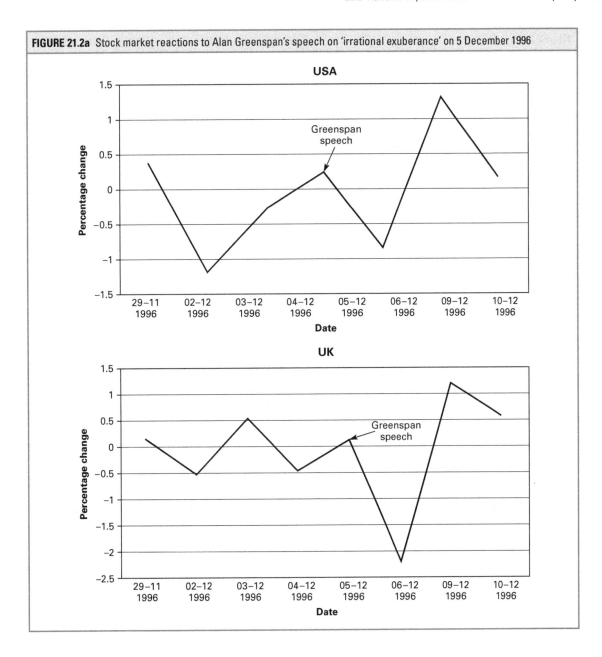

FIGURE 21.2a Stock market reactions to Alan Greenspan's speech on 'irrational exuberance' on 5 December 1996

where ε is a stochastic 'white noise' variable with zero mean. Suppose further that dividends are initially taxed at the proportional rate τ_0. According to (51), the rational expectation of the after-tax dividend received at the end of period $t + n$ is then given by:

$$D_{t+n,t}^e = (1 - \tau_0)\bar{d}, \tag{52}$$

as long as the dividend tax rate is expected to stay constant. Inserting (52) into (50) and collecting terms, we get:[9]

---

9. In deriving (53), we have used the general formula:

$$1 + a + a^2 + a^3 + \ldots = \frac{1}{1-a} \qquad \text{for } -1 < a < 1.$$

In our particular case we have $a = 1/(1 + r)$.

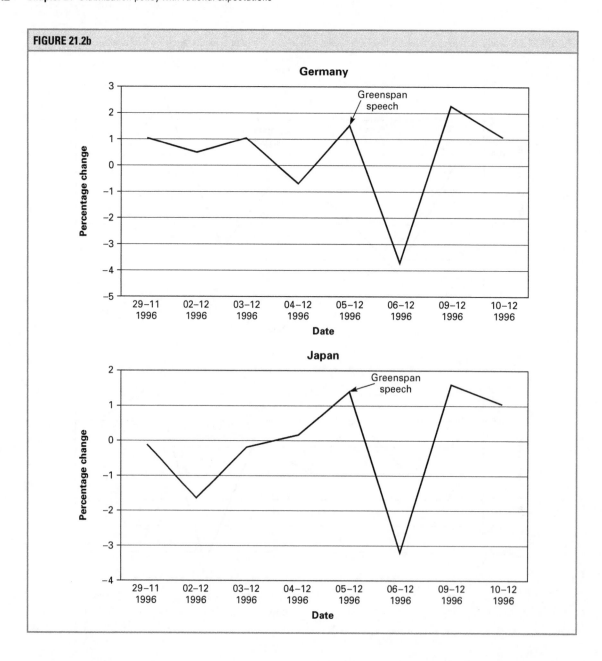

$$V_t = \frac{(1-\tau_0)\bar{d}}{r}. \tag{53}$$

Now suppose that at time $t = t_0$ the government suddenly announces that it will permanently reduce the dividend tax rate to a lower level $\tau_1 < \tau_0$ from some future time $t_1 > t_0$. Thus the actual net dividends accruing after time t_1 will be:

$$D_t = (1-\tau_1)(\bar{d} + \varepsilon_t) \qquad \text{for } t \geq t_1. \tag{54}$$

For the time periods from $t = t_0$ and up until $t = t_1 - 1$ the expected net dividend will still be given by (52) (with $t + n \leq t_1 - 1$), since the dividend tax cut does not take effect until period t_1. However, from (54) it follows that the rational expectation of net dividends paid out from period t_1 and onwards will be:

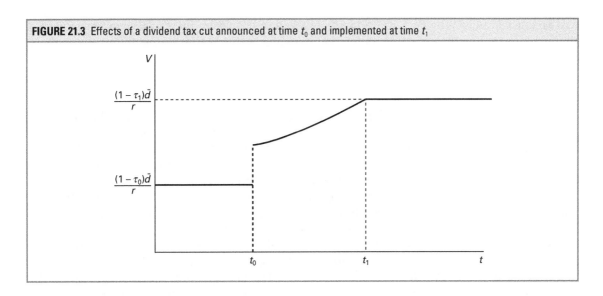

FIGURE 21.3 Effects of a dividend tax cut announced at time t_0 and implemented at time t_1

$$D^e_{t+n,t} = (1-\tau_1)\bar{d} \qquad \text{for } t+n \geq t_1 \text{ and } t \geq t_0.$$ (55)

Inserting (52) for $t_0 \leq t+n < t_1$ and (55) into (50), we obtain the value of the stock market in the time interval between t_0 and t_1:[10]

$$V_t = \frac{(1-\tau_0)\bar{d}}{1+r} + \frac{(1-\tau_0)\bar{d}}{(1+r)^2} + \dots + \frac{(1-\tau_0)\bar{d}}{(1+r)^{t_1-t}} + \frac{(1-\tau_1)\bar{d}}{(1+r)^{t_1+1-t}} + \frac{(1-\tau_1)\bar{d}}{(1+r)^{t_1+2-t}} + \dots \quad \Leftrightarrow$$ (56)

$$V_t = \left(\frac{\bar{d}}{r}\right)\left\{\left[1 - \frac{1}{(1+r)^{t_1-t}}\right](1-\tau_0) + \left[\frac{1}{(1+r)^{t_1-t}}\right](1-\tau_1)\right\} \qquad \text{for } t_0 \leq t \leq t_1.$$

We now have a complete picture of the evolution of the stock market. Before time t_0 the value of the market is given by (53). Between the time of the policy announcement and the time when the tax cut takes effect, the market value is given by (56), and from the time the tax cut is implemented we have

$$V_t = \frac{(1-\tau_1)\bar{d}}{r} \qquad \text{for } t \geq t_1,$$ (57)

by analogy to (53). Figure 21.3 illustrates the evolution of the stock market implied by these three equations.

Note that the market value of shares immediately jumps at time t_0 when the new information about future tax policy becomes available to the market, but *before* the new policy has actually been implemented. As the government announces its intention to change the future tax rules, investors start to anticipate higher future after-tax dividends, and this expected rise in future earnings is immediately capitalized in stock prices as a result of the forward-looking behaviour of the market. The magnitude of the initial jump in stock prices

---

10. To derive (56), we use the formula in the previous footnote plus the general formula:

$$1 + a + a^2 + a^3 + \dots + a^{n-1} = \frac{1-a^n}{1-a}.$$

In the present case we have $a = 1/(1+r)$ and $n = t_1 - t$.

can be derived by setting $t = t_0$ in (56) and subtracting (53) from the resulting expression to find the rise in the value of the stock market between time $t_0 - 1$ and time t_0:

$$V_{t_0} - V_{t_0-1} = \frac{(\tau_0 - \tau_1)(\bar{d}/r)}{(1 + r)^{t_1 - t_0}}. \tag{58}$$

This result is quite intuitive: the larger the future tax cut $(\tau_0 - \tau_1)$, the greater is the expected rise in future net dividends, so the greater is the initial rise in stock prices.

On the other hand, the longer it takes before the dividend tax is cut (the greater the difference between t_1 and t_0), the more heavily the market discounts the rise in expected future earnings, so the smaller is the initial upward jump in stock prices.

The magnitude $1 - \tau$ is sometimes called 'the retention ratio' because it measures the fraction of the pre-tax dividend which the shareholder is allowed to retain for himself. From (56) we see that between the time of announcement and the time when the tax cut takes effect, shares are valued as if the current retention ratio were a weighted average of the lower initial retention ratio $1 - \tau_0$ and the new higher retention ratio $1 - \tau_1$ which will prevail after time t_1. According to (56) the weight $1/(1 + r)^{t_1-t}$ given to the new retention ratio will be heavier, the shorter the time interval $t_1 - t$ between the current period t and the time when the dividend tax is cut. Again this is intuitive: the sooner the dividend tax will be cut, the more heavily the tax cut is capitalized in stock prices. After the initial jump in stock prices at time t_0, the value of the stock market will therefore gradually rise as the date t_1 for the tax cut moves closer. When that day arrives, the tax cut has already been fully capitalized by the market, so from time t_1 and onwards there is no further increase in stock prices, as illustrated in Fig. 21.3.[11]

The general lesson from this analysis is the following:

ANNOUNCEMENT EFFECTS OF POLICY CHANGES

In an asset market with a flexible asset price and forward-looking expectations, an announced change in a policy instrument affecting the return to the asset will cause an immediate 'jump' in its price even if the policy change does not take effect immediately. The magnitude of the initial price jump will be smaller, the smaller the change in the policy instrument and the longer the time span until the policy change takes effect. Following the initial jump, the asset price will gradually adjust to its new long-run equilibrium value during the time interval between the announcement and the implementation of the policy change. As a consequence, no further price jump will take place when the new policy takes effect.

For concreteness we have focused on the effects of anticipated changes in future economic policy. However, the method of analysis described in this subsection can also be used to study the effects of anticipated changes in other economic variables which are relevant for the valuation of assets with fully flexible prices. In all such cases the general rule is that asset prices 'jump' immediately at the time when new information becomes available, and after that time the asset price moves gradually and continuously towards its new long-run equilibrium value. In Exercise 5 we invite you to explore announcement effects in a simple model of the housing market.

---

11. Of course, in practice the change in stock prices after time t_0 will influence aggregate private investment and consumption and this in turn may have feedback effects on corporate earnings and dividends which will also affect the evolution of stock prices. These complications are ignored here.

21.3 Do people have rational expectations?

Arguments for and against the REH

The REH assumes that people's expectations accord with the predictions of the relevant economic model. The hypothesis does not postulate that ordinary people literally apply complicated economic models to form expectations about future economic conditions. This would obviously be a highly unrealistic assumption. But as we mentioned earlier, the economic forecasts produced by professional economists are widely publicized by the media and are thereby available to the general public. By using this information, people should be able to form unbiased forecasts of, say, the rate of inflation.

Critics have pointed out that economic experts have different views on how the economy works. Hence they often differ in their forecasts of future economic developments, so it is not obvious on which forecast ordinary persons should base their expectations. This is probably one of the most compelling criticisms of the REH. We know that the available economic models are wrong to some extent, since even the brightest economic experts do not fully understand how the economy works.

A related objection to the REH is that it takes time for people to learn enough about the structure of the economy to be able to form rational expectations. Learning from one's past forecast errors and correcting them accordingly is a time-consuming process. Similarly, identifying the economic experts who make the most reliable forecasts of the relevant economic variables may take time. In the meantime, many agents are in a process of learning about the economic environment, and during this period they are likely to commit systematic forecast errors.

Defenders of the REH argue that since economic agents have an incentive to avoid making forecasting errors, it is not attractive to assume that their forecasts differ systematically from the forecasts of the preferred model of the analyst. Such an assumption would imply that the analyst could permanently hide his supposedly superior information from other agents, even though they would benefit from getting access to it. In the context of economic policy making, if policy makers applied an economic model which assumes that private sector expectations differ systematically from the model's predictions, they would effectively be assuming that they could permanently fool the public. It may be a risky strategy to base economic policy on the premise that policy makers are systematically wiser than the private sector. As Abraham Lincoln said long before the rational expectations hypothesis in economics was suggested: 'You can fool all of the people some of the time; you can even fool some of the people all of the time, but you can't fool all of the people all of the time.'

Thus, although nobody really knows the 'true' structure of the economy in all of its detail, and although for this reason agents cannot literally calculate the true objective mean values of economic variables, defenders of the REH argue that it is not safe for the macroeconomic analyst to assume that the private sector is ignorant of the information embodied in his preferred economic model. From this perspective one may apply the REH as a sort of *robustness check* in economic policy evaluation: By asking whether the economic policy considered will have the desired effects if agents form their expectations in accordance with the economic model used by the policy adviser, one can check whether a proposed policy will work even if people fully understand its effects. Undertaking such a check seems useful even if expectations may not be fully rational in practice.

The importance of expectations for consumer behaviour

In the end, however, 'the proof of the pudding is in the eating': whether the REH is a fruitful hypothesis depends on the extent to which it helps us understand observed economic behaviour. In the rest of this chapter we will therefore discuss some empirical evidence bearing on the REH.

In Chapter 14 we have already encountered one version of the REH in the form of the so-called Efficient Markets Hypothesis. This hypothesis says that financial asset prices always reflect the best possible forecasts of the future cash flows from the assets, given all the relevant information currently available. As we explained in Chapter 14, the Efficient Market Hypothesis implies that stock prices will be less volatile than the present value of actual future dividends. In Chapter 14 we saw that this prediction seems to be rejected by the data displayed in Fig. 14.5.

Let us next investigate whether the implications of the REH for the most important component of aggregate demand – private consumption – are consistent with the data for aggregate consumption. This will give us an opportunity to revisit the theory of consumption developed in Chapter 15 and to illustrate the surprising consequences of the REH for consumer behaviour.

To simplify the exposition, we will follow the procedure in Chapter 15 and split the consumer's time horizon into two periods, period 1 ('the present') and period 2 ('the future'), but it should be stressed that all our results carry over to a setting with many periods. Applying the notation from Chapter 15, the representative consumer enjoys instantaneous utility $u(C_1)$ from consumption in period 1 and instantaneous utility $u(C_2)$ from consumption in period 2. But since the consumer is impatient, the present value of future consumption is only $u(C_2)/(1 + \phi)$ in utility terms, where ϕ is the exogenous rate of time preference, so from the perspective of the present the consumer's actual lifetime utility is $u(C_1) + u(C_2)/(1 + \phi)$. As an extension of the analysis in Chapter 15, we will now explicitly allow for the fact that the consumer does not know his future income with certainty. Thus he does not know in period 1 exactly how much he can afford to consume in period 2, so the best thing he can do is to choose his present consumption C_1 so as to maximize his *expected* lifetime utility, taking his intertemporal budget constraint into account.

We will denote the *expected* instantaneous utility of future consumption by $E_1[u(C_2)]$, where the subscript '1' below the expectations operator E indicates that the expectation is formed in period 1. Thus the consumer's expected lifetime utility is $u(C_1) + E_1[u(C_2)]/(1 + \phi)$. If he decides to save an extra euro in period 1, he incurs a current utility loss equal to the marginal utility of current consumption $u'(C_1)$. But if the real interest rate is r, he will be able to increase his consumption in period 2 by $1 + r$, and this will increase the expected lifetime utility from future consumption by the amount $(1 + r)E[u'(C_2)]/(1 + \phi)$, where $E[u'(C_2)]$ is the expected marginal utility of consumption in period 2.[12] For the consumer's choice of C_1 to be optimal, he must be indifferent between consuming an extra euro and saving an extra euro in period 1, implying:

$$u'(C_1) = \left(\frac{1+r}{1+\phi}\right) E_1[u'(C_2)]. \tag{59}$$

Equation (59) is a straightforward extension of the Keynes–Ramsey rule derived in Eq. (9) of Chapter 15. According to (59) the marginal utility of an extra unit of current consumption (the left-hand side) must equal the expected marginal utility from an extra unit of saving (the right-hand side) for the consumer to be in optimum.

For concreteness, let us assume that the instantaneous utility function takes the quadratic form:

$$u(C_t) = C_t - \frac{a}{2}C_t^2, \qquad t = 1, 2, \tag{60}$$

---

12. Although we allow for uncertainty about the consumer's future labour and transfer income, we assume for simplicity that the real return on saving r is known with certainty. This will be the case if the consumer invests his saving in a risk-free indexed bond.

which implies that (expected) marginal utility decreases linearly with the (expected) level of consumption:

$$u'(C_1) = 1 - aC_1 \quad \text{and} \quad E_1[u'(C_2)] = E_1[1 - aC_2] = 1 - aE_1[C_2].$$ (61)

In the benchmark case where the real interest rate equals the rate of time preference $(r = \phi)$, it then follows from (59) and (61) that:

$$C_1 = E_1[C_2]$$ (62)

In other words, the consumer's expected future consumption level will correspond to his current consumption, since the assumption $r = \phi$ implies that he prefers to smooth his consumption perfectly over time.

So far we have made no specific assumption about the formation of expectations. The result $E_1[u'(C_2)] = 1 - aE_1[C_2]$ holds whether or not expectations of future consumption are rational. To explore the implications of expectations formation for consumption behaviour, we need to introduce the consumer's budget constraints. As you recall from Eqs. (3) and (4) in Chapter 15, these are given by

Budget constraint for period 1: $\quad V_2 = (1 + r)(V_1 + Y_1 - C_1),$ (63)

Budget constraint for period 2: $\quad C_2 = V_2 + Y_2,$ (64)

where V_t is real financial wealth at the start of period t, Y_t is after-tax labour and transfer income in period t, and where we assume that all payments are made at the beginning of each period. Using (63) to eliminate V_2 from (64), we obtain the consumer's intertemporal budget constraint:

$$C_1 + \frac{C_2}{1+r} = V_1 + Y_1 + \frac{Y_2}{1+r},$$ (65)

stating that the present value of lifetime consumption (the left-hand side) must equal the present value of the consumer's lifetime resources (the right-hand side). Even if he does not have rational expectations, the consumer knows that over the life cycle he cannot spend beyond his means, so in period 1 he expects that his lifetime consumption is subject to the constraint:

$$C_1 + \frac{E_1[C_2]}{1+r} = V_1 + Y_1 + \frac{E_1[Y_2]}{1+r},$$ (66)

which is obtained by taking expectations of (65), assuming that the consumer knows his current income and wealth $V_1 + Y_1$ but not his future income Y_2. Inserting (62) into (66) and using (63), we get:

$$C_1 + \frac{C_1}{1+r} = V_1 + Y_1 + \frac{E_1[Y_2]}{1+r} \quad \Leftrightarrow$$ (67)

$$C_1 = \overbrace{(1+r)(V_1 + Y_1 - C_1)}^{=V_2} + E_1[Y_2] = V_2 + E_1[Y_2],$$

which may be subtracted from (64) to give:

$$C_2 - C_1 = Y_2 - E_1[Y_2].$$ (68)

Thus the rise (fall) in consumption over time equals the amount by which the consumer underestimated (overestimated) his future income when he formed the expectations governing his first-period consumption.

From (68) we may derive the implications of alternative hypotheses regarding expectations formation. Suppose first that expectations are *static*, implying that expected future income equals actual current income:

$$E_1[Y_2] = Y_1. \tag{69}$$

According to (68) and (69) the change in consumption over time will then be equal to the change in income:

$$C_2 - C_1 = Y_2 - Y_1. \tag{70}$$

Suppose alternatively that expectations of future income are *rational*, being an unbiased prediction of the actual future income so that:

$$E_1[Y_2] = Y_2 - x, \qquad E[x] = 0, \tag{71}$$

where x is a stochastic variable with zero mean, reflecting that agents do not make systematic forecast errors. Substituting (71) into (68), we get:

$$C_2 - C_1 = x. \tag{72}$$

Following a similar procedure, one can show that the results in (71) and (72) also hold for a consumer who lives for many periods. Thus we have:

Static expectations: $C_t - C_{t-1} = Y_t - Y_{t-1},$ $\qquad$ (73)

Rational expectations: $C_t - C_{t-1} = x_t,$ $\qquad$ $E[x_t] = 0.$ $\qquad$ (74)

Notice the striking result in (74): *under rational expectations the change in consumption over time is entirely unpredictable.* According to the REH, the best forecast of consumption tomorrow is the level of consumption observed today. Indeed, current consumption is the only unbiased forecast of future consumption. Because (74) implies that consumption may change by any amount in any direction, it is said that consumption follows a *random walk*. This implication of the REH was first derived in a seminal paper by American economist Robert Hall.[13]

Testing the random walk hypothesis

In summary, under rational expectations the change in consumption over time equals the *unpredictable* part of the change in income, whereas under static expectations the change in consumption equals the *total* change in income, including that part of the income change which could have been predicted by a forward-looking consumer. In another influential paper, economists John Campbell and Greg Mankiw proposed a simple way of testing the empirical relevance of these two competing hypotheses on consumption behaviour.[14]

13. See Robert E. Hall, 'Stochastic Implications of the Life Cycle-Permanent Income Hypothesis: Theory and Evidence', *Journal of Political Economy*, **86**, December 1978, pp. 971–987. At the time the random walk hypothesis was so provocative that when Hall first presented his paper, one prominent economist told him that he must have been on drugs when he wrote the paper.

14. See John Y. Campbell and N. Gregory Mankiw, 'The Response of Consumption to Income – A Cross-Country Investigation', *European Economic Review*, **35**, 1991, pp. 723–767.

Campbell and Mankiw assumed that a fraction λ of aggregate income accrues to consumers who behave in accordance with (73), as if they have static expectations. The remaining fraction $1 - \lambda$ of total income was assumed to accrue to consumers with rational expectations whose consumption follow a random walk. From (73) and (74), the change in total consumption will then be given by:

$$C_t - C_{t-1} = \lambda(Y_t - Y_{t-1}) + (1-\lambda)x_t, \qquad 0 \le \lambda \le 1. \tag{75}$$

This equation spans the two alternative hypotheses on expectations: if $\lambda = 1$ all consumers have static expectations, and if $\lambda = 0$ they all hold rational expectations. Using data on consumption and income, Campbell and Mankiw provided an econometric estimate of the magnitude of the parameter λ in a number of countries. Their results are summarized in Table 21.1, where the figures in brackets indicate standard errors.[15]

In all of the countries the magnitude of λ was found to be significantly greater than 0, ranging from about 0.2 to 0.4. In other words, a large part of consumption seems to be undertaken by consumers who are not forward-looking. This is clearly at odds with a strict interpretation of the REH. On the other hand, forward-looking consumers do seem to account for the bulk of consumption in most countries, so the REH certainly cannot be dismissed as being irrelevant. Rather, it appears that consumers are divided into two groups; one which is forward-looking, and another which is backward-looking. Note that consumers obeying (73) do not necessarily all have static expectations. It is also possible that they are simply myopic, living from 'hand to mouth', immediately consuming all of their current income without caring about the future. Indeed, this is the interpretation adopted by Campbell and Mankiw. However, in both cases the fact remains that these consumers do not behave as predicted by the REH.

TABLE 21.1 The proportion of consumers with static expectations (λ)

Country	Sample period	Estimate of λ (standard errors in bracket)
Canada	1972(1)–1988(1)	0.225 (0.107)
France	1972(1)–1988(1)	0.401 (0.208)
Sweden	1972(2)–1988(1)	0.203 (0.092)
United Kingdom	1975(2)–1988(2)	0.351 (0.117)
United States	1953(1)–1985(4)	0.357 (0.173)

Source: J.Y. Campbell and N.G. Mankiw, 'The Response of Consumption to Income', *European Economic Review*, 35, 1991, p. 736.

15. Campbell and Mankiw actually measured the changes in income and consumption in logarithms and included a constant term on the right-hand side of Eq. (75) to capture long-term growth. Since periods with surprise increases in income probably often coincide with periods with rapid growth in total income, the explanatory variable $Y_t - Y_{t-1}$ is likely to be positively correlated with the error term x_t. Readers trained in econometrics will know that the estimation method of Ordinary Least Squares will then generate an upward bias in the estimate for λ. To deal with this problem, Campbell and Mankiw used the method of Two-Stage Least Squares. The first stage of this estimation method involved the use of lagged changes in consumption (which are necessarily uncorrelated with x_t) in an OLS regression to predict $Y_t - Y_{t-1}$. In the second stage, the estimated values of $Y_t - Y_{t-1}$ were used as the explanatory variable in (75) to estimate the value of λ in another OLS regression.

Of course, the results of this analysis should be interpreted with some caution. First of all, to derive the random walk hypothesis, we assumed a quadratic utility function (Eq. (60)) combined with rational expectations. Thus the econometric study by Campbell and Mankiw is really a joint test of a hypothesis on expectations formation and a hypothesis on the form of the utility function. In principle, if the estimated value of λ deviates significantly from 0, it could be because the utility function is not quadratic rather than because expectations are not rational. However, one can actually derive the random walk hypothesis using approximations to more general utility functions, so the assumption of quadratic utility is not as critical for the findings of Campbell and Mankiw as it may seem.

As another potential objection, a positive value of λ may indicate that some consumers are *credit-constrained* rather than myopic. If a forward-looking consumer expects his future income to be higher than his current income, he may want to borrow against his anticipated future income in order to smooth his consumption over time. But in the absence of collateral, his bank may be unwilling to accommodate his credit demand for fear that he may default on the loan if his future income turns out to be lower than expected. Then the best thing such a credit-constrained consumer can do is to consume all of his current income ($C_t = Y_t$), implying $C_t - C_{t-1} = Y_t - Y_{t-1}$, as if expectations were static.

Although the hypothesis of credit constraints may sound plausible, there are some arguments against this interpretation of the empricial findings of Campbell and Mankiw. Up until the 1980s, governments in the OECD countries typically intervened in financial markets in an effort to regulate the volume of credit. During the 1980s these capital market regulations were lifted in most countries. If liquidity constraints were widespread, one would expect such capital market liberalization to increase the volume of credit, thereby relaxing the credit constraints of many consumers. Presumably this would mean that our parameter λ should decrease, if this parameter mainly reflects credit constraints rather than myopic or backward-looking behaviour. However, Campbell and Mankiw found no cross-country evidence of a statistically significant drop in λ in the latter part of their sample period where capital markets had been liberalized. In a careful analysis of macroeconomic data from Sweden, economists Jonas Agell and Lennart Berg likewise failed to find any significant effect of financial deregulation on the value of λ.[16] This suggests that, at least when the economy is not in a financial crisis, consumption is not significantly constrained by credit rationing.

One can also approach the issue of liquidity constraints from another angle. If such constraints are important, one would expect that current consumption will tend to be governed by current income for households without liquid assets, whereas households with significant liquid assets will be able to smooth their consumption over time, because they can simply sell their assets rather than asking the bank for a loan. However, using microeconomic data on income and consumption in the United States, economist John Shea found no evidence of a significant difference between the consumption behaviour of households with and without liquid assets.[17]

Since all of this evidence suggests that liquidity constraints are not a very important determinant of consumption in 'normal' times, our preferred interpretation of the study by Campbell and Mankiw is that many consumers behave as if they have static expectations or as if they are simply myopic. At the same time a large part of total consumption seems to be governed by forward-looking rational expectations. In summary:

16.   Jonas Agell and Lennart Berg, 'Does Financial Deregulation Cause a Consumption Boom?' *Scandinavian Journal of Economics*, **98**, 1996, pp. 579–601.

17.   See John Shea, 'Union Contracts and the Life-Cycle/Permanent-Income Hypothesis', *American Economic Review*, **85**, 1995, pp. 186–200.

EXPECTATIONS, CONSUMPTION AND THE RANDOM WALK HYPOTHESIS

For consumers with static expectations (or myopic consumers who live 'from hand to mouth'), the change in consumption from one period to the next equals the total change in income. For consumers with rational expectations the change in consumption only equals the **unpredictable** part of the change in income. Hence the REH implies that consumption will follow a random walk. Empirical evidence from a number of Western countries suggests that about 25 to 40 per cent of consumers behave as if they have static expectations (or are myopic), while the remaining fraction of consumers behave in accordance with the REH.

Towards a more general theory of expectations

Thus both of the competing hypotheses on expectations formation which you have encountered in this book – backward-looking expectations and rational expectations – appear to have some empirical relevance. One might therefore specify the expected inflation rate as:

$$\pi_t^e = \lambda \pi_{t-1} + (1-\lambda)\pi_{t,t-1}^e, \qquad 0 \le \lambda \le 1. \tag{76}$$

Here π_t^e is the average expected inflation rate calculated across the entire population, and $\pi_{t,t-1}^e$ is the rationally expected inflation rate, based on all information available up until the end of the previous period. Equation (76) assumes that a fraction λ of the population has static expectations, while the remaining fraction has rational expectations. If we go back to our AS–AD model (1)–(5) and replace (5) by (76), we obtain a model with partly rational expectations. To solve such a model, one still has to go through the three steps used to solve a model with purely rational expectations. Making the first two steps,[18] we find the expected inflation rate for those agents who have rational expectations:

$$\pi_{t,t-1}^e = \pi^* + \left(\frac{\lambda}{\lambda + \gamma \alpha}\right)(\pi_{t-1} - \pi^*), \qquad \alpha \equiv \frac{\alpha_2 h}{1 + \alpha_2 b}. \tag{77}$$

The rational agents know that the expectations of the backward-looking agents have some influence on the actual inflation rate via the expectations-augmented Phillips curve. Hence the rational forecast of inflation stated in (77) accounts for the fact that the expectations held by the backward-looking agents are not anchored by the central bank's inflation target. This is why the term $(\pi_{t-1} - \pi^*)$ enters the right-hand side of (77) with a positive coefficient which is larger the greater the fraction of the population with backward-looking expectations.

Using (76) and (77), one can show that our AS–AD model with partly rational expectations can be reduced to the following two difference equations in the output gap, $\hat{y}_t \equiv y_t - \bar{y}$, and the inflation gap, $\hat{\pi}_t \equiv \pi_t - \pi^*$:

$$\hat{y}_t = \left(\frac{\lambda}{\lambda + \gamma \alpha}\right)\hat{y}_{t-1} + \frac{z_t}{1 + \gamma \alpha} - \frac{\lambda z_{t-1}}{\lambda + \gamma \alpha} - \frac{\alpha s_t}{1 + \gamma \alpha}, \tag{78}$$

$$\hat{\pi}_t = \left(\frac{\lambda}{\lambda + \gamma \alpha}\right)\hat{\pi}_{t-1} + \frac{\gamma z_t}{1 + \gamma \alpha} + \frac{s_t}{1 + \gamma \alpha}, \qquad z_t \equiv (1 + \alpha_2 b)v_t. \tag{79}$$

The model analysed in Chapter 18 is the special case of (78) and (79) where $\lambda = 1$ (if you compare (78) and (79) to Eqs (41) and (42) in Chapter 18 and set $\lambda = 1$ and $\phi = 0$, implying

---

18. Here we maintain our previous assumption that the expected inflation rate π_{t+1}^e entering the monetary policy rule (4) is the private sector's expected inflation rate determining the real interest rate in (2).

that all of the population has static expectations, you will see that the two sets of equations are exactly identical). The model set up in Section 21.2 of this chapter is the other special case where $\lambda = 0$ (in this case (78) and (79) collapse to (35) and (34), given that $\alpha \equiv \alpha_2 h/(1 + \alpha_2 b)$ and $z_t \equiv (1 + \alpha_2 b)v_t$). In the more general case where $0 < \lambda < 1$, (78) and (79) still have the same general form as the difference equations in the output and inflation gaps implied by our AS–AD model with purely static expectations. From an empirical perspective the model (78) and (79) with $\lambda > 0$ has the attractive property that it generates persistence in the output and inflation gaps, that is, the current gaps depend positively on their own lagged values. As you recall from Chapter 13, real-world macroeconomic time series do display such persistence.

Note that substitution of (77) into (76) yields:

$$\pi_t^e = \varphi\pi^* + (1 - \varphi)\pi_{t-1}, \qquad 0 \leq \varphi \equiv \frac{\gamma\alpha(1 - \lambda)}{\lambda + \gamma\alpha} \leq 1. \tag{80}$$

This shows that, in an economy with partly rational and partly static expectations, the average expected inflation rate is a weighted average of the central bank's inflation target and last period's actual inflation rate. When all agents are rational ($\lambda = 0$), we have $\varphi = 1$ and $\pi_t^e = \pi^*$, and when they all have static expectations ($\lambda = 1$), we get $\varphi = 0$ and $\pi_t^e = \pi_{t-1}$.

Equation (80) was derived on the assumption that a part of the population forms rational expectations in accordance with (77). As we have discussed, this assumption that (some) people behave as if they know the entire structure of the economy is indeed a strong one. But there is an alternative interpretation of (80) which does not require that agents are quite as sophisticated as postulated by the REH: even if the forward-looking part of the population may not always have sufficient information to be able to form the strictly rational expectation given by (77), these people may at least be informed about the central bank's inflation target π^*. Therefore, if the central bank has credibility (an issue to which we return in the next chapter), it may make good sense for agents to assume that, on average, the inflation rate will correspond to the target rate of inflation. Thus we may interpret the parameter φ in (80) as the fraction of the population which is informed about (and has confidence in) the central bank's inflation target. Since this is also the long-run equilibrium rate of inflation, this forecasting behaviour may be called 'long-term rational expectations' or 'weakly rational expectations'. We will return to this hypothesis in Chapters 24 and 25 when we consider the open economy.

A MORE GENERAL THEORY OF EXPECTATIONS ❗

If some consumers have static expectations while others have rational expectations, the expected inflation rate will be a weighted average of last year's actual inflation rate and the central bank's target inflation rate. The weight placed on the target inflation rate may be seen as an indicator of the fraction of the population which is informed about the inflation target, even if these people do not have strictly rational expectations.

21.4 Summary

1. The assumption of backward-looking (static or adaptive) expectations is hard to reconcile with rational behaviour because it implies that economic agents may make systematic forecast errors.

2. As an alternative to backward-looking expectations, economists have developed the rational expectations hypothesis (REH) according to which an agent's subjective expectation of an economic variable equals the objective mathematical expectation of the variable, calculated on the basis of all relevant information available at the time the expectation is formed.

3. The REH assumes that the information available to agents includes knowledge about the structure of the economy. Hence rational expectations are *model-consistent*: they correspond to the predictions of the relevant economic model. This does not require that ordinary people are able to solve economic models, since the average person may rely on the publicly available forecasts of professional economists.

4. The REH has led to the Lucas Critique which says that an econometric macro model which was estimated under a previous economic policy regime cannot be used to predict economic behaviour under a new policy regime. The reason is that a change in the policy regime will affect private sector behaviour, including the way in which expectations are formed.

5. Some macroeconomic models with rational expectations have led to the Policy Ineffectiveness Proposition (PIP) which claims that systematic demand management policy cannot affect real output and employment because the private sector will fully anticipate the effects of systematic policy on the rate of inflation.

6. The PIP is nowadays considered unrealistic, since the central bank can typically change its policy in reaction to new economic developments occurring after nominal wages have been temporarily locked into existing contracts. Because nominal wages and prices only respond to economic shocks with a lag, systematic monetary policy can affect output and employment, even if the policy is fully anticipated by rational agents. The optimal monetary stabilization policy involves a trade-off between stabilizing inflation and stabilizing output. The greater the variance of demand shocks relative to the variance of supply shocks, the more the central bank should raise the interest rate in response to a rise in the inflation gap.

7. When aggregate demand depends on expected future income, the current output gap will vary negatively with expected future real interest rates. If the economy ends up in a liquidity trap where the nominal interest rate hits its zero bound, the central bank may therefore still be able to stimulate aggregate demand by promising to keep future nominal interest rates lower and to keep future inflation rates higher than prescribed by the monetary policy rule it has previously followed. However, such an announced policy may lack credibility and may therefore be ineffective.

8. Under rational expectations the announcement of future changes in economic policy will influence the economy already at the time of announcement, even before the new policy is implemented. In particular, the flexible prices of financial assets such as stocks will 'jump' instantaneously at the time of announcement and will then gradually adjust towards its new long-run equilibrium value as the date of implementation of the policy change comes closer.

9. The REH has been criticized for being unrealistic because economists differ in their views of the workings of the economy, making it difficult for the average person to base their expectations on expert forecasts. Defenders of the REH argue that it is not safe to base economic policy evaluation on the assumption that policy makers are systematically better informed than the private sector. Hence policy makers should assume that the knowledge embodied in their economic models is also available to the private sector, as implied by the REH.

▶

10. When consumers with rational expectations seek to smooth their consumption over time, private consumption will follow a random walk, changing only as new information about future incomes becomes available. The random walk hypothesis implies that the current consumption level is the best forecast of future consumption (adjusted for underlying trend growth) and that consumption changes only in response to unpredictable changes in income. By contrast, under static expectations the change in consumption corresponds to the change in the consumer's total income. Empirical evidence suggests that a large part of aggregate consumption follows a random walk, consistent with the REH, but at the same time many consumers behave as if they have static expectations.

11. In an economy where some consumers have rational expectations and others have static expectations, the average expected inflation rate may be written as a weighted average of the central bank's inflation target and last period's inflation rate. The weight given to the inflation target may be interpreted as the fraction of agents informed about the monetary policy target, even if these people do not have all the information needed to form strictly rational expectations regarding the short run.

21.5 Exercises

Exercise 1. Issues in rational expectations

1. Define and explain the concept of rational expectations and discuss the arguments for and against this hypothesis.

2. Explain the Policy Ineffectiveness Proposition and discuss its relevance.

3. Explain the content of the Lucas Critique and its implications for the evaluation of the effects of economic policy.

4. Discuss whether the central bank can pull the economy out of a liquidity trap by promising to keep future nominal interest rates low and/or by promising higher future inflation.

5. Explain the content of the random walk hypothesis for private consumption. Explain the difference between the dynamics of private consumption under static and under rational expectations.

Exercise 2. Monetary and fiscal policy under rational expectations

Suppose that the central bank does not always react systematically to changes in macroeconomic conditions so that monetary policy may be described by the interest rate rule:

$$r_t = \bar{r} + h(\pi_{t,t-1}^e - \pi^*) + a_t, \qquad h > 0, \tag{81}$$

where a_t is a 'white noise' stochastic variable reflecting the non-systematic part of monetary policy. Equation (81) states that the central bank bases its policy decisions on the *expected* inflation gap, since it does not have full information on the current inflation rate at the time when it sets the interest rate. For simplicity, we assume that the bank does not react to the expected output gap.

As usual, the economy's demand and supply sides are described by:

Goods market equilibrium: $\quad y_t - \bar{y} = z_t - \alpha_2(r_t - \bar{r}),$ \hfill (82)

SRAS: $\quad \pi_t = \pi_{t,t-1}^e + \gamma(y_t - \bar{y}) + s_t,$ \hfill (83)

where z_t and s_t are white noise reflecting demand and supply shocks.

1. Assume that expectations are rational and find the model solution for real output by going through the three steps in the solution procedure described in the main text. On this basis, show that the variance of output is given by:

$$\sigma_y^2 \equiv E[(y_t - \bar{y})^2] = \sigma_z^2 + \alpha_2^2 \sigma_a^2, \tag{84}$$

where σ_z^2 and σ_a^2 are the variances of z and a, respectively. Is monetary policy 'effective' in this model? What would be the effect of greater predictability of monetary policy? Would greater predictability be desirable? Discuss.

The variable $z_t = \alpha_1(g_t - \bar{g}) + v_t$ includes deviations of public spending from trend as well as the private demand shock variable v_t. Suppose now that fiscal policy reacts to the expected inflation and output gaps in the following systematic way, reflecting an intended countercyclical and anti-inflationary policy:

$$g_t - \bar{g} = c_\pi(\pi^* - \pi_{t,t-1}^e) + c_y(\bar{y} - y_{t,t-1}^e) \quad \Leftrightarrow$$

$$z_t = \alpha_1 c_\pi(\pi^* - \pi_{t,t-1}^e) + \alpha_1 c_y(\bar{y} - y_{t,t-1}^e) + v_t. \tag{85}$$

Here we assume that v_t is white noise. To focus on fiscal policy, suppose further that monetary policy is passive, keeping the real interest rate at its natural level:

$$r_t = \bar{r}. \tag{86}$$

2. Assume rational expectations and demonstrate that the Policy Ineffectiveness Proposition holds in the model consisting of Eqs (82), (83), (85) and (86). Explain why fiscal policy is ineffective. Suppose instead that the fiscal authorities can react on current information on the actual output and inflation gaps whereas nominal wages are pre-set at the start of each period when inflation expectations can be based only on the information available up until the end of the previous period. Thus (86) is still valid, but (85) is replaced by:

$$z_t = \alpha_1 c_\pi(\pi^* - \pi_t) + \alpha_1 c_y(\bar{y} - y_t) + v_t. \tag{87}$$

3. Show that the Policy Ineffectiveness Proposition no longer holds in the model consisting of (82), (83), (86) and (87) even if expectations are rational. Explain why fiscal policy is now effective.

Exercise 3. Nominal GDP targeting with rational expectations

You are now asked to study the properties of an economy where the fiscal and monetary authorities pursue a target for the growth rate of nominal GDP. Specifically, we assume that

$$\overbrace{y_t^n - y_{t-1}^n}^{\substack{\text{actual growth rate} \\ \text{of nominal GDP}}} = \overbrace{\mu + \eta(\bar{y} - y_{t-1})}^{\substack{\text{target growth rate} \\ \text{of nominal GDP}}} + v_t, \qquad \eta > 0, \tag{88}$$

where y_t^n is the natural log of *nominal* GDP, and where the stochastic white noise variable v_t reflects that the authorities cannot perfectly control the growth in aggregate nominal demand. The first expression on the right-hand side of (88) shows that policy makers try to speed up the growth in nominal GDP if the previous period's real output y_{t-1} has been below the trend level of real output, and vice versa. Thus the authorities follow a countercyclical demand management policy, but since they can only observe output with a lag, they react to the previous period's activity level rather than to current activity.

In our previous notation, $y_t^n \equiv p_t + y_t$, and $\pi_t \equiv p_t - p_{t-1}$, where p and y are the logs of the price level and of real output, respectively. By definition we thus have:

$$y_t^n - y_{t-1}^n = \pi_t + y_t - y_{t-1}. \tag{89}$$

Equations (88) and (89) describe the economy's demand side. The supply side is given by the AS-curve:

$$\pi_t = \pi_{t,t-1}^e + \gamma(y_t - \bar{y}) + s_t, \tag{90}$$

where the stochastic supply shock variable s_t is white noise.

1. Find the solutions for real output and inflation on the assumption that expectations are rational. Does the Policy Ineffectiveness Proposition hold in this model? Explain your results.

   Suppose next that the authorities can react to current output so that the policy rule (88) is replaced by

$$y_t^n - y_{t-1}^n = \mu + \eta(\bar{y} - y_t) + v_t. \tag{91}$$

2. Find the solution for real output and check whether the Policy Ineffectiveness Proposition holds. Which of the scenarios (Question 1 versus Question 2) do you consider to be more realistic? Give reasons for your answer.

Exercise 4. Output persistence under rational expectations

In the main text we noted that our basic AS–AD model with rational expectations does not generate any persistence (autocorrelation) in the deviations of output from trend, in contrast to what we observe empirically. This exercise asks you to show that persistence in output will emerge if we allow for autocorrelation in our supply shock variable. Thus we now describe the economy by the following equations, where we assume for simplicity that the central bank only reacts to the inflation gap:

SRAS: $\qquad \pi_t = \pi_{t,t-1}^e + \gamma(y_t - \bar{y}) + s_t,$ $\qquad\qquad\qquad\qquad$ (92)

Goods market equilibrium: $\qquad y_t - \bar{y} = z_t - \alpha_2(r_t - \bar{r}),$ $\qquad\qquad$ (93)

Monetary policy rule: $\qquad r_t = \bar{r} + h(\pi_t - \pi^*), \qquad h > 0,$ $\qquad\qquad$ (94)

Supply shock: $\qquad s_t = \omega s_{t-1} + c_t, \qquad 0 < \omega < 1,$ $\qquad\qquad$ (95)

Demand shock: $\qquad z_t = \rho z_{t-1} + x_t, \qquad 0 \le \rho < 1.$ $\qquad\qquad$ (96)

The stochastic variables c_t and x_t are assumed to be white noise. When they form their inflation expectations for the current period, $\pi_{t,t-1}^e$, the information set available to private agents includes knowledge of the model (92)–(96) *plus* information on the shocks observed during the previous period, s_{t-1} and z_{t-1}. However, the private sector's information set does *not* include information on the 'innovations' to the shocks, c_t and x_t.

1. Show that the rational expectations solution for the output gap in the model (92)–(96) is given by:

$$\hat{y}_t \equiv y_t - \bar{y} = \beta(x_t - \alpha_2 h c_t) - \frac{\omega s_{t-1}}{\gamma}, \qquad \beta \equiv \frac{1}{1 + \gamma\alpha_2 h}. \tag{97}$$

Try to explain why the output gap is affected by s_{t-1}, but not by z_{t-1}.

2. Show that output displays persistence by using (95) and (97) to write the solution for the output gap in the form:

$$\hat{y}_t = a\hat{y}_{t-1} + \varepsilon_t \tag{98}$$

where $0 < a < 1$, and where ε_t is a (composite) white noise variable. Write the explicit expressions for a and ε_t. (Hint: start by lagging (97) by one period and then use the fact from (95) that $\omega s_{t-2} = s_{t-1} - c_{t-1}$ to write s_{t-1}/γ as a function of $\hat{y}_{t-1}$, x_{t-1} and c_{t-1}. Then insert the resulting expression for s_{t-1}/γ into (97) and collect terms.) Discuss whether output persistence can be said to be endogenous or exogenous in this model.

Exercise 5. Policy announcement effects in the housing market

In the main text we saw that when expectations are forward-looking, announcements of future policy changes will have an effect on the stock market right from the time of announcement. Here we ask you to analyse announcement effects on the housing market. We consider a representative consumer who owns a fixed stock of housing yielding a flow of housing services whose real rental value h_t fluctuates stochastically around the constant mean value $\bar{h}$. We therefore assume that, during any period, the homeowner expects that the real value of his housing service will be $\bar{h}$. The homeowner pays a property tax which is levied in the real amount τ_t per square metre. For simplicity, the property tax is thus assumed to be unrelated to the market value of the house, but the tax may vary over time. Suppose that the consumer owns one unit of housing with a market price Q_t at the beginning of period t. Suppose further that, at the start of period t, the market price at the start of the next period is expected to be $Q_{t+1,t}^e$. If the real interest rate is r (assumed for convenience to be constant), the current market price of housing must then satisfy the following arbitrage condition for consumers to be willing to own the existing stock of owner-occupied housing:

$$\underbrace{rQ_t}_{\substack{\text{opportunity cost of} \\ \text{home-ownership}}} = \underbrace{\bar{h} - \tau_t}_{\substack{\text{after-tax value} \\ \text{of housing} \\ \text{service}}} + \underbrace{Q_{t+1,t}^e - Q_t}_{\substack{\text{expected capital} \\ \text{gain}}}. \tag{99}$$

The left-hand side of (99) measures the consumer's opportunity cost of owning his home rather than selling it at the going market price and investing the proceeds in the capital market, in which case he would earn an interest on the proceeds from the sale. The right-hand side of (99) is the return to home-ownership, consisting of the after-tax value of the housing service yielded by the consumer's housing wealth plus the expected capital gain on that wealth over the period considered. Rearranging (99), we get:

$$Q_t = \frac{\bar{h} - \tau_t + Q_{t+1,t}^e}{1+r}. \tag{100}$$

Rational homeowners know that an arbitrage condition similar to (100) must also hold in future periods; they just do not know with certainty what the future property tax will be. At the start of period t, the expectations of future housing prices will thus be given by:

$$Q_{t+1,t}^e = \frac{\bar{h} - \tau_{t+1,t}^e + Q_{t+2,t}^e}{1+r}, \qquad Q_{t+2,t}^e = \frac{\bar{h} - \tau_{t+2,t}^e + Q_{t+3,t}^e}{(1+r)^2}, \dots \text{ etc.} \tag{101}$$

where $\tau_{t+n,t}^e$ is the property tax rate expected in period t to prevail in period $t + n$. We assume that agents do not expect the real price of housing to rise systematically at a rate in excess of the real interest rate, so the expected housing price satisfies the boundary condition:

$$\lim_{n\to\infty}\frac{Q^e_{t+n,t}}{(1+r)^n} = 0.\tag{102}$$

1. Explain more carefully why the arbitrage condition (99) must hold for the housing market to be in equilibrium. Explain the economic mechanism which establishes this equilibrium.

2. Show by using (100)–(102) that the current market price of housing is:

$$Q_t = \frac{\hbar-\tau_t}{1+r}+\frac{\hbar-\tau^e_{t+1,t}}{(1+r)^2}+\frac{\hbar-\tau^e_{t+2,t}}{(1+r)^3}+\ldots = \sum_{n=0}^{\infty}\frac{\hbar-\tau^e_{t+n,t}}{(1+r)^{n+1}},\tag{103}$$

where the last equality in (103) exploits the fact that $\tau^e_{t,t}=\tau_t$, since the homeowner is assumed to know the current property tax rate from the start of the period. (Hint: you may use the same procedure as the one we used to derive the fundamental stock price (6) in Chapter 14.) Give a verbal interpretation of the result in (103) and compare with the expression for the fundamental share price given in Eq. (6) in Chapter 14.

Now assume that the real property tax is kept constant at the rate τ_0 in the periods between 0 and t_0:

$$\tau_t = \tau_0 \quad \text{for } 0 < t < t_0.\tag{104}$$

At the start of period t_0, the government suddenly announces that it will cut the property tax to the lower constant level τ_1, taking effect from the start of the future period t_1. In other words,

$$\tau_t = \tau_1 < \tau_0 \quad \text{for } t \geq t_1 > t_0.\tag{105}$$

3. Use (103)–(105) to show that:

$$Q_t = \frac{\hbar-\tau_0}{r} \quad \text{for } 0 < t < t_0,\tag{106}$$

$$Q_t = \frac{\hbar}{r}-\frac{1}{r}\left\{\left[1-\frac{1}{(1+r)^{t_1-t}}\right]\tau_0+\left[\frac{1}{(1+r)^{t_1-t}}\right]\tau_1\right\} \quad \text{for } t_0 \leq t \leq t_1,\tag{107}$$

$$Q_t = \frac{\hbar-\tau_1}{r} \quad \text{for } t \geq t_1.\tag{108}$$

(Hint: follow the same procedure as the one we used to derive announcement effects in the stock market, including the formulae in Footnotes 9 and 10.) Draw a diagram to illustrate the evolution of the housing price from time 0 onwards. Give an interpretation of (107) and explain why the housing price reacts already at the time the future change in tax policy is announced. Would the same results emerge if expectations were static?

4. Use (106)–(107) to derive an expression for the size of the price jump $(Q_{t_0}-Q_{t_0-1})$ between period t_0-1 and period t_0 when the future property tax cut is announced. Explain the factors determining the size of the initial price jump.

Limits to stabilization policy

Credibility and uncertainty

Do monetary and fiscal policy makers have the ability to stabilize the macro economy, thereby reducing the social costs of business cycles? In the two previous chapters our answer to this basic question in macroeconomics has been: yes. However, our analysis was based on some important simplifying assumptions. First of all, we assumed that policy makers have *perfect information* about the current output and inflation gaps. Second, we assumed that their policy actions have *predictable and well-known quantitative effects*. Third, in the case with forward-looking agents we postulated that any policy rule announced by policy makers is always considered fully *credible* by the public, implying, for example, that policy makers never have any problem convincing the public that they will stick to an anti-inflationary policy. Taken together, these assumptions are very optimistic and not very realistic. In this chapter we shall study the problems of stabilization policy when these strong assumptions are replaced by more realistic ones.

We will start by studying the problems of establishing the *credibility* of an anti-inflationary monetary policy. This part of our analysis will show how our AS–AD model combined with the hypothesis of rational expectations may provide a theoretical case for *delegation* of monetary policy to an *independent central bank*, as a lot of countries have actually done in recent years. The subsequent part of the chapter investigates how *uncertainty* about the current state of the economy limits the scope for stabilization policy.

Policy rules versus discretion: the credibility problem

The time-inconsistency of optimal monetary policy

In the previous chapter we saw how changes in the rational expectations of the private sector may sometimes offset the intended effects of stabilization policy. Another basic discovery made by the rational expectations school in macroeconomics was the insight that it may not be possible to implement an optimal economic policy because it lacks *credibility*. For example, when the previous chapter derived the rational expectations solution for expected inflation, $\pi^e = \pi^*$, it was assumed that private agents are confident that the central bank will always stick to the announced monetary policy rule with a target inflation rate, π^*. But such credibility of economic policy may be difficult to achieve when policy makers can undertake *discretionary* policy changes *after* private agents have formed their expectations.[1]

---

1. Remember from Chapter 20 that when policy is discretionary, policy makers do not follow a fixed policy rule like the Taylor rule. Instead, they can adjust their instruments in any way they believe will serve the goals of stabilization policy in a particular situation.

If monetary policy makers announce that they will keep the inflation rate down to a certain target level, the private sector may not consider such a statement to be credible if the central bank can boost output and employment by generating unanticipated inflation.

We will now use our AS–AD model to illustrate the credibility problem arising under discretionary policy with rational expectations. To simplify (without invalidating our qualitative conclusions), we will set the aggregate supply curve parameter $\gamma = 1$. For the moment, we will also abstract from demand and supply shocks ($v_t = z_t = s_t = 0$). The expectations-augmented Phillips curve may then be written as:

$$\pi_t = \pi_{t,t-1}^e + y_t - \bar{y}. \tag{1}$$

and the goods market equilibrium condition simplifies to:

$$y_t - \bar{y} = -\alpha_2(r_t - \bar{r}). \tag{2}$$

As before, we assume that the central bank can observe the expected rate of inflation (say, through consumer surveys or by observing the difference between the interest rates on indexed and non-indexed bonds) when it sets the nominal interest rate. Thus the central bank can set the *real* interest rate r_t after the private sector has formed its expectations of inflation. It then follows from (2) that the central bank can control the current output gap $y_t - \bar{y}$. According to (1) it can therefore determine the actual inflation rate, π_t, through its choice of $y_t - \bar{y}$, for any given expected inflation rate $\pi_{t,t-1}^e$.

We assume that monetary policy makers would like to minimize the social loss function:

$$SL_t = (y_t - y^*)^2 + \kappa\pi_t^2, \qquad \kappa > 0. \tag{3}$$

According to (3) society loses welfare when output deviates from its target level y^* and when inflation deviates from its target rate which we now take to be zero for simplicity. The quadratic form implies that large deviations of output and inflation from their respective targets cause disproportionately larger losses than small deviations. The parameter κ indicates the strength of the social preference for price stability relative to output stability. Note that in the case where the target level of output equals natural output ($y^* = \bar{y}$), Eq. (3) is just a version of the social loss function (1) in Chapter 19 where the target inflation rate has been set at zero and the coefficient on the output gap has been normalized to one (so that $\kappa = a_\pi / a_y$ in the notation of Chapter 19).

As we explained in Chapter 19, when product and labour markets are imperfect and the government has to rely on distortionary taxes to raise revenue, the natural level of output is lower than the 'efficient' output level that policy makers would ideally like to target. Hence we assume that

$$y^* = \bar{y} + \omega, \qquad \omega > 0. \tag{4}$$

The parameter ω reflects the magnitude of the distortions in labour and product markets (including tax distortions). The less competitive these markets are, the lower is the normal rate of utilization of economic resources, and the greater is the difference between trend output and the efficient (desired) output level y^*.

From (1) it follows that $y_t = \bar{y} + \pi_t - \pi_{t,t-1}^e$, so according to (4) we have $y_t - y^* = \pi_t - \pi_{t,t-1}^e - \omega$. Substituting this into (3), we get:

$$SL_t = (\pi_t - \pi_{t,t-1}^e - \omega)^2 + \kappa\pi_t^2. \tag{5}$$

Now suppose for a moment that the central bank follows a Taylor rule with a zero inflation target:

$$r_t = \bar{r} + h\pi_t + b(y_t - \bar{y}) \tag{6}$$

The public is assumed to have rational expectations and to know the policy rule (6). Recalling that $v_t = s_t = 0$, it then follows from Eqs (34) and (35) in the previous chapter that the economy will end up in the following equilibrium:

Equilibrium under the Taylor rule: $\pi_t = \pi^e_{t,t-1} = \pi^* = 0, \qquad y_t = \bar{y}.$ (7)

But would the central bank actually want to stick to the Taylor rule? To investigate this, suppose the central bank were to deviate from the rule by generating surprise inflation after the private sector has formed its expectations $\pi^e_{t,t-1} = 0$. How would social welfare be affected by such a policy of 'cheating'? Calculating the derivative of the social loss function (5) with respect to the inflation rate at the initial point where $\pi_t = \pi^e_{t,t-1} = 0$, we find:

$$dSL/d\pi_t = -2\omega < 0. \tag{8}$$

Starting from the Taylor rule equilibrium (or any other equilibrium where $\pi_t = \pi^e_{t,t-1} = 0$), the social loss can thus be *reduced* if the central bank decides to drive output closer to its desired level y^* by generating surprise inflation. The reason is that if $\pi_t = \pi^e_{t,t-1} = 0$ so that $y_t = \bar{y}$, Eqs (3) and (4) imply that the marginal social cost of a slight rise in inflation is zero, whereas the marginal social benefit from a slight rise in output is positive. *Hence a central bank which can engage in discretionary policy will not want to stick to a policy rule that generates price stability*. Indeed, for any given expected inflation rate, the central bank will want to set the actual inflation rate such that the social loss function (5) is minimized. The first-order condition for the optimal choice of the rate of inflation is $dSL_t/d\pi_t = 0$ which implies:

$$\underbrace{2(\pi_t - \pi^e_{t,t-1} - \omega)}_{\substack{=y_t-y^*=\text{marginal} \\ \text{reduction in } SL \text{ due to} \\ \text{higher output}}} + \underbrace{2\kappa\pi_t}_{\substack{\text{marginal} \\ \text{increase in } SL \\ \text{due to higher} \\ \text{inflation}}} = 0. \tag{9}$$

If the central bank has led the public to believe that it will ensure price stability $((\pi^e_{t,t-1} = 0)$, it follows from (9) and (1) that the economy will actually end up in the

'Cheating' outcome with surprise inflation: $\pi_t = \dfrac{\omega}{1+\kappa}, \qquad y_t = \bar{y} + \dfrac{\omega}{1+\kappa}.$ (10)

If SL_R is the social loss incurred in the Taylor rule equilibrium (7), and SL_C is the social loss in the 'cheating' outcome (10), we can use (3), (4), (7) and (10) to calculate the social welfare gain from cheating:

Temptation to cheat $\equiv SL_R - SL_C = \dfrac{\omega^2}{1+\kappa}.$ (11)

Equation (11) is intuitively appealing: the greater the difference between natural output and desired output, ω, the greater is the temptation to create surprise inflation in order to raise output above the natural rate. On the other hand, the stronger the social aversion to inflation, κ, the smaller is the gain from surprise inflation.

The important point is that the policy maker has no incentive to actually implement the policy $\pi_t = \pi^* = 0$ if he can make the private sector believe that he will do so. In other words, over time the policy maker will not want to act in a manner consistent with the rule he previously announced. Economists therefore say that a rule-based equilibrium like (7) with zero inflation is *dynamically inconsistent* or *time-inconsistent* when policy makers have discretion.[2]

THE PROBLEM OF TIME CONSISTENCY

When the socially desired output level exceeds natural output and the initial inflation rate is zero, policy makers will have an incentive to boost output by creating surprise inflation. A promise by the central bank to maintain price stability is therefore said to be time-inconsistent when the bank can act in a discretionary manner, since it will not be optimal for the central bank to avoid inflation once private agents have formed their expectations and negotiated nominal wage contracts on the assumption that prices will be kept stable.

Time-consistent monetary policy

Of course, rational agents who know the preferences of policy makers will realize that the central bank will not really want to implement the policy $\pi_t = 0$. This is the *credibility problem*: if the central bank cannot make a *binding commitment* to stick to the Taylor rule or some other rule ensuring price stability, the announcement that the bank intends to follow a policy of price stability will not be credible and will hence fail to eliminate expectations of inflation. This is because private agents know that the central bank will have an incentive to deviate from price stability in an effort to stimulate output and employment. More precisely, rational agents will recognize that the central bank will set the interest rate so as to achieve the inflation rate implied by the first-order condition (9). Thus neither the rule-based equilibrium (7) nor the 'cheating' outcome (10) will be realized, since these outcomes are not true rational-expectations equilibria when agents know that policy makers have discretion and seek to minimize the social loss function (5). Instead rational agents will form their expectations on the basis of (9), implying that $\pi_{t,t-1}^e - \pi_{t,t-1}^e - \omega + \kappa \pi_{t,t-1}^e = 0$, or $\pi_{t,t-1}^e = \omega/\kappa$. Inserting this solution for the expected inflation rate into (9) and using (1), we obtain the

Time-consistent rational expectations equilibrium:

$$\pi_t = \pi_{t,t-1}^e = \frac{\omega}{\kappa}, \qquad y_t = \bar{y}. \tag{12}$$

The equilibrium in (12) is said to be *time consistent* because policy makers have no incentive to deviate *ex post* from the inflation rate $\pi_t = \omega/\kappa$, given that this rate of price increase is derived from the first-order condition (9). In the time-consistent equilibrium expectations of inflation have driven the actual inflation rate up to a level which is so high that policy makers do not wish to generate further (surprise) inflation, even though they have the ability to do so through discretionary policy.

The results in (12) illustrate the unfortunate implications of the credibility problem under discretionary monetary policy. Though the realized inflation rate permanently exceeds the target inflation rate by the amount ω/κ, inflation is fully anticipated, so no output gains are obtained in return for the excess inflation. Clearly this outcome is worse than the

---

2. The problem of time inconsistency was first analysed by the Nobel Prize winners Finn E. Kydland and Edward C. Prescott, 'Rules Rather than Discretion: The Inconsistency of Optimal Plans', *Journal of Political Economy*, **88**, 1977, pp. 867–896. The problem was later elaborated in another famous paper by Robert J. Barro and David B. Gordon, 'A Positive Theory of Monetary Policy in a Natural Rate Model', *Journal of Political Economy*, **91**, 1983, pp. 589–610.

outcome (7) which would emerge if the central bank could make a binding commitment to stick to a policy of price stability. Let SL_D denote the social loss in the time-consistent equilibrium with discretionary policy. Inserting (4) and (12) into (3), we find that:

$$SL_D = \overbrace{\omega^2}^{\substack{\text{social loss} \\ \text{due to} \\ \text{inefficiently} \\ \text{low output}}} + \overbrace{\frac{\omega^2}{\kappa}}^{\substack{\text{social loss} \\ \text{due to} \\ \text{inflation}}}. \tag{13}$$

The second term on the right-hand side of (13) could be eliminated if the central bank could somehow commit itself to a rule of price stability (to check this, you should use (3), (4) and (7) to show that $SL_R = \omega^2$). This term therefore represents the welfare loss from the inability to commit. We see that the presence of market distortions (ω) and the resulting temptation to generate surprise inflation in order to boost output creates an *inflation bias* under discretionary monetary policy.

The points made above are illustrated graphically in Fig. 22.1. The concentric ovals are social indifference curves showing alternative combinations of output and inflation which generate a constant social loss. The equation for the indifference curve corresponding to the social loss $\bar{C}$ is found by setting the expression on the right-hand side of (3) equal to the constant $\bar{C}$.[3] The minimum social loss (= 0) is achieved at the 'bliss' point E^* where $y = y^*$ and $\pi = 0$. Larger ovals further away from E^* correspond to higher levels of social loss. The *first-best* optimum E^* cannot be attained in an equilibrium where expectations are fulfilled, since it follows from (1) that $y = \bar{y}$ when $\pi^e = \pi$ (to put it another way, monetary policy cannot eliminate the market imperfections reflected in $\omega = y^* - \bar{y}$). The *second-best* optimum E_R is the equilibrium which emerges when the central bank can make a binding commitment to a policy of price stability. In that case the private sector will rationally expect stable prices, and the economy's short-run aggregate supply curve will be given by the curve $SRAS(\pi^e = 0)$ corresponding to a zero expected rate of inflation. However, if the central bank can engage in discretionary policy so that the policy rule $\pi = 0$ is not truly binding, it will have an incentive to create surprise inflation to move the economy from point E_R to the 'cheating' outcome E_C where the SRAS curve is tangent to a social indifference curve. Point E_C represents the lowest possible level of social loss, given a zero expected inflation rate. The trouble is that rational private agents anticipate the central bank's incentive to cheat, so according to (12) they will expect an inflation rate equal to ω/κ under discretionary policy. The actual short-run aggregate supply curve will then be given by the curve $SRAS(\pi^e = \omega/\kappa)$ in Fig. 22.1, and the economy will end up in the time-consistent rational expectations equilibrium E_D. This is a *third-best* optimum where the social loss is minimized given the private sector's positive expected inflation rate.

The model of inflation summarized in Fig. 22.1 is often referred to as the *Barro–Gordon model*, named after its inventors (see the reference in Footnote 2). It has had a strong influence on the way economists think about monetary policy, and it helps to explain why many economists have come to favour binding policy rules over discretionary policy. In particular, the Barro–Gordon model has motivated economists and policy makers to think about ways of securing commitment to policy rules in order to overcome the problem of inflation bias in monetary policy.

---

3. Along a social indifference curve we thus have $dSL = 0$. According to (3) this implies

$$(y - y^*) \cdot dy + \kappa\pi \cdot d\pi = 0 \quad \Leftrightarrow \quad \frac{d\pi}{dy} = \frac{y^* - y}{\kappa\pi}$$

Thus the slope of the indifference curves becomes 0 when $y = y^*$, whereas the slope tends to infinity when inflation tends to 0, as illustrated in Fig. 22.1.

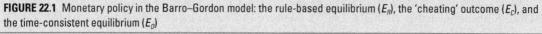

FIGURE 22.1 Monetary policy in the Barro–Gordon model: the rule-based equilibrium (E_R), the 'cheating' outcome (E_C), and the time-consistent equilibrium (E_D)

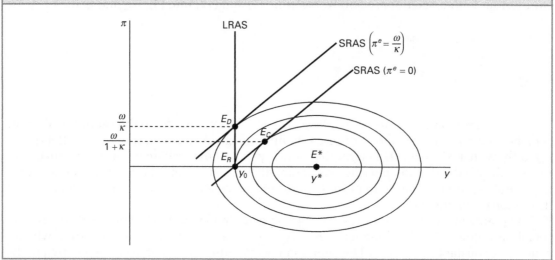

TIME-CONSISTENT MONETARY POLICY

When the socially desired output exceeds natural output and monetary policy makers have discretion, rational private sector agents will anticipate that the central bank has an incentive to create surprise inflation if the private sector were to act on the assumption that prices will be stable. The private sector will therefore expect a positive inflation rate. A time-consistent macroeconomic equilibrium is reached when the expected and actual inflation rate is so high that the central bank no longer has an incentive to generate surprise inflation. In the time-consistent equilibrium output will be at its natural rate. A lower social loss could be secured if the central bank could convince the private sector that it will stick to a policy of price stability, but under policy discretion an announced policy of price stability will lack credibility because it is time-inconsistent.

22.2 Dealing with inflation bias: reputation-building and delegation of monetary policy

Building a reputation

One situation where a rule-based policy of price stability may be sustainable is when policy makers rely on *reputation*. The analysis in the previous section implicitly assumed that policy makers are short-sighted, caring only about the economic outcome in the current period. In that case it is always rational for them to 'cheat' by creating surprise inflation if the initial inflation rate is (close to) zero. Hence rational agents will never consider an announced policy of price stability to be credible if they believe policy makers to be myopic. However, policy makers who interact with the private sector period after period will have an incentive to consider the implications of their current actions for the future behaviour of private agents. For example, if the creation of surprise inflation implies that the policy maker will face higher expected inflation rates in the future, he may prefer to stick to an announced policy of price stability. In this way he will earn a reputation for being a reliable protector of monetary stability, and this will keep future expected and actual inflation rates down.[4]

To illustrate how such a mechanism of reputation-building might work, suppose that the public believes the announcements of the central bank as long as the bank does not generate any unanticipated inflation. Thus, if there were no inflation surprises last period ($\pi_{t-1} = \pi_{t-1,t-2}^e$), the central bank has credibility in the current period. Monetary policy makers can use such credibility to eliminate expectations of inflation by announcing that they will follow a policy rule ensuring an inflation rate π_R equal to zero. We then have:

$$\pi_{t,t-1}^e = \pi_R = 0 \qquad \text{if } \pi_{t-1} = \pi_{t-1,t-2}^e. \tag{14}$$

If the central bank 'cheats' in some period $t-1$ by deviating from price stability, it loses its credibility for the subsequent period t. The public will then form its expectations for period t on the assumption that the central bank will pursue the optimal discretionary policy yielding the inflation rate ω/κ derived in (12) above. Hence we have:

$$\pi_{t,t-1}^e = \pi_D = \frac{\omega}{\kappa} \qquad \text{if } \pi_{t-1} \neq \pi_{t-1,t-2}^e, \tag{15}$$

where π_D is the optimal inflation rate under discretion. Knowing that this is the public's expected inflation rate, the best thing the central bank can do in period t is to announce and implement the policy $\pi_D = \omega/\kappa$. In this way it regains credibility in the next period by carrying out its announced plan in the current period. We may say that the public is playing 'tit-for-tat' against the policy maker. If the policy maker behaves well by sticking to his promises, he is 'rewarded' by zero expected inflation in the next period, enabling him to avoid the social loss associated with inflation. If the policy maker 'misbehaves' by creating surprise inflation, he is 'punished' by high expectations of inflation in the next period.

Suppose we start out in a period in which the policy maker has inherited credibility from the past. The policy maker must then decide whether to stick to the policy $\pi_R = 0$ generating the current-period social loss SL_R associated with the rule-based equilibrium (7), or whether to cheat in order to reduce the current-period social loss to the lower level SL_C associated with the 'cheating' outcome (10). If the policy maker decides to cheat, the net social gain in the current period will be $SL_R - SL_C$. At the same time the cheating will generate a net social loss of $SL_D - SL_R$ in the next period where the economy will end up in the third-best equilibrium (12), whereas it could have ended up in the second-best equilibrium (7) if the policy maker had not cheated in the current period. If the policy maker has a positive rate of time preference ρ, he will discount next period's social loss when comparing it to this period's social gain. Instead of Eq. (11) which is relevant only for a myopic policy maker, we then get the following modified expression for the

$$\textit{Temptation to cheat:} \qquad \overbrace{SL_R - SL_C}^{\substack{\text{current-period} \\ \text{gain from} \\ \text{cheating}}} - \frac{\overbrace{(SL_D - SL_R)}^{\substack{\text{next-period} \\ \text{loss from} \\ \text{cheating}}}}{1+\rho}. \tag{16}$$

Our previous expression (11) for the temptation to cheat is just the special case of (16) occurring when the policy maker is very short-sighted. In that case his rate of time preference ρ approaches infinity so that the second term on the right-hand side of (16) vanishes.

If the expression in (16) is positive, the policy maker will always want to cheat. The rule-based policy of price stability will then be unsustainable, and the economy will end up in

---

4. This idea was developed in another influential paper by Robert J. Barro and David B. Gordon, 'Rules, Discretion and Reputation in a Model of Monetary Policy', *Journal of Monetary Economics*, **12**, 1983, pp. 101–121. The simplified version of the dynamic Barro–Gordon model presented below is heavily inspired by Ben J. Heijdra and Frederick van der Ploeg, *Foundations of Modern Macroeconomics*, Oxford University Press, 2002, Section 10.1.3.

the third-best time-consistent equilibrium in every period, just like before. But if (16) is negative, the policy maker has no incentive to deviate from price stability, and the rule-based second-best equilibrium will then be sustainable and implemented every period. Inserting (3), (4), (7), (10) and (12) into (16), we find that the temptation to cheat may be written as:

$$SL_R - SL_C - \frac{(SL_D - SL_R)}{1+\rho} = \frac{\omega^2(\rho\kappa - 1)}{\kappa(1+\kappa)(1+\rho)}. \tag{17}$$

Equation (17) shows that the policy maker will not want to cheat if his discount rate ρ is sufficiently low, that is, if he cares sufficiently about the future. With a low discount rate the short-term gain from cheating will be outweighed by the future social loss from the inflation that follows from the loss of credibility. We see from (17) that a low value of the inflation aversion parameter κ also helps to increase the likelihood that the policy maker will not want to cheat. The reason is that a low value of κ generates a high rate of inflation in the third-best equilibrium emerging when the policy maker has lost credibility. Hence a low value of κ implies a high value of SL_D (see (13)) which makes the policy maker more eager to avoid a loss of credibility. Finally, it follows from (17) that the magnitude of the market distortions (ω) does not influence the *sign* of the expression for the temptation to cheat, since a higher value of ω increases next period's loss as well as this period's gain from cheating.

DEALING WITH INFLATION BIAS THROUGH REPUTATION-BUILDING

If the public believes in an announced policy of price stability as long as the central bank does not in fact generate surprise inflation, policy makers may be able to establish credibility by building a reputation for sticking to a policy rule of price stability. Policy makers will stick to such a rule only if the short-run gain from creating surprise inflation is smaller than the discounted future social loss from the higher expected future inflation that follows from 'cheating' the private sector. If the time horizon of policy makers is too short and their discount rate consequently too high, a rule-based policy of price stability will be unsustainable, and the economy will end up in the third-best time-consistent equilibrium emerging under policy discretion.

Delegation of monetary policy

The insight from the preceding analysis is that the inflation bias in monetary policy may be eliminated by the policy maker's incentive to build a reputation, provided he places sufficient weight on the future. But casual observation suggests that governments are often very preoccupied with the short term, perhaps because they are mainly concerned about winning the next election.[5] In other words, governments often seem to act as if they put little weight on the more distant future, indicating a high discount rate. For this reason many economists doubt that the incentive for reputation-building will be sufficiently strong to eliminate the inflation bias if monetary policy is controlled directly by the government. As an alternative way of offsetting the inflation bias, it has therefore been suggested that politicians should *delegate* monetary policy to an *independent central bank* with a strong mandate to resist inflation.

In practice, central banks can be more or less independent of the government. In Table 22.1 the degree of central bank independence (CBI) is measured in three main dimensions.

---

5. Of course, if voters actually care about the (more distant) future, politicians seeking re-election should also support policies which place a reasonable weight on the future. If actual policies nevertheless seem to be biased towards the short run, there must be some kind of imperfections in the political process whereby voter preferences get translated into political outcomes. Such imperfections are one of the subjects of the theory of Political Economy which we shall have to leave for another course.

TABLE 22.1 Indices of central bank independence

Measure	Alesina	Grilli, Masciandaro and Tabellini	Eijffinger and Schaling	Cukierman
Maximum total score	1	1	1	1
Personnel independence	0.5	0.375	0.4	0.2
Financial independence	0.25	0.3125		0.5
Policy independence of which	0.25	0.3125	0.4	0.3
Instrument independence		0.1875		0.15
Goal independence		0.125		0.15
Germany	1	0.8125	1	0.66
Canada	0.5	0.6875	0.2	0.46
Japan	0.75	0.375	0.6	0.16
United Kingdom	0.5	0.375	0.4	0.31
United States	0.75	0.75	0.6	0.51
European Central Bank	1	0.875	1	0.94

Source: Adapted from Table 2.2 in Sylvester C.W. Eijffinger and Jakob de Haan, *European Monetary and Fiscal Policy*, Oxford University Press, 2000. The various indices have been normalized so that the maximum total score equals 1 (full central bank independence).

Personnel independence reflects the degree to which government officials are represented on the governing board of the central bank; the extent to which board members are appointed by the government; the length of the term of office of the governor(s), etc. The *financial independence* indicator focuses on the stringency of limitations on the ability of the government to borrow from the central bank, and the *policy independence* indicator measures the degree to which the central bank can set its policy instruments (*instrument independence*) and its policy goals (*goal independence*) without having to take instructions from the government. The upper part of Table 22.1 shows the values of the various indicators assigned to a central bank which is deemed to be fully independent. The weights have been normalized such that the maximum total independence score which can be assigned to a central bank is unity. The column headings refer to the authors of four different studies of CBI (there are several other such studies, but the ones shown here are quite representative), and the lower part of the table reports the estimated total degree of CBI in various countries. All authors seem to agree that the European Central Bank and the German Bundesbank are very independent, and that the US Federal Reserve Bank also has quite a high degree of independence. The central banks of Canada, Japan and the UK seem to occupy a middle ground, although there is somewhat less agreement on the ranking of these banks (which is not surprising, since the interpretation of central bank statutes and legislation leaves room for judgement).

We will now show how the delegation of monetary policy to a (more or less) independent and 'conservative' central bank may help to reduce the inflation bias.[6] Suppose the governor of the central bank considers the loss from instability of output and prices to be given by the loss function:

$$SL_B = (y_t - y^*)^2 + (\kappa + \varepsilon)\pi_t^2, \qquad \varepsilon > 0, \tag{18}$$

---

6. This idea was originally put forward by Kenneth Rogoff, 'The Optimal Degree of Commitment to an Intermediate Monetary Target', *Quarterly Journal of Economics*, **100**, 1985, pp. 1169–1189.

where ε measures the degree to which the inflation aversion of the central banker *exceeds* the inflation aversion of the government. We may say that the parameter ε is a measure of the central banker's degree of 'conservativeness' (his 'excess' aversion to inflation, taking the preferences of the government as the benchmark).

Let β be an index of CBI which can assume a value between 0 (no independence) and 1 (full independence). The parameter β measures the degree to which the government has *delegated* monetary policy to the central bank. The greater the value of β, the greater is the weight of the central banker's preferences in the determination of monetary policy. Since the government's loss function is still given by (3), we may then assume that monetary policy is determined by minimization of the modified loss function:

$$\tilde{SL} = (1 - \beta) \cdot SL + \beta \cdot SL_B = (y_t - y^*)^2 + (\kappa + \beta\varepsilon)\pi_t^2, \qquad 0 \le \beta \le 1, \tag{19}$$

reflecting a compromise between the government and the central bank. The loss function (19) is similar to (3) except that the inflation aversion parameter κ has been replaced by $\kappa + \beta\varepsilon$. All the results from the previous section therefore carry over if we just substitute $\kappa + \beta\varepsilon$ for κ. From (12) we then obtain the *time-consistent rational expectations equilibrium with delegation of monetary policy*:

$$\pi_t = \pi_{t,t-1}^e = \frac{\omega}{\kappa + \beta\varepsilon}, \qquad y_t = \bar{y}. \tag{20}$$

A comparison of (12) and (20) reveals that *by delegating monetary policy authority to a central banker who is more conservative than itself, the government can reduce the inflation bias in discretionary monetary policy*. Indeed, by appointing a very conservative central banker who cares only about price stability ($\varepsilon \to \infty$), the government can move from the third-best equilibrium (12) with positive inflation to the second-best equilibrium (7) with zero inflation. The reason is that a policy maker who is extremely averse to inflation has no incentive to cheat, since cheating involves the creation of inflation. The paradox is that, by voluntarily tying its own hands and delegating monetary policy to a policy maker whose preferences deviate from its own, the government can achieve an outcome which is more desirable from its own viewpoint. To see this, we may insert the results from (20) into the *government's* loss function (3) and use (4) to get the *social loss with delegation of monetary policy*:

$$SL = \omega^2 + \frac{\kappa\omega^2}{(\kappa + \beta\varepsilon)^2}. \tag{21}$$

Clearly this loss is smaller when policy is (partly) delegated to a conservative central banker ($\beta\varepsilon > 0$) than when monetary policy only reflects the government's own preferences ($\beta\varepsilon = 0$).

Note that *two* conditions are required to obtain this beneficial outcome:

1. The central bank must have some independence ($\beta > 0$).
2. The central banker must be more conservative than the government ($\varepsilon > 0$).

If the central bank has no independence at all, the preferences of its governor are irrelevant, since they will be completely overruled by the government. And if the central bank has the same preferences as the government, it will obviously make no difference whether policy is made by the bank or by the government itself.

This analysis suggests that, other things equal, we should expect to observe a lower average rate of inflation in countries with a higher degree of central bank independence.[7]

---

7. The usual caveat 'other things equal' is important here, since the government of a country with a more independent central bank might want to appoint a less conservative central bank governor when there is a trade-off between fighting inflation and minimizing the variability of output. Below we will explain the circumstances in which such a trade-off will arise.

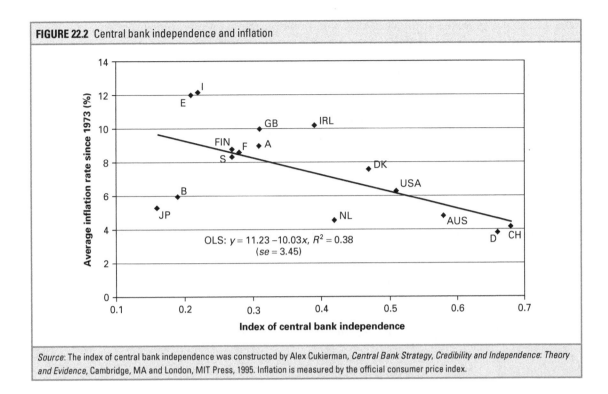

FIGURE 22.2 Central bank independence and inflation

Source: The index of central bank independence was constructed by Alex Cukierman, *Central Bank Strategy, Credibility and Independence: Theory and Evidence*, Cambridge, MA and London, MIT Press, 1995. Inflation is measured by the official consumer price index.

A number of empirical studies have indeed found a clear negative correlation between CBI and inflation, using alternative indices of CBI. Figure 22.2 summarizes the findings from one such study.

Influenced by this experience, many countries have moved towards a much higher degree of central bank independence over the past two decades. For example, the constitutional framework for the European Monetary Union aims to secure a maximal degree of independence of the European Central Bank. In specifying the mandates for their central banks, governments in recent years have also been keen to stress that central bankers should act 'conservatively' by pursuing price stability (defined as a low rate of inflation) as their main goal.

DEALING WITH INFLATION BIAS THROUGH DELEGATION OF MONETARY POLICY TO AN INDEPENDENT CENTRAL BANK

If the government cannot firmly commit to a monetary policy rule of price stability, it can reduce the inflation bias arising under policy discretion by delegating monetary policy to an independent and 'conservative' central bank which places more weight on the goal of price stability than the government itself. In this way a more favourable macroeconomic equilibrium can be established even though the central bank does not minimize the 'true' social loss function. The prediction that countries with more independent central banks will experience lower average inflation is borne out by the evidence.

Credibility versus flexibility

So far our analysis might seem to indicate that the greater the degree of central bank independence and/or the stronger the conservatism of the central bank, the better is the macroeconomic outcome. Unfortunately things are not that simple when we allow for the possibility of aggregate supply shocks. To demonstrate this, let us replace the simple deterministic AS curve (1) by the more realistic supply curve:

$$\pi_t = \pi^e_{t,t-1} + y_t - \bar{y} + s_t, \qquad E[s_t] = 0, \qquad E[s_t^2] = \sigma_s^2, \tag{22}$$

where s_t is a stochastic supply shock variable with zero mean and constant variance σ_s^2. We continue to assume that monetary policy is (partly) delegated to an independent and conservative central bank, so monetary policy is still determined by minimization of the modified loss function (19). Using (22) to eliminate y_t from (19) and recalling that $y^* = \bar{y} + \omega$, we may rewrite (19) as:

$$\tilde{SL} = (\pi_t - \pi^e_{t,t-1} - s_t - \omega)^2 + (\kappa + \beta\varepsilon)\pi_t^2. \tag{23}$$

Assuming that policy makers cannot credibly commit to a rule of price stability, they will set the inflation rate so as to minimize the loss function (23), given the private sector's expected rate of inflation, and given the current-period supply shock s_t which we assume to be observable at the time monetary policy has to be decided. Thus the first-order condition for the solution to the policy makers' problem under discretion is:

$$d\tilde{SL}/d\pi_t = 0 \quad \Rightarrow \quad 2(\pi_t - \pi^e_{t,t-1} - s_t - \omega) + 2(\kappa + \beta\varepsilon)\pi_t = 0$$

$$\Leftrightarrow \quad \pi_t = \frac{\pi^e_{t,t-1} + s_t + \omega}{1 + \kappa + \beta\varepsilon}. \tag{24}$$

Rational private agents know that policy makers will set the inflation rate in accordance with (24), so the expected inflation rate is found by taking expected values on both sides of (24), remembering that $E[s_t] = 0$:

$$\pi^e_{t,t-1} = \frac{\pi^e_{t,t-1} + \omega}{1 + \kappa + \beta\varepsilon} \quad \Leftrightarrow \quad \pi^e_{t,t-1} = \frac{\omega}{\kappa + \beta\varepsilon} \tag{25}$$

Substituting (25) into (24), we get:

$$\pi_t = \frac{\omega}{\kappa + \beta\varepsilon} + \frac{s_t}{1 + \kappa + \beta\varepsilon}, \tag{26}$$

and inserting (25) and (26) into (22) we find:

$$y_t = \bar{y} - \left(\frac{\kappa + \beta\varepsilon}{1 + \kappa + \beta\varepsilon}\right)s_t. \tag{27}$$

We may now substitute (26) and (27) into the *government's* loss function $SL = (y_t - y^*)^2 + \kappa\pi_t^2$ to obtain (using $y^* = \bar{y} + \omega$):

$$SL = \left(\left(\frac{\kappa + \beta\varepsilon}{1 + \kappa + \beta\varepsilon}\right)s_t + \omega\right)^2 + \kappa\left(\frac{\omega}{\kappa + \beta\varepsilon} + \frac{s_t}{1 + \kappa + \beta\varepsilon}\right)^2$$

$$= \left(\frac{\kappa + \beta\varepsilon}{1 + \kappa + \beta\varepsilon}\right)^2 s_t^2 + \omega^2 + 2\omega\left(\frac{\kappa + \beta\varepsilon}{1 + \kappa + \beta\varepsilon}\right)s_t + \kappa\left(\frac{\omega}{\kappa + \beta\varepsilon}\right)^2 + \frac{\kappa s_t^2}{(1 + \kappa + \beta\varepsilon)^2} \tag{28}$$

$$+ \left(\frac{2\kappa\omega}{\kappa + \beta\varepsilon}\right)\left(\frac{s_t}{1 + \kappa + \beta\varepsilon}\right).$$

To find the *average* loss experienced by the government, we calculate the *mean* value of the expression in (28), using $E[s_t] = 0$ and $E[s_t^2] = \sigma_s^2$. We then get:

$$E[SL] = \omega^2 \left[1 + \frac{\kappa}{(\kappa + \beta\varepsilon)^2} \right] + \sigma_s^2 \left[\left(\frac{\kappa + \beta\varepsilon}{1 + \kappa + \beta\varepsilon} \right)^2 + \frac{\kappa}{(1 + \kappa + \beta\varepsilon)^2} \right]. \tag{29}$$

The value of $\beta\varepsilon$ will be higher the greater the degree of CBI (β) and the stronger the conservativeness of the central banker (ε). We may say that $\beta\varepsilon$ measures the 'effective degree of central bank conservativeness'. If there are no supply shocks, that is, if $\sigma_s^2 = 0$, we see from (29) that a higher effective degree of central bank conservativeness will always reduce the government's loss. This is in line with our previous analysis. However, in the presence of supply shocks ($\sigma_s^2 > 0$) a higher value of $\beta\varepsilon$ will not necessarily reduce the expected social loss. Taking the partial derivative of the expression in (29) with respect to $\beta\varepsilon$, we find after some manipulations that:

$$\frac{\partial E[SL]}{\partial(\beta\varepsilon)} = -\frac{\omega^2\kappa}{(\kappa + \beta\varepsilon)^3} + \frac{\beta\varepsilon\sigma_s^2}{(1 + \kappa + \beta\varepsilon)^3}. \tag{30}$$

If the variance of the aggregate supply shocks is high (if σ_s^2 is large), this expression may well be positive, implying that more CBI and/or a more conservative central bank will actually *increase* the government's social loss from instability of output and prices. To understand why, note from (26) that changes in s_t will only be allowed to affect prices to a limited degree when $\beta\varepsilon$ is high. Hence the supply shocks must be absorbed mainly by changes in output (you can verify from (27) that the coefficient on s_t in the solution for output will indeed be larger the larger the value of $\beta\varepsilon$). If the government is not too concerned about price stability so that κ is relatively small, it will incur a welfare loss if the central bank pursues price stability at the expense of output stability.

Thus governments are faced with a trade-off. They may reduce the inflation bias by delegating monetary policy to an independent central bank which is given a mandate to pursue price stability. But if the central bank adheres rigidly to its goal of price stability, the result may be greater instability of output in periods when supply shocks are important. Recent experience in the Euro area suggests that this dilemma is not just a theoretical possibility. In Fig. 22.3 we show the evolution of oil prices, consumer prices and real domestic demand in the EMU countries during the latest decade. The rate of oil price inflation has been smoothed (by taking four-quarter moving averages) and plotted with a one-year time lag, because it takes time for oil price changes to feed into consumer prices and nominal wage rates. Thus the oil price change plotted for 2007 and 2008 actually reflects the development of the oil price in 2006 and 2007. Figure 22.3 indicates that the euro area (which is a net importer of oil) was hit by a negative supply shock in 2007 and 2008 in the form of a sharp increase in the price of oil. In part because of this, the European Central Bank was unable to keep the inflation rate in the euro area below the level of 2 per cent deemed consistent with 'price stability', despite the fact that domestic aggregate demand started to fall. Many observers thought that the ECB should have lowered its interest rate as demand growth began to weaken after the onset of the financial crisis in the summer of 2007, but the bank apparently feared that this would have driven the expected and actual inflation rate further above the target level at that time. As a newly established central bank, the ECB was keen to build up a reputation for sticking to its prime goal of price stability and hence felt unable to pursue a more expansionary interest rate policy.

We may say that policy makers face an unpleasant trade-off between *credibility* and *flexibility*. To reduce the variability of output, policy makers might like to react to shocks in a flexible manner by allowing a greater rise in inflation when the economy is hit by an inflationary supply shock than when it is hit by an inflationary demand shock. But if the

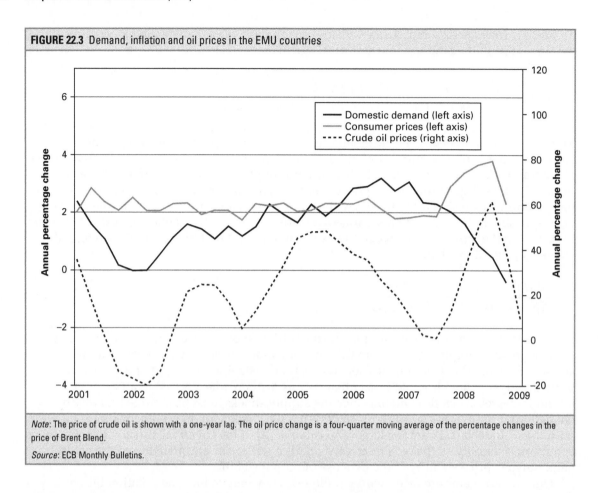

FIGURE 22.3 Demand, inflation and oil prices in the EMU countries

Note: The price of crude oil is shown with a one-year lag. The oil price change is a four-quarter moving average of the percentage changes in the price of Brent Blend.

Source: ECB Monthly Bulletins.

central bank does not take a tough anti-inflationary stance regardless of the cause of a rise in inflation, it is in danger of losing its credibility as a protector of price stability.

THE TRADE-OFF BETWEEN CREDIBILITY AND FLEXIBILITY

Delegating monetary policy to an independent and 'conservative' central bank will enhance the credibility of the monetary policy maker's commitment to the goal of price stability. However, if the economy is exposed to supply shocks with a high variance, a strong central bank emphasis on securing low inflation may increase the variance of output to such an extent that social welfare falls. Thus there is a trade-off between preserving flexibility (allowing a rise in inflation when a negative supply shock occurs) and strengthening the credibility of the central bank's commitment to price stability.

22.3 Groping in the dark: the implications of macroeconomic measurement errors

So far our discussion of stabilization policy has implicitly assumed that policy makers have full information on the current state of the economy, that they can instantaneously react to changes in macroeconomic conditions, and that they can fully predict how the economy will react to any change in policy. None of these assumptions is very realistic, and the present section will discuss the implications of relaxing them. Specifically, we will describe

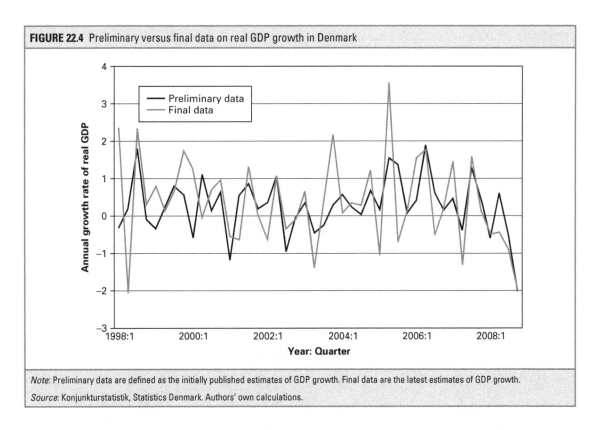

FIGURE 22.4 Preliminary versus final data on real GDP growth in Denmark

Note: Preliminary data are defined as the initially published estimates of GDP growth. Final data are the latest estimates of GDP growth.

Source: Konjunkturstatistik, Statistics Denmark. Authors' own calculations.

the difficulties of stabilizing the economy when there is uncertainty about the current state of the economy and when economic policy changes only take full effect with a time lag. We start by focusing on the former problem.

Measurement errors

In the real world macroeconomic policy makers have imperfect information about the current state of the economy when they have to make their policy decisions. This is because economic data typically only become available with a certain delay, and because the data are frequently revised – sometimes substantially so – at a later stage when statisticians have had time to check the numbers more carefully. Figure 22.4 illustrates this trivial but nevertheless important point. The figure shows the initial preliminary estimates of real GDP growth published by Statistics Denmark compared with the final official growth figures in the national income accounts when all revisions to the data have been completed. Ideally, the latter time series reflects the 'true' historical rate of growth, but the problem for policy makers is that they typically have to base their judgements and policy decisions on the preliminary estimates even though they know that these estimates may be subject to substantial revision.

To estimate the current output gap, policy makers not only need reliable information on *actual* current output; they also face the difficult problem of estimating current *potential* output which we have also referred to as *trend output* or *natural output*. As you recall from Chapter 13, there are several ways of estimating potential output and they typically yield different results, leaving uncertainty regarding the true level of natural output.

The implications of measurement errors for stabilization policy

A dramatic example of the problems raised by macroeconomic measurement errors is given in Fig. 22.5. The dotted graphs show the preliminary data which were available to policy makers in 'real time' when they had to make their policy decisions, while the solid graphs

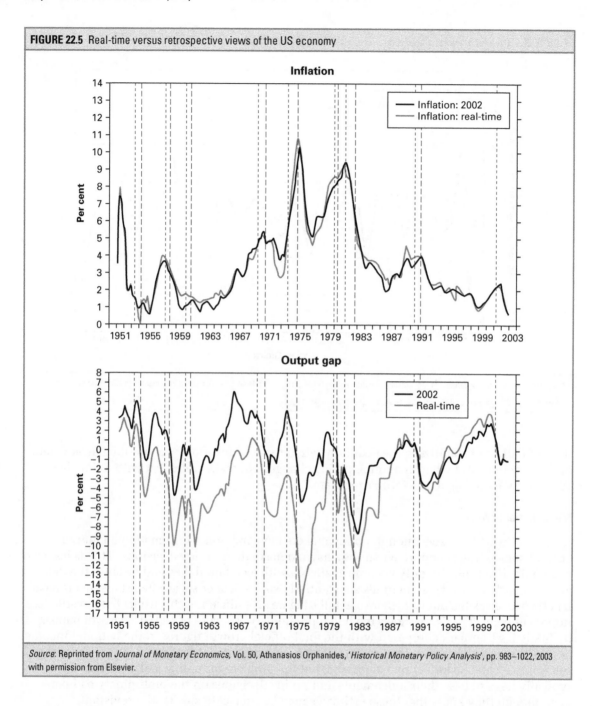

FIGURE 22.5 Real-time versus retrospective views of the US economy

Source: Reprinted from *Journal of Monetary Economics*, Vol. 50, Athanasios Orphanides, '*Historical Monetary Policy Analysis*', pp. 983–1022, 2003 with permission from Elsevier.

represent the revised data available in 2002. The upper part of Fig. 22.5 illustrates the sharp increase in the rate of inflation in the USA in the late 1960s and in the 1970s. The lower part of the figure gives a hint why policy makers failed to prevent this episode which is nowadays referred to as the Great Inflation. Assuming that the more recent revised numbers are the more correct ones, we see that during the 1960s and 1970s policy makers significantly overestimated the amount of slack in the economy. For example, in 1975 monetary and fiscal policy makers believed that US output was more than 16 per cent below its potential level, whereas the data available today indicate that output was in fact less than 5 per cent below potential in 1975. In particular, policy makers at the time were slow to recognize the increase in the natural unemployment rate and the slowdown in the trend rate of productivity growth which took place in the 1970s. For that reason they relax monetary and fiscal policy to fight the massive perceived slack in the economy, but because potential output was considerably lower than estimated at the time, the rate of inflation ended up at a much higher level than intended.

In Chapter 20 we presented evidence to suggest that the Great Inflation in the USA was due to a failure of monetary policy to follow John Taylor's prescription of raising the real interest rate in response to a rise in inflation. In that analysis we had the benefit of hindsight by being able to use the revised macroeconomic data which are available today. However, recent research has shown that monetary policy in the 1970s actually followed a standard Taylor rule fairly closely, given the real-time data available when monetary policy was made.[8] Thus the Great Inflation did not arise because policy makers were unusually 'soft' or irresponsible; the problem was that the data available at the time indicated a very large negative output gap which called for an expansionary monetary policy.

What are the implications of measurement errors for the optimal monetary stabilization policy? We will now use our AS–AD model to analyse this question. We start by specifying the actual output gap and the actual inflation gap as:

$$\hat{y}_t \equiv y_t - \bar{y},$$ (31)

$$\hat{\pi}_t \equiv \pi_t - \pi^*.$$ (32)

Suppose now that the *estimated* output gap $\hat{y}_t^e$ and the *estimated* inflation gap $\hat{\pi}_t^e$ deviate from the respective true gaps by some random measurement errors μ_t and ε_t:

$$\hat{y}_t^e = \hat{y}_t + \mu_t, \qquad E[\mu_t] = 0, \qquad E[\mu_t^2] = \sigma_\mu^2,$$ (33)

$$\hat{\pi}_t^e = \hat{\pi}_t + \varepsilon_t, \qquad E[\varepsilon_t] = 0, \qquad E[\varepsilon_t^2] = \sigma_\varepsilon^2$$ (34)

The variable μ_t captures errors in the measurement of actual as well as potential output, while the variable ε_t represents errors in the measurement of the actual inflation rate. The constant variances σ_μ^2 and σ_ε^2 reflect the degree of uncertainty in measurement. Operating in 'real time', the central bank must base its interest rate policy on the *estimated* rather than the actual output and inflation gaps. Hence we assume that the central bank follows a Taylor rule of the form:[9]

$$r_t = \bar{r} + h\hat{\pi}_t^e + b\hat{y}_t^e \quad \Rightarrow \quad r_t = \bar{r} + h\hat{\pi}_t + b\hat{y}_t + h\varepsilon_t + b\mu_t.$$ (35)

In Chapter 13 we saw that demand shocks seem to be the main driver of business cycles in most countries. To keep the exposition simple, we will therefore abstract from aggregate supply shocks. As we have seen earlier, if the private sector has rational expectations and the central bank has full credibility, the expected inflation rate will be equal to the central bank's inflation target π^*. We may then specify the aggregate supply curve as:

$$\pi_t = \pi^* + \gamma(y_t - \bar{y}) \quad \Leftrightarrow \quad \hat{\pi}_t = \gamma\hat{y}_t.$$ (36)

Allowing for demand shocks z_t, the goods market equilibrium condition may be written as:

$$\hat{y}_t = z_t - \alpha_2(r_t - \bar{r}), \qquad E[z_t] = 0, \qquad E[z_t^2] = \sigma_z^2.$$ (37)

8. This is documented by Athanasios Orphanides, 'Historical Monetary Policy Analysis and the Taylor Rule', *Journal of Monetary Economics*, **50**, 2003, pp. 983–1022.

9. If μ_t reflects errors in the measurement of potential output, these errors will generally cause the central bank to mis-measure the equilibrium real interest rate $\bar{r}$. For simplicity we abstract from this complication here. In Exercise 4 you are invited to analyse the case where $\bar{r}$ is mis-measured.

Equations (35)–(37) constitute a complete AS–AD model which may be solved to give the following expression for the output gap (you may want to derive this result as an exercise):

$$\hat{y}_t = \frac{z_t - \alpha_2 h\varepsilon_t - \alpha_2 b\mu_t}{1+\alpha_2(b+\gamma h)}. \tag{38}$$

This expression shows that a negative bias in the measurement of the output gap ($\mu_t < 0$) or an underestimation of the inflation rate ($\varepsilon_t < 0$) will tend to generate a positive actual output gap (and hence a positive inflation gap) by inducing the central bank to set a lower interest rate, thereby stimulating aggregate demand. As we have seen above, there was in fact a negative bias in the estimated output gap in the USA during the Great Inflation of the 1970s.

Assuming that the stochastic variables z_t, ε_t and μ_t are all uncorrelated, and recalling that they all have zero mean values, it follows from (38) that the variance of the output gap is:

$$\sigma_y^2 \equiv E[\hat{y}_t^2] = \frac{\sigma_z^2 + \alpha_2^2 h^2\sigma_\varepsilon^2 + \alpha_2^2 b^2\sigma_\mu^2}{[1+\alpha_2(b+\gamma h)]^2}. \tag{39}$$

Equation (39) shows that errors in the measurement of macroeconomic data contribute to macroeconomic instability because they make the central bank set the 'wrong' level of interest rates which is not adequately tuned to the true state of the economy.

From (36) we see that a monetary policy minimizing the variance of the output gap will also minimize the variance of the inflation gap in the present model without aggregate supply shocks. To minimize the social loss from variability in output and inflation, the central bank should therefore choose those values of the policy parameters h and b which will minimize the expression in (39). The first-order conditions for the solution to this optimization problem are:

$$\frac{\partial\sigma_y^2}{\partial h} = 0 \quad \Rightarrow \quad h\alpha_2\sigma_\varepsilon^2[1+\alpha_2(b+\gamma h)] - \gamma(\sigma_z^2 + \alpha_2^2 h^2\sigma_\varepsilon^2 + \alpha_2^2 b^2\sigma_\mu^2) = 0, \tag{40}$$

$$\frac{\partial\sigma_y^2}{\partial b} = 0 \quad \Rightarrow \quad b\alpha_2\sigma_\mu^2[1+\alpha_2(b+\gamma h)] - (\sigma_z^2 + \alpha_2^2 h^2\sigma_\varepsilon^2 + \alpha_2^2 b^2\sigma_\mu^2) = 0, \tag{41}$$

from which one can show that:

$$\frac{h}{b} = \frac{\gamma\sigma_\mu^2}{\sigma_\varepsilon^2}. \tag{42}$$

Thus, the greater the uncertainty σ_μ^2 in the measurement of the output gap relative to the uncertainty σ_ε^2 in the measurement of inflation, the larger is the central bank's optimal response to the estimated inflation gap relative to its optimal response to the estimated output gap. Using (41) and (42), one can also show that:[10]

$$b = \frac{\sigma_z^2}{\alpha_2\sigma_\mu^2}, \tag{43}$$

$$h = \frac{\gamma\sigma_z^2}{\alpha_2\sigma_\varepsilon^2}. \tag{44}$$

---

10. We are assuming that the values of b and h implied by (43) and (44) do not lead to a violation of the non-negativity constraint on the nominal interest rate.

These results are quite intuitive since they show that monetary policy should react more cautiously to the measured output and inflation gaps the greater the variances σ_μ^2 and σ_ε^2, that is, the greater the average errors in the measurement of the gaps.

As we have noted, policy makers in the USA (and elsewhere) tended to overestimate the size of the negative output gap for several years during the 1970s. This suggests that measurement errors are likely to display some degree of persistence. We may formalize this by assuming that the measurement errors μ_t and ε_t are given by the autoregressive processes:

$$\mu_t = \rho\mu_{t-1} + d_t, \quad 0 < \rho < 1, \quad E[d_t] = 0, \quad E[d_t^2] = \sigma_d^2, \tag{45}$$

$$\varepsilon_t = \theta\varepsilon_{t-1} + k_t, \quad 0 < \theta < 1, \quad E[k_t] = 0, \quad E[k_t^2] = \sigma_k^2, \tag{46}$$

where the parameters ρ and θ quantify the degree of persistence in the measurement errors, and where d_t and k_t are stochastic white noise variables. By successive substitutions, we find from (45) and (46) that

$$\mu_t = d_t + \rho d_{t-1} + \rho^2 d_{t-2} + \rho^3 d_{t-3} + \ldots \tag{47}$$

$$\varepsilon_t = k_t + \theta k_{t-1} + \theta^2 k_{t-2} + \theta^3 k_{t-3} + \ldots \tag{48}$$

Since d_t and k_t are white noise variables, it follows from (47) and (48) that $E[\mu_t] = E[\varepsilon_t] = 0$, as we assumed in (33) and (34). Recalling that $0 < \rho < 1$ and $0 < \theta < 1$, we also see from (47) and (48) that:

$$\sigma_\mu^2 \equiv E[\mu_t^2] = \sigma_d^2(1 + \rho + \rho^2 + \rho^3 + \ldots) = \frac{\sigma_d^2}{1-\rho}, \tag{49}$$

$$\sigma_\varepsilon^2 \equiv E[\varepsilon_t^2] = \sigma_k^2(1 + \theta + \theta^2 + \theta^3 + \ldots) = \frac{\sigma_k^2}{1-\theta}. \tag{50}$$

Inserting these expressions into (43) and (44), we obtain:

$$b = \frac{\sigma_z^2(1-\rho)}{\sigma_2\sigma_d^2}, \tag{51}$$

$$h = \frac{\gamma\sigma_z^2(1-\theta)}{\alpha_2\sigma_k^2}. \tag{52}$$

Quite intuitively, we see that the greater the degree of persistence in the measurement errors (the higher the values of ρ and θ), the smaller are the optimal values of b and h, that is, the more cautiously monetary policy should respond to the measured output and inflation gaps.

Let us sum up the insights from this analysis:

OPTIMAL STABILIZATION POLICY IN THE PRESENCE OF MEASUREMENT ERRORS !

Errors in the measurement of output and inflation gaps contribute to macroeconomic instability and reduce the scope for activist stabilization policy. The greater the variance of and persistence in the measurement errors, the smaller is the optimal response of the policy interest rate to variations in the measured output and inflation gaps.

The difficulties of fine tuning aggregate demand

Apart from the problems caused by measurement errors and a possible lack of credibility, the scope for stabilization policy is also limited by the existence of time lags, that is, the delay from the time when the need for a change in some policy instrument arises until the time when the policy change achieves its maximum impact on the economy. In Chapter 20 we saw that the so-called outside lag in monetary policy could in principle be dealt with through a policy of inflation forecast targeting. However, the analysis in Chapter 20 was based on the optimistic assumptions that policy makers know the structure of the economy, including the exact length of the outside lag, and that there are no errors in the measurement of current macroeconomic conditions. In practice, there is uncertainty about the true structure of the economy, about current business cycle conditions, and about the length of the outside lag which may vary from one situation to another. For these reasons few economists nowadays believe in the possibility of 'fine tuning' aggregate demand through macroeconomic stabilization policy. We do not know exactly when and by how much a change in monetary (or fiscal) policy affects the economy. The inevitable time lags and our imperfect understanding of the economy imply a real danger that an over-ambitious stabilization policy actually ends up *de*stabilizing the economy, because it only takes full effect long after the economic shock it was meant to offset, or because its effect turns out to be stronger than intended. Many economists therefore believe that monetary policy, and in particular fiscal policy, should only be used actively when the economy is hit by significant shocks which are expected to last for some time.

22.4 Summary

1. With rational expectations monetary policy may suffer from a credibility problem when the socially desired output level exceeds the natural level and the central bank can act in a discretionary manner after the private sector has formed its expectations. If monetary policy makers announce that they will keep the inflation rate down to a certain target level, the private sector may not consider such a statement to be credible when the central bank can boost output and employment by generating unanticipated inflation. The problem is that a rule-based policy of price stability is not time-consistent.

2. In a time-consistent rational expectations equilibrium with discretionary monetary policy, rational private agents anticipate the central bank's incentive to stimulate output by generating surprise inflation. The expected and actual inflation rate then becomes so high that the central bank does not wish to generate additional (unanticipated) inflation. The end result is an equilibrium with inflation above the target rate and an output level equal to the (suboptimally low) natural rate. Hence monetary policy suffers from an inflation bias under discretionary policy. A socially superior outcome could be achieved if the central bank could credibly commit to pursuing a rule-based policy of price stability.

3. If the policy maker cares sufficiently about the future, he may not have an incentive to generate surprise inflation in the short run, because he realizes that this will cause an unfavourable upward shift in the expected inflation rate in the longer run. In such a case the inflation bias in monetary policy may be held in check by the policy maker's desire to build up a reputation as a defender of price stability.

4. The inflation bias may also be reduced by delegating monetary policy to an independent and 'conservative' central bank which puts more emphasis on price stability than the government itself. However, if the variance of supply shocks is high and the central

▶

bank emphasis on price stability is strong, the result of such delegation may be that the variance of output increases to such an extent that social welfare falls. Thus there is a trade-off between gaining credibility in the fight against inflation and preserving the flexibility to allow inflation to rise when the economy is hit by a large negative supply shock.

5. Errors in the measurement of macroeconomic data such as the output and inflation gaps imply that monetary policy makers sometimes set the 'wrong' level of interest rates which is not adequately tuned to the true state of the economy. In this way measurement errors contribute to macroeconomic instability. The greater the average magnitude of the measurement errors, and the higher the degree of persistence in these errors, the smaller is the optimal interest rate response of the central bank to changes in the estimated output and inflation gaps.

22.5 Exercises

Exercise 1. Time-consistent monetary policy

When we analysed the credibility problem under discretionary monetary policy, we assumed for simplicity that the policy maker's target rate of inflation (π^*) was zero. Now we assume that, instead of being given by Eq. (3) in the main text, the policy maker's loss function is:

$$SL = (y_t - y^*)^2 + \kappa(\pi_t - \pi^*)^2, \qquad \pi^* > 0. \tag{53}$$

1. Discuss reasons why it may be reasonable to have a positive target rate of inflation (recall the arguments made in Chapter 19).

   Suppose that there are no stochastic demand and supply shocks so that the economy may be described by the following equations:

   Aggregate supply: $\pi_t = \pi_{t,t-1}^e + y_t - \bar{y}$,   (54)

   Goods market equilibrium: $y_t - \bar{y} = -\alpha_2(r_t - \bar{r})$,   (55)

   Announced monetary policy rule: $r_t = \bar{r} + h(\pi_t - \pi^*) + b(y_t - \bar{y})$,   (56)

   Target output: $y^* = \bar{y} + \omega$, $\omega > 0$,   (57)

2. Explain briefly why it may be reasonable to assume that target output exceeds trend output, as we have done in Eq. (57).

3. What levels of output and inflation will emerge if private agents have rational expectations and if they believe that the central bank will stick to the announced monetary policy rule (56)? Will the monetary policy maker actually want to stick to this rule if he can act in a discretionary manner? Explain.

4. Derive the 'cheating' solutions for output and inflation if the public believes that the central bank follows the rule (56) whereas the bank actually follows the optimal discretionary policy. Compare your results with Eq. (10) in the main text and explain the difference.

5. Explain the concept of time consistency. Derive the time-consistent rational expectations equilibrium values for output and inflation. Compare your results with Eq. (12) in the main text and explain the difference. Draw a diagram analogous to Fig. 22.1 and illustrate the Taylor rule equilibrium (where the private sector believes that the policy maker will follow

the rule (56)), the 'cheating' outcome, and the time-consistent equilibrium in the present situation, where $\pi^* > 0$.

Exercise 2. Inflation bias and delegation of monetary policy

When we discussed the effects of delegating monetary policy to an independent central bank, we assumed that the central banker had the same output target y^* as the government. However, central bankers often claim that they are not targeting an output level above the natural rate, since they know that this will only lead to inflation.

Against this background you are now asked to analyse the effects of delegating monetary policy in a setting where the central bank targets trend output $\bar{y}$, whereas elected politicians have a more ambitious output target $y^* > \bar{y}$. Thus we assume that the government's loss function is:

$$SL = (y_t - y^*)^2 + \kappa\pi_t^2, \qquad \kappa > 0, \tag{58}$$

where

$$y^* = \bar{y} + \omega, \qquad \omega > 0, \tag{59}$$

while the central bank's loss function is given by:

$$SL_B = (y_t - \bar{y})^2 + \kappa\pi_t^2. \tag{60}$$

Note that the government and the central bank are assumed to have the same degree of aversion to inflation (κ).

The central bank has been granted a degree of independence β from the government. Hence monetary policy is determined by minimization of the following loss function, representing a compromise between the preferences of politicians and the preferences of the central bank:

$$\tilde{SL} = (1 - \beta)SL + \beta SL_B, \qquad 0 \le \beta \le 1. \tag{61}$$

Finally, the rate of inflation is given by the SRAS curve:

$$\pi_t = \pi_{t,t-1}^e + y_t - \bar{y}. \tag{62}$$

By controlling the (real) interest rate, monetary policy can control the output gap $y_t - \bar{y}$ and hence indirectly the rate of inflation.

1. Use the procedure described in Section 22.1 to derive the time-consistent rational expectations equilibrium emerging when monetary policy is determined by minimizing (61). Compare the solutions for output and inflation with Eq. (12) in Section 1 and comment on similarities and differences.

2. What is the socially optimal degree of independence for the central bank (the optimal value of β)? Give reasons for your answer. How may central bank independence be achieved in practice?

Exercise 3. The implications of macroeconomic measurement errors

In (43) and (44) in the main text we derived the following formulae for the optimal values of the monetary policy parameters b and h when there are errors in the measurement of the output and inflation gaps:

$$b = \frac{\sigma_z^2}{\alpha_2 \sigma_\mu^2}, \tag{63}$$

$$h = \frac{\gamma \sigma_z^2}{\alpha_2 \sigma_\varepsilon^2}. \tag{64}$$

Give an intuitive interpretation of these results in which you explain the role of all the parameters σ_z^2, σ_μ^2, σ_ε^2, γ and α_2.

Exercise 4. Optimal stabilization policy with measurement errors

In Section 22.4 we noted that when policy makers err in measuring the output gap, they are also likely to mismeasure the equilibrium ('natural') real interest rate. Suppose therefore that the economy is described by the following system, where $\bar{r}^e$ is the *estimated* equilibrium real interest rate, $\hat{y}_t^e$ and $\hat{\pi}_t^e$ are the *estimated* output and inflation gaps, and where the measurement errors a_t, μ_t and ε_t are stochastic white noise variables:

Aggregate supply: $\quad \hat{\pi}_t = \gamma \hat{y}_t, \quad \hat{\pi}_t \equiv \pi_t - \pi^*, \quad \hat{y}_t \equiv y_t - \bar{y} \tag{65}$

Goods market equilibrium: $\quad \hat{y}_t = z_t - \alpha_2(r_t - \bar{r}), \quad E[z_t] = 0, \quad E[z_t^2] = \sigma_z^2, \tag{66}$

Monetary policy: $\quad r_t = \bar{r}^e + h\hat{\pi}_t^e + b\hat{y}_t^e, \tag{67}$

Estimate of $\bar{r}$: $\quad \bar{r}^e = \bar{r} + a_t, \quad E[a_t] = 0, \quad E[a_t^2] = \sigma_a^2, \tag{68}$

Estimate of $\hat{y}_t$: $\quad \hat{y}_t^e = \hat{y}_t + \mu_t, \quad E[\mu_t] = 0, \quad E[\mu_t^2] = \sigma_\mu^2, \tag{69}$

Estimate of $\hat{\pi}_t$: $\quad \hat{\pi}_t^e = \hat{\pi}_t + \varepsilon_t, \quad E[\varepsilon_t] = 0, \quad E[\varepsilon_t^2] = \sigma_\varepsilon^2. \tag{70}$

Equation (65) assumes that the central bank's inflation target is credible so that rational agents have the expected inflation rate $\pi^e = \pi^*$. For simplicity, the model abstracts from supply shocks and from persistence in the measurement errors. Note that since (65) implies that the variance of the inflation gap (σ_π^2) is proportional to the variance of the output gap (σ_y^2), an optimal policy which minimizes the social loss function $SL = \sigma_y^2 + \kappa\sigma_\pi^2$ must minimize the variance of the output gap $\sigma_y^2 \equiv E[\hat{y}_t^2]$.

1. Solve the model (65)–(70) for the output gap and show that the variability of output is given by:

$$\sigma_y^2 = \frac{\sigma_z^2 + \alpha_2^2(h^2\sigma_\varepsilon^2 + b^2\sigma_\mu^2 + \sigma_a^2)}{[1 + \alpha_2(b + \gamma h)]^2}.$$

Comment on this expression and explain the effects of the measurement errors, in particular the effect of the error in measuring the natural rate of interest.

2. Use the procedure described in Section 22.3 to show that the optimal values of b and h are given by the expressions

$$b = \frac{\sigma_z^2 + \alpha_2^2\sigma_a^2}{\alpha_2\sigma_\mu^2}$$

$$h = \frac{\gamma(\sigma_z^2 + \alpha_2^2\sigma_a^2)}{\alpha_2\sigma_\varepsilon^2}.$$

Compare these expressions to those given in Eqs (43) and (44) in the text and give an intuitive explanation for the differences.

PART 7

The Short-run Model for the Open Economy

CHAPTER

23

Aggregate demand and aggregate supply in the open economy

In Part 6 we focused on the closed economy. Understanding the workings of the closed economy before moving on to study the open economy is useful because most of the key mechanisms in the closed economy are also present in the open economy. However, in some important respects openness to international trade in goods and capital does change the way the macroeconomy works. For this reason openness may significantly affect the scope for and the effects of macroeconomic policy. It is therefore time now to put the spotlight on the open economy.

One key insight to emerge from our study of the open economy is that the short-run macroeconomic dynamics and the effects of monetary and fiscal policy will depend on the exchange rate regime. In Chapter 24 we will consider a fixed exchange rate regime where the central bank intervenes in the foreign exchange market to keep the nominal exchange rate fixed. Chapter 25 will study a flexible exchange rate regime where the exchange rate is determined by the forces of supply and demand in the foreign exchange market.

In the present chapter we derive some important economic relationships prevailing under both exchange rate regimes. The analysis will allow for the possibility that the exchange rate may change over time, as it typically does under flexible exchange rates (outside long-run equilibrium). If the exchange rate is actually fixed, one can simply set the nominal exchange rate equal to a constant in all the relationships presented in this chapter without invalidating any of our conclusions.

Back in Chapter 4 we documented the trend towards increased international trade and financial integration over the past half-century. In Section 23.1 we present some further evidence on the ongoing process of globalization and we lay out the key assumptions regarding the open economy. Section 23.2 then considers the implications of capital mobility for the formation of nominal and real interest rates, and Section 23.3 uses these insights to highlight how government attitudes towards capital mobility and the choice of exchange rate regime have changed over time. Following this, Section 23.4 explains how international trade and capital mobility affects the economy's aggregate demand curve, and Section 23.5 discusses the modelling of the aggregate supply side in the open economy. Section 23.6 confronts the aggregate supply curve with the aggregate demand curve to characterize the long-run equilibrium in the open economy.

The analysis in this chapter will set the stage for the next two chapters where we will use our AS–AD model for the open economy to highlight the characteristics of alternative exchange rate regimes, as a prelude to the discussion of the choice of exchange rate regime at the end of Chapter 25.

23.1 Globalization and the small specialized economy

The internationalization of the economy

During the past half-century there has been a tremendous increase in cross-border economic transactions. In the first decades after the Second World War this process of international economic integration mainly took the form of an increase in the volume of international trade. Thus, while the Western countries liberalized their international trade regimes by reducing tariffs and eliminating quantitative restrictions on imports, they maintained substantial restrictions on the private export and import of capital. One motivation for this policy was that capital controls made it easier for governments to defend the fixed exchange rate parities under the so-called Bretton Woods system of fixed exchange rates established after the Second World War. Another motivation was that capital controls were necessary to implement the regulations of borrowing and lending which were seen by most governments as an essential part of their monetary policies.

However, during the 1970s the Bretton Woods system of fixed exchange rates broke down, and quantitative restrictions on international capital flows and on domestic credit came to be seen as increasingly ineffective and harmful to economic efficiency. In the 1980s and 1990s a large number of countries therefore abolished their capital controls. At the same time the rapid improvements in communication and information technologies significantly reduced the transactions costs associated with international investment. As a result, the last two decades of the twentieth century witnessed a truly dramatic increase in international capital mobility.

Table 23.1 gives an impression of the strong increase in foreign trade relative to total output in the OECD area since 1960. Figure 23.1 shows a time series for the sum of total foreign assets and liabilities relative to total foreign trade for an aggregate of industrial countries for which data are available. The fact that this ratio has increased markedly indicates that international capital flows have grown even faster than foreign trade in recent years.

The small specialized economy

In this chapter we will show how our AS–AD framework can be extended to allow for international trade in goods and capital. Specifically, we will explain how one can model aggregate demand and aggregate supply in an open economy with free capital mobility. Our analysis will be based on three key assumptions. The first one is that the domestic economy is so *small* that it cannot significantly affect macroeconomic conditions in the rest of the world. For example, if a purely domestic recession strikes our small open economy, this will not affect its export market since foreign economic activity will remain the same. The reason is that if the domestic economy is small, its imports are only a very small fraction of total foreign output, so even if imports fall due to the domestic recession, this fall in demand will hardly be felt by the rest of the world. For most countries the assumption that the domestic economy is small relative to the world economy is a reasonable first approximation. Exceptions could be an economically very large country like the USA or a large region like the euro zone.

Our second key assumption is that the small domestic economy is *specialized* in the sense that the goods produced domestically are *imperfect substitutes* for the goods produced abroad. This means that the price of domestic goods can vary relative to the price of foreign goods. Indeed, as we shall see in the next two chapters, the endogenous adjustment of the relative price of domestic goods is a basic mechanism through which the small specialized economy adjusts to a long-run macroeconomic equilibrium.[1] The manufactured goods that

---

1. The assumption that foreign and domestic goods are imperfect substitutes distinguishes our open economy AS–AD model from the open economy growth model set up in Chapter 4. In that chapter we made the simplifying assumption that domestic goods were perfect substitutes for foreign goods.

TABLE 23.1 Ratio of foreign trade to GDP, 1960–2008

	1960	1970	1980	1990	2000	2008
Australia	0.14	0.14	0.17	0.17	0.22	0.24
Austria	0.24	0.30	0.37	0.39	0.51	0.56
Belgium	0.39	0.50	0.58	0.70	0.84	0.92
Canada	–	0.21	0.27	0.26	0.43	0.34
Denmark	0.34	0.29	0.33	0.33	0.41	0.54
Finland	0.22	0.25	0.32	0.24	0.38	0.42
France	–	0.15	0.22	0.22	0.28	0.28
Germany	–	0.21	0.27	0.30	0.34	0.44
Greece	0.14	0.13	0.26	0.23	0.30	0.28
Ireland	0.33	0.39	0.53	0.55	0.91	0.75
Italy	0.13	0.16	0.23	0.20	0.28	0.29
Japan	0.10	0.10	0.14	0.10	0.10	0.17
Luxembourg	0.85	0.87	0.94	1.02	1.41	1.65
Netherlands	0.46	0.45	0.52	0.53	0.65	0.73
Norway	0.37	0.37	0.40	0.37	0.38	0.38
Portugal	0.18	0.24	0.30	0.36	0.37	0.38
Spain	0.08	0.13	0.16	0.18	0.31	0.29
Sweden	0.22	0.24	0.29	0.29	0.43	0.50
Switzerland	0.26	0.30	0.34	0.34	0.41	0.51
United Kingdom	0.21	0.22	0.26	0.25	0.29	0.30
United States	0.05	0.05	0.10	0.10	0.13	0.15

Note: Foreign trade is measured as the average of exports and imports.

Source: OECD Economic Outlook database.

make up the bulk of exports in most industrialized countries are typically somewhat differentiated from the manufactured goods produced in other countries. Hence our assumption that countries specialize in the production of different goods also seems plausible.

Reflecting the deep international integration of capital markets prevailing today, our third key assumption is that *international capital mobility is perfect*. You may recall from Chapter 4 that under perfect capital mobility financial investors can instantaneously and costlessly switch between domestic and foreign assets. Further, in the absence of any country-specific risks, the assumption of perfect capital mobility is usually taken to mean that domestic and foreign financial assets are seen as perfect substitutes. From these assumptions it follows that domestic and foreign financial assets must yield the same expected rate of return.

Since foreign and domestic assets are usually denominated in different currencies, and since market exchange rates may fluctuate, investment across borders normally involves exchange rate risk as the domestic-currency value of a foreign asset may vary in a stochastic manner. In these circumstances domestic and foreign assets can only be perfect substitutes if investors are *risk neutral*, caring only about the expected (average) asset returns and not about the stochastic variability of returns.

A more realistic assumption would be that investors are risk averse. In a country with a net savings surplus (a current account surplus) and a consequent need to invest part of national savings abroad, the expected return on domestic investment would then tend to be lower than the expected return on foreign investment to induce domestic savers to incur the exchange

FIGURE 23.1 Foreign assets and liabilities relative to foreign trade

Note: The countries included in the sample are: USA, UK, Austria, Belgium, Germany, Italy, Netherlands, Norway, Sweden, Switzerland, Canada, Japan, Finland and Spain.

Source: Figure 2.4 of Philip R. Lane and Gian Maria Milesi-Ferretti, 'International Financial Integration', *IMF Staff Papers*, 50, Special Issue, 2003, pp. 82–113.

rate risk associated with investment abroad. By analogy, in a country with a net savings deficit (a current account deficit) and a consequent need for capital imports, the expected return on domestic investment would tend to exceed the expected return on investment abroad to provide an incentive for foreign investors to place part of their savings in the domestic economy. The resulting international rate-of-return differentials would represent risk premia needed to compensate for exchange rate risk. In the analysis in the rest of this book we could have included an exogenous (positive or negative) risk premium on international investment (as we did in Section 4.4), but this would not have affected any of our qualitative results. We have therefore chosen to simplify the exposition and combine the assumption of perfect capital mobility with an assumption of risk-neutral investors so that domestic and foreign assets become perfect substitutes. This means that there can be no cross-country differences in expected asset returns. In fact, as we shall see below, differences in expected rates of return on financial investment do tend to be quite small across Western countries.

THE SMALL SPECIALIZED ECONOMY

In a small specialized economy domestic economic developments do not significantly affect the world economy, but the price of domestic goods can vary relative to the price of foreign goods because the domestic economy specializes in the production of goods that are imperfect substitutes for goods produced abroad. Reflecting the deep international integration of capital markets, it is also often assumed that small economies are faced with perfect capital mobility, meaning that financial investors can instantaneously and costlessly switch between domestic and foreign assets. With risk-neutral investors perfect capital mobility also means that domestic and foreign financial assets are seen as perfect substitutes. Together these assumptions imply that the expected rates of return on financial assets are equalized between the domestic and the foreign economy.

The next section derives some important implications from our key assumptions for the formation of nominal and real interest rates in the open economy.

23.2 Capital mobility, interest rate parity and purchasing power parity

Capital mobility and nominal interest rate parity

As already mentioned, foreign and domestic assets must yield the same expected rate of return when capital mobility is perfect. For example, if domestic bonds had a lower expected return than foreign bonds, investors would immediately sell domestic bonds in order to buy foreign bonds, thus driving down domestic bond prices and pushing up foreign bond prices until the expected rates of return are equalized. Given that this arbitrage can occur instantaneously and costlessly, the expected returns must be equal at any point in time.

Let us be more precise. Following common European practice, we define the *nominal exchange rate*, E, as the number of domestic currency units needed to buy one unit of the foreign currency. If i is the domestic nominal interest rate and i^f is the foreign nominal interest rate, perfect capital mobility implies the arbitrage condition:

$$1 + i = (1 + i^f)\left(\frac{E_{+1}^e}{E}\right), \tag{1}$$

where E is the nominal exchange rate at the start of the current period, and E_{+1}^e is the nominal exchange rate expected to prevail at the beginning of the next period. The left-hand side of (1) measures the amount of wealth accruing to an investor at the end of the current period if he invests one unit of the domestic currency in the domestic capital market at the beginning of the period. As an alternative to such a domestic investment, the investor could have bought $1/E$ units of the foreign currency at the start of the period for the purpose of investment in the foreign capital market. At the end of the period he would then have ended up with an amount of wealth $(1/E)(1 + i^f)$ in foreign currency. At the start of the period when the investment is made, the investor expects that this end-of-period wealth will be worth $(E_{+1}^e/E)(1 + i^f)$ units of the domestic currency. Thus equation (1) says that domestic and foreign investment must generate the same expected end-of-period wealth and hence must yield the same expected rate of return.[2]

If we take natural logarithms on both sides of (1) and use the approximation $\ln(1 + x) \approx x$, we get:

$$i = i^f + e_{+1}^e - e, \qquad e \equiv \ln E, \qquad e_{+1}^e \equiv \ln E_{+1}^e. \tag{2}$$

The magnitude $(e_{+1}^e - e) \times 100$ is the expected percentage rate of depreciation of the domestic currency against the foreign currency. This is the expected *capital gain* on foreign bonds relative to domestic bonds over the period considered. Thus Eq. (2) says that if the domestic currency is expected to depreciate by x per cent, the domestic nominal interest rate must exceed the foreign nominal interest rate by x percentage points to make domestic and foreign assets equally attractive.

Equation (2) (and its approximate equivalent (1)) is known as the condition for *uncovered interest rate parity*. The term 'uncovered' refers to the fact that the investor has not covered his risk: when he invests in the foreign capital market, he expects a capital gain $e_{+1}^e - e$, but this gain is uncertain, so he is exposed to risk. If he wants to cover his risk at the time of investment, he can use the *forward market* for foreign exchange. In this market he can sell

---

2. As already mentioned, (1) also covers the case where exchange rates are completely fixed, as indeed they are if the countries considered belong to a monetary union with a common currency. In that case we simply have $E_{+1}^e/E = 1$.

an amount of foreign currency $(1/E)(1 + i^f)$ for delivery one period from now at the forward exchange rate $\tilde{E}_{+1}$ currently prevailing in the market. The one-period forward exchange rate $\tilde{E}_{+1}$ is the domestic-currency price of one unit of foreign currency delivered one period from now. Since $\tilde{E}_{+1}$ is known at the start of the current period when the foreign investment is made, the investor knows for sure that he will end up with $(\tilde{E}_{+1}/E)(1 + i^f)$ units of the domestic currency at the end of the period if he covers his foreign investment via the forward market. For domestic and foreign investment to be equally attractive, we thus have the arbitrage condition:

$$1 + i = (1 + i^f)\left(\frac{\tilde{E}_{+1}}{E}\right). \tag{3}$$

Taking logs on both sides of (3), we get the approximate relationship:

$$i = i^f + \tilde{e}_{+1} - e, \qquad \tilde{e}_{+1} \equiv \ln \tilde{E}_{+1}. \tag{4}$$

Equations (3) and (4) are known as the condition for *covered interest rate parity*. Is it possible for covered and uncovered interest rate parity to hold at one and the same time? According to (2) and (4) the answer is 'yes', provided

$$\tilde{e}_{+1} - e = e^e_{+1} - e \quad \Leftrightarrow \quad \tilde{e}_{+1} = e^e_{+1}. \tag{5}$$

The term on the left-hand side of the first equation in (5) is the *forward foreign exchange premium*, defined as the (percentage) difference between the price of forward exchange (the price of foreign exchange for delivery one period from now) and the current *spot* exchange rate E (the price of foreign exchange for immediate delivery). Equation (5) says that if the spot exchange rate is expected to increase by $(e^e_{+1} - e) \times 100$ per cent over the next period, then the forward foreign exchange premium should also equal $(e^e_{+1} - e) \times 100$ per cent. When investors are risk neutral, this condition must hold. To see this, suppose that $\tilde{e}_{+1} < e^e_{+1}$. In that case it would be possible to score an expected profit by buying foreign exchange in the forward market today and then selling the foreign currency in the spot market when it is delivered one period from now. Similarly, if $\tilde{e}_{+1} > e^e_{+1}$ risk-neutral investors will want to sell foreign exchange in the forward market today and buy foreign exchange in the spot market one period ahead when the foreign currency is to be delivered, thus scoring an expected profit of $\tilde{e}_{+1} - e^e_{+1}$ at the time of delivery. To rule out such arbitrage opportunities for pure profit making, Eq. (5) will have to be satisfied, so covered and uncovered interest rate parity will hold simultaneously *when investors are risk neutral*.

Equations (2) and (4) suggest that when exchange rates can vary a lot, the interest rates of different countries can also deviate substantially from each other. However, when countries move towards greater fixity of exchange rates, the expected exchange rate changes should tend towards zero, forcing national interest rates into equality. Figure 23.2 confirms this hypothesis. Around the mid-1990s the exchange rates within the European Monetary System could in principle vary within an exchange rate band of ±15 per cent around the central parity, and countries like Italy and Spain with a history of devaluations against the German mark had relatively high nominal interest rates, reflecting the perceived probability of devaluation of the Italian and Spanish currencies. At the same time countries like Germany, Netherlands and France, whose currencies were perceived to be strong, had nominal interest rates below the average EU level. However, when financial markets became convinced that political leaders in Europe were determined to establish a monetary union with completely fixed exchange rates (and ultimately a common currency), the nominal interest rates of the different EU countries quickly converged, as fears of substantial exchange rate movements vanished.

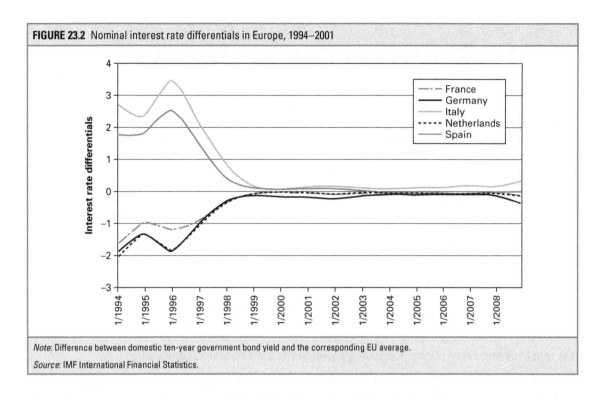

FIGURE 23.2 Nominal interest rate differentials in Europe, 1994–2001

Note: Difference between domestic ten-year government bond yield and the corresponding EU average.

Source: IMF International Financial Statistics.

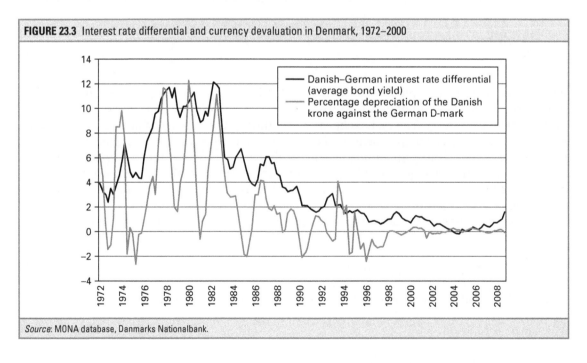

FIGURE 23.3 Interest rate differential and currency devaluation in Denmark, 1972–2000

Source: MONA database, Danmarks Nationalbank.

Figure 23.3 tells a similar story about Denmark. From the early 1970s to the early 1980s, the Danish krone was devalued against the German mark on numerous occasions, and expectations of future devaluation kept the Danish nominal interest rate far above the German interest rate. But as the policy of systematic Danish devaluations was abandoned after 1982 and the krone became a much more stable currency, the Danish interest rate gradually converged towards the German level.

INTEREST RATE PARITY

The hypothesis of *uncovered* interest rate parity assumes that investors are risk neutral. In that case perfect capital mobility implies that foreign and domestic financial assets must yield the same expected rate of return. Hence the domestic interest rate must equal the foreign interest rate plus the expected percentage rate of depreciation of the domestic currency (positive or negative). The condition for *covered* interest rate parity is a pure arbitrage condition ruling out the possibility of making risk-free gains via the foreign exchange market. Under covered interest parity, the domestic interest rate equals the foreign interest rate plus the percentage difference between the forward market exchange rate and the spot market exchange rate. If investors are risk neutral, the conditions for uncovered and covered interest parity will both hold.

We have so far focused on the implications of capital mobility for the cross-country relationship between *nominal* interest rates, but the aggregate demand for goods and services depends on the *real* interest rate, defined as the nominal interest rate minus the (expected) rate of inflation. To see what international economic integration implies for the cross-country link between real interest rates, we must therefore explore the link between national inflation rates created by international trade. This is the agenda for the next subsection.

The real exchange rate, relative purchasing power parity and real interest rate parity

A country's international competitiveness is often measured by the price of foreign goods relative to the price of domestic goods.[3] This important variable is called *the real exchange rate*, E^r, defined as

$$E^r \equiv \frac{EP^f}{P}, \tag{6}$$

where P^f is the price of foreign goods denominated in foreign currency, EP^f is the price of foreign goods measured in domestic currency, and P is the price of domestic goods in units of the domestic currency. The real exchange rate indicates the number of units of the domestic good which must be given up to acquire one unit of the foreign good. The higher the real exchange rate, the cheaper are domestic goods relative to goods produced abroad. The inverse of the real exchange rate $(1/E^r)$ is referred to as the international *terms of trade*, since an increase in the real exchange rate implies a deterioration in the terms on which domestic goods can be traded for foreign goods.

For later purposes it will be convenient to measure the real exchange rate in natural logarithms. We therefore define:

$$e^r \equiv \ln E^r = e + p^f - p, \qquad p^f \equiv \ln P^f, \qquad p \equiv \ln P. \tag{7}$$

The log of the real exchange rate in the previous period is then given by:

$$e^r_{-1} = e_{-1} + p^f_{-1} - p_{-1}, \tag{8}$$

which may be subtracted from (7) to give:

$$e^r - e^r_{-1} = \Delta e + \pi^f - \pi,$$

$$\Delta e \equiv e - e_{-1}, \qquad \pi^f \equiv p^f - p^f_{-1}, \qquad \pi \equiv p - p_{-1}, \tag{9}$$

---

3. Strictly speaking, international competitiveness should be measured by the relative prices of those goods which can be traded internationally. In our AS–AD model we will make the simplifying assumption that all goods can be traded.

FIGURE 23.4 Bilateral exchange rate and relative prices between Denmark and Germany

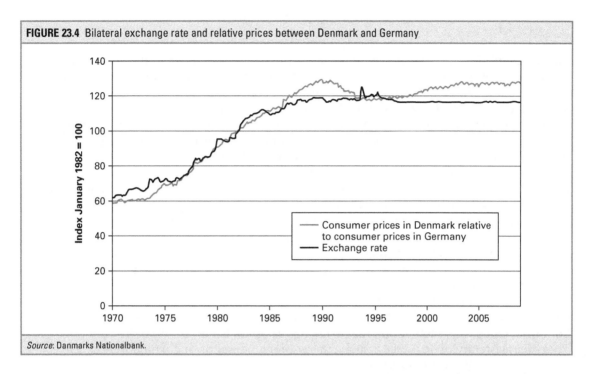

Source: Danmarks Nationalbank.

where Δe is the percentage depreciation of the domestic currency, π^f is the foreign rate of inflation, and π is the domestic inflation rate. According to (9) the percentage depreciation of the real exchange rate is thus equal to the nominal exchange rate depreciation plus the inflation differential between the foreign and the domestic economy.

The definitional relationship (9) has an interesting implication when we combine it with the concept of a long-run macroeconomic equilibrium. As we shall see below, the real exchange rate is an important determinant of the trade balance. For the economy to be in long-run equilibrium, the real exchange rate therefore has to be constant (otherwise the trade balance would keep on changing over time). If we insert the long-run equilibrium condition $e^r = e^r_{-1}$ into (9), we get the *long-run equilibrium condition*:

$$\Delta e = \pi - \pi^f. \tag{10}$$

This condition is known as *relative purchasing power parity*. It says that, over the long run, a country's rate of nominal exchange rate depreciation must correspond to the excess of the domestic over the foreign inflation rate. In this way the country's international competitiveness (its real exchange rate) is kept constant over time. Relative purchasing power parity (RPPP) will play an important part in our characterization of long-run equilibrium in the open economy.

Figure 23.4 shows that the hypothesis of RPPP provides a reasonably good description of the long-run relationship between price levels and the nominal exchange rate between Denmark and her largest trading partner, Germany. For many years the Danish price level increased relative to the German price level, but this loss of Danish competitiveness was more or less offset by a corresponding depreciation of the exchange rate until some time in the 1980s when Denmark switched to a fixed exchange rate policy vis-à-vis Germany.

Combined with our assumption of perfect capital mobility, relative purchasing power parity implies that in the long run the domestic real interest rate is tied to the real interest rate abroad. This may be seen as follows: in a long-run equilibrium the rate of exchange depreciation must be correctly anticipated, that is, the expected rate of depreciation must equal the actual rate, $e^e_{+1} - e = \Delta e_{+1}$. Hence we may write the condition for uncovered nominal interest rate parity as $i = i^f + \Delta e_{+1}$, and the condition for relative purchasing power parity may be rewritten as $\pi_{+1} = \pi^f_{+1} + \Delta e_{+1}$. Subtracting the latter from the former equation gives:

$$i - \pi_{+1} = i^f - \pi_{+1}^f. \tag{11}$$

The left-hand side of (11) is the *ex post* domestic real interest rate, and the right-hand side is the foreign real interest rate measured *ex post*.[4] In a long-run equilibrium where inflation is correctly anticipated, the *ex ante* real interest rates (based on expected inflation rates) are identical to the *ex post* rates, so in the long run the real interest rate in the small domestic economy will be equal to the exogenous foreign real interest rate. In other words, while capital mobility establishes a link between the *nominal* interest rates at home and abroad, the combination of capital mobility and foreign trade also implies a long-run link between the domestic and the foreign *real* rates of interest. The relationship (11) is known as *real interest rate parity* and it will play an important role in our analysis of the open economy.[5]

If real interest rate parity holds, the difference between the *ex post* real interest rates across any two countries in the world economy should tend to fluctuate around a zero mean value. Figure 23.5 suggests that this is indeed the case. The figure shows that long-term real interest rate differentials have fluctuated quite a lot over time – indicating that the economy can fluctuate substantially around its long-run growth trend – but the real interest rate differential displays a clear tendency to revert towards a mean value of zero, as implied by the hypothesis of real interest rate parity. Note that our derivation of (11) did not rely on any specific assumption regarding the exchange rate regime. Thus real interest rate parity should hold in the long run whether nominal exchange rates are fixed ($\Delta e = 0$) or flexible ($\Delta e \neq 0$). This is consistent with Fig. 23.5 which covers a long period during which international exchange rate regimes have varied considerably.

PURCHASING POWER PARITY AND REAL INTEREST RATE PARITY

The real exchange rate is the price of foreign goods relative to the price of domestic goods. In a long-run equilibrium the real exchange rate must be constant. This means that relative purchasing power parity (RPPP) must hold in the long run. Under RPPP the rate of nominal exchange rate depreciation equals the difference between the domestic and the foreign inflation rate. When combined with uncovered interest rate parity, RPPP implies real interest rate parity, that is, in the long run the domestic real interest rate must correspond to the foreign real interest rate, regardless of the exchange rate regime. The long-run prediction of real interest rate parity is supported by empirical evidence.

23.3 Capital mobility and exchange rate regimes: past and present

The macroeconomic trilemma and its historical resolution

The link between capital mobility and the formation of interest rates leads to a fundamental macroeconomic 'trilemma', also known as the 'Impossible Trinity'. The trilemma arises because a macroeconomic policy regime can include at most two out of the following three policy goals:

---

4. The definition of the real interest rate given here is the so-called real producer rate of interest, defined as the nominal interest rate minus the rate of increase of the price of domestic goods. This is the rate of interest which determines the profitability of investment from the viewpoint of domestic firms. From the viewpoint of consumers, the relevant real interest rate is the so-called real consumer rate of interest, defined as the nominal interest rate minus the rate of increase of consumer prices (which include the prices of imported consumer goods). By focusing on the real producer rate of interest, we are implicitly assuming that the interest rate affects aggregate demand mainly through its impact on business investment decisions, whereas household savings are relatively insensitive to interest rates.

5. In Chapter 4 we directly assumed real interest rate parity. We have now provided a deeper understanding of this 'law' for the long run.

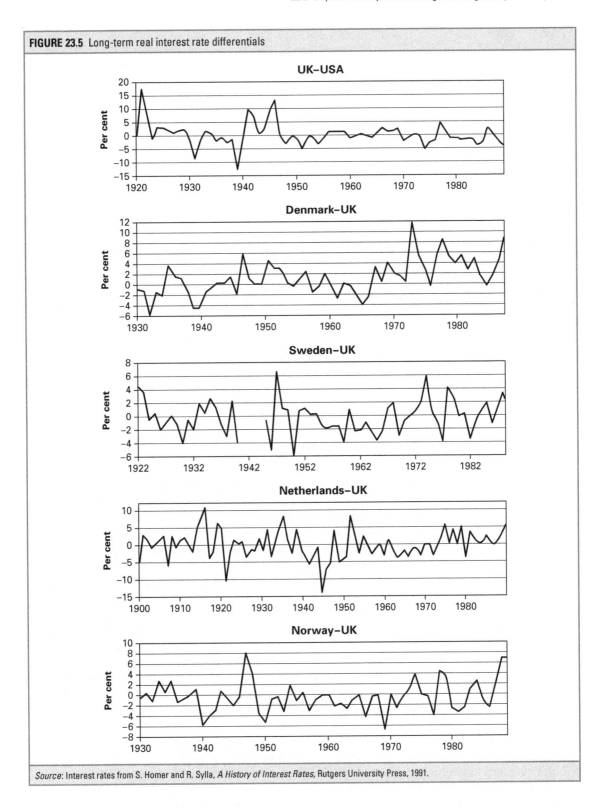

FIGURE 23.5 Long-term real interest rate differentials

Source: Interest rates from S. Homer and R. Sylla, *A History of Interest Rates*, Rutgers University Press, 1991.

1. free cross-border capital flows,
2. a fixed exchange rate, and
3. an independent monetary policy.

TABLE 23.2 The trilemma and major phases of capital mobility

| Era | Resolution of trilemma – Countries choose to sacrifice: | | | Notes |
	Activist policies	Capital mobility	Fixed exchange rate	
Gold standard	Most	Few	Few	Broad consensus
Interwar (when off gold)	Few	Several	Most	Capital controls especially in Central Europe, Latin America
Bretton Woods	Few	Most	Few	Broad consensus
Float	Few	Few	Many	Some consensus; except currency unions, currency boards, dollarization, etc.

Note: For an explanation of the concepts of 'currency boards' and 'dollarization', see the next subsection.

Source: Reprinted from Table 1, Chapter 3: 'Globalization and Capital Markets', by Maurice Obstfeld and Alan Taylor, in Michael D. Bordo, Alan M. Taylor and Jeffrey G. Williamson (eds), *Globalization in Historical Perspective*. The University of Chicago Press, 2003. © 2003 by the National Bureau of Economic Research.

The Impossible Trinity is easily understood by going back to the condition for uncovered interest parity (UCP) which assumes perfect capital mobility. As you recall from Eq. (2), this condition may be stated as

$$\text{UCP:} \qquad i = i^f + e_{+1}^e - e.$$

If a country fixes its nominal exchange rate while at the same time allowing free international capital flows, it follows from UCP that the domestic nominal interest rate i becomes tied to the foreign nominal interest rate i^f, since credibly fixed exchange rates imply that the expected rate of nominal exchange rate depreciation, $e_{+1}^e - e$, becomes zero. Alternatively, if a country wants to be able to set its own interest rate independently of the foreign interest rate while allowing capital mobility, it follows from UCP that it must also allow its exchange rate to vary. As a final alternative, since UCP is enforced by capital mobility, a country must impose capital controls if it wants to pursue an independent interest rate policy while at the same time fixing its exchange rate.

Over the years countries have resolved the fundamental macroeconomic trilemma in different ways. Table 23.2 provides a simplified summary of the historical experience with the trilemma, drawing on a study by economists Maurice Obstfeld and Alan Taylor. Historically the developed countries in the world have made several attempts to establish an international monetary system based on fixed exchange rates. One important and interesting example of a fixed exchange rate regime was the classical gold standard which had its heyday from around 1870 up until the outbreak of the First World War in 1914. During this period almost all advanced countries made their currencies convertible into gold at a fixed price. All agents in the private sector could thus exchange domestic currency for gold with their central bank at the quoted official price. This convertibility of currency into gold implied that exchange rates could only fluctuate within a fairly narrow band determined by the cost of shipping gold from one country to another. If the market exchange rate of some foreign currency were higher than the official gold price of that currency plus the cost of transporting gold, a domestic resident could gain by buying gold from the domestic central bank at the official domestic-currency price of gold, shipping the gold abroad, selling it to the foreign central bank at the official foreign-currency price of gold, and then selling the acquired foreign currency in the market in return for domestic currency. Thus the demand for a currency tended to disappear at the same time as the supply of that currency tended to increase strongly if its market price (the exchange rate) became so high that it became profitable to transport gold across borders as part of the above-mentioned arbitrage activity. By a similar mechanism, the supply of a currency tended to disappear at the same time as the demand for it tended to infinity if it became so cheap that it was profitable to buy the currency in the market, sell it to the foreign central bank in return for gold, ship the gold home and sell it to the domestic central bank in return for domestic currency (convince yourself of this).

One intriguing feature of the classical gold standard was that it tended to be self-regulating. Countries with a weak domestic currency (i.e. countries where the price of foreign currency was high) tended to experience an outflow of gold which reduced the domestic monetary base, thereby driving up the domestic interest rate. Indeed, under the gold standard central banks typically raised their interest rates as soon as there was a slight tendency for gold to flow out of the country. Hence it became more profitable for foreign and domestic portfolio investors to invest in domestic interest-bearing assets, and this tended to increase the supply of foreign currency as well as the demand for domestic currency. By lowering domestic economic activity, the higher interest rate also tended to lower the demand for foreign currency for the purpose of importing foreign goods. In this way the outflow of gold tended to eliminate the excess demand for foreign exchange. In countries with a strong domestic currency and an inflow of gold, the resulting downward pressure on interest rates meant that similar forces worked in the opposite direction to eliminate the excess demand for the domestic currency.

During the era of the classical gold standard up until the First World War, there was a broad consensus among Western governments about the desirability of fixed exchange rates and free international mobility of capital. Thus governments were willing to subordinate their monetary policies to the goal of protecting their gold reserves rather than using monetary policy to stabilize the domestic economy. Under the dominant laissez-faire philosophy of that time, policy makers did not perceive a need for activist stabilization policies since they tended to believe strongly in the self-regulating forces of the free market. But despite the self-regulating forces of the gold standard, the system broke down under the pressure of the First World War. Many governments found it impossible to finance the war effort without resorting to the age-old practice of printing money, so they abolished the convertibility of their currencies into gold in order to be able to expand the money supply.

After the First World War most countries tried to restore the gold standard, but the system broke down again during the Great Depression of the 1930s when many countries started to use monetary policy to stimulate the domestic economy. To be able to do so, either they had to impose capital controls, or they had to abandon their fixed exchange rates and adopt a policy of devaluation or of flexible exchange rates. The latter route was chosen by a large number of countries which were thereby able to recover more quickly from the depression than the countries that stuck to the gold standard.

After the Second World War very few countries were willing to give up the possibility of pursuing an activist monetary stabilization policy, but at the same time they feared a return to the beggar-thy-neighbour policies of the 1930s where countries had tried to gain competitiveness at each other's expense through large aggressive devaluations. As a consequence, a new international system of fixed exchange rates was established as part of the so-called Bretton Woods agreement. Under this system countries pegged their currencies to the US dollar, allowing their exchange rates to fluctuate within a narrow band of ± 1 per cent against the dollar. The dollar itself was made convertible into gold at a fixed price and became the main international reserve currency used by central banks, reflecting the dominant role of the USA in the world economy. Countries were supposed to devalue their currencies only in the event of a so-called 'fundamental disequilibrium' on their balance of payments, and the International Monetary Fund was established to provide international credit to countries which ran into temporary balance-of-payments crises. To secure some scope for an independent monetary policy, the great majority of countries during the Bretton Woods era imposed substantial restrictions on international capital flows.

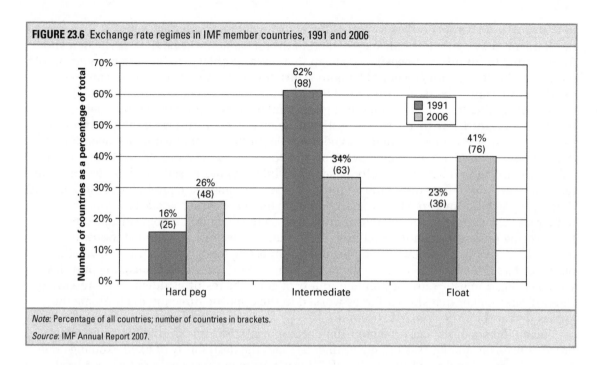

FIGURE 23.6 Exchange rate regimes in IMF member countries, 1991 and 2006

Note: Percentage of all countries; number of countries in brackets.

Source: IMF Annual Report 2007.

However, over time capital controls became harder to maintain, as communication and information technologies developed and the volume of international trade transactions increased. The fixed exchange rates of the Bretton Woods system came under speculative attack in the late 1960s as international capital flows expanded, and the system broke down in a massive wave of speculation between 1971 and 1973. This illustrated the weakness of a fixed exchange rate regime where the exchange rate can be adjusted and capital can move across borders. Under such a system speculation is virtually risk-free: if an investor moves out of a currency which is expected to be devalued, he will obviously gain from this move if devaluation actually occurs, and if the exchange rate is maintained he will lose nothing except a small transaction cost. A system of fixed but adjustable exchange rates with free capital mobility is thus highly vulnerable to speculative attacks.

Since the collapse of the Bretton Woods system the major currencies in the world have been floating against each other, as the most important countries remained unwilling to give up an independent monetary policy. At the same time the member states of the European Union have made repeated efforts to create exchange rate stability within Europe. During the 1970s most of the EU countries made a half-hearted attempt to keep their bilateral exchange rates within a fairly narrow band called the 'currency snake' (because the band could fluctuate vis-à-vis the currencies of third countries), and from 1979 they established a more ambitious system of fixed but adjustable exchange rates in the form of the European Monetary System. In 1999 these efforts culminated in the formation of the European Monetary Union; the ultimate fixed exchange rate arrangement where member countries have irrevocably fixed their bilateral exchange rates by giving up their national currencies in favour of a common currency, the euro.

The recent polarization of exchange rate regimes

In Fig. 23.6 we have grouped the various exchange rate regimes currently found in the world into three categories denoted 'hard peg', 'intermediate' regimes, and 'float'.[6] The exchange rate arrangements described as hard pegs include situations where countries have no

---

6. Figure 23.6 is updated from Stanley Fischer, 'Exchange Rates Regimes – Is the Bipolar View Correct?' *Journal of Economic Perspectives*, **15**, Spring 2001, p. 4.

national currency, either because they are in a currency union like the European Monetary Union, or because they have 'dollarized' by formally adopting the currency of some other country, typically the US dollar. A hard peg can also take the form of a *currency board* where the central bank is obliged by law to exchange domestic currency for a specified foreign currency at a completely fixed exchange rate, and where domestic currency can only be issued against foreign currency so that the domestic monetary base is fully backed by foreign exchange reserves.

The 'floating' group contains economies whose systems are described by the International Monetary Fund as either 'independently floating' or as a 'managed float'. Under independent floating the exchange rate is market-determined. To the extent that the central bank intervenes in the foreign exchange market by buying or selling domestic currency against foreign currency, such interventions aim only to moderate undue fluctuations in the exchange rate, but do not seek to establish a particular level for the exchange rate. Under a managed float the central bank influences the movements of the exchange rate through active intervention in the foreign exchange market without specifying, or precommitting to, a predetermined path for the exchange rate. This is sometimes referred to as 'dirty' floating.

The 'intermediate' group consists of economies with a variety of exchange rate arrangements falling between the hard pegs and the floating group. For example, some countries have set a central parity for the exchange rate against a particular foreign currency or against a basket (a weighted average) of currencies, but the actual exchange rate is then allowed to fluctuate within a fixed band around the parity. Other countries operate a 'crawling band' where the band for the exchange rate is allowed to move over time, or a 'crawling peg' where the exchange rate is temporarily fixed, but where it is allowed to shift gradually over time.

Table 23.3 summarizes the exchange rate regimes prevailing in some of the richest countries in the world at the beginning of the twenty-first century.

Going back to Fig. 23.6, we observe a remarkable polarization of the choice of exchange rate regimes in recent years. In 1991 almost two-thirds of all countries had some form of intermediate exchange rate arrangement. Fifteen years later a lot of countries had moved either towards a hard peg or towards floating. This is not coincidental, since almost all of the serious foreign exchange crises that occurred in the 1990s involved some form of

TABLE 23.3 Exchange rate regimes in developed market economies 2006

Euro area		Other	
	Exchange arrangement		**Exchange arrangement**
Austria	No separate legal tender	Australia	Independent float
Belgium	No separate legal tender	Canada	Independent float
Finland	No separate legal tender	Denmark	Pegged rate in horizontal band
France	No separate legal tender	Hong Kong SAR	Currency board
Germany	No separate legal tender	Japan	Independent float
Greece	No separate legal tender	New Zealand	Independent float
Ireland	No separate legal tender	Norway	Independent float
Italy	No separate legal tender	Singapore	Managed float
Luxembourg	No separate legal tender	Sweden	Independent float
Netherlands	No separate legal tender	Switzerland	Independent float
Portugal	No separate legal tender	United Kingdom	Independent float
Spain	No separate legal tender	United States	Independent float

Source: IMF Annual Report 2007.

intermediate exchange rate regime. This was true of the crisis in the European Monetary System in 1992–93 and of the crises in Mexico in 1994, Thailand, Indonesia and South Korea in 1997, Russia and Brazil in 1998, and Turkey in 2000.[7] The background for these crises was the huge increase in international capital mobility during the 1990s which greatly increased the scope for speculative attacks against 'soft' fixed exchange rate regimes. Alerted by the numerous foreign exchange crises during the 1990s, many countries with a preference for stable exchange rates moved towards a hard peg, whereas countries with a preference for monetary policy autonomy moved towards floating. Indeed, it is now widely believed that intermediate exchange rate regimes tend to be unsustainable in the long run in the modern world of high capital mobility.[8]

THE MACROECONOMIC TRILEMMA AND ITS RESOLUTION THROUGH HISTORY

The link between capital mobility and interest rate formation leads to the 'Impossible Trinity': a macroeconomic policy regime can include at most two out of the following three policy goals: 1) free capital mobility, 2) a fixed exchange rate, and 3) an independent monetary policy. Under the classical gold standard prevailing prior to the First World War and during part of the interwar period, countries chose to sacrifice an independent monetary policy. Under the Bretton Woods system of fixed exchange rates established after the Second World War countries sacrificed free capital mobility, but as capital controls became increasingly hard to maintain, the major countries in the world decided instead to sacrifice the goal of a fixed exchange rate. However, recent decades have seen a polarization of exchange rate regimes, with countries moving either towards free floating or towards a 'hard peg' with completely fixed exchange rates.

23.4 Aggregate demand in the open economy

Drawing on the analysis in Section 23.2, we will now study the determinants of aggregate demand in an economy which is open to trade and capital mobility.

The trade balance and the real exchange rate

In the open economy, the condition for equilibrium in the goods market is:

$$Y = D + G + NX, \tag{12}$$

where Y is real GDP, D is total private demand for goods and services, G is public demand for goods and services, and NX is the trade balance, defined as exports minus imports (net exports). Thus net exports add to the total demand for domestically produced goods. All of the components of demand on the right-hand side of (12) – including the trade balance – are measured in units of the domestic good. In other words, we are using the domestic good as our *numeraire* good. If the *quantity* of imported foreign goods is M, the nominal value of imports measured in domestic currency units will be EP^fM. Given that one unit of the

---

7. Argentina was also hit by a serious crisis in 2001 even though the country had a currency board. However, the Argentinian currency board had a 'soft' element since it allowed foreign exchange reserves to fall below the level of the domestic currency base in exceptional circumstances.

8. Denmark is a rare example of a country with an 'intermediate' exchange rate regime which has nevertheless escaped serious speculative attacks on its currency for many years. The Danish exchange rate parity against the German D-mark – and later on against the euro – has been unchanged since 1987, and except for a short time during the EMS crisis in 1993, the market exchange rate of the Danish krone has been kept very close to the central parity. The stability enjoyed under the Danish fixed exchange rate regime is often ascribed to the fact that fiscal policy has generally been quite disciplined in Denmark since the early 1980s.

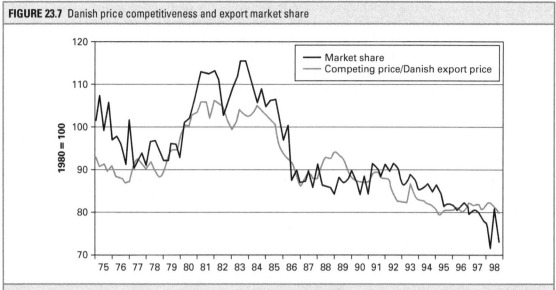

FIGURE 23.7 Danish price competitiveness and export market share

Note: The market share is calculated as the total volume of Danish exports less exports to Germany divided by a weighted average of the imports of the remaining 21 recipient markets. Price competitiveness is the market deflator in DKK divided by the Danish export price.

Source: Chart 2 of Heino Bohn Nielsen, 'Market Shares of Manufactured Exports and Competitiveness', Danmarks Nationalbank, Monetary Review – 2nd Quarter 1999, pp. 59–78.

domestic good sells at the price P, the volume of imports measured in units of the domestic good will then be $EP^f M/P \equiv E^r M$. If the quantity of domestic goods which is exported abroad is denoted by X, we thus have:

$$NX \equiv X - E^r M. \tag{13}$$

It is reasonable to assume that the volume of exports, X, depends positively on the international competitiveness of domestic producers. For example, Fig. 23.7 shows that the market share of Danish exporters tends to vary positively with the price charged by foreign competitors relative to the price charged by Danish exporters. In our stylized model this price ratio is captured by the real exchange rate E^r. It is also natural to assume that the export volume depends positively on total output Y^f in the rest of the world, since higher economic activity abroad leads to a larger export market for domestic producers. Hence we may write $X = X(E^r, Y^f)$, where X varies positively with both E^r and Y^f.

In Chapter 16 we saw that total private demand for goods in the closed economy depends on domestic output Y, the tax rate τ, the real interest rate r, and the state of confidence (the expected future growth rate) ε. In the open economy all of these variables are also likely to affect imports, since some of the goods demanded by the private sector are imported from abroad. In addition, the quantity of imported foreign goods will depend negatively on the real exchange rate, since a higher relative price of foreign goods will reduce domestic consumer demand for foreign goods, partly because a rise in the price of imported goods reduces the purchasing power of domestic nominal incomes (the income effect), and partly because a higher price of foreign goods induces consumers to substitute towards domestic goods (the substitution effect). We may therefore specify the import function as $M = M(E^r, Y, \tau, r, \varepsilon)$, where M varies negatively with E^r, τ and r, and positively with Y and ε.

With these specifications of exports and imports, it follows from (13) that net exports are given by:

$$NX = X(\underset{+}{E^r}, \underset{+}{Y^f}) - E^r M(\underset{-}{E^r}, \underset{+}{Y}, \underset{-}{\tau}, \underset{-}{r}, \underset{+}{\varepsilon}), \tag{14}$$

where the signs below the variables indicate the signs of the partial derivatives. We see that a rise in Y or ε will raise the level of imports, because an increase in these variables will stimulate total private demand for goods and services. On the other hand, a rise in τ or r will reduce imports by dampening total demand for goods.

A crucial question is how a change in the real exchange rate will affect the trade balance. To investigate this, we calculate the partial derivative of the net export function (14) with respect to E^r:

$$\frac{\partial NX}{\partial E^r} = \frac{\partial X}{\partial E^r} - E^r \cdot \frac{\partial M}{\partial E^r} - M. \tag{15}$$

Let us denote the initial magnitudes of X, M and E^r by X_0, M_0 and E_0^r, respectively. As a benchmark case we will assume that the trade balance is initially in equilibrium so that $X_0 = E_0^r M_0$. We may then rewrite Eq. (15) as:

$$\frac{\partial NX}{\partial E^r} = M_0 \left(\frac{\partial X}{\partial E^r} \frac{E_0^r}{X_0} - \frac{\partial M}{\partial E^r} \frac{E_0^r}{M_0} - 1 \right) \quad \Leftrightarrow$$

$$\frac{\partial NX}{\partial E^r} = M_0 (\eta_X + \eta_M - 1), \qquad \eta_X \equiv \frac{\partial X}{\partial E^r} \frac{E^r}{X} > 0, \qquad \eta_M \equiv -\frac{\partial M}{\partial E^r} \frac{E^r}{M} > 0, \tag{16}$$

where η_X is the elasticity of exports with respect to the real exchange rate, and η_M is the numerical elasticity of imports with respect to the real exchange rate. Equation (16) shows that a *real depreciation* of the domestic currency – that is, a rise in the real exchange rate E^r – will improve the trade balance provided the sum of the relative price elasticities of export and import demand is greater than 1 ($\eta_X + \eta_M > 1$). This important result is called the *Marshall–Lerner condition*, named after its discoverers. Numerous empirical studies for a large number of countries suggest that the Marshall–Lerner condition is almost always satisfied, at least when the time horizon is one year or longer, so that economic agents have had time to adjust to the price change. In the following, we will assume that this condition is in fact met.[9]

The aggregate demand curve in the open economy

We are now ready to derive the aggregate demand curve for the open economy. Recalling the factors influencing the trade balance and the private demand for goods, we may restate the goods market equilibrium condition (12) as:

$$Y = D(Y, \tau, r, \varepsilon, E^r) + NX(E^r, Y^f, Y, \tau, r, \varepsilon) + G$$

$$= \tilde{D}(Y, \tau, r, \varepsilon, E^r, Y^f) + G, \qquad \tilde{D} \equiv D + NX. \tag{17}$$

The magnitude $\tilde{D} \equiv D + NX$ measures the total private demand for domestic goods emanating from the domestic as well as the foreign private sector. Notice from (17) that the real exchange rate E^r influences D due to the income effect mentioned earlier: when the price of imports increases relative to domestic prices, the purchasing power of domestic money incomes is eroded, and this will, *ceteris paribus*, reduce total private demand for goods because domestic residents become poorer.

While an increase in domestic economic activity Y will stimulate total private demand for goods, D, it will also increase imports and hence reduce the trade balance NX. Thus it would seem that the sign of the partial derivative $\tilde{D}_Y \equiv \partial \tilde{D}/\partial Y$ is ambiguous. However, since only a

---

9. In the very short run η_X and η_M may actually be so small that the Marshall–Lerner condition is violated, reflecting that firms and households do not instantaneously adjust their patterns of demand and supply to a relative price change. Thus the trade balance tends to follow a 'J-curve' pattern over time, following a real depreciation: in the very short run, the trade balance tends to deteriorate due the worsening of the terms of trade, but as the quantities of exports and imports start to adjust, the trade balance gradually improves.

fraction of total demand for goods will be directed towards imports, the rise in imports will be less than the rise in total demand for goods. Hence we have $\tilde{D}_Y \equiv \partial D/\partial Y + \partial NX/\partial Y = \partial D/\partial Y - E^r(\partial M/\partial Y) > 0$. Maintaining our assumption from Chapter 16 that $\partial D/\partial Y < 1$, it then follows that:

$$0 < \tilde{D}_Y \equiv \frac{\partial D}{\partial Y} + \frac{\partial NX}{\partial Y} < 1. \tag{18}$$

The fact that only a fraction of total demand is directed towards imports also implies that:

$$\tilde{D}_r \equiv \frac{\partial D}{\partial r} + \frac{\partial NX}{\partial r} < 0. \tag{19}$$

$$\tilde{D}_\varepsilon \equiv \frac{\partial D}{\partial \varepsilon} + \frac{\partial NX}{\partial \varepsilon} > 0. \tag{20}$$

$$\tilde{D}_\tau \equiv \frac{\partial D}{\partial \tau} + \frac{\partial NX}{\partial \tau} < 0. \tag{21}$$

Finally, we assume that:

$$\tilde{D}_E \equiv \frac{\partial D}{\partial E^r} + \frac{\partial NX}{\partial E^r} > 0. \tag{22}$$

Recall that $\partial NX/\partial E^r > 0$ when the Marshall–Lerner condition is met. However, because of the negative income effect of a higher real exchange rate, we have $\partial D/\partial E^r < 0$. The assumption in (22) that $\tilde{D}_E > 0$ thus requires that the Marshall–Lerner condition is satisfied with a certain margin so that $\eta_X + \eta_M$ is sufficiently greater than 1. Empirically this has turned out to be a reasonable assumption (except for the very short run where the price elasticities in export and import demand are small, due to inertia in consumer reactions to relative price changes).

Using the above definitions of and assumptions on partial derivatives, and following the procedure for log-linearization explained in Section 16.2, the appendix to this chapter derives the following log-linear approximation to the goods market equilibrium condition (17), where we have kept the tax rate constant for simplicity:

$$y - \bar{y} = \beta_1(e^r - \bar{e}^r) - \beta_2(r - \bar{r}) + \beta_3(g - \bar{g}) + \beta_4(y^f - \bar{y}^f) + \beta_5(\ln \varepsilon - \ln \bar{\varepsilon}). \tag{23}$$

The notation $\bar{x}$ indicates the initial long-run equilibrium value of variable x. The variables y, y^f and g are measured in natural logarithms, and all the β coefficients are positive.

We will now show that (23) implies a negative relationship between domestic output and the domestic inflation rate, just as we found in the closed economy. First we recall from (9) that

$$e^r = e^r_{-1} + \Delta e + \pi^f - \pi. \tag{24}$$

Second, we note from the condition for uncovered interest parity (2) that the domestic (*ex ante*) real interest rate is given by

$$r = i - \pi^e_{+1} = i^f - \pi^e_{+1} + \Delta e^e, \qquad \Delta e^e \equiv e^e_{+1} - e. \tag{25}$$

We may choose our units of measurement such that the real exchange rate $\bar{E}^r = 1$ in the initial long-run equilibrium, implying $\bar{e}^r \equiv \ln \bar{E}^r = 0$. Further, we know from the condition for real interest rate parity (11) that the domestic long-run equilibrium interest rate, $\bar{r}$, equals the foreign equilibrium real interest rate which we denote by $\bar{r}^f$. Inserting (24) and (25) into (23) along with $\bar{e}^r = 0$ and $\bar{r} = \bar{r}^f$, we then obtain the following preliminary expression for the aggregate demand curve for the open economy:

$$y - \bar{y} = \beta_1(e_{-1}^r + \Delta e + \pi^f - \pi) - \beta_2(i^f - \pi_{+1}^e + \Delta e^e - \bar{r}^f) + \tilde{z}, \tag{26}$$

$$\tilde{z} \equiv \beta_3(g - \bar{g}) + \beta_4(y - \bar{y}^f) + \beta_5(\ln \varepsilon - \ln \bar{\varepsilon}). \tag{27}$$

Equation (26) is preliminary since it does not constitute a complete theory of aggregate demand until we have described the formation of inflation expectations (π_{+1}^e) and exchange rate expectations (Δe^e). In the next two chapters we shall argue that these expectations are likely to depend on the exchange rate regime, and we shall therefore postpone the specification of expectations until then. However, remembering that $\beta_1 > 0$, we can already see from (26) that an increase in domestic inflation will, *ceteris paribus*, reduce aggregate demand for domestic output. The reason is that *higher domestic inflation erodes the international competitiveness of domestic producers* by reducing the real exchange rate. Thus, a rise in π raises the relative price of domestic goods, thereby reducing net exports. To see that this is indeed the mechanism, note that the term $(e_{-1}^r + \Delta e + \pi^f - \pi)$ on the right-hand side of (26) is simply the (log of the) current real exchange rate, e_r. In the appendix we show that the response of aggregate demand to the real exchange rate depends on the price elasticities of export and import demand $(\eta_X$ and $\eta_M)$ which are incorporated in the parameter β_1. The higher the value of these elasticities, the stronger is the reaction of net exports to a change in the real exchange rate, and the flatter is the aggregate demand curve in (y, π) space.

A second important observation is that the preliminary AD curve defined by (26) will change position from one period to the next whenever relative purchasing power parity fails to hold, that is, whenever the economy is out of long-run equilibrium. This follows from (24) which shows that the real exchange rate will change over time whenever $\Delta e \neq \pi - \pi_f$. Hence the value of the lagged real exchange rate, e_{-1}^r, appearing on the right-hand side of (26) will also change from one period to the next when the rate of exchange depreciation deviates from the inflation differential between the domestic and the foreign economy, and this will cause the AD curve to shift even if the other variables on the right-hand side of (26) are constant.[10] In the open economy, shifts in the AD curve are thus an inherent part of the adjustment to long-run equilibrium. This contrasts with our AS–AD model of the closed economy where the adjustment took place solely through shifts in the AS curve. In summary:

AGGREGATE DEMAND IN THE OPEN ECONOMY

This varies negatively with the rate of domestic producer price inflation because a higher domestic inflation rate raises the price of domestic goods relative to the price of foreign goods, thereby eroding the competitiveness of domestic producers and reducing nex exports. Whenever the rate of nominal exchange rate depreciation deviates from the differential between the domestic and the foreign inflation rate, the real exchange rate will change from one period to the next, and the aggregate demand curve will therefore also shift over time until a long-run equilibrium satisfying Relative Purchasing Power Parity is reached.

23.5 Aggregate supply in the open economy

To complete our AS–AD model for the open economy, we need to confront the aggregate demand curve with the aggregate supply curve. Modelling aggregate supply in the open economy requires some care because of the possibility that wage formation may be influenced by changes in import prices, and hence by changes in the real exchange rate. To illustrate this possibility, suppose that consumer preferences are given by a Cobb–Douglas utility

---

10.   The fact that the AD curve will be shifting over time as long as $\Delta e \neq \pi - \pi^f$ explains our earlier claim that a long-run equilibrium requires relative purchasing power to hold.

function defined over domestic goods and imported goods. One can then show that the consumer price index will take the form:

$$P^c = (EP^f)^\psi P^{1-\psi} = (E^r)^\psi P, \qquad 0 < \psi < 1, \tag{28}$$

where the fixed preference parameter ψ is the share of imported goods in consumer budgets, and EP^f is the price of these goods measured in domestic currency units. We see from (28) that the consumer price index will move whenever there is a change in the real exchange rate $E^r \equiv EP^f/P$. If wage setters seek to achieve a certain level of the *real consumer wage*, defined as the nominal wage rate W deflated by the consumer price index P^c, a change in the real exchange rate will then obviously induce wage setters to change their nominal wage claim.

However, if wage setters focus instead on *relative* wages, trying to maintain some target ratio between their own wage rate and the average wage level in the rest of the economy, a change in the real exchange rate caused by a change in import prices will not influence wage setting, since a movement in import prices does not disturb the existing pattern of relative wages.

The theories of wage formation developed in Chapters 11, 12 and 17 all imply that wages are set as a mark-up over the representative worker's 'outside option' which includes the rate of unemployment benefit. Whether wage setters focus mainly on real or on relative wages therefore depends on the rules for indexation of nominal unemployment benefits. If nominal benefits are indexed to *consumer prices* so as to keep the real unemployment benefit constant, it follows from (28) that a change in the real exchange rate will affect the nominal unemployment benefit. Hence it will also affect domestic nominal wages and prices because a higher nominal unemployment benefit will drive up nominal wage claims and lead to higher domestic prices through the mark-up price setting of firms. This means that the position of the economy's aggregate supply curve will depend on the level of the real exchange rate.

However, if nominal unemployment benefits are instead indexed to *nominal wages*, nominal benefits will not automatically change when the real exchange rate changes. In such a setting we shall see that it is rational for wage setters to focus on their *relative* wage position even if they only derive utility from their own real income. When benefits are indexed to wages, the real exchange rate will not directly influence the formation of domestic wages and prices, and the aggregate supply curve for the open economy will have the same form as the SRAS curve for the closed economy.

We shall now substantiate this claim by deriving the aggregate supply curve for an open economy where unemployment benefits are indexed to wages, as is the case in most countries where benefits are either linked to the unemployed worker's own previous wage or to the general wage level (which amounts to the same thing in our representative agent model). We will base our analysis on the theory of efficiency wages developed in Chapter 11, but we emphasize that the same end result can be derived from the model of trade union wage setting presented in Chapter 12.[11]

Efficiency wage setting and aggregate supply

We will consider a simplified version of the so-called 'shirking' model of efficiency wages introduced in Chapter 11.[12] The basic idea underlying this model is that work effort generates disutility, so workers have an incentive to 'shirk' on the job (taking coffee breaks, chatting with colleagues, using the office computer to surf the internet, etc.) instead of working hard all the time. To keep the incentive for shirking in check, firm managers therefore have to monitor the work effort of the employees and impose some sanction such as firing a worker who is caught shirking. However, since perfect and constant monitoring is

---

11. We now choose to work with an efficiency wage model rather than a trade union model in order to illustrate that efficiency wage theory offers yet another possible microeconomic foundation for the familiar expectations-augmented Phillips curve.

12. Even if you have not studied Chapter 11, you should still be able to follow the exposition below.

practically impossible or prohibitively expensive, there is always some chance that a worker can get away with shirking without being caught.

To simplify matters, we assume that a worker can either work all the time or shirk all the time. If he works all the time, the expected utility level U_i^w of a worker employed by firm i will be:

$$U_i^w = \left(\frac{W_i}{P^{ce}}\right)(1-\mu), \qquad 0 < \mu < 1, \tag{29}$$

where W_i is the nominal wage rate paid by firm i, and P^{ce} is the expected consumer price level so that W_i/P^{ce} is the expected purchasing power of the money wage offered by firm i. Equation (29) assumes that the worker's utility varies in proportion to his real wage. It also assumes that the disutility of work is given by $\mu \cdot (W_i/P^{ce})$, where μ is a parameter reflecting the worker's preference for 'leisure on the job'. The higher the worker's income, the more highly he thus values leisure on the job, so the more income he is willing to sacrifice in return for the benefits from coffee breaks, internet surfing, etc.[13]

If the worker chooses instead to shirk all the time, he faces a probability θ of being caught by the manager and fired for poor work performance. In that case he must look for a job elsewhere in the labour market, but since there is unemployment, he cannot be sure to find one. We assume that the worker expects to be able to obtain the utility level υ if he is fired due to shirking. The variable υ is referred to as the worker's 'outside option', i.e., his fall-back position if sacked (we will discuss the determinants of υ in a moment). The probability that the worker is not caught shirking is $1 - \theta$. In that situation the worker's utility will simply be his real consumer wage W/P^c, since he obviously does not incur any disutility from work effort when he is shirking. Overall, a shirking worker's expected utility will thus be given by:

$$U_i^s = (1-\theta)\left(\frac{W_i}{P^{ce}}\right) + \theta\upsilon, \qquad 0 < \theta < 1, \qquad \theta > \mu. \tag{30}$$

A utility-maximizing worker will choose to shirk if $U_i^s > U_i^w$ and will choose to work when $U_i^s < U_i^w$. In the borderline case where $U_i^s = U_i^w$, the worker is in principle indifferent between working and shirking, but we assume that in this case social norms induce him to work.

When workers choose to work, their output per person is determined exogenously by the firm's level of technology. It is now easy to derive the cost-minimizing wage rate which the employer will want to offer. If the wage is so low that $U_i^s > U_i^w$, workers will produce nothing and the employer will make a loss as long as the wage rate is positive. Firing the shirking workers will not solve the problem since newly hired workers will have an incentive to shirk as well, assuming that they have the same preferences as those who were fired. On the other hand, if the wage is so high that $U_i^s < U_i^w$, the employer is paying more than necessary to induce work effort without obtaining a higher labour productivity in return (since the productivity of a non-shirking worker is exogenously determined by technology). Hence the cost-minimizing wage rate is found where the *non-shirking condition* $U_i^w \geq U_i^s$ is met with equality. Setting $U_i^w = U_i^s$ and using (29) and (30), we thus obtain the cost-minimizing wage rate offered by firm i:

$$\overbrace{\left(\frac{W_i}{P^{ce}}\right)(1-\mu)}^{U_i^w} = \overbrace{(1-\theta)\left(\frac{W_i}{P^{ce}}\right) + \theta\upsilon}^{U_i^s} \quad \Leftrightarrow \quad \frac{W_i}{P^{ce}} = \left(\frac{\theta}{\theta-\mu}\right)\upsilon. \tag{31}$$

We see that the expected consumer real wage is set as a mark-up over the representative worker's outside option υ. The mark-up factor $\theta/(\theta - \mu)$ is positive and greater than 1, given our

---

13. If we did not allow the valuation of leisure to rise with the worker's income level, the incentive to shirk would tend towards zero as the real wage grows over time due to increasing productivity. Assuming that the demand for leisure varies positively with income is equivalent to assuming that leisure is a 'normal' good.

assumption in (30) that $\theta > \mu$. A higher value of θ reduces the firm's optimal wage rate, because a higher risk of being fired for shirking strengthens the incentive to work, thereby lowering the wage rate which is necessary to induce effort. On the other hand, the stronger the preference μ for 'leisure on the job', the higher is the wage rate which must be paid to secure effort.

Let us now specify the representative worker's outside option, i.e., the utility he expects to obtain if fired for shirking. For an average worker who is sacked, the probability that he will be able to find a job elsewhere in the labour market is given by the employment rate $1 - u$, where u is the rate of unemployment. If he succeeds in finding a job, it follows from the analysis above that he may expect to obtain a utility level $U^s = U^w = (W^e/P^{ce})(1 - \mu)$, where W^e is the expected average money wage level in the labour market. On the other hand, the worker faces a probability u of remaining unemployed, in which case he expects to be able to collect a nominal unemployment benefit B_e with an expected real purchasing power B^e/P^{ce}. We may therefore specify the representative worker's outside option as follows:

$$\upsilon = (1-u)(1-\mu)\left(\frac{W^e}{P^{ce}}\right) + u\left(\frac{B^e}{P^{ce}}\right). \tag{32}$$

The rate of unemployment benefit is assumed to be indexed to the general wage level, with a constant replacement ratio c which is known to all agents. The expected benefit rate is then given by $B^e = cW^e$. We impose the restriction that $0 < c < 1 - \mu$, since otherwise the expected real wage net of the disutility of work, $(W^e/P^{ce})(1 - \mu)$, would be lower than the expected real rate of unemployment benefit, cW^e/P^{ce}, so that unemployed workers would have no incentive to look for a job.

Inserting (32) and $B^e = cW^e$ into (31), and multiplying through by P^{ce}, we find the optimal nominal wage rate offered by firm i:

$$W_i = \left(\frac{\theta}{\theta - \mu}\right)[(1-u)(1-\mu) + cu]W^e. \tag{33}$$

We see that the (expected) consumer price level P^{ce} does not affect wage formation.[14] As (33) makes clear, the individual employer seeks to maintain a certain relationship between his own nominal wage rate and the expected general nominal wage level. A change in consumer prices does not disturb this relationship, since it affects workers inside and outside each firm in the same manner. Thus our efficiency wage model implies 'relative wage resistance' in the sense that individual firms resist a change in the ratio of their own wage to the general wage level. However, the model does not imply 'real wage resistance', since a rise in consumer prices does not automatically lead to a rise in nominal wages.

If we make the *symmetry assumption* that expectations as well as the parameters θ and μ are the same across all firms, (33) implies that all employers will set the same wage rate. Hence we have $W_i = W$, where W is the general level of nominal wages. From (33) we then get:

$$W = M^w(1 - \mu - \gamma u)W^e, \qquad M^w = \frac{\theta}{\theta - \mu} > 1, \qquad \gamma \equiv 1 - \mu - c > 0. \tag{34}$$

To establish the link between wages and domestic prices, we now consider the representative firm's price-setting behaviour. For simplicity, suppose the production function is linear and that one unit of labour produces a units of output, where a is the exogenous level of average and marginal labour productivity. The representative firm's average and marginal unit costs will then be W/a. According to the theory of price formation

---

14. This result relies on our assumption that the nominal rate of unemployment benefit is indexed to the nominal wage level. If benefits were instead indexed to the consumer price level, (expected) changes in P^c would affect the workers' outside option and thereby influence wage setting. In reality, most countries index unemployment benefits to wages rather than to consumer prices.

developed in Chapter 17, a monopolistically competitive firm will set its price as a mark-up, M^p, over its marginal labour cost. Since all firms pay the same wages, using the same technology and charging the same mark-up, the price of domestically produced goods charged by the representative firm will then be:

$$P = M^p \cdot \frac{W}{a}, \qquad M^p > 1. \tag{35}$$

Let us assume that M^p is constant over time whereas labour productivity fluctuates around some trend level $\bar{a}$. Equation (35) then implies that, on average, the relationship between the general wage level and the domestic price level is $W = \bar{a}P/M^p$. Suppose that, by experience, wage setters are aware of this average relationship between wages and prices. Suppose further that, at the time when the individual firm sets its own wage and price for the next period, it expects the general domestic price level to be P^e during that period. It is then reasonable to assume that the representative individual firm will expect the general wage level to be:[15]

$$W^e = \frac{\bar{a}}{M^p} \cdot P^e. \tag{36}$$

Using (35) and (36) to eliminate W and W^e from (34), taking natural logarithms on both sides of the resulting equation, and exploiting the approximation $\ln(1 - \mu - \gamma u) \approx -\mu - \gamma u$, we get:

$$\overbrace{\frac{a}{M^p}}^{W} \cdot P = M^w (1 - \mu - \gamma u) \overbrace{\frac{\bar{a}}{M^p}}^{W^e} \cdot P^e \;\Rightarrow\; p \approx p^e + m^w - \mu - \gamma u + \ln \bar{a} - \ln a, \tag{37}$$

$$p \equiv \ln P, \qquad p^e \equiv \ln P^e, \qquad m^w \equiv \ln M^w.$$

If we subtract p_{-1} on both sides and use the concept of the natural unemployment rate $\bar{u}$, we may rewrite the price setting equation (37) in terms of the actual and expected domestic inflation rate:

$$\pi = \pi^e + \gamma(\bar{u} - u) + \ln \bar{a} - \ln a,$$

$$\pi \equiv p - p_{-1}, \qquad \pi^e \equiv p^e - p_{-1}, \qquad \bar{u} \equiv \frac{m^w - \mu}{\gamma}. \tag{38}$$

We see that (38) is an expectations-augmented Phillips curve. From this we may derive an aggregate supply curve. Denoting the total labour force by N and the trend level of output by $\bar{Y}$, we introduce the following definitions and approximations from Chapter 17:

$$Y \equiv a(1 - u)N \;\Rightarrow\; y \equiv \ln Y \approx \ln a + \ln N - u, \tag{39}$$

$$\bar{Y} \equiv \bar{a}(1 - \bar{u})N \;\Rightarrow\; \bar{y} \equiv \ln \bar{Y} \approx \ln \bar{a} + \ln N - \bar{u}. \tag{40}$$

Inserting (39) and (40) into (38), we end up with a short-run aggregate supply curve of the form:

$$\text{SRAS:} \qquad \pi = \pi^e + \gamma(y - \bar{y}) + s, \qquad s \equiv (1 + \gamma)(\ln \bar{a} - \ln a), \tag{41}$$

---

15. Equation (36) may seem a roundabout way of forecasting W (by first estimating W/P and then forecasting P). However, recall from Chapter 17 that the mark-up price-setting behaviour of the representative firm i was derived from a demand curve of the form $Y_i = (P_i/P)^{-\sigma}(Y/n)$. To forecast its own demand, the firm thus has an incentive to form an estimate of the general price level, P, and then it may as well use this estimate to forecast the general wage level, exploiting its knowledge of the average relationship between W and P. Moreover, even if the firm forms a direct estimate of W, (36) will still hold provided the firm's (separate) expectations about W and P are consistent with its knowledge of the average ratio of wages to prices.

where s is a supply shock variable capturing productivity shocks.[16] Equation (41) shows that our theory of efficiency wage setting leads to an aggregate supply curve of exactly the same form as the SRAS curve for the closed economy.

As we mentioned, our aggregate supply curve (41) is based on a theory of 'relative wage resistance', because wage setters tend to resist changes in their relative wage position as long as the level of economic activity is unchanged. As you recall, this result is based on the assumption that unemployment benefits are indexed to wages. If nominal benefits are instead indexed to consumer prices, wage setting will be characterized by 'real wage resistance' in the sense that wage setters will resist changes in their real consumer wage at any given level of activity. The position of the SRAS curve will then be influenced by the real exchange rate, as we have already explained. Here we will stick to the assumption that benefits are indexed to wages, partly because this is the most common practice in the real world, and partly because it leads to a simpler specification of aggregate supply which is directly comparable to the SRAS curve for the closed economy. In Exercise 3 we ask you to explore the alternative case of real wage resistance.

THE AGGREGATE SUPPLY CURVE IN THE OPEN ECONOMY

When unemployment benefits are linked to the general wage level, wage setting will be characterized by 'relative wage resistance' in the sense that individual wage setters will wish to maintain a certain level of their own wage rate relative to the general wage level. An efficiency wage model (or a trade union model) of wage setting then leads to a short-run aggregate supply curve for the open economy of exactly the same form as the SRAS curve for the closed economy. If unemployment benefits were instead indexed to the consumer price level, the position of the SRAS curve would be affected by import prices and hence by the real exchange rate.

23.6 Long-run equilibrium in the open economy

Conditions for long-run equilibrium

As noted earlier, a complete AS–AD model which is able to describe the *short-run* dynamics of the open economy must include a theory of the formation of inflation and exchange rate expectations, and these expectations are likely to depend on the exchange rate regime. In the next two chapters we will study expectations formation and short-run macrodynamics under alternative exchange rate regimes. However, at this stage we can already characterize the *long-run* equilibrium on which the small open economy will converge if it is stable.

We have seen earlier that the real exchange rate must be constant in a long-run equilibrium. Otherwise the AD curve (26) would keep on shifting over time. We have also seen that constancy of the real exchange rate implies relative purchasing power parity, which leads to real interest rate parity when capital mobility is perfect. In the long run the domestic real interest rate is thus tied to the exogenous foreign real interest rate, regardless of the exchange rate regime:

$$r = r^f. \tag{42}$$

Moreover, we know that $r \equiv i - \pi^e_{+1} = i^f + \Delta e^e - \pi^e_{+1}$. Inserting these relationships plus (42) into (26), we obtain the open economy's *long-run aggregate demand curve* (LRAD):

---

16. For simplicity, we have assumed that the wage and price mark-ups m^w and m^p are constant. If they are fluctuating over time, the supply shock variable s would also include the cyclical components of m^w and m^p.

$$e^r = \frac{y - \bar{y} - z}{\beta_1}, \tag{43}$$

$$z \equiv -\beta_2(r^f - \bar{r}^f) + \beta_3(g - \bar{g}) + \beta_4(y^f - \bar{y}^f) + \beta_5(\ln \varepsilon - \ln \bar{\varepsilon}).$$

The LRAD curve specifies the relationship between real output and the real exchange rate which is consistent with long-run equilibrium in the market for domestic goods. Unconventionally, the curve is *upward-sloping* in (y, e^r) space since a real exchange rate depreciation (a rise in e^r) increases total demand for domestic goods by improving the international competitiveness of domestic producers. To maintain equilibrium between the demand for and the supply of domestic goods, domestic output must therefore increase. The exogenous variable z captures demand shocks stemming from the foreign and the domestic economy. By construction, z is zero in the initial long-run equilibrium.

To determine the long-run equilibrium values of output and the real exchange rate, we must combine the LRAD curve with the economy's long-run aggregate supply curve (LRAS). In a long-run equilibrium inflation expectations must be confirmed ($\pi^e = \pi$), and productivity must be at its normal trend level ($\ln a = \ln \bar{a}$). Inserting these conditions into the SRAS curve (41), we get the LRAS curve:

$$y = \bar{y}. \tag{44}$$

This shows that the long-run aggregate supply curve is vertical in (y, e^r) space, given the assumption of relative wage resistance underlying the SRAS curve (41). In the long run output will be at the natural level given by (40), corresponding to the natural rate of unemployment $\bar{u} \equiv (m^w - \mu)/\gamma$.

Figure 23.8 illustrates the long-run equilibrium in the open economy. Output is determined exclusively from the supply side, and the equilibrium real exchange rate is found where the upward-sloping LRAD curve crosses the vertical LRAS curve. A permanent shock to aggregate demand – that is, a shift in the LRAD curve generated by a permanent change in z – will be fully absorbed by a change in the equilibrium real exchange rate, leaving the long-run output level unaffected.

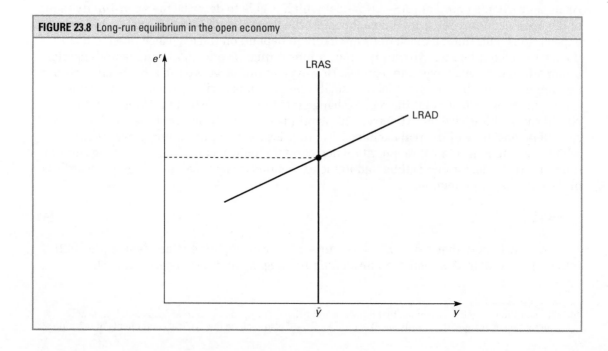

FIGURE 23.8 Long-run equilibrium in the open economy

The long-run neutrality of the exchange rate regime

Our analysis of *long-run* equilibrium in the open economy has one striking implication which is worth emphasizing: *the long-run equilibrium values of 'real' variables such as the real interest rate, the real exchange rate and real output are all independent of the exchange rate regime*. This follows from the simple fact that we did not have to make any assumption regarding the exchange rate regime when we derived the long-run equilibrium values of r, e^r and y. The analysis in Fig. 23.8 is valid regardless of whether exchange rates are fixed or flexible.

Our analysis thus suggests that the exchange rate regime is *neutral* in the long run, since it has no impact on the long-run equilibrium values of real variables. This is a parallel to the long-run neutrality of money in the closed economy. In a closed economy setting, the authorities can control the nominal money supply M (or at least the monetary base), but in the long run they cannot control the real money supply M/P, because the price level is endogenous. Similarly, in the open economy policy makers can choose to fix the nominal exchange rate E rather than allowing it to float, but they cannot fix the long-run value of the real exchange rate, EP^f/P.

The idea of long-run neutrality of the exchange rate regime is well illustrated by the experience of Denmark and Sweden, two neighbouring countries heavily engaged in trade with one another. As shown in Figure 23.9, it took about 1.40 Danish kroner to purchase one Swedish krona in early 1982. By July 2009, the price of one SEK was only a little over 0.70 DKK. Over the period considered the Swedish currency thus depreciated by a dramatic 50 per cent in nominal terms against the Danish currency. This reflected that Sweden pursued a policy of devaluation during part of the 1980s and later shifted to a floating exchange rate regime, whereas Denmark continued to fix its exchange rate vis-à-vis the German mark and later against the euro. Yet we see that the purchasing-power-parity adjusted GDP levels in the two countries started out and ended up at almost exactly the same level in the two countries. This is consistent with our theory that the choice of exchange rate regime does not affect real economic outcomes over the long run.

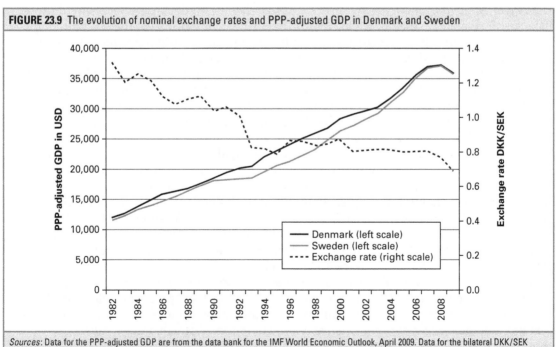

FIGURE 23.9 The evolution of nominal exchange rates and PPP-adjusted GDP in Denmark and Sweden

Sources: Data for the PPP-adjusted GDP are from the data bank for the IMF World Economic Outlook, April 2009. Data for the bilateral DKK/SEK nominal exchange rate were provided by Danmarks Nationalbank.

One should not conclude from this analysis that the choice of exchange rate regime is unimportant. As we shall see in the next two chapters, the mechanisms through which the economy adjusts towards its long-run equilibrium are different under fixed and flexible exchange rates. The choice of exchange rate regime may therefore make an important difference for the *short-run* and *medium-run* dynamics of the macro economy. Indeed, we shall see that this choice will determine whether or not monetary policy can be used as a tool of short-run stabilization policy.

Moreover, there is not general agreement among economists that the exchange rate regime is really neutral in the long run. Some believe that the choice of exchange rate regime may have important structural effects in the long run. For example, some researchers have argued that the lower volatility of exchange rates under a fixed exchange rate regime may significantly promote international economic integration by reducing the degree of risk and uncertainty relating to cross-border economic transactions. In the next chapter we shall see that there is indeed some evidence supporting this view.

LONG-RUN EQUILIBRIUM IN THE OPEN ECONOMY

The long-run aggregate demand curve (LRAD) in the open economy shows the relationship between domestic GDP and the real exchange rate consistent with long-run equilibrium in the market for domestic goods. The LRAD curve is upward-sloping because a rise in the real exchange rate improves the competitiveness of domestic producers, thereby boosting demand for domestic goods via an increase in net exports. Under relative wage resistance the open economy's long-run aggregate supply curve (LRAS) is vertical at the natural rate of output. A long-run equilibrium is found where the LRAS and LRAD curves intersect. The resulting equilibrium is independent of the exchange rate regime, implying that the choice of exchange rate regime cannot affect real economic variables in the long run.

Wealth effects and the balance of payments in the long run

Whenever an open economy is running a surplus (deficit) on the current account of the balance of payments – that is, whenever it is exporting (importing) capital – it will accumulate (decumulate) foreign assets. When the current account imbalance stems from private sector transactions, it will therefore generate a change in the private sector's aggregate net wealth. In Chapter 15 we saw that changes in private wealth are likely to affect private consumption. In an economy with no long-run growth, a 'true' long-run equilibrium would then require that the real (inflation-adjusted) balance on the current account be zero. Otherwise real private wealth would be changing over time, inducing changes in aggregate demand which would be incompatible with long-run equilibrium.

However, in an economy with secular growth the real balance of payments must deviate from zero in the long run to allow real private wealth to grow in line with output and income (see Exercise 5). Moreover, real-world experience suggests that it takes a very long time before the economy fully adjusts to wealth effects stemming from current account imbalances. The Danish experience is a good example of this. As shown in Fig. 23.10, Denmark ran a persistent current account deficit from the late 1950s to around 1990. The deficit was so high that the ratio of foreign debt to GDP was rising throughout most of this period. On the other hand, since 1990 Denmark has run a persistent current account surplus. The fact that the economy seems to respond very slowly to current account imbalances in the short and medium run indicates that it may be a reasonable simplification to ignore current account dynamics unless one wants to focus on the very long run. To keep matters simple, our model of the open economy therefore abstracts from wealth effects stemming from current account imbalances, just as we have previously ignored changes in private wealth arising from possible imbalances on the government budget.

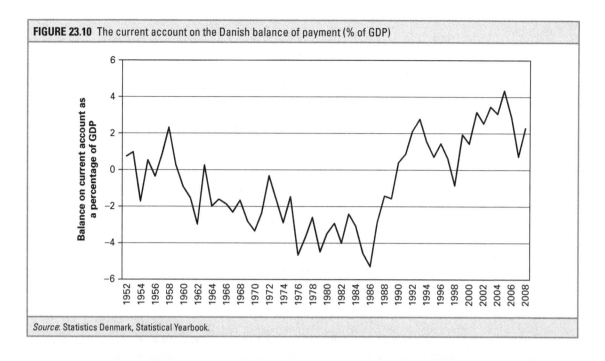

FIGURE 23.10 The current account on the Danish balance of payment (% of GDP)

Source: Statistics Denmark, Statistical Yearbook.

23.7 Summary

1. This chapter develops a model of aggregate demand and aggregate supply for an open economy. The economy is assumed to be so small that it cannot significantly affect macroeconomic conditions in the rest of the world. It is also assumed to be specialized in the sense that the goods produced domestically are imperfect substitutes for the goods produced abroad. This means that the price of domestic goods can vary relative to the price of foreign goods. A third important assumption is that capital is perfectly mobile across borders.

2. Under perfect capital mobility the arbitrage behaviour of risk-neutral investors will enforce uncovered nominal interest rate parity. This implies that the domestic nominal interest rate will be equal to the foreign nominal interest rate plus the expected percentage rate of depreciation of the domestic currency against the foreign currency. If a group of countries moves towards credibly fixed exchange rates, the interest rate differentials between them will therefore tend to vanish.

3. In the forward market for foreign exchange investors can buy or sell foreign currency for future delivery. The arbitrage behaviour in the forward market enforces covered nominal interest rate parity. This means that the domestic nominal interest rate equals the foreign nominal interest rate plus the forward foreign exchange premium. The latter is defined as the percentage difference between the forward exchange rate and the current spot market exchange rate. Covered and uncovered interest rate parity will hold simultaneously if the forward exchange premium equals the expected rate of change in the exchange rate over the period considered. This equality must hold if investors are risk neutral.

4. The link between capital mobility and interest rate formation means that macroeconomic policy choices are subject to the macroeconomic trilemma. The trilemma arises because a macroeconomic policy regime can include at most two out of the following three policy goals: (i) free cross-border capital flows, (ii) a fixed exchange rate, and (iii) an independent monetary policy. Under the classical gold standard before

the First World War most countries chose to sacrifice monetary autonomy. Under the Bretton Woods system of fixed exchange rates between 1945 and 1971 most countries maintained restrictions on international capital flows, but since the early 1970s the largest economies have abandoned fixed exchange rates while allowing capital mobility and pursuing independent monetary policies. More recently the majority of EU member states have adopted a common monetary policy and a common currency as a means of ensuring irrevocably fixed exchange rates in a common market with free capital mobility.

5. The various exchange rate regimes currently found in the world can be categorized into hard pegs, intermediate regimes, and floating. Under a hard peg the exchange rate is fully fixed, and the national currency may even have been abandoned as in the case of membership of a monetary union. Under floating the exchange rate is market-determined, although the central bank may sometimes intervene in the foreign exchange market to moderate exchange rate fluctuations. The intermediate exchange rate regimes fall between the hard pegs and the floating regimes by allowing some exchange rate flexibility within a (possibly shifting) band around the parity. In recent years there has been a worldwide tendency for countries to move away from intermediate regimes towards a hard peg or towards floating exchange rates.

6. The real exchange rate is the price of foreign goods relative to the price of domestic goods. The real exchange rate is inversely related to the international terms of trade. The percentage change in the real exchange rate equals the percentage rate of depreciation of the nominal exchange rate plus the difference between the foreign and the domestic rate of producer price inflation. In *long-run* equilibrium the real exchange rate must be constant, implying that relative purchasing power parity (RPPP) must hold. Under RPPP the rate of depreciation of the nominal exchange rate equals the difference between the domestic and the foreign inflation rate.

7. When capital is perfectly mobile, relative purchasing power parity implies that in the long run the domestic real interest rate is tied to the foreign real interest rate. This long-run relationship is referred to as real interest rate parity and tends to hold empirically.

8. The trade balance is the difference between exports and imports of goods and services, also denoted net exports. When the Marshall–Lerner condition is met, a depreciation of the real exchange rate will improve the trade balance. The Marshall–Lerner condition requires that the sum of the numerical price elasticities of export and import demand exceeds unity.

9. The short-run aggregate demand curve in the open economy implies a negative relationship between the rate of domestic producer price inflation and the aggregate demand for domestic goods. The reason is that higher domestic inflation will, *ceteris paribus*, erode the international competitiveness of domestic producers. The higher the price elasticities of export and import demand, the stronger is the reaction of net exports to a change in the real exchange rate, and the flatter is the aggregate demand curve in the output-inflation space. When the economy is out of long-run equilibrium, the short-run aggregate demand curve will gradually shift as the real exchange rate changes over time.

10. The properties of the short-run aggregate supply curve in the open economy will depend on whether there is relative wage resistance or real wage resistance. Under real wage resistance wage setters have a target for the real consumer wage, defined as the nominal wage rate deflated by the consumer price index. Real wage resistance implies that the short-run aggregate supply curve will shift when the real exchange rate changes, as workers respond to changing import prices by adjusting their nominal wage claims. Real wage resistance will exist when nominal unemployment benefits are indexed to consumer prices.

11. Under relative wage resistance individual wage setters seek to maintain a certain relation between their own wage rate and the wages set in the rest of the economy. Such behaviour emerges when nominal unemployment benefits are indexed to nominal wages, and it leads to an aggregate supply curve of the same form as the SRAS curve for the closed economy. The specification of aggregate supply adopted here assumes relative wage resistance since indexation of unemployment benefits to wages is the most common international practice.

12. The open economy's long-run aggregate demand curve (LRAD) shows the relationship between real output and the real exchange rate which is consistent with long-run equilibrium in the market for domestic goods. The LRAD curve is upward-sloping in the output–real exchange rate space since a real exchange rate depreciation increases total demand for domestic goods by improving the international competitiveness of domestic producers.

13. Under relative wage resistance the open economy's long-run aggregate supply curve (LRAS) is vertical at the natural rate of output. The long-run equilibrium level of output is then uniquely determined by the position of the LRAS curve, and the long-run equilibrium real exchange rate is found where the LRAD curve intersects the LRAS curve.

14. Our AS–AD model of the open economy implies that the long-run equilibrium values of the real interest rate, the real exchange rate and real output and employment will be independent of the exchange rate regime. In the long run the exchange rate regime is thus neutral with respect to real variables. The proposition that the exchange rate regime is neutral in the long run should be seen only as an approximation, since the exchange rate regime may have some influence on the degree of international economic integration.

15. When there are wealth effects on aggregate demand, the accumulation of net foreign assets via the current account on the balance of payments will influence the evolution of the economy. In a long-run equilibrium without secular growth, the current account balance measured in units of domestic output must then be zero to ensure constancy of the real stock of net foreign assets. However, the evidence suggests that in practice it takes a very long time for current account imbalances to adjust via wealth effects of domestic demand, suggesting that these effects are quite weak. To simplify the analysis, our AS–AD model of the open economy therefore ignores wealth effects stemming from the current account.

23.8 Chapter Appendix: deriving the aggregate demand curve for the open economy

This appendix shows how to derive the log-linear approximation to the goods market equilibrium condition given in Eq. (23) of the main text. Our procedure will be similar to the one which was used to derive the aggregate demand curve for the closed economy in Chapter 16.

We start by restating Eq. (17):

$$Y = \tilde{D}(Y, \tau, r, \varepsilon, E^r, Y^f) + G \qquad (45)$$

Assuming that we start out in a long-run equilibrium, and using the notation for partial derivatives introduced in Eqs (18)–(22), we calculate the total differential of (45) (keeping the tax rate τ constant for simplicity) to get the linear approximation

$$Y - \bar{Y} = \tilde{D}_Y(Y - \bar{Y}) + \tilde{D}_r(r - \bar{r}) + \tilde{D}_E(E^r - \bar{E}^r) + \tilde{D}_\varepsilon(\varepsilon - \bar{\varepsilon}) + \tilde{D}_{Y^f}(Y^f - \bar{Y}^f) + (G - \bar{G}) \quad \Leftrightarrow$$

$$Y - \bar{Y} = \left(\frac{\tilde{D}_E}{1 - \tilde{D}_Y}\right)(E^r - \bar{E}^r) + \left(\frac{\tilde{D}_r}{1 - \tilde{D}_Y}\right)(r - \bar{r}) + \left(\frac{\tilde{D}_\varepsilon}{1 - \tilde{D}_Y}\right)(\varepsilon - \bar{\varepsilon})$$

$$+ \left(\frac{\tilde{D}_{Y^f}}{1 - \tilde{D}_Y}\right)(Y^f - \bar{Y}^F) + \left(\frac{1}{1 - \tilde{D}_Y}\right)(G - \bar{G}), \tag{46}$$

where long-run equilibrium values are indicated by a bar above the variables. It is natural to assume that, other things equal, an increase in world economic activity will increase the domestic economy's export market in proportion to the domestic economy's initial weight in the world economy. In that case we have:

$$\tilde{D}_{Y^f} \equiv \frac{\partial NX}{\partial Y^f} = \frac{\bar{Y}}{\bar{Y}^f}. \tag{47}$$

When a relationship like (47) holds for all countries, it simply means that an increase in world output Y^f does not in itself change the individual country's share of the world market.

Our next step is to rewrite (46) in terms of *relative* changes of the various variables (except the real interest rate which is already expressed in percentage terms). Doing this, and using (47), we get:

$$\frac{Y - \bar{Y}}{\bar{Y}} = \left(\frac{\bar{E}^r \tilde{D}_E}{\bar{Y}(1 - \tilde{D}_Y)}\right)\left(\frac{E^r - \bar{E}^r}{\bar{E}^r}\right) + \left(\frac{\tilde{D}_r}{\bar{Y}(1 - \tilde{D}_Y)}\right)(r - \bar{r}) + \left(\frac{\bar{\varepsilon}\tilde{D}_\varepsilon}{\bar{Y}(1 - \tilde{D}_Y)}\right)\left(\frac{\varepsilon - \bar{\varepsilon}}{\bar{\varepsilon}}\right)$$

$$+ \left(\frac{1}{1 - \tilde{D}_Y}\right)\left(\frac{Y^f - \bar{Y}^f}{\bar{Y}^f}\right) + \left(\frac{\bar{G}}{\bar{Y}(1 - \tilde{D}_Y)}\right)\left(\frac{G - \bar{G}}{\bar{G}}\right). \tag{48}$$

Using the definitions

$$y \equiv \ln Y, \qquad y^f \equiv \ln Y^f, \qquad e^r \equiv \ln E^r, \qquad g \equiv \ln G,$$

and remembering that the relative change in some variable x is approximately equal to the change in the natural logarithm of x, we may write (48) as:

$$y - \bar{y} = \beta_1(e^r - \bar{e}^e) - \beta_2(r - \bar{r}) + \beta_3(g - \bar{g}) + \beta_4(y^f - \bar{y}^f) + \beta_5(\ln\varepsilon - \ln\bar{\varepsilon}) \tag{49}$$

where

$$\beta_1 \equiv \frac{\bar{E}^r \tilde{D}_E}{\bar{Y}(1 - \tilde{D}_Y)}, \qquad \beta_2 \equiv \frac{-\tilde{D}_r}{\bar{Y}(1 - \tilde{D}_Y)}, \qquad \beta_3 \equiv \frac{\bar{G}}{\bar{Y}(1 - \tilde{D}_Y)}, \qquad \beta_4 \equiv \frac{1}{1 - \tilde{D}_Y}, \qquad \beta_5 \equiv \frac{\bar{\varepsilon}\tilde{D}_\varepsilon}{\bar{Y}(1 - \tilde{D}_Y)}$$

We see that (49) is identical to (23) in the main text.

As we shall see in the next two chapters, the magnitude of the parameter β_1 is crucial for the speed with which the economy adjusts to long-run equilibrium. It is therefore useful to express β_1 in a form which will enable us to estimate its likely magnitude. According to (16) and (22) we have:

$$\tilde{D}_E \equiv \frac{\partial D}{\partial E^r} + \frac{\partial NX}{\partial E^r}, \qquad \frac{\partial NX}{\partial E^r} = M_o(\eta_X + \eta_m - 1).$$

Furthermore, let us specify the numerical elasticity of total private demand with respect to the real exchange rate as:

$$\eta_D \equiv -\frac{\partial D}{\partial E^r}\frac{\bar{E}^r}{\bar{D}}.$$

Using these relationships, and choosing units such that the initial real exchange rate $\bar{E}^r = 1$, you may verify that the expression for β_1 may be rewritten as:

$$\beta_1 = \frac{(M_O/\bar{Y})(\eta_X + \eta_M - 1) - (\bar{D}/\bar{Y})\eta_D}{1 - \tilde{D}_Y}. \tag{50}$$

This specification of β_1 will be used in the next two chapters.

23.9 Exercises

Exercise 1. Important concepts in the theory of the open economy

1. Explain what is meant by a 'small specialized economy'.

2. Define the concept of perfect capital mobility and explain the conditions for uncovered and covered interest rate parity. Which assumption is necessary for both parity conditions to hold at the same time? Are these parity conditions short-run relationships or long-run relationships?

3. Define the concepts of the real exchange rate and the international terms of trade. Explain the conditions for relative purchasing power parity (RPPP) and real interest rate parity. Are these conditions short-run relationships or long-run relationships?

4. Explain the Marshall–Lerner condition. Is fulfilment of this condition sufficient to ensure that a real exchange rate depreciation will raise the demand for domestically produced goods?

5. Suppose that individual domestic exporters are each selling a differentiated product and that each of them therefore has a monopoly position in the international market (and thus faces a downward-sloping demand curve). Give a theoretical reason why, in these circumstances, the Marshall–Lerner condition must necessarily hold. (Hint: a monopoly firm will produce and sell up to the point where marginal revenue equals marginal cost. What does this imply for the size of the price elasticity of demand in the firm's optimum?)

6. Explain the concepts of relative wage resistance and real wage resistance and how these phenomena are related to the rules for indexation of unemployment benefits.

Exercise 2. Alternative monetary and exchange rate regimes

1. Explain the classification of alternative exchange rate regimes used by the International Monetary Fund. Discuss briefly why there has been a polarization of the choice of exchange rate regimes in recent years.

2. Explain the nature of the macroeconomic 'trilemma'. Why is the trilemma inescapable, and how have countries tended to deal with it over time?

Exercise 3. Permanent shocks under relative wage resistance

In this exercise you are asked to undertake a graphical analysis of the long-run effects of permanent shocks in a small open economy with relative wage resistance. The conditions for long-run equilibrium in such an economy were summarized in Eqs (43) and (44) in the text, and the long-run equilibrium was illustrated graphically in Fig. 23.8. You may use this diagram along with (43) and (44) as a basis for answering the following questions.

1. Suppose the foreign real interest rate permanently increases. Give a graphical illustration of the long-run effects of this demand shock on the real exchange rate. Explain the effect.

2. Assume that the domestic government permanently increases public consumption. Illustrate and explain the long-run effect of this policy change on the real exchange rate.

3. Suppose that domestic productivity permanently increases so that the supply shock variable $s = (1 + \gamma)(\ln \bar{a} - \ln a)$ permanently declines from zero to some negative amount. Illustrate and explain the long-run effects of this productivity shock on domestic output and on the real exchange rate.

Exercise 4. Permanent shocks under real wage resistance

This exercise invites you to study the long-run effects of permanent shocks in an open economy with real wage resistance and to compare these effects with those emerging under relative wage resistance. For this purpose you must first derive the aggregate supply curve under real wage resistance and characterize the economy's long-run equilibrium under this wage setting regime.

Consider a representative monopoly trade union which sets the nominal wage rate W with the purpose of achieving a target real consumer wage. The nominal wage rate is set at a time when the union does not have perfect information on the average consumer price level. According to (28) in the main text the actual consumer price level is $P^c = (E^r)^\psi P$, where E^r is the real exchange rate and P is the price of domestically produced goods. Hence the expected consumer price level is $P^{ce} = (E^{re})^\psi P^e$, where E^{re} and P^e are the expected levels of E^r and P. We assume that the nominal rate of unemployment benefit is indexed to the consumer price level, so the real rate of unemployment benefit, b, is unaffected by changes in P^c. The union aims to obtain an expected real consumer wage which is a mark-up, m^w, over the real unemployment benefit. Thus the nominal union wage claim is given by:

$$W = m^w b P^{ce} = m^w b (E^{re})^\psi P^e. \tag{51}$$

It is reasonable to assume that the union will moderate its wage claim when the rate of unemployment (u) rises. We may model this by specifying the union mark-up factor as:

$$m^w = \omega(1-u)^\gamma, \qquad \omega > 0, \qquad \gamma > 0, \tag{52}$$

where ω and γ are constants.

The representative domestic firm uses a linear production technology by which one unit of labour produces a units of output. Hence the marginal cost of production is W/a, and the firm sets its price as a mark-up, m^p, over marginal cost:

$$P = m^p \cdot \frac{W}{a}, \qquad m^p > 1. \tag{53}$$

Finally, we assume that the real unemployment benefit is tied to the 'normal' level of productivity, that is, the trend value of a, denoted $\bar{a}$:

$$b = \bar{c} \cdot \bar{a}. \tag{54}$$

This specification assumes that, over the long run, the unemployed are allowed to share in the real income gains generated by productivity growth.

1. Show by taking logarithms that Eqs (51)–(54) lead to an expectations-augmented Phillips curve of the form:

$$\pi = \pi^e + \gamma(\bar{u} - u) + \psi e^{re} + \ln \bar{a} - \ln a,$$

$$\bar{u} \equiv \frac{\ln(m^p \omega \bar{c})}{\gamma}, \qquad \pi \equiv \ln P - \ln P_{-1}, \qquad \pi \equiv \ln P^e - \ln P_{-1}, \qquad e^{re} \equiv \ln E^{re}, \tag{55}$$

where π and π^e are, of course, the actual and the expected domestic inflation rate, respectively. (Hint: use the approximation $\ln(1-u) \approx -u$.) Explain in economic terms why the (log of the) expected real exchange rate, e^{re}, appears in (55).

2. Use (55) along with Eqs (39) and (40) in the main text to show that the short-run aggregate supply curve under real wage resistance takes the form:

$$\pi = \pi^e + \gamma(y - \bar{y}) + \psi e^{re} + s, \qquad s \equiv (1 + \gamma)(\ln \bar{a} - \ln a), \tag{56}$$

where s is a supply shock variable reflecting productivity shocks.

3. Derive the long-run aggregate supply curve (LRAS) in an open economy with real wage resistance by inserting the long-run equilibrium conditions $\pi^e = \pi$ and $e^{re} = e^r \equiv \ln E^r$ into (56). Draw the resulting LRAS curve in a diagram with y along the horizontal axis and e^r along the vertical axis, and give an economic explanation for the slope of the LRAS curve. Draw the long-run aggregate demand curve (the LRAD curve given by Eq. (43) in the text) in your (y, e^r)-diagram. Explain the slope of the LRAD curve and identify the economy's long-run equilibrium. Will y necessarily be equal to $\bar{y}$ in long-run equilibrium? Make a graphical comparison of the long-run equilibrium under real wage resistance and under relative wage resistance.

4. Assume that the domestic government permanently increases public consumption. Illustrate the long-run effects of this policy change on domestic output and on the real exchange rate under the two alternative scenarios of real wage resistance and relative wage resistance. Compare and explain the effects.

5. Suppose that domestic productivity permanently increases so that the supply shock variable $s \equiv (1 + \gamma)(\ln \bar{a} - \ln a)$ permanently declines from zero to some negative amount. Illustrate the long-run effects of this productivity shock on domestic output and on the real exchange rate under the two alternative scenarios of real wage resistance and relative wage resistance. Compare and explain the effects.

Exercise 5. The open economy with wealth effects on aggregate demand

In this exercise you are asked to study an open economy with relative wage resistance and wealth effects on private consumption demand. We noted in the text that imbalances on the current account of the balance of payments may affect aggregate demand by changing the private sector's stock of wealth and the associated amount of capital income accruing to domestic residents.

To concentrate on the role of the current account in the process of wealth accumulation, we will ignore other sources of changes in private wealth. Thus we will identify private wealth with the private sector's stock of net foreign assets, denoted by F and measured in units of domestic output (just as we have measured the trade balance in units of domestic output). *Ceteris paribus*, a rise in F will generate an increase in private consumption. Hence we must respecify our previous goods market equilibrium condition (17) in the following way, where we do not explicitly include the exogenous confidence variable ε and the exogenous foreign activity level Y^f:

$$Y = D(Y, \tau, r, E^r, F) + NX(Y, \tau, r, E^r, F) + G,$$
$$D_F = \frac{\partial D}{\partial F} > 0, \qquad \frac{\partial NX}{\partial F} < 0, \qquad D_F + \frac{\partial NX}{\partial F} > 0. \tag{57}$$

By stimulating private consumption, a rise in net foreign assets will cause a deterioration of the trade balance, because part of the rise in consumer demand will be directed towards imports. However, since the marginal propensity to import is less than 1, the net effect of a rise in F on the demand for domestic goods is positive, as indicated by the last inequality above.

By definition, we have:

$$F = \frac{EF^f}{P}$$
(58)

where F^f is the nominal stock of net foreign assets denominated in foreign currency. As an accounting identity, we also have:

$$E_{+1}F^f_{+1} - EF^f = P \cdot NX + \left(i^f + \frac{E_{+1} - E}{E} \right) EF^f$$
(59)

This equation says that the increase in the *nominal* stock of net foreign assets (the left-hand side) arises through a nominal surplus on the trade balance, $P \cdot NX$, through interest earnings on the existing foreign assets, $i^f \cdot EF^f$, or through exchange rate gains on the current asset stock, $((E_{+1} - E)/E)EF^f$. Dividing by $P_{+1} \equiv (1 + \pi_{+1})P$ in (59) and using (58) plus the approximation $\Delta e_{+1} = (E_{+1} - E)/E$, we find that the increase in foreign assets measured in units of domestic output is given by:

$$F_{+1} - F = \frac{NX + (i^f + \Delta e_{+1} - \pi_{+1})F}{1 + \pi_{+1}}.$$
(60)

We can now characterize the long-run equilibrium in the open economy with wealth effects. Since we are abstracting from long-term growth, a long-run equilibrium requires that the stock of net foreign assets be constant, since aggregate demand would otherwise keep on shifting over time. We also know that relative purchasing power parity and real interest rate parity must hold in the long run. Moreover, if we assume relative wage resistance, we know that the long-run equilibrium level of output is an exogenous constant, $\bar{Y}$. Hence we have the long-run equilibrium conditions:

$$F_{+1} = F, \qquad Y = \bar{Y}, \qquad r = r^f,$$
$$\Delta e_{+1} = \pi_{+1} - \pi^f_{+1} \Rightarrow i^f + \Delta e_{+1} - \pi_{+1} = i^f - \pi^f_{+1} = r^f,$$
(61)

which may be inserted into (57) and (60) to give:

$$\bar{Y} = D(\bar{Y}, \tau, r^f, E^r, F) + NX(\bar{Y}, \tau, r^f, E^r, F) + G,$$
(62)

$$NX(\bar{Y}, \tau, r^f, E^f, F) + r^f F = 0.$$
(63)

Equations (62) and (63) determine the long-run equilibrium values of the two endogenous variables E^r and F. Notice from (63) that in the long run the current account has to balance in real terms to ensure constancy of the real stock of net foreign assets.

1. Use Eqs (62) and (63) to illustrate the economy's long-run equilibrium in a diagram in which F is measured along the horizontal axis and E_r is measured along the vertical axis. The equilibrium combinations of F and E_r implied by (62) may be termed the 'GME curve' (GME for Goods Market Equilibrium). Show that the slope of the GME curve is:

$$\left(\frac{dE^r}{dF} \right)_{GME} = - \left(\frac{D_F + \frac{\partial NX}{\partial F}}{D_E + \frac{\partial NX}{\partial E^r}} \right) < 0,$$
(64)

which is seen to be negative since we assumed in the main text that $D_E + (\partial NX/\partial E^r) > 0$. Give an economic explanation for the negative slope.

The equilibrium combinations of F and E^r implied by (63) may be denoted the 'CAB curve' (CAB for Current Account Balance). Show that the slope of this curve is:

$$\left(\frac{dE^r}{dF}\right)_{CAB} = -\left(\frac{r^f + \dfrac{\partial NX}{\partial F}}{\dfrac{\partial NX}{\partial E^r}}\right) \tag{65}$$

Empirically, a value of r^f in the region of 5 per cent per annum is plausible. In many empirical studies based on annual data the magnitude of the derivative D_F in the numerator of (64) is also estimated to be close to 0.05. Assuming $D_F \approx r^f$, you can now determine the sign of the slope of the CAB curve and say whether it is steeper or flatter than the GME curve. (Hint: what is the sign of the derivative $D_E \equiv \partial D / \partial E^r$?)

Identify the long-run equilibrium values of F and E^r in your diagram.

2. Suppose the domestic government permanently raises public consumption. Give a graphical illustration of the long-run effects of this policy change on net foreign assets and the real exchange rate. Explain the effects.

3. Assume that the foreign real interest rate permanently increases. Illustrate and explain the long-run effects of this demand shock on net foreign assets and on the real exchange rate.

4. Assume alternatively that the domestic economy is hit by a positive supply shock which permanently increases domestic potential output $\bar{Y}$. Illustrate and explain the long-run effects of this supply shock on net foreign assets and on the real exchange rate.

Exercise 6. The sustainable balance of payments

In Exercise 5 we saw that in an economy with wealth effects on aggregate demand and with no real growth in the long run, the current account must balance in real terms in the long run to keep the stock of private wealth constant. However, if there is secular real growth, a long-run equilibrium no longer requires constancy of real private wealth; it only requires that real private wealth grows at the same rate as real GDP. This means that the real balance on the current account no longer has to be zero in the long run, although there is a limit to how much it can deviate from zero. You are now asked to illustrate these points by some simple numerical examples.

Consider an open economy where real GDP is expected to grow at an average annual rate of 2 per cent in the long run. Suppose that this economy starts out with a stock of net foreign debt equal to 25 per cent of GDP. Suppose further that the average inflation rate at home and abroad is expected to be 2 per cent per annum. Assume finally that the international real interest rate is 4 per cent per annum.

1. What is the magnitude of the nominal current account deficit relative to nominal GDP which the country can afford to sustain without increasing the ratio of foreign debt to GDP?

2. What is the magnitude of the real current account deficit (the deficit measured in units of domestic goods) which the country can afford to sustain without increasing the debt–GDP ratio?

3. What is the magnitude of the nominal trade balance relative to nominal GDP which the country must sustain to maintain a constant ratio of foreign debt to GDP?

CHAPTER 24

The open economy with fixed exchange rates

The AS–AD model of the open economy developed in the previous chapter implies that the long-run equilibrium values of real variables such as real output, the real interest rate and the real exchange rate are unaffected by the exchange rate regime. In this and the next chapter we shall see that a country's choice of exchange rate regime is nevertheless a fundamental economic policy choice because of its influence on the economy's short-run dynamics. First of all, the choice of exchange rate regime will determine whether monetary policy can be used as a tool of macroeconomic stabilization policy. Second, the exchange rate regime will affect the way in which the economy adjusts to its long-run equilibrium and how it responds to exogenous shocks in the short and medium term.

The rest of this book will elaborate on these points by analysing the workings of the macroeconomy under alternative exchange rate regimes. The present chapter focuses on a *small specialized economy* with *fixed exchange rates* and *perfect capital mobility*. We start by studying the characteristics of fixed exchange rates as an economic policy regime and by discussing why a country might want to adopt a fixed nominal exchange rate. We then adapt the AS–AD model of the open economy set up in Chapter 23 to analyse how the economy adjusts to long-run equilibrium under fixed exchange rates. The final parts of the chapter use our AS–AD model to study the effects of macroeconomic policy under fixed exchange rates.

24.1 Fixed exchange rates as an economic policy regime

Under a fixed exchange rate regime the central bank fixes the nominal price of (some) foreign currency in terms of domestic currency. This official price of foreign currency is referred to as the exchange rate parity. In the purest version of a fixed exchange rate regime, the central bank stands ready to buy and sell unlimited amounts of foreign currency at the exchange rate parity so that the nominal exchange rate is completely fixed. In practice, most countries with 'fixed' exchange rates have allowed the market price of foreign currency to fluctuate within some band around the exchange rate parity. Of course, the wider the band within which the exchange rate is allowed to vary, the closer the 'fixed' exchange rate regime comes to a regime with freely floating exchange rates. Moreover, many countries with 'fixed' exchange rates have occasionally changed the official exchange rate parity, in effect following a policy referred to as fixed but adjustable exchange rates. The difference between fixed and flexible exchange rates is therefore a matter of degree, and the precise dividing line between the two types of regime is not clear-cut.

In Chapter 23 we described the different types of exchange rate regimes found in the world and mentioned some important historical examples of fixed exchange rate arrangements with varying degrees of 'fixity' of the exchange rate. For analytical purposes the present chapter will start out by focusing on the theoretical benchmark case where the nominal exchange rate is completely fixed. Later in the chapter we will consider a regime with fixed but adjustable exchange rates.

The impotence of monetary policy under fixed exchange rates and free capital mobility

Under a regime with fully fixed exchange rates and free capital mobility it becomes impossible to use monetary policy for the purpose of stabilizing the domestic economy. The previous chapter already made this point, but it is sufficiently important to warrant a restatement. Recall from Chapter 23 that when international capital mobility is perfect, the following condition for uncovered interest parity must hold:

$$i = i^f + e_{+1}^e - e, \qquad e \equiv \ln E, \qquad e_{+1}^e \equiv \ln E_{+1}^e. \tag{1}$$

Here i is the domestic nominal interest rate, i^f is the foreign nominal interest rate, E is the nominal exchange rate (the price of foreign currency in terms of domestic currency), and E_{+1}^e is the nominal exchange rate expected to prevail in the next period. Hence $e_{+1}^e - e$ is the expected percentage rate of depreciation of the domestic currency against the foreign currency, that is, the expected capital gain on foreign bonds relative to domestic bonds over the period considered. Thus $i^f + e_{+1}^e - e$ is the total expected return on foreign assets which must equal the return i on domestic assets when the two asset types are perfect substitutes. Under a so-called hard peg where the exchange rate is credibly fixed, the expected exchange rate change will be zero, that is, $e_{+1}^e - e = 0$. It then follows from (1) that:

$$i = i^f. \tag{2}$$

In other words, *under fixed exchange rates and perfect capital mobility the domestic nominal interest rate is tied to the foreign nominal interest rate.*

As far as the market-determined interest rates are concerned, the equality in (2) is enforced by the arbitrage between domestic and foreign assets described in the previous chapter.

When it comes to the short-term domestic interest rate set by the central bank, Eq. (2) is enforced by the need to protect the country's foreign exchange reserves. If the central bank tries to keep the domestic short-term interest rate below the foreign short-term interest rate, capital will flow out of the domestic economy. As investors sell domestic currency and buy foreign currency to invest in foreign assets, the central bank will have to sell foreign currency and buy domestic currency to maintain the fixed exchange rate. In this way the country's foreign exchange reserves will be exhausted if the central bank insists on keeping the domestic short-term interest rate below the foreign level. Indeed, the market will most likely interpret such an interest rate policy as a signal that the central bank is not committed to defending the exchange rate. In that case expectations of a future devaluation will arise, and a speculative attack on the domestic currency will occur, leading to an even faster depletion of foreign exchange reserves. Once the reserves are gone, the central bank can no longer intervene in the foreign exchange market to keep the exchange rate fixed, and the domestic currency will have to fall.

On the other hand, if for some reason the central bank keeps the domestic short-term interest rate above the foreign short-term interest rate, a massive inflow of capital from abroad will occur. This will swell the foreign exchange reserves and create a constant upward pressure on the exchange rate. The huge capital inflow will also lead to a large expansion of domestic bank credit and a rise in domestic asset prices which will generate strong inflationary pressures.

The upshot is that if the central bank wishes to maintain a fixed exchange rate, it cannot set a short-term interest rate which deviates from the short-term interest rate abroad. The situation in Denmark illustrates this point very well. The Danish krone is pegged to the euro, and whenever the European Central Bank decides to change its leading interest rate, the Danish central bank interest rate is almost always changed by exactly the same amount within the same hour.

Monetary policy thus becomes *impotent* under fixed exchange rates and perfect capital mobility. When the exchange rate is fixed, the central bank cannot pursue an independent interest rate policy aimed at managing aggregate demand. Instead, monetary policy is fully bound by the commitment to defend the exchange rate. In contrast, if a country is willing to accept exchange rate variability, it can set its interest rate independently of the foreign interest rate, as indicated in Eq. (1).

In principle, a country with a fixed exchange rate can also pursue an independent monetary policy if it is able to maintain effective control over private cross-border capital flows, thereby preventing the arbitrage which would otherwise drive the domestic interest rate into equality with the foreign interest rate. However, nowadays practically all the developed countries in the world have abandoned capital controls, partly because they are difficult to enforce, and partly because they are considered undesirable, since they prevent investors from seeking out the most profitable investment opportunities and from diversifying their portfolios to hedge against country-specific investment risks.[1]

The case for fixed exchange rates

If capital controls are ineffective or are seen as undesirable, the price of maintaining fixed exchange rates is the loss of monetary policy autonomy. Given this fact, why would a country nevertheless choose a fixed exchange rate regime? Advocates of fixed exchange rates usually point to the disadvantages of exchange rate uncertainty and to the benefits of using a fixed exchange rate as a nominal anchor in the fight against inflation. Let us briefly consider these arguments.

1. The first argument is that the large exchange rate movements often observed under floating exchange rates may hamper international trade and investment by creating exchange rate uncertainty. To be sure, short-term foreign exchange risk can be covered through the forward exchange market at a modest transaction cost, but the opportunities for covering long-term foreign exchange risks are much more limited, and this might discourage long-term trade contracts and long-term international investments if the exchange rate is highly unstable.

2. A related argument starts from the observation that exchange rates often seem to 'overshoot' their long-run equilibrium values under floating exchange rates, as we shall see in the next chapter. The concern is that such excessive exchange rate movements may cause an unintended redistribution of real income across different sectors in the economy. For example, a sharp appreciation of the domestic currency will erode the international competitiveness of the domestic export industry and of domestic industries which are competing against imports. As a consequence, profits and employment in those sectors will be squeezed, whereas sectors relying on imported inputs and selling their output in the domestic market without any competition from abroad will benefit from the appreciation. If the resulting redistribution of income is significant, it may cause social tensions.

3. Another main argument is that a fixed exchange rate can provide a *nominal anchor* which may help to bring down inflation. In the longer term a country can only maintain a fixed exchange rate against a foreign trading partner if the domestic inflation rate does not systematically exceed inflation in the foreign country. Policy makers may therefore signal a commitment to keep the domestic inflation rate low by announcing that they will peg the domestic currency to the currency of a foreign country with a history of low

---

1. In Chapter 4 we offered a more extensive discussion of the long-run benefits and risks associated with free capital mobility.

inflation. If this commitment is credible, it will keep domestic inflation expectations in check, and this in turn will make it easier to keep the actual inflation rate low. Thus, by pegging to a stable foreign currency, domestic policy makers may 'import' some of the credibility and discipline of foreign policy makers who have been successful in fighting inflation. Such a strategy is most likely to be credible and to succeed if the political costs of giving up the peg to the foreign currency are perceived to be considerable.

The belief that pegging to a stable foreign currency can help to bring down domestic inflation motivated many previous high-inflation countries in Europe to tie their currencies closer to the German D-mark after the mid 1980s. After a setback caused by the speculative attacks on the European Monetary System in 1992–93 (to which we shall return later in this chapter), this policy of pegging to the D-mark gradually led to lower exchange rate variability which did in fact drive national inflation rates in the EU closer to the low German level, as shown in Figs 24.1a and 24.1b.

The evolution of international trade following the formation of monetary union in Europe may cast some light on the hypothesis that credibly fixed exchange rates tend to stimulate trade. In the third and final phase of the European Monetary Union (EMU) the member countries adopted a common currency, the euro, thereby effectively locking their exchange rates for good. Figure 24.2 shows estimates of the effects of the introduction of the euro on export volumes in various groups of countries, based on an empirical trade model which controls for a number of other factors affecting exports in order to isolate the trade effect of the euro.[2] The group of 'hard peg' countries consists of those EMU countries that pursued a consistent fixed exchange rate policy vis-à-vis the German D-mark during the 1990s. The group of 'Other EMU countries' includes countries that are full members of the EMU but allowed much more exchange rate variability against the D-mark prior to the formation of monetary union. The figure also includes the three non-EMU countries, Denmark, Sweden and the UK. The latter two countries have allowed their currencies to float since the early 1990s, whereas Denmark followed a 'hard peg' policy vis-à-vis the D-mark during the 1990s and continued this policy by pegging the Danish krone to the euro after the formation of the EMU. All effects in Fig. 24.2 measure the *additional* rise in exports compared to the increase in exports from a 'control' group of seven OECD countries outside the EMU (see the definition of the various country groups in the note to the figure). An asterisk above a column means that the relevant export effect is statistically significant.

Figure 24.2 indicates that the introduction of the euro has boosted the exports of countries that pursued a consistent fixed exchange rate policy before the formation of the EMU, whereas the trade effects for the other countries have so far been much more modest and statistically insignificant. The fact that the two countries with floating exchange rates (Sweden and the UK) have not reaped any (significant) trade gains from the euro might be seen as evidence that fixed exchange rates tend to stimulate trade by eliminating exchange rate uncertainty. However, it is not clear why EMU membership has not yet given any significant boost to the exports of the group of 'other' EMU countries. One possibility is that since these countries have a history of volatile inflation rates, there is still considerable uncertainty regarding the evolution of their *real* exchange rates. If that is the case, such uncertainty may still hamper the development of long-term trade relations until these countries have established a sufficiently long track record of real exchange rate stability.

Two other surprising results stand out from Fig. 24.2. The first one is that the formation of the EMU seems to have boosted exports to countries outside the euro zone by as much as it boosted exports from one EMU country to another. This may be because the introduction

---

2. Among other things, the analysis controls for the effects on trade of GDP, the real exchange rate, and tariffs. The trade impact of factors such as geographical distance and cultural similarity is captured by dummy variables. The study underlying Figure 24.2 was based on the methodology in Harry Flam and Håkan Nordström, 'Euro Effects on the Intensive and Extensive Margin of Trade', IIES Seminar Paper No. 750, December 2006, Institute for International Economic Studies, University of Stockholm. An updated data set for the study was also provided by these authors.

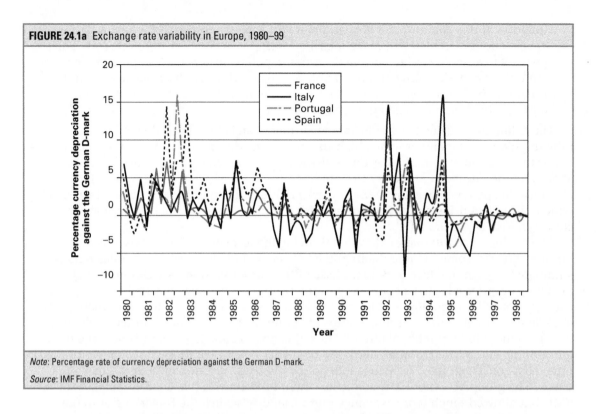

FIGURE 24.1a Exchange rate variability in Europe, 1980–99

Note: Percentage rate of currency depreciation against the German D-mark.

Source: IMF Financial Statistics.

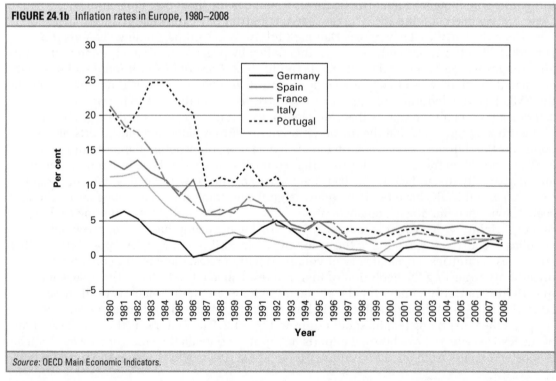

FIGURE 24.1b Inflation rates in Europe, 1980–2008

Source: OECD Main Economic Indicators.

of a common currency made euro area exporters more competitive by reducing the cost of cross-border production, including the cost of using inputs from suppliers in other parts of the euro zone. The other striking result in Fig. 24.2 is that Danish exports seem to have benefited as much from the euro as the exports from the EMU countries themselves. Through

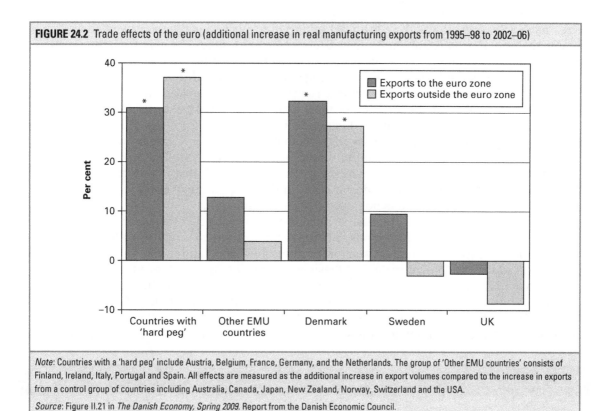

FIGURE 24.2 Trade effects of the euro (additional increase in real manufacturing exports from 1995–98 to 2002–06)

Note: Countries with a 'hard peg' include Austria, Belgium, France, Germany, and the Netherlands. The group of 'Other EMU countries' consists of Finland, Ireland, Italy, Portugal and Spain. All effects are measured as the additional increase in export volumes compared to the increase in exports from a control group of countries including Australia, Canada, Japan, New Zealand, Norway, Switzerland and the USA.

Source: Figure II.21 in *The Danish Economy, Spring 2009*. Report from the Danish Economic Council.

its long-standing policy of firmly fixed exchange rates against the core countries of the euro zone, it appears that the Danish economy works very much like the economies of those countries.

Although the evidence in Fig. 24.2 suggests that fixed exchange rates and/or a common currency could have significant positive effects on foreign trade, the resulting effect on real national income may be small. This can be illustrated by a numerical example based on Fig. 24.2. According to the figure the euro boosted total Danish exports by about 30 per cent. In contrast, the 'other' EMU countries without a history of exchange rate stability only experienced a 12 per cent increase in their exports to the euro zone and almost no increase (relative to the control group countries) in their exports to non-EMU countries. Suppose now that the Danish export performance would have been similar to that of the 'other' countries if it had followed a similar historical exchange rate policy. Since exports to the euro zone make up about half of total Danish exports, the increase in Danish exports would then have been only 12/2 = 6 per cent. The export gain from the Danish fixed exchange rate policy may then be estimated as 30 − 6 = 24 per cent. Presumably this increase in exports arose because the absence of exchange rate uncertainty works like a reduction in the costs of doing international trade. The long-run price elasticity of Danish exports has been estimated to be around 3, so to generate a 24 per cent increase in exports, the fixed exchange rate policy must have worked like a drop of 24/3 = 8 per cent in the production costs of the Danish export sector. This may be seen as a productivity gain that allows a 24 per cent increase in imports via higher exports, thus supporting a higher Danish standard of living. As an alternative to increasing exports and imports, some of the resources of the export sector could have been reallocated to the domestic import-competing sector and used to replace the additional imports by increased domestic output. But in that case these resources would not have been 8 per cent more productive, since this productivity gain arises from (increased) exchange rate stability and hence accrues only to firms engaged in cross-border trade. It is therefore reasonable to assume that if the additional imported goods had had to be produced at home, the cost of production would have been 8 per cent higher. The gain from the Danish fixed exchange rate policy may then be estimated as the resulting increase in foreign trade (24 per cent) times the cost savings from being able to import additional goods rather than having to produce them at home (8 per cent) times the ratio of the Danish export sector's value-added to GDP (33 per cent), that is, $0.24 \times 0.08 \times 0.33 \approx 0.6$ per cent of GDP.

Although there are of course many uncertainties involved in the chain of reasoning leading to this estimate, it nevertheless suggests that the real income gain from the additional trade generated by exchange rate stability is fairly small even if the trade effects are significant. Though our numerical trade example modifies our earlier result that the exchange rate regime does not affect 'real' economic variables in the long run, it gives reason to believe that this neutrality assumption is not a bad first approximation.

The discussion above also illuminates the trade-offs involved in the choice of exchange rate regime: by fixing the exchange rate, a country may eliminate nominal exchange rate uncertainty and provide a nominal anchor for domestic prices, and it may also reap some gains from additional foreign trade. But these benefits can only be achieved by sacrificing monetary policy autonomy, and giving up an independent monetary policy may weaken a country's ability to pursue an effective macroeconomic stabilization policy. Given this difficult trade-off, it is hardly surprising that different countries with different economic histories and different economic structures have chosen different exchange rate regimes.

FIXED EXCHANGE RATES AS AN ECONOMIC POLICY REGIME

Under fixed exchange rates and perfect capital mobility a small open economy cannot pursue an independent monetary policy, since the domestic interest rate will have to equal the interest rate on assets denominated in the foreign currency to which the domestic currency is pegged. On the other hand, a fixed exchange rate may provide a 'nominal anchor' that helps to reduce domestic inflation if the domestic currency is pegged to the currency of a foreign country with a record of low and stable inflation. By reducing/eliminating exchange rate uncertainty, a fixed exchange rate regime may also stimulate foreign trade, although the resulting real income gain is likely to be limited even if the increase in trade is large.

24.2 Macroeconomic adjustment under fixed exchange rates

Inflation and real exchange rate dynamics

Before analysing the effects of economic policy in an open economy with fixed exchange rates, it is useful to study the dynamic process through which such an economy adjusts to long-run equilibrium. As we shall see in this section, the evolution of the *real* exchange rate plays a key role in the macroeconomic adjustment process. From the previous chapter you will recall that the real exchange rate is defined as $E^r \equiv EP^f/P$, where E is the nominal exchange rate, P^f is the foreign price level measured in foreign currency, and P is the price of domestic goods. When the nominal exchange rate is fixed, it follows that the percentage change in the real exchange rate (the change in the log of the real exchange rate) is given by:

$$e^r - e^r_{-1} = \pi^f - \pi,$$

$$e^r \equiv \ln E^r, \qquad \pi^f \equiv \ln P^f - \ln P^f_{-1}, \qquad \pi \equiv \ln P - \ln P_{-1},$$

(3)

where π^f and π are the foreign and the domestic inflation rate, respectively. Thus the real exchange rate can only remain stable over time if the domestic inflation rate corresponds to the foreign inflation rate. Since a constant real exchange rate is one condition for long-run equilibrium, it follows that the domestic inflation rate will converge on the foreign inflation rate if the long-run equilibrium is stable (as indeed it will be under the assumptions made below).

We will now illustrate the role of the identity (3) in our AS–AD model of the open economy with fixed exchange rates.

Aggregate demand and aggregate supply

In Eq. (26) of the previous chapter we presented the general expression for the aggregate demand curve in the open economy. Allowing for the possibility of exchange rate flexibility, that equation included both the actual rate of nominal exchange rate depreciation which affects the country's international competitiveness, and the expected rate of nominal exchange rate depreciation which influences the domestic rate of interest. Under a policy regime where nominal exchange rates are credibly fixed – that is, where the public believes in the government's declared commitment not to devalue the currency – the expected as well as the actual rate of nominal exchange rate depreciation will be zero. Inserting this condition ($\Delta e = \Delta e^e = 0$) into Eq. (26) of the previous chapter, we get the following expression for the goods market equilibrium condition in an economy with credibly fixed exchange rates:

$$y - \bar{y} = \beta_1(e^r_{-1} + \pi^f - \pi) - \beta_2(i^f - \pi^e_{+1} - \bar{r}^f) + \tilde{z}, \tag{4}$$

where $\bar{r}^f$ is the initial foreign real interest rate, π^e_{+1} is the expected rate of domestic inflation between the current and the next period, and $\tilde{z}$ is a demand shock variable. From (3) we see that the magnitude $e^r_{-1} + \pi^f - \pi$ in (4) is simply the current real exchange rate, e^r. Thus aggregate demand varies positively with the competitiveness of domestic producers, measured by the current real exchange rate. We also see that total demand varies negatively with the real interest rate, $i^f - \pi^e_{+1}$.

In modelling aggregate supply, we will rely on the hypothesis of relative wage resistance explained in the previous chapter. As you recall, this hypothesis leads to a standard aggregate supply curve of the form:

$$\pi = \pi^e + \gamma(y - \bar{y}) + s. \tag{5}$$

To complete our AS–AD model with fixed exchange rates, we now only need to specify the formation of inflation expectations.

Expectations formation under credibly fixed exchange rates

As a starting point for doing so, let us return to the idea presented at the end of Chapter 21 that some people are backward-looking whereas others are forward-looking. Specifically, suppose the population is divided into two groups. The first group (Group 1) has purely backward-looking expectations and simply believes that this period's inflation rate will equal the rate of inflation observed in the previous period. This is, of course, the familiar hypothesis of static expectations.

The second group of people (Group 2) is more sophisticated. This group realizes that under fixed exchange rates domestic inflation cannot systematically exceed foreign inflation for a long period of time, since this would undermine the international competitiveness of domestic producers and lead to an ever-increasing trade deficit. An ever-growing trade deficit would ultimately force the domestic authorities to bring down domestic inflation in order to protect the country's foreign exchange reserves. Similarly, Group 2 people also understand that if domestic inflation were systematically lower than foreign inflation, the persistent fall in the relative price of domestic goods would lead to ever-increasing demand for domestic output which would ultimately pull up the domestic inflation rate. In short,

Group 2 agents realize that on average the domestic inflation rate will have to equal the foreign inflation rate, but they do not have enough information to predict the short-run fluctuations of the inflation rate. Instead, they assume that the domestic inflation rate for the current and next period will be at its average level given by the foreign inflation rate. We may say that these individuals have 'weakly rational' expectations, since they hold correct beliefs about the long-run equilibrium inflation rate but cannot perfectly predict the short-run inflation rate.

If Group 2 constitutes a fraction φ of the total population, these assumptions imply that the average expected inflation rate will be:

$$\pi^e = \varphi \pi^f + (1 - \varphi)\pi_{-1}, \qquad 0 \leq \varphi \leq 1. \tag{6}$$

In Exercise 6 we ask you to study the general case where $0 < \varphi < 1$. However, in the following we will consider the special case where all agents have weakly rational expectations, $\varphi = 1$, so that $\pi^e = \pi^e_{+1} = \pi^f$, where foreign inflation is assumed to be constant at the level π^f. We will concentrate on this case because it greatly simplifies the graphical exposition of our AS–AD model and allows us to focus on the role of real exchange rate dynamics in the adjustment to long-run macroeconomic equilibrium.

The assumption that $\pi^e = \pi^e_{+1} = \pi^f$ may be seen as a compromise between the case of purely backward-looking expectations and the strong postulate of strictly rational, forward-looking expectations. Our hypothesis on expectations formation is a simple way of formalizing the idea that, under credibly fixed exchange rates, the authorities have implicitly adopted an inflation target equal to the foreign inflation rate, and this inflation target serves as an anchor for domestic inflation expectations.

The complete AS–AD model with fixed exchange rates

Inserting $\pi^e = \pi^e_{+1} = \pi^f$ into (4) and (5), isolating π on the left-hand side of (4), and remembering that $r^f = i^f - \pi^f$ is the foreign real interest rate, we may now state our complete model of the open economy with fixed exchange rates as follows:

AD: $\qquad \pi = e^r_{-1} + \pi^f - \left(\dfrac{1}{\beta_1}\right)(y - \bar{y} - z),$

$$z \equiv -\beta_2(r^f - \bar{r}^f) + \beta_3(g - \bar{g}) + \beta_4(y^f - \bar{y}^f) + \beta_5(\ln \varepsilon - \ln \bar{\varepsilon}), \tag{7}$$

SRAS: $\qquad \pi = \pi^f + \gamma(y - \bar{y}) + s,$ $\qquad\qquad\qquad\qquad\qquad\qquad$ (8)

Real exchange rate: $\qquad e^r = e^r_{-1} + \pi^f - \pi.$ $\qquad\qquad\qquad\qquad\qquad$ (9)

Equation (7) is a restatement of the aggregate demand curve. Since $\beta_1 > 0$, we see that a higher domestic inflation rate will, *ceteris paribus*, be associated with lower aggregate demand for domestic output. In the closed economy the negative impact of inflation on demand stems from the fact that higher inflation induces the central bank to raise the real interest rate. In the open economy with fixed exchange rates this mechanism is suppressed, because the domestic interest rate is tied to the foreign interest rate via perfect capital mobility. Instead, the reason for the negative slope of the AD curve (7) is that higher domestic inflation erodes the international competitiveness of domestic producers by reducing the real exchange rate. Thus, a rise in π raises the relative price of domestic goods, thereby reducing net exports.

The variable z in (7) captures so-called real shocks to aggregate demand. In the open economy, these shocks include changes in foreign real output, y^f, and in the foreign real interest rate, r^f, as well as changes in domestic real government spending, g, and in domestic private sector confidence, ε. A change in any of these variables will cause a shift in the aggregate demand curve. In addition, (7) shows that the domestic economy may be exposed to a so-called nominal shock in the form of a change in the foreign inflation rate, π^f. Such a shock will also shift the AD curve. In addition, a foreign inflation shock will shift the short-run aggregate supply curve (8) by changing the expected rate of domestic inflation.

From short-run to long-run equilibrium

As the economy enters the current period, last period's real exchange rate e^r_{-1} is a predetermined constant. The current rates of output and inflation, y and π, are then determined simultaneously by the AD curve (7) and the SRAS curve (8), given z and π^f and the supply shock variable s. The current level of inflation in turn determines the current real exchange rate via (9). If $\pi^f \neq \pi$ it follows that $e^r \neq e^r_{-1}$, and the economy will then enter the next period with a new predetermined real exchange rate. According to (7) this means that the position of the AD curve will shift from the current period to the next one. This will generate new short-run values of output and inflation during the next period which in turn will change the level of the real exchange rate, and so on.

Figure 24.3 illustrates this dynamic adjustment process. The bracket attached to each AD curve in the figure indicates the previous period's real exchange rate which determines the position of the AD curve for the current period, according to Eq. (7). In period 1 the AD curve has the low position AD_1 determined by the real exchange rate in period 0, e^r_0. The weakness of aggregate demand in period 1 means that the economy is in recession, with low levels of output and inflation (y_1 and π_1). But this is only a short-run equilibrium: since domestic inflation is lower than foreign inflation, the real exchange rate increases during period 1 so that $e^r_1 = e^r_0 + \pi^f - \pi_1 > e^r_0$. Thus the international competitiveness of domestic producers improves by the amount $\pi^f - \pi_1$ during period 1, and according to (7) and (9) the AD curve shifts upwards by a corresponding distance as the economy moves from period 1 to period 2. As a result, domestic output and inflation increase to the levels y_2 and π_2 in period 2.

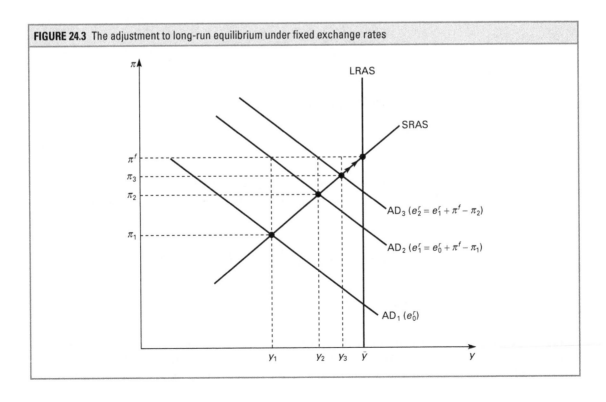

FIGURE 24.3 The adjustment to long-run equilibrium under fixed exchange rates

However, since domestic inflation is still lower than foreign inflation in period 2, there is a further gain in domestic competitiveness, so the AD curve shifts upwards by the distance $\pi^f - \pi_2$ between periods 2 and 3, causing a further rise in output and inflation in period 3, and so on. In this way the gradual improvements in domestic competitiveness will continue to pull the economy up along the short-run aggregate supply curve until domestic output reaches its trend level, $\bar{y}$. At that point domestic inflation catches up with foreign inflation so that no further changes in the real exchange rate will take place, that is, the economy will be in long-run equilibrium. Provided the supply shock variable s is zero, output will be at its trend level $\bar{y}$ in this long-run equilibrium, since it follows from (8) that $y = \bar{y}$ when $\pi = \pi^f$ and $s = 0$.

Notice the difference between the dynamic adjustment mechanism in the closed and in the open economy. In the closed economy a recession will lead to falling inflation which induces the central bank to cut the real interest rate so that aggregate demand recovers. Thus economic policy is crucial for the dynamic adjustment of the closed economy. In the open economy with fixed exchange rates a recession drives domestic inflation below foreign inflation, causing a gradual recovery of demand by lowering the relative price of domestic goods. This endogenous adjustment of the real exchange rate will pull the open economy towards long-run equilibrium even if economic policy remains passive.

Stability and speed of adjustment under fixed exchange rates

What determines the speed of adjustment to long-run equilibrium in the open economy with fixed exchange rates? To investigate this, we will now solve the model analytically. We start by defining the output gap, $\hat{y}$, and the inflation gap, $\hat{\pi}$, in the usual manner:

$$\hat{y}_t \equiv y_t - \bar{y}, \qquad \hat{\pi}_t \equiv \pi_t - \pi^f. \tag{10}$$

We may then rewrite the model consisting of (7), (8) and (9) as:

$$\hat{\pi}_t = e^r_{t-1} - \left(\frac{1}{\beta_1}\right)(\hat{y}_t - z_t), \tag{11}$$

$$\hat{\pi}_t = \gamma \hat{y}_t + s_t, \tag{12}$$

$$e^r_t = e^r_{t-1} - \hat{\pi}_t. \tag{13}$$

Now insert (12) into (11) and solve for e^r_{t-1} to get:

$$e^r_{t-1} = \left(\frac{1+\gamma\beta_1}{\beta_1}\right)\hat{y}_t + s_t - \left(\frac{1}{\beta_1}\right)z_t \tag{14}$$

Substituting (14) and the analogous expression for e^r_t into (13) along with the expression for $\hat{\pi}_t$ given in (12), we get the following first-order linear difference equation in the output gap:

$$\overbrace{\left(\frac{1+\gamma\beta_1}{\beta_1}\right)\hat{y}_{t+1}+s_{t+1}-\left(\frac{1}{\beta_1}\right)z_{t+1}}^{e^r_t} = \overbrace{\left(\frac{1+\gamma\beta_1}{\beta_1}\right)\hat{y}_t + s_t -\left(\frac{1}{\beta_1}\right)z_t}^{e^r_{t-1}} - \overbrace{(\gamma\hat{y}_t+s_t)}^{\hat{\pi}_t} \quad \Leftrightarrow$$

$$\hat{y}_{t+1} = \beta\hat{y}_t + \beta(z_{t+1}-z_t) - \beta_1\beta s_{t+1}, \qquad \beta \equiv \frac{1}{1+\gamma\beta_1}. \tag{15}$$

Equation (15) has the same structure as the difference equation for the output gap in the closed economy given in Eq. (19) in Chapter 18. Indeed, the only difference between the two equations is that the parameter α in the closed economy model is replaced by the parameter

β_1 in the open economy model. This reflects the difference in the macroeconomic adjustment mechanisms: in the closed economy, the parameter α incorporates the central bank's interest rate response to changes in the inflation gap and in the output gap as well as the interest elasticity of aggregate demand for goods. In the open economy, the parameter β_1 includes the price elasticities of export and import demand which determine the effect of a change in domestic inflation on the demand for domestic goods.

When $z_{t+1} = z_t = s_t = 0$, the solution to (15) is:

$$\hat{y}_t = \hat{y}_0 \beta^t, \qquad t = 0, 1, 2, \dots \tag{16}$$

We see from (15) that the parameter $\beta \equiv 1/(1 + \gamma\beta_1)$ is positive but less than 1. According to (16) this ensures that the economy will indeed converge towards a long-run equilibrium, provided the shock variables z and s stay constant over time. In other words, the open economy with fixed exchange rates is *stable*. The speed of convergence to long-run equilibrium will be higher, the smaller the value of β. Hence the adjustment to equilibrium will be faster the greater the value of β_1, that is, the larger the price elasticities in foreign trade. This is intuitive: if exports and imports are very sensitive to relative prices, a negative demand shock which drives domestic inflation below foreign inflation will lead to a large increase in net exports which will quickly pull the domestic economy out of recession. The magnitude of the price elasticities in foreign trade will depend on the structure of product markets. If competition in international markets is tough, the price elasticities will tend to be large, and the economy's adjustment to equilibrium will then be relatively fast.

Let us consider a numerical example to get a feel for the likely order of magnitude of the open economy's speed of adjustment. In the appendix to Chapter 23 we showed that

$$\beta_1 = \frac{(M_0/\bar{Y})(\eta_X + \eta_M - 1) - (\bar{D}/\bar{Y})\eta_D}{1 - \tilde{D}_Y}, \qquad \eta_D \equiv -\frac{\partial D}{\partial E^r}\frac{E^r}{D},$$

where η_D is the numerical elasticity of total private demand for goods with respect to the real exchange rate, $M_0/\bar{Y}$ is the ratio of imports to GDP, and $D/\bar{Y}$ is the ratio of total private demand to GDP (which in turn equals one minus the ratio of government consumption to GDP when foreign trade is balanced). Empirical studies indicate that if the length of the time period is one year or longer, the sum of the relative price elasticities in export and import demand are almost always greater than 1. For concreteness, suppose that

$$\eta_X + \eta_M = 3, \quad \eta_D = 0.3, \quad M_0/\bar{Y} = 0.3, \quad \bar{D}/\bar{Y} = 0.8, \quad \tilde{D}_Y = 0.5.$$

These parameter values are not implausible for a relatively open economy. The justification for the choice of the value of η_D is that if about 30 per cent of demand is directed towards imports, then a 1 per cent rise in the relative price of imported goods should erode the real purchasing power of domestic consumers by about 0.3 percentage points and lead to a similar percentage fall in demand. In Chapter 18 we saw that a realistic value of the Phillips curve parameter is $\gamma = 0.3$ when the length of the time period is one year. Using these parameter values, we find that:

$$\beta = \frac{1}{1 + \gamma\beta_1} \approx 0.82.$$

From the analysis in Chapter 18 we know that the number of time periods t^h which must elapse before half of the economy's adjustment to long-run equilibrium is completed is given by:

$$t^h = \frac{\ln 2}{\ln \beta} = -\frac{0.693}{\ln \beta}.$$

For $\beta = 0.82$ this implies that $t^h \approx 3.49$. In other words, given the parameter values assumed above, it will take about three and a half years before the economy has moved halfway back towards the long-run equilibrium after it has been disturbed by a shock.

MACROECONOMIC ADJUSTMENT UNDER FIXED EXCHANGE RATES

If exchange rates are credibly fixed, the expected domestic inflation rate is likely to equal the average foreign inflation rate. In that case the aggregate supply curve will not shift during the adjustment to long-run equilibrium. Instead, adjustment will take place via shifts in the aggregate demand curve. When the domestic economy is in recession (boom), the domestic inflation rate will be lower (higher) than the foreign inflation rate. Hence domestic competitiveness will gradually improve (deteriorate), and the AD will shift upwards (downwards) from one period to the next. In this way the economy will move up (down) along the SRAS curve until a long-run equilibrium is reached where output is at its natural rate and the domestic inflation rate equals the foreign inflation rate. For realistic parameter values, our AS–AD model suggests that it could take 3–4 years for the economy to complete half of the adjustment back to long-run equilibrium after the occurrence of a shock.

24.3 Fiscal policy

We will now use the AS–AD model developed above to study the effects of macroeconomic policy under fixed exchange rates. As we have already seen, when fixed exchange rates are coupled with high capital mobility, there is no role for an independent monetary policy. This leaves fiscal policy and discretionary changes in the exchange rate parity as the two major remaining instruments of macroeconomic stabilization policy. In Section 23.4 we shall consider the effects of exchange rate policy. The present section focuses on fiscal policy. We start by analysing the repercussions of a fiscal policy shock before moving on to consider the effects of a systematic countercyclical fiscal policy.

Unsystematic fiscal policy: a temporary fiscal shock

Figure 24.4 illustrates how an open economy with fixed exchange rates will react to a temporary fiscal expansion. In period 0 the economy is in long-run equilibrium at A_0 where output is at its trend level and domestic inflation equals foreign inflation. Suppose then that the government temporarily increases its spending in period 1, but cuts spending back to its original level from period 2 onwards. In period 1 when the government raises its spending so that z goes up, the AD curve shifts up from AD_0 to AD_1, and the economy moves to a new short-run equilibrium A_1 where domestic output and inflation is higher. In period 2 when the government cuts back its spending to its original level, one might think that the AD curve would simply fall back to its original position AD_0 so that long-run equilibrium would be restored from period 2 onwards. In fact, however, the AD curve for period 2 will fall to the position AD_2 *below* the original aggregate demand curve. The reason is that the higher rate of inflation in period 1 reduces the real exchange rate in that period (since $e_1^r = e_0^r + \pi^f - \pi_1$) so the economy enters period 2 with a weaker international competitiveness. In formal terms, the lagged real exchange rate, e_{-1}^r, in Eq. (7) falls by the amount $\Delta \pi_1 \equiv \pi_1 - \pi^f$ between period 1 and period 2, thereby pulling down the aggregate demand curve by a similar vertical distance. As a result, the economy falls into *recession* in period 2 when the temporary fiscal stimulus has vanished and has left the economy with an inflated cost and price level.

From period 2 onwards, we see from Fig. 24.4 that domestic inflation is below the foreign inflation rate. This generates a gradual improvement of domestic competitiveness which pulls domestic output and inflation back towards their long-run equilibrium levels through successive upward shifts in the AD curve.

FIGURE 24.4 Effects of a temporary fiscal expansion

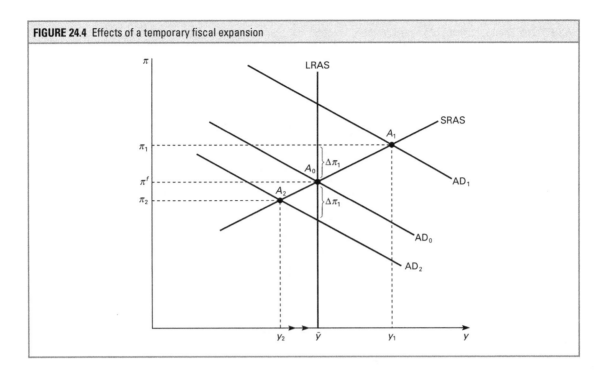

When the economy has moved all the way back to point A_0, all real variables (including the real exchange rate) are back at their original levels. The interesting point is that the temporary fiscal expansion takes the economy through a boom–bust cycle where a short-lived economic expansion is followed by a protracted period with below-normal activity. Of course, a similar adjustment pattern would occur if our demand shock variable z temporarily increased due to some event other than a change in fiscal policy.

Systematic fiscal policy

The analysis above focused on a fiscal policy *shock* rooted in exogenous political events. It is also of interest to study the effects of a *systematic* fiscal policy which follows a *fixed policy rule*. For example, suppose that fiscal policy is *countercyclical* so that public spending is raised above trend when output is below the natural rate, and vice versa. In that case we have:

$$g - \bar{g} = a(\bar{y} - y), \qquad a > 0, \tag{17}$$

where the policy parameter a indicates how strongly fiscal policy reacts to changes in the output gap. Inserting (17) into the definition of z given in (7), we obtain a new equation for the AD curve:

$$\pi = \pi^f + e_{-1}^r - \left(\frac{1 + \beta_3 a}{\beta_1}\right)(\bar{y} - y) + \frac{\hat{z}}{\beta_1},$$

$$\hat{z} \equiv -\beta_2(r^f - \bar{r}^f) + \beta_4(y^f - \bar{y}^f) + \beta_5(\ln\varepsilon - \ln\bar{\varepsilon}). \tag{18}$$

We see that a countercyclical fiscal policy involving a positive value of a makes the AD curve *steeper* compared to a passive policy where $a = 0$. The implications of this are illustrated in Figs 24.5 and 24.6 where we assume that the economy starts out in long-run equilibrium in period 0.

Figure 24.5 shows the short-run effects of a negative demand shock which lowers our variable $\hat{z}$ from zero to some negative amount in period 1, thereby shifting the AD curve (18)

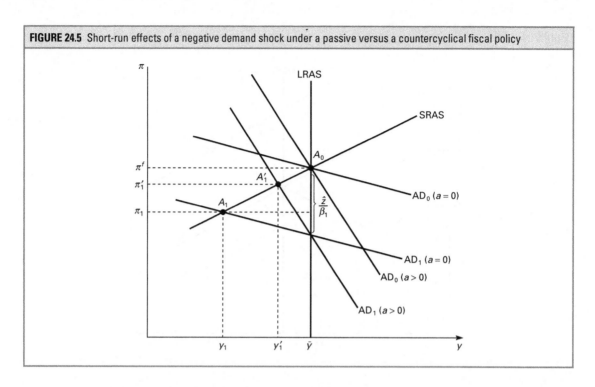

FIGURE 24.5 Short-run effects of a negative demand shock under a passive versus a countercyclical fiscal policy

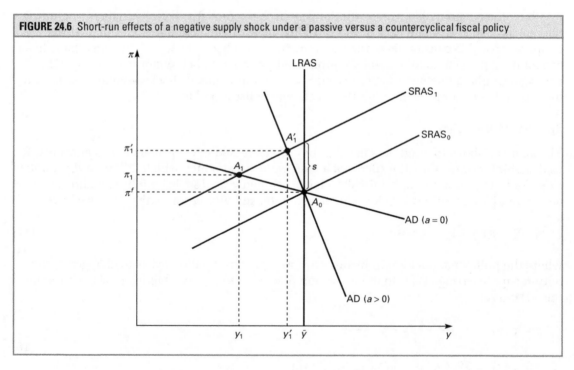

FIGURE 24.6 Short-run effects of a negative supply shock under a passive versus a countercyclical fiscal policy

downwards by the vertical distance $\hat{z}/\beta_1$. In the case of a passive fiscal policy ($a = 0$) the economy will then end up in the short-run equilibrium A_1 in period 1, but with an active countercyclical policy ($a > 0$) the new short-run equilibrium will be given by point A_1'. In this case we see that the steeper slope of the AD curve ensures a smaller drop in output as well as inflation. Of course, this is because the countercyclical policy implies an offsetting rise in public sector spending when the exogenous fall in aggregate demand reduces the level of output.

Figure 24.6 illustrates the case where the SRAS curve shifts upwards due to an unfavourable supply shock. Again we see that the steeper AD curve implied by a countercyclical fiscal policy will ensure a smaller drop in output, but at the same time it will imply a larger increase in domestic inflation. Thus policy makers face a trade-off between reducing the volatility of output and reducing the variance of inflation when the economy is exposed to supply shocks. This dilemma is well known from our analysis of the closed economy.

The countercyclical fiscal policy also involves another dilemma: although it reduces the short-run output fluctuations caused by exogenous shocks, it also reduces the economy's speed of adjustment back to long-run equilibrium. If we replace our previous AD curve (7) by (18) and follow the same procedure as the one used to derive Eq. (15), we find that the dynamics of the output gap under the countercyclical fiscal policy are given by:

$$\hat{y}_{t+1} = \hat{\beta}\hat{y}_t + \frac{\hat{z}_{t+1} - \hat{z}_t}{1 + \gamma\beta_1 + \beta_3 a} - \frac{\beta_1 s_{t+1}}{1 + \gamma\beta_1 + \beta_3 a}, \qquad \hat{\beta} \equiv \frac{1 + \beta_3 a}{1 + \gamma\beta_1 + \beta_3 a}. \tag{19}$$

As you can easily verify, the coefficient $\hat{\beta}$ on the lagged output gap is *larger* the greater the value of a, that is, the stronger fiscal policy reacts to the output gap. A more vigorous countercyclical policy will therefore slow down the convergence towards long-run equilibrium. The reason is that once output starts to move back towards the natural rate after having been pushed into recession by a negative shock, fiscal policy is automatically tightened under a countercyclical policy. Obviously this will reduce the speed at which aggregate demand and output are able to increase.

Yet a countercyclical fiscal policy will also reduce the initial displacement from long-run equilibrium when the economy is hit by a shock. With a quadratic social loss function of the form assumed in our analysis of stabilization policy in Part 4, governments are presumably willing to accept some reduction in the economy's speed of adjustment if they can thereby avoid large deviations of output from trend. This is because large deviations from the natural rate cause a disproportionately greater social loss than small deviations. But our analysis shows that governments cannot have it both ways: they cannot reduce the short-run impact of shocks through countercyclical policy and at the same time increase the economy's speed of adjustment.

In closing this discussion of fiscal policy, we should remind you of the warnings given in Chapter 20. The simple policy rule (17) assumes that fiscal policy makers can instantaneously react to the current output gap. This may not be very realistic, since the so-called inside lag in the fiscal policy process may sometimes be quite long due to the parliamentary procedures needed for approval of fiscal policy changes. Because of time lags, there is a danger that fiscal policy measures which were intended to be countercyclical end up being destabilizing because of inappropriate timing.

FISCAL POLICY UNDER FIXED EXCHANGE RATES

A positive but temporary fiscal shock will generate a boom–bust pattern of adjustment: the initial impact on economic activity will be positive, but the resulting rise in domestic inflation will reduce domestic competitiveness so that activity will fall below normal when the fiscal stimulus is withdrawn. As the recession drives domestic inflation below foreign inflation, competitiveness is gradually restored and domestic activity gradually returns to the natural rate. A systematic countercyclical fiscal policy reduces the fluctuations in the output and inflation gaps resulting from demand shocks. When the economy is hit by supply shocks, a countercyclical fiscal policy reduces the volatility of output, but at the same time it increases the volatility of inflation. A countercyclical fiscal policy rule also reduces the speed of adjustment to long-run equilibrium.

24.4 Exchange rate policy

So far we have analysed a so-called hard currency peg where the government does not use changes in the nominal exchange rate as an instrument of economic policy. We will now consider a 'softer' type of fixed exchange rate regime where the authorities may occasionally adjust the exchange rate. This is sometimes referred to as fixed but adjustable exchange rates. In practice, most countries with such a policy regime have tended to *devalue* their currencies from time to time in order to compensate for the impact of high domestic inflation on international competitiveness or to stimulate domestic economic activity.

When analysing the effects of exchange rate policy, it is crucial to distinguish between *anticipated* and *unanticipated* devaluations. When a devaluation is foreseen by the private sector, it will already have an anticipation effect on economic activity before it occurs, whereas an unanticipated devaluation will have no impact until it is implemented.

We will start by considering an unanticipated devaluation since this provides a useful benchmark when we move on to analyse the more complicated case of a devaluation which is (partly) anticipated.

An unanticipated devaluation

Suppose the economy starts out in a long-run equilibrium like the one illustrated by point A_0 in Fig. 24.7. Suppose further that the government finds that the unemployment rate corresponding to this equilibrium is too high and needs to be brought down quickly before the next election. As a 'quick fix', policy makers may then engineer a short-run improvement in international competitiveness through a devaluation of the domestic currency. Let us assume that the devaluation is undertaken at the start of period 1. Given that the devaluation is unanticipated, it will not affect the *expected* exchange rate for period 1. When the devaluation occurs, the government solemnly declares that this is a unique, one-time event which will never be repeated; from now on the government is fully committed to a solidly fixed exchange rate. Suppose the public actually believes the government. With these assumptions, the devaluation will never cause the expected rate of exchange rate depreciation $e_{+1}^e - e$ to deviate

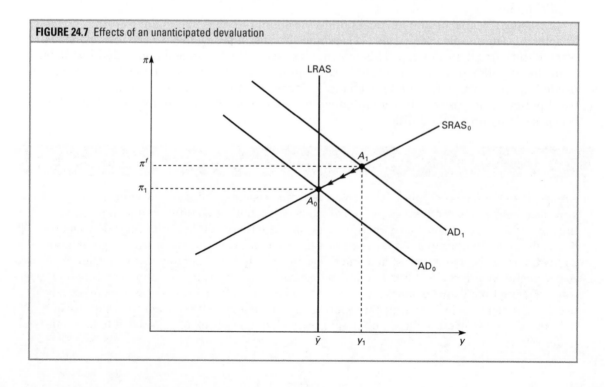

FIGURE 24.7 Effects of an unanticipated devaluation

from 0, so according to the uncovered interest parity condition (1) the domestic nominal interest rate will remain equal to the foreign interest rate both before and after the devaluation. Moreover, since the public expects no further devaluations in the future, the expected domestic inflation rate remains equal to the foreign rate of inflation, so there is no change in the domestic real interest rate and no upward shift in the aggregate supply curve.

Given these very optimistic assumptions (which will be relaxed later on), the only short-run effect of the devaluation is to stimulate aggregate demand by raising the real exchange rate. In period 1 which starts right after the devaluation occurs, the real exchange rate will be $e_1^r = e_0^r + \Delta e + \pi^f - \pi_1$, where $\Delta e \equiv \ln E_1 - \ln E_0 > 0$ is the percentage rate of devaluation. Setting $z = 0$, we may then use (7) to write the AD curve for period 1 as:

$$\pi_1 = e_0^r + \Delta e + \pi^f - \left(\frac{1}{\beta_1}\right)(y - \bar{y}), \tag{20}$$

which shows that the AD curve shifts upwards in period 1 when the devaluation occurs. The economy therefore moves to a new short-run equilibrium like point A_1 in Fig. 24.7, where domestic output has increased due to the gain in competitiveness generated by the devaluation. However, the new short-run equilibrium A_1 also implies that domestic inflation rises above the foreign inflation rate, so from period 2 the real exchange rate starts to fall over time as the excess domestic inflation gradually erodes the initial gain in competitiveness.[3] Hence the AD curve starts to shift down from period 2 onwards. This process will continue until domestic inflation has been brought down in line with foreign inflation, that is, until the economy has moved all the way down the SRAS curve to the initial long-run equilibrium A_0 in Fig. 24.7.

We see from this analysis that a devaluation will be entirely *neutral* in the long run. In other words, a devaluation will have no impact on the long-run equilibrium value of any real variable. To verify that a devaluation of the *nominal* exchange rate cannot influence the long-run equilibrium value of the *real* exchange rate, recall that in long-run equilibrium $e^r = e_{-1}^r$, $\pi = \pi^f$ and $\bar{y} = \gamma^{-1}s$, where s is a permanent supply shock. Inserting these conditions into (7) and rearranging, it follows that the long-run equilibrium value of the real exchange rate is given by:

$$e^r = \frac{\gamma^{-1}s - z}{\beta_1}, \tag{21}$$

which is seen to be independent of the nominal exchange rate. Thus, in the long run the real exchange rate is affected only by the *permanent* supply and demand shocks, s and z.

The preceding analysis shows that policy makers may *temporarily* drive output above its natural rate through an unanticipated devaluation. However, since exchange rate policy cannot permanently influence real output and employment, it may be more natural to use it as an instrument for *speeding up the economy's adjustment* to long-run equilibrium and then use structural policy to steer the natural rate of employment towards its desired level.

Figure 24.8 illustrates how an unanticipated devaluation may be used to shorten the length of a recession. In period 0 the economy is in deep recession in the short-run equilibrium A_0. In the absence of policy intervention, the economy would gradually pull itself out of the recession and move up the SRAS curve towards the long-run equilibrium $\bar{A}$, because an output level below the natural rate keeps the domestic inflation rate below the foreign inflation rate so that international competitiveness is gradually improving. However, this self-regulating market mechanism may work very slowly. Indeed, for plausible parameter values we have seen that it may take around three to four years for the economy to move just halfway towards long-run equilibrium. If the economy starts out very far below the natural

---

3. From period 2 onwards the evolution of the real exchange rate is once again given by (13).

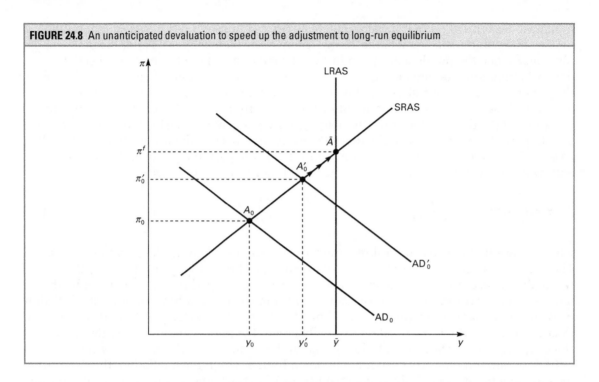

FIGURE 24.8 An unanticipated devaluation to speed up the adjustment to long-run equilibrium

rate of employment, such a long period of adjustment may be politically unacceptable. To speed up the adjustment process, policy makers may therefore decide to devalue the domestic currency in period 0. If the devaluation is unanticipated, the economy will then jump immediately from the short-run equilibrium A_0 to the new short-run equilibrium A_0'. In this way the policy makers save the time it would otherwise take to move from A_0 to A_0' through a gradual gain in competitiveness generated by a protracted period of high unemployment which keeps domestic inflation low. Still, the conclusion remains that the devaluation only brings a temporary stimulus to economic activity, since the economy will ultimately end up in the same long-run equilibrium $\bar{A}$ whether or not the currency is devalued.

An anticipated devaluation

Our analysis of an unanticipated devaluation serves as a useful theoretical benchmark, but in the real world devaluations rarely take the private sector by complete surprise. This is especially true in countries that have devalued on several previous occasions. In such countries the government's declared commitment to a 'fixed' exchange rate will typically lack credibility, and expectations of a future devaluation may easily arise whenever the state of the macroeconomy provides (or is believed to provide) a temptation for policy makers to devalue the currency. Thus, if the authorities devalue the domestic currency from time to time, households and firms will start to incorporate the risk of future devaluation into their forecasts of inflation and asset returns. A realistic analysis of exchange rate policy must include such effects on expectations.

To illustrate this point, we will now consider an economy which is in long-run equilibrium in period 0 and which undertakes a devaluation in period 2. We may assume that the decision to devalue is motivated by the policy makers' desire to bring about a quick expansion in a situation where the natural unemployment rate is unacceptably high. However, our qualitative results would still be valid if we assumed instead that the economy starts out in a short-run equilibrium where output is below trend.

Because the country considered has devalued previously on several occasions, we assume that fears of a future devaluation arise in the private sector in period 1 already. The economy therefore goes through three stages of reaction to the devaluation. The first stage may be termed 'the anticipation stage' where the emergence of devaluation expectations starts to affect the real economy even before the devaluation occurs. The second stage may be called 'the implementation stage' and includes the short-run effects of the devaluation occurring in the period when it is implemented, while the third and final 'adjustment stage' includes all the subsequent macroeconomic adjustments which take the economy back to the long-run equilibrium. We will consider each of these stages in turn.

Stage 1: The anticipation effects of a devaluation
The anticipation stage coincides with period 1 where expectations of a future devaluation have arisen but where the devaluation has not yet been implemented. The actual percentage rate of devaluation implemented in period 2 is Δe_2. We introduce a parameter ϕ to indicate the ratio between the rate of devaluation which is expected to occur in period 2 and the rate of devaluation that actually occurs. In period 1, the percentage devaluation which is expected to take place in period 2 ($e_2^e - e_1$) is therefore given by:

$$e_2^e - e_1 = \phi \Delta e_2, \qquad 0 \le \phi \le 1, \tag{22}$$

where e_2^e is the log of the nominal exchange rate expected to prevail in period 2. In the borderline case where the parameter ϕ is equal to 0 the devaluation is completely unanticipated, whereas $\phi = 1$ reflects the opposite borderline case where the devaluation is fully foreseen. In principle, it is of course possible that the private sector overestimates the rate of devaluation so that $\phi > 1$, but this case will not be considered here.

Since perfect capital mobility implies that the expected returns to domestic and foreign assets must be the same, it follows from (22) and the arbitrage condition (1) that the domestic nominal interest rate in period 1 will be:

$$i_1 = i^f + e_2^e - e_1 = i^f + \phi \Delta e_2. \tag{23}$$

Thus the domestic interest rate must equal the foreign interest rate i^f (assumed to be constant throughout our analysis) plus the expected exchange rate gain $\phi \Delta e_2$ on foreign assets.

A devaluation raises the price of imported goods, and we will assume that households and firms expect this to lead to a temporary increase in the domestic inflation rate. As we shall see, our analysis of the implementation stage will in fact justify such an expectation. Specifically, we assume that investors in period 1 expect the inflation rate for period 2 to be:

$$\pi_2^{eb} \equiv p_2^{eb} - p_1 = \pi^f + \theta_2 \phi \Delta e_2, \qquad 0 \le \theta_2 \le 1. \tag{24}$$

The superscript *eb* in (24) indicates that the expectation is formed *before* the magnitude of the devaluation is known with certainty. The parameter θ_2 measures the extent to which the anticipated devaluation in period 2 is expected to drive the domestic inflation rate for period 2 above the foreign inflation rate. In general, we assume that $\theta_2 < 1$ so that the devaluation is not expected to be fully reflected in the domestic inflation rate in the short run. Since the domestic real interest rate in period 1 depends on the expected rate of price increase between periods 1 and 2, it follows from (23) and (24) that:

$$r_1 \equiv i_1 - \pi_2^{eb} = r^f + \phi(1 - \theta_2)\Delta e_2, \qquad r^f \equiv i^f - \pi^f. \tag{25}$$

We see that when the anticipated devaluation is not expected to be fully and immediately passed through to the domestic inflation rate (that is, when $\theta_2 < 1$), *the domestic real interest rate will rise above the foreign real interest rate before the devaluation*, provided the devaluation is at least partly anticipated so that $\phi > 0$. To see how this will affect the macroeconomy, we note from Eq. (23) in the previous chapter that when there are no other shocks than those

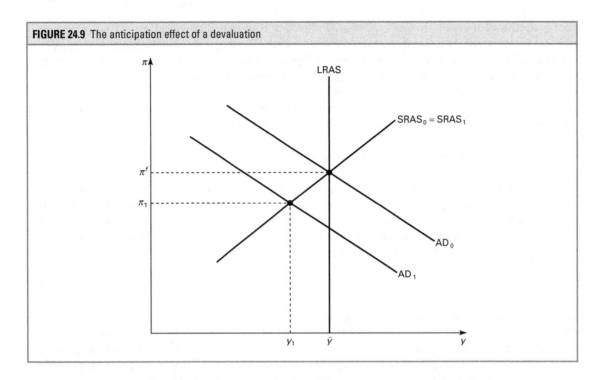

FIGURE 24.9 The anticipation effect of a devaluation

arising from exchange rate policy (i.e., when $g = \bar{g}$, $y^f = \bar{y}^f$, and $\varepsilon = \bar{\varepsilon}$), the equilibrium condition for the goods market in period 1 can be written as:

$$y_1 - \bar{y} = \beta_1 e_1^r - \beta_2 (r_1 - r^f), \qquad (26)$$

where we have chosen units such that the initial real exchange rate $\bar{e}^r = e_0^r = 0$, and where we have assumed that in the initial period 0 (before the fear of devaluation arises) the economy is in a long-run equilibrium with $\bar{r} = r^f$. From (9) we have $e_1^r = e_0^r + \pi^f - \pi_1 = \pi^f - \pi_1$, given $e_0^r = 0$. Inserting this along with (25) into (26) and rearranging, we get the following expression for the aggregate demand curve for period 1:

AD curve for period 1: $\pi_1 = \pi^f - (1/\beta_1)(y_1 - \bar{y}) - (\beta_2 \phi / \beta_1)(1 - \theta_2) \Delta e_2.$ (27)

In period 0 when there is no expectation of a future devaluation and the economy is in a long-run equilibrium with $e_{-1}^r = z = 0$, it follows from (7) that the equation for the AD curve is simply $\pi_0 = \pi^f - (1/\beta_1)(y_0 - \bar{y})$. Comparing this expression to (27), we see that *the aggregate demand curve will shift downwards in period 1* when expectations of a future devaluation emerge, because the fear of devaluation pushes the domestic real interest rate above the foreign real interest rate. The downward shift in the AD curve between periods 0 and 1 is illustrated in Fig. 24.9.

Since the devaluation does not occur until period 2, it does not affect the short-run aggregate supply curve for period 1, because the position of this curve depends only on the expected increase in prices from period 0 to period 1. The reason is that wages are reset each period, so wage setters do not have to worry about the expected inflationary impact of the devaluation already in period 1, since this effect can be accounted for when wages are reset at the start of period 2.[4] Hence we see from Fig. 24.9 that the downward shift in the AD

---

4. We assume that wages and prices for period 1 are set at the start of the period right before the expectations of a future devaluation emerge, so wage setters do not take into account that the anticipated devaluation will influence domestic inflation already in period 1 by affecting the position of the AD curve for that period.

curve will cause output in period 1 to fall to the level y_1, while inflation in period 1 will fall to π_1. In other words, when the private sector starts to expect a future devaluation, *the fear of devaluation will push the economy into recession* because it feeds into the domestic real interest rate.

Stage 2: The implementation effects of an anticipated devaluation
Suppose now that the domestic currency is actually devalued by the amount Δe_2 at the beginning of period 2, right before wages and prices for that period have to be set, and just before the investment decisions for period 2 are made.[5] Since workers and firms are thus able to form their expectations for period 2 after the magnitude of the devaluation has become known, the setting of wages and prices for period 2 will be based on an expected inflation rate equal to:

$$\pi_2^e \equiv p_2^e - p_1 = \pi^f + \theta_2 \Delta e_2. \tag{28}$$

In the absence of supply shocks ($s = 0$) the relationship between domestic inflation and output is given by the SRAS curve, $\pi_2 = \pi_2^e + \gamma(y_2 - \bar{y})$. Inserting (28) into this expression, we get the SRAS curve for period 2:

$$\pi_2 = \pi^f + \theta_2 \Delta e_2 + \gamma(y_2 - \bar{y}). \tag{29}$$

Compared to the SRAS curve for period 1, Eq. (29) contains the additional term $\theta_2 \Delta e_2$. This shows that *the short-run aggregate supply curve will shift upwards in the period when the devaluation occurs*, as illustrated in Fig. 24.10.

But what happens to the aggregate demand curve? The AD curve for period 2 is given by the general expression:

$$y_2 - \bar{y} = \beta_1 e_2^r - \beta_2 (r_2 - r^f). \tag{30}$$

Accounting for the effect of the devaluation, the real exchange rate for period 2 is:

$$e_2^r = e_1^r + \Delta e_2 + \pi^f - \pi_2. \tag{31}$$

We assume that the implementation of the devaluation in period 2 eliminates any fears of a further devaluation in the near future. When the exchange rate is expected to stay constant between periods 2 and 3, perfect capital mobility ensures that $i_2 = i^f$. If investors expect that the devaluation which occurred in period 2 will continue to have some impact on domestic inflation in period 3 so that $\pi_3^e = \pi^f + \theta_3 \Delta e_2$ (where θ_3 could be zero), the domestic real interest rate for period 2 will then be:

$$r_2 \equiv i_2 - \pi_3^e = i^f - \pi^f - \theta_3 \Delta e_2 = r^f - \theta_3 \Delta e_2, \qquad 0 \le \theta_3 \le 1. \tag{32}$$

Substituting (31) and (32) into (30), we obtain the AD curve for period 2:

$$\pi_2 = \pi^f + e_1^r + \Delta e_2 - (1/\beta_1)(y_2 - \bar{y}) + (\beta_2 \theta_3 / \beta_1)\Delta e_2. \tag{33}$$

Comparing (33) to the AD curve for period 1 given in (27), recalling that the AD curve for period 0 is $\pi_0 = \pi^f - (1/\beta_1)(y_0 - \bar{y})$, and noting that $e_1^r = e_0^r + \pi^f - \pi_1 = \pi^f - \pi_1 > 0$ (since domestic inflation fell below π^f in period 1), we see that *the devaluation will cause the AD*

---

5. Alternatively, we might assume that the devaluation occurs right after the decisions on wage and price setting and investment for period 2 have been made. This would slightly complicate our analysis but would not change our qualitative conclusions.

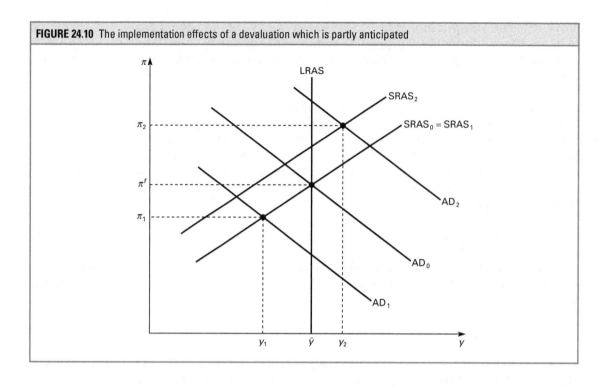

FIGURE 24.10 The implementation effects of a devaluation which is partly anticipated

curve in period 2 to shift upwards to a position above the AD curves for periods 0 and 1, as shown in Fig. 24.10. There are two reasons for this. First of all, the temporary drop in domestic inflation in period 1 as well as the devaluation in period 2 improve the international competitiveness of domestic producers, thereby inducing domestic and foreign consumers to substitute domestic for foreign goods. This expansionary effect is captured by the term $e_1^r + \Delta e_2$ in (33). Second, both the elimination of the fear of future devaluation and the expected inflationary effect of the devaluation cause the domestic real interest rate to fall. The vanishing fear of future devaluation is reflected in the fact that the AD curve for period 2 does not include the negative term $-(\beta_2 \phi / \beta_1)(1 - \theta_2)\Delta e_2$ which appeared in the AD curve for period 1, and the impact of higher expected domestic inflation on the real interest rate in period 2 is captured by the term $(\beta_2 \theta_3 / \beta_1)\Delta e_2$ in (33).

Although the SRAS curve also shifts upwards in period 2, the effect of the devaluation on the AD curve is sufficiently strong to ensure that output increases *above* the trend level in period 2, given the assumptions we have made. To prove this, you may solve (29) for $\pi^f - \pi_2$ and insert the resulting expression into (33) to get:

$$y_2 - \bar{y} = \left(\frac{\beta_1}{1 + \gamma \beta_1}\right) e_1^r + \left(\frac{\beta_1(1 - \theta_2) + \beta_2 \theta_3}{1 + \gamma \beta_1}\right)\Delta e_2. \tag{34}$$

Since e_1^r and Δe_2 are both positive, and since $0 \leq \theta_2, \theta_3 \leq 1$ by assumption, it follows from (34) that $y_2 - \bar{y} > 0$, as illustrated in Fig. 24.10.

The basic insight from this complex analysis is that *anticipated devaluations may generate a 'bust–boom' movement in the domestic economy*. Before the adjustment of the exchange rate, when fears of a future devaluation build up, the impact on the economy is likely to be contractionary, as the perceived risk of devaluation and the associated capital outflow drives up the domestic real interest rate. But when the devaluation has occurred, the economy will expand, as domestic competitiveness improves and the domestic real interest rate falls (assuming that the exchange rate adjustment does not foster expectations of further imminent devaluations).

Stage 3: The longer-term adjustment to an anticipated devaluation

While the devaluation will stimulate the economy in the period in which it occurs, its effects in the subsequent periods depend on the exact way in which the AD curve and the SRAS curve will shift over time. After the devaluation (in period 2), we see from Fig. 24.10 that the domestic inflation rate is higher than the foreign inflation rate. This will gradually erode the domestic economy's initial competitive gain from the devaluation. Hence the AD curve will gradually shift downward due to a falling real exchange rate e^r. *Ceteris paribus*, this will tend to push domestic output and inflation back towards their original levels, $\bar{y}$ and π^f. As domestic inflation falls due to falling aggregate demand, and as the devaluation becomes an event of the past, firms and households will most likely reduce their estimate of the effect of the devaluation on next period's domestic inflation rate. This fall in expected inflation will cause the SRAS curve to shift downwards, back towards its original position. At the same time the lower expected rate of inflation and the associated rise in the domestic real interest rate will push the AD curve further down. As a result of these shifts in the two curves, the domestic inflation rate will continue to fall back towards the foreign inflation rate, and the downward-shifting AD curve will help to pull output back towards the natural rate.

Thus, although the devaluation does indeed raise the real exchange rate e^r in the short run, it will be followed by periods in which the domestic inflation rate exceeds the foreign inflation rate, and this situation will continue until the real exchange rate is back at its original level. Depending on the specific dynamics of expected domestic inflation, one can even imagine that output and inflation may fall below their original levels for a while before the economy ends up in the original long-run equilibrium.

A final word of caution

Although plausible, the devaluation scenario described above is not the only possible one. The exact short-run effects of a devaluation will depend on the specific way in which private sector expectations are affected, and this in turn may depend very much on the specific historical and political context. In Exercise 4 you are invited to consider another possible devaluation scenario involving different effects on our expectations parameters ϕ and θ.

THE EFFECTS OF DEVALUATION

In the long run a devaluation is neutral towards 'real' economic variables. An unanticipated devaluation will temporarily stimulate economic activity by improving domestic competitiveness, but over time the gain in competitiveness is eliminated by the higher domestic inflation generated by higher activity. Moreover, a devaluation is hardly ever completely unanticipated. A (partly) anticipated devaluation will tend to depress domestic activity before it occurs by driving up the domestic real interest rate. When the devaluation is undertaken, the domestic interest rate falls and competitiveness temporarily improves, thereby stimulating domestic activity, but the gain in competitiveness is gradually eroded by higher domestic inflation, and in the long run the economy returns to the natural rate of output and employment.

Empirical illustration: the EMS crisis of 1992–93

The dramatic crisis in the European Monetary System (EMS) in 1992–93 provides some empirical support for our stylized analysis of an anticipated devaluation. Under the EMS system introduced in 1979, the participating EU countries had obliged themselves to keep their bilateral exchange rates within a band of ±2.5 per cent around the fixed exchange rate parities. Germany also participated in this arrangement, but the independent German central bank (Bundesbank) had indicated from the beginning that it would not compromise on its strong historical commitment to maintain a low German inflation rate.[6] As a consequence, German monetary policy continued to be directed mainly towards the goal of domestic price stability, so the EMS system effectively implied that the other EU countries pegged their currencies to the D-mark and hence had to subordinate their interest rate policy to the policy followed by the Bundesbank. For a while during the 1980s this arrangement worked quite well in the sense that the other EU countries were able to bring down their rates of inflation significantly by voluntarily subjecting themselves to the German monetary discipline (see Fig. 24.1b above). Indeed, around 1990 Finland, Norway and Sweden all decided to unilaterally peg their currencies to the ECU (a unit of account consisting of a basket of EU currencies) in an effort to import the low rate of inflation prevailing in the EU area.

However, the reunification of East and West Germany in late 1990 initiated a strong construction boom concentrated in the former DDR and led to massive debt-financed income transfers from the German federal government to the new *Länder* in the East. Not surprisingly, this fiscal expansion tended to create excess demand in the German economy and induced the Bundesbank to raise its leading interest rate in order to stop German inflation from rising. This tightening of German monetary policy forced the other member countries in the EMS system to raise *their* interest rates to defend their exchange rates against the D-mark even though their economies were not exposed to any expansionary forces like those felt by the reunifying Germany. As a result of having to mimic the tight German monetary policy, the rest of the EU therefore fell into a recession which deepened as the high German interest rates persisted.

During the summer of 1992, a growing number of international financial market participants began to doubt that this situation would remain politically acceptable to the non-German members of the EMS. Speculations arose that several EU countries would be tempted to devalue their currencies against the D-mark in order to escape from the recession. These speculations were strengthened when Danish voters rejected the Maastricht Treaty on European Monetary Union in June 1992, and when French voters only barely accepted the Treaty with a very narrow majority in September of the same year. Given this voter scepticism, would European politicians remain committed to the creation of a monetary union with completely fixed exchange rates, or would they fall back on their earlier practice of using devaluations as a temporary relief during economic recessions?

As doubts about the policy makers' commitment to fixed exchange rates were growing, the currencies of most EMS member countries came under violent speculative attacks in September 1992. Within a few days Finland, Italy and the UK had to drop out of the EMS system and allow their currencies to float, and the Spanish peseta had to be devalued. A further devaluation of the peseta and the Portuguese escudo followed in November, and Sweden and Norway had to move to a floating exchange rate in November and December 1992, respectively. The spring of 1993 saw yet another round of devaluations of pesetas and escudos as well as a devaluation of the Irish pound. In the summer of 1993 the crisis culminated in a massive attack on practically all the remaining currencies in the EMS, so on 2 August the EU finance ministers felt forced to widen the exchange rate band around the EMS parities to ±15 per cent, effectively giving up fixed exchange rates for the time being.

The diagrams in Fig. 24.11 show the evolution of short-term interest rates, nominal exchange rates against the D-mark and industrial production from month to month in a number of European countries in the period from the start of 1992 until the end of 1994.

We see that, before the devaluations/switches to floating exchange rates, all countries had to raise their interest rates sharply in reaction to mounting expectations of a future devaluation/depreciation of their currencies. The high interest rate policy prevented output from growing and even forced a decline in industrial production in several countries. When

---

6. In the aftermath of the two world wars of the twentieth century, Germany had experienced two episodes of devastating hyperinflation. Because of this traumatic experience, German voters and policy makers have given high priority to the goal of price stability in the postwar period.

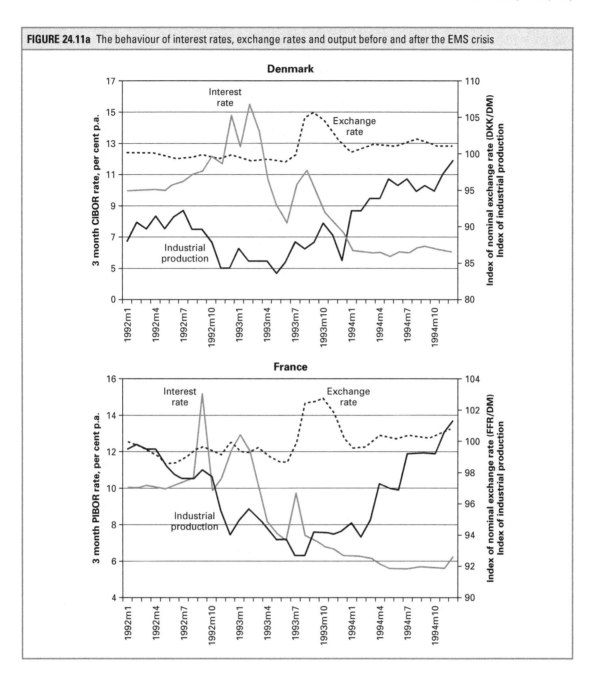

FIGURE 24.11a The behaviour of interest rates, exchange rates and output before and after the EMS crisis

the previous exchange rate parities were abandoned and the currencies were allowed to fall, interest rates could be lowered, and output started to increase in all countries. This accords with our graphical analysis of an anticipated devaluation in Fig. 24.10.

The vulnerability of a fixed exchange rate regime

The EMS crisis in 1992–93 illustrates that a fixed exchange rate regime coupled with free capital mobility is vulnerable to speculative attacks. When financial investors believe that some currency X may soon be devalued, they have an incentive to borrow a large amount in this currency, exchange it into some other currency and convert the funds back into currency X at a later time when a devaluation may have occurred. If currency X has actually been devalued in the meantime, this transaction will generate an exchange rate gain, and if no

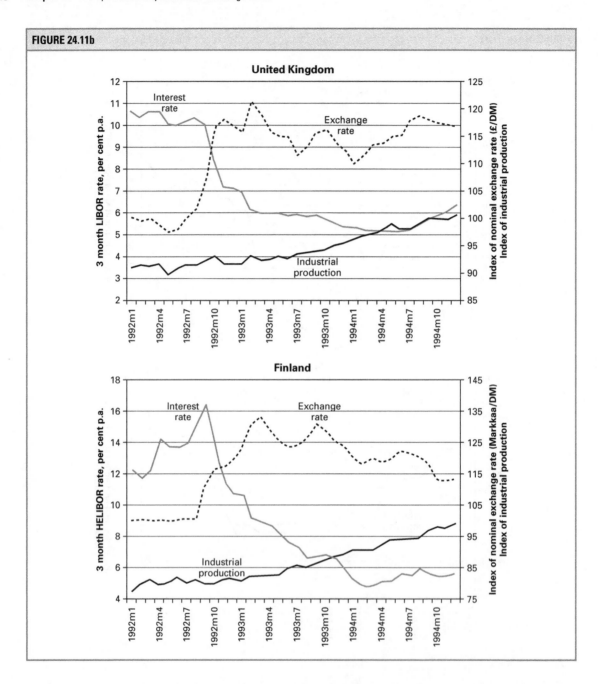

FIGURE 24.11b

devaluation occurs, it will only generate a small transaction cost. Thus speculation against a fixed exchange rate is virtually a one-way bet: you have a chance of scoring a large gain at the risk of losing very little.

An expectation that currency X could be devalued may therefore generate an extremely large additional supply of X, imposing a strong downward pressure on the exchange rate (an upward pressure on E). To be sure, the central bank issuing currency X may try to reduce the attractiveness of speculation by raising its interest rate and thereby increase the cost of borrowing in currency X. However, if the market believes that a large devaluation is just around the corner, it may take an extremely high interest rate to offset the expected gain from speculation against the currency. For example, on 16 September 1992 the Swedish central bank raised its overnight lending rate to 500 per cent in an attempt to ward off a speculative attack on the Swedish krona. Very few governments can live with the economic

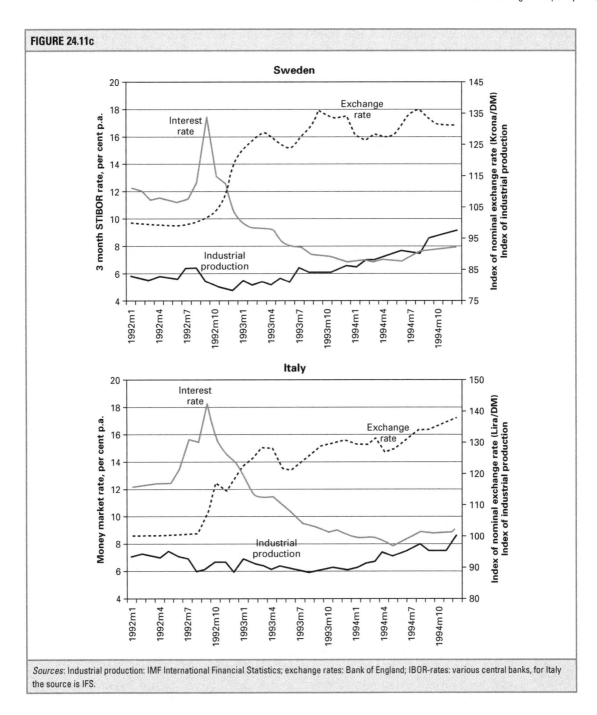

FIGURE 24.11c

Sweden

Italy

Sources: Industrial production: IMF International Financial Statistics; exchange rates: Bank of England; IBOR-rates: various central banks, for Italy the source is IFS.

and social consequences of such exorbitant interest rates for very long.[7] This is why a speculative attack may become *self-fulfilling* in the sense that it may force a government to let the currency fall even if policy makers would not have devalued if the attack had not occurred. The sustainability of a fixed exchange rate regime is therefore crucially dependent on the credibility of the government and the central bank. This credibility in turn depends

---

7. In September 1992 the Swedish central bank did, in fact, win the first battle against the speculators, but on 19 November of the same year a renewed speculative attack forced the bank to abandon its fixed exchange rate and allow a sharp depreciation of the krona.

on the ability of policy makers to avoid large macroeconomic imbalances which are seen by the market as providing a temptation to devalue the currency. The historical experience shows that a speculative attack can occur very suddenly once the markets start to doubt a government's political will to defend its exchange rate.

The vulnerability of a fixed exchange rate regime to speculative attacks is an important reason why many countries have moved towards flexible exchange rates in recent years when growing capital mobility has increased the scope for currency speculation. In the next chapter we shall study how the macroeconomy works under flexible exchange rates.

24.5 Summary

1. In an open economy with credibly fixed exchange rates and perfect capital mobility monetary policy is impotent in the sense that the domestic interest rate has to follow the foreign interest rate as a consequence of the condition for uncovered interest parity. Despite the loss of monetary autonomy a country may nevertheless choose a fixed exchange rate regime to reduce the uncertainty associated with exchange rate fluctuations. There is some evidence that elimination of exchange rate uncertainty stimulates foreign trade. By pegging the domestic currency to the currency of a country with a history of low inflation, domestic policy makers may also succeed in bringing down the expected and actual rate of domestic inflation.

2. If exchange rates are credibly fixed, private agents are likely to realize that the domestic inflation rate cannot systematically deviate from the foreign inflation rate for an extended period of time. Our AS–AD model for the open economy with fixed exchange rates therefore assumes that the expected domestic inflation rate is tied to the foreign inflation rate. On this assumption the economy's short-run aggregate supply curve will not shift during the adjustment to long-run macroeconomic equilibrium. Instead adjustment will take place through shifts in the aggregate demand curve as the international competitiveness of domestic producers changes over time whenever the domestic inflation rate deviates from the foreign inflation rate.

3. A temporary fiscal expansion will generate a boom–bust cycle: at first output expands, but when the fiscal stimulus disappears the economy falls into a recession because of the loss of international competitiveness incurred during the previous expansion. The economy then gradually recovers from the recession as international competitiveness is gradually restored through a low domestic rate of inflation.

4. A systematic countercyclical fiscal policy will reduce the short-run output fluctuations generated by exogenous shocks to aggregate demand and supply, but it will also reduce the economy's speed of adjustment towards long-run equilibrium, since a countercyclical fiscal policy rule implies an automatic tightening of fiscal policy as the economy recovers from a recession, and an automatic relaxation of fiscal policy when the economy starts to move back towards a normal activity level following a boom.

5. An unanticipated devaluation will temporarily stimulate domestic output, but in the long run the economy settles in an equilibrium where all real variables are unaffected by the devaluation. Hence a devaluation is neutral in the long run because the initial gain in international competitiveness is gradually lost again due to the higher domestic inflation rate following the devaluation. However, in a domestic recession, an unanticipated devaluation may speed up the adjustment to a normal activity level.

6. In practice, a devaluation is often (partly) anticipated. In that case it will generate a bust–boom cycle: before the devaluation the economy will be pushed into recession because the fear of a future devaluation generates a capital outflow which drives up the

domestic real interest rate. When the devaluation occurs, output expands, even though domestic inflation also rises, in part because of a higher expected rate of inflation. Over time, the higher inflation rate gradually eliminates the gain in domestic competitiveness stemming from the devaluation, and the economy returns to the original long-run equilibrium.

7. A fixed exchange rate regime is vulnerable to speculative attacks in a world of high capital mobility. The vulnerability stems from the fact that currency speculation is virtually without any risk under such a regime. The historical experience shows that a speculative attack can occur very suddenly once financial markets start to doubt a government's commitment to defend its fixed exchange rate.

24.6 Exercises

Exercise 1. Issues in the theory of the open economy with fixed exchange rates

1. Explain why monetary policy is impotent in an open economy with perfect capital mobility and (truly) fixed exchange rates. Discuss some reasons why a country might nevertheless want to adopt a fixed nominal exchange rate.

2. Explain the basic macroeconomic adjustment mechanism under fixed exchange rates and compare to the basic adjustment mechanism in the closed economy.

3. Explain why a devaluation is neutral in the long run.

4. Explain why a system of fixed but adjustable exchange rates may lead to anticipation effects in advance of a devaluation. Explain the nature of these anticipation effects and how they are likely to affect the economy.

5. Explain why a system of fixed exchange rates is vulnerable to speculative attacks. Explain briefly what is meant by a 'self-fulfilling' speculative attack.

Exercise 2. Temporary and permanent shocks in the open economy with fixed exchange rates

This exercise asks you to undertake a graphical analysis of the effects of temporary and permanent shocks, using the AS–AD model for the open economy with fixed exchange rates summarized in Eqs (7)–(9) in the text. In all scenarios you may assume that the economy starts out in long-run equilibrium in period 0.

1. Do a graphical analysis of the effects on output and domestic inflation of a *permanent fiscal expansion*. Illustrate and explain the short-run effects as well as the economy's adjustment over time. Explain the macroeconomic adjustment mechanism under fixed exchange rates and make sure that your diagram indicates precisely how much the AD curve shifts from one period to the next (indicate the position of the AD curves for periods 0, 1, 2 and 3, and use arrows to indicate the movement of the AD curve after period 3). What happens to the real exchange rate in the long run?

2. Illustrate the effects on output and domestic inflation of a *temporary negative demand shock* which lasts for one period. Explain the short-run effects as well as the economy's adjustment over time. (Hint: it may be useful if you go through the analysis in Fig. 24.4 once again.)

3. Illustrate the effects on output and domestic inflation of a *temporary positive supply shock* which lasts for one period. Explain the effects in the short run and over time. Do the effects of the shock go away as soon as the shock has died out?

4. Suppose now that *the positive supply shock is permanent*. Illustrate and explain the evolution of the economy from the initial long-run equilibrium to the new long-run equilibrium. What happens to the real exchange rate in the long run?

Exercise 3. The effects of a global recession

You are now asked to use the AS–AD model of the small open economy with fixed exchange rates to analyse the domestic effects of an international recession. In Questions 1–3 you may assume for simplicity that the global recession only affects foreign output, y^f, and the foreign inflation rate, π^f, but *not* the foreign real interest rate, r^f. In all questions you may also assume that the domestic economy starts out in long-run equilibrium in period 0.

1. Suppose that the foreign economy is hit by a negative *demand* shock which generates an international recession in period 1. The recession lasts for one period only (which may be thought of as a year), so all foreign macroeconomic variables return to their original values from period 2 onwards. Use the AS–AD diagram to illustrate how the domestic economy is affected over time by the temporary global recession. Explain the effects in period 1 as well as the subsequent adjustments. (Hint: start by explaining how y^f and π^f are affected by the global recession.)

2. Suppose alternatively that the international recession lasts for *two* periods so that y^f and π^f only return to their original values from period 3 onwards. Illustrate and explain the dynamic effects on the domestic economy in this scenario and compare with the scenario in Question 1 where the recession lasted only one period.

3. Now assume instead that the international recession is triggered by a negative *supply* shock which occurs in period 1. Suppose further that y^f and π^f return to their normal values from period 2 onwards. Illustrate and explain the effects of the global recession on the domestic economy in the short run and over time. Compare to the effects found in Question 1. (Hint: start by explaining how y^f and π^f are affected in period 1 when the international recession originates from a negative supply shock.)

4. Discuss briefly how the answers to Questions 1–3 are likely to be modified if we allow for the possibility that the international recession may affect the international real interest rate, r^f, and the confidence variable ε. (Hint: how are foreign monetary policy and domestic confidence likely to react to the recession?)

Exercise 4. The effects of a fully anticipated devaluation

In this exercise you are invited to study the effects of a devaluation in the borderline scenario where the devaluation which occurs in period 2 is fully and correctly anticipated already from period 1, and the private sector expects that the rate of domestic inflation in period 2 will rise by the same amount as the percentage rate of devaluation (and that domestic inflation will fall back to the initial level π^f from period 3 onwards).

1. Use the AS–AD diagram for the open economy to illustrate the effects of a fully anticipated devaluation. (Hint: what are the values of the parameters ϕ and θ in this scenario?) Will the devaluation have any effects on real economic variables? Will there be any difference between the short-run and the long-run effects of the devaluation? Discuss the realism of the assumptions underlying this scenario.

Exercise 5. The open economy with fixed exchange rates and rational expectations

The model in the main text of this chapter assumed a form of 'weakly' rational expectations where the expected domestic inflation rate is anchored by the foreign inflation rate, $\pi^e = \pi^f$, provided the exchange rate is credibly fixed. In this exercise we assume instead that expectations are *strictly rational* in the sense defined in Chapter 21. Thus the expected domestic inflation rate, $\pi^e_{t,t-1}$, is the expected inflation rate for period t predicted by our AS–AD model, given all the information available up until the end of period $t-1$. The model of the small open economy with fixed exchange rates consists of the following equations, where the stochastic demand and supply shock variables are white noise, and where the foreign inflation rate, π^f, is assumed to be constant:

Goods market equilibrium: $y_t - \bar{y} = \beta_1 e_t^r + z_t,$ $E[z_t] = 0,$ $E[z_t^2] = \sigma_z^2,$ (35)

SRAS: $\pi_t = \pi_{t,t-1}^e + \gamma(y_t - \bar{y}) + s_t,$ $E[s_t] = 0,$ $E[s_t^2] = \sigma_s^2,$ $E[z_t s_t] = 0.$ (36)

Real exchange rate: $e_t^r = e_{t-1}^r + \pi^f - \pi_t.$ (37)

1. Show that under rational expectations the solutions to the model (35)–(37) are given by:

$$y_t - \bar{y} = \frac{z_t - \beta_1 s_t}{1 + \gamma\beta_1},$$ (38)

$$\pi_t = \pi^f + e_{t-1}^r + \frac{s_t + \gamma z_t}{1 + \gamma\beta_1}.$$ (39)

(Hint: solve the model by the procedure outlined in Section 2 of Chapter 21.) Discuss whether this model has plausible persistence properties. (Hint: does the model display persistence in output?)

Now suppose instead that a fraction λ of the population has 'weakly' rational expectations, expecting the domestic inflation rate to equal the foreign inflation rate, while the remaining fraction has strictly rational expectations. The average expected inflation rate is then given as:

$$\pi_t^e = \lambda\pi^f + (1-\lambda)\pi_{t,t-1}^e,   0 < \lambda < 1.$$ (40)

and the SRAS curve becomes:

$$\pi_t = \pi_t^e + \gamma(y_t - \bar{y}) + s_t,$$ (41)

where π_t^e is given by (40). The agents with rational expectations form their expectations for period t knowing that the structure of the economy is given by the equations (35), (37), (40) and (41), and using all information available up until the end of period $t-1$.

2. Show that the rate of inflation expected by the 'strictly rational' part of the population is:

$$\pi_{t,t-1}^e = \pi^f + \left(\frac{\gamma\beta_1}{\lambda + \gamma\beta_1}\right)e_{t-1}^r.$$ (42)

3. Show by using (42) that the output gap may be written as:

$$y_t - \bar{y} = \left(\frac{\lambda\beta_1}{\lambda + \gamma\beta_1}\right)e_{t-1}^r + \frac{z_t - \beta_1 s_t}{1 + \gamma\beta_1}.$$ (43)

Use this result along with (37), (40), (41) and (42) to show that the output gap $\hat{y}_t \equiv y_t - \bar{y}$ evolves according to the difference equation:

$$\hat{y}_{t+1} = \left(\frac{\lambda}{\lambda + \gamma\beta_1}\right)\hat{y}_t + \left(\frac{1}{\lambda + \gamma\beta_1}\right)z_{t+1} - \left(\frac{\lambda}{\lambda + \gamma\beta_1}\right)z_t - \left(\frac{\beta_1}{1 + \gamma\beta_1}\right)s_{t+1}.$$ (44)

(Hints: use (40), (41) and (42) to find an expression for $\pi_t - \pi^f$. Use this expression along with (43) to rewrite (37) in terms of $\hat{y}_{t+1}, \hat{y}_t$ and the shock variables z_{t+1}, z_t and s_{t+1}. Then collect terms to get (44).)

4. Does the model with $0 < \lambda < 1$ have more plausible persistence properties than the model with strictly rational expectations where $\lambda = 0$? How is the economy's speed of adjustment

to long-run equilibrium affected by a higher degree of rationality in expectations formation (a lower value of λ)? Try to give an economic explanation for your answer.

Exercise 6. Simulating an AS–AD model for an open economy with fixed exchange rates and a mixture of backward-looking and forward-looking expectations

This exercise invites you to undertake computer simulations with the following generalized version of our model of the small open economy with fixed exchange rates, where we apply the usual notation:

Goods market equilibrium: $\quad y_t - \bar{y} = \beta_1(e_{t-1}^r + \pi^f - \pi_t) - \beta_2(i^f - \pi_{t+1}^e - \bar{r}^f) + H\tilde{z}_t,$ (45)

SRAS: $\quad \pi_t = \pi_t^e + \gamma(y_t - \bar{y}) + s_t,$ (46)

Expectations: $\quad \pi_t^e = \varphi\pi^f + (1-\varphi)\pi_{t-1}, \quad 0 \le \varphi \le 1.$ (47)

Real exchange rate: $\quad e_t^r = e_{t-1}^r + \pi^f - \pi_t.$ (48)

Equation (47) gives the average expected domestic inflation rate, assuming that a fraction φ of the population has 'weakly rational' expectations which are anchored by the foreign inflation rate, π^f, whereas the remaining fraction of the population has static expectations, expecting that this year's inflation rate will correspond to the inflation rate observed last year, π_{t-1}. In the special case where $\varphi = 1$, we obtain the basic model analysed in the main text of this chapter.

1. Discuss briefly whether Eq. (47) is a plausible specification of expectations. (Hint: for this purpose you may want to go back to the last subsection of Section 21.3.)

2. Show by means of (45) and (47) that the equation for the aggregate demand curve is:

$$\pi_t = \pi^f + \left(\frac{\beta_1}{\tilde{\beta}_1}\right)e_{t-1}^r - \left(\frac{1}{\tilde{\beta}_1}\right)(y_t - \bar{y} - z_t),$$ (49)

$$\tilde{\beta}_1 \equiv \beta_1 - \beta_2(1-\varphi), \qquad z_t \equiv -\beta_2(r^f - \bar{r}^f) + \tilde{z}_t.$$

Before implementing the model on the computer, it is useful to reduce it to two difference equations in the output gap and the inflation gap. Defining $\hat{y}_t = y_t - \bar{y}$ and $\hat{\pi}_t = \pi_t - \pi^f$, the model consisting of (46)–(49) may be summarized as:

AD: $\quad \hat{\pi}_t = \left(\frac{\beta_1}{\tilde{\beta}_1}\right)e_{t-1}^r - \left(\frac{1}{\tilde{\beta}_1}\right)(\hat{y}_t - z_t),$ (50)

SRAS: $\quad \hat{\pi}_t = (1-\varphi)\hat{\pi}_{t-1} + \gamma\hat{y}_t + s_t,$ (51)

Real exchange rate: $\quad e_t^r = e_{t-1}^r - \hat{\pi}_t.$ (52)

From (50) and (52) it follows that:

$$\hat{\pi}_t - \hat{\pi}_{t-1} = \left(\frac{\beta_1}{\tilde{\beta}_1}\right)\overbrace{(-\hat{\pi}_{t-1})}^{=e_{t-1}^r - e_{t-2}^r} - \left(\frac{1}{\tilde{\beta}_1}\right)[\hat{y}_t - \hat{y}_{t-1} - (z_t - z_{t-1})],$$ (53)

while (51) implies that:

$$\hat{\pi}_t - \hat{\pi}_{t-1} = -\varphi\hat{\pi}_{t-1} + \gamma\hat{y}_t + s_t.$$ (54)

It also follows from (51) that

$$\hat{y}_t = \gamma^{-1}\hat{\pi}_t - \gamma^{-1}(1-\varphi)\hat{\pi}_{t-1} - \gamma^{-1}s_t. \tag{55}$$

3. Equate (53) and (54) to find an expression for $\hat{\pi}_t$ and substitute the resulting expression into (51) to show that the model may be reduced to the following second-order difference equation in the output gap:

$$\hat{y}_{t+2} - a_1\hat{y}_{t+1} + a_0\hat{y}_t = \beta(z_{t+2} - z_{t+1}) - \beta(1-\varphi)(z_{t+1} - z_t) - \tilde{\beta}_1\beta s_{t+2} + \beta(\tilde{\beta}_1 - \beta_1)s_{t+1},$$

$$\beta \equiv \frac{1}{1+\gamma\tilde{\beta}_1}, \qquad a_1 \equiv \beta[2-\varphi+\gamma(\tilde{\beta}_1 - \beta_1)], \qquad a_0 \equiv \beta(1-\varphi). \tag{56}$$

Furthermore, insert (55) into (53) and show that the model may alternatively be condensed to the following difference equation in the inflation gap:

$$\hat{\pi}_{t+2} - a_1\hat{\pi}_{t+1} + a_0\hat{\pi}_t = \gamma\beta(z_{t+2} - z_{t+1}) + \beta(s_{t+2} - s_{t+1}). \tag{57}$$

Verify that (56) collapses to Eq. (15) in the main text in the special case where $\varphi = 1$. (Hint: remember to use the definition of $\tilde{\beta}_1$.)

You are now asked to simulate the model (56) and (57) on the computer, say, using an Excel spreadsheet. Recall that:

$$\tilde{\beta}_1 \equiv \beta_1 - \beta_2(1-\varphi).$$

Using the definitions given in the appendix to Chapter 23, and assuming that trade is initially balanced and that the marginal and the average propensities to import are identical, one can show that:

$$\beta_1 = \frac{m(\eta_X + \eta_M - 1) - \eta_D(1-\tau)}{1 - D_y + m},$$

where $m \equiv M_0/\bar{Y}$ is the initial ratio of imports to GDP, η_X and η_M are the price elasticities of export and import demand, $\tau \equiv (\bar{Y} - \bar{D})/\bar{Y}$ is the net tax burden on the private sector, $\eta_D \equiv -(\partial D/\partial E')(E'/\bar{D})$ is the elasticity of private domestic demand with respect to the real exchange rate (reflecting the income effect of a change in the terms of trade), and D_Y is the private marginal propensity to spend.

Under the assumptions mentioned above, one can also show from the definition of β_2 in the appendix to Chapter 23 that

$$\beta_2 \equiv \frac{\eta(1-\tau)(1-m)}{1 - D_Y + m}, \qquad \eta \equiv -\frac{D_r}{(1-\tau)\bar{Y}},$$

where η is the change in private demand induced by a one percentage point change in the real interest rate, measured relative to private disposable income (we already encountered this parameter in Chapter 18). Given these specifications, your first sheet should allow you to choose the parameters γ, φ, m, η_X, η_M, τ, η, η_D and D_Y to calculate the auxiliary variables β_1, β_2, $\tilde{\beta}_1$ and β (from which your spreadsheet can calculate the coefficients a_1 and a_0 in (56)).

You should construct a deterministic as well as a stochastic version of the model. In the deterministic version you just feed an exogenous time sequence of the shock variables z_t and s_t into the model. In the stochastic version of the model, the shock variables are assumed to be given by the autoregressive processes

$$z_{t+1} = \delta z_t + x_{t+1}, \quad 0 \le \delta < 1, \quad x_t \sim N(0, \sigma_x^2), \quad x_t \text{ i.i.d.} \tag{58}$$

$$s_{t+1} = \omega s_t + c_{t+1}, \quad 0 \le \omega < 1, \quad c_t \sim N(0, \sigma_c^2), \quad c_t \text{ i.i.d.} \tag{59}$$

so your first sheet should also allow you to choose the autocorrelation coefficients δ and ω and the *standard deviations* σ_x and σ_c. We suggest that you simulate the model over 100 periods, assuming that the economy starts out in long-run equilibrium in the initial period 0 (so that all of the variables $\hat{y}$, $\hat{\pi}$, e^r, x, c, z and s are equal to zero in period 0 and period −1). From the web page for this book http://highered.mcgraw-hill.com/sites/0077104250/student_view0/index.html you can download an Excel spreadsheet with two different 100-period samples taken from the standardized normal distribution. Choose the first sample to represent the stochastic shock variable x_t, and the second sample to represent the shock variable c_t. To calibrate the magnitude of the shocks x_t and c_t, you must multiply the samples from the standardized normal distribution by the respective standard deviations σ_x and σ_c.

Apart from listing the parameters of the model, your first sheet should also list the standard deviations of output and inflation as well as the coefficient of correlation between output and inflation and the coefficients of autocorrelation for these variables (going back four periods) emerging from your simulations of the stochastic model version. It will also be useful to include diagrams illustrating the simulated values of the output gap, the inflation gap, and (using (52)) the real exchange rate.

For the simulation of the *deterministic* version of the model, we propose that you use the parameter values:

$$\varphi = 0.1, \quad \gamma = 0.2, \quad m = 0.3, \quad \eta_X = \eta_M = 1.5,$$
$$\tau = 0.2, \quad \eta = 0.5, \quad \eta_D = 0.3, \quad D_Y = 0.8.$$

4. Use the deterministic model version to simulate the dynamic effects of a *temporary negative demand shock*, where $z_1 = -1$ in period $t = 1$ and $z_t = 0$ for all $t \ge 2$. Illustrate the evolution of the output and inflation gaps in diagrams and comment on your results. Does the model embody a theory of business cycles? Discuss. (Hint: is the adjustment to long-run equilibrium monotonic or cyclical?)

5. Now use the deterministic model to simulate the dynamic effects of a *temporary negative supply shock*, where $s_1 = +1$ in period $t = 1$ and $s_t = 0$ for all $t \ge 2$. Illustrate the evolution of the output and inflation gaps in diagrams and comment on your results. Is the adjustment to long-run equilibrium monotonic or cyclical? Illustrate the importance of expectations formation for the economy's dynamic properties by varying the value of the parameter φ.

6. Simulate the stochastic version of the model, setting:

$$\varphi = \delta = \omega = 0.5, \quad \sigma_x = \sigma_c = 1,$$

while maintaining the other parameter values given above. From this starting point, try to adjust the values of φ, δ, ω, σ_x and σ_c so as to achieve a better match between the model-simulated standard deviations and coefficients of correlation and autocorrelation for output and inflation and the corresponding data for the Danish economy presented in Tables 13.2–13.4. For your information, the standard deviation of the cyclical component in the Danish inflation rate was 0.0074, according to the quarterly data underlying Tables 13.3 and 13.4. (When trying to reproduce the observed correlation between output and inflation, you should focus only on the *contemporaneous* coefficient of correlation. Moreover, note that our simplified model cannot be expected to reproduce the data with great accuracy.) Assuming that your parameter values are plausible, what are the implications of your analysis for the relative importance of demand shocks and supply shocks as drivers of the Danish business cycle?

The open economy with flexible exchange rates

25

As we have seen, a fixed exchange rate regime is vulnerable to speculative attacks in a world with high capital mobility. In recent years many governments have learned this lesson the hard way. We have already reported how the fixed exchange rate regime of the Europan Union (the European Monetary System) came under heavy attack in 1992–93. A few years later, a number of other countries which pegged their currencies to the US dollar were attacked by currency speculators. This happened to Mexico in 1994, to the East Asian countries in 1997, to Russia in 1998, to Brazil in 1999, and to Argentina in 2000–01, just to mention the most spectacular examples.

Countries have reacted in different ways to the growing vulnerability of fixed exchange rate regimes arising from the growing mobility of capital. Contrary to the prediction of many observers at the time, the EMS crisis in 1992–93 strengthened the resolve of European political leaders to move towards the ultimate fixed exchange rate regime by forming a monetary union where the use of a common currency rules out the possibility of currency speculation.

However, during the 1990s a minority of Western European countries as well as a large number of emerging market economies and developing countries reacted to the growing frequency of speculative attacks against fixed exchange rates by moving towards flexible exchange rates where currency speculation is much more risky because there is no fixed exchange rate parity against which to speculate. Thus these countries have followed the lead of big economies like the USA and Japan which have allowed their currencies to float right from the breakdown of the Bretton Woods system of fixed exchange rates in the early 1970s.

Against this background the present chapter studies the workings of an open economy with flexible exchange rates. We continue to focus on a small specialized economy, and in line with the previous chapter we assume perfect capital mobility, since significant capital controls are nowadays very rare among developed countries.

The first section of the chapter defines the characteristics of a flexible exchange rate regime and describes how a number of Western countries have designed their monetary policies under this regime. This part of the chapter also highlights the role of exchange rate expectations under flexible exchange rates. In the second section we adapt our AS–AD model to a regime with flexible exchange rates and identify the similarities and differences in the macroeconomic adjustment process under flexible and fixed exchange rates. The third section of the chapter then studies how an open economy with flexible exchange rates reacts to demand and supply shocks and compares these reactions to those occurring under fixed exchange rates.

25.1 Flexible exchange rates as an economic policy regime

Inflation targeting as a nominal anchor

A crucial characteristic of a flexible exchange rate regime is that it allows the domestic central bank to pursue its own monetary policy even if capital mobility is perfect. This follows from the condition for uncovered interest parity with which you are already familiar:

$$i = i^f + e^e_{+1} - e, \quad e \equiv \ln E, \quad e^e_{+1} \equiv \ln E^e_{+1}. \tag{1}$$

According to (1), the domestic central bank may set the domestic nominal interest rate, i, independently of the foreign nominal interest rate, i^f, provided the bank is willing to accept whatever magnitude of the expected percentage exchange rate depreciation, $e^e_{+1} - e$, which is necessary to make the holding of domestic and foreign interest-bearing assets equally attractive.

Since the expected change in the exchange rate depends on the current level of the (log of the) exchange rate e, we see from (1) that the domestic central bank can pursue a fully independent interest rate policy only if it is willing to leave the determination of the exchange rate completely to the forces of the market. Obviously this means that the exchange rate cannot serve as a nominal anchor, in contrast to a fixed exchange rate regime where pegging to the currency of a low-inflation country can help to keep the expected and actual domestic inflation rate low.

As an alternative way of providing a nominal anchor for inflation expectations, many countries with freely floating exchange rates have therefore adopted a monetary policy regime of *inflation targeting*. Under inflation targeting policy makers specify a target for the rate of inflation which is considered to be consistent with an acceptable degree of price stability. Monetary policy is then given the task of ensuring that the actual inflation rate stays close to the target. Typically the target inflation rate is quite low, say, 2 per cent per annum. Realizing that monetary policy cannot perfectly control the rate of inflation, inflation targeting countries also specify a 'tolerance band', that is, an acceptable range of fluctuation of the actual inflation rate around the target rate. Indeed, some countries only specify a target *range* for the inflation rate without explicitly setting a particular target *rate*.

To make the policy goal of a low inflation rate as credible as possible, most inflation-targeting countries have delegated monetary policy to an independent central bank. In Chapter 22 we saw that such delegation may be a way of overcoming the credibility problem arising from the possible inflation bias in monetary policy. As you recall, an inflation bias may exist when policy makers with a short time horizon are tempted to stimulate output by creating surprise inflation.

More generally, the creation of an independent central bank may be a means of convincing the public that the goal of price stability will not be compromised by a government trying to manipulate monetary policy to its own short-term political advantage. However, to ensure that monetary policy makers can be held accountable for their actions by democratically elected politicians, many inflation-targeting countries require the central bank to justify its policy decisions at regular intervals in reports to the government and/or parliament and to the general public. Through such a reporting procedure to promote transparency in monetary policy making, it becomes easier to check whether the central bank adheres to the goal of price stability in a satisfactory manner. This may strengthen the credibility of the inflation target and at the same time make the delegation of monetary policy democratically acceptable.

Table 25.1 lists a number of countries which have practised explicit inflation targeting over the last one or two decades. We see that all of these countries have chosen inflation targets of 2–3 per cent, with a typical tolerance band of ±1 per cent. In recent years many disinflating countries in Eastern Europe and the developing world have also adopted inflation targeting. These countries are in the process of gradually reducing their inflation targets down to the level chosen by the 'best-practice' countries listed in the table.

TABLE 25.1 Inflation targets in different countries (for 2008)

	Target inflation rate (%)	Tolerance band (% points)	Actual average inflation rate 2003–07 (%)
Australia	2.5[a]	2–3	2.7
Canada	2.0[a]	1–3	2.2
Czech Republic	3.0[a]	2–4	2.1
New Zealand	2.0[a]	1–3	2.6
Norway	2.5	1.5–3.5	1.5
Poland	2.5	1.5–3.5	2.0
Sweden	2.0	1–3	1.3
United Kingdom	2.0	1–3	2.0

[a] Inflation target implied by midpoint of tolerance band. Only the tolerance band is publicly announced.

Source: Secretariat of the Danish Economic Councils.

Although the European Central Bank (ECB) has not officially adopted inflation targeting, it has announced that it aims to keep inflation in the euro area below but close to 2 per cent. The ECB bases its monetary policy on an analysis of a wide range of economic and financial variables, but the purpose of this analysis is to evaluate whether a change in the interest rate is needed to maintain a low and stable rate of inflation. In several important ways the ECB's monetary policy regime is therefore similar to a regime of inflation targeting.

In the USA, the official goal of the Federal Reserve System is to promote maximum employment, stable prices and moderate long-term interest rates. However, at least since the early 1980s the actions of the Fed have revealed that it attaches great weight to the maintenance of a low and stable rate of inflation, so although the USA is not officially an inflation targeting country, US monetary policy also bears some similarity to inflation targeting.

Monetary policy under inflation targeting

In theory one may distinguish between 'strict' and 'flexible' inflation targeting. Under strict inflation targeting, monetary policy aims exclusively at fulfilling the inflation target, whereas flexible inflation targeting implies that monetary policy also reacts to the evolution of real output and employment. In practice, inflation-targeting central banks have tended to adhere to a flexible regime. In Exercise 3 we will ask you to analyse such a regime of flexible inflation targeting, but the main text of this chapter will simplify by considering a regime of strict inflation targeting. As we shall see later, even strict inflation targeting may reduce the volatility of output compared to a regime with fixed exchange rates, provided business cycles are driven mainly by demand shocks.

Specifically, we will assume that the inflation-targeting domestic central bank sets the interest rate in accordance with the policy reaction function:

$$i = r^f + \pi^e_{+1} + h(\pi - \pi^*), \qquad h > 0, \tag{2}$$

where π^* is the target inflation rate, π is the actual current inflation rate, and π^e_{+1} is the expected rate of inflation between the current and the next period. As before, Eq. (2) assumes that the central bank can observe the public's expected inflation rate, say, through consumer and business surveys, or by observing the difference between the interest rates on indexed and non-indexed bonds. Through its control over the nominal interest rate, i, the central bank can therefore also control the *ex ante* real interest rate, $i - \pi_{+1}^e$, in the short run. However, the bank also recognizes that in long-run equilibrium the domestic *ex post* real interest rate must equal the foreign real interest rate, r^f, as we have shown in Chapter 23. Thus the policy rule (2) says that the central bank raises the domestic real interest rate above its equilibrium level when the inflation rate exceeds its target, and vice versa. Note that this is just a special version of the Taylor rule where the coefficient on the output gap has been set at zero.

In practice, aggregate demand and inflation only react to a change in the interest rate with a certain time lag. Inflation targeting central banks must therefore base their interest rate policy on a *forecast* for the inflation rate expected to prevail one or two years ahead, as we saw in Chapter 20, and as we will explain in more detail later in this chapter. However, since there is some persistence in the inflation rate, a rise in the current inflation rate, π, will typically increase the central bank's forecast of future inflation, thereby triggering a rise in the interest rate, as assumed in (2).

Specifying the inflation target

Table 25.1 shows that smaller Western inflation targeting economies have chosen roughly the same inflation target of 2.0–2.5 per cent. In recent years the euro area and the USA have also experienced a rate of inflation very close to this level. This suggests that Western inflation targeting economies tend to choose an inflation target which is equal to the average rate of inflation in the OECD area, either because they see the foreign inflation rate as an appropriate nominal anchor, or simply because there is a strong international consensus on what the appropriate level of inflation is. In other words, it seems realistic to assume that the target inflation rate is roughly equal to the foreign inflation rate π^f:

$$\pi^* = \pi^f. \tag{3}$$

Apart from the empirical justification, there is also a theoretical rationale for this choice of inflation target. As you recall from Chapter 23, a long-run equilibrium requires fulfilment of the condition for *relative purchasing power parity* to ensure constancy of the real exchange rate:

$$\Delta e \equiv e - e_{-1} = \pi - \pi^f. \tag{4}$$

In the long run an inflation-targeting country which manages to keep the domestic inflation rate equal to the foreign inflation rate will therefore also be able to maintain a stable nominal exchange rate, since $\pi = \pi^f$ implies $\Delta e = 0$ according to (4). The international experience suggests that although inflation-targeting countries do not pursue a specific target for the nominal exchange rate, and although over the medium term the exchange rate can move quite far away from its historical average, countries usually try to avoid policies which lead to a systematic depreciation or appreciation of their currencies over very long periods of time. Equation (3) combined with (4) is our way of modelling this apparent policy preference for long-run stability of the nominal exchange rate.

Inflation expectations under inflation targeting

Let us now consider the formation of inflation expectations under inflation targeting. From the monetary policy rule (2) it follows that the economy can only be in long-run equilibrium when the inflation rate equals its target rate, since the real interest rate, $i - \pi_{+1}^e$, will only attain its long-run equilibrium value, r^f, when $\pi = \pi^*$. In parallel to the previous chapter, we will assume that agents are 'weakly' rational in the sense that they can form a correct estimate of the long-run inflation rate even though they do not have enough information to predict the short-run fluctuations in inflation. Under inflation targeting, agents thus understand that on average the inflation rate has to equal the central bank's official inflation target. Using (3), we therefore assume that:

$$\pi_{+1}^e = \pi^e = \pi^* = \pi^f, \tag{5}$$

where the foreign inflation rate, π^f, is assumed to be constant. Equation (5) is the simplest way of formalizing our assumption that the central bank's inflation target has credibility. It is the natural analogue to the analysis in the previous chapter where our specification $\pi_{+1}^e = \pi^e = \pi^f$ reflected the assumption that the central bank's commitment to a fixed exchange rate was credible.[1]

Exchange rates and interest rates

Consider next the formation of exchange rate expectations. From (1) we see that these expectations are crucial for the link between interest rates and exchange rates. Whereas the central bank's official inflation target provides a natural anchor for inflation expectations, there is no similar policy-determined focal point for exchange rate expectations, since there is no official exchange rate target under freely floating exchange rates. Our theory of exchange rate expectations is therefore based on a different line of reasoning than the one underlying our simple theory of inflation expectations. Specifically, we will adopt a hypothesis of 'regressive' exchange rate expectations which has often been used in the literature on the open economy. This hypothesis postulates that the exchange rate is expected to rise if it is currently below its perceived normal level, and vice versa. If the expected exchange rate for the next period is e_{t+1}^e and the perceived 'normal' exchange rate is $\bar{e}_t$, the hypothesis of regressive expectations thus says that:

$$e_{t+1}^e - e_t = \theta(\bar{e}_t - e_t), \qquad \theta > 0. \tag{6}$$

In other words, agents believe that there is some normal or average level towards which the exchange rate tends to move over time.[2] The perceived normal exchange rate is likely to depend on the actual exchange rates observed in the past, with greater weight being attached to the more recent observations. As a rough approximation capturing this idea, we will assume that the 'normal' exchange rate is simply identified with last period's observed exchange rate:

$$\bar{e}_t = e_{t-1}. \tag{7}$$

We emphasize that none of the results derived in this chapter depend crucially on this strong simplification. In Exercise 1 we ask you to derive a very similar AS–AD model from an alternative theory where the perceived normal exchange rate is simply treated as exogenous. However, the link between interest rates and exchange rates implied by (7) does find some empirical support, as we shall see in a moment.

---

1. A more general assumption than (5) would be

    $\pi^e = \varphi\pi_{-1} + (1-\varphi)\pi^*, \quad 0 \leq \varphi \leq 1,$

    reflecting the idea from Chapter 24 that a fraction φ of the population has static expectations while the remaining fraction has weakly rational expectations. The main text of this chapter focuses on the limiting case where $\varphi = 0$ whereas Exercise 4 asks you to explore the more general case where $0 < \varphi < 1$.

2. We do not restrict the value of the parameter θ in (6) to be less than 1. If $\theta > 1$, agents expect that the exchange rate will tend to *overshoot* its normal level in the short run. As we will explain later in this chapter, exchange rates do in fact tend to overshoot their long-run equilibrium values in the short term. The regression results reported below are also consistent with the hypothesis that $\theta > 1$, since the estimated value of θ^{-1} in Eq. (10) is smaller than 1.

Inserting (7) into (6) and dropping the time subscript for the current period for convenience, we get:

$$e_{+1}^e - e = -\theta(e - e_{-1}), \tag{8}$$

which says that if the exchange rate was rising (falling) between the previous and the current period, it is expected to fall (rise) over the next period. From (8) and (1) it then follows that:

$$\Delta e \equiv e - e_{-1} = -\theta^{-1}(i - i^f), \tag{9}$$

which shows that when the domestic interest rate is raised above the foreign interest rate, the domestic currency will appreciate, and vice versa. The reason is that when i is raised above i^f, domestic assets tend to become more attractive than foreign assets, other things being equal. To maintain a capital market equilibrium where all assets are equally attractive, it is therefore necessary for the domestic currency to appreciate, since this will create an expectation that the domestic currency will *depreciate* over the next period (see (8)) so that the higher interest yield on domestic assets is offset by an expected exchange rate loss.

Equation (9) was derived from (1) which assumes that investors are risk neutral and that foreign and domestic bonds are perfect substitutes. But suppose that financial investors are risk averse and that foreign and domestic bonds are considered to have different risk characteristics because they are issued in different political jurisdictions using different currencies. In equilibrium the expected returns to domestic and foreign bonds must therefore differ to compensate for the different risk characteristics of the two assets. Let us call this difference the 'risk premium', and let us assume that it consists of a 'systematic' component, $\bar{v}$, plus a stochastic component, ε, which fluctuates around a zero mean value, reflecting random shifts in the market's evaluation of the riskiness of the two assets, or shifts in the 'appetite' for risk-taking. Using (8), the arbitrage condition (1) then modifies to:

$$i = i^f + e_{+1}^e - e + \bar{v} + \varepsilon \quad \Leftrightarrow \quad \Delta e = \theta^{-1}\bar{v} - \theta^{-1}(i - i^f) + \theta^{-1}\varepsilon, \qquad E[\varepsilon] = 0. \tag{10}$$

Note that the systematic component $\bar{v}$ in the risk premium can be either positive or negative. For example, if the risk characteristics of domestic bonds are seen as more attractive than those of foreign bonds – say, because historically foreign bond prices have been more volatile than the prices of domestic bonds – $\bar{v}$ will tend to be negative. Since the mean value of ε is assumed to be zero, (10) still predicts that on average the relationship between the interest rate differential $i - i^f$ and the percentage change in the exchange rate Δe should be negative, although in periods with large temporary increases (decreases) in the risk premium one may observe positive (negative) values of $i - i^f$ as well as Δe.

In Fig. 25.1 we have plotted monthly observations for the percentage depreciation of the bilateral exchange rate (Δe) against the corresponding bilateral short-term interest rate differential $i - i^f$ for a number of countries with floating exchange rates. According to (10) the observations for each pair of countries should be scattered around a downward-sloping straight line. As one would expect given the simplistic theory of expectations formation (7) which is embodied in (10), the negative relationship between $i - i^f$ and Δe observed in Fig. 25.1 is far from tight. A regression analysis nevertheless shows that the line of best fit through the observations does indeed have a negative slope which is statistically significant for all the countries considered.

Of course, it is possible that a more sophisticated theory of expectations formation could have given us a better fit, but the theory specified in (6) and (7) has the advantage of being very simple. Hence we shall stick to it, since its prediction of a negative relationship between the interest rate differential and the change in the exchange rate seems to be empirically correct on average. To keep the exposition as simple as possible, most of our analysis will be

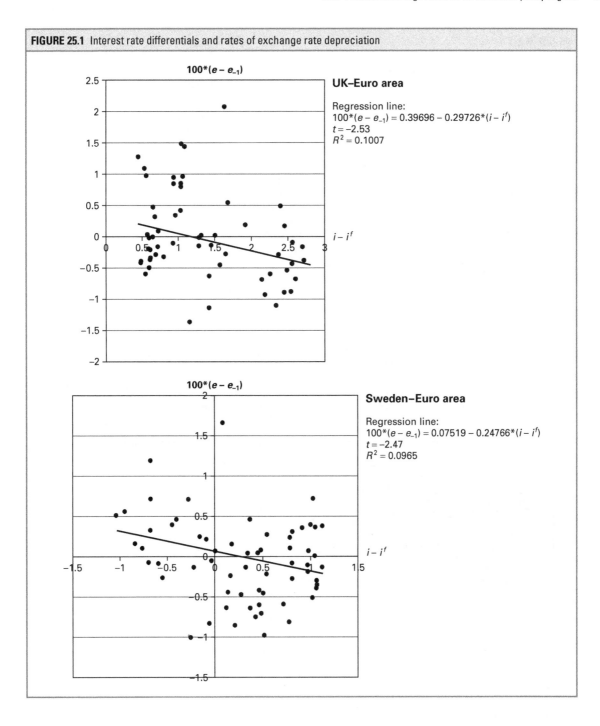

FIGURE 25.1 Interest rate differentials and rates of exchange rate depreciation

UK–Euro area

Regression line:
$100*(e - e_{-1}) = 0.39696 - 0.29726*(i - i^f)$
$t = -2.53$
$R^2 = 0.1007$

Sweden–Euro area

Regression line:
$100*(e - e_{-1}) = 0.07519 - 0.24766*(i - i^f)$
$t = -2.47$
$R^2 = 0.0965$

based on the deterministic equation (9), but later on we will also discuss some implications of the more general stochastic relationship (10).

'Dirty' floating

The specifications above relate to a regime of 'clean' floating where policy makers do not in any way try to influence the market-determined exchange rate. Yet historically many countries have practised so-called 'dirty' floating by intervening in the foreign exchange market in order to reduce the fluctuations in the exchange rate. The exchange rate can

FIGURE 25.1 *Continued*

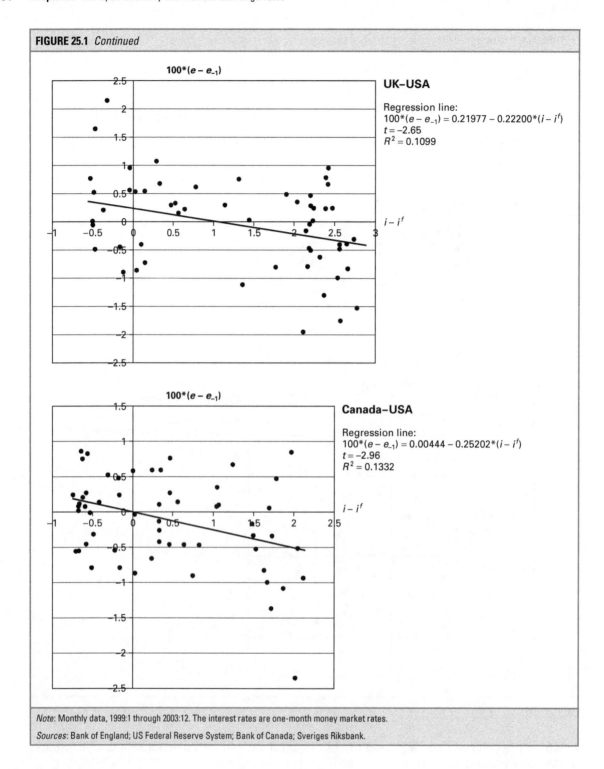

Note: Monthly data, 1999:1 through 2003:12. The interest rates are one-month money market rates.

Sources: Bank of England; US Federal Reserve System; Bank of Canada; Sveriges Riksbank.

usually be controlled over a few days by relying on 'sterilized' foreign exchange market interventions where the central bank buys or sells foreign exchange without changing the interest rate. The evidence shows, however, that to have a persistent effect on the exchange rate, foreign exchange interventions must be 'unsterilized', that is, they must involve a change in the interest rate which supports the movement in the exchange rate that the central bank is trying to achieve.

To model a policy regime where inflation targeting is supplemented by unsterilized foreign exchange intervention to smooth fluctuations in the exchange rate, we might modify the monetary policy rule (2) in the following way:

$$i - \pi_{+1}^e = r^f + h(\pi - \pi^\star) + \lambda(e - e_{-1}), \qquad h > 0, \qquad \lambda > 0. \tag{11}$$

According to (11) an observed depreciation of the exchange rate $(e > e_{-1})$ induces the central bank to raise the domestic interest rate. In this way the bank may generate a capital inflow which will increase the supply of foreign exchange and the demand for domestic currency, thereby moderating the depreciation. By analogy, when the bank observes a tendency for the domestic currency to appreciate $(e < e_{-1})$, it reduces the interest rate to induce a capital outflow which will increase the supply of domestic currency and the demand for foreign currency. Such a policy is sometimes described as 'leaning against the wind', because the central bank goes against the tendencies in the foreign exchange market.

In Exercise 2 we will ask you to show that the AS–AD model emerging under the policy of dirty floating specified in (11) is qualitatively similar to the model implied by the clean floating regime (2), although the quantitative properties of the model will be affected by a policy of leaning against the wind. In the rest of the chapter we will maintain the assumption of clean floating, partly because it slightly simplifies the exposition, and partly because many countries with flexible exchange rates have in fact moved towards 'cleaner' floating by significantly reducing the frequency of their foreign exchange market interventions in recent years.

Let us sum up what we have learned so far:

FLEXIBLE EXCHANGE RATES WITH INFLATION TARGETING   ❗

To provide a nominal anchor for inflation expectations, many countries with flexible exchange rates have adopted explicit inflation targets, typically around 2–2.5 per cent on an annual basis. The fact that so many countries have announced similar inflation targets suggests that they seek to keep domestic inflation close to the average foreign inflation rate to avoid a systematic depreciation or appreciation of their exchange rates over the longer run. Our AS–AD model of the open economy with flexible exchange rates therefore assumes that the expected inflation rate equals the target inflation rate which in turn equals the (average) foreign inflation rate.

THE LINK BETWEEN EXCHANGE RATES AND INTEREST RATES   ❗

The hypothesis of regressive exchange rate expectations says that the exchange rate is expected to rise when it is currently below its perceived normal level, and vice versa. The perceived normal exchange rate is likely to depend on the actual exchange rates observed in the recent past. When regressive exchange rate expectations interact with the condition for uncovered interest rate parity under flexible exchange rates, the domestic exchange rate will tend to appreciate when the domestic interest rate is above the foreign interest rate, and vice versa. There is some evidence to support this hypothesis.

25.2 Macroeconomic adjustment under flexible exchange rates

We are now ready to set up our version of the AS–AD model for the open economy with flexible exchange rates. After having done so, we will study the economy's adjustment to long-run equilibrium and compare the adjustment process to the one characterizing a fixed exchange rate regime. Through this comparison we will gain a deeper understanding of the special features of the two alternative exchange rate regimes.

The aggregate demand curve

As you recall from Eq. (26) of Chapter 23, the goods market equilibrium condition for the open economy may be written as:

$$y - \bar{y} = \beta_1(e^r_{-1} + \Delta e + \pi^f - \pi) - \beta_2(i^f - \pi^e_{+1} + e^e_{+1} - e - \bar{r}^f) + \tilde{z},$$

$$\tilde{z} \equiv \beta_3(g - \bar{g}) + \beta_4(y^f - \bar{y}^f) + \beta_5(\ln\varepsilon - \ln\bar{\varepsilon}), \tag{12}$$

where we have used the usual notation. To derive the AD curve under flexible exchange rates, we start by noting from (1) that $e^e_{+1} - e = i - i^f$. Inserting this along with (9) into (12), and using the fact that $i^f - \pi^e_{+1} = i^f - \pi^f = r^f$, we then get:

$$y - \bar{y} = \beta_1(\overbrace{e^r_{-1} - \theta^{-1}(i - i^f)}^{\text{exchange rate channel}} + \pi^f - \pi) - \beta_2(\overbrace{i - i^f}^{\text{interest rate channel}} + r^f - \bar{r}^f) + \tilde{z}. \tag{13}$$

Equation (13) illustrates the two channels through which monetary policy affects aggregate demand under flexible exchange rates. One channel is the familiar interest rate channel which also operates in the closed economy: when the interest rate rises, there is a direct negative effect on private investment and possibly also on private consumption. The strength of this effect depends on the parameter β_2 which captures the interest sensitivity of aggregate demand. The second channel in the monetary transmission mechanism is the exchange rate channel: when the domestic interest rate increases relative to the interest rate abroad, there is a tendency for the domestic currency to appreciate. This leads to a loss of international competitiveness which reduces net exports. The greater the value of the parameter β_1, that is, the higher the price elasticities of export and import demand, the stronger is this effect of monetary policy through the exchange rate channel. By increasing the response of the exchange rate to a rise in the domestic interest rate, a lower value of the parameter θ will also strengthen the impact of monetary policy on aggregate demand through the exchange rate channel.

The second step in the derivation of the AD curve is to note from (2), (3) and (5) that:

$$i = \overbrace{r^f + \pi^f}^{=i^f} + h(\pi - \pi^f) \implies i - i^f = h(\pi - \pi^f). \tag{14}$$

Substituting (14) into (13) and using the definition of $\tilde{z}$, we get an expression for *the AD curve under flexible exchange rates*:

$$y - \bar{y} = \beta_1 e^r_{-1} - \hat{\beta}_1(\pi - \pi^f) + z, \qquad \hat{\beta}_1 \equiv \beta_1 + h(\beta_2 + \theta^{-1}\beta_1),$$

$$z \equiv -\beta_2(r^f - \bar{r}^f) + \beta_3(g - \bar{g}) + \beta_4(y^f - \bar{y}^f) + \beta_5(\ln\varepsilon - \ln\bar{\varepsilon}). \tag{15}$$

For comparison, Eq. (7) in Chapter 24 gives the analogous expression for *the AD curve under fixed exchange rates*:

$$y - \bar{y} = \beta_1 e^r_{-1} - \beta_1(\pi - \pi^f) + z. \tag{16}$$

We see that the AD curve has the same structure under the two exchange rate regimes. Under both regimes the demand shock variable z includes the same disturbances, and a rise in the domestic inflation rate lowers aggregate demand. However, since $\hat{\beta}_1 > \beta_1$, we see from (15) and (16) that a rise in domestic inflation causes a *larger* fall in aggregate demand under flexible than under fixed exchange rates.

By taking a closer look at the expression for $\hat{\beta}_1$ in (15), we can identify the various effects generated by a rise in domestic inflation under a floating exchange rate. First, there is a direct effect as the rise in π reduces net exports by eroding the economy's international competitiveness. This direct effect – which is the *only* effect arising under *fixed* exchange rates – is reflected in the term β_1 in the expression for $\hat{\beta}_1$. However, under floating exchange rates a rise in π generates two additional effects stemming from the fact that a flexible exchange rate provides scope for an independent domestic monetary policy. As domestic inflation rises, the central bank reacts by raising the domestic interest rate. This creates additional downward pressure on aggregate demand, partly through the interest rate channel (reflected in the term $h\beta_2$ in the expression for $\hat{\beta}_1$), and partly through the exchange rate channel (captured by the term $h\theta^{-1}\beta_1$ in the definition of $\hat{\beta}_1$). This explains why the AD curve is *flatter* under flexible than under fixed exchange rates. As a consequence, the economy will respond differently to exogenous shocks under the two exchange rate regimes, as we shall see later on.

Nominal and real exchange rate dynamics

As was the case under fixed exchange rates, we see from (15) that the AD curve under flexible exchange rates includes the lagged value of the real exchange rate, e_{-1}^r. As long as the economy is out of long-run equilibrium, the dynamics of the real exchange rate will therefore cause the short-run AD curve to shift from one period to the next. Under flexible exchange rates, these shifts in the AD curve are driven by the identity:

$$e^r = e_{-1}^r + \Delta e + \pi^f - \pi. \tag{17}$$

Substituting (14) into (9), we find that the dynamics of the *nominal* exchange rate are given by the relationship:

$$\Delta e = -h\theta^{-1}(\pi - \pi^f), \tag{18}$$

which may be inserted into (17) to give the dynamics of the *real* exchange rate:

$$e^r = e_{-1}^r + \overbrace{\pi^f - \pi}^{\substack{\text{direct effect on} \\ \text{competitiveness}}} + \overbrace{h\theta^{-1}(\pi^f - \pi)}^{\substack{\text{monetary policy} \\ \text{effect}}} \tag{19}$$

Thus the real exchange rate will depreciate (that is, e^r will rise) whenever the foreign inflation rate exceeds the domestic inflation rate. Part of this real depreciation is due to the direct effect on competitiveness. The other part is due to a monetary policy effect: when domestic inflation falls below the inflation target π^f, the central bank cuts the domestic interest rate, inducing a depreciation of the nominal exchange rate.

The complete AS–AD model with flexible exchange rates

We may now summarize our complete AS–AD model of the open economy with flexible exchange rates. Following the previous chapter, we continue to use a specification of the aggregate supply side based on the hypothesis of relative wage resistance. Rearranging (15) and (19), we then end up with the following model:

$$\text{AD:} \qquad \pi = \pi^f + \left(\frac{\beta_1}{\hat{\beta}_1}\right)e_{-1}^r - \left(\frac{1}{\hat{\beta}_1}\right)(y - \bar{y} - z), \tag{20}$$

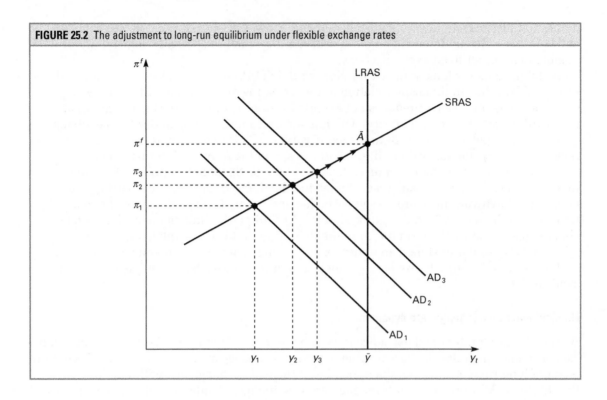

FIGURE 25.2 The adjustment to long-run equilibrium under flexible exchange rates

SRAS: $\pi = \pi^f + \gamma(y - \bar{y}) + s,$ (21)

Real exchange rate: $e^r = e^r_{-1} + (1 + h\theta^{-1})(\pi^f - \pi).$ (22)

The structure of this model is similar to the structure of the model with fixed exchange rates (you may want to compare with Eqs (7)–(9) in Chapter 24). At the start of each period, the previous period's real exchange rate e^r_{-1} is predetermined, so the current rates of output and inflation are determined by the intersection of the aggregate demand curve (20) and the short-run aggregate supply curve (21), where the position of the AD curve depends on the lagged real exchange rate, the foreign inflation rate π^f and the real demand shock variable z, while the position of the SRAS curve depends on π^f and on the supply shock variable s. The current level of inflation then determines the current real exchange rate through (22). If $\pi^f \neq \pi$ it follows that $e^r \neq e^r_{-1}$, and the economy will then enter the next period with a new predetermined real exchange rate, causing a shift in the position of the AD curve. This will generate new short-run values of output and inflation during the next period which in turn will change the level of the real exchange rate, and so on.

Figure 25.2 illustrates this adjustment process in a case where the economy starts out in recession at the output level y_1 and a corresponding domestic inflation rate π_1 below the foreign inflation rate. From (22) and (20) it then follows that the AD curve will shift upwards by the vertical distance $[\beta_1(1 + h\theta^{-1})/\hat{\beta}_1](\pi^f - \pi_1)$ between period 1 and period 2. The definition of $\hat{\beta}_1$ given in (15) implies $\beta_1(1 + h\theta^{-1})/\hat{\beta}_1 < 1$, so the upward shift in the AD curve will be *smaller* than the distance $\pi^f - \pi_1$. The new AD curve generates a new short-run equilibrium in period 2 where output is y_2 and inflation is π_2. Between period 2 and period 3, the AD curve shifts upwards again by the distance $[\beta_1(1 + h\theta^{-1})/\hat{\beta}_1](\pi^f - \pi_2) < \pi^f - \pi_2$, causing a further rise in output and inflation to y_3 and π_3, and so on, until the economy reaches the long-run equilibrium at point $\bar{A}$. Since $e^r = e^r_{-1}$ in long-run equilibrium, we see from (22) that the domestic inflation rate must equal the foreign inflation rate in the long run. As noted earlier, the central bank's inflation target will thus be realized, and the nominal as well as the real exchange rate will stay constant. According to (21) the condition $\pi^f = \pi$ also implies that output will equal its natural rate $y = \bar{y}$ in a long-run equilibrium without supply shocks $(s = 0)$.

The speed of adjustment under alternative exchange rate regimes

From the previous chapter you may recall that under fixed exchange rates the *vertical shift* in the AD curve from one period to the next equals the *full* distance $\pi^f - \pi$. Hence one might be tempted to conclude that the adjustment towards long-run equilibrium is faster under fixed than under flexible exchange rates. However, this would be wrong since we have also shown that the *slope* of the AD curve is *flatter* under flexible than under fixed exchange rates. It is easy to visualize from Fig. 25.2 that with a flatter AD curve, a given vertical shift in this curve will cause output and inflation to move closer towards their long-run equilibrium values. Thus we cannot say *a priori* whether the economy's speed of adjustment is faster under fixed than under flexible exchange rates.

Let us now identify the parameters which are crucial for the relative speed of adjustment under the two exchange rate regimes. For this purpose we introduce our familiar 'gap' variables:

$$\hat{y}_t \equiv y_t - \bar{y}, \qquad \hat{\pi}_t \equiv \pi_t - \pi^f, \tag{23}$$

and write the model (20)–(22) as:

$$\hat{\pi}_t = \left(\frac{\beta_1}{\hat{\beta}_1}\right)e^r_{t-1} - \left(\frac{1}{\hat{\beta}_1}\right)(\hat{y}_t - z_t), \tag{24}$$

$$\hat{\pi}_t = \gamma \hat{y}_t + s_t, \tag{25}$$

$$e^r_t = e^r_{t-1} - (1 + h\theta^{-1})\hat{\pi}_t. \tag{26}$$

Using (25) to eliminate $\hat{\pi}_t$ from (24) and solving for e^r_{t-1}, we get:

$$e^r_{t-1} = \left(\frac{1 + \gamma\hat{\beta}_1}{\beta_1}\right)\hat{y}_t + \frac{\hat{\beta}_1 s_t}{\beta_1} - \frac{z_t}{\beta_1}. \tag{27}$$

By substituting (27) and the corresponding expression for e^r_t into (26) along with the expression for $\hat{\pi}_t$ given in (25), you may verify that the evolution of the output gap under *flexible exchange rates* is given by the following difference equation:

$$\hat{y}_{t+1} = a\hat{y}_t + \frac{z_{t+1} - z_t}{1 + \gamma\hat{\beta}_1} - \frac{\hat{\beta}_1(s_{t+1} - s_t)}{1 + \gamma\hat{\beta}_1} - \frac{\beta_1(1 + h\theta^{-1})s_t}{1 + \gamma\hat{\beta}_1}, \tag{28}$$

$$a \equiv \frac{1 + \gamma h\beta_2}{1 + \gamma h\beta_2 + \gamma\beta_1(1 + h\theta^{-1})} = \frac{1 + \gamma h\beta_2}{1 + \gamma\hat{\beta}_1} < 1. \tag{29}$$

For $z_{t+1} = z_t = s_t = 0$ the solution to (28) is:

$$\hat{y}_t = \hat{y}_0 a^t, \qquad t = 0, 1, 2, \ldots \tag{30}$$

From (29) we see that the coefficient a is positive but smaller than 1. According to (30) this guarantees that the economy with flexible exchange rates is stable and converges monotonically on its long-run equilibrium, as illustrated in Fig. 25.2 above.

For comparison with (30), we recall from the previous chapter that the solution for the output gap under *fixed exchange rates* is:

$$\hat{y}_t = \hat{y}_0 \beta^t, \qquad \beta \equiv \frac{1}{1 + \gamma \beta_1} < 1. \tag{31}$$

The speed of adjustment to long-run equilibrium will be lower (higher) under fixed than under flexible exchange rates if the coefficient β in (31) is larger (smaller) than the coefficient a in (30). From the definitions of a, β and $\hat{\beta}_1$ we find that:

$$\beta - a = \frac{\gamma h \beta_1 (\theta^{-1} - \gamma \beta_2)}{(1 + \gamma \hat{\beta}_1)(1 + \gamma \beta_1)}. \tag{32}$$

The presence of the monetary policy parameter h in the numerator of (32) shows that the difference in the speed of adjustment under the two exchange rate regimes arises from the fact that only a flexible exchange rate leaves scope for an independent monetary policy. In general (32) does not allow us to say which exchange rate regime implies the fastest convergence on long-run equilibrium, thus confirming our earlier conclusion. The reason is that the macroeconomic adjustment process under flexible exchange rates includes one mechanism which makes for faster convergence, but another mechanism which makes for slower convergence than under fixed exchange rates. On the one hand, when domestic inflation falls below its steady-state level π^f under flexible exchange rates, the central bank reacts by cutting the domestic interest rate, thereby inducing a nominal exchange rate depreciation which helps to pull domestic inflation back up again by stimulating aggregate demand. This mechanism – which is reflected in the term θ^{-1} in the numerator of (32) – tends to speed up the adjustment to long-run equilibrium and is obviously absent under fixed exchange rates. On the other hand, as inflation rises back towards its steady state level, the central bank also reacts by gradually raising the domestic interest rate under flexible exchange rates, thereby *dampening* the increase in aggregate demand which is pulling the economy back towards long-run equilibrium. This mechanism clearly tends to *slow down* the adjustment process under flexible exchange rates and is captured by the term $-\gamma \beta_2$ in the numerator of (32).

The relative magnitude of the parameters θ and $\gamma \beta_2$ will determine whether the net effect of these two offsetting mechanisms is to speed up or to delay the convergence to long-run equilibrium under a flexible rate regime compared to a fixed exchange rate regime. To recap:

MACROECONOMIC ADJUSTMENT UNDER FLEXIBLE EXCHANGE RATES

A rise in domestic inflation causes a greater drop in aggregate demand under flexible than under fixed exchange rates, so the AD curve is flatter under flexible rates. Under both regimes higher inflation induces a fall in demand arising from reduced competitiveness, but under flexible exchange rates with inflation targeting the higher inflation also triggers a rise in the domestic interest rate. This has a negative direct effect on demand as well as a negative indirect effect from the resulting appreciation of the domestic currency. Over time the economy with flexible exchange rates adjusts towards long-run equilibrium via successive shifts in the AD curve, as the real exchange rate continues to adjust so long as domestic inflation deviates from foreign inflation. As a matter of theory one cannot say whether the speed of adjustment will be higher under flexible than under fixed exchange rates.

However, even though we cannot say for sure whether deviations of output and employment from their natural rates will last longer under fixed than under flexible exchange rates, theory *does* allow us to predict the relative magnitude of the short-run fluctuations in output and inflation occurring under the two exchange rate regimes when the economy is hit by shocks. This is the topic for the next section.

25.3 A floating exchange rate: shock absorber or an amplifier of shocks?

An important issue is whether a flexible exchange rate can help to absorb shocks to the economy so that short-run fluctuations in output and inflation are reduced, or whether the response of a floating exchange rate will actually tend to amplify the effects of shocks on output and inflation? We will now use our AS–AD model of the open economy to analyse this question.

The short-run effects of aggregate supply shocks

We start by considering the short-run effects of aggregate *supply shocks* under alternative exchange rate regimes. In the previous chapter we saw that the numerical slope of the aggregate demand curve is $1/\beta_1$ under fixed exchange rates, while Eq. (20) above shows that the numerical slope of the AD curve is $1/\hat{\beta}_1$ under flexible exchange rates. Since $\hat{\beta}_1 > \beta_1$, it follows that the AD curve is *flatter* under flexible than under fixed exchange rates. The reason is that under flexible exchange rates a fall in the rate of domestic inflation will not only stimulate aggregate demand by the direct impact on competitiveness; it will also induce the central bank to lower the interest rate, thereby boosting investment and generating a depreciation which further strengthens international competitiveness.

In Fig. 25.3 the curves 'AD(fix)' and 'AD(flex)' represent the AD curves under fixed and under flexible exchange rates, respectively. Suppose now that the economy is hit by a negative supply shock which shifts the SRAS curve upwards. As illustrated in the figure, this will have a larger negative short-run effect on output and a smaller positive impact on inflation under flexible than under fixed exchange rates.

The explanation for the different effects of supply shocks under the two exchange rate regimes is that whereas the interest rate stays constant under fixed exchange rates, under

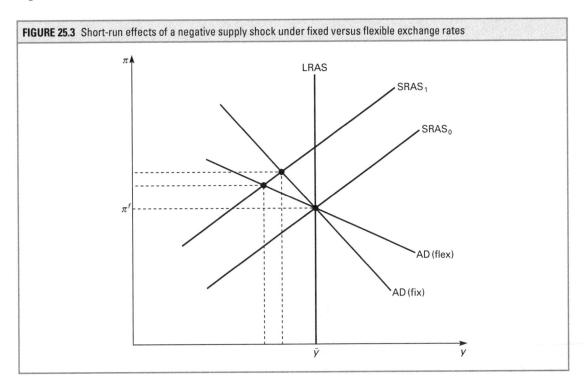

FIGURE 25.3 Short-run effects of a negative supply shock under fixed versus flexible exchange rates

flexible exchange rates the inflation targeting domestic central bank responds to higher inflation by raising the interest rate, thereby depressing aggregate demand via the interest rate channel and the exchange rate channel.

Thus we conclude that under a flexible exchange rate regime with strict inflation targeting, adjustments in the interest rate and in the nominal exchange rate help to dampen the fluctuations in inflation arising from supply shocks, but only at the cost of increased fluctuations in the level of output compared with a fixed exchange rate regime.

The short-run effects of aggregate demand shocks

Let us next compare the short-run effects of aggregate *demand shocks* under the two exchange rate regimes. This is not so easily done by a graphical analysis, since the *vertical shift* in the AD curve generated by a given shock to aggregate demand will be different under the two regimes at the same time as the *slope* of the AD curve differs across regimes. It is therefore more convenient to resort to a mathematical analysis. Solving (25) and (24) for the short-run values of the output and inflation gaps, and using the definition of $\hat{\beta}_1$ stated in (15), we get:

$$\textit{Flexible exchange rates:} \quad \hat{y}_t = \frac{z_t}{1 + \gamma\beta_1 + \gamma h(\beta_2 + \theta^{-1}\beta_1)}, \tag{33}$$

$$\hat{\pi}_t = \frac{\gamma z_t}{1 + \gamma\beta_1 + \gamma h(\beta_2 + \theta^{-1}\beta_1)}, \tag{34}$$

where we have set $e_{t-1}^r = s_t = 0$, since we are now focusing on demand shocks, and since the value of e_{t-1}^r is immaterial for the present short-run analysis. In a similar way, we find from Eqs (7) and (8) in the previous chapter that the short-run solutions for the output and inflation gaps under fixed exchange rates are (for $e_{t-1}^r = s_t = 0$):

$$\textit{Fixed exchange rates:} \quad \hat{y}_t = \frac{z_t}{1 + \gamma\beta_1}, \tag{35}$$

$$\hat{\pi}_t = \frac{\gamma z_t}{1 + \gamma\beta_1}. \tag{36}$$

From these expressions we see that the demand shock variable z_t has a *smaller* short run effect on output as well as inflation under flexible than under fixed exchange rates. Under the latter regime, the impact of a positive demand shock is dampened only by the loss of competitiveness occurring as higher domestic activity drives up the domestic inflation rate. This dampening effect is reflected in the term $\gamma\beta_1$ in the denominators of (35) and (36). But under flexible exchange rates the rise in domestic inflation generated by a positive demand shock also induces the central bank to raise the interest rate, causing a further dampening of the rise in output and inflation through the interest rate channel and the exchange rate channel. This shock-absorbing effect of the change in the interest rate and in the nominal exchange rate is captured by the term $\gamma h(\beta_2 + \theta^{-1}\beta_1)$ in the denominators of (33) and (34).

This analysis suggests that if demand shocks are the dominant source of macroeconomic fluctuations, a country wishing to minimize the variability of output and inflation may be better served by a flexible than by a fixed exchange rate, because a floating exchange rate allows the interest rate and the nominal exchange rate to help absorb demand shocks, thereby reducing the need for adjustments in output and inflation.

Table 25.2 summarizes our results regarding the differences in the short-run effects of demand and supply shocks under the two exchange rate regimes. Because of the qualitative similarities in the structure of the open economy under the two regimes, the qualitative

TABLE 25.2 Short-run effects of shocks under flexible exchange rates, compared to the effects under fixed exchange rates

Short-run fluctuations in	Type of shock	
	Demand shock	Supply shock
Output	Smaller	Larger
Inflation	Smaller	Smaller

medium-term and long-term effects of demand and supply shocks are similar under fixed and flexible exchange rates. In particular, the dynamic, qualitative effects of temporary and permanent fiscal policy shocks under flexible exchange rates correspond to those found in the previous chapter. Hence we will not repeat the graphical analysis of such shocks in the present chapter. However, notice that since our variable z_t includes fiscal policy shocks, the mathematical analysis above implies that fiscal policy has a smaller quantitative impact on economic activity under flexible than under fixed exchange rates.

Is the exchange rate really a shock absorber?

Table 25.2 suggests that a floating exchange rate can help to cushion the economy against demand shocks and that it also helps to reduce fluctuations in the inflation rate under an inflation-targeting regime. However, based on empirical observations some economists have questioned whether a flexible exchange rate is really an effective shock absorber rather than an independent source of shocks. To illustrate how a floating exchange rate could be a source of shocks, note from Eq. (10) that when financial investors are risk averse and foreign and domestic bonds have different risk characteristics, the change in the nominal exchange rate may be written as:

$$\Delta e = \theta^{-1}(i^f - i + \bar{v} + \varepsilon). \tag{37}$$

Experience shows that risk premia in financial markets can vary quite a lot, as some unexpected economic or political event motivates international investors to revise their evaluation of the relative riskiness of assets issued in different countries. For a given stance of domestic and foreign monetary policy – that is, for given values of i and i^f – we see from (37) that fluctuations in the (stochastic component of the) risk premium ε must generate fluctuations in the exchange rate which may in turn contribute to instability in output and inflation. If the shifts in risk premia are frequent and significant, a floating exchange rate may thus become a source of macroeconomic instability rather than an absorber of shocks arising elsewhere in the economy.

If a floating exchange rate tends to act as an absorber of shocks to real output and employment, we should observe a negative correlation between exchange rate volatility and output volatility. In Fig. 25.4 we measure exchange rate volatility, σ_e, as the standard deviation of each country's nominal effective (i.e. trade-weighted) exchange rate, while output volatility, σ_y, is measured by the standard deviation of the rate of growth of industrial production. The diagram is based on monthly data for 17 OECD countries for the period 1975–2002. This period was divided into 28 two-year intervals for which the standard deviations were calculated, giving a total of 28 × 17 observed combinations of exchange rate volatility and output volatility. Fitting a regression line through the data, we find that higher exchange rate volatility does tend to be associated with lower output volatility, but this relationship is driven very much by a few outliers in the data representing periods when output volatility was unusually high. Moreover, the regression explains very little of the

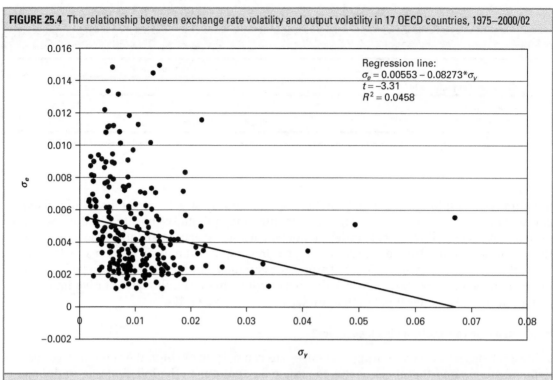

FIGURE 25.4 The relationship between exchange rate volatility and output volatility in 17 OECD countries, 1975–2000/02

Regression line:
$\sigma_e = 0.00553 - 0.08273 * \sigma_y$
$t = -3.31$
$R^2 = 0.0458$

Note: Exchange rate volatility is measured by the standard deviation of the nominal effective exchange rate. Output volatility is measured by the standard deviation of the change in the log of seasonally adjusted industrial production. The regression line was estimated using standard OLS.

Source: IMF International Financial Statistics.

total variation in the data, so the main impression is that higher exchange rate flexibility has at best a very weak stabilizing influence on output.[3]

Using a statistical technique called vector autoregression analysis (VAR), several economists have tried to evaluate more carefully whether the exchange rate is mainly a source of shocks rather than a shock absorber. A VAR analysis allows the researcher to estimate that part of the current movement in variables such as output and inflation which is due to new shocks occurring in the current period. These shocks may then be categorized into different types using basic assumptions (so-called identifying restrictions) from economic theory. For example, we know from theory that only supply shocks can have a permanent effect on output, so an estimated shock which has a permanent statistical effect on output is categorized as a supply shock. As another example, a so-called real demand shock (e.g. a permanent fiscal shock) is a disturbance which has a lasting statistical effect on some real variable other than output (such as the real exchange rate), whereas a so-called nominal shock has no permanent effect on any real variables. A shock to the nominal exchange rate arising from a temporary shift in risk premia is an example of a nominal shock.

The economists Michael Artis and Michael Ehrmann have carried out a comparative VAR analysis of data for industrial output, inflation, domestic and foreign short-term interest rates and nominal exchange rates for Canada, Denmark, Sweden and the UK for the period 1980–98. The purpose of their analysis was to evaluate the role of the exchange rate as a shock absorber or source of shock. Their main results are summarized in Table 25.3 which

---

3. The idea for the simple analysis in Fig. 25.4 came from a paper by Robert P. Flood and Andrew K. Rose, 'Fixing Exchange Rates – A Virtual Quest for Fundamentals', *Journal of Monetary Economics*, **36**, 1995, pp. 3–37. Based on a more sophisticated analysis of the data, these authors also concluded that there is no clear trade-off between reduced exchange rate volatility and macroeconomic stability.

TABLE 25.3 Proportion of the variance of output, inflation and nominal exchange rate explained by different types of shocks, 1980–98

Country	Variance of	Percentage of variance explained by			
		Supply shocks	Real demand shocks	Foreign and domestic monetary policy shocks	Exchange rate shocks
Canada	Output	15.5	83.4	1.0	0.1
	Inflation	53.9	1.8	24.6	19.7
	Exchange rate	4.1	0.7	87.9	7.3
Denmark	Output	90.6	5.9	3.0	0.5
	Inflation	3.0	0.3	54.9	41.8
	Exchange rate	3.1	1.3	51.7	43.9
Sweden	Output	55.2	41.8	2.3	0.7
	Inflation	50.7	15.9	32.6	0.8
	Exchange rate	1.2	0.6	2.3	95.9
United Kingdom	Output	83.9	11.6	3.1	1.4
	Inflation	7.0	17.1	43.1	32.8
	Exchange rate	1.5	1.5	36.2	60.8

Note: Variance calculated over one-year horizon.

Source: Michael J. Artis and Michael Ehrmann, 'The Exchange Rate – A Shock-Absorber or Source of Shocks? A Study of Four Open Economies'. Centre for Economic Policy Research. Discussion Paper No. 2550, September 2000.

shows the proportion of the short-run variance of output, inflation and exchange rates which can be ascribed to the different types of shock. A monetary policy shock is an 'unsystematic' movement in the short-term nominal interest rate, that is, a movement which cannot be predicted from a monetary policy rule such as Eq. (2). These shocks as well as exchange rate shocks are categorized as nominal shocks.

Over the period considered, all of the four countries have allowed considerable variation of their bilateral exchange rates against their major trading partner (Germany in the case of Denmark, Sweden and the UK; the USA in the case of Canada). This is also true for Denmark, even though that country held its exchange rate against Germany within a rather narrow band towards the end of the period. It therefore makes sense to study the role of the exchange rate as a potential shock absorber in these countries.

If the nominal exchange rate is mainly an absorber of shocks to the real economy (output) rather than an independent source of shocks, then most of the movements in the exchange rate will be driven by the same types of shock as those causing variations in output. This hypothesis finds little support from the results reported in Table 25.3. The bulk of the short-run variance in output is explained by supply shocks or by real demand shocks, but these shock categories explain less than 5 per cent of the variance of the exchange rate in all countries.

However, Table 25.3 indicates that a substantial part of the variability in inflation has been created by monetary policy shocks which also seem to explain quite a lot of the variance in the exchange rate in Canada, Denmark and the UK. This suggests that nominal demand shocks arising from unsystematic monetary policy have been absorbed by changes in exchange rates as well as by adjustments in goods prices.

Still, the most striking result in Table 25.3 is the very high proportion of the variance in the exchange rate which is explained by shocks to the exchange rate itself, particularly in Sweden and the UK. This suggests that, rather than reacting to shocks originating elsewhere

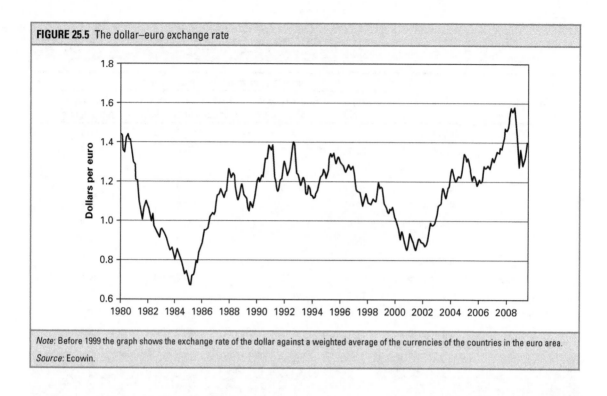

FIGURE 25.5 The dollar–euro exchange rate

Note: Before 1999 the graph shows the exchange rate of the dollar against a weighted average of the currencies of the countries in the euro area.

Source: Ecowin.

in the economic system, the exchange rate moves mainly in response to shocks to the foreign exchange market such as shifts in risk premia. In Denmark and the UK, and to a smaller extent in Canada, the exogenous exchange rate shocks seem to have generated a large part of the variance in the inflation rate, so while the exchange rate may have absorbed part of the monetary policy shocks to inflation, it may also have been a breeder of inflation shocks itself. At the same time we see from the table that exchange rate shocks appear to have had very little influence on the variance of output.

Results like those reported in Table 25.3 should be interpreted with great care because of the inherent difficulties of separating the effects of shocks from the underlying systematic movements in economic time series. In particular, identifying shocks to the nominal exchange rate is very hard because economists have had great difficulty in modelling the determination of floating exchange rates. But with this proviso, Table 25.3 suggests that exchange rates tend to move in response to shocks other than those that drive output fluctuations and that a large part of exchange rate variability originates from disturbances to the foreign exchange market itself. A number of other empirical studies have found similar results. This does not support the idea that the exchange rate plays an important role as a shock absorber.

Exchange rate overshooting

On top of the short-run fluctuations, floating exchange rates also tend to undergo rather large swings in the medium term. For example, Fig. 25.5 illustrates the large medium-run movements in the exchange rate between the US dollar and the euro (a weighted average of the euro area currencies before 1999). Such large swings in floating exchange rates may seem hard to rationalize. After all, the hypothesis of relative purchasing power parity formalized in Eq. (4) says that over the long run the movement in the exchange rate should just offset the difference between national inflation rates. Since these differences tend to be small across developed countries (and are, indeed, nowadays close to zero), the large medium-run exchange rate swings might seem to reflect an irrational overreaction in foreign exchange markets.

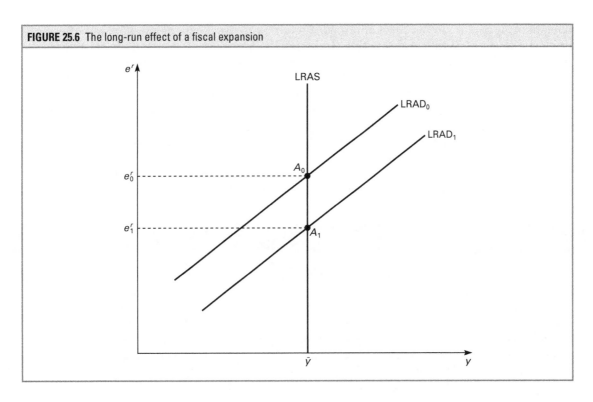

FIGURE 25.6 The long-run effect of a fiscal expansion

In a seminal contribution, the late German-American economist Rudiger Dornbusch showed that rather than reflecting irrationality, the apparent 'overshooting' of flexible exchange rates may be compatible with rational behaviour in foreign exchange markets.[4] Dornbusch used the example of a monetary policy shock to make his point, but here we will illustrate that exchange rate overshooting may also occur in response to other disturbances such as a fiscal policy shock.

Inserting (6) and (5) into (1), we may write the condition for uncovered interest parity as:

$$r_t = r_t^f + \theta(\bar{e}_t - e_t). \tag{38}$$

Following Dornbusch, we now assume that the expected 'normal' exchange rate $\bar{e}_t$ in (38) corresponds to the economy's long-term equilibrium exchange rate. In other words, financial investors have correct (rational) expectations of the economy's long-term equilibrium nominal exchange rate. Suppose now that the domestic government engages in a permanent fiscal expansion. Figure 25.6 shows how this will affect the economy's *real* exchange rate in the long run, using the analytical apparatus from Chapter 23.

As you recall, LRAD is the long-run aggregate demand curve which is upward-sloping since a real exchange rate depreciation (a rise in e^r) stimulates the demand for domestic output by improving the country's international competitiveness. The LRAS curve is the long-run aggregate supply curve. A permanent fiscal expansion shifts the LRAD curve to the right.[5] This implies a new long-run equilibrium at point A_1 where the real exchange rate has appreciated.

Under a floating exchange rate, part of this real appreciation will occur through an appreciation of the long-run *nominal* exchange rate $\bar{e}_t$. We can now see how exchange rate

4. See Rudiger Dornbusch, 'Expectations and Exchange Rate Dynamics', *Journal of Political Economy*, **84**, 1976, pp. 1161–1176.

5. In Chapter 23 we showed that the LRAD curve is given by the relationship $e^r = \beta_1^{-1}(y - \bar{y} - z)$. A permanent fiscal expansion implies a permanent rise in z so that aggregate demand permanently increases for any given level of the real exchange rate e^r, thereby shifting the LRAD curve to the right.

overshooting occurs. In the short and medium term, the fiscal expansion drives up the domestic levels of output and inflation, inducing the domestic central bank to raise the domestic real interest rate r_t. At the same time rational investors correctly anticipate that the long-run equilibrium exchange $\bar{e}_t$ rate has fallen. It then follows from (38) that the current exchange rate e_t has to fall by even *more* than $\bar{e}_t$ to maintain uncovered interest parity. In other words, in the short run the exchange rate must 'overshoot' its new long-run equilibrium value in order to generate *expectations of a future depreciation* of the domestic currency so that domestic assets are no more attractive than foreign assets, despite the fact that the domestic interest rate has risen.

This analysis suggests that overreactions in the exchange rate relative to its long-run equilibrium may be an unavoidable feature of a flexible exchange rate regime. In summary:

THE ROLE OF EXCHANGE RATE FLUCTUATIONS UNDER FLEXIBLE EXCHANGE RATES

A flexible exchange rate can help to absorb the effects of shocks to the economy, but shifting expectations and risk premia in foreign exchange markets mean that exchange rate fluctuations can also be an independent source of shocks. There is some evidence to suggest that the exchange rate is indeed a source of shocks, although the impact on real output seems to be limited. In the medium term, flexible exchange rates tend to undergo rather large swings, indicating that they often 'overshoot' their long-run equilibrium values. Such apparently irrational behaviour is in fact compatible with rational expectations.

Some economists see the phenomenon of overshooting as an argument in favour of fixed exchange rates, whereas others argue that the benefits from an independent national monetary policy outweigh the costs of exchange rate overshooting under floating exchange rates. These observations take us into the great debate on the choice of exchange rate regime.

25.4 Fixed versus flexible exchange rates

For many decades economists have debated the pros and cons of fixed versus flexible exchange rates. This controversy will surely continue, but going through the main arguments will help us understand some of the factors determining whether a particular country is better served by one or the other exchange rate regime. Indeed, our analysis will suggest that different exchange rate regimes may be suitable for different countries, depending on their individual circumstances.

As we have seen, our simple AS–AD framework implies that the exchange rate regime is *neutral* in the long run. For the moment we will maintain this assumption. If the exchange rate regime cannot influence the long-run equilibrium values of any real variables, the main issue in choosing between fixed and flexible exchange rates is whether the short-run fluctuations in output and inflation will be systematically smaller under one regime or the other. Related to this is the question whether the economy's speed of adjustment to long-run equilibrium will be faster under one regime or the other. The analysis in this chapter suggests that the answers to these questions depend on the nature of the shocks hitting the economy and on the parameters of the aggregate demand curve. In particular, we found that when demand shocks are dominant, the short-run instability of output will be smaller under flexible than under fixed exchange rates, but when supply shocks are the dominant drivers of business cycles, output will be less unstable under a fixed exchange rate. Since the nature of shocks and the economy's capacity to absorb them may vary over time and across countries, there is no reason to believe that all countries will prefer the same exchange rate regime at all times.

In the following we will elaborate on the factors determining which exchange rate regime offers the best potential cushion against short-run macroeconomic instability.

The exchange rate regime as a framework for monetary policy

Under free capital mobility we have seen that the choice of exchange rate regime is intimately linked to the choice of monetary policy regime: if a country faced with high capital mobility wants to pursue an independent monetary policy, it must adopt a flexible exchange rate. It is therefore useful to consider the goals and targets for monetary policy, for once these have been decided, they will dictate the choice of exchange rate regime in a world with mobile capital.

In recent years a widespread consensus has emerged that – at least in 'normal' times when securing financial stability is not an overriding concern – the prime goal of monetary policy should be to secure a low and stable rate of inflation. This is based on the view also embodied in our AS–AD model that in the long run monetary policy can only influence nominal variables, but not real variables. Of course monetary policy can affect real variables like output and employment in the short and medium term. However, if the public believes that price stability (a low and stable inflation rate) is the prime goal of monetary policy, an expansionary macroeconomic policy can actually become a more powerful tool in a recession, since it is easier to stimulate aggregate demand without igniting inflation expectations when the central bank's commitment to long-run price stability is credible. Making low and stable inflation the main official goal of monetary policy is therefore seen by most economists and policy makers as the best contribution monetary policy can make to economic stability.[6]

If this is indeed the main goal of monetary policy, it might seem most logical to adopt an inflation targeting regime and let the exchange rate float to enable monetary policy to concentrate on the domestic goal of price stability. But monetary policy cannot directly control the inflation rate, since it only works indirectly and with a time lag through its influence on aggregate demand (and possibly its impact on expectations). As an alternative to inflation targeting with flexible exchange rates, a country may therefore choose to peg its exchange rate to the currency of a country with a record of low and stable inflation. Let us consider this option more closely before returning to inflation targeting.

A fixed exchange rate as an intermediate target for monetary policy

A fixed exchange rate may be seen as an *intermediate target* for monetary policy. A fixed exchange rate regime means that the *instruments* of monetary policy – the short-term interest rate and foreign exchange market interventions – become fully and exclusively dedicated to achieving the intermediate target of a fixed exchange rate. However, this intermediate target is adopted with the purpose of realizing the *ultimate policy goal* of price stability. By credibly pegging to a hard foreign currency, a country can import a low and stable inflation rate from abroad, since the domestic inflation rate must equal the inflation rate of the hard-currency country over the long run for the fixed exchange rate to be sustainable.

In general, the rationale for adopting an intermediate target for monetary policy is that the central bank cannot directly control the ultimate goal variable such as the rate of inflation. It may then be useful to choose an intermediate target variable which is easier to control by means of the monetary policy instruments and which is systematically related to the ultimate goal variable. Ideally, an intermediate target variable should have a *high correlation with the goal*, so that achieving the intermediate target is an effective way of fulfilling the ultimate policy goal. The intermediate target should also be *easier to control than the goal* – otherwise there is no point in adopting the target rather than focusing directly

---

6. We should not exaggerate the degree of consensus on this point. Economists do disagree on the extent to which monetary policy can affect the economy in the short and medium run, and therefore they also disagree on the extent to which stabilization of the real economy should be included in the official goals of monetary policy.

on the goal. Finally, it should be *easy for outsiders to observe* whether the intermediate target is achieved, since this makes it easier for the political authorities and the general public to hold the central bank accountable for its actions.

A fixed exchange rate regime has obvious advantages by the last two criteria. In normal times when the country is not exposed to a speculative attack on its currency, it is easy for the central bank to control the exchange rate via foreign exchange market interventions combined with an interest rate policy that follows the policy of the foreign anchor country.[7] When the exchange rate is only allowed to move within a narrow band, it is also easy for outsiders to observe whether the intermediate target is achieved or not: either the exchange rate is (roughly) fixed, or it is not.

However, a fixed exchange rate is not necessarily closely correlated with the ultimate goal of low and stable inflation. As you recall, the evolution of the (log of the) real exchange rate e^r is given by:

$$e^r = e^r_{-1} + \Delta e + \pi^f - \pi, \tag{39}$$

where $\Delta e \equiv e - e_{-1}$ is the rate of exchange rate depreciation, π^f is the foreign inflation rate, and π is the domestic inflation rate. From (39) we see that under fixed exchange rates ($\Delta e = 0$) the domestic inflation rate may be written as:

$$\pi = \pi^f - (e^r - e^r_{-1}). \tag{40}$$

A low and stable domestic inflation rate thus requires a low and stable inflation rate in the foreign anchor country *plus* stability of the real exchange rate, i.e., $e^r = e^r_{-1}$. The first condition will be met if the anchor country is indeed committed to low and stable inflation, but this does not in itself guarantee stability of the real exchange rate. Such stability depends on the similarity between economic conditions at home and in the foreign anchor country. To illustrate this point, Fig. 25.7 shows the case of a negative supply shock which permanently reduces the natural level of output. As a result of the shock, the long-run aggregate supply curve of the domestic economy shifts to the left. If the supply shock is 'asymmetric' – that is, if it only affects the domestic but not the foreign economy – there will be no shock to net exports since foreign economic activity will be unchanged. The LRAD curve will then be unaffected, and the domestic economy will end up in a new long-run equilibrium at point A_1 where the real exchange rate has appreciated relative to the original equilibrium point A_0.

However, suppose instead that the supply shock is 'symmetric', affecting the foreign economy to the same extent as the domestic economy. Then foreign economic activity will decrease, and this will shift the LRAD curve to the left by reducing net exports from the domestic economy. If the long-run aggregate demand curve shifts to the new position LRAD′, the domestic economy will end up in a new long-run equilibrium at point A'_1 where the real exchange rate is unchanged. In practice, the shift in the LRAD curve may not be exactly sufficient to ensure an unchanged real exchange rate, but a symmetric shock will always imply a smaller change in the equilibrium real exchange rate than an asymmetric shock.

If the foreign and the domestic economies are closely integrated and have very similar structures, it is more likely that a shock affecting one country will have a roughly similar impact on the other country. For example, if the negative supply shock is a permanent increase in the relative price of imported oil, the two countries will be affected equally if they are equally dependent on imported oil. In that case the effect of the shock would be described by the movement from point A_0 to point A'_1 in Fig. 25.7. But if the domestic economy is frequently hit by asymmetric shocks, then it may need frequent adjustments of its real exchange rate, and under a fixed nominal exchange rate this can happen only through fluctuations in the domestic rate of inflation. For instance, in the case of a negative

---

7. We use the term 'anchor country' for convenience; of course this 'country' could be a region such as the euro zone.

FIGURE 25.7 The long-run effects of an asymmetric versus a symmetric negative supply shock

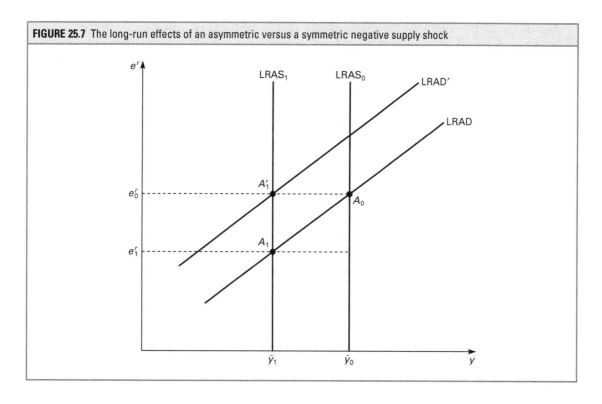

asymmetric supply shock, the real appreciation implied by the movement from the original equilibrium A_0 to the new equilibrium A_1 in Fig. 25.7 can occur only through an adjustment period in which the domestic inflation rate exceeds the foreign inflation rate.

To sum up the argument so far, a close correlation between the intermediate target of a fixed nominal exchange rate and the ultimate goal of a low and stable inflation rate seems to require that the domestic economy is hit by roughly the same type of shocks as the foreign anchor economy – and that the two economies react in roughly the same way to the shocks – so that large and frequent adjustments in the real exchange rate are not needed.

But this argument needs to be modified. Consider again our example of a negative asymmetric supply shock which shifts the LRAS curve to the left. If the domestic government wants to neutralize the impact of this shock on the equilibrium real exchange rate, it can permanently tighten fiscal policy since such a permanent negative demand shock will shift the LRAD curve to the left. By an appropriate dose of fiscal contraction, the domestic government can thereby move the economy from the equilibrium A_0 to the new equilibrium A_1' in Fig. 25.7. In this way it can avoid the temporary rise in domestic inflation which would otherwise be needed to take the economy to the alternative equilibrium A_1. In general, by assigning to fiscal policy the task of minimizing fluctuations in the real exchange rate (keeping the domestic inflation rate close to the foreign inflation rate), a country with a fixed nominal exchange rate should be able to avoid substantial fluctuations in the rate of inflation even if it is hit by asymmetric shocks.

Sceptics argue that it is unlikely that fiscal policy will be able to live up to such a task. First of all, the required frequent changes in taxes or public spending may have undesirable side effects on resource allocation and income distribution and may therefore be politically difficult to implement. In particular, in cases when a fiscal contraction is needed, this may be very hard to carry out because of its political unpopularity. Second, usually there are long lags in the fiscal policy process, as we explained in Chapter 20, and this may make it very difficult to achieve the appropriate timing of temporary fiscal measures intended to offset the effects of temporary shocks.

For these reasons many economists believe that fiscal policy is not a very effective instrument of stabilization policy, at least when it comes to dealing with shocks of a shorter duration. To the extent that fiscal policy does not succeed in minimizing fluctuations in domestic inflation, a fixed exchange rate regime may then imply that monetary policy becomes *procyclical*, that is, destabilizing. To see how this may happen, let us return to the idea presented in Chapter 24 that only a fraction φ of the population has 'weakly rational' expectations ($\pi^e = \pi^f$) while the remaining fraction may have static inflation expectations ($\pi^e = \pi_{-1}$). The average expected inflation rate will then be given by:

$$\pi^e = \varphi\pi^f + (1-\varphi)\pi_{-1}, \qquad 0 \le \varphi \le 1. \tag{41}$$

In Chapter 24 we focused on the benchmark case where $\varphi = 1$, but suppose instead that $\varphi < 1$. An asymmetric negative demand shock which forces the economy into recession will drive down the domestic rate of inflation. According to (41) this will reduce the expected inflation rate in the subsequent period. But since the central bank has to keep the domestic *nominal* interest rate equal to the (unchanged) foreign nominal interest rate to defend the fixed exchange rate, it follows that a fall in the expected inflation rate will drive up the domestic *real* interest rate in a time of recession. Obviously this will further depress aggregate demand, which is exactly the opposite of what is needed during a recession. By analogy, under a boom which raises the actual inflation rate, the real interest rate for the following period will fall when the nominal interest rate has to be kept constant to fix the exchange rate and part of the population has backward-looking expectations.[8]

The vulnerability of a fixed exchange rate regime to speculative currency attacks also tends to increase the risk that monetary policy becomes procyclical. For example, if the economy is in a deep recession with mass unemployment, international investors may begin to speculate that the authorities will feel tempted to devalue the currency in order to escape from the recession. If such expectations become widespread, a speculative attack may occur, forcing the domestic central bank to raise the domestic interest rate to defend the currency. Clearly this procyclical policy will only tend to deepen the recession.

This line of reasoning combined with scepticism regarding the scope for fiscal stabilization policy explains why quite a few economists believe that business fluctuations will tend to be larger under fixed than under flexible exchange rates, other things equal.

The alternative: flexible exchange rates with inflation forecast targeting

Given these difficulties with a fixed exchange rate as a framework for monetary policy, many countries have recently adopted flexible exchange rates combined with inflation targeting to secure an anchor for inflation expectations. Under inflation targeting, the central bank's inflation forecast effectively becomes an intermediate target for monetary policy.[9] As we explained in Chapter 20, the reason is that monetary policy only affects the inflation rate with a certain time lag which is typically between one and two years. The lag arises from the fact that it takes time before aggregate demand reacts to a change in the interest rate, and it also takes time before a change in demand achieves its maximum impact on inflation. The central bank must therefore set the interest rate today knowing that this will not significantly affect the inflation rate until $1\frac{1}{2}$–2 years from now. Hence monetary policy must

---

8. This argument against fixed exchange rates is sometimes referred to as the 'Walters Critique' because it was formulated by the late British economist Alan Walters who served for a time as an economic policy adviser to former Prime Minister Margaret Thatcher. See Alan Walters, *Britain's Economic Renaissance*, Oxford, Oxford University Press, 1986.

9. This interpretation of inflation targeting regimes as well as several other points made above are well explained in the highly readable article by Lars E.O. Svensson, 'Exchange Rate Target or Inflation Target for Norway?', in Anne Berit Christiansen and Jan Fredrik Qvigstad (eds), *Choosing a Monetary Policy Target*, Oslo, Scandinavian University Press (Universitetsforlaget AS), pp. 120–138.

be based on a *forecast* of future inflation over a time horizon corresponding to the time it takes for a change in the interest rate to influence the inflation rate. If the inflation forecast exceeds (falls short of) the target inflation rate when the interest rate is held constant, then the interest rate must be raised (lowered) until the inflation forecast corresponds to the target. In this sense the inflation forecast is used as an intermediate target for monetary policy, that is, inflation targeting implies inflation forecast targeting.

Of course, the *realized* future inflation rate will typically deviate from the inflation forecast since the central bank does not have perfect knowledge of the way its policy affects the economy, and new unpredictable shocks may hit the economy between the time the interest rate is changed and the time it attains its impact on the inflation rate. However, provided the central bank optimally uses all relevant information in producing its forecast, inflation forecast targeting will make the deviations of actual inflation from the target rate of inflation as small as existing economic knowledge permits. This is why advocates of inflation targeting believe that this monetary policy regime makes it easier to achieve the goal of low and stable inflation than a fixed exchange rate regime.

Moreover, the inflation forecast is obviously easier for the central bank to control than the inflation rate itself, and it is also easy for the public to observe, provided the central bank publishes its forecasts. From these perspectives the inflation forecast seems to be an attractive alternative to a fixed exchange rate as an intermediate target for monetary policy.

However, those who are sceptical of flexible exchange rates have pointed to a number of potential problems with this regime. First of all, in practice central banks do not target the rate of *producer* price inflation (our variable π), as we have so far assumed for simplicity. Instead, they target the rate of *consumer* price inflation which is a weighted average of the inflation rate for domestic and imported goods. Thus, if the share of imports in private consumption is ψ, the rate of consumer price inflation (π^c) targeted by the central bank is:

$$\pi^c = \psi \cdot \overbrace{(\Delta e + \pi^f)}^{\text{inflation rate for imported goods}} + (1-\psi) \cdot \overbrace{\pi}^{\text{inflation rate for domestic goods}}, \qquad 0 \leq \psi \leq 1. \tag{42}$$

As we saw in Section 25.3, under the floating regime the nominal exchange rate (and hence Δe) may be subject to considerable exogenous shocks which cannot be offset easily by monetary policy in the short run. Such nominal exchange rate shocks will contribute to volatility in the targeted rate of inflation through their impact on the prices of imported consumer goods, according to (42).[10]

Second, in Section 25.3 we found that aggregate demand shocks have a smaller impact on the economy under flexible than under fixed exchange rates. On the one hand this means that the economy may be less vulnerable to shocks under flexible rates, but it also implies that fiscal policy (which is included in our demand shock variable z) becomes a less effective tool of stabilization policy. The greater scope for monetary policy under flexible exchange rates is therefore achieved at the expense of the effectiveness of fiscal policy.

Third, apart from being volatile in the short run, we have seen that floating exchange rates may undergo very large fluctuations in the medium run because they tend to overshoot their long-run equilibrium values. Both types of exchange rate instability may hamper international economic transactions by increasing their riskiness. It may also cause an unintended redistribution of real income across different sectors in the economy, as we explained in Chapter 24.

Let us sum up some of the main arguments from the discussion above:

---

10. The extent to which exchange rate fluctuations actually contribute to inflation instability depends on the degree to which changes in the exchange rate are passed through to domestic consumer prices. The empirical evidence suggests that some foreign producers of imported goods follow a 'pricing-to-market' strategy, preferring to keep their prices relatively stable measured in the local currency of their export market. In that case exchange rate fluctuations tend to be absorbed by fluctuations in profit margins rather than in domestic consumer prices.

FIXED VERSUS FLEXIBLE EXCHANGE RATES

A low and stable inflation rate is widely regarded as the prime goal of monetary policy. This ultimate goal may be served via the intermediate goal of keeping the nominal exchange rate fixed against a foreign anchor country with a history of low and stable inflation. However, if the domestic economy is often hit by asymmetric shocks, it will frequently need to adjust its real exchange rate in which case a fixed nominal exchange rate cannot ensure a stable rate of inflation. In principle the need for substantial changes in the real exchange rate can be eliminated through adjustments in fiscal policy, but skeptics argue that time lags and political constraints prevent fiscal policy from playing such a role. The ultimate goal of low and stable inflation may alternatively be served via a regime of flexible exchange rates and inflation targeting where keeping the inflation forecast equal to the target inflation rate becomes an intermediate goal of monetary policy. Such a regime allows an independent monetary policy, but this benefit comes at the cost of reduced effectiveness of fiscal policy and greater exchange rate uncertainty which may hamper cross-border transactions.

The concern about the impact of exchange rate uncertainty amounts to saying that nominal exchange rate stability should not only be considered an intermediate target; it may also be a legitimate ultimate policy goal itself. We shall now elaborate on this argument which takes us into the theory of optimum currency areas.

The theory of optimum currency areas

In Chapter 23 we presented evidence suggesting that greater exchange rate stability may indeed stimulate international trade by reducing its riskiness. A stable exchange rate could also increase economic welfare by reducing the risk associated with cross-border investment. According to the theory of optimum currency areas the choice of exchange rate regime then becomes a matter of trading off such microeconomic benefits against the potential macroeconomic costs of fixing the exchange rate.[11]

The theory of optimal currency areas may be summarized using Fig. 25.8. The diagram illustrates a country's total costs and benefits (relative to GDP) of moving from a flexible to a fully fixed exchange rate, possibly by adopting the same currency as the major trading partners. The horizontal axis measures the country's degree of economic integration with its trading partners measured, say, by the ratio of foreign trade and investment to GDP. The BB curve indicates the *microeconomic benefits* from exchange rate stability. One such benefit is that a credibly fixed exchange rate reduces the riskiness of foreign trade and investment. This is welfare-improving when economic agents are risk averse. Further benefits are gained if exchange rate stability is achieved through a common currency. In that case society saves the real resources (mostly labour time and computer software) which are needed to exchange one currency into another and to keep books in different currencies. It has also been argued that the adoption of a common currency will generate a welfare gain from stronger international price competition because a single currency facilitates the comparison of prices across borders. Moreover, by increasing the volume of transactions carried out in the same currency, a monetary union tends to increase the liquidity of the markets for financial assets and paves the way for more competition and greater economies of scale in the financial sector.[12]

---

11. The theory of optimum currency areas was pioneered by the later Nobel Prize winner Robert A. Mundell in 'A Theory of Optimum Currency Areas', *American Economic Review*, **51**, 1961, pp. 657–665. This theory has played an important role in the economic debate on monetary union in Europe.

12. A 'liquid' market is a market with a large and fairly steady volume of day-to-day transactions. In a liquid market, a seller in need of cash can normally expect to be able to sell his asset without having to accept a significant cut in its price.

FIGURE 25.8 The costs and benefits of a common currency

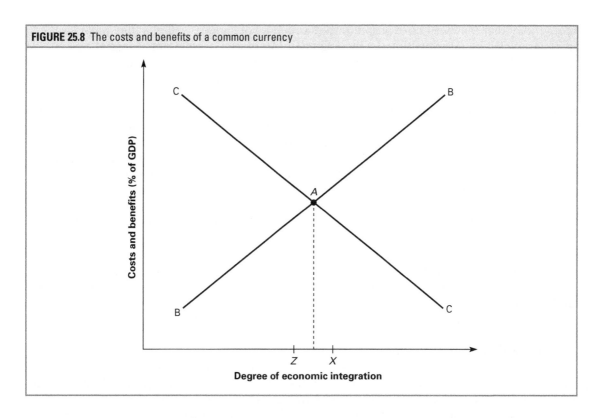

The greater the volume of international transactions relative to the size of the economy, the larger are the microeconomic benefits from a stable exchange rate and a common currency relative to GDP. This is why the BB curve slopes upwards in Fig. 25.8. Since several of the benefits mentioned above can only be reaped by adopting a common currency, the position and positive slope of the BB curve will be higher when the fixed exchange rate is achieved by entering a monetary union.

The CC curve in Fig. 25.8 indicates the *macroeconomic costs* of switching from a flexible to a fully fixed exchange rate, measured as a percentage of GDP. The fact that this curve lies above the horizontal axis reflects the assumption of optimum currency area theory that the short-run volatility of output and inflation will tend to be lower under flexible than under fixed exchange rates. As you recall from the previous chapter, this is consistent with our AS–AD model if the shocks to the macroeconomy mainly originate from the demand side. More generally, the assumption of positive macroeconomic costs of fixing the exchange rate is based on the idea that the ability to pursue an independent monetary policy under flexible exchange rates makes it easier to stabilize the economy. But as indicated in the diagram, these macroeconomic costs will be smaller relative to GDP the more the domestic economy is integrated with the economies of its trading partners.

There are four reasons for the negative slope of the CC curve. First, the value of nominal exchange rate flexibility is greater the more often the country is exposed to *asymmetric shocks* requiring a significant adjustment of its real exchange rate. Remember from the analysis in Fig. 25.7 that when a shock hits the domestic country and its trading partners symmetrically, there is no need for a real exchange rate adjustment. Moreover, in the case of symmetric shocks a common interest rate policy will be equally appropriate for the domestic and for the foreign economy (assuming that the two countries or regions have roughly the same social preferences for output stability relative to inflation stability), so there is no need for nominal exchange rate flexibility to allow for different national monetary policies. Now comes the point: as the domestic and the foreign economies become more integrated, it is more likely that they will be exposed to the same type of shocks.[13] Hence they have less need for exchange rate flexibility as the degree of international economic integration increases. For this reason the macroeconomic cost of moving to a fixed exchange rate will fall as we move to the right on the horizontal axis in Fig. 25.8.

The second reason for the negative slope of the CC curve is that if the domestic country allows its nominal exchange rate to depreciate in order to absorb, say, a negative asymmetric shock to its export demand, the increase in import prices stemming from the depreciation will be transmitted more quickly to the domestic wage and price level the larger the ratio of imports to GDP. The gain in competitiveness obtained through a flexible exchange rate will therefore be more short-lived – and consequently the cost of giving up exchange rate flexibility will be smaller – the more the domestic economy depends on international trade.

Third, as the domestic and foreign economies become more integrated in terms of trade and investment, the international mobility of labour is also likely to increase, since cross-border economic transactions tend to reduce the information barriers and cultural barriers to migration. Higher international labour mobility means that if the economy is hit by a negative asymmetric shock which creates unemployment, some domestic workers will emigrate to look for jobs abroad. Hence it becomes less urgent to deal with the unemployment problem through a depreciation of the domestic currency, so the cost of giving up exchange rate flexibility falls to the extent that increased economic integration implies increased labour mobility.

The fourth potential mechanism generating a negative slope of the CC curve is more speculative and much less certain to occur: if deeper economic integration also leads to more political integration (think of the EU context, for example), and if political integration motivates the trading partners to engage in joint supranational activities financed through a common budget (again, think of the EU budget), then such a budget may be used as a means of transferring resources from countries benefiting from positive asymmetric shocks to countries hit by negative shocks. Such transfers would reduce the need for nominal and real exchange rate adjustments to counter asymmetric shocks. However, there is of course no guarantee that increased economic integration will automatically induce the integrating countries to implement such an international transfer mechanism.

At a level of economic integration corresponding to point A in Fig. 25.8, the microeconomic benefits from a fixed exchange rate/common currency are just offset by the macroeconomic costs. At a higher degree of economic integration, the domestic country would benefit in economic terms from fixing its exchange rate or from entering a currency union with its trading partners (remember that the position of the BB curve will be higher and its slope steeper in the latter case). At lower degrees of integration, the macroeconomic costs of exchange rate fixity exceed the microeconomic benefits.

Optimum currency area theory does not offer a quantitative method for estimating whether a particular country is to the right or to the left of the critical point A in Fig. 25.8. But the theory does help us to focus on the factors which are important for evaluating whether fixing the exchange rate or joining a currency union is a good or a bad idea. The theory also has one important qualitative long-run implication: if international economic integration continues to deepen in Europe and elsewhere, then a growing number of countries should find it in their economic interest to form/join a currency union with their most important trading partners. Thus the theory suggests that more European countries will want to adopt the euro as time goes by.

---

13. Actually this relationship is not self-evident, since increased international trade may lead different countries to specialize in different types of production subject to different industry-specific shocks (so-called inter-industry trade). However, most of the trade among the OECD countries takes the form of intra-industry trade, that is, exchange of different variants of the same type of products. For example, France may export Citroen cars to Germany while Germany exports BMWs to France. Hence both France and Germany are vulnerable to shocks hitting the car industry.

In the reasoning above we have taken the degree of international economic integration as given, but of course the adoption of a common currency may in itself tend to increase the degree of integration by stimulating cross-border trade and investment. Hence one may conceive that a country which starts out from a point like *Z* in Fig. 25.8 may end up at a point like *X* after having joined a currency union with its trading partners. In other words, even though union membership seems to imply an economic loss *ex ante*, it turns out to generate a net economic gain *ex post*. Much of the economic debate on the Economic and Monetary Union in Europe can be understood in this way. Those economists who were/are sceptical about EMU membership have tended to argue that economic integration among the (potential) EMU countries has not yet proceeded far enough to justify the adoption of a common currency, at least as far as the more peripheral EU member states are concerned. By contrast, those in favour of monetary union have tended to argue that, in so far as the preconditions for successful monetary unification are not already present, the adoption of a common currency will in itself promote economic integration to the point where the economic gains outweigh the costs.

THE THEORY OF OPTIMUM CURRENCY AREAS

The theory says that the choice of permanently fixing the exchange rate (possibly by joining a currency union) involves a trade-off between microeconomic benefits and macroeconomic costs. The microeconomic benefits increase with the degree of economic integration between the domestic and the foreign economy, since the gains from exchange rate stability increase with the volume of cross-border transactions. At the same time the macroeconomic cost of sacrificing exchange rate flexibility falls with the degree of economic integration because 1) tighter integration with the foreign economy reduces the likelihood that the domestic economy is hit by asymmetric shocks; 2) nominal exchange rate changes become a less effective means of changing the real exchange rate when the ratio of foreign trade to GDP goes up; and 3) higher international labour mobility (and possibly international transfers) can serve as a substitute for exchange rate changes as a means of absorbing asymmetric shocks. When the degree of economic integration becomes sufficiently deep, a country can therefore gain economically from fixing its exchange rate against (and possibly entering a currency union with) its main trading partners.

25.5 Summary

1. A crucial characteristic of a flexible exchange rate regime is that it enables the domestic central bank to pursue an independent monetary policy even if capital mobility is perfect.

2. Under a floating exchange rate regime the nominal exchange rate cannot serve as a nominal anchor for inflation expectations. To provide an alternative nominal anchor, many countries with flexible exchange rates have adopted a monetary policy regime of inflation targeting where the central bank seeks to keep inflation within a narrow band around some target rate which is typically set to 2–2.5 per cent. Under strict inflation targeting the central bank's interest rate reacts only to deviations of inflation from the target, whereas flexible inflation targeting implies that the central bank also reacts to the evolution of output and employment. The fact that inflation-targeting countries in the OECD have chosen roughly the same inflation target suggests that these countries try to avoid a systematic depreciation or appreciation of their nominal exchange rates over the longer run.

3. Most inflation-targeting countries have delegated monetary policy to an independent central bank to strengthen the credibility of the inflation target. When the target is credible, it will serve as an anchor for domestic inflation expectations. The model in

this chapter assumes that agents have weakly rational expectations in the sense that the expected inflation rate equals the central bank's inflation target. Given that countries choose (roughly) the same inflation target, this means that the expected domestic inflation rate is (roughly) equal to the foreign inflation rate.

4. Under flexible exchange rates and perfect capital mobility the difference between the domestic and the foreign nominal interest rate is given by the expected rate of change in the nominal exchange rate. According to the hypothesis of regressive exchange rate expectations, the exchange rate is expected to rise if it is currently below its perceived normal level, and vice versa. The perceived normal exchange rate is likely to depend on the actual exchange rates observed in the past. The model in this chapter makes the simplifying assumption that the perceived normal exchange rate equals last period's actual exchange rate. From this assumption plus the assumption of uncovered interest rate parity it follows that a positive differential between the domestic and the foreign interest rate will cause an appreciation of the domestic currency, whereas a negative interest rate differential will generate a depreciation. The empirical evidence lends some support to this hypothesis.

5. Under 'clean' floating the central bank does not intervene in the foreign exchange market. Under 'dirty' floating the central bank intervenes with the purpose of reducing fluctuations in the exchange rate. In the case of 'sterilized' interventions the central bank buys or sells foreign currency without changing the interest rate. To have a lasting impact on the exchange rate, interventions have to be 'unsterilized', involving a change in the interest rate which supports the movement in the exchange rate that the central bank is trying to achieve. When the central bank systematically raises (lowers) the interest rate in response to a depreciation (appreciation) of the domestic currency, it is said to follow a policy of 'leaning against the wind'.

6. In a flexible exchange rate regime monetary policy affects aggregate demand both through the interest rate channel and through the exchange rate channel. The interest rate channel is the direct impact of a change in the interest rate on investment and consumption demand. The exchange rate channel is the impact through the foreign exchange market: when the interest rate is lowered, there is a tendency for the exchange rate to depreciate so that net exports increase.

7. Under flexible exchange rates a fall in the domestic rate of inflation boosts aggregate demand through three effects. First, there is a direct positive effect on net exports as domestic competitiveness improves. Second, a lower rate of inflation induces an inflation-targeting central bank to reduce the interest rate, thereby stimulating investment and consumption. Third, the lower interest rate causes a depreciation which gives a further stimulus to net exports. The latter two effects are absent under fixed exchange rates. Hence the aggregate demand curve is flatter under flexible than under fixed exchange rates.

8. The AS–AD model for the open economy has a similar structure under fixed and under flexible exchange rates, but the quantitative properties of the economy will differ under the two regimes. *A priori* one cannot say whether convergence on long-run equilibrium will be faster under one or the other regime.

9. Under flexible exchange rates with strict inflation targeting, supply shocks will cause larger short-run fluctuations in output but smaller fluctuations in inflation than under fixed exchange rates. Our AS–AD model also predicts that demand shocks (including fiscal policy shocks) will generate smaller fluctuations in output as well as inflation under flexible than under fixed exchange rates, because a floating exchange rate allows the central bank to counteract demand shocks through its interest rate policy.

10. When domestic and foreign assets have different risk characteristics and financial investors are risk averse, fluctuations in required risk premia can cause fluctuations in nominal exchange rates under floating exchange rates. Empirical evidence suggests that exchange rates tend to move in response to shocks other than those that drive output fluctuations and that a large part of exchange rate variability originates from disturbances to the foreign exchange market itself. This does not support the idea that the exchange rate plays an important role as a shock absorber.

11. Floating exchange rates tend to undergo large swings in the medium term and often seem to 'overshoot' their long-run equilibrium values. Such apparently irrational behaviour may be quite compatible with rationality. For example, financial investors may correctly anticipate that a permanent positive demand shock requires a long-term appreciation of the exchange rate. If the central bank raises the domestic interest rate above the foreign interest rate in response to the shock, the exchange rate will then have to appreciate even more in the short run than in the long run to generate market expectations of a future depreciation so that domestic assets are no more attractive than foreign assets.

12. There is currently a widespread consensus that the ultimate goal of monetary policy should be to maintain a low and stable rate of inflation. A country may adopt a fixed exchange rate as an intermediate target for monetary policy with the purpose of achieving the ultimate goal of low and stable inflation. However, under fixed exchange rates stable inflation requires not only a stable inflation rate in the foreign anchor currency country; it also requires stability of the real exchange rate. This may be hard to achieve if the domestic economy is often exposed to asymmetric demand and supply shocks.

13. As an alternative to a fixed exchange rate, a country may adopt a flexible exchange rate with an inflation target to serve as a nominal anchor. Under inflation targeting the central bank's inflation forecast effectively becomes an intermediate target for monetary policy, since the central bank can only affect inflation with a time lag of $1\frac{1}{2}-2$ years. If the inflation forecast exceeds (falls short of) the target inflation rate when the interest rate is held constant, the interest rate must be raised (lowered) until the inflation forecast corresponds to the target.

14. Proponents of flexible exchange rates with inflation targeting argue that this policy regime will make the deviations of actual inflation from the target rate of inflation as small as existing economic knowledge permits. They also point out that a fixed exchange rate regime is vulnerable to speculative currency attacks. Proponents of fixed exchange rates argue that a floating rate may be an independent source of shocks and that a stable exchange rate should be seen as a goal in itself, since exchange rate uncertainty may hamper international trade and investment.

15. The theory of optimum currency areas sees the choice of exchange rate regime as a trade-off between the microeconomic benefits and the macroeconomic costs of a fixed exchange rate. One microeconomic benefit is that a credibly fixed exchange rate reduces the riskiness of foreign trade and investment. Further benefits are gained if exchange rate stability is achieved by entering a currency union where the adoption of a common currency reduces international transactions costs, improves market transparency and increases the liquidity of financial markets. The macroeconomic costs arise from the fact that a fixed exchange rate/common currency excludes the possibility of an independent national monetary policy to stabilize the domestic economy.

16. The microeconomic benefits of a fixed exchange rate/common currency increase with the degree of international economic integration whereas the macroeconomic costs decrease with economic integration. When integration proceeds beyond a certain point, it therefore becomes optimal to switch from a flexible exchange rate to a fixed rate/

common currency. It has also been argued that even if joining a currency union is not optimal *ex ante*, it may become optimal *ex post* because the adoption of a common currency will in itself promote economic integration.

17. Optimum currency area (OCA) theory suggests that the macroeconomic costs of giving up exchange rate flexibility within a group of trading partners will be relatively small if there is a low frequency of asymmetric shocks, a high degree of labour mobility across countries, and an international transfer mechanism securing a transfer of resources from countries hit by positive shocks to those hit by negative shocks. OCA theory also implies that the microeconomic benefits of a fixed exchange rate/common currency will be greater the greater the volume of trade and investment across borders.

25.6 Exercises

Exercise 1. The aggregate demand curve under flexible exchange rates

The derivation of the AD curve in the main text assumed that the expected 'normal' exchange rate is equal to the actual exchange rate observed during the last period. This exercise asks you to demonstrate that under certain assumptions, one can derive a similar AD curve under flexible exchange rates by simply assuming that the expected normal exchange rate is exogenous.

We start by assuming that the real interest rate affects aggregate demand mainly through its influence on business investment. Assuming that it only takes one period for firms to adjust their capital stock to its desired level K^d, and abstracting from depreciation on the existing capital stock, total gross investment in the current period, I, will equal the desired increase in the capital stock:

$$I_t = K_t^d - K_{t-1}^d. \tag{43}$$

Reflecting the underlying growth in aggregate demand, the desired capital stock varies positively with time, but at the same time it varies negatively with the real interest rate. Adopting a linear specification for convenience, we thus have:

$$K_t^d = at - br_t \quad \Rightarrow \quad I_t = a - b(r_t - r_{t-1}), \tag{44}$$

where a and b are constants. In other words, the *level* of investment depends on the *change* in the real rate of interest. Dropping the time subscripts for the current period, we may therefore approximate the goods market equilibrium condition by:

$$y - \bar{y} = \beta_1 e^r - \beta_2(r - r_{-1}) + \tilde{z},$$
$$\tilde{z} \equiv \beta_3(g - \bar{g}) + \beta_4(y^f - \bar{y}^f) + \beta_5(\ln \varepsilon - \ln \bar{\varepsilon}), \tag{45}$$

where we apply the usual notation (the constant a has dropped out because (41) considers a deviation from trend, and the parameter b is incorporated in β_2).

Now suppose that the central bank targets the foreign inflation rate by raising the real interest rate when domestic inflation is above foreign inflation, and vice versa:

$$r - r_{-1} = h(\pi - \pi^f). \tag{46}$$

In addition we have the condition for uncovered interest rate parity:

$$i = i^f + e_{+1}^e - e, \tag{47}$$

where we assume that exchange rate expectations are regressive:

$$e_{+1}^e - e = \theta(\bar{e} - e), \qquad \theta > 0. \tag{48}$$

Here we treat the expected normal exchange rate, $\bar{e}$, as an exogenous variable, although it may change from time to time.

By definition, the *ex ante* domestic real interest rate is $r \equiv i - \pi_{+1}^e$. The central bank has credibility, so the expected domestic inflation rate equals the central bank's inflation target, that is, $\pi_{+1}^e = \pi_{+1}^f = \pi^f$. Hence we have:

$$r = i - \pi^f. \tag{49}$$

Finally, we have the familiar definition of the foreign real interest rate,

$$r^f \equiv i^f - \pi^f, \tag{50}$$

and the bookkeeping identity for the current real exchange rate:

$$e^r = e_{-1}^r + e - e_{-1} + \pi^f - \pi. \tag{51}$$

1. Use Eqs (45)–(51) to show that the aggregate demand curve takes the following form:

$$y - \bar{y} = \beta_1 e_{-1}^r - \hat{\beta}_1(\pi - \pi^f) + z, \qquad \hat{\beta}_1 \equiv \beta_1 + h(\beta_2 + \beta_1\theta^{-1}), \tag{52}$$

$$z \equiv \beta_1\Delta\bar{e} + \beta_1\theta^{-1}\Delta r^f + \beta_3(g - \bar{g}) + \beta_4(y^f - \bar{y}^f) + \beta_5(\ln\varepsilon - \ln\bar{\varepsilon}). \tag{53}$$

where $\Delta\bar{e} \equiv \bar{e} - \bar{e}_{-1}$ and $\Delta r^f \equiv r^f - r_{-1}^f$ (Hint: as an intermediate step, use (47)–(50) to derive an expression for $r - r_{-1}$ in terms of $e - e_{-1}$, $\Delta\bar{e}$, and Δr^f. Then insert (46) to obtain an expression for $e - e_{-1}$ in terms of $\pi - \pi^f$, $\Delta\bar{e}$, and Δr^f.) Make a brief comparison between these results and the AD curve (15) in the main text.

2. Suppose that expectations of a permanent weakening of the domestic currency arise. How will this affect the aggregate demand curve? Give some examples of economic events which might generate expectations of a permanent depreciation of the domestic currency.

Exercise 2. 'Leaning against the wind' under flexible exchange rates

This exercise invites you to explore the implications of a monetary policy regime where the central bank follows a policy of 'leaning against the wind' by setting the interest rate in accordance with the following policy rule, explained in the section on 'dirty floating':

$$i - \pi_{+1}^e = r^f + h(\pi - \pi^*) + \lambda(e - e_{-1}), \qquad h > 0, \qquad \lambda > 0. \tag{54}$$

Because of perfect capital mobility and risk neutrality, the condition for uncovered interest parity must hold:

$$i = i^f + e_{+1}^e - e, \qquad e \equiv \ln E, \qquad e_{+1}^e \equiv \ln E_{+1}^e. \tag{55}$$

We also continue to assume regressive exchange rate expectations so that:

$$e_{+1}^e - e = -\theta(e - e_{-1}), \tag{56}$$

and we maintain the assumption that the central bank's inflation target is credible and equal to the foreign inflation rate:

$$\pi_{+1}^e = \pi^e = \pi^* = \pi^f. \tag{57}$$

The goods market equilibrium condition corresponds to Eq. (12) in the main text, repeated here for convenience:

$$y - \bar{y} = \beta_1 \overbrace{(e^r_{-1} + \Delta e + \pi^f - \pi)}^{e^r} - \beta_2 (i^f - \pi^e_{+1} + e^e_{+1} - e - \bar{r}^f) + \tilde{z}, \tag{58}$$

$$\tilde{z} \equiv \beta_3(g - \bar{g}) + \beta_4(y^f - \bar{y}^f) + \beta_5(\ln \varepsilon - \ln \bar{\varepsilon}).$$

Finally, we continue to work with an aggregate supply curve of the form:

$$\pi = \pi^e + \gamma(y - \bar{y}) + s. \tag{59}$$

1. Discuss briefly why the authorities might want to adopt a policy of 'leaning against the wind'.
2. Use Eqs (54)–(59) to show that the economy's aggregate demand curve takes the form:

$$\pi = \pi^f + \left(\frac{\beta_1}{\tilde{\beta}_1}\right) e^r_{-1} - \left(\frac{1}{\tilde{\beta}_1}\right)(y - \bar{y} - z), \qquad \tilde{\beta}_1 \equiv \beta_1 + \frac{h(\beta_1 + \theta \beta_2)}{\theta + \lambda}, \tag{60}$$

$$z \equiv -\beta_2(r^f - \bar{r}^f) + \beta_3(g - \bar{g}) + \beta_4(y_f - \bar{y}_f) + \beta_5(\ln \varepsilon - \ln \bar{\varepsilon}).$$

(Hint: follow the procedure described in Section 25.2.) Explain the economic mechanisms underlying the negative slope of the AD curve. Explain how the policy of leaning against the wind affects the slope of the AD curve.

3. Derive the equations determing the change over time in the nominal and in the real exchange rate. Does the policy of leaning against the wind amplify or dampen the impact of the inflation gap $\pi - \pi^f$ on nominal and real exchange rates? Explain. (Hints: use (54)–(57) to express $e - e_{-1}$ in terms of $\pi - \pi^f$ and the parameters h, θ, and λ.) Give a graphical illustration of the economy's adjustment to long-run equilibrium and explain the adjustment mechanisms.

4. Does leaning against the wind slow down or speed up the economy's speed of adjustment to long-run equilibrium? (Hint: derive a difference equation of the same form as (28) in the main text and investigate by differentiation how the parameter λ affects the coefficient a on the lagged output gap.) Try to provide an economic explanation for your result.

5. Use the procedure described in Section 25.3 of the main text to investigate how the policy of leaning against the wind affects the economy's short-run reaction to supply and demand shocks. Does leaning against the wind amplify or dampen the short-run effects of the shocks? Give an economic explanation for your findings.

6. Demonstrate that if the policy of leaning against the wind is very aggressive (so the parameter λ tends to infinity), the economy will work approximately as if the exchange rate were fully fixed. (Hint: compare the difference equation derived in Question 4 for the case of $\lambda \to \infty$ with the corresponding difference equation for the output gap under fixed exchange rates, given in Eq. (15) of Chapter 24.) Give an intuitive explanation for your finding.

Exercise 3. A flexible exchange rate regime with flexible inflation targeting

In the main text we assumed that the domestic central bank pursued so-called strict inflation targeting, reacting only to changes in the inflation gap. This exercise studies a regime of so-called flexible inflation targeting where interest rate policy follows a standard Taylor rule with a positive coefficient on the output gap. Our open economy with flexible exchange rates is thus described by the following equations (in our usual notation):

Goods market: $y - \bar{y} = \beta_1(\overbrace{e^r_{-1} + e - e_{-1} + \pi^f - \pi}^{e^r_t}) - \beta_2(i - \pi^e_{+1} - \bar{r}^f) + \tilde{z},$ (61)

Inflation expectations: $\pi^e_{+1} = \pi^e = \pi^f,$ (62)

Monetary policy: $i = r^f + \pi^e_{+1} + h(\pi - \pi^f) + b(y - \bar{y}),$ $b > 0,$ (63)

Uncovered interest rate parity: $i = i^f + e^e_{+1} - e,$ (64)

Exchange rate expectations: $e^e_{+1} - e = -\theta(e - e_{-1}),$ (65)

Foreign real interest rate: $r^f = i^f - \pi^f,$ (66)

SRAS: $\pi = \pi^e + \gamma(y - \bar{y}) + s,$ (67)

Real exchange rate: $e^r = e^r_{-1} + e - e_{-1} + \pi^f - \pi.$ (68)

1. Use Eqs (61)–(66) to show that the economy's aggregate demand curve is given by:

$$\pi = \pi^f + \left(\frac{\beta_1}{\hat{\beta}_1}\right)e^r_{-1} - \left(\frac{1 + b(\beta_2 + \theta^{-1}\beta_1)}{\hat{\beta}_1}\right)(y - \bar{y}) + \frac{z}{\hat{\beta}_1},$$ (69)

$$\hat{\beta}_1 \equiv \beta_1 + h(\beta_2 + \beta_1\theta^{-1}), \quad z \equiv -\beta_2(r^f - \bar{r}^f) + \tilde{z}.$$

(Hint: follow the procedure used in Section 25.2 to derive the AD curve.) Explain in economic terms how the central bank's reaction to the output gap affects the slope of the AD curve.

2. Use a (y, π) diagram to undertake a graphical analysis of the way the economy reacts to demand and supply shocks in the short run (i.e. in the first period), assuming that the economy is in long-run equilibrium in period 0. Illustrate and explain what difference it makes for your results that b is positive rather than zero. Can you think of a situation where policy makers would not want to choose a positive b?

3. Use (62)–(66) to show that

$$e^r = e^r_{-1} - (1 + \theta^{-1}h)(\pi - \pi^f) - \theta^{-1}b(y - \bar{y}).$$ (70)

Explain in economic terms why positive inflation and output gaps generate a real exchange rate appreciation (a fall in e^r).

Defining $\hat{y}_t \equiv y_t - \bar{y}$ and $\hat{\pi}_t \equiv \pi_t - \pi^f$ and using (62), (67), (69) and (70), we may summarize our model as follows:

AD: $\hat{\pi}_t = \left(\frac{\beta_1}{\hat{\beta}_1}\right)e^r_{t-1} - \left(\frac{1 + b(\beta_2 + \theta^{-1}\beta_1)}{\hat{\beta}_1}\right)\hat{y}_t + \frac{z_t}{\hat{\beta}_1},$ (71)

SRAS: $\hat{\pi}_t = \gamma\hat{y}_t + s_t,$ (72)

Real exchange rate: $e^r_t = e^r_{t-1} - (1 + \theta^{-1}h)\hat{\pi}_t - \theta^{-1}b\hat{y}_t.$ (73)

4. Use (71)–(73) to show that the model may be condensed to the following difference equation in the output gap:

$$\hat{y}_{t+1} = a\hat{y}_t + \beta(z_{t+1} - z_t) - \beta\hat{\beta}_1(s_{t+1} - s_t) - \beta\beta_1(1 + \theta^{-1}h)s_t,$$

(74)

$$\beta \equiv \frac{1}{1 + \gamma\hat{\beta}_1 + b(\beta_2 + \theta^{-1}\beta_1)}, \qquad a \equiv \beta[1 + \beta_2(b + \gamma h)].$$

Is the economy's long-run equilibrium stable? Does an increase in the value of b have an unambiguous effect on the economy's speed of adjustment? Try to give an economic explanation for your conclusion on the latter question. (Hint: it may be helpful for you to reconsider our explanation for the result found in equation (32) in the text.)

Exercise 4. Simulating an AS–AD model for an open economy with flexible exchange rates and a mixture of backward-looking and forward-looking expectations

Following up on Exercise 6 in the previous chapter, this exercise seeks to deepen your understanding of the workings of an economy with flexible exchange rates by asking you to implement the following model on the computer:

Goods market: $\quad y_t - \bar{y} = \beta_1(\overbrace{e_{t-1}^r + e_t - e_{t-1} + \pi^f - \pi_t}^{e_t^r}) - \beta_2(i_t - \pi_{t+1}^e - \bar{r}^f) + \tilde{z}_t,$ (75)

Inflation expectations: $\quad \pi_t^e = \varphi\pi^f + (1 - \varphi)\pi_{t-1}, \qquad 0 \le \varphi \le 1.$ (76)

Monetary policy: $\quad i_t = r^f + \pi_{t+1}^e + h(\pi_t - \pi^f),$ (77)

Uncovered interest rate parity: $\quad i_t = i^f + e_{t+1}^e - e_t,$ (78)

Exchange rate expectations: $\quad e_{t+1}^e - e_t = -\theta(e_t - e_{t-1}),$ (79)

Foreign real interest rate: $\quad r^f = i^f - \pi^f,$ (80)

SRAS: $\quad \pi_t = \pi_t^e + \gamma(y_t - \bar{y}) + s_t,$ (81)

Real exchange rate: $\quad e_t^r = e_{t-1}^r + e_t - e_{t-1} + \pi^f - \pi_t.$ (82)

Equation (76) gives the average expected domestic inflation rate, assuming that a fraction φ of the population has 'weakly rational' expectations which are anchored by the central bank's inflation target, $\pi^* = \pi^f$, whereas the remaining fraction of the population has static expectations, expecting that this year's inflation rate will correspond to the inflation rate observed last year, π_{t-1}. In the special case where $\varphi = 1$, we obtain the basic model analysed in the main text of this chapter.

1. Show by means of (75)–(80) that the equation for the aggregate demand curve is:

$$\pi_t = \pi^f + \left(\frac{\beta_1}{\hat{\beta}_1}\right)e_{t-1}^r - \left(\frac{1}{\hat{\beta}_1}\right)(y_t - \bar{y} - z_t),$$

(83)

$$\hat{\beta}_1 \equiv \beta_1 + \beta_2 h + \beta_1\theta^{-1}(1 - \varphi + h), \qquad z_t \equiv -\beta_2(r^f - \bar{r}^f) + \tilde{z}_t.$$

(Hint: use the procedure followed in Section 25.2 to derive the AD curve.)

To facilitate implementation of the model on the computer, we now want to reduce it to two difference equations in the output gap and the inflation gap. Defining $\hat{y}_t \equiv y_t - \bar{y}$ and $\hat{\pi}_t \equiv \pi_t - \pi^f$, and using (76)–(80) to derive $e_t - e_{t-1} = -\theta^{-1}(1 - \varphi + h)$, the model consisting of (81)–(83) may be summarized as:

AD: $\qquad \hat{\pi}_t = \left(\dfrac{\beta_1}{\hat{\beta}_1}\right)e^r_{t-1} - \left(\dfrac{1}{\hat{\beta}_1}\right)(\hat{y}_t - z_t),$ $\qquad\qquad$ (84)

SRAS: $\qquad \hat{\pi}_t = (1-\varphi)\hat{\pi}_{t-1} + \gamma\hat{y}_t + s_t,$ $\qquad\qquad$ (85)

Real exchange rate: $\qquad e^r_t = e^r_{t-1} - [1 + \theta^{-1}(1-\varphi+h)]\hat{\pi}_t.$ $\qquad$ (86)

From (84) and (86) it follows that:

$$\hat{\pi}_t - \hat{\pi}_{t-1} = \left(\dfrac{\beta_1}{\hat{\beta}_1}\right)\overbrace{[1+\theta^{-1}(1-\varphi+h)](-\hat{\pi}_{t-1})}^{=e^r_{t-1}-e^r_{t-2}} - \left(\dfrac{1}{\hat{\beta}_1}\right)[\hat{y}_t - \hat{y}_{t-1} - (z_t - z_{t-1})], \quad (87)$$

while (85) implies that:

$$\hat{\pi}_t - \hat{\pi}_{t-1} = -\varphi\hat{\pi}_{t-1} + \gamma\hat{y}_t + s_t. \qquad\qquad (88)$$

It also follows from (85) that:

$$\hat{y}_t = \gamma^{-1}\hat{\pi}_t - \gamma^{-1}(1-\varphi)\hat{\pi}_{t-1} - \gamma^{-1}s_t. \qquad\qquad (89)$$

2. Equate (87) and (88) to find an expression for $\hat{\pi}_t$ and substitute the resulting expression into (85) to show that the model may be reduced to the following second-order difference equation in the output gap:

$$\hat{y}_{t+2} - a_1\hat{y}_{t+1} + a_0\hat{y}_t = \beta(z_{t+2} - z_{t+1}) - \beta(1-\varphi)(z_{t+1} - z_t) - \hat{\beta}_1\beta s_{t+2} + \beta h\beta_2 s_{t+1},$$

$$(90)$$

$$\beta \equiv \dfrac{1}{1+\gamma\hat{\beta}_1}, \qquad a_1 \equiv \beta[2-\varphi+\gamma h\beta_2], \qquad a_0 \equiv \beta(1-\varphi).$$

Furthermore, insert (89) into (87) and use the definition of $\hat{\beta}_1$ to show that the model may alternatively be condensed to the following difference equation in the inflation gap:

$$\hat{\pi}_{t+2} - a_1\hat{\pi}_{t+1} + a_0\hat{\pi}_t = \gamma\beta(z_{t+2} - z_{t+1}) + \beta(s_{t+2} - s_{t+1}). \qquad (91)$$

Verify that (90) collapses to Eq. (28) in the main text in the special case where $\varphi = 1$. (Hint: remember to use the definition of $\hat{\beta}_1$.)

You are now asked to simulate the model (86), (90) and (91) on the computer to study the dynamics of output, inflation and the real exchange rate under flexible exchange rates. We proceed in a manner identical to the procedure followed in Exercise 6 of the previous chapter, but in case you haven't solved that exercise, we repeat all the steps here.

Using the definitions given in the appendix to Chapter 23, and assuming that trade is initially balanced and that the marginal and the average propensities to import are identical, one can demonstrate that:

$$\beta_1 = \dfrac{m(\eta_X + \eta_M - 1) - \eta_D(1-\tau)}{1 - D_Y + m},$$

where $m \equiv M_0/\bar{Y}$ is the initial ratio of imports to GDP, η_X and η_M are the price elasticities of export and import demand, $\tau \equiv (\bar{Y} - \bar{D})/\bar{Y}$ is the net tax burden on the private sector,

$\eta_D \equiv -(\partial D/\partial E')(E'/\bar{D})$ is the elasticity of private domestic demand with respect to the real exchange rate (reflecting the income effect of a change in the terms of trade), and D_Y is the private marginal propensity to spend.

Under the assumptions mentioned above, one can also show from the definition of β_2 in the appendix to Chapter 23 that:

$$\beta_2 \equiv \frac{\eta(1-\tau)(1-m)}{1-D_Y+m}, \qquad \eta \equiv -\frac{D_r}{(1-\tau)\bar{Y}},$$

where η is the change in private demand induced by a one percentage point change in the real interest rate, measured relative to private disposable income (we introduced this parameter in Chapter 18). Given these specifications, your first sheet should allow you to choose the parameters γ, φ, h, θ, m, η_X, η_M, τ, η, η_D and D_Y to calculate the auxiliary variables β_1, β_2, $\hat{\beta}_1$ and β (from which your spreadsheet can calculate the coefficients a_1 and a_0 in (90)).

You should construct a deterministic as well as a stochastic version of the model. In the deterministic version you just feed an exogenous time sequence of the shock variables z_t and s_t into the model. In the stochastic version of the model, the shock variables are assumed to be given by the autoregressive processes:

$$z_{t+1} = \delta z_t + x_{t+1}, \qquad 0 \le \delta < 1, \qquad x_t \sim N(0, \sigma_x^2), \qquad x_t \text{ i.i.d} \tag{92}$$

$$s_{t+1} = \omega s_t + c_{t+1}, \qquad 0 \le \omega < 1, \qquad c_t \sim N(0, \sigma_c^2), \qquad c_t \text{ i.i.d.} \tag{93}$$

so your first sheet should also allow you to choose the autocorrelation coefficients δ and ω and the *standard deviations* σ_x and σ_c. We suggest that you simulate the model over 100 periods, assuming that the economy starts out in long-run equilibrium in the initial period 0 (so that all of the variables $\hat{y}$, $\hat{\pi}$, e^r, x, c, z and s are equal to zero in period 0 and period −1). From the web page for this book http://highered.mcgraw-hill.com/sites/0077104250/ student_view0/index.html you can download an Excel spreadsheet with two different 100-period samples taken from the standardized normal distribution. Choose the first sample to represent the stochastic shock variable x_t, and the second sample to represent the shock variable c_t. To calibrate the magnitude of the shocks x_t and c_t, you must multiply the samples from the standardized normal distribution by the respective standard deviations σ_x and σ_c.

Apart from listing the parameters of the model, your first sheet should also list the standard deviations of output and inflation as well as the coefficient of correlation between output and inflation and the coefficients of autocorrelation for these variables (going back four periods) emerging from your simulations of the stochastic model version. It will also be useful to include diagrams illustrating the simulated values of the output gap, the inflation gap and the real exchange rate.

For the simulation of the *deterministic* version of the model, we propose that you use the parameter values

$$\varphi = 0.5, \quad \gamma = 0.2, \quad m = 0.3, \quad \eta_X = \eta_M = 1.5, \quad \theta = 2,$$
$$h = 0.5, \quad \tau = 0.2, \quad \eta = 0.5, \quad \eta_D = 0.3, \quad D_Y = 0.8.$$

3. Use the deterministic model version to simulate the dynamic effects of a *temporary negative demand shock*, where $z_1 = -1$ in period $t = 1$ and $z_t = 0$ for all $t \ge 2$. Illustrate the evolution of the output and inflation gaps in diagrams and comment on your results. Investigate how the economy's adjustment to the shock depends on the conduct of monetary policy by varying the value of the parameter h. Try to explain your findings.

4. Vary (one by one) the parameters φ and θ to explore how the economy's dynamic reaction to the temporary demand shock depends on the way expectations are formed. Try to explain your results.

5. Now use the deterministic model to simulate the dynamic effects of a *temporary negative supply shock*, where $s_1 = +1$ in period $t = 1$ and $s_t = 0$ for all $t \geq 2$. Illustrate the evolution of the output and inflation gaps in diagrams and comment on your results. How do the results depend on the monetary policy parameter h? Does monetary policy face a dilemma? Explain.

6. Simulate the stochastic version of the model, setting $\delta = \omega = 0.5$, and $\sigma_x^2 = \sigma_c^2 = 1$, while maintaining the other parameter values given above. From this point of departure, try to adjust the values of φ, δ, ω, σ_x^2 and σ_c^2 so as to achieve a better match between the model-simulated standard deviations and coefficients of correlation and autocorrelation for output and inflation and the corresponding data for the UK economy presented in Tables 13.2–13.4. For your information, the standard deviation of the cyclical component in the UK inflation rate was 0.0086, according to the quarterly data underlying Tables 13.3 and 13.4. (When trying to reproduce the observed correlation between output and inflation, you should only focus on the *contemporaneous* coefficient of correlation. Moreover, note that our simplified model cannot be expected to reproduce the data with great accuracy.) Assuming that your parameter values are plausible, what are the implications of your analysis for the relative importance of demand shocks and supply shocks as drivers of the UK business cycle?

Exercise 5. Symmetric versus asymmetric shocks and the need for (real) exchange rate flexibility

1. Explain why a low and stable domestic inflation rate under fixed exchange rates requires a stable real exchange rate as well as a low and stable inflation rate in the foreign anchor country.

2. Explain the difference between symmetric and asymmetric shocks in open economies. Illustrate the effect on the long-run equilibrium exchange rate of a permanent positive supply shock when the shock is asymmetric and compare with the effect of a symmetric shock. Explain why a fixed nominal exchange rate may be problematic in the scenario with an asymmetric shock.

3. Discuss the potential role of fiscal policy in a country with fixed exchange rates exposed to asymmetric shocks.

4. Assume that a group of countries with fixed but adjustable exchange rates and strong international trade links are exposed to a symmetric negative demand shock. What would happen if all (or most) countries tried to escape from the resulting recession by devaluing their currencies? What would be the most rational economic policy response from an international perspective?

Exercise 6. Optimum currency area theory

1. Explain and discuss the nature of the microeconomic benefits from a fully fixed exchange rate/common currency and how these benefits depend on the degree of international economic integration. What difference does it make whether the exchange is fixed or whether national currencies are abandoned in favour of a common currency?

2. Explain and discuss the nature of the macroeconomic costs of a fully fixed exchange rate and how these costs depend on the degree of economic integration.

3. Many economists have argued that even though a fixed exchange rate/common currency among a group of countries may not seem optimal *ex ante*, it may nevertheless turn out to be optimal *ex post*. Explain and discuss this argument.

4. Discuss the relevance of optimum currency area theory for (the debate on) monetary integration in Europe.

Appendix: Basic regression analysis

This appendix gives a brief introduction to regression analysis as used in this book. It can in no way substitute for a real (introductory) course in econometrics,[1] but it should enable the reader to understand the estimations undertaken in this book. Our appendix presupposes some basic knowledge of probability theory and statistics such as empirical and theoretical distributions and their means and variances.

1   Model and data

Assume that according to some economic theory, *ceteris paribus* one economic variable x affects (or explains or causes) another economic variable y according to the following linear relationship:

$$y = \beta_0 + \beta_1 x, \tag{1}$$

where β_0 and β_1 are parameters. We call x the independent or explanatory variable and y the dependent or explained variable.

For example, x could be household income and y could be household consumption, or x could be the length of an individual's education in years and y could be the individual's hourly earnings.

The meaning of the *ceteris paribus* assumption above is that other variables believed to affect y are held constant. In economics, where data rarely come from laboratory experiments, it is most often *not* possible to hold other variables constant. The economist may then wish (and have) to include as many important explanatory variables as possible. This often leads to an equation with several explanatory variables such as:

$$y = \beta_0 + \beta_1 x + \beta_2 z. \tag{2}$$

In our earnings and education example, an important additional explanatory variable would be experience (years in the labour market).

The linear form of (1) or (2) may seem special, but y and/or x and z could, for instance, be the logs of some underlying economic variables. For instance, in estimations of earnings and education relations in labour economics, the y in (2) is typically the log of hourly earnings, so β_1 and β_2 are semi-elasticities (giving the percentage increase in earnings resulting from an additional year of education or experience). If both the dependent and the independent variables are measured in logarithms, the parameters are elasticities. The linear form may therefore not be as restrictive as it first appears.

We assume that the economist collects data in the form of coupled observations of x (and z) and y, or of variables that come as close as practically possible to the theoretical variables x, y and z. The data set is thus of the form (x_i, y_i) or (x_i, z_i, y_i), where i is an index for observation number running from 1 to n.

1. For a real guide to econometrics we can refer the reader to Jeffrey M. Wooldridge, *Introductory Econometrics: A Modern Approach*, Thomson, South-Western, 2003, or to James H. Stock and Mark W. Watson, *Introduction to Econometrics*, Addison Wesley, 2003.

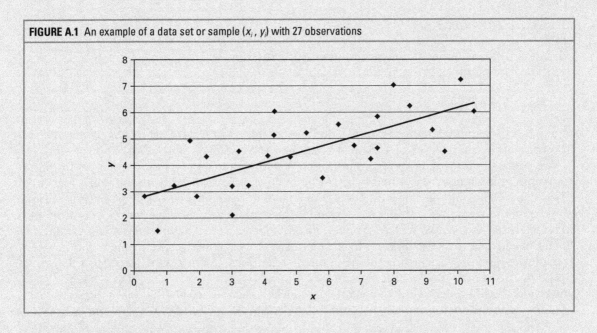

FIGURE A.1 An example of a data set or sample (x_i, y_i) with 27 observations

Such a data set can be a 'cross-section' where the index i runs across entities such as persons or firms or countries. For instance, for each person i in a group of persons, the economist observes average hourly earnings, education level and experience in some specific year. Alternatively the data set can be a 'time series', where the index i goes across time, so, for instance, the data set contains for each year i between 1960 and 2008 aggregate income and aggregate consumption of a specific country. The index i can go across both time and entity. In that case the data set can be a 'pooled cross-section' reporting, for instance, for two different years the average hourly earnings, education levels and experiences of a number of people, but the people need not be the same in the two years, or it may be a set of 'panel' or 'longitudinal' data where, in the earnings and education example, the people for whom earnings, etc., are observed would be the same in the two years.

We assume throughout that for any collected data set not all observations of an explanatory variable are identical, and in the case of several explanatory variables the observations of x_i and z_i are not perfectly correlated, that is, they are not situated exactly on a straight line.

A data set for the case of one explanatory variable is illustrated in Fig. A.1 where there are 27 observations (x_i, y_i). Note that the points are not situated exactly on a straight line, but rather as a cloud seemingly clustered around a line. In practice, data always involve some 'disturbance' because of measurement errors and because in practice it is not possible to include literally *all* factors affecting the dependent variable.

If our model is strictly speaking (1) and our data set is as illustrated in Fig. A.1, the model is immediately rejected: according to our model the points should be exactly on a straight line, but they are not. Thus we have to modify our model for it to be consistent with the data. We therefore assume that y is a *random* variable and that it is only the conditional *mean* value of y that is given from x as $\beta_0 + \beta_1 x$. This amounts to saying that:

$$y = \beta_0 + \beta_1 x + u, \tag{3}$$

where u is a random 'disturbance' or 'error term' that can also be thought of as the unobserved influence of omitted explanatory variables. For our exposition (which does not aim at maximal generality) we will from the beginning impose the following strong but classical conditions on the distribution of u: the distribution of the error term u is independent of x and follows for any given x a normal distribution with mean zero and variance $\sigma^2 > 0$. In standard notation:

u is i.i.d., $u \sim N(0, \sigma^2)$, $\qquad\qquad\qquad\qquad\qquad\qquad\qquad\qquad\qquad\qquad$ (4)

where i.i.d. means 'independently and identically distributed'.

In the case of multiple explanatory variables our model is:

$$y = \beta_0 + \beta_1 x + \beta_2 z + u, \qquad\qquad\qquad\qquad\qquad\qquad\qquad\qquad (5)$$

where u is now independent of x *and* z, and we combine again with (4) for the full model. The name for our model is the 'classical linear regression model'.

We assume that the data set (x_i, y_i) or (x_i, z_i, y_i) is the outcome of a random sample from the true 'population model' described by (3) or (5) and (4): somehow realizations x_i of x (and z_i of z) occur. This could be deterministically in a laboratory experiment where one can control x and z, but in most applications in economics the explanatory variables are not controllable in which case observations such as x_i and z_i are best viewed as realizations of random variables.[2] Each time an x_i (and z_i) has been realized, a value y_i of y is generated according to our model: it is picked randomly according to one of the distributions $N(\beta_0 + \beta_1 x_i, \sigma^2)$ or $N(\beta_0 + \beta_1 x_i + \beta_2 z_i, \sigma^2)$. This is how the data set or sample, (y_i, x_i) or (y_i, x_i, z_i), $i = 1, \ldots, n$, has been generated. The data set is thus to be considered a stochastic variable that takes different contents with different probabilities, and repeated sampling would yield different data sets.

2   OLS estimators

The economist (econometrician) wants to use the data set to estimate the parameters β_0, β_1 (and β_2) of the model. Because of the randomness of the data set, one can only arrive at the correct values by accident: different samples will, for any given estimation procedure, yield different estimates. To distinguish estimates from true parameter values we use the notation $\hat{\beta}_0$, $\hat{\beta}_1$, $\hat{\beta}_2$ for our estimates. Given a specific sample, how should one arrive at a reasonable value of, say, $\hat{\beta}_1$?

Consider the simple linear regression model with one explanatory variable. Given $\hat{\beta}_0$ and $\hat{\beta}_1$, the estimated value of y for a given observation x_i of x would be $\hat{y}_i = \hat{\beta}_0 + \hat{\beta}_1 x_i$. The observation of y coupled with x_i is y_i, so the residual (the difference between the observed and the estimated value of y, given x_i) would be $\hat{u}_i \equiv y_i - \hat{y}_i$. The so-called ordinary least squares (OLS) criterion says that $\hat{\beta}_0$ and $\hat{\beta}_1$ should be set such as to minimize the sum of squared residuals over the data sample:

$$\min Q(\hat{\beta}_0, \hat{\beta}_1), \quad \text{where } Q(\hat{\beta}_0, \hat{\beta}_1) \equiv \sum_{i=1}^{n} \hat{u}_i^2 = \sum_{i=1}^{n} (y_i - \hat{\beta}_0 - \hat{\beta}_1 x_i)^2. \qquad (6)$$

By minimizing the sum of the *squared* residuals, rather than just the sum of the absolute values of the residuals, one puts particular emphasis on avoiding large (as opposed to small) residuals. This makes intuitive sense, but there are also some more basic reasons for adopting the OLS criterion, as we shall explain below. To understand this explanation, we must first derive the implications of the OLS criterion. Note that the data sample is considered fixed here and the variables to be chosen are $\hat{\beta}_0$ and $\hat{\beta}_1$. The first-order conditions, $\partial Q/\partial \hat{\beta}_0 = 0$ and $\partial Q/\partial \hat{\beta}_1 = 0$, for this minimization are:

$$\sum_{i=1}^{n} (y_i - \hat{\beta}_0 - \hat{\beta}_1 x_i) = 0, \qquad\qquad\qquad\qquad\qquad\qquad\qquad\qquad (7)$$

$$\sum_{i=1}^{n} x_i(y_i - \hat{\beta}_0 - \hat{\beta}_1 x_i) = 0, \qquad\qquad\qquad\qquad\qquad\qquad\qquad\qquad (8)$$

---

2. These random variables are assumed to have finite (well-defined) means and variances. For the present purposes we do not need to be more specific about their distributions than that.

and because of the quadratic form of Q, these conditions are also sufficient for a (global) minimum. Equation (7) can be written as:

$$\sum_{i=1}^{n} y_i = n\hat{\beta}_0 + \hat{\beta}_1 \sum_{i=1}^{n} x_i.$$

Dividing here on both sides by n and letting averages be denoted by bars ($\bar{x} \equiv (1/n)\sum_{i=1}^{n} x_i$ and $\bar{y} \equiv (1/n)\sum_{i=1}^{n} y_i$) gives $\bar{y} = \hat{\beta}_0 + \hat{\beta}_1 \bar{x}$ or:

$$\hat{\beta}_0 = \bar{y} - \hat{\beta}_1 \bar{x}. \tag{9}$$

Inserting this expression for $\hat{\beta}_0$ in the second first-order condition (8), gives:

$$\sum_{i=1}^{n} x_i (y_i - \bar{y} + \hat{\beta}_1 \bar{x} - \hat{\beta}_1 x_i) = 0,$$

or

$$\sum_{i=1}^{n} x_i (y_i - \bar{y}) = \hat{\beta}_1 \sum_{i=1}^{n} x_i (x_i - \bar{x}). \tag{10}$$

From this we can find $\hat{\beta}_1$ directly, but we prefer to write it slightly differently. Since obviously $\sum_{i=1}^{n}(y_i - \bar{y}) = 0$ (show this), we have:

$$\sum_{i=1}^{n} x_i (y_i - \bar{y}) = \sum_{i=1}^{n} x_i (y_i - \bar{y}) - \sum_{i=1}^{n} \bar{x}(y_i - \bar{y}) = \sum_{i=1}^{n}(x_i - \bar{x})(y_i - \bar{y}),$$

and therefore in the special case where $x_i = y_i$:

$$\sum_{i=1}^{n} x_i (x_i - \bar{x}) = \sum_{i=1}^{n}(x_i - \bar{x})^2.$$

Inserting the latter two into (10) gives:

$$\hat{\beta}_1 = \frac{\sum_{i=1}^{n}(x_i - \bar{x})(y_i - \bar{y})}{\sum_{i=1}^{n}(x_i - \bar{x})^2}. \tag{11}$$

The formula in (11) is our *estimator* (our general formula for estimation) of the slope β_1 in the simple linear regression model. An *estimate* is a particular value for the slope computed from a specific data set. An estimator for β_0 follows by inserting the estimator $\hat{\beta}_1$ into (9). Most often our main interest is in the slope estimate (a constant measurement error on x will simply be included in the estimate of the intercept, but will not affect the slope estimate).

Once one has fed the data set into a spreadsheet on a computer, it is easy to compute the estimates $\hat{\beta}_1$ and $\hat{\beta}_0$. Standard programs give the estimates and other relevant information of the estimation at the press of a key. For the example in Fig. A.1, the OLS estimates are $\hat{\beta}_0 = 2.736$ for the intercept and $\hat{\beta}_1 = 0.342$ for the slope.

If there are several explanatory variables as in (5), the first-order conditions for minimizing the sum of squared residuals, $Q(\hat{\beta}_0, \hat{\beta}_1, \hat{\beta}_2) \equiv \sum_{i=1}^{n}(y_i - \hat{\beta}_0 - \hat{\beta}_1 x_i - \hat{\beta}_2 z_i)^2$, are:

$$\sum_{i=1}^{n}(y_i - \hat{\beta}_0 - \hat{\beta}_1 x_i - \hat{\beta}_2 z_i) = 0, \tag{12}$$

$$\sum_{i=1}^{n} x_i (y_i - \hat{\beta}_0 - \hat{\beta}_1 x_i - \hat{\beta}_2 z_i) = 0, \tag{13}$$

$$\sum_{i=1}^{n} z_i (y_i - \hat{\beta}_0 - \hat{\beta}_1 x_i - \hat{\beta}_2 z_i) = 0, \tag{14}$$

etc. for even more explanatory variables. These systems of equations become more tedious to solve the more explanatory variables there are, but simple computer routines can solve such systems. So again, having typed in the data, the press of a key will give the estimates.

As a further step before explaining the rationale for the OLS estimators, it is useful to show how one can get an indication of the goodness of fit of an estimation.

3 The goodness of fit

Now that we have our estimates for $\hat{\beta}_0$, $\hat{\beta}_1$ and $\hat{\beta}_2$, we can write down the OLS regression line (or function):

$$y = \hat{\beta}_0 + \hat{\beta}_1 x + \hat{\beta}_2 z.$$

For the example in Fig. A.1 this 'line of best fit' is the line indicated in the figure:

$$y = 2.736 + 0.342x.$$

One can compute the observed values of residuals as $\hat{u}_i = y_i - \hat{y}_i$, where $\hat{y}_i = \hat{\beta}_0 + \hat{\beta}_1 x_i + \hat{\beta}_2 z_i$, for each observation i. A property of our estimation is that $\sum_{i=1}^{n} \hat{u}_i = 0$, as you may see directly from the first of the first-order conditions above, (7) or (12). We can view each observation y_i of the dependent variable as the sum of the predicted or fitted value, $\hat{y}_i$, and the residual, $\hat{u}_i$, that is, $y_i = \hat{y}_i + \hat{u}_i$. Averaging on both sides gives: $\bar{y} = \bar{\hat{y}}$, so the sample average of the dependent variable equals the average of the fitted values.

As a measure of the total variation of the dependent variable in our data set (the variation we seek to explain) we may use the 'sum of squares, total':

$$SST \equiv \sum_{i=1}^{n} (y_i - \bar{y})^2.$$

As a measure of the variation explained by our line of best fit we may use the 'sum of squares explained', defined as:

$$SSE = \sum_{i=1}^{n} (\hat{y}_i - \bar{\hat{y}})^2 = \sum_{i=1}^{n} (\hat{y}_i - \bar{y})^2,$$

while letting the 'sum of squares of residuals' measure the variation not explained:

$$SSR = \sum_{i=1}^{n} \hat{u}_i^2.$$

Each of these sums of squares is positive, and one can show that $SST = SSE + SSR$. As a single numerical measure of how good the fit of the 'line of best fit' actually is, one often uses the so-called R-squared or coefficient of determination, which measures the fraction of the total variation of the dependent variable in the sample that is explained by the explanatory variables according to the estimation:

$$R^2 \equiv \frac{SSE}{SST} = 1 - \frac{SSR}{SST}.$$

This R^2 is a number between 0 and 1. If all the observations y_i are exactly on the line of best fit, $y_i = \hat{y}_i$ for all i, then $R^2 = 1$, indicating the best possible fit. If, on the other hand, R^2 is close to 0, very little of the variation in y is explained by x (while the residuals 'explain' all the variation). Generally R^2 is considered an index of the goodness of fit.[3] The R-squared is typically included in the output of standard computer programs. For the example in Fig. A.1 we have $R^2 = 0.53$.

Many packages report an 'adjusted R-squared' as well. The R^2 just defined necessarily increases as more explanatory variables are added even if these do not help to increase the explanatory power of the regression very much. To compensate for this tendency the adjusted R-squared is defined as:

$$\bar{R}^2 = 1 - \frac{n-1}{n-k-1}(1-R^2),$$

where k is the number of explanatory variables. Increasing k makes R^2 go up which tends to increase $\bar{R}^2$, but the adjusted R-squared includes a 'cost' of adding new explanatory variables. Evaluating the goodness of fit by the adjusted R-squared rather than the R-squared tends to favour parsimonious theories that include only few, important explanatory variables. A value of 1 for $\bar{R}^2$ still corresponds to a perfect fit while a negative value (which is now possible, for instance if $R^2 = 0.2$, $n = 21$ and $k = 5$) corresponds to a poor fit.

It is important to emphasize that an estimation that yields a low R^2 (or $\bar{R}^2$) may still be very useful in the sense that it may give an accurate estimate, $\hat{\beta}_1$ say. If important explanatory variables have been left out (perhaps because they are difficult to observe or measure), but the assumptions of the linear regression model nevertheless hold, then an estimation based on a good (large and well dispersed) sample may give a sharp estimate of the model's parameters and yet explain only a tiny fraction of the variation in the dependent variable. However, our basic model assumptions, in particular that the mean of the disturbance u is zero (and its variance constant) *independently of* x, are less likely to be fulfilled if important explanatory variables have been left out (try to explain why). This is why we said above that the econometrician may wish to include as many important explanatory variables as possible.

In conclusion, the econometrician would usually like to see a high R^2, but should not necessarily dispose of an estimation if the R^2 is low.

4 OLS estimators are BLUE

The OLS estimators are themselves random variables since different data samples occur with different probabilities and yield different estimates. Note that there are two sources of randomness: the draw of the sample values of the independent variable(s), e.g. $(x_1, \ldots, x_n) \equiv \mathbf{x}$ and, given this draw, the randomness of the dependent variable due to the randomness of the error terms.[4] We now establish some properties of the OLS estimators as random variables, with the purpose of explaining the rationale for the method of Ordinary Least Squares.

Consider the slope estimator $\hat{\beta}_1$ of the simple regression model stated in (11). Since $\sum_{i=1}^{n}(x_i - \bar{x}) = 0$, we can write this as:

$$\hat{\beta}_1 = \frac{\sum_{i=1}^{n}(x_i - \bar{x})y_i}{\sum_{i=1}^{n}(x_i - \bar{x})^2} = \sum_{i=1}^{n}\frac{(x_i - \bar{x})}{s_x^2}y_i, \tag{15}$$

where we have used the definition $s_x^2 \equiv \sum_{i=1}^{n}(x_i - \bar{x})^2$. It appears from (15) that $\hat{\beta}_1$ is a linear combination of the observations y_i of the dependent variable given $\mathbf{x}$. We say that $\hat{\beta}_1$ is a

3. One can show that R^2 as defined is the square of the coefficient of correlation between y_i and $\hat{y}_i$, which explains the name R-squared and again indicates that R^2 measures the goodness of fit.

4. If the sample values x_i can be controlled, the randomness of samples comes solely from the error terms. As we mentioned, most often in economics the sample values of the independent variables must be considered random variables.

linear estimator. From (9), $\hat{\beta}_0$ is also a linear estimator. It can be shown that the OLS estimators for the model with multiple explanatory variables are linear as well. There could be (and are) other linear estimators of $\hat{\beta}_1$ where the coefficient w_i on each y_i would not be exactly $(x_i - \bar{x})/s_x^2$ as in (15), but a w_i depending in some other way on the sample values x_i.

Since $\hat{\beta}_1$ is a random variable we can ask: what is its mean value? According to our model each observed y_i can be expressed in terms of the observed x_i as:

$$y_i = \beta_0 + \beta_1 x_i + u_i, \tag{16}$$

which is just a repetition of our model restricted to observed values of x. Note that the β_0 and β_1 occurring here are not estimates, but true values, of the parameters, and likewise the u_i are not the residuals $\hat{u}_i = y_i - \hat{y}_i$ defined above (that can be computed using the estimates $\hat{\beta}_0$ and $\hat{\beta}_1$), but the true realizations of u. Inserting (16) into (15) gives:

$$\hat{\beta}_1 = \frac{\sum_{i=1}^{n}(x_i - \bar{x})(\beta_0 + \beta_1 x_i + u_i)}{s_x^2}$$

In the numerator we may use that $\sum_{i=1}^{n}(x_i - \bar{x})\beta_0 = 0$ and $\sum_{i=1}^{n}(x_i - \bar{x})x_i = \sum_{i=1}^{n}(x_i - \bar{x})^2$ as well as $s_x^2 \equiv \sum_{i=1}^{n}(x_i - \bar{x})^2$ to get:

$$\hat{\beta}_1 = \beta_1 + \frac{\sum_{i=1}^{n}(x_i - \bar{x})u_i}{s_x^2} = \beta_1 + \sum_{i=1}^{n}\frac{(x_i - \bar{x})}{s_x^2}u_i. \tag{17}$$

Given the observations x_i, the estimator $\hat{\beta}_1$ is equal to the true β_1 plus a linear combination of the true error terms u_i. It is only because the error terms are typically not zero that the estimate $\hat{\beta}_1$ does not deliver β_1 exactly. However, since the *expected* value of each error term u_i is (assumed to be) zero, taking expected values on both sides of (17) conditional on $\mathbf{x}$ (that is, taking the sample values x_i as given so they are not random) gives: $E(\hat{\beta}_1 \mid \mathbf{x}) = \beta_1$. Since this holds for any given $\mathbf{x}$, we also have without conditioning on $\mathbf{x}$:

$$E(\hat{\beta}_1) = \beta_1. \tag{18}$$

Likewise one can show that $E(\hat{\beta}_0) = \beta_0$. On average across a large number of samples the estimators $\hat{\beta}_0$ and $\hat{\beta}_1$ will thus correspond to the true values of the parameters β_0 and β_1. We therefore say that $\hat{\beta}_0$ and $\hat{\beta}_1$ are *unbiased* estimators. To arrive at this result we did not use all the distributional assumptions stated in (4), only that the mean of u given any x is zero: $E(u \mid x) = 0$. It can be shown that also with multiple explanatory variables the OLS estimators are unbiased.

Next turn to the variance $var(\hat{\beta}_1)$ of the slope estimator in the simple regression model. We should emphasize that by $var(\hat{\beta}_1)$ we mean the variance of $\hat{\beta}_1$ *conditional on* $\mathbf{x}$ (we could have called it $var(\hat{\beta}_1 \mid \mathbf{x})$ to stress this fact). The term β_1 in (17) is a non-random constant, and given $\mathbf{x}$ so is each coefficient $(x_i - \bar{x})/s_x^2$ on u_i. Since the u_i are independent and all have variance σ^2, it follows from the usual computational rules for variances that:

$$var(\hat{\beta}_1) = \sum_{i=1}^{n}\left(\frac{(x_i - \bar{x})}{s_x^2}\right)^2 \sigma^2 = \frac{\sum_{i=1}^{n}(x_i - \bar{x})^2}{s_x^4}\sigma^2 = \frac{\sigma^2}{s_x^2}, \tag{19}$$

and the standard deviation of $\hat{\beta}_1$ is:

$$std(\hat{\beta}_1) \equiv \sqrt{var(\hat{\beta}_1)} = \frac{\sigma}{s_x}. \tag{20}$$

The two latter equations have an intuitive content: the larger σ^2 is, the more spread out around the true straight line the observations y_i will tend to be given the x_i, and therefore the less precise an estimate derived from the observations will be. On the other hand, the greater the dispersion of the x_i (the larger s_x is), the more precise is the estimate (just draw a figure where the x_i are very close to each other and see how easily a fitting line can be twisted). This warns us, in so far as we have any influence on the sample values x_i, to try to have these 'well spread out'.

With more explanatory variables one can again find the variances of the OLS slope estimators given the sample values of the independent variables. These look a bit more complicated because they have to take account of any correlation between the independent variables. However, independently of the number of explanatory variables the following important result about OLS estimators known as the Gauss-Markov theorem holds: *Among all linear and unbiased estimators, the OLS estimator has the smallest (unconditional) variance. In other words, the OLS estimators are Best Linear Unbiased Estimators, or BLUE.* This is an important motivation for the criterion of 'least squares'. We give here a nice and simple proof of the Gauss–Markov theorem for the slope estimator of the simple linear regression model.

Consider an arbitrary linear estimator of β_1 : $\tilde{\beta}_1 = \sum_{i=1}^{n} w_i y_i$, where the weights w_i depend on $\mathbf{x}$. As above, we may rewrite the expression for $\tilde{\beta}_1$ using $y_i = \beta_0 + \beta_1 x_i + u_i$ to get: $\tilde{\beta}_1 = \beta_0 \sum_{i=1}^{n} w_i + \beta_1 \sum_{i=1}^{n} w_i x_i + \sum_{i=1}^{n} w_i u_i$. Taking expected values on both sides conditional on $\mathbf{x}$, remembering that $E(u_i) = 0$, gives: $E(\tilde{\beta}_1 \mid \mathbf{x}) = \beta_0 \sum_{i=1}^{n} w_i + \beta_1 \sum_{i=1}^{n} w_i x_i$. Insisting that $E(\tilde{\beta}_1 \mid \mathbf{x}) = \beta_1$ for any values of the true parameters β_0 and β_1, that is, insisting on (conditional) unbiasedness, requires that for any $\mathbf{x}$:

$$\sum_{i=1}^{n} w_i = 0 \quad \text{and} \quad \sum_{i=1}^{n} w_i x_i = 1. \tag{21}$$

Conditional on $\mathbf{x}$, the variance of $\tilde{\beta}_1$ is: $var(\tilde{\beta}_1) = \sigma^2 \sum_{i=1}^{n} w_i^2$. Hence, the linear and unbiased estimator that gives the smallest variance (given $\mathbf{x}$) is one that minimizes $\sum_{i=1}^{n} w_i^2$ subject to the two restrictions in (21). The Lagrangian for this problem is: $La \equiv \sum_{i=1}^{n} w_i^2 - \lambda_1 \sum_{i=1}^{n} w_i - \lambda_2 (\sum_{i=1}^{n} w_i x_i - 1)$, where λ_1 and λ_2 are the Lagrange multipliers. The first-order conditions resulting from differentiating with respect to λ_1 and λ_2 and the w_i are the two equations in (21) repeated and: $2w_i - \lambda_1 - \lambda_2 x_i = 0$, $i = 1, \ldots, n$, which can be rewritten as:

$$w_i = \frac{\lambda_1}{2} + \frac{\lambda_2}{2} x_i. \tag{22}$$

Inserting this expression for w_i into each of the equations in (21) gives:

$$n \frac{\lambda_1}{2} + \frac{\lambda_2}{2} \sum_{i=1}^{n} x_i = 0 \quad \text{and} \quad \frac{\lambda_1}{2} \sum_{i=1}^{n} x_i + \frac{\lambda_2}{2} \sum_{i=1}^{n} x_i^2 = 1. \tag{23}$$

From the first of these, $\lambda_1/2 = -(\lambda_2/2)\sum_{i=1}^{n} x_i/n = -(\lambda_2/2)\bar{x}$. Inserting this expression for λ_1 into the second equation in (23) gives:

$$\frac{\lambda_2}{2} \left(\sum_{i=1}^{n} x_i^2 - \bar{x} \sum_{i=1}^{n} x_i \right) = 1.$$

Here $\sum_{i=1}^{n} x_i^2 - \bar{x}\sum_{i=1}^{n} x_i = \sum_{i=1}^{n} x_i x_i - \sum_{i=1}^{n} x_i \bar{x} = \sum_{i=1}^{n} x_i(x_i - \bar{x}) = \sum_{i=1}^{n} (x_i - \bar{x})(x_i - \bar{x})$, so:

$$\frac{\lambda_2}{2} = \frac{1}{\sum_{i=1}^{n} (x_i - \bar{x})^2}.$$

Inserting this expression for $\lambda_2/2$ into the expression for $\lambda_1/2$ we found above $(\lambda_1/2 = -(\lambda_2/2)\bar{x})$ gives:

$$\frac{\lambda_1}{2} = -\frac{\bar{x}}{\sum_{i=1}^{n}(x_i - \bar{x})^2}.$$

Finally, inserting the expressions for $\lambda_1/2$ as well as $\lambda_2/2$ into (22) gives:

$$w_i = \frac{x_i - \bar{x}}{\sum_{i=1}^{n}(x_i - \bar{x})^2},$$

and this is exactly the value of w_i in the OLS estimator (just compare to (15)). Hence, conditional on $\mathbf{x}$, the OLS estimator $\hat{\beta}_1$ has smallest variance among all linear, unbiased estimators. Since this holds for any given $\mathbf{x}$, the variance of the OLS estimator is also smallest unconditionally. This finishes our proof.

Note that we have still not used all of our assumptions on the distribution of u. The additional assumption used above is that the variance of u is σ^2 independently of x, whereas normality of the distribution of u has still not been used. It will be now.

5 Inference

We know that the mean of the slope estimator, $\hat{\beta}_1$, of the simple regression model is β_1, and the variance (given $\mathbf{x}$) is σ^2/s_x^2 (the standard deviation is σ/s_x). Furthermore, the expression in (17) shows that $\hat{\beta}_1$ is the sum of a fixed term (β_1) and a linear combination of the error terms u_i, where the weights are fixed given $\mathbf{x}$. This means that given $\mathbf{x}$, the estimator $\hat{\beta}_1$ is normally distributed (applying for the first time that the u_i are normally distributed): $\hat{\beta}_1 \sim N(\beta_1, \sigma^2/s_x^2)$. Consequently, the transformation defined by:

$$\upsilon = \frac{\hat{\beta}_1 - \beta_1}{\sigma/s_x} = \frac{\hat{\beta}_1 - \beta_1}{std(\hat{\beta}_1)} \tag{24}$$

has the standard normal distribution: $\upsilon \sim N(0, 1)$. This is potentially useful for statistical inference. For instance, let $\upsilon_{0.975}$ be the 97.5th percentile for the standardized normal distribution, that is, the particular number such that according to $N(0, 1)$ the probability, $\Pr(\upsilon < \upsilon_{0.975})$, of drawing a value of υ below $\upsilon_{0.975}$ is 97.5 per cent. This percentile is known to be 1.960. Since $N(0, 1)$ is symmetric around zero, the probability of a random draw ending between $-\upsilon_{0.975}$ and $\upsilon_{0.975}$ is 95 per cent, that is,

$$\Pr(-\upsilon_{0.975} < \upsilon < \upsilon_{0.975}) = 0.95.$$

Since $\upsilon \sim N(0, 1)$, we have:

$$\Pr\left(-\upsilon_{0.975} < \frac{\hat{\beta}_1 - \beta_1}{\sigma/s_x} < \upsilon_{0.975}\right) = 0.95 \Leftrightarrow$$

$$\Pr\left(\hat{\beta}_1 - \upsilon_{0.975}\frac{\sigma}{s_x} < \beta_1 < \hat{\beta}_1 + \upsilon_{0.975}\frac{\sigma}{s_x}\right) = 0.95.$$

This says that there is a 95 per cent probability that the true value of β_1 lies between $\hat{\beta}_1 - \upsilon_{0.975}\sigma/s_x$ and $\hat{\beta}_1 + \upsilon_{0.975}\sigma/s_x$, and the interval reaching from the lower to the upper of these values is called the 95 per cent *confidence interval* for β_1. Likewise, substituting the 99.5th percentile $\upsilon_{0.995}$ (known to be 2.576) for $\upsilon_{0.975}$ gives the 99 per cent confidence interval for β_1. Hence, given the estimate $\hat{\beta}_1$ and the standard deviation σ/s_x, we can identify a confidence interval so that with probability 95 per cent (or 99 per cent) the true value of β_1 lies in the interval, given the assumptions of our model. Such a statement is, of course, very useful, in particular if the confidence interval is narrow. However, in practice we almost never know the true variance σ^2, so we cannot compute the above confidence intervals. We must estimate σ^2 from the data to do any statistical inference analysis.

The error terms $u_i = y_i - \beta_0 - \beta_1 x_i$ cannot be observed because the true parameter values β_0 and β_1 are unknown, but the residuals $\hat{u}_i = y_i - \hat{\beta}_0 - \hat{\beta}_1 x_i$ can be computed and are estimates of the u_i. Since $\sigma^2 = var(u) = E[u^2]$, one might think that the estimator for σ^2 should be $\sum_{i=1}^{n} \hat{u}_i^2 / n$, but because of the intricate matter of 'degrees of freedom', which is beyond the scope of this appendix, the estimator $\hat{\sigma}^2$, that ensures unbiasedness ($E[\hat{\sigma}^2] = \sigma^2$) is:

$$\hat{\sigma}^2 = \frac{\sum_{i=1}^{n} \hat{u}_i^2}{n-2} = \frac{\sum_{i=1}^{n} (y_i - \hat{\beta}_0 - \hat{\beta}_1 x_i)^2}{n-2}. \tag{25}$$

For a given sample the estimated variance $\hat{\sigma}^2$, and hence the estimated standard deviation $\hat{\sigma}$, can be computed. The latter is reported by standard computer programs, for instance under the name of 'standard error of regression'. For our example, $\hat{\sigma} = 0.989$. Since $std(\hat{\beta}_1) = \sigma / s_x$, the natural estimator for $std(\hat{\beta}_1)$ is:

$$se(\hat{\beta}_1) = \frac{\hat{\sigma}}{s_x}.$$

This can be computed, which is always done by standard packages, and it is reported as the 'standard error of the estimate $\hat{\beta}_1$'. (Sometimes it is less precisely referred to as the 'standard deviation of $\hat{\beta}_1$' although strictly speaking it is an *estimate* of the standard deviation). In our example $se(\hat{\beta}_1) = 0.064$. With more than one explanatory variable there are similar formulae for the standard errors of the OLS estimates. In the regressions of this book the computed standard errors are widely reported and used for the purposes described in the following.

In view of what we did above it is now natural to define the transformed variable:

$$t = \frac{\hat{\beta}_1 - \beta_1}{\hat{\sigma} / s_x} = \frac{\hat{\beta}_1 - \beta_1}{se(\hat{\beta}_1)}, \tag{26}$$

which is almost the same as υ, but with the estimate $\hat{\sigma}$ substituted for σ (or the standard error $se(\hat{\beta}_1)$ substituted for the standard deviation $std(\hat{\beta}_1)$). The variable t is not normally distributed (note from (25) that the y_i enter into $\hat{\sigma}$, as they do into $\hat{\beta}_1$, so even given $\mathbf{x}$, the variable t is not just a normally distributed variable times a constant plus a constant). However, t is clearly a random variable since it depends on the random realizations of y. Given the properties of the random variable y_i implied by our modelling assumptions, and given $\mathbf{x}$, the variable t defined by (26) has been shown to follow the so-called t-distribution with $n - 2$ degrees of freedom. The t-distribution is 'spread out' compared to $N(0, 1)$, and more so the fewer degrees of freedom there are, but it approaches $N(0, 1)$ as the number of observations n goes to infinity. For any given number of degrees of freedom, the t-distribution is fixed and known and symmetric around zero. In particular its different percentiles are known and can be found in statistical tables. If the 97.5th percentile of the t-distribution with $n - 2$ degrees of freedom is $t_{0.975}$, then analogously to the above:

$$\Pr\left(-t_{0.975} < \frac{\hat{\beta}_1 - \beta_1}{se(\hat{\beta}_1)} < t_{0.975}\right) = 0.95 \quad \Leftrightarrow$$

$$\Pr(\hat{\beta}_1 - t_{0.975} se(\hat{\beta}_1) < \beta_1 < \hat{\beta}_1 + t_{0.975} se(\hat{\beta}_1)) = 0.95.$$

Hence, the 95 per cent confidence interval for β_1 goes from $\hat{\beta}_1 - t_{0.975} se(\hat{\beta}_1)$ to $\hat{\beta}_1 + t_{0.975} se(\hat{\beta}_1)$, and likewise the 99 per cent confidence interval goes from $\hat{\beta}_1 - t_{0.995} se(\hat{\beta}_1)$ to $\hat{\beta}_1 + t_{0.995} se(\hat{\beta}_1)$. These intervals can be computed since they depend on $\hat{\sigma}$ (or $se(\hat{\beta}_1)$) rather than on σ (or

$std(\hat{\beta}_1)$). One or both of these intervals are usually included in the output of standard regression packages along with the estimated coefficients and their standard errors, etc. In our example the 95 per cent confidence interval for (the estimate $\hat{\beta}_1 = 0.342$ of) β_1 is [0.209; 0.474], while the 99 per cent confidence interval is [0.163; 0.521].

If you look into an old-fashioned statistical table listing percentiles for the t-distribution as depending on degrees of freedom, you will see that already for 25 degrees of freedom (corresponding to 27 observations in the simple regression model), $t_{0.975}$ is close to two (2.060), for 50 degrees of freedom it is very close to two (2.009) and for 60 degrees of freedom it goes below two, from there falling further towards its boundary value of 1.960. As long as we have a reasonable number of observations, we can use the rule of thumb that the 95 per cent confidence interval is the estimate plus or minus two of its standard errors. In our example, where $\hat{\beta}_1 = 0.342$ and $se(\hat{\beta}_1) = 0.064$, you will see that the 95 per cent confidence interval stated above is pretty close to being given this way.

If there is more than one explanatory variable, the 95 per cent confidence interval for each estimate $\hat{\beta}_j$ still goes from $\hat{\beta}_j - t_{0.975}se(\hat{\beta}_j)$ to $\hat{\beta}_j + t_{0.975}se(\hat{\beta}_j)$, just with the modification that the number of degrees of freedom of the relevant t-distribution is the number of observations n minus the number of explanatory variables k minus one, that is, $n - k - 1$, specializing to $n - 2$ for $k = 1$. Hence, as long as the number of observations exceeds the number of explanatory variables to a reasonable degree, $t_{0.975}$ will still be close to two, so the rule of thumb just described still holds.

The standard errors $se(\hat{\beta}_j)$ and the associated confidence intervals are useful since they provide us with interval estimates of the parameters. Standard deviations and confidence intervals are particularly useful for hypothesis testing.

Assume that according to our theory, explanatory variable number j affects the dependent variable and that we have arrived at an estimate $\hat{\beta}_j > 0$, say. We may be in doubt whether β_j is really zero (explanatory variable j does not affect y after all) and we just arrived at a $\hat{\beta}_j \neq 0$ by accident. We would therefore like to test the hypothesis that variable j has no influence on the dependent variable, $\beta_j = 0$, against the 'two-sided' alternative that variable j has some (positive or negative) influence, $\hat{\beta}_j \neq 0$. Now, if zero is *not* in the 95 per cent confidence interval, then there is a less than 5 per cent probability that $\beta_j = 0$ at the same time as we drew the sample leading to $\hat{\beta}_j$, $se(\hat{\beta}_j)$ and the associated confidence interval. We therefore reject the hypothesis $\beta_j = 0$ (against $\hat{\beta}_j \neq 0$) at the 5 per cent significance level. Likewise, if zero is not in the 99 per cent confidence interval, we reject that $\beta_j = 0$ (in favour of $\hat{\beta}_j \neq 0$) at the 1 per cent significance level. Of course, the 1 per cent level gives a stronger rejection than the 5 per cent level. In our example, we must reject $\beta_1 = 0$ both at the 5 and at the 1 per cent level.

We may have theoretical reason to believe in a particular value b_j for β_j, and would like to test the hypothesis $\beta_j = b_j$ against $\beta_j \neq b_j$, where this time we may want *not* to have the hypothesis rejected. If b_j is *not* in the 95 per cent interval, then we *must* reject $\beta_j = b_j$ (in favour of $\beta_j \neq b_j$) at the 5 per cent level, while if b_j *is* in the 95 per cent interval then we *cannot* reject $\beta_j = b_j$ (against $\beta_j \neq b_j$) at the 5 per cent level.

We are often interested in testing the idea that $\beta_j > 0$ (or $\beta_j < 0$) since our theory most often gives an indication of the sign of an influence, so the 'null hypothesis' $\beta_j = 0$ should be tested against the 'one-sided' alternative $\beta_j > 0$ (or perhaps $\beta_j < 0$). If $\beta_j = 0$ is true, then (from the analogue of (26)) the random variable

$$t = \frac{\hat{\beta}_j}{se(\hat{\beta}_j)} \tag{27}$$

should follow a t-distribution with $n - k - 1$ degrees of freedom. We can compute the actual t-value following from (27) and our estimates $\hat{\beta}_j$ and $se(\hat{\beta}_j)$. Note that this is just the number of standard errors that the estimate $\hat{\beta}_j$ lies away from zero, which is exactly the 't-value' reported by standard packages along with the parameter estimates etc. In our example, the

t-value is 5.323. Let the 95th percentile of the t-distribution with $n - k - 1$ degrees of freedom be $t_{0.95}$. If the hypothesis $\beta_j = 0$ is true, then the probability that the t-value exceeds $t_{0.95}$ is only 5 per cent, so if $t > t_{0.95}$ we reject $\beta_j = 0$ against $\beta_j > 0$ at the 5 per cent significance level. From a table one can see that even with few degrees of freedom, $t_{0.95}$ is below two and $t_{0.99}$ is below three. Therefore, as rules of thumb, when the number of observations exceeds the number of explanatory variables just moderately, if the t-value is above two (below minus two) we can reject $\beta_j = 0$ against $\beta_j > 0$ ($\beta_j < 0$) at least at the 5 per cent level, while if the t-value is above three (below minus three) we can reject $\beta_j = 0$ against $\beta_j > 0$ ($\beta_j < 0$) at least at the 1 per cent level. In our example therefore, $\beta_j = 0$ is rejected against $\beta_j > 0$ at a significance level even stronger than the 1 per cent level.

Along with the t-value of an estimate $\hat{\beta}_j$, standard software packages for regression analysis usually report a P-value which is the probability mass in the tails of the relevant t-distribution: if $\hat{\beta}_j$ and (hence) the t-value are positive, the P-value is the probability according to the t-distribution with $n - k - 1$ degrees of freedom that a random draw of t ends above the t-value or below minus the t-value, that is, it is the significance level at which one will just (or just not) reject $\hat{\beta}_j = 0$ against $\hat{\beta}_j \neq 0$ (and similarly for $\hat{\beta}_j < 0$). In our example, the P-value for $\hat{\beta}_j$ is $1.62 \cdot 10^{-5}$, so not to reject $\hat{\beta}_j = 0$ would require an extreme significance level of at most 0.00162 per cent.

You have probably realized that the estimated standard errors $se(\hat{\beta}_j)$ (along with the parameter estimates themselves) gives us the information needed for inference analysis. This is why we focus so much on standard errors in the estimations in this book.

6 | A final warning concerning causality

We were very explicit above saying that the economist's theory implies that x influences y, not the other way round. Very often, however, the economist will be in doubt. For instance, if x is national income and y is national consumption (and our data set is a time series), there may be reason to believe that x affects y because when people earn more they can spend more, but also that y affects x because national consumption is a large part of aggregate demand which affects aggregate income according to short-run macroeconomic theory. From the econometrics presented in this appendix one cannot draw conclusions about the direction of causality. Finding a well-fitting and significant regression line, $y = \hat{\beta}_0 + \hat{\beta}_1 x$, by the techniques we have explained does not exclude that it is really y that affects x or that there are causal relationships in both directions. If, on the other hand, x is household income and y is household consumption (and our data set is a cross-section, say), there may not be a similar problem of 'reversed causality', since we may have no reason to believe that high family spending should cause high family income, but may have reason to believe that high family income results in high family spending.

Even if we do have reason to believe that x affects y (according to a linear relationship) and have no reason to believe that y affects x, we can still not be sure that a nice (significant, etc.) result from an OLS regression of y on x indicates that x really causes y. This is because of the possibility of 'spurious correlation': it may be that a third and omitted variable really explains both x and y, say, affecting both positively, so a close relationship between x and y may not indicate any causality. The earning and education example is illustrative here. There may be little reason to believe that earnings affects education level and good *a priori* reason to believe that education level affects earnings. Nevertheless, finding a tight relationship between education and earnings (perhaps including other explanatory variables such as experience) could simply be an indication that 'innate capability' (a variable that it is difficult to measure and include) explains both education level and earnings, affecting both of these positively, without education itself having any impact on earnings.

There are econometric techniques to test for causality (or endogeneity), but they are too advanced for this appendix.

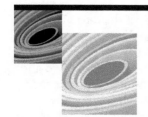

Index